OPERA IN LONDON
Views of the Press
1785–1830

Theodore Fenner

Southern Illinois University Press

Carbondale and Edwardsville

Copyright © 1994 by the Board of Trustees,
Southern Illinois University
All rights reserved
Printed in the United States of America
Edited by Carol Besler
Designed by Ed King
Production supervised by Natalia Nadraga
97 96 95 94   4 3 2 1

Publishing expenses have been supported by a grant
from the National Endowment for the Humanities, an
independent federal agency.

Library of Congress Cataloging-in-Publication Data

Fenner, Theodore.
    Opera in London: views of the press, 1785–1830 / Theodore Fenner.
      p.   cm.
    Includes bibliographical references and index.
    1. Opera—England—London—18th century. 2. Opera—England—London—19th century. 3. Operas—Reviews. I. Title
ML1731.8.L7F4 1994
782.1′09421′09033—dc20   93-16279
ISBN 0-8093-1912-8   CIP
                                                                       MN

The paper used in this publication meets the minimum requirements of
American National Standard for Information Sciences—Permanence
of Paper for Printed Library Materials, ANSI Z39.48-1984. ∞

To my brothers,
Jim & Dick

Contents

Illustrations *ix*
Preface *xi*
Abbreviations *xv*

PART I. The Periodical Press

Overview *1*

Appendixes

1. Leading Journals and Their Critics *51*
2. Reviews by Leading Critics *54*

PART II. Italian Opera

Introduction *65*
The Theatres *70*
The Audience *85*
The Operas *94*
The Performances *158*
Themes and Currents *257*

Appendixes

3. Seasonal Listing of Performances and Reviews *276*
4. Comic and Serious Productions: Premieres and Revivals *302*
5. New Productions, Performances, and Ratios *304*
6. Productions by Composer: In Three-Year Periods *306*
7. Operas by Composer: With Librettist *308*
8. Operas by Librettist: With Composer *312*
9. The Minor Singers *316*

PART III. English Opera
Introduction   *345*
The Theatres   *358*
The Audience   *365*
The Operas   *370*
The Performances   *513*
Themes and Currents   *582*

Appendixes
10. Annual Listing of Performances and Reviews   *608*
11. New and Revived Operas: Productions and Performances   *633*
12. Premiere Productions: By Theatre and Type   *635*
13. Operas by Known Playwrights: Major and Minor Theatre Performances   *636*
14. Productions by Composer: In Three-Year Periods   *637*
15. Productions by Librettist: In Three-Year Periods   *638*
16. Operas by Librettist/Dramatist: With Composer   *640*
17. Operas by Composer: With Librettist/Dramatist   *644*
18. English Adaptations: With Composer and Arranger   *648*
19. The Minor Singers   *649*

Notes   *679*
Selected Bibliography   *733*
Photographic Credits   *745*
Index   *749*

Illustrations

Frontispiece
Theatre Royal, King's Theatre

Between pages 12–13
James Henry Leigh Hunt
William Hazlitt

Between pages 88–89
Domenico Cimarosa
Wolfgang Amadeus Mozart
Vincente Martín y Soler
Johann Simon Mayr
Gioacchino Antonio Rossini
Lorenzo da Ponte

Between pages 98–99
Giuseppe Viganoni
Diomiro Tramezzani
Giuseppe Naldi
Giuseppe Ambrogetti
Manuel del Popolo Vincente García
Giovanni Battista Velluti
Domenico Donzelli
Gertrude Mara
Brigida Banti
Elizabeth Billington
Angelica Catalani
Teresa Bertinotti-Radicati
Joséphine Fodor-Mainvielle
Teresa Giorgi Trombetta Bellochi
   (Belloc)
Henrietta Sontag
Giudetta Pasta
Maria-Felicia García-Malibran

Between pages 372–73
Theatre Royal, Drury Lane
Theatre Royal, Covent Garden
Wolf's glen scene in *Der Freischütz*
John Gay
James Cobb
William Dimond
Prince Hoare
Frederic Reynolds
James Robinson Planché
Thomas Augustine Arne
Dr. Samuel Arnold
William Shield
Henry Rowley Bishop
Charles Incledon

Between pages 514–15
John Braham
Henry Phillips
Nancy Storace
Lucia Elizabeth Vestris
Buy a Broom sheet music cover
Mary Anne Paton
Catherine Stephens
Carl Maria von Weber

Preface

LITTLE IS KNOWN about opera in London during the forty-five years covered by this study. In part this is due to the destruction of opera scores and librettos when the King's Theatre burned in 1789 and when Covent Garden and Drury Lane burned in 1808 and 1809, respectively. Full scores of Italian and English operas of the period were almost never published, and surviving vocal scores are often unreliable.[1]

To be sure, many of the Italian operas mounted by the King's Theatre—the only house in England that produced them—saw their genesis on the Continent, where the productions of Mozart and Rossini, for example, have been thoroughly scrutinized. But many minor Italian opera composers of the period have been neglected, and even the names of some operas first performed in London have until now remained only titles. Moreover, the development of English opera and its relationship to Italian opera at the King's Theatre have been little studied or understood, even by recent musicologists, and many of the fine performers of the period—some outstanding—are unknown.

Some of the 425 Italian and English operas cited in this study would doubtless reward further individual study, and it is my hope that the light I have shed on them will be useful to future investigators. My own interest lies less in scores and librettos, however, than in how the English press and the public of the time related to them. Fortunately, evidence for this aspect of the period is ensured by the survival of a large number of reviews of performances of both Italian and English opera in the London periodical press, and from them I have chosen to present a chronicle—told as much as possible in the words of the reviewers—of the operatic world of London: the many operas, composers, librettists, playwrights, and performers during the period. I have traced developments in the theatres and audiences as well as shifts in musical taste—attitudes and opinions on many aspects of opera. I have included critical commentary from other contemporary sources—histories, memoirs, and biographies of operas, musicians, librettists, and playwrights—as well as recent commentary from musicologists.

This forty-five-year period, 1785–1830, was selected not for any particular musical development but because it documents the "rise" of musical journalism in London during the period of English Romanticism.[2] While opera had been reviewed sporadically in London periodicals after mid-century, it was not until the 1780s that it began to be reviewed with some consistency and regularity by the periodical press. Initially, for the most part, weak and insipid, these reviews gradually grew in competency until, by the 1820s, they were in full flower.

In Italian opera Dennis Arundell has presented many excerpts of reviews in his *Critic at the Opera* (1957), but his coverage is much too broad and sporadic for a close examination of one period. William Smith, in his *Italian Opera and Contemporary Ballet in London, 1789–1820* (1955), has provided a useful chronicling of King's Theatre productions, but his accompanying reviews are usually mere snippets. On the other hand, Frederick C. Petty, in *Italian Opera in London, 1760–1800* (1980), has supplied a large gathering of reviews for his period. He has brought a wide range of reading to bear on different aspects of opera in London but has not followed a similar pattern with the reviews, which, though well annotated, are merely set forth chronologically. While it is an advantage in some instances to see a whole review, much of this early criticism is too trivial to warrant any quotation at all, let alone a complete perusal; moreover, in his approach commentary on particular composers, singers, and other aspects of opera becomes completely scattered.

In English opera Allardyce Nicoll, in volumes III and IV of *A History of English Drama* (1956–65), presents much information on the genre but only insofar as it is related to English drama generally; he is not interested in English opera developments. But the late Roger Fiske, in *English Theatre Music in the Eighteenth Century* (1986), is very sympathetic to English opera and has provided a fine study of it up to 1800. Neither Nicoll nor Fiske, however, explores the views of the press. Charles Gray, in his *Theatrical Criticism in London to 1795* (1931), does so and touches on part of our period in English opera as well, but he, too, is not specifically interested in English opera; moreover, his study does not concentrate on the contents of the periodicals he discusses.[3]

In gathering my primary sources,[4] I am obligated for their courtesy and cooperation to the librarians at Columbia University (Butler and Department of Music); Yale University (Sterling and Beinecke); Harvard University (Widener); Cornell, Hamilton, Temple, and Duke universities; as well as at the Boston Athenaeum and the New York Public Library (Main Branch, Newspaper Annex and Lincoln Center, Music). I am also indebted to librarians in London at the British Library as well as their Newspaper Library (Colindale Avenue). I am also indebted to many librarians at the

Crumb Library of the State University College, Potsdam, for their unfailing courtesy and diligence in obtaining access to material at widespread locations.

I wish to thank Dr. David Ossenkop, associate librarian at the Crane School of Music, State University College, Potsdam, for his critical reading of the typescript and his expert comments. I am also indebted to the late Dr. Roland Gibson for his careful proofreading of the text. I am especially grateful to the publisher's readers for their excellent suggestions for improving earlier versions of the manuscript. None of my readers, of course, are responsible for errors I have failed to expunge. I must also express my deep obligation to Professor Carl Woodring—joined in memory to the late Paul Henry Lang—for strong support as my former mentors at Columbia University in interdisciplinary studies.

I wish to acknowledge the welcome financial assistance for this fifteen-year study from the American Council of Learned Societies for a grant in 1982, and from the Carl and Lily Pforzheimer Foundation for a grant in 1984. Special thanks for their support of my research are also due to Karl Krober, Professor of English, Columbia University, and to Donald H. Reiman, Librarian, Carl H. Pforzheimer Library, New York City.

Finally, my deepest appreciation goes to my wife, Lee Ullmann Fenner, for her perceptive editorial suggestions, her assistance in proofreading, and her strong and sympathetic support over the fourteen years of this study.

Abbreviations

Books

Boaden   *Memoirs of John Philip Kemble* (1825)
Burney   *General History of Music* (1776–89)
"Chronicles"   "Chronicles of Italian Opera" by S. D.
D.N.B.   *Dictionary of National Biography*
Fiske   *English Theatre Music of the Eighteenth Century*
Genest   *Some Account of the English Stage* (1832)
Highfill   *Biographical Dictionary*
Hogarth   *Memoirs of the Musical Drama* (1838)
Kelly   *Reminiscences* (1826)
L.S.   *London Stage, Part 5*
Mt-E   Mount-Edgcumbe, *Musical Reminiscences* (1834)
N.   Nicoll, *A History of English Drama*
N.G.   *New Grove Dictionary of Music and Musicians*
N.O.   *New Grove Dictionary of Opera*
NOHM   *New Oxford History of Music*
O.E.D.   *Oxford English Dictionary*
Parke   *Musical Memoirs* (1830)
Petty   *Italian Opera in London, 1760–1800*

Periodicals

(d) daily; (t) triweekly; (w) weekly; (m) monthly.

Advertiser, see PA
AR   *Analytical Review* (m)
At   *Atlas* (w)
Ath   *Athenaeum* (w)
BC   *British Critic* (m)
BS   *British Stage* (m)
BWM   *Bell's Weekly Messenger*
C   *Morning Chronicle* (d)
Ch   *Champion* (w)
Chronicle, see C

Cr   *Courier* (d)
CR   *Critical Review* (m)
D   *Diary* (d)
DA   *Daily Advertiser* (d)
DM   *Drama Magazine* (m)
E   *Examiner* (w)
EM   *European Magazine* (m)
Gazette, see LG
G   *Daily Gazetteer* (d)
GA   *General Advertiser* (d)
Inquisitor, see TI
H   *Morning Herald* (d)
Har   *Harmonicon* (m)
Herald, see H
LC   *London Chronicle* (t)
LitC   *Literary Chronicle* (w)
LG   *Literary Gazette* (w)
LM   *London Magazine* (m)
MM   *Monthly Mirror*
MR   *Monthly Review*
NM   *New Monthly Magazine*
O   *Oracle* (d)
OPA   *Oracle and Public Advertiser* (d)
P   *Morning Post* (d)
PA   *Public Advertiser* (d)
Post, see P
QMM   *Quarterly Musical Mag. & Review*
Register, see UR
Sp   *Spectator* (w)
T   *Times* (d) (= *Universal Register*)
TB   *True Briton* (w)
TC   "Theatrical Cutting"
TI   *Theatrical Inquisitor* (m)
TO   *Theatrical Observer* (d)
UM   *Universal Magazine* (m)
UR   *Universal Register* (d) (= *Times*)
W   *World* (d)
WH   *Walker's Hibernian Magazine* (m)

PART I
The Periodical Press

Overview

SINCE THE DISCUSSION of operas and performances in parts II and III rests very largely on the criticism that appeared in more than thirty periodicals during our forty-five years of coverage—criticism written by perhaps a hundred reviewers—we need first to examine in some detail the world of these reviewers: their identities wherever possible, the kinds of publications for which they wrote, the coverage they provided of both Italian and English operas, the quality of their criticism, and some of the circumstances that gave rise to the proliferation of these newspapers and journals during these years.

Though newspapers existed in London long before 1785, many of them had been highly ephemeral, single-folio productions. There were, however, a number of exceptions, such as the long-lived triweekly *London Chronicle* (see below), which carried some reviews as early as 1757. Fine opera criticism could also be found in the monthly *British Review* by 1760.[1] Not until the latter part of the century, however, did a number of newspapers and journals of some size and longevity begin to spring up and increase their circulations. Between 1776 and 1800, for example, there were at various times nearly sixty different newspapers carrying news of the theatre; many magazines of the period also had reviews though some were even more short-lived than the newspapers.

The annual circulation of newspapers reflects this change: seven million in 1758, twelve million in 1776, and twenty-four million in 1811.[2] Similarly, London dailies grew from eight morning papers in 1784 to fourteen in 1790 and to eighteen in 1813, while the first evening papers were also established.[3] The growth of weeklies was even more astonishing—from a single weekly in 1778 to sixteen by 1813.[4] By 1810 the circulation of the Sunday press exceeded that of the dailies.[5] Circulation, however, remained modest. Even by 1790 some of the dailies printed only about 2,000 copies, though many papers could make a profit with fewer than this (Williams, p. 185). Readership was of course much higher, for at taverns and country inns, many hands shared one paper. And after 1800 one could find subscription reading rooms. The *Monthly Magazine* pointed out in 1800 that newspapers and other periodicals were bought by "the middling orders of society, by the literati, and sometimes by the loftiest of our nobility."[6] By 1820 the circulation of the *Times* was 7,000; the *Morning Chronicle*, 2,100; and the evening *Courier*, 5,100.

In part this development was due to an increasing population: in the seventy years between 1751 and 1821 the British population doubled from seven to fourteen million, and this increase occurred largely in towns (Williams, p. 135). Moreover, due much to the growth of Methodism and Sunday schools, there was an increase in the literate population from an estimated one-and-a-half million in 1780 to seven or eight million in 1830.[7]

Under George III there was a large increase in the number of laws seeking to control the press, including imposition of taxes on each number sold, each advertisement carried, and even on the newsprint. Moreover, the government attempted to manipulate the press by placing its own lucrative subsidies and advertising with journals that were willing to publish material favorable to the administration.[8] Yet the papers increased in power and strongly resisted these measures.[9] After 1815, according to Alexander Andrews, the newspaper "was no longer a luxury—it had insensibly grown into an actual necessity of life."[10] But owing to increased prices forced on the papers, by 1830 a middle-class household with an annual income of £200-£300 could not afford a daily paper at 7*d*. (Williams, p. 190).

The typical daily of the period had four four-column pages, nearly two pages of which were given over to advertising. During session, reports of the parliamentary debates took one page or more. The balance was filled with a leading article (editorial), news paragraphs (domestic and foreign), trials, police reports, shipping news, market news, and the like, including theatricals. The weeklies and monthlies were largely made up of articles and reviews of all kinds.

The need for advertising lay behind the establishment of many of the papers. Thus the *Public Ledger* (1760) was a general mercantile organ, the *Morning Advertiser* (1796) was established by the licensed victualers, the *Day* (1798) by the auctioneers, and the *Traveller* (1800) by the commercial travelers. Some were on that account politically neutral.[11] But by the 1770s and 1780s most papers took on varying degrees of political coloration; indeed, some were launched as vehicles for or against the governing ministry, which led, on occasion, to a good deal of internecine warfare. On the whole, the more politically liberal organs tended to be more independent in their views, including their opera criticism.

CRITICISM AND CRITICS

In a review of London newspapers in 1821 the conservative monthly *British Stage* (Mar., pp. 61–69), describing the *Times* as "preeminent in circulation and baseness," called their politics "radical" following the "Manchester business,"[12] though press historians agree that the *Times* was then pro-government, though moving slowly to the left. They called the *Morning Chronicle* an "avowed Whig organ," and Bourne (II, 12) found it the "boldest of the independents" from 1820 to 1830. Oddly enough they noted that the *Morning Post*, once a mouthpiece of Whig opposition, was now a supporter of the Tories and adopted an "outrageous tone of ultra-loyalty" that was "disgusting," while its theatricals were "contemptible." Of course they had much praise for the right-wing evening *Courier* and *New Times*, while the generally left-wing Sunday papers were a "national disgrace."

In a later survey William Hazlitt, whose politics tended toward the radical, had quite different views.[13] Noting that literary criticism had "never flourished in Periodicals as now," he called the *Chronicle* the best "both for amusement and instruction"—they "held fast to party and principles" and did not "overwhelm" readers as did the *Times*, which was "too heavy, full, detailed" as well as "pompous, dogmatical, full of pretensions." The *Courier* was a paper "of shifts and expedients, of bare assertions and thoughtless impudence." He went on to praise the *Examiner* as "the ablest and most respectable of the weeklies" and admired both the *London Magazine* and the *New Monthly*, the latter being "remarkable for its delicacy."

Occasionally other writers could find something commendatory to say about competing critics or periodicals. In 1796, for example, the *True Briton* acknowledged the presence of "the best musical critics" among writers for the press (Feb. 10). In 1801 the *Monthly Mirror* found the *Chronicle* reviewer to be "one of our best diurnal critics" (Dec.). In 1821 the *London* (Jan.) was effusive over the value of the new *Quarterly Musical Magazine* "to music, and musical men." And in 1829 the *Examiner* (Mar. 8) commended the criticism of the *New Monthly*, though noting "a tendency towards an overestimation of merit" (in which I concur). Leigh Hunt, too, during his days with the weekly *Examiner*, occasionally sought a friendly colloquy in print with his "brother critics"—few responded.

But on the whole, a considerable amount of sharp criticism was leveled from time to time by one periodical against another—arising from the very strong competition between rival journals (Bourne, II, 27). Some of this criticism was of course politically motivated: it prompted an attack on

Hunt by the *Theatrical Inquisitor* in 1812 (Nov.) and in 1819 (Oct.); it also underlay a good deal of sniping by the *Chronicle* at the conservative *Courier* from 1811 to 1813, though the *Chronicle* occasionally attacked the moderate *Times* as well (all seemed jealous over its rapid growth). Sometimes the criticism was precise and probably justified, as when the *Theatrical Observer*, reporting the *Chronicle*'s assertion that playwright William Dimond's muse "had slept for 16 years," replied by citing several recent successful productions of his (Jan. 21, 1829). At other times it was vague and appeared to arise from competitive instincts, as when the *Post* accused the other morning papers of "malicious satisfaction" in trying to weaken the popularity of a ballet at the King's Theatre (Apr. 18, 1795).

But most of the criticism emanated from the weeklies and monthlies and was directed toward the dailies, a rather unfair situation, since the former had great advantage over the latter in meeting their deadlines.[14] In 1786 the *Chronicle* denied an assertion by an unidentified daily that the critic for the *General Advertiser* was writing its reviews (Jan. 4). In 1810 Henry Robertson of the *Examiner* noted that the papers "have extolled" Guglielmi's one-act *Atalida* "beyond all bounds." In 1813 the *Inquisitor* wrote: "As to the criticism of the papers, we must declare that we think them in general scarcely deserving of notice." Noting their discrepancies in reporting the height of one performer, they asked: "Do any two of them agree? Do they look with the same eyes?" (Oct.).

In 1819 Thomas Kenrick in the *British Stage* (May), complaining of the power of the daily press, stated that his journal's reputation would suffer if it disagreed with the newspapers on Italian opera, yet he found the *Post* written in a style of "bombastic fustian," and he described the monthly *European Magazine*, "once respectable," as "trash." In 1827 Edward Holmes, in the weekly *Atlas*, criticized the *Chronicle* for its "flippant ignorance" in its review of Pasta's appearance in *Romeo e Giulietta* (May 13). And William Ayrton in the monthly *Harmonicon*, which frequently attacked the music criticism of the daily press, asserted in 1830 (VIII, 178) that "not one musical critic in five has the slightest knowledge of the elements or even the language of the art in which he sits on judgment." Also in 1830, the *Examiner*, after quoting a paragraph of criticism of the dailies, criticized them for limiting their reports largely to the singers and for trivial critiques even on them (Jan. 10).

Surprisingly, we find very few references to absentee reviewing. In 1789 the *Times* carried a paragraph, "Theatrical Criticisms," signed by one Ned Shuter, reprimanding a reviewer for "Puppy-print," claiming he had reviewed Mrs. Billington in a performance she had not even attended because of illness (Dec. 22). And in 1808 Henry Robertson (E) complained of reviews of Italian opera written by absent reviewers (Jan. 17). Frederic Reynolds, a very successful playwright-librettist, made a similar charge in his autobiography. Even Lord Campbell admitted, in his autobiography, that just before quitting the *Chronicle* as a reviewer in 1805 he — "for the first time in my life" — wrote a "conjectures" criticism of *Romeo and Juliet* and was almost discovered because of a last-minute change in the edition being performed![15]

Bass singer Henry Phillips tells us in his *Recollections* that, according to Nicholas Mori, husband of the King's singer Signora Mori, praise in the London papers was "a necessity of life" to her. Phillips also stated that singer Braham, who would seem to have had little cause for complaint, was quite sensitive to adverse criticism; he told Phillips that "any new idea or reading is sure to be seriously criticised, until the performer has convinced all parties that he is correct." And Phillips pointed out that about 1815 Braham even wrote to James Perry, then editor of the *Sun*: "I would wish to hint in your valuable paper, at the *degraded state* of musical criticism, when one of the greatest beauties of musical performance, namely, what the Italians call posta di voce, which may be interpreted as the swelling and diminution of the voice, ... is compared to a *Mail Coach Horn!*"[16] Nevertheless, Braham was an ardent collector of newspaper cuttings extending over most of his long career![17] Even Thomas Dibdin, successful playwright, quoted full reviews from five periodicals in his *Reminiscences* (II, 221) to allay the charge that his *Family Quarrels* (1802) was anti-Semitic.

But it was the theatre managers — especially the playwright-managers — who were most concerned with press notices. The great Sheridan was a case in point. Michael Kelly tells us (pp. 340–41): "No man was ever more ... frightened at criticism than he was.... He dreaded the newspapers, and always courted their friendship. I have many times heard him say: Let me but have the periodical press on my side, and there should be nothing in the country which I would not accomplish." His love-hate relationship is best expressed in his burlesque of Mr. Puff in his play *The Critic* (1781).

George Colman the Younger, playwright and owner-manager of the Little Theatre, had a similar relationship. In 1777 he complained of "the severity of London critics," naming specifically William "Memory" Woodfall, "whose opinion contributes to fill me with apprehensions," though they became friends.[18] About 1786 he wrote to O'Keeffe about the latter's play: "the papers will perhaps, for a time, prevent the applause and attraction" but that will come back later.[19] James Boaden, a playwright and journalist, informs us that in a prologue written about this time Colman "repelled a malignant insinuation" by George Steevens in the *Public Advertiser*.

In 1788 Colman's comedy *Ways and Means* "encountered some opposition," he noted. "The epilogue, written by myself, was taken in high dudgeon by the newspaper writers, whom it somewhat impolitely ridiculed, and they joined common cause, by endeavouring to run down the piece, with much acrimony, in almost all their journals" (Peake, II, 212–13). The epilogue read, in part:

> I am a critic, my masters! I sneer, splash, and vapour,
>   Puff parties, damn poets; in short *do* a paper.
>   My name's Johnny Grub—I'm a vender of Scandal.

Yet he was prompt to quote from a "critic of the day" on Master Braham's debut at Covent Garden! In *Critical Essays* (1807, p. 89) Hunt cited another prologue to Colman's *Five Miles Off* (1806), which was critical of his reviewing in the *News* and which actor John Fawcett "spoke right in my teeth" (Hunt was sitting in a box adjoining the stage), but Hunt was only amused, looking "upon Mr. Colman as a great monkey pelting me with nuts, which I ate."

Later playwrights were also uneasy with critics. In 1789–90 Charles Dibdin, though he "laughed at newspaper criticism," undertook to publish the weekly *Bystander* "to promote his reputation as a composer of musical drama."[20] In his preface to *Kais* (1808), Isaac Brandon castigated the *Examiner* and *Bell's Weekly Messenger* (Adolphus). Reynolds cited Arthur Murphy's contempt for press reviews, though "he made *money* on plays."[21] But Reynolds, who showed like contempt, acknowledged the power of the press in launching the career of Edmund Kean, whose Shylock was deemed unsuccessful by the audience (II, 396). In his *Reminiscences* (1822), Thomas Dibdin also noted the power of the press and was pleased to cite the *Herald*'s kind reviews of a Covent Garden production.

A later playwright, Edward Fitzball, writing in 1859, thought the current scene much improved: "Thirty years ago the mass had to be told what they might like, what they might not, according to the opinions, or pretended opinions of certain charlatans. The public is now, every man his own critic [and] a manly and noble system of truth and liberality has sprung up amidst the reviewers of the present day."[22] Yet elsewhere he was pleased to offer quotations from favorable *Times* reviews for his *Pilot* (1825) and *Devil's Elixir* (1829), and he noted twice how well 1822 reviewers had written of him! Alfred Bunn, also discussing the mid-Victorian theatre, complained, however, that "if you omit [orders for] a paper or periodical of the vilest description, your reputation is assailed by it, and your exertions misrepresented in the most shameless and mendacious manner."[23]

Many of these complaints are weakened by direct contradictions—for example, that all reviewers agreed, or that none of them agreed, with each other. Except in attacks on theatre managers (T, Sept. 19, 1811), however, it is not surprising that critics, in their reviews, seldom alluded to puffery—attempts to solicit the favor of their readers through inordinate praise.

Although it is largely true, as Charles Beecher Hogan asserts (L.S., I, xci-xciii), that the public, not the reviewers, determined the fate of the play—especially at the "giving out"[24] of a performance—the consensus of the above opinions makes it clear that the power of the press nevertheless exerted a strong influence on the playgoing public. Cecil Price, writing of the Garrick period, agrees that the theatre managers attempted to control the press. But "what was too often forgotten was that publicity, however artful and seductive, could rarely persuade people to attend plays that were known to be caviare to the general. . . . On the other hand, a new piece that enthralled an audience drew crowds without the help of newspaper puffing." Yet he goes on to quote from the diary of Tate Williams, manager of the York Theatre, who in 1790 pointed out in his memoirs (iv, 82) that the "authority" of the dailies had superseded the "critics in the pit"—i.e., the reaction of the audience.[25] In 1788 the *Universal Magazine* (Mar., lxxxi, 140) had noted that "the public is no longer the judge. . . . The newspapers decide on dramatic [and musical] merit with absolute authority."

PUFFERY

Leigh Hunt, in an often-quoted passage, was outspoken about the problem in his *Autobiography* (p. 155):

> Puffery and plenty of tickets were . . . the system of the day. It was an interchange of amenities over the dinner table; a flattery of power on the one side, and puns on the other; and what the public took for criticism of a play was a draft upon the box-office, or reminiscences of last Thursday's salmon and lobster-sauce. The custom was to write as short and as favourable a paragraph on a new piece as could be; to say that Bannister was "excellent" and Mrs. Jordan "charming"; to notice the crowded house or invent it, if necessary; and to conclude by observing that "the whole went off with éclat."

Nor was Hunt the first to voice the complaint. As early as October 1776, a critic for the older *London Magazine* had written:

> The news-paper *critics* are another great cause of the degeneracy of the stage, for as the established morning papers are connected with the managers, this insect tribe are connected with the players. . . . Editors

of papers and persons connected with the second-rate performers; and scribblers looking for favours, or for a dinner, from every person concerned or connected with the theatres, from the managers down to the lowest frequenters of Jupp's, these are the authors of the theatrical critiques or criticisms. . . . If the independents were capable of giving an able judgment, the news-paper printers would refuse their productions. (Quoted by Gray, pp. 136–37)

There is other evidence. Nicoll (III, 12) found puffing "common" in the "low and servile state" of the press in the eighteenth century. It was common knowledge that actor and theatre manager David Garrick "bought" the press and owned some newspaper shares in the *Public Advertiser*, but there was some adverse criticism anyway (Gray, p. 201). (Winesanker [p. 89] asserts he also "shared in the management" of the *Daily Gazetteer*, *Morning Post*, and *St. James's Chronicle*.) After retiring from the stage, Garrick even wrote some theatrical criticism himself.

The *History of "The Times"* (I, 47–49), which finds occasional "articles of dramatic criticism" in London newspapers after 1765, admits that most of them were sheer puffery; although they cited the *Public Advertiser* in the 1770s as one of the first to provide special treatment of dramatic intelligence, they do not find "candid" criticism before the advent of Leigh Hunt in 1805.

Peake admitted that "Memory" Woodfall, of the *Advertiser*, was a great friend of both Colmans, yet contrasted his fine criticism with the "frothy nonsense" in the "modern press." And O'Keeffe (I, 141) likewise admitted Woodfall was a friend of Charles Stuart (brother of the influential Peter and Daniel, also newspaper editors), who was "of much use for his influence in the newspapers" (I, 141). The journalist John Taylor,[26] writing of Michael Kelly's first appearance at Drury Lane, admitted he did not admire Kelly's singing, but didn't want

> to say anything injurious to a young man who came to London with high musical fame, and of whose private character I had heard a good report. I was the more disposed to decline criticising his performance, on account of [Sheridan], with whom I was intimate and who expected much advantage from [Kelly's] talents. I therefore requested Mr. Richardson to give an account of Kelly's first appearance; the interest he took in the theatre, as well as his own benignant temper, induced him readily to undertake the task, and his report was highly favourable.

In 1784 the *New Spectator* claimed that "no small sum has been spent in puffing [the music of Rauzzini's *La Regina di Golconda*] in the newspapers."[27] Somewhat later the *Diary* complained that Thomas Harris, manager of Covent Garden Theatre, had paid the *Times* £100 for good criticism of a production.[28] Lorenzo da Ponte tells us that librettist C. F. Badini, his predecessor as poet at the King's who "had learned English well," was employed as a critic "on a number of newspapers [including *Bell's Weekly Messenger*], whose opinions are accepted as good in London, perhaps to a greater extent than in any other country."[29] Da Ponte also asserted that the success of William Taylor, the King's manager, depended on it, adding that James Perry of the *Chronicle* was Taylor's "agent and friend."

Da Ponte was probably wrong about Perry, however, though John Campbell, the critic for his theatricals from 1800 to 1805, showed the low state of journalistic criticism. He wrote to his father in 1802: "From reading the 'Star,' the 'Sun,' &c, you will see what miserable Grub street generally appears under the head 'Theatres.' There are a few cant terms upon which different changes are rung to answer private ends" (*Life*, I, 118). In fact Campbell left journalism in 1805, fearing that it would damage his reputation as an upcoming jurist (I, 183). And some years later (c. 1840) he pointed out that

> no one in the present day can form a notion of the importance then attended to the drama. . . . Dramatic criticism was accordingly very much attended to. . . . I took great pains with my articles on plays and players. . . . It was pretty well known from whom the dramatic articles came, and I sometimes found myself treated with a most unaccountable deference by first-rate performers and popular dramatists. The plaudits or hisses of the audience, and overflowing houses or empty benches, certainly depended a good deal on the word of the anonymous critic of the Morning Chronicle. (*Life*, I, 113)

Later accusations dropped sharply, though in 1811 the *Inquisitor* charged the *Post* with puffery, and in 1815 (Oct.), after printing identical paragraphs of criticism on the same date for the *Post* and the *Day*, the *Inquisitor* complained that the Covent Garden managers have "transmitted a *circular* to divers of our intelligent and independent morning prints, accompanied with *the usual fee*." Moreover, by the late 1790s the practice of "undercharging" the King's for its advertisements in their papers "in exchange for free seats" began to be challenged by the *Times* and *Chronicle*.

It must be pointed out, however, that much of what was called puffery appeared not in the reviews at all but in the form of "paragraphs" mingled in with the highly heterogeneous general news sections of the newspapers. These would largely deal with forthcoming events—productions, actors, and singers—not too different from the quite acceptable "publicity" of our own day. Parke cited an instance (c. 1827) where puffery appeared by error in the theatre advertisement rather than in the "news."

Such a puff is perfectly exemplified by this unidentified Theatrical Cutting of 1788 (probably from the *Post*) concerning the forthcoming production of Paisiello's *La Frascatana*:

> The amateurs of music, who may desire to seek amusement at the Opera House this evening will not be disappointed; the Frascatana to be performed, will prove highly entertaining. . . . The parts allotted to some of the principal performers being so well adapted to their abilities, must of course excite the admiration of every one the least interested in the well chosen music. The comic song, composed by Signor Sacchini, which will be introduced by Signor Morigi, and the song Paterio, at the conclusion, will prove highly diverting.[30]

Another source of puffery annoying to the press were the playbills. In 1823, for example, the *Herald* quoted from one on the Planché-Bishop *Cortez* at Covent Garden: "'Whereas, the vocabulary of eulogies has been exhausted in the announcement of the success of the new performers,' &c. &c. It required great obliquity, or obtuseness of perception, not to have seen that this is a broad sneer upon its own inditers. . . . It is a fact disgraceful to the national stage . . . that the two great theatres have recourse to a system of puffing" (Nov. 7).

No doubt many more such comments are to be found in the papers *outside* of the reviews. The question remains, how much puffing got *into* them? Reviews of the King's premiere of Paisiello's *La Discordia Conjugale* are perhaps a case in point. On December 30, 1791, the *Herald* carried a notice: "In this opera the genius of Paisiello is exerted with admirable effect, as it abounds in whimsical, characteristic, and original music. The accompaniments are rich and fanciful." This reads like a review and has the characteristics Hunt posited for puffs of extreme brevity and trite praise. It was, in fact, a puff, appearing some three months before the premiere. The *Herald*'s actual review (Apr. 2), though considerably longer, still smacked of puffery:

> The long-promised Opera of La Discordia Conjugale was at length produced at this Theatre on Saturday, and very well received by a large and brilliant circle. The music is wholly by Paisiello, and is considered as scientific, original, and a work of much ingenuity. The general effect is spirited and exhilarating.
>
> The piece was originally performed at Naples where it was much admired, and indeed it was one of the most successful Operas ever exhibited at that place.

> Its dramatic merit is of the usual level, and is little more, intrinsically, than a channel for the music. . . .
> The two songs of Casentini, particularly the first in the second act, went off admirably. The Duet in the second act was delicious. Lazzarini's songs were finely-composed. The Sestetto in the first act, and the quartetto in the second, were happily admired. The whole of the music is thought to be the best that Paisiello has ever composed.

The April 2 reviews by the *Diary* and the *Times* were also brief and trite. The *Oracle*'s review had equally high praise but, though somewhat shorter, had touches of particularity that suggest it was a bona fide review:

> There are some single airs of enchanting simplicity. A whimsical duo between Cipriani and Casentini, and a duet solus in falsetto and bass by the Signor [are] pleasant enough. Lazzarini, however, has the grand song allotted to him in the second act. A more delightful air and one better given we have not of late heard. It was loudly called for a second time and sung with additional beauty. The sestetts or finales were original and [had] very rich harmonies indeed.

How much puffery is present in the April 2 accounts? They all meet Hunt's criteria. The *Diary* and *Times* reviews are uncharacteristically brief and might pass for puffs, though it must be remembered Paisiello operas *were* very popular at the time; moreover, a certain amount of puffery did get into the *Times*'s reviews in the 1790s. In the present instance, however, only the *Oracle* offers anything like serious criticism. Though the other specimens are clearly marginal, my guess is that there is no puffery in them but that they suffer from the prevailing triteness and insipidity that marked many of the earlier reviews. The source of this triteness was owing less to the coffers of the theatre managers than to the lack of any genuine interest on the part of Johnny Grub in the operas themselves. I have endeavored in this study to edit out such marginal criticism wherever it occurs.

ANONYMITY

Although we still accept without question anonymous delivery of the "facts" in the daily news dispatches of our papers, we have long been accustomed to the reassurance of a byline for most other events. But all the reviews cited herein were written anonymously, and some of the best writers of the period, including Leigh Hunt and William Hazlitt—and occasionally Charles Lamb and even Samuel Taylor Coleridge—wrote anonymous reviews of stage performances.

It should be pointed out that anonymity in the periodical press was not adopted to protect negatively critical reviewers from reprisal: the entire journal—not just the criticism—was written anonymously. The advantage of anonymity to the publisher or editor was that it permitted him to use his limited contributions in various styles for various departments. Another advantage was that it enabled the editor to deny responsibility for writing regarded by the government as politically subversive. But of course the practice did enable reviewers to feel freer in making their comments. Unlike other editors, Charles Wentworth Dilke, who edited the *Athenaeum* in the 1830s, thought anonymity a safeguard for independent criticism.[31] Actually most contemporary insiders would have known at any time who was contributing what to whom.

It is facile to point out that this anomynity led to some of the abuses just discussed—absentee reviewing, copying, puffery, and the like; yet such abuses could just as easily have taken place with signed critiques. No contemporary writer ever thought that anonymity in any way compromised the criticism in any journal. One contemporary historian felt anonymity no bar to progress in the press. In 1853, in his *History of English Literature* (p. 404), the Reverend William Spalding declared:

> The remarkable advancement which newspapers have made, alike in ability of thought and writing, and in the extent of their influence on the minds of the public—the extraordinary amount of active speculation and spirited composition which their *anonymous* [my emphasis] authors have lavished on them during the last thirty years, would fully justify expressions of surprise like those which escaped from us, when we observed, in the early part of the century, similar phenomena in the larger periodicals.

What can be deplored is the fact that the low salaries[32] and irregular assignments contributed to the pluralism among critics in the press (staff writers were something of a novelty before 1800), for many of the reviewers moved from journal to journal as opportunities arose or faded; even the best writers, like Hazlitt and Hunt, were at times forced to scrounge for work.

While it is true, as the *New Grove* ("Criticism") asserts, that "since the value of a criticism depends in part on the reader's knowledge of the critic's standpoint, the unsigned article is improper," the identity of a regular *reviewer* is less important, since the regular reader of any periodical becomes quickly acquainted with the particular facets of that reviewer's taste and approach. Indeed, style is more important than name, especially when nothing further than that can be ascertained about the critic's background.

1. James Henry Leigh Hunt (1820); engraved by J. C. Armytage from an unfinished miniature of Joseph Severn

2. William Hazlitt, self-portrait

REVIEWS AND REVIEWERS

Yet we rejoice when a critic can be identified by name. Sometimes the name of the editor is sufficient; Leanne Langley points out that in roughly half of the musical journals whose editors can be identified by name, the editors "served as principal writers" in their journals.[33] Sometimes (quite rarely) reviewers can be identified by a symbol or by initials following the review (this was characteristic of the *Examiner*). Often contemporary histories, biographies, memoirs, and the like will supply a missing name or date for a given journal (the D.N.B. is an indispensible aid).

Still further assignations can be made through a detailed analysis of the style and content of all the reviews for each newspaper and journal, as we will see from later discussions. Such an analysis reveals that most reviewers can be characterized by a more or less distinctive style of writing and attitude toward their subject matter — to the extent that their reviews can be identified over a given span of months or years and can even be traced among more than one newspaper or journal. From this evidence we can often supply a name based on the independent findings of the historians.

But even if no name is forthcoming, we can still characterize many of these reviews and give them a nameless identity, such as critic A, B, or X. We can also see that, despite the pluralism cited earlier, many journals had but one writer doing the reviewing for either Italian or English opera over a considerable period of time: the assignments were not as scattered as the poor condition of Johnny Grub might suggest — in fact, Johnny Grub types were beginning to fade out after 1800.

In addition, we find that most or all newspapers had two reviewers — one for the playhouses and another for Italian opera. But there were exceptions, such as the *Chronicle* from 1826 to 1830, when John Payne Collier provided splendid reviews for both English and Italian opera. Weeklies or monthlies, which did not have to provide day-to-day coverage, could get by with only one reviewer, but the better journals still had one critic for Italian and one for English opera.

Coverage of Italian opera was excellent in the *Times* and good in the *Chronicle* and in most weeklies and monthlies, but it was poor in the remaining newspapers. Coverage of English opera was good to excellent throughout. The *Times* was far better than any other periodical in providing reviews for revivals and debuts; such reviews were of course much briefer than those for a premiere.

Often the "benefits," to which leading performers were entitled, were not reviewed before 1800. Bagster-Collins and the *Times* thought this was because usually there was no novelty in the performance. But another reason was to refrain from comment out of fairness to the person whose benefit it was. Thus the *London Chronicle* wrote in 1791: "We have been induced to deviate from our practice of being silent upon benefit productions, from understanding this opera [*Cave of Triphonius*] belongs to the house" (May 5). Later in our period, most journals did review benefit performances.

The length of reviews increased from 1785 to 1800, then leveled off till the 1820s, when those in the journals expanded considerably. In 1785, for instance, an average review of Italian opera was only about three hundred words, whereas they often ran to seven hundred words by the end of the century. English opera reviews were somewhat longer, mainly because there was more interest in the plot of those operas than in Italian operas. Sometimes, indeed, the plot occupied as much as 85 or 90 percent of the review! Without a printed text, which was not usually available for some time after the premiere, the reviewer had to construct it out of the dialogue heard in the theatre (TO, Jan. 14, 1824). It was a chore for many reviewers (some weeklies and monthlies borrowed the plots, with due credit, from the dailies), but the public seemed to demand them. Often the plot was printed in smaller type than the rest of the review.

Sometimes in the review and sometimes following it, reviewers would insert lyrics from English opera songs (at sale in the theatres). Newspapers may at times have indulged in the practice as space fillers, as Gray states, but I believe that readers were interested in them as well as in the plots. True, they tended to fade out after 1800, but the *Chronicle* and other newspapers continued to reprint specimens as late as the 1820s.

Length of reviews also depended on what was reviewed: a three-act opera deserved more attention than a one-act afterpiece. Also a premiere deserved more space than a revival or, say, the debut of a performer. Although Gray has pointed to overly critical comments in the latter part of the eighteenth century on the debuts of young performers by reviewers who were in league with the established ones, this situation did not prevail in opera criticism. What I do find is that quite often when a critic is much irritated with some aspect of the opera performance, that annoyance tends to color the rest of the review. Perhaps this is a common failing in criticism.

Another factor that affected length of reviews was style. In 1785 periodical reviews were usually short and simple reports. They sometimes opened with brief observations on the house, a new performer, or other matters of particular interest, then moved toward comments on the libretto (including a précis for English opera), followed by remarks on the music. They usually concluded with a brief discussion of the outstanding performers, and sometimes of minor ones as well. Of course, the straightforward report could also be quite detailed, depending on the amount of close observation by the critic. From 1795 to 1805 reviewers brought more attention to bear on their subject, and some reviewers in certain journals, such as Hunt in the *Examiner* and John Taylor in the *Monthly Mirror*, brought an essay style into their criticism. Thus, the first paragraph or two were often explorations of musical ideas related to the opera rather than strictly reportorial. The essay approach (examples will be found in appendix 2) gradually expanded until the 1820s, when writers were learning to include a good deal of interesting material along with their reports on operas. Indeed, writers such as Hazlitt in the *London* so overwhelmed their reviews with general observations, the opera itself was all but lost sight of.

Another important characteristic of reviews was the extent to which reviewers brought negative criticism to bear on their discussions of librettos, music, and performers. Except for occasionally adverse comments on some singers, negative criticism is almost entirely absent from the early reviews, as we have seen. In Italian opera criticism, for instance, there was little sustained adverse criticism until Henry Robertson's reviews began in the *Examiner* in 1808. Much briefer but also negative English opera criticism could be found in the *Monthly Mirror* beginning in 1811, though Hunt had been a sharp critic of English opera as early as 1804. Again, by the 1820s, strongly negative comments were much in evidence. On the other hand, few of the early reviewers—and even some of the later ones—were capable of expressing any genuine pleasure in their musical experiences, even when their reviews were generally positive.

Max Graf[34] adopts the thesis that music criticism wrongly took the side of the public against the artist after the mid-nineteenth century, whereas critics were supportive of the composer before then. This is certainly not true of most of the later criticism in our period. I do agree with Dennis Arundell that Italian opera criticism, which became "rather more of a professional matter" than earlier criticism, was "fundamentally right in spite of prejudicial mistakes due to the taste of the day."[35]

Of course, we need to emphasize that very few of our critics were trained musicians. William Ayrton (*Harmonicon*) and Edward Holmes (*Atlas*) were musicians, and so was Thomas Busby—unfortunately his *Monthly Musical Journal* was short-lived. Richard Mackenzie Bacon (*Quarterly Musical*) was not a musician, though he was a gifted writer on music. But even Ayrton was not without faults as a music critic. In English opera perhaps not much expertise was needed to make intelligent comments on the songs or the singing. Italian opera was something else, and sometimes the early reviewers made only vague reference to the music or left their judgment "to the cognoscenti," as we shall see. But even here, especially in the later reviews, our nonmusician critics fared quite well. Doubtless, some musical training would have improved them. Leigh Hunt (*Examiner*), a talented piano player, no doubt benefited from his close association with the Novello circle and their love of singing glees together. And Thomas Massa Alsager (*Times*) loved music and gave musically significant performances in his home. No doubt others had some musical interests as well.

While Dr. Langley is more concerned with musical essays in the journals for our period, she asserts that

> it is difficult to gauge the real quality of the performance on the basis of these contemporary reviews, for not only were the performance standards of the time very different from modern ones, but the opinion of the writer was also inextricably linked to his familiarity with the music, the composer, the performer(s), as well as his own skill as a listener. (Pp. 78–79)

Certainly the listening is critical. Paul Henry Lang[36] has pointed out that since newspapers stress reporting, the aim of their nonmusician critics was primarily to report on the performance; the main consideration here rested in *judgment* rather than in knowledge. Something of this is evident in Dr. Charles Burney's "Essay on Musical Criticism." For him, the critic meant "not a professional musician, still less a journalist, but a judicious listener."[37] Hunt made much the same point in a debate with composer John Barnett in the *Tatler*, as we shall see. Fortunately, in some of our criticism, the role of a "judicious listener" could be, and was, combined with that of the journalist.

For a closer look at the more important periodicals quoted in these pages, we turn to an account of their individual accomplishments in musical journalism.

THE NEWSPAPERS

Morning Chronicle (1769–1862)[38]

This newspaper achieved some reputation in the 1770s, when it was edited by William "Memory" Woodfall, who got his nickname from his ability to attend the parliamentary debates and later write them out verbatim without notes (Bourne, I, 193).[39] He also "set great store on his dramatic criticism" (Gray), though it dropped off by 1780, and he left the *Chronicle* to found a new daily—the *Diary*. But under the brilliant James Perry (1756–1821),[40] who with James Gray (also spelled Grey) became coproprietor and coeditor in 1789, the *Chronicle* achieved its greatest influence and made Perry a rich man, and it led all the London papers in influence until he retired due to ill health in 1817. (Perry himself wrote little for the paper.) John Black, who cared little for theatrical criticism, served as editor until 1821, and W. J. Clement served from 1822 to 1834.

Italian opera criticism. It is difficult to ascertain the *Chronicle*'s contribution before 1800 because of gaps in the runs. Reviews that do survive show a competency somewhat above that of other newspapers. The number for February 16, 1786, is signed by "Crito," suggesting that a probably unpaid correspondent provided early coverage. Later ones in the 1790s were somewhat improved, but trivial reviews are often in evidence before 1802. From that point on, though, the criticisms take on some substance. They are often brief, but reviewers were not afraid of negative criticism, and gradually, through 1806, they introduced essay-type passages that carried the criticism well beyond the bare bones of mere reportage. (By 1804 reviews of the King's Theatre were appearing in columns with other news, often under the caption "The Mirror of Fashion.") Reviews of premieres before 1811 were generally only one-quarter to one-third of a column; after that they often reached nearly a full column of somewhat smaller type. We cannot ascertain names of critics in that period.

Though Bourne states that William Ayrton (for other details on this important critic see *Harmonicon*, below) reviewed operas for the *Chronicle* between 1813 and 1826, Ayrton probably would not have written for the paper in 1817 and 1821, when he was music director at the King's Theatre. Inspection of reviews and comparison of styles during this period indicate quite clearly that he did indeed review Italian opera from 1813 until 1826, except for 1817 and 1821. Langley (p. 295) asserts that Ayrton was an "honorary" critic and was not paid for his criticism, and she points out that he may have been brought to the *Chronicle* by his friend John Dyer Collier.[41] Ayrton's first review was that of March 26, 1813, in which he strongly inveighed against the King's management for mounting a Pucitta opera instead of one of the many neglected masterpieces available. His prose style was strong and clear—always to the point, which was often incisive but rarely witty. He was generally upbeat on audiences; he often sharply condemned Rossini's operas; and he skillfully handled the musical and historical background on operas, though he never indulged in technical terms. Ayrton was especially alert to librettos and condemned "those extravagancies in which Italian Opera too commonly abound" (Feb. 28, 1820). (See appendix 2 for an extract of an Ayrton review.) The advent of Ayrton's reviewing reveals a sharp upturn in the preceding period in the *Chronicle*, and by mid-1826 their criticism fell into the competent hands of John Payne Collier (see below).

English opera criticism. Beginning in 1785 the English opera reviews in the surviving numbers of the *Chronicle* were much more frequent than those on Italian opera. There is no doubt that they were written by the regular dramatic critic — some early reviews even show some antipathy toward Italian opera. They were also generally longer, for they usually included a long discussion of the plot. Though triteness crept in, these reviews were surprisingly well written; they were witty on occasion and dealt carefully with the music and the singers. Most reviews were favorable — see especially that for *Lodoïska* (1794) — but occasionally negative criticism also appeared. Sometimes an accompanying song was included — a practice that continued into the 1820s. In style the reviews from 1785 to 1796 were consistent and written largely by one critic — Perry's coeditor, James Gray, who died in 1796 (Christie, p. 316). They were the product of a "learned and sensible man" and an "able writer" (Taylor, I, 238).

Reviews from 1800 to 1805 show a different hand; they were written by John Campbell — later Lord Campbell — who was then a young law student (C. H. Gray). Of Scottish ancestry, he had attended St. Andrews, came to London in 1798, and wrote briefly on literature for the *Oracle*. Robert Spankie, then editor of the *Chronicle*, hired him in 1800 when he entered Lincoln's Inn. By 1802 he was also doing some court reporting (*Life*, I, 65–67). These reviews were on the whole longer than those of his predecessor; they were also well written and on occasion speculated on such matters as John Bull's attitudes toward foreigners and on the problems of operas as mere vehicles for the music. Campbell was capable of sharply negative criticism, though he displayed no antiopera bias and gave fine details on the dramas; he was, however, quite weak on music and singing.

We find some triteness in the reviews of 1806 and 1807. Beginning with a sharply negative review of *Kais* in mid-1807, however, we find another strong critic writing for the *Chronicle*. This is probably the work of John Dyer Collier (1762–1825), who had met financial reverses in his wool trade business and about 1793–94 turned to letters, moving into the Lamb and Coleridge circles. After a stint on the *Monthly Register* and the *Critical Review*, he came to the *Times* in 1804 and after a few years there, began writing for the *Chronicle* about 1809. It is possible that he held the post of drama critic there until 1818 when he left London, though occasionally reviews by others, including Hazlitt in 1813–14, were also published.[42] Collier's reviews were characterized by the best writing yet in the *Chronicle*: careful attention to detail — on music and singing as well as on the drama — and a flexible critical stance capable of strong censure as well as praise. Only rarely did he dwell on broad problems such as the character of national taste in music (1817). He was quick to condemn operas that were mere vehicles to music, but he was sensitive to the intent and special appeal of some productions, such as Thomas Moore's *M. P.*, which was a "delightful trifle."

He was succeeded by a less competent hand. The reviews of this writer, beginning about 1818, were unusually brief and generally weak on music and singing. The quality of writing was on the whole mediocre and reflected conditions under editor Black cited above. This writer (perhaps there was more than one) lasted until mid-1826.

But there is no doubt that subsequent reviews—through 1830—were written by a single and highly gifted critic. Not only was the writing competent—it had a distinct literary flavor and was spiced with wit—but very careful attention was paid to all aspects of the opera, including music and singing. These reviews are undoubtedly the work of Collier's son, John Payne Collier (1789–1883), who followed his father's footsteps. (See appendix 2 for an extract from one of his reviews.) He had been appointed by John Walter II, to succeed Collier's father at the *Times* sometime before 1809 (probably 1807) and remained there until about 1820, when he had a disagreement with the editor (Barnes) and, like his father, switched to the *Chronicle*, writing parliamentary debates and leading articles, and then turning to dramatic and literary criticism (Bourne, II, 14, 67). He had already served as foreign correspondent for them in 1813–15; in 1816–17 he contributed articles to the *Critical Review*. During the Victorian years he made a name for himself as a Shakespearean scholar; he remained with the *Chronicle* until 1847.

Of the dailies, only the *Times* gave the *Chronicle* any competition, and the latter's criticism of both Italian and English operas is, in my opinion, generally superior to that of the *Times*.

Morning Post (1772–1937)

This journal was established by twelve proprietors, including John Wheble as publisher and John Bell, who later for many years edited his own *Bell's Weekly Messenger*. William Bate (later Dudley) was editor of the *Morning Post*, and his opinions reflected the leisure class of the fashionable West End.[43] But they also rendered the journal a "retailer of coarse gossip" and "a shameless organ of the King's party" (Bourne, I, 222). The *Post's* theatrical criticism was important from the beginning and was written mainly by Bate himself (Gray). (As we shall see, Bate later became a successful playwright.) Garrick made some contributions, as noted earlier, and Hindle (pp. 51–52) believes that Joseph Richardson, one of the proprietors and another successful playwright, also wrote some of the early criticism. In any event Bate was removed from the scene by a libel against the Duke of Richmond, and when he got out of jail, about 1780,++ he began another newspaper, the *Morning Herald*. At the *Post* he was supplanted for some years by William Jackson, a "very able writer" (Taylor, II, 266) who was in turn succeeded by John Taylor, who served two years as editor and dramatic critic. Still another writer, C. F. Badini—occasional librettist at the King's Theatre—may have written some of the reviews about 1784; he was probably brought there by his friend Bell.

But the paper went into a decline, probably because of its politics, and in 1795 Daniel and Peter Stuart bought it and proceeded to divest it of its "ferocious politics" (Hindle, p. 77). The Stuarts soon claimed independence for the paper, now Whiggish, and induced many men of literature to make contributions. But the Stuarts sold the paper for considerable profit in 1803, and it once more began to decline. By 1819 it had become "extremely Tory" (Hindle, pp. 43, 68–69), yet it still had a circulation of 4,500—more than any other newspaper at the time (Andrews, I, 227).

Documentation of the paper's coverage and reviews is most difficult owing to the scattered nature of surviving numbers in our period before 1795 and after 1804. But we can determine that in 1795 the paper had but one review of the King's Theatre and meager coverage of the playhouses—they were generally brief and trivial. Beginning in 1798 much more attention was being paid to the theatres, but, despite other changes made by the Stuarts, these reviews continued to be quite weak. Out of twenty-odd reviews of the King's from then until 1805, for example, less than half a dozen have any real value. Most of them, appearing under the rubric "The Fashionable World," showed more interest in the boxholders than in the performances. Reviews of English opera did fare somewhat better; there was even some negative criticism, and a few were well written and fairly lengthy, yet even in these reviews there was little criticism of the music and singing.

Morning Herald (1780–1869)

As noted above this journal was edited for some years by Bate, who continued to stress the fashionable and who had shifted his political sympathies from the King to the Prince of Wales (one A. Chalmers was a later editor). The *Herald* had some influence, but its circulation was only 1,500 in 1820; this increased to 5,000 by 1830, when it became a bit too liberal for the Tories, but gained considerable influence. Inspection of scattered numbers during 1785–1807 and 1822–23 indicates rather poor theatrical coverage in the early years, with many unreviewed premieres in both English and Italian opera; moreover, the writing is generally rather trite, and its pronounced emphasis on the attendance of the upper orders shows an appeal to the fashionable. By 1821, however, the right-wing *British Stage* called it the best daily, and the 1822–23 reviews of both English and Italian opera do show much improvement.

Public Advertiser (1752–1794)

Among the older newspapers, this journal carried excellent theatrical criticism in the 1770s and 1780s under the editorship of Henry Sampson Woodfall, brother of "Memory" Woodfall, who may have written some of it. Charles Este as "Clio" and George Steevens,[45] who wrote reviews between 1780 and 1794 (when it merged with the *Oracle*), were outstanding critics for the journal. Gray states that by 1792 it had the best theatrical criticism of the dailies, and Bourne (I, 219) found that the paper exhibited "careful and unusually intelligent dramatic criticism." Certainly many of their reviews of the King's collected by Petty confirm their strength in the early 1780s.

Oracle, Gazetteer, and Courier

Under various titles in different periods (see the bibliography), the *Oracle* was established in 1789 as a rival to the *World*, edited by E. Topham. Conducted for a time by James Boaden (1762–1839), who was also a playwright—his first successful musical piece was produced at Covent Garden in 1793—the *Oracle* carried some of his fine criticism of operas under the pseudonym of "Thetis." Charles Este also reviewed opera for the *Oracle*, probably between 1794 and 1796, as well as for the *Times* (see below). Other reviews of this rather scattered publication were poorly organized, yet some managed to convey much honest observation.

The *Daily Gazetteer* (1735–97) was edited from 1783 to 1789 by James Perry and had some good reviews of both Italian and English opera in the late 1780s and 1790s but their criticism was quite uneven in quality and their coverage rather poor.

The *Courier and Evening Gazette* (1798–1842) was edited briefly by Perry. It became a leading Tory paper under T. G. Street in 1809 (Baer, p. III) and achieved some prominence under the ownership of Daniel Stuart. But many of the reviews were merely reprints of the morning papers; indeed, as it is possible that all their reviews were borrowed, we cannot characterize the reviewing.

[Daily] Universal Register (1785–1787) and the Times (1788–)

John Walter I (1738–1812), who inaugurated the *Register*, found the *Times* a more appropriate title three years later. He justified his aim to make the paper "a complete chronicle of accurate and interesting news" (Bourne, I, 258), for the *Times* had by far the best coverage of all the newspapers. In 1789 he was imprisoned for sixteen months and fined £250 for libels against the Duke of York. But he was no independent, and he actually "respected" theatrical puffs as sources of revenue.[46] Joseph Farington stated in his *Diary* (I, 156) that Harris, manager of Covent Garden Theatre, paid Walter an annuity of £100 so "that his Play House will be recommended in that paper." Moreover, the paper fell off badly; in 1797 circulation had dropped to 1700.

But it soon revived after 1803 when Walter II (1776–1847) filled his father's shoes and immediately strove for the paper's political independence. He deplored his father's attitude on puffery—a shift that nearly severed their relationship—and "consistently managed the theatrical criticism of the *Times* for seven or eight years" (*History*, I, 88). He also abjured free tickets from playhouse managers. It is even possible he wrote some criticism himself—he was himself author of at least one play. In general the paper supported the Tory government until 1812 and did not move toward open opposition until the Manchester Massacre of 1819. Much of its strength lay in its staffing, which was notable by 1810. Walter II was also successful in introducing a system of packet boats that could penetrate the Continental blockade to bring in early news of the Napoleonic wars, and Henry Crabb Robinson became an expert foreign correspondent for the journal. Under the editorship of Thomas Barnes and Edward Sterling, the *Times* increased its political clout, gained further independence, and moved toward its later reputation as the "Thunderer." By the introduction of a steam press in 1814, it was able to increase its circulation, which for a time far surpassed its closest competitors.

Italian opera criticism. In 1785 Charles Este also began reviewing Italian and English opera for the *Register* and continued with the *Times* more or less regularly to about 1792. (They were quite possibly unpaid contributions—a not uncommon practice in earlier years.) His Shandean style is instantly recognizable, not only for his penchant for using dashes for periods but mainly for his characteristic wit and tongue-in-cheek observations. True, his reviews were uneven and marred by occasional triteness, but he usually made his points deftly and could sometimes be quite negative. Best of all was his ability to convey his enjoyment of opera—something that far more professional reviewers who succeeded him could not do.

Critic A, who covered opera in 1787–88 and occasionally in 1790–91, was a straight reporter who gave fair coverage of performances but was much too brief; yet he sometimes provided interesting details and favored music that, as he stated, "did not cover the voice." It is difficult to characterize most reviews for 1789–98; undoubtedly they were the work of more than one writer. They were generally brief and trite, though there were exceptions.

A new critic—call him critic B—appeared in 1796 and wrote until 1805, with a few late reviews up to 1808. He produced demonstrably better writing than the foregoing critic, with longer reviews and attention to plots, toward which he could be quite harsh. He occasionally had good detail and even paid attention to the scenery. It is not likely that John Dyer Collier wrote these; he was at the *Times* from about 1804 to 1807, mainly as a law reporter; nor do our sources cite any dramatic criticism by him for this journal. Trite reviews do show up now and then during these years—no doubt by other hands.

A new critic appeared suddenly in 1810 and stayed until early 1812. His writing is excellent—better than B's—and he is the first *Times* critic to bring a measure of competence to its Italian opera reviews. Most of them were medium to very long; there were intelligent comparisons between prima donnas, and the plots were frequently criticized. He gave considerable attention to the acting as well as the singing and provided fine details on other parts of the performances. He gave thorough coverage to all the King's performances, including revivals. Yet his judgments on some composers seem inconsistent and even perverse. This criticism was undoubtedly written by the Reverend George Croly, an Irish Protestant graduate of Trinity College who came to London in 1810 and did some writing for the *Times*. He also contributed to the *Literary Gazette*. Henry Crabb Robinson thought him talented and eloquent but wanting in delicacy and discrimination of judgment—a sentiment I find unduly harsh. We do know that Croly left the *Times* about 1814 and that he was drama critic for Stoddart's *New Times* after the latter broke with Walter in 1817.

In 1809 Barron Field introduced Thomas Barnes (1785–1841) to Walter. Along with Leigh Hunt, Lamb, and Coleridge, Barnes was a "Blue Coat boy"—a graduate of Christ Hospital academy—and an early member of Thomas Hill's open house gatherings of literati. Field's father had close connections with that school, and Field was already writing theatricals for the *Times* (see below); Barnes succeeded him in that capacity about 1810. In 1811 Barnes was reporting on Parliament, and in 1812 he wrote a series of literary portraits for John Scott's new weekly, the *Champion* (see below), and later produced a number of "Parliament Portraits" and reviews for

Hunt's *Examiner*. Barnes's reviews of the King's Theatre, which began about 1812, reflected his strong personality. He was the first, after Henry Robertson, to bring an essay-like approach to Italian opera criticism. He devoted nearly the whole of some reviews to a single theme, such as a comparison of Mozart and Rubens or a discussion of England and the arts. Most of his reviews were quite long, and he was particularly excellent on singers.

In 1817 Barnes was appointed editor by Walter, a post he held the rest of his life. He made the *Times* the dominant London daily, in part because he took great pains to hire good writers.[47] One of them was Thomas Massa Alsager (1779–1846), whose family owned a clothworking trade in Southwark. The *History of the "Times"* (I, 415) states merely that Alsager joined the paper as city correspondent in 1817 and that by 1821 he had become an expert on the money market; there is no doubt that the *Times* saw him primarily as a financial writer. But music was always important in his life. As David B. Levy states, Alsager had an acute musical sensibility.[48] In 1832 he gave, at his home, the first English performance of Beethoven's *Missa Solemnis*, and in his later years he did much to champion the music of the later Beethoven. He was a good friend of Ayrton and Hunt.

Levy has positively identified a few of his reviews (i.e., April 14 and 16, 1817; May 17, 1817; and June 10, 1834), and stylistic comparison of these reviews with other anonymous reviews in between these dates suggests that Alsager did, in fact, write most of them. The major improvement Alsager brought to his reviews was an increased emphasis on the music, now discussed with more intelligence and significance. His reviews were also longer (by 1819 the *Times* was printing all its reviews in small type), and he showed a strong interest in all details of performances. Though his writing was excellent, his prose style was not in any sense literary, and he seldom attempted essay-like passages. He was a judicious writer, capable of strong support or sharp rebukes, but on the whole I find him a bit too easygoing on the singers, in comparison with his fellow critics on the *Chronicle*. Excerpts from one of his reviews may be found in appendix 2.

English opera criticism. Early reviews (1785–87) of English opera were quite uneven in quality. There was a good deal of triteness and they were rather short, but now and then one was fairly well written, including a fine tribute to William Shield's music and a very negative review of playwright John O'Keeffe.

From early 1787 to mid-1792, and including one review in late 1785, the reviews were written by Charles Este, whose writing we have already discussed in Italian opera criticism. In his English opera criticism, he usually paid little attention to the plots, though on occasion he was quite negative on them. He did give attention to characters and situations but was often rather trite on the performers.

Aside from a change in style, a new critic—call him critic C—who reviewed from 1792 to 1794, gave much more attention to opera plots, which he often found wanting in point and sentiment. Though he was weak on the music, he did occasionally have good details on the singing. Reviews in late 1794 and especially 1795 were a mixed lot—probably by several hands. Many were quite trivial and most were brief, though a few were mildly negative.

Reviews from 1796 to 1806—apparently the work of one critic (call him critic D)—were generally longer, better written, and showed a strong interest in plot and dialogue, toward which he could be sharply negative. Critic D also objected to the trite characters found in English operas. He tended to scant the music and performers in his early reviews but was much improved later on. Possibly these reviews were the work of critic B, the critic of Italian opera for the *Times* during this period (the styles are similar), or possibly they were produced by Walter II.

New winds of journalism were evident by 1805. Barron Field (1786–1840), another Blue Coat boy who became well acquainted with the Lambs and Hunts and their literary circles, was appointed to the *Times* that year, and the *History* (I, 89–91) cites Hunt's influence on him about that time. It is not clear, however, whether he began writing theatricals before 1807; several of them can be identified as his that year, as well as three in late 1808 and one in 1809, when he, like Campbell, resigned from the paper and began his studies at the Inner Temple; he was called to the bar in 1814. He also contributed essays to Hunt's *Reflector* in 1811.

Meanwhile, Hunt wrote two reviews of English opera for the *Times* in 1807—August 14 and 17—while William Hazlitt wrote several more in October, November, and early 1808. What these reviews displayed in common was a command of writing skill far superior to that of previous critics and a very strong emphasis on the essay style. But several of Hazlitt's "reviews" were merely excuses to discuss the decline of the drama. Playwrights like Cherry, Reynolds, Morton, and Dibdin—as well as melodrama in general—were severely castigated. Accordingly, little attention was paid to the music or other details of the performance.

Times criticism in late 1809 and 1810 tended to be brief and rather trivial. But in 1811 and 1812 several good reviews appeared. Though there was little reference to the music, a number were sharply negative on plots and songs, and several had essay-type passages similar to Barnes's Italian opera criticism; I believe he was also writing some English opera criticism for the *Times* as well during these years.

In 1813 and 1814 reviews again tended to be brief and weak, but in 1815 a new hand was in evidence. Reviews tended to be longer and better written, though not in any sense literary. All aspects of the performance were noted and excellent details provided on singing and acting. The music also received adequate emphasis. Occasionally the author touched on wider themes relevant to the occasion, but in general his attention was concentrated on the performances, for which he provided good coverage. It is true that Hazlitt wrote numerous reviews of English operas between April and December of 1817, but I believe that the reviews just described were the work of Edward Sterling (1773–1847), and except for 1817 they continued from 1815 right on to 1830 and later. Sterling, another Irish Protestant and quondam reformist, was, like Hunt, a "highly independent" writer (D.N.B.), and his liberalism is evident in an 1822 review of *Maid Marian*, with its scorn for the "un-Holy Alliance." He may have submitted some theatrical criticism to the *Times* following Croly's departure, but he was not on the staff there until about 1813 (*History*, I, 144, 170). By 1829 he was also writing leaders, one of which won the epithet "The Thunderer" for the paper. He left the *Times* in 1840 after a disagreement with Barnes. Excerpts from one of his reviews will be found in appendix 2.

The *True Briton* (1793–1803) was owned by John Taylor (1757–before 1832), an oculist by profession (appointed to the Prince of Wales, no less), who was much more interested in journalism and the theatre. As noted earlier, he edited and wrote reviews for the *Post* for two years, and he also for a time owned the evening *Sun* (1792–1876). In later years he also wrote "Sketches" of theatrical figures for the *Mirror* and he may have contributed to the *London*. (Stylistically, the sketches are not unlike the undocumented miscellany that fills his autobiography.) Not surprisingly Taylor was politically conservative, and editors for the *Briton* included, besides himself, John Heriot and "John Gifford" (i.e., James R. Green), who founded the *Anti-Jacobin Review* (see below). The *True Briton*, which merged with the *Oracle and Daily Advertiser* in 1803, provided good coverage of the theatres, and now and then we come across exceptional reviews of ballet and English opera; but for the most part their criticism was trivial.

A few other dailies and even triweeklies occasionally carried useful opera criticism, though their coverage was usually scant.[49]

OTHER PERIODICALS

Weeklies were sometimes thought of, and referred to, as "weekly newspapers." Some were intended largely for rural distribution. Many carried features similar to the dailies, but there were far fewer ads. The weeklies were often more sharply political than newspapers and had numerous literary features and articles that found no space in the dailies. This greater degree of specialization among the weeklies brought a narrow focus congenial to those with special interests. The same could be said of the monthlies — the main difference here being that, as "magazines," they contained a much greater amount of literary and other material and had the space for very long articles. It should be pointed out, though, that despite the greater room in the weeklies and especially in the monthlies, reviews of performances in them were often not as long as those found in the newspapers, yet some, like the *London* and the *New Monthly*, were exceptions.

Accordingly, journals other than newspapers are discussed chronologically, except that they are divided into three categories depending on the amount and type of stage criticism they usually carried.

Periodicals on Literature and Drama

We have only minor interest in this category, since these journals usually carried no stage criticism at all. Some *did* carry reviews of printed English opera librettos; there must have been, therefore, a fair number of readers who actually enjoyed reading these librettos (or at least reviews of them), though most of them were meant to serve merely as "vehicles" for musicals. It is no wonder, then, that these librettos were often highly castigated by the literary reviewers for such publications. Some, like the *Anti-Jacobin Review and Magazine* (1798–1821), were obviously politically motivated,[50] and their reviews were quite hostile toward the librettos, but the *British Critic* (1793–1826), a strongly Tory journal that sometimes carried essays on music by John Wall Callcott, was among the best of this class on the theatre. This group also includes Ralph Griffith's leading and highly influential *Monthly Review* (1750–1844), for which the music historian Charles Burney wrote some criticism during its early years; the liberal *Monthly Magazine and British Register* (1796–1826), which was occasionally quite positive toward the librettos; and Thomas Christie's *Analytical Review* (1788–99), which attracted the revolutionary literati and which provided fair reviews: Thomas Busby wrote some of its criticism (Winesanker, p. 92), probably in the form of articles (no reviews of his have been identified in the numbers scanned). These monthlies, along with eight others as well as three weeklies and even some annuals — many of brief duration — also reviewed librettos.[51]

But a few literary journals did include some stage criticism of English operas along with their libretto reviews. Perhaps the most interesting was *Walker's Hibernian Magazine*, published in Dublin (1771–1811); they were not hostile toward opera and occasionally even published printed music for the songs in English operas, but their reviews were quite weak. There were some fair reviews in the right-wing *Satirist, or Monthly Musical Meteor* (1807–94) and in the *Critical Review* (1756–1817), which merged with the *Monthly Review*. The *New Lady's Magazine* (1782–95) even had some Italian opera reviews and an essay on Thomas Dibdin's musicals, written, perhaps, by his stepbrother, Charles Dibdin, who was an occasional critic for some journals. Two other short-lived monthlies complete this group: the *Literary Magazine and British Review* (1788–94) and the *Register of the Times* (1794–96). Though reviews garnered from some of these journals are included in appendix 10, only a few are useful enough to warrant reference in the text.

Periodicals on the Stage

A number of periodicals specialized largely or even exclusively in the theatres and regularly carried reviews of performances. Three of them were dailies—the *Theatrical Observer* (1821–30), the *Theatrical Examiner* (1823–31), and the *Tatler* (1830–32). The first two were issued in small, single sheets (later doubled), one side of which carried theatre playbills, and the other very brief reviews; they were intended to be taken to the theatre. Extant numbers of the *Theatrical Examiner* are too few to ascertain much of its character. Files for the *Theatrical Observer*, however, are complete, and they occasionally included reviews of the King's Theatre. Because space was limited, reviews sometimes carried over to two or three consecutive numbers; though brief, they were fairly well written and could be sharply critical, but much of the material dealt only with the performers. Discussion of the *Tatler*, which was written entirely by Hunt, is deferred to our account of him in connection with the *Examiner*. An excerpt from an essay in this journal may be found in appendix 2.[52]

The *Drama; or Theatrical [Pocket] Magazine* (1821–26), issued in a size convenient to take to the theatre, was short-lived. Their reviews of opera and ballet are surprisingly well written, with a refreshing spirit of humility (they cited their own "slight and imperfect notices"), and some of their comment is pungent and telling, but on the whole the "notices" are too brief to have much value for their period.

Although in some ways the writing in *The British Stage and Literary Cabinet* (1817–22), also short-lived, was rather weaker than that in the *Drama*, it provided much longer and more detailed reviews and included many very useful "Dramatic Sketches" of the performers, together with engraved likenesses of performers, playwrights, and composers. It also occasionally carried printed music, though its reviews in this department were trivial. Until 1820 it was edited and mostly written by Thomas Kenrick, and it provided strong coverage of Italian opera and ballet as well as of the playhouses, and it even included news and reviews of the provincial theatres. At first, Kenrick's reviews were weakened by much trite praise, but he or another reviewer soon developed in judgment and became capable of making nice distinctions. He showed no bias in his reviews of Italian opera; they were not as full as those of the *Times*, for example, but some included detailed observations. But by far the most important journals in this class were the *Mirror* and the *Inquisitor*.

Monthly Mirror **(1795–1811).** What the *Mirror* primarily reflected was an interest in both the London major and minor theatres and the provincial playhouses; not only were performances there reviewed, but an article profiling a performer or dramatist appeared as the lead story every month. The journal was launched by Thomas Hill (1760–1840), bibliophile and bon vivant. At his Sydenham home he gave famous dinners for a wide circle of friends including Thomas Campbell, Edward DuBois, Barron Field, Cyrus Redding, the Hunts, Theodore Hook, comedian Charles Mathews, and many others.

Most important of these to Hill was DuBois (or Bois) (1774–1850), who became the first editor of the *Mirror* and who wrote most of its reviews. For each theatre every month there was listed, by day, all the productions, including benefits and any changes of importance. (There were also reviews on some books and printed librettos.) From the first number it was obviously written by a man fully at home in the theatre. DuBois got his early experience writing theatricals for Perry in the *Chronicle*. For a time he had Theodore Hook as assistant; Thomas Campbell also wrote for the journal.

DuBois's early reviews tended to be quite brief and occasionally trivial, but after 1800 they strengthened considerably. Their brevity is due in part to a lack of interest in plots, which were not treated in any detail. Instead they danced around the operas rather than plodding through them item by item as most dailies did, thereby providing much delightful wit and insight though at times sacrificing much relevant detail. Reviews were of course quite often negative; they showed some of the bias of literary reviewers toward operas but no strong antipathy. DuBois impugned spectacles generally, which he felt robbed dramas of any importance, and he often touched the heart of a problem in a pithy phrase or sentence. He was against dullness anywhere—even in the music. As Hunt pointed out (*Autobiography*, pp. 21–22), DuBois "had no faculty for gravity" though he was capable of being an excellent scholar. He "held his editorship . . . very cheap"—half his jokes "were written for his friends, and must have mystified the uninitiated."

The *Mirror*'s memoirs and sketches were written by John Taylor, who, as we have seen, edited and wrote for the *Post*, the *True Briton*, and other journals. Written in a lively manner, they contained much information on playwrights, actors, and singers. Taylor continued his work for Hill after the *Mirror* was absorbed by the *Theatrical Inquisitor*.

Italian opera was seldom covered by the *Mirror*, though there were reviews of the King's in 1797, 1800, and 1806; however, they were very brief. By 1800 we find a few very long reviews including much detail on plot, but they did not last long, and DuBois's facile hand soon reappeared. His witty comments on composer William Shield in 1807 were picked up and used by Hunt in the *Examiner* the following year.

***Theatrical Inquisitor and Monthly Mirror* (1812–1820).** Since the style and contents, including the sketches, remained the same for some time, I find no reason for the change in title aside from a possible desire to emphasize the journal's largely exclusive attention to the stage, or perhaps it simply reflected a change in management. But gradually changes there were. In 1813 we find a review signed "H," and in 1814 one signed by "Ed." and one by "D." The reviews were also changing style: they were much longer, included discussions of plots, and introduced essay-type passages that were not, however, well integrated with the rest of the review. We note a particular emphasis on the performers that continues through 1820. Also, beginning in 1817, there was a sharp increase in the number of reviews of Italian opera. Thus it is impossible to know who was writing the very uneven reviews after 1814. Some may have been by John Litchfield, a later editor on the *Mirror*. Certainly DuBois was not forgotten by Hill, who vested all his stock in his editor, making him a wealthy man. In 1821 this journal was absorbed by another, the monthly *London Magazine*, but the form and contents changed radically and it will be treated separately below.

Periodicals on Literature and the Stage

The best reviews in our period came from a rather large group of periodicals that specialized in *both* literature and the stage.[53] They were about evenly divided between weeklies and monthlies. Because writers from two musical journals also wrote for some of these, they have been included, chronologically, in this section.

***European Magazine* (1782–1826).** Founded and edited by James Perry, who, as we have seen, became an able editor of the *Morning Chronicle*, the

European provided an "extraordinary range" of literary, historical, and miscellaneous subjects, including articles on music by Thomas Busby and Dr. Samuel Arnold.[54] But this brilliance was short-lived, as Perry remained with the journal only one year. Under the heading "Theatrical Journal," good coverage of the playhouses, including English opera, was provided, but the quality was abysmal. From 1789 to 1796, for example, the reviews were brief, trite, and invariably positive. By 1808 there was somewhat more detailed criticism and occasional reference to performers, but not until 1813 was there any negative criticism at all. In 1823–24 there were reviews of the King's, but most were copies of the *Times*. A new series was announced for 1825, and some good reviews appeared, but the next year the journal was absorbed by the *Monthly Magazine and British Register*.

***Bell's Weekly Messenger* (1796–1896).** The earliest weekly of this type—periodicals on literature and the stage—was the long-lived *Bell's Weekly Messenger*, which had a large country distribution. It was launched by John Bell, a book publisher, and John Edmund Cox; it was edited by Bell. A man of "meagre education," Bell nevertheless had great taste (Andrews), and he no doubt wrote some of its theatrical reviews. Sometime between 1804 and 1808 C. F. Badini, quondam librettist at the King's Theatre, was editor for Bell and very likely wrote much of its criticism. Surviving numbers from 1804 to 1814 have reviews of only the playhouses. Reviews from 1808 to 1810 were quite good—thoughtful and detailed. But reviews from 1811 to 1814 were briefer and less competent; critiques on the music were generally trivial.

***Examiner* (1808–1881).** The best known of the weeklies, at least under the direction of the brothers John (1775–1848) and Leigh Hunt (1784–1859) from 1808 to 1821, was the Sunday *Examiner*. John usually wrote the leading articles and served as general manager. Leigh wrote the "Theatrical Examiner," "The Round Table," and other literary features. A third brother, Robert, reviewed art exhibitions.[55]

Both John and Leigh held radical political views and were frequently in trouble with the law. In 1812–13 they were imprisoned for a satirical attack on the Prince of Wales and had to rely on friends, such as Barnes and Hazlitt, to write the features and publish the journal. (Another "warm friend" who assisted Leigh Hunt at this time was James Perry of the *Chronicle*, who was himself under attack by the government.) The paper handily survived this difficulty, but by 1821 it was again in trouble. Leigh, in too ill health to survive another imprisonment, was invited to go to Italy both for his health and to edit a new journal, the *Liberal*, which would include contributions by Percy Bysshe Shelley and Lord Byron (both then in Italy) in addition to himself and others. But Leigh had scarcely set foot in Genoa when Shelley was drowned at sea, and Byron soon left the Hunt family in the lurch economically by enlisting in the cause of Greek independence. It was several years before the Hunts could return to London, and by that time there was no place for Leigh on the *Examiner*. Eventually he made a rather precarious living in journalism, mostly writing and editing journals for others. Meanwhile John Hunt was again imprisoned for libel, and again the journal survived his absence. But in 1830 he sold his shares in the paper.

Despite his radical politics, Hunt was a product of the middle class. Son of liberal Unitarians and educated at Christ Hospital, he displayed wide literary interests early, and while yet a boy he published a volume of poetry of some worth. By 1804 he was making contributions to the weekly *Traveller*, and by 1805 he was writing dramatic criticism for his brother's weekly *News*. In 1807 he published *Critical Essays*, probably based largely on his *News* criticism (none of it survives). In 1811 he published a long satirical poem that created much ill will for him among the right-wingers. By the advent of the *Examiner* he was becoming well known—a member of Lamb's literary circle and of Vincent Novello's musical circle. Haydon[56] thought that by 1816 Hunt had already "raised the ranks of newspapers" by his example, and Bourne (I, 378) states that the *Examiner* "at once took ranks above all the other weekly periodicals [there were thirteen in 1814], and contained such careful and scholarly writing as only appeared occasionally . . . in the best of the daily papers."

Hunt insisted on the absolute independence of criticism. Despite his politics, he had planned for criticism of Italian opera from its inception. For several years it was conducted as an unpaid contribution in the form of a series of letters written by his friend Henry Robertson, whom he had met about 1800 and who by 1823 was treasurer of Covent Garden theatre (he remained there most of his life). Robertson, a tenor, and his brother Francis, a bass, were—along with Hunt, Shelley, and others—part of the musical evenings at the Novellos. Robertson's coverage of the King's Theatre, very full from 1808 to 1810, dropped to two reviews each in 1811 and 1812 and to one each in 1813 and 1814. With his first review he made an astonishing improvement in the criticism of Italian opera and ballet in London periodicals: nothing like the fullness and depth of reporting had yet been seen. Though lacking Hunt's remarkable literary and critical talents, he had his own essay-like style—straightforward, blunt, persistent, and thorough—which he brought to bear on the operas and performances. During the early years, for example, he roundly condemned the trivial operas that Madame Catalani introduced at the King's, and though on occasion he did praise her singing, he was the only reviewer who dared deliver negative criticism on this darling of the upper orders.

During Hunt's imprisonment and subsequent illness, his friend Thomas Barnes, as noted earlier, wrote reviews of the King's for the *Examiner*; he, too, proved a competent critic, though his essay style sometimes took him afield from the performances. Intermittently, from 1814 to 1817, William Hazlitt (1778–1830) also wrote a few reviews of the King's for the journal. A man of letters, like Hunt, he wrote for many publications during his rather brief lifetime—including the *Chronicle* and the *Times*, as we have seen—as well as the *Atlas* and others. He was a "good hater," and his highly charged prose vented itself against many persons and ideas—mainly political. As an essayist-reviewer on opera and ballet, however, his criticism often lacked relevance to the performances: he never seemed comfortable among the upper orders at the King's, for instance, and would rather pursue such topics as the musical taste of the English people than the performance at hand. His best criticism was for the *Atlas* (see below).

Beginning in 1817 and continuing with excellent coverage through 1819, Hunt reviewed Italian opera, along with the dramatic criticism of the playhouses he had been providing since 1808. Apparently ill health prevented his writing any review of the King's in 1820 (Robertson returned for a final contribution that year), and he wrote only one review—his last for the journal—in 1821. By 1817 he felt the new musical prominence of the King's, with its resounding premiere of *Don Giovanni* followed by exciting new operas by Rossini, was now too important to be left to other hands. Unlike Hazlitt, Hunt responded warmly to the King's Theatre and its audiences, and his vigorous prose gave life to the performances and performers as no one had before. He was fully capable of dealing with the new music, and his penetrating comment extended even to the inner nature of some characters, especially that of Don Giovanni. He was of course not without faults: like other writers he was at first put off by Rossini's "borrowing" from Paisiello's *Barbiere*, though he rectified this attitude in later reviews. In general he was more favorable toward Rossini than other critics.

Hunt's reviews of English opera offered very extensive coverage and brought to his task both wit and humor usually missing in other critics (the *Mirror* was an exception). Foremost among the journalists of his time in literary criticism, he was of course concerned by the direction of the stage and its deleterious effect on English drama. Yet he harbored no strong prejudices against English opera per se, and if he frequently had to render negative judgments on many of them, they were not unrelieved by insights into the genuine values such works could occasionally demonstrate.

In both his Italian and English opera reviews Hunt was quite capable of dealing with general ideas in powerful prose pssages, yet he seldom did so at the expense of the salient details in the work under consideration. But his usual critical manner eschewed analysis; it rested on a series of loosely related perceptions imaginatively developed; the impression he captures has a vitality and strength that lie beyond the art of analysis. His writing illustrates a thorough command of tone and style, which he perfectly accommodated to his shifts in subject. His prose is punctuated by wit, clarity, and brilliance. He always kept his readers in view though he was never condescending. He brought to the *Examiner* a natural musical aptitude, a conviviality wedded to utilitarian ideals, a broad cultural commitment, and a journalistic competence that gave him exceptional qualifications for the role of opera critic.[57]

Hunt's criticism for the short-lived monthly *Companion* (1828) is somewhat disappointing: he buried his critiques in long, rather rambling essays that drained them of much of their usual wit and panache. But in 1830 he inaugurated the *Tatler*, called "A Daily Journal of Literature and the Stage," though in fact it concentrated almost wholly on the stage. His criticism regained its wonted power: that he could sustain it for two years singlehandedly is a remarkable testimony to his energy and gives the lie to Dickens's caricature of him as Skimpole in *Bleak House* (1853). Again and again we find him confuting the settled opinions of even the best critics on Italian and English operas and performers in the 1820s by the skill, the aptness, and the logic of his penetrating comparisons.

John Hunt was fortunate in the men he chose to carry on the "Theatrical Examiner" following Leigh's departure for Italy. From 1822 until February of 1828 the King's Theatre reviews were signed by X. (Hazlitt undertook some Theatrical Examiners in March of that year but they ceased by June.) X came back for two more reviews in 1829, then dropped out once more. From his first review of April 1822, X shows himself a worthy follower of Robertson and Hunt. He adapted an essay-type style to many of the reviews with marks of ready wit and a trenchant dismissal of works and performers that were inferior. He was generally unhappy with Rossini, especially in his melodramatic operas for which his "tricksome passages" were unsuitable. Indeed, few operas during this period pleased him greatly except for revivals of Mozart—if well produced. He often found space for comments on ballet and sometimes devoted a whole column to it. He was also capable of changing his opinion, finding later revivals of Rossini's *Otello* much more effective than the premiere. He was usually apt in his scrutiny of the cast, with a wide range of positive or negative reactions carefully grounded in particular observations. Thomas Alsager has been suggested as the author of the X contributions, but he had an altogether different style and his attitude toward Meyerbeer's *Crociato*, for example, was quite opposed to that of X.

Reviews of the King's from April 1829 to December 1830 were unsigned, but the six examples we have were also quite competent and somewhat similar to X's work. On one occasion he was liberal enough to cite for his readers "a beautiful as well as scientific critique" on Cimarosa's *Matrimonio Segreto* in the *Atlas*.

Meanwhile the reviews of English operas as well as dramas were the work of a critic known as Q, and they extended from May 1822 through December 1827. Hazlitt, who had contributed a review on May 7, 1826, took over the dramatic criticism from March 23 to June 25 of 1828, though most of his contributions were more essays than reviews. (A few unsigned reviews appeared early in 1823.) In any event, possibly Q was miffed by the intrusion, for he wrote no more. Q's reviews were on the whole long—sometimes very long, necessary in part because of his interest in plots (usually set in smaller type). He seldom attempted an essay approach, yet his writing is quite good—sometimes excellent. His remarks on singers are particularly fine, and he often has competent comments on the music (including overtures) and songs that are well supported by detailed observations. (See appendix 2 for an extract from his criticism.)

From March to June of 1828, Hazlitt again reviewed for the *Examiner*, providing many fine, essay-type passages and displaying his usual wit and pungency. Excellent reviews followed in 1828, 1829, and 1830, but they are not collected in the P. P. Howe edition and may not be by Hazlitt.

Champion (1814–1822). Another Sunday paper with somewhat radical interests was the *Champion*—"Late Drakard's Paper"—that had many of the features of the *Examiner*, but their reviews suffered from a lack of direction. The proprietors were S. Clayton Jennings and, from 1814 to 1817, R. D. Richards. In 1818 when their Italian-opera reviewing commenced, Jennings's place was taken by John Thelwall. There was a column for "Review of Literature, Arts, Amusements, &c, &c," and reviews of all theatres, including the King's, were placed under "Dramatic Review." But coverage of these theatres was rather scant for most of the years; moreover, attributions are so scattered as to render any authorship of most of them questionable. From 1814 to 1818, for instance, only one English opera review, in 1815, was signed "G"; other reviews in the same number were not identified at all (Hazlitt contributed one review on November 6, 1814). In

1819 we find an article under "Parliamentary Reform" signed "J. T."—undoubtedly Thelwall—and his initials follow one review in 1819 and one in 1821, both on English operas.

Contents of reviews merely add to the puzzle. A King's review in 1815, for instance, cited the lack of musical taste in English audiences (essay-type approaches are found in some of these reviews); in the same year, G wrote a long essay on Italian versus English opera, upholding the practice of spoken dialogue in the latter. Much the same approach is made in another review of English opera in 1816, which would argue for the same authorship, but the review carred no initials at all. The two reviews by Thelwall were very well written, but so were many of the other reviews from 1819 to 1822 that also contained good details on the performances. But side by side with these were others that were inferior.

Literary Gazette (1817–1862). In contrast to the politically liberal *Examiner* and *Champion*, the mildly right-wing weekly *Literary Gazette* was established by publisher Henry Colburn, with the assistance of William Jerdan in 1817. The emphasis of this journal was clearly on literature, and though some attention was given to the arts, they generally achieved only secondary importance (Langley). The journal was soon brought under the control of Jerdan, who remained coproprietor and sole editor from mid-1817 to December 1850. Indeed, Colburn remained proprietor only until 1827, when Jerdan's ultraconservatism offended him and he withdrew to assist in establishing the *Athenaeum* (see below). Jerdan did some of the writing for the *Gazette*, but most was solicited from outside contributors (see Langley, pp. 484–85).

He could hardly have done better than he did in calling on Richard Mackenzie Bacon (1775–1844) to review operas for 1817–18.[58] In 1817 he provided fine coverage of Italian opera, with seven reviews that ran from long to very long and that contained excellent writing. His style—clear, strong, and self-assured, with brief and pointed sentences interlarded with long, complex ones capable at times of achieving lofty rhetoric—corresponds very closely to that of his *Quarterly Musical* (see below) and, except in wit and in conveying the life of the performances, was comparable to Hunt's—even better in some of the details on performances. Most of his commentary was positive, but he was also capable of very acerbic criticism on both the music and the performances. He reviewed two English operas that year, but his criticism was very negative, as one might expect from a critic who often denounced the medium in the *Quarterly*. Yet in 1818 when he produced three reviews, he could be quite positive on two of Bishop's operas. That year he began the *Quarterly*, so it is understandable that his coverage for the *Gazette* suddenly dropped off, though by 1820 he was also contributing to the *London*. (For an excerpt from his criticism, see appendix 2.)

From mid-1818 to 1830, however, the coverage was generally poor and reviews of the King's became quite rare; there were none at all from 1828 to 1830. Reviews of English opera were also poor. They tended to be brief and at times trivial, and there was no particular consistency in style. There were, of course, exceptions, such as the excellent review of *Oberon* at Covent Garden in 1826 and Kramer's "tasteless" adaptation of Mozart's *Seraglio* in 1827. It is impossible to identify any of these reviewers. Thomas Billington, Thomas Greenwood, or a Miss Wilkinson, "who was a sometime help, as a musical critic," were possible musical contributors, but no doubt some were by Jerdan; he tells us that he produced reviews "critical of the arts" himself, though he did have "several able coadjutors."[59]

Quarterly Musical Magazine and Review (1818–1828). The *Quarterly Musical* was the first English journal of music to achieve a position of authority. It was edited by Bacon, who also contributed to the *Gazette* and the *London*. In it he displayed, according to Fuller-Maitland, "a remarkable critical faculty."[60] Its coverage of music was of course wider and much lengthier than that in the *Harmonicon* (see below), and it even contained some printed music. Each issue also provided a goodly number of articles submitted by unpaid correspondents. Bacon, incidentally, was not a musician, and he pointed out that he was unconnected with any musicians except through his publication (QMM, IV, 371). Yet he was catholic enough to include a contributed article on the weakness of reviews by amateurs! Bacon also for a time owned and edited the weekly *Norwich Mercury* (1797–1842), but he apparently had to depend on the assistance of English composer William Horsley (who probably also contributed a number of important reviews), his daughter Jane M., and musician Edward Holmes in writing the criticism of performances. (William Ayrton did a review of *Gazza Ladra* for the *Quarterly*, III, 252–63 — Langley.)

In its initial number Bacon deplored the want of "the real faculty of discrimination" in contemporary reviewing though the critics were "fully conversant with the murderous art of dealing out keen and cutting dispraise," from which he exempted only some critiques in the *Times*, *Chronicle*, and of course the *Gazette* — though even they were often "too vague and loose." But Bacon's criticism in the *Quarterly* was sometimes too rambling (his writing for the *Gazette* was tighter); moreover, he was quite capable of dispensing some sharply negative criticism himself.

The journal did not carry any reviews per se; the critiques were buried in articles such as "The State of Music in London," which contained one long, continuous narrative, or the "Public Establishments for Music in London," which was followed by comments on the "King's Theatre," and the like. Much of the criticism is also to be found on various articles on the singers—both those at the King's and those at the playhouses.

Although Bacon emphasized Italian opera productions in his journal, he did give some attention to English opera, which he disliked: "But after all, what is the English Opera? A jargon of speaking and singing, that depresses all sensibility rather than elevates the mind to any perception of the force of character or the kindling of sentiment" (VI [1824], 176–77). Yet he provided excellent critiques on the most important singers in the playhouses and even occasionally reviewed some of the more outstanding English operas on which he could sometimes be quite positive.

After a decade or so both the *Harmonicon* and the *Quarterly Musical* failed, "and English criticism followed the rest of English society into respectability" (N.G.).[61]

***London Magazine* (1820–1829).** Bad luck haunted the *London*[62] in later years, but for a time it outshone everything else. It was begun by Robert Baldwin and others as an attempt to provide "a genuinely impartial literary journal" (Langley, pp. 499–501); yet Baldwin chose the gifted John Scott (1783–1821)—who as noted above had edited the *Champion* and who was certainly a liberal—as editor. He drew together a fine group of writers whose contributions, particularly in literary criticism (about half the contents of each number), imparted a brilliance to the first year and a half of publication. Ironically, Scott had attacked the satiric scurrilities of the Tory *Blackwood's Edinburgh Magazine* and became embroiled in a controversy with its editor, John Gibson Lockhart; Scott was killed by a friend of Lockhart's in a duel in mid-1821. John Taylor and James Hessey took over the editing, but they had trouble building a readership.[63] Though some fine work continued to be published (Taylor stayed on until 1824), it was soon evident that the journal was in trouble and its quality slowly deteriorated. The appointment of Henry Southern as editor (1825–27) did little to stem the decline. By 1829 they wound up with a "journal of facts"—clearly a last gasp.

The *London*'s Italian opera criticism appeared in the "Report of Music" columns—a long (usually five- or six-page) article that also included reviews of concerts, oratorios, provincial music festivals, printed music (sometimes in a separate "New Music" column), and general information and gossip on the world of London music. All this was woven together in an essay-style report written with considerable musical sophistication. The essay form makes it difficult, at times, to identify specific productions, but it permitted a refreshing breadth of musical outlook into the various facets of operas and performances. Again Richard Mackenzie Bacon—whose capacity for work seems equal to that of Hunt—wrote the report from January 1820 to May 1824, in addition to his *Quarterly* journalism. In these reviews Bacon's attention to the plots varied considerably: sometimes there was no reference to them at all; elsewhere he had long accounts of and commentary on them and relatively little on the music. There was always close attention to the performers. As elsewhere Bacon displays spirited writing and, like Hunt, takes considerable pleasure in the performances — an element too often missing in other reviewers; yet he could be quite negative at times.

The coverage through 1825 was excellent, but it fell off sharply after this. After 1824 there were changes—to a single column per page format, with headings such as "Italian Opera" or "Opera" or "Music of the Month." There was also a hodgepodge of writing, musical gossip, and chitchat.

English opera was to be found under the heading "The Drama," though at first it was found under the broader heading, later dropped, of "General Reporter." This column was written in 1820 by Hazlitt. As against his critiques on straight drama, his reviews of English opera had weaknesses. His prose is of course solid and at times brilliant, and he took advantage of the essay style in this journal to render penetrating insights on much that he touched. But this was achieved at the cost of providing salient details on the operas under consideration. He was at times good on the singers, but he had little to say of the music and often ignored it altogether. Like Bacon he varied in his interest in plots, but unlike Bacon he seldom delivered negative reports on the operas; indeed, a few of his brief reviews border on the trivial.

After Hazlitt's departure, coverage of English opera continued to be strong, and beginning in 1821 there was a movement away from freewheeling essays toward the conventional-type review. Although some brief and trite reviews occurred during these years, most of them were fairly competent, and occasionally the writing was excellent with telling details on operas and singers. I find, however, little consistency in these reviews and conclude that they were the work of various hands. Possibly some were by the ubiquitous John Taylor or by Thomas Noon Talfourd, who may have written for the journal in 1824—but I do not recognize the style of either critic in its pages. Coverage in 1826 and after disintegrated almost entirely.

New Monthly Magazine and Literary Journal (1821–1884). There were two forerunner journals—the *New Monthly Magazine* (1814–15) and the *New*

Monthly Magazine and Universal Register (1818–20). The latter was established as a politically moderate organ to counteract the "poison" of the Jacobin *Monthly Magazine*. In this form it presented a "straightforward chronicle of events in the English business and literary worlds" (Langley, pp. 502–5). By 1821 publishers Henry Colburn (who was still copublisher of the *Gazette* but was losing interest in that journal) and Frederic Shoberl (who left the *New Monthly* wholly to Colburn) changed its title and format. As a continuation of the old *New Monthly* it now comprised a "Historical Register," which included a miscellany of news and reviews, and "Original Papers," which contained articles by such writers as Lamb, Hunt, Hazlitt, Stendhal, and many others. Although the new editor was the poet Thomas Campbell, who was "not the man to lead in anything bold or novel,"[64] he did establish a good foundation for the journal, which in Victorian times acquired an eminent reputation in literature. Later editors included Bulwer-Lytton, Theodore Hook, and Thomas Hood. By 1822 it was carrying excellent reviews of English opera in the "Drama" columns and, by 1824, of Italian opera in the "Music" columns.

On the whole its criticism of the King's Theatre from 1824 to 1830, which included ballets as well as operas, ranks among the best that was being produced in our period. From a musical point of view it even excelled that of Hunt, except for the latter's brilliance. Unfortunately it must remain unidentified, and we are obliged to call him critic Z.[65] The writer provided excellent coverage of Italian opera and often included very detailed attention to the performers on both singing and acting. His reviews ran from long to very long. He was not afraid to use technical musical terms, but they are so clear in their context as to make them largely self-explanatory. He paid considerable attention to plots, including commentary. At times he could be very negative on both operas and performers, but his critiques always seem fair and balanced. He often indulged in essay-type passages to explore all sorts of musico-dramatic ideas, such as changes in musical styles, problems with encores, and historical background, in which he was well versed (he cited twenty-five years of experience in opera). His writing was excellent: clear, concise, intelligent, and capable of subtle distinctions. He never attacked other critics and was the only critic to do justice to the castrato Velluti.

The English opera reviews were written by Thomas Noon Talfourd (1795–1854), who had written briefly for the *London*; the dramatic department was "entirely under his direction for several years" (D.N.B.). Talfourd, who became a judge and was knighted, was a lifelong friend of Hunt and Lamb. His reviews began in 1822, and except for 1824 and 1825 he provided good coverage of the playhouses. His critiques are only moderate in length, though occasionally essay-type passages expanded them. His tone is easy, informal, and open. His writing is marked by genial affability that invites the confidence of his readers—a "light, topical humour" was regarded as the best approach for selling the magazine—and that conveys a strong sense of the critic's enjoyment of opera. He took pains to "place" each work—what type and what historical or literary connections characterized the piece. He was particularly good on singers, and he was quite capable of being sharply negative on occasion, although sometimes he was also too easily pleased—a characteristic that was noted by Hunt.

Moreover, he often became apologetic about his competence when reviewing an opera with more than ordinary musical interests. He would seek assistance from his "musical ally"—critic Z, who reviewed the musical aspect of the opera in his "Music" section. On the other hand, on two occasions Talfourd wrote on the acting skills of Giuditta Pasta.

Harmonicon (1823–1833). The *Harmonicon*, established by one W. Clowes, was edited and largely written by William Ayrton (1777–1858). He was the son of an eminent musician who gave him his training. Ayrton married the daughter of composer Samuel Arnold, and Ayrton's son married Thomas Alsager's eldest daughter. Ayrton had considerable influence on the music of his time, not only through his writings but through his association with various musical organizations; for example, he was founder, treasurer, and director of the Philharmonic Society (1812). His circle of friends included Vincent Novello, Lamb, Alsager, Hazlitt, Henry Crabb Robinson, John Payne Collier, and Talfourd. As we have seen, he wrote music criticism for the *Chronicle* between 1813 and 1826, which overlapped his work on the *Harmonicon* by three years. He was also editor of the *Music Library* from 1834 to 1837, and he made contributions to the *Examiner* from 1838 to 1851.[66]

Two features of the *Harmonicon* are of interest to us: the "Review of Music" and the "Drama," which remained the journal's "two stablist departments" (Langley, p. 338). The former could be quite lengthy; it frequently included several pages of printed music and dealt with a single work, usually an opera. The textual part of this section treated extensively all aspects of the work except the performance. The "Drama" section, on the other hand, dealt mainly with opera and concert performances. (At times there was even a "Foreign Musical Report" on performances in Vienna, Berlin, and elsewhere.) There was not always a neat division—sometimes an outstanding performer was discussed in the "Review," and quite often the "Drama" discussed the music of an opera, though in much less detail. Of course, far more operas were discussed in the "Drama" than in the "Review."

Others contributed some of the articles to the journal, such as John Parry and George Hogarth, who was for a time associate editor and contributed essays after 1826; Hogarth was later (1829–30) a staff writer for the *Edinburgh Weekly Journal*.[67] It is doubtful, though, that such contributions extended to the criticism. More likely Edward Taylor, who was also writing for the *Atlas* and the *Spectator* (see below) during these years, wrote some of the late reviews (D.N.B.). His work for the *Atlas* preceded that for the *Harmonicon* (Har, VII, 134). In any event analysis of style and content of the "Drama" criticism clearly indicates most if not all the critiques were by Ayrton.

Ayrton's coverage in the "Drama" section of Italian opera was of course excellent, while that of English opera was more comprehensive than might have been expected in a musical journal. But his reviews in this department were all too brief—briefer than those in the rest of the press and briefer than his own contributions to the *Chronicle*. After 1824 he lengthened them by including extensive accounts of the plots—so extensive, in fact, that on occasion they occupied as much as 85 percent of the review.

As exemplified in his *Chronicle* reviews, Ayrton's style is terse, clean-cut, direct, and under strong control; not a word is wasted, and each sentence is a kind of pronouncement—almost dogmatic in effect.[68] There are no shades in his writing. Though a musician, Ayrton generally eschews the use of musical terms in his "Drama" criticism. He could be sharply negative, and he understood well the power of irony in rendering stinging indictments on composers, librettists and performers; yet he could be favorable toward such a light, breezy piece as Kenney's *Sweethearts and Wives*!

His criticism displayed other characteristics. Beginning about 1826, when his criticism for the *Chronicle* ceased, he began very frequently to call his readers' attention to the poor reviews of operas elsewhere in the periodical press, particularly in the newspapers. He once cited the *Examiner* and the *Atlas* as being quite exempt from these strictures. On one occasion he was extremely contemptuous of the "paragraph-mongering" *Chronicle* for their comments on the choruses in an English opera, though earlier he had even lifted verbatim from that journal a comment that he explained was "well noted"—and he did not cite his source. On another occasion he excerpted a complete review from the newly established *Spectator*. In his later reviews he also frequently took the management of the King's Theatre to task, with good reason, for the poverty of good operas and good voices there.

More serious objections from a musician of Ayrton's prominence are apparent in his approach to some masterworks. At a performance of *Arthur and Emmeline*, for instance, he found Purcell's accompaniments too thin and was glad that the adaptor had boosted them by adding brass, woodwinds, and a drum.[69] Similarly, at a production of Mozart's *Seraglio* as an English opera, he was full of praise for Kramer's revision of the score and his introduction of choruses—"better than the opening of the original work." Other contemporary critics had a more enlightened view of these productions (see part III). Although on the whole Ayrton's criticism did contribute to the quality of London periodical reviewing, it must be regarded as something of a disappointment considering his background.[70]

***Atlas* (1826–1869).** The *Atlas*, a radical Sunday organ like the *Champion* and the *Examiner*, became an exponent of the Benthamite school, which was known for its "educated radicalism" (Bourne, II, 19). (The radicals were, of course, becoming less "radical" and more mainstream as Britain moved toward the Reform Bill of 1832.) The *Atlas* contained foreign and domestic news, articles on science, and literary and music criticism. Robert Stephen Rintoul, a Scottish journalist, served as editor for the first two years and had the assistance of Hazlitt and Albany Fonblanque (Langley, pp. 527–30). Fonblanque was a witty writer on politics and economics; he edited the *Examiner* from 1830 to 1847. In 1828 Rintoul left after a disagreement, and Robert Bell, another outspoken journalist who had written widely on the Catholic emancipation issue, became editor.

Almost from the beginning the *Atlas* could claim a professional musical critic on its roster—Edward Holmes (1797–1859). Holmes met Hunt through his first music teacher, Charles Cowden Clark, and remained a fast friend for many years. Both men were part of the Vincent and Mary Novello circle. Vincent (1781–1861) was organist, choirmaster, composer, and publisher, as well as a teacher of young Holmes. In June of 1827 Holmes and Mary Novello made a musical tour of Germany, the immediate outcome of which was Holmes's *Ramble among the Musicians of Germany . . .* (1828). Holmes later wrote a *Life of Mozart* (1848), which Max Graf called "the most useful, complete, and trustworthy biography then in existence" (p. 178). Following his stint on the *Atlas*, he wrote for the *Musical Times*. Hunt called him "the best musical critic which this nation has yet produced" (*Autobiography*, p. 430). Holmes had high standards of scholarship and an "alert intelligence"; he gave music criticism "technical authority and intellectual respectability" (N.G.).

Holmes's initial criticism was in his "Music and Musicians" column of the *Atlas*, which included essays on musical topics as well as occasional reviews of operas and concerts. The column began in late 1826 and continued until 1838 when Holmes apparently left the journal. But we find that after September 1828, he wrote no more reviews for that column—at least until 1831; instead, his reviews of both English and Italian operas were placed in the "Theatricals" column. In both columns Holmes gave almost as much attention to English opera as to Italian; from December 1827 to August 1830, he wrote eleven on the former and fourteen on the latter.

Holmes's style is unmistakable. It is literary in quality, as would befit a member of the Hunt-Novello circle and a student, along with Keats, at the Enfield Academy. His style is equable, moving easily with well-balanced periods; and it is marked by humor, wit, and apt figures of speech. Holmes liked to include brief quotations of English or Italian poetry, and he occasionally provided a musical quotation. He always included some musical terms—for instance, he nearly always mentioned the key signatures of arias—but he used them so skillfully they were never a handicap for nonmusician readers. He occasionally discussed plots, though they were kept to a minimum, and he widely employed an essay-type style that moved easily from central to peripheral matters without eclipsing any details of the performances. He could be very negative on occasion, though his strictures were well supported. As Langley writes (p. 114), Holmes "delighted in elegance of language" and (unlike Ayrton) in expository argument; he was affirmative and constructive. (See appendix 2 for an excerpt from his criticism.)

Hazlitt, whose career we have traced to the *Chronicle*, the *Times*, the *Champion*, the *Examiner*, and the *London*, produced his best opera criticism for the *Atlas*. From May 1827 to May 1828, he wrote six reviews of English operas and three of Italian operas. (During 1828 he was also writing for the *Examiner*, but these were all essays on the theatre—not reviews of performances—and the *Examiner* was a sister journal.) He brought to his criticism the same qualities observed earlier—hard-biting prose, abundant wit, hilarity and verve—in short, gusto. But his essay style—which included fine passages on such matters as "the *stew* of English opera"—still occasionally departed from attention to performance details. In fact, his reviews for the *Atlas* were longer and gave somewhat more serious attention to the music than is to be found in his earlier writing.[71] Occasionally in these reviews Hazlitt referred readers to the "Music and Musicians" column for further coverage on the music, and there, in the same number, we find Holmes's supplemental comments, though he too sometimes discussed the drama. This, of course, made for some awkwardness, and it is my guess that for this reason Holmes, following Hazlitt's departure, wrote his further reviews for the "Theatrical" column.

Thus between them Hazlitt and Holmes provided excellent coverage of opera criticism for the journal. To be sure, I do find a very few reviews—

three or four in 1828 and 1829 — that were not written by either. Possibly they were the work of Edward Taylor (1784–1863), who earlier had failed in business. He became a vocalist, chorus master, and friend of Ludwig Spohr. He "went into music" about 1827 and wrote music criticism for the *Atlas*, the *Harmonicon*, and the *Spectator* (D.N.B.).

Athenaeum and Literary Chronicle (1828–1921). James Silk Buckingham, who according to Jerdan was "not very business-like" and Henry Colburn, whom we last found at the *New Monthly*, launched the weekly *Athenaeum* in 1828. In Victorian times it became an "outstanding popular literary journal" with mildly liberal principles.[72] From 1828 to 1830, responsibility for its musical journalism was shared by J. Augustine Wade, Robert Bell, and Neville Butler Challoner, but apparently Wade (c. 1796–1845) wrote most of the early reviews of operas and concerts. A native of Ireland, Wade was an English opera composer (see part III) and a conductor in London. (The well-known writer Henry Chorley, who wrote strong music criticism for the journal for thirty years, did not join the *Athenaeum* until 1834.)

Wade provided excellent coverage of Italian opera after early 1829. He was well experienced, citing changes in opera that took place twenty years earlier. His literary style relied heavily on the essay-type approach, but he was also careful about details of performances. In his first review he showed his independence by chastising all the critics in London for their disparaging attitude toward Rossini. He wrote more on the singers than on the music, though he made fine observations on the latter as well. The reviews were generally medium to long, and his somewhat saturnine tone is one of considered judgment — not to mention academic. In his second review, for instance, he wrote: "We can say with perfect security that the three hours of the performance . . . were distinguished by more villainous singing than the most speculative man could have supposed practicable in so short a space of time." But he was capable of commendatory as well as negative reactions.

Fairly good coverage of English opera also began early in 1829. The hand of Wade can be traced in some of them, but most were written by others; indeed, a number are quite brief, even trivial, though most were well written. In some, elaborate accounts of the plot occupy as much as 90 percent of the reviews; sometimes the plot was admittedly lifted from the daily journals.

Spectator (1828–1928). Our last journal, the *Spectator*, was published on Saturdays and was, like the *Athenaeum*, a vehicle for educated readers, but like the *Atlas*, it was a liberal organ and supported the Reform Bill of 1832. It was launched by Rintoul following his disagreement at the *Atlas*. Its features included "News of the Week," "Parliament," "Topics of the Day," "Literary Spectator," and "The Music of the Season." Reviews of operas had no special rubric; each received its own title. English opera coverage fared well after late 1828; Italian opera reviews commenced in April of 1830. Both were written by the same critic. After an initial review, in which a long preamble was quite inappropriate to the rest of the review, the writing was fair to good. Reviews were of moderate length. The author was not afraid to mete out negative criticism — even of an artist like Malibran — and he was quite opposed to Rossini in both English adaptations and Italian opera. Rintoul brought with him several writers from the *Atlas*, including Edward Taylor, who as we have noted had earlier written for the *Harmonicon* as well. Taylor wrote musical pieces for the "Topics of the Day" column (Langley, pp. 543–44), and he is likely the author of this criticism. (In the 1840s Holmes wrote on music for the *Spectator*, and his friend Thornton Hunt, Leigh Hunt's eldest son, was a staff writer there.)[73]

A final word on contemporary opera criticism in books. William Parke, in his *Musical Memoirs*, discusses performances of both Italian and English opera from 1784 on, and as a musician and oboist in the band at the King's, he should certainly have been able to provide much interesting background on the period. But his book is a disappointment, for I found so much of his material drawn *verbatim* from the dailies — mostly from the *Times* — that it is hard to believe he did not write the whole book out of the newspaper clippings he evidently saved. Thus it is not a memoir at all, though the book has some value in presenting secondhand views not disclosed elsewhere.

Richard Mount-Edgcumbe, who wrote only on Italian opera, did present a memoir, and his fine and detailed reminiscences of King's productions are an invaluable resource, even though some are marred by an insufferable snobbery, and though his later views remained incorrigibly old-fashioned.[74]

George Hogarth, too, was not above the biases of his age, but his *Memoirs*, which dealt with both Italian and English opera developments, is on the whole well balanced and well written, and it sometimes provides penetrating socio-musical evaluations.

James Boaden, both critic and librettist, has fascinating details on the singing and acting in English operas in his *Memoirs* of Kemble.[75] Michael Kelly's high-spirited *Reminiscences*, written for him by Theodore Hook, is a useful resource for personalities and events in both Italian and English opera during our period, though it is occasionally inaccurate. Also his criticism of performances are, like Parke's, often as banal as those in the early newspapers.

THE RISE OF OPERA CRITICISM

Gray asserts (p. 309) that "after 1795 it is clear that there is no further development in newspaper criticism"—a remark that applies in no way to opera criticism. Certainly it is obvious from our detailed survey that criticism of both English and Italian opera underwent very significant development right up to 1830. When we look back over the outstanding reviewers of opera discussed in the previous pages—Ayrton of the *Chronicle* and *Harmonicon*; John Payne Collier of the *Chronicle*; Alsager and Sterling of the *Times*; Hunt, Robertson, and critics X and Q of the *Examiner*; Bacon of the *Gazette, London,* and *Quarterly Musical*; Kenrick of the *British Stage*; Talfourd and critic Z of the *New Monthly*; Holmes of the *Atlas*; and Hazlitt of several journals—we are struck by the fact that all of them, with the major exception of Hunt and Robertson, wrote after 1813— most of them after 1820. What can account for this sudden explosion of critical talent, new journals, and quickening interest in opera?

The question looms even larger when we consider the mediocrity of reviews early in our period. At its worst, for example, were these thoughtless and trivial comments on Gertrude Mara as Dido in 1786: "She warbled five songs besides a *Terzetto*, in every one of which, she displayed all the energy that can possibly be called forth in a musical performance" (*Public Advertiser*); "Madam Mara was encored in several songs, and she executed them with the most affecting pathos. She has the happy talent of agitating the bosoms of her audience, and of exciting emotions of sympathy" (*Gazetteer*). Consider, also, this *complete* review in the *Times* of a new Italian opera by Giovanni Paisiello:

> The new Opera of La Discordia Conjugale, in which Negri was to have made her first appearance at the Pantheon, went off extremely well on Saturday.
>
> The Music in general is very fine, and the accompanyments have all the richness for which Paisiello is so celebrated.
>
> The performance was done great justice to; but particular praise is due to the exertions of Lazzarini, Cipriani, and Cassentini.
>
> The galleries were by no means deficient in number, nor the boxes in brilliancy. (Apr. 2, 1792)

Admittedly these comments are worse than average for the time. But many reviews before 1800 were meager and thin, ground out by otherwise harmless drudges. On the other hand, *some* good reviews were to be found in earlier years, even before 1785. In 1788, for example, the press was generally quite negative on Sarti's *Giulio Sabino*. Nor were *all* the reviews of the 1820s outstanding: the *European* and the *Literary Chronicle* were quite untouched by the new criticism.

But the rise in Italian opera reviewing remained sluggish. There was some progress in the 1790s, both in the newspapers and in the *Mirror*, and some excellent criticism appeared in 1802. But the average reviews of Italian opera remained for the most part mediocre until 1808, when Robertson's reviews for the *Examiner* began to appear. A similar pattern appears in English opera criticism, which shows that although some noteworthy passages appeared in the press in nearly every year until 1808, the level of reporting remained relatively weak. For instance, we find several examples of sharply negative criticism even before Hunt's 1805 *News* criticism. This is especially evident in the 1802 reviews of Thomas Dibdin's *Cabinet* and *Family Quarrels* by John Campbell in the *Chronicle* and by DuBois in the *Mirror*. That criticism was not sustained, but we can see that the *enfant terrible* was not without precedent in his crusade to improve the stage, including English opera.

After 1808 other journals were also showing strength: in Italian opera strong reviews by the newspapers in 1811 probably owe their strength to Robertson's example—they certainly do in ballet criticism. In reviews of English operas the newspapers provided excellent negative criticism of the *Armourer* as early as 1793 and thoughtful reviews of *Up All Night* in 1809. By 1810 good criticism appeared in the newspapers and in *Bell's* on *Gustavus Vasa* and *Oh! This Love*; there was also a savage indictment of Mrs. Mountain's acting by DuBois in the *Mirror*. In 1811–12 there was competent negative criticism in the newspapers; these probably owe much to Hunt. By 1815 Sterling (*Times*) was as opposed as Hazlitt (*Examiner*) to the *Unknown Guest*. With the addition of good reviews from Kenrick (*British Stage*) and Bacon (*Literary Gazette*), the rise in English as well as Italian opera criticism was well under way.[76]

Yet the rest of the press was slow to echo Hunt's interest in discussing the librettos, and often even the music was ignored—the performers got most of the attention. There were no positive references to Hunt in the other journals except by his friend Talfourd, who alluded to him in a review in April 1826: "Where are the young Templars [Barron Field], who, under the guidance of Mr. Chitty, then called 'Mr. Town,'[77] decided the fate of the players and plays? . . . Where are the critics, sour and severe, who were confessedly hard to please; whose approbation was worth having; and who gave a lustiness and flavour to the opinion of the mass? Alas! their voice is nearly extinct; we, who profess to follow them, and sit in the boxes by favour of the managers!" The last is an allusion to Hunt's well-known refusal to accept managerial "courtesies."

In opera criticism both Robertson and Hunt exercised some influence, as we have noted. Students of Hunt's dramatic criticism have attributed to him the much greater objectivity of such criticism in the press by 1832,[78] though Hunt himself was ambiguous about that influence. But it would be presumptuous to suppose that they helped spawn the appearance of the new weeklies and monthlies, starting in 1817, that contributed so significantly to that rise. It is more likely, rather, that Hunt and Robertson appeared merely at the leading edge of an emerging sensibility that became manifest not only in the press but in the growing number of readers who were no longer satisfied with the earlier platitudes.[79] The thirst for a deeper theatrical and operatic experience, evident in the later developments of Italian and especially English opera, was one of the many manifestations of Romanticism, and the *Examiner*, with respect to opera, became the first substantial exponent of this rising tide.

Along with the widening spheres of Romanticism, a more immediate cause for the astonishing growth after 1815 was the cessation of the Napoleonic wars and the lifting of the Continental blockade that year. Feelings long repressed by wartime conditions could now be aired freely, England was again open to Continental influences, and the time was ripe for liberals to gain renewed vigor: the movement toward the Reform Bill of 1832 was accelerating.[80] Some journals were now even providing reviews of operas in Paris and Vienna. In Italian opera (and ballet) a great welcome was given to the several brilliant new voices (and dancers) then available from Paris. This led directly, as we shall see, to the enormously influential premiere of Mozart's *Don Giovanni* in 1817, which in turn helped launch a movement toward adapting operas to the English musical stage—bringing it closer to the ideal of opera. These developments stimulated public interest in opera, and the stronger opera critics that were then being appointed to both the newspapers and the new journals helped satisfy the public's curiosity and provide a new richness to the operatic life of London.

In the ensuing criticism—part II deals with Italian opera, part III with English—I have chronicled the works of individual composers and librettists under "Operas" and of performers under "Performances." "Theatres" and "Audiences" also receive separate treatment. Other perennial interests are discussed in the "Themes and Currents" sections.

The reviewers, we will find, differed on many of these works and performers. Sometimes the differences can be ascribed to opposed political coloration, to an animus between competing organs, or simply to differing degrees of critical acumen. In a number of instances, these pro and con stances can be attributed only to honest differences of opinion—a situation not unknown in today's criticism. A detailed examination of both book and score would be required for any attempt to reconcile opposing views; unfortunately, such examinations lie well beyond the scope of this already very lengthy study. In general, therefore, we have given greater weight to those reviewers with some history of outstanding critical ability.

To minimize the enormous amount of documentation that would otherwise be needed, I have provided appendix 3 for part II and appendix 10 for part III. The reader need know only the name and year of the opera performance (always given in the text) to find, in those appendixes, a listing of all the periodicals that carried reviews of that performance, together with the dates of the reviews.[81] In further simplification of the documentation, since my remarks on the operas are drawn from *all* the reviews of a performance, I have not cited particular journals for these comments except when they are quoted at length or where further amplification is desirable. Thus I have often consulted far more reviews than those indicated by references in the text.

In the four-page dailies, reviews (usually headed by the name of the theatre, though in the *Chronicle* often buried in a column of unrelated paragraphs) were almost always placed on page three, though occasionally on page two. Page numbers have been supplied for most weeklies and monthlies.[82]

Though sometimes a different approach is dictated on occasion, my policy has been to quote reviews chronologically. The newspapers usually lead off, followed by the weeklies and monthlies. This places the emphasis, as it should be, on those critics closest to the immediate event and deprived of whatever advantages later critics might derive from earlier opinions. Criticism from books published during or shortly after this period is cited separately; again, to avoid unwieldy documentation, I include the reference to these frequently but briefly quoted authors — most of them cited in the Abbreviations — directly in the text; their memoirs or histories are, of course, fully annotated in the bibliography. Criticism from our own time is sometimes briefly cited at the beginning or end of discussions of composers or librettists in the text, but most are placed in the notes.

Quotations with usage no longer acceptable pass unchallenged if supported by the *Oxford English Dictionary*. For greater clarity to the modern reader, however, I have normalized the italics or small capitals usually employed for names of performers or titles of operas. Such names and titles do, in other respects, follow the exact usage and spellings of the sources, including the occasional insertion of English words in Italian opera titles and the deletion of most diacritical marks from Continental terms. The large number of errors in their citations of Italian arias has, however, prompted me to correct them silently.[83]

Appendix 1

Leading Journals and Their Critics

IO—Italian Opera; EO—English Opera; sc.—scattered reviews

Morning Chronicle
    IO   sc. 1785–1801
           1802–1812: ?
           1813–1816, 1818–1820, 1822–1826: William Ayrton
           mid-1826–1830: John Payne Collier
    EO 1785–1796: James Gray
           1800–1805: John Campbell
           mid-1807–1818?: John Dyer Collier
           1813–1814: William Hazlitt
           1819–1825: ?
           mid-1826–1830: John Payne Collier

Morning Post
    IO   1784: C. F. Badini
    EO 1772–1780: William Bate; Joseph Richardson
           c. 1787: John Taylor

Morning Herald
    IO   ?
    EO 1780-?: William Bate

Public Advertiser
    IO and EO   c. 1780–1794: Charles Este; George Steevens

Oracle (title varies)
    EO sc. 1791–1805: James Boaden ("Thetis")
         sc. 1791–1794: Charles Este

Times (Universal Register)
    IO   sc. 1785–1792: Charles Este
         sc. 1787–1791: Critic A
         1789–1798: John Walter II?
         1796–1805; sc. to 1809: Critic B
         1810–1811: George Croly
         1812–? : Thomas Barnes

           1817–1830: Thomas Massa Alsager
    EO   1787–mid-1792: Charles Este
           1792–1794: Critic C
           1796–1806: Critic D
           sc. 1807–1809: Barron Field; Leigh Hunt; William Hazlitt
           1811-1812?: Thomas Barnes
           1817, May-June: William Hazlitt
           1815–1830: Edward Sterling

British Stage
    EO and IO   1817–1822: Thomas Kenrick

Monthly Mirror
    Mostly EO   1795–1811:
           Reviews: Edward DuBois
           Memoirs and Sketches: John Taylor

Theatrical Inquisitor and Monthly Mirror
    Mostly EO   1812–1820: DuBois and others; some possibly by John Litchfield
    IO   1817–1820: ?

Bell's Weekly Messenger
    EO   1796–1803: John Bell?
           sc. 1804–1808: C. F. Badini

Examiner
    IO   1808–1810; sc. 1811–1814; 1819: Henry Robertson
           1814: Thomas Barnes
           1816–1817: William Hazlitt
           1817–1821: Leigh Hunt
           1822–mid-1829: Critic X
           mid-1829–1830: ?
    EO   1808–1811: Leigh Hunt
           1812–1813: Thomas Barnes; William Hazlitt; Charles Lamb
           1814–1821: Leigh Hunt
           1822–1827: Critic Q
           1828: William Hazlitt

Champion
    IO and EO   1814 (Nov.): William Hazlitt
           1814–1822: Some by John Thelwall?

Literary Gazette
    IO and EO   1817–mid-1818: Richard Mackenzie Bacon
        1818–1830: Thomas Billington? Thomas Greenwood? Miss Wilkinson?

Quarterly Musical Magazine and Review
    IO and EO   1818–1828: Richard Mackenzie Bacon

London Magazine
    IO   1820–May 1825: Richard Mackenzie Bacon
    EO   1820: William Hazlitt
        1821–1825: John Taylor? Thomas Noon Talfourd?

New Monthly Magazine
    IO   1824–1830: Critic Z
    EO   1824–1830: Thomas Noon Talfourd

Harmonicon
    IO and EO   1823–1833: William Ayrton
        1830–1833: Edward Taylor?

Atlas
    IO and EO   1826–1830: Edward Holmes*
    EO   1827–1828: William Hazlitt**

Athenaeum
    IO   1828–1830: J. Augustine Wade
    EO   1829–1830: A few by Wade

Spectator
    IO   1830: Edward Taylor?
    EO   1828–1830: Edward Taylor?

Tatler
    EO   1829–1832: Leigh Hunt

*Holmes:
    EO—1827: Dec. 2; 1828: Aug. 3, Aug. 24, Sept. 7, Dec. 7; 1829: Jan. 18, Aug. 30, Oct. 25; 1830: Feb. 7, Feb. 14, May 9.
    IO—1828: Jan. 20, Feb. 10, Feb. 24, July 27; 1829: Mar. 8, June 21; 1830: Feb. 14, Feb. 21, Mar. 14, Mar. 21, Apr. 4, Apr. 18, Apr. 25, Aug. 1.

**Hazlitt:
    EO—1827: May 6, July 25, Nov. 11, Dec. 2; 1828: June 1, Sept. 7.
    IO—1827: May 13, June 10; 1828: May 4.

Appendix 2

Reviews by Leading Critics

Listed chronologically, by type

ITALIAN OPERA

Richard Mackenzie Bacon

From the *Literary Gazette* of March 15, 1817, on a revival of *La Molinara*

... the incidents and dramatic situations which form the slight plot of this Opera, are strung together in a natural way, a spirit of cheerful *naiveté*, richly tinged by comic humour, commands the attention of the audience from beginning to end, and the easy and frequently droll language, truly Neapolitan, is eminently calculated to augment this favorable impression. ...

Although the general complexion of the music in La Molinara is, as it should be, of light cast, it nevertheless contains sufficient evidence of science to convince the Connoiseur that where it does not smell of the lamp, it is not for want of oil. Operas are not composed for professors alone; in Italy, above all, they are written to please the population at large, from the accomplished amateur down to the mechanic, whose ear is by no means insensible to the beauties of good music. — It has of late become fashionable to decry *indiscriminately* the best musical productions of the Italian School. This we consider not only as indicative of a want of good taste, but as a piece of ingratitude toward a country from which, as in the other Fine Arts, we have derived, either at first or second hand, the greatest portion of our musical treasurers. ... Mozart himself became Mozart only by his stay in Italy; it was there that the spark of his transcendent genius was lighted into a flame, the ardent fire of which consumed itself at a time when admiring Europe had scarcely beheld its transient lustre. ...

William Ayrton

From the *Chronicle* of January 19, 1818, on *Figaro*

... of all the productions of its composer, *Figaro* comes nearest to the incomparable *Don Giovanni*, and is perhaps only rendered inferior to it by the nature of the subject, which did not afford that scope and opportunity for the mysterious and sublime. ... The general character of *Figaro* is beauty—beauty in all its forms of softness, grace, and proportion; neither, as these qualities are corporeal rather than mental, is it wanting in the deeper infusion of character and sensibility. If we can imagine a being to whom by long habit music has become a language, the depository of the purest breathings of genius, that being is Mozart, and his *Figaro* the most striking example. Both operas are perfect in their kind; they stand at the head of dramatic music, and will long serve like the pillars of Hercules, to mark out the *ne usque* to future travellers in the same region.... Signora Corri, the new singer, is not of a very prepossesing appearance; her figure is *petite*, and her countenance is not remarkable for intelligence; but her voice is good, her musical talent still better, and, last of all, she is quite at home in Mozart's music. Her intonation is not of that fine quality for which Mad. Fodor is so remarkable; she does not, like that lady, fasten on a passage and make it part of herself, but sometimes, like an unskilful fencer, pauses at the onset, and fears to make the attack; the notes seem to come from her because she dares delay them no longer, not because she gives them willingly....

Naldi does not, we think, understand the character of Figaro. There is nothing of the buffoon about him; he is a wily knave, who has got the length of his master's foot, and absolutely overawes him by the superiority of his intellect, qualifying and concealing all under the humility of his exterior. There is a rude familiarity about Naldi's manner which is extremely repulsive. His singing is also liable to censure; he appears to labour under a flutter and indecision which makes him not exact in the time, too soon or too late for the orchestra, to the great distress of all who know the opera, that is, all who pretend to study music....

Thomas Massa Alsager

From the *Times* of January 10, 1820, on *Cenerentola*

[The Cinderella story], having travelled across the Alps, and become divested of those infantine associations, which tend so strongly to bias the judgment towards excessive admiration or excessive contempt, has found its true level, and become popular as a pleasing *jeu d'esprit* of the imaginative power.... [The story] has been deprived, however, of its fairy agency, and an opportunity thereby lost, which Rossini, who is the composer of the music, might have profited by, to invent a style characteristic of that aerial race.... As an Italian comic opera, according to the modern practice, can no more exist without its buffoon, than a pantomime without its clown, a personage has been introduced ... the very prototype of folly and absurdity.... The character of course was assigned to Ambrogetti, whose talents can make any thing appear respectable. The music ... comprises many pieces of great beauty and felicity of comparison. Overtures, in general, [Rossini] least excels in, and that to *La Cenerentola* is no exception. The first movement, an *andante*, commences with a pleasing subject, but the *allegro* has neither continuity of plan nor distinctness of character. . . .

With the aid of all the musical beauties contained in this Opera, it is not likely, however, without very essential alterations, to become a favourite in this country. The composition wants variety of style and aims too exclusively to please the refined and experienced student. The excessive length is sufficient to weary even that class of auditors. There is no prominence of individual effect. . . . Half the songs and recitatives . . . are worse than useless, as they merely serve to overwhelm the principal character, Cinderella, in a mass of dramatic insipidity. . . .

Critic X of the *Examiner*

From the *Examiner* of April 14, 1822, on *I Due Pretendi Delusi*

The selection of new operas this season appears to be regulated by some persons devoid of the commonest appreciation of merit. . . . *I Due Pretendi Delusi*, by one Mosca . . . is a change from bad to worse. A more miserable string of common-places never yet proceeded from the head of a musician, and the wearied ear, always anxiously listening to catch some faint touches of melody or originality, is not once relieved from disappointment. . . . What can induce the manager to neglect the rich stores of music and rake up such trash, with equal labour and expense, is inconceivable, unless he is controlled by the caprice of the great, by those smatterers and dabblers in music, whose vanity prompts them to rely on their own incapability, and then persist in forcing their favourites upon us, lest the withdrawing them should impugn the profundity of their judgment. There is no doubt that the opera is chiefly supported by people of fashion, and that those of real musical taste are in comparison few; but it will be found out in time, that the latter have eventually the most importance; that they give the tone and zest to the entertainment: deserted by them, it will depend solely on that fickleness, that can at one time prefer Mosca and Pacini to Mozart and Rossini, and that is just as likely soon to decry operas altogether with as much zeal as it now upholds them. With people of sense and real taste it is otherwise, their opinions are grounded on more firm principles, and their pleasures do not depend on the mere fashion of the day. . . .

Critic Z of the *New Monthly Magazine*

From the *New Monthly* of February 1828, on Meyerbeer's *Margherita d'Anjou*

... in "Margherita d'Anjou" there is little originality; but the airs are written in a good style, and with a due regard to the sense of the text. There are perpetual reminiscences of Rossini, and many of the passages are plagiarisms from Mozart. The accompaniments are of various degrees of merit: some are full, and richly wrought up, while others are comparatively thin and naked. The choruses, "Zitti, zitti, la Regina," and "Che bell' alba, che bel giorno," deserve praise for something better than their effectiveness and ingenuity; they are exceedingly sweet and graceful. But the choral and orchestral effects of Meyerbeer in other parts of the opera, are generally produced rather by the mere force of numbers, than by learning and contrivance. Trumpets and trombones, we would venture to hint, may be made more important than mere accessories to the strength of an opera. . . .

The orchestra is fuller of strength and talent than we ever remember to have seen it. . . . We doubt, however, whether the arrangement is a good one, which has assembled all the wind instruments in one corner of the orchestra; a measure by which, we fear, both effect and precision will be hazarded. . . .

ENGLISH OPERA

Edward Sterling

From the *Times* review of October 14, 1818, on *The Barber of Seville*

. . . the present drama is nearly a counterpart of the celebrated *Il Barbiere di Siviglia*, which proved so attractive during the last season at the King's Theatre. Two or three additional characters have been introduced. . . . But it is not merely the drama that has been transfused; an attempt has also been made to naturalize the musical compositions of the Italian school, to apply English words to them, and withal to preserve their original beauty unimpaired. Of this part of the work, all the praise, or all the censure, appertains to Mr. Bishop, the composer to this theatre, who . . . has certainly done more on this occasion than ever was done in a similar way before. . . .

On the whole, we have seldom enjoyed a higher musical treat at an English theatre, while the audience appeared to participate in the same pleasure, and to feel the superior refinement of the composition. The part of Rosina was sustained by Mrs. Dickons. . . . As an English singer, there are few, if any, superior to this lady; her style is bold and determined, her taste is correct, and her execution possesses singular neatness and articulation: she seldom or never offends the ear by any of those deviations from strict tune, which ruin the notes of so many of our native warblers; her shake is close and distinct, and her expression admirably dramatic and characteristic. A slight tremour agitated her voice in her first song . . . but she soon recovered herself completely and retained her self-possession throughout the piece. . . .

Critic Q of the *Examiner*

From the *Examiner* of December 8, 1822, on *Maid Marian*

We never witnessed a more easy and felicitous assumption of the mirthful tone of the old ballads than the frisky narrative of Mr. Peacock, or a more successful endeavour to unite poetry to the character of the homely ballads, which, like the poems of Ossian, enshrine so much true and interesting matter of fact. . . .

Upon such materials the dramatist could construct nothing of *serious* interest: its essence is mirth and forest freedom; and Mr. Planche has contrived, in many respects, to preserve the spirit of the tale. The frank and boisterous Friar Tuck, most admirably performed by Mr. C. Kemble, was the very essence of a conventional wag of six feet high, who could devour venison in all forms, drink canary at all times, and fight with every or anybody on all occasions. . . . Matilda, in both original and copy, is a jocund and spirited huntress; not exactly the character for Miss Tree, who is so essentially feminine, and does her spiriting so gently. Her playful naiveté in the management of the humorous Baron her father . . . was however an attractive substitute; and we know not whether her arch yet composed call upon the *Coeur de Lion* to surrender to her single arm, was not more piquant than a similar modest demand from a more perfect Amazonian. . . .

[Bishop's overture] was a beautiful, if not altogether an original composition. The celebrated overture to Anacreon of Cherubini, and both the Prometheus and the Fidelio of Beethoven have paid tribute, we believe. It is evident, indeed, that no small portion of this kind of freedom has been taken throughout; and as to thefts from himself, Mr. Bishop, like the eminent composer Rossini,—to whom he has been compared—has been most unsparing. . . . In glees and choral composition, Mr. Bishop is always more than usually at home; and in *Maid Marian* he has fully kept up his character. A sestette, commencing "O bold Robin Hood," is a spirited proof of this truth. Upon the whole, Mr. Bishop has supported his reputation, which is certainly that of the leading *native* operatical composer of the day.

John Payne Collier

From the *Chronicle* of May 1, 1826, on *Aladdin*

Another "grand romantic fairy Opera" (as Weber called his *Oberon* . . .) was produced at Drury-Lane, on Saturday night, under the title of *Aladdin*, the whole of the music composed by Mr. H. R. Bishop. Whether any contest for superiority between these two Composers were or were not intended, certain it is that the Public has presumed the existence of "rival bating envy" on one side or the other; and as Bishop has been the last to enter the lists, it was perhaps not a very unfair conclusion to suppose that he desired to prove by *Aladdin* that he was an equal competitor. After weighing, as well as we can, the merits of the two musical productions, and making allowances for all the disadvantages of a first representation, we cannot help saying that Bishop seems to have been "pricked on by a most emulate pride," and that he has, in some degree, disappointed even those who were anxious to be satisfied. If we do not much mistake, Bishop's chief error will be found to consist in this, — that he has (perhaps unconsciously) made the laboriously scientific stile of his rival the object of his imitation, instead of endeavouring to produce something essentially different. . . . Music & poetry have many things in common, and we know that Moore, while the sweetest song writer in our language (Burns alone excepted), has failed in attempting the more sustained flight of the would be epic. We do not mean, by this illustration, to say that Bishop is not competent to the invention and arrangement of the music of an English Opera: far from it — On the contrary, he has several advantages over Weber, independent of the important one, of an acquaintance with the language which he clothes with music. Weber has, as it were, to dress his words by conjecture, & it is almost a matter of chance whether the apparel will exactly fit. But Bishop's principal advantage, of course, is a knowledge of and long accordance with the English taste, be that taste bad or good; and when we heard that his production was full of melodies, we concluded that he relied most upon them, and that he has not gone out of his usual path, to follow that of Weber. . . .

Horn has a difficult part to perform and sing, and the whole weight of the first act (and no light weight neither) rests very much upon his shoulders. He gave great effect in the air, "The hour is come," but the contest between his voice and the orchestra, towards the close, was decidedly in favour of the latter. . . .

As originally written, there was comparatively little music in the third act, and most of that little, from some cause or other, was omitted. It contains, nevertheless, the most graceful and touching air of the whole opera, "In my bower a lady weeps," sung by Miss Stephens. . . . All the latter part of the Opera was huddled up in confusion, and it was evident that something had occurred to disconcert previous arrangements. Horne fell on a wrong part of the stage, and was obliged to shuffle himself to the trap-door by which he was to descend, like most defeated enchanters, to Tartarus. Miss Stephens was obliged to come in without her disguise. . . .

Edward Holmes

From the *Atlas* of August 3, 1828, on *Tit for Tat*

... the introduction of this opera has gratified us more than we can express: first, we have the purity of Mozart's music, free from interpolations—which have hitherto been found necessary to gild the pill for the vulgar; secondly, the pleasant sight of singers content with the simplicity of the text, and taking pains to give it correctly; but most of all, a mixed audience appearing to relish the best parts of Mozart, and *encoring* such compositions as the terzetto, "Soave sia il vento," and the quintetto, which precede it. The English words have been adapted to these, as well as a great deal of accompanied recitative, very cleverly; the rhythm is preserved, without any bungling accentuation. It has been thought by some that this opera, from the conclusion of the grand *finale* in D, is unworthy of Mozart's genius. The first act contains such a tissue of exquisite movements as the author never surpassed; yet, though the discrepancy must be acknowledged, there is to the end melody enough to keep the attention awake, with every now and then a choice harmony, or a modulation that startles us with its beauty. . . .

Much credit is due to Mr. Wagstaff, the leader. . . . The parts were well kept under, sustained, and smooth; but the time of the beautiful movement "Di Scivir mi ogni Giorno," was mistaken, and the piece played so fast as to destroy its pathetic character. . . .

Leigh Hunt

From a *Tatler* review of September 27, 1830, on *The Marriage of Figaro* in English

[Miss Paton] evidently does not understand Mozart;—we do not mean his notes, but his spirit. She knows nothing about it; she does not understand the song she is singing, probably does not think of it. She forsakes even the measure; lengthens the time as she pleases; and without attending to the nature of demands of the passage, makes any note wait for her at her pleasure, while she indulges the house with a circuit through the commonplaces of ornament. . . . Lowness and softness are not simplicity, though they may occasionally be proper to it. Simplicity consists in a feeling of the sufficiency of truth and nature, and in knowing how to dress it accordingly. A girl, speaking sincerely to her lover, and engrossed by her fondness for him, expresses herself with simplicity, though her simplicity may be as full as it can hold of natural eloquence. If she declaims, or puts on mincing airs, or is thinking how finely her ear-rings or her tresses are dangling about, she is in a state of artifice and affectation. Now Miss Paton, on the stage, is thinking, not of the sentiment (which should be the singer's love), but purely of shewing herself off by means of it. A very fine shew she makes: but it is not love: it is not Mozart or Paesiello: it is Miss Paton, practicing.

PART II
Italian Opera

Introduction

THE KING'S THEATRE

SITUATED IN THE HAYMARKET, the King's Theatre was built in 1704–5 by John Vanbrugh and was intended as a theatre for Thomas Betterton's players. Despite alterations in 1707–8 and later, however, it was never suitable for that purpose; Colley Cibber stated in 1740 that he could not hear one word in ten. It was named the Queen's Theatre in 1702 on the accession of Queen Anne, the King's Theatre in 1714 (George I), and Her Majesty's Theatre in 1837 (Queen Victoria).

Its initial offering was Johann Jacob Greber's *Gli amori piacevole d'Ergasto*—the first opera performed wholly in Italian in London. There followed productions of other operas in Italian, in English "after the Italian manner," and in a mixture of Italian and English. But after 1710 productions were confined mainly to Italian opera, and exclusively so after the Licensing Act of 1737. Indeed, on at least two occasions—at the production of a revival in April 1800 of Giovanni Paisiello's *Nina* when the recitative was *spoken*, and at a production of "some scenes" in German from Mozart's *Die Zauberflöte* in 1829—the theatre violated its franchise.

With the arrival of George Frederic Handel in 1711, Londoners could enjoy the flowering of baroque opera. Moreover, under the auspices of the Royal Academy of Music—underwritten by a group of noblemen—Italian opera became a "plaything of the aristocracy" from 1720 to 1728 and indeed "has remained so since."[1] Handel and his supporter, John Jacob Heidegger, opened the Second Academy in 1729, and it lasted until 1733. But the competing "opera of the nobility," founded that year under the direction of Giovanni Battista, began to provide strong competition, and Handel turned to another musical form—the oratorio—and a new middle-class audience at Covent Garden Theatre. They became very popular, though he continued to compose some operas into the early 1740s.

RESISTANCE TO ITALIAN OPERA

While the upper orders relished the opera and welcomed prima donnas to their private musical entertainments, almost from the beginning we find a growing antipathy toward Italian opera among the middle classes. National bigotry and the jealousy of English musicians deserve much of the blame. As early as 1707 critic John Dennis wrote, "Let us take heed that, as we have taken the opera from the nations which we despise, it render us not contemptible to those very nations."[2] Even at its beginning, Italian musicians (with a sprinkling of French, Spanish, and Germans) were resented in England, where they earned at least twice as much in fees and salaries as local musicians. By mid-century, this trickle swelled to a great migration, and criticism was redoubled, but to little effect.

What added to the intensity of feeling was the presence—indeed, the prominent roles—of Italian castrato singers. They reigned there almost from its beginnings until late in the eighteenth century when the growth of comic opera (in which they seldom appeared) forced their demise. As early as 1703, a character in Thomas Baker's *Tunbridge Walks* speaks of going "to hear a parcel of Italian eunuchs, like so many cats, squall out somewhat you don't understand," and later critics found strong moral objections to their presence. Nothing more outraged the doughty sensibilities of John Bull—the "average" Englishman—and he delighted at hearing them burlesqued in English operas.

But the greatest objection to Italian opera was its foreign tongue. The influential critic Joseph Addison, who had earlier failed in his attempt to write an opera in English after the Italian manner (*Rosamond*, 1707), sharply chastised audiences who would "ease themselves entirely of the Fatigue of Thinking" by attending operas they could not understand (*Spectator*, no. 18). Jonathan Swift also condemned "Italian effeminacy, and Italian nonsense" (*Intelligencer*, no. 3); Dr. Samuel Johnson called Italian opera "an exotick and irrational entertainment" ("Life of Hughes"); and Lord Chesterfield admitted to his son: "Whenever I go to the Opera, I leave my sense and reason at the door with my half guinea, and deliver myself up to my eyes and ears." The dramaturgy of opera librettos was likewise condemned, but some exceptions were made for Metastasio.[3]

Though reviewers of Italian opera after 1785 show bias only toward the "Italian cabal" at the King's Theatre, as we shall see, criticism of the Italian influence still lingered. A foreign observer stated in 1791 that London was a "PERU" to foreign musicians;[4] in 1800, the *Dramatic and Literary Censor* (July 7) presented a vicious personal attack on Joseph Mazzinghi, a permanent English resident and composer of both Italian and English operas;

and in 1809, an anonymous pamphleteer thought all Italian singers — "spies, incendiaries, and parasites" — should be banished.[5] Yet resistance waned in later years and by 1814 anecdotalist Allatson Burgh could write: "The English have not only manifested a liberal spirit with regard to Italian Opera, but also good taste and good sense; for it is universally allowed, that the Italian tongue is more sonorous, more sweet, and of more easy utterance than any other modern . . . language."[6] Of course even the middle and lower classes thoroughly relished Italian opera arias — when they were fitted with English words and sung in English operas, as large numbers were after 1760.

LATER DEVELOPMENTS IN ITALIAN OPERA

By 1785, the beginning of our period, not only had late baroque opera been long dead, but even the Metastasian opera seria that followed it was in decline. To be sure, Handel arias borrowed by English operas or sung at concerts were still enjoyed, as were excerpts from his oratorios at the Lenten "Oratorios."[7] But as a composer of dramatic music he was at this point less well known than Purcell (Fiske, p. 275).

These changes came about gradually. Librettists Apostolo Zeno, whose reforms began about 1700, and Pietro Metastasio, who followed about 1730, brought a new order and purity to the loose baroque style. As opera seria, it was purged of all comic elements (though it had to end happily); it had a logical movement from problems to solutions, and the action was clearly divided into recitative and aria. The old *da capo* aria, in which the singers were expected to supply their own musical embellishments in the repetition, was strengthened, but there were fewer choruses. The musical structure permitted changes to be made by substituting or eliminating arias, though the drama might suffer.[8]

Thus the way was open for the expansion of pasticci — popular earlier in the century — in which an existing score could be interspersed by a compiler, an existing libretto reset with arias of a different origin, or existing arias grouped by a librettist with a specially written text. This practice was confined largely to commercial houses and arose from the power of the impresarios to diminish the risk of failure, for example, by selecting arias that had already won favor with the public. Pasticci had another advantage in achieving a variety not necessarily found in the work of one composer. Poor protection of copyrights at the time simplified such proceedings.

It cannot be overstressed, then, that most of the *opere serie* we are dealing with in this study were pasticci, compiled not only for the reasons just given but also because, to permit sufficient time for the requisite ballet in London, full-length operas imported from Italy had to be cut considerably by both the house composer and the house poet. Only those works by a few maestros who happened to be in charge of producing their own operas at the King's escaped these tamperings, which were also exacerbated by prima donnas whose "right of the book" gave them the privilege of substituting arias of their own choice whenever they saw fit. Thus, Sacchini's *Armida*, produced in London in 1791, retained few of its original numbers; it was assembled from at least three operas based on the Rinaldo and Armida story. Some later operas, such as those by Mozart and Rossini—especially when mounted by William Ayrton—managed to escape most of this mangling.

The popularity of Metastasio's own librettos was so great that it persisted long after operatic tastes had otherwise considerably changed. A glance at appendix 8 will show that his librettos were far more popular than any others in this period (this listing does not even include the many adaptations by others of his librettos). Nevertheless, by mid-century reform was in the wind, for the Metastasian format now seemed too mechanical and undramatic. The first came from Gluck and his librettist Calzabigi,[9] who in their *Orfeo* (1762) abandoned conventional virtuosity in the *da capo* aria and sought to emphasize dramatic truth through simplicity and musical expression.

More pervasive were similar reforms stemming from Naples, which had always been responsive to popular taste, and eventually Neapolitan opera took hold even in Venice as well as throughout Europe generally. It was signaled by a shift away from counterpoint and toward simplicity, with stronger emphasis on melody. There was an accompanying concentration on the words, with simple, heartfelt arias preferred to bravuras. This new *style galant* also sought for greater orchestral and choral effects.

But along with the new sentimentality in serious opera, we find an even more important mid-century development—the rise of comic opera or opera buffa. For by 1740 the buffa and comic intermezzi (purged from opera seria) were combined into one general type of comic opera. Its heroines were sung by women (never by castrati), and the bass voice (seldom used in seria) was introduced, leading to ensembles at the end of each act. The Romantic tenor voice also began to appear, though stylistically it was similar to the castrato. To reach the high notes many tenors and some baritones in England used falsetto extensively, for which they were criticized by Haydn.

Attempts were made to carry on the action of the drama in the finales, but this aim was not fully achieved before Mozart (Grout, I, 249). Through Goldoni the new comic operas became more like dramas than low-class farces and always had three acts. Characters were drawn mainly from the peasant or middle classes, and the plots, which frequently involved parody of opera seria, were both more realistic and more romantic. Popular Italian songs were often introduced, and recitative was much curtailed, though there was no spoken dialogue. The first comic opera appeared in London in 1748, but the genre did not become established there until 1760.

A COMMERCIAL HOUSE

As a commercial house, the King's was dependent almost solely on its box office receipts, including the leasing of its boxes, and it frequently had financial difficulties — a problem it shared with other commercial houses on the Continent. Owing to its insularity, the King's was at a disadvantage with respect to Continental houses — courtly or commercial — in producing its operas. As the *London Magazine* noted in 1820:

> The cities of Italy and Germany, be it observed, are not, like ourselves, content with the old [operas] till heaven pleases to send the new: — they address their efforts to rear a successive race of composers, whom they encourage; and the public exercise of art is with them, a constant theme of discussion, and object of exertion: composers travel from city to city, they are sought according to the report of their merit, and Managers engage a composer to write expressly for themselves. Those of the King's Theatre of England, on the contrary, wait patiently . . . till the continental cities have approved, and perhaps nearly forgotten, the compositions which we of the second table receive with the humility which becomes us. (July)

It is true that London had to wait fifteen years after its Continental premiere for the first hearing of a Mozart opera (though even Continental performances of his operas waned quickly after his death). But considering its distance from Italy, the King's did not do too badly. In the period from 1785 to 1800, for example, London waited an average of eight years following the European premieres of some sixty-five operas. If we eliminate nine of these operas that had delays of from seventeen to twenty-five years, however, the average of the others drops to six years. Moreover, in the same period, the King's presented twenty-four European premieres by sixteen composers, ten of whom were at various times in residence there.

The Theatres

PERFORMANCES

THE KING'S THEATRE PRESENTED approximately sixty nights of opera and ballet each season on Tuesday and Saturday evenings. The season normally lasted from December to July but could start in November and end in early August.[1] Beginning usually in March, benefit performances for star singers and dancers were given on Thursdays, and they could keep all receipts beyond a "house charge"; indeed, sometimes the benefit exceeded the salary of the star for the entire season. Aside from the boxes, which were subscribed for the first fifty nights, the theatre in 1785 could accommodate five hundred in the pit at 10s. 6d. per ticket, three hundred in the first (crown) gallery at 5s. per ticket, and two hundred in the second gallery at 3s. per ticket.[2] In the 1820s the boxes provided more than twice the receipts from the pit and galleries. Boxes in the upper tier could be taken by the night; their four seats sold for one guinea each.

The house was lit by wax candles (increasingly displaced by oil lamps) inside and outside the boxes and in the lobbies and passageways. A large chandelier was suspended over the pit. These remained on throughout the performances and provided plenty of light for reading librettos. The stage had twice that amount of light, using oil lamps for footlights and stage-lights; these had reflectors behind and sliding doors in front to control the amount of light during the performances; men adjusted them and reset additional moveable lamps as needed.[3] Illumination by gas was introduced in 1818 (see below).

The house was unheated, though there were stoves in the lobbies and salons. Fruit women offered refreshments for sale as well as translations of the librettos, which were often faulty and poorly written. In 1828 Thomas Alsager (*Times*) objected to the new practice of striking a heavy wooden block on the floor three times backstage to signal the commencement of a performance: "This practice is taken from the theatres of Paris, where, we recollect, it always appeared to us a very clumsy piece of scenic arrangement. The small bell formerly used here ... is surely ... a much less Turkish mode" (Feb. 11).

Though Italian operas in London had fewer rehearsals than at Continental theatres, the King's did hold them as long as a month in advance — sometimes longer. In 1795, for example, Gluck's *Alceste* had "30 full and regular rehearsals" (MC, May 4). A week before the premiere, a full dress rehearsal was open to subscribers only, and it was most often attended by "ladies of fashion" (*Times*, Apr. 5, 1790). Nevertheless, productions at the Kings were deplorable. After severe cutting the works often became unintelligible,[4] and the extraneous musical borrowings were ubiquitous. In Paisiello's *Il Re Teodoro* (1788), for example, historian Charles Burney thought the added airs by Corri, Mazzinghi, and Storace destroyed its unity of style, though the public wanted none of them omitted. Indeed, conductors and impresarios all over Europe were also responsible for the mangling of texts.[5]

THE MANAGEMENT[6]

1785–1800

Although Richard Brinsley Sheridan, proprietor of Drury Lane Theatre, and Thomas Harris, manager of the rival Covent Garden Theatre, were competitors with different politics, they actually had a friendly relationship, and in 1778, at the suggestion of George III, they bought the King's Theatre for £22,000. But it lost money, and in 1781 Sheridan sold his shares to his friend William Taylor, a banker's clerk then only twenty-six, for £12,333, while Harris's shares were sold to Gallini.[7]

"Sir" John (Giovanni Andrea Battista) Gallini (Florence, 1728–1805) studied dancing in Paris as a *soi-disant* impoverished youngster and came to London in about 1757. He made rapid progress as a dancer at the King's: by 1762 he was appointed dancing master there and published two books on dancing. He became wealthy, perhaps because of his marriage into English nobility, and he won a knighthood of the Golden Spur from the Pope (Gallini had no right to the "Sir" but assumed it anyway). A born entrepreneur, he increased his wealth by promoting various concerts and masques in London, and in 1780 he purchased a mortgage of £12,000 on the King's from a banker.

But Taylor, by this time indebted for £16,000, was jailed and his creditors forced the appointment of trustees to run the theatre, including Gallini, and by 1785 Gallini took over as manager and tried to improve performances at the King's. That year the *Advertiser* thought better musical values were to be found at the opera house than at concerts (Feb. 28). Early in 1786 the *Chronicle* stated that if Gasparo Pachieratti and Gertrude Mara were hired for the season, "serious opera would then be in a style of perfection far beyond any thing we have heard for many years" (Jan. 4). These singers were indeed hired by Gallini, resulting in several outstanding seasons. The 1787 season was "never so conspicuous" for its success in Italian opera UR, July 2). With the further acquisitions of Jean Georges Noverre as balletmaster (he had served in that capacity in 1781–82) and of Nancy Storace and Giovanni Morelli for comic opera, the King's "now muster[ed] greater strength" than shown for years, and the management was called "extremely liberal" (T, Apr. 30, 1789).

But even as Gallini took over the management, there were problems with creditors: "the business," said the *Universal Register*, "wears a very mysterious aspect" (Sept. 26, 1785). Some of the mysteries came to light three years later in a legal motion to remove Gallini from his post, with the charge that he "had shared in the emoluments resulting from the benefits of some of the performers" (T, July 3, 1788). The Lord Chancellor refused the motion but did require him to deposit some of his profits with the court, while the *Times* thought that only the sale of the opera house, under chancery, would solve the creditors' problems.

Gallini also encountered difficulties with his audiences in 1789 when the poor quality of dancers early that season brought about a riot, during which the scenery sustained considerable damage (T, Feb. 9). A month later the audience again became unruly, and after appeals by Gallini for patience, and with apologies in French by Noverre for his inadequate company, a crowd led by Lord Barrymore and other aristocrats "came forward on the stage, and with great *sang froid* broke every lamp in the orchestra," though the better part of the audience hissed their actions. "Those who read this paper," the *Times* continued, "will certainly not accuse us of having spared Gallini. . . . But what passed on Saturday, was not the mode to correct [the management], nor would such conduct have been tamely permitted at any other than the Italian theatre" (Mar. 9).

But a far worse disaster lay just ahead. On the night of June 17, 1789, while dancers were practicing on the King's Theatre's stage, some fireworks that were being prepared for a performance the following night caught fire and the whole building was soon engulfed in flames. No lives were lost, but the amount of damages was well over £40,000, of which only about £8,000 was covered by insurance. Arson was rumored but never proved. Aside from creditors the chief loser was a descendant of Sir John Vanbrugh and Taylor.

Despite the loss the company was able to finish out its season at Covent

Garden Theatre where the acoustics were perfect for opera, and the *Times* called for a new opera house to be built in "accord" with it (July 1, 1789). The following season the company had to be content with the Little (Haymarket) Theatre across the street, but this summer theatre was much too small: it was impossible to see the stage from the gallery, and there was little room for the orchestra (T, Jan. 8 and 9, 1790).

Meanwhile a good deal of dissension arose about using the old site, and there were even doubts whether Italian opera would ever really take root in the city. Moreover, the "supporters of English opera pleaded for the establishment of the native production in place of the fashionably exotic" (Smith, p. 11). Yet some of the nobility forged ahead, and the cornerstone for the new building, designed by Michael Novosielski, was laid April 3, 1790, by the Earl of Buckingham.

But within weeks after the fire, the Duke of Bedford, the Earl of Salisbury, and other nobles, with the support of the Prince of Wales, wanted to freeze out Taylor and establish a "court opera house" along the lines of European court opera houses. They engaged James Wyatt, the original architect, to remodel the Pantheon as an opera house (it was built in 1772 as a place to hold masquerades and concerts) and spent some £34,000 on the venture.[8] (Salisbury had to remain anonymous since he was the Lord Chamberlain — in charge of licensing.) The committee then engaged Robert Bray O'Reilly — really just a caretaker — to hire performers and inaugurate a season of Italian opera and ballet. The theatre opened as the "King's Theatre, Pantheon" under O'Reilly's direction in February 1791. Of course they had no difficulty obtaining a license, but they were much disappointed in being unable to engage either Giovanni Paisiello as house composer (Adalbert Gyrowetz, who composed much ballet music, ultimately took on that task) or some of the singers they wanted.

Without a license Gallini's 1790 season at the Little Theatre was not wholly a disaster: he was able to produce ballets and concerts, and some of the latter, conducted by Haydn and featuring his music, were very popular; together with the Salomon concerts at Hanover Square Rooms, they provided stiff competition for the Pantheon, which was already in debt because of the high salaries for singers and dancers (MC, Aug. 17).[9]

Shortly after the beginning of the 1791–92 season, the Pantheon also burned (Jan. 14) under mysterious circumstances, with a loss of £60,000. Arson was suspected but never proved, and the insurers never settled the claim. (It was rebuilt in 1795 as an assembly hall and came to an end in 1814.) Curtis Price[10] points out that the contract for the Pantheon had a potentially damaging clause stipulating that the committee was responsible for "dismantling" the theatre, which would have added enormously to their already heavy investment, raising the possibility that this may have had something to do with the fire. In any event, to obtain their agreement to transfer their allegiance and support back to the newly rebuilt King's Theatre, Bedford and Salisbury were granted no less than twenty-four boxes in the new theatre for their use, rental, or resale to compensate for their loss of between £30,000 and £40,000 in the Pantheon affair. But this represented a tremendous burden on the management of the new theatre, the effects of which lasted into the 1840s.

Still another remarkable aspect of this situation was the perserverance of Taylor in rebuilding the King's.[11] Discredited, penniless, and without a license after the fire, he was by January 1790 personally liable for £99,000 in unpaid opera debts. But he used his only advantage adroitly; since his innumerable creditors could not agree on what should be done, he was eventually able to get them to accept his "Plan," by which £70,000 could be raised through sales of stock in the new theatre and through the long-term rental of boxes. The sum was sufficient to begin construction, and at the same time Gallini[12] yielded up his mortgage, leaving the indefatigable Taylor again in charge; with the help of the Prince of Wales, he was again granted a patent.

With the 1792–93 season, opera performances were resumed at the new theatre. The new King's was the largest opera house in Europe, except for La Scala in Milan. The *Times* found it much too large and hard to hear in, even in boxes nearest the stage (Mar. 23, 1791), though others thought the acoustics good; the stage space was restricted, in any case. But since it was built in great haste, workmanship was poor, and the house needed much rebuilding in 1825.

Taylor now managed affairs somewhat better, and at the 1794 season opening, the *Chronicle*, noting its previous annoyances with him, now praised him for his "uncommon perseverance, zeal, and integrity" and declared that the theatre "in chastity and elegance of design, extent, and convenience of arrangement has not its superior in Europe" (Jan. 13). Further improvements were pointed out by DuBois the following season (MM, Nov.). And in 1798 the King's was the "best attended in years" (MM, July), Brigida Banti being the great attraction.

There was difficulty, though, in balancing the serious and comic strengths—for example, the company lacked a first-rate serious lead in 1795 and a comic lead in 1798. In 1796 Taylor began having trouble with his patrons. On February 6, a riot nearly erupted, but "whether this dissatisfaction arose from the supposed inactivity of the manager, or from the unmannerly intrusion of several persons on the stage, we cannot say" (DuBois, MM, Feb.). Taylor was in any event obliged to apologize to his subscribers. In 1797 there were economic troubles about which DuBois badgered Taylor: "We hear with regret that the pecuniary concerns of this house are very irregularly conducted" (Apr.). "There is a confusion pervades the management of the Opera, which, while it exists, will deprive the town of the variety of new operas and ballets to which it is entitled. Why these continued broils between Mr. Gallet [the dancing master] and Mr. Taylor?" (May). "The whole concerns of their magnificent theatre, for want of system and regularity, are rapidly going to destruction" (June). Ultimately Taylor could not pay the orchestra's salary (Smith, pp. 40, 41).

By 1798 the company had recovered, but in 1799 Taylor was again criticized for penny-pinching: "The liberality of Mr. Taylor, the Manager, cannot be praised with respect to the splendour or elegance of the dresses and decorations. They were strongly expressive of 'cold economy,' and the attendants were not only too few in number, but too squalid for the affected importance of the occasion" (*Times*, Jan. 23).

Despite the prevalence of pasticci, one occasional practice of the management during this period deserves mention. To indulge the craving for novelty, the manager, undoubtedly with the connivance of the musical director, very frequently cited advertised performances as "new" or "entirely new" (they almost never referred to Continental premieres) with reference to operas that had been previously performed at the King's, deceiving not only audiences but sometimes the reviewers as well. Giovanni Paisiello's operas, for example, often had several titles for the same work. His *Re Teodoro*, first given by the King's in 1788, was offered as "new" in 1795 under the title *Conte Ridicolo*. In 1793 the King's revived this opera as "new" under the latter title—perhaps with some justification in this case, however, for the alterations by Stephen Storace were extensive. The *Diary* critic recognized it as a revival but did not protest. In 1795 the King's called Paisiello's *L'Amor Contrasto* new—it fooled the *True Briton*—though it was the same opera as his *La Molinarella* (later amended to *La Molinara*), which had its King's premiere in 1791. Other composers' works met similar treatment. P. A. Guglielmi's *Pastorella Nobile*, first given in 1792 and revived in 1801 as "new," was assumed to be so by the *Times*. But when Pasquale Anfossi's *Viaggiatori Felici*, first at the King's in 1782 and revived in 1785 and 1786, was again produced as "new" in 1803, critic B of the *Times* was alert to the deception: "Surely the Manager must have supposed the public extremely ignorant with respect to the state of the Italian stage as connected with this country, to have represented a Comic Opera as a new Piece, which was acted, if not on the same boards [a reference to the 1789 fire], at least on the same scite, so far back as nearly twenty years ago."

The office of music director was an ephemeral one and shifted almost from season to season depending on which composers the King's could acquire for residency. Luigi Cherubini, Antonio Sacchini, and Anfossi had served in that capacity in earlier years. In 1791 Joseph Mazzinghi, Paisiello, and Giovanni Giornovichi were announced as the house composers, and the following year Mazzinghi, Guglielmi, and Paisiello were announced as house composers (however, there is no evidence Paisiello ever came to London). In 1793 Storace and Vincenzo Federici—the latter also serving as house poet—were house composers, and the next year Storace was slated as manager, along with Michael Kelly, while Federici was appointed director of music. In 1795 Francesco Bianchi and Martín y Soler presided at the harpsichord at their own operas. Bianchi and Mazzinghi were house composers for 1796 and 1797. And in 1799 and 1800, Federici was "director, at the harpsichord."

Michael Kelly became stage manager in 1793—the season of his premiere there as singer—and he continued in that capacity for thirty years, sometimes accepting a benefit in lieu of salary. In 1794 Lorenzo da Ponte[13] was appointed house poet, a post he retained for ten years at £250 a season. Famous for his libretto in Mozart's *Don Giovanni*, he wrote some fourteen librettos in London for operas by Martín y Soler, Mazzinghi, Bianchi, and Winter. Apparently, the King's listed no other house poets until 1816.

1800–1815

In 1803 when Taylor's "Rights to the Site" of the King's expired, he was forced to yield one third of his interest to one Francis Goold for £13,335. Goold began to assert his management the following season. The press praised him in 1804 for his fine productions of Winter's *Il Trionfo dell' Amor Fraterno* and *Il Ratto di Proserpina*. But the theatre lost £3,000 that season, and DuBois commented with tongue-in-cheek: "Mr. Goold means to reimburse himself by having no comic operas next season" (MM, Aug.). Yet in his production of Winter's *Zaïra* in 1805, he "carried his liberality farther in this point than any of his predecessors within our memory" (*Times*, Jan. 30); the *Chronicle* thought the liberality was due to "the addition of the Directors" (Jan. 30). Still Goold ran into problems in June when he had to close the theatre by midnight, depriving the audience of their ballet. In the ensuing riot, seats were torn up, chandeliers smashed, and musical instruments destroyed (*Times*, June 17).

It became necessary in 1806 to raise the subscription, which prompted the *Chronicle* (Dec. 15) to discuss in some detail the financing of the King's. The basic problems, they said, were the short season, the limit of two performances a week (except for benefits), and the limited audience: "A successful piece at Drury-lane or Covent-garden will command fifty or sixty distinct Audiences—the Opera has but one or two" and thus is "altogether dependent on the favour of the higher orders." Even with the appearance of a popular prima donna, "the infrequency of the performance makes it impossible for the Theatre greatly to profit from the fashion."

Continuing financial problems stemming from the Pantheon affair prompted Goold to request a "distinguished" committee[14] to examine the "whole state of the Opera affairs"; they certified to the theatre's loss of £15,261 in the previous four operas and recommended an increase in the subscriptions but not in the price for the pit and gallery. This presumably would set the King's on an even keel. Although the 1806–1807 season was profitable—the theatre received £23,000 from subscriptions and £7,000 from the pit and gallery—Goold had contracted with Angelica Catalani in 1807 for the sum of 2,000 guineas, plus two benefits, "one of which was insured to produce a thousand" (MM, June). "How we are ruined!" exclaimed the *Sun*.[15] Indeed, in 1807–1808 her salary was increased to 3,000 guineas, and the burden of it became almost intolerable in later seasons; Mount-Edgcumbe thought her demands did permanent harm to the King's and tended to exclude from the boxes "persons of moderate income."

Goold died in January 1807, and the financial burden again devolved on Taylor, though Edmund Waters, executor of Goold's estate, attempted to assert his claims on the theatre when two sets of performers were engaged. A fracas took place, and Waters was arrested for assaulting the dancer James D'Egveille, Taylor's acting manager, who was subsequently convicted of assaulting Waters (*Survey of London*, XXIX, p. 236). Further expenses were incurred in 1808 when the theatre was lavishly refurbished and redecorated. Discontent over Catalani's salary became critical in 1809, when she threatened to leave the King's to sing at Covent Garden. The *Times* complained bitterly: "We have always viewed with regret . . . the sums of money which are likely to be taken out of it by those rapacious foreigners. . . . We deem it not improbable that some attenpt will be made to introduce this woman upon the English stage, to raise the price of admission; thus at once insulting the sense and plundering the pockets of the British audience" (June 7).

Several seasons depended almost exclusively on Catalani, the British blockade of the Continent (1806–12) making it very difficult for the management to recruit there, though Lisbon and St. Petersburg were accessible. In 1808, for example, she sang all but four nights; as a result, "towards the close of the season, empty benches and a miserable box account, told the manager his error" ("Chronicles"). Other seasons were nearly as bad. In 1810, when Taylor was back in charge, Pucitta's *La Vestale* was produced "under the pretense of being for the benefit of Madame Catalani. This was however nothing but one of Mr. Taylor's schemes to deceive the public, in order that he might ensure to himself a full house." (E).

In 1812 several disgruntled patrons of the King's, unhappy with the management and the 300-guinea "or upwards" subscription price for boxes,[16] again briefly established a rival opera company at the rebuilt Pantheon, led by Teresa Bertinotti, who found it difficult to work with Catalani. But the license covered only one-act burlettas or dancing (though no *ballet d'action*), the productions were not attractive, and the orchestra was very poor; moreover, the Pantheon was declared unsafe (Smith, pp. 113–14). But the net result was that Taylor, who had lost £6,000 that season, had to lower his prices.

In 1813 Taylor was placed "under the rules of the King's Bench," and the sheriff took possession of part of his property against these liabilities. Catalani refused to sing some performances as her salary was in arrears, leading to great discontent in the audience. These conditions culminated in a riot when members of the audience even disarmed soldiers sent on the stage to restore order (*Times*, May 31). The artistic fallout of this situation, as well as frustration by the long domination of Catalani, is evident in Ayrton's review of Pucitta's *Boadicea* in 1813:

> When it is considered that there are many of the greatest masters which have never been performed in this country [including the "choicest" productions] of Piccini, Paisiello, Cimarosa, Winter, Gluck &c. which have been performed in London and heard with rapture, that are now forgotten, and would be completely new to the present age; is it not, under these circumstances, astonishing that a Manager should be so defective in his public duty, and so blind to his own interest, as to bring out an opera that he surely must be aware does not possess any one merit? (*Chronicle*, Mar. 26)

Meanwhile Waters vigorously pressed his claims against Taylor. The courts finally gave him their support, and in 1814 he bought out Goold's interest for £35,000, making him coproprietor with Taylor and a mortgagee of Taylor's share. Waters continued as theatre manager until 1820.

From 1802 to 1804 William Jewell was named acting stage manager; he became treasurer from 1805 to 1807 and again after 1812. The indefatigable Kelly seems to have had his hands on the reins during some of these years and was named acting manager from 1805 to 1807 and in 1809. Peter von Winter was music director from 1803 to 1805; Giocomo Ferrari was director at the harpsichord in 1808, and Pucitta and P. C. Guglielmi directed their own operas in 1809. The latter was apparently music director in 1810 and Pucitta in 1811.[17]

1815–1830

A radical change in the interior lighting of the King's took place in 1818. From the relatively dark interior that had hitherto prevailed, there was now a blaze of light—from gas. Alsager was enthusiastic: "The new method of lighting the house answers perfectly: every object, either on the stage or in different parts of the theatre, is as distinct as in the clearest daylight.... The beautiful form of the interior, by banishing the chandeliers, which projected from the boxes, is now seen to the utmost advantage" (T, Jan. 12). Leigh Hunt, who also admired the new lighting, noted that the gas chandeliers had been withdrawn from the boxes at Covent Garden: "The light is found, as we expected, too powerful for the complexion, when brought so near; and certainly there is no reason why the ladies' faces should suffer for it" (E, Jan. 25).

Another change to the theatre in 1829 caused much dissension: the installation of what were called "stalls"—seats with backs on them in place of the simple benches—in the first third of the pit nearest the stage. "Some of these stalls were quietly smuggled in during the last season; and as the subscribers to the pit were simple enough not to complain, success has emboldened the impresario" (Alsager, T, Jan. 26). There were no comments on what would seem to be the great advantage of stalls—seats with backs. Rather the complaints focused on the fact that the management was charging an additional 4s. for these seats and that the establishment of this special section would have a detrimental effect on the rest of the pit audience. There were letters to the *Times* (Jan. 30), including a rebuttal by manager Pierre Laporte (Jan. 31), and a near riot in the theatre (Feb. 2), but this new order prevailed, and ultimately they spread to the rest of the "pit," which thus became the "stalls" ("orchestra" in the United States).

At first Waters showed signs of success after replacing Taylor as director of the theatre, though Taylor continued to harass him. Funds were insufficient for new singers in 1815, but Waters did refurbish the theatre, and Alsager (T, Jan. 26) noted the first full house of the season: "We conceive the overflow to have arisen from the circumstances of the general management having for some time given such satisfaction as to bring the Opera more and more into fashion." The 1816 season was even more lucrative, but in addition to better singers, Alsager credited the Peace of Amiens (1815), which brought back a "multitude of military and naval officers," "numerous foreigners," and "our native gentry who have returned from abroad" (T, Aug. 12).

But Waters's greatest contribution was in hiring William Ayrton as the musical director for 1817. He brought to the King's a new musical sensibility—his greatest achievement. Alsager took notice of the system, "commenced last season, of studying to make the whole drama as perfect as possible, rather than particular parts prominent and the rest detestable; . . . it affords at once the truest gratification to an audience, and the surest means for the improvement of music" (T, Jan. 19, 1818). For the first time, too, Ayrton brought an increased respect to the intentions of the composer, at the expense of leading singers accustomed to doing pretty much what they wanted. In this he was not altogether successful. When he forbade Crivelli and Fodor from tamperings with Mozart, they appealed to Waters, who stood behind them. "Mr. Ayrton bowed and retired: responsibility without power come not within his bargain"; he even had to sue Waters to collect his salary—this for producing "a more profitable season than had been known for years" ("Chronicles"). The King's was so popular in 1817 that at some performances "not a single box" was unoccupied—a "rare occurrence" (BS, May). In fact, the appeal of opera to the middle classes was so great that the King's "has been extremely prejudicial to the other houses, particularly on Saturday evenings when the [playhouse] managers, even after the issue of abundance of orders, have scarcely been able to produce a respectable attendance" (BS, Mar.).

After Ayrton's resignation, Waters coasted along for a couple of seasons, but in 1820 his mismanagement produced another fiscal crisis. He could not pay the orchestra, and they refused to play. The house closed early that season—the subscribers were still owed several performances—and Waters fled to the Continent to escape his creditors (Taylor died in debtors' prison in 1825). The *Inquisitor*, however, blamed not Waters for this situation but rather "the cruel and capricious views of a party" among the nobility to establish a separate opera house, and the leading singers Madame Fodor and Signora García "were driven out of the country by the senseless objections and unwarranted influences of this party" (July 1820). These managerial problems had already been anticipated by Bacon in the *Quarterly Musical* (Jan. 1819):

> The immense sums annually paid in support of the Opera, entitle the public not only to a fine establishment, but to the very finest in Europe. It is perfectly clear that a far better performance might be given for the sum, or that the price of admission might be greatly

reduced, because the enormous expenditure entailed upon the concern by former pecuniary mismanagement, and by the present eternal litigations in the courts of law and equity, consume an uncommonly large proportion of the funds. (I, 259)

(For other interesting details on these managerial problems at this period, see "A brief statement of facts concerning the King's Theatre," TI, June 1818, 22–27.)

In 1821 John Ebers (c. 1785–1830), a bookseller, was brought in as manager, and except for one season, he remained at the King's until 1827 when he went bankrupt. Although he made a financial investment in the theatre, he was given the sum of £4,000 by the Committee "as an encouraging douceur to undertake the enterprize" (*London*, Apr. 1821). At least the King's was at this point in conscientious hands, but Ebers, who reported that the theatre lost £7,000 in 1821, struggled unsuccessfully for seven years to balance the books.

Ebers brought Ayrton back as music director in 1821; he took the post only on the assurance that his musical authority would not be countervened. Together with extensive redecorating and a strong roster of singers, the season succeeded in bringing back the most "polished" society it had seen in years (*Chronicle*, Mar. 12). Ayrton was praised by Alsager for making "our Italian theatre what it ought to be—a school of the fine arts, to form a point of attraction to the upper classes, as well as to the numerous foreigners who visit this city" (T, Aug. 20). But in 1822 Ayrton was "expelled," probably by the committee, and was replaced by a Sr. Petracchi, from La Scala, Milan (LM, Feb. 1822). In the King's season advertisement for 1823, no one was credited with musical direction, and Alsager fulminated at length against the management for the "dilapidation and decay" and underhandedness in dealing with the performers, especially the orchestra, which was forced to accept "terms degrading to their rank in the profession" (T, Jan. 6 and 27). Of course Ayrton agreed the season was not favorable: "People of rank have suffered much—or is it they are apathetic?" (Har, Jan. p. 28).

Giovanni Battista Benelli, formerly a theatrical agent, was part of the "new management" for the 1823–24 season (LM, Sept. 1823; T, Jan. 26) and was praised for his liberality (NM, Mar. 1824). He did not act under Ebers but was actually "manager and licensee" (Bacon, QMM, VI, 514–26), and Ebers sold his interest to him for £10,000. Yet the arrangements are not clear, for Ebers returned as manager for the 1825–27 seasons.

Again in 1824 Bacon complained (LM, Feb.) about the rise in the rent of boxes that season, claiming that the theatre took in £70,000 a year, while the engagements of principal performers were less than £15,000. But Weinstock tells us Benelli ended up in debt £25,000 for the season. He paid Rossini £1,000 for his appearances, and the singers cost him £10,950. He called in Catalani to "save the season" but this got him even deeper in debt. Yet in May of that year critic X of the *New Monthly* thought the house "restored in a state of efficiency and splendour" thanks to Ebers's "inconceivable efforts." Those efforts included bringing Ayrton back once more as musical director—not for the season but for producing a single opera—Meyerbeer's *Il Crociato*, which was carefully produced and proved very successful. Even then he was unable to control Malibran, who insisted on inserting an aria from another opera.

Criticism of Ebers mounted, however, in his last years at the King's. He engaged Carlo Coccia, opera composer, as musical director for three years, but Coccia ran into much difficulty and resigned the post after 1825. In that year, as the *Chronicle* wrote (Mar. 21), the theatre was "scarcely five and thirty years old—hardly out of its swaddling clothes—when one of its sides falls into decrepitude, threatens to sink under a kind of hemiplegia, and is superannuated before it has even arrived at the aduliscence of an edifice." The whole north wall had to be entirely rebuilt at a cost of £4,000–£5,000, the expense of which was not paid off until 1845. The company was forced to conclude its season at the Little Theatre. "This summer theatre," Ayrton reported, "is certainly not favourable to music, owing to the number of breaks in the front of the boxes, and the many cavities, in which the sounds are lost" (Har, III, 70).

In 1826 Bacon in the *London* (Feb.) wrote: "We thought last year that matters were pretty nearly at the worst at the King's Theatre, but we were in great error, for the proprietor has, by a vigorous effort, made a surprising progress from bad to worse." Not only were many favorite singers let go, but the controversial castrato singer Velluti (see "The Performances," part II) was appointed music director that season, and he kept performing "his" opera exclusively—*Crociato*. Bacon again observed, "A foreigner who has been so short a time in our country, can hardly be supposed to understand our traits" (*London*, Mar.). Ebers reported that Velluti, "being accustomed to the careful and gradual getting up of the operas in his own country, could not be reconciled to the more rapid preparations of the King's Theatre." Yet the opera was so successful it helped to rescue an all but depleted treasury.

In the 1827 season Nicholas Bochsa was named director, but the season had hardly started before he, too, fell afoul of criticism from the *Chronicle* (Dec. 4, 1826; Jan. 1, 1827), and Ayrton (Har, V, 18) castigated his production of Spontini's *La Vestale*.[18] There were other problems. Critic X of the

Examiner complained: "If Mr. Ebers will be foolish enough to engage actresses of high salaries, and stipulate that they should only play such characters as they themselves choose, on his head must be the blame" (Mar. 25, 1827). By his own account, in 1823 Ebers paid Alberico Curioni £900 as primo tenore serio and Mathieu Porto £800 as primo buffo—these amounts fall within the limits proposed for these categories by an "impartial observer" (*Literary Gazette*, Jan. 6, 1827). But the same year he paid García-Malibran £1,400 and Violetta Camporese £1,920—much above the proposed limit of £1,000 for a prima donna assoluta—though of course far less than the sum paid Catalani in 1808. But Ebers apparently far exceeded even these salaries in 1826. He engaged Guidetta Pasta for £2,300 for the 1828 season but explained that she had "a great effect on the fulness of the house."

Ebers protested that there had been no "superfluity" of orders; in his first season his "free list" was limited to £50, plus £50 for newspapers. But that he, like other managers, finally indulged in papering the house is evidenced by Ayrton in 1823 (Har, I, 41), when he noted a claque at work: "The system of *orders* acts injuriously in this theatre as it does in other places. When will the public resist this sort of tyranny over their judgments?"

Ebers complained throughout his book about the impossibility of managing the King's and proved himself no exception. The King's lost £44,000 under his regime. Nevertheless, he was able to sell his interest in the theatre in 1824 for £10,000 to Benelli, who was praised for his liberality (NM, Mar. and June). In 1828 Pierre Laporte took over as manager and stayed until 1841 though he too had to continue under the impossible load of the King's finances.

At the conclusion of the 1828 season, Holmes confirmed its success: "There has been variety in singers and performances, and improvement in the steadiness of band and chorus" (*Atlas*, July 27); Wade (*Athenaeum*) agreed. But Alsager, noting the exhorbitant rent[19] placed on the managers by the assigners of the lease (Messrs. Chambers), was worried about the future: "It has unfortunately happened, during a long series of years, that this theatre has been generally regarded as a foreign concern, with which national feeling was in no way to be connected; but this indifference has of late years been gradually converted into interest in proportion with the progress of musical taste, and it is with reference to that taste alone that all arrangements ought in future to be made" (T, Aug. 4).

In addition to the flap over the new stalls, the 1829 season got off to a bad start when Bochsa fired several favorite first-desk players in the orchestra, especially Lindley and Dragonetti, and substituted French players at considerably lower salaries. Ayrton and Alsager objected furiously, though Wade thought the money saved might be better used elsewhere. Views also differed on the season as a whole. By March Ayrton found "not a single performance has yet been given that would not produce an outcry in a barn!" (Har, VII, 97); by June critic X of the *New Monthly* protested strongly at the absence of new operas, and in the same month critic X of the *Examiner* (June 21) remarked on the ineptness of the management in its Mozart productions.

There was another feature of Bochsa's reign, starting in 1827, that drew criticism from the press: the growing number of presentations of one- or two-act operas cut down from three acts. It is not clear whether Bochsa seized on this device as an attempt to introduce more variety in the performances or to cope with the indispositions of his prima donnas. Of a truncated *Ricciardo e Zoraide* of Rossini, Alsager thought it would be better to omit it altogether, "considering the strength of the company" (T, Mar. 28, 1827). Critic X of the *New Monthly* thought the practice "ought to be exploded for ever" (July 1, 1827). In 1829 they also complained that the one-act *I Messicani* was expanded to two acts while the two-act *Ricciardo* was compressed into one, "and yet performed with a long interval of rest . . . so that . . . our notions of *acts* are actually at this moment in a sadly unsettled condition" (May; see also Har, VII, 98). Meanwhile in the *Athenaeum* Wade complained about the "bits and pieces" of operas produced that season. Similarly, there were complaints of omitted scenes: "Much discontent was manifested by the audience" for the omission of "the whole of the 7th scene" of Rossini's *Semiramide* (T, June 3, 1829). In 1830 critic X of the *New Monthly* thought that one-act versions were offered because of the unusually strong roster of singers that season: very few operas were written for more than "*one* first-rate singer" (June 1).

The Audience

THE MAIN INTEREST of the boxholders—the principal source of revenues for the King's—lay less in the performance than in the aristocratic society around them. Fashion there was the "ruling god," as Michael Kelly explained, since Saturday night performances were much better attended in the boxes than those on Tuesday nights, regardless of who was performing. In fact the nobility did not usually arrive until the performance was well under way, and the chattering and closing of box doors created disturbances as great as those at the playhouses. Each lady regarded her box as an extension of her drawing room—complete with servants who "kept places" in the boxes or waited out the performance in the upper gallery, which had the best acoustics in the house (*Survey of London*, III, p. 231). Visiting between boxes was *de rigueur*, even during the performances, and card games whiled away the *longueurs* during the recitative, though the guests occasionally paused to listen to a favorite prima donna sing a favorite aria. Indeed Christian Goëde,[1] though not always the best observer, called the patrons "destitute of all sympathy and enthusiasm" for Italian opera. Not all occupants of some boxes could see the stage anyway, so the men sitting in the back often wandered down to the "fop allies"—open spaces on each side of the pit where assignations were frequently made.[2]

Ernest Walker[3] tells us that the attitude of the English public toward music "demanded at all costs that it should not be bored," which led to pasticci, borrowings, and ornamental singing. But even in Italy, card games were played to fill in for the "monotony of the recitative," and there was much chatter and visiting during the performance.[4] Boxholders were quick to enlist fashionable prima donnas for their private concerts, and some kept in touch with the latest opera events on the Continent during their tours, passing along news of promising new singers and productions to the impresario at the King's, who, of course, also made his own trips to Paris and Italy to canvass promising musicians. All this changed somewhat during our period. Because of rises in the price of boxes, they became no longer a "home" to be loaned to friends, and unwanted tickets were sold.[5]

Indeed by 1834 Henry Chorley reported that the "air of a private society" at the King's had all but disappeared.

During the early years of our period, opera reviewers on the whole had little to say about the King's fashionable audience. The *Post* and occasionally the *Herald* dutifully recorded the presence of the nobility,[6] even if nothing was said about the performance. But other newspapers were even mildly negative on occasion. The *Times* complained in 1788: "Indeed, of late, the eminent composers are not very solicitous about the excellence of their overtures, which may be ascribed to the attention of people of fashion, who seldom come to the theatre early enough to hear them" (Jan. 17). In 1811 Robertson wrote in the *Examiner*: "Our nobility seem willing to endure every species of managerial imposition and insult, rather than forego [the opera];—so powerful is the force of fashion" (Mar. 24). And in 1813 the *Theatrical Inquisitor* complained: "It is almost impossible for a modest woman, under the present system of management, to appear at the opera, unless she has a box of her own; noise and confusion reign triumphant over the pit, and behind the scenes dirtiness and disorder, rule predominant" (Apr.).

Yet the decorum of the boxholders themselves was less than exemplary. The lack of attention they habitually gave performances is suggested by an incident at Catalani's debut: "Once indeed, while she was on the stage, there was some chattering in one of the boxes, which appeared to embarrass her a little; but it was immediately silenced by the imperative interference of the whole pit" (T, Dec. 16, 1805). As the *Times* declared, the audience at the King's was "not of the most polished kind" (Dec. 19, 1796). In 1792 the *Herald* wrote: "The *fop-allies* leading to the Pit were quite 'filled and dammed up' with legions of the well-dressed *Insipidi*" (Apr. 2). Even the normally well behaved "amateurs" hissed on occasion (P, Jan. 21, 1788; Mar. 25, 1789). When Mara arrived at the King's in 1786, numbers who could not get seats in the pit threw apples and oranges, then got on stage and produced a riot (T, Mar. 15). Indeed, in 1811 the *Chronicle* noted that the audience was "of the most promiscuous character we ever saw; for women of notorious infamy were placed in the boxes of the highest distinctions" (Jan. 28). (Rather severe attacks were leveled against the fashionable in later years; closely related to questions of public taste, they are discussed in "Themes and Currents," part II.)

Another source of irritation came from the presence of persons on the stage during the performance. Although this was occasionally a problem at the playhouses, it was much more severe at the King's. The manager was usually blamed, probably because at times he actually sold seats there for 10*s*., but at other times he was almost helpless in dealing with the situation.

Occasionally the management had sentinels on duty for that purpose, but they were not very effective. An advertisement in 1788 requested all persons to keep clear of the stage during the ballet to avoid possible accidents from moving machinery, opening trap doors, and the like (T, Jan. 29). The next year "Queen Charlotte caused two sentinels to be posted . . . so that no person was admitted to approach behind the stage but the performers. This unusual prohibition very highly disgusted John Bull" (*Post*, May 13). At a 1794 ballet, "some of our young Sprigs of Fashion made a point of sporting their persons so prominent on the Stage, as to spoil the effect of the representation" (T, Mar. 4). In 1796 there were "such crowds at the side scenes as almost to prevent the working of the machinery" (T, Apr. 18). And in 1800 DuBois declared: "We were happy to find the stage clear of a race of locusts, with which it has been too long infested, and we sincerely hope their flight is final" (*Monthly Mirror*, Apr.). The presence of any audience on the stage was forbidden by the Lord Chamberlain in 1813.

In the pit sat the town bucks, who came to meet acquaintances or make assignations. Most of the pit, however, was filled with the intelligentsia, professional men, writers, critics (who had passes from the manager), and other music lovers.

The galleries were the only part of the house where formal dress was not required. The lower or crown gallery (admission 5s) accommodated merchants, tradesmen, and other less affluent music lovers of the middle class. From its inception at least some of the middle classes attended the King's. If the average weekly wage of a clerk at the time was 10s,[7] Italian opera would not be beyond his reach, but it would require careful saving, and the lower prices at the playhouses would be more inviting.

The "gallery gods" in the three-shilling upper gallery were mostly sailors, prostitutes, and servants, whose livery was occasionally soiled by their neighbors. This motley group occasionally grew rowdy and threw fruit at, or even emptied buckets of water on, the occupants of the pit, and sometimes thrown objects caused injuries to them and members of the band.

The galleries were often frequented by claqueurs, many of whom represented an Italian cabal and supported only Italian-born musicians. Others were on the manager's "free list," which included his friends, authors, composers, and selected members of the press. One correspondent characterized them in a letter to the *Post* in 1778: "The managers, conscious of their own inattention to insure success, think to command it be cramming the upper part of the house with a set of miscreants (the sweepings of every Italian warehouse in town, etc. etc.) whose only payment is by palms of hands, and lungs."[8] This cabal was fully active as early as 1765, when it caused the failure of Thomas Arne's *Olimpiad*, and J. C. Bach came under attack in the 1770s and 1780s (Petty). But even Italian-born Antonio Sacchini and Venanzio Rauzzini fell afoul of their machinations in the same period.

Twice they gave support to Francesco Bianchi: once in 1790 for *Villanella Rapita*, when there was no support "for this poor opera" except for "a few followers in the gallery" (T, Mar. 8)—though in fact the opera was moderately successful—and once in 1799, at the premiere of his *Ines de Castro*, when the house was ill-attended save for the gallery, which was "almost filled with foreigners" who "seem to be introduced for the sole purpose of applauding the performances, and whose ill-timed approbation interrupted the business of the scene" (T, Jan. 23). Da Ponte reported "hands paid to applaud" Bianchi's *Aci e Galatea* in 1795.

In 1800 DuBois noted that "the Italians manage to keep things snug *en famille*," citing Haydn's "Scena di Berenice," which had been written for Brigida Banti, but "the Italian *junto* would not allow it to be performed at the opera" (MM, Feb. 1800). As A. C. Dies, Haydn's biographer, asserted, there was "a strong counter-party in London, mostly Italians, the *spiritus rector* of which was . . . [Felice] Giardini."[9] It was perhaps also due to this cabal that Mozart was not performed in 1794 despite the urging of da Ponte and Banti.[10] Predictably, the cabal initially caused trouble for German Mara and Irishman Kelly, as noted below. But it was also in evidence in 1794 at the premiere of the new buffo, Luigi Bonfanti, who was hissed by the gallery, which was "more than half filled with the lower sort of foreigners" (T, Dec. 9). Yet the gallery represented a small portion of the audience; and while it proved on occasion to get its way, there is no doubt that really popular composers such as Sacchini and Martín y Soler, and performers such as Mara and Kelly, could prevail over them.

In 1800, for instance, they were defeated in an attempt to thwart the operas of Winter, though a reference in 1813 shows them still active; they could then be found in the pit as well as the gallery. As the *Chronicle* wrote that year, Pucitta's *Boadicea* "was received without the slightest approbation, except for a few *foreigners* posted advantageously in the pit, and several who were stationed in the gallery. These foreigners are chiefly distinguished by the shabbiness of their dress, and their clamorous applause which they bestow, without any regard to justice or propriety" at the direction of the management. In 1825 the *London Magazine* instructed the claqueurs to attend rehearsals so they would at least know *where* to applaud (May), and in 1827 Hazlitt cited the "claqueurs, and unshaved, unshorn, uncombed, unwashed, undressed, block-whiskered, gratuitously admitted host of Italians [who call] for the performer to come on and make a bow for their noise" (*Atlas*, May 13). But "even the *claqueurs* could not be rallied in support of" some operas (Har, V, 171; VII, 97).

3. Domenico Cimarosa

5. Vincente Martín y Soler (c. 1787)

4. Wolfgang Amadeus Mozart, aged twenty-six; after an unfinished painting by Joseph Lange

6. Johann Simon Mayr

7. Gioacchino Antonio Rossini

8. Lorenzo da Ponte

With a real hit on his hands, the manager would give an opera a run of perhaps several weeks. Usually, however, variety and availability of singers determined the sequence of productions through the season. The musical preferences of the audience became known throughout the performance by means of the encore, meant in its sense of "again," not "more"; that is, the piece should be repeated—indeed it might even be repeated a third time, though the *da capo* aria itself involved repetitions! (Sometimes overtures were encored as well.) The practice had started before 1715, when the management forbade it (unsuccessfully),[11] and in 1736 no encores were requested owing to the length of the performance. But this was a Continental practice as well. Royal theatres had better control. In 1737 the San Carlo Royal Opera House did not permit encores except by permission of the king or his deputy.[12]

The press carefully noted encores, even in the later years when many of the critics were protesting this "barbaric" practice, for they represented a kind of statistical proof of the popularity of the opera. In 1791 the *Times* reviewer wrote: "John Bull will perhaps think it extraordinary that during the evening there did not occur one *Encore*" (Dec. 19). Surely the manager monitored singers' encores as well, though house attendance was a better clue to the success of any particular performance.

It took an extraordinary prima donna to defy this practice, as Mara did on a couple of occasions. The first was a concert at Oxford in 1785, when she refused an encore and was hissed by the audience on her appearance the following day (*Herald*, July 2). That event was recalled the next season by a *Times* reviewer, who wrote: "That Mara merits all the applause she can have, nobody can doubt. We did maintain it, when much opposition was in our teeth from the *barbarous* Sophs of Oxford. Nothing, therefore, but our zeal for *order* can be thought of, when we would check applause from being clamorous in the middle of an air. The airs . . . should not be bravo'd, &c. till the symphony be closed. They order this matter better in Italy." Again in 1793 at the King's, Mara "pleased too much by her wonderful exertions . . . and being unable to repeat [the aria] incurred censure of a discontented few" (*World*, Feb. 6). The *Times* decided "she was very properly hissed for refusing" (Feb. 6) but the *Chronicle* was more enlightened: "She was inhumanly encored in a most difficult song . . . and because she did not obey the summons of some twenty inconsiderate voices, she was cruelly hissed in the *finale*." After 1800 there was a gradual diminution in references to encores, though in 1808 Catalani was given a *double* encore, and "they afterwards became fashionable with regard to singers, particularly at the playhouses" (Parke).

Indeed by 1817 and the premiere of *Don Giovanni*, there was growing antipathy to it. On that occasion Alsager found that the interruption by applause of a fine passage—"however judicious in itself"—"is perfectly ruinous to the effect" (T, Apr. 16). At a later performance that season the *Inquisitor* (Aug.) put the blame on none less than "our *cognoscenti*," who, "assisted by a translation of the Opera, rattle their canes and their snuff-boxes, at every favourite, attract the attention of many silent observers by jargon and grimace, insist upon the repetition of some particular tune, and then walk out to avoid it. Such is a fair specimen of English taste." Kenrick, at the same opera two years later, wrote: "Most of the songs were encored. . . . We suppose the call generally proceeds from gentlemen who visit the house only once in a season, and who are therefore determined to have as much as possible for their money, regardless of the fatigue it may occasion the performers" (BS, Apr.).

In 1825 critic X of the *New Monthly*, at a production of *Così*, complained of the "many fatiguing *encores* . . . . These wanton and selfish calls exhaust the singers and cloy the hearers. . . . There is a point of saturation" (June). There were occasional encores for the chorus (T, May 2, 1829) and even an oboe player (T, July 27, 1830). On one occasion Malibran refused to comply with an encore, but subsequently gave in to the system (T, May 11, 1829).

Catalani, singing but one encore during a performance, accepted the plaudits after the final curtain; this may have been the first of such curtain calls at the King's (T, Mar. 1, 1824).[13] When Pasta attempted the same thing the following month, Alsager (T, Apr. 26) objected: "This foreign foppery ought to be discouraged." His objections were repeated in 1828 (Aug. 4), when Sontag "felt too much exhausted to comply" with an encore "and the call was then changed for that of her reappearance after the dropping of the curtains" (T, May 6, 1829). Occasionally the audiences were chastised for *not* encoring the *best* numbers in operas (C, Feb. 19, 1823; T, Apr. 26, 1824). In 1829 Alsager (Apr. 27) reprehended Malibran for ignoring the applause of the audience when she first appeared on stage, pointing out that such applause was customary in England though not on the Continent.

In 1787 the Prince of Wales headed a list of "Musical Amateurs," which included ten members of the nobility,[14] though in 1790 the *Times* cited the Duke of Leeds as "without exception the first Gentleman Amateur in this kingdom" (Jan. 38). Thus at any time there were probably a couple of dozen "amateurs"—all from the nobility and all boxholders—who did provide the upper orders with more than a modicum of interest in the performances. Their views on operas and singers seemed to be well known to, and were reported by, the press. Their behavior during performances was carefully monitored to note their degree of enthusiasm, or lack of it, and their views on forthcoming productions were also known and perhaps solicited in the green room. No instances are reported of divided opinions among the amateurs—they were not necessarily amateur *performers*, for they were also referred to as connoisseurs, cognoscenti, and dilettanti—though their views were sometimes contrasted with those of the reviewers.[15]

In 1786 the *Chronicle* referred to them as the "first judges" (Feb. 16); in 1789 the *Post* called them the "proved judges" (Jan. 26); and in 1795 the latter cited the "refined taste of the Italian cognoscenti" (Feb. 2). This adulation is further evident in the very frequent citation by reviewers of their opinions on the music and performances; scarcely a production in the early years does not elicit such comments. Their expectations were not disappointed in Andreozzi's *Principessa* (T, 1801) or Bianchi's *Alzira* (C, 1801), and they were indebted to Josephina Grassini for producing the former's *Vergine* (T, 1804) and to Goold for producing Winter's *Trionfo* (T, 1804). There was "not an *amateur* who did not leave the theatre with some degree of regret" after hearing Elizabeth Billington (T, Feb. 25 and March 29, 1805), and Fioravanti's *Capricciosa* was a "high treat to the connoisseur" (C, 1809).

But after 1809 references to amateurs were less frequent—again, I think, showing a growing independence of the press. In 1812 the *Chronicle* (Mar. 5) spoke twice of the "audience" where they would previously have written "amateurs" or "cognoscenti." And in 1813 the *Chronicle* actually undertook instruction to the amateurs: "We wish to excite the attention of all connoisseurs to these sublime productions" of Mozart (Mar. 1).

To be sure, in 1816 the *Times* (probably not Alsager) was deferential at a performance of *Figaro*, which was "held up by amateurs more competent than we are to pronounce its praise" (June 24). And in 1824, at the premiere of Rossini's *Zelmira*, Ayrton noted that "many beauties that did not escape the observation of discriminating judges, were, however, unobserved by most of the audience" (C, Jan. 26, 1814). But in 1817 Bacon had pointed out that "Operas are not composed for professors alone; in Italy, above all, they are written to please the population at large" (*Gazette*, Mar. 15). In 1824 they dismissed "the intricacies of composition—very fine, the connoisseurs say, but very wearisome and . . . very unintelligible to an English audience" (Jan. 31). In 1827 the *London* observed: "Formerly the amateurs were a very small body; now every body has a taste for music—a very bad taste undeniably, but still a taste. . . . But a large portion of the audience will probably . . . attain to a moderate degree of discretion formerly limited to a select few" (June, pp. 152–53).

In fact by 1829 critic X of the *Examiner* doubted whether there were *any* competent judges at the opera. Complaining of poor Mozart performances "with scandalous slovenliness" in the chorus, "fine airs omitted, others transferred, and whole parts transposed," he wrote:

Mr. Laporte, or his blessed understrappers, perhaps judge, and we think they judge correctly, in setting down one half of the audience at the Italian opera as wholly incompetent to give an opinion upon music, and the other half as utterly indifferent to everything within the walls except the drama, and the exhibition of their own precious persons, which passion almost absorbs the other. The conductors, who are shrewd observers, and moreover *are* judges of good music . . . have only to remark the utter ignorance manifested by their auditors when they determine upon any liberty with a composer . . . and they might . . . safely perform an opera backward, as schoolboys do the Lord's Prayer, to raise the Devil.

Commentators spoke occasionally of the lack of knowledge of Italian on the part of the audience. This ignorance was not universal, though Bacon in the *Gazette* was probably accurate in citing, in 1817, "the imperfect knowledge with a great part of the audience." But in the same year in the *Chronicle*, condemning the shifting of an aria in Mozart's *Tito*, Ayrton wrote that this offered "an insult to the understanding of the audience, who surely may be presumed to know enough of the language to enable them to discover so palpably absurd and ludicrous a transposition." As early as 1807 the *Chronicle* pointed out that tenor Giuseppe Siboni "labours in vain to make himself understood"—a desideratum the reviewer obviously thought important.

Some of the upper classes knew Italian; an author who was certainly no partisan of the fashionable pointed out in the *Gazette* in 1826 that "families of rank have travelled on the Continent, especially in Italy" and many "have an intimate knowledge of the Italian language and music." Certainly many "professors of music" among the audience knew Italian, as well as some of the "cognoscenti," though th *Inquisitor* in 1816 cited the latter as "rattling their translations." In 1815 the *Times* tells us that the quality of those translations was "a matter certainly not unimportant to one half of the audience."

Interest of the middle classes in Italian opera had long been whetted by airs borrowed from them for English operas, and in 1816 the *Times* (May 20) reminded its readers that the music of *Cosa Rosa* was well known, although it had not been performed at the King's since 1805. But an even more powerful force was at work during these years—the large-scale introduction of fortepianos (as they were first termed) into middle-class homes, where the family daughters followed the rage to perform on them and piano teachers were inundated with pupils.

Substantial improvements in the piano were made in the 1790s by John Broadwood, who produced seven thousand square and one thousand grand pianos between 1782 and 1802. By 1820 "the pianoforte was tending to become a piece of furniture by owning which a lower-middle-class family could appear a shade less lower." In the same period there was a large increase in the number of music shops and published piano renditions of favorite numbers.[16] Burgh (I, iv) claimed daughters of mechanics would feel deprived without a pianoforte.

In this manner, the family came to know Italian arias sometimes even before they were heard at the King's, as the *London* (Aug. 1825) wryly commented anent a performance of *Crociato*: "But after [an] unpromising beginning, perhaps we enjoy the more keenly those compositions in which Meyerbeer discovers his genius; these pieces are already so hackneyed, that we need not particularize them; we have, indeed, seen them advertised under the title of The Beauties of Meyerbeer; and by this time all the pianofortes in the united kingdoms have resounded with them." Surely the interest of such families in the performances at the King's, and in the reviews of them, increased during this period, when, as we shall see in "Themes and Currents," part II, the press largely agreed on the improvement of public taste in all classes.

Anther factor contributing to the spreading interest of Italian opera was the enormous popularity of Mozart and Rossini, along with the brilliance of such divas as Sontag, Pasta, and Malibran in the late 1820s. Whatever the cause the resulting increase in attendance of the middle classes at the King's is evident. To be sure in 1818 Bacon, in the *Musical Quarterly*, reported but few of the middle class at the King's (I, 218). Perhaps less reliable was Kenrick, who observed in the *British Stage* of July 1817 that the great popularity of *Don Giovanni*, which "all" the middle classes attended, had a serious effect on the attendance at the playhouses. By 1821 Ebers found that lovers of opera were "now of a numerous class," and in 1823 the *European*, noting a similar trend, thought it arose "from the general spread of knowledge, and the love of intellectual amusement among the mass of the people" (Jan.). In 1830 Alsager pointed out, at the premiere of the English version of Rossini's *Gazza Ladra*, that the music was "all familiar to the public" (T, Feb. 5).

The Operas

BY 1760 few if any European opera houses still patronized opera seria exclusively, and at the King's comic opera had achieved a parity with it by 1765.[1] From 1788 to 1794 the comic mode even became predominant, and the most important composers produced there before 1800 — Sacchini, P. C. Guglielmi, Sarti, Fioravanti, Cimarosa, and even Paisiello — wrote both types. Indeed many of the serious operas, such as those of Sacchini, were considerably "re-formed" from the older Metastasio type. In his seria *Pirro* (1787), for instance, Paisiello first introduced an action finale, and in *Elfrida* (1792), also a seria, he refused to write ornamented vocalizations.

Comic operas also became more innovative. As early as 1784, in Paisiello's *Il Re Teodoro*, a "dramma eroicomico," and in Gazzaniga's *Don Giovanni Tenorio* (1787), a "tragi-comedy," we find a shift toward the semiserious opera (the term did not come into use until 1800). In these types a heroic (sometimes historical) figure becomes the prototype. Part of this development merged into other new opera types — the *farsa sentimentale* and the *melodramma sentimentale*. The latter trend can be seen in the theme of madness, which occurs in Paisiello's late opera *Nina*, an opera that had a strong influence on Paer's *Griselda*, *L'Agnese*, and *Camilla*. For a time, semiseria opera represented no synthesis but rather "a haphazard product of several strains" and had little effect on the music until the appearance of Mayr and Rossini, who occasionally used the same music for both comic and serious elements (*NOHM*, VIII, 337, 391).

Patrick Smith[2] has noted that the eighteenth-century libretto did not attract first-class minds, that their names seldom appeared on the printed librettos, and that they were somewhat superseded by the growing importance of music vis-à-vis words. But by the 1780s a new Romantic influence was making itself felt in the librettos,[3] many of which were based on Revolutionary "rescue" themes, such as Paer's *Camilla*, Cherubini's *Lodoïska*, and of course Beethoven's *Fidelio*. This trend is also evident in librettos borrowed from Sir Walter Scott. Romantic aspects are strongly evident in parts of Rossini's *La Gazza Ladra* as well as in act I of his *La*

Donna del Lago (via Scott's romance) and in act III of his *Otello* (much abetted by Pasta's performances). The libretto of Mayr's *La Rosa Bianca* also reflected the new mode. Meyerbeer's *Il Crociato*—a hit in London—showed "every Romantic effect except the supernatural" (*NOHM*, VIII, 126). Not all these developments, however, were welcomed by the critics, as we shall see.

A more gradual but pervasive effect (especially felt in London in the operas of Mozart) was the growing German influence in instrumentation. To be sure, Salieri (Vienna), Paer and Morlacchi (Dresden), Spontini (Berlin), and German composers like Mayr, Winter, Weigl, and Meyerbeer—not to mention Mozart—all studied in Italy, and the Italian school, which "never allowed lyric drama to be threatened by the eloquence of the orchestra,"[4] was generally sustained in Germany until the advent of Weber. Nevertheless, an increasing emphasis was placed on combining Gluck's dramaturgical theories with the symphonic ideal of Haydn, and this was clearly perceived as a German development in London. Thus the musical taste of the listeners at the King's Theatre, where all these composers were heard, was polarized for many years between the influence of the German school and the Italian, with the former influence gradually gaining ground in popularity and triumphing in the operas of an Italian—Rossini!

During the forty-five years covered by this study, the number of operas presented each season (see appendix 4) varied from as few as 5 in 1792 to as many as 16 in 1828 and 1830, for an average of about 10. Similarly the number of performances ranged from as low as 39 in 1826 to as many as 85 in 1805, with an average of 65.6. Negative variations were due to such factors as the loss of the theatre by fire in 1789, extensive reconstruction in 1825, competition from the Pantheon in 1792 and 1812, and of course from financial problems throughout the period but especially in 1828–29. Positive variations were due to particularly remarkable prima donnas, such as Catalani in 1805–6, and an unusual contralto, such as Grassini, who followed her.

An overall decline will be noted after 1794 in the popularity of comic operas—they were all but washed out after 1821—and their seasonal average of 1.9 contrasts with that of 2.4 for serious operas, which included an increasing number of tragicomic and melodramatic types as the period advanced. Matters of taste aside, it must be remembered that the repertory changed from season to season—sometimes radically—depending on the ability of the impresario to provide singers suited to serious or comic roles.

But opera revivals were equally important to every season, with averages for the entire period of 32.6 for premieres and 32.8 for revivals. Despite the popularity of new serious over new comic productions, the seasonal average of serious revivals—2.7—was less than that of comic revivals—3.5.

Yet relatively few premiere operas were revived. Of a total of eighty-two new operas from 1785 to 1800, for example, only thirty, or about 39 percent, were ever revived. And only seven had four or more revivals up to 1830: Cimarosa's *Il Matrimonio Segreto*, seven, and *Il Capriccio Drammatico*, four; Paisiello's *Elfrida*, seven, and *Nina*, five; Gluck's *Alceste*, six; Bianchi's *Semiramide*, six; and Martín y Soler's *La Scuola de Maritati*, four.

With their thirst for novelty, opera-goers were rather hard on composers. Of the forty-six represented in our period (see appendix 6), twenty-eight, or a little over half, had four or fewer productions, while at the other end of the scale only five composers had twenty-five or more productions. Rossini's startling total of seventy-one—due in part to many one-act productions—was achieved in fifteen years, while Mozart's forty-three were compiled in twenty-four years; but interest in Cimarosa and Paisiello continued through much of the period despite profound changes in musical taste.

Obviously some premiere productions met with success while others did not, and normally this could be determined by the number of performances for each production during its first season. A production with nine performances ("nine days' wonder") was considered a success at the playhouses, which not only had a much longer season but had six performances a week rather than two, or sometimes three, as at the King's. Though we have little interest in the "gross receipts" at the King's,[5] its manager had to pay attention to its economic viability. While the number of productions of opera and ballet—new or revived—offers a clue to the impresario's willingness to provide a certain amplitude and variety in any season, the number of performances provides an indication of the popularity of these productions and the overall strength of the season. (We can present no figures on *attendance*—the bottom line for the impresario; but, even if the boxes were paid for by season, news of a popular production would help fill up the pit and gallery, from which receipts were about half that of the boxes.) The number of performances can also provide something of an index to the taste of the audience for the various types of productions and the appeal of the singers.

Listed in appendix 4 are the season totals for the number of new operas and their performances, and from them we can calculate a rough index to the popularity of premiere productions for each season. For the entire forty-five-year period, that ratio is 7.6—the average number of performances for each new production. From this we would conclude that any premiere production should, *mutatis mutandis*, require only slightly fewer performances—say six—to be considered successful or popular.[6] This average varies, of course, among the seasons, moving from a high of 12 or 13 in some seasons to a low of 1.5 in 1829, which indicates something of the difficulties the company was then experiencing.

With respect to particular operas, we can unequivocally identify which new operas were hits at the King's. But a drop below six performances does not necessarily reflect negatively on the work or even its popularity. Often new operas opening late in the season, when many of the box patrons had retired to their country estates, did not do well. Benefit operas too—frequently mounted after March—are difficult to classify; some—often the choice of the one benefited and sometimes planned in haste—were not expected to have more than a single performance. Moreover, performers' voices were often subject to hoarseness in the damp English climate, and an otherwise fine opera would have to be postponed and perhaps even abandoned, just as injuries to ballet stars affected the production of new ballets. But the quality and power of the singers, the attraction of the music, and the attention given to costumes and scenery all had an effect on the popularity of a given production.

The composers as well as their operas are discussed more or less chronologically with respect to their premieres at the King's, though a different order is sometimes prompted by the material. It should be kept in mind that, until Mozart and Rossini, the "right of the book" was fully exercised by leading singers—abetted by most musical directors—and that scarcely an opera was performed without borrowings from an average of three or four other composers (space doesn't warrant listing them all).

Certain themes run through some of the criticism and are briefly pointed out in passing, but they—together with themes from "The Performances" in part II—are not fully elaborated until the following section, "Themes and Currents." We can, however, offer here a preamble to the repertory as a guide to the high points of the ensuing discussion.

Among the older composers—both recently in London—Sacchini, who had only one success after 1785, drew fair support, while Anfossi was regarded by some critics as brilliant and original, though the coolness of the audience was noted. Sarti's operas—still being produced in 1808—received very high praise for an early comedy and for three later works, but two operas in between were "mechanical" or had no "character" and were only moderately popular. Two of Salieri's comedies were also highly praised, though one failed.

There was little admiration for some of the "French" composers; Gluck's *Ifigenia* pleased only the press, for example, though his *Alceste* was a popular and critical success in 1795. Two comedies by Cherubini, regarded as "original" by the press, received strong support, though one failed.

Almost all of Cimarosa's productions were comedies, and most succeeded with both the critics and the public. But two comedies and one seria succeeded despite negative reviews, as did two comedies with mixed reviews. Two late seria operas also got mixed notices, one of them (1817) with very strong critical support despite changes in musical taste.

Operas by Guglielmi, Federici, Mazzinghi, and Martín were generally admired by the press, especially a pastoral by the latter, which failed. One of Bianchi's pastorals, also praised, likewise failed—the genre was now too old-fashioned. Also Bianchi's first opera, a comedy, was panned by critics; but with the assistance of claques it succeeded at the boxoffice. Of his other nine operas (the last six were all serias), three drew positive reviews, and two others outstandingly favorable ones—all were successful, as were four serias that received mixed notices.

Paisiello was also very popular with both the critics and the public. His ten comedies, produced between 1777 and 1799—some with revivals after 1815— were well supported by the critics; four of them received very high praise and long runs. Of his four serias, one received harsh reviews but succeeded, while another was praised but failed. Toward some late revivals, reviewers were generally critical, though there were a few exceptions. Both the press and the public were kind to Von Winter's few operas at the King's, and some critics welcomed the advent of a new German influence in his music.

Guglielmi, Portugal, and Pucitta had the powerful aid of Catalani behind their productions. For that reason, however, the critics tended to dismiss some of them. Guglielmi's operas got mixed or adverse notices and just succeeded. Some of Portugal's, too, had the support of the press, and one (1811) was even highly praised; the public response varied considerably. Pucitta, however, ran afoul of the critics in two of his comedies, though they were popular; one seria, with fair reviews, also succeeded. His last two serias drew mixed notices and were marginal failures.

Of the composers after 1815, Paer received very strong support from the critics for his five melodramatic operas, though three of them were marginal successes. An 1820 revival also drew high praise. Mayr's only comedy had the support of both critics and patrons, as did one seria. But another seria had only fair praise and fair attendance. A late seria (1828), confronted by changes is taste, drew mixed notices and failed. Of Meyerbeer's two serias, one got mixed reviews but succeeded, and the second got positive reviews but failed. (The failures were due to faulty performances.)

Late operas by Coccia, Bochsa, and Bellini all failed, and all drew negative reviews. One opera by Spontini failed because of performances, but another succeeded; both got quite favorable notices.

The contributions of Mozart and Rossini to the King's are so enormous as to defy any sort of summary.

9. Giuseppe Viganoni

10. Diomiro Tramezzani

11. Giuseppe Naldi as Figaro in *Le Nozze di Figaro*

12. Giuseppe Ambrogetti as Don Giovanni (c. 1824)

13. Manuel del Popolo Vincente García

14. Giovanni Battista Velluti

15. Domenico Donzelli

17. Brigida Banti (c. 1795)

16. Gertrude Mara (c. 1791)

18. Elizabeth Billington

19. Angelica Catalani (c. 1807)

21. Joséphine Fodor-Mainvielle

20. Teresa Bertinotti-Radicati

22. Teresa Giorgi Trombetta Bellochi (Belloc)

23. Henrietta Sontag

24. Giudetta Pasta as Tancredi

25. Maria-Felicia García-Malibran (c. 1835)

HANDEL

A taste for the older composers was fast fading at the King's even before 1785. Indeed only one opera of George Frederic Handel (1685–1759) was revived after 1760—*Giulio Cesare in Egitto* in 1787—but it probably bore little resemblance to the 1724 original. Dr. Arnold, musical director, selected music from three other Handel operas as well as from *Cesare*. Both Mara and male alto Giovanni Rubinelli had sufficient voice and style for this music, but the other parts were "miserably executed, and the effect was absolutely ludicrous" (Mt-E). Yet the opera was quite popular, being repeated eleven times that season. Rubinelli, one of the last castrati in London, left the King's at the end of it, and no further Handel revivals were risked. Handel's music was of course still very popular at concerts and the "oratorios."[7]

BACH

Johann Christian Bach (1735–82), who became as English as Handel, suffered a similar fate. His last opera for the King's—and his best—*La Clemenza di Scipione* (1778), a late Metastasio work, was generally praised by the press.[8] The opera received eight performances, but there were no revivals of Bach operas until 1805 when Elizabeth Billington, the great English soprano, brought out *Scipione* for her benefit. The *Times* called the opera "the work of a great genius, uniting at once all the science and energy of the German school with the delicacy and expression of the Italian," and DuBois in the *Mirror* asserted that the music was "bold, expressive, and tasteful." Critics agreed that the work was produced with "classical correctness" and splendor. The opera received thirteen performances that season and five the following, yet no other Bach revivals were attempted.[9]

SACCHINI

In 1778 Bach's name was linked to Sacchini's as the very best of the current composers of opera seria (PA). Antonio Sacchini (1730–86), who began writing operas in Naples about 1761 and had his first big success in *Olimpiade* (1763), was one of the most popular composers at the King's, though that popularity was largely limited to his residence in London from 1772 to 1781.

Gertrude Mara was probably responsible for the 1786 revival of *Perseo*.[10] One reviewer (TC, Mar. 22) wished "that more of Sacchini's songs had been preserved. They have not mended the opera by the adoption of other compositions." In 1791 Joseph Mazzinghi, then musical director, undertook a revival of *Armida*, which had premiered in 1775.[11] The opera opened the season at the Pantheon,[12] but even the superior performance by Mara in the title role could not obtain more than five hearings for it.

Nevertheless, still another serious opera, Sacchini's last, was produced in 1797—the London premiere of *Evelina* (with a subtitle "The Triumph of the English over the Romans"). The story, based on "the history of the ancient Prince of Wales" (MM), was no doubt partly responsible for the work's popularity—thirteen performances that season and five the next—with the further appeal of an elaborate production and the support of Banti in the title role. Critic C (T) noted that although Sacchini's music was famous, this work alone was "capable of stamping with solid reputation a name totally unknown." An unidentified reviewer (TC) enjoyed the delightful choruses of the Druids. Parke noted the "elegant and finished" style of the opera.

Concerning Sacchini's work as a whole, Burney wrote, "This composer has a taste so exquisite, and so totally free from pedantry, that he was frequently new without effort," and he described his accomplishments as "rich and ingenious." George Hogarth felt that Burney's appraisal was just.[13]

ANFOSSI

Pasquale Anfossi (1727–97) had two enormous successes in London—*Viaggiatore Felice* in 1782 and *Trionfo* in 1783, with 28 and 18 performances and highly favorable reviews (see Petty, pp. 199–202). They no doubt prompted the composer to conduct his operas there in 1783 and 1784. Yet his later operas were largely disappointments. His *Il Curioso Indiscreto* opened the 1785 season with mixed notices; it was moderately successful. His serious *Nitteti* was revived; the *Herald* praised the overture, a brilliant first act, and several arias[14] in which Anfossi "has given the greatest proof of his taste and abilities." But Este in the *Advertiser* (Mar. 4) noted: "The music . . . boasting equally a good deal of contrivance and effect, passed by neglected, without a single hand in favour of Anfossi." It received but five performances.

In his *Didone Abbandonata* (1786), Mara sang the lead at her King's debut. The libretto, adapted by Badini from Metastasio, was praised by the *Universal Register*, which pointed out that "a considerable part of the dialogue is a literal translation of the finest passages of the Aeneid, which gives it a degree of energy and excellence, but rarely to be found in [opera]." The music possessed a "delicacy of turn and originality of stile." The work received eight performances but failed the following year.

L'Englese in Italia followed later that season. The *Herald* protested the Italian allusions lost on English ears and was not too happy with some of the music. The work was repeated only once.

In 1795 Brigida Banti brought out Anfossi's *Zenobia in Palmira*, which he had written for her in Venice (1789). Though the arias were well adapted to her voice, none was encored (T); yet the work succeeded.

SARTI

The last of the older composers, Giuseppe Sarti (1729–1802), also fell in popularity after some initial success. In fact his first King's premiere in 1784—*I Rivali Delusi*—had a phenomenal success, receiving twenty-one performances that season. It was revived six times the next season and again in 1793 under the title *Le Nozze di Dorina*. Revised by Storace it contained at this point additional music by himself and Martín; the *Chronicle* was enthusiastic and this version had ten performances.

This success was followed in 1784 by another comedy, *Le Gelosie Villane*, which had greatly increased Sarti's reputation. An unidentified review (TC) stated: "Comic operas are certainly the favourites of the town, but the *Gelosie Villane* . . . has the highest right to preference, not only on account of the music, but because there is in the opera itself a plot tolerably well supported, and the jealousy of the villagers displayed all that colouring of living and ludicrous comic which becomes the situation of various personages." For some reason the opera failed that season, but it played fourteen times when it was revived in 1794 in a two-act version by da Ponte under the title *I Contadini Bizzarri*.

Sarti's first serious opera at the King's was *Giulio Sabino*, produced in 1788. Although Cherubini's setting of the same libretto[15] had failed badly two years earlier, Sarti's received eleven performances, owing to the great strength of Luigi Marchesi, who made his King's debut in this production. It was Sarti's most successful serious opera on the Continent (Loewenburg)—and his *chef d'oeuvre* (Mt-E)—but for some reason it was not revived at the King's; moreover, the reviewers remained generally unimpressed. The music was "rather sweet and agreeable than august and impressive. . . . There is nothing that lingers on the ear and hangs about the heart" (P, Apr. 7). The opera "exhibits little taste or originality and shews that [Sarti] has given himself no great concern about the affections" (P, Apr. 14). The *Advertiser* placed Sarti in the "second class of musical writers," while the *Times* thought a great part of the music was very insipid, excepting only a first-act duet, "Oh Dei, da tanti affanni miei" (Apr. 14). The *World* agreed: "That Sarti should know the use of an orchestra, and so now and then form a pretty accompaniment of showy structure, certainly can never be doubted. But the difference between *Mechanism* and *Passion* is vast.... In England—as they feel they judge—they have the credit of neglecting science, when it strays from the confines, and ceases to be SUBORDINATE to SENSATION."

Sarti's later operas brought a reversal; they won some critical plaudits, but achieved only moderate popular success. (An exception was *Idalide*, which the King's mounted in 1791; it had nine performances[16] and was revived in 1796.) When *Ipermestra* appeared in 1798, critic B (T) found the language "happily suited to the characters," but the music "possesses so great a range of variety that it cannot lay claim to any distinctive excellence or character of style." It had but three performances, probably owing to an inadequate cast.

Yet the next year the King's mounted *Medonte*[17] for the season's opening with Banti. Critic B was now impressed: "The music of Sarti has been justly distinguished for a variety of expression admirably suited to the subject matter of the different scenes.... In *Medonte* he has happily succeeded in displaying the most delicate touches of exquisite softness with the spirit and rapidity of impassioned feeling." But the opera, too, had only five performances, probably because Banti, who was praised by the critics, had been ill and could not continue

Sarti's last serious opera at the King's (1800) was *Alessandro e Timoteo*, based on the "Alexander's Feast" theme, and again critic B was enthusiastic: "In the simple movements of Sarti, he is of all the modern composers perhaps unequalled." And the *True Briton* stated: "The music of Sarti exhibits contrivance, taste, and learning to a high degree, but perhaps it may be '*caviare* to the million.'" "It will be received by every amateur as an uncommon musical feast," reported the *Chronicle*. Though no arias[18] were encored, the *Post* thought they "were, perhaps, never surpassed in brilliance or sweetness." They added that "the opera on the whole [was] much indebted to the dancing incidental to the piece"—a rare mention of dancing *in* operas. Perhaps it was this that made the work quite successful, though it was never revived.

Not until 1808 was the King's to produce its last Sarti opera, the comic *I Contrattempi Amorosi*. It had but three performances, possibly because Catalani was "extremely imperfect in her part." Robertson (E) wrote that Sarti's compositions "have long been celebrated for elegance and refinement, and [this opera] abounds with beautiful airs, enlivened and enriched with sportive and scientific accompaniments. The opening quartetto and finale cannot be heard too often."

The *New Grove* finds Sarti's melodic style often pedestrian; the quality of his music did not deserve his success—an evaluation with which the King's opera-goers, in contrast to the reviewers, would apparently have concurred. The *Dictionary of Opera*, however, states that "historians have been unduly harsh in assessing" him.

GLUCK, CHERUBINI, AND "FRENCH" COMPOSERS

In the 1780s, the works of several composers who had strong connections with French opera were performed at the King's. The first of these was Antoine-Frederic Gresnich (1755–99), a Belgian composer who had a single opera performed at the King's. At the persistence of Mara, he came to London in 1786 and wrote *Alceste* for her, which opened the 1787 season. Este in the *Register* (Dec. 25) reported that the music "partakes more of the uniform sweetness of Sacchini, than of the rich variety of Haydn. Its peculiar excellence is, that, to speak technically, it does not *cover* the *voice*. The accompaniments . . . are made properly subservient, and by that means contribute very powerfully to the general effect"; the *Herald* (Jan. 1) admired "the ingenious variety that runs through all the airs."[19] But two weeks later Este took exception to its Neoclassical chill: "Plot, intrigue, distress, and all the *busile* of tragedy, [in] which John Bull so much delights—Alceste has not an atom of. The hero and heroine walk coolly into the Temple of Hymen, the disappointed lover coolly gives up his mistress, and the piece concludes with a grand chorus. This may suit the languor of *soft Italia*, but in the land of beef and liberty, something of characteristic opposition is wanting—to keep the audience 'tremblingly alive'" (Jan. 8).

Nevertheless, the opera was given ten times that season. The N.O. view that "he was hailed by the press" cannot be sustained. Gresnich was subjected to attacks by the cabal and even before the end of January fled England despite his enjoyment of the protection of the Prince of Wales. This "agreeable melodist" in the tradition of Grétry (N.G.) departed for Lyon and Paris, where he composed nearly 20 *opéras comiques*.

André E. M. Grétry (1741–1813), another Belgian composer who studied in Rome and finally achieved great success in France, also had only a single opera performed at the King's—his comic *Zémire et Azor*,[20] produced as *Zemira ed Azor* in 1779; it received eleven performances but scant notice. The work was revived in 1796 but for some reason failed badly. Although it "abound[ed] with delightful music" (T; C), not even the presence of Banti or the debut of young Braham could save it.[21] Yet it was revived the next year for four more performances. In 1786 Grétry's fine rescue opera, *Richard Coeur de Lion*, adapted by John Burgoyne into an English opera, was extremely successful.

A thoroughly French composer represented by a single, fairly successful opera at the King's was Pierre-Alexander Monsigny (1729–1817). His *La Belle Arsène* was produced as *La Bella Arsene*, a heroic opera, in 1796. Little was thought of the libretto—a Spanish story that da Ponte had adapted from Favart. But the *Times* found the "new" music "light and pretty and very much in the stile of our country," and especially admired the choruses under the direction of Michael Kelly. The *Chronicle* called the opera "pleasing but not great. It is gay and slight but not striking." The work received seven performances but was never revived. Monsigny was not prolific but had a certain depth and originality, and his writing was richer than Grétry's (N.G.).

Another "French" composer at the King's—and a far more original one—was the German-born Christoph Willibald Gluck (1714–87). *Orfeo*, the first work in his new style, reached England in 1770—in the form, however, of a pasticcio that included seven arias by J. C. Bach;[22] two by P. A. Guglielmi; and one by the First Man, Guadagni, with additions to the libretto by G. C. Bottarelli. Charles Burney (II, 877) deplored this destruction of the opera's "unity, simplicity, and dramatic excellency"; nevertheless, it was highly successful, with thirteen performances that season and six the next. In 1773 *Orfeo* was presented "as originally performed" but received only a single performance. The pasticcio, on the other hand, was given ten performances in 1785 in a production by Anfossi that by this time included several Handel arias. One unidentified report the following year (apparently not a review) shows some feeling for the power of Gluck's music: "Gluck is the Michael Angelo of musick, and is as happy in painting difficult attitudes and situations of the mind as that painter was of the body. In scenes of great distress . . . Gluck shines. He is at once poet, painter, and musician, and gives a strength and colouring to passion, which has seldom been equalled but never surpassed" (TC, Oct. 27).

London had to wait ten years for another Gluck opera *Alceste*, which received a careful production in 1795 for Banti's benefit. The *Chronicle*, declaring it was identical to the Paris production under Gluck (Apr. 28), was impressed by its thirty London rehearsals (May 4) and accorded it a glowing review (May 1): "It was "a piece of a kind so different from the common race of Operas that it requires to be judged of only by a master in the science. Its character is dignity and pathos. There is a solemn air in the music finely adapted to the subject, and the passion is carried to a height that is irresistible in its effects on our emotions." The work was given fourteen times.

Ifigenia in Tauride (*Ifigénie en Tauride*) was produced in 1796 in a da Ponte translation with the support of Banti. The *Chronicle* wrote: "The new opera was heard with utmost attention. The music is so sublime and elevated that it requires a scientific ear to feel all its beauties. It is perhaps too *recherché* to be popular." They were right; it received but five performances and was never revived. Indeed not until 1830 did any reviewer even mention the composer. But that year Holmes (*Atlas*) remembered with pleasure Gluck's artistry: "Gluck, whose modulation in recitative shows how profoundly he possessed the feeling for harmony, has, in his classical operas, *Iphigenia* [sic] and *Alceste*, created an interest throughout with little contrast of situation or character; but even he was obliged to give, in some flowing and tender melody, a relaxation to the ear" (Feb. 21).[23]

Gluck's disciple, Luigi Cherubini (Florence, 1760–1842), also had a disappointing response in London despite his presence there in 1784 when he won the favor of the Prince of Wales' circle. Most of the operas he wrote for the King's, where he shared musical directorship with Anfossi, were not mature productions. The first, *Demetrio* (1785) — the *Alceste* story[24] altered from Metastasio's by Badini — was a pasticcio, with only six interpolated numbers by Cherubini.[25] The *Advertiser* found Cherubini a composer who had "genius" but noted: "In the Opera he shall next produce, our recommendation is, to collate less, to compose more. The compiled music of Demetrio does not excel in . . . the *power* of *pleasing*. His own music pleased enough, which is the rather unexpected from its extreme difficulty." Yet the pastiche received eight performances.

Three months later, Cherubini produced a two-act buffa, *La Finta Principessa*. The *Chronicle*, pleased with the composer's turn to the comic, observed that none of his "airs excited very much cheerfulness. On the contrary, the best of these were rather softening and pensive, but they were worked up with much art and delicacy of effect. . . . The subjects of at least five of his airs were perfectly novel as well as beautiful to an excess." The *Post* heard "in most of his airs a considerable degree of originality, the surest evidence of genius," though the finales were weak.[26] These plaudits fell on a deaf public, however, perhaps because, as the *Herald* noted, the lively Italian dialogue "was lost on the audience." The work had scant success and was never revived.

Two weeks later Cherubini again reverted to a pasticcio, *Artaserse*,[27] to which he contributed an overture and six numbers (Selden). Despite (or perhaps because of) Thomas Arne's very popular setting of the story at the playhouses, King's audiences were unimpressed; the opera played only six times.

In 1786 Cherubini returned to serious opera in *Il Giulio Sabino*, which received but a single performance, although it was later successful on the Continent. No reviews survive, but Burney tells us that the opera "was murdered at its birth for want of capital singers." No wonder the composer settled in Paris in the spring of that year, though not before contributing some fine music to Paisiello's *Il Marchese Tulipano* (see below).

In 1789 the King's mounted another of Cherubini's serious operas, *Ifigenia in Aulide*, and this time the opera had a strong cast. Este, in the *Times* (Jan. 26), was not partial to the composer: no airs were encored because "of their extreme length,—and the sameness of stile." But other reviewers quite disagreed. "This opera is infinitely superior to any that has lately been produced," wrote the *Gazetteer*, calling his songs "striking and elegant. . . . The more this opera is heard it will be the more admired." The duet "Almen del tuo tormento" was especially praised (C). The *Post* (Jan. 26) found the music "highly grand, impressive, and affecting," yet complained that "the accompaniments were too complicated and overpowered the airs."[28] The work had eight performances.

On the whole, the press commended the originality they detected in these early operas, most of which drew support from the public as well.

In Paris, Cherubini's *Lodoïska* (1791), a "rescue" opera set in Poland, was one of the first Romantic operas.[29] Its popularity reached England in the form of an English opera of that title, translated by John Kemble, in 1794; and at least some of the music from Cherubini's most highly praised opera, *Les deux journées* (Paris, 1800), in which his use of melodrama was "successful and exciting" (*NOHM*, VIII, 44), was incorporated into Holcroft's *The Escapes* in 1801 (see part III).

To "French" music generally, it should be noted, the English were generally indifferent, if not hostile. Although this is not evident in the reviews just cited, the *Times* spoke, in 1785, of the "depraved taste of French music" and Mount-Edgcumbe reflected this attitude years later when remarking on the advent of "Grand Operas": "To all ears but French, they can only give pain"; he elsewhere exclaimed "that human ears can bear it is marvellous."

SALIERI

Among the somewhat younger Italian opera composers[30] was Antonio Salieri (1750–1825), who, like Sarti, never came to London, though he too had some successes there. His first London production was the comic *La Scuola dei Gelosi*, produced in 1786. The *Herald* (Mar. 13) was delighted: "It is the first lyric drama that may be termed strictly good, whether we advert to the poem itself [by Mazzolà], the music or the performance."[31] The *Post* called the work a "masterly composition" that "does great honour to Salieri." The opera, though very successful, was never revived.

Not until 1798 did the King's mount another Salieri comedy—*La Cifra*. The opera "approaches, as nearly as the genius of Italian compositions of this nature will admit, to the bustle and eccentricities of most of our modern comedies," wrote the *Times*. "The plot [by da Ponte] is not devoid of interest, but the incidents are too crowded to arrest the attention. The music is light and pleasing [with] much original melody." The *Oracle* also found the music "scientific and original," while the *Chronicle* heard "much novelty" in the overture, and the music throughout was "light and easy, but without gaiety or much animation." Despite some encores the work failed completely, probably because of the cast, which was found somewhat inadequate.

In 1802 the King's produced its last Salieri opera, the comic *L'Angiolina*. Critic B (T) heard a certain coolness in the music that "is more distinguished for taste and neatness of effect, than for any of those movements which astonish the ear, or find the way to the heart. There is little to censure; but there is also little that calls for the warmth of panegyric." Yet this opera succeeded, thanks to the fine singers. Salieri's chief work, *Tarare*, based on Beaumarchais' play, was highly successful in Paris (1787), but the Italian version—*Axur, Re d'Ormus*—was never produced at the King's. In 1825 it was successful as an English adaptation.[32]

CIMAROSA

Few of the composers discussed thus far achieved anything like lasting appeal with London audiences. To some extent this changed with Cimarosa, who may be ranked next to Paisiello in overall popularity in London before Mozart and Rossini. Domenico Cimarosa (1749–1801), with conservatory training, produced his first successful opera at Naples in 1772 and by the 1780s was known throughout Italy. He was at St. Petersburg from 1787 to 1791 and was active later in Vienna and again in Italy; he never came to England. Altogether, he wrote some eighty operas.

Cimarosa's first King's production, in 1785, was the comedy *Il Pittor Parigino*. There was some disagreement with respect to the libretto by Petrosellini, but the *Post* especially admired "the fine *obbligato* movements" and the *Herald* found the music in a style entirely new" and "extremely pleasing."[33] "The overture has great merit, and some of the songs[34] are, if not the best, equal at least to what we have hitherto heard of the kind." The work succeeded.

In 1787 another comedy, *Giannina e Bernardone*, was offered as a pasticcio. The *Register*'s critic A thought it entirely too long and was glad to see cuts made (Jan. 15), and in a final notice, he found Cimarosa improved on repetition; his work "beat Paisiello's *Il Tutor Burlato* out and out" (Mar. 15). It did, playing nine times to *Tutor*'s three.

La Locandiera, originally entitled *L'Italiana in Londra* but in this version set in Amsterdam,[35] was given the following year under Mazzinghi's direction. The *World* thought the music "at once very ingenious and very gay," and the *Times* agreed.[36] But the *Post* (Jan. 16) was negative: "The music, though light and airy, discovers nothing of striking or novel merit and certainly does not proceed from a very refined or prolific imagination. . . . It is easy to trace many of its best passages in other compositions." Burney's view (II, 901) supports that of the *Post*; he was disappointed in the work, partly owing to the poor performers: "Much of the music seemed feeble, common, and not of the newest taste." It was barely successful and was never revived.

L'Olimpiade, Cimarosa's first opera seria to reach England (1788), had the support of Marchesi, but the reviews were trivial. Hogarth thought the work among Cimarosa's best. It played ten times but was not revived. The following season brought another comedy, *La Villana Riconosciuta*; it was hissed off the stage. Part of the problem was unsuitable performers, but the *Times* now found "very little grandeur or originality in the composition," while the *World* fulminated: "La Villanova [*sic*] Riconosciuta is called Cimarosa's music. Be it whose it will, it is bad music, and it is worse sung."

But in 1790 Cimarosa had another popular though not critical success—the comic *La Ninetta*. It was given in the Little Theatre after the King's burned, and that small theatre prevented the reduced orchestra's "giving the proper effect to some very pretty music" (T, Jan. 8). An unidentified reviewer (TC) was unimpressed: the opera "is of insupportable dulness" and "Cimarosa's music was never less brilliant. . . . The only *encore* of the night was of an air despicably sung, and certainly the audience meant the encore in derision." The *Advertiser* agreed that the opera had not "much attraction" and the performance was poor. Yet the work was repeated eleven times that season—the third highest rating for any of Cimarosa's operas.

The comic *Le Trame Deluse* was mounted in 1792. The work, though too long, did "great credit to the fancy and genius of Cimarosa"; the airs were beautiful and the concerted numbers had "infinite ingenuity" of composition (T). The rest of the press was also supportive. The work played seven times but was not revived.

The year 1794 saw the King's premiere of the first of his operas to have revivals there: *Il Matrimonio Segreto*, which was adapted by Mazzinghi. Bertati's libretto was based on the perennial favorite of the English playhouses, *The Clandestine Marriage* (1776), by Colman the Elder and Garrick; it was further altered for this performance by da Ponte. This opera, by the way, drew the little press comment we have on that librettist, who was resident poet that season. Este (T) wrote with characteristic irony that "if Mr. da Ponte (the poet) means that the audience should not *forbid* the *banns*, he must shorten his marriage ceremony considerably; and in order to do so, he has only to take away a few airs and graces from the underlings, and leave the management of the plot [to the principals] — and it cannot be in better hands than those of Morelli, Rovedino, and the pretty Casentini." But a casual approach to librettos was, as we have noted, common at the time; the press usually had little to say on opera plots, and few protests are heard about distortions of them — let alone of the music — created by the frequent interpolations and cuts. The work was given a lavish production, and the band was augmented for the occasion. The reviewers were generally supportive.[37] Although the work was barely successful that season, it was given seven more times in 1798, and it had more revivals (in six seasons to 1830) than any of his other operas.

Reviews of these revivals in later seasons are of particular interest in showing not only a shift in musical taste but also the growing competence of the reviewers. Of the 1818 revival, Alsager (*Times*) wrote: "Our predilection for the German school, and Mozart in particular, may serve in some degree to explain [the cool reception of Cimarosa's operas]: Cimarosa, little skilled in, or little solicitous about the effects of the orchestra . . . has placed all his attraction on the stage: we can form no judgment of the true effect of his operas, unless the singers are all of a superior stamp." The *Inquisitor* declared: "Cimarosa is doubtless a great master the music of this opera is dull and heavy and totally deficient in that playful sprightliness and captivating melody which are necessary to support a comic opera." And Leigh Hunt "missed . . . what in an Italian composer of celebrity we had a right to look for — sentiment in general, and beautiful melodies in particular. . . . The most admired air in the piece, *Pria che spunti in ciel l'aurora*, is to us, we must confess, a great deal too literal" (E). In the *Tatler* (February 28, 1831), however, he reconsidered these views, calling it the best comic opera after Mozart.[38]

At an 1829 revival Alsager (T) remarked on "that delightful suavity which is the chief characteristic of Cimarosa's music." Ayrton (Har) pointed out that in this kind of opera everything depends on the cast, and in this revival, fortunately, the cast was perfect. But critic Z (NM) explored changes in musical taste, on which he had mixed views:

To speak conscientiously, *some* of the [vocal] pieces exhibited, in part at least, indications of a taste not only gone by, but the absence of which we see no reason to regret. There is here and there a simplicity which borders upon insipidity. But . . . Cimarosa's accompaniments are full of elegance and variety, without ever obscuring the vocal parts. . . . All we have to wish, for the good of the art, is, that good sense may soon bring us back to the observance of such models.

Somewhat less popular was the musical farce *Il Capriccio Drammatico*. It also came to the King's in 1794 in an adaptation by da Ponte. The work, which had eight performances, received little comment in surviving reviews; at a 1798 revival, however, critic B (T) showed alarm about recent musical developments: "The music of Cimarosa is happily adapted to the subject, and is completely devoid of the difficulties and desultory transitions which have of late years been so assiduously sought after, to the detriment of true harmony. Cimarosa seems, at least in this composition, to have carefully studied the first principles of his art, and has accordingly displayed a just combination of sound and sense." And at an 1808 revival Robertson was completely positive: "Cimarosa, I think, may be placed above every other Italian composer. . . . With the sportive fancy and elegance for which the Italian music is remarkable, he combines the ability and grandeur of the German school" (E).

In 1796 the King's mounted another Cimarosa opera—*I Traci Amanti*—but it proved to be no favorite. Though the *Chronicle* was positive, other reviewers disagreed. The *True Briton* said that the opera "shews great science and contrivance, but there are no airs in the piece that much engage the ear or haunt the memory." The *Times* regarded the music as "by no means provincial" but it was "neither striking nor novel." The *Monthly Magazine* concurred: the opera had "little [stage] business and no great musical excellence." It received seven performances and was never revived.

I Due Baroni arrived in 1803. The humorous allusions in the plot, by Palomba, were lost on the *Post*, but the music was something else: "Its airs, its recitatives, have both a power that seems to equal the praise of the musical composer with that of the noblest of poets. Tenderness, grace, airy lightness, elegance of artifice and a comic expression . . . are the most eminent characteristics of this music." Critic B (T) agreed, but for the *Chronicle* the whole opera was a disappointment: It "is unsufferably long, frigid, and unmeaning. There is not a single air that dwells upon the memory—not a scene that has the slightest exhilaration." The piece did not quite succeed.

Cimarosa's last comedy at the King's, *Le Astuzie Femminili*, was produced in 1804. Critic B now found Palomba's plot good: "The dialogue possesses the merit of neatness, and the characters are distinctly marked.... The poetry is certainly superior to the generality of compositions of this class which have been represented for several years." Moreover, in the music, "we find all the characteristics of Cimarosa's taste and playfulness. There is, indeed, nothing to astonish, but there is scarcely an air that does not please."[39] Yet the work played only seven times and had no revivals.

Finally, two more of Cimarosa's serious operas made late appearances at the King's. *Gli Orazi e I Curiazi*, which Kelly and Hogarth (I, 165–67) regarded as Cimarosa's best tragedy,[40] appeared in 1805, in a fine production. It received nine performances that season and eleven in 1806; it also had revivals in 1814, when Hunt (E, June 5) reported that Grassini alone tried to do justice to the composer's ideas, and in 1815. Not until 1829, however, do we get reviews of some substance. In that year Alsager (T) was unhappy with both the libretto and the music, though he admired some airs,[41] and the *Chronicle*, discussing a poor performance, found the music too tame after Rossini. Critic Z (NM) thought that "Cimarosa's forte lay obviously not in serious drama."

But Ayrton (Har) admired the overture, which was "by far the best instrumental work of Cimarosa," and the accompanied recitative—"Qual pallor! qual silenzio"—was "a masterly piece of musical declamation." Critic X (E), in a brief notice, was quite positive: "The whole opera is one finely-sustained flight of martial enthusiasm, relieved toward the close with exquisite passages of deep pathos and tenderness." Wade (Ath) was also supportive. Thus some of the most competent critics were unwilling to dismiss the old-fashioned music.[42]

Cimarosa's final work at the King's—*Penelope*—did not appear until 1817. At this premiere, in which Pasta made her debut, the reviewers were again at loggerheads. The *Times* reviewer (perhaps Alsager) suffered from "weariness" stemming from "a *tristesse* pervading this entire Opera, which will prevent its becoming a favorite." But the *Chronicle* wrote: "This is certainly one of the composer's best works.... The music altogether is admirably adapted to the sense and passion of the scene; it corroborates the poetry, and adds a force and sentiment to it which renders it highly interesting." And Bacon (LG) declared: "The melodies, whether of tender or pathetic import, are uncommonly fine; the accompaniments exhibit the utmost richness and elegance, and frequently an abundant store of harmonic science." The opera, which played six times, was regarded by Hogarth as one of Cimarosa's best. He found in his serious operas a "noble simplicity" and "strong expression" in which "dramatic truth is never sacrificed to vocal display."

But vocal strength was always important to Cimarosa's operas, and the absence of it accounted for a poor showing in some seasons. It is interesting to see in the late reviews a tendency to regard him as a great classic who was once powerful, whereas the early reviews are often mixed or negative. But changes in taste also divided the later reviewers. On the whole press and public showed remarkably congruent attitudes toward these operas.

GUGLIELMI, FEDERICI, AND MAZZINGHI

Before turning to Cimarosa's only real competitor, Paisiello, we shall take a brief look at several minor composers whose works appeared mainly before 1800. The oldest and perhaps the most important of these, Pietro Alessandro Guglielmi (1728–1804), offered some challenge to Cimarosa and Paisiello (N.G.), but his popularity in London was quite episodic. He was music director at the King's between 1767 and 1772, and during that period he produced eleven operas of his own, both serious and comic. It is astonishing that although there were no productions at all from 1773 to 1790, his *La Bella Pescatrice* had a run of twenty-two performances in 1791 and several revivals. The reason for its popularity is not clear from the reviews. At a rehearsal the *Gazetteer* (Jan. 22) predicted the success of the trio "Lo caro mio tu sei," stating that "with all the graces of the Italian music, it is not without that prevalence of *subject* which is so acceptable to the English ear." At the premiere (Mar. 2) they found the work "most powerfully *comic*, and the whole is less intricate than Italian compositions in general." Reviews of the 1792 revival were also positive. (Fiske finds the work "more perfect" than any other comic opera at the King's in the 1790s.)

The opera's popularity prompted another premiere in 1792—*La Pastorella Nobile*. The *Times* stated it had "some very excellent music" and one or two laughable situations; the overture and first-act finale were excellent.[43] The *Gazetteer* was also supportive, but the *Oracle* (possibly Boaden) thought the music was marked by prettiness rather than originality. Though the opera failed, it had a brief revival in 1801. Two later operas had marginal success at the King's in 1797 and 1807. His son, P. C. Guglielmi, had even less popularity at the King's in 1809 (see below).

Vincenzo Federici (1764–1826) was born in Italy and apparently at age sixteen came to London, where he settled, supporting himself by giving music lessons and serving as *maestro al cembalo* at the King's from 1790 until 1800 or 1802. His authority there was at times sufficient to frustrate da Ponte, who called him "a veritable emporium of inequities." His first work at the King's, *L'Usurpator Innocente*, a serious opera based on an adaptation of Metastasio's *Demofoonte*, was mounted in 1790 and became a one-season hit. Reviews were mixed, and it was mainly because of Mara's strength that the work received fifteen performances; it was never revived.

Although Joseph Mazzinghi (1765–1844) wrote only one opera for the King's, he adapted a great many. Eldest son of Tommaso Mazzinghi, a Corsican wine merchant in London, he studied with J. C. Bach and Sacchini. He was organist at the London Portugese Chapel from 1786 to 1788, and in 1789 became musical director at the King's, writing much ballet music and adapting several operas and librettos. When the score for his *La Locanda* was destroyed in the Pantheon fire, he quickly reconstructed it from memory. But "he trifled with his genius" (*Thespian Dictionary*) and never achieved front rank.

In 1790 he was briefly ousted in favor of old Guardini, and in 1791 he was named house composer for the Pantheon, probably because he was a favorite of the Prince of Wales. In 1793 he was replaced by Storace; by 1798 he was out of the King's for good. After that, he gave music lessons, wrote music for several English operas (see part III), and composed much instrumental music for amateurs as well as a number of arias that were introduced into the operas of others. His only "complete" opera was *Il Tesoro*, a comedy mounted in 1796. The *Chronicle* found it "a work of very considerable merit. The arias have . . . ease and familiarity, and yet they are scientific and elegant." And *Bell's Weekly Messenger* noted "masterly pieces" in the work, though they were disappointed by the overture. But the opera was a failure. Perhaps the cabal was at work with this native son, as it seems to have been with Martín. But his own operatic music was "slight" (N.O.).

MARTÍN Y SOLER

Vincente Martín y Soler (1754–1806), who came to London in 1794 and was known to the English as Vincenzo Martini, was a Spanish composer who found early success writing operas in Italy and later at St. Petersburg. His *opere buffe* have been called equal in quality to those of Cimarosa and Paisiello (N.G.). By far his most popular opera everywhere was *La Cosa Rara* (whose libretto was by da Ponte), which came to the King's in 1789. The *Herald* saw him as "more indebted to genius for his success than to science" and praised his "originality and lively imagination."[44] The *London Chronicle* was also positive, declaring the second-act sextet "one of the finest compositions we ever heard." There were ten performances, and it was revived in 1805, 1806, and 1816.[45]

Martín was brought to London by the buffa Anna Morichelli late in 1794, according to da Ponte. Earlier that year the King's had produced his *Il Burbero di Buon Cuore*, which included a duet by Haydn, composed perhaps for the occasion.⁴⁶ The opera was a total failure, though it succeeded elsewhere.

Interest quickened the next season, however, with the first performance of *La Scuola dei Maritati*, his first opera written for the King's. (The libretto, by da Ponte, was *not* based on *The Taming of the Shrew*.) The *Chronicle* found the work quite suited to British taste: "It is the sure test of good music when it is seized on by the popular ear, and . . . comes at length into the streets. It is a curious proof of the power of this great master, that so perfectly has he adapted his airs to the character of a nation where he has been so short time a resident, that many pieces of his first essay will assuredly come to the barrel organ" (Feb. 2). But the music for *Maritati* does not seem to have wandered into English opera as it had from *Cosa Rara*. The work played twelve times that season and had four revivals. In 1802 the *Times* flatly asserted that "no modern composition is equal to it."

Martín lost no time mounting another first performance the same season; *L'Isola del Piacere*, a serious opera, failed, however—possibly, as da Ponte claimed (p. 258), because Sga. Banti insisted on inserting a "mad scene" for the second act, which was "quite inappropriate." The composer left for Russia the next year, but the year after (1797) his pastoral opera *L'Arbore di Diana*⁴⁷ was produced at the King's. The *Chronicle* praised especially the first-act finale and the quartet at the beginning of the second, the latter being "one of the most elegant and masterly compositions we ever heard," and they predicted great success for the work. Critic B (T) was also supportive, adding that the composer "has so happily blended in this instance the *lively* and the *tender*, that it would be difficult to characterise this composition by the name of any peculiar style." There was a strong cast; nevertheless, the work was a marginal failure, perhaps because pastorals were no longer fashionable.⁴⁸

Except for his *Cosa Rara*, Martín, who was very successful on the Continent, did not succeed in London despite support from the press, and again one must speculate about the effect of the cabal; da Ponte reported that *Scuola* succeeded despite the cabal against it.

BIANCHI

The one composer besides Cimarosa and Paisiello who had some clear successes in the 1790s was Francesco Bianchi (1752–1810), who altogether composed over one hundred works for the stage. He was brought to London in 1795—perhaps by Banti, as da Ponte reported, to write serious operas for her. For several years he acted as musical director at the King's, though in 1794 he shared that post with Martín, and he remained in London the rest of his life. Henry Bishop was his most successful pupil.

He was preceded to London by his most popular opera (Loewenberg), *La Villanella Rapita* in 1790, but it proved to be an unfortunate choice for the King's. It had suffered many changes during its several European productions and was apparently produced at the King's as something of a pasticcio by Storace. Although the *Herald* commended Storace for introducing numbers by Mozart and Martín,[49] they thought the finales "very short of Paisiello" and "contained the music of three or four masters, sadly combined." Este, in the *Times* (Mar. 1), was excoriating: "Dear bewitching VARIETY seems to be the goddess of Gallini's idolatry, and [the opera] had not anything very *ravishing* to recommend it" besides the title. A week later they referred to the "noisy plaudits of a 'few followers' in the gallery." In this case the claque may have had some success, for despite the poor reviews, the work played nine times, though it was not revived.

In 1794, with Bianchi now at the King's, Banti chose his *Semiramide* for her debu. The *Times* (Apr. 28) reported that the only encore of the evening was a second-act cavatina,[50] but he praised the music both at this production and at a revival next year. The opera was a great success, due in large measure to Banti, with twelve performances that season, eleven in 1795 (strongly praised), and six later revivals, outlasting even Banti's long reign.[51]

In 1795 Bianchi produced his pastoral opera *Aci e Galatea*. The *Herald* reviewer declared that "the overture was in the grand style of Haydn, but softened in the exquisite manner of Sacchini. . . . The chorusses all discovered a great depth of musical knowledge." The *True Briton* was pleased by the effect of a second orchestra behind the scenes. But an unidentified reviewer (TC) found the recitative "sometimes heavy and tedious," and "the dialogue and airs of the inferior characters inspire languor." Haydn witnessed the opera at the King's that year, stating that after the third performance "everyone was dissatisfied" with the production. It was "very rich in parts for the wind instruments" but "one would hear the principal melody better if it were not so richly scored."[52] This from the father of the "German school"! Despite Banti's best efforts, it did not succeed and had no revivals—perhaps again because pastorals were thought to be passé.

The following year Bianchi's *Piramo e Tisbe* was an even worse failure. It was "laid aside," we are told, "to give room for Cimarosa's new Comic Piece"—*I Traci Amanti* (TB). But his seria *Antigona*, written for the King's and produced the same season, was a resounding success, although the two reviews we have were only mildly favorable. It ran for thirteen performances that season but failed in a 1798 revival.

In 1797 Bianchi produced a one-act comedy, *Il Consiglio Imprudente*, which succeeded. The *Chronicle* was supportive, admiring especially the first duet and the fugue at the close of the finale, which was also applauded by *Bell's* and the *True Briton*. The latter also pointed out that the occasion marked "banishing buffoonery and nonsense from the Comic Opera" and provided "what is more creditable and fully consistent with the Comic Character—*Elegance of Sentiment*." In fact, they added, the opera "abounds" with "finished passages" that "shew sentiment to be the prevailing feature through the whole."

Another premiere that season, *Merope*, adapted by da Ponte from Voltaire's tragedy, got routine praise from the *Chronicle* and the *Herald*, but not from the *Monthly Magazine*, whose "English" bias is as obvious as it is rare in Italian opera reviewing: "We were led to expect a very grand, scientific and impressive performance, from the united efforts of so glorious a triumvirate [Voltaire, da Ponte, and Bianchi], but the whole was 'stale, flat, and unprofitable.' Indeed, we by no means think serious opera, founded on superstitious circumstances, congenial to the constitutional habits of honest John." The work played ten times that season and twice more in 1798.

Cinna, another seria, premiered in 1798[53] to glowing notices; the *Post* and the *Chronicle* (Feb. 21) thought the work surpassed Bianchi's previous productions: "While he captivates by the simplicity of his melodies, his harmony, though rich and various, never overpowers the song." A week later critic B (T) stated that Bianchi "has not confined himself to any particular style, but occasionally blends in the most captivating manner, the richness of harmony with the simple grandeur of sound [for "melody"?]." The reviewer then touched on the heart of opera: "But his chief excellence consists in giving on almost every occasion, suitable expression to the various emotions and passions." The public also responded to the opera, which was repeated ten times that season against strong competition from Paisiello.

In 1799 another seria, *Ines de Castro*, which introduced a melodramatic flavor to the King's, was brought forward. The *Courier* noted that the plot had been altered to give it a happy ending, "but it is easy and natural. Bianchi delights in subterranean horror, and he has a very fine sense of this sort, in which the catastrophe is brought about with masterly art, both in musical force and stage effect."[54] Critic B (T), however, was outraged over the liberties taken by the librettist, Luigi de Sanctis: "A subject originally fruitful in producing pathetic effect was, by the bungling hand of the Italian author, debased into an absolute *burlesque*, the ridicule of which was increased by the ludicrous action and *mock-heroic* deportment of the singing, rhyming and chiming heroes and heroines of the piece." Nor were they happy with the music. Yet such burlesquing may have appealed to the public, for the opera had seventeen performances and was revived the next year for three more.

In 1801 Bianchi mounted two more operas, both serious. The first, *Alzira*, generated some interesting comments. The *Chronicle* wrote: "In no instance has Bianchi so eminently succeeded in rousing the passions and in agitating the heart. The choruses have the sublimity of Handel, and the airs are as beautiful in melody as in science." Critic B thought the work would add to Bianchi's reputation: "It does not, perhaps, abound in those instances of the sublime which occur in his *Semiramide*, but it is superior in correctness, and the corresponding arrangement of all the parts. . . . His most elaborate passages are distinguished for truth of expression and natural feeling." The work turned out to be as popular with the public as with the press: it had fifteen performances and was revived the next year for five more.

Armida, which premiered in 1802, was regarded as one of Bianchi's best by da Ponte.[55] The *Post* review was favorable: The music "was always correct, and in some passages, very pathetic." But critic B held otherwise: "If a modern Italian Opera could be considered as a legitimate object of criticism, we should be disposed to speak of this in terms of more than usual severity for it is certainly one of the worst which has of late been exhibited. The music was neither appropriate nor striking; it cannot even claim the praise due to originality, but on the contrary it is tame and spiritless." Nevertheless, with Banti in the title role, the opera was quite successful.

Bianchi's last opera at the King's, also serious, appeared in 1805—*Erfile*. Critic B by this time apprehensive of the power of a prima donna, wrote: "The great vocal talents of Mrs Billington may procure for [the opera] a temporary currency, to which it is not entitled from its intrinsic merit. There is no *ensemble* in the composition, all the characters being sacrificed to the principal one." But the *Daily Advertiser* (Feb. 20) was more positive: "Mr. Bianchi's bent, in this as in all his former musical efforts, is directed toward the tender and pathetic, and if he does not ravish or surprise us by novelty and boldness of composition, he seldom fails pleasing us by the softness and sweetness of his melodies." The performance was not helped by Billington's weakness as an actress, and the opera was barely successful.

From 1802 to 1807 Bianchi shuttled back and forth between London and Paris, composing operas and directing them (N.O.), but it is not clear how he avoided the blockade. Despite his successes Bianchi's personal life was tragic, for he committed suicide in 1810 following the death of his five-year-old daughter. But in his settings of da Ponte's librettos composed for the King's, the enthusiasm of most of the press as well as the public—this despite keen competition from Paisiello—testify to a remarkable strength in this composer.

PAISIELLO

With Giovanni Paisiello (1740–1816), we come to the most popular composer at the King's before Mozart. That popularity began in 1776 and continued steadily until 1802. He had premieres as late as 1808 and 1809, and revivals as late as 1825. He showed much promise as a pupil in the Naples Conservatory, and with the assistance of Giuseppe Carafa, he had his first operatic success at Bologna in 1764. A composer of some eighty operas, along with much sacred and instrumental music, he had established strong competition with Piccinni in Naples by 1766. (The latter's *Buona Figuola* enjoyed frequent revivals at the King's.) In that year he turned down an offer to come to London and instead went to the court of St. Petersburg at Catherine's invitation. He wrote operas there until 1784 when he returned to Naples and became composer of operas for Ferdinand IV. Napoleon admired his music, and the composer came to Paris in 1802, receiving many French awards; but his public reception there was lukewarm, and he returned to Italy in 1803, losing his French pension after Waterloo.

His first opera at the King's was the comic *La Frascatana*, produced in 1777. This turned out to be a great favorite, with nineteen performances that season and many successful revivals through 1808.[56] Astonishingly, no adequate review of this opera survives until its final revival by Madame Catalani, when Robertson, in his first review for the *Examiner*, declared: "The music of Paisiello is remarkable for its extreme elegance, the great beauty of the melodies, and that degree of science which tends to enrich the composition without fatiguing the ear. It is at once calculated to charm the professor and the amateur."[57]

Paisiello's *Le Due Contesse*, which premiered at the King's in 1778, was nearly a failure, and not until 1786 was another Paisiello opera mounted: *Il Marchese Tulipano*. Reviews were mixed. The *Chronicle* thought the work "seldom rose much above mediocrity," but the *Advertiser* (Jan. 25) was positive, and the *Herald* pointed out that Sestini's first aria, "Saper bramate," occurred originally in Paisiello's *Barbiere di Siviglia* and was the source of the English song "For Tenderness Form'd."[58] The opera was repeated nine times but was not revived.

In 1787 *Il Tutor Burlato* received its first performance at the King's.[59] Lord Cowper, an amateur, brought the score there from Florence (H, Feb. 19, 1787). Unfortunately, the male lead, Andrea Morigi, in jail because of debts (T, Feb. 19), had to miss the opening, and Domenico Cremonini was obliged to *read* the part. Although the piece was reputed to be Paisiello's masterpiece (H), and although Morigi's role was sung by Vincenzo Calvesi at the second performance, it could not survive this disaster, and it played only three times.

But the production later that season of *Gli Schiavi per Amore* fully restored Paisiello's popularity. The production had the support of Nancy Storace, who was obliged to repeat some arias three times. An unidentified review (TC) called it "much superior" to Piccinni's *Buona Figliuola*. And critic A (UR, July 2), noting the remarkable popularity of the work, wrote: "The taste of the public for the Italian opera has never been so conspicuous. . . . The audience appeared to be not unusually but almost unprecedently possessed of the musical mania."[60] (Burney noted the "many gay and agreeable airs" in the opera.) It had an astonishing success—nineteen performances—and was followed in 1789 by thirteen more. It had two more revivals: in 1790 (when it failed) and in 1797.

For the 1788 season opening, Mazzinghi directed a new type of comic opera—*dramma eroicomico*: Paisiello's *Il Re Teodoro in Venezia*. Kelly, who had sung in the opera's Vienna premiere (Mozart was present at that performance), again sang the lead (I. L. Hunt, pp. 33–34). The English subtitle was "Theodore, King of Corsica at Venice"; Giovanni Casti took the main incidents from Voltaire's *Candide* and added the "historical" interest and a touch of realism (Patrick Smith). Critic A (T, Dec. 25) strongly objected to the denigration of this historical person, whom Casti's libretto showed dying miserably in Fleet Street prison,[61] and whose real-life son was still living in England. He also noted (Dec. 10) that six principal singers were required at the Vienna premiere and that several airs, except those belonging to Morigi and Nancy Storace, had to be dropped. Yet they called the music "extremely good" and pointed out that it had more ensembles, "most of which display much *science*, and less *airs*, than any piece in our recollection."[62] But there were not too few arias for the operagoers, for the work received thirteen performances and was revived three more times in 1795, when the *Chronicle*, surprisingly, still found it "too learned and too long for an English audience." Hogarth thought both *Schiavi* and *Re Teodoro* delightful for "originality, gaiety, and elegance," and though both he and Burney deplored the "unwarranted" substitutions, "yet music lovers want none omitted."

In 1789 *Il Barbiere di Siviglia* was brought out for Nancy Storace's benefit (and for only three other performances), which accounts for an absence of reviews, and though it was revived for seven seasons through 1808, it failed at every revival. In 1798 the press rendered the music trite praise. The failure of this opera is curious, for it gave to English music the great favorite "For Tenderness Form'd," and the story was well known to the public through a production of Goldoni's popular *Spanish Barber* (1777). Moreover, not a little jealousy was generated against Rossini on the appearance of *his Barbiere* in 1818.

In 1791 Paisiello had another failure in *Pirro*, his first serious opera in London. Unfortunately no reviews survive.[63] It was revived by Catalani in 1809 but failed again, although the *Times* then called it "perhaps the composer's *chef d'oeuvre*."

But in *La Molinarella*, produced at the Pantheon later that season, he had another hit. The libretto, by Palomba, was based on Bickerstaffe's *Maid of the Mill* (1763) and included the arias "La Rochelina" (already famous at the playhouses as "Whither my Love" in Storace's *The Haunted Tower* [1789]) and "Nel cor più non me sento" (the origin of "Hope told a flattering tale"). Both songs ranked close to "For Tenderness Form'd" in popularity. The *Times* thought the opera might "prove rather *caviare* to the general," but the *Post* predicted the opera would be a favorite. It was, running ten times that season with several revivals as late as 1818, under the titles of *L'Amor Contrasto* or, more commonly, *La Molinara*.

Not until the 1817 revival—a fine production—do responsive reviews appear. Alsager (T) praised the manager for the revival as an attempt "to refine the taste for music among the upper classes of the country," and they noted that the operas of Mozart and Paisiello "address themselves as much to the judgment as to the senses," though Mozart was much superior. "Paisiello is full of sweetness and of delicacy, but with little force, and with less variety. *La Molinara* is one of the most pleasing of his works; it is . . . soothing but never astonishing or elevating." The *Chronicle*, noting the opera's popular music, expressed wonderment at its having lain dormant fourteen years. It "is an Opera of the pure Italian school, whose merit [lies] in the beauty and originality of its melodies, and in the adaptation of the sound to the sense."

Hunt (E) wrote that the opera was "very pleasing and in some respects very original . . . [and] at times [Paisiello] equals [Mozart] in expression, that is to say, the air is quite suitable to the sentiment intended to be conveyed. . . . This is perhaps the highest character that can be given to any one particular point." Yet he felt that Paisiello's inspiration flagged at times and complained of the poor dialogue of the libretto. Bacon (LG) had no caveats: "Replete with the most enchanting simplicity, [Paisiello's melodies] are nature and sweetness itself. On the other hand, the comic songs are equally models of humorous composition. . . . Comic songs are by no means the easiest compositions; Mozart himself can boast of but few happy efforts in that line" (Mar. 15). He later (Mar. 22) reported: "The incidents and dramatic situations . . . command the attention of the audience from beginning to end, and the easy and frequent droll language, truly Neapolitan, is eminently calculated to augment this favorable impression." But at another revival the next year the *Inquisitor* pointed out: "The Italian language is not sufficiently understood in this country for the merit of a Comic Opera to be appreciated; La Molinara contains a great deal of humour, which never seems to be felt by the audience."

Still another comic opera, produced in 1791, was *La Locanda*, written for the King's (now at the Pantheon) by the composer.[64] The *Post* cited its warm reception and thought the music, "in many parts exquisite," would "add to his fame." But the *Times* wrote that the opera, "with all its fascinations, is yet infinitely too tedious in representation"; except for the finale, it has "few claims to dramatic merit." Opening late in the season, it nevertheless had eight performances and chalked up twenty-two more in 1792.

In that year the King's (now at the Little Theatre) produced *La Discordia Conjugale*, the plot turning upon the jealousy of an old man with a beautiful young wife. The reviews all spoke of its warm reception; the *Diary* thought the airs well adapted to the performers and the "accompanyments original, pleasing, and brilliant," while the *Herald* (Apr. 2) considered the opera "scientific, original, and a work of much ingenuity" and later called it "too good for the multitude" (Apr. 11). Yet it received eight performances; obviously the musical taste of the public was again somewhat higher than the press believed.

In 1793 there were two more Paisiello operas. The first, a serious work, was *I Giuochi D'Agrigento*. It had a splendid production (T), and much praise was given to the songs[65] and the performances, but the opera had only slight success. The second was a fairly successful and frequently revived comedy, *I Zingari in Fiera*. The *Times* (June 3) observed that almost every song was encored,[66] and the music and acting were "far superior to the trash that is usually introduced into Italian Opera"—an unusual remark, for only one previous reviewer had shown similar objections toward Italian opera.

In 1794 *La Serva Padrona* was produced. Although it succeeded then and was revived in 1799, no reviews survive.

Paisiello's popularity in London continued with the production of *La Modista Raggiratrice* in 1796. Critic C (T) thought it equal to any of his other works—the performers did it justice, and it was warmly received, most of the principal arias being encored.[67] The *True Briton* stated that the music "possesses all the fine, fancy, and harmonious contrivance" of the composer. The work succeeded and was revived seven times each in 1795 and 1819. In the latter year, when it had a fine production,[68] the *Inquisitor* confirmed that in this work Paisiello could "write the most exquisite melody with the necessary portion of comic effect." For Kenrick (BS), however, the libretto lacked something in probability or interest: "To the beauty of the music alone does it owe its present revival." And Hunt (E), who showed mixed feelings about the older style, was not even happy with the music: "The accompaniments are more than usually light, and there is a want of abundance in it altogether amounting to the bald."

In 1797 still another hit was produced: *Nina*, based on a libretto by Giuseppe Carpani—further adapted by Lorenzi and da Ponte—which Grout calls the best example of sentimental comedy of the whole period. The theme of madness, with melodramatic overtones, assured the success of the work.[69] The *Oracle* (probably Boaden) provided unusual insights: "Paisiello has executed no work of greater simplicity, delicacy, and expression. If we were to judge of Italian taste by most of the operas performed among us, we should be under a delusion, for the integrity of their composition is generally violated by some ranting bravuras, [with?] which some German cooks *appear* to suit the principal singer. Nina, however, has not an air which does not rise out of character and situation." Critic B declared that *Nina* "is unmatched in the magic power it has over the human breast, with respect to the tender simplicity, delicacy of expression, and pathetic effect. The string of sensibility seldom ceases to vibrate to the electric touch of this exquisite composer." Only DuBois (MM) thought the work could "never be a favourite." But indeed it was: the work had ten performances that season and several revivals up to 1828.

At an 1825 revival, Alsager (T) wrote: "There is a melodious quietness in the whole of the music of this opera, which works upon one's feelings in a deeper degree than the efforts of more splendid composers, who are rather anxious to take the heart by storm than to tap it by gently working on its finer sensibilities" (May 27). And Ayrton (Har) stated that *Nina* "is full of beauties of the gentle kind; its melodies are original, pure, and delightful, and every note in the opera is appropriate to the words." But the *London* observed that after Mozart and Rossini, "it sounds tame and occasionally insipid."

One of Paisiello's most popular operas at the King's—ranking close to *Frascatana*—was not comic but the serious opera *Elfrida* (libretto by Calzabigi) produced in 1798. It achieved sixteen performances that season, sixteen in 1799 (including four in a one-act adaptation), and had six more revivals through 1813.[70] Reviews of the premiere were scant and trivial, but at an 1811 revival, Croly (T) had nothing but praise for the composer's music; he regretted, however, "the impediments which the Composer generally throws in his own way by the choice of subject. . . . The most exquisite music, and its most felicitous execution, are made insipid and unpopular, by being wasted on subjects[71] which would disgust even the judgment of the lowest loungers at an Opera." The opera was produced once in 1813 for Catalani, but Barnes (T), showing the continuing shifts in taste even before the full impact of Mozart, now questioned the music: "The taste and tenderness of the Composer are not sufficiently relieved, the ear becomes insensibly weary of its perservering softness and laborious simplicity; and no skill of execution can redeem the whole from dulness."[72]

Paisiello's last opera at the King's was *Didone [Abbandonata]*, produced in 1799. The work was barely successful, but was revived for Catalani in 1808. Robertson (E) wrote: "The music . . . abounds with spirited passages, but [the composer's] genius does not appear suited to the grand character of the music; there is too much playfulness for dignity, too much beauty for sublimity."

Altogether, the public strongly supported most of his sixteen comic operas — some in spite of adverse criticism — and even one or two serious ones. Moreover, Paisiello's popularity was remarkably well sustained in revivals after 1815, despite a strong shift in musical taste.[73]

Our chronology follows, by and large, that of the premieres at the King's. Thus we find that many of the composers discussed after 1800 fall between the death of Mozart and the advent of Rossini — a period when no composer was "an artist of the first rank, and few even aspired to the second. . . . Failure of the music to engage the drama on its own level was the besetting weakness of the whole period" (*NOHM*, VIII, 376, 386). Operatic fare at the King's, accordingly, fell into the doldrums with a string of mostly forgettable operas and composers, of whom only Winter, Paer, Mayr, and perhaps Pucitta deserve some emphasis. But this decline must also be attributed, in part, to diva Angelica Catalani, who pretty much dominated affairs at the King's for upwards of ten years.

WINTER

The new century at the King's opened with operas by Peter von Winter (1754–1825). He studied violin in Mannheim and played in the court orchestra there as well as at the court in Munich, where he met Mozart. Though he wrote his thirty operas in many operatic styles, he "could not put the stamp of his personality on them" (N.G.). Nevertheless, some made a lasting impression on a few London critics.

His first work at the King's was the comic *I [Due] Fratelli Rivali* (1800). The only surviving review, which reported that the work was well received, went on to lambaste the "*Italian junta*," which was, however, ineffective

(MM). The work played six times and was never revived. But Winter himself came to the King's in 1803, at the invitation of Kelly (then acting as impresario), and composed four serious operas to librettos by da Ponte. The first was *La Grotta di Calipso*, written for Billington that season. It had thirteen performances and three more in 1804. The only review of the premiere rendered trite praise to Winter and Billington, adding that the "well told" story "does great credit to da Ponte" (P). But at an 1804 revival, the *Post* stated that "the merits of the music of *Calypso* have been long acknowledged."

In 1804 Winter produced *Il Trionfo dell'Amor Fratero*. The story, drawn from Greek mythology (Castor and Pollux) had "several incidents which, although not strictly classical, may be fairly allowed" (T). The *Chronicle* noted with approval the introduction of German music: "The German masters, if they have not all the melody of the Italian, yet have great powers of emotion, and they make even the instruments of the orchestra greatly contribute to the influence of the voice on the soul. This is admirably proved in the Opera." And critic B was most enthusiastic. "Winter," he wrote, "has in his present work exceeded all his former productions, by a display of unexpected originality; by the happiest combinations of sounds, bearing a just relation to the passions he has to imitate; and by a depth of science, which surmounts the greatest difficulties of the art, and softens them into the most affecting and natural impressions. The whole may be considered as a grand union of the sublime, the pathetic, and the gay and lively." The opera, well produced with a strong cast (Billington and Braham), was repeated twelve times and was revived the next season for eight more.

Still later that season, Winter produced his biggest success, *Il Ratto di Proserpina*—a classical pastoral reminiscent of Gluck's *Orfeo*—which was composed for Billington and Josephina Grassini.[74] The opera was "one of the most splendid productions we ever witnessed on the stage" (P). The *Chronicle* agreed: "It is a grand and sublime production, and in every point—in the composition both of Music and Poetry, by Winter and Da Ponte—in Decoration, by Marinari—in the lead of the Orchestra, by Weichsel—in the Dancing, by Des Hayes—and still more in the united vocal talents of the two principal women, is altogether without a parallel." It played fifteen times and had successful revivals the next two seasons and in 1815.[75] Parke called the music "masterly."

In 1805 Winter brought out his final opera for the King's, a seria written for Grassini—*Zaïra*.[76] Criticism was scant but favorable, and the work was given nine times that season, four the next, and eight in 1816. Despite these successes Winter returned to the Continent at the end of that season.

The influence of Winter, perhaps not fully realized by surviving reviews, is apparent in the recollections of this period by S. D. ("Chronicles"): "The engagement of this eminent composer, whom the death of Mozart had left without a rival in Germany, does infinite credit to Kelly.... For [four] seasons... the frequenters of the Opera had really good music. It is only surprising (if one did not know how completely first singers rule both managers and public) that the *platitudes* of Portogallo were endured by those who had listened to the *music* of Winter." And he added that "the engagement of Winter laid the foundation stone of a better style of music on our King's Stage." In 1813 the *Chronicle* called for a revival of Winter's operas since the King's had acquired Madame Ferlendis, a contralto; it will "afford an opportunity of hearing music again which is too good to be allowed to be forgotten" (May 18). Robertson praised Winter on several occasions in the *Examiner*, though he never had an opera of his to review, and in 1819 Hunt wrote: "What would we not give to have Winter's *Ratto di Proserpina* again, with all the voluptuous pathos and Greek beauty" (E, Aug. 22).77

P. C. GUGLIELMI AND PORTOGALLO

Pietro Carlo Guglielmi (1772–1817) — called Guglielmi *le fils* — was the son of Pietro Alessandro Guglielmi, but he lacked his father's "musical intelligence and originality" (N.G.). Born in London, he was apparently in Naples by 1782, and in Madrid in 1794, when his first opera was produced. He did not return to London until early in 1809, though his first opera at the King's was produced in 1806 — *I Due Nozze ed un Sol Marito*, which was chosen by Guiseppi Naldi for his King's debut.78 Almost all critical attention was on the performance. The opera was successful and was briefly revived in 1813, when Barnes (T) wrote: "Dull as the plot and dialogue of operas generally are, '*Due Nozze*' excels all that we have seen of unrelieved stupidity."

In 1809 Guglielmi directed the King's premiere of his *La Serva Raggiatrice*, apparently based on his *La serva bizzarri* (Naples, 1803), which failed badly. But he was more successful with *Sidagero*, produced the next month for Diomiro Tramezzani's debut. The music, Robertson wrote, "gives me no reason to congratulate the musical world on his arrival in our country, being destitute of any striking traits of originality or science, likely to improve the present degenerated taste" (E). In its 1813 revival, the opera was found to have "no merit.... The music is uniformly feeble" (T).

A revival of his *La Scommessa* opened the 1810 season. Robertson thought a worse opera had never been produced at the King's. The music was "languid and monotonous," (C) though it was "much applauded" (T, Jan. 8). Despite poor performances, however, the work was given eight times. *Romeo e Giulietta* was produced two months later. The plot followed Shakespeare "with as much closeness as was consistent" for two acts, wrote Croly (T), adding: "The general style of the composition is vigorous and pure, with occasional displays of taste and science of no common order." But Robertson gave the work short shrift, noting that Guglielmi "had found a suitable librettist in Buonaiuti," for the music was "in perfect union" with the author's "contemptible language." Yet it played six times. Guglielmi returned to Naples in the spring of 1811.

Marcos Antonio Portugal (1762–1830), known as "Portogallo" in London (he never went there), wrote both seria and buffa operas, though London was mainly interested in the former. His first opera at the King's was the comic *I Due Gobbi*, selected by Viganoni for his 1796 debut; it received mixed notices. The *Chronicle* thought it had "a great deal of very charming music, enlivened by variety, and recommended by its popular and easy character," but the *Times* declared that the opera "has very little in it either of music or any other allurement." The public sided with the *Times*: it was barely successful. Nevertheless, his seria *Fernando nel Messico*, which received trite praise in 1803, had twelve performances that season and was revived the next for four more.

In 1806 the King's produced his seria *Argenide e Serse*—a critical and popular success. "For grandeur and effect" the music "cannot be exceeded. The accompaniments are rich and beautiful, the airs are full of taste and science" (T). The music was "uncommonly fine" (C), and the overture was "grand and impressive" (*Courier*). The next year Catalani made her debut in Portogallo's *Semiramide*, which he had composed for her and considerably revised for this production. Most of the critical attention was on Catalani. The opera was successful and had four revivals. At an 1811 revival, Croly (T) was impressed: "The most distinguished days of the Italian school never produced a work with more of the power and vigour of genius. The recitatives have a rich and bold expression, which makes a striking contrast with the usual tameness of recitative; and the bravuras were composed for Catalani's voice. There cannot be, in our opinion, a higher panegyric." Still later in 1807, Catalani produced his *La Morte di Mithridate*. The opera "combines more musical beauties for a Performer, than any that we know," wrote the *Chronicle*.[79] But other critical attention was again glued to the performance. The work was repeated nine times and revived once in 1809.

Portogallo's last opera at the King's was another seria, *Barsene, Regina di Lidia* (not listed in N.O.), produced by Mme. Sessi for her benefit in 1815. The *Chronicle* wrote: "The music very much resembles most of the composer's other works—it is without fault and without vigour; but it contains some good points." The opera played eight times. In 1811 Portogallo went to Rio de Janeiro, where he died.

PUCITTA

Vincenzo Pucitta (1778–1861), the last of the "Catalani composers," had a curiously mixed career in London. Pucitta wrote about seventeen operas between 1800 and 1807—mostly comedies and farces for Milan and Venice. Brought to London in 1809 by Catalani to write both seria and buffa for her (he also accompanied her on tours), he conducted his operas at the King's that season and in 1811 was music director. In 1814 he took the same post at the Théâtre Italien in Paris but was so much disliked that Catalani had one of his operas advertised without his name.

His first King's premiere—the comic *I Villeggiatori Bizzarri*[80] (libretto by Buonaiuti)—was produced in 1809 for the debut of his wife. Robertson (E) was dismayed by the libretto: "To attempt the reformation of the *Poets* of this theatre would be a hopeless task; ... their writings abound with the grossest absurdities.... [Moreover] Signor Pucitta's compositions possess neither novelty nor science, they are generally pleasing and lively, but without much variety; old Italian passages occur every minute, and it is easy to judge by one bar what will occur in the next." The opera was, however, a great success, with twenty performances but no revivals.

The premiere of the strongly melodramatic (heroicomic) *La Caccia d'Enrico IV* followed two months later. The *Chronicle* stated: "The music has the charm of adaptation to the subject.[81] Every idea of the poet is feelingly expressed by the musician; it is intelligible even to the untutored ear." But critic B (T) deplored the libretto: "The construction of the piece [is] absurd to the last degree." And Robertson stated that the poet "should remember that [librettos] would not be tolerated for a moment were it not for the music that accompanies them and in some degree conceals their absurdity. The opera is from beginning to end a composition that a boy of twelve or thirteen years of age would blush to own." Nevertheless, with Catalani at her zenith, the piece was a hit, with fourteen performances that season and two revivals. At an 1812 revival the *Times* (possibly Barnes) admitted that the music was "generally pretty, but some of the chorusses deserve a higher praise."[82]

In 1810 Pucitta produced his best serious opera (Loewenberg) and his first seria for Catalani: *La Vestale*. Robertson (E) now found Pucitta's music at least a relief from "the unexampled dulness of Guglielmi. Pucitta has but little genius, and less science, yet he is not without merit; the airs . . . are generally graceful, and supplanted by playful accompaniments that evince considerable fancy and knowledge of the effect of the different instruments." Despite its lateness in the season, the opera was given eleven times and had two revivals. The following season the *Times* (Mar. 25) called it "by far the best of Pucitta's operas. The music, [though] without any of those striking excellencies which we have a right to expect from Italian genius, never offends."

In 1811 Pucitta produced a semiserious opera, *Le Tre Sultane*, that received mixed notices. The *Times* found the music "beautiful, and might have almost told the story without the aid of language," and the *Herald* wrote that it had "one feature throughout, which is not very common in this age, we mean originality." But Robertson noted that Pucitta "has not only carefully avoided giving the other singers any opportunity of shewing their talents, but has even appropriated to them, in some parts, passages similar to [Catalani's], that an immediate comparison of their powers may be formed. Such malignant and contemptible artifices should be disdained by her." The *Chronicle* agreed, calling the opera a *"frippery* of compositions. . . . [It] is the degradation of genius to condemn [Catalani] to such uses." The work barely succeeded.

Pucitta's serious *Boadicea*, on a British subject,[83] premiered in 1813. Produced in the immediate wake of Mozart's *Tito* and *Figaro*, it suffered sharp competition. Barnes (T, Mar. 24) found the plot "not destitute of interest," while the music was "delicate and tasteful," and he went on to praise "the finale of the first act—a bold, deep, scientific harmony,—and the prayer at the opening of the second." But Ayrton (C) was quite acerbic:

> The whole of this drama is without plot, incident, or interest. . . . [The opera] does not contain one piece—not a fragment—that is even well *selected*, for to originality it has not the slightest pretence. The overture is made up of shreds and patches. . . . Many of the airs are of the bravura species, as old and very much in the worst style of Porpora and Hasse. Those of a more tranquil and sober cast . . . resemble the tunes that pass through the noses of parochial performers into our parish churches.

The work failed. In 1814 his *Adolfo e Chiara* had but two performances, but his revival of *Aristodamo* the same season was quite a success.

Pucitta frequently drew sharply mixed reviews, but the public showed strong support for most of his operas, owing, no doubt, to Catalani's power. In 1819 Pucitta successfully toured Germany and Austria with Elizabeth Feron, his English pupil. But the French disliked him immensely (N.O.).

PAER AND MAYR

Fernando Paer (1771–1839) perhaps ranked closer to Mozart than any other composer represented at the King's before 1815. He was maestro di capella at Parma, and his *Ero e Leandro* (Naples, 1794), performed by Billington, was his first big success. He lived in Paris after 1807, where Napoleon admired his music. Liszt was one of his pupils in composition. He dominated Italian opera between 1800 and 1810. Many of his operas (he wrote about forty) combined pathos and comedy; these semiseria, in which "tragic and comic elements appear side by side," were like *opéras comiques* but with sung recitative (N.G.). Despite fine critical support, his operas were not very successful in London.

His first opera at the King's, produced in 1807, was the one-act *dramma giocosa Il Principe di Taranto*; it had thirteen performances but little critical comment until its revival in 1810, when Robertson thought it displayed "a scientific taste in the disposition of the accompaniments and the construction of the harmony, as well as a considerable elegance in the melodies."

Camilla, a rescue opera thought to be his masterpiece (N.G.), came to the King's in 1812. The strongly melodramatic character of the work is evident from a description of Catalani in one scene: "Pale and emaciated with confinement, but at the sight of her child suddenly returning to smiles and loveliness, and the natural joy of a mother's heart,—then shut up once more in the dungeon,—with her child dying before her for food,—crying out for help to the walls and echoes, sinking feebly beside the body,—screaming distractedly with a voice which had forgot all its music" (T). The *Times* found the music was equally touching: Paer "found materials for the finest interest of the stage in the part, and he had the judgment which would not [enfeeble] it by superfluity of composition. The splendor and sparkling of the art would have been a most unsuited ornament to the deep and impressive interest of the character, and bravuras and brilliancy would have been only burthensome." But the public apparently wanted bravuras, for the work had only six performances. It was revived in 1819 for a single performance, but Alsager (T) stated that the "best pieces" were, "apparently, left out intentionally and nothing remains but an unbroken chain of dry, unmeaning recitative."

Paer's setting of Metastasio's *La Didone Abbandonata* was mounted in 1814. Barnes (E) was not happy with the libretto, whose "poetry is generally of a mediocre kind, displaying tolerably smooth versifications, tolerably pretty sentiment, and tolerably elegant diction." But he found that Paer's music, "for sweetness, variety, and the unlimited profusion of the most delicate graces, is scarcely surpassed by the best compositions of Mozart."

Ayrton (C) agreed that it was, "beyond all comparison, the best composition of this author that we have yet heard. It is full of the elegant, flowing melody that characterizes the Italian School, and is not deficient in the rich harmony, the simple and illustrative accompaniment, which acknowledges a German as its parent." Yet again the opera barely succeeded with the public.[84]

The King's opened the 1816 season with *Griselda*, selected by Josephine Fodor for her debut. It was the first opera to bring Paer fame. "The story of *Griselda*"—well known through Boccaccio and Chaucer—"is extremely well adapted to be the vehicle of music of a soft and melting character" (T—Barnes?). And Ayrton (C) wrote: "To the admirers of the Italian school, this opera will afford a luxurious treat; it is replete with beautiful melodies, the accompaniments are appropriate and judicious, and the sense throughout is well illustrated by the sound." This critical success had but eight performances, yet it was revived the next year, when Bacon (LG) observed: "The Music of this Opera is at first somewhat languid and heavy, but improves greatly in its progress . . . so that, taken as a whole, *Griselda*, although not the best of Paer's works, is certainly a fine composition."[85]

Paer's last opera at the King's was the seriocomic *L'Agnese* (libretto by Buonavoglia), which was produced in 1817. The opera ran into strong competition from *Don Giovanni*. It carried a heavy dose of melodrama and was acted to the hilt by Violante Camporese and Giuseppe Ambrogetti.[86] The *Chronicle* noted that, unlike most Italian operas, *Agnese* was "compounded of a regular dramatic poem, action essentially necessary to the piece and music; the latter of which is not more conducive to the effect of the whole than the acting." Bacon (LG), however, questioned whether such a story was "a proper subject for the pen of a dramatic poet, and above all for a musical piece."

"The music," the *Chronicle* wrote, "is one of the best efforts of this master. . . . Every part of it is appropriate; the passion throughout is well considered, and every sound is either an echo, or a judicious introduction to the sense."[87] Alsager (T) was only somewhat less enthusiastic:

> Paer's music is not of the highest order: it is perhaps neither very original, nor very profound; its character is sweetness, pathos, and a peculiar facility of adaptation to scenic representation. . . . Paer is remarkable, too, for his great judgment: he undertook perfectly what we may call the modelling of an opera; he knows where to employ the *recitativo parlanti* . . . where an increased interest requires the recitative accompanied, and where the subject should rise into the full melody, into regular rhythm and movement.

Bacon (LG) thought the music inferior to his previous operas but admitted he may have been adversely influenced by his dislike of the story.[88] Despite this favorable criticism and a fine production, the work had but five performances, which were "suspended on account of some similitude which was thought to exist between the situation of Hubert [i.e., insanity] and that of his late majesty [George III]" (BS, May, 1821). It was also unsuccessfully revived in 1820 and 1821, when the critical support continued. Bacon (LM, Aug. 1820) praised Paer's "exquisite" melodies: "He is not, however, of the latest school of instrumental effects. His accompaniments are subordinate to the voice. . . . His Opera is strictly vocal, yet he employs the orchestra with great and adequate effect. He apparently has unlimited command of beautiful strains of melody,—short, but never to be forgotten." Thus the press showed itself to be well in advance of the public in its appreciation of this fine composer.[89]

Johann Simon (Giovanni Simone) Mayr (or Mayer) (1763–1845) composed some sixty serious and semiserious operas, four of which appeared at the King's (he turned down offers to come to London). Basically he was of the late Neapolitan school (Lang), though occasional richness (especially in the woodwinds) suggest a Germanic influence (N.G.). His reputation was early eclipsed by Rossini; Gaetano Donizetti was his most famous pupil.

Mayr's first opera at the King's—*Il Fanatico per la Musica* (1806)— became an immediate hit, with many revivals to 1830. The hilarious plot,[90] providing a tour de force for musical versatility and inviting interpolated numbers, overshadowed its merits as a composition. The *Chronicle* wrote: "Il Fanatico per la Musica is the most incomparable Opera we ever witnessed. It produced convulsive bursts of laughter by the drollery and humour of Signor Naldi, while the musical merits of the work, heightened by the exquisite performance of Mrs. Billington, engaged the liveliest interest of the audience." Such buffoonery, however, did not wear well, and although the opera was revived every season to 1813, as well as in 1817, 1819, 1824, and 1829 (often cut down to one act), it never received more than a few performances. Indeed, the work could hardly be discussed apart from the virtuosity of its performers. In 1819 the *Inquisitor* was not even sure of the name of the composer. But in 1824, when the opera was "altered by Rossini" (EM), Alsager (T) could still "laugh at the eccentricities of Don Fedro," which were "cloathed by Mayr in harmonies of a very appropriate and expressive character." Yet in 1829 he reported: "The music of this opera is of a tame and insipid character, which must long since have consigned it to utter oblivion, had not its chief merit rested on its qualities as a farce" (T).

Mayr's first serious opera at the King's—*Adelasia e Aleramo*—was produced in 1815. The *Times* (Jan. 11) found it had "the same insipid order of plot as the multitude of Italian dramas" but thought some of the music pleasing. The choruses were also praised (May 8). The opera received a good production and played eleven times but was not revived.[91]

His next opera, also a melodramatic seria, did not appear until 1826 — *Medea in Corinto*, his "undoubted masterpiece" (Commons), which was produced for a Pasta benefit. Alsager (T) thought the libretto, by Romani, had insufficient incidents to form an effective plot. The music, however, was "highly creditable to the genius of Mayer. It places his character, as a composer, in a more lofty and commanding situation than it had before attained, at least in this country. . . . The music . . . is remarkable for its wild and powerful harmony." Critic Z (NM), even more enthusiastic, found Rossini wanting by comparison. "The music deserves, in every respect, the term of a classic work." The opera had nine performances and three revivals.[92]

Mayr's last opera at the King's — *La Rosa Bianca e la Rosa Rossa* — was produced in 1828. For the *Chronicle* the opera "afforded no striking dramatic or musical effects."[93] Alsager (T) tended to agree: "It is extremely pleasing throughout, without exhibiting any striking traits of genius." The *Examiner* concurred.

These reviewers found the libretto, mainly a love story, only vaguely historical,[94] but it had too much history for Hunt: "Song is for passion in its own shape, and not mixed up in the pretenses of history. Great writers . . . have rarely laid their scenes in the midst of these impertinances. . . . We do not want a singing Earl of Derby, singing footguards, and a warbling sheriff. [But] the music is so good that we expect it every minute to be better. There is now and then a very delicate commentary of accompaninent, throwing out little unexpected passages both learned and to the purpose" (*Companion*). Holmes (At) agreed with Hunt, whom he quoted; Mayr, he declared, "has married the German and Italian schools without constraint or affectation." Critic Z (NM) also noted that Mayr's music, "while tinged with the harmonic richness of his own country, limits the display of it to what he knows to be acceptable to the Italian ears."[95] Apparently the indisposition of Maria Caradori-Allan doomed the work to only three performances; it was not revived. With this exception, then, both the press and the public supported Mayr's operas. Ebers called Mayr's music "elegant and pleasing" and "old-school Italian" — "a sop to the older amateurs."[96]

MOZART

Wolfgang Amadeus Mozart (1756–91) had been dead fifteen years before his first opera appeared at the King's — and twenty-five years before his music began to enjoy popularity there. The Italian cabal was one impediment, as da Ponte reported, but there were others. Catalani and other prima donnas, for instance, were averse to singing his music, which did not lend itself to elaborate ornamentation. Also, the King's did not have adequate baritones for *Don Giovanni* until much before 1817.

But Mozart had not been totally neglected in London.[97] Some of his arias were introduced in Gazzaniga's *Vendemmia* (1789), Fabrizi's *Due Castellani Burlati* (1790), and Guglielmi's *Pastore Nobile* (1792). And "all of the music deserving celebrity in [Bianchi's *La Villanella Rapida*] is by Mozart—and it is to the praise of Storace that many of these have been introduced" (H, Mar. 1, 1790). Hunt as a schoolboy (1791–94) first heard Mozart when the band at St. James's Park played "Non più andrai." By 1800 Mozart was "the delight of every amateur circle" ("Chronicles").

It may seem strange that when London did first turn to a Mozart opera in 1806, they selected *La Clemenza di Tito*, an opera seria long out of fashion elsewhere. "Chronicles" tells us that *Tito* was produced at the suggestion of the Prince of Wales, and that the score was supplied out of his library. But undoubtedly some of the credit for the production must be allowed to Billington, who chose it for her benefit. Buonaiuti "skilfully curtailed much of the recitative" of this production (C).

The premiere was recognized as unusual: "Every part of the Theatre overflowed—and upon no occasion was the patronage of the public so properly bestowed," for, the *Chronicle* continued: "We never witnessed on [sic] any Theatre so exquisite an Opera. . . . [*Tito*] combines every essential beauty. It has the poetry of Metastasio, and the grand instrumental harmony of the German School softened and refined by the vocal beauty of the Italian. It is the least complicated of all his operas. . . . It is a *chef d'oeuvre* of art, and cannot fail to be popular." The *Post* stated that Weichsell, the leader, "exerted himself with the whole orchestra to render every justice to one of the greatest composers the world ever produced." In 1829, however, Ayrton (Har) wrote: "So little attention was paid to the instrumental accompaniments at this period [i.e., 1806], that in the grand aria of Vitelli 'Non più di fioni,' a tinkling harp was substituted for the impressive and wailing tones of the Corni di Bassetto obbligato."[98] Hogarth (II, 360), also writing of this production years later, declared that the Italian singers "neither relished nor understood the music and found the study of one of Mozart's concerted pieces a more laborious task than that of half a dozen whole operas of the Italian school." The opera had only six performances.

When *Tito* was revived in 1812, it proved to be surprisingly popular, with sixteen performances. The *Chronicle* wrote: "Mozart is without comparison, as we think, the Shakespear of the lyric drama, the man above others who gives the passion of poetry to music, and quickens by its influence all the best emotions of the soul. It is not the man of science only, but the man of nature also, who is moved and gratified by the eloquence of Mozart." The *Times* review (Mar. 5) by Barnes raised some Romantic objections to the libretto: the subject was "so bare, that nothing like the interest of a plot could be felt through it"—"such was the taste of the stage in countries where the decay of political freedom spread through all the departments of intellectual effort the same spirit of tameness, weakness, and monotony." Moreover, Barnes had difficulty coming to terms with Mozart's music, which "probably bears the exclusive impression of science too strongly and too unremittingly for the general ear; . . . and taste, nature, and simplicity might, in some instances, at least, be advantageously substituted for chromatics and cadences, the crashing of disjointed harmonies, and the array of scientific discordance."99 Robertson, too, was unhappy with the libretto though he thought Mozart triumphed over it: "There is but one scene which deviates from sameness, but of this one [when Vitellia plots with Sextus against Titus], Mozart has taken glorious advantage. It is here that the genius of Mozart is powerfully called into exertion, and springs forth into the sublimest flights of imagination" (E).

At *Tito*'s revival with the same cast the next year, Ayrton (C) was moved to a remarkable panegyric on Mozart, nor had he any caveats on the drama, which was "the most perfect that we have seen represented upon the Italian stage."

At an 1817 revival, the *Chronicle* (July 14) complained of alterations: "One beautiful air is omitted, another of no merit is added, and a recitative and aria were moved by the prima donna, Mme. Fodor, from the end of the third to the middle of the second act, despite the protests of Ayrton, the musical director." Fodor, in a letter to the *Chronicle*, tried to justify her alterations, and Hunt, in a later review, recounted the controversy and came down decisively on the side of the *Chronicle*. But he found a lack of inspiration in Mozart's music, and like Barnes he placed the blame squarely on Metastasio's libretto and its Neoclassical taste: "Poor Dr. Burney was taken in, as the phrase is, by his smirking manners and his cheap sentimental common-places. . . . He seems to us to have been a very middling poet, and a cold, servile, over-prudential man" (E).

In 1818 *Tito* had three more performances and was "deservedly a favourite in this country" (TI), but after the advent of Rossini, it quickly dropped in popularity. In 1828 Alsager (T) still called the work "an opera of the highest merit," but critic Z (NM) demurred: "To be candid, this opera has lost some part of its former attraction; partly owing to the revolution effected of late in musical taste [i.e., Rossini], and partly to the nature of the composition itself. Although the last opera which Mozart wrote, it is far from his best. It was the song of the dying swan." Hogarth (II, 260) called *Tito* "the noblest serious opera in existence." Apart from the libretto, the press was nearly unanimous in its praise of this opera in both premiere and revival performance—an enthusiasm also shared by the public.

Following the King's premiere of *Tito* in 1806, Mozart again returned to limbo for another five years, though in the interval there were some "amateur" productions of his operas.[100] Robertson, in his 1808 and 1809 reviews, belabored the King's for its neglect of Mozart, and critic William Gardner, in the *Monthly Magazine* (March 1811), deplored the lack of talent or ability at the King's to perform him. But that very month the King's did perform Mozart again—*Così Fan Tutte*. It was given by Madame Bertinotti-Radicati for her benefit, and S. D. ("Chronicles") gave her full credit:

> Madame Bertinotti, the new [first] woman, can hardly be blamed for patronizing her own husband's opera; but had her musical airs been as red as scarlet, she would have atoned for all by affording the English public, at her benefit, the opportunity of hearing a comic opera by Mozart. . . . Now, at length, they looked forward to see the Italian spell broken, and the works of the immortal German and his school naturalized in the London Opera-house.

The performance had problems. "It was not the best the house could afford," and Bertinotti, as Fiordiligi, omitted "Come scoglio" and "Per pietà," introduced "Porgi amor" from *Figaro*, and robbed Dorabella of "E amore un ladroncello"; similar changes were made for Cauvini, who sang Fernando ("Chronicles"). Robertson (E), who also thought Bertinotti could not be "too much praised" for the production, wrote: "[*Così* is] one of the most masterly works of the great Mozart. To convey by words an idea of the electrical effect this music produces, is impracticable, and to recommend any particular [number] would be useless, where the whole is one collected mass of excellence. It is only by hearing such music that an adequate conception can be formed of the exquisite beauty and variety of the airs, the uncommon richness of the harmony, or the genius displayed in the accompaniments." It quickly became a success and had twelve performances that season—more than in any of its several revivals up to 1830.

It was revived in 1816 for Fodor's benefit, and Ayrton (C) deplored its neglect for seven years.[101] At its revival in 1817 Alsager (T) called it "perhaps the gayest of Mozart's compositions . . . . The music is highly dramatic, particularly in the part of Don Alphonso . . . which is marked throughout by a strong vein of sarcasm. We also highly admire the discrimination that is shown in the two female characters, Fiordiligi and Dorabella, which are in a style essentially different."

At an 1818 revival the *Inquisitor* was apparently the first to point out that *Così* "is almost entirely composed of concerted pieces; and the harmony of this is as delightful as any which was ever produced either by Mozart or any other master." And Hunt was first to comment on the plot, which had "the advantage of being simpler and more obvious in its incidents,—of telling its own story better, than any we have ever witnessed." Regarding the music, he exclaimed: "What an inexhaustible succession of beautiful airs and harmonies is there in Mozart! One combination after another does not start out with a more sparkling facility in the far-famed Kaleidoscope. . . . What do we not owe to an art and a master like this, who as it were spoke music as others speak words" (E).

The success of *Così* in 1811 prompted Giuseppe Naldi to bring out *Il Flauto Magico* the following month for his benefit.[102] "An apology was made by Naldi, that it could not be given with adequate *spectacle*," for the stage "wants *depth* for perspective" (C). But there were other production problems. As "Chronicles" wrote much later, "this opera required singers [Naldi] could not command, a chorus such as had never been heard within the walls of the King's Theatre, and a judgment he did not possess. He had a charming Pamina in Bertinotti, but where was his Sarastro? where his Regina di Notte?"[103] Yet the *Chronicle* thought "the Overture was given with all its genuine effect, and it was impossible quite to destroy the beauty of the Airs as they did of the Chorus; but even with all the faults of the performance it was a grand treat to the musical ear." Robertson agreed about the overture, and Bertinotti was "the only performer competent to her part" (he was silent on Naldi). But he deplored the plot: "The pleasure that the wonderful music of this gives, receives a serious drawback from the almost unprecedented absurdity of its plot and language, which are so incoherent, that they can scarcely be imagined the work of an ideot; and it does not reflect a little discredit on the taste of the [Germans], that this opera, sublime as its music is, should not only be tolerated, but even enthusiastically admired by them." The work, not surprisingly, received but two performances.

It was not revived until 1819 when it proved to be quite popular and brought a number of fine reviews. Ayrton (C) found the drama "absolute nonsense . . . and should have been re-written, and made, at least intelligible." But Alsager (T) did "not consider this a point of great importance: the greater part of the incidents and situations are easily comprehended; and perhaps even the difficulty itself, from its novel nature, forms an agreeable exercise to the understanding." Hunt agreed:

> We do not participate in the objections made to the nature of the story, which because it is a fairy tale[104] is thought frivolous. Alas, how

frivolous are most of the grave realities of life. . . . It anticipates for us something of the good, which the human mind . . . is so anxious to realize, — something of a brighter and more innocent world, in which the good-natured and flowery will is gratified; and the evil spirit . . . is always felt to be the weaker of the two, and sure to be found so at last. (E)

Hunt also praised "the bird-like hilarity of *Gente e qui l'uccellatore* . . . the abundant pomp and solemnity of all the grand melodies and harmonies connected with the Priests . . . and then again, the delicate and tricksome stepping of the return of the Genii, *Gia fan ritorno*." Then follows a masterly passage: "But the whole opera is one continued and deep river of music, breaking into every possible turn of the course and variety of surface, and exhibiting every aspect of the heavens that lie above it. Mozart's genius is here in it's most romantic and passionate character, undoubtedly. We can hardly say it is his best. . . . It is, we suspect, too poetical to be so; — too much referring to indefinable sentiments and sensations out of the pale of common experience." All reviewers agreed the opera was much too long, the cast uneven, and the chorus execrable. In addition the machinery failed to operate correctly, and the "two whirling globes . . . emulated the singing and the orchestra with a noise, of which none but tin heads could have been capable" (E). Astonishingly, it had fifteen performances.

In 1829 "some scenes" of "Zauberflöte" were given in German[105] for Sontag's benefit (she sang Pamina). Holmes (At) wrote: "What extraordinary thought, what grace, and what power of writing are shown in the overture! As for the body of the work . . . all is so flowing, so fertile in subject, and so fitting, that it could only be the work of *the* one magic hand." He and Alsager praised the performance, but critic X (E) quite disagreed: "We did not think to find Mozart's own countrymen (for it was a German company who exhibited), so untender of his memory as to leave out the finest of his airs, and to execute those they admitted inefficiently." That Sontag "should think of altering whole passages, so that the original phrase was lost . . . was perfectly monstrous."

Again, apart from the libretto, the press was unanimous in its support of this opera.

In 1812, the year after the premieres of *Così* and the *Flute*, Mozart's *Le Nozze di Figaro*[106] bowed at the King's for Naldi's benefit, and no doubt he was again largely responsible for the production. Joseph Fischer was engaged to sing the Count since Tramezzani refused to play a comic role, and Maria Dickons was brought over from Drury Lane to fill the role of another first woman, the King's having only Catalani ("Chronicles").

Robertson (E) wrote that the libretto, "in its quick succession of incidents, gives full scope to the fancy, which teemed with delightul combinations of sound, and sprung from subject to subject with inexhaustable freshness, vigour and originality. Every air, and almost every close, has strong character of novelty." The opera had strong support from Catalani and Dickons (Naldi was not even mentioned) and played eight times.

It was revived in 1813 when Naldi was again influential, but again the production faltered. Ayrton (C, Mar. 11) was acerbic: "Is it not surprising that in the first city in the world—that in this metropolis, unequalled for its wealth and for the encouragement which it holds out to musical merit, an Opera of such undisputed excellence should be performed in a manner that would disgrace a minor theatre in the suburbs? . . . The Orchestra alone did its duty well." Yet in 1816 it was revived again in a much stronger production, and Alsager (T) argued for its appeal to a wide public. The work then had only four performances, but in 1817 and 1818 it played eleven and twelve times, respectively. In 1817, the *annus mirabilis* of Ayrton, the *Chronicle* had to admit that the performers—Fodor, Camporesi, and Ambrogetti—were superb. Bacon (LG) thought that the many intrigues of the plot and the large cast "render it unfit for an Opera," yet its melodies "are at once so original, so ravishingly sweet, that the heart partakes the delight of the ear." Moreover, the concerted numbers "appear to us the highest efforts of a rare combination of genius and science" (Feb. 8). Despite the glowing premiere of *Don Giovanni* that season, Kenrick (BS, May) declared: "No novelty, be its merits what they may, will be able to efface 'Figaro' from the recollection of the public. . . . Never was any Opera more generally or more deservedly popular than this." In 1818 and 1819 arguments continued over which opera of Mozart's was the best (C; BS). Against the torrent of Rossini productions in the 1820s, *Figaro* held up very well, with revivals nearly every season right through 1830.

Not until 1817 did the King's have two baritones sufficient for the production of *Don Giovanni*, and William Ayrton, director that season, was determined to give it a superior production. He soon ran into difficulties, however:

> Scarcely . . . had [Ayrton] assumed the operatic helm, when storms lowered around him. He stood pledged to the public to bring out the long-desired Don Giovanni of Mozart. This was more than Italian patience could bear. Intrigues of every kind were resorted to; nay, if all that was whispered at the time might be true, even representatives of royalty "mingled in the dance" and denounced the theatrical damnation of Don Juan. . . . Honestly supported alone by Ambrogetti, and with only open enemies or concealed intrigues in the rest of his *corps operatique*, the manager firmly persevered; Don Juan was brought out;

the real lovers of music sustained it against the cabal, and it ran ten nights without interruption. ("Chronicles")

Ebers also confirms the interference of the "vexatious cabal."

On April 12 *Don Giovanni* opened to an enthusiastic house. It had a total of twenty-six performances that season, exceeding all former premiere runs at the King's. Reviews were still being written as late as mid-August: "This Opera [the *Chronicle* asserted] is at once the greatest work of Mozart, and the finest specimen that exists of dramatic music In the last scene, the burst of the whole orchestra upon the entrance of the stone figure is tremendous; which with the wind instruments ascending the musical scale in various keys, in mysterious progressions and wailing sounds, renders the whole almost petrifying."

The production was superb in all its parts. Particular praise was bestowed on the arias and performances, but two "errors" in the "conduct of the drama" were noted: "Don Juan, in his attempt on Zerlina, should carry her into the adjoining apartment" for "she invokes help by her shrieks, at a time when she is surrounded by the peasants, and consequently in no sort of danger." Also, in the supper scene, "the musicians and servants remained on the stage all the time the spectre is addressing Don Juan, whereas it is evident they should fly in alarm."

The weekly and monthly press were equally adulatory. Bacon (LG) pointed out the difficulty of performing Mozart: "The Opera of Don Juan, more than any other vocal drama, abounds in such scientific and profound harmonies, and parts dove-tail into each other with such peculiar nicety as to time, that none but accomplished musicians are equal to its execution." The King's company generally had sufficient skill for the task, though at times "the notes of the singers do not yet float, as they ought, in exquisite well-measured sweetness, correctness and purity of tune; and their only support, the wind instruments, have been out of tune in both representations" (Apr. 19).

In the next number, however, Bacon took some exceptions to da Ponte's drama — "the mixture of the tragic with the comic." He goes on to say, "The music, if it be good, renders the impression of every scene too strong and deeply rooted to admit of sudden and continued transitions from the serious to the ludicrous." Mozart remained blameless, however, for "there are not four bars in this Opera, which do not express the sense of the text." Kenrick (BS), however, welcomed the tragicomedy: "From the commencement to the conclusion the music is in the highest degree characteristic and expressive; nothing can be more gay and enlivening than that of the comic portions of the Opera, nothing more solemn and appalling than that of the serious scenes. It is a perfect whole." (May).

Hunt admired the music but had objections to the stone Commendatore in the final scene of the opera:

> The whole is too loud and crashing, and of too vulgar a description of the terrible. We know not that an apparition of stone has any particular claims to be noisy and bullying. The terror of spectral visitations consists in ghostliness, obscurity, and sepulchral hollowness, like the Ghost in *Hamlet*, — in short, in the quietest possible exhibition of power [as in the cemetery scene], which is always awful in proportion to it's ease, and to it's contempt of human vehemence. (E, Aug. 3)

Two weeks later he wrote a full essay developing his thoughts on the portrayal of the ghost in the final scene, drawing inferences from Wieland, Schiller, Ariosto, Homer, the authors of *Psalms* and *Kings*, Milton, Shakespeare, and others to buttress his case.[107] The *Inquisitor* (Aug.) quite agreed: "'The Examiner' has treated this objection with less freedom than discernment, but still urged enough to convince those who are inclined to decide for themselves that the immortal composer must have 'waxed desperate with imagination,' when he wantoned in such glowing and excessive frivolity." During the next three years, the work was performed fifteen, twelve, and nine times, respectively, and was revived nearly every year to 1830, but critics thought the later performances had deteriorated.

The impact of *Don Giovanni* on London in 1817 was unprecedented. Bacon (LG, May 10) crowed: "The interest excited by *Don Giovanni* remains as undiminished as it is unparalleled in the annals of the King's Theatre. The musical public cannot resist the temptation of hearing again that which afforded them such delight, and as the Opera has become the general topic of conversation in polite circles, fashion contributes in no small degree to the constant succession of full houses." Still, *Don Giovanni* was only the crest of the Mozartian wave that lasted from 1816 to 1820, when his operas averaged nearly 50 percent of all performances:

	1816	1817	1818	1819	1820	Total
Don Giovanni	—	26	15	12	9	62
Figaro	4	11	12	5	4	36
Così	9	2	5	—	—	16
Magic Flute	—	—	—	15	6	21
Tito	8	4	3	—	—	15
Total Mozart	21	43	35	32	19	150
Total Performances	65	64	62	69	52	312
Percent Mozart	32%	67%	56%	46%	37%	48%

After 1820 the Rossini fever took over for some years, but by 1825 the public was glad to have Mozart back again (Parke). Mozart's influence was also strongly felt in English opera.[108]

Rossini, whose operas at the King's were offering a challenge to Mozart's by 1819, is discussed last. Meanwhile works of other composers at the King's offered little challenge to the popularity of either Mozart or Rossini. Some of them were found to be tame imitators of the latter, and most of their operas failed. They included Giovanni Liverati, Giuseppi Mosca, Giovanni Pacini, Niccolo Antonia Zingarelli, Saverio Mercadanti, Pietro Generali, and Francesco Morlacchi. These composers had from one to three of their works produced, but most of them failed (Morlacchi's was an exception), and reviewers were mostly quite critical, seeing several as poor imitations of Rossini. Even Liverati and Mercadanti, who came to London for their premieres, had no better of a reception.

MEYERBEER

An important exception to these composers was Giacomo Meyerbeer (1791–1864), né Jacob Liebman Beer, son of a Jewish banker. Meyerbeer achieved early success as a pianist and composer of piano music. (He was in London briefly in 1815.) He spent nine years in Italy, wrote several successful operas beginning in 1817, and was soon held by many to be an equal to his friend Rossini. The great success of *Crociato* in 1814 gave him confidence to go to Paris where he achieved spectacular success in Grand Opera,[109] with his *Robert le Diable* (1831), *Les Huguenots* (1836), and *Le Prophète* (1849).

The King's mounted the seria *Crociato in Egitto* (libretto by Rossi)[110] in 1825 in a production carefully supervised by Ayrton (Hogarth); in fact, the preparations required postponement of the opening. But there was another reason for the great anticipation: the appearance in the lead role of Giovanni Velluti, Europe's last castrato and the first to sing at the King's in nearly thirty years. Critical reactions to him ranged from contempt to sympathy, as we shall see, and in some instances this colored views of the opera. Alsager (T), though overcome with disgust, made brief but favorable mention of the work (July 1). The *Post*, however, thought the opera overrated: "It is delightfully rich in melody, and its vocal as well as its instrumental harmonies command high admiration. But it certainly cannot be said that Meyerbeer compares with Rossini in his production of orchestral effects."[111] Critic X (E) agreed, adding that "Meyerbeer has concocted from various sources what to us appears to be one of the dullest operas ever represented." And Bacon (LM) thought so too: "The opera opens with a chorus of slaves who sing vehemently of their country, and hammer at blocks of stone, and we cannot decide whether the singing or the hammering was the more fatiguing to the ear. . . . Yet on the whole we cannot but regard Il Crociato in Egitto as an unequal production, and we are particularly struck by the absence of *style* in it."

Despite these disclaimers at its premiere—and the flap over a castrato—the public was supportive: the work played eleven times and had several revivals, including eleven performances in 1827. In 1826 Alsager (T) thought even better of the work and of Velluti: "The numerous beauties which this fine work discloses—the extraordinary tenderness of some of its strains—the martial boldness of others—the scientific harmony which pervades the concerted pieces—and the magnificent grandeur of its chorusses, merited in every respect this honour." And in 1828 critic X (E) shifted his opinion, calling it "unquestionably a masterly composition. . . . Almost every scene exhibits a richly-coloured musical picture" (Apr.). But Holmes (At) delivered an astonishingly virulent anti-Semitic attack on the work.[112]

For the 1828 season opening, the King's produced another Meyerbeer opera, *Margherita D'Anjou*, also a seria. Alsager (T) took exception to the historical deviations made by the librettist, Romani,[113] and thought the opera "very inferior" to *Crociato*. "There are, however, . . . many good dramatic situations, and they have been handled with a due conception of the passions which were to be expressed by the composer. The concerted pieces are numerous and for the most part effective."[114] Ayrton (Har) also dismissed the libretto with contempt and found the opera much weaker and more immature than *Crociato*. He too admitted, however, that some numbers revealed "a strong wish in the author to extricate himself from the bondage of the fashionable school." Critic X (E) was positive: "The composer has succeeded in producing excellent theatrical effect. . . . The words are well adapted to musical expression, and Meyerbeer seems to have felt their sentiment strongly." The *New Monthly* agreed, but Holmes (At) thought quite otherwise. He not only felt *Margherita* preferable to *Crociato* but complained: "With Meyerbeer, any tune fits any words; his operas do not so much express sentiments, as they furnish a certain quantity of tunes to a drama." In any event, the cast, except for Caradori, was ineffective, and the opera had only four performances.

Meyerbeer's phenomenally successful *Robert le Diable* had to wait until 1847 for its King's debut, and the *Huguenots* until 1845, though on the English stage there were no fewer than five versions of *Robert* by 1832, followed by productions of the *Jewess* in 1835, the *Huguenots* in 1836, and the *Prophet* in 1849.

COCCIA, BOCHSA, SPONTINI, AND BELLINI

Except for Bellini these late composers met with little success in London. Carlo Coccia (1782–1873), musical director at the King's for two seasons, produced his only opera to be seen there—*Maria Stuarda*—in 1827. He wrote it for Pasta, and she sang in the London premiere. Holmes's review (At), the first in print, stated that "upon the whole, the Opera is considerably above mediocrity, and if it cannot be said that Coccia is a very original thinker in music, he shows such a decided judgment in availing himself of the conceptions of others, as, combined with his own resources, his intimacy with orchestral powers, and especially consummate skill in the management of the chorus, demand our approbation." Alsager (T) agreed, and Ayrton (Har, p. 149) wrote: "The general character of this opera is undeviating correctness. The most scrupulous attention is paid to the sentiments of the poet. . . . [Coccia] has proved himself throughout a man of good sense and equally good taste."

But the *Chronicle* was not impressed: "We have *allegros* perpetually occurring in the most serious parts of the drama, and there is moreover a fearful portion of passages which are neither grave nor gay, but simply soporific." And critic X (E) thought the work "a complete failure." It is difficult to account for such divergence among good critics. In any event none of the reviewers support the claim made by Ebers (p. 342) that "never was an opera so 'translated' from its original mould and features. Scarcely a single part in the piece escaped unchanged" by the singers. Despite the presence of Pasta, the work received but four performances.

No more successful was Nicholas Charles Bochsa (1789–1856), French composer, although as we have seen, he was musical director at the King's from 1827 to 1830 through the influence of George IV. His *I Messicani*, a pasticcio, was condemned by the press and had but three performances.

Gaspare Spontini (1774–1851) had but one opera produced at the King's—*La Vestale*—in 1827. Reviewers condemned the inadequate performances, but critic X (NM) was quite enthusiastic about the music, which he considered "highly dramatic throughout, the harmonies are rich and scientific, and the instrumentation is excellent; several of the chorusses combine simplicity with grandeur of effect, and the marches . . . are vigorous and imposing." Ayrton (Har) agreed, but thought the King's inadequate for a French Grand Opera. The work received only six performances and was not revived.[115]

The young Vincenzo Bellini (1801–35) had no better luck at the King's with his *Il Pirata* (1830), though the reviews were mixed. The *Chronicle* found the drama[116] well constructed, and the music contained "a profusion of *cantaline* [for "*cantilena*"?], extremely sweet and pleasing, and there are passages in the opera by no means deficient in grace, but yet of no very grand or imposing character." Alsager (T) agreed and Holmes (At) was more positive: "Bellini has been able to vary his *motivos* so well, that notwithstanding the melancholy feeling which pervades them there is no monotony of subject. . . . He uses the same forms a little too often—at times dwells too long on the same key; . . . but against these defects we may set the beauty of his vocal phrases, his admirable style of recitative, melodious basses, and effective instrumentation." Ayrton (Har), on the other hand, deplored Bellini's stylistic debt to Rossini, though he "does now and then make attempts to release himself [especially in the choruses] from the fetters which fashion has forged and indolence riveted." The other weeklies and monthlies were also generally negative. The work had only five performances, plus two in a one-act version.[117] But the ultimate success of the composer at the King's is indicated by the premieres there of *La Somnambula* in 1831, *La Straniera* in 1832, *Norma* and *I Capuletti ed i Montecchi* in 1833, and *I Puritani* in 1835. An English version of the *Puritani* appeared in 1843.

In considering the King's productions of these late composers it should be kept in mind that partly because of the disorganized theatre management, the tremendous appeal of Madames Pasta and García (whom the public was avid to see in as many roles as possible) and the culmination in the popularity of Rossini, we find a number of anomalous seasons after 1824—especially 1825 and 1828–30—where only two or three new operas were presented (sometimes *none* of which were successful). In compensation there were an enormous number of revivals (sometimes over fifteen in just *one* season), primarily of Rossini operas cut down to one or two acts. Such a scattered approach to opera productions could hardly have fostered the attention needed for the adequate preparation of new works of any kind.

ROSSINI

Gioacchino Antonio Rossini (1792–1868), whose first comic opera was produced in 1810, and first seria in 1813 (both in Venice), did not have long to wait either for international fame or for his first London production. That appeared in 1818—*Il Barbiere di Siviglia*—just two years after its Rome premiere. The choice was an odd one, since it overlooked his more popular previous operas. Moreover, *Barbiere* had run into difficulties in Italy because the initial reaction of critics was that Rossini had somehow plagiarized Paisiello's *Barbiere*, which was still quite popular and its composer still living and highly respected. Such protests were unusual; perhaps the growth of Romanticism was generating a new respect for artistic property.

Alsager (T, Mar. 11) wrote of the opera: "Taken as a whole perhaps, it bears the mark of haste, and still more of extravagance; but we are persuaded that all persons who have carried the study of music to the least degree of refinement must have been delighted and astonished by the occasional touches of genius, the variety and originality of his style. The general character of Rossini's music is extreme ornament . . . but his resources in that line . . . seem almost unlimited." Ayrton (C) was also enthusiastic:

> In this new Opera there are some very original ideas, and some very striking effects. . . . The first thing wherein the author manifests his talent is in . . . *Una voce poco fa*, which is new and the accompaniments very clever. . . . ["La calunnia"] is singularly ingenious, and is one of the most accurate descriptions that musical language is capable of affording. . . . The finale to the first act is extremely good, quite *a la Mozart*, and that is the highest commendation that can be bestowed upon it.[118]

But the opera, he added, had "too much of the same colouring throughout" and "has been over-rated." Bacon (LG) called the work "vocal without extravagance, rich without losing sight of the most touching simplicity, and various without embarrassing the ear by its complication." Indeed, it had "all the qualities of musical genius," and he pronounced Rossini Mozart's successor.

But on further reflection he stated (QMM): "[Rossini's] great fault (as a writer of Comic opera at least) is a disposition to spin out his pieces, by repetition, to too considerable length. . . . Little that we have seen of his, will live, we think, beyond the hour." The *Inquisitor* thought the work "marked by sprightly playfulness" and the accompaniments were "triumphant, full, ingenious, and highly effective," but it lacked "the soul-touching of Paisiello." Astonishingly, the *News*[119] found "no originality" in his music, and chastised his "impudence" in repeating Paisiello's story. Hunt (E, Mar. 22) also deplored Rossini's "taking up" Paisiello and explained the latter's superiority:

> Paisiello's compositions are special instances of this power of expression. His melodies are exquisitely graceful, touching, and original; and his recitatives always appear to us as so extremely to the purpose, as to be superior even to those of . . . Mozart.

> In neither of these main qualities, will Signor Rossini's Opera, in our opinion, bear any comparison. We should be loth to speak so decidedly after only one hearing; but what renders an Opera most delightful . . . is a succession of beautiful airs; and of these the new *Barbiere di Siviglia* appears to us to be destitute. [Moreover] the recitative is singularly bald and common-place. You might always know the comment which the fiddle-bow was going to make.

Despite these mixed notices the opera chalked up thirteen performances and remained one of Rossini's most popular in the repertory, with eight revivals through 1830. When Hunt returned to the opera the next year (1819) he declared he "ought to have remembered that something like this [borrowing] was an old Italian custom, at least in books." He added: "The more we hear this opera, the more highly we think of it. All works of genius require, as it were, to be *read* with attention, — painting and music as well as poetry. At the first hearing of an opera, one misses nine out of twenty parts of it, from the mere hurry of its passage. It is like dashing in a post-chaise through a fine landscape." By 1831 Hunt thought this the best of Rossini's operas, though he still preferred Paisiello's *Barbiere* (*Tatler*).

Later the same season (1818) the King's followed with a production of Rossini's first serious opera, *Elisabetta, Regina d'Inghilterra*. Performed in Naples in 1815,[120] the opera was his first "world success" (Loewenberg). But London did not care for it — in part *because* of the English story (Stendhal admired it, however). As Ayrton (C) declared: "It will afford no pleasure to a British audience to see the weak part of this otherwise sagacious Sovereign's character exhibited before them." Regarding the music, he noted the Germanic influence on Rossini,[121] who "is entitled to the credit of duly appreciating, and boldly adopting, a style in which Handel, the Bachs, Haydn, and Mozart have shone so resplendently." He continued: "The present Opera is not destitute of traits that manifest some imagination, but it possesses still less of originality than his [*Barbiere*]. His *score* displays numberless examples of either haste, carelessness, or want of knowledge, the effect of all which is forcibly felt by the auditors . . . for music appeals to the judgment through the ear."

The *Inquisitor* admired some of the music but thought his style "peculiarly adapted to give effect to a Comic opera. It does not possess that dignity and pathos which are desirable in a serious drama."[122] His worst defect is his want of originality: . . . when you have heard one of his operas you have heard all." But Alsager (T) was quite positive: the music was "very beautiful; it is in a distinct style from *Il Barbiere di Siviglia*, but not at all inferior to it."[123] The work played only four times, however, and was never revived.[124]

The King's opened its 1819 season with another comedy, *L'Italiana in Algieri*. Alsager (T) sorely lamented Anelli's libretto, which contrived "to mutilate the beautiful story of Roxalana, from the tales of Marmontel, a subject that has frequently been dramatised, but never till now, perhaps, has experienced such ill treatment." The opera "contains some beautiful airs, and many original and happy passages; but as a whole it is extremely equal" and by the end of the second act "becomes feeble and languid to a degree" (Jan. 27). Ayrton (C) was even more severe: "The music is of a very inferior description," except for one duet, "Se inclinassi a prender moglie." "This is the first opera that raised the fame of its composer in Italy, and it is a proof of the declining taste for the art in that country." The opera "must ultimately fail here; we now understand what is really good music—what has either originality, taste, or effect—and this has not one of these qualities."

Two days later, Alsager confirmed that the opera had not improved; nevertheless he proceeded with a remarkably sympathetic analysis of the impact of the composer. He declared him

> a real curiosity; a being *sui generis*; who can neither be praised, censured, or imitated, without danger. The German critics censure him with freedom and even severity, while he draws crowds to their theatres.... They try him by the rules of art, which he disdains, and are not be to driven from their cold, calculating task, by the glowing warmth of his native genius. They complain of consecutive fifths and octaves, and unresolved discords, while the spirittancy [*sic*], and varied contrasts of his works are too evanescent for their perceptions.

Though Hunt agreed that the libretto left much to be desired, he found the opera "of a piece" with the *Barbiere*: "The author seems to delight in expressing a precipitate and multitudinous mirth; and sometimes works up and ferments a passage . . . till orchestra and singers all appear drunk with uproariousness. . . . He carries this feeling, we think, to a pitch of genius" (E). Despite a fine cast and fair production, the work had but seven performances, though it was given three revivals.

Late in 1819 the King's produced another comedy—Rossini's one-act farce, *L'Inganno Felice*—his first great success in Italy. Ayrton (C) was dismayed: "In this fatiguing work, it is impossible to point out a solitary proof of talent, or any thing, however trifling, that excites the faintest emotion of pleasure; either in the music, or in the mode of performing it—in the story, or in the management of it; and we will not further occupy the attention of our readers upon so unworthy a subject." The *Champion*, too, was disappointed: "It is a very dull and serious affair," unrelieved by

Rossini's usual vivacity. Hunt, however, thought that although the piece would not bear comparison with *Barbiere*, it was noteworthy in some ways and worth going to hear (E). And the *Inquisitor* was quite positive, declaring that the "delightful little opera . . . has formed a most agreeable addition to the stock of acting operas." The opera, not produced until July, was not thought to warrant a revival the next year but was brought back in 1827; it was also produced by the Royal Academy of Music in 1829 and 1830. In 1827, when it failed, Ayrton (Har) thought it one of Rossini's worst productions, admiring only the trio, "Quel sembiante."

But Rossini was redeemed from these failures by the production of *La Cenerentola* in 1820. True, Ayrton (C) was not impressed. The poor production did not help: "None of the pageantry that should have graced it is introduced." Instead, we find "empty boards, old dresses, and worn-out scenery"; they even omitted Cinderella's glass slipper. "Of the music, all that is *bona fide* Rossini's may be known immediately, for it consists of his everlastingly-repeated passages"; there were also borrowings from Mayr and Carafa. Bacon (LM), too, was cautiously negative: "With more of sprightliness than diversity, profundity, or originality, there is [in Rossini's music] perhaps enough to captivate and enliven, without sufficient intensity either to affect the feelings or excite any deep and lasting interest."

But Alsager (T), as we might expect, saw it quite differently. The music "comprises many pieces of great beauty and felicity." The overture did not excel, but there followed a procession of highly praised numbers.[125] Yet the opera, he thought, "wants variety of style" and—lasting nearly four hours—was much too long. Robertson, in his last review for the *Examiner*, gave Rossini the strongest support yet:

> [The music] runs on in his usual pleasant strain with all sorts of quips, cracks, and quaintnesses, flippant divisions, and rapid utterance, but it breathes at the same time the air of Italy, seems tinged with its sunshine, and overflows with sparkling and bouyant hilarity. Perhaps the secret of the English indifference, which his operas too often experience, may in some measure be that we, grave fellows as we are, do not bring sufficient liveliness with us to enter into his high spirits, which have upon our gravity the effect of an ill-timed pun.

The work achieved nine performances despite a poor production and mixed reviews. After lying dormant for five years, it had several revivals. In 1829 Wade (Ath) was enthusiastic: "Once more 'Cenerentola'! There is something so agreeable in this opera, that we can never witness it without being put in good humour, nor think of it without being inclined to prattle about it." But Ayrton (Har) still thought the work "not worth criticism," and in 1830 he maintained that "one air and the quintet are the only pieces in it at all bearable."

A more popular serious opera ("melodrame-eroica") came along later that year—*Il Tancredi*.[126] Alsager (T) trumpeted its success: "It possesses, we think, greater richness, variety and originality, than any opera by Rossini that has reached this country." The first big recitative and aria of Tancredi—"In che accendi"—though well known from concert performances, "form perhaps one of the most striking displays of art ever contrived to bring on a principal singer. The symphonies are well adapted to the situation and breathe a soft melancholy, in perfect accordance with the feeling." Ayrton (C), now moderating his views of the composer, thought Rossi's libretto, "abridged from Voltaire's tragedy," was "therefore more consistent and intelligible than the generality of Italian operas"; indeed, the whole work was "a very superior production," and "if not equal to the *Barbiere*, it is because the author is rather under restraint when setting a serious drama to music." But the most supportive account of the opera was written by Bacon (LM).

The opera had fourteen performances, assisted by a fine cast. It was revived eight more times through 1830, though usually, after 1825, only the first act was revived. In 1825 Alsager wrote: "There is a melodious quietness in the whole of the music of this opera, which works upon the feelings in a deeper degree than the efforts of more splendid composers, who are rather anxious to take the heart by storm, than to tap it by gently working on its finer sensibilities." Only Hunt, in 1828, was less than enthusiastic: *Tancredi*, he wrote, was "crammed . . . as full of common-places and old threadbare recitative, as nine-tenths of it can hold. It is theatrical clothesman's music. But there is good in the remainder; and the fine air, *Di tanti palpiti*[127] is part of it" (*Companion*).

With the opening of his melodrama *La Gazza Ladra* in 1821, the popularity of Rossini began to snowball. Alsager (T) noted its success in Italy, "notwithstanding the difficulty and complexity of the music," which required sixty rehearsals for its Venice production.[128]

> We can convey [he continued] in no manner more strongly our sense of the skill manifested by Rossini in the music of *La Gazza Ladra*, than by saying that he has imparted by it a species of tragic dignity to this humble tale ["The Maid and the Magpie"], and rescued it from all our former associations. We regard him indeed, on this occasion, partly as a new composer, for, though much of the former leven of caprice, extravagance, and inappropriate accompaniment still remain, he has evidently chastened his style by a careful study of the old masters, producing [an]

intermixture of their classic construction with the free graces of the moderns.

The *Chronicle* found this the best of his operas yet seen. Especially praiseworthy was the "*Funeral March* and Chorus, together with the Prayer at the beginning of the second *finale*"—"Mozart himself would have been proud of such a scene." Hunt, too, was quite positive: "We were afraid that Rossini, accustomed as he is to write in a hurry, under various other disadvantages, found original airs too great a demand upon his spirit, and so took refuge in a multitude of voices. But *La Gazza Ladra* undeceived us,—delighted us."

The *Gazette*, however, was not so pleased: the music was generally "brilliant and tasteful; but with more of noise than force, and more of elegance than expression . . . and the whole composition has the character of hurry." Bacon (LM) also remained unimpressed: "*La Gazza Ladra* affords another proof that science and interest are not synonymous terms; for we think the music is deficient in . . . those bright melodies which fill the fancy, and attach themselves to the memory."

The cast, chorus, and orchestra drew strong praise, and the work had fourteen performances that season despite the mixed reviews. It had five brief revivals through 1830, and in 1827 it was presented eight times. Mount-Edgcumbe thought the opera represented all the worst features of the composer, and Stendhal (Coe, pp. 123, 268) called it "a black and platitudinous melodrama" and thought it "noisy and overorchestrated." The *New Oxford* (VIII, 406) calls it one of Rossini's "most artistically successful and satisfying works," and N.O. finds in it his "richest expression" of blended seriocomic elements.

The second King's premiere that season, also successful, was the buffa *Il Turco in Italia*. The *Chronicle* noted that the story[129] was "founded on a style of manners not tolerated in this country, but the moral, buried under the double veil of the language and the music, is never intruded into notice." The music was "charming; full of the lightness and fancy of Rossini," but there were borrowings from himself—the finale to act one of *Cenerentola,* and parts of *Italiana*—as well as from other composers, including Carafa and Fioravanti. Alsager (T) also enjoyed the opera: "The music, if not the best, may rank amongst the most pleasing of Rossini's compositions." But Bacon (LM), who found Romani's plot absurd, declared that "nothing can be much more meagre and gaudy than its music. . . . It abounds in florid passages, but has neither agreeable melodies, nor the peculiar expression, of most of his pieces." The cast was superior and the work "caught on" (LG, June 9), receiving twelve performances. It was revived for eight more in the next season as well as in 1824 and 1827. In 1822 Alsager still thought the opera "not equal in musical merit to the others composed by Rossini, yet it abounds with masterly and well-harmonized pieces." Mount-Edgcumbe regarded *Il Turco* as one of the few Rossini operas "exempt from censure."

In 1822 the King's produced the tragico-sacra *Pietro l'Eremita*, which had premiered in Naples (1818) as *Mosè in Egitto* (libretto by Tottola). Though initially written as an oratorio—the biblical subject was chosen so it could play through Lent—it was really a three-act opera and a great success. Rossini wrote the music first, giving the librettist the meter and the number of verses needed; he added the famous prayer, "Dal tuo stellato soglio," in 1819.[130] Alsager observed that

> a singular confusion of old facts with new names have rendered this drama one of the most curious perversions of history ever exhibited on the stage. By substituting Pharaoh for Noraddin, Moses for Peter the Hermit, and the Israelites for the Christians, we have the exact counterpart of that most venerable piece of Scripture history. . . . The opera is, in fact . . . the Oratorio of *Mose* . . . which has been for some time known in the country, and justly esteemed as a masterpiece of [Rossini]. . . . But absurd as the [re]construction is, those who hear the music will incline to pardon that and much greater offences against good taste. Since Mozart, there has been no musical drama so striking in merit performed in this country.[131]

Bacon also had objections to the drama, yet he too found the music "of a very rich and eloquent description, and the chorusses and accompaniments full and effective; but the quantity of unnecessary recitative . . . gave the entire [work] a weary length of performance and weakened the effect." Ayrton (C), however, objected to the music as well: though "scientifically written," it was "exceedingly heavy, and wants colour and originality."

Despite these critical disclaimers, *Pietro* was extremely successful and had three revivals through 1830, including eight performances in 1827. By 1825 Ayrton (C) displayed a more positive view of the opera. Alsager (T) and critic Z (NM) thought it the best and most effective of Rossini's serious operas. Mount-Edgcumbe declared the opera a "profanation."

Still later that season (1822) the King's brought out *Otello* for Violante Camporesi's benefit. There was considerable interest in the libretto by Beria di Salsa. Alsager found the plot "not essentially different from Shakespeare's tragedy. Moreover, he said, "so well does the music harmonize with the pervading sentiment of the situations, that the mere theatrical effect is far greater than might be expected, and some of the scenes . . . were listened to with a breathless attention, scarcely ever paid in this house to acting." Bacon (LM) was also impressed: "A scream of horror from all the dramatic personae concludes the piece, in a manner quite new to the Italian stage.[132] It is difficult to say which is the most powerful agent in this very effective drama, the music, the situation, the singing, or the acting; but we never felt so thoroughly disposed to admit the supremacy of musical tragedy as upon this occasion."

Produced late in the season, the work had but one performance beyond the benefit, but it soon gained a firm place in the repertory, with six revivals through 1830. In 1823 the *Drama Magazine* noticed "more spirit and originality" in *Otello* than in Rossini's other works. At later revivals, however, most critics grew cool toward it. In 1825 the *London* thought that, despite the acting of Pasta, the opera "drags and goes off heavily," and "intrinsically it has little to recommend it." In 1828, when the opera had fourteen performances, the critics made clear that it was Pasta's "electric" portrayal of Desdemona that drew the rapt audiences. Holmes (At) complained that only Pasta's last scene made "three barren acts endurable" and went on to chide: "Is Rossini so heartless as to suppose that a generous woman is to be stabbed to this tune of all others?"—and he quoted the musical passage. "For such a strain, it would be more fitting that Desdemona should sit while Otello exhibited the shuffling step of a hornpipe." And in 1830 Holmes again found the work tiresome, and Wade (Ath) thought Rossini should stick to comedy:[133] "In the excesses of grief we find his singers or characters *tittering* passages of the drollest kind. . . . Sometimes, as, for instance, in the celebrated 'Ma maca [sic] la voce,' the words assert one thing and the music another" (July 24). Hogarth also thought the libretto "absurd," and Stendhal found it "shallow" and the music "noisy." London's first English version did not arrive until 1844.

No less than three new serious Rossini operas came out in 1823. The first, *La Donna del Lago*, adapted by Tottola from Scott's *Lady of the Lake* (1810), was enormously popular, although the daily reviewers were beginning to sound a bit weary of Rossini premieres. The *Herald* was enthusiastic. "The whole finale of the first act is animated with the true soul of music. . . . The chief beauty of [the opera] consists in the numerous and brilliant chorusses, which have all a fine sylvan character in their arrangement, and a wildness appropriate to the local scenery."

But other reviewers were rather negative. Ayrton (C) thought the story "tolerably well dramatized" and grudgingly observed that the opera "has rather less of its Author's mannerisms than his other compositions show, but . . . it offers scarcely any thing that is new, either in melody or effect." And later, in the *Harmonicon*, he wrote that the strength of the opera depended on the chorus, which was inadequate, and it required two tenors of great compass, which it also lacked. He added that "many violations of the rules of musical grammar are obvious in this opera, to the critic who diligently examines the work." Alsager (T) was also lackluster: "The opera showed neither more care or less genius than" Rossini's other operas. Moreover, Scott's poem was "nearly deprived of all interest," although it has incidents "admirably suited to dramatic effect." Bacon (LM), too, was unimpressed; he thought the story was "robbed of every particle of its original brightness," while the music "merits very little encomium," though it "is light and airy, and some of the parts are certainly even graceful."

The press were poor prognosticators: the opera received an astonishing nineteen performances and was revived every season through 1829, when the production was badly mangled (NM), and critic X (E) thought the opera "contemptible."

Lago was followed by the serious opera *Ricciardo e Zoraide*. Alsager found the libretto, by Beria di Salsa, "crude and uninteresting—the situations[134] forced and unnatural—the sentiments trifling, and the style bombastic," while the music was of "unequal merit." "It is not rich in melodies . . . but many of the concerted pieces are elaborately beautiful." Bacon (LM) agreed, but the *Herald* found the plot "sufficient for an opera" and the work was "deeply impressed with Rossini's genius."[135] The opera had twelve performances and three revivals. There were "considerable alterations and additions" made by Rossini at the King's in 1824—"generally for the better" (NM).[136]

Although the critics, if not the audiences, were growing weary of Rossini, still another of his operas was brought forward as late as July of that season (1823)—*Matilde e Corradino*, a "melodrame giocoso" partly composed by Pacini (Weinstock, p. 105). Alsager thought it "above the ordinary run of such productions." The music was largely "pillaged from himself" and thus "more of an ingenious *cento* than an original production," yet it was "very spirited." Bacon (LM) thought the libretto[137] even more absurd than that of *Ricciardo*, but "Rossini has contrived to find pegs to hang some beautiful music upon. It is indeed amongst the most spirited of his works," and "the concerted pieces are polished and effective."

There was time for only three performances that season, and it was not revived until 1830, when it played seven times. In that year Alsager thought the best and most original parts were the concerted numbers. Wade (Ath) agreed, adding that "they have the liveliness of Rossini's early style, and are yet not deficient in the skill that gives his later compositions the character of learning." But Holmes (At) did not concur: "The music is like that of a common theatrical journeyman; ... there is not a single bar of melody to reward the patience with which the opening has been endured."

With the production of two more new operas in 1824, the Rossini avalanche was finally slowing down. The first was the melodrama *Zelmira*, for the London production of which Rossini, now at the King's with his wife, had given considerable attention (he was roundly applauded when he took his seat at the pianoforte, but later admitted it "went against the grain being a paid accompanist"—see Scott, "Rossini in England," *Opera*, 27 [May 1976], 434). Ayrton (C) thought the opera "may be ranked with most of his best works,"[138] though "not by any means exempt from his mannerisms." It "contains several pieces that could only have emanated from genius." But it was too long and carried "the extravagant use of noisy military instruments." He noted that many pieces were obliged to undergo adaptation to accommodate specific singers, and though made by the composer himself, "yet it takes from them much of the force and freshness of a *prima intenzione*." Alsager thought the libretto[139] absurd but did admire the precipitate beginning: "The whole of this introduction is a happy effusion of genius, full of affect, and distinguished by vigour and originality. . . . Altogether, [the opera] is one of the finest works of Rossini; . . . the principal movements are original, varying in character and well contrasted, and his vigour continues unimpaired to the close."[140]

But most critics were quite negative. The *Gazette* thought the work "dull and dreary": "It was . . . erroneous to take [Rossini] out of his popular sphere, and present him in the first instance as a competitor of the German school, where he is inferior." And critic X (E) was quite harsh: "It is, in our opinion the very worst of his works that has yet been produced. We are now more than ever convinced, that his talent lies more in the comic than in the serious vein; and cannot but protest against the light style in which he treats the deepest feelings of our nature.[141] Tripping, divisions and rapid execution are his modes of expressing the emotions of terror and pity." Critic Z (NM) was struck by "the stunning noise of the accompaniments. Trombone, trumpet, kettle-drums, drum, &c. are seldom at rest."[142] Moreover, Rossini "has of late shewn a partiality to military bands *on the stage*, and in 'Zelmira' that musical auxiliary is seldom off the boards."

On this opera the public apparently agreed with the critics, despite the participation of Rossini and his wife.[143] The work had a scant seven performances and was revived only briefly in 1826 and 1828. On the latter occasion Holmes (At) fulminated against negative reviews he had seen, yet he went on to deplore Rossini as "the head of a poor school content with ruling supreme over triplets and dance subjects."

Quite late that season (1824), the King's produced, for Garcia's benefit, the tragic melodrama *Semiramide*. Alsager found "more interest than usual" in the subject, with which King's audiences were of course familiar: "The music of this opera is of an elevated and heroic character. Rossini felt that the personages introduced were "the honourable of the earth" — princesses, princes, and warriors; and he has endeavoured very successfully to give them strains befitting their proud and lofty fortunes. We think, however, that the opera never will be popular."[144] After a second hearing, critic Z (NM) wrote: "The score is powerfully written; many of the harmonic combinations are of a superior stamp and deeply impressive." But the opera was "very deficient in point of good and original melodies. . . . Rossini's style seems to have undergone a striking change of late; he is more learned, more stern, and less gay and melodiously pleasing."

The opera had only five performances that year despite a fine production, but there were several revivals. In 1825 the *London* thought the opera "grievously long and tedious," and in 1830 Holmes (At) wrote: "This opera, like most of the author's attempts in the serious style, and at German harmonies, possesses a monotony of character in the subjects of its musical scenes, which nothing but great excellence of dramatic representation . . . can render tolerable." From 1827 to 1829 the opera had that support, with either Pasta or Sontag in the lead.

The impetus behind Rossini's great popularity in London finally abated, and it was two years before another new opera was presented: the serious *Aureliano in Palmira* (1826). It had, however, only three performances late in the season, and no reviews have survived. Oddly, Mount-Edgcumbe regarded it as Rossini's best opera. In 1829 the King's mounted his last opera in our period—*Il Conte Ori*—an *opéra comique* first produced as *Le Comte Ory* in Paris the preceding year. Alsager wrote: "The musical part of the construction abounds in choruses and concerted pieces, which bear the stamp of the composer's genius, and evince his reliance on their striking character for a favourable impression on his audience. Not only are their leading subjects extremely pleasing, but the orchestral accompaniments are arranged with a skill almost sperior to that which he has hitherto displayed."

But other critics remained quite negative. The opera contained scarcely an aria—"a sin against Italian taste," wrote Ayrton (C), adding that the opera "abounds in *morceaux d'ensemble*, and exhibits a succession of ever-changing motivos, with many *pezzi concertati*, the orchestra overpowering instead of supporting the voice." And in the *Harmonicon* he regarded it as "beyond comparison the worst work of Rossini." Critic X (E) found the plot absurd, while the music, though it had "some lively passages," was mostly borrowed from Rossini's previous works. Holmes (At) heard only "scattered *prettinesses*." Wade (Ath) thought it "pregnant with the master's most besetting sins," though some choruses were "stamped with the impress of Rossini's constitutional vivacity." But all reviewers agreed that this was just about the worst vocal production they had ever heard at the King's. The opera had but a single performance.

Nothing like a Rossini cabal or claque is evident during these years. Alsager was consistently supportive of Rossini's music, but there was no settled view of the composer by other reviewers. The press did, however, reflect quite closely the taste of the public based on number of performances and revivals. *Barbiere, Tancredi, Gazza Ladra, Turco,* and *Otello* won fair praise in the press and were highly popular, though the public was also pleased with *Pietro, Donna,* and *Ricciardo,* on which the press had mixed opinions. As noted earlier, *Cenerentola* remained highly popular despite strong condemnations of the critics. There was also a general agreement between the dailies on the one hand and the weeklies (except the *Athenaeum*) and monthlies on the other, though on *Zelmira* they differed widely. Only four operas—*Elisabetta, Iganno, Ori,* and *Aureliano*—were clearly failures all around. The glut of Rossini productions, strongly felt by 1823, produced negative reactions, as we have seen. As late as 1829, critic Z (NM, May) was still complaining: "Rossini for ever! *Toujours perdrix!!* the usual round of the old never-to-be-hummed favourites; such as 'La Donna del Lago' (we are almost sick of spelling the name!) . . . and so on, till the Rossinian wheel has once more made its full rotation." But on February 25 of the same year, Wade (Ath) made the most vigorous attack yet on the composer's detractors (Alsager of course was not among them):

> To us there is nothing more disgusting than the general outcry which the musical criticals of this musical country have taken it into their heads to raise against the merits of Rossini as a composer.
>
> > "Mongrel puppy, whelp and hound,
> > And cur of low degree,"
>
> are all joining in the chorus; and the sound of his own swan-like ministrelsy is likely to be overwhelmed by the barking of these furious little animals. . . . The malcontents try to assume a plausible excuse for themselves. Rossini, they say, has no learning, is no musician, titillates the ears, and leaves no impression, &c . . . . Poor Rossini! The noise of these worthies from their attics will doubtless extend, fatally for your fame, to all the distant corners which have hitherto rung so loudly with your applause.

Other contemporary sources also had contradictory views. For example Ebers stated that *Pietro* "at once" established Rossini's reputation in

England, yet *Turco* was nearly as popular the preceding season and the *Barbiere* was already solidly in the repertory. And Mount-Edgcumbe, who wrote mostly grudging, negative asides, did admit that Rossini had "genius and invention," though was "not guided by good taste." But he also asserted that most of his operas failed — a patent untruth. Edwards, writing later in the century, asserted that *Otello* and *Pietro* were "welcomed by amateurs but not by the public," which also was not true, at least by 1830. Chorley stated that the "purists" (c. 1825) could not see the real genius of Rossini, just coming into vogue: they could not accept German science and therefore had to dismiss Rossini as merely tuneful.[145] But this view, too, is far from unanimous in contemporary reviews.

Rossini's *L'Assedio di Corinto* was produced at the King's in 1834 and was adapted to the English stage two years later. *Guillaume Tell*, his last opera, did not appear until 1838, though it was adapted as an English opera (*Hofer*) in 1830 (see part III).[146]

With respect to Italian operas generally during this 1785–1830 period, it must be admitted that on the whole critics' responses were not far from those of the audience, and where there are discrepancies, the problem often lay in the performances. But there were a few occasions, such as with some operas by Gluck and Cherubini, where the taste of the critics was more responsive than that of the patrons. Occasionally librettos received considerable attention from the press and negative views of them — including those of the audience — sometimes colored their responses to the operas. To all listeners, the arias were of course the high points of the operas, and all too often, in lieu of analysis, reviewers were reduced merely to citing the ones that moved them. But we might note, finally, that no opera could succeed without the strong support of the performers, who often got more attention than the operas themselves.

The Performances

IT WAS FOR AND AROUND the leading singers that eighteenth-century composers largely wrote their operas, yet some prima donnas dominated even the most famous. At the King's Theatre, for example, Handel was himself a "captive of a custom that was largely the result of the virtuosity—and vanity—of the pampered Italian singer."[1] In 1725 party rivalry in the pit and boxes was so great between two rival prima donnas that opera performances had to be suspended for a time.[2] In 1763 Thomas Gray wrote to Count Algarotti that no one "could govern the Italian *virtuosa*, destroy her caprice and impertinence, without hurting her talents, or command those unmeaning graces and tricks of voice to be silent."[3] The castratos may have received less attention, but they earned substantially more. By 1785, however, the prima donna had largely usurped the fading castrati in power and popularity. In place of Signora or Madame, her surname was often prefaced, before 1800, by the English definite article—an adaptation of the Continental custom.

Her special forte was in vocal ornamentation, which came into favor early in the century. Prima donnas inserted flourishes in the *da capo* return whether they agreed with the accompaniment or not, and Handel tried to insist on control over embellishments by writing them out at times (as did Rossini).[4] Although this excessive practice declined somewhat all over Europe in the latter half of the century, Burney complained that "so changed is the style of Dramatic Music, since Handel's own period, that almost all his songs seem scientific"—i.e., contrived.[5]

Even more harmful was the prima donna's almost dictatorial power over the arias to be sung.[6] This right was sometimes contested between leading singers, as it was in 1790 between Luigi Marchesi, a castrato, and Gertrude Mara (W, Jan. 12). Females were not the only offenders. In 1820 Ebers, the King's manager, complaining that he had no power in such cases, declared: "Let a new opera be intended to be brought forward, Signor This will not sing his part, because it is not prominent enough; so, to enrich it, a gathering must be made of airs from other operas, no matter whether by the same composer or not, nor whether there be any congruity between" them.[7]

Furthermore, favorite singers could command very large fees. In 1789 Marchese was paid £1,500 plus a benefit and free apartments. (He received £600 for a single concert.) The same year Cecilia Giuliani earned £891 and a benefit, but five others received only £150 to £225 and no benefit. The next year Mara was paid £850.[8] By 1796 Brigida Banti was being paid 1,500 guineas plus a benefit, and Giuseppe Viganoni earned £1,000 in 1797. But even these figures pale beside the enormous sums paid Angelica Catalani. And in addition to her salary, she received twice as much for her concerts. Ronzi de Begnis was paid only £1,400 in 1823.[9] Most musicians also gave private music lessons, and some famous singers earned as much as a guinea a lesson.[10]

Aside from the deleterious effects of English weather on Italian singers (Ebers, p. 304), their main concern was with the public. If the audience had not welcomed their borrowed songs, they would not have sung them. Not all prima donnas became the darlings of the aristocracy, with all the perquisites that that could bring. And, as we shall see, many singers did not succeed with the public at all (lack of sufficient vocal power was the single most important factor) and lasted only a season or two—indeed, sometimes for only one or two performances.

They were also usually very careful to appear as scheduled—some actually leaving sickbeds to do so—owing to the quick wrath of the audience if they felt they were being skimped on the performance. More than one serious riot took place at the King's over just such incidents. One Italian singer refused to go to England to sing, declaring: "For were I to take it in my head not to sing, I am told the people there would certainly mob me, and perhaps break my bones."[11]

From 1785 to about 1815 the King's had some forty male and female singers, the males dropping sharply before 1800 as the castratos disappeared. Perhaps part of the decline resulted from the blockade during the war years, though the greatest damage was in ballet—the King's relied strongly on obtaining dancers from Paris. After 1815 the numbers jumped enormously to about twenty-eight males and forty-one females just in those fifteen years, in addition to about half a dozen who sang at the Academy of Music in the late 1820s. Singers were of course very sporadic at the King's—especially so after 1815, when about one third of the men and nearly half of the women sang for one season only (indeed, some are too fugitive even to be listed). Occasionally an outstanding singer would have a brief season for reasons of his own. But most were dropped by the management and little is known about many of them—sometimes not even their first names. (The more important minor singers are discused in appendix 9.)

No doubt the excessive turnover late in our period reflected the problems of management already cited. The *Examiner*, however, found the rule of fashion at the King's much to blame when they complained about this situation in 1828, stating that they did "not understand the heartless fashion of sending away old and tried favourites for the mere sake of novelty. But we have long decided that the leaders in fashionable life, who have too much influence in this establishment, are utterly destitute of taste and discrimination" (Jan. 20).

It may be useful here to provide a preamble summarizing the highlights of the more important singers of Italian opera in our period. Early on, among the men, we find the castratos dying out at the King's, though there were still kind words for Rubinelli and especially Marchesi. Babbini, a tenor, proved too weak a singer, while Kelly, also a tenor, was apparently past his prime and ran afoul of the cabal. But Morelli, a buffo, who sang from 1785 to 1807, was warmly applauded right up to his last year. There was some disagreement about Viganoni, a tenor, though most critics remarked on his taste and style. After 1800, Braham, a tenor, was much admired, except for his florid style, but he apparently felt more comfortable in English opera. Diomiro Tramezzani filled the need for a "good tragic tenor," though he proved he could perform well in comedy too. Naldi, the first good buffo after Morelli, brought a fine talent in musicianship and comic acting to the King's, though at times critics' opinions differed on his effectiveness. There was some disagreement, too, over Crivelli, whose performances strengthened in later seasons, but he was never very popular. Ambrogetti, a buffo, was perhaps the best singing actor at the King's, and he contributed much to the success of Mozart's operas. In later years García, a tenor, drew mixed reviews; most critics praised him highly, but some thought him vulgar in acting and over-ornamented in singing. Velluti, a castrato, ultimately managed to bring most critics and patrons to his support after a nearly catastrophic beginning. De Begnis, a baritone, was an accomplished singer and actor for six years, while Zucchelli, a bass, though weak at first, was accorded high praise in later seasons. Donzelli, a tenor, was recognized as outstanding in his earliest appearances, and he went on to a long career at the King's.

Among the women Mara did not quite reach top rank, and she ran into problems of her own making. Storace, a buffa, injected new energy into her roles up to 1793, but her métier lay in English opera. Banti, plagued by illness, nevertheless called forth the highest plaudits for her acting and singing. Billington, like Storace, Dickons, and Vestris, found a home in both Italian and English opera. Grassini, who brought new interest to the contralto voice, was an admired and beloved performer, but Catalani, who followed her, swept all others aside as an *assoluta*. Vestris, a contralto, was a great hit in trouser roles and a fine singing actress, but her true home was also in English opera. Fodor, who with Banti and Catalani had one of the best voices during our period, was particularly successful in her Mozart roles. Camporese was something of a classical singer and too "cold" for some critics. Ronzi de Begnis won wide respect for her Rossini roles, while Caradori, weak at first, grew into a fine, though not a first-rate, performer.

With respect to the last women singers—Sontag, Pasta, and García-Malibran—the critics were rapturous, and it is astonishing to see how the artistry of these divas seemed to draw forth spontaneously some of the finest reviews of all our singers.

THE LEADING MALE SINGERS

The most significant change regarding the male singers early in our period was the fading out of the castratos. Aside from Velluti (1825–26), Agrippino Roselli was the last, leaving the stage in 1800. Castratos had, of course, been on a decline for some years, and in 1796 the *Chronicle* no doubt reflected current views in asserting that singer John Braham would "chace the castratos from the English stage" (Nov. 28). There were still adherents to the old style, however. James Boaden, who "was not meanly qualified" to enjoy Italian opera, pointed out the consequences of this change in serious opera, which "must decline if not supported on the plan of its composition. If the chief male have a Soprano part assigned him by the composer, it is no use to prattle about manliness, *such* creatures, and so forth. The usual recourse since has been either transposition or consigning the hero to a female, and in consequence the effect is beyond measure weakened."[12]

Rubinelli

Giovanni Rubinelli (1753–1829), a male contralto, sang leading roles in operas by Anfossi and Paisiello at Naples and Rome. He came to London in 1786, making his debut the next season as Icilius in *Virginia* by Tarchi, who had composed this part for him. The *Advertiser* found him "a musician of the first class. . . . His voice and his science, though both preeminent, are now forced beyond their proper rank, which, in a musician, is the rank of subserviency to the feelings. The music that is not felt is no music." An unidentified review (TC) called him "a most enchanting performer. His voice, without one idle note, or impertinent antick in the play of it, has the compass, the clearness, and variety of tone needful to do all that could be wished.... He has a hold, rather a strong one, upon the heart. We felt it in most of his music [especially in "La mia sposa" and "Idolo mio, questa alma Amante"]. The sudden shift to the lower notes in the second line—the address to Lucius—and the apostrophe to other faithful lovers, 'Fide amanti voi vedete'[13]—are among the most beautiful and delightful excitements we recollect from any musick."

The *Herald* called "his figure good, his acting chaste and expressive, and his manner of singing incomparable, having all the beauties of Paccierotti without any of his faults," and they admired his competency in different styles (May 5). Two unidentified reviews (TC) of him as Rinaldo in *Armida* the following month were somewhat less enthusiastic: "Rubinelli has less of, what there should be, pathetic impression, than in the former Opera of *Virginia* [sic]," but the best aria of the latter opera "lost none of the charm it could pretend to from [Rubinelli's] manner of giving it" (June 3).

He was praised in *Alceste, Cesare,* and *Vestale* in 1787; in 1788 his place was taken by Marchesi (UR, Feb. 7, 1787), but he continued to sing elsewhere until 1808. Burney called him tall and majestic with a true and full contralto. Though his "shake" (i.e., trill) was "not sufficiently open," he had fine articulation, and his embellishments were in good taste. Mount-Edgcumbe reported a voice "of fine quality but limited compass. It was full, round, firm and steady in slow movements, but had little agility."

Marchesi

More lasting in popularity than Rubinelli was Luigi Marchesi (1755–1829), who had himself castrated against family wishes and who both composed and played the horn. He was singing female roles in Rome in 1773, and his first big opportunity came in Naples in 1778. He later sang in Venice and Milan and began an association with Bianchi and Sarti. He went to St. Petersburg with Sarti in 1785 (N.G.). From 1788 to 1790, he sang at the King's, making his debut as the lead in *Giulio Sabino* (1788). At a rehearsal he "displayed amazing powers in cantabile" singing, and some spectators were reduced to tears by his "pathetic strains" (H). At the premiere he was greeted with hisses from the gallery, but he at length prevailed. The *Times* declared that, since the great Farinelli, no performer at the King's was "so truly entitled to commendation unlimited—his voice ... is harmony itself; the lower notes have more perfection. His acting, too, is much superior to what we have been used to" (Apr. 7). And they felt the "insipid" music could be supported only by his distinguished talents (Apr. 14).

The *Gazetteer* was more specific: "His voice is exquisitely fine, particularly his lower tones, from which he makes the most beautiful transitions to the higher notes. The nasal intonation so frequent in the Italian school . . . is a fault from which Marchesi is totally free. If he has a fault, it is that he embellishes with too many graces. . . . His *forte* seems to be the pathetic." And the *Advertiser* added: "The connoisseurs were convinced that his style of singing was peculiar to him and superior to what has ever been heard. How much more will they be surprised when on the following nights they will hear him vary his music . . . which he has been known to do for many running nights with the greatest of ease." Mount-Edgcumbe was somewhat disappointed in this performance, for "I had repeatedly heard Paccierotti sing [the songs] in private, and I missed his tender expression . . . and lamented that their simplicity should be injured as it was, by an over-flowery style."

Later that season Marchesi appeared as the lead in *Olimpiade*, to which he contributed some of his own arias. The *World* thought that "his former failures of impression were the fault of Sarti rather than his own . . . . There were the sweetest captivations of the first style in his simple and broken close on 'respondi mori' and on 'piagendo parti'" (June 9). Boaden, who tells us Marchesi had a compass of three octaves, thought that he had "laboured to astonish" in *Sabino* but to "delight" in *Olimpiade*.

In 1789 he was "wonderfully great" as Achilles in *Ifigenia in Aulide*: "His recitative was given with all the energy and passion of a perfect tragedian, and his airs were executed with a precision and taste that conferred a credit on the composer and did honor to himself" (H). He also "exhibited all the merit which raised his character last year, and with such excellence, it was surprising that he had no encore" (P, Jan. 26). The *Times* agreed. Later that season, as Poro in *Generosta*, he had "never sung with better effect, as the airs were finely adapted to his powers" (P).

As Pyrrhus in *Andromaca* (1790) — apparently his last performance at the King's — he showed further abilities: "Signor Marchesi sung three airs of his own composition; and if we judge from the enrapturing impression they made on the audience, which of the two, his merit as a singer, or his skill as a composer, should be the greatest object of admiration, we are at a loss to determine" (PA).[14]

Marchesi returned to Italy as one of the greatest castratos of the age. Allatson Burgh thought Marchesi, who was among his first recollections, a fine actor as well as singer. Burney found him elegant and refined; he had beauty of person and was a fine actor. Burney had no complaint about his "many embellishments," but Mount-Edgcumbe, complaining of his bravura in Sarti's "simple" songs, admitted that his flowery style "was absolute simplicity to what we have heard in later days."

Babbini

The first tenor singer in our period was Matteo Babbini (1754–1816), who trained in Italy and sang in Russia, Austria, and Germany. He went to England in 1785–86 for two seasons, apparently as a replacement for Angelo Franchi, who had received favorable notices for his King's appearances in 1783 and 1784. Babbini's debut as Artabano in *Artaserse* stirred this gossipy response from Este (UR):

> Babooni! *Babooni! all the world running after Signor Babooni; not a monkey of fashion, or an old Tabby* of the *Ton*, but flew to the opera to see Signior Babooni. Signior Babooni is a tenor, and a good one—but there is one material objection—his voice is *natural*—for Signior Babooni, in spite of his voice is a man. He must be excluded from *toilette* conversations to *midnight* revels, &c. . . . His person is diminutive, his countenance shrivelled, and as to grace and action, Signior Babooni has yet to acquire both.

But the *London Magazine* had a more sober view: "Though this performer cannot be said to possess a very great compass of voice, this defect is supplied by a taste and manner of singing superior to any of his predecessors in that walk. Add to this a good figure, a style of acting seldom met on the Italian stage, ever true to the character he represents; and we shall have conveyed an idea, though still very imperfect of the merit of Signor Bab[b]ini" (Petty, p. 227). The *London Chronicle* also agreed that his singing and acting were admirable. He was also praised by Mount-Edgcumbe for his singing in *Giulio Sabino*, which had but one performance and no reviews.

He sang Gianetto in *Viaggiatori Felici* at the end of that season, and the *London* was again enthusiastic: The singer's "first appearance in the comic [role] was a masterly piece of acting. . . . His caricature of the depraved taste of French music was much admired and repeated with additional merit" (Petty, p. 228). In 1786 Babbini "sang with exquisite taste" as Giorgino in *Marchese* (H, Jan. 26), and the audience was pleased with his acting and singing (UR), but the *Chronicle* thought all singers deficient. Later that season an unidentified reviewer (TC) admired his singing the role of Ubaldo in another serious opera, *Armida*, but the *Herald* thought the opera so bad the singers "are packing up for Italy in hopes of absolution from the Pope."

Babbini remained at the King's throughout 1789, according to Mount-Edgcumbe, who found him "unequal to producing much effect, from the weakness of his voice." Burney called him sweet but not powerful, with a "fine style." He also stated that Babbini was eclipsed by Rubinelli in 1786, which, if true, shows the strong competition in opera seria between a castrato and a tenor even at that time.

Morelli

A stalwart buffo who sang at the King's between 1787 and 1807 was Giovanni Morelli, who has been overlooked by N.O. and N.G. He had made a name in *La Serva Padrona* and came to London, where he settled in 1787. That year he sang in the Handel Commemoration and made his debut at the King's as Bastiano Ammazzagatte in Paisiello's *Schiavi*, where his duet with Storace was encored, though he otherwise went unnoticed. The next season he sang Taddeo in *Teodoro* at the season opening and "afforded a fresh proof, if any were yet wanting, of his comic talents," and his first aria, "Chene [*sic*] dici tu Taddeo," "richly merited the warm and unanimous *encore* it received" (T). A week later, the *Times* offered further observations: "Morelli's acting seems wholly under the guidance of good sense, he despises the grimace and buffoonery so peculiar to the foreign schools, and which indeed predominates too much in our ears. . . . [He is] the best comic actor we have seen." As Don Polidoro in *Locondiera* the following month, he sang a duet with Storace, "Con quelle tue manine," which was the only piece encored (P, Jan. 16) and was "by far superior to anything of the kind we ever had on stage" (H). As Don Pancrazio Garofano in *Cameriere* the same season, he could not be "too much commended for the admirable manner in which he portrayed the Neapolitan coxcomb" (T).

Despite this warm reception, Morelli was absent from the King's until 1791 (possibly returning to Italy). On his reappearance that year as Pistofolo in *Molinara*, "his powers appeared to be greatly improved indeed. He sung most exquisitely, and was greatly applauded" (P). He next appeared in 1793 as Almaviva in a revival of *Barbiere*. In a cautionary technical note by the *Oracle* (Boaden?), astonishing for those years, he was told, when he next sings the trio, "not to oppose a ninth against the octave of his closing note, but to drop the fifth at once upon it without any discordant grace, which, though it glides to the close, glides out of the way."

Morelli received warm praise in *Dorida, Matrimonio, L'Amor Contrasto*, and *Scuola* in 1794 and 1795, and he also sang successfully in *Due Nozze* (1805 and 1806) and *Virtuosa* (1807). Burney called him a fine and flexible bass, and Boaden reported he had an astonishing depth of tone and was a consummate actor such as the King's seldom witnessed. Mount-Edgcumbe, an utter snob, said he had a voice of great power and quality, but "having been a *running footman* to Lord Cowper at Florence, he could not be a great musician." His place was finally taken by perhaps a better buffo, Giuseppe Naldi, who helped him financially, for he had lost both voice and money (Boaden).

Kelly

The most colorful male singer in the 1790s was surely Michael Kelly (1762–1826), a triple-threat man—in both English and Italian opera—as singer, composer, stage manager, and even chorus director at the King's (his activities as a composer were confined to English opera). In addition, from 1802 to 1811, he was a music publisher, though he went bankrupt the latter year. The eldest of fourteen children of a prosperous Dublin wine merchant, he had music lessons as a child, singing under Passerini and Rauzzini, and piano lessons under Michael Arne. At the age of seventeen he went to Italy to study, partly under the patronage of Sir William Hamilton; his four years in Vienna, singing under Mozart and others, were the crown of his travels. He was a close friend of Stephen and Nancy Storace, who were also in Vienna at the time, together with the composer Thomas Attwood, who also studied under Mozart. This foursome returned to London in 1787, and that season Kelly made his debut at Drury Lane.

He did not make his King's debut until 1793, when he appeared as Figaro in *Barbiere*: his second-act duet with Nancy Storace received commendation (T, Jan. 28), but he otherwise went unnoticed (perhaps the cabal was at work). The following month, as Eraclide in *Giuochi*, he had a bravura aria "in which he displayed all the powers of his skill and voice with admirable effect" (H). The *Oracle* also praised him as a singer and as a stage manager: "No Italian opera in our remembrance has ever been got up with so much splendor." (Kelly assumed his duties as stage manager that season, a task he sustained for thirty years, and in some seasons he acted as impresario as well.)

He was at Drury Lane in 1794 but returned to the King's in 1795, when he ran afoul of the cabal while singing Arsace in *Semiramide*. As the *Chronicle* observed: "A little miscreant Italian cabal, who have endeavoured to derange the performances at this Theatre, attempted to hiss Mr. Kelly, who had generously come from the Drury Lane Theatre, that the serious opera might not be interrupted. The liberal feelings of the English subscribers overpowered the noise, and Mr. Kelly received the applause which his spirit deserved." The *Times* praised his singing and acting.

The next season he was praised as manager in *Bella Arsene*: "The greatest treat for the ear were the choruses under the direction of Mr. Kelly; they were given with such judgment and accuracy as proves the utility of a separate direction for this department" (T). He also assisted, as manager, in calming the audience, which was threatening a riot, apparently over "the unmannerly intrusions of several persons on the stage" (MM). He was listed as a singer with the company that season but does not seem to have performed. Thereafter he sang mainly at Drury Lane.

He was not listed again until 1806, when he sang a minor role in *Cosa Rara*; the *Herald* stated that he played Corrado "with much skill and effect." But the "Chronicles" wrote that "the audience were so attuned to good humour that even Kelly's cracked tenor, in a characteristic air of an old *Podesta*, was honoured with an encore." In 1806, in his capacity as stage manager, he was responsible for the "judicious" curtailment of an opera (C, Dec. 29)—obviously a useful function about which he tells us almost nothing in his *Reminiscences*. But as a singer and composer, he was far more welcome on the English stage. Mount-Edgcumbe, whose bias is again evident, admitted he was "not a bad singer" but he had "so much of the English vulgarity of manner, that he was never greatly liked" at the King's.

Viganoni

Giuseppe Viganoni (1754–1823), also overlooked by N.O. and N.G., was, however, much admired at the King's Theatre, especially for his taste. He had made his debut in Brescia in 1777 and sang in several Italian cities before coming to the King's in 1782 for two seasons. Back in London in 1796, when nobody seemed to recall his previous appearances there (even the ads called him new), he made his second King's debut in *Due Gobbi*, and "was most flatteringly received. His voice, though not powerful, is of the sweetest tenor kind, equally flexible to all the tender modulations, as to the most rapid divisions. His 'Io parto mio bene!' was given with wonderful expression" (TC). The *Times* remarked with surprising bias that he appeared "quite an unique for the Italian stage, since he actually appeared like a man and a gentleman" and showed much "natural taste." As Gianferrante in *Modesta*, he was encored in all his songs (T).

The next season he was highly commended as Capitano in *Amor* for "the care which he bestows on the most trifling scenes, and [for] his exertions to prevent that languor which is but often inseparable from recitative." Moreover, he helped the music "pass current with an audience whose musical taste is not of the most polished kind" (T, Dec. 7). As Arvino in *Evelina*, he "increases in public estimation, as possessing considerable science, and an exquisite taste" (MM, Jan.). In 1800, as Don Pietro in *Ines*, he "accompanied his singing" with acting that was "natural and impassioned" (T).

In 1801's and 1802 Viganoni sang frequently but received little comment. In 1803 he performed a duet with a Signora Gerbini in *Viaggiatori*, which "was executed with great ability and effect" (P). The next season, in *Vergine*, his duet with Grassini was "deservedly encored"—"we cannot speak too favourably of the delicacy and finished style in which [he] executed his airs" (T). In a revival of *Calypso*, he was "not exactly suited to the serious cast of the Opera" but nevertheless "communicated real pleasure by the neatness and delicacy of his style" (T). His appearance in *Astuzie* was "among the happiest performances of the evening," and in *Trionfo* his "refined taste" was "manifested to every possible advantage" (T).

He sang in 1805—his last season—but went unmentioned in the press. On December 16, 1805, the *Times* stated that he had retired to Bergamo "in wealth." Mount-Edgcumbe thought his voice neither strong nor fine but that he excelled in musical taste and versatility in both serious and comic roles. The "Chronicles," uniquely negative, thought him "devoid of force, animation or genius."

Braham

Undoubtedly the most outstanding English male singer on any London stage during the first three decades of the nineteenth century was the tenor John Braham (1774–1856). He sang mainly in English opera, and he made his debut in both English and Italian opera in 1796. But he was always a rather marginal figure at the King's, singing there, after a brief introduction, only occasionally from 1804 to 1806, plus a few later performances. Reviews of him there were never as strong as those of his English opera performances.

His origins are obscure, but he was apparently the son of a Portugese Jew. The composer and singing teacher Michael Leoni (Meyer Lyon), who was said to have been Braham's uncle, admired the boy's voice, trained him, and supervised his appearances as boy soprano at Covent Garden in 1787. Braham later studied with Rauzzini and sang at Bath, where he met Nancy Storace, forming a long-lasting liaison. In 1816, the year before Nancy's death, he married Frances Elizabeth Bolton, by whom he had two sons (both singers) and a daughter. He last sang in public in 1852 at age 78. Though he sang in London synagogues, he never objected to performing in the theatre Friday evenings. He had a vocal range from A to E (N.G.), and he was also a composer and pianist.

His London debut as an adult, in Drury Lane in April 1796, met with critical acclaim (see part III), but at his King's debut later that year (the 1797 season) in *Zemira ed Azor*, he was welcomed mainly as a displacement for the castratos: "When he has learnt to moderate his decorations, and to suffer the exquisite melody of his voice to be felt unencumbered by the weight of ornament, he will gratify the most scientific as well as the natural ear. . . . He sustained the part so well that we trust . . . he shall induce us to *chace* from an English stage the degrading and disgusting form of a *Castrato*" (C). In *Evelina* later that season, "though possessing a sweet and powerful voice, he has yet not sufficient voice to fill the vast extent of this capacious theatre" (MM). Parke asserted (c. 1796) that he "should have studied acting."

Following a singing tour of the Continent, Braham returned to English opera in 1801, and to the King's in 1804, when he appeared in only one opera—*Trionfo*; but the initial criticisms persisted: "Braham is indeed incomparable in this Opera. We sigh only for more simplicity. He would be a most captivating artist, even to the untutored ear, if he would shew a little of the cloth upon which he lays his embroidery" (C).

The next season in *Cosa Rara*, he was fine in a duet with Billington (T). In 1806 he again appeared in both English and Italian opera. In *Argenida* that year, he "would be much greater if he would attempt to do less" (C). His role as Orazi in Cimarosa's opera was "well adapted to his powers" (H), and he "confined himself within moderate bounds" (C). He was much applauded in *Cleopatra*, and the house was "enraptured" (T) with his performance as Sesto in *Tito*, in which he sang "admirably" (P) and was "loudly encored" (DA).

It is not clear what prompted him to leave the King's at the end of 1806. He stayed away ten years. The challenge of performing Mozart may have induced him to return in 1816, when the press was much more positive. At a revival of *Tito* that year, the *Times* welcomed him as a "fine acquisition" to the house and declared that he "fully sustained" his reputation. The *Chronicle* was even more enthusiastic, noting that the connoisseurs were out "to enjoy the high gratification of hearing the most exquisite tenor singer that our day, or probably any other, has produced. He resumes his station at this Theatre, with his vocal powers in their fullest vigour, with an accumulation of that experience which is one of the best sources of good taste, and with an augmentation of his abilities as an actor that immediately struck the whole audience with surprise." The *Post* agreed: he was never "in finer voice, and his acting throughout was chaste and impressive." As Ferrando in *Così* later that season, he "sung with a taste and tenderness of passion that no other singer can arrive at," though his rendition of "Un aura amorosa" received lackluster applause (C).

Despite this critical warmth, the audience apparently remained cool, for he sang no more at the King's. Robertson seems to have been the first to have fully appreciated him in Italian opera; in 1808 he wrote that Braham "is the only singer we now have that is fit to perform the principal characters at this theatre, where the lofty music and noble band seems to inspire him with an ardour and animation that are never observable in his efforts at Drury Lane," and he even praised his acting (E, Jan. 17 and 31). S. D. of "Chronicles" wrote that Braham was then "the first tenor singer in England" despite a voice no longer fresh.[16] Of his singing at the King's in 1816, "Chronicles" again asserted: "In fact, if Europe does contain a superior voice, or, when he pleases, a more finished singer, either English research has failed in discovering, or English gold has been powerless to lure it across the seas." But as Mount-Edgcumbe noted, "The fact is, that [Braham] can be two distinct singers, according to the audience before whom he performs, and that to gain applause he condescends to sing as ill at the playhouse as he has done well at the opera."

Tramezzani

In view of his very considerable talents and his six-year period as reigning tenor at the King's, it is astonishing that little is known about Diomiro Tramezzani (c. 1776–?), overlooked by N.O. and N.G. He was a fine singing actor who studied under Marchese, made his stage debut in 1800, and by 1806 was singing successfully at La Scala, Milan, and elsewhere in Italy. He was later very successful for two years at Lisbon, coming from there to the King's in 1809. Fétis said he was "called" to London, but Mount-Edgcumbe states he "happened to be in London without any engagement with the Opera," which stood in sore need of a good tragic tenor ("Chronicles"), and he was immediately engaged. He could accompany himself on the guitar and composed at least one opera, *L'Ingiusta Gelosia*, which had a single performance at the King's in 1810.

Tramezzani made his King's debut late in the 1809 season in *Sidagero*. "He is a fine and skilful singer," wrote the *Chronicle*, "as well as a graceful actor. The quality of his tone is good, and the simplicity of his stile has that charm and influence on the feelings which taste and nature never fail to produce. His figure is also highly in his favour, and his deportment is grand. He was honoured with universal applause." The *Times* reported that he possessed "a voice of much mellowness and perfect execution" but that it "wanted sweetness." Robertson saw in him a "superior talent to any that has appeared on the Opera stage, Braham excepted. . . . His figure is manly, his action dignified, and his voice possesses a rich mellowness and strength of tone . . . nor is he deficient in talent as an actor—his general conception of character is just, and will be much improved when he restrains the violence of acting so prevalent among foreign performers." Yet

Parke cited his "great histrionic powers" as well as singing of the "first order."

The next season *Scommessa* was "brought forward to shew Signor Tramezzani's talent for comedy, and having once shewn it, it is to be hoped he will remain satisfied, and desist from repeating a performance for which he is so ill calculated" (E). Parke said he was applauded in the role, and the *Chronicle* and *Times* (Jan. 8) reported some good singing but preferred to see him in tragedy. Their preferences were granted the next month, when he appeared in *Romeo*. "Tramezzani, in Romeo, sustained the burthen of the piece; and his fine performance of the part—his sudden alterations from rapture to despair—the deep, rich, melancholy power of his tones—the sad and stern energy of his countenance, exhibited a rank of talent which must place him high among the first tragic actors of the age" (T). In *Atalida* his performance with Catalani excelled: "It was, in truth, a rapturous display of the powers of dramatic music, or of the combination of singing and acting. Great as they both are separate, they acquire new force by emulation" (C). Robertson found no objections to him in *Figliuola*; indeed, he "acted with more than his usual spirit; his action was free and playful, and his singing, as it always is, full of feeling" (E).

As the Sultan in *Zaira* at the 1811 season opening, Tramezzani gave "a noble piece of representation, but his voice was rather hoarse, and he probably did not exert all his powers" (T). His acting in *Semiramide* "deserved all the plaudits which it received" (T), and in *Vestale* he "distinguished himself by a great display of theatrical talent" (T, Mar. 25). In 1812, as Sesto in *Tito* (with Catalani), he "was uncommonly splendid.... We never heard an air sung with such pure taste as that with which he concluded" (C; T). Robertson (E) declared, however, that he and Catalani "did much for the composer, and but little for the poet; both seemed to revel in a continual grin." Later critics of that performance had mixed views. Hogarth (II, 375) thought he took the part "unquestionably to the detriment of the music," but "Chronicles" recorded that the tenor sang his part well and played it better. At the oratorios that year he was "too elegant" for Hunt (E, Feb. 20).

In 1813 he sang in the ill-fated *Boadicea*, when neither he nor Catalani "could warm or animate the audience into any sympathy or emotion" (C). In *Eroina* he was "remarkably animated" in the recitative, and his acting was "admirable" (C). But Tramezzani's most important appearance in 1813 was in the role of the Count in *Figaro*. As noted, he had received equivocal notices in comic roles, and he left to the "celebrated" Joseph Fischer, Jr., the King's debut of that role in 1812. But Fischer was something less than a success (see appendix 9), and Taylor pressed Tramezzani to appear in *Figaro* and also in Pucitta's comic *Enrico IV*. The singer declined because, as the manager announced, it did not accord "with his dignity." The singer protested in a letter to the editor of the *Inquisitor* (Apr.), claiming his contract called only for serious roles. The editor supported his claim for an additional £200 to sing the role, and he finally agreed, "with the view of obliging the public" (C, Apr. 26; Smith, p. 124).

The *Chronicle* (Mar. 11) thought Tramezzani's talent would "qualify him well for either department of the Opera," and they later stated: "We are persuaded that Tramezzani will not now repent of performing in this opera. We never heard him to more advantage" (June 4); the *Times* concurred. Thomas Barnes called him "a good actor, and [he] sings with exquisite taste and sweetness . . . but his face is vulgar [Mt-E disagreed] and incapable of any expression except a grim ferocity to designate courage . . . and a grin of a most teeth-displaying expansion to express joy or tenderness" (E, May 9). In 1814 Barnes gave him trite praise in *Didone* (E); this was probably his last performance at the King's.

Ayrton, at an 1829 revival of *Gli Orazi*, declared, "We shall never forget the effect produced by Tramezzani" in the role of Orazio (Har, VII, 232). Mount-Edgcumbe wrote that he was "one of the most agreeable tenors I ever remember to have heard. He was a very handsome person and was full of animation and feeling. His voice was of the sweetest quality, of that rich, touching, *cremona*[17] tone peculiar to the Italians," and he called him a "great favourite." Baugh gave him high praise but said he occasionally sang out of tune. Tramezzani returned to Italy in 1814 and sang at Turin and Milan from 1815 to 1817, after which Fétis lost track of him. In January 1823, the *London Magazine* reported he had gone "mad."

Naldi

Much is known about Guiseppe Naldi (1770–1820), a bass, who made his debut in Milan in 1789. After singing in several other Italian cities, he went to Lisbon in 1803, and from there went to the King's in 1806, replacing the aging Morelli.[18] He was also a composer, "having produced several very pleasing and elegant compositions" (BS, Feb. 1818), and Robertson (E, Jan. 3, 1810) also spoke of the "good taste" of his music. He could play the cello and other instruments, and he was also a lawyer (Kelly).

Billed as "the most celebrated Buffo Caricato in Europe," he made his King's debut in 1806 in *Due Nozze*. The *Times* found his performance "equal in every respect to the reputation he acquired in Portugal. His voice is rich, and of great compass; and in point of taste and science, he is far before any comic singer who has appeared here for a considerable time. He appears to be a finished actor, possessing all the humour without the extravagances of the Italian school." The *Chronicle* called him "an accomplished musician. His skill and taste in his art place him at the head of his profession." And the *Post* declared that he "possesses a fine full baritone voice, of great compass, and uncommon flexibility. He seems to be a thorough musician, and sings with great taste; besides which he is an excellent actor."[19] But his forte in humor was not recognized until two months later in *Fanatico*: "It was utterly impossible to resist the effects of Naldi's Comedy. It not merely enraptured the spectators, but at times distracted the orchestra, and the whole theatre (audience and performers) joined in a general roar, while he, the author of the commotion, was apparently unconscious of the effects he produced" (C).

The work "has been greatly heightened by many introduced pieces by Signor Naldi [his own compositions?]. His acting throughout of the enraged musician was full of character and truth, and the whole of his performance was unique" (P).

His humor was again evident the next season in *Principe*: "Signor Naldi was extremely great in the whimsical part of Don Scoto, and kept the house in a continued laugh throughout all his scenes" (C). And in *Virtuosa* he "repeatedly convulsed the House with laughter, from the whimsicalties of his attitudes and features" (H). In 1809, in *Capricciosa*, he "was received with the warm welcome which he deserves; for his comedy is a high treat to the Connoisseur" (C) and was "hailed with loud applause" (T). In *Villegiatori*, the "Taming of the Shrew story," as the *Times* noted, "furnishes very good opportunities for displaying [his] exquisite humour." But Robertson found him "neither sufficiently stupid nor vulgar, and his countenance and deportment appear incapable of conforming themselves to the characters of low comedy. When he plays a peasant he looks like a gentleman in common clothes, and his features are seldom divested of the sensible expression which is natural to them" (E).

Yet at a revival of *Fanatico* in 1810, Robertson thought his talents "exactly suited to the character of Don Febeo." Fioravanti's *Matrimonio* gave him no opportunities for displaying his humor (E). In 1811 he "sang with more than usual spirit" as Don Alfonso in the premiere of *Così* (E). Later, as we have seen, he brought out the *Magic Flute* for his benefit; however, he was virtually ignored in the reviews.

In 1813, when he offered *Figaro*, also for his benefit, he played the title role "with much spirit and humour" (T). He sang in the 1814 season without press comment, dropped out in 1815, but was back in 1816 in *Griselda*, when Ayrton (C) "felt heartily rejoiced to see [him] again resume his place in this establishment. His absence made a vacancy that no other could supply—a comic opera loses half of its support without him; his humour is genuine, but never descends to any thing low. . . . His knowledge of the stage and of music render him one of the most important characters that tread upon these boards." The *Times* agreed; his song "Alla Natia" was "a rich treat both for composition and execution." In *Cosa Rara*, his duet with Fodor, "'Pace, caro mio sposa,' . . . produced an effect which has never been surpassed upon the Italian stage" (T).

But in 1817 and 1818 (his last season) Naldi produced some baffling contradictions among his critics. On his singing in 1817, for instance, both Alsager (T) and Bacon (LG) changed their minds in different performances, and on his acting in both years, they again changed their opinions, while Hunt, who also waffled, thought him much improved in 1819.

For example, as Figaro in 1817 he sang "Non più andrai" with "extraordinary spirit and energy" (T); but Bacon (LG) thought that both in acting and singing, "he fell short of the life and vigour of Beaumarchais' delineation of the character" and even his "Non più andrai" "was sung in too formal and slow a manner." (It is interesting to note, here and elsewhere, that leading singers were held accountable for tempo.) In *La Molinara* he was "excellent" (C); his Pistofolo "abounded with drollery; the scene between him and Rospolone . . . we have seldom seen surpassed, even upon an English stage" (BS). But again Bacon disagreed: "Neither his comic humour, quaint and formal as it is, nor his voice, if such it may be called, were" comparable to those of Ambrogetti. He added: "In the musical efforts of Mr. Naldi . . . we observe more and more an unpardonable *nonchalance*. He oftener speaks than sings, and in his Recitativos we seldom know in what key he means to be, till Mr. Dragonetti's chord on the double bass conveys to us the desired information. He [also] delights in adding a syllable more to a word, than it has with every body else; as *paderrone*, etc." With respect to his acting in the role, Hunt (E) agreed: "We either do not understand the style of humourous Italian acting, or in his hands it is somewhat too manual and pantomimical for us." Hunt, however, found it "a pleasure to hear him pronounce Italian."

In a performance as Leporello in the premiere of *Don Giovanni* "his drollery produced many bursts of laughter" (C). It "was a piece of comic and assured extravagance" (T, Apr. 14); he "acted and sang with great spirit, but we have heard him more accurate in his execution" (Apr. 16). Even Bacon (LG) relented somewhat: "He did not spare his comic powers, which infused life and spirit into all his scenes," though he was "a little ludicrous" in addressing the statue. But Hazlitt, echoing Hunt, wrote: "His humour is coarse and boisterous, and is more that of a buffoon than of a comic actor" (E, Apr. 20). And Kenrick (BS, June) stated: "His *nonchalance* also in the presence of the Spectre, in the last act, borders on absurdity." Later that season, as Pasquale in *Agnese*, he was "occasionally a little inattentive to the musical effect," according to Alsager (but Bacon now thought him successful). And he failed to please in a revival of *Così* (T).

In 1818 again there were mixed feelings about his Figaro. Alsager (T) wrote (pace Hazlitt): "There is nothing of the buffoon about him; he is a wily knave, who has got the length of his master's foot, and absolutely overawes him by the superiority of his intellect. . . . There is a rude familiarity about Naldi's manner which is extremely repulsive." Yet Hunt's impression of the singer had now improved: "Naldi . . . appears to have got rid, at least in this character, of the extremes to which we ventured to object last year. . . . He does not fling himself so much about the stage" (E).

When he sang Figaro in the premiere of *Barbiere* that year, Alsager (T, Mar. 11) reported that in singing concerted numbers with Fodor and García he "exposes himself to all the cruel affects of immediate comparison"; but on his acting Bacon (LG) now was positive: he "was unusually arch and animated. He was in perpetual movement, and he moved without his old perpetual *grimace*." Kenrick (BS) agreed. But of his performance in Cimarosa's *Matrimonio*, Alsager (T) was acidulous: Naldi, as Geronimo, has "ingeniously contrived to retain nothing of the old humourous citizen but feebleness and imbecility; his singing and his acting might fairly dispute the palm; we cannot decide so knotty a point." In the growing negative criticism of Naldi, most of which centered on his acting, some discrepancies are apparent, such as whether he was too much of a buffoon or not enough of one. But clearly he had lost much of the confidence of the press.

Following his departure in 1819, the *Inquisitor* (Mar.), in still another *volte-face*, regretted the loss of Naldi in the role of Leporello and Figaro, though his voice "has for a long time been unequal to the music of this opera." In his "Dramatic Sketches" on Naldi (BS, Feb. 1818), Kenrick thought him overpraised as an actor: "Accustomed as we are to the bustling comic performers of our English Theatres, Naldi's style of acting often appears excessively tame and spiritless." In 1828 Ayrton (Har, VI, 214), speaking of the role of Don Alfonso in *Così*, wrote: "Naldi was perfect in this character, for craft was natural to him; he did not act, but merely unfolded it." Mount-Edgcumbe called him an excellent actor and musician but regarded his voice as weak and uncertain. But (*pace* N.O.) not all reviewers praised his acting.

Naldi went to Paris in 1819 and there, two years later, at the home of his friend García (see below), he was killed while demonstrating a steam-cooking apparatus.

Crivelli

In 1817 Ayrton brought to the King's several outstanding male singers, most of whom remained there several seasons. One of these, Gaetano Crivelli (1768–1836), a tenor and a native of Brescia, made his debut in 1794. He was singing at La Scala, Milan, in 1805, and at Paris in 1811. He made his King's debut as Ulysses in *Penelope*. His voice was "a clear and strong tenor but destitute of compass and flexibility. Some of his tones are excellent, but once or twice, where he attempted to force a passage, he cracked the note and spoiled the effect. . . . This person acts with extraordinary simplicity, energy, and feeling. His face is prepossessing, and his figure manly" (T). The *Chronicle* was even more enthusiastic: "Signor Crivelli is a singer of the highest merit, and in the grand style, with a powerful, expressive, and extremely musical voice, and his acting is of the most judicious kind." The *Gazette* described him as "of the middle size, *embonpoint*, with a head somewhat large." They noticed "a habit, rather unpleasing, of turning up and shutting his eyes," but this was "overbalanced, by dignified deportment, a noble simplicity of action, impressive delivery, and above all, by a fine body of voice."

As the marquis in *Griselda* two weeks later, he displayed "a manliness and magnificence in his manner which preposses every spectator; and his voice on Saturday afforded proofs of richness, softness, and flexibility, for which we had not given him credit when we heard him before" (T). He "gave an importance to [the marquis] which most largely contributed to improve the effect of the Opera" (C). The *Herald* reported that "his deep tenor voice" was "always attractive, and it seemed particularly in unison with those feelings of manly affection, which he had to express upon this occasion." Bacon (LG) was, however, disappointed: "He was not in such fine voice" as in *Penelope*, "and in his singing as well as acting, a sameness and languor were observable."

At the premiere of *Don Giovanni*, Crivelli "gave a force and dignity to the character of Ottavio; . . . his voice, which flows so naturally from his manly chest, is music itself" (C). Though he was "correct enough," the *Times* found him "overpowered by superior organs" (Apr. 14); yet two days later they thought he had "one of the finest tenor voices we have ever heard." The *Gazette* (Apr. 19) admired his "fine manly voice" and "great musical talent." Yet he "seemed to us to indulge too much in the interpolation of embellishments," which "had more than once the effect of absolutely encroaching on the measure, and obliging the orchestra to slacken time." Also, occasionally, "when addressed by others, he appeared, above all, inanimate" and "actually seemed asleep."

Late that season he succeeded as Titus in Mozart's opera—"the character which he considers his best" and a role hitherto "consigned to second-rate performers": "The Imperial purple should, on the stage, be allowed to flow only over a majestic figure; and Titus, being also a cool, sedate character, is exactly calculated to exhibit the manly person of Crivelli, and his tranquil but dignified manner. . . . He was received with the loudest plaudits, and he did not fail . . . to act that character with the utmost propriety and judgment" (C, July 14). But the *Inquisitor* expressed disappointment in the singer: his Titus was only "a decent specimen of mediocrity."

In March 1818 his Ottavio was still admired by Kenrick (BS): "His *Dalla sua pace* and *Il mio tesoro* are master-pieces." And in April, the *Inquisitor* reviewer now thought the role of Titus "could not have been placed in better hands. We never before have seen this part represented with so good effect. . . . He gave to it all the dignity and energy which both the poet and composer intended." In May he sang Leicester in *Elisabetta*; his airs were "well executed" (T) and he "appeared to great advantage" (C). "We never saw this respectable performer to so great perfection . . . whilst his chaste and tasteful execution of the music left us nothing to desire" (TI). His illness interrupted the run of the opera and perhaps prompted him to quit London, but late in the season he returned to his role as Ottavio. The *Inquisitor* (Aug.) wrote: "Crivelli, in quitting an English audience, was resolved, in his last display, to shew his power, and sung the few airs assigned to him with a sweetness and energy truly delightful. We do not know how it happens, that this singer, who is allowedly the first tenor in Europe, should be so little appreciated as he has been in this country. The audience did not take the least notice of his last appearance."

And exactly a year later, the *Inquisitor* observed that the "insensibility" of the "frequenters of the opera" "to the powers of Crivelli . . . is a lasting stigma on their want of taste" (TI). Mount-Edgcumbe thought him an "excellent tenor of the old school" and noted his "sonorous, mellow voice" but added that he was "dull." The "Chronicles" stated that he "*had been* a good singer; in 1817 he still retained his taste, but not his powers"—an evaluation that most reviews contradict.

Ambrogetti

By far the most successful of the 1817 male newcomers was Giuseppe Ambrogetti (1780–after 1833), a basso cantante, about whom very little is known. He made his Paris debut as Don Giovanni in 1807 and his King's debut as Almaviva in *Figaro*.

"[He] may be considered a very important acquisition," wrote Alsager. "With a masculine figure and a strong countenance, this singer possesses a contre-tenor voice, deep, flexible, and mellow. He fills the theatre with apparent ease; some of his tones are extremely powerful, his ear true, and he crowns the whole by a free and natural style of acting." And the *Chronicle* wrote: "His voice is termed, in musical language, a baritone, or a high bass; it is smooth, very pleasing, and sufficiently powerful. To these qualities he adds a purity of style, and a judgment—we might indeed say an elegance—in spite of his person, which inclines to corpulency—in acting." Bacon (LG, Feb. 8) found his "*baritono* or low tenor" voice "strong and full-bodied; his person somewhat corpulent, but well-proportioned; his countenance manly and impressive, and his action graceful, spirited, and dignified." And Kenrick wrote that his voice, "naturally fine, has received every improvement and embellishment which art is capable of imparting, and a more scientific singer has seldom appeared upon any stage" (BS, Mar.).

As Don Rospolone in *Molinara*, "besides a respectable skill in music, [he] showed a power of humour which would bear comparison with any comic actor of the day," Alsager declared. "He appears also to possess one faculty which few comedians exhibit—that of the most striking and even broadest expressions of the ludicrous, without degenerating into vulgar or offensive caricature." Bacon agreed: "As a *buffo caricato*, Signor Ambrogetti may challenge competition without any apprehension. . . . He knows how to draw the difficult line between comic humour and vulgarism; and in the height of his drolleries, he is neither an idiot nor a baboon, he still looks the gentleman" (Mar. 22). Hunt called him "a clever singer with a good voice" but found his humor largely "unaccountable" (E).

His biggest success that season was in the role of Don Giovanni. Alsager wrote: "Ambrogetti acquitted himself with extraordinary energy; and with respect either to vocal or dramatic action, we have rarely seen any performance more powerful than his." He later added: "'Finch'han' was sung with great effect; . . . his volubility and his articulation are surprising" (T, Apr. 14, 16). The *Chronicle* was equally delighted: "His gaiety, activity, address; his power of commanding his countenance, his by-play, and attention to all the *minutiae* of the scene, render him the first performer in his department that has been seen on the Italian stage." Bacon added: "His every motion and expression were those of the gay, abandoned, irreclaimable sensualist; and the musical execution of his part was equally excellent and unrivalled throughout. His fine full-bodied voice, joined to the most distinct articulation and to consummate histrionic abilities, gave effect to every piece. . . . 'La ci darem' la mano' he acted with an amorous warmth of the highest colouring, yet within just bounds of propriety" (LG,

Apr. 19). Kenrick (BS) was also quite positive, and "Chronicles" thought him a perfect Don Giovanni. Hazlitt alone was critical: "We neither saw the dignified manners of the Spanish nobleman, nor the insinuating address of the voluptuary. He makes too free and violent a use of his legs and arms. He sang the air *Fin ch' han dal vino* . . . with a sort of jovial, turbulent vivacity, but without the least "sense of amorous delight." His only object seemed to be, to sing the words as loud and as fast as possible" (E, Apr. 20). And later Hunt probed deeply into the characterization:

> [Ambrogetti] is always ready and energetic; and perhaps, considering he is so active, makes even his robustness contribute to a certain air of the imposing, defying, and sensual. We do not think he succeeds in the serenade . . . but then he succeeds as much perhaps as Don Giovanni should; for Mozart in this instance has outrun his character, as Shakespeare was accustomed to do; and made his profligate hero say more than he intended. The song is too sincerely amorous, and would suit Romeo better than a rake. (E, Aug. 3)

In May Ambrogetti excelled in quite a different opera—*Agnese*—playing to the hilt the melodramatic role of Hubert—Count Uberto. Alsager wrote: "Ambrogetti seemed to have abandoned for the occasion all idea of fine singing; it was throughout a voice choked with emotion, distorted with frenzy, or sinking under insupportable anguish. We shall not soon forget the fixed look with which, at his first appearance, he advanced to the front of the stage—his eye intensely marked the brooding of a distempered mind; subsequently . . . his endeavor to recollect the words of a song . . . were no less admirable" (T). The *Chronicle* agreed, and "Chronicles" tells us: "The *vraisemblance* was too harrowing. Ambrogetti had studied the last degrading use of humanity in the hospitals . . . and had studied it too well."

The following season (1818) he returned as Almaviva and deserved "great praise for the spirit and correctness" of his performance. "His recitative is the best we have ever heard, and our operas would go off with infinitely greater effect if his example was generally imitated" (T; C). And he repeated his role in *Molinara*, "though he exhibited in it, to our opinion, more trick and grimace than quite becomes so excellent a musician" (T). Later he excelled as Bartolo in *Barbiere* (T, 3), and "made it the most important personage in the piece" (BS, Apr.). In that opera, "Chronicles" recalled,

> his great point was in the sestett in the second act, when Bartolo overhears the Count, disguised as a music-master, avow himself to

Rosina. In this, the sarcasm with which he announced his discovery—"Il suo travestimento! su Alonso! bravo! bravo!" followed by the burst of uncontrollable rage ... every feature swelling with passion, and seizing on the chairs to drive the intruder from the house, absolutely electrified the audience.

Ambrogetti was less successful as Count Robinson in *Matrimonio*. Alsager wrote: "Disliking perhaps his prototype and his associates ... [he] burlesqued, and played the buffoon, till the semblance even of humanity scarcely remained.... We regret to see this judicious actor and singer betray so evident an anxiety to force applause, at whatever cost" (T, June 1). But Kenrick (BS, July) thought the "excess ... far preferable to the lifeless performances which we formerly were accustomed to on this stage."

At the opening of the 1819 season, he sang Thaddeus in *Italiana* but appeared "as an actor rather than as a musician," for the part was "unworthy of him" (T, Jan. 30). He pleased Alsager as the schoolmaster in *Modista*, but Bacon advised him "most earnestly to refrain from mixing English phrases with his Italian dialogue. Though we may be a little Bœotian, our taste is above *that* trick which is quite out of place." In *Camilla* he "was sadly degraded by a wretchedly unmeaning part" (T). But in the *Magic Flute*, Alsager wrote, he "played and sung Papageno with so much spirit and animation, that he deserves our best praise: he was literally the life of the piece, and one cannot think a better Papageno could be found" (T). Ayrton (C) reported, however, that although he "was all life and activity, his airs did not tell, and his duet ... 'Papageno' was spoiled, as were other pieces, by being executed too slow." Hunt quipped, "He looks too beef-eating for a bird-catcher" (E).

Ambrogetti completed the season with two more one-act performances. The first was in *Fanatico*: "We never saw an actor who so fully possessed the power of making something out of nothing; for this, the insipidity of the Italian writers affords him ample scope; and no performer that ever was seen in this country, imparted to the flatness of the Italian comedy so much spirit and vivacity.... His performance in this opera was one of his happiest efforts" (TI). And in a new kind of melodramatic role in *Inganno*, "he was as eminently successful, as powerful in this, as he has been in every other line of character" (TI).

At the 1820 season opening, Ambrogetti again sang Almaviva and, as Ayrton (C) noted, "was graceful and attentive as ever, but we thought, less passionate." But Bacon (LG) found him "expending as much animal spirit as would serve for two characters." In *Cenerentola* he sang Don Magnifico and "afforded some excellent, though rather tedious foolery" (T). Ayrton

(C) thought nothing could be made of the part, and "in his efforts to succeed, he approached, upon one or two occasions, very near to the confines of buffoonery." But Bacon found him "great in his part," and the *Inquisitor* was exultant.

He again won plaudits as Count Uberto in *Agnese* (T). Bacon (LM) called it "the finest piece of acting we ever beheld," Kemble and Kean notwithstanding—the role "stamps him in our opinion the very first actor of the age." The *Inquisitor* asserted that, without Ambrogetti, *Agnese* "can never be rendered a source of delight to those by whom its power has been the most vividly appreciated."

In 1821 Ambrogetti was apparently having vocal problems, for the next year critic X (E) congratulated him "on the restoration of his voice"; as Almaviva, his "acting and high spirits [were] the same as ever." The *Times* found him "gay and spirited, but not quite enough of the gentleman," though still "a great favourite" with the public. But Bacon (LM) thought his acting of Almaviva "as excellent as" his singing was "execrable. He is certainly the very worst singer that ever took the rank that he maintains with so much popularity."

He appeared in the comic role of Brant in *Barone*, which "he rendered highly amusing" (T), though Kenrick (BS) thought he perhaps "went a little beyond it at times. It is Ambrogetti's peculiarity that he can seldom assume a vigour beyond the occasion, without breaking out into something which borders rather too closely on the tricks of a vulgar stage."

There is no further mention of him at the King's, and if the public did not desert him, his voice did. Two years later Bacon (LM) wrote that "never, perhaps, did any man maintain as high a place in a musical theatre with so little real musical qualifications" (June, 1824). Mount-Edgcumbe thought him an excellent actor, though deficient in voice. Ebers mentions that Ambrogetti was "privately a miserable hypochondriac," which perhaps accounts for his great success as Uberto. In 1833 he joined the Trappists in France. Hunt (*Autobiography*, p. 128) thought his "great big calves seemed as if they ought to have saved him from going into La Trappe." It was rumored that he was in Ireland in 1838 (N.G.).

García

Manuel del Popolo Redríguez Vicente García[20] (1775–1832), a Spanish tenor and composer, and father of the more famous singer Malibran, was quite successful at the King's, though his voice was past its prime. He first sang in Spain in 1798 and was successful in Paris from 1808 to 1811. He also composed some forty Spanish operettas, nine Italian, and seven French. Later he went to Italy, where Rossini wrote for him the parts of Almaviva in *Barbiere* and Norfolk in *Elisabetta*.

He drew rather mixed notices during his first season at the King's in 1818. Alsager wrote of his debut as Almaviva: "His voice is a pure tenor, somewhat on the decline, but of great flexibility, strength, and compass. His style is the florid, and carried to a degree which probably has never been exceeded; but his singing is the perfection of that style, and considered as a mere exhibition of art, cannot but produce high gratification" (Mar. 11).

Two days later Ayrton (C) remarked: "His personal appearance is not very favourable, and his acting wants elegance; but his voice has great compass and equal flexibility, and was once, we can easily imagine, very musical: at present it is hard, and wants . . . tenderness." But Bacon (LG) seemed almost to describe a different performer: García "is a tall and dashing figure, with a great deal of action, and a voice of singular sweetness and flexibility. . . . His swaggering, drunken, sportive dragoon, was one of the most amazing caricatures we have seen." The *Inquisitor* seemed to have it all together:

> The figure of this gentleman is rather tall and elegant, but we cannot think his countenance prepossessing; its openness approaches to impudence. . . . His acting is spirited and characteristic, but it always betrays a coarseness. . . . His voice is a fine tenor, of considerable compass; but we sometimes thought it rather harsh. . . . In the upper tones it is peculiarly sweet, but not powerful. His execution is rapid, brilliant, and extremely neat.

The next month García appeared in a serious role—Sesto in *Tito*. Ayrton (C) was now quite negative. Recalling the singer's defects as Almaviva, he wrote: "How much more glaring must [they] have appeared in a serious part, where elegance and dignity are so much more essential and when accompanied, as they were in the present instance, by the most violent distortions of figure . . . and countenance! As a singer, we have still more cause of complaint; [in "Come ti piace"] it was almost impossible to discover the original air." The *Inquisitor*, too, by this time found him, "by nature, utterly disqualified for the personation of a serious character," though they were "highly gratified by some of his singing."

Later that season, Alsager (T) wrote that, in *Elisabetta*, "he found in Norfolk a character not quite important enough for him, [though] his airs were extremely well executed," but the *Inquisitor* thought his "horrible grimace, redundant gesture, and general boisterousness of manner, produce an effect unpleasing in the highest degree." Yet Alsager thought that

García, in *Così*, was "the best Fernando that has ever fallen under our observation: those who know the general power and excursive talent of this accomplished singer, will alone be able to appreciate the spirit, fidelity, and absence of meretricious ornament that distinguished his performance.... But he is too good a musician not to feel that to graft his eccentricities on Mozart would be a step little short of profanation." Ayrton (C) still had mixed mixed feelings on his singing, but the *Inquisitor* thought it "unexceptionable," though they still found the same defects of gesture and grimace.

In 1819 the same critics continued with mixed notices as García performed in *Italiana* and *Modesta*. But he drew more consistent praise in *Camilla* and *Barbiere*. When he turned to Tamino in *Il Flauto* at the end of that season, there were no demurs. Alsager (T) wrote: "The songs were given in his usual masterly manner"; in the long recitative before the Temple of Wisdom "we have seldom heard a more noble and commanding effect produced by the human voice." Even Ayrton (C) now agreed, as did Kenrick (BS): "He has never since his arrival in this country been heard in a part so adapted to display the full extent of his powers," though his acting generally "is by no means to our taste."

García concluded the season with some "fine singing" in Rossini's *Inganno*: "We are very glad to find that the public have become more sensible of the want of this fine singer; he daily increases in popularity, and the frequenters of the opera seen now disposed to repair the injustices which they last season did him" (TI; BS, July).

In 1820 García was ousted by the "management cabal" and went back to Paris, much to Alsager's regret (T, Jan. 10). But he returned to the King's in 1823 as Otello. The *European* noted that he had formerly been "admired for his roulades, but in the Opera of *Otello*, the music was more pathetic than florid, and he infused into his under-tones, particularly when he had to hold long on a note, more of feeling than we have lately been accustomed to hear." *Drama Magazine* commended his acting as "dignified and commanding" and reported that "his voice, when in its proper order, is a very sweet and perfect tenor, perhaps not inferior to any in Europe." Ayrton (Har) was more positive: "His voice has extensive compass, considerable power, is round and clear. Its flexibility is remarkable, but betrays him into ... an exuberance of ornament." Bacon (LM) agreed. He was also "very successful" as Agorante in *Ricciardo*, where his "very florid style of singing" was "well adapted to Rossini's no less florid style of composition" (T, June 6, Aug. 6).

In 1824 García sang Ilo in *Zelmira* and was "as great as ever" (T), and even Bacon (LM) now found him extraordinary: "As a singer, his force, energy, execution, and expression, exceed, far exceed all his competitors;

and his acting is not less remarkably excellent to those who are acquainted with the natural language of passion of the Italians. His voice has certainly lost the freshness and quality that belong to youth alone, but his genius and his volume are improved by maturity and exercise." He was "the only singer who appeared to great advantage," declared critic X (E), and his "wonderful powers of voice" were united with "exquisite taste and profound knowledge." And critic Z (NM) could "scarcely speak in terms of sufficient praise"—"excepting always his predilection for embellishments."

He repeated his role as Otello "with great force and feeling" and "displayed musical and scenic powers of the first order" (T). The *Examiner* agreed: "The vigour and animation, in which he is unrivalled, suit well with the impetuous Moor. There seems no limit to the splendour of his voice."[21] And he again succeeded as Don Giovanni. Alsager stated that "his picture of the thoughtless daring libertine was gay, without vulgarity— impassioned without extravagance." His "Finch'han dal vino" "was full of mirth and jollity; but they were the mirth and jollity of a gentleman." Bacon (LM) was again positive: he "supported the character with all his animation, and with a superiority of manners that set him above his great competitor [Ambrogetti]."

García excelled as the Indian King in *Semiramide* (T), but the highest praise for him that season came from Bacon (LM), who noted he made "a great deal indeed" of his small role in *Romeo*: "His singing always reminds us of the soaring of the lark. His soul is in every note—he seems let loose from earth, and the more boundless his flight, the more full of ecstasy is his song.... In his final aria, 'Misero che faro,' the words 'misero' and 'mia figlia' were uttered with a tone and emphasis that touched the very soul."

In 1825, his last year at the King's, García was not in good voice for *Adelina* (C; LM). As Almaviva in *Barbiere* he was "irresistibly droll in the scenes of broad humour," but on the whole he "makes the count vulgar" (LM). At this point Alsager thought that, as Fernando in *Così*, "he contrived to mingle more vulgarity than was desirable in his representation." The *New Monthly* agreed—but his "vocal exertions" were generally "of the highest order.... His command over passages of great rapidity is complete." Bacon (LM), now losing patience with him, found that his Don Giovanni "went off very languidly, though, whenever an opportunity offered, he endeavoured to inspirit it by a boisterous rant."

Final notice of him in *Crociato* provided a comment on his abilities as a composer: "Why," Alsager asked, "did the Manager suffer Signor Garcia to interpolate a tolerably good air of his own for Meyerbeer's aria 'Pace ci reca'? He should assert his authority and insist that the players should perform that which was 'set down for them'" (T).

He was a successful teacher of voice in London (his daughter, Malibran, and Marie Lalande were his outstanding pupils), but apparently not long after his retirement from the King's, he went on a concert tour of the United States and Mexico. He was prematurely reported to have died in Mexico in 1829 from "inflammation of the lungs" (T, Jan. 23), though his actual death at Paris in 1832 may have resulted from the same disorder.

In sum, we find that reviewers differed mainly on the degree of their aversion to, or approval of, García's ornamental style of singing and of his Italianate stage mannerisms. He was one of the few male singers who received only moderate praise on first appearance at the King's but who finally won over most critics to his style and gained increasing critical acclaim. S. D. ("Chronicles") observed, as of 1818, that "he was half worn out," and added that "if he had ever possessed the power of sustaining a note, it was by now entirely gone and he endeavoured to conceal the defect by the utmost profusion of florid ornament. It must be acknowledged, however, that, in the novelty, variety, and taste of his divisions, he has been excelled by no tenor of our time."

Velluti

Certainly the most controversial singer at the King's was Giovanni Battista Velluti (c. 1790–1861), who sang there in 1825, 1826, and 1828. A castrato, Velluti (his name was often mispelled as Velutti by reviewers) made his debut in 1801 and thereafter sang at Naples, Rome, Milan, and Venice. He also performed in Turin in 1811 and Vienna in 1812. As mentioned previously, London had not heard a castrato since the last days of Roselli (around 1800). Thus, a generation of opera-goers had no experience whatever with this "exotic" singing.

No wonder Velluti caused a great stir when he made his London debut, late in the 1825 season, as Armand in the King's premiere of Meyerbeer's *Crociato*, which had been written for him. On the day of that premiere (June 30), the *Times* ran a "paragraph" against him—in the news section— which probably expressed typical John Bull reactions: "Our opinion was, that the manly British public, and the pure British fair, would have been spared the disgust of such an appearance as that of Velluti upon any theatre of this metropolis. His shameless patrons have dared to insult, not only the British nation, but even humanity itself, by thrusting forward this non-creature upon the stage. . . . Humanity itself should rise against such a violation of decency—such an outrage upon feeling."[22]

The next day their reviewer—not Alsager—went on to attack the aristocracy for supporting the singer. In the pit were many professors of music, anxious to analyze Velutti's talents, and many Italians; who during the evening, with, as we think, very bad taste, applauded him whether he sang well or ill.... Those high and no doubt honourable personages [in the boxes], many of whom have passed a considerable portion of their lives in Italy, far from their own sturdy, rough-toned peasantry, may delight in such forced fruits, such costly exotics ... but they never will suit the unsophisticated taste of the people who for years fought the battles of Europe, and came from the contest victorious.[23]

Velluti was described as tall and his face "distinguished by a melancholy placidity.[24] It speaks of a heart that knows no joys.... [His voice] is the most unequal, as well as the most unnatural, that we ever heard.... At times it burst upon us with all the discordance of a peacock's scream." There were some hisses and other disturbances, but the reviewer acknowledged that in general he received "nearly unanimous applause." Critic X (E), though also showing bias, was quick with a rejoinder: "After the absurd ravings of a leading journal, many people anticipated a disturbance, but the excessive virulence evidently defeated its object.... We must, however, confess that the performance was very revolting. A hero, a valiant crusader, a soldier, a victor, and a lover, venting his emotions in a squalling treble ... was more than we could endure."[25]

The *Literary Chronicle* agreed. But Bacon, who had already condemned the shabby treatment of Velluti by the King's "corps vocale" (LM, July), mounted the strongest attack yet on the *Times* and gave his support to the singer. Pointing out that "no one but Velluti knew anything about the manner in which the opera should be produced, and [that] he had to direct every particular," Bacon observed: "We had been warned that we should not be pleased with Velluti's voice on first hearing it, and that, like olives, it would be disliked at first but extremely relished after a few trials; we did not, however, actually dislike it at first, and we liked it better on a second hearing.... That he is a perfect master of the science it is easy to perceive, and his execution is wonderful" (Aug.).

Ayrton (Har) reported that "his voice had the compass of two full octaves, from the G above the treble clef, to the G above the bass [the *New Monthly* stated "from a to ā"]. It is powerful, and in its softer tones is sweet; but when strained[,] is harsh and painful. His style of singing is of the best school; expression is its characteristic; *roulades* ... he appears to despise." But critic Z (NM), obviously a well-seasoned listener, was most enthusiastic of all. To be sure, there were faults of intonation, particularly in the lower register, but "what a style of singing! how simple, how pure, how impassioned! We at once recognized the model upon which Pasta formed her style. Here is no interlarding of meretricious ornament to cloak imperfections, no feverish feats of *bravura*. . . . Every thing Signor Velluti utters is chaste, tranquil, and distinctly articulated. . . . [He is] far superior to any male soprano we have heard, Marchesi not excepted."[26] Even his acting was "of a superior order, pathetic, impassioned, yet chaste and graceful."

Velluti continued in only that role the rest of the season, and at the 1826 opening of the same opera, the *Times* critic somewhat moderated his views: "There are parts of his voice . . . which we dislike, as to our ears, they sound harshly. . . . His tones, with this exception, are perfect, his science of the very first order, and his expression admirable." But Ayrton (Har) now was sharply negative: "Signor Velluti produces no effect this season. . . . We do not find that [his taste] possesses the charm of variety; he is a mannerist. . . . From the commencement of the present season, he has sung so extremely out of tune, so flat, that many ears could not bear it."

Alsager praised him in *Tebaldo*: "In the two fine scenes with Isolina, his expression of the pangs attendant on a violent passion . . . was equal to any thing we have seen him undertake. . . . In the scene where Tebaldo recognizes his father . . . [he] not only sang, but acted, extremely well." But Ayrton (C) declared that in a duet "the *Soprano* is so capricious in his time, that the other voice cannot keep with him," though one aria was sung "with great feeling, and less out of tune than most other songs that fell to his lot." Critic X (E), still showing some bias, was also critical: "What taste indeed can be expected from a man who sings as miserably out of tune." Even Bacon (LM) had become disenchanted: "We have heard Velluti and nothing but Velluti for months past, and we like him less than we ever did. His voice is like a sharp, harsh and ill-governed instrument . . . and bitterly does it grate on our musical nerves, like the scraping of a slate pencil" (Mar.).

This was Velluti's last regular season at the King's, to the relief of most critics. But the strength of his coterie among the aristocracy was evident when, in 1828, he was brought back for a benefit in still another production of *Crociato*. It was in response to "extravagant eulogies respecting his talents" that Alsager produced a long and thoughtful critique on the singer and his style (July 25), noting, first, that the change in the style of contemporary opera was totally unsuitable to the capabilities of "*soprani*" in general, and, second, that Velluti's voice, having suffered the "ravages of time," was no longer a fit musical instrument. Yet Holmes (At), in his only comment on the singer, was quite supportive: "Signor Velluti affected us powerfully with pity and horror; the middle parts of his voice have a more awful quality of tone than we have ever yet heard from any thing human."[27]

Mount-Edgcumbe noted that he was past his prime at the King's, with a failure in the middle tones, though the upper ones were "still exquisitely sweet"; there was also "a deficiency in spirit and variety." He thought the singer had overcome much of the prejudice against him.

De Begnis[28]

A fine singing actor with a long tenure at the King's was Giuseppe de Begnis (1793–1849), a baritone. He began his music studies at seven years of age and made his opera debut in 1813 at Modena. Soon singing throughout Italy, he married Giuseppina Ronzi in 1816, and by 1819 he was singing with her in Paris. The couple came to London in 1821 from the Théâtre Italien, and both made their King's debuts in the premiere of *Turco*.

Most of the critical attention was on Ronzi, but Giuseppe, who sang Don Geronio, was found by Alsager to be "a valuable player, both as an actor and a singer. His talent for humour, and in the discrimination of character, is of the first order; and he seldom or never descends to that low buffoonery, too much tolerated at this theatre, which is always appealing to the audience. . . . His voice is a *barytone*, not powerful, but extremely pure and flexible." The *Champion* also noted that "his humour seems to spring from the circumstances he is placed in; he does not appear to watch for the moment when he may throw in a prepared grimace." The *Gazette* thought his voice "of no prominent quality," but Kenrick (BS) found him a "good singer and a valuable addition to the company." Bacon (LM) reported he had "a free full toned voice, and a good manner. He is a far better singer than Ambrogetti." He was also excellent as Leporello (T).

The de Begnises were welcomed back the following season in their *Turco* roles (T). They reappeared in the premiere of *Pretendenti*, when Giuseppe was called "an actor of great skill, as well as an excellent musician; every look and action was intelligible" (T). In 1823 he sang Fernando in *Gazza*, but Bacon (LM) was not impressed: "He is a comic singer and nothing else. In rapid notation he is supreme; but the moment he attempts serious music, we perceive all the havoc which comic singing is almost certain to produce. . . . Though a musician, he cannot sing, in the true sense of the word." For their benefit, the de Begnises sang in *Matilda*, where, as Alsager wrote, Giuseppe's "broad farce is a very perfect specimen of the *buffo* style of acting." *Drama Magazine* reported his acting "was neither buffoonery, grimace, nor caricature, and still it was pregnant with the richest humour. Some of the proudest of our native comedians might study it with the certainty of advantage."

In 1824 Giuseppe performed in *Fanatico* "with considerable humour"

(T; LitC). As Bartolo in *Barbiere* he "gave much satisfaction," although he was not equal to Ambrogetti (NM). He was also effective as Leporello in *Don Giovanni* (T, May 7). Later Alsager wrote: "This gentleman has much of the humour of Naldi, and he has the advantage of a more pleasing and flexible voice than that celebrated *buffo* possessed" (T, Aug. 16). Toward the end of the season he was "a vivacious Figaro" (T).

In 1825 Giuseppe made a successful Don Simone—a pedantic schoolmaster—in *Adelina* (T, Mar. 21; C). He was also "respectable" as Almaviva in *Figaro*, though it was "not one of his happiest performances" (LM). Indeed, Bacon declared it "the worst of all his characters" (QMM, VII, 188). But he made an excellent Alfonso in *Così* (T), and in 1826 he was again successful as Don Magnifico in *Cenerentola* (NM).

In 1827 Giuseppe was very effective as Mustapha in *Schiava*, and according to Alsager, he "hit off to the life the busy, bustling dealer in shoes. . . . His by-play in the scene with Zulma merits the warmest praise" (T, Dec. 29, Jan. 1). The *New Monthly* and the *Chronicle* agreed, but the latter noted "there are some errors in point of good-taste . . . the occasional introduction of English words, for instance, is not merely absurd, but there is no humour in it." As Gottardo, the magistrate, rather than as Fernando (*Gazza*), he was "exceedingly good" and "proved that his powers were fully adequate to the delineation of serious feeling" (Alsager, Feb. 5). Ayrton (Har) thought that he did well and that his voice "told in the concerted pieces."

In 1828 he was instructing the pupils of the Royal Academy of Music in acting (T, Dec. 19). In 1829 he sang Don Febeo in *Fanatico* for that company, and his personation "was the best of the kind witnessed for a long time in this country" (T). The de Begnises were separated, apparently in 1826. Ronzi retired to Italy, but Guiseppe remained at the King's, where Hogarth reported he was still singing buffo roles as late as 1838.

Porto

Mathieu Porto, a bass not cited by N.G. or N.O., is known to have sung in Pavia in 1802, Milan in 1805, and then in Venice and Rome. He sang at Paris from 1810 to 1814, then returned to Italy. He was back in Paris in 1819, though he had little success there.

He made his King's debut in 1823 as Podesta in *Gazza*, when he displayed a bass "of some depth and firmness, but not remarkable for clearness or flexibility" (EM). But Bacon (LM) was more enthusiastic: Porto "has a fine, mellow, and powerful voice. Indeed, as a singer, he is justly equal in his deportment to any other man we have had for some years. . . . Rossini's music . . . is not calculated for the round heavy staccato execution of the legitimate bass. . . . It is, however, only just to Signor Porto to say, that he succeeded far better than his predecessors."

As Douglas in *Donna del Lago*, "his style" was "more dramatic and effective than at first" (T). The *Herald* agreed: "Signor Porto now displays the style to which he is properly suited. He must leave grimace and low comedy for parts of great solemnity. The deep tones of his bass voice came out fully rounded, and with an energy arising from feeling and unaffected expression." Ayrton, however, found his voice "unsuited to Rossini's rapid turns and divisions, and awkward skips." As the count in *Elisa* he was only "passable" (T), though the *Herald* thought the character was "represented with great truth." In *Figaro* he "infuses a good deal of buoyancy and spirit into his representation of the intriguing Count. He sings with much ease and expression; and, in the concerted pieces particularly, acquitted himself in masterly style" (EM). As Ireano in the premiere of *Ricciardo*, he was supportive (T), and as Elmiro in *Otello* he "sustains the various concerted pieces admirably well" (Har, I, 85).

The next season, as Basilio in *Barbiere*, his "execution of the elaborate air 'La Calunnia' was exceedingly fine" (T). The *New Monthly* agreed, but "once or twice in attempting to transpose an octave lower to 'show off,' he got out of his depth . . . and nothing but indistinct rattles were audible. He was not equal to Angrisani." In *Don Giovanni* he was "a livelier Masetto than we expected" (EM).

In 1825 he was satisfactory in the title role of *Pietro* and, "with his slow-moving, deep-toned voice, gave a very solemn effect to the music" (C; Har; LM). The *New Monthly* asserted: "We do not undervalue the merits of this gentleman, but sublimity of conception or elevated feeling are not among their number." On his other roles, the *London* was negative.

In 1826 he was again praised as Pietro, delivering his denunciation of vengeance "in a most powerful and impressive manner" (T). He was absent from the King's in 1827, but the next year—his last there—the critics (E; NM; Har) welcomed him back in *Margherita*. He was unsuccessful as Rodolph in *Rosa Bianca* (C), but as Publio in *Tito* he was "very effective" (Har, VI, 94). He was "respectable" as the Sultan in *Crociato* (NM), and he sang and acted well as Masetto in *Don Giovanni* (At). Porto returned to Italy after that season, wanting "too much money" to be acceptable (Ebers).

Zucchelli

Carlo Zucchelli (usually spelled Zuchelli by reviewers), a bass, was born in London (1793–1879) to an Italian father and an English mother. He accompanied his family to Italy in 1803 and was singing in public by 1814. In 1816 he made his debut in Ferrara and sang in operas by Rossini and Guglielmi in Vienna. Later, at La Scala, he sang more Rossini roles, and the composer thought his Don Magnifico, in *La Cenerentola*, the best he had heard.

He made his King's debut in 1822 as Noraddin in *Pietro l'Eremita*. Alsager wrote: "His voice is not so mellow as some [basses] we have heard but possesses great depth, compass, and flexibility. He sings perfectly in tune, and has the faculty for making himself heard distinctly over the orchestra, yet without the least apparent effort. He is evidently a good musician." Critic X (E) was similarly impressed but warned him against "too exuberant embellishment." Bacon (LM) noted his "tremendous volume and extensive compass" but reported him "more defective in his shake than any performer we ever heard."

Zucchelli could have hardly been deterred by such notices; nevertheless, he spent the next three years singing at Paris. He returned to the King's in 1827 as the Caliph in the premiere of *Schiava*, and, as Alsager wrote, "he proved himself to be a vocalist of great feeling and judgment. Hope and love, jealousy, disappointment, and ultimately, joy, were expressed by him, naturally and eloquently" (Jan. 1). The *Chronicle* wrote: "He is a most accomplished and scientific singer; his voice has a higher compass than the ordinary bass and is equally effective in solos and in concerted pieces. His execution has nothing of the heaviness and monotony which so often characterizes bass singers." The *New Monthly* concurred.

As Fernando in *Gazza* he "described the sufferings of the unhappy father with great truth," and the duet "Per questo amplesso" between him and Fanny Ayton "was well worthy of the long-continued applause that was bestowed on it" (T, Feb. 2). He again gave strong support to the role of Noraddin (T, Mar. 19, 21; Har) and sang "in the most finished and exquisite manner" (E, Mar. 25). The press "deeply regretted" his departure for Paris after these performances.

In a season review, Bacon stated: "He may now without doubt or hesitation be considered to rank with the first singers of his class in Europe. His scale of two octaves is most perfectly formed, its tone not more remarkable for its vast volume than for its smoothness, roundness and liquidity" (QMM, IX, 51).

Zucchelli was back the next season, however, as Assur in *Semiramide*, the production of which had been delayed for him, and he filled the role adequately (T). As Don Giovanni he was "eminently successful" (T). Critic Z (NM) gave highest praise to his voice in the role, but added: "His conceptions of characters, however, whether of the serious or comic kind, generally fall short of the demands of the part. In the former there is a want of inward emotion; and in humorous parts one misses the genuine comic vein.... His Don Giovanni wanted the unction, the light-heartedness, the gentlemanly *enjouement* of the debauchee which is essential to the part."

Holmes (At), on the other hand, was quite harsh: "If Signor Zuchelli thinks himself qualified to remodel Mozart's melodies, he is one of the most fatuous of men." Further, he "had no requisites either of person or manner for the accomplished libertine, and seemed fitter to scare away ladies than to bring them to his love."

In 1829 Zucchelli sang Figaro in *Barbiere*, but "his translation to such a *buffo* part was certainly not to his advantage," especially after the performances of Pellegrini and de Begnis, Alsager observed. Wade (Ath) agreed: "He is too cumbrous a creature for the agile and vivacious 'factotum della citta.'" But Wade found him "admirable" as Don Magnifico in *Cenerentola*. His performance "combines the highest musical taste and talent, with a liveliness of dramatic powers not very often excelled" (May 13). His buffo burlesquing as the Count in *Matrimonio* was highly entertaining, especially in the comic duet "Se fiato in corpo avete" with Galli (T; Ath; Har). His performance in *Italiana* "threw much additional vigour into the entire opera," and as Wade wrote, he "added a fresh laurel to his wreath; ... we should not willingly think that it will be his last" (Ath, Aug. 5).

Zucchelli continued his Paris-London shuttle until 1825, when he returned to Italy, retiring from the stage in 1842. Ebers found him good in both comic and serious roles, and Mount-Edgcumbe wrote that he "possesses the most soft, mellow and flexible bass voice I almost ever heard." "Chronicles" asserted that "no bass that has been heard in England has ever united so many perfections in an equal degree."

Curioni

It is astonishing that we should know so little about Alberico Curioni (c. 1785–1832), a tenor. In Naples he created the role of Alberto in Rossini's *Gazza Ladra* in 1816, and he came to the King's from Barcelona, singing leading roles there from 1821 to 1830 and perhaps later.

At his 1821 debut as the lead in *Tito*, Alsager thought his voice "of excellent quality in the lower and middle notes" but the upper register had a "certain hardness," and he lacked flexibility. He was sparing of ornaments but had a "coldness of manner or want of enthusiasm" in his songs. Kenrick (BS) was also disappointed in him, but Bacon (LM, May) reported: "He has a good figure, a very pleasing, fair, English physiognomy; possesses graceful action, a voice powerful and of excellent quality, and a manner purely Italian." (See also QMM, III, 381.)

As Don Narcissus in *Turco* later that season, he "was quite at home in the part; his melodious voice sounded most charmingly" (C). Alsager thought him even improved over his Titus, but Bacon (LM) changed his mind on his voice, which now seemed "not very powerful, nor very extensive. . . . He adds a note or two of falsetto without any very disagreeable effects." Though not equal in science to Crivelli or García, he was "a singer of unquestioned ability."

In 1822 Curioni played the lead in *Barone di Dolsheim*. The *Champion* was negative—"his cold, listless manner disgusts us"—but Alsager reported he "sustained the character well" and sang one song "with considerable effect." For the *Examiner*, "it was quite a pleasure to hear Curioni's beautiful voice again." In *Pretendente* Alsager thought he performed "with feeling and just expression. . . . With more force and bolder display, he would be a very valuable singer." And Bacon (LM) reported he sang "remarkably well; indeed he has scarcely had fair play since his engagement in England." As Orosmanes in *Pietro* he "distinguished himself particularly" (T); he "was as agreeable as the nature of his part would allow" (C) and was "very successful" (LM). He ended the season as Otello in the King's premiere, and as Alsager wrote, he "sang throughout in a fine sustained style, and acted with a feeling and energy which would have entitled him to high rank as an actor" (T). Bacon (LM) agreed his acting was "superb" and his singing "had more of true feeling than we ever remember to have witnessed since the days of Tramezzani."

At the opening of the next season, he returned to *Tito* and, according to Alsager, "gave the recitative with much effect. . . . As a tenor of the first class his voice wants power and volubility, but he is unquestionably a performer of very considerable merit." But he again made substitutions for some of the original songs, which was "unworthy of his high reputation" (EM). As Uberto in *Donna del Lago*, he "exhibited much energy; and his voice, which is acquiring greater strength, filled the house more completely than usual" (T), but Ayrton (Har) thought the part too high for him. In *Ricciardo*, although he sang the title role "occasionally out of tune," he was applauded "chiefly on account of his cadences, several of which were full of expression" (T). He also sang an excellent Roderigo in *Otello* (Har).

In 1824 Curioni appeared in *Fanatico* with satisfaction (T), but as Antenore in *Zelmira* he had difficulty with one aria and "could not therefore cause it to be felt and understood by the audience" (T). As Argerio in *Tancredi* he performed with "very tolerable justice" (T). Welcomed back for a late re-engagement in 1825 after a trip to Paris, he was again effective as Orosmane in *Pietro* (T), relieving the management "from many difficulties" (C; Har).

In 1826 Curioni excelled as Adrian in *Crociato*, the king in *Donna del Lago*, Bremondo in *Tebaldo*, and Almaviva in *Barbiere*, drawing plaudits from Alsager, Ayrton, and the *Examiner*. Bacon alone faulted his acting: In a sketch of him that season he wrote that Curioni's voice was "pure to the most polished degree . . . [but] he is less dramatic than any stage singer we ever heard, taking into account that he is always expressive" (QMM, VIII, 340–42).

Curioni opened the 1827 season as Lucinius in *Vestale*. Alsager wrote that "many passions are to be described" in his scene with Julia, and that "he entered fully into each of them: love, apprehension, and terror, were alternately portrayed with great truth" (Dec. 4). But the *Chronicle* reported that he "laboured under an inauspicious hoarseness, & went through his part with more than his usual carelessness, and less than his usual redeeming spirit and animation." Others (LitC; LG; NM) praised him highly, but the *Examiner* thought he lacked energy where it was needed, while Ayrton (Har) reported that "though he alone . . . has the power of giving sufficient strength to the music, and did not spare himself now, yet it was evident that he did not enjoy his part." He again excelled in *Schiava* (T; C; NM), *Gazza* (T), and *Pietro* (T; C). But he went through the role of Ricciardo "in a careless or slovenly manner. Perhaps he was affected by the mediocrity which met him at every turn" (T). In *Maria Stuarda* he "simpered through the part of Leicester as if he felt it to be totally beneath his merits" (E; NM).

Later reviewers became more critical of his acting. At the 1828 opening he sang the Duke of Lavarenne "in good voice" in the premiere of *Margherita* and had "a degree of animation somewhat unusual with him" (T; E). He also "played and sang with unusual energy and ability" as Otello (T; C), but "his acting, though spirited, characteristic and natural, was natural only inasmuch as it was Italian. The attitudes and gestures would have been extravagant in any other country" (LitC). Holmes (At) thought him "not effective" as Vanaldo in *Rosa*, but the *New Monthly* wrote: "We are glad to observe, he seemed to be pleased with [the role]; for he sang well and with his usual fervour." Hunt pointed out that Curioni, "who has a manner of feebleness and indifference in general, seems inspired when he comes to sing with Pasta" (*Companion*). But Ayrton (Har) thought he strained his voice until it "became hard and disagreeable."[29]

In 1829 the criticism deepened. Curioni sang Conte Ori in the premiere of Rossini's opera, and Alsager wrote: "Nearly the whole weight of the perfomance fell upon Signor Curioni, who . . . appeared to exert himself to the utmost for the purpose of saving the piece from disgrace. . . . But his efforts were indifferently supported and his pains ill requited" (T). The

Chronicle, however, reported that "with all proper sense of Curioni's merits," "he is heard to infinite disadvantage" following Donzelli, and the *Examiner* found him "more feeble and inefficient than we ever heard him before." Holmes (At) noted his singing was by this time out-of-tune and added: "We warned him a long time ago of forcing his voice, but he has persisted in bawling and hallooing, till he has . . . destroyed the justness of his intonation." He also sustained the role of Curiazio in *Orazi* (T, July 31, Aug. 3) and sang "with evident care, judgment, and good expression" (E).

In 1830 he again succeeded as Idreno in *Semiramide* and "went through his task with good taste and judgment" (T). But Wade (Ath) denounced "his old *nonchalant* style," while Holmes (At) again dismissed him for imperfect intonation. But in *Otello*, Alsager pointed out, "the able manner in which he fills this character [of Rodrigo] has the effect of raising it far above the inferior station assigned to it in the drama," and Wade (Ath, Feb. 20) agreed that he "shone beyond his wont. . . . His notorious defect is, that having heard him once you have heard him always." Holmes (At) growled that he "should endeavour to renovate his voice in Italy—it has become a mere thread." Wade (Ath, May 8) agreed that he had "less voice than ever," and he also thought that, as the Count in *Barbiere*, Curioni was "becoming more and more careless and ineffective: he not only sings wofully flat, but also disregards the meaning of the author." Despite these detractions, he remained popular with the public. Alsager noted the "testaments of approbation which were repeatedly bestowed" on him as Leporello (June 7), adding that he "was greeted with loud plaudits from all parts of the house on his first appearance on the stage." (Critics in this period never seemed to object to the transpositions necessary for such shifts in roles.)

Mount-Edgcumbe found him no great singer though his voice was "very sweet and pleasing." Parke noted the decline in his vocal powers (1830). "Chronicles" observed that he had "considerable talent as an actor when he pleases." Curioni was an honorary member of the Royal Academy of Music.

Donzelli

Domenico Donzelli (1790–1873), a tenor, had been a boy soprano and later studied with Bianchi, making his debut in Bergamo, his birthplace, at age eighteen. He was soon singing in Rossini operas throughout Italy. By 1825, when his voice was heavier and larger, he was admired as Otello in Paris.

He made his King's debut in 1829 as Roderic in *Donna del Lago* and was an instant hit. Alsager (T, Feb. 2) wrote: "His voice is a *tenore* of great compass, commanding much variety of inflection, and every kind of modification suggested by his musical taste and discrimination. . . . There is an equality of richness in his high and low notes, and in his attempts to reach still higher ones . . . the *voce di testa* which is thereby called into action produces a far more pleasing effect [than the usual falsetto]." Wade (Ath, Feb. 4) agreed, adding: "He has a *portamento di voce*, which appears almost irreconcilable with sweetness,—a vigour and massiveness of tone, which would be supposed refractory to all tune; he gives the broad effect so well, that you would despair of the graces, and wreaths, and harmonizing tints; yet it is all, and more than all, displayed in the happiest variety, and to the utmost extent."

In *Italiana* two weeks later he was "nearly, very nearly perfect" (Wade). Next month, in Bochsa's heartily disliked *Messicani*, Alsager noted his lungs were "kept in violent exercise throughout this opera. Both himself and the adapter seem to have had a notion that pulmonary effort is a principle requisite of the music. . . . Signor Donzelli may appear to momentary advantage by his 'splendid bursts' . . . but nothing can be more insufferably tiresome to the auditor than their frequent repetition." The *Examiner*, however, praised "the grandeur of his voice, and the judgment with which he used it."

Donzelli next appeared as Otello and, according to Alsager, "both acted and sang with all the spirit with which he might have been expected to infuse into the part" (T, Apr. 27), though the *Examiner* would "advise Otello to be a little more sparing of the power of his magnificent voice, which was, at times, more prominent than was conducive to the general effect." As Agorante in a revival of *Ricciardo*, he "sang in his usual grand and masterly style" (NM). Still later in the season, he sang Almaviva in a *Figaro* produced for Malibran's benefit. Wade noted that he "has not, perhaps, in Mozart's operas, so many opportunities of displaying the peculiar power of his voice, as in Rossini's; but, after all, it is not much to his disadvantage . . . that he is thereby restrained from over exerting his own voice. . . . We never heard him finer than in the few words in which he asks Figaro whether he knew who wrote the letter" (Ath). And Ayrton declared he was "really admirable; if he did but abstain from now and then using his falsetto, quite needlessly, he would be perfect in the part" (Har, VII, 178).

As Paolino in *Matrimonio*, Donzelli "took pains to give the beautiful cavatina, *Pria che spunti*, in that peculiar elegance of execution which it requires," wrote Alsager. Critic Z (NM), who thought "all was perfection," in his performance, explained that the aria just cited "lost somewhat in interest by a transposition from E flat to the key of D natural." Ayrton declared he was "in every way all that could be wished" (Har), but Wade (Ath) thought he gave "a cumbrous character to the music, which is quite foreign to it."

As Don Ottavio in *Don Giovanni*, Donzelli was "excellent in every respect" (Ath); he pleased in *Cenerentola* (Ath), and he concluded the season as Marcus Horatio in *Orazi*, when critic X (E) observed: "One of the most remarkable qualities in this extraordinary singer is, that . . . he always appears to have a *corps de reserve*,—that he does not put forth *all* his might: . . . he knows how and when to subdue it; his piano and crescendo—in common terms, his 'swell,' is as perfect as we ever heard. And, to crown all, he evidently loves the highest class of music, and sings as he loves it."

So concluded Donzelli's first season, remarkable no less for appearing in some thirteen major roles—an achievement none of the reviewers noted, and not even equaled by Catalani. The 1830 season, however, produced a growing criticism of him in many of these same operas, along with continuing praise. Notices of his Otello, for example, were mixed. He "sang and played" with "taste and admiration" (T), and his voice was "prodigious as ever; but we would that he were something more sparing of his *fortissimo*" (At). Wade (Ath) agreed, but reported that "the first gasp of English air has, we fear, clogged the machinery of his voice in some slight degree. . . . His *ad. lib.* passages were not so free and vigorous as they might be in the soft atmosphere of sunny Italy" (Feb. 20). As Ramiro in *Cenerentola* he was "justly admired" (Ath); his voice was superb, although his acting style "disclosed on this occasion a want of force and refinement" (T). On the other hand, Wade (Ath, June 19) wrote that he "sings more and *shouts* less in this opera than in any we have yet heard him in."

Donzelli sang Claudio in the premiere of *Elisa*, but the music "did not afford to his talents much opportunity for display" (T; C). Indeed, Wade was "almost glad" of the absence of that opportunity since "he substitutes for [display] an abundance of grace and tenderness and exquisite modulation of tone, with a delicacy of finish which we never before noticed in him." As Corradino in *Matilda*, he was "magnificent" (T; E). Ayrton thought his exertions did much to save the opera, and "if he had a little more light and shade" he would be even better. Wade agreed. As Gualtiero in *Pirata* he was superlative (T), though the *Chronicle* thought the part "too high for him and notwithstanding the skilful transposition to which it had been subjected, he did not do it uniform justice."

Donzelli again sang Paolino, though this buffo role was "not very suitable to [his] dignified style of singing and acting," according to Alsager; but Wade found his voice "delicious"—"particularly when it goes in sixths with the soprano" (June 12). In his last opera that season, as Don Alfonso in *Donna Caritea*, he "carried his pulmonary vigour to an excess production of downright bellowing," and he was warned against the possible "deterioration, perhaps destruction of an organ so liberally gifted by nature" (NM).

In the thirties Bellini wrote Barole for him in *Norma*; he was also acclaimed in many Donizetti operas. He retired from public singing in 1844 and remained for some years in London, though he died in Bologna. Chorley said he had "one of the most mellifluous, robust low tenor voices ever heard" but displayed no great dramatic power.

THE LEADING FEMALE SINGERS

Most of the attention of the press was, of course, on the prima donna assoluta. Of the twenty-one women singers before 1800, however, only two—Mara and Banti—had any staying power with the public and clearly deserved that rank. Storace, perhaps more popular, did not achieve it.

Mara

Gertrude Mara, née Schmeling (1749–1833), neglected in infancy, suffered from rickets and never fully recovered; she also had plain features and protruding teeth. She first showed talent on the violin and became something of a prodigy in Vienna. In 1759 she came to London and played before the queen. At Leipzig she began singing lessons and had a successful debut at Dresden in 1767. She also sang in Berlin, the Low Countries, and Vienna, where she failed to impress Mozart.

She returned to London in 1784 to sing in concerts, and she made her King's debut two years later in *Didone*. There were protests by the cabal over this German singer, but her performance was "a triumph of genius and merit over obloquy and prejudice." The *Chronicle* contined: "To a voice in which strength, sweetness and compass form an unprecedented union, this incomparable performer has added a profound acquaintance with the science of her profession. . . . [She] delivered the recitative with a force of expression that produced the strongest interest of character." And the *Register* noted that "She exhibited a degree of delicacy and feeling, exquisitely characteristic and pleasing." Despite Anfossi's presence, she substituted several of her own selected arias for his (Boaden).

The next month she sang Andromeda in *Perseo* and received high praise for a second-act bravura, "Non è la mia speranza," and a second-act duet (P; TC). She introduced her own selections in *Armida* and showed great versatility: "Mara in her first and yet more in her last Bravura, was almost miraculous. And yet . . . we still prefer the simple melody of the last air she had to sing [by Schuster]. In calm and mellow composure, it was in music what the best of Claude is in painting" (TC, June 3).

The following season (1787), the *Herald* confessed that to speak of Mara's performance in *Alceste* "would only be repeating what has been said an hundred times of her abilities; yet, in our opinion she was even above herself" in "Deh s'affretti" and "Luci del caro bene" (Dec. 25). But after the second performance, they did have reservations: "With regard to execution, and *bravura*, this lady is perhaps the ablest singer in Europe; but the German school, in which she has been tutored, has not used her to *spin out* her voice—*filar la voce*, as the Italians term it, that is, to warble a number of notes, without break or division, though the modulation may be varied, which is the chief secret of *cantabile*" (Jan. 1). After a brief illness (UR, Jan. 29), she sang "incomparably well" (Mt-E) as Cleopatra in *Cesare*, and she executed a bravura in *Vestale* with "great power" (UR, May 3).

We find no evidence in earlier reviews of her for the *Register*'s assertion, at the beginning of her second season, that "from the ill-treatment Madam Mara received the last season in her engagement at this House, she has seceded, and has a weekly concert of her own, which has been very liberally subscribed to" (Nov. 7, 1787). She also turned to English opera, making her Drury Lane debut in *Artaxerxes* (Apr. 7) with an overwhelming reception. She apparently went to Italy for a time (H, Apr. 7, 1790), but in 1790 she was persuaded to return to the King's and was given a "hearty welcome" as Dircea in *Usurpator*. The *Herald* noticed a change in her: "Madam Mara, in her excursion to the Italian regions, has acquired a peculiar suavity in the expressions of her note[s], which added to the amazing extent of her powers, makes her to feast the ear with celestial nectar in every modulation, and may entitle her to the appellation of the OPERATICAL HEBE." She was also praised in *Andromica* (PA, May 31).

In 1791 she drew praise at a rehearsal of *Armida* at the Pantheon (P, Feb. 10): "She sung [a bravura] with all its requisite fire and force, and seemed to exert herself to the utmost of her abilities. We cannot omit observing, that she totally laid aside those cadences which are now so much hackneyed at every musical assemblage by her numerous imitators, and gave new graces to each passage" (T, Feb. 11). After a "dangerous" illness, she returned to the stage (T, Apr. 11) and succeeded in *Idalide*, where her "beautiful air, to Haydn's favourite movement of 'Ah che nel petto,' was superlatively scientific and affecting" (T). She sang under Haydn at the Salomon concerts that year.

In 1792 the Pantheon could not produce opera seria that season, and the King's did not renew her contract, but she was engaged by Covent Garden to sing an all-sung English opera devised for the occasion—*Didi, Queen of Carthage*; unfortunately, reviewers were silent on her performance. In 1793 she returned to the King's and appeared as Aspasia in Paisiello's seria, *Giuochi*. She was generally applauded but was hissed when she refused to take an encore (W). She received routine praise in *Teodolinda* and in *Odenato* (T).

Mara's abrupt departure that year resulted from her "elopement" with a young flute player. In 1796, however, DuBois (MM), in a review of her in Arne's *Artaxerxes* at Covent Garden, observed: "Madame Mara having compromised with her husband in a way the most unexceptionably just and moral—that is, on the principle of *snacks* [i.e., to share or divide profits, etc.]—is not again at full liberty to proceed in the exercise of her talents. Madame Mara retains all of her sweetness, but has lost much of her power; she still continues to interest, but no longer astonishes. The house was indifferently attended" (May). Apparently her audiences there, too, had deserted her.

Eventually she went off with her husband to Russia and settled in Moscow. Unfortunately, during the Napoleonic invasion, her property there was destroyed, and she was left penniless. Her voice, too, was gone. One of the saddest events in this chronicle is her attempt to earn money by a reappearance on the concert stage in London in 1820 at age seventy-one. She was eagerly anticipated, for, as Bacon noted, there were many "who remember with a degree of admiration, never effaced by the brightest prodigies that have since risen upon our horizon, the dignity of the finest singer the world ever saw in the genuine great style" (LM, Feb.). But the disappointment at the concert was inevitable: "We delight not to dwell on the ruins of departed greatness, and could have been far better pleased to have retained no recollections but of the power, the grandeur, and the pathos of the art as it was once manifested in the performances of Mara" (LM, Apr.). Kenrick (BS, Apr.) was not quite so bleak: "The power and sweetness of her voice seems to be gone; but the correctness of her taste is as apparent as ever. . . . Her step is firm, and her person erect; [but] it was altogether a melancholy sight to see a woman of her advanced years thus obliged to exert herself when the power of pleasing was no longer hers."

To Burney she "seemed a divinity among mortals." Mount-Edgcumbe and Boaden agreed she was no actress (she sometimes "sang while seated"), but the former called her voice "clear, sweet, distinct," and her agility and flexibility revealed her "a most excellent bravura singer." Parke adds that she occasionally marred her performances with "symptoms of caprice and hauteur."

Storace

The most colorful buffa of this period was Anna Storace (1765–1817), better known as "Nancy."[30] Sister of opera composer Stephen, she had singing lessons from Sacchini and Rauzzini, and first sang in public when she was twelve. She went to Italy for training in 1778 and for the next ten years sang there and in Vienna. She had a disastrous marriage and later became consort to the English tenor, Braham, to whom she bore a son in 1801. Her figure, which was short and plump, and a certain roughness in her voice led her to comic roles; she was Mozart's Susanna at the premiere of *Figaro* and was also his first Fiordiligi in *Così*. Indeed, she was more acclaimed abroad than in London (N.G.), where she returned in 1787. She sang in English opera as well.

Storace made her King's debut in 1787 as Gelinda in *Schiavi*, where her duet with Morelli, "Piche, cornacchie e nottole," and her cavatina, "Chi mi mostra," brought encores (UR, Apr. 30, July 2). One unidentified reviewer (TC) proclaimed that she and Morelli "will perhaps ever stand unrivalled on the Italian stage." The following season she also succeeded as Lisetta in *Teodoro*, when the *Times* pointed out her aptitude for the comic: "Storace did strict justice to the jealousy, the ambition, and returning love . . . of Taddio's daughter" (Dec. 10). They added that "the rapidity and articulation with which she executed the different arduous and masterly divisions forced them on the imagination," and they found her master of pathos as well in "Come obbliar potrei" (Dec. 17). The *Advertiser* stated that she "has baffled the efforts of the musicians to make her sing out of tune, quick or slow, as they fiddled, she modulated" (Jan. 17). As Madame Brilliante in *Locandiera*, she again displayed her abilities as a comic singing-actress, in company with Morelli: "So well did their unison [in "Con quelle tue manine"] in the acting accord, that they both seem to have been under the guidance of one mind" (T, Jan. 17). Next came her brother's *Cameriera*, and although the work failed, she received a "warm" encore for performing an inserted number, "Beaux yeux," and made an "extremely sprightly and entertaining Violetta" (T).

In 1789 she sang at Drury Lane but in 1790 returned to the King's company at the Little Theatre as Mandina in Bianchi's *Villanella Rapita*, in which "all the music of the opera deserving celebrity is by Mozart—and it is to the praise of Storace that so many have been introduced. To the merit of this favorite singer, all the success the Opera experienced is also to be attributed." Specially mentioned were "Bella rosa porporina" and "Dite almeno in che maniera"; the latter quartet was "a beautiful composition, and Storace's superiority in it very conspicuous" (H). A last-act duet with

Fausto Borselli gained an encore (T, Mar. 8). She sang Rosina in the premiere of *Barbiere* "with great taste and animation" (Parke).

In 1791 and 1792 she returned to Drury Lane, but in 1793 she was back for a revival of *Barbiere* and was praised for a duet she sang with Kelly, perhaps their first performance together (T, Jan. 28, 30). She next appeared as Lucrezia in *Zingari*, and she, Kelly, and Rovedino performed a "charming trio in the last act" (P). Her part was "full of spirit and frolics, which she hit off admirably" (Parke). She dropped out of the King's until 1797, when she appeared as Amore in *Arbore*. The role was "peculiarly adapted to her stile of singing and acting" (T, Apr. 19). "In order to give Storace an opportunity of displaying the graces of her person as well as the charms of her voice, the celebrated air of the *Negro Dance* in *Paul et Virginie* was introduced, and, executed as it was, it could not fail of complete success" (C; T).

After this season her career was devoted almost exclusively to English opera. She did reappear at the King's in 1806, when she was "all life and spirit" in *Cosa Rara* (T); and in *Due Nozze* she was described as "better in this piece, though with less provision being made for her by the composer, than we ever saw her" (C). Though obviously endowed for both stages, her greatest contributions appear to have been in English opera. Burney called her a lively, intelligent performer but with a voice unsuited "for delicate, tender passages" (the *Times* thought otherwise). Mount-Edgcumbe noted "she had a harshness in her countenance, a clumsiness of figure, and a vulgarity of manner"; yet she could sing "in every style," and was an excellent actress—unrivalled in buffo operas.

Banti

With Brigida Giorgi Banti (1756–1806) we come to probably the greatest natural musician and singing actress before Catalani. Her father was a Venetian gondolier and street singer. By age twenty she had made her Paris debut in playhouses, singing songs between acts, and she later studied with Sacchini but was "too lazy" to be a good pupil. In London in 1779, she was briefly regarded as a "bad singer with a beautiful voice" (N.G.). While there she married a principal dancer at Covent Garden and they departed for Italy.

By the time she returned to London in 1794, she had achieved a formidable reputation. Replacing Mara as First Woman, she made her debut in *Semiramide*. Despite a cold (English weather did not agree with her), the *Times* thought that

> there was yet a sufficient sample . . . to enable us to form a decided judgment in her favour; for, with all the exquisite taste and science of

Mara, she is fortunate enough to possess a voice which must put all modern competition to defiance.

In the accompanied recitative, the style and manner of Banti was shewn off to as much advantage as indisposition would allow; but her first air of "Ah non rai," proved alone sufficient to establish her fame. (Apr. 28)

At a later performance, Banti's rendition of "La Rachelina" "produced one of the most enthusiastic encores we ever heard" (T, May 5). The *Oracle* agreed; she was "the finest singer in the world. Among the vocal tribe, the rarest union is that of sweetness and force. Mara has one, Storace the other. Both are sound musicians. Banti has more of both force and sweetness than either and as much science and self-possession as both." Mount-Edgcumbe, who saw that production, reported that "her acting and recitative were excellent," and her last-act death scene was "incomparably fine." At a revival of the opera the next season, she was "never more herself" (T); and the *Chronicle* reported: "The tender flexibility, the melifluous tones and the extraordinary powers of her voice, were all produced with that feeling and judgment which have so often charmed. Her manner of dying is finely pathetic, and her whole deportment very superior to tragic actresses of Italy, whom we have had the opportunity to see." As a singer and actress she was "inimitable" in *Serva Padrona* (C, June 4).

Banti opened her 1795 season in *Zenobia*, which had been composed for her in Venice. She was now in fine voice and made a "triumphal entry." The music "afforded ample scope for [her] brilliancy of voice and expression" (T). In *Aci e Galetea* she was applauded for a first-act duet, her aria "Del mio bene a seno amato" proving a great favorite. It "was given by Banti in a very capital and finished stile" (TC). Near the close of the season, she was praised in *Alceste* (C, May 1), and in a revival the next year Gluck's music and Banti's execution "formed a sort of terrestrial paradise" (T, June 20).

In 1796 Banti appeared in *Arsene*, in which her "voice never betrayed more striking or melifluent tones" (T), and she drew encores for duets with Roselli and Morelli (P). She then appeared in *Piramo* and *Antigona*, but both works failed. In *Ifigenia*, she received encores in "both her songs" (T), but again became ill (T, May 9.) In the 1797 season, she sang in her first comedy, a revival of *Zemira*, "with all that incomparable power and taste which make her voice the wonder of the world" (C). She performed well in *Evelina* and in *Nina* (T, May 1). Burgh (III, 325) states that in the latter opera she and Vignoni "delighted the audience, particularly that part who understood the Italian language, by their admirable and natural acting."

She opened the 1798 season in *Ipermestra* and was "in exquisite tone," excelling in a first-act trio (T), but the work failed. In *Cinna*, which *was* very successful, she had an encore of a cantabile aria in the second act (P), and in a trio with Rovedino and Viganoni, she "was particularly happy in her execution. . . . Her '*ad libitum*' in another air . . . was a brilliant display of taste and science" (T). She later appeared in *Elfrida* and in *Antigona*.

In 1799 she was again plagued with illness, but at the season opening of *Medonte*, her voice did "not seem to be in the least affected by her late indisposition" (T). Almost immediately, however, she again became ill, and Maria Bland, who sang mainly in English Opera, was brought in, but not before the cancellation of several advertised performances, which irritated the subscribers and the *Times* critic. Banti again appeared as Selene in *Medonte* on December 22, and on December 24 the *Chronicle* lamented "the late illiberal and unmanly attack upon this lady" by the *Times*, adding: "We cannot join in those wretched cabals, who, under the name of public criticism, direct their impotent malice against the private interests of individuals." Later that season, in *Ines*, Banti had encores in a trio, "Ah, se Re, sa giusto sei," and in an invocation, "Grand Dio, che regoli." A second-act air of hers was "in a singular style: she is accompanied by the Hautboys and Tenors only; the Violins are mute. It had a very fine effect" (Cr).

In 1800 she appeared in a revival of *Semiramide*, and DuBois (MM) gently chastised her: "Madame Banti's performance in this opera is all the connoisseur can wish, but we cannot pass unnoticed a habit, peculiar to this lady, of conversing *mezza voce* with the performers in the orchestra, instead of attending to the business of the scene. Such disrespect to the audience would, in an English theatre, be treated, as it merits, with universal reprobation. Madame Banti's good sense will profit by this hint." As Taido in *Alessandro*, she was in excellent voice and her airs excited loud applause, though none were encored (P; T).

In 1801 she sang in a revival of *Alceste* and was "in full voice" (T). She substituted for Madame Bolla, who was ill, in *Consiglio*, but her comic acting was faulty: "Her step was too measured, her gesticulation too violent, and in the archness and bye-play of the part, she was evidently deficient. In the airs she was however deservedly applauded" (T). In March she sang in *Alzira*, and one aria displayed "all her volume of voice, unaccompanied at intervals by the Orchestra; the richness of its variety and pathos enchanted the Theatre (C).

Early in the 1802 season Banti was again ill, forcing the substitution of another opera; to placate the subscribers, the management circulated a medical certificate on her health when the doors opened (T, Jan. 11). In February she appeared as Zerlina in *Mitridate* and "evinced considerable feeling" (T, Feb. 24). She "was in excellent voice, and executed [her arias] with such taste and beauty, as to call down reiterated plaudits throughout the whole performance" (P).

The next month she prevailed on Elizabeth Billington to join with her in producing *Merope* for their joint benefit. So avid was the opera-going public to see and hear both divas, several were injured in the rush to get seats.

"To be sure of grasping all the money, the Signor [Banti] had the pit door barricaded, and posted himself there with assistants. . . . At their unlocking, the rush was so great that crash went the barricado, and that with Signor Banti was carried in the van of the crowd to the extremity of the pit, recovering his legs and eyes, he surveyed around, and in disappointed anguish exclaimed, by Gar, by Gar, de pit full, de gallery full, all overflowing, and no money in de box" ("Veritas," pp. 26–27). The *Post* was able to observe that Banti "appeared quite at ease in male attire" (P). And the *Chronicle* wrote: "The duet between [Billington] and Banti was a most wonderful effort of the art; the exquisite nature of the one with the perfect science of the other, made its influence irresistible over the heart." This was virtually Banti's swan song at the King's. She did another *Alceste* in May, and in June she appeared in the premiere of *Armida* (the last of the Bianchi-da Ponte operas for Banti). She "entered completely into her part, and by the charming animation of her countenance and action, as well as the powers of her voice, made it very interesting. She was repeatedly encored" (P). But she retired at the end of that season.

According to Mount-Edgcumbe, she left the King's because of her health and her loss of the public, though the press offers no hints of the latter or, apart from her illnesses, of a diminution of her powers (she died in Bologna only four years later). Banti was the most "delightful" singer Mount-Edgcumbe had ever heard: she sang "with more pathos and true feeling than any of her competitors," and, when young, she had no superior in bravura. "She had an extensive compass without a fault—rich lower tones, a powerful mid-range, and highs without shrillness." Burgh (III, 340) stated that "her voice was so expressive, and her intonation so perfect, that she reached, not merely the ear, but penetrated to the heart of every attentive hearer." S. D. ("Chronicles") thought she exhibited "no exuberance of execution, but much feeling."

Backstage, Banti was something less than perfect. Da Ponte (*Memoirs*) called her ignorant, stupid, and insolent; when vexed, "she became an asp, a fury, a demon of Hell, capable of upsetting an empire, let alone a theatre." In 1797 she had Wilhelm Cramer, long the admired leader of the orchestra at the King's, replaced by Giovanni Viotti. She even appropriated the unburned candle ends after performances, customarily a perquisite of the poor candlesnuffers ("Veritas," pp. 20–21).

Billington

Because of Catalani's reign at the King's from 1806 to 1813, some of the female performers early in the century appear peripheral. Nevertheless, a few were outstanding, such as Billington, who already had considerable experience on the English stage before her 1802 debut at the King's. Elizabeth Billington (1765–1818) was the daughter of Carl Weichsell, a prominent oboist in London, and her mother was a well-known singer. As a child, she studied singing and composition with J. C. Bach; before age twelve she produced two keyboard concertos. She married James Billington, a singing teacher and double bass player, in 1783. For several years she sang and played the harpsichord, with her brother on the violin, in afterpiece concerts at Covent Garden. She had a very high vocal range and accurate intonation.

Billington made her King's debut in *Merope*. "Banti prevailed on Mrs. Billington to perform with her on the night of her benefit, leaving to the latter the choice of the opera, and the principal character" (Mt-E). The *Chronicle* called the principals "the two most accomplished singers in the world" and reported that "Mrs. Billington has not been heard before in England to advantage.... The Duet between her and Banti was a most wonderful effect of the art; the exquisite nature of the one, with the most perfect science of the other, made its influence irresistable over the heart." The next day critic B (T) agreed, adding: "The sublime and impassioned music of Nasolini gave her full scope for the exercise of her great and commanding talents, and we confess, that her science, her pathos, and expression, even exceed the high character we had before conceived of them. The English Opera does not allow her sufficient range for the exertion of the incomparable powers of her voice."

At the next season's opening (1803) Billington repeated her role as Merope, and critic B (T) wrote: "Her deportment, action, and grand manner, which, on the English stage, went somewhat beyond the natural delineation of the character, are here suited to the subject.... The recitative was raised from its customary level ... and her *Cavetina* ... was embellished by graces all intimately connected with the theme of the composition" (Dec. 6). The *Post* found that her "extraordinary powers" embraced" a great variety of movements from the highest and most rapid flights of the *bravura* to the most soft and simple measure." Though her appearance in *Fernando* brought a disappointingly small audience, she was encored in two airs and "displayed her great powers with much effect" (P). Her arias and duets in *Calypso* were "loudly encored" (P).

At a repetition of *Calypso* in 1804, critic B (T) wrote: "This unrivaled singer displays her accustomed powers, science, and taste. But however admirable the execution of the different airs was, it is in her delivery of recitative, that she soars above all competition. She rejects the common modulation and the trite cadenzas which too frequently tire the ear and ennobles the sentiment expressed by the Author, with a richness of tone, a spirit and animation, that elevates her to the summit of the art." And the *Post* wrote: "In the part where she held a distinct and clear *nota termina*, her firmness of tone and perfect intonation was truly sublime." At the premiere of *Trionfo*, her "powers of voice, her exquisite feeling, and the delicacy with which she conveyed the sentimental passages, was truly fascinating" (T).

At the premiere of *Proserpina* in 1805 she was "in excellent voice, and sung with all the taste and delicacy, expression and neatness of execution, that have long placed her above the reach of competition" (T). "Never was her excellence in all the varieties of the art more clearly demonstrated than last night" (C). Yet her performance in *Erfile* convinced critic B to evoke the first shadow of criticism: "Were the acting powers of Mrs. Billington equal to her vocal, the impression of those united qualities would have been irresistible; as it is, there is always . . . a considerable *drawback* upon the performance of this distinguished singer." But critic B forgot those objections afer *Scipione*, which offered her "unparalleled powers of execution. . . . The highest treat . . . was the introduction of that exquisite *aria* 'Si ti perco', which Mrs. Billington executed with all that neatness, taste, expression and fire which in this particular song lifted her some years back to that proud height on which she is placed." The *Post*, also supportive, ranked her "the first bravura singer in the world," and the *Mirror* echoed their praise.

In 1806 Mrs. Billington again excelled in *Proserpina* and in *Cosa Rara* (T). As Serse in *Argenide*, she sang "with the most perfect truth and taste" (C); as Vitellia in the premiere of *Tito*, she received high praise from all reviewers; and she was effective at the premiere of *Fanatico* (C). This was her last performance at the King's; her place there was filled the next season by Catalani. Comparisons were inevitable. Upon Catalani's first appearance, the *Times* wrote: "For neatness and rapidity of execution, she is almost equal to Billington" though a better actress (Dec. 15, 1806). When Bertinotti (see below) appeared in 1810, her similarity to Billington in voice and manner were noted (T, Dec. 24).

Billington returned to the concert stage and to English opera, where she was so popular that she sang alternately at both Drury Lane *and* Covent

Garden theatres, although, since she apparently never sang in new works, her performances usually went unrecorded in the press. She retired in 1817. Boaden wrote that she exhibited "the steady composure which always attends great talent. She presented herself well to the audience, her self-possession sustained her through the protracted exertion of vocal power, accompanied by but little action." S. D. ("Chronicles"), in a retrospective, wrote (pp. 11–12):

> Her voice was not so remarkable for its compass . . . as for its unusually high position in the scale, E on the first line of the violin clef was her lowest *good* note; but, on the other hand, she soared to, and could hold, the highest C that a flute or violin player can produce on his instrument. [Her execution], certainly, never has been equalled since her time. . . . Billington was a breathing violin — Catalani a living organ. . . .
>
> On the stage, it must be admitted, Billington was wanting in almost every quality necessary for an actress. *Embonpoint* deprived her of elegance, and even ease of motion . . . and she was wholly incompetent to the expression of any strong emotion.

Mount-Edgcumbe agreed: "With all those great and undisputed excellencies something yet was wanting; for she possessed not the feeling to give touching expression,[31] even when she sung with utmost delicacy and consummate skill. Her face was handsome and her countenance full of good humour, but it was incapable of change, and she was no actress."

Grassini

Josephina Grassini (1773–1850), an Italian contralto, made her debut in Parma in 1789 and later sang in many Italian cities as well as in Paris. Contraltos, a neglected department of the King's, were not fashionable there.[32] Nevertheless, her 1804 debut in *Vergine* was a popular and critical triumph. Critic B (T) wrote:

> Signora Grassini is unquestionably a singer of the first order. . . . All her natural tones and modulations are excellent, and it is only when she rises into that which she exclusively possesses . . . a falsetto, that she is least successful. The transitions are too abrupt; they may surprise, but they cannot delight the ear. . . . In several passages she succeeded in touching the heart. [She] has a commanding person . . . and as an actress she possesses no inconsiderable merit.

The *Chronicle* agreed: "Her tone approaches to the tenor of a man — strong, full, and sweet. . . . She sings entirely from the breast. She affects none of the German instrumentality, which makes the nose supply the deficiency of the throat." Later that season she sang in *Proserpina*; "The affecting *contralto* of Madame Grassini," wrote the *Chronicle*, "maintains the strongest influence on the heart."

When she repeated the role at the opening of the 1805 season, the *Times* declared: "The grace and dignity of Grassini in *Proserpina* could not have been exceeded even by the majestic gesture and motion of a [Sarah] Siddons," the great English tragedienne. She next appeared in *Zaira*, which Winter had composed for her. Critic B (T) wrote: "Nothing could have exceeded her pathos and expression; she was in excellent voice, and the power, the clearness, and the exquisite delicacy of her tones, rendered her performance irresistably affecting. . . . [Her acting] was as chaste, dignified, and impressive, as any we have witnessed at either of our national theatres." The *Chronicle* concurred, adding: "That most rare and valuable talent, by which, with a few simple notes, she makes a deep and lasting impression on the heart, she displayed in this Opera to uncommon advantage. . . . Her acting gives to this Opera a charm peculiarly its own."

She and Billington opened the 1806 season in *Prosperina* and again won plaudits. But a few days later, she fell ill and another opera had to be substituted (T, Dec. 16). Meanwhile, Billington became ill, and Grassini got out of a sickbed to sing in *Orazi*—she had sung in its Venice premiere—"so as not to disappoint the subscribers" (C), and performed well despite occasional lassitude (Cr). A week later she again sang the part "with her usual pathos and feeling" (H). Later that season, she sang in *Cleopatra*, which Nasolini had written for her. The *Times* wrote: "A delicate softness predominates, upon which the highly cultivated taste of an Italian amateur would hang in extacy [*sic*]; but it wants the animation and variety which keeps alive the attention of an English theatre." The work would likely have failed badly except for her.

At the end of 1806 Grassini returned to Paris, where she was a favorite of Napoleon, but she came back to the King's for the single season of 1814, replacing Madame Ferlendis in *Orazi*. On that occasion Robertson (E) wrote that

> her powers have rather been improved than impaired. Her refined expression and commanding abilities have long been wanting [at the King's].
>
> Madame Grassini is the finest specimen of that class of singing which sets execution at defiance and relies entirely on feeling. Her first objective seems to be, the doing justice to the composer, by strictly preserving his ideas in their original purity.

The *Inquisitor* was also enthusiastic: "She displayed throughout this arduous and varied character, the most exquisite pathos, and the most impressive energy." Grassini's last opera was the King's premiere of Paer's *Didone*, but she failed to please the *Chronicle*, who reported that she "appeared, not the graceful contr'alto she had left us but an ambitious first soprano. Her success was, to say the best of it, only negative." The following year she returned to Italy and retired there in 1823.

Parke admired her "highly finished cadences" and her acting ability. Kelly said she "possessed a fine counter-tenor voice, the lower tones of which were sublimely pathetic." And Mount-Edgcumbe found her an "excellent actress.... Her style of singing was exclusively cantabile ... which bordered a little on the monotonous. . . . She had entirely lost all its upper tones, and produced little more than an octave of good natural notes." He added that she was feted by society. Hogarth called her "strikingly beautiful — tall and commanding, graceful with a noble head and black eyes" but also noted her limited range. "Chronicles" stated that she "never attempted what was beyond her power" and that "in the expression of the subdued and softed passions, she has never been excelled."

Catalani

The 1807 season was remarkable if only for the debut of Angelica Catalani (1780–1849), an Italian soprano who made her first appearance in Venice in 1797 and was soon admired by audiences in Madrid, Lisbon, Naples, and Paris. Her effect on the finances of the King's Theatre has been cited. Her artistic impact was no less astonishing.

At her debut in *Semiramide*, the house was completely filled, and "the great expectation which her fame had raised was not disappointed. . . . The compass of her voice exceeds any ever heard in this country" (H, Dec. 15).[33] Critic B (T) agreed, adding that "the tone of it is rich, mellow and substantial. There is no labour in her singing; she filled the whole of this immense theatre with as much apparent ease as if she had been practicing in her drawing room. For neatness and rapidity of execution she is almost equal to Billington, while in her voice, feeling and deportment, we discover the combined excellencies of a Banti, a Mara, and a Grassini." Particularly impressive was a bravura at the end of the first act: "For strength and variety of expression, for fire and feeling, and a degree of effort in some sort *electrical*, we have never heard it equalled." They also found her a fine actress. The *Chronicle* noted that she combined the talents of the finest lyric performers.

In her next opera, *Serse*, "curiosity was ... warmly excited to see Catalani in the same character in which Mrs. Billington had so eminently succeeded,—There was however no room for comparison, for the manner in which Catalani delineated the part was so different, that she made it perfectly new" (C). The *Times* repeated its praise for her delicacy, taste, execution, compass, quality of voice, and energy of manner. And the Herald (Mar. 16) noted: "The more this Lady appears before the Public, she exhibits increased powers and additional graces." In *Mithridate*, "the difficulties she has to execute, and the graceful manner in which she triumphed over them, were sources of high gratification to the skilful few—and by her exquisite delicacy and emotion in the touching passages, she equally affected the untutored crowd" (C).

In 1808, the second of the "Catalani seasons," she sang in all but four of the fifty-two performances. In *Semiramide*, on opening night, attempts were made "by a few of her envious countrymen to counteract the kind reception she met with from the British public," but they were soon drowned out by the applause. Her voice "appeared still more powerful than last year . . . her intonation more firm and perfect, and her executions more correct" (C). In his first review for the *Examiner*, Robertson rendered the first negative criticism of the diva in *Frascatana*:

> We have hitherto seen her small but elegant figure possessed with a load of regal ornaments, and a constant smile on her face, which neither the sorrows of Semiramis, nor the misplaced love of Cleopatra, could repress. . . . In the light music of *La Frascatana*, Catalani is divested of that profusion of ornament, with which she disguised the music of the operas produced last season. . . . But she has now employed her amazing powers to more advantage.

Hogarth (II, 164) called Frascatana one of her most charming roles.

She next returned to tragedy in *Didone*, and the *Times* wrote: "We witnessed last night a display of mimic talent which would have done honour to a tragedian"; she even "rivalled Mrs. Siddons." The *Chronicle* reported: "Nothing could transcend the graceful and impassioned action of Catalani." In an inserted aria by Piccinni, "Se il ciel divide," she proved superior to the passion of Mara and Banti. "The precision of Mara, perhaps, was wanting, because, in a song of such impetuous passion, there is grandeur and pathos in rising above the mere point of accuracy. It was a scream, indeed, with which she flew into the flames; but it was a scream that went to the heart." Even Robertson (E), who disliked the opera, admitted that she "shewed more propriety of action as Dido than she has ever before exhibited in the serious opera," but "she should avoid those screechings which make us feel for the safety of her lungs." Absent for several performances, she returned, none the worse for her illness, as

Sesostris, a trouser role, in *Festa*, though the *Times* thought she would have been better in a comic role. Robertson now complained:

> Madame Catalani becomes more and more a singer of mere trick. There is nothing pleasing in the retention of a note till she is breathless as the exhausted receiver of an air pump, nor in chromatic runs which are introduced on every occasion of joy and sorrow. As an actress, she has no talent for serious opera. Her mouth is distended in a perpetuity of grin, which is moderated neither by affliction or death.

Late that season she appeared in *Virtuosa* and introduced an aria from *Il Flauto Magico*,[34] which was "rapturously applauded" (T). And she concluded the season in *Contrattempi*, in which Robertson admitted she "sung with much taste and more than usual simplicity," though she was "extremely imperfect in her part."

Catalani's demands for 1809 were so exorbitant that Taylor was obliged to continue without her. She subsequently entered into a contract with Covent Garden (T, June 7, 1809), but this venture was unsuccessful—"John Bull exercised his veto" ("Chronicles").[35] But in 1810, after a late start, she again returned to the King's in *Fanatico*. The *Post* thought she was "in excellent voice, and never displayed her great and admired powers with more happy effect." Robertson now admitted that, "as a singer" she was "every thing that could be wished for," but added: "It is to be regretted that her acting does not keep pace with her vocal abilities, and that her unrestrained vivacity often leads her into absurdities and impertinencies" (Mar. 11). Yet her acting in *Atalida* was acclaimed by the *Chronicle*: "No acting of Mrs. Siddons, in the most pathetic movements of a scene, where the tones of the voice were heightened in their effect by the language of poetry . . . could surpass in force of emotion, or in delicacy of taste . . . the execution of Catalani and Tramazani [*sic*]." But Robertson vehemently protested:

> The Daily Papers . . . have not scrupled to assert that Madame Catalani's performance is equal to the noblest exertions of Mrs. Siddons! . . . If a deaf man was to be present at the performance of Madame Catalani, he would, from her gestures and countenance, pronounce that she was performing a comic character, for joy is the only passion she attempts to express; even the dose of poison is drunk as unconcernedly as if it was a glass of lemonade. (E)

Robertson returned to the attack in reviewing her performance in *Vestale*: "If a total disregard of the calamities of life is characteristic of fortitude, Madame Catalani is of all actresses the most heroic; . . . she seems to scorn all feeling, to 'smile at death and laugh at woe.'" But in the

1811 season, Croly (T) took up the challenge: "We have always considered this extraordinary woman's talents as an actress in no degree inferior to her powers as a singer." And at a revival of *Elfrida* later that season, he provided another long and diffuse argument on her acting.

By 1812, albeit another "Catalani season" in which she sang every night but two, she was constrained by popular will to sing in *Tito* and *Figaro* ("Chronicles"). She "detested Mozart's music, which kept the singer too much under the controul of the orchestra, and too strictly confined to time, which she is apt to violate."[36]

Regarding her Vitellia in *Tito*, the *Chronicle* noted that, in singing Mozart, "she reaches a higher point than that of merely astonishing by her voice." And "Chronicles" asserted she "was, perhaps, the best Vitellia we have ever seen or heard." But Robertson again disagreed: "Catalani and Tramezzani did much for the composer, and but little for the poet; both seemed to revel in a continual grin." In *Camilla* she again showed her penchant for melodrama: "Pale and emaciated with confinement, but at the sight of the child suddenly returning to smiles and liveliness . . . —then shut up once more in the dungeon . . . crying out for help to the walls and echoes . . . —screaming distractedly with a voice which had forgot all its music . . . [she would] produce a picture of passion, original and powerful almost beyond the hopes of [a painter's] art" (T). She played Susanna in *Figaro* and appropriated to herself Cherubino's "Voi chè sapete," though "never has it been so delightfully sung" ("Chronicles").

Her reign came to an end in 1813. In the opening premiere, *Il Furbo*, her voice was good though lacking its accustomed power (T). She excelled in singing and acting in a revival of *Tito* (C). And Ayrton (C) declared she again sang Susanna with "her usual and unequalled brilliancy . . . but she so amply supplied with embellishments Mozart's music, that it had, at least, the merits of being quite novel" (C). At the premiere of *Boadicea*, her vocal powers "were enfeebled by being lavished on a restless succession of unimportant bravuras," but she "exhibited her usual mime of impressive action, with unequalled voice" (T). Ayrton (C) was moved to ask: "Is it possible that Madame Catalani prefers such music as this to the compositions of Mozart?" And at the premiere of *Eroina* he wrote: "We must recommend [Catalani] to look rather more grave when she exclaims:—

'Addio, per sempre addio,
Speranze del tuo cor!'

The smile of happiness and content is surely not well adapted to these lines"—perhaps a bow to Robertson. Yet he added: "The acting of Catalani and Tramezzani was admirable."

The riot over Catalani's absence, noted earlier, took place in May. She did return for two performances, the last being *Figaro*, where she was, "as usual, a perfect Syren: the music and the singer were worthy of each other" (T). But she was not re-engaged.

"Since that period she has led the life of a kind of prima donna—errant, starring it throughout Europe . . . staying everywhere just time enough to let the wonder work its wonders, and nowhere long enough to allow of her pretensions being fairly weighed."[37] Clearly not everyone deplored her departure. In July 1817 the *Inquisitor* wrote: "As a singer of taste and science her attributes were contemptible, but in bursts of impassioned grandeur, and vocal magnificence, she was heavenly, matchless, and irresistible. Her powers rolled down upon criticism in a flood of wonder." At the same time, the *Chronicle*, decrying Joséphine Fodor's ornamentation as Vitellia, claimed: "She could have been drawn into it only by the praises bestowed on the capricious liberties which Madame Catalani had taken before with the part" (July 18, 1817).

Catalani returned to the King's for several performances in 1824,[38] starting with a revival of *Fanatico*. Her appearance drew an overflow crowd, and she was moved to tears by her warm reception. Alsager (T) wrote: "Some slight change has taken place in the personal appearance of Madame Catalani; her figure is not so light, so sylph-like, as we recollect it to have been; but her genius and her voice, although the latter has lost some of its compass, are unimpaired. . . . There was no elaboration of ornament. . . . [Her] performance altogether, was a highly intellectual treat." Critic Z (NM) agreed: "Madame Catalani appeared to us to have considerably improved in point of scenic demeanour; she participated more in the business of the play, little as that business was, and identified herself more with the rest of the performers."

As Susanna in *Figaro*, "she played it, we think, with as much *naivete* and spirit as ever," Alsager wrote. "There is an easy buoyancy—a playful grace—about her performance, that is absolutely enchanting. . . . In the course of the evening she introduced a popular air of Mozart's, with difficult variations by Paer, which she executed very beautifully." But at the season's close, critic X (E) protested vigorously: "Madame Catalani did her utmost to spoil two [revivals], by all sorts of omissions, additions, and alterations, and to convince the public that her powers will not bear to come in contact with the grace, feeling, and fine taste of Ronzi and Pasta" (Aug. 22). Yet two years later he could not forget her: "What has become of Madame Catalani that we now never hear of her? Has she flown on one of her own fluttering airs, or on the sunbeam of a smile, to some other sphere? We know not: but we miss at the Opera the divine expression of her face, the breathless exultation of her tones, her winning grace, her matchless power" (May 7, 1826).

Later critics tended to support Robertson's early evaluations. In 1830 S. D. ("Chronicles") stated: "The period is now, perhaps, arrived, when the merits of this extraordinary performer may be coolly and impartially scanned. During her reign not one [outstanding] female performer [except Dickons] was permitted on the Opera boards: foils, not companions, were what she sought. . . . Not one classic opera owes its naturalization on the English stage to her patronage."

Hogarth claimed that she was intelligent but uneducated, even in music, and had no feeling for her art. Mount-Edgcumbe considered her the last great singer he had ever heard, and he believed that her uncommon voice "was capable of exertions almost supernatural." Yet "her taste is vicious, her excessive love of ornament spoiling every simple air." He found her more pleasant in her comic roles, but also noted her majesty in serious opera and found her face and figure suited both. He summarized Banti as "all feeling," Grassini as "all grace," and Catalani as "all fire." Burgh (III, 360–61) thought her equal in comic or tragic roles—"no one has ever surpassed her"—but he deplored her attempts at ornamenting Mozart. Stendhal (Coe, p. 337), quipped: "God somehow forgot to place a heart within reasonable proximity of this divine larynx."

The public regarded Catalani personally very highly, blaming her husband for her excessive salary demands. Kelly declared: "No woman was ever more charitable or kind-hearted." In 1807, however, the *Chronicle* cited her "illiberal refusal" to sing at the Middlesex Hospital benefit (June 26).

Dickons

Another major English opera singer capable of performing at the King's was Maria [Martha Francis] Caroline Dickons (née Poole) (1776–1833). She was playing Handel's concertos on the pianoforte by age six and singing at Vauxhall by eleven (TI, "Sketch," Feb. 1819). Later Venanzio Rauzzini, at Bath, became her teacher. She sang at the Ancient Concerts in 1792 and made a successful debut as Ophelia at Covent Garden in 1793, primarily to sing Purcell's "Mad Bess" song. This was followed by many successes in English opera up to 1812.

In June of that year she was engaged by the King's to sing the countess in the premiere of *Figaro*, which required two first women, and they had only Catalani. S. D. ("Chronicles") wrote: "As a singer, she was distinguished more by the extent of her voice, and its finished execution, than by its tone, which was rather thin and reedy. As a musician, she was second to no singer but Billington. Thus qualified, she was a dangerous rival to be admitted near the throne of Catalani." And he added: "The result did anything but confirm the Italian's pretentions to unapproachable supremacy." The *Sun* reported that, as the countess, she "seemed to be animated with a spirit of rivalship, which produced exertions far beyond what we have ever witnessed, even from this charming singer. And Robertson (E) wrote that she "gives a gratifying instance of good taste, in abstaining considerably from that excess of ornament in which she too often indulges.... Her acting too gives her a decided superiority to all but Madame Catalani[!] and ought to afford the Italians an instructive lesson of the advantages which even a foreigner can obtain over them, by a proper attention to the business of the piece."

She remained at the King's two more seasons. In 1813 she appeared in P. C. Guglielmi's *Due Nozze*. With little more than a day's notice, she sustained the part of Giaconda "in a manner which reflected the highest credit upon herself.... Her acting and singing throughout was excellent" (C). "She sung last night better than usual: her stile appeared more refined, and her voice more flexible" (T). She repeated her role of the countess, but the *Chronicle* (Mar. 11) declared, "Mrs. Dickons should not appear upon the Italian stage. She did not seem to understand the character of the music allotted to her." But at a still later performance, the *Times* stated that she "seems to improve every time she comes before the public; ... she executed a duet with Catalani with the most finished skill and elegance."

Though she was on the King's roster for 1814, it is not clear whether she sang there. If not, it may have been due to a "dreadful fever" that she suffered and that "well nigh proved fatal" (TI, Feb.). At any rate, Catalani was no longer at the King's, and she and Dickons—far from being rivals—toured the Continent together, "from which step [Dickons] received infinite benefit," singing successfully at the Théâtre Italien in Paris as well as in Milan and Venice. But she sang no more at the King's, where Mount-Edgcumbe thought she had "little effect." By 1815 she was back in English opera, where she remained for a long and successful career.

Vestris

One of the most flexible singers of either sex during our period was Lucia Elizabeth Vestris, née Bartolozzi (1797–1856), granddaughter of the celebrated engraver Francesco Bartolozzi, who came to England from Italy. Her German mother was "one of the most accomplished Piano-forte players of her day" ("Chronicles"). Elizabeth had "only a few" singing lessons from Corri, according to Kenrick (BS, Jan. 1821).

A contralto, Vestris (as she was known throughout her career) made her London debut at the King's in 1815 as Proserpina in Winter's opera, in a performance for the benefit of her husband, Armand Vestris. A dancing master, he was an illegitimate son of Gaetano Vestris, known to Parisians as "le dieu de la dance." The role was "a most arduous undertaking for a novice," the *Times* (perhaps Barnes) reported:

> This lady, not more than sixteen years of age [she was eighteen], has a form of perfect symmetry, with a beautiful countenance, capable of the most animated expression—into which spirit and energy may be called upon when she will—but in which, while unexcited, feminine delicacy predominates. Her voice is a *contra alto* of the finest order. Young as she is, it has all the mellow richness of Grassini's . . . and it indisputably possesses a greater compass. . . .
> The wife of Vestris may naturally be presumed to move with grace, but there is a keeping in her movement,—an adaptation of it to the sense . . . which appeared to us to complete the image of the most faultless and bewitching *debutante* that we have ever seen. (July 21)

The *Inquisitor* was similarly impressed: "There is a chasteness in her acting which seldom fails to please; . . . we scarcely ever remember to have seen so much ease and simplicity evinced on a first appearance" (July). "Each time she repeated the performance with increased success. . . . She is already a perfect mistress of her art" (Aug.).

The following season she repeated the role and "was better heard than she was last season" (T). As Zaira in Winter's opera, Alsager reported, she "sung with more power than usual, and the audience seemed to hear, with as much surprise as pleasure, the spirit and expression which reigned through some of her songs, particularly the air 'Ah mia vita, caro bene.'" Later that season she sang Dorabella in *Così* and, Ayrton noted, "played her part with a delicacy and playfulness that were excessively charming" (C). And she played Susanna in *Figaro* "with considerable comic talent"; she has "made a sensible progress in strength of voice . . . [and] sung delightfully some very trying passages in the course of the opera" (T).[39]

In 1817 she followed her husband to Paris, where he pursued his dancing career, but he soon abandoned her and she returned to London, making her debut in English opera at Drury Lane in 1820. Though her success there was also instantaneous and though she remained in the playhouses to the end of her career, she did occasionally return to the King's.

In a "Dramatic Sketch," the *British Stage* (Apr. 1821) described her as "short in stature but well-formed; her face is handsome, and her arch dark eyes are capable of the most animated expression. She has moreover a bewitching mouth . . . and takes care to play off the charms of her lips upon the hearts of the youngsters in the boxes, without mercy."

In 1821 she sang the "trouser" role of Pippo in *Gazza Ladra*. Alsager (T) wrote: "We have seen Madame Vestris when in better voice and spirits; but there was still much left to admire. No singer of the age surpasses her in the purity of her intonation, or in passages of simple pathos and sensibility. . . . The Italian stage, where she was first naturalized, is her true sphere, and the interest of her reputation, with the gratification of the public, will be best consulted by her never again quitting it." The *Chronicle* agreed, but Bacon (LM) found her voice "scarcely entitled to the high commendations lavished on it" in Italian opera. And Kenrick (BS), noting that the alternative arrangement between King's and Drury Lane was concluded "after much angry bickering," wrote: "We cannot agree in opinion with those who think the Italian Stage is her proper sphere. To us she appears completely cast into obscurity by the simple brown doublet, and subdued style of acting, which she is there compelled to assume. The effrontery, slang, feathers, and switch of [the English opera] *Don Giovanni* suit her far better." But S. D. ("Chronicles") thought that "her Pippo was a delightful treat, and has never since her retirement from the Italian stage been adequately represented."

In 1823 she successfully sang another trouser role as Malcolm in *Donna del Lago* (T; C). Ayrton (Har) noted that she "performed her arduous task with the greatest ability; her powers of execution were never before so much put to the test." She also succeeded as Zemira in *Ricciardo* (T). As Eduardo in *Matilda*—another trouser role—she acted and sang "delightfully" (T) and "eminently well" (Bacon).

In 1824 Alsager reported that she "sustained the character of Rosina pleasingly" in *Barbiere*; but critic Z (NM) strongly disagreed:

> And Madame Vestris, as *prima donna* in Rosina! There's courage! We have a very high regard for this lady's musical talents, and we have observed their improvement of late years with sincere gratification, but we owe it to candour to declare, that, in our opinion, neither her musical acquirements, considerable as they are, nor her voice, nor her histrionic talents could justify the manager for introducing her in the part of Rosina. . . . A tame infantine simplicity pervaded the whole tenor of her deportment.

But Ayrton (Har) offered two views, noting that "none can excel her in the part, as to appearance and acting; but much of the music" was "entirely out of her compass, and in the concerted pieces she was scarcely heard." In a small part (Emma in *Zelmira*), she sang well (LG) but was miscast: she "was never made to mourn" (LitC).

In 1825 she triumphed in another trouser role—Arbaces in *Semiramide*. Alsager wrote: "The idea of a successful warrior being represented by a woman is somewhat laughable. Madame Vestris however . . . strutted as boldly, and hummed as loudly, as many of our 'mannish cowards' do in bond-street." The *London* agreed that she did "ample justice to the part in every respect; indeed, the opera owes much of its interest to her graceful personation. . . . It is, in truth, a very delightful performance." Of her Zerlina in *Don Giovanni*, however, the *London* thought that "in singing she was unequal to the part, but in smiling she far exceeded it. . . . A lady should not show her teeth to the public as she would show them to a dentist." She also played Susanna "with no great effect; indeed this lady seems to us altogether out of her element on the Opera stage." And Bacon thought her Susanna "ruined" the opera (QMM, VII, 188). Nor was her voice "equal to the music" of Rosina in the *Barbiere* (LM, Apr.). As Dorabella in *Così* later that season, she "was occasionally pleasingly arch, and throughout gave ample proof of her musical talent" (NM).

After 1825 her appearances at the King's diminished. In 1827 she again performed Pippo (*Gazza*) well and, Ayrton thought, "animated every scene in which she appeared" (Har). Her "just intonation, and smooth yet firm notes, cannot be too highly valued" (T). In 1829 Wade (Ath) deeply regretted that an engagement in Dublin prevented her appearance as Cherubino.

Although Vestris seldom sang leading characters at the King's, we must bear in mind that after 1820, all her King's appearances took place while she was engaged for leading roles in English operas. Storace, Billington, and Dickons, it will be recalled, sang briefly in English operas, but no other King's singer during any of these years, including Braham and Kelly, began to match Vestris's record in holding forth on both stages almost simultaneously. The King's critics were kind to her, even when it became apparent that her voice lacked sufficient volume for that theatre. Even Mount-Edgcumbe noted her fine singing and acting at the King's, though at first she gave "higher promise" there than she later attained.

Fodor

In Joséphine Fodor-Mainveille (1789–1870), the King's had a genuine prima donna assoluta. She was raised in St. Petersburgh, though her musical education had "chiefly been cultivated in Russia, under the guidance of her father," Monseiur Fodor, "who ranks high in the world as a performer on the violin" (TI, Jan. 1816). She played the harp and piano as a child and gave concerts at age twelve. She made her debut as a singer in 1810 at the Imperial Theatre in St. Petersburgh. Married in 1802, she sang at Stockholm and Copenhagen and made her Paris debut in 1814.

At her King's debut in 1816, Fodor sang Griselda at the premiere of Paer's opera. Alsager wrote:

> [Her] stature is about the middle standard. Her face is more English than foreign . . . and the expression of her countenance combines the charms of spirit, sensibility, and good nature. Her figure has a roundness approaching to the *em bon point*. . . . This lady's voice, though less powerful than [Catalani's] is considerably more so than Grassini's in her best day. It possesses, undoubtedly, greater compass than force: but her upper notes are distinguished for a clearness and thrill of tone which we have scarcely heard equalled, except by the flageolet; and she sends them forth with such easy flexibility, that they seem to float and riot in the highest regions of the air.

Ayrton (C) agreed, saying that she was "one of the most delightful performers that have adorned this stage" and "must be placed in the very first rank of vocal talent." The *Post* also concurred, adding: "Her taste is chaste, her execution correct, easy and elegant, and her science evidently profound. To the brilliance of ornamental flights, she joins the still greater charm of feeling." The *Inquisitor* found her "perfectly devoid of affectation in her style of acting and singing."

She next sang Ceres in *Proserpina* and gave the audience "a much higher idea of her vocal power" than in *Griselda*, wrote Alsager. "In point of knowledge, and in the more popular requisites of sweetness, flexibility, and compass of voice, we cannot imagine any thing more perfect." As Vitellia in *Tito* she sustained the part "with an energy and justness of acting that gained the warmest tokens of approbation" (C). She showed insufficient volume as Amazilia in *Selvaggi* (T), but as Lilla in *Cosa Rara* she sang "Nel cor più mi sento" "with exquisite delicacy and animation."

Ayrton (C) praised her for reviving *Così*—not revived since its 1811 premiere—for her benefit: "The character of Fiordiligi in this opera is exactly suited to Madam Fodor's powers, and she supported it with the most consummate musical ability. . . . [She] is daily gaining in the public estimation, and we do not fear contradiction, when we say that she is the best qualified . . . *prima Donna*, that has been on this stage since Mrs. Billington's retirement." (The omission of Catalani in this comparison shows how far her reputation had sunk by this time.) Hazlitt, however, thought her voice did not "harmonize with this composer. It is hard, metallic, and jars like the reverberation of a tight string" (E, Aug. 4). Fodor concluded the season with a performance of the countess in *Figaro*; she "adds to profound knowledge a refined and exquisite taste . . . [T]he purity, delicacy, and expression [of "Voi chè sapete," which she also appropriated] was deeply felt by the audience" (T).

In 1817 Alsager found her "as successful as ever in the pathos of her acting" the role of Griselda, and in "the delicacy, brilliancy and purity of her songs." The *Herald* stated that "her undertones are remarkably firm, deep, and mellow; her ascents to the highest notes of the scale are executed with equal facility and sweetness." Bacon (LG) wrote that she "unites almost every kind of excellence of which the art she professes is susceptible."

As Rachelina in *Molinara*, her "execution accorded with the character of the composer. Like her author, she made no effort to surprise: but all was natural, simple, graceful," wrote Alsager. But Hunt quite disagreed: she "overwhelmed [the air "Nel cor più mi sento"] in such a load of variation as to do away all features of it. It was no longer a pretty little complaint, but a piece of flowery giddiness" (E).

Fodor next appeared as Zerlina in the premiere of *Don Giovanni*, and "the charming *naivete* with which she performed this part . . . produced thunders of applause (C); her duet "Là ci darem" was "quite enchanting" (T, Apr. 14). Bacon (LG, Apr. 19) noted that she "was every thing the character required, alternately innocent, arch, and flirting," adding later that "in her acting there is a freshness, a *naivete*, a sprightliness which must be seen to be appreciated," while her songs are "aided by a voice, the clear intonation and command of which exceeds the present tones of a first-rate flute" (Apr. 26). Hazlitt agreed: "There is a clear, firm, silvery tone in her voice . . . which accords admirably with . . . the rustic character of Zerlina" (E, Apr. 20). And even Hunt admitted she sang "with the truest taste and simplicity" (E, Aug 3). Kenrick (BS, May) noted: "The sprightliness and simplicity of the country girl sat as naturally upon her as if she had passed all her life amid the plains and shepherds." No one thought her embonpoint a detraction in the role.

She later succeeded in *Sbaglio* (LG; BS) and *Così* (T). But when she again turned to Vitellia in *Tito* at the end of the season, she created problems for Ayrton by insisting, over his objections, in changing the sequence of arias in the opera. As discussed earlier, she was backed by the Committee, and Ayrton resigned.

In 1818 Fodor sang Susanna in *Figaro*, which she performed "admirably" (T). Hunt praised her "animal spirits" in the role (E), and Kenrick (BS) found her "as sprightly a Susannah as we ever witnessed." But Ayrton (C) found her miscast: much of the spirit of the "airy, the witty, the half-intriguing soubrette" was "surrendered in this representation." She was again effective as Rachelina (T; TI), as Griselda (T), as Vitellia (TI), and as Rosina, when she sang "with the sweetness so peculiar to her, and so exactly applicable to the character" (BS). When she "appeared to great advantage" in the title role of *Elizabetta*, Alsager wrote: "She was dressed with great elegance and correctness in the old English costume, and, when seated on the throne, really looked like a queen. Her singing was in her best style." But again Ayrton (C) disagreed, believing she could not act—even her dress was "extremely unbecoming." The *Inquisitor* also thought "her good-humoured countenance is incapable of expressing the rage and vengeance of a disappointed and vindictive lover."

Later that season she was "brilliant" in *Matrimonio* (T), and her Fiordeligi was "one of the pillars of her fame" (T) and "has always afforded us infinite pleasure" (C). On her conclusion of the season with yet another performance of Zerlina, the *Inquisitor* (Aug.) wrote: "She has now, for three years, been a favourite, and during all this time she has progressed in public estimation; why she is permitted to leave us, we cannot conjecture. . . . Madame Fodor was altogether overcome by [the cordiality of the audience]; it was many minutes before the cheers of the audience and her own feelings would permit her to proceed with the part." The *Inquisitor* did not explain that she had been ousted by the "management cabal," as we saw in "The Theatres," part II.

Mount-Edgcumbe admitted Fodor's voice had sweetness, though she never pleased him: she "sang through her teeth." But "Chronicles" thought her only slightly less eminent than Billington and Catalani. From London she went to Italy and was very successful in Venice. She returned to Paris, but tragedy struck her there while singing *Semiramide* in 1825 under Rossini's baton: she suddenly, and permanently, lost her singing voice.

Belloc

Madame Fodor was supplanted, in 1819, by (Maria) Terese Giorgi Belloc, née Trombetta (1784–1855), a French mezzo-soprano, who was derided by some English critics for Italianizing her name as Bellochi (the Italian cabal was apparently still influential). She made her debut in Turin in 1801 and later sang in Parma and Trieste. She became specialized in Rossini roles and in 1803 was singing *Nina* and *Griselda* in Paris; she later appeared in Venice and at La Scala, Milan.

She made her debut in the King's premiere of *L'Italiana*, and Alsager wrote: "Her talents are of an order that place her in the first rank of her profession; nature has gifted her with an agreeable and able voice, and its cultivation has been carried to the highest perfection. . . . [She] possesses an unusual compass, and her lower and upper notes are equally grand" (T, Jan. 27). Ayrton (C) concurred, but he added: "She has to contend against two adversaries—the want of youth and figure. . . . Her acting is purely Italian and may appear to English spectators unrefined; but it is full of animation, and her attention to the . . . bye-play is very conspicuous." The *Inquisitor* and *Gazette* were also supportive. Belloc succeeded in *Raggiratrice* (T; TI) and displayed "great talents," while Kenrick (BS) observed that she paid "more attention to the *acting* . . . than is common."

As Zerlina she "presented a union of vocal and dramatic talent, such as we have rarely seen surpassed; . . . [she] exhibited so lively a portrait of the simple, yet artful peasant girl . . . that her every look and every motion were filled with meaning" (T). But Hunt disagreed, declaring that in "sheer vivacity" she "revels and enjoys herself at will. . . . But when she is grave she is undone. . . . In Zerlina, we have no hesitation if giving the palm, every way, to Madame Fodor" (E). Alsager thought her Susanna was "on the whole, less perfect than we had anticipated; an anxiety to render the part extremely *piquante* as a piece of acting, too frequently diverted her attention from the music" (T). The *Chronicle* agreed, but added that she "makes the character too broad, it wants refinement, there is too much *buffa* in it. . . . There is also a want of propriety in the rude slap of the face given to Figaro." But again Hunt disputed his "brother-critic" about the slap:

> We doubt whether he does not reason too much from English premises on this occasion. Beaumarchais undoubtedly says that . . . she is not to have "the gaiety bordering on effrontery too common to the ladies' maids of these degerate times"; but after the cold tea of the ordinary English character, the winy vivacity of a French *soubrette* may appear somewhat extravagant, eve in it's [O.E.D.] most reasonable state of fermentation. [And the slap] is expressly enjoined by the French author: "*Susanne lui donne un soufflet*";—a plain, unsophisticated box on the ear. (E)

As Rosina she was "a less agreeable actress than our favourite Fodor," according to Kenrick (BS). As Pamina in the *Flute* she produced a "ruinous effect" by altering the notes in her duet, "*La dove prendi*," which was too high for her voice (C), and her acting was "quite broad" (BS). But in *L'Inganno Felice*, which was written for her, she "displayed more feeling than she has in any former performance, and indeed more than we suspected her of possessing" (TI). Thus concluded a very full first season.

She opened the 1820 season as Susanna and "succeeded better in the part . . . than she has hitherto done" (C; LG). As Cenerentola she was "in charming voice" (T; LG) but did not "look the character" (C). Others disagreed. She "never displayed her talents to better advantage," and "the introduction of this opera will tend to raise as high a character for her in musical-taste as that she before possessed as a singer" (T; BS). It was, however, a trouser role, which her contract with the King's specifically excluded, so in repeat performances the manager was obliged to pay her an extra hundred guineas a night (BS, June; LM, July).

Despite the support of some reviewers, Belloc never became popular in London. "Chronicles" is more negative on the singer than most other critics: she "had few pretensions to the rank of prima donna" and her voice was "of limited compass, neither distinguished by beauty of tone nor constant truth of intonation: she had no great facility of execution, and no shake at all." Mount-Edgcumbe thought her excellent in *Tancredi* but found her voice coarse, and she displayed "a plainness of person."

Camporese

A very popular singer at the King's was Violante Camporese (1785–1839), a soprano. "Chronicles" reported that she was married to one Giustiniani, of "a Roman princely family." She had little stage experience before her King's debut in 1817, having previously only sung in concerts, as first singer of the Chapel Royale in Paris, and in some operas in the private theatre of the Tuileries, where she studied under Crescenti.

Camporese made her King's debut as Penelope in Cimarosa's opera. Alsager wrote: "This lady has a tall and slender person, a countenance expressive of tragic dignity, and features, for a female, rather strongly marked. . . . [She] executed some of her songs in a very successful manner." The *Chronicle* agreed, declaring that she "possesses one of the richest voices that we have ever heard; it is full, and penetrates, without any painful effort, every part of the Theatre. Her singing is in the best, but true Italian style, with sufficiency of ornament to render it delicious to the ear. . . . Her acting is admirable, just as much as should be admitted into the lyric drama." Bacon (LG) noted but one flaw: "The higher notes appeared somewhat weak, and occasionally uneven, owing to a habit of 'mincing' the sounds, to which, at times, even Catalani was subject."

A month later she played Susanna, and "though she does not vie with her attractive predecessor [Vestris] in archness or playfulness of manner, she more than compensates that inferiority by a voice of superior richness and extent," wrote Alsager. The *Chronicle*, too, praised her comic performance, and "her singing was delightful—her round, rich voice, flowing uninterruptedly from the chest . . . gave the most delicious effect."

Later that season Alsager wrote that Camporese "gave us great pleasure" as Donna Anna; "her acting was very good, and her singing chaste, unaffected, and full of feeling" (Apr. 16). The *Chronicle* agreed she was "full of pathos; the music of this part is well calculated for her rich voice and grand style." And in two scenes, she "surpassed all her former efforts on these boards," especially in the duet "Fuggi, crudele, fuggi!" Bacon (LG, Apr. 19) wrote: "It was here we saw, for the first time, tears in the pit of the King's Theatre"; the *Inquisitor* (Apr.) thought the performance "a musical treat but rarely equalled."

For her benefit Camporese appeared as the lead in *Agnese*, when her value to the King's was "felt more and more at each successive appearance," and musically she "surpassed all we had before heard from her" (Bacon, LG). "Nothing can exceed the purity of tone and truth of feeling which pervades this vocal performance," and her acting was "profound" (T; C; BS).

As Dorabella (*Così*) she was full of "life and spirit" (T). She rounded out her first season as Sextus (*Tito*). The *Chronicle* wrote: "The merits of this lady, as a musician and actress, are now beginning to be well understood.... Her energetic, though graceful, action,—the admirable expression which she threw into her intelligent countenance,—and the pathos which she infused into the whole character, produced an effect which we have never witnessed since the best days of Grassini" (July 14). The *Inquisitor* was "positively astonished by the tasteful variety of action that [she] exhibited. It left competition at an immeasurable distance." But Hunt was not satisfied with her acting (E), and in 1818 he recalled her as "rather a correct and powerful than delightful singer" (E, Jan. 28).

For some reason she bowed out at the King's at the end of Ayrton's 1817 season and did not return until he did, in 1821. In the interim she sang at La Scala as well as in some London concerts, but Alsager (Mar. 14, 1821) made it clear that the King's was the only "area that calls forth all her powers."

In 1821 she performed Ninetta in the King's premiere of *Gazza*. Alsager noted that in 1817 she had been "esteemed in the first rank but in the interval has still more improved both the extent of her voice and perhaps the character of her style." The *Chronicle* also found her powers "extended by practice, and she now stands almost without a rival.... Her performance of 'Di piacer' was quite astonishing." Hazlitt (LM) acknowledged she was not handsome, "but never, surely did any face possess such power of instantly expressing, by sudden and beautiful transitions, the passing emotions.... Indeed, while Camporese was upon the stage ... we scarcely saw or heard anything else." As Amenaide in *Tancredi*, she was "delightful," and she again "excelled" as Zerlina (T).

In his 1821 season review, Bacon reported Camporese had "a pure, genuine, fine Italian style"; her "tone however wants, to our ears, that delicacy and richness which are essential to expression." Her voice was "also deficient in compass," but her acting was "natural and striking" (QMM, III, 380).

In 1822 Camporese again performed admirably as Susanna (T; LM), and in *Dolsheim* she delivered her appeal to the king "in a very striking manner. It was one of those touching situations in which she peculiarly excels: the audience felt it and warmly applauded" (T). Kenrick (BS) had "seen her in no part in which she displays so much power," and the *Gazette* emphatically agreed. Critic X (E) wrote: "How much might most of our English singers gain by carefully studying the style of this delightful performer, who gives herself up to all the force and feeling that the situations require, instead of coldly uttering their unimpassioned tones as if they scarcely felt or understood the words they utter!"

As Agia in the premiere of *Pietro*, she was "particularly in her element," and "her tenderness and pathos in acting drew repeated plaudits" (T). But Ayrton (C) thought that, "except now and then, her voice seemed as if enfeebled by too much use." Critic X agreed: she "would do well to scream less; her voice sounded unusually harsh and metallic." Yet Bacon noted that she "gave magnificent proof of her expressive power" (LM). A month later, she took her "farewell benefit" as Desdemona and "was almost as delightful as an actress as she was a singer" (T).

But her "farewell" was a year premature. In 1823 she was back at the King's as Sesto in *Tito* and was "unrivalled" (T). Her Desdemona was "equally great, both in acting and singing" (Har). And for her benefit and final appearance she sang Zaraide in the premiere of *Ricciardo* and, Alsager noted, "never acted with more spirit—she never sang with more fascinating skill."

S. D. ("Chronicles"), who did not admire her in the comic roles she "insisted on playing," wrote: "She expressed her feelings as her education told her they ought to be expressed" and she always had her auditors' "judgment in her favour. . . . Her execution was not distinguished, except by the good sense which prevented her ever tasking it beyond what it could securely accomplish." Mount-Edgcumbe found her a good actress with genteel manners and thought she performed Sesto better than Braham or Tramezzani.

De Begnis

Of the many women singers who came to the King's in the early 1820s, the most successful was probably Giuseppina Ronzi de Begnis (1800–1853),[40] an Italian soprano who married Giuseppe de Begnis in 1816, the year of her debut in Bologna. In 1818 she sang Ninetta (*Gazza Ladre*) under Rossini, and she appeared at the Théâtre Italien in 1819 and 1820.

As we have seen, she and her husband made their King's debuts in 1821 as Fiorilla and Geronio, respectively, in the King's premiere of *Turco*. Alsager wrote:

> She has not so fine nor so powerful a voice [as Fodor], but her singing is more characteristic and expressive; and as an actress she is greatly her superior. The *forte* of Signora de Begni seems to be placed in subtle and varied expression. [Her voice, however] is deficient in volume . . . and in high passages . . . does not always escape harshness. . . . [Her countenance] is pleasing; she can boast the great feminine attraction of a finely moulded hand and arm.

Ayrton (C) added that she was "remarkable for the delicate tone of her voice, which is of an excellent quality, and exactly suited for the comic opera. Her execution and science are indisputable." And the *Champion* wrote: "Her vivacity and her archness, joined to a naivete so unaffected, have fixed her, we think, at once, in public favour." Though deficient in volume, her voice "vibrates with something like sharpness on the ear," yet it has "a pervading natural sweetness and purity of intonation truly pleasing." But Bacon (LM) thought her "below the first rank," with a thin voice imperfectly produced. And in his 1821 season summary, he was quite critical, saying that her voice "can scarcely be said to be distinguished by any eminent properties" and that its tone "appears thin and its power feeble," though her acting was "lively and attractive" (QMM, III, 381).

The next season she repeated her role as Fiorilla and, as Alsager observed, "possessed, as acting, the arch playfulness of the best specimens of the French stage, and as singing, the grace and delicacy that distinguishes the finest form of expression in the schools of Italy." She sang Emilia, the heroine in *I Pretendenti*, and played the coquette admirably. Her scolding was impressive, and her scenes with Don Fausto "were *naif* and simple in the highest degree without being in any way alloyed with vulgarity" (DM, Apr.). She then appeared as Fatima in *Pietro*. Alsager (T) noted only that she "loses nothing by her transition to the serious drama"; Ayrton (C) added that "her mode of performing" the role "shewed the greatness and versatility of her talents." The *Gazette* agreed.

In 1823, as Amenaide in *Tancredi*, Ronzi performed admirably despite a recent indisposition (T). She next sang Elena in *Donna del Lago* and her acting was superior: "If her figure derogated in a slight degree from the portrait drawn by [Walter Scott], her excellent acting and singing removed every other impression" (T; C). Ayrton (Har) wrote that her "great flexibility and compass of voice, her knowledge of music, and her animated style of acting, qualify her admirably for the character." The *London* found her one of the few "effective" performers in the piece.

She also sang the countess in *Figaro*, and the *European* thought her superb. As Matilda in Rossini's opera she was "particularly happy.... The lady improves every time we hear her, having changed her manner, and attained much nearer to the great style of singing since she came to England" (LM). "She played with a good deal of spirit. Some of her scenes were marked with a coquettish delight, which was not the less delightful, from the contrast it afforded to the usual languid and voluptuous repose of her manner" (DM). At the end of that season, Bacon was enthusiastic about her, especially in *Donna del Lago*: "Never perhaps did any singer so rapidly improve in a change of style as this lady.... She has corrected the imperfection of her tone" and "has shewn as much versatility of talent as acuteness of sensibility" (QMM, V, 263).

In 1824 Ronzi was warmly welcomed back as Fiorilla (T), and according to critic X (NM), she "lost nothing in her personal charms.... Such playfulness, such naïveté, such knowingness in handling and mastering a connubial appendage like Don Geronio! The treat is exquisite." She repeated her Donna Anna in "the finest style" (T), and when she returned to Amenaide in *Tancredi*, she "imparted to the music all that passionate feeling and power of expression, in which she takes the lead of almost all the singers of the present day" (T). She has "such beautiful execution, and is so superior as an actress that we thought she altogether made" a greater impression than Pasta (E). As the countess in *Figaro*, "her lady-like and elegant demeanour" was "in perfect union with the character," and her airs "were given with a pathos and feeling which thrilled through the heart" (T). She concluded the season "with much success" singing Giulietta to Pasta's Romeo in Zingarelli's opera (LM).

In 1825, her last season at the King's, Ronzi sang Adelina in Generali's opera. Alsager wrote: "She was in fine voice.... Her expression throughout was of the finest order" and was seconded by "fine and appropriate action." She then sang a "perfect" countess (LM) and was superior as Agia in *Pietro* (Har). But at her benefit (last act of *Romeo*, first act of *Pietro*) she omitted a favorite duet and "did not even do what properly fell to her part"; moreover, she was said to be sparing her voice "for a grand private concert" after the opera. Though a great favorite, "she must not trespass too much on the patience and good nature of the public" (LM, July).

The *London* (Mar. 1826) tended to blame Velluti's musical directorship for her resignation, but her separation in 1825 from her husband, who remained at the King's, was the more likely reason. Whatever the cause, it was still a matter of gossip in 1828 (LM, May). She returned to Italy, singing in Naples for several years, though she did return to London in 1843 to sing *Norma* in English at Covent Garden. Meanwhile she was not soon forgotten. She had made Fiorilla so much her own, it was difficult for anyone to succeed her (E, May 6, 1827), and her former personations of Giulietta (At, May 13, 1827) and Matilda (Ath., Apr. 3, 1830) presented the same problem to later singers.

Ebers found Ronzi the last of the great artists in opera buffa: "Her beauty came on the spectator at once, electric and astonishing." Mount-Edgcumbe also had high praise for her singing and acting. S. D. ("Chronicles") recalled her "extreme versatility" in singing both comic and tragic roles, and added: "Alas! that her career has been so short, for never was so much and so varied talent united in one woman. . . . Within the last ten years we have admired the acting of Pasta, the beauty and astonishing execution of Sontag, and the varied talents and wonderful voice of Malibran; but, take her for all in all, we have not met and shall not soon see Ronzi's 'like again.'"

Caradori

Maria Caterina Rosalbina Caradori-Allan (1800–1865), born of Alsatian parents (her father, Baron de Munck, was a colonel in the French army) took her mother's name and was entirely taught by her. Her husband was secretary of the King's Theatre. She had never been on a stage before her King's debut in 1822 ("Chronicles"), when she appeared in the season opening as Cherubino. Alsager (T) wrote: "Amid all the disadvantages of her situation—youth, timidity, inexperience—we think we discern qualities in her which, if fully developed, will lead to public favour and reputation. . . . It is a *soprano* in class, but with something of the mellowness that belongs to the *alto* voice. . . . Its range is something under two octaves; but the purity and just intonation of her upper notes prove that she can command much more of the scale in *alt* when restored to her self-possession." She gave signs, too, of being an intelligent actress. For Bacon (LM) and the *Examiner*, she was a welcome addition: "Her voice is like her person, slender; but has the tones of extreme sweetness and expression that go at once to the heart," and it was "completely free" of "all show of difficulty or exertion" (LM). Her airs "were given with a pathos in complete accordance with the depth of passion that Mozart has so beautifully infused into them" (E).

She next sang Batilde in *Barone*, and "her solas [*sic*] were so gracefully light and articulate, that there was no wish for their abbreviation," and in her singing "there is occasionally a murmuring richness, admirably adapted to accompaniment, and her modulation can scarcely be more perfect" (LG). Her Emilia in *Otello* was "full of the promise of something still more advanced in the science" (T).

In 1823 Caradori appeared as a stand-in for Ronzi as Vitellia in *Tito*, but she was no "prima donna," and her ill-advised substitution "spoiled the whole opera" (T; EM). As Carlotta in *Elisa*, she had the best executed aria in the opera (DM; LG), but in a repeated Cherubino she was "rather too bashful and retiring for such a part" (EM). She was again delightful as Emilia (Har; DM), but "was wholly unfitted for her role in *Matilda*: "Her mouth seems formed for the sweet smiles of tranquil and confiding love, and wholly incapable of expressing the anguish and the rage of disappointed jealousy" (DM). In 1824 she sang Zerlina with "unaffected simplicity" (T). Bacon (LM) agreed, adding: "Signora Caradori is now known as a singer of exceedingly high finish and very delicate taste, though her volume is very inadequate."

In 1825 she repeated her Cherubino at the season opening, but though she sang with sweetness, critic Z (NM) pointed out she was "insipidity personified. . . . Cherubino is a little devil." She sang Carlotta, a peasant girl in *Adelina*, but the role was "beneath her rank" (NM). She "sustained the character . . . with unusual strength and animation; her thorough acquaintance with music was obvious in every scene" (C; T). The *London* (May, June) also agreed, but still found her voice too weak for the theatre, while the *New Monthly* still thought her too "ladylike."

Perhaps these criticisms were brought home to the singer, who seems to have undergone a transformation later that season. For her benefit she sang Fiordiligi (*Così*) and "executed the music . . . with a delicate precision throughout" (T). Critic X (NM) reported: "She gave Mozart's music not only as he wrote it, but we are confident as he wished it to be sung, introducing embellishments where there were legitimate opportunities for employing them, limiting their duration judiciously, yet infusing into their delivery a gracefulness and a perfection of finish."

As Palmida in *Crociato* she "astonished" by her "brilliance" (T) and "outstripped all our expectations. We now only know the extent of the treasure we possess. . . . The accession of physical strength, too, in [her] voice appeared to us remarkable. . . . What would the Opera have done this season without [her]?" (NM). In a sketch of the singer that season Bacon wrote that her "intonation is far more correct than usually appertains to the performers of the King's theatre. . . . In point of conception, Madame Caradori tempers the warmth of Italian sensibility with a chastity that is all but English.... She reads music with the utmost ease and accuracy—a circumstance that adds very much to her usefulness as well as to her reputation as a professor" (QMM, VII, 347).

In 1826 she appeared as Ellen in *Donna del Lago* and "displayed to full effect [her] power and taste," and in a trio she sang "with a force and expression which showed that she fully entered into the pathetic energy of the strains to which she gave utterance" (T; LG). But the *Examiner* thought her still lacking in "animation and strength of voice," and the *London* (Mar.) declared: "It is the fashion with the newspaper people to be in raptures about her, which is particularly silly and ill-judged. She is really a very tasteful and sweet singer ... with an inexhaustable fund of good nature, [but] as an actress, she is insipid to the last degree."

As Rosina in *Barbiere*, Caradori performed with "much archness in her scenes with her antiquated lover" (T). The *New Monthly*, noting her "great advances, not only in the strength of her voice, but also in dramatic action and expression," found her a strong Rosina and regretted she did not appear more frequently in operas. She was again charming as Fatima in *Pietro* (T) and was successful as Susanna in *Figaro* (NM). In Mayr's *Medea*, the role of Creusa was "worthy of her talents" (T), and her performance was "effective" (NM).

She opened the 1827 season as the lead, Julia, in *Vestale*: "She has a great deal to do and she does it exceedingly well"; she "executed with great spirit" a "long and animated *scena*" at the end of the last act, and "appealed very powerfully to the heart" (T, Dec. 1, 4; C; NM). "The execution, feeling, and pathos of Caradori, may almost be equal to Pasta" (LitC). But the *Examiner*, noting she "bears the whole weight on her shoulders," found she had "neither the power nor energy requisite to a just representation of La Vestale"; Ayrton (Har) and the *Gazette* concurred. Caradori also played the lead, Zora, in *Schiava* and "added very much to her previous reputation, both as an actress and a singer. There is a modest dignity in her manner ... that must please every heart" (T, Jan. 1). Her part was "arduous and difficult, but ... her strength and spirits seemed to augment in proportion with her exertions" (NM).

She sang the minor role of Fatima in *Pietro*, for which she was applauded (T; E). She wound up the season playing Amenaide to Pasta's Tancredi in a one-act version, and her songs "were distinguished by the most passionate tenderness" (T). She also played Giulietta to Pasta's Romeo: "We must frankly confess that we cannot be reconciled to her in the part" after seeing Ronzi in it. "She is too cold and inanimate [and] looks almost a denizen of the grave" (At). Hunt agreed (*Companion*).

In 1828, her last season, Caradori sang the lead in the premiere of

Margherita. Alsager (T) wrote: "In the few scenes where Margaret soars above the weakness of her sex . . . [she] acted with commensurate energy." Even Holmes (At) could not fault her. The *New Monthly* also thought she acted with "unusual energy" and executed the "extremely difficult" music "with equal science, taste, and spirit." But the *Examiner* again thought her too weak—"her voice loses its sweetness as it augments its power"—and out of her class; Ayrton (Har) agreed. Seldom were these fine critics further apart.

She next sang Clotilda in *Rosa*, and though ill, she "gave true feeling to the music she had to execute" (E). Yet the part was of "great importance" and the performance suffered (C). She was much improved in her performance of Vitellia, though still not up to the demands of the role (Har; NM). Alsager thought her a perfect fit for the character of Palmida in *Crociato*, although she was still suffering the effects of illness (NM, Apr.). Finally, for her benefit, she sang a "very successful" Zerlina (T), but she did not please Holmes (At) because of her overornamentation.

In "Musical Chit Chat" the *London* wrote: "We beg that . . . Madame Caradori [will not] forsake Mozart to indulge the public with specimens of difficult *solfeggi*" (May 1828). Perhaps this was a hint that she intended to quit the King's for the concert stage. She seems to have sung there no more. We know only that she was married to an Englishman (Allan) and died in England in 1865. Ebers thought her a "perfect" singer except for her somewhat restricted volume, but Mount-Edgcumbe didn't even cite this defect; he thought her a "faultless" singer and a better Cherubino than Vestris or even Pasta. "Chronicles" agreed, calling her "the long admired, the deeply missed and regretted."

In the 1820s the King's was particularly ruthless with many of its lesser female singers. Five sang but one season each, while six more sang only two or three seasons each (see appendix 9). No doubt Bacon had many of them in mind when, in 1821, he exclaimed on the current lack of top-flight vocal artists in Europe: "The really great style of singing has almost ceased to exist. . . . The age of expression is gone!—and that of tinsel execution has followed. . . . We shall not again listen to genuine expression . . . till a composer, who can unite dignity and strength with melody, and a singer, who can command by pure tone . . . shall happily arise" (QMM, III, 382–83). By the late 1820s, however, such singers, if not composers, did happily arise.

Sontag

Henrietta Sontag (1806–54), a German soprano, sang at the King's only two seasons, and although she got off to a rather shaky start, not even Catalani seems to have created so much enthusiasm in such a brief period of time. The daughter of actors, she was on the stage at age six; she attended the conservatory at Prague and made her mature debut in Paris in 1821 and in Vienna in 1822. Her first hit was in *Donna del Lago* in 1823. Weber wrote the title role of *Euryanthe* for her (1826), in which she triumphed in Leipzig, Berlin, and Paris.

She made her King's debut in 1828[41] as Rosina in *Barbiere*, and Alsager (T) wrote that her performance "confirmed much that has been said and written of her the last two years." Her beauty was not at all "extravagant," as had been reported, but she was "extremely elegant and delicately formed" and had a pleasant expression. Her tone was "extremely clear and melodious" but not uncommonly powerful. She was "more florid than any other singer in Europe," yet her ornaments were not overdone, owing to her "highly cultivated musical taste." In that respect she was comparable to Catalani, and Rosina was the perfect role for her. Her "motions," however, were "not easy or natural. Of dramatic expression she exhibits no traits."

Critic Z (NM), anxious to avoid any bias owing to the "universal *furore*" over her,[42] declared her not to be "the delicate, the aerial, the *mignonne* beauty, which report had almost universally described her to be," but was more like a "stout healthy country lass," though not unattractive. She was no actress at all, even in this undemanding role, and her stage deportment was awkward, such as "the constant motion of the head . . . from one side to the other, whilst singing, and the frequent raising and shutting of the eyelids." Her voice was "not a powerful one" and, when forced, was "not of an agreeable *timbre*." The sound was good but lacked "inward emotion and feeling." Yet "she sings perfectly in tune, and the flexibility, the precision of intonation, are wonderful certainly"; her range—from middle C to high E—was extraordinary. The *London* admired her vocal dexterity and intonation and preferred the quality to the quantity of her sound.

Sontag next turned to Donna Anna, but Alsager found her acting "stiff and inanimate." She was judicious not to introduce ornamentation, "but the necessary consequence of this was that her voice had to stand on its natural merit . . . and thus completely failed to make an impression." Holmes (At) agreed her performance "wanted soul and tenderness"; she also forced her voice unnaturally (Wade, Ath). But critic Z (NM) prefaced his long review of this performance with an account of the new middle and even lower classes being attracted to the King's by the spells of the "Coblenz Sorceress" and her social success:

> She is courted by the highest of the land, mixes with lords and dukes on terms of equality. . . . St. James's-street is thronged with equipages to

make kind calls and inquiries; and the cards that are left form daily Mont Blancs on the idol's table.

Under aspects like these, a critic has to mind what he is about. Parties run high, and opinions are found to be vastly at variance, even in the same family. The Gluck and Piccini times are come again. . . .

In Donna Anna she sang the part, note for note, as written by Mozart, with scarcely any addition of her own. . . . [But] the composition, poetry, and the scene altogether require a manifestation of intense feeling. . . . This was, and we fear ever will be, beyond the sphere of Madamoiselle Sontag's intellectual organization.

As Elena in *Donna del Lago*, she enjoyed "the most unequivocal success," for "the part abounds in opportunity for the display of vocal talent" (T). But her singing was still deficient in expression; moreover, her German style led to her placing false emphases in her delivery (NM). She next turned to Desdemona, playing opposite Pasta's Otello. She was "invested with a magic pathos, and her talents are demanded for a complicated exercise of passion and sentiment, simple feeling and rapid utterance: and all this by the side of the inimitable Pasta" (LitC). And critic Z (NM) even got the drama critic (Talfourd) to review her; he noted that she acted "in a natural and affecting style, though without aiming at energy. . . . In the youthful grace and innocent looks of Sontag, we find all that is necessary to the perfection of the dramatic picture."

Sontag's next role was Angelina in *Nina*, and she "delighted the audience with the execution of the beautiful music," going through her final bravura "with her usual felicity and precision." Only her coiffure was objectionable (T). She excelled as the lead in *Medea* (T), and as Palmida in *Crociato*, where Holmes (At) thought she "sang well." She finished her first very full season as Tancredi, which was "as good as ever"; but Holmes's further comments on her singing some numbers in German following a performance of *Tancredi* are of particular interest:

It is our opinion that the frequenters of the Opera have only seen the *real* Madamoiselle Sontag twice this season; once at Pixes' benefit, in *Der Freischutz*,[43] and again in the Emmeline of [Joseph Weigl's] *Die Schweitzer Familie*. The German opera makes her appear as one transformed — all her usual coldness of manner is forgotten. [In these characters] she appears as a dramatic singer, with voice, looks, and action wholly subservient to the business of the scene.

In a sketch of her that season, Bacon wrote wrote: "Mademoiselle Sontag performs with a simplicity and ease that are perfectly captivating. Not only are all passages alike to her, but she has appropriated some that were hitherto believed to belong to instruments. . . . The ear is never disturbed by a harsh sound—the notes trickle and sparkle like the diamond drops of the brightest fountain" (QMM, IX, 479–86).

Returning to the King's in May of 1829, she first sang Angelina in *Cenerentola*, and Alsager pronounced her voice the best it had ever been— "perfect." Others agreed: "It is . . . evident . . . that her early inclination for embellishments, for *rifiorimenti*, is fast on the wane" (Ayrton, Har). In point of acting, she held her own with Malibran in the role, and according to Ward, she gave to her part "that interest which she has never yet failed to infuse into whatever character she has supported" (Ath, May 13). Her voice "is more emphatic and pathetic; it is less German, and more Italian." Her acting as well, though still too mild, had improved: "There is truth and nature in all she undertakes" (NM).

She next sang in a one-act *Semiramide*, but "no freak, fondness, or folly, could tempt the most abandoned of Bedlamites to image her the mother of Madame Pisaroni" (Holmes, At). Neither could she rival Pasta in the role, though she did better than expected, and her singing style was improved (Ayrton, Har). She then sang the countess in *Figaro*, "and certainly this exquisite songstress gave no needless exertion to throw into her part more than was required. The exercise of her musical powers, however, lost none of its effect from the tameness of her acting" (Wade, Ath). Ayrton (Har) thought she "quite mistakes the character of the music," and "her 'Porgi amor,' among other things [was] very censorable; even in this fine air she introduces her eternal descending run of semitones."

This was followed by her benefit: it consisted of an act of *Tancredi* and "some scenes" from *Zauberflöte*, the latter performed in German by the entire cast.44 As Amenaide in the former and Pamina in the latter, she performed "with very great ability" (T; C). Wade (Ath) thought nothing could exceed the sweetness of" her duet with Malibran in *Tancredi*. And Holmes thought Pamina "admirably suited to her person, voice, and style of singing." But critic X (E) criticized her for introducing, in "O! cara armonia," "that eternal *chromatic* descent, which after all has no better effect than that of *retching* set to music."

Sontag then sang Carolina in *Matrimonio* and was praised for her concerted numbers with Malibran (T). Ayrton (Har) wrote: "The gentleness, not without a sufficiency of feeling, with which Mdlle. Sontag both acted and sung her part; the knowledge of music and pure taste she showed throughout, particularly in the duets, rarely departed from the simplicity of the original." She performed Donna Anna but seemed ill or in low spirits (Ath, June 10). Later she performed Zerlina, and the part was "well adapted to her powers." She drew a packed house, and "never, certainly, was there a stronger body of votaries to the lady's cause, more zealous in their admiration" (Wade, Ath, July 29).

Two days later she gave her farewell appearance as Desdemona; the audience was, however, strangely unresponsive. Under the circumstances of her departure, Wade forbore criticism of her role but went on to say: "Her personal character and situation, the suddenness and universality and . . . the short life of her public renown, will separate her from the crowd of her predecessors, not one of whom has excited such individual sympathy, or has raised herself to the highest pinnacle of fame, with such modesty of deportment. . . . A bright, brief meteor,—her radiance will long live after her" (July 29).

Parke reported her arpeggios superior even to Catalani's. Mount-Edgcumbe found her voice "of great extent, brilliant clearness, and correct intonation," though shrill when forced. He did not think her lavish in ornamentation but noted a want of feeling and expression. Hogarth agreed she had no depth for tragic roles.

The king of Prussia gave her a patent of nobility, under which she was obliged to renounce the stage (1830). But in the late 1840s, needing money, she returned to the stage in London, Paris, and the United States, with her powers undiminished (N.G.).

Pasta

Giuditta Pasta, née Negri (1797–1865), studied in Milan and made her debut there in 1815; in Paris the next year (where Ayrton discovered her); and at the King's in 1817, when she appeared as Telemachus in Cimarosa's *Penelope*. The *Chronicle* wrote that Pasta, "with a most interesting voice, an excellent and pure manner, and a beautiful person, produced the happiest effect, and made a most brilliant and successful debut." And Hazlitt confessed: "We received most pleasure from Madame Pasta's Telemachus. There is a natural eloquence about her singing which we felt, and therefore understand. . . . Her voice is good, her action is good; she has a handsome face, and *very* handsome legs" (E). And Bacon agreed she "appears to us a meritorious singer. The air, 'Ah! per noi bella Aurora,' with its recitativo, she gave with correctness and considerable feeling" (LG).

Later that season, as Lisetta in Paer's *Griselda*, she "bore her part with considerable effect in several scenes" and got an encore in a duet with Fodor (T). The *Herald* perceptively noted her acting: "This lady has already become a general favourite. She was very happy in her delineation of the ignorant, affected, and arrogant domestic. Her style of acting is formed from the purest example—nature. She never for a moment ceases to interest; and whether she stands or moves, she is still graceful, and invested with the character committed to her care." As Cerubino she was "quite fascinating; but she sang her first air too slow" (C). The *Gazette* (Feb. 8) agreed, adding that her performance was not lively enough, though it had "a vein of infantine innocence." And Kenrick (BS, Mar.) reported this was her best role yet: "Her arch countenance and well-turned figure, are excellently adapted to the character." Thus S. D. ("Chronicles") was right in asserting, in 1817, that "some few persons saw in her the germ of future excellence."

But still later that season, as Vespina in *Agnese*, she "had very little to do and that little she entirely spoiled; her performance was without meaning and without effect" (T), and she was only "tolerable" (TI). Neither was Pasta strong enough to characterize the shrew in *Sbaglio* (LG). Finally, she sang Servilio in *Tito* without critical comment. (In 1818 Hunt recalled her performance of Cherubino as being "not very clever" [E, Jan. 25].)

Perhaps the later reviews prompted Pasta to seek further experience; in any event, she pursued her vocal studies in Venice and other Italian cities in 1819 and 1820. In 1821 she made a "triumphant" return to the Théâtre Italien as Desdemona and other Rossini heroines. In 1824 she returned to the King's as Desdemona, and Alsager (T) was on guard: "She is, undoubtedly, much improved since we last saw her, but we do not think that her improvement warrants the excessive praises which have been showered on her by our Gallic neighbours. Her powers of voice are very considerable; but her tones are deficient in . . . full and rich melody. . . . Some of her notes are, indeed, sharp, almost to harshness." Fortunately, he added, she avoided overornamentation. The *Examiner* was more positive, saying that after a shaky start she "soon showed a mastery of her art, a decision arising from musical knowledge, and an originality in ornament and expression, that fixed her at once, in our estimation, as a singer of very high order. Her acting, admirably kept pace with her singing." Critic Z (NM) provided more detail, reporting that her voice, a mezzo soprano,

> commands two octaves, but two or three of the highest notes of this range are forced and not agreeable [and] occasionally notes escape in the lowest half octave, which are husky and harsh. . . . [But she] appears to us to be somewhat indifferent to tempo: the orchestra has to watch and indulge her much. . . . Her residency in France, where tempo is generally secondary consideration,[45] may have had some influence in this particular. . . . [Her acting] is natural and unaffected.

But Bacon (LM) was more perceptive:

> She has contrived to make mind superior to matter; she has set a great example of what industry and study can effectuate; and, in spite of a voice contracted in compass, volume, and even quality, there are few singers who have made more successful or more touching appeals to the feelings than Madame Pasta. . . . Her scale is of different qualities, by which she contrives with singular art to vary the lights and shades of her tone and expression. Her sensibility is as exquisite as her judgment is mature. . . . Her comparatively plain style is not the effect of want of science, but of a purity of thought and expression which are her own.

Pasta next sang Tancredi and fully acquitted herself. Alsager now wrote: "Her forte is not power, nor that breadth of style which is deemed essential to a singer of the first class; but an insinuating softness and delicacy of expression, which produces an affect not easily conceived by those who have not heard this delightful performer. . . . Her acting was less forceful than the character required, but was judicious and graceful." And the *Examiner* added: she "has a sweetness and liquidity about [her voice] that is quite enchanting."

For her benefit performance, she sang Romeo (Zingarelli), but the press, annoyed with the opera, found little to praise except her pathos in the last scene (T; Har). There her "triumphs, both as an actress and as a singer, were certainly very complete. It is impossible to imagine more beautiful and more perfect expression" (LM). To conclude the season, she represented Semiramide "with admirable effect . . . and looked 'every inch a queen'" (T).

Early in 1825 Pasta sang in Paris, returning to the King's in midseason for a "term of eight nights" (LM, June), and repeated her triumphs as Desdemona and Semiramide, to which she added the character of Nina in Paisiello's opera. Of the latter Alsager wrote (May 27): "We think it could be sustained with more force or feeling. Abstraction of mind was finely depicted in the early part of the performance. . . . Her singing was very delightful." Hazlitt also commended her characterization:

> Poor Madame Pasta thinks no more of the audience than Nina herself would, if she could be observed by stealth. . . . She gives herself entirely up to the impression of the part, loses her power over herself, is led away by her feelings either to an expression of stupor or artless joy, borrows beauty from deformity, charms unconsciously, and is transformed into the very being she represents. She does not act the character—she *is* it, looks it, breathes it. . . . This alone is true nature and true art. The rest is sophistical.[46]

She again succeeded as Romeo, with which she concluded her brief season. The *London* wrote: "As a piece of acting, nothing can be conceived more finished or more deeply affecting than [her final scene]. How different from the whining or bellowing scene we are accustomed to witness in Romeo and Juliet, as commonly performed on our [English] stage."

Astonishingly, in an 1825 season review, the *Quarterly Musical* delivered a minority report. They thought her "greatly over-rated, both as an actress and as a singer." Only her execution was "unquestionably of the highest order." She "has not that delicate apprehension of the nicer shades of the workings of passions that enables her to portray them justly and strikingly" (QMM, VII, 193–94). (Most likely, this review was *not* written by Bacon, for in his 1826 season review, he shows quite opposing sentiments.)

In 1826 Pasta sang in Naples but again returned to London later that season to sing Medea in the premiere of Mayr's opera, sustaining the role "with great force and dignity" (T). Critic X (E), in a passage reminiscent of Hunt at his best, wrote:

> Madame Pasta is the reigning favourite, nor undeservedly so. She has . . . sound taste and judgment, and a thorough and predominate feeling of her part. Her voice is *veiled*: her features want play and animation: her limbs are heavy; but she is always in tune, her movements are unaffected, unconscious, and there is a settled and increasing purpose in every look, tone, and gesture, that from the ground of the utmost simplicity mounts in the end . . . to the highest grandeur and even sublimity. (May 7)

Critic Z (NM) noted her fine acting but averred: "Such is the effect of Madame Pasta's histrionic exertions that amidst them we often lose sight of the singer."

In his 1826 season review Bacon quite reversed the *Quarterly*'s 1825 review of Pasta, writing: "It appears to us that Madame Pasta goes on to enrich her style continually by those finest touches of art which demonstrate the extremest finish, that her faculty of transition is increased, her ornaments still further diversified, and her sotto voce execution more touching than ever" (QMM, VIII, 136).

Again in 1827 Pasta did not appear until late in the season, when she sang in the first act of *Tancredi* and in the last act of *Romeo*. Alsager noted she was very warmly greeted and delivered a "highly intellectual performance. . . . It is not that she coldly understands the fine music of Rossini, and executes it correctly—no, she binds her soul to the character, and seems to feel deeply the sentiments which she utters with heart-touching eloquence of harmony" (May 7). Plaudits continued from the *Examiner* and from Holmes (At), who wrote: "Language cannot convey an idea of the delicate beauties which she throws into the dying scene of Romeo—every action, every gesture, every tone, has the charm of soul—of a mind penetrated with the genius of romance. . . . Noisy applause never follows it; shaded countenances, and a short silence of emotion, are its apter tributes."

Later that season she again triumphantly repeated her role as Semiramide (T; At). Still later Alsager (T) noted that her performance as Mary Stuart in the premiere of Coccia's opera "may fairly be ranked with any of her preceding efforts, and were we to study for a month, we could not confer upon it a praise more ample or more emphatic. She threw a lovely dignity around the feeling of the forlorn Queen." Holmes (At) agreed: "We often hear the remark . . . that Pasta is a better actress than singer. To be sure she is; and were she ten times the musician and vocalist she is, yet would her histrionic powers leave her other accomplishments behind. . . . We have seen nothing comparable to [her Mary] since Mme. Siddons." She performed "in a manner very nearly approaching perfection" (Har). In the September number, Talfourd, the *New Monthly*'s drama critic, wrote a long and remarkable account of Pasta as an actress—most assuredly a triumph of Romanticism on the stage—from which a brief excerpt must suffice:

> No acting within our remembrance has been more worthy of critical attention. . . . She has no trace of the personal grandeur of Mrs. Siddons, nor the tremendous energy which that mighty woman was wont to put forth in her prime . . . but her style is, we dare to affirm, higher and purer. . . . She is the only artist we ever saw on the stage in whom Nature uniformly spoke and wrought through Art, as the medium of development and expression. . . . But Pasta's acting is throughout the spontaneous development of a refined and elevated nature.

In 1828 Pasta sang the full season, beginning with Zelmira, a character which "affords a much greater scope [than Tancredi] for the exercise of her dramatic as well as vocal powers," and though the story "bears little dramatic interest . . . that little is made immense by Madame Pasta's acting" (Alsager). It was nothing "short of perfection" (At). She again sang a moving Desdemona despite the haste with which the production was mounted (T, Feb. 6, 11). Holmes wrote: "With what a look did she, turning to Otello, accompany these words, 'Ingrato! perfido!'—her eyes condensed all their meaning—her relapses into tenderness, her gradual desperation and flight from the dagger, on discovering his fixed resolve, were beyond praise" (At).

She distinguished herself in the trouser role of Enrico in *Rosa*, introducing two "beautiful airs" of Carafa,[47] redeeming much in a dull opera (E) and giving genius to a basically weak character (NM). Hunt agreed:

> Her part is one of the least effective ones she has had; but everything becomes elevated by that fine face of hers, and that voice breathing the soul of sincerity.... Even a break now and then in her voice [is no hindrance]. She slides over it as if it were a molehill under her chariot wheels, and abates nothing of her triumphant progress; nay, adds a grace and a dignity on the strength of it, as if it were a new proof how indifferent to the spirit of the passage was the ground the most material to those who can look no higher.... When she opens her arms in a transport of affection, leaning at the same time a little back, and breathing and looking as true as truth could wish, her heart seems to come forward for one as real, and her arms to wait the sanction of its acknowledgment. (*Companion*)

Later that season she sang another trouser role—Armondo, a part composed for Velluti, in *Crociato*—and made "the most remarkable difference" in execution owing to its "regularity and precision in time"; and her conception of the character was "entirely her own" (T). But the *New Monthly*, with apologies to their "brother critics," begged to differ, finding Velluti clearly superior in the role. Ayrton (Har) also admitted that Pasta was unsatisfactory.

In June she again returned to Nina, with Sontag, and was most successful (T). She wound up the season as Medea, when her powers earned "more than their usual triumph." Indeed, Alsager took the occasion to attribute to Pasta's performances an elevation in public taste for Italian opera: "This lady is in fact the founder of a new school, and after her, the possession of vocal talent alone ... is insufficient to secure high favour, or to excite the same degree of interest for any continuance of time."

Pasta sang at Vienna in 1829[48] and at Paris in 1830, returning to the King's in 1831, where she sang, off and on, until 1837. Her success in *Anna Bolena* (1830) "made Donizetti's career" (N.G.). By 1840 her voice was almost gone. Mount-Edgcumbe called her a first-rate performer, even though her voice was not of the finest quality and her figure was short and lacking in grace. Hogarth and Chorley declared her intonation insecure, but that was forgotten in the passion of her performance. And Chorley added: "There was a breadth, an expressiveness in her roulades, an evenness and a solidity in her shake, which imported to every passage a significance totally beyond the reach of lighter and more spontaneous singers.... Her audience was held in thrall, without being able to analyze what made up the spell, what produced the effect, as soon as she opened her lips.[49]

García-Malibran

Our final singer is Maria-Felicia García (1808–36), a mezzo-soprano, daughter of the great tenor, who gave her solid training but treated her harshly (Hogarth). As a child she appeared in *Agnese* at Naples in 1814. Brought to London by her father, she sang in the King's chorus in 1824, and she and her father gave private recitals. The *London*, in May of that year, wrote: "At this moment there are no performers so highly in vogue in the private parties of people of fashion, as singer Garcia and his daughter. They sing some Spanish things, exquisite in their kind. Mademoiselle Garcia frequently takes the vocal part, and her father accompanies her on the guitar. The airs have a burden in which the company often joins."

She made her debut at the King's in 1825, in the role of Rosina (*Barbieri*). Then only seventeen, she was probably "too injudiciously put forward" (Mt-E), but because of the illness of Ronzi and Caradori, together with Pasta's return to Paris, the opera house needed her in order to present any opera at all. Ayrton (C) wrote: "This *debutante* possesses a low voice . . . of good quality, but not yet arrived at its full strength. . . . She has every indication of being a good musician, and though young, never for a moment loses her self-possession. Her style is as florid as the nature of her voice will permit; but the latter is not very flexible. . . . Altogether she is an interesting performer of much promise." The *London* (July) thought the daily reviewers, except the *Chronicle*'s, too prodigal in their praise. "She has considerable capacities, but her style is at present encumbered with ornament," like her father's; "if she will consent to simplify her manner a little, she will be a valuable acquisition." Critic Z (NM), on the other hand, was most enthusiastic:

> Mademoiselle Garcia trod the boards with a confidence and ease seldom witnessed on a first *debut*, and evinced the germ of comic powers, which bid fair to expand into a first-rate perfection. . . .
>
> Her voice is a mezzo soprano, mastering a scale of two octaves without effort (a to ā). . . . The lower half of this compass is of sufficient power and roundness, but the upper notes [want] strength and vibration. . . .
>
> Art has done, we might almost say, wonders in her case . . . perhaps too much [owing to her father's training]. In this respect we must do [her] the justice to say, the taste and delicacy of her passages, their

gracefulness, the plenitude of musical feeling displayed in their execution, astonished, and, we willingly own, delighted us.

The next month she sang in *Crociato* and "sustained the character of Felicia most charmingly" (T, July 1); she "bids fair to arrive quite at the summit of her profession" (E). But the *New Monthly* now thought her performance unequal to her Rosina—she "inclines more to the comic"—while the *London* chastised her for "venturing to attempt Madame Pasta's graces." They also blamed her for introducing, against Ayrton's explicit instructions, an aria written by her father.[50]

At the end of that season, father and daughter traveled to New York, where their opera venture failed. There she met and married Malibran, a merchant twice her age, who soon went bankrupt. The marriage proved a disaster as well, and she went to Paris in 1827, making a very successful debut at the Theâre Italien the next year and singing in many of the roles Pasta had made famous.

As Madame Malibran, she returned to the King's in April of 1829 and sang Desdemona. Since her 1825 debut, her voice, Alsager noted, "has acquired no addition of power: but it now possesses a far more extensive compass. It reaches to the deepest notes of a rich *contr'alto*, and to the highest of a *mezzo soprano*" (Apr. 22). He thought her personation an imitation of Pasta's—although "with such additional exaggerations of passion and so superabundant a vehemence of action, for the evident purpose of producing stage effect, as to be sometimes outrageously at variance with theatrical decorum. . . . The great tendency of all her efforts appears to be that of producing astonishment: hence the stern energy in which the character is conceived, in admitting no display of tender emotion, fails to awaken sympathy" (Apr. 27).

But critic X (E) disagreed: she was now, "we could almost say, perfect, both as an actress and as a singer. . . . She has . . . formed herself upon [Pasta's] style altogether, but not so as to become a mere servile imitator. . . . The performance throughout abounded with instances of the finest perception of character of a finely-regulated mind and of grace and picturesque action not to be surpassed." Comparing Pasta and Malibran in the role "without invidiousness," Wade (Ath) stated: "It seems to us that the performance of Madame Pasta was distinguished by a few noble and intense traits;—the effects of Madame Malibran are obtained by a multitude of fine and minute touches."

A week later Malibran returned to her role of Rosina. Alsager noted the part "was rendered highly interesting by the gay and lively manner in which [she] went through it, and still more by the native truth with which she, above all the other ladies who have appeared at this theatre, was able to represent the Spanish *Donzella*." And Ward (Ath) agreed she was an "almost perfect" Rosina: "Her singing, though scarcely of the highest order, was everywhere free from fault,—tempered, expressive, and clever. Her acting is arch in the extreme. . . . A simplicity half assumed, a gentleness that is always on the verge of something more impassioned . . . this and much more is represented by her with a fidelity not even equalled by Mademoiselle Sontag."

She followed this with Ninetta in *Gazza Ladra*. Ayrton (Har) thought that her singing, "though it manifests cosiderable genius and practical knowledge," was "often exceedingly outre; and her acting,—though it exhibits much feeling, and an active mind, is too frequently extravagant." Ward (Ath, May 20) admitted that "Di piacer" was "sung with effort but not with effect," though, "as usual with Madame Malibran," she "substituted for the difficult portions in which she might have failed, other embellishments, of which she felt herself mistress." But her acting was beyond reproach; it was "by far the most vivid representation of the character itself which we have seen, or hope to see, or fancy that we can see. It is as impassioned a piece of acting as any that an English audience of this generation can remember."

Several serious and comic roles quickly followed. In *Semiramide* she sang "with accuracy and effect," but her acting could not quite match that of Pasta (T). For her own benefit she sang Susanna, with Sontag singing the countess. Alsager wrote: "It cannot now be doubted that she possesses great aptitude for both the serious and comic style of performance [but] we believe . . . her talents are more suited to the comic. . . . Her personation was the best of that character which has for years been seen on this stage." Moreover, she displayed "a more intense feeling of the beauty of the music" than Sontag (Ath; E).

Malibran also sang Zerlina in Donzelli's benefit. Wade wrote: "On former occasions, we deemed the dramatic style of this lady somewhat too fervid and Asiatic, and her action too vehement and redundant; but [she now] revealed herself to our wondering eyes as the perfection of the vain and playful coquetting of low life" (Ath, June 10). But Ayrton (Har) complained that she made her Zerlina "sing like an educated lady, and act like a vulgar peasant." She then turned to Tancredi, and Ward declared: "The performance of this character is distinguished by all the life, and force, and variety which belong almost exclusively to Madame Malibran. No torpor nor feebleness vitiates the prevailing vigour of her style. . . . How singularly [Pasta] filled the soul of her auditory; and yet, how neat a rival, how bewitching, how talented, how wonderful!" (Ath).

The following month she sang in *Matrimonio*, performing the role of Fidalma, an old lady, in "high comic humour," despite suffering from an arm injury she had received in performing Romeo too vigorously in Paris. But others found her part unsuccessful (Ath; Har; NM).

She did not appear until May of the 1830 season, when she sang Cenerentola, and Ward noted that "some little of that redundant gesticulation and excessive vivacity, which were formerly the subject of complaint . . . have been evidently discharged from service; and her high animal spirits . . . are subjected to a control which till now they seemed to disdain. [Her voice also had] a greater command and flexibility" (Ath, May 1). Malibran next returned to Desdemona, and Ward again thought her "magnificent in the extreme. In point of vigour, and force, and variety, and the skilful union of dramatic and vocal excellence, this character will, we believe, rank pre-eminent amongst the representations hitherto given to us by Madame Malibran, and we are not sure that any of her predecessors in it have done it equal justice" (Ath, May 8).

But later criticism was somewhat negative. At her repetition of Tancredi Ward "had difficulty in not comparing her unfavourably with Mad. Pasta, in all the tragic characters which they have in common supported," and he preferred to see her "in characters of the mixed kind, which give her scope for the exercise of her mercurial powers." Alsager noted that her performance of Zerlina was "by no means an accurate one. She mistakes an awkward sprightliness, and an incessant rapidity of motion, for the amiable *naïveté* of an interesting country girl" (T, June 7).

Her repetition of Angelina (*Cenerentola*) was a disaster because of her indisposition (Ath, June 19); moreover, some of the music had to be transposed for her (Har). But she performed Orazi in a revival of Cimarosa's opera "with superior judgment" (T), and her acting was "of the very highest order" (Ath). By the end of the season, when she sang the trouser role of Don Diego in *Caritea*, the press in general was strongly supportive, and Holmes (At) was positively euphoric: "She stakes her whole reputation on a note, and is determined either to be the greatest singer in the world or none at all. Her late progress in the florid style has been such as to beat Madlle. Sontag fairly out of her field: her divisions are the triumph of execution, and show the perfection of human ear and taste. There is no doubt but she unites more extraordinary qualities and greater perfection than any female singer that has lived."

In the 1830s Malibran sang variously in London and Paris as well as in Italy. She was never taken up by English society the way Sontag was, despite her success there. Also in the 1830s she had an affair with Belgian violinist Charles de Beriot, but neither that nor the birth of illegitimate children interfered with her career. In 1835 she finally obtained a divorce from Malibran and married de Beriot. At the height of her powers, she died as a result of being thrown from a horse in Manchester in 1836.

Hogarth called Continental critics "bumpkins" for regarding her Ninetta and Zerlina as "too real" (II, 242–43). Chorley wrote that "there was something feverish, meteoric, ever changing into a new surprise, both in her nature and in her art," although she did not establish any new opera or character on the stage. Edwards (II, 259) thought she surpassed Pasta even in roles created for the latter by Bellini. Phillips considered her the greatest singer of his time.

CHORUS, ORCHESTRA, COSTUME, AND SCENERY

Though considerable praise (and some blame) was bestowed on *composed* choruses throughout our period, there were relatively few references to the *performances* of the chorus. We have noted its "precision" under the guidance of Mara in *Perseo* (GA) in 1786. It was also praised under the direction of Samuel Arnold and Michael Kelly in 1796. It was well managed in 1794 (T, Apr. 28) and "sang delightfully" in a Sacchini revival (TC, Jan. 12, 1797).

On one early occasion when the chorus was expected to *act* (*Don Giovanni Tenerio*, 1794), however, the result was unsatisfactory: "The Italian gentry must *pantomime* it more—they really stand as dull as some of our own actors, with one eye upon the Prompter, and the other upon the leader of the Band, beating time with both hand and foot like children in the science" (O, Mar. 3). The press offered no objection, as Burney did, to the poor Italian diction of the English singers in the chorus.

The singing of the choruses in *Trionfo* (1804) was praised (T), and in 1807 the choruses of *Semiramide* "were given with correctness and effect" (H). But later criticism was generally negative. In 1811 the *Times* was happy that the chorus, in *Elfrida*, "a barbarous and wearisome superfluity, has been almost totally dispensed with." In 1818 Ayrton (C) compared them to a detachment of Chelsea Pensioners, and the next year he complained that the choruses in the *Flute*, though augmented, were "productive only of mortification" (May 27). In 1820 their "execution was faulty" at the premiere of *Tancredi*. In 1822 this "ragamuffin set" could be taken for "the Newgate Gang in the Beggar's Opera" (E, Apr. 14), and they could not "keep strict time" (E, Apr. 28). In 1823 the press found the chorus untrained at the premiere of *Donna del Lago*; even the chorus at the Drury Lane was better (E, Feb. 23; LG, Feb. 19). In 1824 the *New Monthly* wrote: "We have often had bitter occasion to declare against the wretchedness of the chorus, bawled out as they were, against tune and time by awkward, vulgar-looking beings" (May). In 1827 they were a "half-paid handful of starvelings." As Ayrton explained, the chorus was poor because English singers don't know Italian and "are paid so ill they cannot afford to give their parts the necessary time and attention" (Har, V, 127).

Yet in Ayrton's 1821 season, an improvement was noted: the chorus was "particularly an object of attention, and consists of thirty-six carefully selected voices" (LM, May; T, Mar. 12). And in *Conte Ori* (1829) the chorus was actually encored — "an honor scarcely ever bestowed on a chorus" (T). Chorley later wrote that "the rueful, shabby people who used to shout their easy Italian tones out of tune, in meagre, motionless semi-circle — so many scare crows instead of singers—" were replaced by "earnest" singers in *Fidelio* in 1832.

The King's orchestra was considered better than that at the Paris Opéra, though it was somewhat smaller (Petty, p. 54). The band pit at the old King's had a capacity of only about thirty-five players, but more room was provided when the house was rebuilt in 1792 (L.S.). Indeed, in 1796 the *True Briton* complained: "The Band was so large that its effects must necessarily be powerful. We were, therefore, not surprized that some of the . . . Airs . . . were overborne by the Accompaniments" (Mar. 3). By 1817 the orchestra there had nine first violins, nine second, four tenors (violas), four cellos, five double basses, two oboes, two clarinets, one horn, two bassoons, two trumpets, one trombone, and drums — for a total of forty-two players (QMM, I, 789–90). In 1795 we find a second orchestra behind the scenes, and in 1824 there was a band on the stage.

The orchestra had two conductors. One, called the conductor, was usually either the composer of the opera or the house composer. He was in charge of the singers and always sat at the keyboard, accompanying them in all the *secco* passages of recitative. The other, called the leader, was actually the first violinist — our concertmaster. His responsibility was the orchestra, and he conducted all orchestral passages even when the composer was at the keyboard. He usually marked time with his bow, keeping his violin ready for "emergencies" (N.G.). By the late eighteenth century, the conductor used a scroll of paper or a stick — later the baton. This dual system worked well in the early eighteenth century but later led to conflicts and many poor performances. Weber was one of the first modern conductors.

Leaders and composers were paid much less than star singers. Piccinni was offered only £400 for an eight-month engagement (he declined), and in 1797 Bianchi received £600 as house composer. Composers could usually earn extra money by publishing their songs, though the Pantheon's contracts stipulated that any music "heard in the theatre" was the property of the theatre. Da Ponte tells us he was paid £250 in 1797 as house poet, but he also made profits on the sales of his librettos, which he estimated at £500 per annum.

As leaders, Giardini, Viotti, and Salomon received from £300 to £400 for the season. Instrumentalists were paid much less; in 1794 the entire orchestra was paid only £50 a night. Like singers, they could supplement their incomes with private music lessons.

The orchestra and leader received considerably more attention from the critics than the chorus. As early as 1778 the *Advertiser* called the orchestra "infinitely superior to any other in Europe." In 1787 the *Times* called their playing "really a treat of considerable magnitude" (Dec. 25), and the next year the *Chronicle* asserted: "A better [orchestra] there cannot be" (Jan. 26). It was "far excelling any in Europe" (TC, June 3). In 1793 the *Oracle* proclaimed that Wilhelm Cramer, the leader, "heads the finest band ever heard" (Jan. 28). Against these panegyrics we must place Haydn's observations, on his second trip to London, that the King's orchestra was "just as mechanical and badly placed as it was before, and indiscreet in its accompaniments,"[51] although Reinhard Pauley[52] states that Haydn was impressed by the size of it in 1791. And in 1788 the *Advertiser* was sharply critical:

> The orchestra . . . has by no means been conducted with that exactness that should be expected from that band. . . . It must be supposed that neither the master of music at the harpsichord, nor Mr. Cramer, the leader, *have influence, or power enough* [my italics] to prevail on the band to play, or rather, to accompany, more correctly. . . . The airs of the tenor and base have been played, or rather accompanied, too fast, and without harmony with the voices of Morelli and Fineschi. (Jan. 17)

Wilhelm Cramer (1745–99), a violinist, was the father of the more famous John Baptist Cramer (1772–1858) and the leader of the opera band for many years until 1796, and he was cited for both his fine conducting and his superior obligato playing on several occasions.[53] As we have seen, Banti succeeded eventually in replacing him as leader with a better musician, Giovanni Battista Viotti (Smith, p. 46). Viotti (1735–1824) was the "most influential violinist between Tartini and Paganini" and a founder of the modern French school of violin playing (N.G.). He was forced to flee to London during the Revolution and spent most of his unfortunate life there. By 1793 Viotti succeeded Salomon as director of the Hanover Square Concerts. In the 1794–95 season at the King's, he became acting manager and director of music, where his "abilities in this line are so well known, that we look upon his engagement as an happy omen of future greatness for the Italian theatre" (C, Dec. 22, 1794). But in February 1798, he was falsely suspected of being a Jacobite and was forced to flee to Germany. He returned to London in 1801 and went into the wine business, which failed in 1818. In 1819 he was named director of the Paris Opéra but was ousted there by favoritism. He returned once more to London in 1823.

Viotti's place as leader at the King's was assumed by Johann Peter Salomon (1745–1815), who came to London and Covent Garden in 1781. As impresario, he arranged concerts for Mara in 1783 and of course the much more famous concerts by Haydn in 1790–91 and 1794–95. He was also one of the founders of the Philharmonic Society and led its first concert. He seems first to have been a violinist in the King's Theatre band before 1796. The *Times* "welcomed the return of an old favourite" (Mar. 5, 1798); in 1800 he conducted the band "in a masterly style" (T, Jan. 13, 1800).[54]

Robert Lindley and James Cervetto, both cellists, and one Holmes, a bassoonist, were praised on several occasions for their solo work,[55] for which they sometimes drew encores. Lindley (1776–1855) had a long career in London orchestras. In his youth he was given free lessons by his friend Cervetto, who was even more successful. Cervetto's career, which spanned fifty-two years, included playing with the Philharmonic after its beginning in 1813. Another friend of Lindley's was the great bass player, Domenico Dragonetti (see below), who gave concerts with Lindley; both players composed for their instruments.

In 1802 Salomon was replaced as leader by Charles Weichsell (1766–?), son of oboist Carl Weichsel (or Weichsell), who came from Saxony, and brother of Elizabeth Billington. He was J. C. Bach's best-known pupil. As a child he played violin sonatas, and about 1790 he married the daughter of bass Carlo Rovedino. In his early years he gave joint recitals with his sister and composed difficult arias for her. He was leader at Covent Garden when his sister sang there, commanding as much as £500 for these performances. He published some violin music about 1805.

At his first appearance as leader at the King's, the *Times* wrote (Dec. 6, 1802): "Mr. Weichsell, in his new situation of Leader of the Band, both in judgment and execution, proved himself fully equal to that ardous task. The whole deportment of the Orchestra was managed with consummate skill." Weichsell was praised for his fine violin accompaniments for his sister as well as for Catalani.[56]

In 1812 Robertson noted that the band at the King's "completely eclipsed its competitor" at the Pantheon (Mar. 8). At a performance of Mozart's *Tito* the same season, he observed that the orchestra was "perfection itself; the spirit and refined taste of Mr. Weichsel, the leader, infuse themselves into every individual" (Mar. 22). At the same performance the *Chronicle* noted: "When [Mozart's] compositions come to be performed by an orchestra as perfect in execution . . . as the band at the Opera always are when they have his works before them, it requires only the addition of a Catalani or Tramezzani to make the enchantment irresistible" (May 5).

In 1809 Robertson chided Guglielmi for "his restoration of the harpsichord to the orchestra, from which it had been with propriety banished since the invention of the grand piano-forte. . . . The clicking of the quills, and the whistling of the cords, render the recitative more than usually unpleasant and tedious" (Dec. 17). In her negotiations for that season, Catalani insisted on replacing Griesbach, first oboe, with her brother, a "very indifferent performer"; thus "the best oboe player in Europe [was] to be turned out to make room for the worst." She also wanted to replace Weichsell. Apparently, she relented on both points ("Chronicles").

In 1813 "Monsieur Ferlendis accompanied his wife upon the teneroon or tenor hautbois, and also upon the common hautbois. The former possesses a richness of tone that may render it useful, but we must express our disapprobation of his semitone passages, which are, almost ever, at utter variance with good taste" (C, May 18).

In later years the press generally continued to be kind toward the orchestra. In 1821 it was "composed of the ablest musicians in England on their respective instruments" (C, Mar. 12). Weichsell was replaced as leader in 1819 by Paolo Spagnoletti (1768–1834), who studied violin at the Naples conservatory at age twelve and came to London about 1802, where he played second violin at the King's. In 1812 he lead the band at the Pantheon, and in 1813 he was a member of the Philharmonic. The *New Monthly* "often praised" him (Mar. 1824). In 1827 he "wrought such an effect by a ritornello, a violin solo . . . that he actually obtained an encore" (Har, V, 38). He was not blamed for unfortunate changes in the orchestration of *Matrimonio* in 1829, for "he is allowed but little control over the orchestral concerns of this theatre" (T, July 20).

While playing under him and Rossini at the opening of the 1824 season, the "orchestra, as if animated . . . to the highest pitch of exertion, struck into the introductory movement in a style, and with a degree of spirit we never recollect to have heard surpassed" (T, Jan. 26). In 1828 the band was "fuller of strength and talent than we ever remember to have seen it," wrote the *New Monthly* (Feb.), but they questioned the seating arrangement, "which has assembled all the wind instruments in the corner of the orchestra; a measure by which, we fear, both effect and precision will be hazarded." Occasionally, however, the orchestra was deemed considerably less than perfect (1818, 1829, 1830).[57]

Individual members other than the leader were also occasionally cited in later years. We have earlier noted praise for Domenico Dragonetti (1763–

1846), double bass, whose playing had charmed both Haydn and Beethoven. He arrived in London in 1794, and "his dog Carlo always accompanied him in the orchestra" (Grove, *Dictionary*, 1890 edition). He was unaccountably absent from the King's for some years but had returned by 1818, when the *Times* (Jan. 12) observed: "We have an acquisition in Dragonetti, one of the most extraordinary performers on the double bass that perhaps ever existed." The next year the *Chronicle* welcomed his return "after a long and regretted absence" (Dec. 20). In 1828 he "played here like an archangel—to descend from the gigantic to the gentle, it did our hearts good to hear how he warmed with his author" (At, Feb. 10). He and others survived changes of personnel in 1824: "Lindley, Mariotti, and Dragonetti, those colossal and unique artists, are with us; and Signor Coccia presides worthily at the pianoforte," but "Mr. Mackintosh, the bassoonist, we looked for in vain," and the new oboist was quite unequal to "our Griesbach" (NM, Mar.). And in 1830 Dragonetti was "a giant in his way"—"delicate and polished" (Ath, June 12).

Other players were less fortunate. "The hideous bassoon still continues to utter its discordant sounds. . . . We recommend as a substitute some aspiring boy, who, with a comb and a bit of brown paper, would supply the place equally well, and at a much smaller expense" (E, May 2, 1824). In 1829 there was, as noted earlier, general consternation at the management's changes in some of the players, which even affected Lindley, and as a result the band was "miserably imperfect" (Har, VII, 178). These instrumentalists were rehired the following season.

Occasional interest in conducting was manifested during the later years. In 1821 the *Times* wrote: "We would recommend to Sig. Scappa, the conductor, who acts as guide to that body, the truncheon used by the *coryphee* of the French stage, rather than to disturb the performance by clapping his hands to keep them from wandering, which was frequently done, not only at the beginning, but several times in the bar" (Mar. 12). Things were not much improved by 1824: "The chorus singers, it seems, are incorrigible, and it would be wise, therefore, in the conductor, to cease from giving notice to the audience by the noisy beating on his book, that his protegees are at fault" (T, Apr. 14).

In the next year, the *Times* (June 13) ran a paragraph, "Orchestral Discipline," commenting on the difference between French and Italian conductors. In Paris, they said, "the leader of the orchestra gives no less than three signals for the commencement of the overture. These signals are not audible, but merely visible." Thus, "the audience listens to the overture, from beginning to end." In Italy, on the other hand, the "first violin . . . gives several loud raps on the tin shade which covers his candle, and then immediately begins the overture... without knowing or caring whether his colleagues be in readiness to follow him."

In 1830 Ward (Ath), a conductor himself, had this comment on conducting at the King's:

> But to our old complaint—the orchestra. Oh! the poor orchestra!—when shall we see it as it should be? We fear never! Poor Spagnoletti! it certainly must cost him more in *bows* than *fiddles*,—for he does nothing all the long night but beat his music-book with them, which, independently of *looking* so badly, has a shocking effect upon the ear. Lindley, too, in his old days is capering more than ever; his twirls and twitterings in the recitatives are sometimes very amusing and droll, but—misplaced! Could not he and the gentleman at the pianoforte contrive to read and play the chords *as they are written, and simultaneously*? for if they would but agree to that, we know Dragonetti would not be far behind hand! (June 26)

In 1835 Thomas Love Peacock deplored the "gesticulations and *tapage*" of the conductors.

Costuming before 1800, still very much the perquisite of individual singers, received some attention from the press. In 1787 the *Register* noted improvements in *Giannina*: "The omission of the prison scene—the preventing of Benini from unnecessarily wearing the breeches—added considerably to the general effect." The *Times*, reviewing *Armida* in 1791, stated that "none of the performers dressed in character" (Feb. 11, 1791). During the war panic of 1792, Cipriani was hissed for appearing as a Frenchman with a national cockade in his hat! In 1794 the *Times* briefly praised the dresses and scenery for the premiere of *Matrimonio* (Jan. 3). In 1797 the *Mirror* reported that at a performance of *Evelina*, "the dress of Madame Banti... was grand in the extreme; it was made, we understand, from a design by Bartolozzi" (Jan.).

Rather more attention was paid to costuming after 1800, when managers sometimes shared with singers the praise or the blame. At Signora Vinci's debut in *Principessa* (1801), "her dress, though very expensive, was neither tasteful nor well adapted to the character; her head-dress was also inelegant" (C, May 6). But in *Zaira* (1805), "the dresses, scenery, and decorations, were all new, and strictly appropriate to the *costumes* and manners of the country in which the action of the Opera is supposed to pass" (T, Jan. 30). In *Contrattempi* (1808) Madame Dussek was taken to task for wearing, in the character of Aeneas, "a nosegay in her breast-plate, and a spy-glass tied with a black ribbon round her neck" (E, July 3). In 1811 librettist Giuseppe Caravita was chastised for not recollecting that no

Roman was allowed to wear a sword in Rome (T, Mar. 25). But in the same season, Catalani "appeared to great advantage in her costume. The white satin robe trailing on the ground, the ruff, the Spanish hat and plume, and, to complete the picturesque dress, the crimson *mantila*, allowed her an opportunity which she seems seldom inclined to adopt for exhibiting a person of great grace and dignity" (T, Apr. 29).

In 1812 Catalani again impressed the *Times*: "Her dress . . . was magnificently arranged; and the glittering diadem,—the head wreathed like an antique bust,—the scarlet tunic,—and the looped and tasselled drapery, gave the full impression of regal grandeur" (Mar. 5). But in 1813 they noted that her dress "was peculiar, graceful, and *out* of character" (Feb. 8). Later that year the *Chronicle* scolded her: "Why does she allow herself to be so ill-advised concerning her dress? Can she for one moment suppose, that a hussar jacket, hanging from one shoulder, with lacings, fur, and all the absurdities that make four of our regiments ridiculous, were known, or were of use, during the time of the Roman Republic?" (Apr. 12).

In the same year Robertson thought the Pantheon showed up Taylor's scrimping: "The dresses and decorations have discarded their former appendages of dust and rags" and the scenery has "brightened up" the performance. (E, Feb. 2). And the *Chronicle* deplored the shabby treatment given *Boadicea*: "If we may be allowed to judge by the scenery, dresses, and decorations, of the estimation in which the Manager holds this opera, we shall conclude that he thinks as contemptuously of it as it deserves. . . . The costume of the British characters and appointments is absurd throughout" (Mar. 26, 1813). No objections were raised regarding women in male attire, the *Times* praising the trouser costumes of Catalani (Apr. 22, 1808) and Ferlendis (May 17, 1813). In 1804 the *Times* censured the costumes of the chorus "for want of classical propriety" (Mar. 26).

Still later, with the growing number of historical operas, an approximation of accuracy in costuming was requisite. In Rossini's opera *Elizabeth*, she "was dressed with great elegance and correctness in the old English costume, and when seated on her throne, really looked like a queen" (T, May 1, 1818). Ronzi, heroine of another English story in *Lago*, wore an "accurate" costume in 1823 (Ebers; C). And care was taken to provide the exact tartans of each character.[58]

On the other hand, in 1825 the *London* (May) thought that *Pietro* owed "none of its success to the pomp of circumstances of dresses and decoration. Indeed, all the proprieties of costume are most daringly violated, and we observe the very newest modes of millinery prevalent in the time. . . . As for the Crusaders, never was there such a ragged regiment, and we are surprised that any Christian manager would suffer those doughty champions of the Faith to appear in such shabby guise." In 1827 de Begnis was blamed for an inaccurate costume in *Gazza Ladra* (Har, V, 58), and in 1830 the *Times* observed that "the curls and whiskers of a modern dandy are not exactly in accordance with the venerable attributes of Desdemona's father" (Feb. 15).

Though scenery and scenic effects were predominant in English opera, this aspect of opera and ballet performances was not overlooked by King's reviewers. In 1787 both the *Gazetteer* and an unidentified reviewer were much impressed with the scenery for Rauzzini's *Vestale*—"the best we ever saw at the Opera." In 1793 the production of *Giuochi* was commended: "No Italian opera in our remembrance has ever been got up with so much splendour" (O). Of the production of *Matrimonio* in 1794 the *Herald* observed: "The scenes, which were entirely new, have never been exceeded in splendour of general effect, nor, we think, equalled in exactness of design and execution. They are really pictures. . . . One, representing the hall of an Italian Villa, shews a ceiling designed like that of the Theatre itself." In *Alzina* (1801), "the prospective is managed with masterly art and gives a depth and distance to the *Stage*, which is perfect illusion" (C).

Occasionally, scenic designers were cited. At the premiere of *Teodoro*, the *Register* reported: "The scene laying in Venice has given Signor Marinaro [Marinari] an opportunity of giving two fine aquatic views of that celebrated city." In the first, "the gondolas and people on the bridge have a very striking and novel effect; the former are worked most ingeniously, and the latter seem absolutely starting from the canvas; the other [scene] gives a view of the grand canal, upon which the gondolas pass" (Dec. 10, 1787). In 1794 Marinari was also praised for his "practical hell" in a ballet sequence in the pasticcio *Don Giovanni Tenerio* (C). For the fine production given *Proserpina* in 1804, which included decorations by Marinari, the *Chronicle* credited the "taste and vigour" of Goold's management, as did the *Times* in 1806 for the production of *Zaira*.

During the brief fling of Italian opera at the Pantheon in 1791, attention was drawn to the new drop curtain created by Henry Tresham, R.A. (c. 1749–1814), who was noted for his portraits and historical pictures. The *Advertiser* reported: "Tresham's beautiful and erudite curtain was submitted to public view and pleased the audience and amateurs alike" (Feb. 12, 1791; T, Feb. 11). Curtis Price ("Turner") has pointed out that no less a painter than Joseph M. W. Turner was painting scenery at the Pantheon at age sixteen. (He even made some sketches of the burned-out theatre the day after the fire.)

But not all criticism was positive. In 1797, for instance, the *Mirror* complained of a lack of variety in the scenery for *Nina*. And later comment by Robertson was mostly critical. Of the production of *Didone* (1808), he wrote: "The new scenery was devoid of that classical grandeur of design and bold execution [of Marinari]. . . . [Augustino] Aglio, the new painter[,] appears to possess but very little architectural knowledge; the rough workings of the brush give a very unfinished effect to his productions."[59] And at *Festa* the same year, he chided the scene painter, who "should have known better than to introduce Roman or Grecian architecture in Egypt" at this early age. "The statue of *Isis* was one of the most ludicrous figures I ever beheld." The *Times*, too, could be critical on occasion. Reviewing *Tre Sultane* (1811), they noted, "In the Scenes which were announced as new we recognized many very old acquaintances"—but they lacked Robertson's bite.

After 1815, critics became still more outspoken on the subject. One occasion was the Ayrton *Don Giovanni* of 1817: "The moonlight view of a cemetery, with the equestrian figure of Don Pedro, is the finest thing that ever was seen upon the stage. The dresses, decorations, &c. are all in the same good style" (C, Apr. 14; BS, May), but "the machinery and chorusses still want reformation" (T, May 28). And in 1822 the *Gazette* thought the scenery in *Pietro* "splendid and appropriate," but the *Examiner* disagreed:

> The close of the opera was most ridiculous, and drew peals of laughter from the audience;—the Red Sea was omitted, we presume by order of the Lord Chamberlain, and was replaced by a most ricketty bridge, [which] with much ado [the performers] passed over, all but two ill-stuffed figures that followed them, and fell into the water below, as a representation of the destruction of the whole host,—a climax never surpassed at a Puppet-show or Bartholomew Fair. (Apr. 28)

At a revival of *Tancredi* in 1824, the *Examiner* exclaimed: "The opera is got up in the most disagreeable manner. The scenery would not be tolerated at the lowest private theatre; the dresses are of the shabbiest description" (May 23). Perhaps the criticism was effective; at the premiere of *Tebaldo* in 1826 Alsager noted that "more attention has been paid to the scenery in the production of this piece than we recollect to have witnessed at this theatre for some years" (Feb. 27). And at Spontini's *Vestale* in 1827, the *New Monthly* (Jan.) was satisfied with the "spectacle." Ebers provided four horses to pull Lecinius's chariot, but "some foolish people in the gallery cried 'Shame,'" and they were thereafter dispensed with.

At an 1830 revival of *Cenerentola* Alsager complained:

> The scenes are in a state of woeful delapidation, dirty, and ill-adapted to what they are presumed to represent. The hall of the Prince's palace

might be converted with equal facility into a barn or a prison; and in the concluding [throne] scene . . . this appendage of royalty is represented by a couple of arm-chairs, elevated on tressels, with a piece of dirty carpet thrown across, and evidently not to be ascended without danger of life and limb. (Feb. 22)

And at the premiere of Mercandante's *Eliza* the next month, the scenery and dresses were "ludicrously shabby" (T).

In the same year, we find a rare comment on the need for rehearsals. Alsager, annoyed with a slovenly performance of *Cenerentola*, pointed out that "it is utterly impossible to do justice [to Rossini's operas] without frequent previous rehearsals" (Feb. 22) But Hogan (L.S., I, cli) notes that in 1795 *Alceste* had thirty full rehearsals. Sometimes final dress rehearsals were open to the public.

Themes and Currents

ALTHOUGH ITALIAN OPERA was widely regarded with distaste by the middle classes, as we have seen, it is surprising to note the rarity of attacks on Italian opera coming from the reviewers, though they could be found in news "paragraphs." There were, of course, exceptions—all before 1800. In the *Register*'s very first review of the King's (Apr. 11, 1785), they stated that the opera "was performed to a crouded audience of dupes to foreign imposition."[1] In 1790 a writer for the *Oracle*, though he admired Cimarosa's music in *Ninetta*, stated: "This *exotic monster*, the Italian opera . . . is, we sincerely hope, near its end. It must be the wish of nature and common sense, to get as speedily rid as possible of a direct insult to both." And in January 1797, DuBois (MM), pleased with Kelly's appointment, asserted that "the active management of the Italian stage ought not to be vested in a foreigner."

The appearance of Billington at the King's in 1802 (*Merope*) prompted a chauvinistic reaction from the *Chronicle*, though it was no attack on Italian opera per se:

> It was altogether a triumph of the musical art in England. . . . The first woman was an Englishwoman. The leader of the band was an Englishman. An Englishman was at the harpsichord. The bassoons (the best in the world) were English. The French horn (also the first in the world) was English. The violincello an Englishman, and the principal clarinets, English. It showed that if the people of fashion would resolve to give their united protection to the Opera, and not divert their patronage to triflings, that can only serve to reduce London to the contemptible state of a mere colony, instead of being a metropolitan seat of the arts, there is no splendour to which we might not bring this as a national theatre. (Mar. 26)

But in his very first review for the *Examiner* (1808), Robertson, claiming his criticism would be "without bias," tackled at once the detractors of Italian opera:

> This building [the King's], sacred to *Apollo*, has always suffered under the imputation of the unmusical and illiberal, who, preferring the jingle of [William] Reeve or the empty rattle of Ware, to the divine strains of Mozart or Cimarosa, have incessantly exclaimed against the encouragement of foreigners, and the ridiculous inconsistencies of Italian opera. With relation to the former, there cannot be any blame in rewarding great talents, though from a foreign country, unless that reward prevents the patronage of similar abilities in those of our own nation. (Jan. 17)

On the nature of opera itself there was also little speculation in the early reviews. One unidentified critic took note that the story of Sacchini's *Mithridate* was "admirably told in the *music*" (1781); the *Times* observed that Bianchi's "excellence" consisted in giving "suitable expression to the various emotions and passions" (1798); and the *Oracle*, as noted, found that Paisiello's *Nina* (1797) "has not an air which does not rise out of character and situation."

In 1800 the *Monthly Mirror* (not DuBois) summarized what they regarded as an ideal opera in reviewing Sarti's *Alessandro*:

> If *scenery*, which displays, in picturesque variety, the grand conception of the artist . . . — if *music*, replete with all that can entrance the mind of the hero it is supposed to subdue, and lead it, in rapid whirl, through all the variety of opposing passions . . . — If *graceful action* . . . is presented with a striking theme: — If all these qualities deserve a warm and marked encomium, such are combined in the serious opera of *Alessandro e Timoteo*, and that encomium must not be withheld. (Apr.)

A similar view comes from a *Chronicle* review of January 16, 1804: "As a school for the arts, an opera is an object of national importance. It presents the most beautiful living pictures to the eye . . . and its powers of creation are unlimited. It thus seeks to present the most captivating forms to the artist, while by the united force of poetry, painting, music and action, it possesses an irresistible influence on our hearts." But in 1808 Robertson again went to the heart of the problem: "The improprieties and absurdities of the representations cannot so well be vindicated, but even these have been exaggerated. The folly of dying in chromatics and sorrowing in semibreves does not appear so great, when it is considered that the action of the drama is merely intruded as an ornament to the music, not the music as a natural accompaniment of the action" (E, Jan. 17).

Thanks to Ayrton's productions of Mozart in 1817, there was a newly recognized integrity in opera as a whole. Alsager wrote: "We take pleasure in noticing that the system commenced last season, of studying to make the whole drama as perfect as possible, rather than particular parts prominent and the rest detestable, continues to be acted on; it affords at once the truest gratification to an audience, and the surest means for the improvement of music" (T, Jan. 19, 1818).

We also find a rising indignation at operatic tamperings by leading singers and an annoyance with the management for permitting it. Sometimes these were simply omissions of difficult arias—the tenor aria "Si, retrovarla io guaro" in *Cenerentola* was one such (T, Feb. 22, 1830). Usually they involved the interpolation or substitution of other arias. In 1825 Alsager complained: "But why, we ask, did the Manager suffer Signor Garcia to interpolate a tolerably good air of his own for Meyerbeer's aria '*Pace ci reca*'?" in *Crociato*. Nor could Ebers control the singers; he complained that Coccia's *Maria Stuarda* (1827) was so altered by them as to be "almost unrecognizable." In the same year Ayrton (Har) complained of "a great quantity of other trash" introduced into Mercadante's *Didone*, and in 1829 he decried Bochsa's *I Messicani* as a pasticcio. At an 1827 performance of *Figaro*, Vestris "incurred the displeasure of the audience by introducing into Mozart's opera that silly trash ballad, 'I've been roaming'" (Parke).

Yet occasionally these tamperings were indulged, even by good critics. In 1828 Alsager spoke only with admiration of two cavatinas, composed expressly for Pasta by Pacini, which she introduced in Rossini's *Zelmira* (Feb. 4). And the following year, finding *Conte Ori* devoid of arias, he even suggested that some should be introduced (Mar. 2). The same year even such a critic as Holmes could find inserted numbers acceptable: "The best interpolation we ever heard was one by Madam Malibran. It was an air from *La Clemenza di Tito*, introduced in Cimarosa's heroic opera of *Gli Orazi*, just in that place where the stilted commonplace of this work, and its dryness of melody, had prepared the ear to relish to the full the flowing *cantilena* of Mozart" (At, Aug. 1). But as early as 1802, the *Times* called special attention of the problem of unity in works that required reduction to provide time for the ballet—a matter on which they explicity disagreed with public taste:

> From the practice which has obtained in the Italian theatre of this country, of compressing the incidents of *three* acts into *two*, the business is so precipitated or mangled, that the events lose all appearance of probability, and the Spectators all chance of illusion. It would be in vain therefore to look for regularity or consistency of plot. . . . However, as the audience consider themselves as indemnified by the pleasure of an additional Ballet, it is not for us to arraign the propriety of the usage. (Mar. 29)

LIBRETTOS

Considering the general ignorance of the Italian language, it is surprising how much interest was manifested in the librettos by the reviewers. Librettos were expected to make sense, even in the early years,[2] and to contribute to the unity of the production. On one occasion, as we have seen, there were even complaints on tamperings with Metastasio. But in several instances reviewers felt that their expectations were unrealistic. In 1790, for instance, the *Advertiser* asserted: "If in a modern English Opera very little merit is found exclusive to the music, in an Italian one anything else ought not to be expected" (Apr. 7). Reviewing *Mithridate* (libretto by Sografi) in 1802, the *Post* was pleased to observe that the plot was "sufficiently well conducted for an Italian opera, in which all that variety of incident, activity of business, and contrast of colours, which constitutes the miscellany of a modern English opera, are never seen, or expected." At the premiere of *Così* in 1811 the *Times* admitted: "Custom has taught us to think little about the dramatic merit of Operas: of the dialogue, therefore, nothing need be said; but it is only justice to say, that the incidents of the fable are very well managed." And in 1813 the *Inquisitor* declared: "The truth is, that without the accompaniments of music, the plot and business of the majority of modern operas would not bear comparison with the spectacles of Astley, or the ballets of the Surrey Theatre" (June). In 1819 Alsager wrote of Anelli's libretto for *L'Italiana*: "We confess . . . no little ill will at the outset toward the writer of this opera, for having contrived in this instance to spoil and mutilate the beautiful story of *Roxalana*" (Jan. 27). And in 1830 he regarded the libretto by Romanelli for *Elisa* "as contemptible as any which has been meant to serve as a mere vehicle for music" (Mar. 15).

Ebers believed that many Italian operas were hurt by poor librettos. Indeed, because of them, Ward (Ath) thought it incumbent on the performers not to be "bound to adapt themselves to any fixed standard of the characters they support. Those characters are and must be modified as they wish them to be; for the trashy language which is put into their mouths will suit one person as well as another unless vivified with a fire which is the artist's own" (May 20, 1829). On only a few occasions, therefore, was the libretto eminently suitable for the music. In 1816, for example, Alsager found Anelli's libretto for *Griselda* "extremely well adapted to be the vehicle of music of a soft and melting character" (Jan. 15), and in 1824 he declared that Rossi's libretto for *Semiramide* "possesses more interest that is usually found in the subjects dramatized by the modern Italian poets" (July 19). In 1820 Ayrton (C) noted that Stephano Vestris's libretto for *Gastone e Bajardo* "is devoid of those extravagances and absurdities in which Italian Opera too commonly abound . . . and evidently comes from the pen not only of a scholar and a man of taste, but of a poet" (Feb. 28). Ebers (p. 59), however, was unhappy with this house poet, who was "forced" on him for several seasons by virtue of his being the father-in-law of Ronzi de Begnis.

From the very beginning of our period, we find occasional comments on the quality of libretto translations sold in the opera house. Early critics were generally upbeat. In 1785, for example, the *London Chronicle* thought the libretto for *Demetrio* was translated by Badini "into intelligible English," and the following year they found *Didone Abbandonata* rendered into "decent and intelligible English." In 1787 the *Advertiser*, reviewing *Marchese Tulipano*, reported that "the English translation presents a poem more regular and ingenious than usual" (Jan. 25). In 1815 the *Times* thought the translation of *Proserpina* "(a matter certainly not unimportant to one half of the audience) is very much above mediocrity" (July 24).

Later comments were more critical. Bacon (LG), in 1817, wrote that the book of *Don Giovanni* "is superior to the versions of the Italian texts that have hitherto been presented to the public," though "there is still room for further improvements" (Apr. 19). In the same year Kenrick (BS) thought the translation of *Sbaglio* "surpassed [the plot] in absurdity," and in 1823 Bacon (LM, Aug.) complained that the libretto translation of *Matilda* "has caught the vapidity" of the original:

> These slovenly translations are by the way a disgrace to the establishment: —e.g.
>
> *Egol.* This is the castle—Where, inaccessible
> He commands—that terrible man,
> Of madmen, the maddest—the most eccentric,
> Who by his followers scarce ever's seen.
> Who, always arm'd—and always fierce,
> With face of terror—threatens all,
> And knows not what—soft pity means.
> *Chorus.* What a strange fellow! Ha, ha ha!

In 1830 Alsager, complaining about inaccurate librettos, wrote: "The English portion of readers of the libretto would be much obliged to the translators if they would give the translations in plain English, and even avoid the form of blank verse, which they usually adopt" (Mar. 29). (This position is similar to Stendhal's—Coe, p. 74n.)

In 1819 Alsager commented on the inherent problem of opera translations, to which he was prompted by a performance of *Il Flauto Magico*. The opera, he wrote, was originally composed to German words, and so extensive has been its career of popularity, that . . . there was no German, possessing the least knowledge of music, that did not retain all of its beautiful airs in his memory. The difficulty of translating an opera, and of applying another language to the same music, where all the niceties of accent are to be preserved, is very great; it was early overcome, however, in the instance of *The Magic Flute*, and its translation into Italian, which in music ranks as a universal language, diffused it over the rest of Europe. (May 27)

RECITATIVE

Sporadically throughout these years we find protests against recitative — that bugbear to English taste. Of the pasticcio *Teodolinda* (1793), the *Times* observed: "It is only a repetition of the same dull recitative that hangs heavy both on the actors and the audience" (Mar. 30). In 1794 Cimarosa's Matrimonio had "the praise of not distressing the audience by too much recitative" (P). In 1795 the recitative in Bianchi's *Aci e Galatea* was "sometimes heavy and tedious" (TC). And in 1797 a reviewer found "languor" was "inseparable from the recitative" in Guglielmi's *Amor*. In 1781 attempts were made by Morigi to "interlace" English with Italian in his recitatives in Anfossi's *Viaggiatori*, and in 1800, Paisiello's *Nina* was presented "as it was originally performed at Paris and afterwards in Vienna, without the recitatives in music, but the words to be spoken in declamation the same as English opera, . . . which will undoubtedly leave it more in the power of the performers to render by their action, the drama itself more interesting to the audience" (C). As Mount-Edgcumbe explained, this "experiment" was illegal, and the patent theatres forced the King's to put an end to it.

After 1800 these complaints diminished somewhat. Billington, as we have seen, succeeded in raising recitative "from its accustomed level" (T, Dec. 6, 1802), and in her recitative she "soared above all competition." In 1804 Grassini "displayed true judgment, taste and feeling in her recitative" (T, Jan. 16 and Feb. 6). To be sure, the *Chronicle* was pleased with the considerable curtailments of the recitative in Winter's *Trionfo*: "The ear of an English audience is not sufficiently habituated to the science to enjoy the charms of difficult execution for a length of time" (Mar. 26, 1804). But in their review of Guglielmi's *Atalida* (1810), the *Chronicle* wrote: "Those who affect to doubt the powers of musical declamation over the heart, and who think that recitative can never be eloquent, have only to sit under the influence of Catalani and Tramezzani in this Opera." Reviewers also gave high praise to the recitative in *Festa* (1808), and in 1813 Ayrton (C) found the recitative sung by Tramezzani in *Così* "one of the finest specimens of musical declamation we ever heard."

In 1817, commenting on the superior recitative in *Agnese*, Alsager observed: "Once allow for the elevation of recitative above ordinary dialogue, and we obtain a natural gradation of sentiment and passion, without that abruptness which attends the transition from speaking to singing, there is then a certain congruity between the parts and the whole, without which no production will bear the scrutiny of taste" (T, May 19). (After 1815 English opera reviewers occasionally argued for the replacement of dialogue with recitative—see part III.)

ACTING

As we have seen, acting in Italian opera became very important in later years. But S. D. ("Chronicles") was not accurate in asserting that "histrionic talent was not then [c. 1800] looked for on the boards of the King's Theatre."[3] As early as 1787, the *Register* acknowledged a need for better acting (Jan. 29) and was grateful to Morelli for omitting the "grimace and buffoonery of foreign schools" (Dec. 17). And Banti's acting was generally admired, though, as we have seen, she had to be chastised for talking to members of the orchestra. Among later divas, critics agreed that Billington and Gerbini were poor actresses; Bolla, Bertinotti, and Ferlendis were good; and Grassini's tragic performances were even comparable to Sarah Siddons's. Among the men, Braham was regarded as a poor actor initially, but he had become more animated by 1816. Tramezzani was a graceful tragic actor who found he could do well in comedy, while there was considerable discussion about the acting skill of Naldi in buffo parts.

Still later, the appearance of such artists as Pasta and Malibran, Ambrogetti and Donzelli, lent a powerful stimulus to reviewers on the art of acting in opera. Some recognized, for example, that Pasta was "founder of a new school" and created the taste by which she was to be appreciated. But well before her appearance, Alsager found a watershed in the Ayron production of *Don Giovanni* in 1817, "since, independently of the improvement it will have effected in the national taste, it serves to mark the introduction of good acting, of pure dramatic effect, hitherto neglected entirely on this stage, or confined to one performer" (May 28). By 1829 even a revival of *Gazza Ladra* could have an outstanding dramatic impact from the entire company. As Ward wrote: "Each of the *dramatis personae* seemed to forget the inveterate maxim, that operatic singers are automatic in all respects but with regard to their throats; on the contrary, arms, legs, gesture, attitudes, expression, feeling, passion, were employed as though probability were considered of some insight, and scenic illusion a matter not too low for even the *artistes* of the King's Theatre" (Ath, Apr. 15). We have already noticed the importance placed on acting in ensembles (C, Mar. 15, 1830). Reviewers were not blinded by the divas; even Pasta was not beyond criticism

ORNAMENTATION

A powerful voice was the single most important asset of singers, and most unsuccessful singers failed for lack of one. Vocal agility and an "expressive manner" were also important in the leading singers.

Shifts in the degree of ornamentation are difficult to detect with any precision. Petty states that vocal embellishments "died a slow death" in London and Europe toward the end of the eighteenth century; yet Mount-Edgcumbe thought Marchesi's embellishments simple compared with later times. In any event we find that some of the male singers had to be cautioned against that practice: Marchesi in 1788 (G and PA, Apr. 7; P Apr. 14); Lazzarini in 1792 (O, June 11); and Morelli in 1793 (O, Jan. 28). Among the prima donnas, certainly Catalani was the worst offender, prompting Robertson to explain, in his review of *Orazi*, that "the mischief of exuberant ornament is, that it levels all music to one character, and produces a fatiguing monotony. It is indeed remarkable that few singers seem aware how impolitic it is to exhibit the whole extent of their talent on every occasion, without accommodating their style to the nature of the composition" (E, June 5). Ayrton (C) seemed reluctant to criticize her for it, even in *Figaro*, but by 1821 she was "florid to the highest degree" in her concerts, and even Mount-Edgcumbe strongly complained. On the other hand, Grassini was praised for setting "execution at defiance," and Bertinotti had no need of "dazzling faculties" and the "modern practice" of exalting powers of execution.

Later critics also showed a certain dichotomy on florid singing. As we have seen, Alsager (T) thought embellishments a "profanation" in performing Mozart (Hogarth agreed, II, 242–43), but critic Z (NM, June 1825) believed there were legitimate opportunities for employing them in *Così*—again Alsager disagreed (May 13, 1825). In 1819 Alsager found that "the greatest defect of Rossini was the extreme florid style of his compositions" (Jan. 30), and Pasta had learned not to "overlay the work of the composer by . . . ornament" (Apr. 26, 1824). But in 1828 he thought Sontag's ornaments not excessive, for they were executed "with taste," and the next year he complimented Malibran on "the introduction of a great deal of tasteful and appropriate ornament" in her role of Desdemona (Apr. 27).

There were also differences of opinion in the press on the ornamentation of the same singer at the same performance. In general, the balcony audience delighted in vocal showmanship,+ while the amateurs remained unimpressed; but when a singer such as García, in his last seasons, succeeded in uniting the press against him for this fault, the public was not slow to follow. Parke, incidentally, noted the difficulty for the instrumentalists in accompanying singers who introduced many embellishments.

Some English opera singers were effective in Italian opera, though none could match Billington. Alsager asserted in 1821 that Vestris "belonged" at the King's (Mar. 12), and Mrs. Gattie-Hughes was welcome there. Yet on the whole, King's critics regarded English opera singers as inferior. Sometimes poor singers at the King's were contemptuously thought not to be worthy even of places at the English theatres (LM, July 1825; T, Aug. 2, 1829), and fine singers such as Camporese were held up as models to English singers, who "utter their impassioned tones as if they scarcely felt or understood the words they utter" (E, Jan. 27, 1822).

In 1825 Bacon explored the difference between the two styles:

> Italians concentrate — the English dissipate their powers. The former rarely quit the music of their own composers — the latter on the contrary aspire to be at once Italian and English singers in all styles, the church, the orchestra, the theatre, and the chamber. Hence, we view with little surprise the diversity of style, or rather the absence of any decided characteristic style in our native vocalists. (QMM, VII, 347)

"SCIENCE"

One interesting clue to shifting musical taste is the use in reviews of the terms "science" and "scientific" with respect to music. Before 1800, for example, the reviews sometimes merely carry an honorific judgment on the degree of knowledge of music that has been acquired by the composer or performer through study. In this sense, Mara was a "scientific" singer (1787), and Sarti's arias were "scientific" (1793). Bianchi had "much taste and performed science" (1795), and a Salieri opera was "scientific and original" (1798). Tarchi's music was "scientific and interesting" and "must therefore have had more admirers" (1789).

Yet in other instances, "science" implied a certain difficulty in music. In 1787 Paisiello's music, although "scientific and solid" was "not altogether so airy and alluring as his former productions"; in 1789 Tarchi's music was "rather scientific than affecting"; and in 1796 Mazzinghi's airs had "the engaging merits of ease and familiarity, and yet they are scientific and elegant." The manifestation of science occasionally implied an absence of melody. Paisiello had "more science and less airs" than heard before (1787), and Cimarosa had "great science" but "no airs." In that respect "science" was more appealing to the more sophisticated listeners. In 1784, for example, Anfossi's opera was "full of science and to the connoisseur has greater recommendations than to the common ear," while Paisiello had "too much science for the many" (1787). In 1798 Bianchi's opera "adds greatly to his fame, not perhaps with the multitude, but with those skilled in the science" (P, Feb. 21). Indeed, at times it appeared that too much science was rather anti-English. In 1788 the *World* stated: "In England they have the credit of neglecting Science, when it . . . ceases to be subordinate to SENSATION" (Apr. 7). Similarly, in 1795, the *Chronicle* asserted: "Whatever we may pretend, we are too ignorant of musical science as a nation, to find pleasure in what produces rapture in an Italian stage" (Apr. 15).

ITALIAN/GERMAN SCHOOLS

We can also see, in these years, a hint of the Italian school/German school dichotomy, with which the press was very much concerned after 1800. As early as 1787, the *Herald* found Mara's German style of singing somewhat inferior to the Italian *cantabile*, and the next year the *Advertiser* pointed out that Storace favored the "German style" over the "usual plan of Italian" composers. By 1800 DuBois (MM) was contrasting Haydn's "masterly style" with the "*monotonous* and *wire-drawn* sing-song of the Italian school."

After 1800 the German school was often regarded negatively and confounded with too much science. It was representative of the "modern school of composers, who fall into the error of astonishing rather than delighting" (T, Mar. 2, 1801). Nasolini, like Bianchi, "does not lavish his powers in the invention of difficulties, which rather surprise than affect" (T, Mar. 29, 1802), and his *Mithridate* was "destitute of all the thunder and crash of our modern compositions of this kind" (T, Feb. 24, 1802). *Vergine* was "distinguished for sound science and correctness of taste" (T, Jan. 16, 1804). And even difficulty was not objectionable in *Trionfo*, for Winter displayed "a depth of science, which surmounts the greatest of difficulties of the art, and softens them with the most affecting and natural expressions" (T, Mar. 26, 1804). We have already observed the *Chronicle*'s ambiguity regarding the Germanic influence in this opera.

A positive shift toward science was noticeable at the revival of Bach's *Scipione*, which was "the work of a great genius, uniting at once all the science and energy of the German school with the delicacy and expession of the Italian" (T, Mar. 29, 1805). Even Robertson looked for a careful balance between the two schools. He found that Paisiello's *Frascatana* had "science" that "enriches without fatiguing the ear" (Jan. 17, 1808), while Cimarosa's *Capriccio* owed its superiority to its link between the two schools (Apr. 10, 1808). In 1811 *Elfrida* "never forsakes its original tenderness" even when "it rises to its richer style" (T, June 26), but in 1813 the same opera was made "dull" by a "laborious simplicity" (T, Feb. 8). We have already noted Barnes's (T) shift on *Tito* in 1812, when it "might have persuaded the admirers of the unmitigated German school, that taste, nature, and simplicity might in some instances, at least, be advantageously substituted for chromatics and cadences, the crashing of disjointed harmonies, and the array of scientific discordance" (Mar. 5). Obviously, Mozart here was no exponent of the German school. Yet eleven days later he wrote: "Whoever wishes to feel the manly delight of manly interest, should turn from the languid elegance of Italy . . . to the rudeness of German genius" (Mar. 16).

After 1815 the press leaned still more strongly toward the German school. These attitudes were intensified by the performances of Cimarosa and Paisiello in 1817 and 1818, just as Mozart was becoming popular. In 1817 Bacon (LG) thought that Cimarosa's *Penelope* "partakes to a certain degree of the common fault of the present Italian School, a want of originality in ideas, and of striking effects" (Jan. 25). Yet two months later he cautioned: "It has of late become fashionable to decry *indiscriminately* the best musical productions of the Italian School. This we consider not only as indicative of a want of good taste, but as a piece of ingratitude toward a country from which . . . we have derived . . . the greatest portion of our musical treasures" (Mar. 15). Of Paisiello's *Molinara* the same year, the *Chronicle* wrote:

> In sublimity the music of Italy, generally speaking, does not succeed in any degree comparable to that of Germany, wherein the orchestra [makes] so important a part in supporting the melody and illustrating the poetry; and not in smothering the one and punning upon the other, as some persons have alleged, whose impatient admiration of that species of music in which they were . . . initiated, prevents them from examining and cultivating the more modern improvements in harmony and instrumental accompaniment. (March 10)

In 1818 Alsager, again reviewing *Molinara*, found Paisiello's resources "too limited, he repeats the same idea too often," though it was not a "fault" that he "does not possess richness of harmony and modulation, since he disclaimed them both upon principle" (Feb. 29; see also Feb. 17, 1819). And at a revival of *Matrimonio* later that season he explained Cimarosa's "cold reception": "Cimarosa, little skilled in, or little solicitous about the effects of the orchestra, except as mere accompaniment, has placed all his attraction on the stage. . . . With the sublime composer of

Don Giovanni and *Figaro*, a different system prevails; and whether we choose to bestow on the orchestra, or the singers, our exclusive attention, we may imbibe a distinct perception of beauty." (In 1829 critic Z [NM, Aug.] quoted Grétry: "Cimarosa put the statue on the stage, the pedestal in the orchestra; Mozart put the pedestal on the stage, the statue in the orchestra.") Other Italian composers were also reflecting this change in taste. At the premiere of Paer's *Griselda* in 1816, Ayrton (C) wrote: "To admirers of the Italian school, this opera will afford a luxurious treat; it is replete with beautiful melodies. . . . Paer, however, has enriched his Opera by more harmony than Paisiello admitted. . . . The former has tasted of the German stream" (Jan. 15; cf. TI, Apr. 1819).

Neither were all reviewers swept away by the German school. In 1818 Hunt had one foot in each school:

> The great excellence of the Italian school (which with all our admiration of Mozart appears to us to be much undervalued now-a-days, partly owing to the undoubted merit in the German school, and partly to a court fashion[5] for that school) consists in fine melody and expression. They take up one passion after another, and give you the genuine elementary feeling of it. . . . Paisiello's compositions are special instances of this power of expression. His melodies are exquisitely graceful, touching, and original; and his recitatives always appear to us so extremely to the purpose, as to be superior even to those of that delightful German by nation, and Italian by nature, Mozart. (E, Mar. 22)

The advent of Rossini in the same year prompted mixed feelings on whether the German influence was going too far. At the premiere of *Elizabetta*, Ayrton (C), who was generally critical of the composer, waxed quite enthusiastic:

> Rossini has had the adroitness to take advantage of this change in the taste of his countrymen, and released them from the thraldom in which the national vanity held their opinion. He has introduced into Italy the German school of accompaniment;[6] but then he is an Italian, and thus a veil is thrown over a truth which would have been intolerable had it been abruptly and undisguisedly exposed to view. Rossini, therefore, is entitled to the credit of duly appreciating, and boldly adopting, a style in which Handel, the Bachs, Haydn, and Mozart have shone so resplendidly. (May 4)

At the 1824 premiere of *Zelmira*, however, he had misgivings, for the accompaniments "are, generally, more powerful than any vocal strength can bear up against; they give no quarter to the voice. Here, then, is the very fault which the Italians have always imputed to Mozart, though very unjustly, and to the school of Germany." In the same year, Alsager found *Semiramide* "too obtrusely and elaborately scientific to please the million," though the work became very popular.

Again in 1829 Alsager (T) wrote in an end-of-season review, of public apathy toward the operas presented: "For, whatever may be alleged to the contrary, the fact is undoubted, that . . . English audiences have never been collected for a long period of time by amusements chiefly depending for their [attraction] upon musical science and elaborate combinations" (Aug. 3). And in 1830, at still another *Matrimonio*, he thought the decline in popularity of Cimarosa's operas was "more ascribable to that frequency of repetition which finally satiates the taste . . . than to any decided superiority in the more complicated compositions of the school by which he has been superseded" (Jan. 25).

Though Mount-Edgcumbe did not speak specifically of the German or Italian schools, this shift in taste undoubtedly lay behind his admission, in 1834, that his taste was "old-fashioned" and that for the past twenty years he no longer took much pleasure in opera, which had undergone a great shift from "the good old style" — by this time obsolete. What he missed was "the genuine, unsophisticated expression of really fine music." S. D. ("Chronicles") dismissed him as "one of that class of dilettanti who took nearly twenty years to consider whether Mozart was worthy of a hearing" — a stricture that editor Ayrton (Har) mitigated in a footnote. But Hogarth, like Mount-Edgcumbe, also regretted the change in taste: "In Italy, all we make account of is melody, and employ modulation only to heighten the expression of words. In Germany, whatever be the case, or from a consciousness of inferiority to us in respect to song, they make little account of melody. . . . Hence, they are obliged to have recourse to elaborate harmonies to supply the defect."

The battle, of course, continued long after 1830. As Grout sums it up, "The old struggle between Latin and German, southern and northern music in opera — the singer against the orchestra, melody against polyphony, simplicity against complexity — was incarnate in the nineteenth century in the works of Verdi and Wagner."

ATTITUDES TOWARD AMATEURS AND PUBLIC

Despite the allegiance of the press to the taste of the amateurs during the early years, there was little marked divergence between the views of amateurs, public, or press. A dozen or so operas by Anfossi, Cimarosa, Cherubini, Tarchi, Paisiello, Bianchi, Martín, and Sarti performed during those years—all of which were praised by amateurs—were also praised by the press, and all but one were successful. The public even supported a few operas, like Cherubini's *Ifigenia*, that were too scientific for the press. One exception that the amateurs did *not* like—Cimarosa's *Locandiera*—received fairly good praise from the press and was supported by the public. Thus, the evidence suggests that the public, no less than the amateurs and the reviewers, learned to accommodate to its taste the growing complexity of music.

Even after 1800, when the reviewers were beginning to express moderate criticism of the public and the amateurs, the evidence shows large areas of unanimity. Of the fifty-odd operas presented, only ten showed a marked divergence between public and press; of these, half were successful, though criticized by the press (three succeeded because of the performers), and half failed, despite praise from the press (including three of Paer's operas and *Figaro*, which, as we have seen, was ultimately very successful). There was also considerable unanimity of opinion, *pace* Robertson, within the press itself.

Yet reviewers showed a growing independence with respect to the public and an increased concern with musical taste. In 1794, for example, the *True Briton* (Dec. 8) wrote: "We are far . . . from thinking that [Paisiello's *Molinara*] is one of his happiest productions, as the greatest part of the Music was heard with very faint applause, and only one song was encored." But three years later the *Times* asserted that the musical taste of the public was "not of the most polished kind," and in 1802 they flatly disagreed with the public's demand for ballet at the expense of the integrity of the operas. In 1813 Ayrton (C) generated a remarkable review (*Boadicea*), deploring the low state to which opera had sunk during the Catalani years and placing the blame on the public, managers, and performers:

> When it is considered that there are many of the finest operas of the greatest masters which have never been performed in this country . . . is it not, under these circumstances, astonishing that a Manager should be so defective in his public duty . . . as to bring out an opera that he surely must be aware does not possess any one merit? . . .
>
> The fault is with the subscribers and with the public, whose apathy in whatever concerns the stage, whether Italian or English, increases daily. . . . Managers and performers now govern the public; they are suffered to controul the taste and judgment of every audience, and they will finally destroy both if some powerful hand is not raised to protect them. This protection may be afforded by the press, and we call upon our brother journalists to aid us in our efforts for this purpose. Our desire is not to injure individuals, but to support the Arts. (Mar. 26)

The same year the *Inquisitor* complained bitterly about both management and audience.

Even in the 1820s, when the press was often outspoken against public taste and the amateurs, there was little real divergence of views. As noted earlier, the opinions of the periodicals on Rossini by and large coincided with those of the public, as determined by the box-office success or failure of his operas. And, despite occasional disagreeements among the reviewers in the face of radical changes in opera styles, they were much more often than not in basic agreement with each other.

After 1817 and *Don Giovanni*, increasing numbers of the unfashionable began to attend the King's. In 1818 the *Inquisitor* pointed out that "the Italian opera of this city is at present in a more flourishing condition than it has been for many preceding years, and the unfounded prejudices against it in the middle and lower classes, are daily disappearing" (May, pp. 338–39). It was perhaps for this reason that later press commentary on the public and musical taste became much more outspoken and led to considerable hostility toward the upper orders there. In 1822, for example, critic X (E) was acerbic:

> What can induce the manager to neglect the rich stores of music and to rake up such trash [as Mosca's opera], with equal labour and expense, is inconceivable, unless he is controlled by the caprice of the great, by those smatterers and dabblers in music, whose vanity prompts them to rely on their own incapability, and then persists in forcing their favourites upon us, lest the withdrawing them should impugn the profundity of their judgment. There is no doubt that the opera is chiefly supported by people of fashion, and that those of real musical taste are in comparison few; but it will be found out in time, that the latter have eventually the most importance. (Apr. 14)

Further attacks on fashion and taste at the King's occurred in passages written by Hunt and Hazlitt in 1828. In the *Companion* for January 30, Hunt wrote:

> The cue of polite life is to take indifference for self-possession; and you are not seated long before you begin to feel that there is an air of neutralization and falsehood around you. The quiet is a dread of committing themselves; — people come as much to be seen as to see; — the performers in the boxes prepare for disputing attention with those on the stage; — men lounge about the allies, looking so very easy, that they are evidently full of constraint; the looks of the women dispute one another's pretensions; . . . in short, you feel that the great majority of the persons around you have come to the Opera because it *is* the Opera, and not from any real love of music and the graces.

Four months later Hazlitt delivered a blistering essay-type review for the *Examiner* (May 4),[7] from which a brief passage must suffice:

> In a word the question comes down to this—*Are the English an essentially vulgar people or not*? If all that they have of their own is vulgar and unworthy of the notice of the upper classes, then the unavoidable inference is that the upper classes themselves are unworthy to see anything better, and are the most vulgar, fashionable audience in Europe. . . . Is Madame Pasta a favourite with the great vulgar? Not in the least. They hear her fame, but not her. What piteous, vacant aspects in the fine gentleman in the pit the first night of Madamoiselle Sontag's appearance! And what would they not have given (before committing themselves beyond an applause which might be construed into a good-natured encouragement) to know what the newspapers would say next day! What then is the amount of this exclusive preference and fastidious superiority of fashionable taste? Mere arrogance and affectation. Look at the men in the pit. Are they in raptures with the ballet or the music? They are solely occupied in thinking how they themselves look. . . . Look at the women in the boxes. Are they at their ease? Or do they not keep one fixed attitude, or else loll, and laugh, and stare without meaning? The great thing is not to seem to take an interest; and this is not difficult, where none is felt.

Hazlitt was seldom comfortable at the King's, or with Italian opera,[8] yet in sharing with Hunt a detestation of upper-class snobbery and hypocrisy, he was also capable of appreciating the artistry of a Sontag or a Pasta, as we have seen. The "question" at the heart of his diatribe is really a *cri de coeur* for *commitment* to the arts and for banishing hypocrisy in *all* society.

But most critics who cited the taste of the audience or the public did not make discriminations of rank. Further, they seemed about evenly divided, during these years, about whether to blame or congratulate their musical taste. Sometimes the same critic shifted his opinions from season to season.[9]

ATTITUDES TOWARD CRITICISM

In the later years, some reviewers occasionally expressed a growing consciousness of their critical faculty and function. We have already noted, in the Hazlitt passages just quoted, the indication that the fashionable have to *read reviews* to know how to respond at the opera house; though the intent was satirical, the remark no doubt reflects the growing influence of reviewers.

In 1829 Ward (Ath) wrote on the increased demands of reviewing:

> As proof of the change which has come upon the constitution of the Italian opera in these latter days, may be mentioned the double duty of him who now undertakes to review its proceedings, compared with that of his predecessors in the office of criticism. It is not now merely a comparison and measurement of one or two songs, which were the permanent trial-pieces of every new singer; it is not enough to say that the prima donna has a delicate soprano, the primo tenore a genuine *voce di petto*. We take into account much more collateral accomplishments. (Apr. 29)

Further problems in musical criticism were cited by critic Z (NM) in 1830, in a critique of *Donna Carita*:

> We have on a former occasion spoken of the difficulties which a modern composer has to encounter in writing an opera, and we candidly own, from our own experience, that when such an opera is written and brought out, even the critic labours under difficulties in forming an unbiassed and correct estimate of the merits of the work. In the first place, musical genius, it can scarcely be denied, is not a characteristic feature of the present age. It is extremely rare, and when it presents itself, it is not of first-rate force.... Hence, it would be too much to require that a modern work should be entirely free from the seducing peculiarities of what is generally termed the Rossinian style and manner, but which... is perhaps as much the style and manner of the age.... Experience has taught us not to be too fastidious about the appropriation of entire ideas and passages. (Sept.)

In 1817 even Bacon (LG), who found the libretto of *Agnese* distasteful, had to warn himself against its influencing his view of the entire work: "Our opinion may possibly have been influenced by the want of relish we felt for the subject; for in music even a small matter will often untune the strings of our susceptabilities." Basic musicianship also needed critical attention, as Holmes (At) observed in 1828: "It is from singers like Madame Schutz and Mademoiselle Sontag, that the English public will learn to appreciate the beauty of concerted music *perfectly* in tune. Hitherto we have not stopped to quarrel about half a note this way or that; it is time that we should."

Changes in musical taste also offered problems for critics, as Ward (Ath) noted in 1829: "It is a very common and very sensible opinion, that musical taste changes its standard at certain intervals of time; no *beau ideal* having a longer period of supremacy than the third or perhaps the half of a single century. The cause for this fact might furnish food for much wise theory" (June 10). A similar problem was noted in 1827 in the *London*'s review of the second edition of Mount-Edgcumbe's *Musical Reminiscences*, published that year:

> When the taste is pliant, it forms itself to the existing model of excellence, and after a time it is incapable of accommodating itself to a departure from the old standard. The senses become comparatively dull, and the judgment, too feeble to traverse new walks, contends that there is no nature beyond the mill-horse round in which it has delighted for half a century. *We*, who are of course the only reasonable men under the sun, do not imagine that ours is *par excellence*, the age of music.[10] (June)

In conclusion, we come to some remarkable passages of Hunt on criticism of both Italian and English opera that provide a link between parts II and III of this study. They occurred in a series of responses to criticism made by English composer John Barnett[11] as correspondent to the *Tatler*. This running debate appeared in five scattered numbers from August 27 to September 12, 1831.[12] The controversy began when Barnett, denying Hunt's implication that his compositions were affected by his becoming the proprietor of a London music shop, went on to assert that the music of Thomas Arne and William Shield—and "all the twaddle of the last century"[13]—was inferior to that of some "modern" composers, citing Henry Bishop, whose music "was worthy of Mozart."

Hunt challenged these assertions and rejected Barnett's contention that only an assiduous study of the masters would make a composer great. It would, Hunt thought, only lead to imitation: "Did Mozart grow great by study? Did the works of Haydn, or Handel, or Gluck, whom he knew how to imitate when he chose, render him the enchanter he was?" Barnett responded by again dismissing Arne as no great genius and implying that if Hunt were more learned in the science of music, he would be in a position to evaluate that music for what it was worth.

The issue was joined. Hunt replied: "There is not a more shallow piece of plausibility, than the proposition, that a critic has no right to speak of an art which he does not profess; or at least, that he has no right, compared with that of anybody who does profess it." Noting that criticism and invention are two distinct things (though often practiced by the same person), he continued:

> Now there are many professors of music, as well as painting who have only become so because they had not modesty or sense enough to perceive that they had no right. The list of existing musical professors is

enormous. There are few of them probably, who do not think themselves qualified to compose; and still fewer, who have any notion of a critic's opinion compared with their own. They fancy that because they can put a few crotchets together, and a few harmonies, they are at liberty to pass censure on men stamped with the love and admiration of their betters.... There is nothing more certain, than that the great majority of these men are no more to be called real musicians, than greengrocers are to be called botanists.

Barnett, who had been slowly giving way, responded once more by admitting "it is not absolutely necessary for a critic to be inventive," but he must be "thoroughly acquainted with the principle of the art he criticizes." Hunt responded that music appeals to people's love, and to their sense of pleasure,

> and where it strikes them, either pleasantly or painfully, they have a right to speak accordingly, whether they understand the theory of the art or not. They have the same right to criticize it, as men have to express their feelings with regard to a face or a flower, or the sunshine, without understanding anatomy or physics; for it is not the means or the process of the mystery which is the thing they are concerned with, but the *result*; and it is in proportion as they can express their feelings as to this result, and give their reasons for what they feel, and why others feel it, that they have a right to be critics.

Barnett failed to substantiate his arguments, and posterity would dispute his judgments on Arne and Bishop (though other contemporaries also saw something of Mozart in Bishop's music). With respect to professional presumption, however, time has been very much on Barnett's side.[14]

Appendix 3

Seasonal Listing of Performances and Reviews

ALL PERFORMANCES are at the King's Theatre (KT), except for a very few at the Pantheon (PAN), Covent Garden (CG), the Little Theatre (LT), or the Royal Academy of Music (R.A.M.). Operas are listed in two groups for each season. First are the King's premieres, in all capitals (or the *earliest* revival after 1784 for which we have reviews, which I have listed in initial capitals) followed by the year of earliest production at the King's. These are listed by date of performance. The second group, placed after the first and indented, lists subsequent revivals alphabetically by title in initial capitals, indicating number of performances and providing a cross-reference to the year (i.e., starting in January) of earliest listing in this appendix.

Following the date of performance (* indicates a first performance) for each entry in the first group are (1) the type of opera, in parentheses (the "-A" that follows either the type of performance or number of performances indicates only one or two acts); (2) the name of the opera as known in London; (3) the number of performances; (4) the names of the composer and librettist; (5) the place and year of the opera's Continental premiere in parentheses, unless its first performance was at the King's; (6) a chronological listing of periodicals by date of review—then, within a given day, alphabetically (periodicals shown in parentheses indicate a verbatim reprint of a review that appeared in the immediately preceding periodical); and lastly, (7) the year(s), in italic of any revivals, followed by the number of performances in parentheses and a listing of reviews, if any. On pagination for journals, see the end of part I and notes.

Abbreviations of opera types:

(c)	comic	(p)	pastoral	(s-s)	semiserious
(ch)	chevalric	(s)	serious	(t-c)	tragicomic
(h)	heroic	(s-c)	semicomic	(t-h)	tragiheroic
(h-c)	heroicomic				

Other abbreviations used:

| ad. | adaptation, or adapted by | l. | librettist | tr. | translator |
| addn. | addition | past. | pasticcio | | |

1784–1785

Dec 18, 1784 (c) *IL CURIOSO INDISCRETO* (18), Anfossi, l. unknown (Rome, 1777). Dec 20 H, P, PA.

Jan 4 (c) *I Rivali Delusi* (6), Sarti, l. Goldoni (Milan, 1782, as *Fra due Litiganti il terzo gode*; Naples, 1784, as *Le Nozze di Dorina*), KT 1784. Jan 6 UC. *1793* (10) as *Le Nozze di Dorina*): Feb 27 C, D, H; Mar 4 T; ll D. *1795* (2).

Jan 8* (s) *DEMETRIO* (8), Cherubini—past., l. Metastasio. Jan 3 H; 10 H, P, PA; 8–11 LC.

Jan 25 (c) *IL PITTOR PARIGINO* (7), Cimarosa, l. Petrosellini (Rome, 1781). Jan 26 H, P.

Feb 26 (s) *NITTETI* (5), Anfossi, l. Andrei, ad. Metastasio (Naples, 1771). Feb 28 H, PA; Mar 4 PA.

Apr 2* (c) *LA FINTA PRINCIPESSA* (6), Cherubini, l. Livigni. Apr 4 C, H, P; 5 UC; 11 UR; LM (II, 302).

Apr 16* (s) *ARTASERSE* (6), Cherubini—past., l. Metastasio. Apr 18 UR; LM (II, 302–3).

May 25 (s) *Orfeo* (10), Gluck—past., l. Jarvis; addn. by Bottarelli; KT 1770, 1771, 1773 ("as originally performed"). May 16 UC. *1786*: Oct 27 UC.

May 28 (c) *La Buona Figliuola* (1-A), Piccinni, l. Goldoni (Rome, 1760); KT 1767. *1789* (1-A): May 30 UC. *1790* (1-A). *1796* (1-A). *1810* (5-A): July 8 E.

May 28 (c) *I Viaggiatori Felici* (7-A), Anfossi, l. Livigni (Venice, 1780); KT 1781. May LM; 28–31 LC. *1786* (6). *1803* (4): Mar 2 P, T.

1786

Jan 24 (c) *IL MARCHESE TULIPANO* (9), Paisiello, l. Chiari (Rome, 1767) as *Le Finte Contesse* Jan 25 PA, 26 C, H, P, PA, UR; 30 H, P.

Feb 14 (s) *Didone Abbandonata* (8), Anfossi—past., l. Badini, ad. Metastasio (Naples, 1785). Feb 16 C, UC, UR; 16–18 LC. *1787* (1).

Mar 11 (c) *LA SCUOLA DEI GELOSI* (11), Salieri, l. Mazzolà (Venice, 1778). Mar 13 H; 15 H, P.

Mar 21 (s) *Perseo* (5), Sacchini, l. Gamerra (KT 1774); ad. Bottarelli. Mar 22 GA, P, UC; 24 UC.

Mar 30 (s) *[IL] GIULIO SABINO* (1), Cherubini, l. Giovannini (Venice, 1780).

May 4 (s) *VIRGINIA* (8), Tarchi, l. unknown (Florence, 1785). May 5 H; 6 PA, W; 8 H, UC. *1787* (6).

May 20 (c) *L'INGLESE IN ITALIA* (2) Anfossi, l. Badini. May 22 G, GA, H.

May 25* (s) *ARMIDA* (6), Mortellari, l. Gamerra. May 29 H, (?) UC; June 3 UC.
  —*I Viaggiatori Felici* (6), Anfosse, see 1785.

1786–1787

Dec 23, 1786* (s) *ALCESTE* (9), Gresnich, l. Badini, ad. Metastasio's *Demetrio*. Dec 25 H, P, UR; 23–26 LC; Jan 2 H; 3 UR; 8 UR; 29 UR.

Jan 9 (c) *GIANNINA E BERNARDONE* (9), Cimarosa, l. Livigni (Venice, 1781). Jan 10 H; 11 UR; 15 UR; 17 UR; 29 UR; Mar 15 UR.

Feb 17 (*?) (c) *IL TUTOR BURLATO* (3), Paisiello, l. Casti? Feb 19 C, G, GA, H, UR; Mar 18 UR.

Mar 1 (s) *Giulio Cesare in Egitto* (9), Handel, l. Haym (Royal Academy, 1724); ad. Arnold. Mar 3 UR.

Apr 24 (c) *GLI SCHIAVI PER AMORE* (19), Paisiello, l. Palomba (Naples, 1786, as *Le Gare Generose*). Apr 26 UR; 30 UR; July 2 UR; 8 UC. *1788* (13): Feb 6 H, P. *1790* (1). *1797* (7): Dec 27, 1798 C, P. *1799* (6).

May 1* (s) *LA VESTALE* (2), Rauzzini, l. Badini. May 2 UC; 3 G, UR; 21 UR.
  —*Didone Abbandonata* (1), Anfosse, see 1786.
  —*Virginia* (6), Tarchi, see 1786.

1787–1788

Dec 8, 1787 (c) *IL RE TEODORO IN VENEZIA* (13), Paisiello, l. Casti (Vienna, 1784). Dec 10 H, T, W; 17 PA, T, UC; 21 UC; 25 T; Jan 4 T, 17 PA. *1795* (3 as *Il Conte Ridicolo*): Apr 15 C.

Jan 15 (c) *LA LOCANDIERA* (7), Cimarosa, l. Petrosellini (Rome, 1778 as *L'Italiana in Londra*). Jan 15 T; 16 P, W; 17 T; 21 H, P, T.

Mar 4* (c) *LA CAMERIERA ASTUTA* (7), Storace, l. unknown. Mar 5 T; 6 PA.

Apr 5 (s) *[IL] GIULIO SABINO* (11), Sarti, l. Giovannini (Venice, 1781). Apr 5 H; 7 G, P, T, W; 8 PA; 5–8 LC; 14 P, T; 16 W.

May 8 (s) *L'OLIMPIADE* (10), Cimarosa, l. Metastasio (Vicenza, 1784). June 9 W; 23 W. *1789* (9).

May 15 (c) *La Frascatana* (6-A), Paisiello, l. Livigni (Venice, 1774); KT 1776, 1777, 1781 (ad. da Ponte). May 15 UC. *1794* (1). *1799* (4): Mar 26 T. *1808* (7): Jan 17 E.
— *Gli Schiavi Per Amore* (13), Paisiello, see 1787.

1789 (at CG after May 11)

Jan 10 (c) *LA COSA RARA* (10), Martín y Soler, l. da Ponte (Vienna, 1786). Jan 12 H, LC; 19 T. *1805* (7). *1806* (3): Dec 16, 1805 T, H. *1816* (4, 3-A): May 20 T.

Jan 24 (s) *IFIGENIA IN AULIDE* (8), Cherubini, l. Moretti (Turin, 1788). Jan 26 G, H, P, T; 28 P; Feb 16 C, P; 23 T; 26 T.

Feb 28* (s) *IL DISERTORE* (8), Tarchi, l. Benincasa, ad. Sedaine. Feb 19 P; 21 P; Mar 2 P, T.

Mar 24 (c) *LA VILLANA RICONOSCIUTA* (3), Cimarosa, l. Palomba (Naples, 1783). Mar 25 P, T, W; 26 P.

May 9 (c) *LA VENDEMMIA* (5), Gazzaniga, l. Bertati (Florence, 1778). May 11 P, T.

June 2 (s) *LA GENEROSITÀ D'ALESSANDRO* (8), Tarchi, l. Badini, ad. Metastasio's *Alessandro nelle Indie* (Milan, 1788). June 3 P, T, W; 8 T. *1790* (12).

June 11 (c) *IL BARBIERE DI SIVIGLIA* (4), Paisiello, l. Petrosellini (St. Petersburg, 1782). *1790* (2). *1793* (4): Jan 28 O, T; 30 T. *1798* (5): May 14 C; June 7 C, P. *1807* (6). *1808* (3; 1-A): Mar 20 E.
— *La Buona Figliuola* (1), Piccinni, see 1785.
— *L'Olimpiade* (9), Cimarosa, see 1788.

1790 (at LT and CG)

Jan 7 (c) *LA NINETTA* (11), Cimarosa, l. Palomba (Naples, 1783, as *Chi dell' altrui*). Jan 8 O, T, UC; 9 PA, W; 7–9 LC; 25 T.

Feb 2 (c) *I [DUE] CASTELLANI BURLATI* (6), Fabrizi, l. Livigni (Bologna, 1785). Feb 3 LC, O, PA, T; 8 T.

Feb 27 (c) *LA VILLANELLA RAPITA* (9), Bianchi, l. Bertati (Venice, 1783). Mar 1 H, T; 8 T.

Apr 6* (s) *L'USURPATOR INNOCENTE* (14), V. Federici, l. Metastasio (*Demofoonte*). Apr 7 H, PA, T, UC; 12 T.

May 28 (s) *ANDROMACA* (6), Nasolini, l. Badini, ad. Racine (Venice, 1790). May 31 PA.
—*Il Barbiere di Siviglia* (2), Paisiello, see 1789.
—*La Buona Figliuola* (1), Piccinni, see 1785.
—*La Generosità D'Alessandro* (12), Tarchi, see 1789.
—*Gli Schiavi Per Amore* (1), Paisiello, see 1787.

1791 (at PAN and LT)

Feb 17 (s) *Armida* (5), Sacchini, l. Gamerra (Milan, 1772); KT 1774, ad. Tonioli; 1780. Feb 10 P; 11 C, T; 12 PA; 18 C; 23 C.

Mar 1 (c) *LA BELLA PESCATRICE* (21), P. A. Guglielmi, l. Zini (Naples, 1789); ad. Mazzinghi. Jan 22 G; Mar 2 C, G, O, P; 7 T. *1792* (10): Apr 13 O; June 11 D. *1794* (4). *1801* (3) ad. da Ponte.

Mar 10 (s) *PIRRO* (3), Paisiello, l. Gamerra (Naples, 1787). Mar 11 G. *1809* (3): June 14 T.

Apr 14 (s) *IDALIDE; OSSIA, LA VERGINE DEL SOLE* (9), Sarti, l. Moretti (Milan, 1783). Apr 15 P; 18 G; May 2 T.

May 14 (c) *LA MOLINARELLA* (10), Paisiello, l. Palomba (Rome, 1789, as *L'Amor Contrasto*; later as *La Molinara*. May 16 P, T. *1795* (4—as *L'Amor Contrasto*): Dec 8, 1794, C, T, TB; 9 T. *1803* (7). *1804* (1). *1817* (4): Mar 10 C, T, 15 LG pl2of; 22 LG p135; 23 E; Apr BS p77f. *1818* (4): Feb TI p118, 2 T; Mar BS p57f.

June 2 (s) *Quinto Fabio* (1), Bertoni, l. Zeno; KT 1780.

June 17* (c) *LA LOCANDA* (8), Paisiello, l. Bertati, ad. *Il Fanatico in Berlina*; addn. by Toniolo. June 17 P; 20 T. *1792* (22). *1802* (7): May 24 P.

1791–1792 (at PAN until January, then LT)

Dec 17, 1791 (c) *LA PASTORELLA NOBILE* (4), P. A. Guglielmi, l. Zini (Naples, 1788). Dec 19 G, H, O, T. *1801* (4): Jan 5 T.

Feb 14 (c) *LA TRAME DELUSE* (7), Cimarosa, l. Diodati (Naples, 1786).
Feb 15 C, H, O, T.

Mar 31 (c) *LA DISCORDIA CONJUGALE* (5), Paisiello, l. Lorenzi and Palma (Naples, 1790); also as *Le Vane Gelosie*. Dec 30, 1791, H; 1792: Apr 2 D, H, PA, T; Mar 31–Apr 3 LC; II H, O.
 —*La Bella Pescatrice* (10), P. A. Guglielmi, see 1791.
 —*La Locanda* (22), Paisiello, see 1791.

1793

Feb 5 (c) *I GIUOCHI D'AGRIGENTO* (6), Paisiello, l. Pepoli (Venice, 1792). Feb 6 C, D, H, O, T, TC, W.

Mar 19 (s) *TEODOLINDA* (9), Andreozzi, l. Boggio (Turin, 1789); ad. Federici. Mar 20 C, T; 30 T; *Thespian* (I, 270).

May 14 (c) *I ZINGARI IN FIERA* (9), Paisiello, l. Palomba (Naples, 1789). May 15 C, P; 18 D; 27 D; June 3 T. *1795* (6): Jan 12 T. *1800* (14; 1-A): Jan 13 C, T, TB; 14 P; Mar MM. *1801* (1). *1803* (3). *1804* (1).

June 11* (s) *ODENATO AND ZENOBIA* (2), V. Federici—past., l. Bandettino.
 —*Il Barbiere di Siviglia* (4), Paisiello, see 1789.
 —*Le Nozze di Dorinda* (10), Sarti, see *I Rivali Delusi*, 1785.

1794

Jan 11 (c) *IL MATRIMONIO SEGRETO* (6), Cimarosa, l. Bertati (Venice, 1792); ad. da Ponte. Jan 13 C, H, P, T. *1798* (3; 3–A): Apr 23 C, T. *1799* (4): Apr 10 C, P, TB, UC. *1803* (6). *1814* (3). *1818* (4): June TI p44If; 1 T; July BS p153f; 7 E. *1829* (2): Har (VII, 204); July 20 T; 22 Ath p471f; Har (VII, 204); Aug NM p344–46; 2 E. *1830* (9–A): Jan 25 T (R.A.M.); May 14 T; 15 Ath p300; 22 Ath; June NM p251f; 12 Ath p385. *1831*: Feb. 28 *Tatler*.

Jan 14 (c) *I Contadini Bizzarri* (14), Sarti, l. Grandi (Venice, 1776, as *Le Gelosie Villane*); KT 1784 (as *Villane*): Apr 16 UC. *1797* (2-A) and *1801* (3) as *Villane*, ad. da Ponte.

Mar 1 (t-c; -A) *DON GIOVANNI TENORIO* (2), Gazzaniga, l. Bertati (Venice, 1787); tr. Mazzinghi. Mar 3 C, O; 4 T.

Mar 1 (c) *IL CAPRICCIO DRAMMATICO* (8), Cimarosa, l. Diodati (Naples, 1786, as *L'Impresario in Augustie*). Mar 4 T, 11 C. *1798*, ad. da Ponte (6–A): Apr 11 H; 16 T; 23 P. *1800* (11-A). *1801* (4-A). *1803* (6-A). *1808* (1-A): Apr 20 E.

Apr 26 (s) *SEMIRAMIDE; LA VENDETTA DI NINO* (12), Bianchi, l. Moretti, ad. Voltaire (Naples, 1790, as *La Vendetta di Nino*). Apr 28 O, T; May 5 T. *1795* (11): Feb 9 C, H, T. *1796* (5): Jan 5 P. *1798* (4): Jan 10 C; 22 C. *1800* (5): Feb MM. *1801* (2). *1805* (11). *1806* (5).

May 17 (c) *IL BURBERO DI BUON C[U]ORE* (4), Martín y Soler, l. da Ponte ad. Goldoni (Vienna, 1786).

May 29 (c) *LA SERVA PADRONA* (7), Paisiello, l. Federico (St. Petersburg, 1781). June 4 C. *1799* (7).
 —*La Bella Pescatrice* (4), P. A. Guglielmi, see 1791.
 —*La Frascatana* (1), Paisiello, see 1788.

1794–1795

Dec 20, 1794 (s) *ZENOBIA IN PALMIRA* (6), Anfossi, l. Sertor (Venice, 1789). Dec 22 C, T.

Jan 27* (c) *LA SCUOLA DEI MARITATI* (10; 2-A), Martín y Soler, l. da Ponte. Jan 28 C; 29 C, T; Feb 2 C. *1798* (7): Jan 24 C, P, T. *1801* (4). *1802* (8): Jan 30 T.

Mar 21 (p) *ACI E GALATEA* (5), Bianchi, l. Foppa (Venice, 1792). Mar 23 C, H, TB; 26 UC.

Apr 30 (s) *ALCESTE, OSSIA IL TRIONFO DELL' AMOR CONJUGALE* (14), Gluck, l. Calzabigi (Vienna, 1767); ad. da Ponte. Apr 28 C; May 2 C; 4 C, TB; June 15 TB. *1796* (1): Jan 20 T, TB. *1797* (4). *1800* (4). *1801* (4): Jan 5 T. *1802* (1).

May 14 (p) *ATI E CIBELE* (1), Cimador, l. Pepoli (Venice, privately performed, 1789).

May 26* (c) *L'ISOLA DEL PIACERE* (4), Martín y Soler, l. da Ponte. May 27 TB. *1801* (1).

May 28* (comic intermezzo) *LE NOZZE DEI CONTADINI* (1), Martín y Soler, l. da Ponte.

—*L'Amor Contrasto* (4), Paisiello, see *La Molinarella*, 1791.
—*Il Conte Ridicolo* (3), Paisiello, see *Il Re Teodoro*, 1788.
—*La Nozze di Dorina* (2), Sarti, see 1785.
—*Semiramide* (11), Bianchi, see 1794.
—*I Zingari in Fiera* (6), Paisiello, see 1793.

1795–1796

Dec 12, 1795 (h) *LA BELLA ARSENE* (8), Monsigny, l. Favart (Fontainebleau, 1773, as *La belle Arsène*), ad. Mazzinghi and da Ponte. Dec 14 C, P, T, TB. 1796: Feb MM.

Feb 9 (s) *PIRAMO E TISBE* (3), Bianchi, l. Sertor (Venice, 1783). Feb 10 C, T, TB; 17 P.

Feb 16 (c) *I TRACI AMANTI* (7), Cimarosa, l. Palomba (Naples, 1793). Feb 17 C, T, TB; MM, *Monthly Mag.* (I, 246).

Mar 15 (c) *I DUE GOBBI* (6), Portogallo, l. Mazzini (Florence, 1793, as *La Confusioni della somiglanza o siano I due gobbi*). Mar 16 C, T, UC; 21 TB.

Apr 7 (s) *IFIGENIA IN TAURIDE* (5), Gluck, l. Guillard (Paris, 1779 as *Iphigénie en Tauride*); ad. da Ponte, Vienna, 1783. Apr 8 C; 11 C, T; *Monthly Mag.* (I, 233).

Apr 16 (c) *LA MODISTA RAGGIRATRICE* (11), Paisiello, l. Lorenzi (Naples, 1787). Apr 18 P, T, TB; *Monthly Mag.* (I, 233). *1797* (3; 2-A): Feb 16 T. *1819* (7): Feb TI p145–47; 17 T; 21 E; Mar BS p77f; 13 LG.

May 24* (s) *ANTIGONA* (12), Bianchi, l. da Ponte. May 25 C; 26 T; June 6 TB. *1798* (2).

June 14* (c) *IL TESORO* (3), Mazzinghi—past., l. da Ponte. June 16 C; 20 T; BWM (I, 63).

July 23 (c) *Zemira ed Azor* (2), Grétry, l. Marmontel, ad. de Beaumont's *La belle et la bête* (Fontainebleau, 1771, as *Zémire et Azor*); KT 1776 (tr. Verazzi), 1779, 1781 (ad. Badini), 1783; ad. and tr. da Ponte. July 25 T, TB; Aug 1 PA. *1797* (4): Nov 28, 1796, C.
   —*Alceste* (1), Gluck, see 1795.
   —*La Buona Figliuola* (1), Piccinni, see 1785.
   —*Semiramide* (5), Bianchi, see 1794.

1796–1797

Dec 6, 1796 (c) *L'AMOR FRA LE VENDEMMIE* (4; 5-A), P. A. Guglielmi, l. Palomba (Naples, 1792). Dec 7 C, T, TB; 17 T.

Dec 20, 1796* (s) *IL CONSIGLIO IMPRUDENTE* (8), Bianchi, l. da Ponte, ad. Goldoni's *Curioso Accidente*. Dec 21 C; 22 TB; 25 BWM p279; 28 T. *1798* (2). *1801* (5): Jan 21 T. *1815* (3).

Jan 10 (s) *EVELINA* [*The Triumph of the English over the Romans*] (13), Sacchini, ad. *Arvire et Evelina*, l. Guillard (Paris, 1788); ad. Federici and da Ponte. Jan: MM p56; 12 UC; 23 T. *1798* (5).

Apr 18 (p) *L'ARBORE* [*L'ALBERO*] *DI DIANA* (5), Martín y Soler, l. da Ponte (Vienna, 1787). Apr MM; 18 UC; 19 C, T, TB.

Apr 27 (c) *NINA* (9), Paisiello, l. Carpani and Lorenzi (Caserta, 1789); ad. da Ponte; one-act as *Nina, Pazza per Amore*, 1825–28. Apr 28 C; 29 OPA, TB; May MM; 1 T. *1798* (4). *1800* (3): Apr 19 C. *1825* (1; 2-A): May 27 T; June 25 T; 27 T; July LM p371f; Har (III, 118). *1826* (1; 1-A). *1828* (2-A): June 27 T.

June 10* (s) *MEROPE* (10), Bianchi, l. da Ponte, ad. Voltaire. June 12 C, H; *Monthly Mag. Suppl.* (III, 371). *1798* (2).
 —*Alceste* (4), Gluck, see 1795.
 —*Le Gelosie Villane* (2), Sarti, see *Le Contadini Bizzari*, 1794.
 —*La Modista Raggiratrice* (3; 2-A), Paisiello, see 1796.
 —*Gli Schiavi per Amore* (8), Paisiello, see 1787.
 —*Zémira ed Azor* (4), Grétry, see 1796.

1797–1798

Nov 28, 1797 (s) *IPERMESTRA* (3), Sarti—past., l. Metastasio (Rome, 1766). Nov 29 P, T, TB; 30 C.

Feb 20 (s) *CINNA* (10), Bianchi, l. Anelli (Naples, 1794); ad. da Ponte. Feb 21 C, H, P; 26 C; Mar 5 C, T.

Mar 10 (c) *LA CIFRA* (3) Salieri, l. Petrosellini (Vienna, 1789), ad. da Ponte from *La Dama Pastorella*, Rome, 1780. Mar: 12 C, OPA, T.

Apr 26 (s) *ELFRIDA* (17), Paisiello, l. Calzabigi (Naples, 1792). Apr 27 C; May 7 C; 14 C. *1799* (10; 4-A). *1800* (3): June 23 H. *1802* (6). *1808* (1). *1811* (8): June 26 T. *1812* (8). *1813* (1): Feb 8 T.

—Antigona (2), Bianchi, see 1796.
—Il Barbiere di Siviglia (5), Paisiello, see 1789.
—Il Capriccio Drammatico (5; 1-A, Cimarosa, see 1794.
—Il Consiglio Imprudente (1; 1-A), Bianchi, see 1797.
—Evelina (5), Sacchini, see 1797.
—Il Matrimonio Segreto (3; 3-A), Cimarosa, see 1794.
—Merope, Bianchi (2), see 1797.
—Nina (4), Paisiello, see 1797.
—La Scuola dei Maritati (7), Martín y Soler, see 1795.
—Semiramide (4; 2-A), Bianchi, see 1794.

1798–1799

Dec 8, 1798 (s) *MEDONTE* (5), Sarti, l. Gamerra (Florence, 1777, as *Re di Epiro*). Dec 10 P, T; 24 C.

Jan 22 (s) *INES DE CASTRO* (17; 4-A), Bianchi, l. de Sanctis (Naples, 1794). Jan 23 Cr, H, P, T. *1800* (3): Mar 19 T.

May 15* (c) *I DUE SVIZZERI* (15-A), Ferrari, l. Buonaiuti. *1800* (7). *1803* (1): Mar 12 T.

May 30 (s) *DIDONE* (5), Paisiello, l. Metastasio (Naples, 1794). May 31 C. *1808* (13): Jan 27 C, T; 31 E.
—Elfrida (10; 4-A), Paisiello, see 1798.
—La Frascatana (4), Paisiello, see 1788.
—Il Matrimonio Segreto (4), Cimarosa, see 1794.
—Gli Schiavi per Amore (6), Paisiello, see 1787.
—La Serva Padrona (7), Paisiello, see 1794.

1800

Feb 18 (c) *I [DUE] FRATELLI RIVALI* (6; 4-A), Winter, l. Botturini (Venice, 1793). Feb MM.

Apr 15 (s) *ALESSANDRO E TIMOTEO* (11), Sarti, l. Torre di Rizzonico (Parma, 1782). Apr MM p238; 16 C, P, T, TB.

May 22* (s) *ZENOBIA* (1) Mount-Edgcumbe, l. Metastasio.

June 17*(?) (c) *IL PRINCIPE SPEZZACAMINO* (1), Portogallo, l. unknown.
—Alceste (4), Gluck, see 1795.

—*Il Capriccio Drammatico* (11), Cimarosa, see 1794.
—*I Due Svizzeri* (7), Ferrari, see 1799.
—*Elfrida* (3), Paisiello, see 1798.
—*Ines De Castro* (3), Bianchi, see 1799.
—*Nina* (3), Paisiello, see 1797.
—*Semiramide* (5), Bianchi, see 1794.
—*I Zingari in Fiera* (14; 1-A), Paisiello, see 1793.

1801

Feb 28* (s) *ALZIRA* (15), Bianchi, l. Rossi. Mar 2 C, P, T. *1802* (5).

Apr 30* (s) *LA MORTE DI CLEOPATRA* (3), Bianchi, l. Buonaiuti.

May 5 (c) *LA PRINCIPESSA FILOSOFA* (14), Andreozzi, l. Sografi (Venice, 1784); ad. Buonaiuti. May 6 C, P, T.
—*Alceste* (4), Gluck, see 1795.
—*La Bella Pescatrice* (3), P. A. Guglielmi, see 1791.
—*Il Capriccio Drammatico* (4), Cimarosa, see 1794.
—*I Consiglio Imprudente* (5; 1-A), Bianchi, see 1796.
—*Le Gelosie Villane* (3), Sarti, see *I Contadini Bizzarri*, 1794.
—*L'Isola del Piacere* (1), Martín y Soler, see 1795.
—*La Pastorella Nobile* (4), P. A. Guglielmi, see 1792.
—*La Scuola dei Maritati* (4), Martín y Soler, see 1795.
—*Semiramide* (2), Bianchi, see 1794.
—*I Zingari in Fiera* (1), Paisiello, see 1793.

1801–1802

Dec 29, 1801 (c) *ANGIOLINA; OSSIA IL MATRIMONIO PER SUSURRO* (8), Salieri, l. Defranceschi, ad. Jonson's *Epicœne* (Vienna, 1800); ad. da Ponte. Dec 30 P, T.

Feb 23 (s) *LA MORTE DI MIT[H]RIDATE* (15), Nasolini, l. Sografi (Trieste, 1796); ad. da Ponte. Feb 24 P, T; Mar 29 T.

Mar 16* (c) *RINALDO D'ASTI* (3), Ferrari, l. unknown. Mar 22 T.

Mar 25 (s) *MEROPE [E POLIFONTE]*. (1), Nasolini, l. Botturini (Venice, 1796). Mar 26 C, P; 27 T; 29 T. *1803* (14): Dec 6, 1802 P, T; 13 P, T.

June 1* (s) *ARMIDA* (7), Bianchi, l. da Ponte. June 2 P, T.
—*Alceste* (1), Gluck, see 1795.

—*Alzira* (5), Bianchi, see 1801.
—*Elfrida* (6), Paisiello, see 1798.
—*Il Fanatico di Berlina* (7), Paisiello, see *La Locanda*, 1791.
—*La Scuola dei Maritati* (8), Martín y Soler, see 1795.

1802–1803

Jan 1 (c) *I DUE BARONI* (5), Cimarosa, l. Palomba (Rome, 1783). Jan 3, C, P, T.

Mar 31 (s) *FERNANDO NEL [IN] MESSICO* (12), Portogallo, l. Tarducci (Venice, 1798). Apr 1 P. *1804* (3).

May 31* (s) *[LA GROTTA DI] CALYPSO* (13), Winter, l. da Ponte. June 6 P. *1804* (3): Feb 4 T; 6 P.
—*Il Capriccio Drammatico* (6), Cimarosa, see 1794.
—*I Due Svizzeri* (1), Ferrari, see 1799.
—*Il Matrimonio Segreto* (6), Cimarosa, see 1794.
—*Merope* (14), Nasolini, see 1802.
—*I Viaggiatori Felici* (4), Anfossi, see 1785.
—*La Molinara* (7), Paisiello, see *La Molinarella*, 1791.
—*I Zingari in Fiera* (3), Paisiello, see 1793.

1804

Jan 14 (s) *LA VERGINE DEL SOL* (19), Andreozzi, l. Casoli (Genoa, 1783). Jan 16 C (Cr), P, T. *1805* (10).

Feb 21 (c) *LE ASTUZE FEMMINILI* (6), Cimarosa, l. Palomba (Naples, 1794). Feb 22 T.

Mar 22* (s) *IL TRIONFO DELL' AMOR FRATERNO* (12), Winter, l. da Ponte. Mar 26 C, P, T. *1805* (8).

May 3* (s) *IL RATTO DI PROSERPINA* (15), Winter, l. da Ponte. May 4 C (Cr), P. *1805* (12): Nov 26, 1804 T. *1806* (9): Dec 9, 1805, H, T. *1815* (7): July TI p57f; 21 T; 24 T; Aug TI p145. *1816* (7): Feb 5 T.
—*Fernando Nel Messico* (3), Portogallo, see 1803.
—*Calypso* (3), Winter, see 1803.
—*La Molinara* (1), Paisiello, see *La Molinarella*, 1791.
—*I Zingari in Fiera* (1), Paisiello, see 1793.

1804–1805

Jan 29* (s) *ZAÏRA* (9), Winter, l. da Ponte, ad. Voltaire. Jan 30 C, T. *1806* (4). *1816* (8): Feb 19 T.

Feb 19* (s) *ERFILE* (6), Bianchi, l. Gamerra. Feb 20 D, DA, PA; 25 T.

Mar 28 (s) *La Clemenza di Scipione* (13), Bach, l. Bottarelli, ad. Metastasio; KT 1778. Mar MM; 29 P, T. *1806* (5).

May 2 (s) *GLI ORAZI E[D] I CURIAZI* (9), Cimarosa, l. Sografi (Venice, 1797). May 3 P. *1806* (11): Jan 8 C, Cr; 13 H. *1812* (2). *1813* (2). *1814* (9): Apr 13 C, Cr, T; June TI p373; 5 E. *1815* (5). *1829* (4; 1-A): July 31 C, T; Aug 2 E; 3 T; 5 Ath p490; Sep NM p390; Har (VII, 232). *1830* (1): June 18 T; 26 Ath p397.
—*La Cosa Rara* (7), Martín y Soler, see 1789.
—*Il Ratto di Proserpina* (12), Winter, see 1804.
—*Semiramide* (11), Bianchi, see 1794.
—*Il Trionfo Dell' Amor Fraterno* (8), Winter, see 1804.
—*La Vergine Del Sol* (10), Andreozzi, see 1804.

1806

Jan 25 (s) *ARGENIDE E SERSE* (9), Portogallo, l. Farrari (Florence, 1797, as *Il Retorno di Serse*; revised as *L'Argenide*, Lisbon, 1804). Jan 27 C, Cr, T; Feb 10 H. *1807* (9) as *Il Retorno di Serse*: Feb 25 C, H, T; Mar 16 H.

Mar 4 (s) *LA MORTE DI CLEOPATRA* (7), Nasolini, l. Sografi (Venice, 1791). Mar 5 C, H, T. *1807* (3; 1-A) July 17 Cr.

Mar 27 (s) *LA CLEMENZA DI TITO* (6), Mozart, l. Mazzola, ad. Metastasio (Prague, 1791). Mar 28 C, DA, P; 29 T, 31 Cr; Apr UM. *1812* (16): Mar 5 C, T; 16 T; 22 E. *1813* (5): Mar 1 C; 8 T. *1816* (8): Mar 4 C, P, T. *1817* (4): July TI p65–67; 14 C; 18 C; 19 LG p43; 27 E. *1818* (3): Apr TI p283–85; 6 C. *1821* (4): May DM; 2 T; June BS p172f. *1823* (1): Jan EM p82; 6 T. *1828* (1): Mar 3 T; Apr NM p153f.

Apr 15 (c) *I DUE NOZZE [ED] UN SOL MARITO* (12; 1-A), P. C. Guglielmi—past., l. unknown (Florence, 1800). Apr MM p166; 16 C, H, P, T. *1813* (3): Feb 1 C; 3 T.

May 1 (s-c) *CAMILLA, OSSIA IL SOTTERRANEO* (2), Fioravanti, l. Carpani and Caravita (Lisbon, 1801).

June 10*? (c) *LA SERVA ASTUTA* (2), unknown composer and librettist.

June 19 (c) *IL FANATICO PER LA MUSICA* (7), Mayr, l. unknown (Venice, 1798, as *Chi originale*). June 20 C, P. *1807* (7): July 17 Cr. *1808* (5). *1809* (1). *1810* (6): Mar 7 P; 11 E. *1811* (4). *1812* (4). *1813* (1). *1817* (1): May 10 LG p249. *1819* (3): July TI p57f. *1824* (6): Mar 1 T; 6 LitC; Apr EM p372; May NM p198. *1829* (at EOH) (6): Feb 4 Ath p77; 7 T.
— *La Cosa Rara* (3), Martín y Soler, see 1789.
— *La Clemenza di Scipione* (5), Bach, see 1805.
— *Gli Orazi ed I Curiazi* (11), Cimarosa, see 1805.
— *Il Ratto di Proserpina* (9), Winter, see 1804.
— *Semiramide* (5), Bianchi, see 1794.
— *Zaïra* (4), Winter, see 1805.

1806–1807

Dec 13, 1806 (s) *SEMIRAMIDE* (17; 1-A), Portogallo, l. unknown, ad. Voltaire (Lisbon, 1801, as *La Morte di Semiramide*). Dec 15 C, H, T; Jan 26 H. *1808* (11): Jan 4 C, T; Aug 7 E. *1811* (3): Feb 6 T. *1812* (2): Jan 16 T; 20 T; Feb 2 E. *1813* (4; 1-A).

Dec 23, 1806 (t-h) *IL PRINCIPE DI TARANTO* (13; 1-A), Paer, l. Livigni (Parma, 1797). Dec 24 P; 29 C. *1810* (4): Jan 17 P; 21 E.

Feb 3*? (c) *ROBERTO L'ASSASSINO* (3), Trento, l. unknown.

Apr 7 (c) *LA VIRTUOSA IN MARGELLINA* (4), P. A. Guglielmi, l. Zini (Naples, 1785). Apr 8 H.

Apr 16 (s) *LA MORTE DI MIT[H]RIDATE* (8), Portogallo, l. unknown (Lisbon, 1806). Apr 17 C, P. *1809* (1).
— *Il Barbiere di Siviglia* (6), Paisiello, see 1789.
— *Il Fanatico per la Musica* (7; 1-A), Mayr, see 1806.
— *La Morte di Cleopatra* (3; 1-A), Nasolini, see 1806.
— *Il Ritorno di Serse* (9), Portogallo, see *Argenide*, 1806.

1808

Mar 1 (c) *IL FURBO CONTRA IL FURBO* (1), Fioravanti, l. Tottola (Venice, 1796). Mar 2 T; 6 E. *1813* (3): Jan 20 T.

Apr 21 (s) *LA FESTE D'ISIDE* (10), Nasolini, l. Rossi (Florence, 1794; reset 1798). Apr 22 DA, T; May 1 E.

May 31 (c) *IL VIRTUOSO IN PUNTIGLIO* (6; 1-A), Fioravanti, l. Balocchi (Paris, 1807); also as *I virtuosi ambulanti*. June 1 T.

June 23 (c) *I CONTRATTEMPI AMOROSI* (3), Sarti, l. unknown (St. Petersburg, 1784); also as *Gli amanti consolati*. July 3 E.
 —*Il Barbiere di Siviglia* (3; 1-A), Paisiello, see 1789.
 —*Il Capriccio Drammatico* (1), Cimarosa, see 1794.
 —*Didone* (13;1-A), Paisiello, 1799.
 —*Elfrida* (1), Paisiello, see 1798.
 —*Il Fanatico per la Musica* (3), Mayr, see 1806.
 —*La Frascatana* (7), Paisiello, see 1788.
 —*Semiramide* (11), Portogallo, see 1807.

1809

Jan 6 (c) *LA CAPRICCIOSA PENTITA* (10), Fioravanti, l. Romanelli (Milan, 1802). Jan 7 C(Cr), T; 15 E. *1815* (6 as *L'Orgoglio Arvilito*): Feb 8 C, T.

Jan 31* (c) *I VILLEGGIATORI BIZZARRI* (20; 1-A), Pucitta, l. Buonaiuti. Feb 1 T; 5 E; 6 T.

Mar 7* (c) *LA CACCIA D'ENRICO IV* (14), Pucitta, l. Buonaiuti, ad. Collé. Mar 8 T; 13 C; 19 E. *1812* (16): Feb 3 T. *1813* (5; 1-A). *1814* (5).

Apr 13 (s) *TERESA E CLAUDIO* (2), Farinelli, l. Foppa. Apr 19 T; 31 E.

May 16* (c) *LA SERVA RAGGIRATRICE* (2), P. C. Guglielmi, l. Buonaiuti; based on *La serva bizzarra*, l. Palomba, Naples, 1803. May 17 T; 21 E.

June 1 (burletta) *AMOR VUOL GIOVENTÙ* (1), P. C. Guglielmi (?), l. Buonaiuti (?).

June 20* (s) *SIDAGERO* (10), P. C. Guglielmi, l. Buonaiuti, ad. Tasso. June 21 T; 26 C; July 2 E. *1810* (14; 1-A): Dec 9, 1809 T. *1811* (1). *1813* (5): July 5 T.

July 11* (c) *LE QUATTRO NAZIONI* (4), Pucitta, l. Buonaiuti. July 12 T; 16 E.
 —*Il Fanatico per la Musica* (1), Mayr, see 1806.
 —*Mitridate* (1), Portogallo, see *La Morte di Mitridate*, 1807.
 —*Pirro* (3), Paisiello, see 1791.

1809–1810

Dec 12, 1809 (c) *LA SCOMMESSA* (8), P. C. Guglielmi, l. Buonaiuti (Rome, 1807, as *La Guerra aperta*). Dec. 13 C, T; 17 E. 1810: Jan 8 T.

Feb 20* (s) *ROMEO E GIULIETTA* (6; 1-A), P. C. Guglielmi, l. Bounaiuti. Feb. 25 E; 26 T.

Mar 20 *(?) (s) *ATALIDA* (11; 1-A), P. C. Guglielmi—past., l. Buonaiuti. Mar 21 C, T; Apr 1 E.

Apr 5*? (c) *L'INGIUSTA GELOSIA* (1), Tramezzani, l. unknown.

May 5* (s) *LA VESTALE* (11; 1-A), Pucitta, l. Buonaiuti. May 13 E; June 25 T. *1811* (7): Mar 25 T; May 20 T. *1813* (5).

May 24* (c) *IL MATRIMONIO PER SUSURRO* (4), Fioravanti, l. Defranceschi and da Ponte (cf. Salieri's *Angiolina*, 1802). June 3 E.
 —*La Buona Figliuola* (5), Piccinni, see 1785.
 —*Il Fanatico per la Musica* (6), Mayr, see 1806.
 —*Il Principe di Taranto* (4), Paer, see 1807.
 —*Sidagero* (14; 1-A), Guglielmi, see 1809.

1810–1811

Dec 22, 1810 (s) *ZAÏRA* (12), F. Federici, l. Bocciardini (Palermo, 1799). Dec. 24 C, P, T; 30 E.

Jan 22* (s-s) *LE TRE SULTANE [IL TRIONFO DI ROSSELANE]* (7), Pucitta, l. Caravita. Jan 23 H, T; 28 C; Feb 3 E.

Mar 5* (s) *PHÆDRA [FEDRA]* (6), Radicati, l. Buonaiuti. Mar 6 C, H; 11 T; 24 E.

Apr 25* (h-c) *CLIMÈNE* (6), Trento, l. Caravita. Apr 29 T.

May 9 (c) *COSÌ FAN TUTE* (12), Mozart, l. da Ponte (Vienna, 1790). May 19 E; June 3 T. *1816* (9): June 8 C; July 15 T; Aug 4 E. *1817* (2): June 13 T. *1818* (5): June TI p443f; 15 C, T; Aug 2 E. *1825* (1): May 13 T; June NM p247–49. *1829*: Dec 14 T (R.A.M. at KT).

June 6 (c) *IL FLAUTO MAGICO* (advt. as *"Die Zauberflote"*) (1; 1-A), Mozart, l. Schikaneder (Vienna, 1791); tr. Gamerra. June 8 C; 16 E. *1819* (15): May TI p381f; 27 C, T; 29 LG p349f; 30 E; June TI p457f; July BS p203f: Aug TI p101f. *1820* (6): Apr TI p225; 24 T. *1829* (scenes in German) (1): June 19 C, T; 21 At p409, E; 24 Ath; Har (VII, 178).
 —*Elfrida* (8), Paisiello, see 1798.
 —*Il Fanatico per la Musica* (4), Mayr, see 1806.

—*Semiramide* (3), Portogallo, see 1807.
—*Sidagero* (1), Guglielmi, see 1809.
—*La Vestale* (7), Pucitta, see 1810.

1812

Apr 16 (s) *GINEVRA DI SCOZIA* (4), Pucitta, l. Rossi (Trieste, 1801).

May 12 (h-c) *CAMILLA* (6), Paer, l. Carpani (Vienna, 1799). May 25 T. *1819* (1): Apr TI p299f; 15 T; May BS p139f.

June 18 (c) *LE NOZZE DI FIGARO* (advt. as "*Le Mariage de Figaro*") (8), Mozart, l. da Ponte (Vienna, 1786). June 19 *Sun*; July 6 T; 12 E. *1813* (5): Mar 11 C; June 4 C, T; 5 P. *1816* (4): June 24 T. *1817* (11): Feb 3 C, T; 8 LG p45f; 22 LG p78f; Mar BS p50f; May BS p102. *1818* (12): Jan TI p48f; 19 C, T; 24 LG p61f; 25 E; Feb BS p34. *1819* (5): Mar TI p218f; 15 C, T; 21 E; Apr BS p112. *1820* (4): Dec 20, 1819 C, T; 25 LG p830; 26 E. *1821* (6): July 23 T. *1822* (6): Jan 14 T; 20 Ch p44, E; Feb LM p194. *1823* (6) Apr EM p371. *1824* (2) May 28 T. *1825* (2): Apr LM p597f. *1826* (1): July NM p278f. *1828* (8). *1829* (1): June 12 T; 17 Ath p380; Har (VII, 178). *1830* (2) Dec 18 Ath p796f.
  —*La Clemenza di Tito* (16), Mozart, see 1806.
  —*Elfrida* (8), Paisiello, see 1798.
  —*Il Fanatico per la Musica* (4), Mayr, see 1806.
  —*Enrico IV* (16), Pucitta, see *La Caccia d'Enrico IV*, 1809.
  —*Gli Orazi ed I Curiazi* (2), Cimarosa, see 1805.
  —*Semiramide* (2), Portogallo, see 1807.

1813

Mar 23* (s) *BOADICEA* (4), Pucitta, l. Buonaiuti. Mar 24 T; 26 C; Apr TI p185–87; 5 T.

Apr 8* (s) *L'EROINA DI RAAB* (7), Ferrari, l. Buonaiuti(?). Apr 12 C; 25 E; June TI p313. *1815* (3): Apr 5 T.

May 13 (c) *LA DAMA SOLDATO* (6), Orlandi, l. Mazzolà. May 17 T; 18 C; June TI p313. *1814* (6). *1815* (3).
  —*La Clemenza di Tito* (5), Mozart, see 1806.
  —*Il Due Nozze* (3), P. C. Guglielmi, see 1806.
  —*Elfrida* (1), Paisiello, see 1798.
  —*Enrico IV* (5;1-A), Pucitta, see *La Caccia d'Enrico IV*, 1809.
  —*Il Fanatico per la Musica* (1), Mayr, see 1806.
  —*Il Furbo Contra Il Furbo* (3), Fioravanti, see 1808.

—*Le Nozze di Figaro* (5), Mozart, see 1812.
—*Gli Orazi ed I Curiazi* (2), Cimarosa, see 1805.
—*Semiramide* (4;1-A), Portogallo, see 1807.
—*Sidagero* (5), P. C. Guglielmi, see 1809.
—*La Vestale* (5), Pucitta, see 1810.

1814

May 26 (c) *ADOLFO E CHIARA* (2), Pucitta, l. unknown (Rome, 1801, as *La burla fortunata*).

June 9* (s) *ARISTODAMO* (13), Pucitta, l. unknown (Naples, 1808). June 10 T; 13 T.

July 7 (s) *LA DIDONE ABBANDONATA* (6), Paer, l. Metastasio (Paris, 1810). July 10 E, 11 C.
—*La Dama Soldato* (6), Orlandi, see 1813.
—*La Caccia D'Enrico IV* (5), Pucitta, see 1809.
—*Il Matrimonio Segreto* (5), Cimarosa, see 1794.
—*Gli Orazi ed I Curiazi* (9), Cimarosa, see 1805.

1815

Jan 10 (s) *ADELASIA E ALERAMO* (11; 1-A), Mayr, l. Romanelli (Milan, 1807). Jan TI p75f; 11 C(Cr), T; 12 C; May 8 T.

Mar 7 (s) *IL RITO* [*RITI*] *D'EFESO* (11), Farinelli, l. unknown (Venice, 1803).

June 3*? (s) *BARSENE, REGINA DI LIDIA* (8), Portogallo, l. unknown. June 5 C.

June 27* (s) *I SELVAGGI* (4; 1-A), Liverati, l. unknown. June 29 T. *1816* (6): Apr 1 T.
—*Il Conciglio Imprudente* (3), Bianchi, see 1797.
—*La Dama Soldato* (3), Orlando, see 1813.
—*L'Eroina di Raab* (3), Ferrari, see 1813.
—*Gli Orazi ed I Curiazi* (5), Cimarosa, see 1805.
—*L'Orgoglio Auvilito* (6), Fioravanti, see *La Capricciosa Pentita*, 1809.
—*Il Ratto di Proserpina* (7), Winter, see 1804.

1816

Jan 13 (s) *GRISELDA; OSSIA LA VIRTU IN CIMENTO* (8; 1-A), Paer, l. Anelli, ad. Goldoni (Parma, 1798). Jan TI; 15 C, P, T. *1817* (4): Jan 27 C, H(TI), T; Feb 1 LG p28f. *1818* (2): Jan 12 T.

Apr 23* (c) *LE ASTUZIE FALLACIE* (2; 2-A), Fioravanti, l. unknown. Apr 24 T.
   —*La Clemenza di Tito* (8; 1-A), Mozart, see 1806.
   —*La Cosa Rara* (4; 3-A), Martín y Soler, see 1789.
   —*Così Fan Tute* (9; 2-A), Mozart, see 1811.
   —*Le Nozze di Figaro* (4), Mozart, see 1812.
   —*Il Ratto di Proserpina* (7; 2-A), Winter, see 1804.
   —*Il Selvaggi* (6; 1-A), Liverati, see 1815.
   —*Zaïra* (8), Winter, see 1805.

1817

Jan 11 (s) *PENELOPE* (6), Cimarosa, l. Diodati (Naples, 1795). Jan 13 C, T; 19 E; 25 LG p14f; Feb BS p27.

Apr 12 (c) [*IL*] *DON GIOVANNI* (26), Mozart, l. da Ponte (Prague, 1787). Apr TI p297f; 14 C, *Sun*, T; 16 T; 19 LG p199f; 20 E; 26 LG p216; May BS p102–5; 18 E; 28 T; June BS p126–28; Aug TI p136f; 3 E; 17 E; Sep BS p197. *1818* (15): Feb TI p119; Mar BS p58; Aug TI p157–59. *1819* (12): Mar TI p217f; 1 C, T, 7 Ch p156f; Apr BS p111f; 4 E; Aug TI p101f. *1820* (9): Apr TI p234f. *1821* (4): May 25 T. *1822* (6). *1824* (5): May 7 T(EM); June LM p673; Aug 16 T. *1825* (1): May LM p12f. *1828* (4): May 2 T; 4 At p281, E; June NM p248–50. *1829* (3): June 10 Ath p364f; July 29 Ath p476; Har (VII, 178). *1830* (4): June 4 T; 5 Ath; 7 T; July 10 Ath p428f.

May 8* (c) *LO SBAGLIO FORTUNATO* (1), Ferrari, l. unknown. May 10 LG p249f; June BS p127f.

May 15 (s-s) *L'AGNESE* (5), Paer, l. Buonavoglia, ad. Opie (Parma, 1809). May TI p380–82; 17 LG p265f; 19 C, T; June BS p108; 9 E. *1820* (4): June 29 C, T; July TI p69–71; 1 Ch; Aug LM p202–4. *1821* (2): May BS p140.
   —*La Clemenza di Tito* (4), Mozart, see 1806.
   —*Così Fan Tute* (2), Mozart, see 1811.
   —*Il Fanatico per la Musica* (1), Mayr, see 1806.
   —*Griselda* (4), Paer, see 1816.
   —*La Molinara* (4), Paisiello, see *La Molinarella*, 1791.
   —*Le Nozze di Figaro* (11), Mozart, see 1812.

1818

Mar 10 (c) *IL BARBIERE DI SIVIGLIA* (13), Rossini, l. Sterbini (Rome, 1816). Mar TI p207–9; 11 T; 13 C, T; 14 LG p173f; 15 *News*; 22 E; Apr BS p82f; 12 E; 13 T; QMM (II, 79). *1819* (9): Apr 13 T; 25 E; June BS p174f. *1822* (6): May 29 T. *1824* (9): Feb 16 T; Mar NM p104f; Har (II, 53). *1825* (7; 1-A): Apr LM p598; June 13 C; July LM p374; NM p295f; Har (III,118). *1826* (5): Mar 13 T; Apr EM p417, NM p151f. *1828* (5): Apr NM p201–4; 16 T; May LM p268; Dec 22 T (R.A.M. at EOH). *1829* (2; 1-A): Apr 29 T; May 6 Ath p285; June NM p250f; Har (VII, 24). *1830* (3-A): Feb 27 Ath p124f; Mar 13 Ath.

Apr 30 (s) *ELISABETTA, REGINA D'INGHILTERRA* (4), Rossini, l. Schmidt, ad. C. Federici, ad. Sophia Lee's *The Recess* (Naples, 1815). May TI p361–63: 1 T, 4 C; June BS p128–30.

—*La Clemenza di Tito* (3), Mozart, see 1806.
—*Così Fan Tute* (5), Mozart, see 1811.
—*Don Giovanni* (15), Mozart, see 1817.
—*Griselda* (2), Paer, see 1816.
—*Il Matrimonio Segreto* (4), Cimarosa, see 1794.
—*La Molinara* (4), Paisiello, see *La Molinarella*, 1791.
—*Le Nozze di Figaro* (12), Mozart, see 1812.

1819

Jan 26 (c) *L'ITALIANA IN ALGIERI* (7), Rossini, l. Anelli (Venice, 1813). Jan TI p65–67; 27 T; 28 C; 30 T; 31 E; Feb BS p44. *1829* (7): Feb 18 T; 23 C; 25 Ath p127; July 3 T; Aug 5 Ath p490; Dec 7 T; 9 Ath (R.A.M. at KT).

July 1 (c) *L'INGANNO FELICE* (4-A), Rossini, l. Foppa (Venice, 1812). July 3 C, 11 Ch p443; Aug BS p239, TI p1oof; 1 E. *1827* (1): Har (V, 172). *1828*: Dec 19 T (R.A.M. at EOH).

—*Il Barbiere di Siviglia* (9), Rossini, see 1818.
—*Camilla* (6), Paer, see 1812.
—*Don Giovanni* (12), Mozart, see 1817.
—*Il Fanatico per la Musica* (1; 3-A), Mayr, see 1806.
—*Il Flauto Magico* (15), Mozart, see 1811.
—*La Modista Raggiratrice* (7), Paisiello, see 1796.
—*Le Nozze di Figaro* (5), Mozart, see 1812.

1819–1820

Jan 8 (c) *LA CENERENTOLA* (9), Rossini, l. Ferretti (Rome, 1817). Jan 10 C, T; 15 LG p56; 16 E; Feb BS p106, LM p169f, TI p114f. *1826* (1): July NM p279. *1828* (1–A): June 27 T. *1829* (3): May 6 T, 13 Ath p302f; June NM p251; July 8 Ath p428; Har (VII, 150). *1830* (8; 1-A): Feb 22 C, T; 27 Ath p124f; Mar 7 At p154; Apr NM p153; May 1 Ath p269; June 19 Ath p330; Har (VIII, 134).

Feb 26* (h-c) *GASTONE E BAJARDO* (5), Liverati, l. S. Vestris. Feb BS; 28 C, T; Mar 11 LG p174f; Apr BS p158, LM p440f, TI.

May 4 (s) *IL TANCREDI* (14), Rossini, l. Rossi (Venice, 1813). May TI p312f; 5 T, 6 Ch p301f; 8 C; June BS p202f; July LM p94f. *1821* (3): Apr 16 T; May LM p568. *1823* (3): Jan 27 T. *1824* (8): May 19 T; 23 E; June LM p672. *1825* (2-A): May 27 T; June LM p290. *1827* (2; 2-A): May 7 T; 13 At p302f. *1828* (1-A): Jan 30 *Companion* p29–31; July 27 At p477. *1829* (1-A): May NM p292f; June 18 Sp p457, 19 T; 21 E; 24 Ath. *1830* (1; 1-A): May 13 At p297; 21 T, 22 Ath.
— *L'Agnese* (4), Paer, see 1817.
— *Don Giovanni* (9), Mozart, see 1817.
— *Il Flauto Magico* (6;1-A), Mozart, see 1811.
— *Le Nozze di Figaro* (4), Mozart, see 1812.

1821

May 10 (c) *LA GAZZA LADRA* (14), Rossini, l. Gherardini (Milan, 1817). Mar 12 C, T; 17 LG p173f; 18 E; Apr BS p105f, LM p449f. *1822* (3). *1823* (3): Jan EM p82f; 18 LitC; Feb LM p225f. *1825* (4). *1827* (8): Feb 5 T; Apr 9 T; May NM p194; July 20 T; Har (V, 57). *1828* (1). *1829* (6; 1-A): Apr 10 T; 15 Ath p238f; May 20 Ath p317; Har (VII, 150). *1830* (1-A): Mar 6 Ath p142.

May 19 (c) *IL TURCO IN ITALIA* (12), Rossini, l. Romani (Milan, 1814). May 21 C, T; 26 LG p334, 27 Ch p334; June BS p173, LM p675–77; 9 LG p363. *1822* (8): Feb 11 T. *1824* (4): May EM p465f; 3 T; June LM 672f, NM p247f. *1827* (4): Feb 28 T. *1830* (2-A): R.A.M. at KT.
— *L'Agnese* (2), Paer, see 1817.
— *La Clemenza di Tito* (4), Mozart, see 1806.
— *Don Giovanni* (4), Mozart, see 1817.
— *Le Nozze di Figaro* (6), Mozart, see 1812.
— *Il Tancredi* (3), Rossini, see 1820.

1822

Jan 22 (s-s) *IL BARONE DI DOLSHEIM* (9), Pacini, l. Romani (Milan, 1818). Jan DM; 22 Ch p58, 23 C, T, TO; 26 LG p61f; 27 E; Feb BS p76–79; Mar LM p287.

Apr 9 (c) *I [DUE] PRETENDENTI DELUSI* (3), Mosca, l. Prividali (Milan, 1811). Apr DM; 10 T, TO; 14 E; May LM p490.

Apr 23 (s) *PIETRO L'EREMITA* (13), Rossini, l. Tottola (Naples, 1818, as *Mosè in Egitto*); 1825 and 1827 as *Peter the Hermit*. Apr DM, LM p391–93 (as oratorio); 24 T; 25 C; 27 LG p266; 28 E; June LM p583f. *1825* (4): Apr 25 C, T; May LM p13f; June LM p291; NM p247; July LM p373f; Har (III, 90). *1826* (2): Apr 3 T. *1827* (8): Mar 16 T; 18 At p168; 19 T; 21 T; 25 E; Apr 23 T; May NM p192f; 6 E; Har (V, 57).

May 16 (s) *OTELLO* (2), Rossini, l. Beria di Salsa (Naples, 1816). May 17 T; June LM p584. *1823* (6): May EM p469; June DM, LM p173f; Har (I, 85). *1824* (6): Apr 26 T; May 2 E; June LM p672, NM p246f. *1825* (8): May 18 T; June LM p291. *1828* (14): Feb 6 C, T; 10 At p92; 11 T; Mar NM p112; May 30 LitC; 31 LG p349; July NM p294. *1829* (6; 1-A): Apr 22 T; 26 E; 27 T; 29 Ath p269f; July 29 Ath p476. *1830* (4; 1-A): Feb 15 T; 20 Ath p109f; 21 At p121; May 8 Ath p254; July 24 Ath.
—*Il Barbiere di Siviglia* (6), Rossini, see 1818.
—*Don Giovanni* (6), Mozart, see 1817.
—*La Gazza Ladra* (3), Rossini, see 1821.
—*Le Nozze di Figaro* (6), Mozart, see 1812.
—*Il Turco in Italia* (8), Rossini, see 1821.

1823

Feb 18 (s) *LA DONNA DEL LAGO* (19), Rossini, l. Tottola, ad. Scott (Naples, 1819). Feb 19 C, H, T; 22 TO (as oratorio at D.L.); Apr LM p464f; Har (I, 41). *1824* (3): June LM p673. *1825* (3). *1826* (1): Jan 30 T; Feb 4 LG p77; 12 E. *1827* (5). *1828* (5): May 12 T; June NM p250–52. *1829* (3): Feb 2 T; 4 Ath p.77; Mar NM p106f; 9 C, T; 11 Ath p158; June NM p251; Aug 2 E.

Apr 12 (s) *ELISA E CLAUDIO* (2), Mercadante, l. Romanelli (Milan, 1821). Apr EM p371; 14 H, T; 19 LG p253; 20 E; May LM p580f; June DM. *1830* (3): Mar 15 C, T, TO; 20 Ath p172; 21 At p186; Apr NM p154f; Har (VIII, 178).

June 5 (s) *RICCIARDO E ZORAIDE* (12), Rossini, l. Beria di Salsa (Naples, 1818). June 6 H, T(EM); July LM p77; Aug 6 T. *1824* (2): Apr EM p372; 5 T; 11 E; May NM p198f. *1827* (5): Mar 26 T; May NM p193–95. *1829* (2-A): Apr 8 Ath p222f; 10 T; May NM p201f.

July 5 (s) *MATILDE E CORRADINO; OSSIA, IL TRIONFO DELLA BELTA* (4), Rossini, l. Ferretti, ad. Hoffmann (Rome, 1821, as *Matilde di Shabran*). June DM; 7 T (EM); Aug LM p205–8. *1830* (7; 3-A): Mar 29 T;

Apr 3 Ath p204; 4 At p218, E; May NM p199f; Har (VIII, 221).
—*La Clemenza di Tito* (1), Mozart, see 1806.
—*La Gazza Ladra* (3), Rossini, see 1821.
—*Le Nozze di Figaro* (6), Mozart, see 1812.
—*Otello* (6), Rossini, see 1822.
—*Il Tancredi* (3), Rossini, see 1820.

1824

Jan 24 (s) *ZELMIRA* (7), Rossini, l. Tottola (Naples, 1822). Jan 26 C, T(EM); 31 LG p76; LitC; Feb LM p208–10; 1 E; Mar NM p103–5. *1826* (2). *1828* (1): Feb 4 T; 10 At p92; Mar NM pmf.

June 21 (s) *ROMEO E GIULIETTA* (10), Zingarelli, l. Foppa (Milan, 1796). June 30 T; Aug LM p203f; Har (II,145). 1825: July LM p371f. *1826* (3). *1827* (2-A): May 7 T; 13 At, E; July 20 T; Har (III,118). *1830* (1-A): May 9 At p298.

July 15 (s) *SEMIRAMIDE* (5), Rossini, l. Rossi (Venice, 1823). July 19 T; Sep NM p390f. *1825* (2): May 21 T; June LM p290f. *1827* (11): May 11 T; 13 At p297; June NM p240f; Har (II, 167). *1828* (6): Apr 21 T. *1829* (5; 2-A): May 20 Ath p317; June NM p251; 3 T; Har (VII, 150). *1830* (6): Feb 8 T; 13 Ath p93f; 14 At p105.
—*Il Barbiere di Siviglia* (9), Rossini, see 1818.
—*Don Giovanni* (5), Mozart, see 1817.
—*La Donna del Lago* (3), Rossini, see 1823.
—*Il Fanatico per la Musica* (6), Paer, see 1806.
—*Otello* (6), Rossini, see 1822.
—*Le Nozze di Figaro* (2), Mozart, see 1812.
—*Ricciardo e Zoraide* (2), Rossini, see 1823.
—*Il Tancredi* (8), Rossini, see 1820.
—*Il Turco in Italia* (4), Rossini, see 1821.

1825

Mar 19 (s-s) *ADELINA* (LT 2-A; KT 1-A), Generali, l. Rossi (Venice, 1810). Mar 19 T; 21 C, T; Apr LM p598–600; May NM p199f; Har (III, 70).

June 30 (s) *IL CROCIATO IN EGITTO* (11), Meyerbeer, l. Rossi (Venice, 1824). June 30 T; July LM p475; 1 P, T; 2 T; 3 E; 9 LitC; Aug LM p516–20, NM p342–46; 15 T; Har (III, 143). *1826* (2): Jan 9 T; Mar LM p315f; Har (IV, 42). *1827* (11). *1828* (5): Mar 17 T; Apr NM p154–56; May NM p200; July 25 T; 27 At p476f.
—*Il Barbiere di Siviglia* (8), Rossini, see 1818.

—*Così Fan Tute* (1), Mozart, see 1811.
—*Don Giovanni* (1), Mozart, see 1817.
—*La Donna del Lago* (3), Rossini, see 1823.
—*La Gazza Ladra* (4), Rossini, see 1821.
—*Nina* (3), Paisiello, see 1797.
—*Le Nozze di Figaro* (2), Mozart, see 1812.
—*Otello* (8), Rossini, see 1822.
—*Peter the Hermit* (4), Rossini, see *Pietro l'Eremita*, 1822.
—*Semiramide* (2), Rossini, see 1824.
—*Il Tancredi* (2), Rossini, see 1820.

1826

Feb 25 (s) *TEBALDO E ISOLINA* (9), Morlacchi, l. Rossi (Dresden, 1820). Feb 27 C(EM), T; Mar 5 E; Apr NM p149–52; Har (IV, 86).

June 1 (s) *MEDEA IN CORINTO* (9), Mayr, l. Romani (Naples, 1813). June 2 T; 3 LG p350; July NM p279f. *1827* (7). *1828* (6; 1-A): July 18 T; Aug 4 T. *1831*: May 13 *Tatler*.

June 22 (s) *AURELIANO IN PALMIRA* (3), Rossini, l. Romanelli (Milan, 1813).
—*Il Barbiere di Siviglia* (5), Rossini, see 1818.
—*La Cenerentola* (1), Rossini, see 1820.
—*Il Crociato in Egitto* (2), Meyerbeer, see 1825.
—*La Donna del Lago* (1), Rossini, see 1823.
—*Nina* (2), Paisiello, see 1797.
—*Pietro l'Eremita* (2), Rossini, see 1822.
—*Romeo e Giulietta* (3), Zingarelli, see 1824.
—*Zelmira* (2), Rossini, see 1824.

1827

Dec 2, 1826 (s) *LA VESTALE* (6), Spontini, l. Jouy (Paris, 1807). Nov 25 LG p249; Dec 1 T; 4 C, T; 9 LitC, LG p780; 16 E. *1827*: Jan NM p13–15; Har (V, 18); Feb NM p56.

Dec 30, 1826 (c) *LA SCHIAVA DI BAGDAD* (9), Pacini, l. Pezzi (Turin, 1820). Dec 29 T; Jan 1 C, T; 6 LitC; Feb NM p56f; Har (V, 37).

June 7* (s) *MARIA STUARDA, REGINA DI SCOZIA* (4), Coccia, l. Giannone. June 10 At p361; 11 C, T; 17 E; July NM p288–91; Har (V, 149, 171).

July 5 (s) *DIDONE* (2), Mercadante, l. Metastasio (Turin, 1823). July Har (V, 171).
—*Il Crociato in Egitto* (11), Meyerbeer, see 1825.
—*La Donna del Lago* (5), Rossini, see 1823.
—*La Gazza Ladra* (8), Rossini, see 1821.
—*L'Inganno Felice* (1), Rossini, see 1819.
—*Medea in Corinto* (7), Mayr, see 1826.
—*Pietro l'Eremita* (8), Rossini, see 1822.
—*Ricciardo e Zoraide* (5), Rossini, see 1823.
—*Romeo e Giulietta* (2), Zingarelli, see 1824.
—*Semiramide* (11), Rossini, see 1824.
—*Il Tancredi* (4), Rossini, see 1820.
—*Il Turco in Italia* (7), Rossini, see 1821.

1828

Jan 12 (s) *MARGHERITA D'ANJOU* (4), Meyerbeer, l. Romani (Milan, 1820). Jan 14 C, T; 20 At p44, E; Feb NM p66f; Har (III, 143, 166) and (IV, 47).

Feb 16 (s) *LA ROSA BIANCA E LA ROSA ROSSA* (3), Mayr, l. Romani (Genoa, 1813). Feb 18 C, T; 20 *Companion* p71–75; 24 At p124, E; 25 TO; Mar NM p112–14.
—*Il Barbiere di Siviglia* (5), Rossini, see 1818.
—*La Cenerentola* (1), Rossini, see 1820.
—*La Clemenza di Tito* (1), Mozart, see 1806.
—*Il Crociato in Egitto* (5), Meyerbeer, see 1825.
—*Don Giovanni* (4), Mozart, see 1817.
—*La Donna del Lago* (5), Rossini, see 1823.
—*La Gazza Ladra* (1), Rossini, see 1821.
—*L'Inganno Felice* (1?), Rossini, see 1819 (R.A.M. at LT).
—*Medea in Corinto* (7), Mayr, see 1826.
—*Nina* (2), Paisiello, see 1797.
—*Le Nozze di Figaro* (8), Mozart, see 1812.
—*Otello* (14), Rossini, see 1822.
—*Semiramide* (6), Rossini, see 1824.
—*Il Tancredi* (1), Rossini, see 1820.
—*Zelmira* (1), Rossini, 1824.

1829

Feb 28 (s) *IL CONTE ORI* (1), Rossini, l. Scribe and Delestre-Poirson (Paris, 1828, as *Le comte Ory*). Mar 2 C, T, TO; 4 Ath p141f; 8 At p153, E; Har (V, 97).

Mar 17* (s) *I MESSICANI* (2-A), Bochsa—past., l. Pistrucci. Mar 22 E; 23 T; 25 Ath p191; Har (VII, 97); May NM p201f.
   —*Il Barbiere di Siviglia* (3), Rossini, see 1818.
   —*La Cenerentola* (3), Rossini, see 1820.
   —*Così Fan Tute* (1?), Mozart (R.A.M. at KT), see 1811.
   —*Don Giovanni* (3), Mozart, see 1817.
   —*La Donna del Lago* (3), Rossini, 1823.
   —*Il Fanatico per la Musica* (6), Mayr, see 1806.
   —*La Gazza Ladra* (7), Rossini, see 1821.
   —*L'Italiana in Algieri* (7), Rossini, see 1819.
   —*Il Matrimonio Segreto* (2), Cimarosa, see 1794.
   —*Le Nozze di Figaro* (1), Mozart, see 1812.
   —*Gli Orazi ed I Curiazi* (5), Cimarosa, see 1805.
   —*Otello* (7), Rossini, see 1822.
   —*Ricciardo e Zoraide* (2), Rossini, see 1823.
   —*Semiramide* (7), Rossini, see 1824.
   —*Il Tancredi* (1), Rossini, see 1820.
   —*Die Zauberflöte* (scenes) (1), Mozart, see *Il Flauto Magico*, 1811.

1830

Apr 17 (s) *IL PIRATA* (5; 2-A), Bellini, l. Romani, ad. Maturin's *Bertram* (Milan, 1827). Apr 19 C, P, T; 24 Ath p252f, Sp p259; 25 At p265, E; May NM p200–202; Har (VIII, 222).

July 26 (s) *DONNA CARITA* (2; 3-A), Mercadante, l. Pola (Venice, 1826, as *Caritea, regina di Spagna*). July 27 T; 28 TO; 31 Ath p477; Aug 1 At p505; Sep NM 378f.
   —*Il Barbiere di Siviglia* (3), Rossini, see 1818.
   —*La Cenerentola* (9), Rossini, see 1820.
   —*Don Giovanni* (4), Mozart, see 1817.
   —*Elisa e Claudio* (3), Mercadante, see 1823.
   —*La Gazza Ladra* (1), Rossini, see 1821.
   —*Matilda e Corradino* (10), Rossini, see 1823.
   —*Il Matrimonio Segreto* (9), Cimarosa, see 1794.
   —*Le Nozze di Figaro* (2), Mozart, see 1812.
   —*Gli Orazi e I Curiazi* (1), Cimarosa, see 1805.
   —*Otello* (5), Rossini, see 1822.
   —*Romeo e Giulietta* (1), Zingarelli, see 1824.
   —*Semiramide* (6), Rossini, see 1824.
   —*Il Tancredi* (9), Rossini, see 1820.
   —*Il Turco in Italia* (2), Rossini, see 1821.

Appendix 4

Comic and Serious Productions: Premieres and Revivals

	King's Theatre Premieres				King's Theatre Revivals				Total	
	Comic		Serious[1]		Comic		Serious[1]			
Year	No. of Operas	No. of Performances	No. of Operas	No. of Performances	No. of Operas	No. of Performances	No. of Operas	No. of Performances	No. of Operas	No. of Performances
1785	3	31	3	19	3	14	1	10	10	74
1786	3	22	3	15	1	6	1	13	8	56
1787	3	31	2	11	0	0	3	18	8	60
1788	3	27	2	21	2	24	0	0	7	72
1789[2]	4	22	3	22	0	0	1	10	8	54
1790[3]	3	26	2	20	3	4	1	12	9	62
1791[4]	3	39	2	12	0	0	2	6	7	57
1792[5]	3	16	0	0	2	32	0	0	5	48
1793	2	15	2	11	2	14	0	0	6	40
1794	5	27	1	12	3	20	0	0	9	59
1795	3	15	4	26	4	15	1	11	12	67
1796	4	27	4	28	2	3	2	6	12	64
1797	2	13	4	36	4	19	1	4	11	72
1798	1	3	3	30	6	30	4	15	14	78
1799	1	15	3	31	5	21	1	14	10	82
1800	2	11	2	12	4	36	4	15	12	74
1801	1	15	2	18	8	25	2	6	13	63
1802	2	11	3	23	3	21	2	12	10	67
1803	1	5	2	28	6	27	1	14	10	74
1804	1	6	3	46	2	2	2	6	8	60
1805	0	0	3	24	2	19	5	42	10	85
1806	3	15	4	24	2	14	4	23	13	76
1807	2	7	3	40	2	14	2	13	9	71
1808	3	11	1	10	4	17	3	25	11	63
1809	6	52	2	12	1	1	2	4	11	69
1810	3	13	3	31	2	11	2	19	10	74
1811	3	19	3	25	1	4	4	19	11	67
1812[6]	2	14	1	4	4	22	3	26	10	66
1813	1	6	2	11	5	18	6	24	14	59

Comic and Serious Productions: Premieres and Revivals cont.

	King's Theatre Premieres				King's Theatre Revivals				Total	
	Comic		Serious[1]		Comic		Serious[1]			
Year	No. of Operas	No. of Performances	No. of Operas	No. of Performances	No. of Operas	No. of Performances	No. of Operas	No. of Performances	No. of Operas	No. of Performances
1814	1	2	2	19	3	14	1	11	7	44
1815	0	0	4	36	3	12	3	15	10	63
1816	1	4	1	9	3	22	4	30	9	65
1817	2	27	2	11	4	18	2	8	10	64
1818	1	13	1	4	5	40	2	5	9	62
1819	2	11	0	0	7	58	0	0	9	69
1820	2	14	1	14	3	19	1	4	7	52
1821	2	26	0	0	2	10	3	9	7	45
1822	1	3	3	24	5	29	0	0	9	56
1823	0	0	4	37	2	9	3	10	9	56
1824	0	0	3	22	5	26	4	19	12	67
1825	0	0	2	14	5	19	5	19	12	52
1826	0	0	3	21	3	8	5	10	11	39[7]
1827	1	9	3	12	3	15	8	53	15	90[8]
1828	0	0	2	7	6	22	8	40	16	69
1829	0	0	2	3	10	34	6	25	18	62
1830	0	0	2	12	7	28	7	35	16	75[8]
Total	86	623	107	848	159	805	122	665	475	2954
(Average)	(1.9)	(13.8)	(2.4)	(18.8)	(3.5)	(17.9)	(2.7)	(14.9)	(10.5)	(65.6)

Notes: 1. Includes semiserious types. 2. At KT and CG. 3. At LT. 4. At PAN. 5. At PAN and LT. 6. Competition from PAN. 7. Season curtailed. 8. Many one-act performances counted as one each.

Appendix 5

New Productions, Performances, and Ratios

Year	Productions	Performances	Performances per Production
1785	6	50	8.3
1786	6	37	6.2
1787	5	42	8.4
1788	5	48	9.6
1789	7	44	6.3
1790	5	46	9.6
1791 (PAN.)	5	51	10.2
1792	3	16	5.3
1793	4	26	6.5
1794	6	39	6.5
1795	7	41	5.9
1796	8	55	6.9
1797	6	49	8.2
1798	4	33	8.3
1799	4	46	11.5
1800	4	23	5.8
1801	3	32	10.7
1802	5	34	6.8
1803	3	33	11.0
1804	4	52	13.0
1805	3	24	8.0
1806	7	39	5.8
1807	5	47	9.4
1808	4	21	5.3
1809	8	64	8.0
1810	6	44	7.3
1811	6	44	7.3
1812	3	18	6.0
1813	3	17	5.7
1814	3	21	7.0
1815	4	36	9.0
1816	2	13	6.5
1817	4	38	9.5
1818	2	17	8.5

Year	Productions	Performances	Performances per Production
1819	2	11	5.5
1820	3	28	9.3
1821	2	26	13.0
1822	4	27	6.8
1823	4	37	9.3
1824	3	22	7.3
1825	2	14	7.0
1826	3	21	7.0
1827	4	21	5.3
1828	2	7	3.5
1829	2	3	1.5
1830	2	12	6.0
Avg.	(4.3)	(32.7)	(7.6)

Appendix 6

Productions* by Composer: In Three-Year Periods

Composers	1785–1787	1788–1790	1791–1793	1794–1796	1797–1799	1800–1802	1803–1805	1806–1808	1809–1811	1812–1814	1815–1817	1818–1820	1821–1823	1824–1826	1827–1830	Total
Anfossi	5	–	–	1	–	–	1	–	–	–	–	–	–	–	–	7
Cherubini	3	1	–	–	–	–	–	–	–	–	–	–	–	–	–	4
Cimarosa	2	4	1	3	3	2	5	2	–	4	2	1	–	–	4	33
Paisiello	2	5	7	5	12	7	4	5	2	2	1	2	–	2	–	56
Tarchi	2	3	–	–	–	–	–	–	–	–	–	–	–	–	–	5
Salieri	1	–	–	–	–	1	–	–	–	–	–	–	–	–	–	2
Sacchini	1	–	1	–	2	–	–	–	–	–	–	–	–	–	–	4
Mortellari	1	–	–	–	–	–	–	–	–	–	–	–	–	–	–	1
Piccinni	1	1	–	1	–	–	–	–	1	–	–	–	–	–	–	4
Gresnich	1	–	–	–	–	–	–	–	–	–	–	–	–	–	–	1
Storace	–	1	–	–	–	–	–	–	–	–	–	–	–	–	–	1
Federici, V.	–	1	1	–	–	–	–	–	–	–	–	–	–	–	–	2
Sarti	–	1	2	2	1	2	–	–	–	–	–	–	–	–	–	8
Martin y Soler	–	1	–	1	2	3	2	1	–	–	1	–	–	–	–	11
Gazzaniga	–	1	–	–	–	–	–	–	–	–	–	–	–	–	–	1
Fabrizi	–	1	–	–	–	–	–	–	–	–	–	–	–	–	–	1
Bianchi	–	1	–	5	8	7	2	1	–	–	1	–	–	–	–	25
Nasolini	–	1	–	–	–	1	1	3	–	–	–	–	–	–	–	6
Guglielmi, P.A.	–	–	2	1	2	2	–	1	–	–	–	–	–	–	–	8
Andreozzi	–	–	1	–	–	1	2	–	–	–	–	–	–	–	–	4
Gluck	–	–	–	3	1	3	–	–	–	–	–	–	–	–	–	7
Monsigny	–	–	–	1	–	–	–	–	–	–	–	–	–	–	–	1
Portogallo	–	–	–	1	–	–	2	4	2	2	1	–	–	–	–	12
Grétry	–	–	–	1	–	–	–	–	–	–	–	–	–	–	–	1
Ferrari	–	–	–	–	1	–	1	1	–	1	–	–	–	–	–	4
Winter	–	–	–	–	–	1	7	2	–	–	3	–	–	–	–	13
Bach	–	–	–	–	–	–	2	–	–	–	–	–	–	–	–	2
Mayr	–	–	–	–	–	–	3	3	1	2	1	–	1	2	–	13
Mozart	–	–	–	–	–	–	–	1	2	4	7	9	7	5	8	43
Guglielmi, P.C.	–	–	–	–	–	–	–	1	5	2	–	–	–	–	–	9
Fioravanti	–	–	–	–	–	–	–	1	1	1	1	–	–	–	–	4
Paer	–	–	–	–	–	–	–	1	2	3	2	2	1	1	–	12
Pucitta	–	–	–	–	–	–	–	–	6	5	–	–	–	–	–	11
Federici, F.	–	–	–	–	–	–	–	–	1	–	–	–	–	–	–	1
Orlandi	–	–	–	–	–	–	–	–	–	2	1	–	–	–	–	3

Appendixes

Composers	1785–1787	1788–1790	1791–1793	1794–1796	1797–1799	1800–1802	1803–1805	1806–1808	1809–1811	1812–1814	1815–1817	1818–1820	1821–1823	1824–1826	1827–1830	Total
Liverati	—	—	—	—	—	—	—	—	—	—	2	1	—	—	—	3
Farinelli	—	—	—	—	—	—	—	—	—	—	1	—	—	—	—	1
Rossini	—	—	—	—	—	—	—	—	—	—	5	11	18**	37**		71
Pacini	—	—	—	—	—	—	—	—	—	—	—	1	—	1		2
Zingarelli	—	—	—	—	—	—	—	—	—	—	—	—	—	2	2	4
Mayerbeer	—	—	—	—	—	—	—	—	—	—	—	—	—	2	2	4
Morlacchi	—	—	—	—	—	—	—	—	—	—	—	—	—	1	—	1
Mercadante	—	—	—	—	—	—	—	—	—	—	—	—	—	—	2	2
Mosca	—	—	—	—	—	—	—	—	—	—	—	—	—	—	1	1
Spontini	—	—	—	—	—	—	—	—	—	—	—	—	—	—	1	1
Bellini	—	—	—	—	—	—	—	—	—	—	—	—	—	—	1	1

*Excludes premieres with less than six performances.
**Includes many one-act versions.

Appendix 7

Operas by Composer: With Librettist

By year of King's premiere or earliest revival

ANDREOZZI: 1793: *Teodolinda* (Boggio). 1801: *La Principessa Filosofa* (Sografi). 1804: *La Vergine del Sol* (Casoli).
ANFOSSI: 1785: *Il Viaggiatori Felici* (Livigni); *Il Curioso Indiscreto* (unknown); *Nitteti* (Andrei). 1786: *Didone Abbandonata* (Metastasio); *L'Inglese in Italia* (Badini). 1795: *Zenobia in Palmira* (Sertor).
BACH: 1805: *La Clemenza di Scipione* (Bottarelli).
BELLINI: 1830: *Il Pirata* (Romani).
BERTONI: 1791: *Quinto Fabio* (Zeno).
BIANCHI: 1790: *La Villanella Rapita* (Bertati). 1794: *Semiramide* (Moretti). 1795: *Aci e Galatea* (Foppa). 1796: *Piramo e Tisbe* (Serto); *Antigona* (da Ponte). 1797: *Il Consiglio Imprudente* (da Ponte); *Merope* (da Ponte). 1798: *Cinna* (da Ponte). 1799: *Ines de Castro* (de Sanctis). 1801: *Alzina* (Rossi); *La Morte di Cleopatra* (Buonaiuti). 1802: *Armida* (da Ponte). 1805: *Erfile* (Gamerra).
BOCHSA: 1829: *I Messicani* (Pistrucci).
CHERUBINI: 1785: *Demetrio* (Metastasio); *La Finta Principessa* (Livigni); *Artaserse* (Metastasio). 1786: *Giulio Sabino* (Giovannini). 1789: *Ifigenia in Aulide* (Moretti).
CIMADOR: 1795: *Ati e Cibele* (Pepoli).
CIMAROSA: 1785: *Il Pittor Parigino* (Petrosellini). 1787: *Giannina e Bernardone* (Livigni). 1788: *La Locandiera* (Petrosellini); *L'Olimpiade* (Metastasio). 1789: *La Villana Riconosciuta* (Palomba). 1790: *La Ninetta* (Palomba). 1792: *La Trame Deluse* (Diodati). 1794: *Il Matrimonio Segreto* (Bertati); *Il Capriccio Drammatico* (da Ponte). 1796: *I Traci Amanti* (Palomba). 1803: *I Due Baroni* (Palomba). 1804: *Le Astuzie Femminili* (Palomba). 1805: *Gli Orazi ed Curiazi* (Sografi). 1817: *Penelope* (Diodati).
COCCIA: 1827: *Maria Stuarda* (Giannone).
FABRIZI: 1790: *I Castellani Burlati* (Livigni).
FARINELLI: 1809: *Teresa e Claudio* (Foppa). 1815: *Il Rito D'Efeso* (unknown).
FEDERICI, F.: 1811: *Zaira* (Bocciardini).
FEDERICI, V.: 1790: *L'Usurpator Innocente* (Metastasio). 1793: *Odenato and Zenobia* (Bandettino).
FERRARI: 1799: *I Due Svizzeri* (Buonaiuti). 1802: *Rinaldo d'Asti* (un-

known). 1813: *L'Eroina di Raab* (Buonaiuti?). 1817: *Lo Sbaglio Fortunato* (unknown).
FIORAVANTI: 1806: *Camilla* (Carpani and Caravita). 1808: *Il Furbo contra il Furbo* (Tottola); *Il Virtuoso in Puntiglio* (Balocchi). 1809: *La Capricciosa Pentita* (Romanelli). 1810: *Il Matrimonio per Susurro* (Defranceschi and da Ponte). 1816: *Le Astazie Fallacie* (unknown).
GAZZANIGA: 1789: *La Vendemmia* (Bertati). 1794: *Don Giovanni Tenorio* (Bertati).
GENERALI: 1825: *Adelina* (Rossi).
GLUCK: 1785: *Orfeo* (past.) (Jarvis). 1795: *Alceste* (Calzabigi). 1796: *Ifigenia in Tauride* (Guillard).
GRESNICH: 1787: *Alceste* (Badini).
GRÉTRY: 1796: *Zemira ed Azor* (Marmontel).
GUGLIELMI, P. A.: 1791: *La Bella Pescatrice* (Zini). 1792: *La Pastorella Nobile* (Zini). 1797: *Amor Fra le Vendemmie* (Palomba). 1807: *La Virtuosa in Margellina* (Zini).
GUGLIELMI, P. C.: 1806: *I Due Nozze ed un Sol Marito* (Unknown). 1809: *La Serva Raggiratrice* (Buonaiuti); *Sidagero* (Buonaiuti). 1810: *La Scommessa* (Buonaiuti); *Romeo e Giulietta* (Buonaiuti); *Atalida* (Buonaiuti).
HANDEL: 1787: *Giulio Cesare in Egitto*—past. (Haym-Arnold).
LIVERATI: 1815: *I Selvaggi* (unknown). 1820: *Gastone e Bajardo* (Vestris).
MARTÍN Y SOLER: 1789: *La Casa Rara* (da Ponte). 1794: *Il Burbero di Buon Cuore* (da Ponte). 1795: *La Scuola dei Meritati* (da Ponte); *L'Isola del Piacere* (da Ponte); *Le Nozze dei Contadini* (da Ponte). 1797: *L'Arbore di Diana* (da Ponte).
MAYR: 1806: *Il Fanatico per la Musica* (unknown). 1815: *Adelasia e Aleramo* (Romanelli). 1826: *Medea in Corinto* (Romani). 1828: *La Rosa Bianca e la Rosa Rossa* (Romani).
MAZZINGHI: 1796: *Il Tesoro* (da Ponte).
MERCADANTE: 1823: *Elisa e Claudio* (Romanelli). 1727: *Didone* (Metastasio). 1830: *Donna Caritea* (Pola).
MEYERBEER: 1725: *Il Crociato in Egitto* (Rossi). 1828: *Margherita d'Anjou* (Romani).
MONSIGNY: 1796: *La Bella Arsène* (Favart).
MORLACCHI: 1826: *Tebaldo e Isolina* (Rossi).
MORTELLARI: 1786: *Armida* (Gamerra).
MOSCA: 1822: *I Pretendenti Delusi* (Prividali).
MOUNT-EDGCUMBE: 1800: *Zenobia* (Metastasio).
MOZART: 1806: *La Clemenza di Tito* (Mazzolà). 1811: *Così Fan Tutte* (da Ponte; *Il Flauto Magico* (Schikaneder; tr. Gamerra). 1812: *Le Nozze di Figaro* (da Ponte). 1817: *Don Giovanni* (da Ponte).

NASOLINI: 1790: *Andromaca* (Badini). 1802: *La Morte di Mitridate* (Sografi); *Merope e Polifonte* (Butturini). 1806: *La Morte di Cleopatra* (Sografi). 1808: *La Feste D'Iside* (Rossi).
ORLANDI: 1813: *La Dama Soldata* (Mazzolà).
PACINI: 1822: *Il Barone di Dolsheim* (Romani). 1827: *La Schiava di Bagdad* (Pezzi).
PAER: 1807: *Il Principe di Toranto* (Livigni). 1812: *Camilla* (Carpani). 1814: *La Didone Abbandonata* (Metastasio). 1816: *Griselda* (Anelli). 1817: *L'Agnese* (Buonavoglia).
PAISIELLO: 1786: *Il Marchese Tulipano* (Chiari). 1787: *Il Tutor Burlato* (Casti?); *Gli Schiavi per Amore* (Palomba). 1788: *Il Re Teodoro in Venezia* (Casti); *La Frascatana* (Livigni). 1789: *Il Barbiere di Siviglia* (Petrosellini). 1791: *Pirro* (Gamerra); *La Molinarella* (Palomba); *La Locanda* (Bertati). 1972: *La Discordia Conjugale* (Lorenzi and Palma). 1793: *I Giuochi D'Agrigento* (Pepoli); *I Zingari in Fiera* (Palomba). 1794: *La Serva Padrona* (Federico). 1796: *La Modesta Raggiratrice* (Lorenzi). 1797: *Nina* (Carpani and Lorenzi). 1798: *Elfrida* (Calzabigi). 1799: *Didone* (Metastasio).
PICCINNI: 1785: *La Buona Figliuola* (Goldoni).
PORTOGALLO: 1796: *I Due Gobbi* (Mazzini). 1800: *Il Principe Spezzacamino* (unknown). 1803: *Fernando nel Messico* (Tarducci). 1806: *Argenide e Serse* (Farrari). 1807: *Semiramide* (unknown); *La Morte di Mithridate* (unknown). 1815: *Barsene* (unknown).
PUCITTA: 1809: *I Villeggiatori Bizzarri* (Buonaiuti); *La Caccia D'Enrico IV* (Buonaiuti); *Le Quattro Nazioni* (Buonaiuti). 1810: *La Vestale* (Buonaiuti). 1811: *Le Tre Sultane* (Caravita). 1812: *Ginevra di Scozia* (Rossi). 1813: *Boadicea* (Buonaiuti). 1804: *Adolfo e Chira* (unknown); *Aristodamo* (unknown).
RADICATI: 1811: *Phædra* (Buonaiuti).
RAUZZINI: 1787: *La Vestale* (Badini).
ROSSINI: 1818: *Il Barbiere di Siviglia* (Sterbini); *Elisabetta* (Schmidt, with Federici). 1819: *L'Italiana in Algieri* (Anelli); *L'Inganno Felice* (Foppa). 1820: *La Cenerentola* (Ferretti); *Il Tancredi* (Rossi). 1821: *La Gazza Ladra* (Gherardini); *Il Turco in Italia* (Romani). 1822: *Pietro L'Eremita* (Tottola); *Otello* (Beria di Salsa). 1823: *La Donna del Lago* (Tottola); *Ricciardo e Zoraide* (Beria di Salsa); *Matilde e Corradino* (Ferretti). 1824: *Zelmira* (Tottola); *Semiramide* (Rossi). 1826: *Aureliano in Palmira* (Romanelli). 1829: *Il Conte Ori* (Scribe and Delestre-Poirson).
SACCHINI: 1786: *Perseo* (Gamerra). 1791: *Armida* (Gamerra). 1797: *Evelina* (Guillard).
SALIERI: 1786: *La Scuola dei Gelosi* (Mazzolà). 1798: *La Cifra* (Petrosellini and da Ponte). 1802: *Angiolina* (Defranceschi).

SARTI: 1785: *I Rivali Delusi* (Goldini). 1788: *Giulio Sabino* (Giovannini). 1791: *Idalide* (Moretti). 1794: *I Contadini Bizzarri* (Grandi). 1798: *Ipermestra* (Metastasio). 1799: *Medonte* (Gamerra). 1800: *Alessandro e Timoteo* (Torre di Rizzonico). 1808: *I Contrattempi Amorosi* (unknown).
SPONTINI: 1827: *La Vestale* (Jouy).
STORACE: 1788: *La Ceneriera Astuta* (unknown).
TARCHI: 1786: *Virginia* (unknown). 1789: *Il Disertore* (Benincasa); *La Generosità d'Alessandro* (Badini).
TRAMEZZANI: 1810: *L'Ingiusta Gelosia* (unknown).
TRENTO: 1807: *Roberto L'Assassino* (unknown). 1811: *Climène* (Caravita).
WINTER: 1800: *I Fratelli Rivali* (Butturini). 1803: *Calypso* (da Ponte). 1804: *Il Trionfo dell'Amor Fraterno* (da Ponte); *Il Ratto di Proserpina* (da Ponte). 1805: *Zaira* (da Ponte).
ZINGARELLI: 1824: *Romeo e Giulietta* (Foppa).

Appendix 8

Operas by Librettist: With Composer

By year of King's premiere or earliest revival

ANDREI: 1787: *Nitteti* (Anfossi)
ANELLI: 1816: *Griselda* (Paer). 1819: *L'Italiana in Algieri* (Rossini).
BADINI: 1786: *L'Inglese in Italia* (Anfossi). 1787: *Alceste* (Gresnich); *La Vestale* (Rauzzini). 1789: *La Generosità d'Alessandro* (Tarchi). 1790: *Andromaca* (Nasolini).
BALOCCHI: 1808: *Il Virtuoso in Puntiglio* (Fioravanti).
BANDETTINO: 1793: *Odenato and Zenobia* (V. Federici).
BENINCASA: 1789: *Il Disertore* (Tarchi).
BERIA DI SALSA: 1822: *Otello* (Rossini). 1823: *Ricciardo e Zoraide* (Rossini).
BERTATI: 1789: *La Vendemmia* (Gazzaniga). 1790: *La Villanella Rapita* (Bianchi). 1791: *La Locanda* (Paisiello). 1794: *Il Matrimonio Segreto* (Cimarosa); *Don Giovanni Tenorio* (Gazzaniga).
BOCCIARDINI: 1811: *Zaira* (F. Federici).
BOGGIO: 1793: *Teodelinda* (Andreozzi).
BOTTARELLI: 1805: *La Clemenza di Scipione* (Bach).
BUONAIUTI: 1799: *I Due Svizzeri* (Ferrari). 1801: *La Morte di Cleopatra* (Bianchi). 1809: *I Villeggiatori Bizzarri* (Pucitta); *La Caccia d'Enrico IV* (Pucitta); *La Serva Raggiratrice* (P. C. Guglielmi); *Sadigero* (P. C. Guglielmi); *La Quattro Nazioni* (Pucitta). 1810: *La Scommessa* (P. C. Guglielmi); *Romeo e Giulietta* (P. C. Guglielmi); *Atalida* (P. C. Guglielmi); *La Vestale* (Pucitta). 1811: *Phædra* (Radicati). 1813: *Boadicea* (Pucitta); *L'Eroina di Raab* (?) (Ferreri).
BUONAVOGLIA: 1817: *L'Agnese* (Paer).
BUTTURINI: 1800: *I Fratelli Rivali* (Winter). 1802: *Merope e Polifante* (Nasolini).
CALZABIGI: 1785: *Alceste* (Gluck). 1798: *Elfrida* (Paisiello).
CARAVITA: 1806: (with Carpani) *Camilla* (Fioravanti). 1811: *Le Tre Sultane* (Pucitta); *Climène* (Trento).
CARPANI: 1797: (with Lorenzi) *Nina* (Pasiello). 1806: (with Caravita) *Camilla* (Fioravanti). 1812: *Camilla* (Paer).
CASOLI: 1804: *La Vergine del Sol* (Andreozzi).
CASTI: 1787: *Il Tutor Burlato* (?) (Paisiello). 1788: *Il Re Teodoro* (Paisiello).
CHIARI: 1786: *Il Marchese Tulipano* (Paisiello).
DA PONTE: 1789: *La Casa Rara* (Martín). 1794: *Il Capriccio Drammatico*

(Cimarosa); *Il Burbero di Buon Cuore* (Martín). 1795: *La Scuola dei Meritati* (Martín); *L'Isola del Piacere* (Martín); *Le Nozze dei Contadini* (Martín). 1796: *Antigona* (Bianchi); *Il Tesoro* (Mazzinghi). 1797: *Il Consiglio Imprudente* (Bianchi); *L'Arbore di Diana* (Martín); *Merope* (Bianchi). 1798: (ad. Petrosellini) *La Cifra* (Salieri); *Cinna* (Bianchi). 1802: *Calypso* (Winter). 1804: *Il Trionfo* (Winter); *Il Ratto di Proserpina* (Winter). 1805: *Zaira* (Winter). 1811: *Così fan Tutte* (Mozart). 1812: *Le Nozze di Figaro* (Mozart). 1817: *Don Giovanni* (Mozart).

DEFRANCESCHI: 1802: *Angiolina* (Salieri). 1810: (with da Ponte) *Il Matrimonio per Susurro* (Fioravanti).

DELESTRE-POIRSON: 1829: (with Scribe) *Il Conte Ori* (Rossini).

DE SANCTIS: 1799: *Ines de Castro* (Bianchi).

DIODATI: 1792: *La Trame Deluse* (Cimarosa). 1817: *Penelope* (Cimarosa).

FARRARI: 1806: *Argenide e Serse* (Portogallo).

FAVART: 1796: *La Bella Arsène* (Monsigny).

FEDERICI: 1818: (with Schmidt) *Elisabetta* (Rossini).

FEDERICO: 1794: *La Serva Padrona* (Paisiello).

FERRETTI: 1820: *La Cenerentola* (Rossini). 1823: *Matilde e Corradino* (Rossini).

FOPPA: 1795: *Aci e Galatea* (Bianchi). 1809: *Teresa e Claudio* (Farinelli). 1819: *L'Inganno Felice* (Rossini). 1824: *Romeo e Giulietta* (Zingarelli).

GAMERRA: 1786: *Armida* (Mortellari); *Perseo* (Sacchini). 1791: *Armida* (Sacchini); *Pirro* (Paisiello). 1799: *Medonte* (Sarti). 1805: *Erfile* (Bianchi). 1811: (tr.) *Il Flauto Magico* (Mozart).

GHERARDINI: 1821: *La Gazza Ladra* (Rossini).

GIANNONE: 1827: *Maria Stuarda* (Coccia).

GIOVANNINI: 1786: *Giulio Sabino* (Cherubini). 1788: *Giulio Sabino* (Sarti).

GOLDONI: 1785: *I Rivali Delusi* (Sarti). 1789: *La Buona Figliuola* (Piccinni).

GRANDI: 1794: *I Contadini Bizzarri* (Sarti).

GUILLARD: 1796: *Ifigenia in Tauride* (Gluck). 1797: *Evelina* (Sacchini).

HAYM/Arnold: 1787: *Giulio Cesare in Egitto* (Handel).

JARVIS: 1785: *Orfeo* (past.) (Gluck).

JOUY: 1827: *La Vestale* (Spontini).

LIVIGNI: 1785: *Il Viaggiatori Felici* (Anfossi); *La Finta Principessa* (Cherubini). 1787: *Giannina e Bernardone* (Cimarosa). 1788: *La Frescatana* (Paisiello). 1790: *I Castellani Burlati* (Fabrizi). 1807: *Il Principe di Toranto* (Paer).

LORENZI: 1792: (with Palma) *La Discordia Conjugale* (Paisiello). 1796: *La Modesta Raggiratrice* (Paisiello). 1797: (with Carpani) *Nina* (Paisiello).

MARMONTEL: 1796: *Zemira ed Azor* (Grétry).

MAZZINI: 1796: *I Due Gobbi* (Portogallo).

MAZZOLÀ: 1786: *La Scuola dei Gelosi* (Salieri). 1806: *La Clemenza di Tito* (Mozart). 1813: *La Dama Soldata* (Orlandi).

METASTASIO: 1785: *Demetrio* (Cherubini); *Artaserse* (Cherubini). 1786: *Didone Abbandonata* (Anfossi). 1788: *L'Olimpiade* (Cimarosa). 1790: *L'Usurpator Innocente* (V. Federici). 1798: *Ipermestra* (Sarti). 1799: *Didone* (Paisiello). 1800: *Zenobia* (Mount-Edgcumbe). 1814: *La Didone Abbandonata* (Paer). 1827: *Didone* (Mercadante).

MORETTI: 1789: *Ifigenia in Aulide* (Cherubini). 1791: *Idalide* (Sarti). 1794: *Semiramide* (Bianchi).

PALMA: 1792: (with Lorenzi) *La Discordia Conjugale* (Paisiello).

PALOMBA: 1787: *Gli Schiavi per Amore* (Paisiello). 1789: *La Villana Riconosciuta* (Cimarosa). 1790: *La Ninetta* (Cimarosa). 1791: *La Molinarella* (Paisiello). 1793: *I Zingari in Fiera* (Paisiello). 1796: *I Traci Amanti* (Cimarosa). 1797: *Amor Fra le Vendemmie* (P.A.Guglielmi). 1803: *I Due Baroni* (Cimarosa). 1804: *Le Astuzi Femmineli* (Cimarosa).

PEPOLI: 1793: *I Giuochi d'Agrigento* (Paisiello). 1795: *Ati e Cibelle* (Cimador).

PETROSELLINI: 1785 *Il Pittor Parigino* (Cimarosa). 1788: *La Locandiera* (Cimarosa). 1789: *Il Barbiere di Siviglia* (Paisiello). 1798: (ad. da Ponte) *La Cifra* (Salieri).

PEZZI: 1827: *La Schiava di Bagdad* (Pacini).

PISTRUCCI: 1829: *I Messicani* (Bochsa).

POLA: 1830: *Donna Caritea* (Mercadante).

PRIVIDALI: 1822: *I Pretendenti Delusi* (Mosca).

ROMANELLI: 1809: *La Capricciosa Pentita* (Fioravanti). 1815: *Adelasia e Aleramo* (Mayr). 1823: *Elisa e Claudio* (Mercadante). 1826: *Aureliano in Palmira* (Rossini).

ROMANI: 1821: *Il Turco in Italia* (Rossini). 1822: *Il Barone di Dolsheim* (Pacini). 1826: *Medea in Corinto* (Mayr). 1828: *Margherita d'Anjou* (Meyerbeer); *La Rosa Bianca* (Mayr). 1830: *Il Pirata* (Bellini).

ROSSI: 1801: *Alzina* (Bianchi). 1808: *La Feste d'Iside* (Nasolini). 1812: *Ginevra di Scozia* (Pucitta). 1824: *Semiramide* (Rossini). 1825: *Il Crociato in Egitto* (Meyerbeer). 1826: *Tebaldo e Isolina* (Morlacchi).

SCHIKANEDER: 1811: (tr. Gamerra) *Il Flauto Magico* (Mozart).

SCHMIDT: 1818: (with Federici) *Elisabetta* (Rossini).

SCRIBE: 1829: (with Delestre-Poirson) *Il Conte Ori* (Rossini).

SERTOR: 1795: *Zenobia in Palmira* (Anfosse). 1796: *Piramo e Tisbe* (Bianchi).

SOGRAFI: 1801: *La Principessa Filosofa* (Andreozzi). 1802: *La Morte di Mitridate* (Nasolini). 1805: *Gli Orazi ed Curiazi* (Cimarosa). 1806: *La Morte di Cleopatra* (Nasolini).

STERBINI: 1818: *Il Barbiere di Siviglia* (Rossini).

TARDUCCI: 1803: *Fernando nel Messico* (Portogallo).
TORRE DE RIZZONICO: 1800: *Alessandro e Timoteo* (Sarti).
TOTTOLA: 1802: *Il Furbo contra il Furbo* (Fioravanti). 1823: *La Donna del Lago* (Rossini). 1824: *Zelmira* (Rossini).
VESTRIS: 1794: *Gastone e Bajardo* (Liverti).
ZENO: 1791: *Quinto Fabio* (Bertoni).
ZINI: 1791: *La Bella Pescatrice* (P. A. Guglielmi). 1792: *La Pastorella Nobile* (P. A. Guglielmi). 1807: *La Virtuosa in Margellina* (P. A. Guglielmi).

Appendix 9

The Minor Singers

A few major singers who had brief tenure at the King's during our period are included in this appendix; all singers are indexed and are here arranged chronologically according to their appearances at the King's.

THE MALE SINGERS

Andrea MORIGI, possibly a nephew of Pietro Morigi, was the oldest of the buffos, having sung in the premiere (1760) of *La Buon Figuliuola* in Rome as well as at the King's (1766). He performed at the King's from 1766 to 1771, 1781 to 1788, and 1793. In the 1785 revival of *Viaggiatori*, Morigi, "the greatest of all buffos," "by his droll caricature entertained those who had less relish for the music, than for humour and buffoonery" (LC) in the role of Palterio. In the title role of *Marchese* (1786), his "song of the floating batteries" was managed with "a good deal of art and effect" (PA). In 1787 he spent a short term in debtor's prison and missed the opening of *Tutor Burlato* (T, Feb. 19), but in later performances as M. Perruque in *Schiavi* (1787, 1788) he won repeated encores (UR; T).

Morigi's competitor was Luigi TASCA, who filled comic bass roles from 1783 to 1786 and whom Burney called an "excellent" buffo with a strong but "stiff" voice. He sang in *Rivali*, *Gelosie* (1784), *Curioso*, *Pittor* (1785), and *Scuola* (1786), when he was "as excellent as ever" (H, Mar. 13).

Giuseppe FORLIVESI apparently made his King's debut in 1788 as second male soprano in *Sabino*. The next season, his last, he was hissed (P, Mar. 25) but also encored in a trio (P, June 3). Burney called him an uninteresting singer with a weak voice.

Among the early tenors was Vincenzo CALVESI, who found success in Venice, Naples, and Vienna, but not in London. At his King's debut as Fenicio in *Alceste* (1787), the *London Chronicle* was sharply negative, while Este (UR) disliked his acting: "Calvesi—did he attend more to the *cunning* of the scene—would be better entitled to a favourable report... —a little more warmth and attention—the eyes less *directed* to the pit, and more to the stage, will be acceptable, good Signor Calvesi" (Dec. 25). Este was "happy to see Calvesi" in *Locandiera* (1788) "sustain the grave part of

Sumers with becoming gravity; this young man sung remarkably well, and seems much improved." This, however, is the last we hear of him.

Antonio BALELLI (fl. 1786–89) made his debut as second male soprano in *Alceste* (1787) "to replace Bartolini" and was "very pleasing (LC), but the *Register* said he lacked "fulness and compass" (Dec. 25). He remained at the King's through the 1789 season (T, Dec. 17, 1788). N.G. calls him a bass, but Highfill points out that his roles indicate a wide vocal range.

Girolamo CRESCENTINI (1762–1846) made his debut in Rome in 1783 and at the King's two years later in *Demetrio*. The *London Chronicle* wrote: "To a melodious voice, though not of the greatest compass, he adds a taste and action which speaks him a perfect master of music, and an actor of refined feelings. He is a pleasing stage figure." He also appeared in *Nitteti* and *Arteserse*, where the *London Magazine and British Register* found him "better than ever." But this was his last mention; he later achieved success in Italy and Paris.

Vincenzo FINESCHI, a second tenor, had little success. At his debut in *Re Teodoro* (1788) he was "too much indisposed" for the critics to comment, but in *Locondiera* the following month, he conveyed "true pathetic taste in all his songs" (T, Jan. 17). He was hired for the 1789 season as well but we hear nothing further of him.

Bernardo MENGOZZI (1758–1800), an Italian composer and singer, was singing in oratorios in Venice by 1784 and married Anna Benini about that time. He made his King's debut in a *mezzo carattere* role in *Tutor Burlato* (1787), when he "seemed to possess a clear and melodious voice, but did not discover so much power in the high notes as in the lower ones." The connoisseurs, however, "appeared quite enraptured with his singing" (H). Yet he sang but one season in London, where the climate impaired his voice.

Lorenzo Angelo CIPRIANI made his debut at the Pantheon in *Pescatrice* (1791), where he was an "admirable Buffo" (P, Mar. 2). In *Discordia* the next season he performed a whimsical duo with Casentini "and a duet solus in falsetto and bass by the Signor [was] pleasant enough" (O). His acting and singing were admirable (LC). He seems to have been dropped the next two seasons but reappeared in 1795 in *Isola* (TB).

Domenico Luigi BRUNI (1758–1821), a male soprano, sang frequently in Italy following his 1772 debut. He sang at St. Petersburg from 1787 to

1790. He sang only one season at the King's (1793) but made a strong impression there. In his debut in Paisiello's *I Giuocchi* (1798), he was "the best singer of his kind within our remembrance, being distinguished from the rest by uniting to their softness and clearness of tone greater strength than they were masters of" (H). And an unidentified reviewer wrote: "His voice is what the Italians call *voce pastore* by which they mean that the sound is thick.... He sings perfectly in time and has the best male figure that we ever saw in a Soprano." Mount-Edgcumbe wrote: "Bruni sang better at the King's than in Florence, but he was still very weak and poor in comparison to his predecessors."

Another male soprano, Agrippino ROSELLI, sang at the King's between 1794 and 1800 and was the last castrato there before Velutti. At his debut as Arsace in *Semiramide* (1794) he "did great justice to a very pretty *cavatina* in the second act and his duet with the Banti was also given with great sweetness and effect" (T, Apr. 28). In a 1796 revival of this opera he was "particularly impressive" (P). In *Bella Arsene* (1796) a first-act duet, "enchantingly sung" by him (as Alcindoro) and Banti, was encored (P). In 1800 he sang Timoteo in *Allessandro e Timoteo* and was slated to sing in Mount-Edgcumbe's *Znobia*, but "his voice and powers were so unequal to its execution that it was found necessary to induce him to give it up, and it was taken by Viganoni, who did it far more justice" (Mt-E). Parke, however, thought Roselli's voice "very superior."

In 1789 Morelli had brief competition from Francesco BENUCCI (1745–1824), an Italian bass who was a leading character buffo in Vienna and elsewhere in the 1770s and early 1780s, and who was probably the finest artist for whom Mozart wrote (N.G.). He was not admired in London, however, when he was probably well past his prime; he sang there but one season (1789). But as Bartolo in Paisiello's *Barbiere* and in Gazzinga's *Le Vendemmia* with Nancy Storace, he introduced Mozart's "Crudel! perchè finora" (*Figaro*), the "first piece of Mozart to be heard on the London stage" (N.O.). See also T, Mar. 25, May 11; and TC, May 30.

Gustavo LAZZARINI (c. 1765–?), a first tenor, was a pupil of Paisiello and sang at La Scala in Lucca. He made his King's debut in 1791 (at the age of about 26) as Ubaldo in *Armida*, where he "certainly stamped his fame by one air in which he was universally encored.... All the embellishments he introduced were so capitally executed that he did not so much as once break the time of the accompanyments; and in his encore, his cadences were entirely new." (T). He received routine praise from the press in several other operas that season and in 1792 (see for 1791: G, Jan. 22; P, Apr. 15; P, June 17;

and for 1792: O, Apr. 13; D, June 11). But he was not sufficiently admired, and he returned to Italy; he retired in 1803.

The buffo Carlo ROVEDINO first sang at the King's in 1777 and remained there through 1780. He sang on the Continent for about a dozen years, returning to the King's in the *Barbiere* in 1793. He also sang in *Zingari* that year, in Bianchi's *Acis e Galatea* in 1795, when he "looked more like a miner about Newcastle, than the King of cyclops" (MH, Mar. 23). He also sang in *Matrimonio* and *Semiramide* in 1796, in *Evelina* in 1797, and in *Cinna* in 1798. He also sang in *Angiolina, Mitridate* and *Armida* in 1802, in *Viaggiatori* in 1803, in *Calypso* and *Astuzie* in 1804, in *Casa Rara* in 1805, and in *Argenide* in 1806. S. D. ("Chronicles"), writing of him about 1800, recalled that he "was as basses went then . . . a very fine basso cantante; he had a good deep voice, but occasionally sang wofully out of tune." Indeed, he sang off and on there—defecting to the Pantheon in 1812—until 1814. Altogether, he sang in some seventy parts (Highfill). Unfortunately, comments from the press—almost invariably positive—were so brief and trite as to provide little appreciation of the singer. But the *Examiner* (H.R.) wrote of his Sarastro in 1811 (June 16) that his "'big voice' has no medium but is always either growling with an undefined rumbling like distant thunder, or bellowing forth with the most dissonant and ear-rending harshness." His wife may have been a dancer active in the late 1770s at the King's and Covent Garden under her maiden name of Rosa Tinte. His daughter Stefania—Mrs. Charles Weichsel in 1804—also sang the King's about 1799 (Highfill). His son, G. ROVEDINO, was a pupil of John Braham and made "a very promising debut" in English opera in 1812 (EM, June); he apparently sang at the King's in 1816.

Antonio BENELLI (1771–1830), a tenor and composer, sang briefly at the King's at the close of the decade. He made his debut at Naples in 1796 and had an opera of his produced there in 1798, the year he arrived at the King's. At his debut as Paolino in *Matrimonio*, he "entered fully into the spirit of this great master and executed the most difficult passages with ease and brilliancy. His voice is fine and flexible, with a sufficient degree of strength." He had a "pleasing deportment" but "occasionally indulges in unnecessary exertions that border upon caricature." In recitative he "displayed great delicacy of expression by impressing the sense of the work on the audience. . . . He varies the graces, which he is at liberty to introduce, according to the spirit of each different cantilena" (T). In 1799 Benelli sang the title role in *Mendonte*; he was "in good voice," had "airs well adapted to [his] powers" (P), and was "honoured" by the audience (T). But he received scant attention from the press in other performances that season or in 1800, when he left London for Dresden, where he sang for twenty years.

A Signor RIGHI, a tenor, is little known though he sang for many years at the King's—seldom with praise. At his debut in *Vergine* (1804), he was thought satisfactory (T), but the *Chronicle* found his voice "extremely feeble." He was applauded in *Argenide* in 1806 (T), but Robertson spoke of his "unpolished rusticity" in *Sidagero* in 1809 (E, July 2). S. D. ("Chronicles") declared (c. 1816) that "he at last found his appropriate place in the third-rate character of Basilio in the Figaro of Mozart." He was on the roster until 1819 and was still there in 1822—a "nondescript" (T, Apr. 14).

Giuseppe SIBONI (1780–1839), a tenor, made his debut at age seventeen and sang at Bologna, Genoa, and Milan. He made his King's debut in the 1806–1807 premiere of *Principe*. The *Post* noted that Siboni, "a singer of the finest celebrity in Italy," had "a pleasing voice, seems to be an excellent musician, and executes with neatness all the difficult passages he sings." But later that season, in *Serse*, he had "too feeble a voice for the King's Theatre. He labours in vain to make himself understood" (C). He was not on the 1808 roster, apparently because of ill health, for he is next mentioned as having recovered from his illness sufficiently to sing in *Pirro* in 1809, his last season in London. Later, Paer wrote several roles for him. Mount-Edgcumbe stated merely that he "sang well but with a thick and tremulous voice."

A Signor PEDRAZZI made his debut in *Serva* in 1809, when he showed "taste" but was "deficient in voice" (T). It was apparently his only King's performance.

In 1811 Signor and Signora CAUVINI made their King's debuts in *Tre Sultane*. The Signor "possessed much taste and execution, but unfortunately a voice of moderate strength," and Catalani overwhelmed him (E). He also sang Ferrando in the London premiere of *Così* and "found the two majestic songs 'Tradito schernito dal perfido cor' and 'Ah, lo veggio quell' 'anima bella' too much for his elegant but very limited voice" ("Chronicles"). His wife also sang in that opera and displayed "much archness and readiness in the various transformations of her character," but we hear from neither again.

Joseph FISCHER (1780–1862), a German bass and impresario, was the son of Ludwig Fischer, a friend and ally of Mozart. Joseph had important roles at the King's in 1812, making his debut as Uberto in *Camilla*: "Mr. Fisher's [sic] voice is a deep bass, and of course perfectly unmanageable in the more delicate expression of Italian music. It sometimes labours into the tenor . . . but its compass is narrow, and its tones few, forced, and feeble."

His "air, manner, and countenance are . . . excellent. He must first abjure playing lovers, heroes, and courtiers." (T). Two months later he sang the Count in *Figaro* at its London premiere, when the *Times* (July 6) reasserted its views. Robertson, too, thought that "unless he could get rid of his voice, his figure, and his rough German accent, he cannot reasonably hope to become a favourite" (E). Yet S. D. ("Chronicles") stated that the singer was "not popular, except with those amateurs who forgot," because of "his perfect knowledge of the proper style of singing Mozart's music, a voice which, though extremely deep, was husky and hoarse-toned."

In 1814 a Signor MARZOCCHI made his debut in *Orazi*; he was adequate to the role and was thought to become a favorite (T; Cr). "His voice is at once sweet and powerful, and there is much force and delicacy in his execution" (P). In *Barsene* the next season, "Marzocchi in particular deserves praise; he is a modest singer, who . . . has merit which a little encouragement would bring forth" (C). But we hear no more of him.

In 1815 a Signor GENI made his debut in *Adelasia*. His voice was somewhat too weak for the King's, "but this singer has obvious qualities which give the best compensation for power—his taste is delicate, his execution finished, and that general spirit of the Italian School thrown over his talent, without which vigour of organ is violence and weariness" (T; TI). The *Chronicle* thought him "a very fine tenor." But five months later, "the tremulous tones of Geni were but indifferent vehicles of the rage of the headstrong Emperor" (T). In 1816 he appeared as Orosmane in *Zaira*; "though Geni may certainly boast no common skill in music, we cannot perceive so striking an improvement in his organic power." (T). In *Selvaggi* he "discovers every day a more consummate knowledge of music, and makes us regret . . . the want of freshness and steadiness in his tones" (T). We hear no more of him.

Also making his debut in *Adelasia* in 1815 was another tenor, Signor GRAAM, who was "promising": "He has some dexterity, a slight shake, and a firm tone" (T). A few days later the *Times* found his voice "harmonious and rich" but it "may be unequal to the volume of this enormous Theatre"—"much of the grace and skill which make the finest captivation of music may be hazarded in the labour to be heard." Yet the *Inquisitor* thought his voice "at once powerful and melodious." And in *Orgoglio* he sang better than ever" (T), yet he lasted only one season.

Of the several minor singers first appearing in 1815, probably Nicholas LEVASSEUR (1791–1871), a French bass, was the best. He made his debut in

1815 in *Adelasia*, his voice "not infrequently deepening into utter indistinctness" (T, Jan. 11), but the *Chronicle* found him the equal to Revedino when the latter first came to England. In 1816, as Almaviva in *Figaro*, Levasseur, "who gradually improves in his acting, but whose visage still preserves its inflexible gravity, ought to borrow from Madame Fodor a few of her supernumerary smiles. Though he made love, however, like a Cynic, he showed himself a good musician, and his voice did more justice than we had expected to the songs of Almaviva" (T, June 24). After 1816 he apparently departed for Paris, where he sang several years at the Théâtre Italien, but he returned to the King's in 1827 for one more season, when he substituted for Zuccelli as Fernando in *Gazza Ladra*. His Fernando "gained him great and well-merited applause. A fine bass, great flexibility and musical cultivation, united to dramatic talents of no ordinary description, and impassioned scenic action, contributed to render the performance highly impressive" (NM, May). As Elmiro in *Otello* in 1829, Levasseur "gave weight and effect to the performance" (T, Apr. 27); he "promises to be more serviceable than all of his forerunners of this season put together" (Ath, Apr. 29). As Basilio in *Barbiere* two days later, he "understood" the role "perfectly," and his voice was "peculiarly suited to the music" (T). As Dandini in *Cenerentola*, however, he was "insufficient" in his acting and, in his duet, "Un segreto," "had little of that effervescence and humour which resulted from the harmonious union of brother wits when Pelegrini had the part" (Ath, May 13). After 1828 he returned to Paris where he sang at the Opéra until 1853.

The only new male in 1816 was Pierre Ignace BEGREZ (1787–1863), a French tenor, who had made his debut at the Paris Opéra the previous season. At his King's debut in *Griselda*, Begrez (he was also known as Begri) had "a very clear, sufficiently strong musical, tenor voice; he sings in good taste, possesses a fine person and address, and is an acquisition of value" (C; TI). But the *Times* wrote that he would "make a respectable assistant, but has not qualities to entitle him to the situation to which he seems to have been appointed." The following month they admitted he sang the role of Nerestan in *Zaira* with "flexibility of voice, and considerable science," though he would do only for "a wide range of second-rate characters." (T). But he "acted with great judgment and vivacity" as Guglielmo in *Così* (C, June 8). In 1817 he "well sustained" the role of Don Calloandro in *Molinara* (C; LG), though "it would have been quite as pleasing a performance had he not been continually convincing us how perfectly he is aware that he has a pleasing person and an excellent set of teeth" (BS). He also performed satisfactorily the role of Ernesto in *Agnese*: "His voice is of very good compass, but wants power" (T; LG). Begrez sang in minor roles in 1818 but in 1819 he "succeeded perfectly" as Monostatos in the *Magic Flute* (T; C). He also did well as Ottavio in *Don Giovanni* (BS). He disappeared from the roster in 1820, but the next year repeated his Ottavio. He was for a time displaced by a Signor Torri. However, he returned in 1822 and sang Lusignano in *Pietro* with distinction and "more power than usual" (T) but was still in a character "inferior to his rank" (C). In April the *London* wrote that Begrez "improves every time we hear him. He not only has a fine voice and a correct ear, but his manner of forming his tone is Italian, and exactly true, his taste is good, and his execution improving every hour. He is unquestionably the best tenor in London by many degrees." Notwithstanding this praise, he no longer sang regularly at the King's. He later sang in concerts and no doubt taught singing in London, where he died.

Carlo ANGRISANI (1765–?), an Italian bass, sang in the leading opera houses in Italy from 1786 to 1796; he later sang in Vienna. He made his King's debut in 1817 in *Penelope*, but with three other new singers to review and on an opening night, comments on him were all but lost. In *Griselda* he was "effective" as the marquis (a dual role) in the "elaborate *Finale*, and other pieces in parts"—less so in single songs (LG). And in *Don Giovanni*, he sang both Masetto and the Commendatore; the former role was satisfactory, but in the latter he was "not sufficiently solemn and emphatic"—a "trifling fault." On the whole he was a "most excellent musician" (T, Apr. 16; LG). Kenrick (BS, May) wrote: "His Masetto is a very amusing and natural piece of acting, nor does he fail to do justice to his supernatural character. He has, however, greatly amended his conception of the latter part since the first evening." The *Inquisitor* (Aug.) praised his "deep solemn tones" as the Statue. In 1818 he "well supported" the character of Bartolo in *Figaro* (T, Jan. 19), and the following season he took the lead and won high praise (T; C; TI; BS). As Sarastro in the *Magic Flute*, he "sang his two airs very finely" (C). He also sang Mithridates, a pharmacist—a character unworthy of him—in *Modesta Raggiratrice* (T). In 1820 the *Times* called his Sarastro "beautiful and even sublime." Orbazzano, in *Tancredi*, "is not a character of vocal importance, but Sig. Angrisani rendered it as prominent as propriety would admit" (TI; C). In 1821 he also excelled in a minor role in *Gazza Ladra* (C). He was still at the King's in 1822; in 1825 he went to New York for a season at the Park Theatre. "Chronicles" spoke highly of his roles in *Don Giovanni*, *Barbiere*, and *Figaro* ("'Non più andrai' had never been sung better"). Yet he seems to have become entrapped by minor roles assigned to him.

In 1819 a Signor PLACCI, a bass, made his King's debut as Mustapha in *Italiana*. "He has some execution, but possesses neither a just intonation nor a voice of much strength or clearness" (T, Jan. 27). The *Chronicle* thought his voice a "barytone," whereas the role called for a "true bass"; but the *British Stage* called him "a sweet, rich tenor, though we think without any considerable compass." Later, the role of Figaro in *Barbiere* was "condemned to be butchered by Placci, who appears to be perfectly incapable of conceiving or giving expression to the admirable pleasantry of the character" (BS). Yet he continued, in 1820, as the valet in *Cenerentola*, where he "showed himself an improving singer and actor" (T), though the *Chronicle* found him "destitute of voice." As the magistrate in *Gazza Ladra* in 1821, "certainly he never appeared to so much advantage" (C). He had "no chance of distinction in his role in *Turco* (T; C), but in 1823 he "looked his character" as a hussar in Pacini's *Barone* (LG). That year he replaced Angrisani as Publio in *Tito* and "gave much reason to regret the loss of his predecessor" (T). He was only "passable" (T) in *Elisa*, but the *Herald* thought the role of the marquis "extremely well represented" by him. "Chronicles" said he "did not rise one degree above mediocrity." He died insane in Bologna (T, Jan. 27, 1829).

Also in 1819 a Signor ROMERO, a Spanish bass (BS, Apr. 1819), came to the King's as *primo buffo* by way of Paris but stayed only two seasons. At his debut as Leporello he presented a "balky" figure unsuited to the role, and he could not act (T); he was hissed at the performance though he sang the music "tolerably well" (TI). Two weeks later he "personated Bartolo very respectably" (T), but the *Chronicle* advised him to return "to the more humble, but less dangerous, situation which he held in the Theatre Favart." He was "very favourable," however, in the serious role of Serastro (T). In 1820 he returned to sing Bartolo, but "he puts us to sleep by his watchman-like tones" (C), and as Alidoro in *Cenerentola* he lacked "the power of using his voice" (C). .

A Signor ALBERT, a French bass-baritone, arrived in 1820 but lasted only part of one season. At his debut as Figaro he was "evidently well skilled in music, but his voice, which is a barytone or low tenor, of very limited compass, is so weak as scarcely to find its way, even in the songs, through the accompaniment of the orchestra" (T). Bacon (LM) was even harsher: "He is a bass, completely realizing the idea of mediocrity in vocal science, in power, compass, and execution, while his unfortunate bulk and obesity unfit him almost for any motion."

Another new singer in 1820 who stayed but one season was Francesco BIANCHI, a tenor, who made his debut as Bajardo in *Gastone*. The *Chronicle* thought him "a singer of the first rank, with a rich, powerful tenor voice," and the *Gazette* was flattering, while the *Times* found him "imperfect in a few of the upper notes, but of a good quality, and his style is highly cultivated, though often so profuse in ornament as to destroy all traces of the melody or subject," and in his acting he displayed "an air of vulgar confidence." In singing the role of Tamino, his "eternal *roulades*, and inattention to the measure of rhythm of the composition, are wholly at variance with the character of Mozart's music" (T). Bacon added: "His science and execution, were the natural organ finer, would carry him to a greater elevation, but as he is, he never rescues his auditors from neutral indifference" (QMM, II, 375).

Signor TORRI, a tenor, made his debut in 1820 as Raimiro in the premiere of *Cenerentola*. Alsager stated: "His style and science, considered as Italian, are not above mediocrity, but the tones and limited compass of his voice render him still less eligible" as a *primo tenore* (T). Ayrton (C) found his voice "very weak, but the quality of the tone is good; . . . his execution is slow and excessively laborious," but it is "more than compensated for by the perfectness of his intonation." The *Gazette* agreed, but thought his acting "above the usual stamp of musical performers," and Bacon (LM) remarked on his considerable "power of executing passages with neatness and velocity." In 1821, still first tenor, he sang Pippo in *Gazza*. "His style is good and is united with an agreeable voice and considerable execution," but he deserved no such "exalted rank" (T), an attitude they reasserted at his repetition of Argirio. We do not hear of him again until 1826, when he reappeared as Roderick in *Donna del Lago*, but his reception was cool: "Had it been a first appearance he could not have been more inefficient as regards the business of the stage and the giving due expression to the composition" (Alsager). "He was not at all improved in his singing." (LG; E). But in a later performance as the Prince in *Cenerentola*, he presented a different view to the *New Monthly*: "We perceived with pleasure that Signor Torri has repossessed himself of his former familiarity with the business of the stage, and of the quantum of vocal power and cultivation which he had previously displayed on these boards." In 1827 he performed Agorante in *Ricciardo*, but "in his hands" it "excited no interest at all" (T). In 1828, his last season at the King's, he sang Ilo in the premiere of *Zelmira*, but "it fell into most incompetent hands" (T) and was too difficult for him (At). But he did very well as Rodrigo in *Otello* (T). As Ottavio in *Don Giovanni*, he "really gave us more pleasure (because [he was] less affected) than the principal singers" (At), but the *New Monthly* at this point thought he had little to recommend him to the audience. Holmes (At, Mar. 8, 1829) regretted that he had been cashiered at the end of the season. Mount-Edgcumbe thought he had a sweet but feeble voice.

Ranieri REMORINI (1783–1827), a buffo, was very successful in Italy (*Spettacolo*) but had only two seasons at the King's before his death. He came to London in 1824 by way of Lisbon, making his debut as Selim in Rossini's *Turco*. "His voice is uncommonly powerful, but rather hard; its range is not extensive, and it is defective in the means of expressing . . . tenderness. . . . On the other hand he has plenty of flexibility, and executes his passages with ease and neatness" (T). He was also successful as Assur in *Semiramide* (T). In 1825 he appeared in *Adelina* and "displayed more force, both in his acting and singing, than we before had given him credit for possessing" (T; C). He was very satisfactory as Noraddin (the part was written for him) in *Pietro*, but at a later performance he twice forgot his lines (T; C; LM, May). In *Così* he "might have succeeded better in Guglielmo had he made himself master of his notes," (T) but the *New Monthly* (July) thought his part "was often too high for the usual range of the bass-voice." The next season, in our last notice of him, the *London* (Feb.) reported that Remorini's loss "will be felt."

Felice PELLEGRINI (1774–1832), a baritone, had his early training at Naples and Milan and was singing in Paris by 1819. He made his King's debut in 1826 as Figaro in *Barbiere* and was very well received: "His person is short and slight. . . . [His] voice is a deep tenor, of very fine quality . . . and his natural taste . . . and knowledge of music [are] excellent. His action is extremely appropriate" (T). But in an attempt at the serious role of Noraddin in *Pietro*, he "was deficient in force and dignity. The general character of his singing was chaste and cold" (T). He played Dandini in *Cenerentola* "with a due degree of comic humour; but . . . the whole of his *vis comica* was not brought into action" (NM; QMM, VIII, 50f). In 1828 he sang in *Margherita*, but his acting was disappointing (T; C). The *New Monthly*, however, thought the part unworthy of him. The *Times* thought his part in *Zelmira* "unfit for the nature of his talents." The *Atlas* called him "droll" in the role of Leporello, but the *New Monthly* thought it "a dry and formal exhibition, inferior to De Begnis and Naldi." In 1829 he sang a very satisfactory Podesta in *Gazza* (T), and, in probably his final appearance at the King's, he "acted Figaro with his usual spirit. We envied him the slap which he received from Susanna" (Ath).

Filippo GALLI (1783–1853), a *basso cantante*, made his debut as a tenor in Naples in 1801 and sang at La Scala, Milan, for many years, as well as in Vienna and Paris. He made his debut as a bass in 1811. Rossini wrote the role of Assur in *Semiramide* for him. He made his King's debut as Fernando in *Gazza* in 1827, and Alsager (T, Feb 5) was glad to see that his great reputation "was not a mere bubble . . . of favouritism but a solid superstructure, resting on the basis of unquestioned ability. Signor Galli's voice is of the purest kind. We have scarcely ever heard a singer who combined, in a more eminent degree, the qualities necessary to constitute a fine bass,— depth, clearness, melody, and flexibility." He followed with a performance of Noraddin in *Pietro* that was "in the highest degree successful (T, Apr. 23); yet the *Examiner* (May 6) found him "a very inadequate successor" to Zucchelli: "his execution was coarse and laboured. . . . He is also sadly deficient in animation." He was inferior to Remorini in *Semiramide* (NM). Again the critics disagreed on his Lord Burleigh in *Maria Stuarda*. Absent in 1828, he returned the next year as Count Ori but was disappointing in that role (E; At), as he was in *Cenerentola* (Ath). Sterling gave him high praise as Robinson in *Matrimonio*, but Ayrton was acerbic. We find no further reference to him, although he remained at the King's until 1833. He later sang in Mexico and Spain, returning to La Scala; he was still singing in public as late as 1840. Parke found his voice "powerful in the extreme but not of the best quality."

A Signor DE (or DI) ANGELI, a bass, took the place of Porto in his King's debut (1827) in *Vestale*, but "touching this person, we would only suggest to the Director, that it will be cheaper and not more afflicting to the ears of Opera-goers, to supply his place with the first bellman he can seduce from that employment" (C); "the less said [of him] the better" (NM). Yet he survived these attacks to return, in 1829, when he sang the buffoon Taddeo in *Italiana*; but his voice was "of a very poor quality" and he was "totally without humour" (C; Ath).

Giulio BORDOGNI (1789–1856), a tenor, made his debut in Milan in 1813 and sang with much success at the Théâtre Italien for some fourteen years; he made his King's debut in 1829 as Giannetta in *Gazza*. His power was not great, but his compass was extraordinary: "There is perfect equality in all the gradations of its scale, but it is chiefly distinguished for flexibility. His style of singing is florid, and he is very apt to indulge in appoggiature" (T; Ath; NM). After a weak start, he did "ample justice" to the role of Almaviva (T), but he displayed a woeful lack of power in *Semiramide* (Ath). He retired in 1833 and taught singing in Paris.

A Signor SANTINI—possibly Vincenzo-Felici Santini (c. 1798–1835)—first appeared at the King's in 1830, making his debut as Assur in *Semiramide*. "He has a deep and sonorous bass voice, which he manages with great facility, and he is an experienced actor as well as singer (T; Ath; Har), but Holmes thought he produced "a very bad tone." As Elmiro in *Otello*, he was "not stately enough" (Ath), but he was very successful as Figaro in

Barbiere (Ath, Feb. 27). In *Gazza* he disappointed the *Athenaeum* but not the *Atlas*. He pleased the *New Monthly* as Dandini in *Cenerentola*, but as the Duke in *Pirata*, he greatly disappointed the *Examiner* and the *Chronicle*.

Luigi LABLACHE (Naples, 1794–1858), a powerful bass and a major singer, was the son of an expatriate French merchant and an Irish woman; he became "the most famous bass of his generation" (N.G. and N.O.). After singing in Naples (1812), Milan (1817), and Venice (1824), he made his King's debut in 1830 (on May 13, not Mar. 30 as in N.G.) as Geronimo in *Matrimonio*. Alsager (T) wrote: "He has a bass voice of great depth, power, and flexibility. Its intonation is remarkably clear and correct, and his articulation so distinct that each of his words is understood in every part of the house. His is the perfect *buffo* style of the Italian stage—comic without extravagance, and humorous without vulgarity." The *Athenaeum* quite agreed (May 15), while the *New Monthly* noted that "the specimen is in every way gigantic—a stature of six feet, a circumference not far short of six feet, a pulmonic apparatus of six-horse power." Even Ayrton called his triumph complete. He followed this success with a performance of Leporello, but "ably as Signor Lablache exerts himself . . . his personal appearance was too strikingly at variance with the well-known requisites of that character" (T, June 4; Ath). Except for 1833 and 1834, Lablache remained at the King's for every season until 1852 (N.G.). He was extolled by Mount-Edgcumbe, Parke, Edwards, and Chorley, who said he could sing over any fortissimo.

THE FEMALE SINGERS

Giovanna SESTINI (fl. 1772–91), a pupil of Dr. Busby, once achieved some prominence, but her voice declined early and by our period was nearly gone. She came to London from Lisbon in 1774 and was probably the wife of Vincenzo Sestini, who was at the King's about that time. (He sang a few seasons there, then became their designer of costumes and decorations from 1785 to 1800 [Highfill].) She made her King's debut in 1775 and sang there fairly regularly until 1791. She also sang frequently in Dublin as well as on the English stage from 1782 to 1789. She was still prima donna at the King's in 1786, and as La Baronessa in *Marchese* that season, she "entered into the spirit of her character with great success" (UR). She was also praised as the Contessa di Bandiera in *Scuola* (H, Mar. 13). She appeared in some four operas in 1787, one in 1788, and two in 1789, when she was billed as a second buffa; she sang in *Figliuola*, and an unidentified review (TC) stated that she had "established her reputation in it, being the best buffa who ever performed the character of Cechina." She was the earliest singer Mount-Edgcumbe could remember; he called her handsome, sprightly, and a great actress, but her voice was "gritty and sharp." She was admired by the public but not by the connoisseurs.

Rochele (Rosina) D'ORTA (later Signora GIORGI) raised little notice at her debut in Sarti's *Rivali* in 1784. In *Curioso* the following season her "Son regina disperata" "was a complete piece of acting and singing" and was warmly received (H); she excelled in an aria and duet in *Pittor* (H) and in two arias in *Finta* (LM), after which we hear no more of her.

Maddalena (Teresa) ALLEGRANTI (1754– after 1801) made her debut in Venice in 1770 and later sang in Mannheim (Charles Burney heard and admired her there, although later he was less enthusiastic) and in Venice. She made her King's debut in 1781 but soon thereafter departed for Dresden and Venice. She returned to the King's in 1799 — brought there, according to da Ponte, by himself — to appear in *Matrimonio*. The *Chronicle* was favorable, but the *Post* regarded her appearance as "a sacrifice of prudence to an extraordinary desire to please. The very severe hoarseness . . . proved it a premature essay." Parke claimed she had "not sufficient perfection left to sustain the important part," and Mount-Edgcumbe was scathing: "Never was there a more pitiable attempt: she had scarcely a thread of voice remaining." Da Ponte's assertion that she was the victim of a cabal lacks other support; in fact, her auditors were friendly, but after three more performances, she gave up and in 1801 retired from the stage.

Adriana GABRIELLI, also known as Ferraresi DEL BENE (c. 1760– after 1800), named after her birthplace in Ferrara, was a pupil of Sacchini and sang in Venice, where Burney noted her unusual voice (1770). In 1783 she eloped with Luigi del Bene, son of a Roman consul. In 1785 she made her London debut as Cleonice in *Demetrio* and received mixed notices. She later appeared as Beroe in *Nitteti* (H) and as Mandane in the English opera *Artaxerxes* (LM). In the pasticcio *Orfeo*, she was "truly above all encomium" as Eurydice (UC). As Bettina in *Viaggiatori* she "showed comic powers of which, to say the truth, we did not before suspect her to be capable" (LC). She was "easy, spirited, and apposite to the character of Flirtilla," and several songs were encored (LM). In 1786, as Vespina in *Marchese*, she again showed herself as effective in comic as in serious roles (H, Jan. 30) and was warmly received (T). As Ernestina in *Scuola* she "was applauded even to the skies, in several of her songs; . . . but her rondo in the second act was such as to raise admiration to a kind of enthusiasm" (H, Mar. 13). Nevertheless, she returned to Florence that year, reaching her pinnacle in Vienna (1788–91), where she was Mozart's first Fiordigli (*Così*), though in other roles, such as Susanna (*Figaro*), he had only qualified enthusiasm for her (N.O.). Parke called her no prima donna.

Marie PIELTAIN (née Chanu), wife of Dieudonne-Pascal Pieltain, a Netherlands violinist and composer who played in various London orchestras, was second woman at the King's in 1789 but made no impression at all. In 1791 she turned to English opera, singing in *The Woodman*, but "the terrors of a first appearance on the English stage, deprived her almost of the power of utterance through the first scene" (C; LC, Feb. 28).

Cecilia GIULIANI (née Bianchi) took the place of Mara in 1788–89, making her King's debut as Epponia in *Sabino*. She had "much merit" but was unequal to Mara; "her voice is extremely thin, and her upper notes have a shrillness" (T, Apr. 7). The *Gazetteer* reported that she had a good figure and an expressive countenance but did not rise above mediocrity. In 1789 she sang the title role in *Ifigenia*, where she "shone more in the recitatives as an Actress than as a Singer," though her singing was an improvement over the previous season (P, Jan. 26). In fact, the *Times* thought she and Marchesi "were every thing Cherubini could have wished" (Jan. 26). She performed satisfactorily in *Disertore* (P), but in *Generosità* her acting was decried: She "was chiefly distinguished by a very disgusting mode of rolling her eyes and distorting her features" (P). Boaden stated that although she was never great, she was always agreeable and true; but Burney declared she lacked a powerful voice, had bad affectations, and sang out of tune. Yet she went on to a brilliant debut at La Scala, Milan, in 1790 and was prima donna in Venice in 1791. Moreover, Fétis found her "remarkable for the purity and flexibility of her voice."

Anna BENINI (fl. 1784–91) sang buffa roles at the King's in 1787. At her debut in the title role of *Giannina*, she "gave great satisfaction. Her voice is silver-toned, and she sings with taste and manner, that discovers her to be well skilled in music" (H). The *Register* said: "She was . . . perfectly at home—shaking hands with the orchestra—all was perfect union" (Jan. 11). She also excelled as Rosina in *Tutor* (H), but the English climate disagreed with her, and she and her husband, the tenor Mengozzi, left for Paris. She was in Venice in 1791. Burney and Mount-Edgcumbe agreed her voice was not powerful, yet the former stated that she sang in tune and in an "extremely graceful" manner, and the latter noted her "finished taste and neatness."

A later buffa was Margherita DELICATI, wife of singer Luigi Delicati, who made her debut as Lila in *Cosa Rara* (1789) and introduced airs by Mazzinghi: "Her voice has great compass, and she sings very well in time, but she wants [a] refined taste and expressive manner" (LC). The next month she substituted in a maternal role for Marie Pieltain in *Disertore*, but "her figure has more of the maternal em bon point" in it than was necessary for the role (P, Feb. 19). She appeared in *Villana* in March but thereafter received no further mention.

Mrs. Augusta Vittorio Correr (née Wynne), daughter of "an English gentleman living in Italy," took the name of Signora ANGELELLI (as a disguise, no doubt, for the cabal) and sang at the King's a single season— 1798. At her debut as Donna Ciprigna in *Scuola*, she succeeded despite a cold. "She is possessed of a voice uncommonly sweet and melodious, which she manages with great judgment and skill. Its principal defect is, it has not sufficient strength.... She evinced a delicate and refined taste in her manner of singing" (P). The *Times* found her especially suitable for light comic parts; but "her fine execution was lost in the big house." The *Chronicle* thought her voice "thin and feeble." She appeared as Eurilla in the premiere of *Cifra*, where her second-act aria (encored) ranked "as a *chef d'oeuvre* in variety and delicacy of expression," although her voice was "still too weak." She appeared in *Capriccio*, in which she was very successful. Her "taste becomes every day more conspicuous. The chasteness and facility of her execution, and the pleasing variation with which she introduces occasional graces in her *cantibile airs*, while melody is strictly adhered to, cannot be too highly praised" (T; P). The King's audience would forgive much else in a singer, but never a lack of sheer vocal power.

Signora Luigi Borghi (née Anna CAS[S]ENTINI), a prima buffa, sang in London for three seasons. In her 1791 debut as Dorinda in *Pescatrice* at the Pantheon, where her husband was acting manager, she was called "an elegant and graceful woman. Her voice has an uncommon sweetness, and from the well-managed swell which distinguishes her modulations, we think she is of the school of Pachierotti" (P). She sang with praise as Rachelina in *Molinarella* (T) and in *Locanda* (P). In 1792, as Donna Aurora in *Discordia*, she rendered her airs "with her usual sweetness and ability" (PA; LC). She sang "with great spirit, character, and precision" (D), and her songs "went off admirably" (H). She did not sing in 1793 but appeared in the 1794 season opening, *Matrimonio*, without significant comment, after which nothing further is heard of her. Parke cited her tasteful singing, unaffected gentleness, and ease, but apparently her voice was too weak.

Another comic singer, Anna MORICHELLI-Bosello (c. 1750–1800), arrived at the King's late in her career. She made her debut in Bologna in 1773 and later sang in Spain and Russia. She came to the King's in 1793 in company with Martín, who wrote comic operas for her (according to da

Ponte, she and Martín were lovers). She made her debut as Angelica in his *Burbero*, which failed; but the *Times* noted that she was "triumphant," that her voice had both power and sweetness, and that as an actress, she had "*expression*—and that is a charm which must ever gain a strong hold on an English audience" (Mar. 21). Parke cited her "admirable" singing and acting in this opera. As Rachelina in *Molinarella* (1795) she "sang and acted most inimitably, and gained an unanimous encore to her first charming air," "La Rachelina" (T, Dec. 9). The *Chronicle* observed: "Her comedy was excellent, and infinitely more in the correct stile, which we admire in England, than her former performances." She received encores as Donna Caprigna in *Scuola* (C, Jan. 28) and as Amelina in *Isola* (TB), but there is no mention of the "mad scene" that da Ponte says she inserted to the detriment of the opera. Not satisfied with her London success, she returned to Italy at the end of the season and in 1798 retired from the stage. Mount-Edgcumbe stated she was "cried up" by a strong party as equal to Banti but claimed she was past her prime, her taste "not true," and her acting affected. Da Ponte disliked her "finely posturing voluptuous indulgences" and noted ironically that she "managed to play the part of a modest and retiring virgin of fifteen."

Marinna LAURENTI, called a "scholar" of Giordini, came to the King's from Rome in 1790 as first buffa and appeared in *Ninetta*, but the *World* found her "not very heavy laden with voice or figure." In *Due Castellani* her voice was good but her manner stiff (PA). Parke said she lacked vocal power. She did not survive beyond one season.

Maria BOLLA was brought to England from Milan as a child and, after remaining six years in a school in Hampstead, returned to Italy. Kelly engaged her for the King's in 1800, when she was about twenty-five years old. (She also sang Lila in the *Siege of Belgrade* at Drury Lane the same season.) She made her debut in *Zingari*, which was "rendered more attractive by the taste and science which she displayed. Her voice combines strength and sweetness, and she threw into the most difficult passages of her airs a grace and animation that few first comic women are capable of expressing. . . . To superior musical talents [she] joins the rare merit of excellent acting" (T). The *Chronicle* thought that "her science and taste, joined with her Comedy, made her an incomparable acquisition," and the *Post* stated, "her voice is strong, clear, and enriched with sweetness and her development easy and her manner full of life and sprightliness." The *Mirror* agreed, but found her embellishments "too frequent and too affected." She sang in several other operas that season, without press comment, and in the next season Banti had to take over her role in *Consiglio* when she became ill

(T). In 1802 she sang in Paris (though still on the King's roster), and in 1804—her last season in London—her singing of an aria in *Astuzie* drew praise (T). Mount-Edgcumbe recalled her as a "pretty, genteel actress" with only a fair voice.

Mariana VINCI, "a Lady of considerable celebrity on the Continent," had recently sung in Lisbon, where she "created the greatest enthusiasm both by her singing, person, and acting" (T). She made her King's debut in *Principessa* in 1801. She "possesses an elegant figure, a pleasing countenance, and with a voice in its upper notes is uncommonly powerful and correct, she has the skill of giving to her *continuata* a force that contributes very much to the expression of the music. Her deportment and action were not altogether easy and graceful" (T). The *Chronicle* found her "a grand and superb figure;—tall and majestic in her deportment." The *Post* was quite carried away: "We never witnessed a debut of more flattering promise. . . . Every point of the Lady's person may stand the test of criticism. . . . Nothing can be more beautiful" than her arms and shoulders, and she has "fine black eyes with teeth of purest white." She sang in *Angiolina* (1802) and "played with much ease and spirit" (P); the *Times* said she was "in excellent voice." But a week later she was ill and another opera was substituted. She sang in other operas that season—her last at the King's— without press comment. Parke said she had skill in expressing a "perfect" crescendo and diminuendo. Mount-Edgcumbe noted, cryptically, that she was a "great" woman, with "great pretensions," but "failing in everything."

Lugia GERBINI, who was tutored by Viotti on the violin, performed in concerts in Lisbon in 1799, and in 1801 she was singing in Madrid. She made her King's debut in *Merope* in 1803 and was "well received" in her trouser role of Timantes. Her voice possessed "a full and mellow tone, not without considerable extent" (T, Dec. 6, 1802), and she "displayed science, and a clear full-toned voice" (P). But soon there were disagreements among critics. In a buffa role in *Due Baroni*, she "struggled thro' her part with vigour, but [was] altogether too cold to create an interest," according to the *Chronicle* critic, who disliked the opera; but the *Times* declared that she "gave her airs with powers of voice, skill, and feeling that were rewarded with general and reiterated plaudits." She was "particularly happy in several difficult passages." In *Viaggiatori*, on the other hand, the *Times* thought her singing and acting "above mediocrity" but they "do not soar much beyond it," while the *Post* found her duet with Vaganoni "executed with great ability and effect," and she "in every instance succeeded in the exertion and effect of her vocal powers." Yet she dropped out at the end of the season. Mount-Edgcumbe called her a bad singer but "a good player on the fiddle."

A Signora GRIGLIETTI made her King's debut as Servilia in *Tito* in 1806. She "is engaging in her person, and has a sweet voice, but she was extremely overpowered by her terrors, and was forced... to retire" (C). (The *Post*, reporting nothing of this, merely asserted, "We have no doubt [she] will prove an acquisition.") In Guglielmi's comic *Due Nozze*, "she was deservedly encored, and she will find, though she does not herself suspect it, that her talents are better adapted to the comic than the serious muse" (C). The *Times*, noting the "Signora" was "rather Miss Grigletti [*sic*], a young lady from Bath," stated she "acquitted herself admirably" as second woman. After a few performances the next season, she bowed out, only to reappear in 1810 on the English opera stage. But in 1812 she returned to the King's as Annio in *Tito*, when her costume had "too doubtful a gender." In 1815, still there, she gave an air in Mayr's *Adelasia* "with great sweetness and effect" (TI). We hear no more of her.

Sophia Giustina CORRI (1775–c. 1830), who played the pianoforte in public at age four, was the daughter of Domenico Corri and wife of the composer Jan Ladislaw Dussek, with whom she gave concerts. Under the name Madame Dussek, she made her King's debut in *Didone* in 1808. "We never had a superior second woman," wrote the *Chronicle*. "She executed her songs with true science. We trust her acting will improve." Robertson was also critical of the "wretched feebleness of her acting" in *Amanti*: "Who but herself would in the character of Eneas wear a nosegay in her breast-plate, and a spy-glass tied with a black ribband round her neck?" (E). She stayed only one season, worn out with "so much fatigue and the cabal" (*Dictionary of Musicians*). She was apparently a better harpist and pianist than a singer. She later became Mrs. John Alvis Moralt.

In 1809 Signora PUCITTA made her debut in her husband's *Villeggiatori*. "Her voice is an alto-tenor, of great sweetness but little strength: she manages it however with the greatest taste and science" (T). Robertson was mildly positive about her, but she soon dropped out.

Mrs. Francesco BIANCHI (née Jackson) married the composer about 1800; after his suicide in 1810, she married John Lacy, a singer. She made her debut at the Ancient Concerts in 1798 and at the King's in *Sidagero* in 1809. Her "propriety of action, and her good taste... triumphed over the defects of a very bad voice" (E); but S. D. ("Chronicles") simply called her "one of the worst female performers who ever trod the Opera stage."

Signora COLLINI, a contralto, made her debut in *Capricciosa* in 1809 as second woman. The *Times* called her "elegant" and a "pleasing comedian" but found her voice "of no great compass or extraordinary strength." The *Chronicle*, noting the difficulty of a debut on the same stage with Catalani, was more indulgent: "She sung with ease, clearness, and taste." Robertson was even enthusiastic: She "possesses a very rich and firm-toned voice . . . clear and powerful; and her action is . . . lively and vivacious. . . . With very little execution, she contrives to attract the attention of the audience by her expressive mode of singing." She excelled in *Sidagero* later that season (T). In *Zaira* the next season, she was "one of the most attractive actresses we have ever seen" (T). As Dorabella in the King's premiere of *Così*, she "displayed very considerable talents, and executed her airs in the most pleasing manner" (T). As Egle in *Flauto Magico* her "deep and powerful voice" had "considerable effect" (E). Yet that was her last season at the King's. Mount-Edgcumbe found her good as a second woman but unequal to the first.

Theresa BERTINOTTI Radicotti (1776–1854) contributed much to London's musical life by virtue of her introducing *Così* to the King's in 1811 — the only season she sang there. By age four she was studying music, and at twelve she made her debut with a children's troup. She made her debut at La Scala in 1794–95 and later sang in Florence, Venice, Milan, and Turin, where she met Felix Radicatti, a composer, whom she married in 1801. They concertized together in Munich, Vienna, and Holland. She made her King's debut in *Zaira*, which Federici had written for her. The *Times* admired her voice but thought her character somewhat unsuitable for opera seria. "Her figure is easy and graceful; rather too easy and too graceful for the heroine of the higher opera. It wants the haughty dignity and regal presence, the bold part and majestic movement, which gives us the idea of the tragic queen. Her voice . . . is exquisitely pure and delicate; and some of the tones are of that touching tenderness, which the ear loves to dwell and hang upon, long after the voice has ceased. . . . She exhibited a perfect knowledge of her art, which delighted the audience." Robertson noted that she "made no pretension to acting," but her voice "is powerful, melodious, and, what we rarely find, perfectly in tune. . . . Her only defect . . . is a piercing shrillness in her upper notes." Later that season, in her husband's opera *Phædra*, she "exerted all her powers to give effect to the Opera, and her powers in the 'Cantabile Style,' are admirable; but we fear no powers are adequate to sustain 'Phaedra' for any considerable length of life" (T). Still later that season she produced, for her benefit, the King's premiere of *Così*, and her superiority in comic roles was confirmed. Robertson declared: "Nothing like the singing of Madam Bertinotti has been heard at the opera for some years, as it left nothing to be wished for. It was, as it has not always been lately, perfectly in tune, and given with a feeling that evinced a proper estimation of Mozart's merit. No meretricious ornaments were added, but every grace was introduced in it's proper situation." The *Times* observed: "Madame Bertinotti, as Fiordiligi, sang with the utmost sweetness. If this lady has not the astonishing powers of some others, she certainly does not lose in the comparison, in respect of melody and truth." Not up to two bravura arias in that performance, however, she substituted two easier ones (Hogarth, II, 189–90). Mount-Edgcumbe also commented on her superiority in that role and stated that she performed much better than Catalani in a revival of *Sidagero*. She concluded her season by performing Pamina in Naldi's ill-fated production of *Flauto Magico*. Robertson stated she "was the only performer competent to her part." She later sang successfully at Lisbon, then settled in Bologna, where she was still living in 1849.

Camilla FERLENDIS (née Barberi), was the wife of Alessandro Ferlendis, an oboist who played in the band at the King's. (In 1777 Mozart composed a concerto for Alessandro's father, Giuseppe, a prominent oboist in Vienna.) A contralto, Camilla sang in Milan, Paris, and Madrid before coming to London, where she made her debut in *Dama Soldata* in 1813. "Her voice is a low soprano, limited in its compass and not very powerful, but the tone is full and she sings without any painful effort. Her power of execution is not great, but she does not often attempt anything that she is not conscious of being able to perform" (C; T). The *Inquisitor* was drawn to her acting: "She trod the stage . . . with an ease, a self possession, and an adaptation of dress, attitude, and voice to the [two] characters she assumed, that place her in the first rank of dramatic excellence." She sang in 1815, her last season, but went unnoticed by the press. Mount-Edgcumbe noted that she was eclipsed by Catalani and was "less liked than she deserved."

Morianna SESSI (1776–1847) made her debut in Venice in 1792 and sang at Vienna after 1793, but she left the stage from 1795 to 1804, following her marriage. She stayed at the King's but one season, making her debut in 1815 as Adelasia in Mayr's opera. She displayed "a good voice, considerable skill and facility in its management, and an evident knowledge of music," though she was well past her prime (T). Her voice was "sound, melifluous, and strong," had "no extravagant ornaments," and was in the "highest class—a musician" (C). But she was a poor actress (TI). She pleased in *Proserpina* but did not please enough (T, Jan. 15, 1816; "Chronicles"). Mount-Edgcumbe called her only a fair singer. Parke thought her voice clear and powerful, though she sang without expression. She retired from the stage in 1836.

A Miss MORI, sister of Nicholas Mori, a London violinist, and wife of one Gasselin, also a singer, made her King's debut in 1817 as Arsinoe in *Penelope* and "was throughout respectable, but not sufficiently animated" (LG). She was praised as Eugenia in *Molinara* (C), but was a "cipher" as Charlotte in *Agnese* (T). In 1819 she was adequate in *Raggiratrice* (TI). In 1820 her acting of Cherubino was "full of boisterous gaiety" (C; LG), and as Clorinda in *Cenerentola* she "executed a difficult bravura very successfully" (T; LG), though the *Chronicle* thought she "attempted too much." She was also successful in *Tancredi* (T; TI). As Zaide in *Turco* (1821) she was "very tolerable" (T) and performed her part "with great spirit and propriety" (C). This was apparently her last season at the King's. In 1825 (Apr.) the *London* recalled that Mori was the best Cherubino they had ever seen. She may have been more successful on the Paris stage, where she appeared about 1830 and from which she retired in 1836.

A Miss HUGHES-GATTIE was born in London in 1788 of a wealthy Welsh family, the youngest of eight children, and was related to Colonel Hughes (M.P. for Wallingford), "perhaps the richest commoner in England" (TI, "Sketch," Mar. 1816). She showed early proficiency in music at "Mrs. Davis's celebrated school at Salisbury," and she had private lessons from H. H. Barthélémon. She also wrote verse and could compose songs for herself. Billington and others who heard her sing in private encouraged her to perform in public, and in 1811 she was induced to sing at an Ancient Concert, where her success was the occasion of ill will expressed by her rivals; she returned her remuneration to the directors and withdrew. Nevertheless, she later studied under Siboni and "rapidly acquired all the refined graces and science of the Italian school" and did further concertizing at the Nobility's Concerts and elsewhere. Catalani, who also tutored her, thought her "the only English singer who could sing Italian music in the genuine manner . . . and with the genuine pronunciation of the Italian school," and she urged her to "tread the stage." She sang in English operas at Covent Garden in 1815, but after some dreadful notices, she retired for a year; in 1817 she made her debut at the King's in *Griselda*. The *Times* was glad to see her "at this theatre, where her knowledge of the Italian school has made her an important acquisition." The *Chronicle* noted her singing of La Duchessa "was applauded in a most flattering manner. . . . She is an excellent musician." The *Inquisitor* wished she had "aimed less at ornament. Her voice is naturally very good, and she ought to rely much more on its intrinsic melody than she does." And the *Gazette* thought her debut "not unfavorable," though there was "a tinge of affectation" in her performance. She next appeared as Donna Elvira in the premiere of *Don Giovanni* and "gave it with the energy which a deserted and vindictive female naturally feels; her singing in this most difficult part was excellent" (C; TI). Her Elvira "was a very spirited performance, and she sang with much judgment and effect" (T, Apr. 16). But the *British Stage* thought her efforts as an actress were "entirely overwhelmed by the superior powers of those who surround her." She did not return to the King's until 1819—"now comically termed Mad. Gatti [*sic*]" (C). She sang Marcellina in *Figaro* and was "all correctness" (C), but the *Gazette* thought her only passable. In 1820 she sang Thisbe in *Cenerentola*, and her musical knowledge "was essential to the concerted pieces" (T; LG). And in 1821—the last we hear of her—she sang Isaura in *Tancredi* "with much ability" (T).

Francesca CORRI-PALTONI (1795–?), daughter of Natale Corri, a music publisher, and niece of composer Domenico Corri and cousin of Sophia Giustina Corri, studied under Catalani in 1815 to 1816 and under Braham. She was married to the tenor Paltoni. She came to the King's in 1818 to replace Camporese but "was certainly not that lady's equal in either style or acting, yet she deserves more popularity than she obtained" ("Chronicles"). She made her debut as the countess in *Figaro* but was "not of a very prepossessing appearance; her figure is *petite*, and her countenance is not remarkable for intelligence; but her voice is good, her musical talent still better, and, last of all, she is quite at home in Mozart's music. . . . [She exhibited] an occasional coldness of manner, rarely the concomitant of genius, which absolutely froze some of the finest passages in the opera" (T; LitC). But the *Chronicle* was more positive, calling her "gifted with a rich and powerful voice. . . . Her intonation is perfect [and] her taste, though certainly not perfect, is much better, that is to say, less exuberant—than we expected to find it." When she, instead of Camporese, attempted Donna Anna, the *Inquisitor* (Feb.) made no such allowances: "'Ah! *what a falling off is there my countrymen!*' It almost staggers our opinion of her." But the *British Stage* differed sharply: "She sang the several airs with great taste and feeling; nor are we certain that Camporese herself excelled her in that exquisitely pathetic Duet *Fuggi, crudele, fuggi*." As Matilda in *Elisabetta*, she "was only fair" (TI). In 1819 she sang Elvira in *Italiana*, but she "does not gain ground in the judgment of the *dilettanti*; she seems to be fluctuating between two schools of music, the English and the Italian, and it is probable will therefore become mistress of neither" (T, Jan. 30). In *Raggiratrice* she "acquired deserved applause" (TI); she "has improved since last season in voice but not at all in her acting, which is cold and awkward" (LG). Again as the countess, she "continues to improve, and gave the very charming and difficult music . . . in a style, that would have done credit to the most experienced artist" (TI; T). As Queen of the Night, she "very neatly and correctly executed" two bravuras (T; LG). Hunt (E) also agreed, but he added: "We cannot say we are ever moved by this inexorably frigid performer." In 1820 she "afforded signs of great improvement" as the countess (LG), and the *London*'s endorsement (Jan.) of her was high. She performed Amenaide in *Tancredi* and was "extremely successful" (T); the *Inquisitor* agreed but added, "The tameness of Miss Corri is her most inveterate enemy, and till she masters the great secret of spirit and animation, no permanent eulogy will attach to her endeavours." This was her last season at the King's.

Isabella COLBRAN Rossini (1785–1845), a Spanish soprano, sang but one season at the King's—1824. She sang in Spain in 1806–1807 and was in Naples over a decade, excelling in tragedy (N.O.). Rossini's operas for Naples (1815–1822) all contained parts for her (they were married in 1822), but her voice had started to deteriorate as early as 1815 and was all but gone before she reached London (N.G.; Weinstock, pp. 49, 128). At her King's premiere in *Zelmira*, it was noted that "she may have possessed the voice and style suited to a *prima donna*, but the period has passed" (T; LitC; LG), and the *London* reported she had been "grossly misrepresented by foreign publications," judging by her performance in London; yet she was "still a great singer in many respects; . . . her execution is neat, though very rapid; and her intonation occasionally only faulty. . . . Her expression is still fine; there are marks of a style originally great." The *Harmonicon* and the *Examiner* were quite harsh. Colbran sang Zoraide in *Ricciardo* and "got through the part respectably" (T), and the *Examiner* now saw some improvement: "Some portion of her fault yet remains; but, where sweetness or expression are required, she shows that she possesses them in a high degree. Great refinement is the characteristic of her singing." (Ebers thought this her best role.) After that season she retired from the stage. In 1837 she was legally separated from Rossini.

Madame CASTELLI, wife of Ignez Castelli, sang sporadically from 1825 to 1838. In May of 1825 (apparently not her debut) she appeared as Despina in *Così*; she "sung with some piquancy of style, and did not forget in her acting the archness and cunning" of the part (T; NM). She sang a not very effective Cherubino in 1826 (NM) and seems to have been absent from the company in 1827. She sang in several secondary roles from 1828 to 1830 but received little attention from the press.

Marietta BRAMBILLA (1807–75), a contralto, who studied at the Milan conservatory (1821–26), made her King's debut in 1827 as Arbaces in *Semiramide*. The *Times* found her voice not of the best quality, though the *New Monthly* was quite favorable and the *Atlas* thought her a very good "second-rate" singer. In 1828 she was "extremely meritorious" in *Margherita* (T; C); she had a "powerful voice" and "much feeling" (E), though the *Atlas* thought her voice "hard." She was "very promising" in *Zelmira* (T; NM) and "extremely pleasing" as Felicia in *Crociato* (T; NM). But she returned to Italy at the end of that season.

Giacinta TOSO-PUZZI, a soprano, also a student of the Milan conservatory, married Giovanni Puzzi, a horn player, in 1827. She was very attractive, had a fine stage presence, and a voice remarkable "in its breadth and fullness" as well as in power, but with limited range, so that she was only moderately effective (T, Mar. 19; NM). But she quite failed as the lead in *Ricciardo* (T). She returned to Milan, probably in 1828 (T, Jan 26, 1829).

Madame SCHUTZ, a German mezzo soprano, who studied voice in Italy as well as Germany and had sung at the Théâtre Italien, made her King's debut as Sesto in 1828. She was slender, elegant, and at home on the stage, and her voice had compass and flexibility, but her style was rather florid. She was well received though no prima donna (T; NM; Har). She later sang Arbases in *Semiramide*, but her voice was not right for the role (T, Apr 21). Her Malcolm in *Donna del Lago*, however, "cannot be too highly spoken of" (T, May 12). Mount-Edgcumbe admired her voice and style, but Parke reported she was deficient in expression. Her husband sang Papageno at the King's in 1829 (C).

Henrietta Clementine Méric, née Lanieraux LALANDE (1799–1867), a French coloratura and pupil of Manuel García, sang in French provincial towns from 1814 to 1822. She later sang in Italy, making her debut in Naples in 1814 and becoming "an idol of the Milanese" (Ath, Apr. 24). English critics were split in their opinions about her. At her King's debut in 1830 as Imogene in *Pirata*, Alsager thought her performance placed her "in a very high rank, both as a singer and an actress." But the *Chronicle* thought her voice had a narrow compass and was "now considerably on the wane." She also "labours under some defect of respiration," but was otherwise "entitled to the highest commendation." As an actress Lalande combined "the gentleness of Sontag and Caradori, with a large portion of the force and power of Pasta and Malibran." Holmes (At) admired the beauty of her high notes, her intonation, and her expressive style. But the rest of the press complained of her shrillness and intonation. She was better than expected as Donna Anna (T, June 4 and 7; Ath) Her singing as Donna Carita in Mercadante's opera had "great effect" (T), and the *Athenaeum* thought her much underrated in London despite "a certain tremulousness" in her voice that "incapacitates it for execution of passages of energy or strength"; the

New Monthly and *Atlas* agreed. Ayrton (Har, VIII, 267) was correct in predicting she would never become popular, and Chorley, who claimed English audiences were averse to her "trembling" tones, reported that she gave little satisfaction.

The Misses CHILD, BELCHAMBERS, and BROMLEY, who sang at the Royal Academy of Music performances from 1828 to 1830, were highly praised in criticism as detailed as that for the King's performers.

PART III
English Opera

Introduction

WHAT IS ENGLISH OPERA?

ALTHOUGH ITALIAN OPERA at the King's Theatre had become somewhat democratized in our period, it still retained too many aristocratic trappings to suit the average Englishman. Yet in his own way, the average Englishman was an avid opera-goer: he simply wanted operas in his own language, with dialogue in place of recitative; and at his own playhouse, where it could thrive alongside the nonmusical but traditional comedies, farces, and tragedies of the English dramatic stage.

This required radical alterations from the prevailing Italian mode of opera. For, whereas Italian opera was all-sung—the action of the story being rendered in sung recitative passages and thus giving paramountcy to the music—in English opera the story line was carried on in spoken dialogue, which emphatically included the dramatic climaxes, and to that extent music took a subordinate role. To be sure, John Bull was passionately fond of singing—especially the light, simple songs in which the words could be easily understood, and he might even enjoy an occasional bravura. But he was far too committed to the tradition of spoken drama to want the story garbled in recitative; for him the drama lay not in the music but in the words and the action.

Since Mozart's *Zauberflöte* or Beethoven's *Fidelio*, no one could sustain the premise that genuine opera must be all-sung. But if we are to accept Edward J. Dent's position that "the fundamental principle of opera" is that "the music itself is the drama" and that it is "a complete work of art in which the music is the most important thing and the creation of a distinguished artist,"[1] very little in English opera from, say, Thomas Arne's *Artaxerxes* (1762) to Benjamin Britten's *Peter Grimes* (1945) could meet these criteria.[2]

Even Eric Walter White's definition of English opera as "a stage action with vocal and instrumental music written by a British composer to an English libretto,"[3] broad as it is, would not quite do. The most famous of all English operas was John Gay's *Beggar's Opera* (1728) for which he himself selected all the music, and many later playwright/librettists followed his example. And what is to be said of an English opera like *Love in a Village*, which has borrowings from sixteen other composers—mostly Italian—even though the compiler is a highly respected musician such as Thomas Arne, while the librettist, Isaac Bickerstaffe, took credit for the musical selections?

Much of the problem of English opera has been seen as the "English" influence. The strong adherence of the English people to a powerful native drama, for instance, has been blamed for their resistance to the "irrationality" of all-sung opera. But the collateral development of native types of opera in France, Germany, and Spain, which also had strong traditions of spoken drama, showed similar resistance to sung recitative. Dialogue was as requisite to *opéra comique* as it was to singspiel and *zarzuela*.

Even the language was blamed. In 1708 critic John Dennis pointed out that the English language, with its strong consonants, "cannot be pronounced without very frequently shutting the mouth, which is diametrically opposite to the expression of music."[4] In Thomas Clayton's preface to *Arsinoe, Queen of Cyprus* (1705), the first all-sung English opera to survive, he wrote: "The musick being Recitative, may not, at first, meet with that general Acceptance, as it is to be hop'd for from the Audience being better acquainted with it" (Fiske, p. 32). Thomas Arne himself argued against recitative in English opera. Still later, Richard Mount-Edgcumbe, a composer and critic, repeated the judgment that "our language" is "unsuited to recitative." Indeed, even Dent has asserted (p. 233): "The difficulty of setting English to music is plainly shown by the extraordinarily small number of English songs, old or new, that can be considered as belonging to the rank of masterpieces."

In 1667 John Evelyn, commenting on recitative in English written "after the Italian manner," stated: "I perceive that there is a proper accent in every country's discourse, and that the setting of notes to words, therefore, cannot be natural to any body else than them."[5] But as early as 1653, Matthew Locke had composed effective recitative in *Cupid and Death*, and in 1689 Henry Purcell showed how music could be perfectly accommodated to English recitative in *Dido and Aneas*.

With closer regard to operas after, say, 1785, we note that in defining opera as simply dependent on the "sufficient importance" of the musical numbers, Donald J. Grout[6] has perhaps justified my including them under the classification of "English Opera" rather than "English Musical Stage," though the few musicologists who have examined surviving scores of some of the works included herein emphasize that most are not operas but "plays with music." But even plays with music varied enormously in musical content. The fact is that most of these works were *called* English operas (a

Introduction

very few were thought *not* to be operas by contemporary periodical critics). With all their musical borrowings (q.v.) their frequent patchwork quality was not without precedent. "It is so easy for writers on opera to praise Italian opera in general, and to blame the English operas . . . for adding and adapting," writes Dennis Arundell,[7] "but this is exactly what the average Italian opera [composer] did" at the time.

But "sufficient importance" of musical numbers implies something about both the quantity and quality of the music. The quantity varied enormously. In 1731, for instance, Theobald's *Orestes*, though called an opera, had but one air in each act! This is of course an extreme example. On the other hand, many operas had a good deal of music. The Macnally-Shield *Robin Hood* (1785), for example, which included glees, ballads, airs, duets, trios, and a concluding finale with chorus, had a total of thirty-one numbers. Similarly, the Burgoyne-Jackson *Lord of the Manor* (1780) had twenty-five numbers, and Brandon's *Kais* (1808) in four acts had thirty-one numbers. Yet some of the "operas" discussed herein probably had fewer than ten numbers in each act. Many of the early nineteenth century "musical dramas" discussed by Bruce Carr[8] had only ten to twenty musical numbers altogether.

As to the *quality* of the music, it also apparently varied greatly. Fiske (pp. 580–81), who has examined surviving scores of eighteenth-century English operas, thinks that at its best it was better than that in many contemporary Italian operas. Most of the songs were strophic, though no doubt many of the borrowed songs, and perhaps a few English ones, were through-composed, i.e., the music is changed for each stanza of the poem.

Much of the music was probably not very dramatic. Nicholas Temperley[9] states that the songs were deliberately adapted to the "general situation" rather than to the particular dramatic context so they would *sell* better as detached songs for use in the concert hall or drawing room. In surveying the use of music in "gothic" operas of the late eighteenth century, Aubrey S. Garlington, Jr.[10] finds no music that attempted to portray the "wild" happenings on the stage—battles, storms, mysterious events—in the gothic operas composed by Samuel Arnold, William Shield, and even Stephen Storace. (Supernatural effects in music had been a feature of Restoration stage music, however.) Only after gothic elements merged into melodrama after 1800 (see below) were conscious attempts made to interpret the drama by appropriate music. In his study of the Victorian musical theatre, George Hauser[11] admits that "musical-dramatic unity was a rare occurrence." Fiske has noted a marked decline in musical quality even before 1800, though David Mayer[12] thinks him too hard on early-nineteenth-century composers.

Theatrical practice in our period distinguished between operas and nonoperas by means of a spoken prologue, which preceded only the latter. Of little use are the type designations assigned to these productions by the playwright or manager. A glance at the prefatory note to appendix 10 will show that they had no fewer than twenty-three opera types, though by far the majority used were "comic opera," "operatic farce," "opera (serious)," and "melodrama" (also termed "musical drama"). No doubt many of these types were thought useful in drawing slight dramatic distinctions between the various productions. But, as a matter of fact, many of them were quite misleading, and several examples of strongly operatic productions that were even designated "dramas" can be found in appendix 10. Often, too, the designation provided in the advertisements and playbills—mostly followed by the critics—differed from that in the printed play.

The presence of nonsingers in the leading roles also could not provide a criterion. Many of the melodramatic types required actors, not singers, as leads; yet many melodramas did have considerable musical content (see below), and sometimes leading singers *were* required (Mayer, p. 119). On the other hand, some comic operas called for singers *only* in the leads, while everybody else was confined to dialogue.

Whatever one's criteria for judging whether a particular work is in some significant way operatic, a score is of course indispensible. Yet in a study embracing over 350 productions of the English musical stage, an examination of even those scores and librettos that survive[13] lies beyond my present reach. In this respect I have had to rely strongly on Roger Fiske's invaluable study before 1800, plus a few other scholars who had studied some of the later scores, though they discuss only a handful of the works cited herein.

In an endeavor to select mainly the more operatic productions of the time, I have eliminated all that large hodgepodge of burlettas, burlesques, musical extravaganzas, and the like that were the nightly fare of the minor theatres in London (they were, in any case, totally ignored by reviewers), and instead, I have concentrated on the productions of the two major theatres, which were considered the only "legitimate" theatres, as well as of the one or two summer theatres (see below). I have also eliminated almost all of the very numerous *anonymous* theatrical productions of this period at all theatres. On the contrary, I have concentrated mainly on the major playwrights who wrote operas, though I should hasten to add that I have also included a number of works that represented only one or two operatic productions of a particular playwright's entire opus if the music appeared at all important. Similarly, I have tried to give more emphasis to the productions of the better known composers, even when some of their works appeared to be more plays than operas. Finally, I have occasionally been guided by the reviews themselves—especially when several are found for a given production—in terms of the extent of their commentary on the music and the singing.

While I have sometimes included marginally operatic productions to discuss some particular aspect of them—usually the singers—I believe that most of the works listed in appendix 10 represent the more clearly operatic productions of the period. On the other hand, I make no claim for appendix 10 as a definitive listing: no doubt I have overlooked some that were actually more operatic than many of those listed and discussed; on the other hand some marginally operatic productions have been included for other reasons. In any event, considerations of space have made it necessary to limit discussions in the text mainly to those operas that received critical commentary of some significance.

EARLY DEVELOPMENTS IN ENGLISH OPERA

While it is true that in a sense English opera had no certain continuity and no unbroken line of tradition, a glance at its early history may throw some light on its later manifestations from 1785 to 1830. English operatic types have been traced to the masque—a late Renaissance development, popular in courtly circles, which combined poetry and dancing with vocal and instrumental music. Perhaps its greatest appeal was in the costumes and the scenic effects, produced with elaborate machinery, on which large sums were expended.

In 1656 the so-called first English opera was produced—*The Siege of Rhodes*, libretto by William Davenant and music (now lost) by Henry Lawes, Henry Cooke, and Matthew Locke. It was all-sung, but it was influenced by the masque tradition rather than by Italian opera. Davenant had experimented with various operatic types during the Commonwealth, when only plays with music were allowed. But the public was apparently unhappy with English recitative, for in Restoration revivals it was spoken, not sung.[14]

From 1660 to 1700, playwrights had come to accept a great deal of music so long as the leading players only *acted*. But something closer to opera was achieved late in that century in collaborations between John Dryden and Henry Purcell. In *King Arthur* (1691), for example—probably more play than opera—Dryden had to "cramp" his verses to accommodate the music, but half the opera was spoken, and the principals did not sing.[15] These collaborators also produced a successful tragic opera, *The Indian Queen*, in 1695. With others, Purcell produced the *Fairy Queen* (1692), based on an adaptation of *Midsummer Night's Dream*; though called an opera, this extremely elaborate production was mainly spectacle in the masque tradition. He also wrote songs for the *Tempest* (c. 1695) and other operatic types.[16] In some of these, the drama retrogressed to the masque style, and songs were given only to subordinate characters, but Price (p. 7) points out that many of his songs in *plays* are more "dramatic" than anything in his semi-operas. Most were successful; *King Arthur* was even revived in our period, and "Fairest Isle, all Isles excelling" was very popular, though not all of Purcell's music was retained.

Most critics in our century have regarded Purcell's *Dido* as the first genuine English opera and have mourned his early death, at age thirty-nine, as a disaster for the genre's failure to achieve "true" all-sung opera after 1695. But both White and Price find in this attitude a skewed understanding of late Renaissance dramatic opera, when composers saw no need at all to forsake the prevailing type of opera, and Price concludes that "dramatic opera never threatened to shed its spoken dialogue" during this period.[17]

Still other "English" problems are evident following the decline of the late great Renaissance composers after 1700, as related to the state of English music generally and to the status of English composers. This decline has been blamed on, among other things, the supremacy of shop-keeping during the eighteenth century and empire building during the nineteenth. According to Lang, the English became "too deliberate and practical" for the "irrationalism which permits the flourishing of music,"[18] and Dent (p. ix) sees this national attitude as a main cause of the failure of English opera: "To the Italian music is a means of self-expression, or rather self-intensification; to the Englishman music is a thing apart, a message from another world."

We have already noted the enormous increase in foreign—mostly Italian—musicians in London in the eighteenth century, many of whom could command exorbitant fees compared to native musicians. No wonder the status of the English composer sank abysmally. Many opera composers in our period were forced by sheer economic survival to become theatrical hacks, grinding out songs by the measure to the tune of the managers and playwrights—and sometimes not well paid even for that. And although operas succeeded mainly on the quality of their music, the playwright/librettists "were not conditioned to accept this view." (Fiske, p. 262). Neither did the generally low state of English drama of the time (see below) encourage the production of librettos that offered them much inspiration. The genius of Thomas Arne, William Shield, and Stephen Storace could occasionally triumph over the system, but that of Henry Bishop, despite all his strength, ultimately succumbed to it.

Following unsuccessful attempts to adapt translations of opera seria to the English stage early in the eighteenth century (White, pp. 137ff.), a new way was prepared for English opera by the increase in the number of songs—many of them ballads—found in both comedy and tragedy at that time. As Allardyce Nicoll explains: "Disintegrating elements everywhere were at work, so that we may explain the development of ballad opera as a perfectly regular development of those comedies and farces which had introduced songs into the midst of the dialogue, fostering the decay of the true comic spirit, by the desire to emulate the success of Italian opera and by the prevalence of burlesque and satirical motives."[19] Accordingly, in 1728, one of the most popular English opera ever written—John Gay's *The Beggar's Opera*, a "Newgate Pastoral"—was produced.[20] Gay selected the music—mostly ballads, but also arias by Purcell, Handel, and others—to which he wrote satirical verses sometimes far superior to the originals.[21] The tunes, with ingratiating variety and catchy melodies, provided just the right setting for Gay's new lyrics. Its immense popularity led to a decade or more of similar productions. But ballad opera "lacked the principle of growth," and by mid-century other changes were in the wind.[22] Elements of opera buffa became evident, not only in outright borrowings from Italian opera (which now became fashionable), but in shifting from broad comedy and burlesque to semiserious sentimental types and simple "half-Italian, half-English music" (Grout, I, 262).

By mid-century, English composers were adopting the new *galant* style, while some opera plots switched from the past to the present. Moreover, "the frequent dulness of sentimental comedy and the excessive chill of Augustan tragedy cried out for something that should be thoughtless and absurd and risible" (Nicoll, II, 208)—a dramatic development that was echoed in operatic farces.

The most successful theatre composer of this period was Thomas Arne. In *Artaxerxes* (1762) he wrote an all-sung serious opera, based on his own adaptation of Metastasio's libretto, in the current Italian musical style. Despite its recitative (much or all of it dropped in later revivals), it became enormously popular and was frequently revived for a hundred years. The experimental *Siege of Rhodes* aside, it became the first successful all-sung English opera—a record that stood until late Victorian times.[23] Arne's most influential operas, though, were of the sentimental type that he wrote for Isaac Bickerstaffe's librettos.

LIBRETTOS

English opera librettos were written mostly by playwrights rather than by librettists (both were cited as "authors" by reviewers); that is to say, they were written principally by dramatists whose output was mainly plays, not operas. This has induced me to designate such an author as a dramatist/librettist in the appendixes, though what they wrote for the musical stage were clearly librettos rather than plays or dramas. To be sure, there were exceptions. Thomas Dibdin's extensive productions were almost all musicals of one heterogeneous type or another; but few of them were strongly operatic. On the other hand, even a composer/dramatist like Michael Lacy, who *did* write operas, worked mostly from translations. Some of these playwrights were quite sensitive to the special requirements of a libretto, and one, William Dimond, even wrote a preface about the problem.

Those concerned about the loss of quality in the dramas of our period, such as some of the literary journals, were quick to seize on published librettos in their reviews to illustrate the depravity of the stage. But even George Hogarth, who was no enemy of English opera and who found composers equally culpable, showed a bias (II, 461–64):

> Sense is sacrificed to sound. Music is degraded into a gratification of the ear, instead of being regarded as a language capable of exalting the sentiment, and deepening the passions of the drama. No man of genius will suffer his poetry to be made the vehicle for unmeaning sing-song; hence the opera is left in the hands of playwrights, and, with few exceptions, is looked upon by people of sense and reflection as a slight and frivolous amusement, unworthy of serious notice.

In 1824 the *Literary Chronicle* related librettos directly to the decline of the drama, stating: "How is it possible that any thing worthy the name of dramatic talent, should be exercised on such as form the groundwork of a popular melodrama. How shall an author write common sense, or an audience listen to it amidst the distractions of music, scenery, and banditti, and goblins, on the one hand; battles, horses, water, conflagrations, blue lights, and red fire, on the other" (Aug. 8).

Two years earlier, the *London Magazine*, on the same subject, deplored "the want of some master-spirit to excite and confront the energies of talent; . . . but mere talent will not do it; it cannot create." And they deplored the theatrical system that produced hacks: "A second fatal absurdity . . . is the idle dogma that none can write a play except the inmates of a play-house. . . . A theatre is the school of the pupil, not the study of the master; and he who writes plays solely from the mere mechanic skill acquired in his visits before or behind the curtain, may be a decent playwright, but he never will be a dramatic poet" (Oct.).

More recent critics have also been hard on English opera librettos.

Cecil Forsyth[24] has condemned most of them generally; excepting only the *Beggar's Opera* and a few other early ballad operas, he finds slack diction, stock characters, and stock situations, and he even cites the "traitorous Italianisms" of Arne's *Artaxerxes*. And Nicoll, who is generally unsympathetic to English opera, finds most of the dramatic elements in opera pretty dull.[25] But Price regards his treatment of opera librettos—at least in the earlier years—as superficial and inadequate, while Fiske (pp. 266–68), also in defense of the librettos, points out that their plots were no sillier than those of the plays of the time. In any event, musicologists who insist on using only the composer's name in discussing English operas do not really understand the genre.

Melodrama, a *locus classicus* of the "decline," needs special mention. The term did not arrive until Holcroft's French adaptation of *A Tale of Mystery* in 1802. Thomas Busby's music[26] rendered it "one of the most popular things in its class," according to Boaden (II, 331), who defined melodrama as "an opera in prose, which is merely spoken," though music introduces the characters. The type is traceable to J. J. Rousseau's *Pygmalion* (1779), which contained spoken passages accompanied by music. Most eighteenth-century melodramas included passages in which music is interspersed with spoken dialogue and passages in which spoken dialogue is actually accompanied by music. The English type often did include much singing. Moreover, "the use of music was neither random nor capricious, but closely related to the nature of the piece and to the effects sought. In many instances music was almost continuous, extending for entire scenes, possibly entire acts" (Mayer, p. 115).

Patrick J. Smith finds that melodrama arose from a decline in French tragedy and a growing influence of the novel.[27] Its spirit, according to E. B. Watson,[28] "is found in a specialized plot that "relies strongly on mechanical contrivance" in which characters "of impossible and conventional vices and virtues act with a kind of mathematical precision. . . . The frank directness with which it produced its effects," mainly through the music, "made its utter unreality seem real for the time being and its excessive artificiality seem simple." Often closely associated with the melodramatic type was a sensational atmosphere, derived largely from adapted Auguste von Kotzebue's plays, which reflected the German *Sturm und Drang* movement and merged it with English gothicism. Thus, the early sentimental plots gave way to siege plots, ghost plots, and spectacular effects of all kinds. Operatic melodramas before 1800 included John O'Keeffe's *Castle of Andalusia* (1782), *Coeur de Lion* (1786—one by Leonard Macnally and one by John Burgoyne), James Cobb's *Haunted Tower* (1789), the younger Colman's *Mountaineers* (1793) and *Iron Chest* (1796), and "Monk" Lewis's *Castle Spectre* (1797).

LIBRETTISTS AND COMPOSERS

By and large, in English opera it was the playwright/librettist rather than the composer who was in command. Early on, as we have noted, some of the former even selected the songs. And Thomas Brinsley Sheridan, playwright and theatre manager, furnished his father-in-law, Thomas Linley the Elder, with the smallest details for the music for his *Duenna*, which had to accommodate the styles of the various singers and precise situations of the drama. He also complained about the difficulty of matching new words to old songs that Linley wanted to introduce.[29] On the other hand, Fiske has shown (pp. 259–63) that the elder Charles Dibdin achieved some parity with his playwright, Isaac Bickerstaffe, in *Lionel and Clarissa* and that Stephen Storace largely asserted control over the introduction of music in his operas. Yet he points out that, despite Storace's contribution of two hours of music to the very popular *Siege of Belgrade* (1791), it was still called Cobb's opera.

True, some house composers had a certain authority. Dr. Arnold, composer for the Little Theatre, remonstrated with George Colman the Elder after the stage manager had dismissed a chorus singer for sending in a double for a rehearsal—"this was Arnold's department." The singer was reinstated.[30] And Henry Bishop, who for years had the powerful post of house composer at Covent Garden, had the authority to order lyrics from librettists. Even after that, in 1833, he wrote playwright Edward Fitzball: "Will you oblige me by writing me a song to the measure and style of the enclosed song? Anything, so that it can have the title of *The Merry Mountaineers*, and so that it can be sung by a female; light and playful. . . . You can take any subject so long as it is graceful and pretty."[31]

The slapdash manner with which some of these operas were put together is evident in this rare account of a musical farce, *Review* (1800), which was still being performed successfully forty years later. The farce

> was written, or rather put together by [the elder] Colman in sudden haste at Dr. Arnold's table in Duke-street. The characters and principal dialogue, &c. of Caleb Quotem [an earlier opera], was transferred, without much addition from a piece called 'Throw Physic to the Dogs,' which had failed a season or 2 before. Songs which Dr. Arnold had by him, ready cut and dried, were adopted and even characters introduced to sing them. (Peake, II, 286)

But at least conferences were necessary! In a 1781 letter to O'Keeffe, Dr. Arnold indicated a need to get together with him before he could furnish airs for the songs in *Banditti*. Even then O'Keeffe took the lead: "Arnold noted down from my voice such airs as I myself chose to introduce, with his accompaniments."[32]

The exigencies of commercial production no doubt foisted much tawdry material on the public. Nevertheless, there were times when careful writing did mark some of the lyrics and librettos, and sometimes the playwrights farmed out their work to specialists in lyrics — not always to the public's or critics' liking. There is good evidence that Bishop's musical inspiration flagged over third-rate librettos. As our critics make clear, composers for the musical theatre had an unenviable lot, and many plays with much fine music failed because of inept librettos.

A playwright's remuneration came from a publisher, a theatre, or sometimes both. He usually earned less from a publisher, but some playwrights, anxious to see themselves in print, published anyway; there was a good market for printed plays, but a play's novelty to a theatre manager would be compromised if publication preceded theatrical production. In turning over the libretto to a theatre manager for an agreed-upon sum, he was virtually ceding him the copyright, which, in either choice, reverted to the playwright after fourteen years; sometimes, however, other arrangements were possible (L.S., p. cxc.). For example, late in the 1790s, Thomas Dibdin got £5 a week from Covent Garden to produce one Christmas pantomime and one one-act piece annually, plus £100 for the copyright of the songs (i.e., lyrics).[33]

This sum varied considerably between playwrights (a more successful one could do better), theatres (the majors paid about twice the amount of the minors), and periods (after the 1790s the majors became more generous). Early on, Dibdin found the £100 he got from the majors was higher than publishers would offer, but in 1797 he got only the "old burletta price" of five guineas for a Sadler's Wells production that earned the house £900 — he sold the songs to a publisher for fifteen guineas (I, 208). In 1796 Covent Garden paid Prince Hoare £210 for a one-act musical farce, and they paid Dibdin £300 each for *English Fleet* (1803), *Thirty Thousand* (1804), and *Two Faces under a Hood* (1807) — all three-act pieces (I, 314, 364, 413). Nicoll states that by 1800 an author could earn as much for a one-act afterpiece as for a main piece, and fewer of the latter were produced.

As noted above, often the copyright arrangement did not prevent librettists from publishing the "Book of Songs" (i.e., lyrics), which were sold in theatres and bookstores. Dibdin earned £150 for the songs from the *Cabinet*: they sold for 10 *d.* each — a "high price." Indeed, for most of his three-act productions he earned between £60 and £100 for the songbooks. James Robinson Planché, a later, prominent playwright, earned £100 on one songbook.

In addition to the above, a playwright earned substantial sums from the theatre, depending on the success of his production. Traditionally, he was paid what amounted to benefits for the third, sixth, and ninth nights after deducting the house costs—usually £64 5s. a night—from the receipts.[34] This scale was also increased in the 1790s following an agreement between the very successful playwright Frederic Reynolds and Covent Garden, whereby he was to receive £300 (i.e., £33 6s. 8d. a night for the first nine nights), plus £100 on the twentieth and fortieth nights, even if they should take place the following season—an arrangement later adopted by Drury Lane and the Little Theatre. For his *Cabinet*, for instance, Dibdin earned £400 for the third, sixth, ninth, and twentieth nights, plus £150 for the copyright (I, 327).

Thus, successful playwrights could earn a good living. Reynolds earned £20,000 over a lifetime on some fifty productions. But by the 1820s, the rates for plays had dropped (N.); in 1829 the *Chronicle* thought playwrights got too little for their labors—only £60 for a "fine tragedy" (Jan. 16).

Composers of operas seemed to make their income mainly from the sale of the published music, and if Parke is a reliable guide, their earnings increased very considerably over the years. James Robinson Planché reported it was the custom for the author to allow the composer to publish the words with the music. O'Keeffe states, however, that he gave Shield £120 for the music to *Fontainbleau*; whether this was in addition to the publishing rights is not clear. Publishers paid Arne sixty-three guineas for *Artaxerxes* (1762); Shield £100 for the two-act *Rosina* (1784); Storace £1,050 for the *Siege of Belgrade* (1791) and £500 for the *Haunted Tower*; and the singer/composer John Braham earned one thousand guineas for his music to Dibdin's *English Fleet* (1803). For his *Cabinet* (1801) Dibdin was given his choice of composers, but they were to be paid by the theatre, "which had never been done before" (I, 314). Michael Balfe, a successful Irish composer of English operas in the 1830s and 40s, depended for his living on the sale of the music for his songs (N.G.).

Thus, the composer's income was based on the popularity of his songs in the opera rather than on the number of nights played. Such popularity was no doubt often ephemeral, and timing of the publications critical. The songs of some composers, like Braham, who could *sing* them, were very popular. In fact, the popularity of the singer who "put over" the songs was an important element in any song's success (see illustration of Vestris selling her "broom" song). But this led to collusions, and in 1827 Edward Holmes (At, Jan. 20) bitterly complained of the system. The selection of a composer is determined not by merit, "but by the interest and strength of

Introduction

recommendations he can bring forward to introduce him."[35] No doubt, some theatrical composers did very well. But John Davy, whose operatic music was praised by the press on several occasions, did not even have enough money at his death to pay for his burial.

Critical coverage of English operas by reviewers for periodicals—linked, as they were, with English drama generally—was somewhat better than that of Italian opera, though commentary on them was also often thin during the early years. And it should be remembered that reviews of *revivals* before the 1820s very seldom dealt with anything but the performers; consequently, for those operas that premiered before 1785, discussion of the works usually depends on much later reviews. Most newspapers reviewed full-length operas regularly, but premieres of one- and two-act afterpieces were sometimes ignored—occasionally even by the *Times*.

The prominence of composers in Italian opera made the roughly chronological treatment of their operas straightforward. But the importance of the dramatist in English opera demands more complex treatment. Reviewers almost always gave primary attention to the playwright and his contribution, while the public thought of a work as the playwright's, not the composer's; this coincides with the views of musical historians that almost all of these works are actually plays with music rather than true operas.

In English opera, therefore, I have been obliged to regard the playwright and composer as a partnership—in that order. Along with chronological considerations, I have tried to discuss together those operas that were produced by the same collaborators—successful teams tended to stick together. But of course there were many exceptions, and where these collaborators had other partners, it has been necessary to divide the discussion of a librettist or composer into two or more parts. To assist the reader in following the continuity, therefore, I have had to encapsulate, in ensuing remarks, any previous discussion of them, though this necessarily involves some small repetition.

The Theatres

WHILE THE King's Theatre had little competition, thanks to its exclusive right to present Italian opera, some playhouses also enjoyed sinecures of their own. Crown patents dating 1662–63 were granted to Thomas Killigrew and Sir William Davenant, respectively, for theatres that later became Drury Lane and Covent Garden.[1] For together, known as the "major" theatres, they exercised a monopoly over productions of all plays in London (the Little Theatre[2] obtained its patent to present summer productions only). But keen rivalry did prevail between the majors, which jealously guarded their dramatic properties and performers, and if one theatre launched an important production or an attractive new performer, the other was quick to follow with competent fare. Moreover, both theatres were prompt to object to any infringement from the Little Theatre if they thought its "summer" season too long. But arrangements could be made for that theatre to offer, in addition to its own repertory, productions borrowed from the two English winter theatres.

The sizes of the majors grew markedly during our period. Drury Lane, with a capacity of about 2,300, was spurred by the enlargement of the King's (following its destruction by fire in 1789) to demolish its building in 1791; the rebuilt theatre opened in 1794 with a capacity of about 3,600; it was again rebuilt following total destruction by fire in 1809. Covent Garden, reconstructed in 1782, had a capacity of about 2,500. It was largely rebuilt in 1792 with a capacity of 3,013 (L.S., p. xliv); it was again partially rebuilt after a fire in 1808. The Little Theatre, with a capacity of about 1,500, was also largely rebuilt in 1820.

The difficulty in seeing and hearing performers of legitimate drama in the altered buildings led to a coarsening of the drama. Audiences toward the back of the houses could not hear the actors or even see their expressions, and henceforth only the broadest effects, such as in pageantry and spectacle—including opera—were satisfactory (N., III, 23). As James Boaden complained (I, 140–41): "Theatres become vast from speculation. . . . The genuine drama is banished; because to give its former pleasure, every word must be distinctly heard, every gesture accurately perceived. Music triumphantly reigns over the subject reason of the country, and her handmaid, procession, fills her court with endless and glaring flippery." Thus the drama suffered inevitable degeneration—a development that dissuaded the more literary playwrights from writing for the stage. In fact, Thomas Harris, long manager of Covent Garden, claimed he made no money on the regular drama from 1809 to 1821; the theatre "subsisted entirely on pantomime, spectacle, and melodrama."[3]

Not everyone perceived this as a decline,[4] but many critics deplored the change, in which music played a central role. In an essay the *Inquisitor* cited critics "who impute the decline of comedy to the rage for music. . . . It is this love of music that encourages many new theatres upon license for music and dancing," though they admitted that the same passion for music in France had led to "the ruin of French comedy" (Oct. 1813). And in 1816 they found the music itself intrusive: "In the orchestra particularly double drums and double trumpets, harps, bugles, cymbals, &c. are deemed indispensible, however trifling the music. . . . When we have a fine ranting dialogue in blank verse to tell one part of the story, and we are left to guess at the sequel by the help only of the fiddles and double basses, &c. in the orchestra, it becomes too ridiculous" (Aug., pp. 116–17).

Moreover, the mounting of operas and spectacles was no doubt more expensive than for most plays, and the managers were insisting on longer runs:

> Expense, in fact, appears now-a-days to have become one of the criterions by which the public estimate dramatic merit; and what is the result of this perverted system?—a splendid monotony,—a cloying repetition of the same gorgeous nonsense,—processions and dances, and dances and processions. . . . Absurdity, not only night after night, but season after season, puts our patience to the test. (LitC, Aug. 28, 1824, pp. 555ff.)

Competition between the majors further intensified after 1800. This was particularly evident in opera: "Braham and Storace, are to play at Covent Garden, against Mrs. Billington, the nights she performs at Drury Lane, and it is reported Madame Mara is to stand forward at Drury Lane when Mrs. B. appears at the other house."[5] Then Billington agreed to sing at both theatres at £2,000 each, ushering in a period of extravagance in pay for singers (Boaden).

Moreover, the majors also faced increasing competition from another direction—the minors. These were smaller theatres springing up in and around London, and their numbers became an important challenge after 1800. Only the majors, of course, had patents to perform "legitimate" drama. But the old division of the majors for the literate and the minors for the illiterate was breaking down. And though the minors were still legally confined to circus acts, pantomime, equestrian events, extravaganzas, burlesques, and, later, to musical plays of all types, drama did creep in. One favorite type was the burletta, originally a skit on the masque, which mocked mythological personages;[6] it later came to designate any short work for the minors that had a number of songs and recitatives. It was supposed to be wholly accompanied by orchestra, but increasingly the music was displaced by spoken dialogue. The majors fought this competition in the courts and through their own spectacles, but their audiences continued to decline, and in 1832 they were "never on an average more than one-third occupied" (*Tatler*, Apr. 11). Not until 1843 were all London theatres placed on a freely competitive basis.

Though Drury Lane was regarded as having a more classical tradition as the home of David Garrick and the great tragedean Sara Siddons, its management nevertheless took full advantage of the increasing public appetite for operas. It was presided over by Richard Brinsley Sheridan (1751–1816)—already a famous playwright of such resounding successes as *The Rivals*, *The School for Scandal*, and his only opera, *The Duenna*. He assumed management of the theatre after buying Garrick's shares for £35,000 in 1776. Not satisfied with this eminence, he was drawn into politics as well, becoming a liberal Whig M.P. in the 1780s and a notable orator. By 1788–89, he left the active management of the theatre in the hands of John Philip Kemble (1757–1823), who played around 120 different roles there between 1783 and 1803. Long a close friend of the Prince of Wales, Sheridan shifted to a Tory position after 1800, alienating his supporters and finally losing his seat over the Catholic emancipation issue. Indeed, he became bankrupt after the theatre burned in 1809, began drinking heavily, lost control of the theatre in 1812, and in 1813 suffered the final ignominy of being jailed for debt. Drury Lane was also hurt by the retirement of Mrs. Siddons in 1812, but drooping affairs there were somewhat restored in 1814 by the advent of the great Shakespearean actor Charles Kean.

Covent Garden was presided over by Thomas Harris (?–1820), who had complete control of the theatre by 1774 and remained there until his retirement in 1809. James Boaden, his treasurer for many years, thought the theatre better managed than its rival, though he acknowledged the superior singing and acting talent at Drury Lane. He also thought Harris more adventurous in encouraging new talent; nevertheless, in 1789 the *Times* noted the dearth of good male singers there (Sept. 24). Certainly he was more responsive than the Drury Lane management to the demand for novelty and, especially, for increasingly spectacular productions. He was also the first to introduce the singing of favorite songs between the acts of plays.

In 1803 John Kemble, who fell heir to his father's estate, purchased a sixth share of Covent Garden for £23,000 and began his management of that theatre (Harris still retained 50 percent of the stock) and was occasionally an actor there as well. But in 1809, to help defray expenses for the rebuilt theatre, Kemble attempted to raise admission prices, sparking three months of public "O.P." protests and riots while the theatre remained closed.[7] He was finally forced to return to the "Old Price" schedule.

In 1817 Kemble retired, and after the death of Harris in 1820, he assigned his shares to his brother Charles (1775–1854), who had also acted at Drury Lane and who took over as manager of Covent Garden in 1822–23. But the whole Kemble family, including Charles's wife Maria Theresa (née de Camp) and his daughter Fanny, never recovered from the "O.P." loss,[8] and the theatre became even further committed to spectacle. The house was even castigated for its mutilation of such old favorites as the *Beggar's Opera* (TI, Oct. 1815). Yet in 1831 Hunt found "much greater musical taste in the Covent Garden management" than in other theatres, with "much Handel, Haydn, and Mozart" in the overtures (*Tatler*, Dec. 7).

Another active playwright/manager was George Colman the Younger (1762–1836), who took over management of the Little Theatre in the Haymarket in 1789 after his playwright father, who had acquired the theatre in 1777 from Samuel Foote, suffered a stroke. Young Colman had been educated at Oxford and the King's College, Aberdeen, and was intended for a law career, but he soon became drawn to the life of the theatre. He wrote his first musical farce in 1784, and later his many fine productions did much to contribute to the success of his theatre. Both as author and as theatre manager, Colman feuded with the critics most of his life, as we have seen. But even Colman had troubles at the Little Theatre, though he claimed it had always prospered under his direction. In 1802 he tried, unsuccessfully, to form his own company and make himself independent of the meddling of the majors, and by 1804 the state of his personal finances forced him to take on partners.

The Lyceum Theatre, first built in 1772, also began competing with the majors in opera. As a minor, it could offer musicals—including "operas"—since they were not classified as "plays." In 1792 Dr. Arnold was frustrated in his attempts to produce English opera there, but in 1809 his son, Samuel James Arnold, was more effective. He extensively renovated the building and wrote many of its productions himself beginning that year. At its 1809 opening, the press was enthusiastic. "The whole interior exhibits a light and beautiful effect; and, from its shape and elegance, far surpasses the Haymarket [i.e., Little] Theatre. The orchestra is numerous and excellent, and the company, both vocal and ballet, highly respectable" (T, June 27).

DuBois (MM), though unhappy with its initial offering, had hopes for the future of opera there (July), and the next month they noted that the singers were "better performers than singers are wont to be" elsewhere. He had to wait until 1812, however, for a license.[9] That year the *Inquisitor* wrote that Arnold, "to his praise be it spoken, can first claim the merit of establishing a native opera in this country, divested of the disgusting appendages of French dancers and Italian singers, affording the talents of many deserving performers and writers an opportunity of ripening into perfection" (Sept.). But, though he was apparently quite successful with the public—his competition was especially harmful to Colman's theatre—the press for a time became disenchanted with the quality of his productions. In 1816 Arnold renamed it the English Opera House, and his productions became decidedly more operatic, especially in the 1820s. The theatre burned in 1830.

Rivalry between the majors seemed to reach its peak in our later years. It "is greater than we recollect in any preceding season. Novelty succeeds novelty with unprecedented rapidity," wrote the *Times* (Nov. 30, 1827). If Covent Garden pulled a coup by bringing Weber from Germany to mount his *Oberon*, Drury Lane anticipated them by producing a different *Oberon* somewhat earlier and following it up with Bishop's only all-sung opera. When Arnold at the English Opera House produced a highly popular *Der Freischütz*, both majors soon followed with their own versions, to say nothing of several others at the minors. In 1816 Drury Lane refused to let their performers appear at Arnold's theatre (T, Sept. 10).

The large size of the majors, even after remodeling to make them somewhat smaller, was a continuing problem (E, Oct. 10, 1819). Another was the increasing prominence of stars. Not only did playwrights weaken their dramas by writing mainly for them (N.), but they were demanding more money than the managers could well afford; sometimes, according to Parke, writing about 1827, the managers replaced very popular singers with unknowns from the provinces to save money.

Indeed, the economics of the winter houses, both of which had rejected the services of Bishop by 1829, had a pernicious influence on the production of good operas, as Holmes complained:

> What hands has not this task of entertaining the public fallen into? Copyists, chorus-masters, fiddlers, persons frequently ignorant of the first principles of composition have, in turn with tradesmen no better informed, supplied the music to our national theatres. . . . One of the worst consequences of the mechanical system by which the theatres are supplied is, that we have now not only no operas, but no consistent and connected melodramatic music. (At, Oct. 25)

Another device of the desperate managers was to paper the houses, which had reached such proportions at Covent Garden in 1829 that their treasury issued 11,083 orders in a period of less than two months (Shaw-Taylor). The *Examiner* complained that year: "The house was visited by a cloud of orders, who settled down, like starlings on a moor, clacking, and grateful, as they had been in a convent granary" (Jan. 18). And Reynolds noted that in 1826 orders were "much more abused" than in earlier days. It took an unusual event, such as the premiere of Weber's *Oberon* in 1826, to suspend them. As the *Literary Chronicle* noted: "The play-bills announced that, 'in order to prevent all interference with the opinion of the public, all orders would be refused, and the free-list suspended,' on the occasion; this is a pretty plain confession for what orders are given, namely, to interfere with the will of the public."

On the other hand, after 1815 the English Opera House and other minors were not only prospering but were at times artistically superior to the majors. For example, though some critics scoffed at Samuel Arnold's earlier attempts to produce operas at the English Opera House, the press sang his praises after 1824 for his contributions to musical taste by mounting a series of new English adaptations of foreign operas. In 1825 the *Gazette*, in a review of *Tarrare*, wrote: "We congratulate Mr. Arnold upon the high character his theatre has attained," and in 1826, in reviewing the opera *The Oracle*, they cited his "cultivated judgment [which] renders him so competent to the task of giving to the public the best music in the best manner."

A good example of the new vigor of the minors is explicit in the *Examiner*'s praise of R. W. Ellison, manager of the Surrey Theatre:

> The evident good taste exerted, to *lead* rather than *follow* the public taste, by bringing forward works of standard merit; the handsome manner in which the scenic and subordinate departments are filled up; the liberal complement of orchestral performers—32 in number—and this at a *minor* theatre; then . . . we have an orderly, silent, and attentive audience, because they are interested in the entertainment set before them. You have not one hundredth part of the gabble and impertinence that assail the ear at the Opera House. (E, Sept. 14, 1828)

THE PERFORMANCES

The major theatres offered performances every night but Sunday, for a total of some two hundred performances each season.[10] The summer season at the Little Theatre lasted from mid-June to mid-September. Plays were also forbidden on Wednesdays and Fridays during Lent, when the "Oratorios" were presented. Performances sometimes lasted five hours or more. There were mixed offerings: a five-act drama followed by a one-act work, often musical; a three-act drama followed by a two-act work; and sometimes *two* five-act works. A tragedy or comedy was often followed by a short farce or musical afterpiece. Sometimes three short plays were presented. "Half prices" (see "The Audience") began at eight or nine and were regarded as a right; riots at Covent Garden in 1763, when the managers tried to halt half prices, resulted in £2,000 in damages.

Seats were unnumbered; the wealthy sent their footmen to "keep places." There were upper and lower tiers of boxes (prostitutes were among the habitués of the upper ones) as well as the pit and gallery (after 1811 Drury Lane had both a lower and an upper gallery). On special occasions, standees were permitted in the pit. Prices were generally 5*s*. for the lower boxes, 3*s*. for the upper boxes and pit, and 2*s*. for the gallery.

Fruitwomen sold playbills (which never carried the name of the author), and, for operas, books of songs and sometimes complete librettos, as well as fruit. "Waiting music" (Fiske) was played by the theatre orchestra half an hour before the performance ("first music"); there was also "second" music, and sometimes dancing, between the acts of plays. (A critic once complained of too much waiting music.) There were no curtain calls, but applause was frequent during the play or opera—sometimes for a line or even a single word. The house was lighted by wax candles, which could be dimmed by raising or lowering the chandeliers.

Plays and operas were performed in front of scenery—there was no box set until the 1830s. Scenery was changed in front of the audience, but it was handled expeditiously: there were five grooves in the floor of the stage into which flats were fitted, and upon the whistle signal of the stage manager, stagehands simply slid one panel in front of another, and complicated sets could thus be changed in a moment. (Cobb's *Siege of Belgrade* had fourteen such sets.)

Sheridan once stated in a letter the importance of having the composer attend rehearsals,[11] and performers could be fined if late for the regular 10:00 A.M. rehearsals (Fiske, pp. 254ff). Nevertheless, they were not taken very seriously (N., III, 40); indeed, the opening night was regarded as an "experimental rehearsal," and often a new five-act play would have only eighteen hours of rehearsal. Consequently, much of the burden fell on the prompter, though the audience frowned on promptings. There was also little direction. "You must paint your own picture," was one stage manager's constant advice (Watson, pp. 41–43). This casual approach was not changed until 1837–39, when Covent Garden fell under the direction of Charles Macready.

The Audience

THOUGH THE traditional rowdy playhouse audiences improved somewhat in the latter part of the eighteenth century, the theatres suffered a gradual withdrawal of a large part of the upper orders. The new lateness of their dinner hour (theatres opened at 6:30) and the fashion of musical parties in their homes have been cited as reasons for this change (L.S., p. ccii). For some it was a welcome escape from too many melodramas at the playhouses (Baer) and from the more boisterous behavior there, though, as we have seen, the King's audience was sometimes not all that refined.[1]

Certainly the playhouse boxholders of that time were not beyond reproach. In their "Observations on the Stage" in 1786, the *Register* complained of chattering in the boxes by "antiquated fusty maidens, whose personal charms failing to attract attention, determine to draw the eyes of the audience upon them by noise." Among complaints of another reviewer in 1791 were: "the beating of box-keepers"; "beaux talking extremely loud [of their] racing, drinking, wenching, sparring"; "Orange Girls presenting their wares out of all time and season"; and "women of high quality mobbing it in the Pitt" (T, Dec. 29). Indeed, as late as 1830, Hunt took refuge in the pit because of the talking that went on in the boxes (*Tatler*, Sept. 25).

Theatrical decorum was not helped by the "half-price" policy that prevailed at all the playhouses.[2] This not only interrupted the performance but introduced an even more unsavory element to the theatre. Young bucks on the town would indulge in the "witty explosion of six-penny crackers" and "guffawed at the screams of the frightened females" (N., IV, 9). There was also a good deal of soliciting for prostitution at the theatres, which may actually have been encouraged by the managers, though it, too, hastened the departure of the upper orders.[3]

As at the King's, the "gallery gods" in the upper gallery were the worst offenders; they dominated the house with their catcalls and frequent throwing of fruit or heavier objects at the pit and stage, sometimes causing injuries. The gallery was also guilty of loud talking and of joining in on the songs and choruses (T, July 28, 1788). Haydn, who saw Henry Bate's opera *Woodman* at Covent Garden in 1791, observed: "The common people in the galleries of all the theatres are very impertinent: they set the fashions with all their unrestrained impetuosity, and whether something is repeated or not is determined by their yells."[4] In 1788 the *Times* spoke of "the ridiculous buffoonery of 'Jemmy lineum tweedle'—which with all its nonsense, was loudly encored by the galleries" (Oct. 23), and in 1791 they declared that Storace's music was "rather too sublime for the taste of the galleries" (Jan. 3).[5]

Nothing was improved after 1800, according to Nicoll: "All contemporaries are agreed on one thing; the spectators at the larger theatres during the first decade of the century were often licentious and debased, while those at the minor playhouses were vulgar, unruly, and physically obnoxious." Indeed, there were by this time frequent disturbances in the upper boxes as well.

The advent of *Freischütz* in 1824 and *Oberon* in 1826 briefly attracted the upper orders to Covent Garden. Their customary absence there was regretted by critic Z of the *New Monthly* (Apr. 1826), for "there is nothing tends so much to lend grace and spirit to intellectual amusements, as the mingling of the aristocracy with the people." By 1826 there was even improvement in the galleries; the *Times*, at the premiere of the *Oracle* at the English Opera House that year, wrote: "The galleries here really listen to serious operas with great attention and patience" (Aug. 8). Perhaps this was because many plebians turned to the minors in the 1830s—the majors had become "too aristocratic" (Baer, p. 175).

The majors, like the King's, also suffered cabals; there were numerous instances of a "party" forming against a piece, and Murphy, Kelly, and Colman the Elder were among those whose plays and operas had been unfairly damned (N., III). Sometimes the "party" was political in nature. Sheridan, for example, was occasionally the indirect target, as in 1785, when *Strangers at Home*, composed by his father-in-law, Thomas Linley the Elder, encountered strong political opposition on Sheridan's account, though that opposition proved ineffectual. Linley's son William was opposed by such a cabal in his ill-fated *Honey-Moon* (1797). Henry Bate Dudley also fell afoul of a political party at Covent Garden and in the press at the opening of his *Woodman* (1791). Sometimes professional jealousy obtruded, as was the case in John Walter II's *Hide and Seek* (1789), though politics also played a role: "The Author and Composer were new to the Stage and . . . 'two of a trade can never agree.' Hide and Seek had . . . not one of the *blue* and *buff*[6] to stand forward as protector, for the Author was . . . too well known to be steadily attached to that side of the political question which supports the King and the Constitution" (T, Mar. 11).

William Parke speaks of "forcers"—dependents of principal singers who were admitted, with orders, "to set the applause and encores going" (II, 148). Mostly, however, the claqueurs were there solely at the invitation of the managers, in papering their houses. The presence of such claques sometimes made the success of a work difficult to tell, for the response of the audience was critical at the time the piece was "given out."

Instances of claques or cabals continued into the new century. At the opening of Prince Hoare's *Chains of the Heart* (1801), a party "malevolently and unjustly withheld" first-night indulgences (MM). At the opening of *Thirty Thousand* in 1804, the *Times* cited a "preconcerted opposition, but on the second night they "were either ashamed of their conduct, or apprehensive of the indignation of the impartial and unprejudiced." Indulgence of orders by the theatre managers seemed to increase. In 1808 the *Times* noted that Drury Lane, "as it always is on occasions when one third of the spectators are admitted gratis, was crowded to the ceiling" (Nov. 11).

At Drury Lane in 1816, the *Times* reported that "a most unprovoked and offensive effort was made by some party, whose members were scattered through the house, to damn this unpretending production" (May 22). And at Covent Garden in 1823, the *Herald* noted that "the senseless clapping . . . to resort to extraordinary means . . . for filling a house, is so offensive to that part of the audience whose applause is of value, that more discretion should be exercised. . . . It is in the musical parts of a performance that they are most injurious and offensive, by interrupting a singer at the moment of the finest and most critical execution" (Nov. 7). (They went on to castigate the "puffery" rampant "at the two great theatres," though the press had little to say on this subject during later years.) Edward Fitzball, a prominent librettist writing of this period many years later, spoke of a cabal at Covent Garden against "any new author" they thought might be successful (Wyndham, I, 370).

The majors had no strong body of "amateurs" such as existed at the King's, though there were occasional references to them at the playhouses, as we have seen. Most of these occurred before 1800, when reviewers were less confident of their own views, as at the King's. Thus, the airs in the *Pirates* (1792) "excited *bravissimos* from the Cognoscenti and repeated plaudits from all the rest of the auditors" (T, Nov. 22). *Sprigs of Laurel* (1793) was "an exquisite treat for the taste of the amateur" (LC). And "Musicians and Amateurs will of course enjoy the 'opera' of *Mahmoud*" (1796) (T).

The practice of encoring for musical numbers at the playhouses was firmly in place at the beginning of our period, but not until 1806 do we encounter the first opposition in the press to its abuse. That year the *Chronicle* growled: "There are always a set in the House who oppose the repetition of any thing that is truly musical; but they never fail to vociferate the repetition of a rattling ballad by a cracked voice, provided that it has been accompanied with a proper quantity of grimace" (Jan. 23). Two years later the *Times* noted its own reservations, as well as some in the audience, to its abuse: *Kais* "was crowned by more decided and unqualified applause than we have of late witnessed. In the first act, indeed, the frequent encoring excited opposition. The impropriety of calling always for a repetition was felt at last." Parke (c. 1808) thought encoring had been beneficial in stimulating competition between performers, though he admitted it "destroys the illusion."

The encore system received some heavy bludgeoning after 1815. It began with Ayrton's review (C) that year, which chastised John Harley at the Lyceum for being overly eager: "He received a very seasonable reproof for too readily yielding to a solitary call of encore. . . . We are sorry to observe the growing practice of cringing to the spectators by incessant bowing to the mere beggary of applause. Is it not highly blameable in an Actor to destroy all the illusion of the scene, by shuffling off his assumed character, and making his reference to the company in his own person?" (Aug. 21). The next year the *Inquisitor* commented on singer Charles Horn's "auditors, who, heedless of any other care but that of their own gratification, compell him nightly to repeat his songs, and, in some instances, to sing them three times over, to the inevitable injury of his powers. . . . Surely it is time that their barbarous practice, . . . which of necessity interrupts and destroys the interest and integrity of the scene, should be subjected to some restraint" (Aug.). (At the King's no critic complained of the effect of the encore on the "integrity of the scene.") In 1817 Alsager protested the "injudicious" practice (T, Oct. 15), as did Hunt in 1819, when Braham sang "Scots wha hae" "three times over, to the irrepressible enthusiasm of the audience" (E, Oct. 10). (Hunt did not wish encores abandoned entirely, however—see *Tatler*, Sept. 21, 1830.) In 1823, at the Covent Garden production of *Cortez*, the *Herald* attributed the practice both to claqueurs and to amateurs, and the same year Ayrton (Har) again scored the practice, which he thought was prompted by composers:

> This encoring is easily brought to pass, and the public will has less to do in it than is imagined. Half a dozen *claqueurs*, judiciously posted by the composer, aided by the good nature of some, the passiveness of others, and assisted by the inclination which a singer most commonly feels to repeat his song, will generally succeed in getting a second hearing for any trumpery that may happen to be put in the hands of a favourite performer. (VIII, 234)

Even overtures began to be encored, possibly beginning in 1822 with Bishop's overture to *Maid Marian*, which was "very novel, if not unprecedented" (C). Other overtures were encored in 1827 and 1830.

On the other hand, at the premiere of the *Libertine* in 1817, Hazlitt, with public taste very much in mind, thoroughly trounced the audience for *not* encoring:

> Almost every thing else was against [the opera], but the music triumphed. Still it had but half a triumph, for the songs were not *encored*; and when an attempt was made by some rash over-weening enthusiasts to *encore* the enchanting airs of Mozart, that heavy German composer, "that dull Bœtian [*sic*] genius," as he has been called by a lively verbal critic of our times, the English, disdaining this insult offered to our native talent, they *hissed* — in the plenitude of their pampered grossness, and "ignorant impatience" of foreign refinement and elegance, hissed! (E)

The Operas

THROUGHOUT the latter part of the eighteenth century, music of all kinds—and especially opera—was growing in popularity. Charles Beecher Hogan (L.S., "Introduction") cites the rapidly increasing interest of London audiences in singing, the popular catch clubs, and the thriving music-publishing business. Songs were especially popular—comic songs; hunting songs; drinking songs; "character" songs; and, especially beginning in the 1790s with the troubles in France, patriotic songs. All these and more got into hodgepodge English "operas" of all types.

This development is evident in appendix 13, which lists the number of such works by known authors produced at the major and minor theatres from 1760 through 1830. The number of musicals at the majors, for example, tripled between 1760 and 1780, gradually leveled off until 1824, then again nearly doubled. Musicals at the minors show a somewhat similar growth, though most of their productions were anonymous. As Robert D. Hume has noted, "The tremendous appeal of musical comedy caused the mainpiece comedy to languish toward the end of the century."[1] By the 1820s half the Drury Lane productions were musical, though not necessarily operatic (QMM, III, 159–62).

The listing of the more operatic productions indicated in appendix 10—the basis for appendixes 11 and 12—is much more restrictive. At the majors, we find in appendix 13 a total of 243 productions during our period, whereas in appendix 11 there are only 158 productions of operas at the same theatres.

The same appendix shows that there was an annual average of about one-and-a-half new operas at Drury Lane and of about two at Covent Garden, with the number of performances identical at 32 each. Appendix 11 also shows that both theatres produced a number of revivals most seasons, with two-thirds at Covent Garden and one-third at Drury Lane. The Little Theatre, as well as the Lyceum/English Opera House after 1808, also added to those productions, with the latter showing a relatively large number of revivals for the period covered. For all theatres, there was a total of 197 new operas and 169 revivals.

The total number of premiere performances at Drury Lane, 1141, divided by the number of productions there, 72, yields an overall ratio of 20 performances per production, with Covent Garden following close at 16.7, showing that the latter did not do quite as well as the former despite the larger number of new operas. No doubt many of these operas—some requiring heavy investment in costumes and scenery, to say nothing of providing adequate singers—were more expensive to produce than a play, which needed only nine nights to succeed ("nine-days' wonder"); a ratio of nearly twice that for operas must have been gratifying to the managers.

A different approach is indicated in the first part of appendix 12, which lists those productions having nine or more performances and those having less. This would suggest that, for all three theatres listed, less than a quarter of new productions failed. More afterpieces than three-act operas were produced, but they also failed more often. Again we must emphasize, as in Italian operas, that the number of performances, while clearly highlighting the hits of any season, do not necessarily reflect on the quality of the work or the performance when they fall below nine—that could be due to many other reasons. But in English opera reviews, as against Italian, we are more apt to discover the reasons for the falling off of any particular production.

With respect to the types of operas encountered during our period (the second half of appendix 12), some of the classifications must be occasionally arbitrary (comments from reviewers on the "type" have proved useful), but we can clearly see that "comic operas" were the most common type, that they and "operatic farces" lost ground in subsequent periods, and that both "musical dramas" and "operas" gained ground considerably in the last period.

Many of the comic operas in the overall period had a strong vein of romance, and almost all had exotic settings, which became more spectacular as the century neared its close. Yet melodramatic works were becoming increasingly popular and provided a somber moderation of the comic impulse; reviewers often welcomed contrasting "gay and grave" songs in the same work.

After 1815 we find a shift: the number of melodramas increased markedly, while the so-called "operas," which were always serious, more than quintupled—sure evidence of the growing strength of Romanticism in English opera. There was also a miscellany of other operas in that period, including "domestic operas" (mostly just melodramas), "operettas" (usually comic and produced mainly at the English Opera House), and a few called "vaudevilles," which were merely comic opera afterieces with French sources.

The rage for novelty in English opera was as strong as that in Italian at the King's. There was, however, one important difference in the taste of

English opera audiences: they fully embraced a few select superhits from the past—especially *The Beggar's Opera*, *Artaxerxes*, and some Bickerstaffe operas of the 1760s—that retained enormous popularity up to 1800 and, for some, well into Victorian times. No Italian opera at the King's began to achieve such success.

Early on, most comic operas included a large number of borrowings from Italian operas—too many indeed to list or even index—which were sometimes "confounded with English property."[2] Few critics complained of this practice, however, and the audiences welcomed the introduction of old tunes that they knew and loved. With the demise of Stephen Storace and the decline of William Shield's influence after 1800, however, there was a gradual reduction in these borrowings, a practice followed by Michael Kelly; indeed, in 1813 the *Chronicle* complained of a lack of Italian opera songs on the English stage. Perhaps this shift reflected a decline in the melodic resources of many Italian operas presented at the King's during the same period, as noted in part II.

Moreover, despite the decrease in borrowings, that trend was so completely reversed that many foreign operas were adapted to the English stage. Though evidence of this change first appears in 1817–19, following the great popularity of Mozart and Rossini at the King's, the movement was given great impetus by the English production of Weber's *Der Freischütz* in 1824. From then until 1830 and beyond, English opera audiences experienced a shift in musical taste and for a time lost interest with the play-*cum*-songs type hitherto common to English opera: they flocked to see productions much closer to genuine opera performed in English. This was a triumph for opera in English, if not for English opera.

Adaptations of ballads and folk songs continued to be popular. On the other hand, there was a decided increase in original music written for English operas, together with an increase in the number of composers who collaborated on various productions. This shift may have resulted in part from the growing melodramatic character of English opera, for which arias were less suitable.

After 1800, there was apparently some loss in the quality of music being written for the stage. George Hogarth (II, 447) thought it an "ephemeral" period in which the productions of Kelly, Reeve, Mazzinghi, Davy, and Braham had "no claim" to a place in the annals of music. Having no doubt seen many of the operas himself, he thought them at best "agreeable trifles" and could not imagine how they satisfied. And Fiske (p. 580) declares that English theatre music reached its all-time nadir during this period, though he admits little of the orchestral music has survived. Yet satisfy they often did, particularly in regard to the music.

26. Theatre Royal, Drury Lane

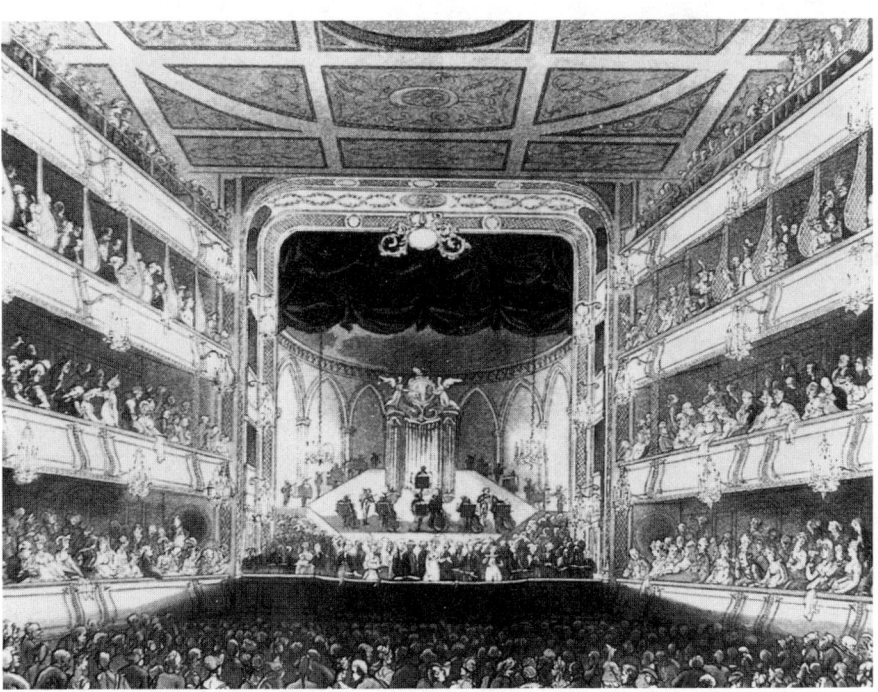

27. Theatre Royal, Covent Garden; drawn by Pugin and engraved by Thomas Rowlandson

28. Detail from the wolf's glen scene in Weber's *Der Freischütz*, Covent Garden (1824)

30. James Cobb; engraved by Ridley

29. John Gay

31. William Dimond; engraved by Freeman from a painting by Bennett

32. Prince Hoare; engraved by Ridley from an original picture by Northcote

34. James Robinson Planché

33. Frederic Reynolds; engraved by Ridley from a miniature by W. Nash

35. Thomas Augustine Arne

36. Dr. Samuel Arnold

38. Henry Rowley Bishop

37. William Shield

39. Charles Incledon as Macheath in *The Beggar's Opera* (1818)

The *Cabinet* (1802), for example, which included several of these composers, achieved high critical and popular reception and did not succeed just because a dog was introduced in the denouement, as Fiske has suggested. In fact, James Boaden[3] pointed out that at just this time "the love of music is now growing fast among us." And Parke, writing of conditions around 1806 (though with hindsight) stated: "Native music in England has now arrived to such a perfection, as to enable the English to vie with the Italian stage," and he chastised the "haut-ton" for admiring only foreign artists.

With respect to revivals, we must again emphasize that, after 1800, our records are based only on those revivals for which we discovered reviews and do not indicate unreviewed performances. Nevertheless, from those records it is obvious that, beginning about 1813, a considerably larger number of revivals *were* reviewed than in earlier years. Since these reviews were almost altogether concerned with the performers — often solely with a leading singer — it certainly reflects a greater interest in singers — especially *new* singers — in the later years. But to the extent that our records do reflect a correlation with all revivals, it suggests that the public, after 1812, exhibited a greater interest in older operas than it had before, and that that interest extended well beyond *Artaxerxes* and *Beggar's Opera* to many older types by Bickerstaffe, Burgoyne, O'Keeffe, Sheridan, Cobb, the younger Colman, and others. Along with the new operas, audiences from 1813 to 1830 also wanted to hear many of those written before 1800 (see listings of revivals for each season in appendix 10).

From appendix 14 we may note the particular strength of operas by Arne, Shield, Arnold, and Storace in the early years, and by Bishop in the later years. But many composers in the middle years are high only because, in many operas, they shared the composership with others. Note that Arne (*Artaxerxes*) and Gay (*Beggar's Opera*), who were responsible for both words and music, are listed as composers rather than as librettists. From appendix 15 we find Cobb by far the most successful playwright, with Bickerstaffe, Reynolds, S. J. Arnold, and T. Dibdin also showing considerable strength.

GAY

In *The Beggar's Opera* John Gay (1685–1732), a poet, playwright, and friend of Pope and Swift, wrote the most popular theatrical production of the century. Previous to his *Beggar's Opera*, Gay had written an excellent libretto for Handel's *Acis and Galatea* (1718) and was familiar with both Italian and English airs. He could play the recorder and knew enough notation to fit his lyrics to the tunes he wanted (Fiske, p. 100).

Gay originally intended the songs to be sung unaccompanied, but at the last minute Johann Christoph Pepusch was called in to write an overture—it was a good one—and to provide accompaniments. The latter were replaced by others, in the *galant* style, composed by Thomas Linley the Elder in 1771, and this version survived well beyond 1830. In fact, almost from its inception, attempts were made to introduce changes in various productions, including the reversal of all male and female roles, a practice that continued in our period (see UM, March 1795, p. 171). (As in Italian opera, the lead singers always felt free to introduce their own favorite songs.)

But it was the lyrics and dialogue that made the work a hit. For even with his title he turned the world upside down: an opera for beggars rather than the aristocracy. The lyrics also aptly satirized Italian opera librettos and parodied the original lyrics, many of which were well known. Bishops might fulminate against its alleged immorality, but the town took the work to heart; its popularity was phenomenal, and it gave rise to a movement of ballad opera that lasted ten years or more.

At an 1812 revival, Leigh Hunt, always on guard with Neoclassical writers, was only mildly supportive of the work: "It is easy to see that the *Beggar's Opera* would long ago have lost its attractiveness, had it not been for the never-dying charm of its simplicity in its songs and music. . . . [The opera possesses] no strong feature of talent, either in the language, manner, or satire, but always true to good sense, with a pleasant feeling for the burlesque, and a vein of ridicule against the vices of high life" (E). But by 1819 his opinions on the book (E) had improved—thanks to critiques on the work by William Hazlitt (see below). And at an 1820 revival, the *Inquisitor* was quite positive:

> The "Beggar's Opera" is the happiest exemplar of low comedy on the stage, the action being vigorous, the allusions keen, and the characters conceived with a singular fidelity to nature. . . . The selection of the music was . . . admirable. All the popular airs seem to have been crowded into its melody, and some of them are of a beauty which, in all the caprices of fashion, will retain its original charm. But . . . the English stage offers no severer trial of combined song and action.

Most of the criticism of revivals dealt with problems in interpretation as a result of basic faults in understanding the work. Thus at an 1802 revival, the *Post* pointed out: "There was a ridiculous contest in the last act, between the advocates for a repetition of the prison scene, and those who were averse to it." At an 1807 revival the *Times* reviewer (almost certainly by Barron Field) declaimed on departures from the original production:

> The introduction to [the opera], from which it derives its name, is omitted. It is recognized as a burlesque by none of the performers ... and we dare say there were not an hundred persons in the house last night, that knew it was written in ridicule of the Italian opera. As it is now performed, therefore, it is a mere low opera.... [Such] an audience have some excuse for not taking the joke of an author [Macheath's song as he is about to be hanged]; and it is for this reason they are not to be abused for surveying Macheath's farewell last night rather with pity than with laughter.

In two 1815 revivals, that of Drury Lane was declared "*perfect*," whereas Covent Garden had produced it "in such a castrated, mutilated state, that we question whether Gay himself" would recognize it (TI). Hazlitt saw the latter production that June, but his comments were centered squarely on Gay: "It is a vulgar error to call this a vulgar play, so far from it that we do not scruple to declare our opinion that it is one of the most refined production in the language.... By the sentiments and reflections which [he] put into the mouths of highwaymen, turnkeys, mistresses, wives, or daughters, he has converted this motley group into a set of fine gentlemen and ladies, satirists, and philosophers" (E).[4]

How far encroaching Victorianism—and its detractors—had come by 1829 is apparent in an *Athenaeum* review of that year, which began with fine irony. Word had gotten out that two singers, for their Covent Garden benefit, had planned a *Beggar's Opera* with male and female roles switched: "The news of this monstrosity struck terror into domestic life; and fathers and brothers began to feel due horror at allowing such exhibitions to shock the eyes of females of respectability. It was feared that much injury would result to society from such a spectacle; and that the moral order of things would be entirely reversed." Yet they seemed to drop their irony for moralism in concluding: "Nothing could be more gross than the exhibition,—nothing more vulgar and inane, and [the promoter] was right in judging that grossness, and vulgarity, and absurdity were qualities that would raise the grin of British box and gallery."

Their moralism[5] again came to the fore in their review of an 1830 revival at Drury Lane, with Vestris in breeches singing Macheath: "We quite agree with the 'unco good' that there are many things shocking in the 'Beggar's Opera.' It is very shocking, for instance ... to see Polly Peacham represented by a ladylike concert-singing refinedly-speaking person, such as Miss [Catherine] Stephens." But at the same performance Edward Holmes (*Atlas*) saw a different Stephens: "Who but this child of nature has ever given us the perfect sentiment of the airs in the old English opera? Who but

Stephens has looked the heroine of them?" And he added: "There is one pleasure yet in the music of the *Beggar's Opera*, which few works of the old school can boast—freedom from interpolation" (but of course there *were* such interpolations!). Moreover, he wanted Linley's old accompaniments updated.

ARNE

Thomas Augustine Arne (1710–78), son and grandson of upholsterers who thought little of his musical interests, had to borrow a servant's livery to gain admission to the upper gallery of the King's! He early became a competent composer in both Italian and English opera, though he had several failures in both. The marriage of his sister Susanna to playwright Theophilus Cibber early on drew Arne to the English stage, and he became associated with a group of musicians aiming to establish English opera "after the Italian manner." His success with the masque *Dido and Aeneas* at the Little Theatre led to his engagement at Drury Lane for composing masques and operas.

DALTON—ARNE

One of the first of these, *Comus* (1738), was an immediate and lasting success, receiving more performances than any other afterpiece between 1775 and 1800. It was based on John Dalton's adaptation of Milton's masque with additional characters; indeed, all the songs were given to subordinate characters. Some of the music of Henry Lawes was retained, but Arne added much, including recitative, final chorus, and concluding dance. George Hogarth thought Arne's music "neither that of the older English masters nor of the Italian composers of the day. It was graceful, flowing, elegant." Thomas Busby found the music "light and airy."

In a 1772 adaptation by Colman the Elder for Covent Garden, the work was cut considerably, including much of the dialogue, and this version prevailed in later revivals.[6] A contemporary judgment on a still different version in 1815, which had restored arias by Handel, with additions by Henry Bishop and an overture by Cherubini, comes from the *Theatrical Inquisitor*:

> Comus, as now represented, has lost much of its poetic beauties; whole speeches have been lopped off; and it is dwindled into a mere vehicle for music and decoration. Much, therefore, is lost, without any thing, in point of interest, being gained. It is not at all the more dramatic for

these barbarous amputations.... It is now a nameless something, dull, and incongruous....

We are still less inclined to pardon Mr. Harris for his monstrous interpolations.... Euphrosyne was not a strumpet; and this is the rank language of the stews....

The opening recitative, composed by Bishop, is uncommonly sweet.... Of Arne's composition we never thought so highly as the fashion now prescribes; by the side of Handel[7] and Cherubini he is poor indeed; but this is, perhaps, no great disgrace.

GARRICK—ARNE/PURCELL

Not quite as popular was Arne's setting of the Garrick version (Drury Lane, 1770) of Dryden's *King Arthur*, music by Henry Purcell (1691). In fact, Arne, a true son of the enlightenment, stated that Purcell's music "was cathedral, and not to the taste of modern theatrical audiences" (Fiske, p. 360), yet he did include some of it and added much of his own.[8] The better critics of the opera in our period were much more interested in Purcell than Arne.

An unknown author—probably John Kemble—made still another two-act version for Drury Lane entitled *Arthur and Emmeline* in 1784, and it is apparently this version that was revived "after sixteen years" at Covent Garden in 1819. Edward Sterling (T) wrote:

> The revival does honour to the establishment, and to the taste of its conductors, who have made it one of the finest specimens of the superb and decorative drama, that has appeared for a long period. [It] will operate, we think, as a stimulus to revive a species of drama much neglected by the moderns, yet capable of being given ... in far greater perfection than at its first invention.... There was something peculiarly gratifying in recurring to the original form in which some of our most popular airs were first introduced.[9]

The *Inquisitor* agreed about the fine production, though they thought this version, which they attributed to Kemble, presented few "points of interest or motives to merriment." Purcell's songs drew praise, and Arne "furnished many popular strains ... but to the common ear, for we cannot call it *taste*, these composers have parted with their charms, and very little sympathy is now aroused by the noblest flights." At the same performance, Hunt termed Garrick's a "dry and pantomimic abridgement" of Dryden: "Managers are generally more cunning than wise in these matters, and finding that dullness cannot do without stage-tailoring, think that genius must be cut and squeezed to it too." He noticed that "a good deal of

Purcell's fine music, too, which though somewhat quaint and crude is full of genius and effect, is unnecessarily missed" (E).

The work was revived at the English Opera House in 1827, in still another adaptation by William Hawes, who suppressed all music except Purcell's, though he included several pieces from his other operas. Thomas Noon Talfourd (*New Monthly*) noted: "The heroic passages [of the drama] are frigid in themselves; but they become animated by Purcell's music, like the singers who give them utterance." Ayrton (Har), noting that Arne's additions to the work were "sunk into oblivion," was unhappy with Hawes for rejecting Purcell's "Two daughters of this aged stream." Other songs from the *Indian Queen, Bonduca,* and *Dido and Aeneas* "blend sufficiently well with the other pieces, and are not inconsistent with the drama." Nevertheless, "Purcell's accompaniments, consisting of little else than stringed instruments, are much too quiet for modern ears; we require the excitement of trombones, horns and drums, with the luxuries of flutes, clarinets and bassoons, all of which have, we think wisely, been added on the present occasion" by William Henry Kearns.

At another English Opera House revival the next year, Holmes (At) provided a different view of the current feeling toward Purcell and Dryden:

> The freshness of the music and poetry in this fine relic of the minds of those congenial spirits Purcell and Dryden, makes our recurrence to them like a pure draught from the fountain-head. Had our glorious musician, Henry Purcell, only written the frost scene[10] . . . he would well have deserved the fine panegyric Dryden put upon his tomb. . . . No English composer ever transfused the spirit of his author so completely as he. His feeling of words is as unexpected by the hearers as it is true, quaint, and poetical. . . . In the song, 'Fairest Isle all Isles excelling,' Purcell has given us a stream of pure and beautiful melody, in this instance surpassing the poet, who at other times goes beyond him in a kind of friendly contention.

Arne wrote a good deal of other music for the theatre, including oratorios, but most of these works were failures (N.G.). Yet aside from *Comus*, Arne had one enormous success that made up for all his shortcomings—*Artaxerxes* (Covent Garden, 1762). He made his own translation from Metastasio, and it was composed "in the Italian style," complete with recitatives. In fact, the critics were alarmed because castratos sang the leads at the premiere in a *playhouse*! The work did contain some arias in the sublimated ballad style, but as Charles Burney observed, he "crouded the airs, particularly the part of Mandane . . . with most of the Italian divisions and difficulties which had ever been heard at the opera." Yet Busby regarded the opera as a "purely English" composition, in which a "strain of rural simplicity" was characteristic, though there was fire and brilliance as well.

From its inception, the opera overwhelmed English audiences, and Garrick mounted three all-sung operas at Drury Lane in a vain attempt to cash in on the vogue. The work soon became a touchstone by which any soprano who hoped for a future on the English lyric stage had to be measured, and the years right up to 1830 are littered with reviews of debutants who failed to measure up and are heard from no more. The most surprising aspect of the work's popularity is, of course, the recitative, for somehow Arne rendered it generally acceptable to his audiences, although as we shall see, they did cause problems at times and, in some performances, were reduced or dropped altogether. (They are no longer extant.)

When Elizabeth Billington appeared as Mandane in 1787, the work had not been given for seven years: "Such were the attractive powers of the music, that many stood in the passage during the whole performance—indeed, when we consider the combination of vocal powers, which supported this excellent composition of Doctor Arne's, we cannot wonder at the avidity with which the public pushed forward to get seats" (UR, Jan. 15). A week later they added: "Recitative Dialogue has generally been found an opiate in its influence on an English audience; but in the performance of the piece before us, as now represented at Covent-Garden, the vocal powers of the principal performers operate like enchantments upon the senses, and keep the soul awake to the sweets of harmony."

In 1813 the *Times* wrote of a Covent Garden revival: "The opera as a drama is, of course, as absurd as any of those composed at a time when it was considered utterly impossible to correct common sense with good music." Yet the music was "admirable in all parts—rich, scientific, and polished." For an 1814 revival there, Bishop "refurbished" the score.[11] At an 1818 revival Sterling (T) wrote:

> It is a curious circumstance attending this opera, that it is the only drama we have on the Italian model, which is generally allowed to be unsuitable to the genius of our language; and that though it has overcome this disadvantage, and gained full possession of the stage, it has had no imitators. Much of its success is to be ascribed to Dr. Arne, who stands nearly at the head of our English composers. . . . We always hear [his music] with pleasure . . . and we even become reconciled to the recitatives.

The public was not to be deprived of any of its airs without protest, as Thomas Kenrick (BS) wrote of the same revival: "Some dissatisfaction was excited by the attempted omission of the Duet *For thee I live my dearest*, and the clamour did not subside till it was given. *Fly, soft ideas* was also omitted, to make way for [Braham's] *Mild as the moonbeam*. This castration of opera is a villainous custom." In a June 1820 review of the opera for *London Magazine*, Hazlitt, who called *Artaxerxes* "the most beautiful Opera in the world, though we have great authorities against us," severely chastised the tenor, John Braham, for omitting "some of the most exquisite airs in Artaxerxes to introduce others of his own composing."

Earlier that year Sterling (T) repeated his dismissal of the revised libretto, saying that the opera "is now compressed into two acts; a license that deserves indulgence, as all the best songs have been retained, and the construction of the opera, in continued recitative, a solitary imitation of the Italian manner, has never been understood or relished by our English audience. It has pleased solely as a musical composition; as a drama it is unintelligible, and therefore tedious." Despite these comments—and the reduction—a good deal of the recitative was retained (QMM, 1820). Its restoration was called "a novelty" by Hunt in an *Examiner* review of the same production: "There is some fine, lasting composition in *Artaxerxes*, particularly in the more tender songs. Arne's genius lay in tenderness and grace, and was a happy follower of the *amoroso* style of the Italians, especially Sacchini's. You can trace the favourite turns of the latter in several of Arne's melodies." Regarding the restored recitative, he wrote:

> Either the novelty pleases, or the public, by favour of Mozart . . . have lately become more susceptible of the delicacies of the art: for the audiences exhibit no symptoms of weariness. . . . But then recitative is so unnatural?—Not so unnatural as we may imagine. Indeed, in some respects it is more natural, in an Opera, than common speech: for grant that beings may sing at all, instead of speak, under the influence of passionate emotions, and it is more natural that they should sing always, than they should burst out into a song occasionally.

He concluded with the idea of speech itself being musical in nature—English as well as Italian. And in 1832 he again came to the defense of Arne's music (*Tatler*).

Allatson Burgh,[12] commenting in 1814 on Arne's achievements, wrote that Arne's style was "so easy, natural, and agreeable to the whole kingdom, that it had a perceptible influence on our national taste." Yet he disliked *Artaxerxes*, noting its "contemptible transitions." Fiske calls it Arne's masterpiece.

BICKERSTAFFE—ARNE

In alliance with Bickerstaffe, Arne exerted an even stronger influence on the direction in English opera. Concerning Isaac Bickerstaffe (c. 1735–1808), the D.N.B. is almost silent, perhaps because of an alleged homosexual offense against a soldier[13] for which he was obliged to flee to Italy in 1772 and live the rest of his life as an impoverished expatriate. He was still being denounced by a Dublin printer in a preface to his librettos in 1791 (White, p. 202). In his youth he had been a page to the lord-lieutenant of Ireland, and as early as 1756 he wrote a tragic opera that was never produced. But from 1760 to 1775, he produced nine librettos, most of which were very popular, and for a time he was included in the Johnson circle.

The first of these was an all-sung afterpiece, *Thomas and Sally* (Covent Garden, 1760), which had several revivals up to 1800, though the *Times* (1789) referred to the "nonsensical jingle" of the songs, and declared that the work was "not well applauded these days." But his next opera, *Love in a Village* (Covent Garden, 1762), was by far his most successful, enjoying an enormous number of revivals until the end of the century; it was still being produced as late as 1840. Even Nicoll (III, 198) thinks the work deserved its success. It was a traditional ballad-type opera, based on Charles Johnson's *Village Opera* (1729), but was "fully composed" by Arne for a wide range of wind instruments, with introductions and postludes (Fiske). Arne wrote some new songs, which Fiske calls outstanding, but for most of the work he used older songs of his own or adapted arias from other English and Italian composers. (One air, by a "Mr. Barnard," was actually composed by George III!) In his preface to *Daphne and Amintor* (1765), Bickerstaffe explained the borrowed music: It was selected for

> the beauty of the airs, and its effect upon the theatre. There are, indeed, some people who may possibly be of the opinion that I ought to have chosen old English and Scotch ballads; or good music composed in the same taste. But, in fact, such sort of compositions scarce deserve the name of music at all; at least they can have little or no merit on the stage, where every thing ought to be supported by a degree of action and character.

(Note that Bickerstaffe takes credit for the selections.) Karl Friedrich Abel composed the overture in the *galant* syle. With this work Arne and Bickerstaffe created a lasting taste for pasticci, though after 1780 musical borrowings in English operas began to decrease.

Early reviews of the opera are confined to the performances. In 1808 Hunt wrote of his distaste for the character Hodge, who "is a mere vehement clown, a perjured swain, who adds blows to unfaithfulness, and threatens to kick his fair one out of doors," while the lyrics given to him are "not worth criticizing as affording opportunities for a singer" (E). In 1816 Sterling (T), reflecting the increasing puritanism of the period, wrote:

"The merit of a few airs has kept alive *Love in a Village*, in spite of the flimsiness of its plot, and the tame vulgarity of its dialogue. Some few excresences of more than ordinary coarseness might, however, with much propriety be lopped away," and the "balderdash song" of Justice Woodcock should be omitted.

In 1817 Sterling noted that the music "is all of the old school, is in many places extremely rugged and difficult of execution; and if not performed with the greatest precision, it fails in its impression." And in 1821 the *Literary Chronicle* admired the "union of the simple and scientific, the pastoral and the refined, which characterizes" the songs of Rosetta, the female lead. In 1827 Ayrton wrote that the opera was sung "in a way that made us wish the spirit of Dr. Arne were present to enjoy the treat," and Talfourd (NM) called the opera "the most English of all English operas, with its gentle interest and unaffected music." But Dr. Burney[14] had years earlier summed up the real importance of the opera: It "betrayed us into a taste for Italian melody, which has been the model of most of our vocal composers . . . ever since."

Strange to say, Arne did not follow up on his great success but instead turned again to Italian opera. His Italian opera *Olimpiade* (1765) failed at the King's, apparently because of the Italian cabal (Busby). He did compose some operas for George Colman the Elder as late as 1773, but he enjoyed no more successes. In his *Autobiography* (p. 43) Hunt called him "a real musical genius, of very pure, albeit not of the very first water."

BICKERSTAFFE — DR. ARNOLD

Bickerstaffe, however, soon produced two more huge successes with other composers — *The Maid of the Mill* (1765) and *Lionel and Clarissa* (1768), both comic operas and both imitative of *Love in a Village*, but they were composed or adapted in the *galant* syle and more difficult to sing (Fiske). For the *Maid*, Bickerstaffe selected some thirty songs with the collaboration of Dr. Arnold. Ranking somewhat below Arne and Shield in theatrical productions was Samuel Arnold (1740–1802), who was later somewhat overshadowed by his better-known son, the playwright and theatre manager Samuel James Arnold. Dr. Arnold learned music as a boy at the Chapel Royal. By 1764 he was a harpsichordist at Covent Garden and was composing pastiche operas. But he was versatile and soon became involved in other projects. With his wife's money, he became a proprietor in Marylebone Gardens and wrote much miscellaneous stage music for their al fresco entertainments, but he was not successful there. He wrote a number of unpublished oratorios for which he obtained his doctorship in music in

1783. In 1777 he joined the elder Colman to write music for the Little Theatre and continued there to the end of his life. But he was also composer and organist at the Chapel Royal (1783), conductor of the Academy of Ancient Music (1789), and organist at Westminister Abbey (1793). He published editions of Handel (1787–93) and directed the chorus at the King's from time to time. "The musical content of his operas is often abysmal," the *New Grove* asserts, "yet he could write well when he took the trouble."

Actually, there was little new music in this opera, though the four numbers by Arnold have been called the "most interesting music in the score" (N.G.). The work included an overture by the Earl of Kelly, finales "in the new Italian style," and borrowings from Galuppi and other Italian comic opera composers as well as from the Paris operas of Monsigny, Philidor, and Duni. Also unusual was Arnold's writing music to accompany the stage action.[15] The work was very popular up to 1800 but seems to have fallen off thereafter; an 1814 revival contained new songs by Bishop. Unfortunately, few reviews survive. In 1798 the *Times* pointed out the need for a competent actor in the male lead, Ralph. "Bickerstaffe has drawn but a faint sketch of rustic humour in the character, and the Actor is necessarily called upon to fill the outlines in a masterly fashion, and to embellish them with a richness of colouring peculiar to his own."[16] Of an 1824 revival Sterling (T) was most unhappy: "It has been almost entirely denuded of the original music, the conjoint work of some of the most eminent composers who flourished at the period when it first appeared . . . and the talent of this house [Drury Lane], either in vocal or the acting department, is not sufficiently vigorous to give due effect to the extensive range of characters, serious and comic, which the opera comprises."

BICKERSTAFFE—CHARLES DIBDIN

For his next opera, Bickerstaffe turned to the versatile Charles Dibdin (1745–1814), composer, dramatist, poet, novelist, actor, singer, and entertainer. The twelfth child of a parish clerk, he was a self-taught composer, singing in the Covent Garden chorus by the age of fifteen, and he early on had roles on the stage, achieving success in character parts. Aside from his stage work, he wrote hundreds of songs, becoming famous for his sea songs during the Napoleonic wars, when they brought more men to the navy than the press gangs (D.N.B.). The strength in his stage composing lay in "dramatically motivated vocal lines" (N.G.).

Their work—*Lionel and Clarissa*, a comic opera on the foibles of the landed gentry—premiered in 1768. Dibdin composed about half of the opera, and he drew on Arne, English folk songs, and Italian opera for the remainder. Not quite as successful as the *Maid* up to 1800, it had even more revivals thereafter.[17] Michael Kelly made his debut in it in 1787, and "Chronicles" alludes to another revival about 1812, but the first reviews of it we have located come from Hunt in 1816: "The piece, like other productions of [Bickerstaffe] has a pleasing mediocrity about it, which is founded in a rich though feeble taste for the theatre. His talent was altogether of a singular description. He seems to have been able to work out nothing out of his own head, but possesses a kind of indolent discernment of simplicity" (E). He added: "There is some very nice music in this piece by old Dibdin, who with his unsophisticated but not very powerful taste, suited his author very happily. But in the performance, a good deal of the music is displaced by inferior composition, apparently according to the caprice of the singer."[18] The *New Oxford History of Music* states that Dibdin "could write fine theatre music but he quarreled with everybody."

SHIELD

The most successful composer of English opera who wrote mainly in our period was William Shield (1748–1829). His father, a singing master, died when William was nine, but he had been taught by age six to play the violin and harpsichord and could "read every cliff" (MM, Jan. 1798). The family fell into poverty, and William was apprenticed to a boat builder for six years; yet he was able to pursue his musical interests on the side, and he studied counterpoint under the famous composer Charles Avison. He soon began composing songs and was engaged as violist at the King's by Giordini in 1773, where he quickly became leader of the viola section, a post he retained for eighteen years.

BATE DUDLEY — SHIELD

In 1778, when Shield was leader of the orchestra at the Little Theatre for one season, he was approached by Henry Bate Dudley (1743–1809) to compose his opera, *The Flitch of Bacon*. Reverend Bate succeeded to his father's rectory, though he lived a life of pleasure in London, where, as noted in part I, he was for many years a newspaper editor, frequently becoming involved in quarrels and duels. To comply with a relative's bequest and to become his heir, he assumed the name of Dudley in 1784. Once a close friend of Garrick's, he began writing for the stage about 1774.

Shield was reluctant to compose the opera because Arnold was the regular house composer, but he finally consented, following the Bickerstaffe-Arne formula: about one-third was borrowed, the rest newly composed. But his orchestration was full of novelty (Fiske). *Flitch* was produced with great success (1778) and was frequently revived up to 1800, but no reviews survive. In the same year, Shield accepted the post of house composer at Covent Garden, taking Charles Dibdin's place and remaining there ten years (though he still retained his post at the King's).

Shield's reputation was thoroughly established by 1791, when he again collaborated with Bate Dudley in a pastoral opera, *The Woodman*. Given Bate's background in journalism, it is no surprise to find reviewers of the *Woodman* hostile to him as was the *Chronicle*'s reviewer — probably James Gray:

> In advising to shelter himself under an assumed name from the efforts of party prejudice the kind anxiety of his friends must have led them to consider that as *probable* which was barely *possible*. Much less knowledge of the world than he possesses, would have been sufficient to convince him, that . . . a consistent attachment to either side is always respected . . . and that the most flagrant dereliction of political principle of which they can be guilty, excites only the silent contempt of the few to whom it happens to be known.

This is a reference not only to his switching political affiliations but also to his assuming a new surname of Dudley, though the doing so was no attempt to conceal his identity. The *Gazetteer*, complaining of the literary borrowings, called the author "very little responsible" for the libretto — chiefly a "musical vehicle." Genest (see below) thought it very poor, but critic C of the *Times* was quite positive: "His sketches, though without any great share of originality, are yet drawn from life and bespeak the hand of a master. *The Woodman* with respect to the simplicity of its characters and plot[19], partakes more of the features of [Mrs. Brooke's] *Marian*, [see below] than any other piece in our recollection."

Regarding the music Gray (C) declared that Shield's talents "have long since justly raised him to a very distinguished situation in the English School. . . . Mr. Shield is always eminently successful in airs that require tenderness and simplicity, and perhaps no English Composer has produced so many pleasing ballads of this description. The pastoral songs in this piece are a fresh proof of the classical delicacy of his taste and the richness of his invention." All reviewers spoke highly of the selected glees, choruses and finale, as well as the three-movement overture, which had "great variety, great spirit, and great novelty" (LC) and included a fine oboe obbligato played by Parke. The work was given a good production. "Notwithstanding all the prejudices of party," it "went off without the slightest opposition" (T) and played twenty-eight times, with six revivals to 1800.

At an 1808 revival, Hunt complained of the libretto's triviality: "Like many other pastoral operas, [it] has a good sort of farmer in it, and a bad sort of country squire, a singing girl or two, some pretty scenery, and a very insipid lover.... One might have dispensed with some allusions and speeches not very edifying to chaste ears." Regarding Shield's music, however, he "could not help admiring the correctness of the public in matters of taste, when I heard some of those fine airs which have become popular and which are indisputably the best in the piece."[20]

Shield was affluent enough later that year to take a trip to France and Italy. His "principal view, in visiting Italy, was to study the mode of teaching singing, for which purpose he had lessons from the best masters at Rome" (MM).

For their final collaboration—*Travellers in Switzerland* (1794), a comic opera—Bate Dudley contrived a book that would give Shield even greater opportunity for the music: there were thirty-four numbers, including more borrowings than in the *Woodman*. But he complained, in the book's preface, about the difficulty of fitting words to the music. Gray (C) had now forgotten his antipathies toward the playwright:

> The adventures of various English people among the mountains of Switzerland are the subject of the story; and the author has rather contrived how to draw out the combined musical and comic talents of the numerous performers of the Theatre [Covent Garden] than to confine himself to a simple and regular fable. Justice must acknowledge he has very successfully hit the mark at which he aimed.... The dialogue throughout is neat, spirited, and frequently humorous.... Terse, concise and efficacious, is the Dramatic poet's motto.

Critic C of the *Times*, on the other hand, was now critical, saying: the opera "has not to boast much artful construction of able or brilliant dialogue. Of character, little of novelty is attempted."

Both had high praise for Shield. He "may be said here to have outdone his usual outdoings. The Overture is a bold and beautiful composition, and the last Movement particularly light and airy," and the "grand and impressive" choruses and the glee "Ye Gentlemen of England" were praised (T). Gray supplied more details on the music:

> The airs, duets, trios, quartettos, and choruses, succeed each other so rapidly . . . that we were really astonished at the power of the composer who was capable of sustaining a task so mighty.... Exclusive of the richness of his melodies, [Shield] is equally a master of harmony, and . . . his accompaniments are as full of invention as his airs.... He

possesses another highly necessary quality, that of knowing and calling forth the powers of his performers.

Obviously Shield had profited by his Italian journey. The production was excellent and the work played twenty-six times. John Genest, a contemporary chronicler of English drama who disliked English opera, called the piece "contemptible clap-trap," but even the literary *Analytical Review*'s critique of the book found the story "well contrived" and several of the characters "drawn from nature." The *Monthly Review* admitted "the dialogue is often terse, and the incidents are amusing"; the *English Review* stated the play had "that degree of elegance and spirit that in general distinguish the productions of Dudley."

But Hunt, at an 1808 revival, again showed his distaste for the playwright: The "unavoidable propensity of the author to low characters sufficiently proves that he cannot be humourous without being vulgar." His greatest objection was Bate Dudley's influence on Shield: "Though Mr. Shield is very deservedly admired by all the lovers of music, yet I have absolutely been sometimes asked where his music is to be found. . . . People are surprised to see the excellent music of Mr. Shield condemned to partial fits of existence and to ultimate death: and they cannot sufficiently lament that he . . . is thus limited to the destiny of a dying and ungrateful muse."

Surprisingly, Bate wrote no more for the stage, devoting his remaining years to editing and managing his church benefices. After his first effort with Bate in 1778, Shield waited five years to write his next opera; his new collaborator was John O'Keeffe, whose earliest operas were composed by Dr. Arnold.

O'KEEFFE—DR. ARNOLD

Born of a Catholic family in Dublin, John O'Keeffe (1747–1833) was educated at a Jesuit school. As a child he had attended Italian opera in Dublin and later became a close friend of many opera singers. Hogarth (II, 95) called him "a passionate lover of music." He completed his first comedy at fifteen and soon became a player on the Dublin stage. He wrote his first opera for Dublin in 1777 and his first London opera in 1781. From then until 1798 he produced over fifty works for the stage, mostly for Covent Garden and the Little Theatre, of which nine were operatic farces and twelve comic operas. Many of his other plays, including pantomimes and burlettas, contained songs. His prolixity was abetted by his method: "If . . . he found he had taken too extensive a survey . . . he would detach any straggling character or incident from his design, and reserve it for another opportunity. By this œconomy, out of those comedies, he produced three good farces."[21] His eyesight began to fail at age twenty-three and was greatly diminished by thirty-eight, yet he continued to act until totally blind at age fifty.

In 1782 O'Keeffe wrote his first comic opera with Arnold—*The Castle of Andalusia*. It was a rewrite of *The Banditti* (Covent Garden, 1781), which had failed.[22] It received thirty-nine performances and several revivals at least until 1817. At an 1815 revival at the Lyceum, Sterling (T) called it "extravagant and incorrigible, if you chose to call it so; but full of that buoyant hilarity and happy foolery which few minds, endowed with healthy spirits, would reject from the list of their joyous recreations."

Arnold's own contributions for Bickerstaffe's *Maid of the Mill* (1765), it will be recalled, were praised more highly than his musical borrowings, and the same was apparently true of *Andalusia*, which had fifteen borrowed numbers—mostly Scottish airs no doubt selected by O'Keeffe. At an 1817 revival, the *European* found that "the music of Dr. Arnold is in itself a sufficient recommendation." Busby called his music for this opera "excellent," though he thought him inferior to Arne. Fiske (p. 453) reports Arnold took "more than usual pains" with the music.

The Siege of Curzola (Little Theatre, 1786), a comic opera based on an episode in Turkish history, was their last collaboration. Genest tells us O'Keeffe wrote the opera for his singer friends Signora Sestini and John Edwin, who had the leading roles. O'Keeffe states he selected most of the airs for Arnold. The *Register* (probably Charles Este) panned the work: "The Opera before us is a composition of absurdities, founded on a collection of scenes, irrelevant to each other, without any claim to originality of character or sentiment, and abounding in palpable plagiarisms, obscene allusions, and vulgarities of action, incident, and language." Este thought he should have stuck to farce. The *Gazetteer* and Gray (C) had similar views, the latter adding: "Perhaps, like Gay, he meant to ridicule the Italian musical drama and to exemplify the maxim of 'No matter how absurdly these things are brought about.' If so, he has been wonderfully successful." The opera played only seven times.

O'KEEFFE—SHIELD

Arnold's later operas were composed for the younger Colman and others (see below). Meanwhile, O'Keeffe's better operas were written for Covent Garden and composed by Shield. The first of these was one of the most popular, *The Poor Soldier* (1783), a rewrite of O'Keeffe's *Shamrock* and an "unbounded success" that had revivals up to the 1820s. Only about half of the seventeen airs were original, the rest selected by O'Keeffe from Irish ballads and airs by Carolan, the Irish bard. He sang the songs to Shield, who wrote only the accompaniments; Shield was paid less for these but made money from the sale of the music.[23] No reviews survive, but in a sketch of Shield in 1798, John Taylor (MM, Jan., p. II) wrote: "One of Shield's most difficult achievements was *The Poor Soldier*, the tunes of which were . . . so wild as hardly to admit of accompanyments, and some able composers, when they first saw them, pronounced the attempt . . . hopeless. Yet he succeeded, and the work will remain among the solid tests of his scientific knowledge and skill." Fiske, however, is critical of Shield's arrangements.

The collaborators' next production for Covent Garden—*Fontainbleau* (1784)—was one of Shield's best efforts.[24] It was very successful, with revivals at least to 1822. A 1785 revival, revised by O'Keeffe, was "much improved," but we have no other comment on the work until 1819, when Sterling (T) wrote of a Drury Lane revival that the opera was "a far more entertaining production than the modern race of operas, and, with all the eccentricity of the author, containing varieties of character as extensive as in his comedies." The *Inquisitor* spoke of "this facetious opera, which the paramount whimsicality of O'Keeffe has endowed with inexhaustible sources of amusement." But nothing was said of the music. At a Covent Garden revival in 1822, Sterling also praised O'Keeffe and found the work well produced, but "little of the original music has been retained." A Rossini aria was one of the substituted songs.

Other collaborations followed. *The Farmer* (1787), a two-act operatic farce, was very successful but was not revived and reviews are trivial. *The Highland Reel*, a comic romance, was offered the next year. The *Advertiser* thought it a "pleasing work" with "excellent music," but the *Herald*, "led to expect a delineation of national manners in which Humour might be combined with novelty," was disappointed: "The author is far from being acquainted with the local manners. . . . The only attempt at Character is made in the Steward."[25] The *London Chronicle* noted that the play "would not bear [the] scrutiny" of "strict rules"; but "there is a romantic air through the whole which, while it is not strictly reconcilable to sound reason, does not fail to interest and to exhilarate the mind." There were original airs by Shield and Domenico Corri (LC) as well as borrowings from Handel, David Rizzio, J. C. Bach, and Grétry, but the greater part consisted of "familiar Scottish airs,[26] to which Shield has set very pleasing accompaniments" (T). Parke's oboe gave "the effect of bagpipes very charmingly . . . and the *pizzicato* accompaniments in the last symphony, made the conclusion very delightful" (H). The *Times* thought it amusing but not as good as the *Castle of Andalusia* or *Fontainbleau*. It too succeeded but was not revived.

O'Keeffe's next opera, the comic *Sprigs of Laurel* (1793), was a patriotic gesture. Both author and composer, anonymous in the advertisements, were guessed correctly by the press. The plot concerned the embarkation of the guards for Holland, under the Duke of York, and included "some little acts of military ardour and some amorous incidents" (UM). The *Times* reported that the work "has this recommendation to public notice, that its subject is the present *popular war* with the French." But Gray (C) declared: "Unfortunately it turns so much upon temporary politics, the most improper of all improper subjects for the Theatre, because [people] wish not to hear the subjects of their serious debates mixed up with their amusements."

The right-wing *True Briton* noted that the piece had "some original merit, much humour, and several points of true wit." But notices from the literary reviewers were mixed. The *Analytical Review* wrote: "This piece seems to owe its success chiefly to it's loyalty; of which it possesses a much larger portion than either of wit, of humour, or of poetry." But the *Critical Review* thought the dialogue "sufficiently sprightly," and "with the assistance of scenery, songs, [and] martial music [the opera] may have as good an effect as a glass of brandy." And the *Monthly Review* asserted that it contained "many strokes of true humour, fancy, and generous sentiment; but we are sorry that its parts are so disjointed . . . that he has [left the text] all but unintelligible"; they also disliked its dabbling in jingoism and politics. Only the *London Chronicle* commented on the music (airs by Handel and Anfossi were among the borrowings): "Shield has added fresh *Sprigs of Laurel* to his well-established reputation as an excellent composer and judicious selector. The music of the Opera in question is infinitely superior in point of melody and appropriation to any that has been heard on the stage for some time past: it is indeed an exquisite treat for the taste of an amateur, and a capital addition to the production of the science."

The opera was successful, with fifteen performances that season and several revivals. The humor was so topical that O'Keeffe had to revise it as *The Rival Soldiers* in 1797, but it was not successful. Under that title, however, Hunt saw the opera in 1818 and wrote that it was "a pleasing specimen, in little, of Mr. O'Keeffe's dramatic spirit. . . . He makes the coarse, selfish, and degrading vices the reverse of tempting, and yet very ludicrous. . . . It is the production of a kind-hearted and chearful man, who believes in the virtues he writes about."[27]

Although by this time totally blind, O'Keeffe continued to rehash his works for a few more musical and nonmusical productions until 1798, but with little further success. C. A. E. Goëde, a rather hostile witness of London performances circa 1821, recalled O'Keeffe's "vile productions." Modern critics have also been hard on this playwright. Nicoll (III, 200–201) attributes to him "the perennial curse of mawkish artificialty which has ever clung to musical comedy" and the "countless inanities in nineteenth century musical drama." But, as we have seen, the contemporary press—even some of the literary journals—in general praised him. No doubt he is to be seen, not read, for he carefully shaped his material for specific performers. And many years later even Hunt and Hazlitt had some praise for his pieces (Fenner, p. 284, n. 15).

BROOKE—SHIELD

An altogether different type of playwright furnished Shield with an early and lasting success. Mrs. Frances Brooke (née Moore, 1724–89), wrote novels, essays, poetry, and biography, as well as four works for the stage. She was best known for the third, *Rosina* (Covent Garden, 1782), a two-act comic-pastoral opera probably based on a French source. The plot, inspired by the Biblical story of Ruth, was rather insipid; nevertheless, Shield's setting, with six true ballads—one a version of "Auld Lang Syne," possibly not Scottish—and the remainder in ballad style, assured the popularity of the work, which had fifty performances through 1800, with subsequent revivals at least to 1830.[28]

At an 1820 revival, Hunt noted that, though the play had "small value as a piece of writing," it was at least unpretentious. "Besides, there is Mr. Shield's music to it, as sweet and pastoral as can well be imagined." Ten years later he made a similar report for the *Tatler*:

> Though the production was poor, the name of *Rosina* sounded as fresh last night, as if our grand mother's [sic] had never heard it.... In [Shield's] musical compositions ... there is always a portion of genius to be found, with still greater evidence of a certain sweetness of nature.... Who would suppose this amiable and lasting composer (for he is among the immortals, if a minor one) could have been denied a burial in Westminster Abbey.

Here Shield's affinity for folk songs must be noted, for it was *Rosina*, more than any other opera, that won him a lasting reputation as a ballad composer. For many years he was an avid collector of folk songs—English, Scottish, Irish, even Russian—and many of his own songs were fine imitations of folk songs. Young (p. 262f.) states that "he believed in folk song not because he rediscovered it, but because it had been a part of his early life. He subsequently lost no opportunity to furnish his audiences with folk music experience in as accurate form as was possible."

It was probably with *Rosina* and *Marian* in mind that Hogarth (II, 441) declared Shield's music "not marked by force or energy.... His melodies, in style, character, and adapted to the accounts of our native speech, are perfectly English." Yet Shield was also quite capable of writing a fine bravura, one of which was even included in *Rosina*. In *Richard Coeur de Lion* he wrote a difficult air for Mrs. Billington at a semitone higher than Mozart's "Queen of the Night" aria. He wrote high notes for men, as well, though the top fifth was understood to be sung falsetto (N.G.).

Another ballad-type opera, Brooke's *Marian*, was produced in 1788. The plot,[29] as the *Times* noted, was meager, but "there are some natural strokes in the dialogue that bespeaks a purity of taste in the author" and on the whole it was entertaining. The *Advertiser* found the plot "simple and elegant in the extreme." Only the overture was singled out for mention, with but trite praise for Shield, whose musical borrowings included Paisiello, Salieri, and Handel's *Athealia*. Parke, however, thought the work contained "almost [Shield's] sweetest music." It played twelve times and had several revivals.

MACNALLY—SHIELD

Shield composed two operas for Leonard Macnally (1752–1820), son of a Dublin merchant. He was called to the bar in 1783, and he practiced law in Dublin, later becoming Barrister at Law in London. He was for a time a government informer reporting on revolutionary activities in Ireland, for which he received a lifelong pension. Author of legal treatises, he produced his first stage work, an opera, in Dublin in 1778.

His first collaboration with Shield was the comic opera *Robin Hood* (Covent Garden, 1784); it was a great hit, with sixty performances to 1789 and fifteen more as an afterpiece before 1800. It was revived in 1813 with additional music by John Addison; Boaden, in 1825, called the music still popular. The familiar legend was reinforced with borrowings from Oliver Goldsmith, but the music, Parke tells us, was the real draw. Shield composed seventeen new airs and adapted twelve old ones, some from an earlier afterpiece. His friend bassoonist Samuel Baumgarten provided the overture, which had "intrinsic merit" (UR).

With his second comic opera—*Richard Coeur de Lion*, (Covent Garden, 1786), also a favorite English story—Macnally was less successful. For starters, the piece had to compete with another opera of the same title, by Burgoyne, with Grétry's music adapted by the elder Linley (both works were taken from Sedaine), which was produced at Drury Lane just a week later. "The anachronisms and improbabilities in the French[30] are avoided, and in their place are substituted humourous characters. . . . [Macnally] has modeled it entirely to our own taste" (LC). Not all went well on opening night, but on the second performance improvements were made: the incidents of the drama were made more relevant to the whole (C), and a song by Richard with "political allusions" was "expunged" (G); moreover, "the feelings of Englishmen are hurt at seeing their Sovereign in imprisonment and in depression. . . . He should by no means appear until rescued" (UR, Oct. 17).

"The musick of this piece, considered altogether, which is beyond dispute one of the richest treats ever offered to the ears of taste and discernment, was last night performed in a very capital style" (C, Oct. 19). It was "rich and various almost beyond precedence" — "at no former time have the English audiences been gratified with chorusses so copious, powerful, and correct as in this Opera" (*Gazette*). Borrowings included airs from Anfossi, Bertoni, Duni, Rizzio, Carolan, Tenducci, Philip Hayes, and John Wilson,[31] in addition to Grétry, and both borrowings and Shield's music drew high praise (LC).

But there were performance difficulties as well. On opening night, Inchbold, who played Richard, lost his voice and had to quit the stage, omitting important scenes (C, Oct. 17) This proved a mortal blow. After four performances, the opera was cut down to an afterpiece, which received thirteen performances despite the competition from the more opulent Drury Lane production (UR, Oct. 23). As Fiske states, Macnally's version was "messed up." After *Richard*, Macnally produced only two more minor works for the stage.

HOLCROFT—SHIELD

In 1784 and 1785 Shield composed two operas, both failures, for Thomas Holcroft (1745–1809), an exceptional, self-made man. Son of a shoemaker and peddler, he moved from stable boy to prompter at a Dublin theatre, then joined a strolling company. Stern and conscientious, he was endowed with much energy but found himself "in continuous struggle against misfortune" (D.N.B.). His first play, an opera, was produced at Drury Lane in 1778. By 1783 he was in Paris as a correspondent for the *Herald* (he also wrote theatrical criticism that year for the *English Review*); while there he made an unauthorized English translation of Beaumarchais's extraordinarily successful *Le Mariage de Figaro*. Produced at Covent Garden in 1784 as *Follies of the Day*, it too became very popular and, long after Holcroft's death, formed the basis for Bishop's highly successful adaptation of Mozart's *Nozze di Figaro* (1819). But his *Follies* had marked him as something of a radical; as revolutionary fears mounted in England, political prejudices toward him increased, and he was obliged to produce his plays anonymously. In 1796 he was indicted for treason as a member of a banned society.

Shield was still house composer for the Little Theatre when he composed Holcroft's comic opera *The Noble Peasant* for production there in 1784; it was never revived. The next year the team produced another comic opera, *The Choleric Fathers*, for Covent Garden. Boaden thought the plot and dialogue careless, and some reviewers agreed, but the critic for *Walker's Hibernian*, reviewing the book, thought Holcroft had "written with great strength and purity"—"the language is correct and nervous," and even the plot[32] was "highly interesting and probable." In any event we are told that subsequent alterations improved the work considerably (H).

Regarding the music, the *Herald* stated: "The overture possesses a majesty that well accords with an opera formed of Spanish materials ... [and] many experimental novelties appear interspersed through [the opera]; some in point of musical expression, and some of instrumental effect." But the *Register* (Este) lavished the greatest praise on the composer in a column devoted to "Shield's Music." After the departure of the celebrated Locke, Handel, and Arne, English music

> was thought to have vanished from England; but happy for all *true lovers of harmony*, it has only a short time lain dormant.... [Shield] by progressive steps stole into esteem with the Public; and possessing the genuine, though latent sparks of *genius*, they have at last blazed forth to *fame*. His late composition of the *Choleric Fathers* would have done honour to any of his famed predecessors, for originality of style, for a bold and masterly expression of the exalted passions, and for its melting delicacy in the pathetic.... The *quartettos, trios*, and *duettos*, are striking proofs of first-rate talents [and] the whole of the music, and particularly the *simple songs*, are better adapted to the taste of the English auditory, than any hitherto brought on the stage.[33] (Nov. 16)

Unfortunately, the opera played only seven times. Discouraged by the failure, Holcroft waited fourteen years to write another opera, as we shall see, though he continued to produce many comedies.

PEARCE—SHIELD

Shield's collaborations with one William Pearce—"a gentleman of acknowledged literary talents" who produced five operas between 1792 and 1795—

were very successful. Their first production was the farcical afterpiece *Hartford-Bridge* (Covent Garden, 1792). The work received a good production and "abound[ed] with bustle, spirit, and entertainment" (LC), and even the literary monthlies had some praise for the drama. The music, partly selected from Haydn and Sacchini and partly composed, was "extremely masterly," and "in both points of view, it does Mr. Shield the highest credit. The overture is a capital composition, and the airs are selected with infinite taste, and the accompaniments far beyond the style of accompaniment attained by several modern masters" (LC).[34] The work had thirty-six performances that season and revivals to 1800.

In 1793 they brought out *The Midnight Wanderers*, another comic afterpiece set in the Pyrenees, which was also given a fine production. The story[35] was "fraught with some whimsicality, but not pregnant with much humour. Several of the observations . . . are apposite and witty, but the plot is rather improbable. . . . The words of the airs are neatly turned" (D, Feb. 26). Other reviewers were more positive. Gray (C) wrote: "The characters have new features . . . and Mr. Pearce . . . thinks that even yet the Music of a Song is not likely to be worse for being set to words that have sense and poetry." The *Thespian* admired the drama and thought the songs "very beautifully written." The *British Critic* agreed, and the *Monthly Review* thought that there was "considerable imagination in some of the incidents . . . but it is rather imagination in embryo than embodied and brought to light," and they preferred *Hartford-Bridge*.

Concerning the music, Gray wrote that the songs "have received, from the natural, modest, original Shield such exquisite airs as will ensure them a permanent place on [sic] the Theatre." In addition to his own songs,[36] Shield drew on Paisiello and Grétry. The work had thirteen performances but only one revival.

Their next collaboration, the following year, was another afterpiece operatic farce, *Netley Abbey*, which had a naval setting. But the drama "was infinitely inferior in every respect" to *Hartford-Bridge*. "Some of the attempts at wit are as coarse as they are stale" and the work "was warmly opposed at its conclusion" (T). Nevertheless, it had ten performances and a few revivals.

HOLMAN–SHIELD

Not until his unfortunately brief collaboration with Joseph George Holman, in 1796, did Shield have another three-act opera to set. Holman (1764–1817), who was raised by an uncle, studied at Oxford but dropped out to become a performer at Covent Garden from 1783 to 1800, where he was highly regarded as actor and singer. *Abroad and At Home* (1796), a comic opera, was his first production, and his fellow performers outdid themselves. The story was "a dramatic compendium of the tricks, dissipation, and chicanery, practiced in the King's Bench prison."[37] Here was something far removed from the namby-pamby sentimentality some critics occasionally complained of. Fiske calls it "the best libretto Shield had to work on for years." Indeed, the shift proved too radical for some reviewers. Critic D (T) reported: "The Opera abounds in those satiric lashes which cut too deep to produce reformation. Vice and folly are very laudably unmasked and stigmatized, but the Author might have more effectively attained his end, by using the ridiculous as his instrument, than by dipping his pen in the gall of indignant reprehension." Nevertheless, he admitted that the dialogue had the merit of originality; the *London Chronicle* agreed, as did Boaden (OPA), who wrote: "This play was designed to depend upon its dialogue . . . the operatical part was an after thought." Many of the songs were well written, though "the more of these are removed the better will the action hold together." But the *Monthly Review* thought that "the songs, though not ill-written, seem quite out of place, and harmonize neither with the plot nor the persons." Moreover, the *Times* reported, "The Music cannot be classed among the happiest compositions of Shield. There are many 'concords of sweet sound,' but there are also many similitudes to former passages. The *Finales* to the second and third acts . . . are but *mediocre*."[38]

Interestingly, this satirical opera, despite these reviews, proved to be very successful, with thirty-two performances and two revivals to 1800. For his next operas—in 1797 and 1800, after Shield had left Covent Garden—Holman turned to Attwood and other composers (see below).

HOARE—SHIELD

Prince Hoare (1755–1834), son of William Hoare, R. A., was early instructed in art by his father. He studied in London and in 1781 was exhibited at the Academy, which appointed him foreign secretary in 1799. Forced to give up painting because of ill health that affected his eyesight, he "withdrew to the seacoast for the benefit of the air" and proceeded to write a tragedy, which succeeded in Bath (1788) and London (1796). He and Michael Kelly were lifelong friends.

He had already produced six operas with Storace (see below) between 1790 and 1795 at Drury Lane and Little Theatre when, in 1796 and 1797, he produced two operas with Shield for Covent Garden. The first was an afterpiece operatic farce, *Lock and Key*, which was "crude and irregular, but his main incidents are provokingly laughable." The overture, by Parke, brought praise; "the rest of the music[39] [is] chiefly by Mr. Shield—*it could have no better name*" (T; TB). Boaden (OPA) noted it produced "broad laugh[s] by the management of its incident, and an additional pleasure by songs serious and ludicrous, set with infinite taste, or selected with much judgment," and the production was superb. It was very successful with thirty-eight performances.

The second opera produced with Shield was a three-act comic opera, *The Italian Villagers*, in 1797. The subject[40] was ably treated and the dialogue was "neat." "Patriotic and impressive sentiments frequently occur, and, on the score of chaste *equivoque* and novel sprightliness, it has no slight claim to approbation" (LC). Boaden wrote that Hoare had "built upon an old foundation"—particularly Shakespeare's *As You Like It*—"it is no bad imitation of the great master. As to the succession of Pantomime tricks, which he has perhaps been compelled to graft upon his old stock, we cannot relish, and will not vehemently decry them." Moreover, "the Songs are written with that dexterity which characterize a man who knows music." And the *London Chronicle* wrote that the music "bespeaks its master. Shield never was more successful than in the present instance. Most of the airs are truly delightful, and the whole is a composition of beauty and taste." It was ably performed, but for some reason it was a box-office flop.

Shield's later efforts with Thomas Dibdin and Frederic Reynolds are discussed below,[41] as are Hoare's later successes with Storace, Dussek, and others.

THE LINLEYS

The Linleys, at Drury Lane, gave Shield and Covent Garden musical competition in the early years of our period. Thomas the Elder (1733–1795), whose music for the *Tempest* has already been mentioned, was the best known. A composer, harpsichordist, and singing teacher, he studied under William Boyce, and from the 1750s to the 1770s, he directed popular annual concerts at Bath. His first theatrical success in London was the *Royal Merchant* (Covent Garden, 1757). Sheridan abducted his daughter, Elizabeth, but Linley finally gave his blessing to the union, and the Linleys were brought into the fold of Drury Lane, of which Linley became part owner; he directed the music there for twenty years. He was also the father of twelve children—all musicians—of whom Thomas the Younger and William achieved considerable note.

SHERIDAN—LINLEYS

No doubt the biggest triumph of both of the Thomas Linleys was the setting of Sheridan's only opera, *The Duenna* (Drury Lane, 1775). No comments (except on performers) occur in reviews before 1813, when the opera was deemed "the most popular in the language [always excepting of course *The Beggar's Opera*], atoning its defects of vigour by a rare and felicitous combination of natural humour, graceful sentiment, and captivating melody" (T). At an 1819 revival, Hunt wrote of the opera: "Coming as it did from the hands of a man of wit, who could not turn his singing characters into mere dolts, [it] might reasonably be represented by persons with very few professed singers among them, but unfortunately the town has come to expect little else in operas besides the mere art of singing [and] they are not readily disposed to let Mr. Sheridan's wit and nature become more prominent than the execution of the songs." The following year DuBois (TI) agreed, speaking of "this admirable opera, so replete with complicated incidents, amusing characters, and lively dialogue." He added: "The original airs have a prescriptive and perennial sweetness which renders their retention indispensible, and this feature of the opera is one which marks its decided superiority, and maintains its primitive success."

As noted earlier, Thomas the Elder disagreed with Sheridan's procedure of selecting the folk airs, but did adapt the tunes,[42] and his main contribution was knowing how to score the ballads in *galant* style (Fiske). Thomas the Younger (1756–78), a greater composer than his father,[43] wrote all the new music. (A friend of Mozart's, he died in an accident at a tragically young age.) *The Duenna* was enormously popular and has been frequently revived right down to our own time.

BURGOYNE

The next production of the elder Linley's was with Burgoyne. Lieutenant-General John Burgoyne (1723–92), known to Americans for his military defeat at Saratoga in 1777 (he never wanted to be sent to America anyway), was better known to Londoners for his popular operas, though his defeat did make him an unpopular figure for a time. Son of a captain and a man of fashion who had fallen on hard times, Burgoyne gained wealth through his marriage, bought a captaincy, and in 1768 became a M.P. He belonged to all the fashionable clubs and participated in amateur theatricals.

Beginning in 1774, he wrote four works for Drury Lane, three of them very successful operas. His first, *Maid of the Oaks* (1774), was composed by F. H. Barthélemon. The second and far more popular was *The Lord of the*

Manor (1780), based on Marmontel and composed by William Jackson.⁴⁴ It had twenty-two performances and seven revivals before 1800 and continued at least until 1830. There were no comments on the opera at any of the revivals, when much of his music was dropped.⁴⁵

BURGOYNE—LINLEY (THE ELDER)

Burgoyne's most popular opera was *Richard Coeur de Lion* (1786), a three-act musical drama that Drury Lane mounted in competition with the unsuccessful Macnally-Shield opera of the same name at Covent Garden. Both dramas followed the Sedaine original, but Burgoyne's was a better adaptation: "We have a chaste copy of the original with only one material alteration . . . which does great credit to the taste and judgment" of the author (C). But the greatest difference was in the music, which in Shield's hands was a pastiche including Grétry, whereas Linley "adapted" all of Grétry's music so that the piece was actually an English version. Gray (C) wrote:

> Though we cannot but think the whole to be a representation rather adapted to the Italian theatre than an English playhouse, yet . . . all who admire a musical piece founded on a simple but a strongly dramatic incident . . . will be highly delighted. . . . The music . . . was, we understand, precisely the same as that performed at the *Comedie Italienne* in Paris, and it deserves every possible praise. . . . Indeed, we scarcely know a passage of it that does not prove the hand of a master.⁴⁶

A *Times* correspondent agreed. But the regular reviewer, in the same number, noted it was rather the adaptation of the words to the music that was the real accomplishment, a task Burgoyne complained of in his preface to the printed play. The work received a splendid production and enjoyed an astonishing run of forty-three performances, with seven revivals before 1800.⁴⁷

After such popularity, it is curious that Burgoyne wrote no more for the stage. Meanwhile, Linley turned to a new dramatist.

COBB—LINLEY (THE ELDER)

James Cobb (1756–1818) was a highly respected member of the East India Company; he displayed no vanity over the success of his stage works (Taylor, I, 312). He was fond of songs, had "a perfect knowledge of music," and played the violin "with no mean degree of execution." We are told by John Taylor that he composed at least one song for every one of his operas

(MM, Jan. 1803). First drawn to the stage by his admiration for the actress Jane Pope, he composed several apprentice pieces, including an opera set by Arnold, *Wedding Night* (1780), which was hissed off the stage. His first success was a farce, the *Humourist* (Drury Lane, 1785).

Cobb soon settled into a long string of operatic successes at Drury Lane, beginning with *The Strangers at Home* (1785), a comic opera composed by Linley. The work had "stronger claims to commendation than most of the comic operas produced of late years" (LC). The characters[48] were not "highly charged with humour; but the dialogue abounds with pleasant thoughts, brilliant witticisms, and beautiful similes" (UR). The *Herald* was less happy: "The first act preserves the business well, but it is rather wire-drawn in the second, and does not wind up with sufficient celerity in the third."

Linley borrowed from Purcell, J. C. Bach, Sacchini, and others, and added music of his own: "The new part of it is like all of Mr. Linley's compositions, masterly. The overture is a charming one . . . and the old tune of Ally Croker has a most improved effect from the new time to which it is now sung" (LC). The *Herald* and *Times* agreed, though the latter thought the overture "not sufficiently bold and vigorous" (Dec. 10). A correspondent (T, Dec. 12) could not praise the opera highly enough, including Linley's use of carillons in the overture, to which some critic had objected. "Linley's music," he wrote, "rises on the public—it was at first '*Caviare* to the million.' To say the truth, Linley, like *Coriolanus*, keeps the vulgar at too great a distance, consequently the *million* will not give him their voice."[49] He went on to note that Linley was the subject of a political cabal: "*Party* has been too much consulted in certain accounts we have lately seen in Ministerial papers. Linley has the honour to be connected with Sheridan by the ties of blood—Sheridan is politically connected with *Opposition*, and therefore it becomes necessary, by way of *opposition*, to cavil at Linley's music. This may be highly politic, but is it fair? We answer no . . . and opposition must be treated by all parties with derision and contempt." Despite the cabal, the work, which had a fine production, played twenty-one times and had seven revivals. An 1789 revival was approved by a full house, and the cast was better than the original one (T). Adolphus (I, 131) states the opera's chief aim was "to exhibit Mrs. Jordan's special charm in a man's dress."

This success prompted another effort, the comic *Love in the East* (1788), by the same team. The story, laid in Calcutta, "did [Cobb] honour for its dramatic structure and animated dialogue" (H). It "abounds with a variety of comic situations[50]—the dialogue is much superior to what we are generally accustomed to; . . . the *true attic* salt pervade[s] the whole performance" (T). The music was also praised as "principally new," and numerous new and compiled airs, including songs by Paisiello and Cimarosa, were singled out as deserving "superior praise" (H).[51] The music was "well-adapted" and the overture and choruses were beautiful (LC; T). Genest grudgingly called the work "indifferent, but good enough for an opera." It had an opulent production but played only nine times. After 1785 Linley, shattered by ill health, gradually relinquished his theatrical work to Storace.[52]

ATTWOOD

Although Thomas Attwood (1765–1838) had far more advantages than Shield or even the Linleys, he never gained their eminence. Son of a coal merchant who played the trumpet in the King's (wind) Band and who also played the viola, Attwood benefited from royal patronage; as chorister in the Chapel Royal, he became page to the Prince of Wales in 1781, receiving training in composition and the organ. Impressed, the prince sent him to Italy and Vienna, where he took lessons from Mozart.[53] If Kelly, who was there at the time, can be believed, Mozart told him that Attwood "partakes more of my style than any scholar I ever had, and I predict that he will prove a sound musician" (I, 225). On his return to England, he found royal pupils, and in 1796 he became organist at St. Paul's. He had a kind and genial disposition and had many friends in the musical world (N.G.).

ROSE—ATTWOOD

Meanwhile, Attwood began writing music for the theatre, his first effort being *The Prisoner* (Drury Lane, 1792), a musical romance—actually more melodrama than opera—by the Reverend John Rose, "one of the masters of Charter House." He produced only four dramas, of which this—his first opera—was the third. The work was said to have been written expressly for the boy singer, Thomas Welsh, then age eleven.[54] The "escape" plot, a story of Spanish jealousy, borrowed from the French and set in South America, was "deeply tragical" and dealt with "chains, imprisonment and death." The melodramatic scenes impressed the *Times* and *London Chronicle* but not the *Chronicle*.

The *Times* praised the songs and the music, which "bespeaks great fancy and genius—the selections from Mozart and Sarti are well adapted to the capabilities of the performers." And the *London Chronicle* called the work Attwood's "corps d'essai" and "a powerful aid-du-camp he has proved himself, since the music is the chief recommendation of the performance."

But Gray (C) wrote: "Had [Attwood] attempted less, he would have been more successful. The overture has neither originality nor spirit, and the ... songs are 'full of sound and fury, signifying nothing.' Some of the airs are however pleasing."[55] Attwood led the band at the premiere. The work proved surprisingly popular, no doubt because of Master Welsh and the melodramatic effects, with twenty-seven performances and a couple of revivals. It led to two final collaborations between them the following year, *Caernarvon Castle*, also a musical drama, and *Fairy Festival* in 1797; both were failures.

BOADEN — ATTWOOD

In 1793 Attwood composed an afterpiece for James Boaden, who, as noted in part I, edited the *Oracle* for a time and wrote some theatrical criticism for it. Boaden published two works on the theatre, and was for many years treasurer of Covent Garden.

Ozmyn and Daraxa (Drury Lane), a not very operatic "musical romance," was his first work for the stage. The plot, set in seventeenth-century Spain, owed something to the picaresque tradition of René LeSage's *Gil Blas*. Some reviewers appreciated its quality; Gray (C), in a brief paragraph, thought "both the dialogue and music are calculated to please the few, than to strike the many. The songs are written with laudable contempt of the prevalent idea that nothing but buffoonery and jingle is necessary in an afterpiece." The *Herald* agreed: "Perhaps it has not enough of what is expected in the English musical drama — ludicrous incidents ... but the language is embellished with elegant imagery, and the course of incidents is ... probable." The *General Evening Post* likewise found "strong markings of character" in the dialogue, and they added that "the music of Atwood is beautiful and appropriate." But the *English Chronicle*, which probably came closer to the public's response, stated that Boaden "seems to have made the Italian school his model, as the piece is merely intended as a vehicle to introduce the pretty music of Mr. Atwood to the Public." Attwood included airs of Giornovichi and Mozart — probably the fandango from *Figaro*. The piece did not succeed, and no doubt both men were disappointed. Boaden went on to write seven more unoperatic melodramas.

From 1793 to 1798 Attwood composed music for a large number of afterpieces at all three theatres, most of which were failures. Samuel Birch wrote most of these trifles — *The Packet Boat* (Covent Garden, 1794), *The Adopted Child* (Drury Lane, 1795), and *Fast Asleep* (Drury Lane, 1797) — though three were successes: *The Mariners* (Little Theatre, 1793), *The Smugglers* (Drury Lane, 1796), and *Albert and Adelaide* (Covent Garden,

1798). The failures, beside the Rose works, included *The Irish Tar* (Little Theatre, 1797), *Britain's Brave Tars!!* (Covent Garden, 1797), and *A Day in Rome* (Covent Garden, 1798). Of these, only the *Mariners*, a musical entertainment, seems to have had more than a modicum of music, some of which was selected.[56]

HOLCROFT—ATTWOOD

As noted earlier, Holcroft produced the highly successful *Folies of the Day*, after Beaumarchais, but after his failure with *Choleric Fathers* in 1785, he avoided the musical stage until 1799. In the interim, however, he had produced a dozen comedies—some, like *The Road to Ruin*, were very successful. In the latter year he produced *The Old Cloathsman* (Covent Garden), a musical farce in three acts. The reviewers were unanimous in their dislike of the flimsy drama. "The characters, dialogue, and poetry are contemptible in the extreme, the fable is poorly contrived, and the incidents injudiciously managed," wrote the *Times*, and they condemned the "rage for sentimental character," which it sought to perpetuate. But they concluded: "The Music displays the talents of Attwood in a very advantageous point of view. It is peculiarly distinguished for appropriate melody," and they regretted its being "lavished on so despicable a subject." DuBois (MM) thought the songs were composed in Attwood's "best manner," noting he had been "extremely unfortunate of late, in his dramatic partnerships." But the *London Chronicle* found that the music "did not display any great degree of merit."[57] Parke's overture drew high praise, but this work failed miserably.

Nevertheless, the partnership continued, and in 1801 they produced *The Escapes*, a musical entertainment afterpiece, also for Covent Garden. Drawn from a French source, the story was largely historical, turning on the disputes between Cardinal Mazarin and the parliament of Paris during the minority of Louis XIV. It was "shot through with the ideals of the French Revolution" (P. Smith, pp. 161–62), but the London critics did not seem at all disturbed by this aspect of the opera. The *Chronicle* thought the drama possessed "great merit. Its simplicity is admirable, and at the same time the attention never flags.... The manners of the time are delineated with great fidelity." And the *Post* found it much superior to "the generality of musical farces ... on which, however worthless, some excellent composer is always found weak enough to throw away his labour."

Attwood adapted four songs—two from Cherubini's *Les deux journées* (Paris, 1800)—and added four of his own. Though "very limited in quantity," the music by Cherubini was "very pleasing" (P; C). The *Times* admired the overture and wrote: "The chorusses [no doubt Cherubini's] are in the first rank of harmony and melody, and many of the movements are not unworthy of the most approved Masters of the present day." The piece proved quite popular. Holcroft went on to produce seven more works for the stage, but none was at all operatic.[58] Attwood also composed operas for Thomas Dibdin (1800) and William Dimond (1806), as we shall see.

HOLMAN—DAVY

Joseph Holman, as noted earlier, wrote the satirical *Abroad and at Home* with Shield (Covent Garden, 1796), which was successful despite lukewarm notices. For his last opera—a three-act comic opera, *What a Blunder!*, produced at the Little Theatre in 1800—he again wrote a superior drama and turned to Davy for the music.

John Davy (1763–1824), an illegitimate child, was born near Exeter and raised by his uncle in Devonshire (*A Dictionary of Musicians*). A prodigy, he was found to be extremely sensitive to musical sounds at age three and was soon taught the cello. At four or five he could play an easy tune after hearing it, and at eight he borrowed some horseshoes from a neighboring blacksmith and contrived a perfect octave on which he played chimes. At twelve he was apprenticed to William Jackson in composition and organ, and later he played violin in the Covent Garden orchestra. He published a set of glees in 1790 and began composing theatre music for Sadler's Wells in 1800. He was thought "well-qualified" as a theatre composer by his "correctness of style" (LitC, Feb. 18, 1824). Taylor (II, 348) stated that his music to *The Blind Boy* was "proof of his science and taste," adding that in his younger days he had been "something of a beau." But he lost heart in his work and drank heavily from 1808 to 1818, when he again returned to composing. His best-known song was "The Bay of Biscay" in Cherry's *Spanish Dollars* (1805), though singer Charles Incledon (a former sailor) provided the nautical air (N.G.).

In *What a Blunder!* the *Times* found "from the commencement to the end an uncommon variety of incident. . . . The great merit of the Author consists in the art with which he arrests the attention until the proper movement for the *eclairissmement*," although there were inconsistencies; "but the complete union of *sound* and *sense* has been rarely exemplified either in the ancient or modern drama." The characters "possess no novelty," but "in the dialogue we were struck with many excellent and edifying passages."[59] DuBois (MM) also wrote a very full and favorable report, adding: "Upon the whole, we are of the opinion that this is a much superior production to the general run of comic operas. It is not a mere vehicle for the music, but has the merit of structure, dialogue, incident, relief, character and situation." As in his previous opera, Holman himself played the leading role "and contributed essentially to the success of his *own* opera." Concerning the music, the *Times* wrote that Davy's "principles are truly scientific, his taste is highly polished. . . . He only wants to study more minutely the nature of dramatic representation, to attain celebrity equal to that enjoyed by the most admired Masters. The Overture was correct and pleasing, but it wanted animation. Many of the airs . . . were distinguished for true melody."

The *Post*, however, heard it otherwise: "So far is the music from being essential to its success, that the Piece, if represented as a plain, broad farce, would go off just as well without it. The music has neither novelty, variety or harmony of movement." DuBois (MM) was cautious: "The style of the airs is uniformly pleasing, but it is deficient in variety and originality. The ear is soothed but not captivated. The stream of melody was too uninterrupted. Mr. Davy should, perhaps, have selected more copiously." But he disagreed with the *Times* about the overture: "There were some beautiful abruptnesses . . . which bespoke the master."[60]

The work played ten times; nevertheless, Holman withdrew from Covent Garden after a conflict with the management.[61] He went to Dublin, and later, in an acting team with his daughter, he toured the United States, where he died. Davy, as we shall see, later composed an opera for Andrew Cherry (1805) and wrote songs for operas by Dibdin in 1802 and 1804.

CADELL—GLUCK

Mrs. Elizabeth Billington, who on other occasions sought to improve the musical taste of the town, gave an all-sung opera, *Orpheus and Eurydice*, for her Covent Garden benefit in 1792. The translation, made by T. Cadell,[62] was apparently based on the pasticcio *Orfeo* by Gluck, and the work included music by Handel, Bach, Sacchini, Weischel, Gyrowetz (the overture), W. Reeve, and probably Mazzinghi—as well as Gluck (about half the score). The Orpheus story, as the *Times* pointed out, was well known to the English stage, and the work "came forward . . . with all those claims to approbation which charming music as charmingly executed could bestow—nor had the performers [which included Mrs. Mountain and Incledon] any reason to complain of their reception—the piece was heard with great attention." The *Times* confidently predicted: "There can be little doubt but Orpheus . . . will very frequently visit the infernal regions during the season" (a puff?). There was, in fact, but a single performance.

COLMAN (THE YOUNGER) — DR. ARNOLD

Early on, as noted, Dr. Arnold had successes with Bickerstaffe in *Maid of the Mill* and with O'Keeffe in *Castle of Andalusia*, though their *Siege of Curzola* failed. But some of Arnold's best work in this period was done in collaboration with the soon-to-be proprietor of the Little Theatre, George Colman the Younger. Several of his early plays for the Little Theatre — mostly farces — had been very popular, and by 1790 the critics saw him as the foremost playwright, second only to Sheridan.[63] Many of his musical works had strong melodramatic appeal.

We have no reviews of his very first opera, *Two to One* (1784), composed by Arnold, which was successful, but the next year they produced an operatic comedy in three acts, *Turk and No Turk*. The *Herald* noted "a great violation of probability in the main structure,"[64] and there were some "indecencies." But many of the incidents "are highly diverting and the dialogue is sprightly throughout." They predicted that Colman "will one day or other hold a distinguished rank amongst our Dramatists." The *Times* agreed: "A vigorous and juvenile spirit breathes through and animates every character." Indeed, the reviewer welcomed it as nothing less than a harbinger of Romanticism: "Critical faults we leave to the pedants. . . . Nature, in first efforts spurns at rules; her effusions are abundant in the comedy before us, and she is no where more pleasing, than in her excursions from the prescribed gardens of art, into the wild flowery fields of imagination." The *Advertiser*, too, declared that the piece was written "with all the vivacity of a pregnant youthful imagination; many of the scenes are highly colored, the wit not sparing, and the humour abundant."

Most of the songs[65] were newly composed, and Dr. Arnold wrote his "best overture" for the work (Fiske). The *Herald* thought the borrowed songs better than the new ones but noted that one song "very ill accords with the measure of the music," and another air was "ill-chosen." The *Advertiser* wrote: "The music in general bore the mark of judgment; but taste, we think, would have been more amplified, had Dr. Arnold availed himself of more old tunes, which would have been no derogation to his acknowledged merit as a composer." The opera had thirteen performances but apparently was not revived.

Two years later Colman and Arnold produced a new opera, *Inkle and Yarico* — one of the first "problem" plays (N.) — which received mixed reviews. The *London Chronicle* wrote: "It is a piece of a higher class than either *Two to One* or *Turk or no Turk*. The tears and applause it drew from a crowded audience are the best proofs of [Colman's] merit." (It is not often we hear of tears at English opera.) The plot[66] combined a love triangle with enlightened views on the sins of slavery, which were beginning to be widely acknowledged. The *Herald* reviewer of *this* opera, however—confused over the author's identity—was quite Neoclassic in his objections: "The *unities* have been very unnecessarily violated in this drama; and however Dr. Johnson may be the apologist for such irregularities, Mr. Colman, *Senior* [*sic*], is too correct a classic not to acknowledge the superior reasoning of *Aristotle*." They also faulted his characterization of Inkle: "He ought to have been represented less under the influence of liberal feelings . . . this would have given his vices the color of education; at present they seem like the workings of the heart." But they thought the other characters were well drawn and the dialogue was "sprightly and animated"; there were, however, too many cheap puns.

Arnold's music, new and "judiciously selected,"[67] (T; LC) included borrowings from Handel and Paisiello; there were many encores and the cast was strong. The opera played twenty-one times and had many revivals for upwards of fifty years. In 1821 and 1822, Miss Kelly, as Yarico, was still moving audiences. (Colman usually retained the right to his plays; he probably lost considerable money by selling this one to Covent Garden.)

Three musical plays by this team were performed at the Little Theatre from 1789 to 1792—*The Battle of Hexam* (1789), *The Surrender of Calais* (1791), and *The Mountaineers* (1793). Only subsidiary characters had songs in these productions (Fiske). Dr. Arnold, often reduced mainly to setting songs selected by playwrights, was a very uneven dramatic composer—Fiske finds much of his music "shoddy"—but at his best he received consistently fair if not high praise from the press. He also composed two operas for his son, James Samuel Arnold, playwright and theatre manager (see below).

KELLY

Michael Kelly's career as singer and stage manager at the King's was discussed previously in part II. This most versatile man also had careers as singer and composer for the English musical stage. But since he often sang his own songs in operas mainly composed or compiled by others, it is not always clear whether press comments applied more to his composition or to his performance. Kelly, by the way, had no training in composition; although he was a trained singer and could read music, he could not harmonize or score his songs but had to sing the airs to a musical amanuensis. He never pretended otherwise.[68] He recounts in his *Reminiscences* (p. 143) that Mozart told him: "Nature has made you a melodist," and there is no need at your age to "perplex yourself" with the "dry bones" of composition; "you can find hundreds of musicians" capable of correcting your work. Mozart wrote a set of variations to an air composed by him (White, p. 217). One of his earliest songs occurred in Cobb's *Love in the East*; the *Herald* declared that "The Guardian, dear Sir," was "one of the most beautiful compositions we ever heard." It was, however, composed by Paisiello.

COLMAN (THE YOUNGER) — KELLY

By the late 1790s Kelly was assuming responsibility for entire operas. His first collaboration with the younger Colman was the dramatic romance *Blue-Beard* (Drury Lane, 1798). Kelly gave Colman £200 for the privilege of writing the music so he could "establish [his] name as a composer." The story was familiar through many dramatizations and pantomimes. Critic D of the *Times* admired the adaptation but found the serious parts "too bombastic." The *Post* also faulted Colman's language while the *Advertiser* noted that much of the stage business was "badly managed."

Regarding Kelly's music (he composed eleven of the fifteen numbers), the *Times* wrote: "We apprehend that Mr. Kelly has not exercised his creative genius to the least advantage, as there is scarcely one original movement throughout the piece he can claim as his own.[69] In the selection of the airs, he has evinced a considerable degree of judgment; and many of them are distinguished for real taste and produce the deepest interest." The *Advertiser* found the music "pleasing, though not all strictly original." And Parke thought the music deserved "great commendation."

The work had a superlative production; it was very successful and was revived for twenty-six years. Concerning his music for this opera, Kelly wrote (I, 348) that "so different is the taste of the French and English that... I did not introduce a single bar from Grétry," whose opera *Bluebeard* was then playing at Paris. Elsewhere (II, 201–2) he stated that he admired Grétry's music but it was "not sufficient for English taste, which, in the musical way, requires more Cayenne than that of any other nation in the world." Fiske (p. 283) remarks on the appearance of the trombone in this work for "spine-chilling effects" — its first such use in English music since Restoration times.

Their next work was *Feudal Times* (1799), a melodramatic afterpiece solicited by Drury Lane following the success of *Blue-Beard*. It had a French source. The *Times* deemed the writing "flimsy" but admired the production; "prodigious" said the *Chronicle* of the spectacle. Adolphus called the play "a farrago, utterly unworthy of the taste and fame of the author" (II, 36), and even Colman thought little of it. The *Times* inconsistently reported that Kelly's music had "much science" but was somewhat devoid of harmony; DuBois (MM) was scathing: "It is dull, frivolous, ill-adapted, and unmeaning.... It is not sufficient that the ear should be stunned ... or perplexed by innumerable *titum-tiddle-dees* and senseless complications." But spectacle carried the day; the work had no fewer than fifty-four repetitions that season.

In 1803 the team again produced an operatic farce afterpiece in *Love Laughs at Locksmiths* at the Little Theatre. It was adapted from *Une folie* by J. N. Bouilly, which Kelly had brought back for him from Paris (the one-year Peace of Amiens made the trip possible); Colman produced it under one of his pseudonyms — Arthur Griffinhoof. The *Chronicle* reported: "Much pains must have been bestowed upon the *adaptation*, as the characters, the sentiments, and the allusions are almost all English. The title will at once intimate that the plot is founded upon the triumph of youthful attachment over aged artifice."

"The music itself," wrote the *Post*, "possesses great merit indeed; but there was no display of vocal talent; the vocal parts, which succeeded most, were those of humour or of acting. A quintetto at the end of the second act, is one of the best ever produced on the stage" (P). DuBois (MM) remarked that "Kelly has been very happy in some of the music," and Hunt praised the music in *Critical Essays* (p. 20). The overture, by Condell, was "very pretty" (C). The work played thirty times, with revivals into the 1820s.

Three years later Colman produced another spectacle for Drury Lane — *The Forty Thieves*, a grand operatic romance that was actually written "to suit the scenery."[70] Nevertheless, Colman's "style and manner" were "easily traced throughout the dialogue" (Cr). The story, adapted from the Arabian Tales, was of course familiar; it was the spectacle that drew the plaudits. Yet the *Times* thought much of the work's success was due to Kelly's music (he wrote nearly all of it), which had "taste, variety and grandeur." The *Herald* declared, "The airs possess a merit which is now rather uncommon, that of being always adapted to the character, and their introduction never retards the progress of the scenic action." But the *Universal* observed that "the music did not boast much novelty." The opera had twenty-five performances.

Thus concluded a series of remarkable successes by this team,[71] and both went on to write more operas with other collaborators, as we shall see, but these did not prove to be as popular.

COBB — STORACE

In Stephen Storace (1762–96) we have a far more capable composer. Son of an English mother and an Italian father (who played the double bass in

Dublin and later with the orchestra at the King's), Stephen studied music in Naples in 1776. Later, in Vienna, he became a friend and probably a student of Mozart. In 1785 he successfully produced two operas there—*Gli sposi malcontenti* and *Gli equivoci*—in which his sister Nancy and Michael Kelly sang the leads. For the King's he produced a single work—*La cameriera astuta*—in 1788, but it failed. He found his greatest success in English opera, which, in his hands, became much more operatic during the few years given him to live.

Following his successful operas with Linley, Cobb wrote several more successful productions for Drury Lane. *The Doctor and the Apothecary* (1788), an operatic farce afterpiece set by Storace, was an adaptation of *Doktor und Apotheker* (Vienna, 1786), by Karl Ditters von Dittersdorf, with whom Storace was acquainted. Though the plot was slight, the situations were whimsical and the language "not deficient in point" (H); however, the *Advertiser* thought the dialogue had "no wit." About one-third of the numbers—two airs, two duets, a trio, and the Finale—were adapted from Ditters; Storace composed about half the opera—the overture, seven airs, and a quintet (White, p. 218). The *Herald* wrote: If the music "cannot be termed first-rate, it is in general various and pleasing." The *Times* predicted the piece would be "highly popular" and had trite praise for the music. The production was good, and even Genest thought the work much better than average. It was very successful, with eighteen performances and seven revivals. Adolphus stated the work succeeded because of "the novel and judicious manner in which the music was selected and adapted [without] overloading any performer."

The next year Cobb and Storace achieved even greater popularity with a three-act comic opera, *The Haunted Tower*. DuBois wrote: "It formed a new era in one walk of the stage: the opera was no longer the mere vehicle of music; it became a new species of the drama, in which an interesting story, regularly developed, is contrasted and enlivened with scenes of comic effect" (MM, Jan. 1803). Hogarth called the work the first "decided step" toward the modern form of opera. The plot,[72] set in England just after the Norman conquest, had elements of suspense with "whimsical characters and situations—and a vein of light humour runs through the dialogue" (H). "Many of the points are happily conceived, introduced with taste and expressed with neatness" (UM). "The neatness of the dialogue . . . both in its comic and serious passages, approaches nearer to Sheridan's Duenna than any other piece in our recollection" (T).

Storace selected songs from Kelly, Linley, Purcell, Sarti, Paisiello, Martín, Pleyel, and others, and he added much of his own.[73] The *Chronicle* thought most of the music "excellent; but some are hacknied tunes." The

Times was more positive: "The overture has many passages which even Gluck might not be ashamed to own; . . . the airs were held in the estimation they deserved, as the frequent encores sufficiently testified." Even the literary *Walker's Hiburnian* admitted that "Cobb has some good things here"—especially the characters; the borrowed music was generally excellent though some of it was "trite."

The cast was strong; Nancy Storace made her English opera debut and joined with Kelly in a lively dance. The opera broke all records, having no less than eighty-four performances in two seasons; on the sixtieth night it "went off with all the fascination, applause, and overflow of the first" (T), and there were frequent revivals at least to the 1830s.

At an 1817 revival Alsager (T) wrote:

> We know not whether it is owing to a dearth of musical talent [today] or to that incessant rage for *novelty* which characterizes the votaries of music . . . that this and other productions of Storace are so seldom brought forward. We think the circumstance, however caused, is to be regretted, and are of the opinion that the operas of this composer deserve to be placed among the most successful efforts of our English musical drama, and that they approach nearer to the delicacy of construction and rich vein of melody of the Italian school than almost any other pieces of the same kind.

But at an 1819 revival, the *Inquisitor* was unhappy with Cobb's libretto, and in 1829 an attempt to revive the work at the Little Theatre failed. Hunt, who reviewed it at an 1832 revival, showed great respect for the composer:

> The composition of the best airs . . . delighted us by its contrast to that unmelodious, unflowing, up and down style, which is too often found in modern musicians, and results from a want of real feeling for the art. Storace does not go hunting for strange combinations and laboured phrases; . . . he resigns himself in good faith to the feeling, and it rewards him by an easy, sweet, and characteristic melody. And his vivacity is of the true character also. (*Plain Dealer*)

In 1791 these confreres were back with another hit, the three-act comic opera *The Siege of Belgrade*. In the story[74] Cobb

> has contrived to blend the grave and the gay most happily—the incidents are in general natural—the situations well contrasted—and the fable is at once artless and interesting.
>
> The Author, and it is much to his credit . . . has carefully studied— *Character*. The Peasant in no one instance galls the kibe of the Court-

ier—the Cottagers speak like Cottagers, and the more elevated Personages of the Drama have sentiments becoming their rank.

Perhaps it will not be deemed as a very high compliment to an Opera . . . that very few Tragedies can boast a situation more truly circling around the heart. (T)

The *Chronicle* found the opera in every way equal to the *Haunted Tower*, and Cobb's dialogue was "always neat, often happily pointed, and never offensive." But the *London Chronicle* dismissed the drama as only "a very pleasing vehicle for the music."

Much of the plot and about one-third of the music came from Martín's *Cosa Rara*; other borrowings were from Salieri, Paisiello, and Kelly. Storace composed sixteen numbers and a three-movement overture, which included quotations from Mozart (Fiske). The *Times* said: "The Music, though rather too sublime for the taste of the galleries, is yet extremely beautiful, and does great credit to the acknowledged taste of Storace." Gray (C) thought the music "well adapted to the taste of an English Audience," and the *Advertiser* gave it high praise. The opera had an astonishing forty-seven performances that season and many revivals to the 1830s.

In an 1811 revival, when new songs by Arne and Shield were introduced, Hunt lamented the use of good music with Cobb's "wretched verse." In 1817 other songs were displaced, and the *European Magazine* thought the opera dull. In 1830 the libretto was entirely reset by John Fane, Lord Burghersh.

Following these extraordinary productions at Drury Lane, Cobb and Storace launched another full comic opera at the Little Theatre, *The Pirates*, which Fiske calls England's first "escape" opera (he also explains Storace's strong influence on its Neapolitan setting). The *Times* wrote: "The author has not much depended on plot[75] for interest. The chief merit is in the Scenery and Music. . . . The Dialogue contained too much pun. There is not that fine stamina of writing that gives vigour to the sentiments of the mind" (Nov. 22); the *London Chronicle* agreed. But Gray (C) noted "the same want of orginality in character with the same sprightliness in dialogue." Then followed an astonishing passage:

> For some time past this [Little] Theatre has with indefatigable industry laboured to create, what we never enjoyed in England, a true full Opera, in which the business should not be suspended during a song from a still-life figure. Here we have a bold . . . successful attempt at an Opera on the Italian model. The finales of the two first Acts, are pieces of action as well as music—The business goes forward, and we have the double charms of vocal harmony and scenic interest.—We were infinitely pleased with the novelty, and do not despair to see an English

lyric school created, under the auspices of the taste and talents which secure to the Theatre the protection of the public, in spite of party.

What is remarkable here is the recognition that the new dynamics given to the English opera stage was generating an operatic spirit never before experienced. Obviously this new approach required singing actors and actresses not common to the English stage; in Kelly and Nancy Storace, this production could provide such expertise.

The music was mostly Storace's but included borrowings from Anfossi, Bianchi, and Guglielmi (the quintet scene from *La Bella Pescatrice*—Pantheon, 1791) as well as two songs (for Kelly) from Storace's own *Gli sposi malcontenti*. The music was thought to be "generally good, and in the chorusses striking" (C). The *Times* (Nov. 22) stated that the airs "were such as do the highest credit to the composer," and four days later, no doubt influenced by Gray, they wrote: "There certainly is no musical comic piece in the English language which comes so near the Italian style as this does, either in magnificence of scenery, or grandeur of musical effect. We have all the excellence of chaste harmony without the horrid accompaniment of nonsensical recitative; so that while all that was valuable on the Italian stage is preserved, nothing which had merit in the English Opera is lost." The work had a fine production and was repeated thirty-six times, with six revivals to 1800. (In 1827 William Dimond wrote a new libretto, *Isidore and Merida*, based on Cobb's story—see below.) Kelly (II, 32) felt the finale to act I was worthy to be placed by the side of Mozart's first finale in *Figaro*. Fiske calls it Storace's best opera.

In 1794 this team returned to Drury Lane with their final production, a full-length comic opera, *The Cherokee*—the first operatic "Western."[76] Critic C of the *Times* wrote: "Action and character, with the *serio-comic*, happily and forcibly blended, create a strong interest, and excite attention and mirth seldom to be found united; hardly indeed to be expected [in opera]. The principal characters possess some bold features of originality—that of *Malooko* is very ingeniously worked up, and his *gunpowder* disposition is formed from *attic-petre*." But other critics were rather negative. The *True Briton* reported: "The dialogue was neat in many parts, but there is too much verbal-trifling, and the comic incidents, are too many, and too feeble." Nor were the songs "in the happiest vein of poetry." And Gray (C) took a hard look at the drama:[77]

> The wild manners of the Indians, were characterized; . . . we could have been well content had the wild manners of these Indians oftener possessed the scene; and that chiefly because they but ill-agreed with the counting-house wit and threadbare incidents with which they were

contrasted. No attempt, indeed, was made to depict the manners of European planters. Instead of an English colony, we continuously imagined ourselves to be on the Stock Exchange.... [Yet] the piece is far from destitute of that kind of merit to which it pretends.[78]

The music, principally by Storace, who took pains with it (Fiske), included borrowings from Anfossi, Mozart, Bianchi, Ditters, and Sarti. The *London Chronicle* found the music "not chosen with [Storace's] usual taste, nor the original imagined with his usual fancy." But the *Times* disagreed: "Description [of it] will be in vain.—It must be heard, and then it will be admired."[79] Gray (C) also concurred: The composer "has laudably, in our opinion, endeavoured to introduce the Italian style of mingling the persons of the Drama in musical conversation; and in this instance has performed his task with great effect."[80] It is astonishing to note that "musical conversation"—something surely approaching recitative—now gets strong approval from a critic of the English stage.

All reviewers spoke highly of the scenic effects—dress and painting. The opera was repeated forty-one times but had only one revival before 1800, mainly because of the lack of a juvenile singer: the opera had to close when Master Welsh's voice broke (Fiske). Meanwhile, Storace turned to other librettists (see below).

COBB—MAZZINGHI/REEVE

Cobb did not write another success until 1798, two years after Storace's death, when the comic opera *Ramah Droog* appeared at Covent Garden. Again his exotic setting and emphasis on spectacle were great draws. The story[81] was related in "scraps," as DuBois (MM) protested: "We cannot say that the interest is powerful, or that the language is remarkable either for elegance, strength, or wit; but the *Irishman* is not without humour; and even the absurdities... are so sanctioned by prescription, that it is perhaps sufficient for us to laugh, without examining too rigidly into the cause of the merriment." The *Times* concurred, adding that "there are no traces of original character to be found throughout the piece." And the *Herald* stated: "The dialogue is certainly not of the finest description of writing, but it forms, on the whole, a very safe vehicle for some of the best music the English stage has for some time been able to boast."

William Reeve (see below) apparently was supposed to compose the music, but Joseph Mazzinghi was brought over from the King's to assist him.[82] (Reeve wasn't even mentioned in the playbills.) The *Times* had curiously mixed feelings on the music: "It is lively, appropriate, and occasionally pathetic. The accompaniments are truly scientific, and the overture is distinguished for the elegance and true taste, which have long graced the works of Mazzinghi. [His music, however, abounds] in an uniform and unwearied exertion to astonish, by a display of laboured brilliancies, which are peculiarly unnecessary." And DuBois (MM) thought Mazzinghi lacked "variety, melody, and simplicity; there is more sound in it than sentiment—more noise than passion—more skill than genius. It is, in short, more instrumental than dramatic." But the *Post* had "nothing to complain of but a superabundance of harmony [for] the audience encored almost every song." Critics might disagree, but the public's vote was clear: the opera was given thirty-five times and had revivals up to 1817.

Mostly adverse views prevailed at the several revivals. In 1800 DuBois (MM), noting the scantness of the work stripped of its attractions, emphasized that "it is some merit, however, to *write up* these things, and few men are better acquainted with the method of disposing the different materials of a modern opera to the greatest advantage than Mr. Cobb." But the *Anti-Jacobin Review* was scathing: "We are . . . sorry to see such [a respectable man] sacrificed to the degraded taste of the million, at a time when men of abilities should endeavour to raise the stage from its present degenerate devotion to extravagant buffoonery or empty *sing-song*." The *Monthly Review* also noted: "There is a roughness in the lyric part which it must be extremely difficult to smooth by good melody. . . . The double-rhymes of Mr. Cobb, and the hobbling lines, render it scarcely possible to give them any cadence either in reading or singing."

At a Drury Lane revival in 1815 Hunt found the work trivial and the music not much better, though the *Inquisitor* thought the music "generally pleasing." In 1817 it was revived "with the greatest magnificence, and cast with all the vocal strength of the company," according to Kenrick (BS), who added: "Some alterations have been made in the music. . . . Though by no means admirers of this system of castrating our operas . . . we think the present alterations are manifestly improvements. . . . The revival of a few of Mr. Cobb's productions, notwithstanding they have to boast of little merit, would be by far more amusing than the continued representation of [our] customary absurdities." Genest, typically, thought the opera "dullest to the last degree," but Boaden declared it had "charm of great value."

Cobb's final opera, *The Wife of Two Husbands* (Drury Lane, 1803), with music by Mazzinghi, was quite successful, but reviews were trite.

COBB—KELLY

In 1802 Cobb produced his only opera with Kelly, *A House to be Sold*, a farcical afterpiece for Drury Lane. The story, adapted from Duval's *La maison à vendre* (Paris, 1800) with many alterations, was in part a spoof on Italian opera (T). The *Post* wrote:

> Where music and scenery come in aid of the writer [Cobb] is but too apt to neglect the duties of his proper department; but in the present case we have a piece perfect in itself, and which might command success without the assistance of any foreign ornament. . . . The dialogue is of the sprightliest cast . . . without a forced conceit, or a puerile pun. It boasts also a very successful attempt at delineation of character, untainted by any caricature.

The other reviewers (except DuBois, who thought it "inflated") were nearly as commendatory.

Kelly, it will be recalled, had produced a number of very successful operas with the younger Colman from 1798 to 1806 in which his music was somewhat disparaged by critics early on, though it was later much admired. His music for the present work also drew high praise. "The whole of [Kelly's] music, except two airs, is original, and does much credit to the taste and science of its author" (H). The *Post* thought the music the opera's "great ornament," and added: "The overture [by Mazzinghi] abounds in sweet and pleasing movements, judiciously varied, and contrasted, not straining at difficulties, and attempting to surprise by execution, but flowing in an easy course, and speaking to the heart. The same character prevails through the airs of the poetry." Kelly's music had "great natural melody" (T). The piece received eleven performances.

Though Cobb lived many more years, he wrote no more for the stage. Perhaps he sensed a waning popularity. No other librettist during our early years, however, enjoyed as much success with the public. To be sure, though his dialogue was frequently termed "sprightly," there were occasional objections to his unmusical language, especially in his songs. DuBois (MM), for example—never a strong admirer of his—wrote (Jan. 1803) that "he has uniformly evinced a strong and inconquerable attachment to the drama: few authors have taken more ardent pains to deserve success, and very few have been more fortunate in its attainment." But in 1807 (Jan.), he spoke of "the vile and degrading office to which the Cobbs, the Cherries, and other of our dramatic poets have submitted, when they have written words to any melody, that the composer might find in his port-folio, ready cut and dry." The fact is that Cobb, like O'Keeffe, had a powerful ability to write for the *stage*—situations and language that encompassed not only the musical elements but the scenic effects as well. And, as we have seen, he also wrote some librettos that could have been successful without musical support.

KEMBLE—STORACE

Storace's accomplishments with Cobb's operas from 1788 to 1794 have already been recounted. Meanwhile, he achieved success with other playwrights as well. One of these was actor and theatre manager John Philip Kemble (1757–1822), whose *Lodoïska* (1794), an afterpiece melodrama, was probably the most operatic. Two versions of the opera were popular in Paris in 1791—Cherubini's and Rodolphe Kreutzer's; Kemble adapted the Kreutzer version. Kelly, who brought both scores to London, thought Kemble's version the best. Storace selected the overture and three other orchestral excerpts from Kreutzer; the quintet and trio in act I were Cherubini's; one song was by Andreozzi. Storace composed the rest. The work was well rehearsed—thirteen times, the last eight with music, plus others for the music alone.

There was as much interest in the spectacle as in the "escape" plot.[83] Gray (C), who was acquainted with both Paris versions, thought Kemble (*not* Storace) erred in following Kreutzer's (at the Théâtre Italien), for Cherubini's, at the Opéra, produced "the most sublimely terrific scene we ever witnessed." Yet some of the Drury Lane scenes drew high praise. Though the piece needed trimming, it "ought to be a first piece" as it "possesses more real interest than most modern three Act Operas" (T). Even the book reviewers commended the drama.

Gray also noted that "there is a great deal of charming music in the Opera, particularly the Overture and the chorusses." But he added: "An Opera of Spectacle should always have good finales, and the stage cannot parallel the conclusion which might have been given to this [second] act by the enchanting sestetto of Cherubini. It is unfortunately left out."

The opera was given twenty-five times and had several revivals. At an 1813 revival, when the decorations were even more lavish than at the premiere, the *Times* found the music "among the most favourite and popular compositions of the late Storace." By 1819, the work had lost its appeal for the *Inquisitor*: *Lodoïska* "periodically contributes to the entertainment of puerile understanding, and girlish curiosity. . . . The scenery is old, and the decorations are incomplete, though vocally, and otherwise, the music is thoroughly calculated to keep its antient hold upon public opinion."

COLMAN (THE YOUNGER) — STORACE

In the last year of his life, Storace composed a musical piece for Colman: *The Iron Chest* (Drury Lane, 1796). (Colman's very successful operas set by Dr. Arnold in 1785 and 1787, and by Kelly in 1798, 1799, 1803, and 1806, have already been discussed.) The work was termed a seriocomic drama, interspersed with songs, but it had Nancy Storace and Kelly in leading roles. The melodramatic plot, based on William Godwin's *Caleb Williams*, involved the Gothic trappings of an old abbey, robber bands, vengeance, and supernatural events. But the *True Briton* was unimpressed: "Throughout the Piece there is an extreme sterility of incident, which renders it uncommonly tedious and uninteresting. . . . The Songs, considered as poetical compositions, are . . . truly contemptible." The *Times* agreed, as did the *Oracle* (Boaden): "Colman seems neither to have understood the plan of Godwin nor the character of his hero." Moreover, "there is no progression of interest . . . no involution of plot. . . . By simplifying the fable he has produced no connection . . . and his characters are remote." They blamed it on "extravagant vanity and managerial impotence." Matters were not helped when Kemble became ill part way through opening night and could not continue.

The *Times* observed: "The whole of the music is of so superior a cast that if Storace had never written a note before, this alone would stamp him with" supremacy. The *Oracle* also noted that the music "had here and there very delightful passages, though it wanted the grace of novelty—it sought to do more than the occasion would allow."

The piece failed at Drury Lane; but Kemble was not the only cause. Storace was already in his final illness, though he wrote his best overture for it (Fiske), and Kelly had to help out on the music. Colman himself was too ill to attend rehearsals and make the necessary cuts. Nevertheless, Colman blamed Kemble for the failure, broke with Drury Lane, and mounted the work at his own theatre later that season. The *Times* was still not impressed with that production: "After much and necessary pruning, the acts still appear tedious. . . . [Colman] too frequently neglects a direct passage to the heart for the temporary pleasure of sporting with the imagination." But the work finally did succeed (thirteen performances) and had revivals for the next forty years. Genest found the play "one of those jumbles of Tragedy, Comedy, and Opera of which Colman junior was so fond, and which every friend of the legitimate Drama must reprobate."

Storace's music made a lasting impression. Parke noted its fine concerted pieces. Boaden stated that "the opening glee will not easily be paralleled," the choruses had great merit, and the finale "seemed built upon the idea of surrounding seraphs whispering peace to a departing spirit." Hogarth (II, 445) observed that the engrafting of pure Italian melody to the accents of English poetry had never been excelled, "permitting the singers to deliver the sounds with perfect distinctness and propriety of pronunciation and emphasis." Colman did not write another opera until he collaborated with Bishop in 1822 (see below).

HOARE—STORACE

Next to Cobb, Storace's most extensive collaborations were with Prince Hoare. His afterpiece operas set by Shield—*Lock and Key* (1796), a box-office success, and *Italian Villagers* (1797), a critrical success—have already been noted. Encouraged by Storace, whom he had met at Florence, Hoare wrote his first opera—a farcical afterpiece, *No Song, No Supper* (1790), though the theatre would not produce it until it had succeeded at Kelly's benefit.[84] For this important premiere, we have only a rather trivial review from the *Times*, which indicated a French source for some of the incidents and noted the good "whimsey" in the piece and the assistance of Storace's "harmony." Storace borrowed one-third of the music: from Grétry (two airs), Giordani, Dr. Harrington of Bath, an air from a Pleyel quartet, and an air, "With plaintive wit"—an old street song (Parke). He also included a trio and sextet from his own *Equivoci*, introduced a glockenspiel, and composed the overture, five airs, a duet, a trio, and two finales. The opera had the support of a good cast, played twenty-five times, and received frequent revivals thereafter (one hundred times through 1796). The *Times* praised the music at an 1803 revival, when a new air by Busby was introduced. The "Bay of Biscay," the most popular song of the opera, was still enjoyed at an 1819 revival, when an air by Braham from *Kais* was also introduced (TI). At an 1830 revival, Hunt wrote: "Storace's music is never to be mentioned without praise." Adolphus[85] said of the opera, "Not a syllable, not a note was uttered in vain."

The next season the team produced another afterpiece entertainment, *The Cave of Triphonius* (1791), which Hoare adapted from Casti's *La grotta di trofonio* (set by Salieri). Rather different from *No Song*, the slender plot, based on the well-known Greek myth, was not devoid of humor: "The Dialogue is as humourous and playful as the Scene, which lies principally among the villagers in Bœotia, would admit," but the piece was much too long (LC). For his music, Storace adapted selections from Salieri, Paisiello, Attwood, Suett, and others. "The music does Storace great credit, particularly the overture and the finale to the first act. The duet in the second act from Paesiello was charming. Suett's melody was pretty, but the words were violently out of place" (LC). The work had a good cast and production, but it failed because of an uninteresting plot, according to Fiske; however, DuBois (MM) stated that "its run was interrupted by the illness of Signora Storace, and the interruption of a dramatic novelty is tantamount to condemnation." (Other works we have noted also failed for similar reasons.)

In 1792 Hoare and Storace produced a serious opera, *Dido, Queen of Carthage*, which is of special interest as one of the few attempts on the English stage to mount an all-sung opera. Indeed, the producers were extraordinarily bold to mount such a work less than three months after the abject failure of the all-sung *Orpheus* at Covent Garden previously noted.

In addition to his own music (about half), Storace drew on Salieri, Paer, Sacchini, Sarti, Giordani, Cimarosa, Joseph Schuster, Andreozzi, and one Rampini. The libretto was a "free translation" of Metastasio[86] and was "chiefly brought forward for the purpose of introducing Mara upon the English stage in a new character. . . . The truth . . . is that in point of poetical merit, it is not a work of much consequence" (H). The *Gazetteer* thought it "so purely an Opera" that they would withhold criticism, yet they went on to note that it "has some fine passages, but upon the whole, is not very striking." The overture was "not the happiest effort of [Storace's] skill, but the composed music was equal in quality to the compiled" (H). Only Gray (C) touched on the recitative: "The general effect fell short in some degree of expectation. Something of this failure may be assigned to the length of the Recitatives, which were protracted even to tediousness, but more to the structure of the Opera. The English ear is too much familiarised to the variety of air and dialogue to relish the sameness of Recitative."

The production was superior and the cast strong. The press indicated a good audience response. The piece was gotten up mainly as a vehicle for Madame Mara, who was available since the King's decided to have no opera seria that season. But even her presence could not save it; the work survived only four performances, though it received one more the following season. There was no criticism of the singing; Mount Edgcumbe (p. 80) stated that Mara "retained only one song of her *Didone* [King's Theatre, Feb. 14, 1786], the brilliant bravura, Son Regina, of Sacchini." Boaden observed that "the lovely power of Metastasio" could not survive "the harshness of another language" and added that "the taste of the people required better situations in the drama." Fiske blames the failure on the old-fashioned libretto, but it is more likely that the recitative did much to make it unpalatable to playhouse audiences.

These collaborators next returned to operatic farce in *The Prize* (1793), an afterpiece for which I find no reviews, although it was quite successful and had several revivals. Later that season they produced *My Grandmother*, another such piece, partly based on *Le Tableau Parlante* by L. Anseaume (music by Grétry). "The songs are written with taste, and set to very lovely and agreeable tunes. . . . [They are] calculated to afford [Nancy Storace] a complete appearance of displaying that mixture of laughable levity, friskiness, and merriment which on the stage gives her so much attraction" (PA). And the *True Briton* thought the music "exquisite," adding that "the piece abounds with humour and comic situation." Even Genest thought it a "pleasing trifle." It nearly equaled *No Song* in popularity. Fiske calls the songs "more substantial and interesting than those of *The Prize*."

In 1795 the team produced a three-act operatic farce, *The Three and the Deuce*, which had a Spanish source. The *True Briton* was mildly favorable, though some of Hoare's "transitions of persons" became monotonous. The *Post* agreed: "The whole groundwork of the piece turns on the Equivoques and Mistakes arising from three Brothers, who are, to use the elegant language of the Author, as like as *three Peas*. . . . Bannister[87] . . . assumes the character of each of the Brothers, outraging in every scene the most distant idea of probability. . . . Nothing could equal the outrageous absurdity of [the opera] but the patient sufferings of an half-consumed Audience." The *Oracle* (Sept. 3 — probably Boaden) wrote: "The knowledge of farce writing is one possessed by very few — Mr. Hoare's productions in this way have usually some very striking incident — some oddity of *equivoque*, and much whimsicality of *character*. But he strung out his fable much too long." The next night (Sept. 4) it was much improved after cuts were made.

Surprisingly, the *Post* and *True Briton* were somewhat negative about Storace's music, but the *Times* thought it excellent: "He blends *Italian science* with *English taste* so happily, that we lose admiration in delight." The *Oracle* claimed his music "will be found *light* and *airy* in the *comic*, *pathetic* and *tasteful* in the serious ballads." The work was repeated twelve times but was not revived.

In 1796 this team produced their last opera, *Mahmoud*, a three-act musical romance, though Storace did not live to see the production. Kelly again had to assist in preparing the performance, and Mazzinghi made the keyboard arrangements. Hoare's story was adapted from incidents in the Arabian Nights and Persian Tales, but in the *Times*'s opinion, "they are put together without method or judgment, and of course fail in points of pleasantry and effect. — Character there is no attempt at," except for Mamoud. DuBois also pointed to absurdities in the plot, and Boaden ("Thestis") was totally dissatisfied:

> This is one of those strange and fantastic medleys called modern Operas, partaking of all the five species of dramatic exhibitions. . . . It

is after the Italian mode, which it forsakes by giving the dialogue for recitative. We have to remark, that the blank verse of the dialogue is frequently nervous, and that the prose, if it have no wit, is also without the affectation of it. The Serious excites neither alarm, nor grief, the comic neither hope nor laughter.

Most reviewers, lamenting the death of Storace, had much praise for his music. The *True Briton* found it, "at times, simple and suitable to the British taste, and occasionally founded upon the model of the Italian school. Many of the airs were *encored*." The *Times* wrote: "The first two acts are almost entirely [by Storace], and it is saying but justly, that the selections in the last Act, though from our first Masters [Sarti, Paisiello, and Haydn] scarcely come near him. The *Finales* would have been sufficient to immortalize his name." Regretting that Storace's demise left the piece without any comic songs, DuBois found "much delightful music in the opera." But Boaden, still negative, reported: "Some incongruous nonsense was applied to [Storace's] lyre, which we were not unhappy enough to recollect. . . . The concerted pieces we have often heard in [Paisiello's] *I Zingari in fiera*, and other Operas of Paisiello and Sarti might claim the greater part."

A strong cast was augmented by the debut of Braham, and the work saw sixteen performances and two revivals before 1800. The entire profits of the opera were assigned by Hoare to Storace's widow. Hogarth thought this Storace's best opera, but Fiske finds it his least interesting.

Storace, who may have died partly from overwork, gave more attention to his mainpiece operas than to his afterpieces, with the exception of *No Song*. He brought a new assertiveness to the role of the composer in English opera. Especially in the *Pirates*, he showed that it was "impossible for an author to produce a good opera without previously consulting the composer; songs must be introduced as the composer pleases" (*Thespian Dictionary*). Yet comparisons with Shield were inevitable, and in 1818 Bacon (QMM, I, 205–6) argued for the superiority of Shield. Storace's best operas (*Pirates* and *Mahmoud*) were "totally neglected," the latter probably because of its "difficulty," while the *Haunted Tower* and *Siege of Belgrade* survived, he believed, because of "their being about the only opera constructed to display the male voice"—especially the tenor. And *No Song* was said to be revived more for its dramatic than musical interest." "Of Storace, as a whole," he concluded, "it must be said, that he had much of science, a wide range of acquaintance with the compositions of foreign writers for the stage, that he was as a composer always natural, sometimes nervous [i.e., forceful], and generally polished, rarely however rising to any high pitch of elegance or originality."[88]

But other contemporary critics were quite positive. Storace was a skillful borrower and "taught the proper use to be made of Italian operas" (Boaden). "Whatever Storace selected, his knowledge of stage effect was so great, that the selections were always appropriate and never failing" (Kelly, II, 32). In his *Autobiography* (p. 43), Hunt wrote that Storace, "an Italian born in England, formed the golden link between the music of the two countries, the only one, perhaps, in which English accentuation and Italian flow were ever truly amalgamated." Adolphus (I, 232–33) declared: "From this period [following Storace], a new style of music prevailed on the English stage." The ballad and Bickerstaffe types "are no longer sufficient to satisfy the scientific ear; and the choicest products of the Italian and German schools are now introduced into our English pieces." (Indeed, he thought English opera had become too operatic, for "an English opera is, properly, a comedy enlivened by music.") Henry Barton Baker also recognized that Storace raised the importance of music vis-à-vis the libretto and that simple ballads in English opera "would no longer do." In a broader sense, as Young (p. 397) has written, he "introduced to the theatre a more cohesive form of opera which . . . allowed a dramatic sense to influence the music," and he "anticipated the gift of Sullivan of lifting insignificance to significance through a perception of the comedy inherent in the commonplace."

HOARE — DUSSEK/KELLY

In 1798 Hoare made a French adaptation called *The Captive of Spilburg* (Drury Lane), a musical drama afterpiece in which he ventured into still another dramatic aspect — melodrama. The plot — "rather too serious for a serious entertainment" (Genest) — was drawn from B. J. Marsollier's *Camille* (Paris, 1791). The *Times* and *Post* agreed that the work was too gloomy, though the story[89] possessed a considerable degree of interest. A drunken scene, provided for comic relief, was unrelated to the drama and "degenerated into downright buffoonery" (T). DuBois was more concerned with overall improbabilities.

Kelly apparently wrote only the music for his own songs. The rest, "entirely new," was composed by Jan Ladislaw Dussek (1760–1812), Bohemian pianist and composer.[90] A pupil of C. P. E. Bach, he worked in London between 1796 and 1802, and he married the daughter of Domenico Corri. Critic D (T) noted that the composer

> has displayed a complete knowledge of the principles of the art. The composition is chiefly of the melancholy cast, and so far it is appropriate to the subject; but even the most pensive habits . . . admit of variety

of movements and diversified expression, which he has not fully succeeded in describing. The melody throughout is natural, and the chorusses are . . . perfect specimens. . . . The overture is entitled to encomium for the delicacy, sweetness and just combination of its movements.

DuBois thought the music "has some learned passages, some skilful combinations, but it is not adapted to the genius of our theatre. The chorusses, however, are full, bold, and in some instances sublime." The cast and production were excellent, and the piece was repeated nineteen times.[91]

HOARE—MAZZINGHI/REEVE

Hoare's last opera, *Chains of the Heart* (Covent Garden, 1801), was a three-act comic opera set by Mazzinghi and W. Reeve, the team that composed songs for Cobb's popular *Ramah Droog* in 1798. But in this production, Hoare ran afoul a remarkable new assertiveness in London reviewers. The drama[92] had "neither much novelty nor much merit. The structure and the dialogue . . . are without any portion of either. In the sentimental scenes there is not one passage of interest, in the lively ones, not a single good point in a continued series of attempts at pun and equivoque. The piece was written, we believe, for the purpose of introducing Signora Storace and Mr. Braham" (P). The *Chronicle* denounced Hoare for treating the book as a mere "vehicle":

> We lament that men who think in this manner should have possession of the Stage. They degrade an art, in which, by the combination of all the powers of the Stage, an expansion is allowed to the fancy that ought to produce the most rapturous effects. . . . It is of the first importance that an Opera should be well-written; for without passion and beauty in the text of the songs, it is not likely that we should find either passion or beauty in the music.

DuBois, calling Hoare "assuredly one of our cleverest and most valuable dramatic writers," declared that he, "like other men of distinguished talent, has condescended to invoke the genius of nonsense" (MM).

Concerning Mazzinghi's music, the *Chronicle* noted a lack of "tune": "It is a severe censure on an Opera, to say that there is not a song in it in which any ear, however quick, or any memory, however retentive, will catch and retain." DuBois, in part agreed: "Though there are learning and spirit, and tasteful combinations in the greater part of the music, and very grand and striking effects in the finales, there is a want of novelty and expression in the airs, which will prevent the music from becoming very popular." Yet the strong support of Braham and Storace secured the success of the piece, which had fifteen performances.

Though Hoare never had the successes of Cobb, he never seems to have had a failure. Like Cobb, he came in for increasing criticism of his later librettos. Nicoll (III, 197) asserts that he "may be completely neglected" as a dramatic writer. But Hoare's range was surely remarkable: he explored a variety of dramatic forms in his operas; he also wrote a successful early tragedy and several comedies—the last produced in 1808. Actually, he was disappointed that his farces were admired more than his paintings.[93]

HOOK

The Reverend Dr. James Hook (1746–1827), son of a cutler, composed a concerto for harpsichord at age six and an opera at age eight. By 1763 he was composing much light entertainment music for London theatre audiences. More elegant than Shield, he was the "only truly *galant* writer in the English tradition" (Young). He was best known for his songs, of which he composed some two thousand for Marylebone Gardens and Vauxhall between 1775 and 1820. But his lack of dramatic sense and "slap-dash methods" limited the success of his operas (Fiske).

Several of Hook's operatic works were collaborations with his playwright son, Theodore E. Hook (1788–1841), between 1795 and 1809. The critics were nearly always negative towards Theodore's "improbable" and "clap-trap" vehicles—the *Siege of San Quintin* (Drury Lane, 1808) was a partial exception—and the music received only routine praise at best. As Hunt wrote anent *Safe and Sound*: "The days seem quite gone by, when Mr. Hook could produce such songs as *Hours of Love, Within a Mile of Edinburgh* &c. His muse has lost her substance and become the mere echo of Vauxhall."

Hook had even less luck writing operas for other playwrights, including William Kenrick (1778) and Robert Houlton (1800). In his later years, Hook gave piano and organ lessons; he retired in 1820.

DIMOND—KELLY

Kelly's indefatigable efforts for the stage in collaborations with Colman and Cobb continued on well into the new century. Between 1797 and 1821, he composed music for some sixty-two productions—more than any other composer except Bishop. Kelly's major productions after 1800 were made in collaboration with William Dimond.

Little is known about this precocious playwright apart from a biographical sketch of him written by John Taylor for the *Mirror* (Dec. 1807). Son of William Wyatt Dimond, one of the patentees of the Theatres-Royal at Bath and Bristol, he was born at Bath about 1785 and was educated by a Dr. Morgan. At age fifteen he was attracted to the literary left-wing Della Cruscans,[94] and he published some "liberal" verses in the *Herald*. Yet his revolutionary ardour did not last long, for he soon wrote *Petrarchal Sonnets*, published under the patronage of the Duke and Duchess of York. He also studied law at the Inner Temple.

In 1803, "despite his youth," Drury Lane accepted his first full-length piece, *Hero of the North* (Gustavus Vasa of Sweden), which was called both a musical drama and a historical play. It was his first of several collaborations with Kelly. The book was called "insipid," but the music possessed "many beauties," and Kelly has "happily combined the science of the Italian school with the taste of an English audience." The work was very successful all season (MM).

Encouraged, Dimond turned the work into a regular opera, now entitled *Gustavus Vasa*, in 1810. Curiously, it was produced at Covent Garden, although it had music by Kelly. "All the features of the story are romantic," wrote the *Times*, but they supplied Dimond with "nothing but the idea of a few caverns, tenanted by a few groups of well-dressed peasants, singing Italian chorusses." Yet "every thing in this Opera seems to have been made subservient to the music and the scenery; and they are both superabundant." Kelly's "composition or compilation was in general tasteful; though we could not discover the propriety of forcing Swedes to sing Italian airs, to the utter neglect of their own national melodies." The audience applauded vigorously but were relieved at the end "from the whole remorseless train of processions and chorusses, peasants and warriors, battles and fêtes-champêtres." Yet the *Bell's* critic, like the audience, delighted in just these things, and the opera had fourteen performances.

Still another adaptation by Dimond was his comic opera *Love, Youth, and Folly* (Drury Lane, 1805), with music by Kelly. It proved a box-office disaster. But Dimond must have felt it had some value, for the next season he recast it as a melodrama, with the title *Adrian and Orrila*; it had songs by Attwood as well as Kelly and was also produced at Covent Garden. A marginal success, it was not very operatic. The *Herald* called it "a play with five acts interspersed with songs," while the *Chronicle* pointed out that Dimond did not "connect the songs properly" with the piece. The *Times* was quite hostile toward Dimond, but both the *Chronicle* and the *Herald* praised the dialogue and the skilfull handling of the plot, while DuBois thought it offered "too little comic relief." The music was called "pleasing and varied," and Attwood's song, "Wine, rosy Wine," was encored.

In 1811 Dimond and Kelly brought out a "dramatic opera," *The Peasant Boy*, at the Lyceum. John D. Collier (C) wrote of Dimond: "This gentleman never writes without exhibiting considerable strength and richness of fancy, with a command of varied imagery and brilliancy of style, which seldom fails to dazzle and extort applause, even when the judgment is not satisfied. We regret, indeed, that he should confine his powers to a species of composition which, even when successful, reflects an equal share of credit on the musician and the painter." The *Universal Magazine* agreed. Kelly's music was admired, and the production, with the able assistance of Fanny Kelly and Henry Phillips, was highly praised (EM). The piece chalked up twenty-four performances. In 1817 this team produced *The Conquest of Taranto* at Covent Garden, but it had no success. Dimond's later collaborators included Bishop, Cooke, and others (see below).

ARNOLD—KELLY/BRAHAM

Samuel James Arnold (1774–1852), son of Dr. Arnold, the composer, wrote many successful musical plays—some more like librettos. He was "educated for an artist" but soon became attracted to the theatre, and by 1794 he produced his first opera, *Auld Robin Grey* (see below). He was for a time manager of Drury Lane and later, as noted, became proprietor of the Lyceum Theatre, later renamed the English Opera House.

His only production with Kelly—joined in this work by the singer and composer John Braham—was *The Unknown Guest*, a melodrama presented at Drury Lane in 1815, which followed several operatic successes with other composers. In a brief note, Sterling (T) found the music good in general but the plot poor and "Braham's voice and Kelly's skill thrown away on an intolerable heavy, intricate, and tedious" vehicle. Hazlitt was blistering: the work "is, we suppose, to be considered a dramatic trifle: it is one of the longest and dullest trifles we almost ever remember to have sat out. . . . The dialogue bears no proportion in quantity to the songs; and chiefly serves as a vehicle to tack together a certain number of unmeaning lines, arranged for different voices, and set in our opinion to very indifferent music" (H). The *Inquisitor* (DuBois?) agreed: "The dialogue never rises above mediocrity, and the plot is neither new nor well-conducted." Moreover, the music "was bad in the extreme; it was fashioned out of the very worst of their former manufactures; it would have disgraced Astley's." Yet the work succeeded.

This was one of Kelly's last productions. The perennial complaint about his borrowing tunes—a practice followed by most composers in this period—was given wide currency by Sheridan's quip that he was an "importer of music and composer of wines" (Kelly, like his father, had been a wine merchant). Although at times critical of him, Hunt wrote in 1817: "We think better of some of Mr. Kelly's compositions than many do. If he stole them, as it is alleged, we should like to see the originals; and then we shall maintain that he has been a very tasteful thief; but till then, we must maintain, that he has sometimes shewn himself a very tasteful composer" (E, Aug. 17). Sometimes Kelly contributed highly praised songs to the works of others, such as *Maid of the Mill* (1798 revival) and *Soldier's Return* (1805). As late as 1825, a chorus from *Blue-Beard* was, according to Ayrton, "of considerable merit" (Har, III, 166); it was still being much applauded in Arnold's *Tarrare*. Hogarth thought that his own airs, "though slight, were elegant" and that his knowledge of Italian and German music "helped enrich English taste."[95] Fiske's judgment in finding Kelly "in no way equipped for composing dramatic music" seems rather harsh, though a few of our critics were at times quite negative about his songs.

ARNOLD—DR. ARNOLD

Dr. Arnold, it will be recalled, composed music for successful operas by Bickerstaffe (1785), O'Keeffe (1782 and 1786), and Colman (1784, 1785, and 1787). Samuel James Arnold's first two operas were composed by his father. The first, *Auld Robin Grey* (1794), produced at the Little Theatre, was a pastoral piece with strong patriotic overtones. It was a slender production but enjoyed a critical and popular success. Their next collaboration in a musical entertainment afterpiece, *The Shipwreck*, produced at Drury Lane in 1796, was also a hit. The *Times*, however, was unimpressed:

> This light piece has little to recommend it, but the music and . . . dialogue. With regard to the plot and novelty of characterization it has not much to boast. . . . The reign of Sentimental Comedy seems to have given way to that of Sentimental Opera, particularly in the representation of British seamen on the stage, and accordingly sentiment is the grappling iron by which Harry Hawser [the hero] strives to fasten on the feelings of the audience.

Yet Dr. Arnold, they added, "has shewn considerable science and taste both in the composition and compilation." Boaden (*Oracle*) thought the dialogue "below criticism," and the songs—"in a literary point of view"—were "contemptible." But he, too, thought the music, "which may be termed an *Olio*, had in several instances a happy effect." DuBois (MM) called the libretto "a compilation principally from *No Song, No Supper* and the inane operas of Mr. Deputy [Samuel] Birch.[96] A string of loyal sentiments, that any child may write, ensured it a good reception, which we hardly think it deserves." It was also dismissed by the literary organs. Only the feeble *Universal* found it "altogether interesting" and the characters "well drawn." Patriotism and sentiment carried the day; it had twenty-one performances.

The next year they produced *The Irish Legacy*, an operatic farce in two acts, for the Little Theatre, but it drew mixed reviews and failed badly despite a strong cast. After 1809, S. J. Arnold wrote mainly for the Lyceum/English Opera House.[97] For these operas he collaborated with a number of composers, never settling with one for more than two consecutive productions. The first of these was King.

ARNOLD—KING

Little is known about Matthew Peter King (1773–1823), who may have been a pupil of Charles Horn (see below). He composed piano sonatas between 1790 and 1800 and wrote several treatises on music. Aside from his operas, he wrote an oratorio, "The Intercession" (Covent Garden, 1816). His music shows the "superficiality" characteristic of lighter English music of the time (N.G.).

In 1809 he and Arnold produced a full-length comic opera, *Up all Night*, for the opening of Arnold's Lyceum. J. D. Collier (C) found the drama slight, the characters common, and the business uninteresting, "but there is a vein of good humour runs through the whole that keeps alive the attention, and the songs are introduced naturally and happily." Yet the music was too derivative: "Perhaps Mr. King could not precisely distinguish between what he invented and what he remembered; but [it] passes muster." The *Times* was more enthusiastic: The songs were "sufficiently well written, and so exquisitely set to music, that we regret Mr. King's talents have been hitherto so little called into *play*." The *European* called it "an interesting and well-constructed opera" with "spirited and well sustained" dialogue, and King's "very pleasing" music "imitated, with much success, the old popular style of English Ballad Opera."

> But on the music Hunt strongly supported Collier's view:
> The music . . . is well suited to the words, not only in its expression, but in its good old age. It is not deficient in taste, and indifferent music will always be more tolerable than indifferent writing, because it appeals to the senses more than to the sense; but we have no hesitation

in saying that neither in the words nor the music of the new opera is there a single idea or turn of composition, that has any claim to originality. (E)

The opera must have been a great success, however, for in 1812 the *Inquisitor* stated that Arnold's "qualifications for writing an opera, no one, who has beheld his 'Up all Night' will doubt." And in 1816 Arnold mounted it again for the inauguration of his new English Opera House.

ARNOLD — KING/BRAHAM

In 1810 this team collaborated on *Plots! or The North Tower*, apparently an unoperatic afterpiece produced at the Lyceum (Sept. 3). But in 1811 they produced a full-length comic opera, *The Americans*, for the Drury Lane company at the Lyceum. With tongue-in-cheek, J. D. Collier (C) noted that

> there was much of business, much of variety, much of ambitious exertion to dazzle and to entrap. We feel no difficulty, therefore, in believing that it is the [creditless] production of some learned Professor of the science of *stage trick*. . . . Without novelty or connection in the plot, the dialogue [is] marked by nothing but trite affectation of vulgar humour, the characters original only in disgusting vice, or not less disgusting folly.

The music, though, was "gay and pleasing." (Braham composed the songs he sang.) The work presumably succeeded for it was revived in 1818. On this occasion, Collier still thought nothing of its "literary merits" but admitted it "acts well." And Sterling (T) noted an innovation in this production:

> The Native Indians are its chief features of novelty, who appear to have been drilled and disciplined into something like the ordinary exhibitions of the drama, without becoming so much sophisticated as to lose that natural and characteristic manner which renders them so curious. These men are evidently quick and intelligent; their motions, nicely adjusted to the airs played by the orchestra, evince a correct ear for music; they appeared to comprehend accurately all that was passing.

The work was "supported by a quantity of good music" (C; EM). This marked King's last production with Arnold. The latter's operas, set by Addison and Horn, are discussed below.

KENNEY — KING

King also set three operas for James Kenney (1780–1849), son of an Irish businessman; little is known about him despite his considerable success.

(His name was almost invariably spelled Kenny by the press.) A frequent guest at poet Samuel Rogers's celebrated breakfasts and dinners, he suffered a nervous tic (douloureux?) and more than once was taken for an escaped lunatic (D.N.B.). Although he received large sums for his stage works, he was not affluent. His first play, *Raising the Wind*, a farce, was produced at Covent Garden in 1803 and was frequently revived.

The next year he produced at Drury Lane his first opera, *Matrimony*, a two-act operatic farce with music by King. Critic D (T) thought that the author had "constructed a very pleasant and amusing entertainment" out of the slender story taken from a French source. "There are but *five* characters in the piece, and the whole business is confined to one scene . . . and yet it afforded as much satisfaction, and involved as much interest as if it had been crowded with *dramatis personae*, or abounded in changes of scenery. It is a chaste and elegant dramatic effect." John Campbell (C) agreed but on the whole found it disappointing: "In an afterpiece we look for broad humourous eccentric characters, and whimsical incidents." DuBois (MM) was also negative, and the *Critical Review*, commenting on the printed play, said: "We have so often complained of transplanting Irishmen into . . . plays borrowed from foreign authors that we grow tired of the fruitless labour. When wit returns to our drama we suppose this and other absurdities may cease."

Several of King's airs were encored and the music "gave promise of great merit" (C; MM). The *Times* wrote: "The music has great and *original* claim to approbation. The general character of it is light and diversified. It abounds with delicate and various accompaniments. . . . The Overture, and the Trios in the second Act, display great taste and science, and were much applauded." The work was a success, owing in part to Mrs. Jordan's performance.

KENNEY—KING/BRAHAM

In 1807 this team produced a full-length comic opera, *False Alarms*, also at Drury Lane. J. D. Collier (C) wrote that "in the development of the story[98] there are several whimsical and striking situations, and the characters are supported with much humour. Indeed it is not often that so much is done for the dramatic part of the entertainment, in pieces that are to be so powerfully recommended by the charms of music and song." The *Herald* and the *European* agreed, and DuBois (MM) went even further, seeing the work as "an attempt to reform the comic opera of our day." Void of "all those meretricious aids of machinery, drums, trumpets, and foppery," the production achieved "something like a *legitimate* English opera," and should be widely imitated. Moreover, "the poetry is of a superior stamp." Kenney has avoided "the vile and degrading office to which the Cobbs, the Cherries, and other of our dramatic poets have submitted"—a phrase Hunt would echo the following year in his *Examiner* criticism.

However, Barron Field (T), admitting Kenney "has a tolerable portion of original humour," found that "in his present Piece it is displayed in the language more than in the character [and] is scattered with many an original and facetious epithet." He also objected to one character who was "continually iterating four unfortunate words"—"*Not by no means*"—"with all the mercilessness of a Reynolds or a Dibdin."

The music was excellent (UM); it "has the character of pleasing simplicity" (EM) and "possesses great merit" (C). Braham composed the music for his own songs as well as two others (T). The biggest hit of the evening was his "Said a Smile to a Tear," in which he accompanied himself on a "grand piano forte" on the stage. Boaden (II, 431) reported cryptically that "his accompaniment was one of those rattles in music called a *battery*—but his touch is very brilliant, like his style of singing, and he was hardly permitted to leave the instrument." Field (T) disliked the song, which drew a "rapturous encore" (C) and remained a favorite for many years.

An even stronger dissent on the songs and the opera appeared in the *Critical Review*. Ostensibly a critique of the printed play, it took notice of the performance as well. It partakes of much of the opera bias of the "literary" organs, but it is of interest for its detail and particularity, which are untypical of such reviews. The reviewer turned against Kenney his own "apology" in the preface for the defects of the play:

> The author from a persuasion of his own imbecility, has introduced every theatrical trap by which crowded houses are usually insured. . . . Bad scenes, bad music executed by an ill-conducted band, shabbiness of costume, arrant nonsense in dialogue were all atoned for by the magic of a female Ferdinand or Theodore.
> . . . The part of Edgar, which means nothing, was properly assigned to Braham, who expresses that meaning to a miracle. This personage has by dint of tagging together parts of old tunes . . . aspired to the name of a musical composer. . . .
> [Braham] has so far entered into his feelings, that a noble emulation for the palm of worthlessness is discoverable, more particularly in one song, between writer, composer and singer. The sickliness or rather the squeamishness of thought, the Monmouth-street finery of diction, of the millinery of sentiment, aided by the trembling nasality and *elegant attitude* of the singer and composer, rendered the following

morçeau absolutely bewitching to the female citizens, who compose so large a portion of our London audiences.

> Said a Smile to a Tear
> On the cheek of my dear,
> And beam'd like the sun in spring weather,
> In sooth, lovely Tear,
> It strange must appear,
> That we should be both here together.

Despite the negative judgments, the opera proved to be very successful.

In 1810 Kenney and King for their final collaboration produced another full comic opera, *Oh! This Love*, for the Lyceum. J. D. Collier (C) found the plot dull: "All these events" of English aristocrats in disguise at Milan, "are brought about in a heavy common-place way, with very little interest either in the incidents or dialogue. . . . So much indulgence has been shewn these vehicles for music, that it becomes at length a species of injustice to be too fastidious with respect to any individual composition of the kind." In a late review, the *Times* noted Kenney had "been most successful where it cost him the least labour." *Bell's* thought "the characters are as much out of life as the action is beyond probability." Hunt agreed; his hopes for Kenney were "dashed," and even his songs were dull (E). And DuBois (MM) complained: "It seems incredible that [Kenney] could possibly write a thing, in which there is nothing worthy to be called dramatic . . . and in which the writing is inferior to any pointless, vulgar effusion from the pen of Mr. Cherry" (see below).

The music, the *Times* wrote, "is in Mr. King's usual style; it is chaste and pure; and peculiarly, in the glees and choruses, reminded us of the powerful and plain harmony of an earlier day." The *Universal* reported it "possesses all the talent, science, and melody of [King's] former compositions." The performers saved the work from failure (BWM).

King, as we have seen, concluded his operatic career with Arnold. Kenney, perhaps stung by the criticism, waited thirteen years to produce another opera.

CHERRY—CORRI

A thoroughly second-rate playwright who also fell afoul of the critics about this time was Andrew Cherry (1762–1812). At age fourteen he played in amateur theatricals at Dublin and went on to become an impecunious strolling player in Ireland. Later he acted at Bath and by 1793 was getting his plays produced. His first operatic farce in London, *Spanish Dollars*, an afterpiece with music by Davy, was apparently a failure at Covent Garden in 1805. But Cherry had quite a success the following year with a three-act "musical entertainment," *The Travellers; or, Music's Fascination* at Covent Garden, with music by Corri.

Domenico Corri (1746–1825), a composer, music publisher, and teacher, studied with Nicola Porpora.[99] Brought to Edinburgh in 1772 by Charles Burney, he settled in London for life in 1790. At least one of his songs found its way into T. Dibdin's *Cabinet* (1802), but the *Travellers* was his best-known opera. In fact, it was he who suggested to Cherry the idea for the opera, in which the national melodies of various kingdoms, from China to England, might be introduced and the progress of music traced (Boaden). The *Times* agreed the idea was a good one. Cherry "has displayed much ingenuity in accommodating his incidents to the labours of the composer. . . . Nor is there that incongruity or glaring violation of probability in the conduct of the plot, that might have been expected in a fable embracing so large a theme." They added that the work was much too long, however, even without the eight encores it was given. DuBois was also positive. To be sure, there were inconsistencies in the plot, "but we shall not try Mr. Cherry by rules which we know he meant to violate." There was also not "much novelty of character or incident." But his opera "is showy, busy, and diversified. The sentiments are put into good language, the songs are pretty well written. . . . What writer of operas can desire more?"

The *Chronicle*, however, saw it quite otherwise: "Mr. Cherry, who has supplied the words, has degenerated into the misery of punning; or into the worse fault of stale and disgusting clap-traps about the eternal bravery of Britons.—The fable is also incessantly broken by new and totally foreign matter. Scene follows scene without harmony or progress. . . . All this heterogeneous trash may be happily cut out." In other respects, however, they greatly admired the opera, which they regarded as primarily Corri's: "He formed the design of a drama on the boldest character of the Opera of his own country, and with an adequate librettist, would have shewn what might not be accomplished with an Opera in England." And the resources of the theatre might "give us, what would be most conducive to the progress of all the arts, a national Opera." (The "literary" reviews were of course scathing on the drama.)

The music, wrote the *Times*, "exhibits much indeed of fancy, taste, science, and variety. . . . The composer has shewn great powers of invention, as well as a thorough knowledge of the science, in imitating characteristic music of the different regions through which the Travellers journey." DuBois, however, "did not notice anything very striking or original in the composition." The production was very strong; the opera had thirty performances, and the libretto was reprinted eight times that year. In fact, when the opera was revived in 1823, Ayrton (Har) wrote that it "has been uncommonly succesful. The managers have spared no expense to give it effect; much of the music is excellent; and . . . it possesses a charm, that, in spite of the almost unparalleled absurdity of the Drama, and the miserable appeal to vulgar minds in which it abounds, draws together large and applauding audiences." The *European* thought "the long and dull opera" had "better success than it merited."

Cherry resumed his partnership with Corri in the production of an operatic farce, *In and Out of Tune*, for Drury Lane the next year.[100] The *Times* reported that "it was decidedly *bad* in plot and dialogue" and was "inexorably condemned," and Hunt found the manners of the stage Negro "disgusting"—"their whole speech and humour consist of the word Massa"; and the "neat" music of Corri, which was reminiscent of Purcell, was "thrown away" (E). The work failed, ending Cherry's stage career; unfortunately, Corri also seems to have composed no more operas.

BURGES—HORN/REEVE

Like Braham and Kelly, Charles Edward Horn (1786–1849) was a singer who also composed for the theatre, though his songs were praised less than his singing. Son of German parentage, he was taught music by his father, Karl Friedrich Horn, and by Rauzzini. He played double bass and cello in London theatres and made his singing debut in 1809. The next year he wrote his first opera, with W. Reeve, for Burges. Reeve, it will be recalled, had joined forces with Mazzinghi in composing songs for operas by Cobb (1798) and Hoare (1801).

Sir James Bland Burges (or Burgess) (1752–1824), a politician who was under secretary of state in 1793 and a supporter of Wilberforce, gave himself up to literary pursuits in the 1790s. His last work and only opera was *Tricks upon Travellers*, a comic opera afterpiece produced at the Lyceum in 1810.

The *Times* reported: "The Opera is not wholly without interest, and one or two of its songs are well-written; but Sir James Burgess has taken the advantage of laying his scene in Spain [then much in the news because of the Spanish Campaign], to imitate a few of the quaint phrases and obsolete allusions of our old dramatists." *Bell's* agreed: "Sir James is too courtly for bufoonery, and somewhat too lofty for mirth. He has very little of the vivacity, or . . . the trick and artifice, of dramatic humours." DuBois was devastating: "The songs are about the pitch of magazine poetry, such as boys and girls, smit with the love of fame—pen under the influence of a [misguided] inspiration."

Bell's thought the music was "extremely good, and many of the songs were rapturously encored." The *Times* agreed; it "will ensure the piece a sufficient run." But Hunt (E) reported that the music's "melodies and harmonies were what the orchestra has been accustomed to ever since it was acquainted with fiddles: — you heard them with that kind of anticipation, with which a two-penny postman walks through his round of streets, knowing every turn and rest that is to come."

ARNOLD — ADDISON

As noted earlier, S. J. Arnold wrote successful operas composed by his father in 1794 and 1796 and by King in 1809 and 1811. Also in 1809, in a serious vein, he produced an "opera" for the Lyceum — *The Russian Impostor*, which he had altered from a play by Henry Siddons.[101] The *Chronicle* found the story "not assisted by language, sentiment, or character. It is one of the many Operas put together in any manner, for the sake of the music."

The music was written by John Addison (c. 1766–1844), double bass player and composer. He was the son of a mechanic, and his wife was a singer at Vauxhall. For some years he directed amateur orchestras at Manchester. Later, in London, he shared the management of Kelly's music-publishing business and played in the King's band and at concerts. The *Chronicle* was impressed with the music: "Mr. Addison does not seem ambitious to display his knowledge as a theorist at the expense of his taste," and the *Times* thought it "elegant and pleasing." But DuBois, in a flippant review, found no science, melody or expression in it. The work, however, proved quite successful. (In 1814 he wrote some of the music for *The Farmer's Wife;* see n. III.)

ARNOLD — HORN/BRAHAM

In 1812 Horn and Braham together composed a three-act operatic romance, *The Devil's Bridge*, by Arnold, for the Drury Lane company at the Lyceum. J. D. Collier (C) found it

> deserving in every respect, of public approbation. . . . It is written with dramatic skill, combining the most lively interest of story with exquisite morsels of music, admirably sung. The situations are striking . . . the dialogue is chaste [i.e., simple] — and the moral is perfect. . . . Every air composed by Mr. Braham for this Opera, we prophecy will become so popular as to be familiar in every social circle, [although in Horn's songs] there was not much scope for the display of musical talent.

Bell's closely echoed Collier's views. But the *Times* (May 8) was unimpressed: "This plot may be any thing or nothing, as it pleases the arranger of the scenery, and the compiler of the music; and we have not now to repeat our weariness of three acts of gloomy tyrants, sentimental rustics, and pining lovers.... The general composition [of Braham's songs] was of too level an order to deserve peculiar praise." Hunt, agreeing with the *Times*, scoffed at the *Chronicle*'s "puff" for Arnold. The opera was in any case a great success (EM). It was revived in 1813, when the *Times* again found the work poor; in 1815; and again in 1816, when it was "received in the best manner" (T).

THOMPSON—HORN

In 1813 Horn got to compose an opera by himself—*Godolphin, or The Lion of the North*, a three-act musical drama by Benjamin Thompson (c. 1776–1816). Son of a merchant, Thompson gave up law to write translations of Kotzebue; one such translation, *The Stranger* (Drury Lane, 1798), was a success. According to the *Chronicle* the present work was "a piece of tedious and uninteresting dialogue, occasionally relieved by songs and chorusses, a single note of which will not be remembered.... The music is to our taste equally trite and common.... Of Mr. Horn, also, we must say that if he looked into the repertories of foreign Theatres, as Storace used to do, he would have provided a better treat for the public." The *Times* agreed: "The dramatic part of productions of this nature is usually considered as a mere vehicle for the songs: but whether the dialogue of Godolphin was meant to convey the songs, or the songs the dialogue, we must, however painful it must be, say that the carriage and its contents were equally wretched, and well worthy of each other." *Bell's* thought the music much better than the words, but the piece was savagely condemned by the *Inquisitor* and others. Despite a very expensive production, it died after three performances.

THOMPSON—PARRY

Undeterred by this failure, Thompson somehow got Drury Lane to produce another opera of his, *Oberon's Oath*, in 1816. It was a musical drama "Fairy Tale" afterpiece, with music by John Parry.[102] J. D. Collier (C) noted "a want of interest or connection" in the piece, which was too long, though he thought the music "pretty and tasteful." Sterling (T) forbore criticism of something so slight as a fairy tale but found the music "rich, spirited, and pleasing, and [it] reflects high credit on its composer." Both reviewers regretted the harsh treatment of the piece by a first-night audience. The play died after five nights; and the author died the same year—the disappointment was said to have killed him.

MOORE

Thomas Moore (1779–1852), an Irish poet and composer, shares with Charles Dibdin, William Linley, J. Augustine Wade, and one or two others in our period the distinction of producing his own opera—words and music—though Moore had some assistance from Charles Horn. Moore studied music as a child and by 1802 had published many very popular lyrics, to which Sir John Stevenson[103] provided the accompaniments. He was probably best known for his series of "Irish Melodies"—folk songs he collected, to which he wrote new lyrics—published between 1808 and 1834, also with Stevenson settings.

His not-very-operatic comic opera, *M.P.; or, The Bluestocking*, was produced at the Lyceum in 1811, with much advance publicity. Opinions were split. The *Times* (perhaps Barnes), probably biased by Moore's Tory politics, was "utterly disappointed" in its expectation: "We cannot attempt to give the *plot* . . . nothing to make a substratum for the pun, and the jest, and the gibe and . . . the clap-trap into which Mr. Moore's sudden affection for Royalty and Regency suffered him occasionally to descend." The songs in the opera are "uniformly flat, feeble, and monotonous," and the music was disappointing, for "we have heard some of Mr. Moore's earlier compositions, and we should not have hesitated to pronounce them among the most touching melodies that we had ever heard."

Hunt also "had a right to expect something good," but "the only part in which the hand of Mr. Moore can be said to be truly visible is in the songs. . . . There is enough of elegance and of poetry to awaken all our regret at the company in which they are found. . . . He may be easily discerned as possessing the true lyric character of old . . . uniting the poet and musician" (E). And *Bell's* wrote that Moore "has not, in the least, deviated from the *namby pamby, unnatural* path of the dramatic writers of the present day," though the dialogue "occasionally discloses a good deal of point" and "the words of the songs also are much superior to the common class of operatic poetry." Yet "the music fails throughout; neither science nor melody rendering any particular part worthy of notice."

But J. D. Collier (C) saw quite a different work. There was no mention of politics; and he *did* give the plot, from which

> it will be seen that Mr. Moore thought only of a light, elegant trifle, over which he might scatter a few of those delicious flowers which

bloom so beautifully in his poetical effusions. . . . The words of his tender songs play round the heart with the finest emotion; and it is here that our British Anacreon is without a rival. His delineation of character is sprightly, and the character of the M. P. unusually bold. . . . It is on the whole, an elegant and most pleasurable *jeu d'esprit*, and in this light alone it ought to be considered.

On the first night some of the songs were hissed; the work failed. Some of Moore's songs and ballads appeared in Terry's *Guy Mannering* (1816) and T. Dibdin's *Gil Blas* (1802).

BRAHAM, REEVE, AND MOOREHEAD

The practice of author-composer teams, shaky at times before 1800, breaks down almost altogether as we consider several Covent Garden productions in which any or all of the above "free-lance" composers (and Davy) were called on to write songs or other theatrical music. Judging from the reviews, these composers do not seem to have been significantly inferior to those thus far considered.

John Braham was nearly as versatile as Michael Kelly, for, in addition to his leading performances in Italian and English opera, he was also, as we have seen, a significant composer of songs. These were not entirely English songs, for he composed at least one aria, which he sang in Portogallo's *Agenide* at the King's in 1806 (Cr, Jan. 27). At first he composed songs only for himself in English operas, working with Reeve and other composers, but his songs met with such success that he began composing them for others as well. We have already noted songs he composed and sang in Kenney's *False Alarms* (1807) and in Arnold's *Americans* (1811) and *Devils Bridge* (1812).

William Reeve (1757–1815) — uncle of actor John Reeve and brother of hosier Thomas Reeve — wrote and composed many burlettas for the minors and was perhaps the most prolific theatre composer in this period, though his talent was negligible (N.G.). Apprenticed to a law stationer, he soon began to study music under one Richardson, an organist at St. James's, Westminister. About 1783 he wrote songs for Astley's Ampitheatre, sang in the Covent Garden chorus, produced burlettas for the Royalty Theatre, and even did some acting. In the following two decades, he helped to produce operas and ballets for Covent Garden. We have already noted his music in Cobb's *Ramah Droog* (1798), Hoare's *Chains of the Heart* (1801), and Burges's *Tricks upon Travellers* (1810).

John Moorehead (1760–1804), an Irish tenor, violist, and composer, played in various provincial orchestras and by 1795 was the principal violist at Sadler's Wells. In 1798 he began playing in the Covent Garden orchestra and also began composing songs. But in 1802 he went insane, was confined, and hanged himself. (His brother, Alexander, leader of the band at Sadler's Wells, met a similar fate the following year.)

THOMAS DIBDIN

All the above composers and others were used by Thomas John Dibdin for his pasticcio operas. Dibdin (1771–1841)[104] had Garrick as his godfather. As a boy, Thomas sang at St. Paul's. Later, apprenticed to an upholsterer, he ran off to play singing roles (he was a "good tenor") in provincial playhouses. He married in 1793, and by 1797 he was writing entertainments for Sadler's Wells, of which his half-brother, Charles Pitt, was manager. Altogether he wrote more than 250 dramatic and musical works for the stage between 1795 and 1837, including the lyrics for some 2,000 songs. This talented man was also very competent in making pencil sketches for scenery and in constructing mock sets.

DIBDIN—MOOREHEAD

In 1799 he produced the first of his many musical works for Covent Garden—a musical entertainment afterpiece entitled *The Naval Pillar*, with music by Moorehead. (Patriotic pieces in those years could hardly fail.) It had no plot but had grand stage effects and "abounds in patriotic sentiment, humorous repartee, and epigrammatic point. The selection of airs was judicious; . . . the overture possesses considerable merit; and that part of the Music which is new, is appropriate to the occasion" (T). DuBois agreed that Moorehead's music was "very ingenious" and the overture had some "fine movements." The piece, which Genest called "contemptible," had a lavish production and played twelve times.

DIBDIN—MOOREHEAD/ATTWOOD

The following year Dibdin wrote a musical drama in three acts, *Il Bondocani; or the Calif Robber*, with six numbers each by Moorehead and Attwood. The piece, based on the Arabian tales, "combines the serious and the comic, the charms of music and the fascination of appropriate scenery with superb decorations" (T). The *Post* thought the plot "far superior to the generality of flimsy productions of the same class. . . . The music, in quantity, [is] just sufficient for embellishment, without retarding the progress of the plot, or disjointing the scenes, and thus frittering away all the interest." DuBois concurred, adding that the music "happily combines scientific and elegant modulation with a striking adherence to the interest of the piece and the *costume* of the country. The chorusses[105] are full and energetic." Even the *British Critic*, reviewing the printed play, was amused: "It is a butterfly, and the wheel will not touch it." The piece was lavishly produced and had twenty-seven performances.

This appears to be about the last of Attwood's contributions to English opera. As noted earlier, he was unfortunate in having collaborated on a number of productions, including those by Samuel Birch, that were either failures or were only marginally operatic. His music received highest praise in Rose's *Prisoner* and Holcroft's *Old Cloathsman*, but even in these some critics were not pleased. In 1816 Daniel Terry produced the very successful *Guy Mannering*, with music by Bishop and songs by Attwood and others, but the songs received only trite praise. And three of his songs were included in an all-sung *Dirce* produced in 1821, but it was too operatic for the playhouse audience and died after seven nights. He even composed some "Celebrated Dances" — published in a pianoforte edition (1793) for James D'Egville's ballet *Le Jaloux Puni*, performed at the King's on June 1 of that year, but reviewers didn't cite the music and apparently he made no further attempts in this direction. Altogether, Attwood seems never to have fulfilled the high promise of his youth.

DIBDIN—MOOREHEAD/REEVE/DAVY/CORRI/BRAHAM

For his comic opera *The Cabinet*, in 1802, Dibdin selected Moorehead as the composer, but he became too ill to carry on, and Dibdin turned to W. Reeve, Davy, Corri, and Braham (Parke reported the music was "entirely new"). The press offered mixed opinions on the drama but admired the music. John Campbell (C) wrote: "Nothing in the form of a drama offered less food for the mind than this theatrical novelty. . . . The author has had in his mind the fable of *The Duenna*, but his imitation resembles the copy of one of Raphael's finest pieces, drawn by a sign painter. [But] many of the airs had uncommon merit. The greater number of them were loudly encored." The *Post* also dismissed the drama, but

> the music is of a description to captivate any audience, without aid or additional ornament. [Braham's airs] are of his own composition, and are admirably adapted to his powers and style of singing. . . . Mr. Incledon's songs are principally the composition of Mr. Davy, who displayed great musical genius. A quintetto of his composition is most

beautiful, and was loudly applauded. Mr. Davy will hereafter rank with composers better known to the public. His songs are charmingly adapted to Incledon's voice.[106]

The *Times* agreed that the plot[107] was mediocre but made the point that "its chief and peculiar merit is the judicious and seasonable manner in which the airs are introduced." The music was "displayed with an effect which could not be justly expected from the union of so many masters." And DuBois reported it "a very agreeable opera" that derives "little or no assistance from . . . bustle and pageantry." Moreover, the piece "is by no means to be regarded as a mere vehicle for the music, but as possessing a considerable portion of dramatic interest, and a vein of sprightliness and humour." Surprisingly, even the reviews of the book were commendatory.[108]

The opera had a fine production and a stellar cast, with over thirty performances that season and the same the next. In fact, it entered the repertory, seeing several revivals up to 1828. In 1807 DuBois credited only Braham with the music, admiring especially his "polacca"—"No more shall sorrow"—and noting his indebtedness to Handel. In 1812 the *Times* thought "the life of the opera" was "to be finally attributed to the exertions of Mr. Braham."

In 1808 Hunt called the opera a "miserable puppet-shew" (E, Jan. 24), but by 1817 he had mellowed: "The *Cabinet* of our old friend Tom Dibdin," he wrote, "was cut down on this occasion, by permission, into a machine of reasonable dimensions [and] we certainly enjoyed it more than we have done on much more imposing occasions. . . . With all our remaining zeal in behalf of a better state of the drama, [we] could not help being a little sorry that we had ever been under the necessity of treating him so roughly" (E).

In 1823 the opera had "never been better performed" (LitC). Yet later criticism that year was sharply negative. Sterling (T) called the opera "the most absurd on the English stage; which is saying a great deal" (Nov. 20), and "one of the most contemptible dramatic abortions that was ever tolerated by a discerning public" (Dec. 12). And the *London* noted "a most evil taste" in whoever revived it, yet "the music is pleasing, and music will float Folly's vessel at any time." In 1828 the exasperated reviewer for the *Examiner* recommended: "In the name of all that is vulgar and commonplace, go and fatten on the *Cabinet* and *English Fleet*."

My own view of the libretto is that, while it is at times simplistic and even banal, it has several amusing incidents and characters. While it is certainly very well adapted to the introduction of the songs, they do nothing to further the plot.

DIBDIN—BRAHAM/REEVE/DAVY/MOOREHEAD

Still later (1802) Dibdin produced *Family Quarrels*, with music by Braham, Reeve, Davy, and Moorehead. The *Chronicle* critic (perhaps Campbell), stung by protests from Harris for his criticism of the *Cabinet*, wrote a long review shot through with irony: "A *strange* Piece made its appearance; but whether it deserves the name of an *Opera* we must leave to others to determine. Let it not be supposed that we are about to be severe." The *Post*, too, was critical: "It is an ungrateful task to be constantly declaiming against the want of plot, interest, and novelty, in modern pieces of this class. If, however, an opera thus defective should succeed by the merit of the music, it is not fair that the writer of the dialogue should engross all the merit.... [In this opera] we find poor and vulgar writing, no interest, no plot, and no pretensions to originality." But DuBois was not altogether ready to fault the playwright: "The public are quite aware of the difficulties which attend this species of composition on the modern stage, where simplicity of fable, and simplicity of music, are no longer sufficient to excite attention. All an author can do now, is to furnish a vehicle for the airs, duets, trios, &c.... For these he must necessarily sacrifice his plot."

And the *Times* was even quite favorable. They added Davy to the list of composers and admired the overture by Moorehead and Davy, but Braham's songs "take the lead in point of novelty, melody, and fine taste, and, enriched by the charms of his voice, they are entitled to rank as masterpieces in the art." Of his duet (with Incledon) they wrote: "A Piece more eminently suited to display the respective powers of these admirable Singers, cannot be composed."

The opera played twenty-two nights. In 1805 the *British Critic*, reviewing the book, found the opera "entertaining on the stage, and by no means disgusting in the closet." But Boaden thought the opera below expectation "even in its humour."

DIBDIN—BRAHAM

In 1803 Dibdin, with an eye still on patriotism, followed with another success, a comic opera called *The English Fleet in 1342*, with music by Braham. The book received mixed notices. The *Chronicle* complained that "such pieces must be looked upon merely as [furnishing a] *canvas* for the musical composer. *The Duenna* should teach us higher notions of *Opera*, and should lead us to expect some gratification to the understanding as well as the ear." The *Post* had "little to say of the wit or elegance of the dialogue," but the songs—"prominently adapted for a train of patriotic sentiments"—

were "happily expressed." And DuBois asserted that Dibdin had connected his comic characters and situations to the main plot "with great address, and has so judiciously balanced the pathetic and humourous scenes, that the effect of the whole is very striking."

The *Times* thought that "in his delineation of Jane of Flanders, the author . . . strictly followed the historians," and was generally favorable toward the piece, but the *Critical Review*, consulting Hume, reported it contained "no particle of history."

The *Times* found the music "generally pleasing," though not original, and the selected overture was too long. The *Chronicle* reported that the music "possesses very great merit," and DuBois thought the choruses "grand and impressive." But the *Post*, declaring that the music had no "very striking or brilliant passages," admitted that the audience responded to it— "and to the public opinion, when fairly ascertained, we are always disposed respectfully to defer." The piece had an excellent production and played thirty-five times; it probably had revivals as well.

DIBDIN—DAVY/REEVE/BRAHAM

Late in 1804 Dibdin produced still another comic opera, *Thirty-Thousand*, which drew a very fashionable audience. The *Chronicle* (perhaps Campbell) thought it even more feeble than his previous operas and, unlike the *Post*, took a tilt at the audience:

> It has long been common to say, of modern plays, that particular parts were written for particular actors. In the present Piece this rule has only been carried the length of writing a particular song, for a particular actor possessed of some powers of voice . . . without the least reference to his powers of acting. The audience never thinks of the characters, the incidents, or the conclusion. Their whole interest is engrossed in the succession of songs, [and Dibdin] has been successful in the highest degree in the songs both of a serious and light description.

All the music, they added, was "highly creditable," and "it is due to Mr. Reeve, as a young composer[109] to state, that he evinces very promising proofs of science." The *Times*, reviewing it the next day, found the work "appeared to gain considerably by the repetition," and, of Braham's song, "The Death of Abercrombie," they wrote: "There is not, perhaps, in the music of the English Opera, any air superior, in point of sympathy and expression, to that most affecting composition." (Davy may have contributed the overture, which received no comment.)

The production was skimpy but the singing satisfactory. There were nine or ten songs, which, with some eleven encores, made the piece much too long (T). It received eleven performances.

DIBDIN—SHIELD/REEVE/BRAHAM

In 1806 Dibdin attempted a musical drama called *The White Plume; or the Border Chieftains*, this time with only Reeve as composer. Based on Sir Walter Scott's *Lay of the Last Minstrel* (1805), it was the first of many operatic productions based on his novels. But Covent Garden could not furnish an adequate vocal heroine (MM), and the piece had but five performances.

Dibdin regained his popularity the following year with a full-length comic opera, *Two Faces Under a Hood*, which he produced with Shield, Reeve, and Braham. The work—"so long expected"—was unanimously condemned as a drama. Gray (C wrote: "It is true indeed, that a musical piece does not require the same rapidity of incident which we admire in some Spanish Comedies; but we think the rules of operatic writing might allow a better train of events than we last night witnessed. It is surely material, that every dramatic production should excite an interest; but the plot of this piece has little operation, either on the feelings or on the fancy."

It had been some ten years since a previous new opera by Shield appeared, but his music had lost no charm for audiences and critics. "Some of the music is pleasant," Gray added, "and some of it original; and we think it will not diminish Mr. Shield's reputation." The *Times* agreed about the drama: "The dialogue of this piece is so pitiful and common place, that nothing but the songs was heard with any complacency; and in those the audience were delightfully lulled by the music of Mr. Shield. . . . We are only sorry that his music is now thrown away on such words. We must be understood, however, to censure Mr. Dibdin only in his serious poetry; his comic has merit." DuBois concurred, adding: "The novelty of [Braham's and Reeve's music] may tickle the ear, and find admirers amongst the 'senceles multitude,' but [Shield's music] rests upon the heart, and will dwell with us when the other is forgotten. . . . In the *finale* to the first act Mr. Shield has introduced a *fugue* with great skill, and the music is altogether a monument of his extraordinary genius, taste, and science."[110] Fiske (p. 559) calls the work "too old-fashioned to have much success"; but despite critical caveats and a production that was only fair, the opera played nineteen times.

Except for an early work of Shield (discussed immediately below) this opera represents the composer's last contribution to English opera. His long string of successes stretched from 1772 or earlier to 1807 and included some twenty-one operas written with some ten dramatist/librettists. Almost all these works were successful, and for the few that were not, critics held the dramatists, not Shield, to account.

True, Shield met with some obstacles. He resigned his Covent Garden post in 1797 after difficulties with Harris over his salary (MM, Jan. 1798). But he continued to play in the King's Theatre orchestra and in the Ancient Music concerts and Ladies Concerts. In later years he became master of the King's music. Perhaps no English composer enjoyed higher regard from his musical colleagues. John Taylor reported in 1798 (MM, Jan.): "Estimable . . . as Mr. Shield must be considered in his profession, he is still more to be admired in his private character. . . . There are few, indeed, that can rival him in sensibility, benevolence, and honour. He is convivial, intelligent, and always ready to exercise the offices of friendship." The humility born of his humble beginnings never deserted him in his success.

After *Two Faces*, Dibdin for a time lost interest in comic operas and did little more for Covent Garden. This prolific playwright had been writing many comedies, farces, and pantomimes, as well as musical burlettas, entertainments, spectacles, extravaganzas, interludes, and musical dramas for that theatre. But after 1810 he mainly wrote these minor musical forms for the Surrey, Royal Circus, and Sadler's Wells (where his half-brother Charles[III] was manager until 1819), though he did have some productions at Drury Lane from 1813 to 1816, as well as at Covent Garden. Two of his late operas with Bishop and Perry are discussed below.

In 1808 W. Reeve was praised for his music to Isaac Brandon's opera *Kais,* which was successful, and in 1815, the year of his death, he contributed songs to Dimond's *Brother and Sister* (see below). But most of Reeve's compositions were written for Sadler's Wells productions. The "promise" of his first attempts at the majors never materialized beyond an occasional plaudit, and even such a collaborator as Braham was clearly superior—at least with the public. Fiske finds Reeve's songs generally poor. The music for several later productions by "Reeve" was presumably composed by his son, George W. Reeve, who had made a favorable debut as a composer in 1813 (TI, Sept.) and composed much for Sadler's Wells.

REYNOLDS—SHIELD

Frederic Reynolds (1764–1841) was a grandson of a wealthy merchant and son of a Whig attorney and solicitor to Lord Chatham. As a child he enjoyed the theatre and had seen Garrick perform. He was educated at Westminister school and the Middle Temple, but he soon abandoned law for drama.

His first successful comedy was *The Dramatist* (1789), and it was followed by his first musical drama, *The Crusade* (Covent Garden, 1790), with music by Shield. He had to adapt his book to the scenery—not to be wasted—for a play that had failed. No wonder the *Times* wrote that Reynolds "seems rather to have aimed at detached scenes—calculated to amuse and surprise—than uniformity of plot. . . . The language, besides having the merit of some striking sentiments . . . has here and there some good points. . . . Shield has been very happy—not only in his own compositions but in his selection from the best masters, among whom Handel and his chorusses cut the greatest figure." Other borrowings were from Cimarosa, Duni, and Martín. Shield introduced some "Turkish percussion" for exotic coloring; the chorus was sung by performers from the Concert of Ancient Music (Fiske). Despite a fine production, the work barely succeeded.

At Drury Lane in 1803, he produced *The Caravan*, a highly successful but not very operatic piece, in which the dog, Carlos, rescues a child from a tank of water (the playwright earned £350 for it). By 1795 he stood "conspicuously forward in the drama of the present day," reported John Taylor in a biographical sketch (MM., Dec.). Reynolds "has no enemies," and backstage objections to his plays "are no sooner started than obviated; he will expunge, correct, transpose, re-write, nay, re-construct, to make the cast of his plays agreeable." Moreover, "success has no power to make him *vain* . . . but merely makes him . . . *more* diffident and unassuming." Indeed, he was becoming a *bon vivante*, counting Morton, Boaden, Andrews, Holman, Cobb, Colman, and other playwrights among his friends, some of whom contributed songs, prologues, and even whole scenes to his plays and operas!

True, by 1800 critics were attacking him on the mannerism of his style and on the similarity of his plots, and he cheerfully admitted there was something to this criticism (*Life*, II, 284). But he soon found himself drawn to operas rather than to dramas, perhaps because, as he frankly admitted, he was better paid for them and they were easier to write.

REYNOLDS—LANZA

In 1806 Reynolds produced a melodramatic "Grand Operatical Entertainment" for Covent Garden called *The Deserts of Arabia*, an afterpiece with music by Gesualdo Lanza. Lanza (1779–1859), a composer and singing teacher, was the son of a Neapolitan composer and came to London as a child. He became well known as a singing teacher[112] and apparently composed just two operas.

The work was clearly operatic, with at least some recitative; not surprisingly it received mixed notices. The *Times* thought no description worthy of a piece "so totally destitute of real merit"; it was, moreover, entirely too operatic:

> In this entertainment there is very little dialogue. The style of the Italian Opera appears to be imitated. The Recitatives and Chorusses were insupportably tedious. . . . We cannot . . . but disapprove of this affectation of the Italian style. For example, when one of the female characters is kneeling by the side of her father, whom she supposes dying, she sings a very long song to express her feelings. Although an Italian audience might conceive this natural, it will be very long before an English audience is reconciled to that mode of expressing strong emotions.

DuBois, agreeing that it was "not well calculated for the English theatre," was only moderately impressed by the piece. The *Herald*, on the contrary, thought it a "most splendid spectacle"; the music was "very beautiful," and several songs were encored. And the *Chronicle* concurred, adding: "As a spectacle, this melo-drame is extremely grand," and Lanza's music, composed "after the manner of the Italian school," was "extremely well adapted to the English stage." The spectacle, no doubt, accounted for its success; the work had fifteen performances despite the recitative. Lanza's second opera, *Outwitted at Last* (Drury Lane, 1817), composed for a libretto by one Earle, failed badly.

BISHOP

Henry Rowley Bishop (1786–1855) was unquestionably the dominant composer of English operas from 1811 to 1830. Son of a watchmaker, he had little formal education. At age thirteen he was selling music, and at fourteen he was writing his first songs; he later studied composition with Bianchi. Early in the century he composed successful ballet music for the King's and for Drury Lane, but most of his theatrical work was confined to Covent Garden. He was early drawn to concerted writing, and he further developed the eighteenth-century glee "with a more elaborate vocal writing and an indispensible instrumental accompaniment."[113]

REYNOLDS—BISHOP/MAZZINGHI

In 1808 Reynolds collaborated with Mazzinghi and possibly Bishop on the music for his melodramatic opera *The Exile, or the Deserts of Siberia*, produced by the Covent Garden company playing at the King's Theatre.

(Nicoll credits the music only to Bishop, but the reviewers do not even mention him.) Mazzinghi, as noted earlier, worked with Reeve in composing songs for operas by Cobb (1798) and Hoare (1801).

There were mixed views on the drama. J. D. Collier (C) was impressed: "The plot,[114] among its other excellencies, has also, in a singular degree, the merits of progression and simplicity: — merits, the more valuable because of late they have been so uncommon." Further, "there are several comic incidents, most skilfully and divertingly managed, which . . . possess in themselves a liveliness and rapidity of thought, that must have been striking even without the advantages of a pathetic contrast." *Bell's* was even more supportive:

> To such plain people as go into a theatre merely for amusement, Mr. Reynolds is certainly a writer of powerful talent: he was the founder of the modern school [and] has had many imitators, though few rivals. . . . [He] possesses in a singular degree the happy power of discovering the public taste, and of adjusting himself by it as by a glass. . . . Accordingly, he has almost totally altered his style; instead of broad merriment, he has given us a serious play, regularly, simply, and interestingly constructed.

But Hunt thought the opera only somewhat better than Reynolds's usual fare: "He has injured [it] by a mean and farcical underplot in order to lengthen it out into a melodrama as long as a play." Neither did he admire the poetry. DuBois agreed, complaining: "But where is he that loves the stage and knows its proper end, who can see the abuse with which it is covered and surrounded?"

The critics in general admired Mazzinghi's music. DuBois found it "very clever and appropriate. The melodramatic part [by Bishop?] is particularly ingenious."[115] Hunt thought that, "though pleasing enough," it "was not so original as might have been expected, and the overture, which was intended I suppose to be adapted to the feelings of the story, was rather too full of starts and surprises, of halting and rushing forward. This is more like the conceits of Beethoven than the surprise and lofty ardour of Haydn."

The work had a strong production and played an astonishing forty-two times, with several revivals. In 1813 the *Times* wrote: "The play itself is an unequal specimen of that style for which our grammars have no name, but which is a compound of the pompous and the absurd." And in 1821 it was "still very popular on account of its splendid spectacle" (T).

No doubt it was this success that prompted Covent Garden to appoint Bishop as musical director and Reynolds as "thinker" of plays — sinecures they retained until about 1824.

In 1812 Bishop and Reynolds turned to a dramatic opera, *The Virgin of the Sun*, based on Kotzebue's drama and on Marmontel's *Incas*. The piece was more melodrama than opera[116] and drew mixed criticism. J. D. Collier (C) thought Reynolds had improved on Kotzebue "in many and material instances. His alterations and insertions are highly dramatic and effective." And *Bell's* reported the characters were "drawn with force and considerable discrimination; and the language, though not very elevated, is simple and occasionally vigorous." But the *Times* (perhaps Barnes) disliked the dramatic treatment: "Those will be least liable to be disappointed who give up all hope of natural situation and genuine feeling,—the fine and felicitous thought, which was at once wisdom and wit. . . . But if they will confess that they are to be amused by glaring sentiments in strong situations,—by the broad coloring that the writer has rather dashed than laid on his canvas, they must subscribe to the popularity of [the piece]."

Bishop's music for the most part received only routine praise. The *Times* (probably Barnes) wrote: "He has considerable science; and some of the chorusses . . . were not unfavourable specimens of his powers as a harmonist; but his airs . . . were remarkably feeble: they were of that humble and mediocre order, which leaves no impression." All reviewers were moved by the scenic effects, which included an earthquake. The work had thirty-three performances, again probably owing mainly to the spectacle.

These successes were broken, in 1817, by their production of another not-very-operatic musical drama, *The Duke of Savoy*, which Reynolds adapted from B. J. Marsollier's *Les deux petites Savoyards*. J. D. Collier (C) found the story "complicated to an unusual degree" and was "somewhat surprised to hear it attributed to the pen of Mr. Reynolds, for though the attempt was not in his usual stile of writing, as it sometimes soared even to the ambition of blank verse, we should have expected . . . a more intelligible plot." Thus the performance suffered; yet the songs were "very pleasing." But Sterling (T) was acerbic, saying the plot was "absolutely unintelligible," and "we consider this melo-drame (or whatever it is to be called) as a masterpiece of insipidity. The music and songs are as commonplace as possible, and the dialogue, sentiments, attempts at wit are . . . completely childish and nonsensical."[117] Hunt concurred, though he had the only good word for Bishop: "We hope . . . that a way will be found to preserve some of the music,—we mean for the stage as well as the shop. It is better than we have had in a long while from Mr. Bishop, and more worthy of his first promise" (E). The monthlies also condemned the drama. Though cast "with the strength of the house," the work failed miserably.

More operatic—and highly successful—were a series of operas adapted from Shakespeare's comedies by these collaborators. The time was propitious. Apart from a general interest in Elizabethan literature, play-goers in this period enjoyed the new scenic arts in Shakespeare productions as well as the first attempts at accuracy in costume at Covent Garden by J. P. Kemble. By 1814 Edmund Kean was revitalizing the tragedies in Drury Lane productions.

Moreover, there was plenty of precedence for operaticized Shakespeare. Impetus for this development started with Shakespeare's perennially favorite songs, stripped of their original music and reset by countless composers, most notably Purcell and Arne. They were not, however, limited to the comedies. We have seen how such tragedies as *Romeo and Juliet* and *Othello* lent themselves to operatic treatment in Italian opera. But the comedies—especially the *Tempest* and the *Twelfth Night*, with their many songs—were the most suitable to operatic adaptations.

During the Restoration and the early eighteenth century, the London stage witnessed a metamorphosis of many Shakespeare plays into masques, burlesques, burlettas, extravaganzas, and other miscellaneous types in which music was an important, if not a primary, element. Even after David Garrick's reforms swept many of these operatic types from the boards by 1776, operatic versions of *Macbeth* and *Romeo and Juliet* continued in popularity, as did the *Tempest* (with thirty-two songs) and *Midsummer Night's Dream* (with thirty-three songs), in addition to many others; meanwhile, the various (nonmusical) farcical and burlesqued adaptations continued apace right through our period, mainly at the minors.

There was of course some protest to all this,[118] though less than might be thought—even from literary critics. Boaden (I, 247) warned that Linley's music for the chorus of witches in *Macbeth* made it "dangerously operatic," and Hazlitt did not want Ophelia's songs *sung*—"no music can add anything to their magical effect." Hunt, however, regarded her song as an opportunity to heighten the characterization, though he admitted that, "in an age that professes to idolize Shakespeare," the role was too often filled with "a mere opera debutante, full of stage attitudes and a ridiculous self-possession" (E, Sept. 25, 1808).

Not since 1777 had London seen a *Midsummer Night's Dream*—in Garrick's version, which failed—and this is perhaps why Reynolds and Bishop turned to it in 1816. Sterling (T) tended to dismiss the play as a curiosity, and he pointed to one interpolation—"to the tune, no doubt, of '*Goosey Gander!*'":

> Whither dost thou wander?
> Lysander, Lysander—
> He hears not!
> Appears not!
> Lysander, Lysander!

"We really believe," he continues, "that Shakespeare might have 'cudgelled his brains,' to the present year, 1816, of the Christian era, without ever being able to accomplish such lines as these." The *Champion* admired the play but, anticipating Charles Lamb's objections,[119] did "not think the *Midsummer Night's Dream* [could] be acted—it is a property of the imagination, and ought not to be trespassed on by machinists and scene painters." They went on to note much of it had been cut, including "much of the fine poetry," and many of the incidents were "entirely altered." Yet they did find some songs delightful. The *European*, too, was pleased by the play's "unfettered imagination." "But on the stage," they added, "this *Dream* wants that species of *substantial* attraction which adapts the drama to a motley audience." Yet they had high praise for the pageantry and noted the addition to the piece of excerpts from Handel's *Acis and Galatea*, finding the music delightful. (Apparently none of Purcell's music to the *Fairy Queen* [1692] was used in this production.) All reviewers noted the fine singing and acting. The work had a run of eighteen performances.

Late in 1819 these confreres again turned to Shakespeare—the *Comedy of Errors*; this time Bishop took credit for the music. The piece was more operatic—"a license to be treated with the greater indulgence," Sterling (T) explained, "as the play never before kept possession of the stage; and becomes, therefore, a fair subject for experiment." He also noted some inept alterations: "What can be more absurd, for instance, than to put songs into the mouth of an Ephesian that relate solely to English customs or English superstitions?" But the music was noteworthy: "Mr. Bishop . . . has added a few airs, and harmonized several others that before only existed in the simple form of melody: he deserves praise for all that he has done," including his selections from Arne, Mozart, Stevenson, and Richard Stevens.[120]

The *Chronicle* reviewer admired it least of Shakespeare's plays; nevertheless, he deplored the interpolations:

> The beautiful little pieces of poetry that appear as gems in *As You Like It*, in *The Merchant of Venice*, in *Measure for Measure*, in *Lear*, *The Tempest*, &c. &c. are torn out of their natural setting, and fixed where they can find neither connexion nor relief. [However,] the pieces thus violently transferred, are chiefly the compositions of Dr. Arne, and are,

most of them, melodies of great beauty . . . as well as Sir John Stevenson's favourite duet, "Tell me where is fancy bred." Some, from the sonnets, are by Bishop, of which "Beauty's valuation," is by far the best. [But the overture,] which is made up of the Airs in *Macbeth*, by Matthew Locke [1672], we object to as another spoilation.

The *Gazette* was also unhappy with Shakespearean tamperings, "but in this case . . . the irregularity of metamorphosing a Comedy into an Opera may at least be tolerated." Hunt thought the play quite unsuitable for an opera: the characters were "anything but harmonious" and the plot has "neither the time, nor temper, nor any thing else, to be dallying with duets and sostenutos" (E). Only the *Champion* was quite delighted with the adaptations and declared: "So much good acting and so much good singing we do not remember ever to have seen united in one performance." In fact, all reviewers praised the performances. The work was a hit, with twenty-seven repetitions and at least one revival, in 1823, when the opera was declared to be "always received with more than passive approbation" (H).

With this encouragement, the collaborators turned, the next year, to *Twelfth Night*. The *Chronicle* again protested:

> Surely this is a Comedy that might be allowed to stand on its own merits . . . without being driven to those aids, the toleration of which either impeaches the judgment of the public, or calls in question the character which our great dramatic bard has so long maintained. Should this inclination for *harmonizing* Shakespeare continue, we must ere long expect to hear *Hamlet* deliver his philosophical soliloquy in a *cavatina*, and *Lear* vent his passion in a *bravura*.

They also objected to the "violent intrusion" in the fourth act of "the Masque from the *Tempest*" (the *Times* agreed). Yet they admired the "bold step" of setting, to a duet by Winter, the parting words of Olivia and Viola in the third act, as well as Bishop's selections from madrigals and glees of Morley, Ford, Ravencroft, and others.[121] Even the conservative *Gazette*, though they could not approve of "this fashion" with Shakespeare "in the abstract," admitted that the work "was so gorgeous and fascinating an exception to the right rule, that we are compelled to pronounce . . . an opinion of the most favourable kind upon its attractions. We certainly never saw any thing upon the stage more rich and brilliant, nor ever heard any thing much more harmonious."[122] Hunt frankly did not know whether "we ought not to resent these 'pickings and stealings'" of Shakespeare, "but the patchwork added to the play is at least made up of himself," and the play "must also be allowed to be more fitted for the introduction of songs."

The opera was a success, with seventeen performances, and revivals the next two seasons. But Genest was outraged: "In the Devil's name, why does not Reynolds turn his own plays into Operas?"

The *Tempest* followed in 1821. The Dryden-Davenant adaptation, first produced in 1667, was offered as a musical in 1673 (in which Dryden's participation is uncertain) and in 1695; Reynolds may have based his adaptation on the latter production. We do not know whether "Dear Pretty Youth," Purcell's only contribution to the work, was retained. Musical selections were borrowed from Mozart, Haydn, Linley, and Braham,[123] among others. In a brief notice, Sterling now appeared quite reconciled to the trend. But *Drama Magazine* strongly opposed the operatic tamperings, as did the *London* in an extended protest. All reviewers expressed admiration for the performances and the production, however, and the work was given fifteen times and was revived the following season.

Still later, in 1821, the team turned to *Two Gentlemen of Verona* — not quite as unpopular a play as *Midsummer Night's Dream*: it had been produced at least as late as 1790. The press agreed the original was a weak play and therefore welcomed this operatizing of the Bard. There was "a constant succession of exquisite singing" (T), though the music had "a too ambitious display of complexity and science" (E).[124] The scenery was splendid, and there was no objection raised to the "very effective" introduction of Cleopatra's barge! The opera was quite a hit, with twenty-nine performances.

Finally, in 1824, they produced the popular *Merry Wives of Windsor* at Drury Lane. It received mixed reviews. William Dowton, as Falstaff, apparently did not sing; but both singing and acting were effective. The work had twenty-four performances.[125]

Following this stint, the indefatigable Reynolds wrote no more operas — he resigned his post at Covent Garden in 1822 — but he produced a series of pantomimes until his death in 1841. He did not need the money: his wealth stemmed from his inheritance and his ownership of a gunpowder mill. He was certainly not admired as a writer by the literati, and Genest declared he had done more to corrupt the public taste than any other playwright. He was not proud of some of his contributions, calling his *Crusade* (Covent Garden, 1790) a "mawkish hotch-potch, a sickening melange." Morton H. Rapp, who has perused many of Reynolds's works, finds them resting on trite, melodramatic plots and stereotyped characterizations; yet he admits the playwright knew how to draw on his actors' talents. Indeed, Reynolds, like Arnold and Dibdin, had a sure grasp of what people wanted in the theatre, and for better or worse he was a force to be reckoned with in the developments of the musical stage.

ARNOLD—BISHOP

In 1810 Bishop collaborated with Arnold on his semicomic *The Maniac; or Swiss Bandetti*, produced by the Drury Lane company at the Lyceum. Arnold, as we noted above, had produced rather poor librettos set by his father in 1794 and 1796, and another set by Kelly in 1815, though all were moderately successful with audiences. In the present instance, J. D. Collier (C) found the drama had "neither prominent character, nor brilliant dialogue, neither interesting plot,[126] nor varied incident"—in short, no originality. The music was "not unworthy" of Bishop's reputation, and the overture was excellent, but some of the many songs were disappointing (the opera had twenty-five set pieces). In a brief notice, however, the *Times* disagreed on the music, which was "of a superior order"; and "the chorusses, in which modern Composers generally fail, are rich and diversified"; moreover, some of the songs had "exquisite tenderness." Hunt (E) thought Bishop's music "wasted on the most paltry songs." DuBois also criticized the drama but found the music "full of exquisite combination, science, and taste.[127] Mr. Bishop is to be envied in every thing." Genest called the piece "insipid" and an "excuse to introduce chorusses." But it had a strong cast and played twenty-six times.

GARRICK—BISHOP AND OTHERS

Garrick's *Cymon*, produced at Drury Lane in 1767 as a "domestic romance," with music by Michael Arne, was revived (Drury Lane company playing at King's Theatre) on Dec. 31, 1791. (Kelly asserted that the piece would be acceptable to Sheridan, who disliked it, only if revised as a spectacle: the theatre was then short on leading performers.) There were no reviews, and playbills indicate the music was by Shaw and Storace (there was no reference to Arne, though the production did contain much of his music); altogether there were twenty-four musical numbers.

That revival was successful, and it was again revived and adapted 1815, at Covent Garden, with nine numbers by Arne and eleven by Storace and Shaw; there were twenty-two numbers in all—some of them, including songs by Paer and Stevenson, reset by Bishop, who wrote the overture. The work still retained its character as a spectacle, and it was introduced by a ballet (TI). The *Times* thought that, "as a written composition, nothing can be much more contemptible than *Cimon*"; fortunately, "the whole weight has been thrown upon the musical composer, the scene painter, and the mechanist." The *Chronicle* thought the work was "much improved" by Bishop's contributions.

MORTON—BISHOP

Thomas Morton (c. 1764–1838), the son of a Durham county "gentleman," was brought up by his uncle after his father's untimely death. Morton was educated in Soho Square Academy under Dr. Barrow," and according to Taylor, he "was a contemporary performer with Mr. Holman, in the private plays, which at one time so much distinguished that excellent seminary" (MM, "Sketch," June 1796). Though Holman was "designed for the *church*, and Mr. Morton for the *law*," both were soon drawn to the theatre.

In 1793 Morton produced an "Interlude"—*The Children of the Wood*—at Drury Lane, with several ballads and new music composed by Dr. Arnold. This heavily sentimental and melodramatic work was enormously popular and had numerous revivals. Nevertheless, Morton did not write another musical until 1811, when he produced the melodrama *The Knight of Snowdon*, based on *The Lady of the Lake*, for Covent Garden, with music by Bishop.[128]

Concerned about early charges of plagiarism, Morton produced most of his works anonymously. In this instance, however, he ran afoul of one critic—perhaps Barnes—for adapting Scott to the stage: "Some such character it certainly was [roared the *Times*] who, conscious of no originality in himself, sought to engraft his name upon the celebrity of another. . . . The dramatist has often deviated from the story of the poem. . . . [We were] ill recompensed for the loss of [the "faithful harper's"] inspired minstrelsy, by the substitution of a bravura from the mouth of a peasant's daughter on the Highland mountains." But on the same day, J. D. Collier (C) saw it quite differently:

> With some few deviations from the original tale . . . the author has adhered with laudable fidelity to the letter of his prototype. In so doing, indeed, few will think he acted wrong, who witnessed the charming effect of the appearance on the sound of Roderick's bugle, of his martial clan concealed in the obscurity of the forest, but intent on their chieftain's call. Never did theatrical contrivance elicit a more sudden or lasting burst of admiration.

"In the musical department," he added, "it is impossible to be too lavish of praise either to the composer or the performers. The overture inspired the house with a delight which continued unimpaired to the final close of the performance."

Slightly later criticism was negative. *Bell's* thought the drama "very clumsy and inartificial; it follows the lagging course of the narrative, and forgets the distinction between action and narration." Moreover, "the dialogue is as vile as it is imprudently introduced. It is emptiness on stilts; a heavy dress of words enveloping very little sense." And Hunt, who admired Scott but deplored most melodramas, dismissed it as "being in a style somewhat more respectable than Mr. Dibdin's productions, but without the least air of novelty, like the generality of Mr. Morton's" (E, Feb. 10). Robertson, too, deviated from his criticism of Italian opera to call it a "contemptible" drama, noting that "the admirable compositions of Mr. Bishop, many of which would have done honour to Mozart, have not been able to protract its existence beyond a very limited period" (E, June 16). But all reviewers *did* agree on the effectiveness of the scenery. The opera had twenty-three performances that season and was revived in 1823, when Bishop added music from Rossini's *Donna del Lago* (LitC).

In 1816 Morton and Bishop produced a musical drama, *The Slave*—"a sort of operatic melo-drame, or colonial tragi-comedy" written for William Macready's talents (T).[129] The work generated considerable controversy among the critics as to the validity of the melodramatic sentiments expressed.

Though noting its enthusiastic reception and Macready's fine (non-singing) performance, Sterling (T) found the work much too long and "almost *unsittable*." "We must not torture the conduct of this story[130] with harsh or subtle criticism"; he added ironically: "That it is unnatural and improbable is sufficiently answered by observing, that it is a melo-drame, an opera, and romance. There is here and there a strong sentence; but the general tone of the serious language is void of elegance and strength [though] the lighter parts have some sprightliness and humour." Hunt (E) was even more negative:

> The play-going reader will see that these characters are all old acquaintances. The serious part of the piece seems compounded out of *Pizarro, Oroonoko*, and Stedman's *Travels in Surinam*; and we are reminded also of Mr. Colman's *Africans* [1808], and other productions relative to negroes and cocknies.[131] Gambia . . . is a kind of African *Rolla*,[132] as far as love and generosity are concerned. . . . The serious part [of the dialogue] consists of common-place sentiment of the most declamatory order, and would be much admired by a girl who had lived servant at a boarding-school.

Still later, the *European* agreed with Hunt: "*The Slave*, as a composition, certainly has one strong feature of *originality*; inasmuch as it is a mixture of tragedy, comedy, opera, and farce. . . . Gambia is a Black man with a white heart, full of declamatory magnanimity, which he pompously pours forth very much after the manner of the pathetically long-winded Selico in *The Africans*." The comic parts, they added, were on the whole trite and vulgar.

On the other hand, J. D. Collier (C) was moved by Morton's social theme: "The great and laudable object of the writer has been to illuminate the generous character of the African—and to place him in situations where not withstanding the disappointment of his most ardent passion, he might make sacrifices and exertions most honourably to the name of man." In this Morton had "eminently succeeded." The *Inquisitor* then got into the fray on the side of Collier, the "Noble Savage," and a full acceptance of the melodramatic mode:

> [Morton] has devoted no mean portion of his intellectual vigour to the part of Gambia, whose form he has endowed with "gigantic strength," and whose soul is elevated to spotless purity. To press a production of this eccentric turn upon the touchstone of truth and probability is to ascribe a perfection it wholly resigns, and urge an ordeal it is entitled to evade. . . . The "Slave" is clearly a better play, in its kind, than any we have had occasion to review.

On the music, however, the press generally agreed, except for Hunt. Sterling thought the songs well written and admired the music by Bishop (with one selection from Boieldieu): the opening quartet was "finely harmonized," "The Mocking Bird" was a "charming bravura," and the final "Sons of Freedom" chorus was most effective. Collier concurred, adding that the finale of the first act was "worthy of Mozart," though in one song, "Wellington," "with recitative of a mixed kind . . . from the heroic to the tender, . . . the transition was too rapid for effect." The *Inquisitor* and *European* also praised Bishop, but Hunt demurred:

> [The music] is not without knowledge, nor unpleasing; but if [Bishop] continues to produce no better, he will not have performed the promise of his youth. There is a sort of small and cold science about his style, which consciously or unconsciously endeavours to conceal its real want of expression, by running to extremes; and the consequence is a fondness for coarse contrast;—he thinks he must shew his sense of every violent and every gentle word that comes across him by an excess of vigour and tenderness; which is as almost absurd in it's way as the man who accompanied the line about "through the long space of ten revolving years," with an action suitable, as he thought, to every word, holding up his finger for "ten," and twisting them round for "revolving."

The critics agreed on the excellence of the cast and the production. The work proved very popular, with thirty-two performances and revivals as late as 1822. In a rare "Review of Music" of the 1817 revival, the *British Stage* gave Bishop very high praise.[133]

In 1820 Bishop composed songs for Morton's final musical romance,

Henri Quatre, which received good notices and ran twenty-eight times, but the musical portion was even more slender than in his other pieces. Morton continued to write for the stage until 1830.

COLMAN (THE YOUNGER) – BISHOP

Among Bishop's later collaborators was Colman, who waited many years to produce another opera following his successes with Arnold (1784–93), Storace (1796), and Kelly (1798–1806). Their collaboration was the musical drama, *The Law of Java*, which opened at Covent Garden in 1822, but its success was marginal, and critics were generally unhappy with the playwright's latest contribution. The *London* took the occasion for a brief reassessment of the playwright: "When George Colman was truly George Colman the younger, he was one of the pleasantest men alive; witty, inventive, original! ... The peculiar forte of George Colman lay in his combination of extravagancies of character, in his *breadth* of humorous dialogue, and in his improbable but laughable situations." But they noted "one species of Drama for which George Colman has a strong predilection, and which we do not very greatly admire, and that is, the sentimental, half humorous, and half musical play," which they blamed on his former ownership of the Little Theatre: "The anxiety to include all the talent of a theatre, must, we conjecture, have been the origin of this grasping and unnatural style of writing." A miscellany of actors "were in the receipt of salaries, and might as well be employed to the utmost, and therefore, desperate blank verse and broad humorous prose were jumbled together to allow of this assemblage of tragic and comic actors on the stage at once." The *Law of Java*, they concluded, fell in this category, as did most of his operas. It "is a musical, serio-comic piece, in three acts, with very many characters, and few incidents. In humour, in spirit, in originality, it is decidedly unfit to be named with the previous works of its author, and we should have been glad to see it published with another name."

Critic Q (E) also thought the tale was not a story for Colman and the work would "bring no sort of accession" to his reputation, though, as a melodrama – "which usually implies extravagant incident and a license to dispense with very nice attention to verisimilitude" – it was "agreeably to the style of the times."

The *Champion* admired Bishop's music, but the *Examiner* thought its "claim is not of the highest order for *him*, either as to taste or originality," though they noted "a passable air or two." The *Gazette* was also unimpressed; the music was a "little less barbarous than the Law of Java itself." All agreed the performances were superior. The opera played eleven times.

DIBDIN—BISHOP

Another of the older playwrights who worked with Bishop was Thomas Dibdin, whose opera *Zuma* was mounted at Covent Garden in 1818—his only work written with this composer. Already discussed were Dibdin's earlier successes with an array of musical collaborators in some seven productions between 1789 and 1806. Considering the rather light character of these earlier productions, it is astonishing to find him now writing a *serious* opera.[134] In his preface to the printed play and in his *Reminiscences*, Dibdin complained about changes in the drama required by Bishop to permit insertions of bravuras and concerted numbers.[135] The reviewers anticipated these complaints. Sterling (T), noting that the work had been "long in preparation," asserted: "As drama, the piece abounds with defects, some radical, others incidental," and one incident "was so palpably absurd, that the indignation of the audience nearly brought the opera to an abrupt termination." Further, "scenes requiring great pathos and power of acting are thrown upon a class of performers who are accustomed to delight us by efforts of a different kind." (This last comment reflects the thinness of the singing casts, as more nonsingers were required for the increasing popularity of melodramas.)

J. D. Collier also dismissed the drama, but Bacon (LG), noting these problems, asserted: "We acknowledge the superiority [of the drama] to most of the things which the name of opera shrouds from criticism under the protection of contempt." For *Zuma* "stands on honourable grounds, without trick, and is at least honestly dull, if dull that can be called, which, to an agreeable plot,[136] and unaffected dialogue, superadds admirable scenery, and the finest music, taken as a whole, which we have heard in this century! . . . [It was] not without scientific ornaments; but free from that taudry overloading, which fritters away the soul of melody in the dilemmas of execution." Both Collier and Sterling concurred on the music, which contained songs by Braham[137] and possessed "considerable merit," especially the concerted pieces and choruses; one air borrowed by Braham— "Aux armes, mes citoyens," the "Marsellaise Hymn"—was encored twice (T).[138] The *Inquisitor* added: "The chorus of friars and nuns, beginning '*Daughter of error, hear,*' was as fine as any we ever heard. . . . The subdued voices of the choristers gradually increasing to a flood of harmony, was in the happiest and most elevated style of that great musician, Bishop." But with the public the music could not compensate for a dull drama; the opera played only six times.

DIBDIN—PERRY

More typical of the playwright was the comic opera *Morning, Noon and Night*, which Dibdin wrote in 1822 for the Little Theatre, with music by Perry. George Frederick Perry (1793–1862), an English composer, sang early in a Norwich choir; studied piano, violin, and composition; and (c. 1818) became leader of the band at the Norwich Theatre-Royal. In 1822 he came to London as music director of the Little Theatre. Aside from several works for the stage, he wrote some oratorios, *The Death of Abel* being the most successful.

For Dibdin, Sterling (T) had some left-handed compliments:

> No man makes up a better bill than Mr. Dibdin; his characters have good names, even if, like modern sign-boards, they have nothing left to them but the names. Then his dialogue will not bear even the touch of criticism; and his incidents generally set common sense as well as probability at defiance. But, with all this, he knows what will do with an audience. He cares little about the means, so that the end be success.

The plot, which was "two-fold, as a plot in an opera ought to be," was "too intricate" to detail. The *Chronicle* and the *Literary Chronicle* agreed, the latter noting how well the characters accorded with the talents of the performers. And the *London* called the piece "nothing more than the residue of some half a dozen former plays that have been melted down for the purpose, and remoulded. It is a piece of lively absurdity, often whimsical, and never dull, dulness being by no means a vice of Mr. Dibdin. . . . There is, besides, . . . a continual change from grave to gay, from dialogue to action, and from both to music." The *Examiner* concurred.

Sterling reported that Perry's music "amounts to something very like a failure. There is not an original air of even moderate value"; the *Examiner* agreed: "Nothing, indeed, sounded original from beginning to end."[139] The work had a good production and played twelve times.

Though Dibdin occasionally continued to write for the majors, his main effort, after 1814, was directed toward the minors, especially the Surrey, of which he became manager that year and for which he produced an enormous number of burlettas, melodramas, spectacles, operatic farces, burlesques, and the like. In 1823 the *Literary Chronicle* noted of the Surrey: "The activity, if not the genius, of Tom Dibdin, still presides over this favourite theatre" (Apr. 5). But about that time he left its management after losing £18,000, which he blamed on competition from the Royal Coburg

Theatre. He also got in trouble with the managements of Drury Lane and the Little Theatre over his *Morning, Noon and Night*, the remuneration for which ended in legal arbitration, and he was even briefly imprisoned. In 1827 his *Reminiscences* were called "two volumes of rubbish" by an *Atlas* reviewer (May 6), though he went on to quote quite a few "amusing" anecdotes from it. No doubt Dibdin's dramatic material was exceedingly thin, as his critics complained, but he had an uncanny sense of the theatrical and knew how to deliver what the broad public demanded for its entertainment.

DIMOND—BISHOP/REEVE

Another of the older playwrights Bishop worked with at Covent Garden was William Dimond, who, as we have noted, wrote several mostly successful operas with Kelly beginning in 1803. In 1815 he collaborated with Bishop and W. Reeve to produce a "slender" two-act operatic farce, *Brother and Sister*, for which C. I. M. Dibdin wrote the lyrics. Both play and music were given only mild praise, but the work was well produced and played seventeen times.

Not until 1824, however, did Dimond and Bishop produce another musical—this time a domestic opera, *Native Land, or The Return from Slavery*. Sterling (T) found its plot[140] "not unsuited to opera, for it is not so interesting as to make the introduction of songs seem impertinent, nor so vapid as to compel the audience absolutely to yawn in the intervals of music." Critic Q (E) thought the dialogue, "if not brilliant or pointed," was "easy and spontaneous . . . and, strange to say, there is poetry in the songs"; but others (LM; NM) thought them "absolute nonsense." With respect to the drama, the *London* confessed: "We have not been so pleased for many a day," and the other monthlies were supportive with the exception of Ayrton, who found the work "not very powerfully written, nor abounding in interest."

There were mixed feelings about the music, much of which Bishop had borrowed from several Rossini operas. "The 'music' is announced to be by Mr. Bishop; 'the selections' from Rossini; but to say the truth, we believe that most of the pieces, by whatever name called, may be traced to the work of that composer" (T). Ayrton also noticed this peculiar attribution, snarling: "Are we therefore to conclude that Signor's compositions are not music?" Critic Q (E) found Bishop's music "decidedly modeled upon [Rossini's] style, and that with no inadequate mastery," while the selections[141] "were highly judicious." And Thomas Noon Talfourd (NM) noted that Sinclair's songs were "well adapted" to his powers.

But Ayrton found Bishop's music "altogether heavy; and, with two or three exceptions, [it] has nothing to very much animate an audience"; yet he highly praised his "Is't art, I pray, or nature" as "most original," and a duet, "Lo! when showers descending," which was "exceedingly beautiful" and "another proof of the merit of these compositions which we affect to despise." However, the selections—from *Ricciardo, Donna del Lago,* and *Turco in Italia*—were "not very handsomely treated. It is said that [Rossini] went to hear it, and hardly recognized himself. The romance, 'Aurora, ah Sorgerai!' [from *Lago*] now set to the words 'Farewell! thou coast of glory!' is sung like a jig, though the movement is marked by the word *andantino*."

The press was generally effusive over the production and performances. The work was repeated twenty times and was revived four years later, when Ayrton still called it a "feeble opera." But Hunt thought it worth going to see "for those who care little about plot or dialogue," and he asserted: "It is seldom that any of Mr. Bishop's music is not worth hearing" (*Companion*, Jan. 16). Genest, *mirabile dictu*, thought the work "very superior," presumably because the drama observed the unities.

DIMOND—COOKE

For his productions at Drury Lane, Dimond turned to other composers. One of these was Thomas Simpson Cooke (1782–1848), an Irish tenor, instrumentalist, and composer, who studied under his father, Bartlett Cooke, an oboe player at the Smock Alley Theatre in Dublin. For several years, beginning at age fifteen we are told, Thomas was leader of the band at Crow Street Theatre in Dublin. There he "became an occasional actor at his own benefits, in comic pieces, most of which were of his own production," in which he was very successful" (TI, June 1814, pp. 240f.).[142]

In 1813 he sang at the English Opera House and in 1815 at Drury Lane, where he filled tenor parts for some twenty years (see appendix 19). This precocious and versatile musician who could play many instruments, served as leader of the band at Drury Lane from 1823 to 1828, as music manager for Vauxhall Gardens from 1828 to 1830, and later led the Philharmonic and Concert of Ancient Music orchestras. He was also an outstanding singing teacher, counting Ann Maria Tree and Miss Povey among his pupils.

As a composer he did not have the stature of Bishop, though he probably stands above most other theatre composers of this period and seems to have served Drury Lane in a capacity similar to Bishop's at Covent Garden. Even by 1814 his compositions were "esteemed among the best productions of the time; and in all the arrangements of harmony that require the superintending hand of skill and taste, there is scarcely a master or professor more competent than Mr. Cooke. [In sum,] so great a stock of musical knowledge and taste—so capable a voice, and so good a conception, have very seldom fitted any man besides Mr. Cooke for eminence in the Operatic Drama" (TI). His first operas for the London stage date from 1815 and continue beyond 1830. He had so many collaborators, however, that even apart from his singing, it will be necessary to follow the thread of his theatrical music through the works of several dramatists.

Cooke's first effort for Dimond appeared in 1822, in a musical drama, *The Pirate*, at Drury Lane. The Honorable George Lambe[143] was one of the compilers. Though "not in any sense an Opera" (E), it is of interest as another adaptation from Scott's novel, "still wet from the press" (T). (Two other versions were already on the boards of the minors!) On the whole, the critics thought the work much too serious, though the selection of characters and incidents was "judicious."

Sterling (T) found "some merit" in Cooke's songs, "but they are too elaborate: in the chorusses he is more successful. We wish he would abandon the wretched taste of constructing an overture out of a medley of Scotch airs. He ranks as a musician, and should have some value for reputation." Critic Q (E) also thought the music—"chiefly selected"—had merit. But the *European* pointed out that the Opera Book attributed "She who walks round ring of green" to Cooke, whereas it was borrowed from Winter's *Proserpina*, which "naturally throws some slur upon the authenticity of the others." The production was only mediocre and the work just managed to succeed.

DIMOND—COOKE/BRAHAM/STORACE

Much more operatic was Dimond's comic opera *Isidore and Merida*, produced in 1827. Dimond wrote a new book for it based on Cobb's *Pirates* (1792). (The reviewers of the original production, it will be recalled, did not think much of the Cobb libretto, but they admired the Italian opera style of the work.) The new work retained some of Storace's music and included borrowings from Mercadante and Balducci as well as new songs composed by Cooke and Braham.

Sterling (T, Nov. 30) declared: "The opera is exceeding heavy, we would almost say stupid; and to be endured must be cut down by an unsparing hand" (it was). He protested "against a tissue of naked absurdities" and found the dialogue equally inferior. Other critics agreed, some recalling that Cobb's dramas had been thought inferior.[144]

Regarding the music, there were some differences. Sterling complained of having no guide to the "profusion of music." "In some of the tender, as well as lively airs, we recognized Storace," and "from their ballad-like simplicity," they suspected the songs were by Braham," while "the frequent appeal to the trumpet and drum, reminded us very strongly of Mr. T. Cooke"; he found the latter's overture "so noisy, that we think even a deaf man could hear it." Ayrton added more details:

> Of Storace's share, we can only speak in high terms of praise, regretting at the same time that more of his compositions are not retained. Mr. Braham has, of course, consulted his own powers in the pieces he has written for himself. . . . Mr. Cooke has been occupied, chiefly in augmenting the accompaniments to the original music, and in bringing to its aid instruments which either were not in the orchestra, or in a most imperfect state, thirty years ago.

He also regretted "the want of a good bass." But Holmes (At) was acerbic:

> Although we know three out of the five [composers] to be as arrant botchers as ever laboured at theatrical journey-work, we will not blame any one of these for making an unconnected piece, in which, after all, they may appear as involuntary contributors. In this light must certainly be considered "the potent, grace, and revered signors;" and as for Mr. Braham and Mr. T. Cooke, as we cannot make an affidavit, or take our corporal oath of the movements they have supplied, we are at a loss how or where to give our judicial thrust.

And he concluded: "We wish there were fewer pieces in one key (C) in this Opera; and also that the ingenious drum behind the scenes were avoided, or at least screwed up to key, and not left to beat an unresolved seventh in the bass."[145] All were agreed on the fine performances and scenery. The opera was repeated eighteen times.

DIMOND—LIVERATI/LEE

In 1829 Dimond produced *The Nymph of the Grotto* at Covent Garden with music by Liverati (whose music, it will be recalled, was not much appreciated at the King's) and George Alexander Lee.[146] It did quite well despite some negative reviews. The *Examiner* found in it "not a particle" of wit, and the *Times* thought the dialogue "sad trash," while the dramatic material was "slender"—but, they added, "the acquaintance of the author with the business of the stage has enabled him to give dramatic effect to the various parts."

They also found the music by both composers "agreeable, but by no means striking," while others thought it "commonplace" (At) and "below mediocrity" (LG), and the *Examiner* "had hoped much better things of Liverati." The scenery and dresses were, however, "magnificent," and they no doubt contributed to the work's success.

Dimond's stage productions (two others are discussed below as English adaptations) virtually ceased by 1830. Heavily committed to English opera of all types, he probably contributed more to melodrama after 1800 than any other dramatist. Reviewers generally had little praise for his language, though they admitted his skill in play construction, and Nicoll noted that this "energetic purveyor" of operas observed the unities.

PLANCHÉ—BISHOP

Among the younger playwrights who worked with Bishop and who also made operatic adaptations of Scott was James Robinson Planché (1796–1880), son of a watchmaker descendant of Huguenot refugees. Privately educated, he was articled to a bookseller, but early turned to amateur acting in a private theatre. At age twenty-one he produced his first stage work at Drury Lane—a burlesque with music by Cooke—and its success launched him on a career as dramatist, for both majors and minors, that lasted into the 1850s and comprised an enormous outpouring of works for the stage (in 1830 he became manager of Adelphi Theatre, which he shared with Vestris in 1831). He must have had some musical training, for at one time he supervised musical arrangements for Vauxhall. Indeed, the great majority of his productions up to 1840 were operas and musical pieces of all types. In addition he developed a strong interest in stage costuming: his production of *King John* in 1823 was influential for the display of his research into historical costuming, and he produced a book on the subject in 1834.

His first work with Bishop was the opera *Maid Marian*, produced at Covent Garden in 1822. The dramatization was based on Thomas Love Peacock's novel of that name. The work drew mixed reviews. Critic Q (E) was quite positive: "We never witnessed a more easy and felicitous assumption of the mirthful tone of the old ballads than the frisky narrative of Mr. Peacock, . . . and Mr. Planché has contrived, in many respects, to preserve the spirit of the tale." And Talfourd (NM) was jubilant: "Its subject seems the fittest for an Opera, which could possibly be chosen. It is the most purely romantic of English stories. . . . The very tale seems as if it would start into music." The *Chronicle* agreed: "Its merits are upon the whole of an order superior" to those in the usual musical piece.

The *Herald* tended to concur, yet thought such a story "loses all its attractions when it is presented on the stage." And Sterling found it "exceedingly languid, except where Friar Tuck, or Baron Fitzwater, is actively employed." He noted "a large portion of playful political satire; from which it is easy to gather that the author is not, on the one hand, a friend of those 'Holy Alliances'[147] which have for their object the destruction of popular rights, nor, on the other, to that wild revolutionary spirit, which would sweep away all distinction between *meum* and *tuum*." The *Gazette* also thought it went over "rather flatly." Hood and his "bold men and true" are "like eagles caged—or as chained lions, when penned within the petty limits of a theatre"; "the characters came poorly off—and the interest continually flagged almost to the Opera's destruction."

Accordingly, some reviewers had more than usual interest in the music. The *Chronicle* merely thought it good vintage Bishop, though they decried the "extravagant use" of drums and trumpets. But the *Herald* heard nothing "very striking or original. Many of the songs were elaborate, and calculated to give a high idea of the composer's science; but there was evidently no effort made to give a predominant character to the music." Moreover, Bishop drew "liberally" on his own previous compositions. Nevertheless, several of the songs "possess no ordinary merit."[148] Sterling (T) agreed, but added a perceptive comment that the music was "not at all in unison with the character of the piece," and "an ambitious display of science is almost everywhere observable."

The *Examiner* and the *Gazette* noted Bishop's borrowings from himself: "Potatoes are excellent; but potatoes and salt for breakfast—potatoes and butter for dinner—and even the change to mashed potatoes and milk for supper, is too much of a good thing" (LG). But again Talfourd was most supportive: "It is good . . . to have the powers of Bishop, incomparably the first of our leading composers, employed on such a subject; and never perhaps were they put forth with more spirit or success. In the gentle breathings of the love-lorn damsel; in her wilder notes stealing from the recesses of the forest, and in the carols of the merry outlaws, he has been almost equally happy."

All concurred on the fine scenery, especially in the banquet scene, which was really "too magnificent for its age" (E), and some noted the excellent costumes but did not remark on their historical accuracy. The opera proved a hit, with twenty-seven performances. Even Genest thought the drama "better than average," while Parke reported "the whole of the music highly meritorious." Loewenberg calls it one of Bishop's best works.

These confreres continued the following year with a musical drama, *Cortez*, in which the chief feature of the production was the introduction of daring horsemanship on the stage of Covent Garden (done in response to a similar recent experiment by its rival). The *Chronicle* wrote that the work "combin[ed] in itself the qualities of melo-drame and serious opera.

... The incidents of the drama[149] are contrived to keep up a constant anxiety for the fate of the principal personages," and "the language affords many opportunities for good declamation, and is altogether executed in a better style than we are accustomed to meet in productions of the same class." But the *Herald* saw "no interest whatever" in the story and was uphappy with the bombastic speeches; the *Gazette* also found the language trite. The *Examiner* thought the "meagre" story was well constructed but admitted they had a "very sovereign contempt" for this "class" of spectacle. The wit of the *London*'s critic was the most telling: "Plot-writing is not particularly our forte, [especially] the dry task of detailing the incidents upon which a modern drama is constructed. A little patriotism — a hair-breadth escape — a heap of love — a battle and a burnt castle — and you have 'a grand romantic play!' The heroes must slap their hearts every five minutes — and the heroines lay their hands upon their left sides, and sing!" Talfourd (NM) agreed the *drama* deserved "little praise," though "as an opera *Cortez* deserves great praise."

With the last comment, most of the press concurred. For example, the *Chronicle* declared that the music "constitutes so remarkable a feature, that even if in other respects the drama was chargeable with deficiency, its success would be insured by the power of harmony alone." The *Gazette* concurred, adding that "the concerted pieces, which are in [Bishop's] very best style," deserved special praise. The *Examiner*, was also impressed, and the *London* averred: "Mr. Bishop revels in the pleasures of tasteful compilation." Ayrton had his kindest words yet for the composer:

> The music is of a superior kind, and announces in every part the scientific composer, — his knowledge of the human voice, — his skill in employing the various instruments of the orchestra, and his thorough acquaintance with the greatest works of the best schools: but it is not music of a popular kind; not a single piece is encored; not one air is carried out of the theatre to haunt the imagination for the next fortnight: the opera has more of knowledge and study in it than fancy, and is addressed rather to the judgment of those who are learned in the art, than to the ear of the multitude, which can only receive impressions from striking melody.

The highest plaudits went to the singing and to the spectacular scenic effects, though some reviewers were disgusted with the on-stage horsemanship. The opera had only twelve performances — probably representing a failure for so expensive a production — followed by five more in a two-act version. Geṇest called it "far from a bad" opera, though "written for horses." Loewenberg calls it a "signal failure despite Bishop's music," but in view of Ayrton's criticism, we must ask whether it was a failure *because* of the music.

After writing several librettos for other composers, Planché returned to Bishop in 1827 for a Little Theatre production of *The Rencontre*, in two acts, printed as a comic opera but designated as a vaudeville (T; E) or as an operatic comedy (At) by the press. Sterling (T) thought the story, evidently a translation, "could not have been more intricate, or more unconveyable. The people of the *dramatis personae* never once know who they are, or each who the other is, for any two minutes consecutively through the piece; and the audience begin to have doubts as to their own identity before the conclusion." Yet it was "bustling and various, and seldom tedious, though now and then extravagant," and there were "touches of point here and there in the dialogue." Most reviewers were delighted with the play; Ayrton observed: "It is one of the pleasantest things we ever saw at this house."

Sterling thought Bishop's music "very light and dramatic in its effect, if not of very highly original character," and many pieces, including the overture, were encored. But Ayrton reported Bishop "has not exerted his talents on the present occasion; except a short trio, we cannot mention anything in the piece worthy of his name." (One song, composed and sung by G. Lee, was encored.) The acting and singing were splendid, however, and the little piece chalked up fifty-nine performances.

PLANCHÉ—LIVERATI

In 1828 Planché attempted a serious opera called *Carron Side*, produced in two acts at Covent Garden, with music by Liverati. It, too, was adapted from a French source—Louis Hérold's opera *Marie* (LitC). Sterling declared it "a production of the kind which are sometimes called operas at our national theatres, but which resemble much more what our neighbors call *vaudeville*.... The incidents of the piece are wove in a manner so skilful as to excite an uninterrupted interest throughout." The *Gazette* thought the plot and incidents "far superior" to the usual opera vehicle, and the songs "are not only beautiful, but full of ... Scots character."[150] For the *Examiner* the dialogue and songs were only "tolerable," but Talfourd (NM) found the work "as pretty a little opera as we have heard for a long time on the English stage: gentle but not dull; with songs in Mr. Planché's neatest style," though some "might have a more direct connexion with the business of the scene"—something "the poet ought never to lose sight of."

Liverati's music—not much admired at the King's—came into its own here. Sterling (T) wrote:

> The music, with which it is abundantly interspersed, is composed by Signor Liverati, who has found it necessary to adapt its composition to the style of Scotch melody, inasmuch as the scene is supposed to be in Scotland. But Signor Liverati has, nevertheless, combined the elegance of the Italian style with the simplicity of Scotch melody, in a manner which we would have supposed to be hardly practical. Without great pretensions to science, it is very ably written, and there is no part of it which is not extremely pleasing.

Its merits were "greatly enhanced" by the performers. The *Gazette* declared the songs "would long be favourites at the pianoforte." Hazlitt (At), too, called Liverati a "skilled musician" but found the music much borrowed. Critic Z—Italian opera reviewer of the *New Monthly*—was, however, most effusive:

> The Scottish part of Signor Liverati's music is as truly Scotch as if it came from the north of the Tweed. The mixture of this style amidst a great proportion of genuine Italian strains, certainly imparts variety to the whole. . . . [Yet] we should have been better pleased if the *whole* of the music had been written in the manner of the Italian school. . . .
> The overture . . . is extremely clever and ingenious. A variety of the subjects in the opera are successively introduced, and linked together with much skill. . . . As to the songs, duets, and concerted pieces, we have listened to them more than once with the highest gratification.[151]

The performances were very fine, but the opera played only seven times, perhaps in part owing to the lateness of the season. In any event, Liverati obviously deserved much credit for his skillful blending of English and Italian musical sources in a production that approached the operatic. Planché was more successful in providing some English adaptations of foreign operas, which are considered below.

TERRY—BISHOP/ATTWOOD/DAVY/WHITTAKER/COOKE

Among the newer playwrights Bishop worked with was Daniel Terry (c. 1780–1829), more actor than playwright. He was educated in a private school and studied under Samuel Wyatt, an architect, but was persuaded to join an acting company under the elder William Macready at Sheffield. At Edinburgh his acting came to the attention of Scott, who wrote some prologues for him. He came to the Little Theatre in 1812, and from 1813 to 1822 acted at Covent Garden, where he made a "graceful figure with a strong, clear voice" and could act "anything but lovers" (D.N.B.). After a quarrel with the management, he performed at Drury Lane from 1822 to 1825; he was also briefly acting manager at the Little and Adelphi theatres, retiring about 1825 due to ill health. He was a strong Tory supporter in 1820 and became a close friend of Scott, who found his architectural knowledge useful in building Abbotsford.

Terry had only a handful of dramatic productions, most written with the help of others. His first, *Guy Mannering*, a melodrama, was written in collaboration with Scott himself and was produced in 1816; this followed by five years Morton's successful *Knight of Snowdon*. Further adaptations of Scott included Pocock's *Rob Roy Macgregor* in 1818, Beazeley's *Ivanhoe* in 1820, Planché's *Maid Marian* in 1822, Pocock's *Peveril of the Peak* in 1826, and Lacy's *Maid of Judah* in 1829.[152]

For *Guy Mannering* Bishop wrote the overture, opening glee and chorus, gypsy solo and chorus, and finale and chorus; additional songs were contributed by Attwood,[153] Davy, John Whittaker,[154] and Cooke. Sterling (T), noting the crowded theatre, asserted that "the name of 'Guy Mannering,' prefixed to a six-penny ballad, would necessarily attract a multitude of readers"; yet no stage presentation of this work could capture "even a faint resemblance to that fervid and ungovernable interest which agitates us through so many pages of the history itself." For example, Meg Merrilies is a creature "impassioned, awful, and irresistible; . . . she borders on the supernatural" and could not be embodied on the stage. The *Champion*, on the other hand, called it "one of the most interesting pieces brought forward of late years." The Dutch character of Hutteralek was "a creature altogether as wild and turbulent as the element on which he lives.—The odd native of the Dutch, English and Scotch language in this character, adds much to its ruggedness." But the "strange and mysterious Meg Merrilies" was the finest character, and "Mr. Terry has certainly succeeded in securing all the interest of the piece, as far as incidents go."

In its "Review of Music," the *Inquisitor* (p. 453) gave trite praise to all the songs,[155] and, of Davy, asked: "Why does he not write more?" Yet reviewers said remarkably little about the music. The *Champion* reviewer, who called it a "musical play," stated: "The music in this play should have been old Scotch airs, than which nothing can be sweeter."

Not only was the opera a hit with eighteen performances, it went into the repertory with frequent revivals at least through 1830. Braham wrote additional music for the 1817 revival, but the "choral beauties" were "barbarously mangled by the paucity and incompetence of the singers" (TI). In April 1819 the *Inquisitor* admitted they "never did greatly admire" the opera. But in October of that year, Drury Lane, in what seems to be an unprecedented maneuver, brought out substantially if not identically the same opera! It seems odd that this astonishing development did not elicit some comment from reviewers, for the majors were highly protective of their properties—especially their hits—and Drury Lane must have forfeited some important tradeoff to its rival in property or performers to acquire the right. Both theatres continued their revivals, Covent Garden's in 1826 and 1827, and Drury Lane's in 1822, 1825, 1828 and 1830 (most of these reviews discussed only the performances).

Terry wrote another musical drama based on Scott's *Heart of Mid-Lothian*, in 1819, but it had little music. In 1818 he also wrote, with John Fawcett, *The Barber of Seville*, which is discussed below.

Guy Mannering was one of the last operas for which Davy composed songs. In *Rob Roy Macgregor* (1818) by Issac Pocock,[156] his music was "selected and harmonized with great taste" (T) and "possessed considerable merit" (C). In *Woman's Will*,[157] his last opera, the music was distinguished "by much bold and original composition." Peake called him an "original composer, on whose melodies subsequent aspirants have worked." In his obituary the *Harmonicon* wrote that his works, though few, "display great talent," and they cited "Just like love," "The Smuggler," "May we ne'er want a friend," and "Bay of Biscay" among his best-known songs. Not only did Davy, though only fifty-nine, outlive the rest of his family, but "owing to an habitual improvidence, the too frequent attendant on genius, poor Davy died in extreme indigence, without sufficient funds to defray the expenses of his funeral."

ANONYMOUS—HORN/BRAHAM/ATTWOOD

In 1821 Horn and Braham produced *Dirce*, an all-sung opera, at Drury Lane. The playbills announced that the work "was brought forward with a view of rendering serious recitative opera a popular species of amusement in England" (DM). Needless to say, it failed. The libretto was a translation, by an unknown hand, of Metastasio's *Demofoonte*, which, as we have seen, had many Italian opera settings. Horn made the musical selections and adaptations from Mozart, Rossini, "and other composers of eminence," including Pleyel's "German Hymn" and an overture by one Vogel (Johann Christoph?). Three of the songs were by Attwood, and both Horn and Braham contributed original songs, with Horn, presumably, writing the recitative.[158]

The *Gazette*, though citing it as a novelty, oddly enough made no mention of recitative; they thought "the whole performance creditable to the actors and the arranger, Mr. Horn." Kenrick (BS) reported the audience seemed to think the story "a dull piece of business, and which scarcely fifty of them perhaps comprehended," while the words of the songs "are sad stuff." Moreover, the translater introduced absurdities "for which Metastasio is not answerable." But they did enjoy much of the music. "The species of performance cannot, however, we are persuaded, ever become permanently attractive at the English Theatres. It has often been tried [since Thomas Clayton's time]; but has never retained possession of the Stage, except in a single instance" (i.e., *Artaxerxes*).

Nevertheless, Bacon, in his "Report of Music" for the *London*, did his best to champion the cause of sung recitative in English opera (further discussed in "Themes and Currents"), concluding that: "At present, the ears of an English audience are not reconciled to recitative, and Poor *Dirce* passed from life to death without distinction, and almost without notice." The opera had a good roster of singers—both composers singing the leading male roles—and even a good production, but it played only seven nights.[159]

This failure may not have come as a disappointment in Horn's career as a song composer; as noted earlier, criticism of his songs for Burges's *Tricks upon Travellers* (1810), Arnold's *Devil's Bridge* (1812), and Thompson's *Godolphin* (1813) ranged from mixed to devastating. Yet songs of his continued to appear in such marginally operatic productions as Hamilton's *Elphi Bey* (1813), Beazley's *Philandering* (1824), Kenney's *Wedding Present* (1825), and Pocock's *Peveril of the Peak* (1826). He fared somewhat better as a singer.

PAYNE—BISHOP

In 1823 Bishop composed his only opera for John Howard Payne (1791–1852), born in New York City, the first American actor and dramatist to attract attention in Europe. Precocious, he was writing five-act plays as well as theatrical criticism in New York by 1805, and he acted there, as well as in Baltimore and Philadelphia, from 1809 to 1812. In the latter year, admirers raised a purse of $2,000 for one year of theatrical experience in London, where he stayed from 1813 to 1832. His seventeen London productions, mostly for the majors, stretch from 1816 to 1832. His only tragedy, *Brutus* (1818), with Keane, was highly successful, but most of his plays were farces, comedies, and melodramas; he wrote two operas as well. He also was an editor of *The Opera Glass* (LitC, Jan. 6, 1827). Nevertheless, his later career was a disappointment, and he finally abandoned the stage altogether.

Payne's first opera (musical drama would have been more appropriate) was *Clari*,[160] a strongly melodramatic story based on his own translation of Marmontel's *Laurette*. The *Herald* had no reservations in its admiration of the dramatic situations and found "a great deal of merit" in the opera. The *Chronicle* noted that the plot,[161] "extremely simple, was also without any pretension to originality, but . . . is full of interest, and though in some parts the dialogue hangs rather heavy, the situations soon awaken the attention." Sterling, less pleased, complained that the melodramatic "distress" was presented "not in dumb show, as on the French stage, but in words fairly and seriously drawn out." Critic Q (E) and Talfourd (NM) were supportive, but the *London* quite condemned it:

> A serious opera from the French is a serious evil. The light gossamer pieces which are woven from that source, on sultry summer nights, look bright and glittering for their hour, and then pass away. But a long solemn heavy drama of three acts, as long as Jenkinson's legs . . . is too much. We can cry our eyes out with any gentlemen living, for three quarters of an hour, at a murder miraculously discovered by a brace of ravens flying over the ruffian's head on the night of Easter Monday, when he has his best clothes on; and can damp as many white pocket handkerchiefs as our betters, at the girl and the spoon, where she is involved in trouble by the natural means of a magpie, who puts the spoon in the spout of the church, until * * *. When the extravagance and pestilent pathos of the French come to be forced upon us for three hours, we beg leave to dry our eyes, pocket our cambric buckets— button up our pockets, and protest as stoutly as we can, against our tears and our money being so plentifully drawn upon.

There were mixed views on the music. The *Chronicle* found little to applaud in it, while Sterling thought Bishop had "judiciously refrained from expending any of his happiest compositions; for, with the exception of ["Sweet Home"], there is not one piece which will linger on the ear." And Ayrton considered the music "unentitled to praise, for it possesses nothing that is distinguished by originality of conception, ingenuity of adaptation, or elegance of effect." The music critic of the *London* noted that "Sweet Home" was "the counterpart of a ballad published by Mr. Parry seven or eight years ago,"[162] and that the opera "does not exhibit one single trait that has not been produced and reproduced over and over again."

On the other hand, the *Gazette* thought it one of Bishop's best compositions, for "there is much variety in the Airs and Choruses, and some of the melodies are uncommonly pleasing." The *Examiner* even found the overture "spirited, without being deeply impressive, and there is much rich combination in the harmonies and accompaniments." A serenade for male quartet was "exceedingly beautiful," as was the "Sweet Home" air. There were also mixed views on the performances, though some singing was praised—Ann Marie Tree was said to have "saved" the piece—and the scenery was splendid. The opera played twelve times and had a revival in

1830. On that occasion Hunt wrote in the *Tatler*: "From the long run it has had, we expected to find *Clari* a better piece than it is, in point of writing. But it has its merits, and those of a popular kind, — appeals to the strongest domestic feelings; and the beautiful air of *Home, Sweet Home*, is worth going to hear, though for the hundredth time" (Sept.15).[163]

SOANE—BISHOP

The success of a large number of English adaptations of foreign operas — some with recitative — encouraged Bishop, in 1826, to bring out his only all-sung opera, *Aladdin*, at Drury Lane, with a libretto by George Soane. (Following disputes with the management, Bishop had deserted Covent Garden at the end of the 1823–24 season.) It was over a year in preparation (EM) and had been commissioned by Robert Elliston, assistant manager, for the theatre; it was intended to compete with Weber's *Oberon* at Covent Garden (see below).

George Soane (1790–1866), son of Sir John Soane, an architect, was a graduate of Pembroke College, Cambridge. With knowledge of French, German, and Italian, he made a number of translations for the stage between 1815 and 1848, including several operas. But the *Inquisitor*'s profile of him in 1820 referred to his many bitter disappointments as a dramatist and cited his plays as "strong and strange examples of wanton perversion, or boundless audacity, and of limited power" (Apr.).

The libretto — "one of the most hackneyed stories, not possessing many dramatic capabilities" — did little for the work; it was characterized by the "hungry Epsom prose" of the dialogue and the "namby-pamby nothingness of the songs" (C), and it was "too contemptible for the lowest booth in Bartholomew fair" (T). Moreover, it was "encumbered with characters who have nothing to do but delay the progress and mar the interest of the story" (LG). The *Examiner* was "astonished [it] should be chosen as the subject matter of an effort so visibly emulative on the part of the Composer" and questioned whether "any power could utterly do away with this disadvantage."

Comparisons with the Weber work were inevitable. John Payne Collier (C) wrote: "Bishop seems to have been 'pricked on by a most emulate pride' [and his] chief error [is] that he has (perhaps unconsciously) made the laboriously scientific style of his rival the object of his imitation, instead of endeavouring to produce something essentially different" (see also appendix 2). Sterling (T), too, was disappointed in the music: despite a poor libretto, "the world of romance was open to the composer, and it was for him to give to the spirits of earth or of air — of flame or of fire — sounds as fanciful as their own creation. Mr. Bishop has not, however, travelled out of the beaten path. . . . If placed by the side of many of Mr. Bishop's preceding compositions, the music of *Aladdin* must suffer in the estimate." He did, however, take care "that the orchestral accompaniments . . . should not overpower and drown" the "human voice."

The *Gazette* found some airs to their liking but thought the performance of four hours' duration "long enough for two operas and dull enough for twenty." The *Examiner* enjoyed the overture (encored) and some numbers but felt that "the grand and highly imaginative is not the proper field of Bishop, whose power seems to be the domestic affections, or higher exhibitions of naïveté and pathos immediately connected with them." Talfourd (NM) agreed and the *European* declared the music "wholly without merit," and if this was Bishop's best effort, "he may go to sleep and make way for others." No one commented on any passages of recitative.

The production was only fair. Notwithstanding all these objections, the opera was not the "complete failure" Loewenberg claims; it managed to eke out ten performances—a very poor showing, to be sure, compared to the concurrent run of thirty-one for Weber's *Oberon*, or even the twenty-eight of the preceding run of Drury Lane's own *Oberon*. Weber, who attended the opening night, called it a very "weak affair."

Though Bishop would continue to have an important influence (Hogarth, II, 452), his reputation suffered a severe blow in the reception to *Aladdin*. If the "public deserted him" (N.G.) on this occasion, it is clear that most reviewers did also. Bacon (QMM, VIII, 140–41), however, pointed out that, in contrast to Weber's *Oberon*, Bishop "was presented with a story completely threadbare" and, with respect to leading characters, "was circumscribed in his range. . . . From this combination of circumstances, Mr. Bishop does not seem to have been permitted to enter upon his task on any thing like equal terms with the German composer."[164]

Yet even in anticipation of *Aladdin*, a *London* critic had written (Jan. 1826, p. 99): "We shall be anxious to hear this performance, and heartily trust it may revive some of his old attraction; for it is not to be denied that the laurels which this gentleman gained by that pretty melo-drame 'The Miller and his Men,' and others of his early compositions, have been gradually fading, and are now almost brown, and one cause of this defect we imagine to have been, that instead of relying on his own resources, he condescended to imitate every popular composer of the day."

Indeed, something of this had been noted much earlier, in perhaps the most perceptive critique on Bishop in midcareer—a retrospective of Bacon (QMM, I, 208–14)—from which brief excerpts must suffice:

[Bishop] produces light, sweet, and strong passages, but they are comparatively short, and in proportion to their brilliance, the lustre is soon impaired. The truth of our observation is shown in the opening of almost every song he has written; the symphonies are universally elegant and pleasing, they lead beautifully to the song, and raise expectation to a very high pitch.—The first strain is as usual almost constantly a repetition of the symphony, but we rarely discover the same traits of continuous production in the passages that follow. Is it that the words fetter the genius of the musician, and that thence the composition languishes, or is it from the effect of exhausted enthusiasm? We observe that in his melo-dramatic music the expression is sharp, short, and decisive, and the effect is very lively and complete. . . . Indeed when we regard the restrictions laid upon the musician by the words, and the trash in the way of poetry which is forced upon the regular composer for a theatre, our wonder is, that he can write at all. . . .

Under all this load, however, Mr. Bishop's songs rarely, we may almost say they never, sink to the level insipidity which is the dull characteristic of by far the greater portion of the writings of most of his predecessors. His airs are light, pleasing, simple and graceful.[165]

His insight on the effect of inferior language on the composer seems justified by the reviews—certainly it was true of the *Fall of Algiers* and *Aladdin*.

In 1830 Holmes (At) stated that Bishop had given up "writing for the stage" (Feb. 14). This was not quite true; he succeeded Tom Cooke as director and composer at Vauxhall Gardens for some years and continued to write for the stage until 1840, but his productions were slender after *Aladdin*. From 1840 to 1848, he conducted the Ancient Concerts, and he was knighted in 1842.[166]

Alfred Bunn, in 1840, blamed Bishop's decline on his emulation of foreign composers: "If he were but *himself*, the stuff is still *in* Bishop; but trying first to be Rossini, and after to be Weber, knocked it all *out* of him."[167] Other writers of those years still had praise for him. Composer John Barnett thought his music "worthy of Mozart"; Allatson Burgh[168] thought it "close to Mozart's in places"; and Hogarth called him "the English Mozart,"[169] adding that "from the very outset" he presented a remarkable contrast to the "flimsy productions" of English opera. Of the music for *Maniac*—"one of his finest"—Hogarth wrote: "The public did not sufficiently understand and appreciate the highly wrought choruses and concerted pieces, and the depth and solidity which characterize this opera."

But Hogarth also thought Bishop's composing for Covent Garden "debased his style" and "thus lowered the character of English music" (II, 453). Edward Fitzball, who had written librettos for him, also alluded to the commercial influence: "Very few know how much music is indebted [to Bishop] for its progress in this country, or half the obstacles he had to contend with. His enthusiasm in his profession was boundless, but his indolence was almost a complete contradiction."[170] Perhaps he could work best only under pressure. Fitzball (p. 196) quoted an undated letter to him from the composer: "I feel very anxious to make a great push and do the whole of the *last* Finale as I first gave it to you . . . —we must try for it. Speed, my boy!—Speed—speed—speed! Mind, though, I am not complaining, for you have achieved wonders."

There is little doubt that theatrical exigencies forced Bishop into hackneyed modes of composition. But he had wedded his talents to a commercial enterprise, and even when he left Covent Garden, the disagreement was over salary. (Drury Lane paid him £20 a week.) Ernest Walker[171] recognized this when he asserted Bishop "squandered his endowments." But Young (p. 466) surely errs in finding Bishop "a quite negligible composer" who "reduced" opera "to its lowest form of light entertainment." (Bishop fell under the onus of Young and other modern critics for his adaptations of Mozart and Rossini—see below.) Holmes, as late as 1830, still placed Bishop, with Shield and Storace, among those who had brought "honour" to English opera and placed the blame for inferior productions squarely on the shoulders of the managers (At, Feb. 14). And Cecil Forsythe found that Bishop "undoubtedly" made improvements in English opera leading to the productions of Barnett and Balfe in the 1830s and 1840s.

KENNEY—COOKE/WHITTAKER/PERRY/NATHAN

Several playwrights who wrote exclusively for Drury Lane or the English Opera House relied on composers other than Bishop for their operas. One of these was James Kenney, who, as we saw earlier, had written successful operas with King in 1804 and 1807 but waited thirteen years to write another one after their critical disaster of *Oh! This Love* in 1810. His patience was rewarded.

For his *Sweethearts and Wives*, produced at the Little Theatre in 1823, he garnered music from Cooke, Whittaker, Perry, and Nathan. Cooke, as noted above, had composed an overture and songs for two operas by Dimond in 1822 and 1829. Isaac Nathan (1790–1864), of Polish-Jewish descent, attended Cambridge and was apprenticed to Domenico Corri in 1809 for singing and composition. He set Byron's *Hebrew Melodies* to ancient Hebrew chants; sung by Braham, they were an instant success. He apparently did little composing of operas apart from his Kenney productions. He also had a music warehouse and publishing business. Ruined by some intrigues involving the royal family, he emigrated to Australia in 1841.

The *Chronicle* thought the plot of *Sweethearts and Wives* "not deficient in either variety or interest," though the incidents were "not very artfully connected" and the dialogue occasionally rambled. The *Herald* admitted its materials were "but slight" and the characters "not very new; but they were so managed and so grouped as to produce what is called effect." Besides, "there was laughter in abundance" and "an agreeable mixture of pathetic interest." Sterling (T) thought Kenney had departed from his former mode as "a very pure writer of comedy" to write a piece "in his very lightest style," primarily for the comedian John Liston, for it relied "upon a little power in the situations, and a great deal of power in the performers." But the *Gazette* found the work "a capital hit"; the *Examiner* admitted Kenney had recaptured his old charm and found "some very delicate and tasteful dialogue" in the piece; and the *London* unabashedly declared: "Kenney is, beyond dispute, the cleverest playwright now in existence:—he understands writing original pieces, translating, or paraphrasing, or adapting French dramas, better than any other English writer."

The piece was not very operatic, as suggested by its label—an operatic comedy. Yet it owed "a great deal of its attraction to the music with which it is embellished." One song, "Mrs. Bell says none shall trick her!", "was set with great judgment—we should suspect by Whitaker" (T). The *Herald* also called the song "exquisitely ludicrous," though the songs were "not many, nor, in general, particularly striking." Another song, "Man was born to sorrow," was "worthy to be sung . . . in purgatory. Some of the notes are the very echoes of grief" (LM). Nathan's song "Why are you wandering here, I pray" was "appropriately set, and is a very good theatrical song" (Har), but he "needed not to have been afraid that the fine selection from Mozart, which forms the Overture, could have been mistaken for his" (LG).

The production was superior and the piece received no less than fifty-one performances the first season, with several revivals. Genest grumbled: "Never has so poor a piece met with such success."

The following year Kenney and Nathan produced "a species of pantomimic comedy" (NM)—*The Alcaid*—for the Little Theatre. But the press was generally critical of both the play and the music, which "betrayed some evidence of hasty composition" (C). Nathan "is one of those composers that require poetry to inspire them" (LM)—like Bishop, we would add. The opera succeeded, though barely, thanks to the singing (LitC).

Thereafter, Kenney's musical productions declined, and the few he did produce were negligible as operas.[172] He did continue, however, to pour forth a continuous stream of dramas—mostly comedies and farces but some tragedies as well—nearly up to his death in 1849.

ARNOLD–COOKE

Operatic successes continued apace at the Lyceum/English Opera House, where Cooke and others composed operas for S. J. Arnold and Beazley.[173] In 1815 Cooke composed the songs for Arnold's comic opera *The King's Proxy*. Sterling pointed out that it was "not a little comical" that the materials for this comic opera were taken from ancient English history (see Pasiello's *Elfrida*). "The death of Athelwold was not in our opinion a very gay occurrence, nor was the ambitious murderess Elfrida a character much calculated to amuse and enlighten us." The *Champion* agreed, saying the story "is so truly tragic, that the endeavour to wrest it into a comical shape has entirely stripped it of its beauties." But J. D. Collier (C) thought it formed "a good fable" that was "managed with dramatic effect."

As for the music, Sterling found Cooke's overture "cold and deficient of merit," while the songs "were in general too much after the manner of jigs and quicksteps, sometimes absolutely out of season," though one song was "harmonized with considerable elegance." But Collier observed that Cooke's music "does him credit; for though a musical ear can discover where he found the idea for almost every air, yet it is so skilfully rehashed that the ragout tastes almost as well as the simple original." The *Champion* thought the music "light, and sometimes pretty" but deplored the many musical "thefts." Even the *Inquisitor* reviewer, who alone disliked the performance, thought some of the songs "extremely pretty," and the following year, in reviewing the printed music to the opera, he declared Cooke "a very extraordinary man . . . for he not only composes *well*, but arranges, or in other words *scores well*, and he can take up any instrument in an orchestra and acquit himself *well* on it." Yet the trite praise they lavished on the songs outdoes any of the "newspaper" adulation the *Inquisitor* constantly complained of.

ARNOLD–HAWES

A number of other Arnold operas followed. Many of them appear from the slender reviews to be musically trivial and probably undeserving of notice. But in 1825 he brought in William Hawes to compose his *Broken Promises*. Hawes (1785–1846), a musician and the father of contralto Marie Hawes, was a Chapel Royal chorister (1795–1801), then a violinist in the Covent Garden orchestra, and later a teacher of singing and a composer. In 1812 he became Master of the Choristers at St. Paul's and, in 1817, of the Chapel Royal. For a time he also ran a music-publishing business. In 1824 he became music director of Arnold's theatre, and in 1830 he was director of the Oratorios at Covent Garden. In addition to his operas, he composed choral and church music.

Called a ballad opera, *Broken Promises* was "a pleasant slight piece, with little plot" but with "agreeable dialogue" (T). The *London* reported that "the situations are evidently arranged by an experienced hand," but the dialogue was "a great deal too sententious." The *Literary Chronicle* found the opera "altogether worthy of the rapturous support it received," adding this revealing note: "We must, however, remark, that as the author has evidently intended to maintain the powers of dramatic illusion in this opera, and has done so for the most part successfully, it is a matter of surprise that he should permit the captain, in the height of distress . . . to while away the single quarter of an hour that precedes the meeting, by turning to the audience and singing a ballad; this, in our estimation, is the greatest blemish in the piece, and might easily be avoided." Thus it is evident that by 1825 English opera had progressed to a point where, even in a light, romantic piece, dramatic allusion was expected to be maintained by the playwright in a work that was intended to be dramatic and not just a vehicle for songs.

Hawes included at least one song of his own—"My morning prayer to heaven is flown"—but borrowed the rest from Weber, Mayr, Cherubini, Berton, Himmel,[174] and Meyerbeer (*Crociato*); he also included two or three Scottish and Irish airs. Ayrton (Har) thought that the Weber and Himmel were "not well chosen, and [that they] fail altogether"; however, he believed the short choruses by Berton "have great merit." The *London* thought all the music "very judiciously selected and arranged." The work was well sung and acted by a fine cast and seemed headed for considerable popularity.

Broken Promises was Arnold's last opera except for two English "versions" discussed below. No doubt he inherited from his father his very strong interest in opera; indeed, he exceeded all other librettists in our period, including Colman, Cobb, Hoare, Reynolds, Dibdin, and Dimond, in the number of his operatic productions—almost all very successful. To summarize, these included operas with Dr. Arnold in 1794, 1796–97, and 1812; with King in 1809 and 1811; with Bishop in 1810; with Horn and Braham in 1812; with Kelly and Braham in 1815; with Cooke and Braham in 1815; and with Hawes in 1825 and 1828. He also had an instinctive knowledge of the musical theatre, marked not only by his successes but also in sensing that, by 1809, London was ready to support a theatre devoted just to English opera. Though not all his works wer *critical* successes, he seemed to reap the highest praise from reviewers for his function as theatre manager, providing strong support of the musical stage over the years at his Lyceum/English Opera House.

A number of English adaptations of foreign operas began to appear soon after the tremendous excitement generated by the King's 1817 production of Mozart's *Don Giovanni*. Operatic adaptations were of course not unknown on the English stage; we have earlier noted that Burgoyne's *Richard Coeur de Lion* (Grétry) in 1786, Cobb's *Doctor and the Apothecary* (Ditters) in 1787, and Kemble's *Lodoiska* (Cherubini) in 1794 were successful adaptations. But this new movement clearly took its genesis from the increasing interest in good music among middle and lower classes, aided by the fad in pianoforte playing and the availability of piano versions of operas in conjunction with the increasingly popular productions of Italian operas at the King's—mainly of Mozart and Rossini. This movement further suggests that a strong appetite was growing among London theatre-goers for something closer to genuine opera on the English stage, though the drama and music of some were badly mangled in the adaptations.

Such productions were not just English operas, of course, but operas in English, and they required different abilities from the adapters. The dramatist worked with a translation of the libretto, converting the recitatives to dialogue; he also had the difficult task of fitting English words to the music. (There were frequent complaints about this difficulty and apologies for the lame verses; of course, earlier dramatists had the same problems with the heavy borrowings from Italian operas, about which Bate Dudley and Cobb had complained.) And he was required to provide dramatic continuity for the inevitable musical cuts and alterations that had to be made, just as at the King's Theatre.

On the whole the musical arranger had an easier task than the librettist, as Ward (Ath) noted at an 1830 adaptation of *Don Giovanni* at the Adelphi: "We are informed that the opera has been *adapted and arranged* by Mr. Hawes. This is a humbug announcement, too frequently to be found in the play-bills now-a-days. In the name of all that's comical, what has Hawes done?—altered the score? no!—changed the melody? no!—corrected the harmony? certainly no! Where then is the *adaptation to the English stage*? Why, the poor scribe who had the trouble of mis-translating the original and dovetailing syllables to notes had all the honour" (July 10).

The task of the musical adapter, however, was no inconsiderable one:

aside from accommodating the music to necessary changes in the libretto, he had to adapt the music to the available cast, with its relatively limited vocal resources. Sometimes there was just no singer available to fill an important role, and the part was simply assigned to an actor, who spoke the lines. It is true that in some instances the musical arranger went further than this, introducing changes in the overture (or substituting another one), rearranging or cutting many passages, and even adding some music of his own. And some alterations were made to accommodate "English musical taste."

Critics of our own time have vigorously protested these alterations, as well they should. Alfred Einstein,[175] for example, after examining a surviving piano score of the *Seraglio*—an adaptation of Mozart's *Die Entführung aus dem Serail* (see below)—expressed outrage at the desecration, which, he noted, went much further than the many deplorable changes in the productions of Mozart at opera houses down almost to our own time.[176] Percy Young voiced similar outrage at Bishop's adaptation of Mozart's *Don Giovanni* (see below). And Gerald Abraham (*NOHM*, VIII, 523) notes Bishop's "shocking English derangements of foreign masterpieces." Indeed, some of Bishop's contemporary critics were also quite negative, as we shall see. But these and other late critics[177] fail to point out that these performances did not take place in an "opera house" but in a "playhouse"— with its English opera tradition of much looser adaptations of all kinds, including a demand to suit "English taste," and its crippling limitations of singers and orchestras to sustain such productions, especially those of Mozart. Had any English person of the time *wanted* to see Mozart or Rossini performed more or less accurately, he would simply have gone to the King's, not to a playhouse.

ENGLISH ADAPTATIONS OF ITALIAN OPERAS

Pocock—Bishop/Mozart

The earliest of these adaptations may be said to have begun with the Pocock-Bishop production of a musical drama, *The Libertine*, at Covent Garden in 1817—only one month after the premiere of *Don Giovanni*— although they had made a partial adaptation of Boieldieu's *John of Paris* in 1814. Billed as a musical drama, the book was not an adaptation of Thomas Shadwell's old play, as Hazlitt thought from the title, but of Da Ponte's libretto: "The plot of the Italian piece is closely followed in almost every instance; Da Ponte's dialogue is literally rendered" (BS, June). Indeed, it was too literal for Sterling: "It is not enough that an opera is done out of Italian, unless it is also done into English."

Vocally the work was a disaster, for the Don was performed by Charles Kemble, who could not sing a note. Nor could the house supply a singer for Don Pedro. "There was some awkwardness necessarily arising from the transposition of the songs, particularly of the duet between Zerlina and Don Giovanni, which was given to Massetto . . . and which by this means lost its exquisite appropriateness of expression" (E; T). Despite such handicaps Sterling (T) and Kenrick (BS, Aug.) thought the music "well arranged" by Bishop, and the overture and many of the airs were retained.[178] Kenrick remarked on the difficulty of fitting English words to some of the arias (especially the "Catalogue") and commended Pocock's libretto, but the *Inquisitor* treated it with contempt.

Accordingly, the performances were scarcely satisfactory, and even Kemble was no Ambrogetti in acting: Hazlitt wrote: "Instead of the intractable, fiery spirit, the unreclaimable licentiousness of Don Giovanni, he was as tame as any saint. . . . Indeed, all the performers seemed, instead of going their lengths on the occasion, to be upon their good behavior, and instead of entering into their parts, to be thinking of the comparison between themselves and the performers at the Opera. We cannot say it was in their favour" (E). Sterling agreed: "Whether it was the effect of the [poor] language, or the fault of the singers, we do not know, but we were upon the whole disappointed." Yet Kenrick found it "very pleasing" on the whole, though "strikingly inferior" to the King's production (June). The adaptation nevertheless had twenty performances.

A good many other musical Dons appeared in subsequent years[179]— mostly in burlesque and mostly at the minors—and some even did not attempt to be operatic. One that did was *Don Juan*, a burletta presented at the Adelphi in 1830, with music arranged by Hawes and the book adapted by John Buckstone.[180] Sterling thought the music well arranged but regarded the text as an extremely poor translation, with "vapid dialogue" and "barbaric versification." The cast, headed by Phillips, sang well, but the theatre was thought too small for such a production.

Holcroft—Bishop/Mozart

In 1819 Bishop again returned to Mozart in his Covent Garden production of the *Marriage of Figaro*. Bishop apparently made his own adaptation of the text. His "poetical talents," the *Inquisitor* had declared (July 1817), "are of an order to supersede half the lyrical stanzas with which his music is generally pestered."

At least in this version *everybody* sang, though some of the parts were poorly performed. In other respects, however, the opera was even more of a departure from Mozart than *Giovanni*. To be sure, the *Inquisitor* thought Bishop's version of the story was "very judicious, and most of the situations pretty well preserved," though the characters were not portrayed "with any great force of coloring." Indeed, "the Character of Figaro, was totally lost, in every respect, both in mirth and in music, which was precisely the case in 'The Barber of Seville.' Mr. Bishop seems to have no notion of this character; indeed the assignment of it to Mr. Liston renders it impossible, that the public should know any thing about it. Figaro is not a buffoon; his merit with his master did not consist in making faces, nor saying funny things, but in a spirit of vivacious intrigue."

The playbill stated that the music was to be "a selection from Mozart's operas"; but the *Inquisitor* pointed out that all Mozart's music in the piece *was* from *Figaro*.[181] In the last act, however, Bishop introduced a duet, "O pescator dell' onda," a popular Italian song, and he inserted a bravura of his own in place of "Dove sono." "This, we think, was a very superfluous exertion of his talents; Mr. Bishop may be assured, that his music will not benefit by a comparison with that of Mozart" (TI). There was also another change: "It was . . . with a feeling amounting nearly to indignation, that we found ourselves deprived of some choice and genuine delicacies, while we were pestered with a low, vulgar song from Fawcett," who played the gardener (it was encored!). "Perhaps, however, Mr. Bishop is not so much to blame in this; he probably had no alternative but to disfigure Mozart, or offend Fawcett" (BS). Moreover, after the third performance, he also substituted his own overture for Mozart's (BS), perhaps owing to the difficulty of the music. To do justice to Mozart's music "requires an orchestra of accomplished professors, well drilled to the task, and certainly, that of Covent Garden theatre, is totally unequal to it" (TI).

Hunt, aghast, was unwilling to excuse Bishop on the grounds of theatrical constraint: "Never, we believe, was there a sadder metamorphosis of French vivacity and Italian singing. . . . What are we to say to an adapter of Mozart, who for some of his pieces substitutes the airs about the street, and in others alters passages to suit the voice of the performer? . . . You can no more alter [Mozart] with impunity than you can put common-places into the songs of [Milton's] *Comus* or [Fletcher's] *Faithful Shepherdess*."

Otherwise the acting and singing were generally praised, the latter prompting the *European* to argue for a latitude of taste: "In the songs the distinction was merely in the wild sweetness of the English style, and the studied beauty of the Italian; the difference between native simplicity and acquired elegance. We cannot now decide by which we were most pleased; but by the performance as a whole, we were more gratified than by any adaptation that we have recently seen." Sterling agreed that the adaptation "shows, that the beauty of [Mozart's] music is perfectly independent of language, and that in any form it cannot but charm and captivate." And though Bishop "has been too sparing of his selections from the original," he "is entitled to great praise for the style of his adaptations."[182]

The scenery was particularly effective, and the work not only played fifteen times but was frequently revived through 1830. In 1828 critic Y (E) was still complaining about the cuts in Mozart and the substitutions: "An Irish melody, a more common-place ballad, and a drinking song that ought never to have emerged from the atmosphere of a pot-house, or a corporation-committee dinner. Since that period [i.e., 1819] the national taste has improved,—although the above disgrace is still tolerated."

Dimond—Kramer/Mozart

In 1827 a Mozart opera that had not even appeared at the King's was Englished—*The Seraglio*,[183]—and produced at Covent Garden. The libretto was prepared by Dimond and the musical arrangements, which were advertised to be by J. B. Cramer (and so recorded by Nicoll), were actually made by Christian Kramer.

Kramer—unrelated to the well-known J. B. Cramer or his brother Franz, both of whom were leaders of the Philharmonic—was not the nonentity Einstein has painted him to be. Ayrton noted he was "master of the King's most extraordinary and perfect band of wind-instruments, in which office he has shewn talents of the highest order, both in arranging music for such an orchestra, and in directing the performance of it so as to produce effects unparalleled by any other military band" (Har, V, 249). The *London* (Apr. 1822, p. 391) noted that Kramer "most skilfully and beautifully adapted" music "for these instruments. The band "is unquestionably the first in Europe, and to Mr. Kramer belongs the highest praise that can be bestowed." Kramer, who published some of his musical adaptations, was named "Master of the King's musick" in 1837.

Sterling found the drama "wrought up with considerable skill"; it was, "though simple, interesting. Some of the acting characters are well drawn." But the *Gazette* thought that, though the dialogue was

> lively, and in some parts tasteful, . . . the songs [i.e., lyrics] are sad things. We have always made great allowances for the obstacles an adapter of words to concerted music has naturally to encounter; but what can be said of such stuff as this, if the printer's devil be blameless:
> Sound our mighty bassa's praises,
> Sing of glory—sing of love—

> Song, the cry of eagle's raises,
> Song, that's murmured by the dove.

The *Examiner* agreed the drama "possesse[d] more interest than belongs to operas in general," but Holmes (At) thought the much-altered story "stupid," and Ayrton reported that the libretto—"almost completely rewritten" by Dimond—was "but a feeble affair." (Einstein concurs.)

With respect to the music, Sterling regarded the later operas of Mozart "as more rich in melodies, more sustained by extensive musical accompaniments," than the *Seraglio*. "Still," he continued, "there is, in every part of the opera, much to delight the scientific ear, though it must be 'caviare to the million.' The serious airs are tender, delicate, and impassioned—the comic are full of laughing spirit—the chorusses are sometimes grand, and always appropriate—and the concerted pieces are beautifully harmonized.... Everywhere we perceive the efforts of a fine genius." Moreover, Kramer performed his task "extremely well." But the *Literary Chronicle* thought the music somewhat disappointing and "not of that decided character which can fix the attention of general hearers"; the *Examiner* agreed.

The *Gazette* pointed out that the "additional airs" composed by Kramer were "anything but improvements, and the arrangements and adaptations grievously unskilful and tasteless.... The mutilation of the beautiful and popular overture is alone a crying sin," though it was encored. Holmes was less critical: "In manufacturing the music for the English stage, the original has been much cut, chipped, and interpolated; but, except in one instance, this delicate task has been not badly executed." He even enjoyed the "fresh treatment and modulations of the overture," but one chorus "doth grievously annoy us with the scent of wrong harmony."

Ayrton, too, was not unhappy with the overture, which was "preceded and much lengthened by a slow movement from the Zauberflote." Kramer, he explained, "has written an introductory chorus, which accords better with the modern style of opera than the opening air of the original work."[184] A second-act recitative and aria for Costanza had "its long, and, to say the truth, rather tiresome symphony, judiciously abridged." Moreover, "the new compositions introduced by Mr. Kramer do him credit as a scientific musician." He only regretted that "at least three exquisite airs in the original work were rejected." But he pointed out that Kramer "has had formidable difficulties to contend against; a weak drama, a most imperfect vocal company, and a feeble band." Later (VI, 24) he regretted the changes in the opera, adding: "but with so imperfect a vocal company, how could it have been otherwise?"

This was also the point of view of Bacon's very long and detailed review commenting on all the changes made in Mozart's score (QMM, IX, 520–29). He regretted many of the curtailments and alterations Kramer had made, yet in each instance he pointed out the limitations of his singers—there was no bass singer, for example, and all Mozart's fine bass songs had to be eliminated. An even more serious matter than these alterations was "the intermixture of dialogue with musical acts" requisite in English opera. The performances got mixed reviews. Hogarth, who found the opera so changed as to be unrecognizable, thought it had failed. But it was a decided success, with twenty-one performances and at least one revival.

Arnold—Hawes/Mozart

Not until 1828 was a Mozart adaptation mounted that had most of the original music intact. This was a production by Arnold for the English Opera House—*Tit for Tat*, based on *Così*. Arnold himself did the libretto, and the music was arranged by Hawes. Sterling wrote: "The adaptation does not differ from the original in any respect besides the language, excepting in the recitative passages, which are spoken instead of being sung. . . . We do not find a single note of new music that has been introduced. . . . *Tit for Tat* . . . is a very close and faithful copy of that excellent opera" (T). Holmes agreed:

> The introduction of this opera has gratified us more than we can express: first, we have the purity of Mozart's music, free from interpolations—which have hitherto been found necessary to gilt the pill for the vulgar; secondly, the pleasant sight of the singers content with the simplicity of the text, and taking pains to give it correctly; but, most of all, a mixed audience appearing to relish the best part of Mozart, and *encoring* such compositions as the terzetto, "Soave sia il vento," and the quintetto, which precede[s] it.

And the *Examiner* chortled: "This is a triumph!", while John Payne Collier (C) thought the production atoned for some of Arnold's musical sins and noted "the extreme difficulty of adapting our harsher tongue to the music." Holmes (At), too, found the adaptations were made "very cleverly; the rhythm is preserved, without any bungling accentuation."

The music was highly regarded. The performances, likewise, were considered far better than those in the earlier Mozart versions (T; LG; NM). Collier averred: "The performers all did their best—some better than we expected," and Ayrton concurred. Even the orchestra excelled: "Much credit is due to Mr. Wagstaff, the leader, for the manner in which he has drilled the band into an accompaniment of this opera. The parts were well kept under, sustained, and smooth. . . . We have not heard of late a theatrical band kept in better order than at the English Opera" (Holmes). The press and public agreed the production was very successful.[185]

Terry—Bishop/Rossini

Close upon the heels of his popular success of *Libertine*, Bishop produced *The Barber of Seville* (1818) at Covent Garden—only seven months after the successful premiere of the first Rossini opera at the King's. It was not, however, intended to be an English adaptation of the opera: it contained only six numbers from *Barbiere*; there were borrowings from Paisiello's *Barbiere*, and Bishop supplied several songs of his own as well as the overture—much to the annoyance of Bacon.[186] Yet the press seemed quite happy with the opera. To be sure, Kenrick (BS) complained that Bishop "has not had sufficient self-denial to let Rossini's music alone," but he nevertheless found it an "agreeable Olio." Sterling declared that Bishop "has certainly done more on this occasion than ever was done in a similar way. . . . On the whole, we have seldom enjoyed a higher musical treat at an English theatre." Bacon (QMM, II, 75) admitted that in the problem of Englishing the opera, Terry "extricated himself with adroitness and success" in some of the numbers, though in others the meanings had been totally altered. He added that these adaptations "are completely against the genius of our language. . . . Nor do we believe that the comic concerted pieces of Italy . . . can ever be successfully transmuted into English."

Mrs. Dickons was warmly welcomed and was generally admired as Rosina, but Jones, as the count, could not sing at all, and his numbers were transferred to Figaro, while Liston, a poor singer, was "obliged to take his part in the singing" (E). The work played twenty nights and was revived twice.[187]

Lacy—Lacy/Rossini

In 1827 London saw a somewhat closer English adaptation of Rossini. His *Il Turco in Italia* (King's Theatre, 1821) was produced as *The Turkish Lovers* at Drury Lane and was Englished by Lacy, who also arranged the music (Braham contributed a few songs).

Michael Rophino Lacy (1795–1867), a violinist and composer, was born in Spain of a Spanish mother and an English father. He was an infant prodigy on the violin. In England at age ten, he could easily converse in Spanish, French, Italian, and English. He studied under Viotti and played at various concerts in London. Encouraged by his father, from 1808 to 1818 he filled "genteel comedy parts in the Provinces, playing the violin in public only at his benefits" (D.N.B.). From 1820 to 1824 he composed, and was leader of, ballet music at the King's. His works for the stage extended from 1827 through 1833 and were produced at both major theatres. Obviously, he combined unusual qualifications for providing operatic adaptations, though he was not always successful.

Of the *Turkish Lovers* Sterling wrote: "To the meagre plot out of which the original has been constructed, additions have been made and it has undergone some alterations suitable to the decorum of the English stage." But the drama was "as heavy and inane as any it has ever been our fortune to sit out." Yet, he continued, "the audience bore all with exemplary patience, disposed to sacrifice sense for the enlivening strains of Rossini. An English auditory are seldom fastidious on such subjects; but so bent were they on preserving the composition entire, that Braham, who . . . ventured to introduce some songs of his own barren and tasteless school, received hints of his transgressions [i.e., hisses!]." This is additional evidence of just how much the taste of the public had improved at this time. Talfourd (NM) concurred, and Holmes (At) thought that of all the English versions to date, "the most successful is the *Turkish Lovers*. In the English representation, the Italian *manner* is preserved, and every character [is] well acted and respectably sung." The opera, however, was barely successful.

Two years later Lacy returned to Rossini with *The Maid of Judah*, produced at Covent Garden. It was a pastiche of Rossini—drawn from several of his operas—rather than an English version.[188] Not all the singers were competent in the music; nevertheless, the public was pleased and the opera had seventeen performances.

In 1830 there were no fewer than *three* English versions of Rossini. The first, *Cinderella*—a "grand comic opera" produced at the Garden and based, of course, on *Cenerentola*—was another Lacy production. Although he made "copious additions to the original fable," they were deemed praiseworthy (T). Wade (Ath) wrote: "Of the several [adaptations] we do not remember any one that has better deserved success." But Holmes (At) thought the effect of the music "un-English." The production was opulent, the singing excellent, and there was "absolute clamour" from the audience at its conclusion. The opera played twenty-two times and was revived the following season. On that occasion Hunt was unhappy with the interpolations: "When [Rossini] writes for any one opera, he writes to suit that particular work; and music characteristic of Turkey and Switzerland must appear out of place in a scene in Italy. There is a very striking instance of this anomaly in the Ball-scene of the present medley, where a dance of soldiers is introduced, and a Swiss air, both of them wholly unsuited to Naples and the fairies" (*Tatler*).

Fitzball—Bishop/Rossini

Bishop made the musical adaptations for Rossini's last two Englished operas. The first, produced at Covent Garden in 1830, was the opera *Ninetta*, based on *Gazza Ladra*, with a libretto prepared by Fitzball.

Edward Fitzball[189] (1792–1873), son of a poor farmer, was apprenticed to a printer but later failed in his own printing business. Encouraged by novelist Amelia Opie, he wrote a play, got it accepted by the Surrey Theatre in 1821, and soon became "unrivalled in every trick and artifice known to the stage" (D.N.B.). He produced a large number of plays, including many musicals, at both majors and minors, and he declared in his autobiography that he had "lent all his genius" to the cause of music.

Sterling was delighted to find the work "all *Gazza Ladra*" and "all familiar to the public" (if the latter was true, many play-goers were also attending the King's at this time—or had piano renditions). Regarding the music, Holmes (At) found the adaptation "as skilful as any that Bishop has yet made for the English stage." Ayrton, too, praised him for adding "no one thing to it." All agreed on the excellence of the performance. The opera was repeated twelve times.

Planché—Bishop/Rossini

Planché and Bishop brought out the opera of *Hofer* at Drury Lane, prompted by the success of *Guillaume Tell* (Paris, 1829), which London was not to hear, in French, until 1845. It was not an English version, however, for Planché, "feeling that the story of William Tell had been dramatized in so many shapes and forms, . . . selected, with much propriety, a portion of the history of Hofer, the celebrated Tyrolean chieftain, who, like the immortal Tell, endeavoured to free his country from foreign thraldom"[190] (T).

The press was unanimous in its praise of Rossini's music. "The whole of the music partakes strongly of the deep, solid, and scientific character of the German school" (T). "The music of course is first-rate, although a little noisy in some of the chorusses. It is of a very varied character . . . and was in general extremely well executed" (C). Holmes (At) concurred: "Mr. Bishop has evidently given his utmost vigilance to the rehearsal of this music, and Rossini is as much indebted to him as are the singers and the musical public. . . . In *Hofer*, or *William Tell*, there are no traces of the same hasty pen which [Rossini's] writings often betray: but, instead, a manifest selection of ideas, much thought and design, yet without stiffness, in the melodies."

The performances were highly satisfactory and the stage production effective. The work played twelve nights and was revived the next season. On the latter occasion, however, Hunt (*Tatler*) was quite negative. He cited the drama as a falsification of the historical Hofer, who "did not throw off a yoke like the greater patriot [Tell]." And he dismissed the "divers attitudinizing scenes in the mountains, with occasional pops of the muskets, and marches of soldiers, [which] show us that the battles are going on; the patriots get the day by dint of the usual hurras, and saying that they do; and triumphant flags, voices and arms are raised in the concluding chorus." Moreover, the verses were so poor as "to render them a *serious* imitation of Swift's Letter of Mary the Cook." And "either Mr. Bishop has not selected well this time, or the music of *William Tell* has scarcely one touch of [Rossini's] genius in it, and is an enormous specimen of his commonplace."

Napier—Hawes/Paer

Two more Italian operas—both, as it happens, written by German composers and neither yet performed at the King's—saw English metamorphoses. In 1827 the English Opera House mounted *The Freebooters*, an English adaptation of Paer's semiserious opera *I fuorusciti di Firenze* (Dresden, 1802). The English book was constructed from Anelli's libretto by one N. Napier, about whom nothing is known. The music was arranged by Hawes.

Sterling (T) found the dialogue barely tolerable, "but the lyrical part is miserable stuff" and "cannot be excused by the plea, that [the librettist] simply adapted the rhymes to the music of a German composer!" Critic Q (E) agreed, but noted a subtle blending of story[191] and song: "A rich vein of sensibility pervades the whole tissue of the composition, the strings which are touched being those that vibrate in every bosom. . . . Paer, in fact, appears to us both in his comic and his serious vein to combine the attributes of taste and feeling with ease, grace, and felicity." Only Ayrton (Har), who thought the choruses "the most meritorious portion of this opera," was not particularly impressed with the music.

The press also remarked on the pains bestowed on the production. Talfourd wrote: "Mr. Arnold has added largely to his claims on the gratitude of the musical world" by producing the opera "on a splendid scale of arrangements, and with a perfection rarely known on the English stage. This is, perhaps, his greatest and most successful effort." Moreover, the star system was suspended: "There is no one performer who could figure as a star. A result so decisive should teach a lesson to our winter managers, that they have a better chance of solid and permanent success, by . . . rendering the dramatic picture equable and complete, than by lavishing high nightly salaries on a few prominent actors, and leaving the general business to incompetent novices." Sterling (T) praised Hawes for his musical direction, and noted that "the united orchestra appeared to be but one instrument" and that the choruses "have been got up with the utmost care." The work was very successful and was repeated in 1828.

Wade

Numbered among the very few capable of writing both the drama *and* the music was Joseph Augustine Wade (c. 1801–45). Largely self-taught, he was given early encouragement by another Irish composer—Sir John Stephenson. Wade wrote an oratorio, *The Prophesy*, in 1824, and produced his first comic opera, *Two Houses of Granada*, at Drury Lane in 1826. The plot of the latter was unclear and tedious (T) and "a failure" (LG), but the music was called "excellent" and it evoked a "tender simplicity" (T); although wasted on the drama, it "met with great success" (LG). Even the *Atlas* thought it "original," while the *Quarterly* noted its "unpretending excellence." The piece was repeated eleven times.

Wade—Weigl

In 1828 Arnold produced at English Opera House a comic opera, *The Pirate of Genoa*, fashioned by Wade from de Gamerra's libretto for Joseph Weigl's *L'amor marinaro*[92] (Vienna, 1797). Weigl (1766–1846), a German composer and conductor, wrote several Italian operas, both comic and serious, that were produced on the Continent, especially at Vienna. He also wrote several *Singspiel*, including *Die schweizerfamilie*, which Planché adapted as *Zella* in 1825; it failed. The present work was Weigl's first success outside Vienna. At least some of its recitative was retained in the adaptation.

Sterling (T) found "a great deal of monotony in the dramatic incidents"; but "it must be remembered that, in recitative, many an insignificant dialogue will pass, which, in words, appears intolerable." And for John Payne Collier (C) there was too much recitative. But the *Examiner* faulted the drama. "It is evident," they wrote,

> that the proprietor is making the experiment, upon how few grains of plot and dramatic interest [the attention of the audience] can exist without "fainting by the way." Like the man in the old story, who tried a

similar experiment upon his horse, he has reduced us very nearly to the same minimum of sustenance; Mr. Arnold, however, must not lose sight of the result of that trial, viz., that just as the horse had attained to the allowance of *one oat* per day, he died. The theatrical man "cannot live by sounds alone."

Both newspapers thought the music first-rate, but Holmes (At) heartily disagreed: "A large portion of it, indeed, consists of *namby-pamby* passages and stale band effects, that have been heard over and over at the Italian Opera, any time the last fifty years. . . . We were heartily tired of his serious songs, which are only dull, and hang upon an audience like a dead weight." Yet the buffo songs were "full of humour and spirit." Ayrton was also displeased. The performances were generally admired and the work was well received.

It will be recalled (part I) that Wade was a competent reviewer of opera for the *Athenaeum* for some years, beginning in 1829. He also published a number of popular songs. But he eventually drank to excess, took up opium, and died insane.

ENGLISH ADAPTATIONS OF FRENCH OPERAS

Arnold—Hawes/Salieri

Given the English antipathy to French music, it is surprising to find English adaptations of several French operas, although one composer was Italian and another Belgian. In 1825 Salieri's *Tarare* (Paris, 1787), Englished by Arnold from Beaumarchais's libretto, was produced at the English Opera House as *Tarrare*, with musical supervision by Hawes. We have met Salieri only as a composer of Italian operas, but in his French operas, which are more interesting, he became a disciple of Gluck (N.G.). This adaptation, however, was much truncated: "The dialogue is curtailed . . . five acts are reduced to two" (T). Perhaps this was because Beaumarchais' libretto was a "heterogenous farrago" that came close to Revolutionary fervor (P. Smith, p. 159). Moreover, it was insurmountably heavy (E; C), and the *European* thought the play "may contest the point of superiority in stupidity with any piece that was ever written."

There were differences with respect to the music. Sterling (T) found that it "maintains the style of Gluck consistently with the terms prescribed by the author. . . . The expression is quite equal to the situation and the passion of the scene." The *Chronicle* considered its musical claims "very high," and the *Gazette* reported "the whole of the music" was "greatly admired." The *Examiner*, more particular, found it "spirited, and indicative of the style of Salieri"; yet, "speaking generally, we encounter but few of those exquisite melodies and passages which haunt the delighted ear for ever afterwards." But the *London* called the work "a decidedly bad Opera, of which the melodies are common-place, and the harmonies thin and monotonous." Ayrton (Har) agreed: after denouncing some other journals for praising the music, he declared: "We cannot point out a single passage that shows a first-rate genius." There were differences, too, about the quality of the performances, but the scenery and costuming were splendid. The opera was, in any case, a "great hit," (NM) and some reviewers congratulated Arnold for his contribution to English musical taste. It was revived the following year.

Payne—Boieldieu

In 1827 Payne brought out at Covent Garden his two-act opera *The White Maid*, based on Boieldieu's *La dame blanche* (libretto by Scribe) as well as on Scott's *Monastery* and *Guy Mannering*. This was apparently a faithful English version, for there was no musical "adaptation" at all, and Payne was "so scrupulous in not altering a single note, that he found himself under the necessity of apologizing for the badness of his verses" (Ayrton).

The scrambling of sources in Scott by Scribe[193] was Sterling's main complaint:

> It is impossible to comprehend the connexion of any two scenes, or scarcely the import even of one, from one end of the opera to the other. . . . [The author or translator] would seem to have selected a single incident, or character, from every one of the *Waverley* novels . . . and then to have jumbled all these well-known personages and materials—placed in new situations [with] a disregard of all common reason. (T)

The *Examiner* agreed, but later reviewers thought otherwise. Talfourd (NM) stated that the work had been "treated with great unfairness by an influential portion of the press. . . . The main defect in the plot of this drama is, that 'The White Maid' turns out to be a hoax. . . . There is not much dialogue; what there is has point and case; but the music . . . is every thing."

Yet there was also a divergence regarding the music. Sterling (T) thought it "not of a high order." He disliked the "constant imitation" of Weber's style,[194] "and the extent to which this is carried . . . is often extravagant, even so far as to be ridiculous." Moreover, the choruses were long and heavy, and there was hardly any melody. But the *Examiner* found the music "decidedly that of a master and a man of talent." And to Talfourd (NM), who did "not profess skill in such matters," the music seemed "very original and impressive," and the auction scene, "which was performed with remarkable precision, was as effective as any thing of the kind we ever heard in an English theatre."

The performances were generally admired, but the taste of the public was apparently closer to that of the daily reviewers, for the work was a marginal failure, playing five times in full, and seven more in a cut-down version.

Fitzball — Bishop/Boieldieu

In 1829 Bishop and Fitzball brought out an English adaptation of another Boieldieu opera, *Les deux nuits*, dubbed *The Night before the Wedding, and the Wedding Night*. This operatic farce was produced at Covent Garden only six months after the Paris premiere of the Boieldieu work. Sterling (T) was unimpressed with the literal translation of Scribe, and the *Examiner* reported the "dullness of the plot amounted to the ingenious, and its tediousness almost to originality."

The music—"by far the greater part" was by Boieldieu—was admired (Ayrton). Sterling enjoyed the choruses and concerted pieces, but "the airs are not very remarkable either for originality or melody." The *Examiner* agreed: "The chorusses are elegant and light, without being trifling; they also display some masterly modulations, interspersed at the same time with flowing and graceful melodies," though two arias were "noisy and blustering." But the production was poor and the opera survived only four performances. As the *Athenaeum* put it: "It is obvious . . . that to render agreeable music popular, it must come forth well attended."

Lacy — Fétis

In 1828 Drury Lane brought out an operetta called *Love in Wrinkles*, which Lacy had adapted from Scribe's *La vieille* (Paris, 1826), with music by Fétis also arranged by Lacy. François-Joseph Fétis (1784–1871), a Belgian teacher, musicologist, and composer, studied at the Paris Conservatoire, where he later taught music. He founded and edited the *Revue Musicale* (1827–33) and edited his invaluable *Biographie Universale*. He composed only a few operas, which were written to make money (N.G.); *La vieille*, however, was the only one to have much success.

Sterling, noting that Lacy had extended the original one act to two, "and so amplified both the dramatic incidents and the music," found the story presented "with considerable elegance and delicacy." But the *Gazette* thought Scribe's libretto "one of the weakest of his thousand and one productions." And J. P. Collier (C) complained that Lacy "does not take sufficient time to do his best, and the Operetta of last night has several French idioms in the dialogue."

Sterling found the music, "from the first note of the overture to the last of the *finale*, an imitation of the Rossini style; but it has the great merit of not betraying the feebleness and servility of imitations. It is very ably arranged, both as to melody and harmony," and one trio in particular was "a masterpiece of vocal composition and of orchestral accompaniment. . . . Mr. Lacy has evidently contributed his own share of airs and duets." Holmes (At) was most enthusiastic: "What was our surprise to hear a whole first act of the most agreeable and lively style of the *good* Italian comic opera; masterly scoring—attractive melodies and harmonies—with real knowledge of stage effect. Truly M. Fetis can do something beside write dissertations upon music, and quote Hesiod." Collier, though, found the music "slight in some places, even to flimsiness," and the *Examiner* thought Fétis's talents "not of a very high or original cast, but . . . his melodies possess much grace and sweetness." Both the acting and singing of Braham gave the performance a boost, and the opera had a run of eleven nights.

Planché—Cooke/Auber

In 1830 still another Englished French opera appeared at Drury Lane: a two-act comic opera, *The National Guard*, adapted by Planché from Scribe's *La fiancée*, set by Auber; it had premiered the previous year at the Paris Opéra Comique. Daniel-François-Esprit Auber (1782–1871) spent his early years in London, where his songs had some success at private concerts. He began writing operas at Paris in 1804 but had little success until 1820. After 1823, he produced over forty operas—mostly *opéras comiques* with Scribe—of which the best was perhaps *La Muette de Portici* (1828), known in England as *Masaniello*,[195] the first of the French romantic "grand operas." But Cooke, who added many selections, used very little of Auber's music, for which Holmes (At) blamed the theatre management:

> In the contest for popularity which subsists between the rival theatres, plans are occasionally resorted to, which are unworthy an honourable strife and abusive of the public confidence. This may be often observed in the adaptation of foreign operas, which, when pared down and altered so as to give scarcely an idea of the original, cannot but be esteemed an injustice to the composer as well as unfair to the visitor, who is attracted by the fame of a popular work.

The rest of the press reflected mixed feelings on the music. The cast was strong, and the work had fourteen performances. At its revival the following season, Hunt (*Tatler*) admired the play; of Auber's music he wrote: "His compositions have not the passion of Italy, nor the rich science of the Germans; yet we fancy we can discern in them something that does considerable honour to the French turn for music. There is a light, conscious art in them, singularly mixed with the simplicity of natural cheerfulness."

ENGLISH ADAPTATIONS OF GERMAN OPERAS

Arnold — Hawes/Winter

In 1826 Arnold and an anonymous translator (perhaps Napier) turned to F. X. Huber's libretto for Peter von Winter's *Singspiel*, *Das unterbrochene Opferfest* (Vienna, 1796), and came up with the semicomic *Oracle; or The Interrupted Sacrifice*. It was produced at the English Opera House with Winter's music arranged by Hawes — some ten years after the last King's performance of a Winter Italian opera. *Opferfest* was Winter's first success and the most popular German opera between *Zauberflöte* and *Freischütz* (Dent).

The uniqueness of the production was emphasized by initial remarks by the stage manager to the audience, pointing out that this was "the first time an attempt has ever been made, upon an English stage, to represent the whole of the music of an Opera decidedly composed for foreign theatres"[196] and requesting the suspension of encores (four times disregarded) owing to the length and difficulty of the work.

J. P. Collier (C), noting it professed to be a "free translation," thought the songs would have better succeeded "if the author had attempted to be more original." But Sterling (T) dismissed the libretto: serious operas "are, in general, very bad tragedies," and this work was no exception. His account of the plot,[197] however, evinces nothing tragic at all. The *Literary Chronicle* found many of the incidents "unnaturally absurd." The *Gazette* agreed about the absurdities — "never did people sing . . . at more improbable moments" — but "it says much for the charm of the opera, that it rarely permits you to perceive" them.

The music was the triumph of the evening. Collier chortled: "The metropolis has been furnished with one of the richest and grandest musical banquets ever provided for it" — language repeated almost verbatim by Ayrton. Sterling agreed, and critic Q (E) wrote: "The chorusses are rich and harmonious, and the bravura parts very grand and various [yet there was] some very impassioned expression, and more than one sweet and pathetic air." Talfourd (NM) thought the effect "more direct and harmonious than that which is left by the 'Freischutz' or the 'Oberon'; there seem to be less violent and startling combinations, and more melody in the concerted pieces." The *Gazette* noted paradoxically: "Not only is it altogether . . . too long; yet as a whole it is not fatiguing . . . and the attention is kept alive from first to last." They also pointed out that one aria was "rather endangered by a startling bit of unusual recitative, very new to English ears." All critics praised the fact that the original music appeared intact; Ayrton (Har, p. 176) was most articulate: "In no opera has so much respect been shown to the original music, which, with some very trifling exceptions, is given without any omission, and what is better, without the addition of any foreign matter, or any violent transposition of the parts. . . . It is by this conscientious respect of the score of a master, and by that alone, that the beauties of his compositions can appear in their true light."

The press also acknowledged the superiority of cast and performance, as well as the highly enthusiastic audience at its conclusion. The work must have been successful for it was revived at Covent Garden the following year. This English version was one of the most genuinely operatic productions yet noted, and its triumph was that it nevertheless attracted strong critical *and* popular support.

Fitzball—Hawes/Ries

In 1829, also under Hawes's musical supervision, the English Opera House produced a musical drama, *The Robber's Bride*;[198] Fitzball had adapted it as a "free Translation" from Ries's *Die Rauberbraut* (words and music), which had premiered in Frankfurt only the previous year. Ferdinand Ries (Bonn, 1784–1838), a pianist and composer, studied piano under Beethoven and concertized about Europe without much success. But he came to London in 1813 to perform with the new Philharmonic Society (which also played much of his music), and by 1824 he had made enough money as performer and teacher to retire to the Continent.

The opera prompted the attendance of "a vast number of musical men . . . of the highest celebrity" (C). And Ayrton (Har) welcomed a new German opera: "Putting Mozart wholly out of the question, who is become a classic, a sort of sacred character, the works of Weber and Meyerbeer have stamped such a value on the modern lyric productions of their country, that whatever now comes from that land, a land overflowing with melody and harmony, is sure of a friendly reception, a patient hearing, and if not a favourable, at least a lenient judgment." But the libretto was weak. J. P. Collier (C) wrote: "More common-place stuff we have seldom seen clothed in tolerably harmonious English," and the *Examiner* declared that the story was "not happily chosen for the structure of a musical work; which, to be lasting, must have a certain fascination for the hearer."

Die Rauberbraut, no singspiel, was almost, if not entirely, all-sung. The press, citing the little dialogue, expressed curiosity about the recitative-like passages and the problems they caused the translator/librettist. Collier thought "the versifier would have done better if he had been content not 'to tag his verses' so frequently. . . . It is a defect . . . of the German that even ordinary topics of conversation are sometimes set, if not to airs, at least to recitative. . . . The manner is too much for the matter."

With respect to the music, the views were generally negative. Sterling (T) wrote: "The music of this opera is of a very lofty character. We fear that it is too scientific to please the million. . . . [It] is rich in concerted pieces, but the melodies are exceedingly few." Collier (C), too, found that while the music "displayed great skill, knowledge, and taste, there is some indication in it of a want of invention, particularly in the airs." Even Ayrton (Har) thought that on first hearing the music, while displaying musical knowledge, lacked "the creative faculty—the power to invent—genius"—a view confirmed after a later hearing. Yet the *Athenaeum* was supportive, while the *Examiner* noted that the "harmonizing and instrumentation" were "learned and full almost to a fault." Ries has, however, "incited our admiration principally by his bold and original treatment of those hacknied subjects of a dramatic composer—Robber Chorusses. . . . It is the first time such a scene on the English stage has been warmly conceived and fitly expressed."

The cast was generally praised, and the chorus and orchestra were deemed particularly effective. Even the audience response was thought, by some, to be quite positive for such a difficult work. And again Arnold came in for kudos for his support of opera. The work may not have succeeded, however; in a late review, Ayrton noted it was on the point of being withdrawn. Yet three months later, in a new season, Covent Garden mounted its own *Robber's Bride* (also called the *Robber's Wife*), a melodrama with a book by Pocock based on "Tales of the Monster Festivals," and with music by Ries (Ath, Oct. 28).

Planché—Marschner

The next month the English Opera House produced *Der Vampyr*, a grand romantic opera, which Planché had translated from W. A. Wohlbruck's libretto for the romantic opera of the same name by Marschner, first performed in Leipzig the previous year. The musical arranger is unknown—perhaps there was none. Heinrich August Marschner (1795–1861), a precocious German composer, was writing his first songs by 1808 and later composed a number of works for the stage at Dresden and elsewhere. A follower of Weber, he called for the support of a national German opera. *Der Vampyr* was his first big success; his later works were overshadowed by Wagner (N.G.).

This was not Planché's first "Vampire." In 1820 he had produced a musical drama, also at the English Opera House, under that title, which he adapted from a French source; it was strong on spectacle but had little music. But the success of *Freischütz* in 1824 brought a renewed interest in diablerie (cf. Meyerbeer's *Robert le diable*, in 1831). In *Der Vampyr*, Planché made a "free translation" of Wohlbruck, which was "highly creditable": Planché "has here, as well as in *Der Freischutz*, proved himself the best opera poet of the day" (T). Ayrton (Har) and the *Examiner* agreed, the latter adding: "He is an adroit and tasteful jeweller; he sets the pearls and diamonds of other men's thoughts. This is not said in any spirit of detraction, but to give him full credit." And Holmes (At) reported that "the English is so well adapted . . . [that] we have not heard any modern opera with greater pleasure." Sterling (T) noted that this work "may, in the truest sense of the word, be denominated an opera. It contains scarcely a dozen lines of speaking dialogue: from the beginning to the end, all the passions and emotions that are called forth are, as in *Der Freischutz*, expressed by the music." Holmes also commented on one narrative scene: "The composer wishing to excite terror, has not attempted to write melody, but adapted something between singing and speaking, and the tale is told to a fearful kind of chromatic ascent."

Concerning the music—only the "greater part of the finale" was omitted (E)—opinions were divided; negative views were in the minority. Ayrton (Har) was the most severe:

> The opera seems to us to be a laboured production—the work of a man who understands the mechanism of the art thoroughly, but who does not possess a genius for original invention. . . . There are very few things in it that we could not trace to some model which appears to have occupied his thoughts; and to the *Freischutz* and *Euryanthe* he has continually made himself a debtor. . . . He leaves no blank—understands not the virtue of repose; each instrument is condemned to incessant toil, and the fatigue of the hearer is little less than that of the performer.

But Holmes (At), who provided more technical terms than most other reviewers were heretofore willing—or able—to introduce, was the most positive, challenging Ayrton's views:

> Although there were three acts, besides an introduction of considerable length . . . no one was tired at the end, and many were longing for more. Can a higher compliment be paid to a composer? . . . Of melody there is abundance, and the musical thoughts are no less original in themselves than in the manner of their expression. . . .
>
> The opening chorus in the unusual key of F sharp minor—the same in which Weber wrote his celebrated incantation scene—probably caused the idea that Marschner has been but an imitator. Except in the choice of an unfamiliar key—which is necessary to give effect to the supernatural and terrible in music—we see little to remind us of Weber; the style is different, and so is the instrumentation. . . . The bridal chorus, in D (9/8 time), is original and leads to a powerful piece of concerted music. . . . The progress of the modulation is rapid here, and every chord raises the expectation of the hearer. Henrika's fear, and the dread of the lookers on, is finely expressed by an agitated and restless bass in C minor. At intervals, the entrance of the chorus "Guard us from the evil eye," has a fine and solemn effect. The harmonies are, throughout, wild and uncommon, and betray great audacity.

Phillips, who performed the vampire, was the hero of the evening; but all performers were highly commended for their singing and acting, the chorus was praised, and even Ayrton noted the excellence of the cast with the "very difficult music." The work was a decided success with the public, too, though its run was cut short by the illness of a principal performer. The following season the piece was greeted with hisses; Hunt was most disappointed. The music, he wrote,

> is disjointed and unmeaning. The author can start, can hurry, can rise into a cry of astonishment, or sink into a grim base . . . but all this is the cant of a German opera. . . . What we require, in order to be touched with what we hear, and to have it 'haunt us like a passion,' is flowing emotion and melody; grandeur of accompaniment sustaining beauty of invention; recitatives full of natural impulse, as if the emotion began with talking to itself out loud, and then the divine air (as in Mozart) giving it its full and flowing way. . . . We have nothing of this rich, flowing, continuous, and substantial syle in the Opera before us. It is a thing of fits and starts, of shreds and patches, and scientific impertinence. (*Tatler*)

Weber

We come finally to our last composer, Weber, and it is a fitting conclusion, for in a sense he virtually gave his life for English opera. Moreover, though

Bishop had planted the seeds earlier, Weber gave a large thrust to the movement for Englished operas through the London production of his singspiel, *Der Freischütz*, in 1824.

Carl Maria von Weber (1786–1826), a sickly child with a permanent limp, studied composition with his father, Franz Anton Weber, also a composer, and with Michael Haydn, under whom he became a chorister at Salzburg. Precocious, he played the piano in public and wrote his first opera at fourteen. After further study at Munich and Vienna (under Abbé Vogler), he traveled extensively in Europe, conducting and producing operas at Breslau, Stuttgart, Mannheim, Darmstadt, Prague, and Dresden, where there was bitter rivalry between him and Morlacchi. His most successful work was *Der Freischütz* (Berlin, 1821), the libretto by Friedrich Kind, in which the German nation "sensed it had found its musical voice" (N.G.).

Logan—Hawes/Weber

So anxious was London to see *Freischütz* that there were actually three main productions of it in 1824—Arnold had the jump on the two majors—to say nothing of the numerous burlesques spawned at the minors. His version, which was a "literal" translation by W. McGregor Logan[199] and was under the musical supervision of Hawes, was the first to appear, on July 22.[200]

The *London*'s reviewer pointed out that the German legend (as in August Apel's original story), on which Kind had drawn for the drama, had a more gruesome ending, and he thought the drama "injudiciously put together," though the translation was "admirable." Talfourd (NM) was more critical of Kind's libretto. But most reviewers were moved by the drama, especially the wolf's glen scene of the second act, which was strongly abetted by all the arts of stagecraft. Sterling (T) wrote:

> Then came the scene of the glen, where Casper was discovered raising the Devil, according to the most approved recipe,—that is, with a circle of black stones, and a skull and hanger. A wild chorus of Spirits is sung while he performs the unholy rites, and the yells of unquiet ghosts and screech-owls accompany it. The Demon appears, and the bargain is made; the materials for casting the bullets rise out of the earth, and Rudolph appears true to his appointment, and undismayed by all the ugly shapes which assail him. As each bullet is cast, the horrors accumulate; dreadful sounds, loathsome birds and reptiles, deformed shapes cluster round the charmed circle, a phantasmagoric hunt is seen . . . in the clouds; until at length the stage looks like the pictures of "the temptations of St. Anthony."

And the *News* reported: "The melting of the lead, amidst the warring of the elements, the frantic demeanour of divers evil spirits, ghosts, goblins, toads, and other reptiles, who shower down fire and change the colour of the moon and the cataract in the glen to that of blood—all these were represented with the entire of the appalling horrors of the *rampant melodrama*" (quoted by Arundell, p. 314). These effects were thought astonishing considering the shallow stage and limited resources of the theatre. Some of the stage machinery and the fireworks failed the first night but were soon put in order.

The heart of the drama, of course, lay in the music. There were detractors; the *Gazette* declared, "We much doubt if there be a single Air that is likely to become popular" and noted that "the audience appeared to be miserably disappointed." The *Observer* thought the music "better fitted to instruct than to please. It is too full of discords and they are sometimes introduced most unfortunately so as to break the chain of melody"[201] (quoted by Arundell).

Most of the press, however, heard it quite otherwise—even with respect to the audience reaction! The *Chronicle* wrote: "In the *Freischutz*, the lively, the tender, the solemn, and the mysterious, all are expressed in the most appropriate tones and harmonies," and "the multitude admire it for the beauties of the melodies." And the *Examiner* responded to some of the objections:

> From the first bar of the overture to the last of the finale, the wild and supernatural is borne continually in recollection, with a variety of combination, which is admirably indicative of the strength and fertility of the mind which could produce it. We have indeed heard this very predominance objected to,—that the melody is broken too much by discords.... We are not of the opinion, and for this reason, that in a piece of this nature, we apprehend the mind of the auditor should never be allowed to subside into common-life impressions.

Ayrton declared the opera "is strictly entitled to the character of originality, and holds forth its author as a man possessing a rich vein of new and beautiful airs, a strong feeling for harmony, united to a deep knowledge of its capabilities, a poetical mind, and a clear judgment"; he continued with a long and detailed analysis of the work and concluded: "It is an intellectual composition, that requires the exertion of intellect to enter into its meaning, and an intimate acquaintance with its various parts to develope [*sic*] all its beauties." But it was the *London* reviewer who most relished the work's musico-dramatic impact:

> It remains but to speak of the music, which, of its kind, is really beyond all ordinary praise or conception. Some of the critics have said it is not so sweet or so good as Mozart's: — Pshaw! it was never intended to be sweet! it is appalling, terrific, sublime! It giveth not "Airs from Heaven," but "Blasts from Hell." From the Overture to the very last note, the composer, Weber, seems to have called upon Zamiel, and to have offered up to him notes which would go into his very soul! There is a depth, a wildness, which frights the mind while it charms the ear; and we will confidently say that no music, not even Mozart's, was ever heard with such breathless attention and earnestness as this extraordinary production of Weber. It is a great work!

Almost everyone praised the production. Somehow, Arnold induced Braham to sing Rudolph (Max), and he outdid himself in the role; the other performers were nearly as effective. The chorus was well rehearsed, the band had been augmented, and no expense had been spared. "Mr. Arnold's very hazardous experiment of giving a popular German opera to an English audience has thus met with the success it merited" (C). It was "received with *real* spontaneous bursts of applause . . . genuine approbation, arising from a feeling of the merits of the composition, and without the assistance of *claqueurs*, or any other sort of artifice" (Har).[202]

Planché — Livius/Weber

In October Covent Garden brought out *their* version of *Freischütz*, which was adapted by Planché, with musical supervision by Livius. Planché, possibly assisted by Washington Irving, made changes in the character of Rudolph (whom he called Wilhelm), which were "very great, as it reduces Wilhelm to a mere spiritless and unadventurous lover, to the loss of all the fine vocal music of the incantation scene." Further, Braham was replaced by Pearman in the role — a "vast disadvantage" (E). There was also a "transposition of the drinking scene"; this "annihilates the design of the fine Bacchanalian song, and the extension of this part, by a very dull dialogue without the smallest pretence to originality, takes much from the interest of the whole opera" (Har). On the other hand, the stage effects were superior: "The scenery is all of it of the most beautiful description: indeed it is hardly possible to praise it sufficiently. . . . The machinery worked well, and fire and brimstone were in great abundance" (LG). This production was immensely successful, with fifty-two repetitions, despite the competition.

Soane—Bishop/Weber

A month later Drury Lane, not to be outdone, opened with *their* version of *Freischütz*—an adaptation by Soane, with the music arranged and directed by Bishop. Billed as an opera rather than as a musical drama, this version had "the whole of Weber's music, as originally performed in Berlin," i.e., it included the *final* Finale dropped in the other productions—the songs were not merely translated but "rewritten," and one or two scenes were added (T). Nevertheless, the *London* was now disappointed: "We are beginning to get very sick of this very good music." And the *Chronicle* questioned some of Bishop's "arrangements," but Ayrton did not protest them, and the *Examiner* even thought them an improvement, for the music "is better adapted to the flow of the melodies and their emphatic parts."

The public, more interested perhaps in the superior stage effects, was even more supportive of this version, which received seventy-two performances. At its 1831 revival, Hunt again rendered a minority report that fully revealed his musical conservatism:

> We hate to differ with the many: we are compelled to speak as we think. We can only say therefore, in self-defence, that . . . we cannot help considering those who think Weber a composer of the highest order, deficient in imagination. His fine movements are the exception. His general character is that of a cold, formal, and literal, not to say sickly composer, who mistakes description for feeling, and thinks he has given us the *effect* of an emotion, by repeating its commonest language. He groans, he sighs, and he shouts, and then waits for our approbation. But this is not sympathy: it is an echo.[203] (*Tatler*)

Dimond—Cooke/Weber

These successes prompted the majors to scramble for further Weber productions,[204] and in 1825 Drury Lane came up with *Abou Hassan*, a two-act comic opera that Dimond apparently adapted or translated (C) from F. C. Hiemer's libretto for Weber's singspiel (Munich, 1811), based on an episode from the *Thousand and One Nights*. The music was adapted by Cooke.

Sterling (T) thought it "a lovely piece. The dialogue runs on glibly, and the jests . . . tell pleasantly." But the *Chronicle* reported that "the best that can be said of [the drama] is that it amuses"; the *Examiner*, too, found it amusing. There were further differences on the music. Sterling thought it was "for the greater part, bold and energetic, sometimes wild in its character," while the *Chronicle* found "nothing of a very striking character" in the music, though some acccompaniments were "finely arranged." Again, the *Examiner* was somewhere in between; the music, they wrote, "if not in the *frappant* style which has produced him so much popularity, is still very attractive." Ayrton merely called the music "light, original, and pleasing," but the *Gazette* and the *London* dismissed it altogether. The opera had but a mediocre production, yet it was quite successful, with thirty-one repetitions.[205]

Soane—Hawes/Weber

Four weeks later Covent Garden produced Weber's *Preciosa* in an adaptation probably by Soane, with music arranged by Hawes.[206] The work, a success in Berlin (1821), was based on a libretto by P. A. Wolff and had an overture and eleven numbers. The work lay on the border between singspiel and a play with music (Loewenburg); it had only one singing character besides the chorus. Sterling wrote: "An attempt to give effect to simple recitation by musical accompaniment, is made in the first act . . . but it was not, we think, successful; the common recitative of the musical drama would have answered better"; the *Examiner* agreed. The *Literary Chronicle* reported: "A more absurd or contemptible production was never offered to the public." The audience was so opposed to it that it closed after a single performance. Parke attributed the failure to "the paucity of the musical effects."

Somerset—Blewitt/Weber

In 1828, two years after Weber's death, still another of his operas—his earliest—was produced: *Sylvana*, a romantic opera based on a text by F. C. Hiemer (Frankfurt, 1810). The English adaptation was made by Charles A. Somerset, with music arranged by Jonathan Blewitt,[207] and produced at the Surrey Theatre. The story, about a dumb girl beloved by a gallant knight, was found absurd (T; C) and a patchwork—"wretchedly written" (At). But the *Gazette* was rather amused, for it included

> a bear, which we were extremely disappointed in finding did not turn out to be the father of the heroine. He was, incontinently, shot. . . . The real human father of Sylvania, however, lived on, a much greater brute and savage than the slain Bruin. . . . We really cannot see why he should

be killed outright: there is the heroine saved when an infant, by the assassin rocking her to sleep instead of throwing her over the precipices, as he was commanded; and why the poor animal should not also be rescued, after tumbling down from the rifle-shot, seems to us to be inconsistent with the good nature of the author, and the character of the symphonies.

All reviewers thought the music compensated for the weakness in the book. J. D. Collier (C) wrote: "The music of *Sylvania*, compared with that of *Der Freischutz*, approaches more the Italian style.... There is the same originality and vigour—the same display of natural and highly-cultivated genius—the same abundance of gay, brilliant, and sparkling combinations in *Sylvania*." The *Gazette* thought the music in the first act "as fine as we have heard in any theatre.... The choruses are equal to any thing Weber ever composed," though the rest was "very wearisome." Holmes (At) wrote: "Weber's *Sylvania* is like the attempt of a young composer just beginning to try his wings—the melody is natural," but the music contains "no hint of that daring novelty, which the composer ventured upon in some parts of his maturer works." The production—orchestra and singers—was extremely poor (At), and the work very likely failed.[208]

Planché—Weber

This brings us to our last opera—and Weber's—*Oberon*, produced as a "New Romantic Fairy Opera" by Covent Garden in 1826. It was, of course, not an adaptation but an original production. London audiences were familiar with the story—Drury Lane had mounted Thompson's unsuccessful *Oberon's Oath* in 1816. Shortly after the English Opera House's opening of *Freischütz*, Charles Kemble wrote to Weber with an offer to compose an opera—on Faust or Oberon—for Covent Garden for the 1825 season, and to come to London to direct it. Though very ill, Weber felt he could only save his family from starvation, after the early death his doctors had predicted, by accepting the offer.[209] The date was unrealistic, of course, but Weber selected Oberon and began studying English. He had 153 lessons from one Cary, an expatriate Englishman residing in Dresden (Langley). The libretto was written by Planché from a translation by William Sotheby of Wieland's poem of that name, which he had drawn, fairly closely, from Lord Berners's translation of the medieval French Romance *Huron de Bordeaux*.

After Weber received the first installment of the libretto from Planché in early 1825, he was concerned because of the radical difference between what it indicated of the nature of English opera and the thoroughly organic style toward which he had been moving in *Der Freischütz* (N.G.). As he wrote Planché, "the intermixing of so many principal actors who do not sing, the omission of the music in the most important moments—all deprive our *Oberon* of the title of an opera, and will make it unfit for all other theatres in Europe."[210] Nevertheless, Weber completed his score by January 1826, and arrived in London March 4, where he reluctantly agreed to make changes and additions in the music for Braham.

In a review of a rehearsal, at which Weber presided at the pianoforte and which was attended by a number of the nobility, Sterling (T) pointed out the choicest parts of the work. On opening night "all orders were suspended," the house was packed, and "many hundreds" were turned away (C; LitC).[211] We are told the crowds flocked to the theatre mainly to see the costumes and stage effects: production costs exceeded £7,000 (N.G.). Weber wrote his wife: "It is quite impossible to describe the dazzling and touching effect of such a complete and cloudless triumph. . . . The splendour and perfection of the scenery passes all description." But he was even more impressed with the stage effects of a rival *Oberon*, which ran simultaneously at Drury Lane.[212]

The *Gazette* thought Planché's dialogue, "if not very powerfully written, is at all events free from affectation; whilst the lyrical compositions are . . . really of a very superior order. . . . Songs written for the stage have been too long notorious for their want of sense and metre, and we consequently hail an attempt to ingraft poetry and meaning upon music." The *Examiner* agreed, but Talfourd (NM, June), who had a theory, did not:

> The most paramount requisite in the poetry for opera songs is simplicity—simplicity of thought, simplicity of diction, simplicity of metre. Next to this, brevity is essential: short songs and short lines! As to the subjects of the songs, the more they have reference to the action of the drama and identify themselves with it, the better. . . . Of their transgression [of these rules] in almost every particular, Oberon furnishes many instances. The lyric texts . . . are often too lengthy, often too descriptive and extraneous; and, wherever this is the case, the composer seems to have laboured, and has invariably proved less successful.

In the matter of language Ayrton alone (Har) pointed to a perceived related defect in the music:

> Though Mr. von Weber had acquired a proficiency in the English language which was quite surprising, the short time that he had devoted to its study being allowed for,[213] yet he had not made himself

master of its accents: hence an abundance of errors arising out of a want of knowledge on this subject, appear in the work. . . . It was the duty of the management to provide a qualified person to assist the German musician in a task which, under his circumstances, it was impossible that he should execute in the manner that the public had a right to expect.

On the work in general, J. P. Collier (C) likened the opera "to an edifice upon the most magnificent scale, with a profusion of the richest ornament," and like the rest of the press, he provided for more musical commentary than usual. He thought that there is "no part of Weber's music which so obviously distinguishes him from other composers as his recitatives, which, while they preserve the narrative style, are full of variety and vigorous expression." And he added, Weber "is, unquestionably, a composer of very original powers, and deals in what has been justly called, the poetry of music. Each note breathes the heart of passion!" Sterling (T) found the work's subject "full of excitement to a mind constituted like that of Weber, which delights in the wild and supernatural. His invocations, choruses of fairies, of the grotesque spirits that attend on the goblin Puck, the rising of sea-nymphs from the ocean . . . all attest his peculiar power in the most striking manner" (Apr. 12). But, he added, *Oberon* "has more, perhaps, in a constant variety of striking and scientifically managed passages than in that simple and definite style of melody which made parts of Der Freischutz so popular" (Apr. 13).

Talfourd, however, regretted there were no *human* passions in the work: "In Oberon, there is no touch of human interest; its marvels are all addressed to the fancy; and the spectator feels no curiosity, from beginning to end, except to see how the next scene will be painted, and to hear how the next song will be adapted to its spiritings." The *European* (June), too, thought the music would suffer by contrast with *Freischütz*: "It has many beautiful and exquisite touches of genius and melody, though the general effect is monotonous and heavy."

In a long and very favorable review, the *Gazette* came up with some interesting comparisons between Weber and Mozart, while the *Examiner* provided apt comparisons of the supernatural in *Oberon* and *Freischütz*. Ayrton (Har), who fully explored the details of the opera, concluded on a positive but wistful note, for Weber was already dead:

> The music of *Oberon*, like that of the *Freischutz*, shews that the composer of it [had] not merely created melodies and discovered new forms of accompaniment, but he studied the passions, their shades and effects, and expressed them with a distinctness and force seldom accomplished

by means of musical sounds. He was, in fact, a well-educated man, of extensive reading and deep thought; . . . even in sickness he showed no symptoms of mental exhaustion, and a very short time before his death he found new musical ideas crowding on him in as quick a succession as when his bodily strength was less impaired.

With respect to the performers, later writers have cited some of the problems faced at the premiere. Sir Julius Benedict, for example, who was twenty-two when he saw the opera in 1826, and who had already conducted opera at Vienna, wrote in 1881[214] that at rehearsals only Braham and Harriet Cause, who was brought in at the last moment to sing the mermaid, were adequate; Paton was "wayward and capricious," Vestris "overweighted" in the part of Fatima, Fawcett had "too little" voice, and Bland had a "bad" voice. But Benedict admitted that things went much better on opening night. John Edward Cox, also in his twenties at the time, wrote in 1872[215] that at rehearsals Weber had to caution Paton not to ornament her singing. But Weber, who was perhaps overanxious to reassure his wife, wrote her that "Paton sang her part enchantingly the first time through." Moreover, he had only praise for the theatre orchestra, and he proudly pointed out that the overture and several numbers were encored. Contemporary reviewers on the whole thought the opera had a strong cast; the *Examiner* wrote: "All of the performers visibly exerted themselves; although some are not well suited with the parts," and Braham "acted as well as he could."

The opera was suprisingly popular, with thirty-one performances and at least two revivals by 1830. The following season, when it was revived under the direction of Sir George Smart,[216] Sterling wrote that *Oberon* "improves upon acquaintance" and "must be placed among the finest even of Weber's compositions." Eric Walter White thinks *Oberon* had a considerable effect on English opera, yet he noted it failed at an 1831 revival. But the influence of *Freischütz* was surely more powerful. Writing of that opera in 1836, Hogarth stated: "No drama produced ever made a greater or more lasting impression on the public." With Weber, English opera finally came to terms with Romanticism. As Nicholas Temperley[217] writes: "Romantic subjects had been common enough in English operas since well back in the eighteenth century, but composers had had almost no success in evolving an appropriate style for them. . . . Instead of the banalities of Bishop [the English] were confronted for the first time [in *Freischütz* and *Oberon*] with music that was as Romantic as the drama." Yet it was Bishop, with all his shortcomings, who launched the movement toward adaptations of foreign operas that led directly to Weber's success in London.

At the conclusion of opening night, "with that bear-like kindness" with which an audience "hugs to death what it embraces, Weber was called on the stage to be applauded. We never saw the shrinking and sensitive character of real genius more pointedly represented than in his bow on this occasion. . . . These braying requisitions are altogether discreditable, and ought to be put an end to" (E). In rapidly failing health, Weber determined to return home to die despite his doctor's warning that he was too ill to travel. On June 5, the day before his projected departure, he died alone in his bed at George Smart's house, where he had been living since his arrival in London.

The Performances

GIVEN THE TWOFOLD NATURE of English opera, the theatres required two casts: one singing and one nonsinging. Usually the leading characters in operas were played by singers, but in some, especially the melodramas, this was by no means the case. And many of the minor comic roles had actors who were not really singers at all but were nevertheless given songs to sing. This occurred, for example, in Arnold's *Up All Night* (1809), when comedian George Bartley, with a "very short allowance of voice," spoiled the songs he had to sing and "was treated with marks of ill humour by the audience" (T). Sometimes a part was just dropped if no substitute was available.[1]

On the other hand, the best music was reserved for the best singers, as Holmes complained in 1829 (At, Jan. 18): "When Miss Paton comes to town, we shall hope to have some music really worth hearing." But for most singers personality had a great deal to do with their success; for years Fanny Kelly—the darling of the stage and never in a heavy singing role—succeeded as a singer of occasional songs with little voice but much histrionic ability. Traditionally, singers were not expected to be as competent in acting as nonsinging performers, though some critics disagreed, and their complaints seem to have been effective in prompting some singers, like Braham, to put more effort into their acting.

Many roles for singers and nonsingers alike were tailored to individual performers by playwrights and composers (N., III, 40). Indeed, leading performers dominated playwrights in their eagerness to play in successful pieces; they also quarreled among themselves about their parts. As Dibdin noted, "if the actors don't like the part, they won't play it"; the work may not be accepted; or the manager may want parts padded to suit actors' whims. And he cited "the old custom of writing almost every song three or four times over, till it suited a situation or a melody approved by the prospective singers, whether or not in harmony with the interests of the story, or the general texture of the piece."[2]

Thomas Linley the Elder believed that no composer could set a song properly unless he knew the character and the performer.[3] When Harris engaged Signora Sestini for Covent Garden, O'Keeffe "matched her with Italian music of the most perfect kind, and good, broken English." And when comic actor John Fawcett wanted to mimic a then-famous buffo at the King's, "Shield got the real music ["Non più andrai"] and supplied me with the measure. I wrote it, and Fawcett sang it with great comic powers."+ Dibdin found he needed to hear the voice of tenor Charles Incledon so as to know how to write better songs for him.

Not all agreed with this tailoring, however. In 1800, the *Dramatic Censor* (June 7) wrote: "We beg leave to ask these [playwrights] what will become of their comedies, when they no longer have a Mr. [W. T.] Lewis to enliven and invigorate their flights and exaggerations. . . . This shows the absurdity . . . of writing plays by an *inverted process*; i.e., of *writing* parts for particular actors, instead of leaving it to the actor to *suit* himself to the part." The *Literary Chronicle* agreed, probing deeper into the problem, which they thought also conributed to the decline of the drama:

> Singers are seldom good actors: indeed it were greatly to be wondered at if they were, when it is considered how little the silly situations in which they are almost invariably placed, while exercising their vocal powers, is favourable to any thing like dramatic propriety. . . . Nor is a piece much improved, when persons who have nothing at all to do with the plot, are brought in merely for the purpose of singing. Another vile practice which has tended considerably to deteriorate both the drama and actors, is the practice of *taking measure*, if we may so term it, of a particular performer, and fashioning parts according to his style and manner of acting. (Aug. 8, 1824)

Performers were paid for each night the theatre was open, whether they were on stage or not. The weekly salary of performers at Drury Lane in the 1801–1802 season was as follows (singers are asterisked): Men—Kemble £56, Bannister £17, King £16, Pope £13, Kelly* £16, Suett* £12, and Sedgwick* £6; Women—Jordan* £31, Crouch* £14, De Camp* £12, Mountain* £12, and Bland* £12. But some performers got less than three pounds.[5] Leading performers also had a benefit night each season, when they had the choice of the work and received the net profits of the performance.

Singers at the playhouses were even more expendable than those at the King's, yet many did have long careers there. But entry was difficult without money and the right connections. Dibdin certainly painted no encouraging picture for them:

> I say nothing of musical pupils forced on the public for any one's real benefit but their own: the audience are disappointed, the theatre pays,

40. John Braham as Don Alphonso in *The Castle of Andalusia*

41. Henry Phillips as Cedric in *The Maid of Judah*, Covent Garden (1829)

42. Nancy Storace; drawn and engraved by Gilray

43. Lucia Elizabeth Vestris, *center*, with John Liston in a scene from *Paul Pry*; from an engraving of a painting by Clint

44. *Buy a Broom*, Cole's Music Store; engraving of a sheet music cover published by John Cole

45. Mary Anne Paton

46. Catherine Stephens

47. Carl Maria von Weber conducting in London

the master profits, and the pupil toils. If the said pupils happen to succeed, the immense expense of a musical education is only to be repaid by the sacrifice of one-half of his or her theatrical appointments for years after success; and this success is so doubtful, that a prize in the lottery, though next to an impossible thing, is certainty compared to the chances of a singer. (II, 396)

Early on, reviewers gave little detail on singers except for a few of the most outstanding ones. Often, too, they failed to mention some of the minor singers at all (see appendix 19). This gradually changed, and after 1815 we find considerably more critical interest—even in the average performers. In part this was due to the increasing number of operatic roles in that period; before 1800, there were less than a dozen male and a dozen female singers of note, but the number about doubled after 1815.

Still, there were many protests from the press in the later years for more and better singers. In 1818, for instance, Kenrick (BS), welcoming Miss Carew to the English Opera House, declared it a "miserable operatic company." In 1822 the *London* (Oct.) noted that "vocal talent" was now "scarce on the English stage," and in 1829 Holmes (At, Oct 25) complained of the inadequacy of singers in English opera. In 1827 a good bass was not to be had. Planché flatly declared that no Covent Garden actors could sing and only Vestris among the singers could act.

THE LEADING MALE SINGERS

Incledon

Of the early male singers, only Incledon and Kelly drew much notice from the press. Charles Incledon (1763–1826), a fine tenor, was also an outstanding comedian. Son of a medical practitioner, at eight he was singing in the Exeter Cathedral choir. In 1779 he went to sea, and his voice attracted the attention of Admiral Pejot, who helped him get started in the theatre. In 1784 he was singing in the provinces, in 1786 at Vauxhall Gardens, and in 1790 at Covent Garden in *Poor Soldier*. For the next thirty years he held a high position with the public. He quarreled with Harris in 1815 and later successfully toured the United States, but his voice was past its prime, and he retired in 1822.

In 1791, as Wilford in the *Woodman*, he "added much to his vocal reputation by the manner in which he executed his songs" (C). He, "beyond comparison, bore away the palm in point of musical excellence. His first two songs . . . were executed with infinite taste and melody" (LC). The same year he sang "admirably" as Somerville in *Magician no Conjurer* and was very successful as Captain Melville in *Just in Time* (C). His "Seaman's Home" in *Midnight Wanderers* (1793) was charmingly sung and "very characteristic" in his role as Julian (H), and as Earl Fitzallan in the *Armourer* that year, he "sung well, but he had no extraordinary scope for the full display of his vocal talents" (C). In *Lock and Key* (1796) he "sang with his utmost ability" (OPA), and he was "unrivaled" (Parke) in the *Beggar's Opera* (1797). He had a "great many" songs and some encores (P) as Frank in the *Old Cloathsman* (1799).

Incledon was "competent" (C) in the *Escapes* in 1801, and in 1802 he sang Davy's "Hunting Song" in the *Cabinet* "with all his fulness and richness of tone" (it was "loudly encored") and gave "unusual force of expression to his airs" (T; P; MM). His duet with Braham in *Family Quarrels* was "alone sufficient to draw crowded audiences" (T) and displayed his "irresistible" powers (P). In 1803 in the *English Fleet*, he was encored "in almost every air" (T); his duet with Braham "excited bursts of applause, which we never saw surpassed in enthusiasm" (C), and his "exertions in voice and action" were much admired (T). In 1804 he again excelled in a revival of the *Cabinet* (P), and in *Thirty Thousand* he "did not appear inferior to himself in whatever he had to do, and we cannot say more of this fine singer" (C; T).

As Edward in the *White Plume* (1806) Incledon sang songs "well calculated to display the characteristic excellence of his style" (C) and "afforded ample scope for the display and development of the great compass and rich volume of his melodious voice: a Recitative was delivered... in an uncommonly impressing and affecting style" (Cr; MM). In 1807 he was effective in *Peter the Great* (C) and in *Two Faces* (MM); in 1808 he was warmly received in the *Exile* (T).

The press was silent on him until 1814, when he was still "in fine voice" and sang "with great animation and effect" (UM) in the *Farmer's Wife*. It may have been following this performance that "his arbitrary employer at Covent Garden, upon the mere grounds of individual offense, deprived the public of that worthy and established favourite," for which action he was advised by the *Inquisitor* to appeal to the Lord Chamberlain (Apr. 1820). In 1815 the *Inquisitor*, however, castigated his Macheath (*Beggar's Opera*): "Although he might have been a good singer formerly," he "certainly could not lay claim to that title of late years, and his acting was ever the acme of everything vile and despicable" (Oct.). But two years later, Kenrick (BS) wrote: "Spite of Incledon's insufferable vulgarity, and the extravagant praise which has been heaped upon his vocal powers, it must be admitted that in the execution of several airs appertaining to the character of Macheath, he has not left his equal behind him" (Oct.).

In 1820, after a successful two-year tour of the United States, he appeared as Artabanes in *Artaxerxes* at Drury Lane. "His reception showed there were many in the theatre in whom the old impressions were not effaced; ... his articulation is less perfect than formerly, but his voice retains much of its original quality and fulness of volume" (T). And the *Inquisitor*, in another *volte-face*, quite agreed: "He still retains that compass, volume, and energy for which his vocal efforts were always so remarkable. His Artabanes is just the same towering performance it has always been considered." This was perhaps his swan song. Haydn, who heard him in 1791, thought he used falsetto to excess.

Kelly

Five years before his King's debut, Michael Kelly, a tenor, brought an exceptional range of singing skill to English opera and was one of the very few early male singers who was not primarily a comedian. He began singing on the English stage soon after his return from Italy, making his debut at Drury Lane—where he remained until his retirement—as Lionel in *A School for Fathers*, an adaptation by Bickerstaffe of his *Lionel and Clarissa*, on April 20, 1787. We find no review of that performance, but a month later he appeared as Young Meadows in a revival of *Love in a Village*. Charles Este of the *Register* wrote:

> His voice and taste are much too good for the generality of an English audience—*caveare* [sic] to the *million*—Two new airs were very happily introduced, to give a sufficient scope for the exertion of his powers. ... [One, "Each anxious hour"] was given in a style that would not have disgraced Rubinelli—we never heard a more general or enthusiastic encore.—Mr. Kelly's endeavours at *expression*—and they are often successful—may have led him into an ill habit—we mean the too frequent application of his hand to his breast.

Yet the *Herald* even praised his acting: "By his energetic manner, he created an interest in the part, which we have never seen it possess in other hands; and his musical ability had claims still stronger on our encomium."

Later that year he appeared in *Artaxerxes*: "Arbaces is so perfectly suited to the talents of Mr. Kelly, that we are astonished he did not fix on it for his *debut*—Never did this operatical *hero* appear with so much eclat—The airs of Arbaces displayed an infinite fund of science, taste and execution" (Este, UR, Oct. 26). In the same opera with Mara the next year, "his performance as an actor ascended very nearly on the scale, to the degree of his musical excellence" (H). As Carlos in *Doctor and Apothecary* (1788) he "never sung so well on the English stage" (H). By 1787 he "had at length brought his manner nearer to the style of the English performers, and he grew into favour with the town" (Boaden, II, 389). In 1789 he sang "very charmingly" as Ferdinand in Kemble's *Tempest* (LC). As Lord William in the *Haunted Tower* the same year, he "was less animated than we have usually seen him" but he had been "lately indisposed" (H).

In 1790 he had an offer from Gallini to sing the next season at the King's Theatre, but he preferred to remain at Drury Lane. He performed Iarbas "extremely well" (LC) in the all-sung *Dido* (1792); he had "all his vocal animation" (H) and sang "with judgment" (LitC). As Marcos in the *Prisoner* later that year, he sang well but "the perpetual rattling of his chains in the prison scene, as an accompaniment to the music, has, in our opinion, a very bad effect" (C). He also excelled as Don Altador in the *Pirates* the next month.

In 1793–94 he was at the King's, but in 1795 he returned to Drury Lane and was encored as Sir Murdock O'Connel in *Jack of Newbury*. In 1796 he was congratulated on his "expressiveness" as Mossafer in *Mahmoud*. Two years later, Kelly sang well as Canesar in *Captive of Spilburg* (T).

As Macheath in *Beggar's Opera* (1802) he had "a whimsicality of manner savouring more of the flash-man [a companion of thieves] than the fine gentleman" (T), and he received a very warm response from the audience (P). In *House to be Sold* the same year, he "did ample justice to his own songs" (C), as he did in *Youth, Love and Folly* in 1805 (C), the last time he comes to notice as a singer. His voice had already deteriorated, and he retired as a performer in 1808. Boaden[6] tells us that at the height of his singing career Kelly's voice had

> amazing power and sturdiness; his compass was extraordinary. In vigorous passages he never cheated the ear with the feeble wailings of falsetto, but sprung upon the ascending fifth with a sustaining energy, that often electrified an audience. [Together with Nancy Storace he] gave a new feature to our amusements. The foreign habits of these accomplished singers enabled them to sing steadily, while moving about the stage, (a difficulty of no mean rank,) and infused a life, a breath into our opera, which before hardly trusted itself to action.

Braham

Like Kelly, Braham sang for a few seasons at the King's, but it was as a singer on the English musical stage that he gained his chief claim to fame. Precocious, he was singing at age thirteen in 1787 at Covent Garden. After later appearances at Bath under Rauzzini's sponsorship, he got a leading role in *Mahmoud* at Drury Lane in 1796 (the year he also made his King's debut). His reception was phenomenal; the *Times* (critic D) exclaimed:

> The whole history of the Stage cannot produce such a debut as Mr. Braham's, in vocal performance; he is the first *tenor* in the world for science, taste, and execution. . . . His forte is of the plaintive kind; by no means inspirited and energetic — very unlike the fire with which Kelly electrifies the house; but that sort of expression which steals upon the heart. He is uncommonly successful in blending the *falsetto* with the natural voice, and his tones, though opposite to shrill, are distinctly heard over every distant part of the house.

The *London Chronicle* reported that the public had "never heard a more accomplished singer" in an English theatre. Boaden ("Thetis" of the *Oracle*) wrote that Braham "is without exaggeration the most finished *tenor* ever heard in this country. . . . His falsetto unites perfectly well with the natural tone, which is not reedy, but clear, mellow, firm, and sweet beyond example. To all this he adds . . . perfect articulation, infinite feeling, and consummate science." DuBois (MM) agreed, as did the *Herald*, though the latter noted that he was an indifferent actor and that his dialogue was "scarcely audible." Of this debut Boaden wrote in 1831 that Braham "presented a perfection of musical science and execution hitherto unconnected with our opera," and for twenty-eight years he had "no shadow of a rival."

Such reviews should have been more than enough to turn the head of any aspiring young singer, yet he went to Italy for further training, and did not return to London until 1801, when he made his first appearance as an adult singer at Covent Garden in the role of Bensalla in *Chains of the Heart*. The *Times* repeated its former plaudits, while the *Chronicle*, noting it was said that he possessed "the finest tenor voice in Italy," agreed that

> its volume, sweetness, and pathos are most wonderful. His natural compass, though limited, has the most ineffable influence on the heart. His full, clear tone, coming directly from the breast, makes the most heart-felt impression on the auditor. . . . [But] when he aims at the fashionable art of execution, his ornaments, instead of embellishing, weaken his cadences, and we sigh for his return to simplicity and pathos. . . . He will find that the part of the audience of England who have cultivated music as a science . . . have more polished taste than is to be found in countries where it is more understood by the multitude. They have not yet degenerated into the love of capricious difficulties.

But the *Post* reviewer admired his most scientific passages, as did DuBois (MM): "He now adds the most consummate science, astonishing flexibility, neatness, and precision in marking the *half-notes* which excites high admiration," and he "has learned to speak with more distinctness and energy, and to deport himself with proper confidence." Parke wrote of this period that he "showed astonishing improvement in his powers" but that he had too much ornament and was not yet generally admired.

From the *London Magazine* we have this portrait (written much later) of the seasoned singer on the English stage:

> In Mr. Braham you see a small, but not inelegantly formed man, with a steadfast countenance. . . . The physiognomy is that of one sobered by fixed, and somewhat severe thought. The demeanour is something dejected and hesitating, rather than informed with any of the superiority of confidence or command. Yet there is a latent fire in the eye, a visible, but unemployed spring and elasticity in the well-compacted, though reduced scale of the whole form, that indicates power when called into action. (July 1821)

Early in 1802 he sang Orlando in the *Cabinet* (for which he also wrote several songs). The *Times* (Feb. 10) reported he "pleases more than on any former occasion by divesting himself of many redundant divisions and luxuriances." He was "inimitable in all his airs, particularly in his 'Beautiful Maid'" (MM; P).

Braham's appearance in the *Travellers* in 1806, following his engagements at the King's, prompted the *Chronicle* to remark:

> Mr. Braham . . . has more power to do good to the stage than any other lyric performer, because he is master of his art. He can fix a just taste, or vitiate the taste of his country; for such is the fascinating power of articulation with his science, that he can make even error rapturous. . . . We submit to every correct ear in the house, whether the affecting simplicity of his first stanza . . . did not strike more powerfully on the affections . . . than the mere shewy execution with which he concluded the song.

His compositions for *False Alarms* in 1807 absorbed all critical interest except for the *Critical Review*, which, in a surprisingly hostile critique, raised a matter little noticed in his earlier reviews: "The part of Edgar, which means nothing, was properly assigned to Braham, who expresses that meaning to a miracle." And they added: "Italians say of Mr. Braham, that whatsoever he touches he absolutely murders." (Quite the contrary was asserted by Boaden, who thought Braham's *acting* in this opera "its prime attraction.")

In 1808 he sang in *Kais*, when the *Times* thought him excellent, but Hunt (E) found him poor in the role, and DuBois (MM) called him "supremely ridiculous." At a revival of the *Cabinet* that year, Hunt remarked: "It is surprising that this beautiful singer exhibits so bad a taste as to scatter his voice into atoms when he might present us with a solid nobility." He has "contributed to deprave the musical taste of this country" (E, Jan. 24).

Later that year Braham appeared as Giovanni in *Jew of Magadore*, but even his fine bravuras could not save the piece (C). DuBois (MM) wrote: "His voice was clearer than usual, and he did not labour to smother the beauty of simplicity, by a load of affecting unimpressive graces" (MM). Still later that year he was drafted by Hook to sing "Scots wha hae wi' Wallace bled" as a "military minstrel" in his *Siege of San Quintin*. "The song is impressive and affecting, but it was here out of its place; all the energy and pathos of Mr. Braham could give no effect to it" (T). But Hunt (E), who wrote that Braham, when not "'most musical' is 'most melancholy,'" thought the song "was sung with a fine fermenting enthusiasm worthy of its author."

In 1811 Braham sang in the *Americans* at the Lyceum, "and never, perhaps, were Braham's exertions heard with greater pleasure. Abandoning the mysterious delicacies of his art, he addressed the unsophisticated sensibilities of his audience" (C). Benjamin Haydon, who attended a revival of the *Siege of Belgrade* that year, confessed in his *Diary* (Mar. 30) that Braham's singing "delighted me. . . . His trillers, shakes and quavers are like those of all other great singers tiresome to me, but his pure melody, the simple song clearly articulated, is equal to anything I ever heard. . . . Indeed, I think Braham a fine actor while singing . . . his whole frame is awakened—his gestures and looks are equally impassioned."

Braham returned the following year as Count Belino in *Devil's Bridge* and sang his songs "with polished sweetness" (C). *Bell's* wrote: "Braham exerted his great powers, both as an actor and as a singer, and proved how excellent is art, when exempt from affectation; and ambitious only of the general effect of truth." Later he sang in two revivals—*Castle of Andalusia*, where he excelled (T), and the *Cabinet*, where his "exertions" rescued the opera from an otherwise poor production, though "the Lyceum was unfavourable to the nature of his voice; its strength required to be softened by distance" (T).

In 1813 the *Inquisitor* disliked his acting in a revival of Gay's *Polly* (July), and in comparing the tenor George Cooke to him, thought that Cooke had "the worst of all possible models. Arms a Kimbo, right arm up, left arm down, toes out, strong shoulders. . . . Messrs. Braham and Cooke have always the appearance of practicing these manoeuvres, without success" (Sept.).

In 1815 Hunt called him "the best singer in England, perhaps in the world," yet "it is curious to note how the orchestra inspires him; and what a difference there is between the tame, indifferent, vapid creatures [sic] that gets rid of his words with a hasty, half-breathing imbecility when speaking, and the first, ardent, intelligent being, that throws them hither and thither with masterly power during a song." He also noted in him a "nasal twang, which to our ears is very offensive," and found his ornaments most excessive: "He lights up, as it were, fifty wax candles to exhibit a nut shell" (E, Feb. 12).

Braham was again singing at the King's in 1816. But he was welcomed back to Covent Garden the next year as Seraskier in a revival of the *Siege of Belgrade*. Sterling (T) wrote:

> This gentleman, with all his faults, for he is not exempt from them, stands at the head of the vocal talent of the country. . . . To the finest tenor voice perhaps in Europe, he has united a profound study of the best models, and incessant application of the principles of his art; his knowledge of music is most perfect and extensive, and from the Italian bravura down to the simple ballad there is no style of singing of which he is not complete master. On the other hand, he is chargeable with too great a redundancy of ornament . . . which sometimes overwhelms composer and author in one undistinguished ruin.

But the *European* admired "his Corinthian richness of ornament." In a "Dramatic Sketch" of him, Kenrick (BS, Dec. 1817) excused his "exuberance of ornament" as "more a compliance with the false taste of the age, than the dictate of his own judgment."

In 1818 he appeared as Mirvan in *Zuma*, singing some of his own songs. It was "impossible to describe the touching power of Braham's notes" in "His dearest mother's joy" (LG), while his singing of the "Marseillaise hymn," "notwithstanding great opposition, was twice[7] encored" (T; C). The *Inquisitor* agreed, but pointed out that Braham "*endeavoured to act!* and never in our lives did we witness anything so ridiculous. Mr. B. is one of those who takes [sic] the direction of *Hamlet* 'suit the action to the word' as literal," and they went on to imitate one of Hunt's apposite metaphors.

In 1819 he performed at Drury Lane as Henry Bertram in a revival of *Guy Mannering*. Sterling wrote: "We have never heard him . . . in more perfect possession of all his powers, both natural and acquired." Still at the Drury in 1820, after another Arbaces, he sang the lead in *David Rizzio*, but he "disappointed us much. . . . He fell into simplicity and insipidity, plump together, ten thousand fathoms down" (Hazlitt, LM, July). Yet in a revival of the *Duenna* that year, he rendered the original songs "in a style of taste, harmony, and intelligence that has never been equalled" (TI).

At a revival of *Artaxerxes* in 1820, Hazlitt (LM, June) was glad Braham had *not* been there, for he "has omitted some of the most exquisite airs in Artaxerxes to introduce others of his own composing; — and where he has not done this, he might as well, for he so overloads, embellishes, accompanies, and flourishes over the original songs, that one would hardly know them again." And he bitterly complained: "Can anything be more tantalising than to hear him sing 'Water parted from the sea?' Instead of one continued stream of plaintive sound, labouring from the heart with fond emotion . . . it was one incessant exhibition of frothy affectation and sparkling pretence."

By 1821 Bacon (QMM, III, 386f) had become quite disenchanted with the singer: "It is our first wish to secure the public taste from the corrupting influence of the example of his faculties in their prostitution and decay. It is our second hope to spare a man who has possessed so many claims to admiration, from the mortification he can but feel at out-staying the period which nature assigns, even to powers so vast and so eminent as his own."

In 1822, at another revival of the *Siege of Belgrade*, he "exhibited all his pathos, and occasional license of ornament. His organ possibly feels the touch of time" (E).[8] He began the 1822–23 season with another *Siege* revival, but "his lower tones are less bold and firm" and "he arrives at the top of his compass with apparent difficulty. He last night laboured to conceal the inroads which time has made on his voice" (T). The *Examiner*, however, dismissing this view, found no "decay of power," but did find "a weariness of a peculiar kind of excellence" — "possibly owing to having seen him so frequently in the same character." And the next month, in another revival of *Guy Mannering*, he was in "musically fine voice" (T). Yet he does not appear to have sung more that season, and in June of 1823, the *London*, in a season review, reported: "Mr. Braham is a ruin, a splendid ruin, indeed, but a complete ruin."

But Braham had no intentions of quitting the stage. Early in 1824 he appeared in Beazley's *Philandering*, but even Braham's powers could do nothing for Horn's music — "the merest common-places that were ever composed" (T). The *Chronicle* and the *Gazette* agreed, but appreciated Braham's attempts at acting.[9] That summer he was appointed general supervisor of the production of *Freischütz* for the English Opera House, and he also sang the role of Rudolph (Max). Sterling (T) found his singing of the difficult music "in every respect excellent," but the *Chronicle* chided him for "introducing some German airs" which "did not accord with the music." The *Examiner* admired him in a first-act "grand scena," which he gave "with all his pristine energy and more than his vocal purity." The *Gazette* and Ayrton (Har) were supportive, and even the *London* reported "he not only sang better than ever on the first night, but acted with a feeling which we never before detected in him." Talfourd (NM) wrote that he "sings with all his heart and all his science, and without the least affectation or superfluous flourishing. In the presence of Weber he forgets even himself, and makes an impression which will never be forgotten by any who hear him."

In 1825, having left Drury Lane,[10] he appeared in the title role of another English adaptation at the English Opera House: *Tarrare*. The *Chronicle* was impressed and Sterling wrote: "In a bold *bravura* . . . he was twice *encored*" and "triumphed in other passages, but with a milder splendor, . . . for he is still the only man of a varied style, and a thorough apprehension of the real purpose of vocal composition on the English stage." And the *Gazette* excepted him from all other performers for being "distinct in his enunciation," while the *Examiner* "never saw this great vocalist more decidedly himself." Talfourd (NM) reported he "really outsings himself; he puts a heart into his very flourishes" and in one passage he "defies the tyrant in recitative." But the *London* reviewer heard it otherwise: "He sang a song about revenge [and] should have danced around the stage on one leg to complete the triumph of absurdity. Mr. Braham sings to the galleries; but in shouting for their amusement he has ruined his voice . . . —his upper notes are perfectly excruciating."

But in 1826 Braham was back at Covent Garden singing Sir Huon in Weber's *Oberon*. "The grand scena" of the first act "could not have been better sung by Braham," the *European* wrote, but he "laboured more with less effect than he commonly and deservedly produces." Later that year he returned to Drury Lane for a revival of *Devil's Bridge*. He "was received with an ardour of applause which we have rarely seen equalled" and was "in extraordinary, fine voice, and sang with more than usual animation." He also sang Don Carlos in *Two Houses of Grenada* and "fully sustained his high character" (T; LG).

In 1827 he sang the sultan in the *Turkish Lovers* and "exerted himself to the utmost in the gallant Turk" (E). Hazlitt (At) wrote: "He sang delightfully, and did not act his part very ill; but had the Sultan been as great a stick as his Grand Visier, Mr. Horn, we would have forgiven him for the exquisite grace with which he sang . . . 'Lightly o'er ocean bounding,' as well as several other morceaux which we could particularize." Later that year Braham appeared in a revival of *Artaxerxes*, but he sang a secondary role rather than Arbaces (perhaps it was by this time too high for him), which he sustained well and "executed the recitative, for the most part, very impressively" (T). He finished the year in the title role of Dimond's *Isidore de Merida* and "beautifully executed" some of his own songs (T; E) and sang "with spirit, and in tune" (At).

In late 1828 he successfully performed in a revival of *Guy Mannering* and *Love in Wrinkles*. Sterling wrote: "Mr. Braham not only sang the music allotted to him with great taste, but played the part with a spirit which we have not for many years seen him exhibit in the dramatic portion of his stage duties." J. P. Collier (C) was also amazed: Braham "begins to find out, after being forty years on the stage, that he is a very good . . . comic performer." In 1829 he appeared in *Casket*, which failed badly. But on May 6 of that year, in our last reference to him, the *Athenaeum*, reviewing an adaptation of *Masaniello* at Drury Lane, thought Braham, in the title role, "acted better than usual, and sang rather less boisterously. Were it possible to fancy that his subdued tones were indicative of a gentler taste, rather than of a weakened organ, his singing would have been more than ordinarily pleasing."[11]

Even after Braham's voice deteriorated in the 1820s, no other male singer could challenge his vocal supremacy. Weber declared him "a singer of the very first rank."[12] He was still active throughout the 1830s, and in fact, he did not make his final public appearance until 1852! In the 1830s he began speculating in theatres and at one time was owner of the St. James's and the Coliseum, but he lost heavily on both and had to tour the United States (1840–42) to recoup his losses (Reilly). He also continued as a singing teacher.

In summing up his career, it is obvious that despite occasional lapses, his acting improved remarkably over the years and that this improvement can be attributed to the periodical criticism, which we know he took seriously. Otherwise, opinion on him was strongly influenced by the degree to which critics welcomed, or derided, his vocal ornamentation, sometimes without respect to the type of song instanced. In this regard, criticism of him offers similarities to the mixed notices García received at the King's.

Horn

Charles Horn, whom we have already discussed as a composer, made his singing debut with Thomas Phillips as Meddle in *Up All Night* (Lyceum, 1809). The *Chronicle* thought he did not have "equal pretensions" to Phillips. "His voice is feeble, though sweet; and his manner uncultivated." Hunt (E) thought his voice and style "delicate and tasteful, though of small power," and he seemed to want confidence. DuBois (MM) was also quite negative.

Despite such notices Horn sang two months later as Albert in *Safe and Sound*. He "so pleased his hearers, that they forgot to inquire" about his role (MM), but he was again overshadowed by Phillips. In 1810, when he began composing songs, Horn again sang with Phillips in Burges's *Tricks upon Travellers* and was commended (T; MM). But he retired as a singer for six years after that performance, continuing his studies under Thomas Welsh; he reappeared in 1816 a much improved performer.

That year he achieved some success as Seraskier in a revival of the *Siege of Belgrade* at Drury Lane. The *Inquisitor* recalled that his voice, "though rather sweet, was extremely feeble, and his acting remarkably tame and insipid; he now, however, seems destined to hold a foremost rank among our vocal performers. His voice, during his retirement, has increased wonderfully in strength and compass, and the various songs allotted to the character were executed in the finest manner. His acting was also considerably improved" (July). And the *Chronicle* reported: "He has passed his time to utmost advantage, and re-appears as a new man,—as a most excellent singer, and very respectable actor."

Later that year he sang in *The Beggar's Opera,* where his "chaste, well-taught and well managed voice lent charms to some of the songs of Macheath. . . . There is a steady *sostenuto* in his tones, and a habit of keeping a strong command over all his powers, which render Mr. Horn one of the . . . most pleasing musicians we have ever listened to. His Macheath, as a piece of acting, requires a longer exercise on the stage" (T). He was also successful that summer in *Love in a Village* (TI, Aug.) as well as in a revival of *Ramah Droog*, though "we still regret that the volume of his voice has been sacrificed to the acquirement of that B. flat, upon which he is so delighted to indulge" (TI, Dec.). In 1817 he sang in, and composed music for, *Elphi Bay* (Drury Lane), which failed. In a "seasonal review" for 1818, Hunt found him "weak, internal, and full of effort" in his singing and "very formal and theatrical" in his acting, and he cared little for his compositions (E, July 12).

After an absence of three years, he reappeared in 1820 at Covent Garden as Young Meadows in *Love in a Village*. Sterling wrote: "His execution, indeed, is of the first order, and finds no difficulty insurmountable," and the *Inquisitor* noted that he was "a vocalist of no common order" and "an indispensible acquisition" for the theatre. The following year he repeated the role successfully for Drury Lane, where he apparently remained. But Bacon (QMM, III, 387) warned: "Mr. Horn is of Mr. Braham's school. The recommendations he possesses incline us to wish he were not so, and at the same time to hope that it is not too late to retrace some of his steps and to return to the domain of natural expression."

In 1823 he sang in *Rob Roy* and "executed his share of the music as well as a correct taste, wedded to a weak and rather husky voice, would permit him" (T, Nov. 17). In 1824 he sang Lord Ainsworth in a revival of *Maid of the Mill*; Sterling (T) wrote:

> There is no character in English opera that more emphatically demands the union, very rarely seen, of the talents of a good actor with those of an excellent singer. Mr. Horn cannot claim any very embarrassing portion of praise as an actor; as a vocalist, his great knowledge of music enables him to do a good deal with a very indifferent voice. . . . He also rejected the old songs, and introduced three of the worn-out common-places of the day.

In another revival of *Lord of the Manor*, his voice was "not rich enough to give due expression to the songs" (EM). When he sang Casper in the Drury Lane *Freischütz*, "his voice has not sufficient vigour and boldness for the strains which Weber has given to this wild and fearful character," yet "his taste, his good sense, and his musical skill carried him through the part . . . creditably" (T; E; LM). Ayrton (Har) noted: "He gave more vigour to the part of [Casper] than we expected."

In 1825 he supported *Fall of Algiers* "in a masterly manner" (LM) and was "more than ordinarily successful" (T). This was followed by his role as Hassan in the Englished *Abou Hassan*, when he "sang tastefully" (T; E). Horn was very active in 1826, singing with "more force than usual" (LG; NM) in *Malvina*. This was followed by his Korasto, in *Benyowsky*, when his voice was "of a very unimpressive and inferior character" (EM, Apr.). But as the Enchanter in *Aladdin*, he "exerted himself most strenuously" and "his voice improves in power," (LG; T) though the *European* was again negative. Finally, late that year, as Don Christobal in *Two Houses of Grenada*, "he sang extremely ill—he appeared to be far from perfect in the words or music of all of the songs with which he was entrusted" (LG).

In 1827 he sang the Vizier in *Turkish Lovers* but was thought "a grand stick" (Hazlitt, At). Later that year[13] he sailed to New York, where he concertized until 1830, when he returned to London as the music director of the Olympic Theatre. But he again visited New York in 1832, lost his voice completely in 1835, and died in Boston in 1849.

Sinclair

Like Horn, John Sinclair (1791–1857), a Scottish tenor, never overcame some difficulties on the London stage. Son of a farmer, he early showed musical talent and studied singing privately. He also acquired great proficiency on the flute and clarinet in a regimental band and soon became a successful music instructor.

In 1810 he came to London, met Thomas Welsh, and through him got an engagement at Covent Garden the next year, making his debut there on September 20 as Carlos in *Duenna*. He was warmly received and

> displayed such a universal compass of voice, combined with such strength, sweetness, and flexibility, as raised him to the highest degree of popular favour. The distinctness of his articulation, the flexibility of his cadenzas, and the rapidity of his shake, were deservedly the theme of universal approbation. . . . His figure is very handsome, and his features, though not prominent or marked, are very pleasing and attractive. (Taylor, "Memoirs," TI, Feb. 1814)

Sinclair does not again come to our attention until 1813, when he repeated that role, but his voice, "originally a fine one, is in danger of being lost in his struggles after effect; and the abandonment of the tasteful and tender stile with which he commenced, promises to be among the more unlucky experiments of the art" (T).

Early the next year, in *The Farmer's Wife*, he was in fine voice (UM), and one of his "beautiful songs was encored" (T; C). He also sang the lead in *John of Paris* and "delightfully executed" his songs (C); he "sustained his vocal reputation with great credit" (EM) and was "very effective throughout the whole Opera" (Ch). But the *Inquisitor* reported that "his stile of speaking completely annihilated the little meaning the text possesses; and his action was more than usually ludicrous and inelegant."

In 1815 he sang a successful *Artaxerxes* (T). Earlier that year Hunt had called him "a pretty singer with a pleasing, sweet voice, and no great powers of any kind" (E, Feb. 12). In 1816 he got mixed notices in *Midsummer Night's Dream* (T; EM; Ch). As Henry Bertram in *Guy Mannering*, he "acted badly and sang worse" (Ch). Still later that year, in the *Slave*, he "made a good Scotsman" (C) and "sang an old Scotch air with infinite taste and feeling" (EM). But again the *Inquisitor* dissented, wishing he "had been pruned away from this piece, which he absolutely encumbers," and the *Champion* noted he "mangled the dialogue" though he "sang his songs prettily."

In a singer's retrospective in 1817, Hunt wrote that Sinclair, "we must confess, grows very tiresome (to use the phraseology of the ladies) with his miminy-piminy affectations, and his *weeths* [withs], *woines* [wines], and *divoines* [divines]" (E, July 13). He reappeared in 1818, "distinguished himself" as Osbaldstone in *Rob Roy Macgregor*, and was "repeatedly encored" (EM; C), though his taste was unequal to his execution (T). Again the *Inquisitor*, while admiring his singing, found him "a very imperfect representative" of the part.

But Sinclair apparently thought he needed more vocal experience, and in 1819 left for the Continent to study singing in Paris, Milan, and Naples. He also sang in some Rossini operas in Italy, where his technique was said to be remarkable, particularly in runs (N.O.). On his reappearance at Covent Garden in November 1823, as Orlando in *Cabinet*, he again generated diverse opinions. Sterling (T) thought

> it must have become evident last night to real judges, that for all the purposes of his art, he might as well have remained in England. His voice has lost perhaps some of that eveness and flexibility which formerly distinguished it, while in style or expression he has gained little or nothing. . . . As an actor, Mr. Sinclair is painfully deficient; such stiffness of manners and absence of all passion are not to be pardoned on a stage where even our musical performers are learning to act with spirit and discrimination.

Ayrton, who thought the role "injudiciously chosen for his re-appearance," did not find much change in the "sweetness and flexibility" of his former voice. He "has power enough for any good purpose" and "his falsetto remains the same; it possesses vast extent" though it was "not very powerful." The *London*, on the other hand, *did* hear a new singer and was most enthusiastic:

> We have never perceived the good effects of pure air and study so finely manifested as in this gentleman's voice. He is now decidedly a masterly and beautiful singer. All the harshnesses and uncertainties of his tones are gone, and the music floats on his voice with a gracefulness and a power perfectly delightful. He glides into the falsetto, without suffering you to distinguish where he quitted his natural tones—and his shake is more rich and gushing—more like an ardent throb of the nightingale than any thing we have yet heard. . . .
>
> He has not, to be sure, improved in his acting, or in his mode of speaking . . . and we cannot but feel surprised that he should still carry Scotland so plainly on the tip of his tongue.

Parke also thought his Italian sojourn beneficial to his voice and style. But Bacon (QMM, VI, 242f) totally disagreed: "Mr. Sinclair has gathered up exotic graces without number and without assimilation; his singing is truly 'an unweeded garden,' or to sum up all in one phrase, it exhibits the very best specimen of the very worst taste it ever fell to our lot to hear." Seldom do we encounter such a marked dichotomy of views among noteworthy critics.

In 1824 Sinclair sang Aurelio in *Native Land* and "relied more than usual on his *falsetto*; and though he displayed skill in managing it, employed it too frequently to satisfy English ears"; his speaking passages were very poor (T). But his songs were "well adapted to his unrivalled powers," and the present role was well suited to him (LG). Ayrton and the *Examiner* admitted he exercised his falsetto "too unsparingly," but the latter admired several of his songs and reported his part "was animated, and [he] acted the Abyssinian like a native of Gondar." Others (EM; DM; LM) were supportive. Parke reported he sang with much effect but "there was a want of variety in his cadences."

Early in 1826 he sang Trumore in a revival of *Lord of the Manor*, and Sterling still found no improvement in his voice: "The utmost that can be said of him is, that he is a pleasing, but certainly not a great singer." Three days later he sang—apparently for the first time at Drury Lane—as Oscar in *Malvina*. "He was a dandy *hero*, and his songs partook of the dandyism of his appearance," Sterling announced ironically, and the *Gazette* declared that more acting is required in the role of Oscar "than he is equal to," while Talfourd (NM) deplored the casting of "Mr. Sinclair, the prettiest of singers, and most mincing of speakers, as the hardy Oscar."

Shortly afterward he sang "Schah of Persia" in *Aladdin*. Sterling was still hostile: "As Dr. Hill's 'tea-spoon' was just enough for patients of every age and constitution, so Mr. Sinclair's flourish and shake are deemed by him to be perfectly in accordance with every species of musical subject." J. P. Collier (C) was also disappointed: "His efforts were, in our opinion, decided failures." And Talfourd (NM) called him "as mincing and insipid as ever."

He made no appearances in 1827, in 1828–29 he was singing at the Adelphi, and in 1829–30 he was back at Drury Lane. At the end of that season he sang in *National Guard* but received little notice. In May, at his last London appearance, he sang Walther in *Hofer*, and J. P. Collier (C) wrote: "We have not heard Sinclair to so much advantage for some years; the airs are well adapted to his voice, and he played with much more spirit than usual: he strutted about the stage with a sword by his side as if he really could use it." Others (E; TO; At) agreed, and Talfourd (NM) declared he "sang with heart as well as voice, and acted feelingly for the first—we hope not the last—time."

But it *was* the last time. That year he visited the United States for a concert tour, after which he retired. Phillips pointed out that Sinclair used falsetto in everything he sang. But it was his personality and mannerisms that most of his critics viewed with distaste.

Duruset

A better performer and a gifted singer was John Duruset ("or Durousset, as the name is more properly spelt"—"Memoir," TI, July 1819), who was born in London in 1796. His French-born father, who had apparently brought his family to London during the Revolution, was a well-to-do picture dealer. Young John was early apprenticed to Domenico Corri, and "his sweet tones, while a boy, were heard with enthusiasm upon many public occasions."

He made his stage debut at the San Souci Theatre as a child singer, and in 1808 he sang at Drury Lane in *Siege of San Quintin*, supplying "powerful support from the manner in which he sustained the duet of 'All's Well' with a youthful coadjutor." Later, at the Lyceum, he sang William in *Rosina* "with critical praise and popular acclamation." For a time, as "Master Duruset," he was hired by Charles Dibdin for Sadler's Wells. In 1810, after a singing tour of the provinces, he was again on the London stage and "attracted the attention of a distinguished peer" under whose patronage he advanced his art (TI).

He first comes to our notice as a young man in 1814, when he was encored for a song in *John of Paris* at Covent Garden, where he sang for most of his career (C; EM). (Reviewers do not specify his range, which must have been considerable for he sang both tenor [falsetto?] and baritone roles.) The next year he performed in *Brother and Sister*; his "abilities as a singer are progressively improving," and he "executed the music attached to the character, in a very commendable style" (EM). But as the Guardian Spirit in *Comus*, he was "surprisingly bad.... Without dignity, without lightness, grossly vulgar, obtrusive, and unmeaning, he is not contented to be wrong, but, as it were, dashes his errors in your face.... Yet ... his voice is good, his form and features well adapted to the stage; with study, properly directed, he might hope for final success" (TI).

But later that year he appeared as the lead in *Cymon* and J. D. Collier (C) noted that he "displayed an ability that charmed every cultivated ear in the House. His simplicity and taste were delightfully shewn in his first air, by Arne, 'You gave me last week a young Linnet.' His melody was perfect; not the slightest effort was made to gain applause by unreasonable decoration.... Both his acting and all his subsequent airs confirmed the impression he had made." The *Inquisitor* by this point agreed he "represented the perfect *natural*, and was in most excellent voice."

In 1816 he sang commendably as Oberon in *Midsummer Night's Dream* (EM). "We were much pleased with his voice;—it gains power, we think, every time we hear it" (Ch). But "he seemed to want both voice and courage" for the "fine and difficult air, 'When smoke upwreathes from humble cots'" in *Your's or Mine?* (T). As Trumore in *Lord of the Manor* "he delivered the speeches, as well as the music of the part, with an effective sensibility," and "his style of singing Lord Byron's beautiful song 'Adieu, Adieu, my native shore' was rich in feeling and expression" (TI). At the end of the year, as an English captain in the *Slave*, he "sung a song with recitative of a mixed kind, in which, however, from the heroic to the tender, the transition was too rapid for effect, and [he] infused into it too much action" (C); moreover, he was "unequal to the character he assumes" (EM) and was "wholly incomprehensible" (Ch).

In 1817, as Masetto in the *Libertine*, Duruset had to sing "Là ci darem" and "Finch'an dal vino," transferred to him because Kemble, the Don, could not sing (BS). He and Catherine Stephens were encored in *Duke of Savoy* and "merited the warmest encomiums, by their rich, zealous, and brilliant expertise" (TI). Singing a duet with Braham in a revival of *Castle of Andalusia*, he "beautifully sustained" his part, and "his mellow notes floated in to bear up the delightful cadence" (EM).

In 1819, in *Figaro*, he took the part of Fiorello, a character added to the drama as servant to the count "for the purpose of atoning for the vocal deficiencies" of the latter. "In the finales, he answered the purpose pretty well; but in the duet of '*Crudel*' he was very deficient" (TI); Sterling, however, thought he sang his songs "in good style." As Antipholis in *Comedy of Errors*, he was "entitled to unqualified applause" (TI), and as Floreski in a revival of *Lodoiska*, he "exalted" the part "to prescriptive repute, by a rare union of science and simplicity" (TI).

In a sketch of him in July of that year, the *Inquisitor* wrote that his "strides . . . to musical pre-eminence have been taken with astonishing vigour," and they thought his performance of Cymon had "established his talents in their proper light, by exhibiting a rare union of vocal accomplishment and histrionic ability." They added: "His voice is full, clear, and vigorous and his style replete with that chastened simplicity which can only result from unwearied cultivation and exalted refinement," and they augured well for his future.

In 1820, at a revival of the old burletta *Midas*,[14] the *Inquisitor* (May) crowed: "In the higher attributes of singing, we do not hesitate to avow our belief, that the stage for many seasons past has not possessed a gentleman as eminently qualified . . . as Mr. Duruset," but they thought he had often been "the victim of managerial indifference" by giving him parts "not only beneath his reputation, but foreign to his talent." In "Pray, goody, please to moderate," he "delivered this exquisite air with an ardour, an intelligence, and a dexterity, that convey the highest compliment to his powers of conception and performance." But in a revival of *Love in a Village* later that year, he did not please as Eustace. Sterling reported: "As we have ever done justice to the merit he possesses . . . we regret to see him yield to an indolence of manner which must endanger his reputation." In 1821 Duruset was "delightful" in a minor role in the *Tempest* (LM). In 1823, singing in *Cortez*, he "affords us more pleasure than any male singer at this theatre; were his voice equal to his taste, he need not shrink from rivalry," reported Ayrton (Har), and the *Examiner* concurred: "One of the airs sung by Duruset was executed with great taste, if not with great power."

By 1826, in our last notice of him, he was still singing minor roles—this time in *Oberon*—as the *European* remarked with sarcasm: "It is a shame that Duruset is kept so much in the back-ground, at least he would make a decent looking fairy, as humanity has no equal for the part compared to the requisites found in a dandy." We know nothing of the rest of his career. Though never a performer of first rank, he did show improvement over the years as both actor and singer, and in some roles he was quite effective.

Sapio

One Mr. Sapio,[15] a powerful tenor, eventually offered a strong challenge to Braham. He was the son of a celebrated Italian singing master who settled in France and married a French woman. At one time the father gave vocal lessons to Marie Antoinette but was forced to flee to England with his family during the Revolution. Young Sapio was born in England and had a classical education, with music as merely an accomplishment. After military service, however, he turned to singing as a career.[16] In 1823 he gave a concert in London and already had a "host of patrons" (LM, June): "He is not only a singer of distinguished ability, but the singer, *par excellence*, of rising estimation."

He had already given concerts the previous year, which prompted an unusual panegyric from Bacon (QMM, IV, 59–64): "Mr. Sapio's voice is a tenor of much compass, and he has the faculty of assimilating his falsetto with ease to the natural voice at their junction. . . . The quality of his tone is full, and it is rendered brilliant by the way in which he brings it forth, namely, very high in the head—perhaps somewhat higher indeed than the Italian method prescribes."

Sapio made his English opera debut late in 1824 at Drury Lane as Saraskier in a revival of the *Siege of Belgrade*, and Sterling stated: "Mr. Sapio's voice is a true tenor, full of richness and expression. His *falsetto* is bold [but] there is an abruptness in his transition [to it]. . . . Mr. Sapio is a very accomplished singer. His style, like that of Mr. Braham, is florid. . . . As an actor, Mr. Sapio may rank with any other operatic performer of the present day. . . . We can award him no higher praise." Of this performance, and a subsequent performance as Prince Orlando in the *Cabinet*, the *London* (Jan. 1825) wrote:

> The brilliancy and power of his voice—the energy of his manner—the nature of the ornament he uses—his facility, and above all the sacrifice of high polish to dramatic effect observable in his concert singing, all fit him eminently for this department. . . . The ease of his manners, his high flow of animal spirits, his gentlemanly bearing, striking features, and well-formed person, are recommendations not commonly to be found among vocalists, who, if they have pleased as singers, have thought themselves privileged to be dull and spiritless actors. [He is] already the best actor of his class that has ever appeared.

Early in 1825 he appeared in *Fall of Algiers*; he "sang with great power and with very great feeling" (T) and "distinguished himself" (LM). In 1826 he sang the lead in a revival of *Tarrare* at the English Opera House and "did ample justice to the fine music of Salieri"; he was "no unworthy successor of Braham" in the role (T). The following month he sang Faulkland in the *Oracle* and had repeated encores despite the manager's request to suppress them (T). "Some of his tones are extremely effective. He fails principally where he directly imitates Braham" (LG). In a fine bravura he "compensated for some deficiency of physical power by great taste and admirable execution" (E).

That fall he transferred to Covent Garden, where he sang the lead in a revival of *Guy Mannering* but was "hardly an equivalent of Braham" (LG). He also sang the lead in *Peveril of the Peak* and "exerted himself a good deal" but was not encored (C). Again the *Examiner* cited his "bounded power, but considerable taste and feeling." The *Literary Chronicle* reported that he took "great liberty with the verse of his songs: when will this gentleman cease to sacrifice sense to sound?" He concluded the year as Sir Huon in *Oberon* and "surpassed the expectations even of his friends by his success." He equaled Braham in the "Battle song" and "looked the part" better than he (C).

In late 1827 Sapio sang Belmonte in the *Seraglio* and "shone more in the concerted pieces than in the solos" (T). Yet Ayrton was aghast: "Mr. Sapio seemed to have lost all his powers; but for his name appearing in the bills, we positively should not have recognized him." Parke, writing of that performance, thought him competent but noted a deficiency in his shake— "a requisite for all good English singers."

In 1828 he sang Captain Lindsey in *Carron Side* but "did not shine in this opera" (At). In a brief retrospective in 1829, Talfourd (NM, Aug.) wrote a sharply negative report on his acting. That summer he performed as Fernando, a military officer, in *Robber's Bride*; he "was in excellent voice and sang, we could almost say, better than we ever heard him before" (T). The *Athenaeum* found his voice as "sweet and expressive as ever" but thought his range too limited for the role. The *Examiner*, however, reported that his voice was "husky and out of tune." He followed this with a minor part in *Vampyr*, which was "not happy"—"His only solo struck us as extremely heavy, and barren of relief" (C), though he was admired in concerted numbers (At). In a final notice of him—as Rudolph in an English Opera House revival of *Freischütz* that year—Ayrton by this time acknowledged that he "was in every way good, except that now and then his high notes bordered on flatness. Next to Braham, he is the best representative of the character we have met with." With few exceptions, Sapio, in English opera, never lived up to the great promise augured by Bacon on the basis of his concert singing.

Phillips

One of the finest basses in our period was Henry Phillips (1801–76), though he had a wobbly beginning. (His *Recollections* provide an interesting background on singing in his time.) Son of a country actor and a German-Jewish mother who had a fine but untrained voice, he had a high, clear, flexible voice as a child, and at age eight he made his stage debut in some songs following a play. He was taught to read music by Michael Leoni and in 1811 was hired by Drury Lane for a boy's part, for which he got 5s. a night. He was then apprenticed to a Mr. Price, chorus master there. After his voice broke, it became a "light baritone." He studied singing with a Mr. Broadhurst and sang in the Lyceum chorus. (For two years he earned money coloring engravings.)

He began learning "all the oratorios" and sang at "city dinners" as well as during intermissions at the theatres. He also began studying Italian opera and performed in it at Bath under John David Loder (1788–1847), who "took great pains to render the orchestra subservient to my mode and style of singing," which raised Phillips's reputation. (He tells us that theatrical basses of that time were cast as "robbers" and wore a "sort of" Spanish costume.)

He made his London stage debut in 1824 in *Artaxerxes* at Covent Garden, but he failed in that role and was hissed. He was reviewed in July of that year, when he performed the role of Casper in the English Opera

House *Freischütz*. As Phillips explained, he was the only one who could sing the role but was regarded as too young to act it; the role was split with a nonsinging actor, Phillips appearing on stage only to sing the songs. Sterling overlooked him until August 16, when he gave him trite praise, but the *Chronicle* right away noticed that Phillips possessed "a fine bass voice" and "acquitted himself very satisfactorily." Ayrton and Talfourd agreed, but the *London* thought him "poor," following, as he did, Braham's "Grand Scena." When the cast was transferred to Covent Garden, Sterling gave him much praise for his drinking song: "He sang and acted both extremely well. It was like a German yager, or hussar, half tipsy, and diverting himself in camp after dinner, with a due mixture of ferocity." And the *Examiner* (Nov. 14) wrote: "Indeed we expect not to see the equal of Phillips in the Circean specimen of unholy inspiration; his style was altogether as unique as the composition itself is eccentric and surprising."

In 1825 he sang the tyrant Atar in *Tarrare* at the English Opera House, "singing in some passages tolerably well, but occasionally his style sank too near to mere growling" (T). The *Chronicle*, however, thought his "fine voice was displayed to great advantage in many passages," and Talfourd (NM) observed that he "walks and commands in high barbaric style, and takes a royal part in the bravuras. He has added much to his power and science since the last season." The *London* agreed: "Mr. H. Phillips is a singer that we always hear with great pleasure: the upper notes of his voice are particularly good—his style is chaste and free from . . . unmeaning flourishes." Ayrton asserted flatly: "Mr. Phillips, both as an actor and singer, is a very superior person."

At the end of that year, Bacon (QMM, VII, 463–67), taking note that he had been very well received in numerous public and private concerts at London as well as in Italian opera in the provinces, wrote:

> His voice presents rather a curious anomaly in description, for it can neither be called base nor barytone, heavy nor light, though it partakes of all these several properties in its tone and compass. Its volume is considerable, but by no means vast, and we conceive it is alike his interest and his inclination to cultivate finish and sweetness rather than grandeur or power. . . . It is in fact a genuine English voice, by which we mean a voice that demonstrates very little of artificial formation, and though sound and good, so far as it goes, there is not enough of supereminent quality to lead one to suppose that nature intended the possessor for a great singer. . . .

He seems to have sung but once in 1826—as Maffera, a Peruvian general, in the *Oracle* at the English Opera House He "was in powerful voice; his recitatives were grand, and his intonation perfect" (LitC), but the *Examiner* found him "scarcely warm" in the part, though "his power in concert was deeply felt, and much and deservedly applauded." Phillips's own self-appraisal echoes the *Examiner*'s view of his acting: "[I] tried to succeed in almost all the operas of that time but invariably failed. I could not act the characters; I could not buckle to the music; I felt a lack of energy, a want of excitement" (*Recollections*, p. 35).

But this phase does not seem to have lasted very long. Early in 1827, still at Covent Garden, he sang Glossin in the *White Maid* and was highly commended (E), and that summer he "distinguished himself" (T) in a revival of *Arthur and Emmeline* at the English Opera House This was followed by his Uberto in *Freebooters*, and he himself admitted he was "very successful in the role." Sterling (T) wrote that "he added immensely to his fame. Nothing can be imagined more expressive than his execution of Paer's music. In the last act, where he recounts the story of his misfortunes, and endeavours to learn the fate of his abandoned daughter, his sorrow was so touching, so natural, as to excite most strongly the feelings of the audience." The *Examiner* found "he was, in fact, everything that could be desired." And Ayrton declared he was the opera's "main support"; his "beautiful voice, pure style, and most pathetic performance of the character . . . sufficiently account for all the applause which the opera receives: he puts the house in so favourable a temper, that the whole appears *couleur de rose*" (Har; NM).

In 1828 he sang Don Alfonso in *Tit for Tat* at English Opera House and was "extremely successful" (T; C). His "rich tones are quite beautiful in the concerted compositions" (LG). The *Examiner* added that "Mr. Phillips possesses in a high degree that accomplishment in a singer, and which has not often been heard since the days of Bartleman[17] — of talking in tone." On the same day, Holmes (At) wrote: "We look upon him to be a worthy scion to the Bartleman stock of singers" — "he promises to be the first singer of his day."[18] Talfourd (NM) thought his "noble, simple, and sustained style of singing is gradually purifying the general taste from the meretricious and tricksy fancies with which it was debauched by Mr. Braham in his lowest mode." Ayrton, while admitting he sang an admirable Alfonso, recommended to him "rather more philosophic deliberations in the dialogue, and more astuteness in his manner."

Phillips followed this with the role of Count Albert in *Sylvania*. Sterling noted he sang two airs "of great beauty," but "they would have been most effective, had they been put into the hands of an able singer"; the *Examiner* agreed, adding that Phillips "introduced" them and they are "pieces of impertinence—first, because they are not required; second, because they are unworthy of the company into which they are thrust." Phillips himself had no compunctions about such insertions, telling us he "always insisted on having a solo ballad inserted for himself." (He was also successful in some songs he composed for himself.)

This was quickly followed by the *Pirate of Genoa*, in which he sang the lead, Captain Tornado. But Ayrton noted he had "hardly a single bar that is worthy of him to sing in this opera; nevertheless, he shews as much zeal as if he had a better part." He was highly praised by J. P. Collier (C), but Sterling's only reference to him was in a trio, the "best vocal piece"—sung by him, Penson, and J. Russell "in a manner so slovenly that it was not even applauded." He received his highest praise of the year in still another performance of Arthur in *Arthur and Emmeline*, when Holmes (At) declared: "Phillips is the only man now before the public who can sing this ["Frost"] scene as the author intended. The continued tremor of voice which is thought necessary to the dramatic effect of this scene, rather annoys our ears—it is like an unresolved discord." Yet, the two passages in it, "as they give the acme of musical expression in their different characters, require the perfection of dramatic singing, of which, in our opinion, Henry Phillips wants but little. Purcell is a most unmerciful author to those who attempt his music without particular study; to succeed but moderately in the highest efforts of his genius is great praise to any singer. We like Mr. H. Phillips because he does his best for the composer and plays no 'fantastic tricks.'"

In 1829 he returned to Covent Garden as Cedric in *Maid of Judah*, for which he was expressly engaged, though he had but one solo to sing. J. P. Collier (C) thought him "an excellent singer," yet added: "He cannot, however, ever expect to be popular, for his style has nothing to recommend it to the multitude, and his voice is of no remarkable compass, while its quality is peculiar." Nevertheless, the *Athenaeum* wrote: "The spirited manner in which he entered into the feeling of his part, has made us desirous of seeing him in other characters." Back at the English Opera House that summer, he appeared as Count Viterbo in *Robber's Bride* and was "in finest voice" (C). Sterling wrote: "Mr. H. Phillips, as the Count, has to execute a great deal of very difficult music, to which he did the most perfect justice. We have not often had a more delightful treat than we received from the pure and pathetic style in which he executed his last air, 'My daughter, yes, my daughter!'" J. P. Collier (C) and *Athenaeum* agreed, the latter adding: "If any exception could be taken to a part of Phillips's performance the other night, it was in adhering now and then a little too formally to the English cadence at the close of his airs, which made some confusion in style."

He followed this with a performance of the lead in *Der Vampyr*. He "had to support the chief brunt of the opera, and got through his task with considerable skill: the whole of the music entrusted to his care was of the most complicated nature; . . . he, nevertheless, received the warmest and most generous tokens of approbation" (C; T). The *Examiner* and Holmes (At) thought him "a little below pitch in some of the high notes." (Noting the progress he had made as an actor, they thought he would make "an admirable Don Giovanni.") Ayrton, too, joined the chorus of praise: "Mr. Phillips developes [sic] more and more talent every time he performs. On his exertions the success of the opera mainly depended: they were as great as [they were] efficient, and we wonder how he found strength to go through so laborious and fatiguing a part." And the *Athenaeum* reviewer, in a whimsical mood, wrote: "Whether thou wilt deem [appropriate] the varying expressions which Mr. H. Phillips throws into his visage when he would alternate between fury and insinuation, it behoveth not us to divine; yet we confess to thee, we deemest them good for a vampyre, they were so unnatural."

In 1830 he appeared as Hofer in Drury Lane—apparently for the first time. J. P. Collier (C) reported: "H. Phillips, by his admirable execution of this difficult music, has raised his name even higher than it was" (T). "He never surprises, but always gratifies; his singing is firm and true, and his taste well regulated." Holmes (At) found his singing and acting "entirely worthy of that excellence which the public have learned to expect from him. All that this performer does is with a view to general effect; where his part is subordinate he keeps it so; where it is principal he does his best for the author." Only Talfourd (NM) hinted at a fault: "He bears himself statelily, and sings in his pure and noble style, but is rather too gloomy for the champion who would rush to the battle-field as to a festival."

Arnold, perhaps picking up the *Examiner*'s assertion that Phillips would make a good Don Giovanni, cast him in that role in a late Buckstone-Hawes adaptation at the Adelphi; but the *Athenaeum* reviewer, who disliked the production, wrote: "Phillips, a very good psalm-singer—a perfect model for a musical parish-clerk—has not a notion of Don Giovanni. We should as soon expect to find Master Slender and 'fat Jack' exchange characters, as this gentleman's solemn monotony of voice and manner accommodated to the hilarious and reckless levity of the libertine Spaniard. He is correct, but tame; he is perfect in the nature of the part, but not in its style." In a revival of *Vampyr* with the English Opera House company at the Adelphi, he "sang beautifully in tune, and with spirit and feeling" (E). But after seeing him in a revival of *Hofer* at Covent Garden that fall—an opera he did not admire—Hunt wrote in the *Tatler*: "He is a better actor than most singers; but that is saying little; and his voice though manly, and seconded by a correct ear and taste, is too much in his throat, seeming to be invested with fat. We miss genius in him, and the power of touching the feelings."

In his *Recollections*, Phillips tells us he never forgot Braham's advice to him: "As you advance you will have twenty blunderbusses continually leveled at your head . . . but have no fear . . . and your enemies will fly before you." He found it only "too true" (p. 65). He went on to sing many more years on the stage as well as at concerts. In 1843 he appeared in "Table Entertainments" but was not successful. In 1846 he made a concert tour of the United States and in 1863 gave a farewell concert.

THE LEADING FEMALE SINGERS

Bland

Marie Therese Bland, née Romanzini (1769–1838), was the daughter of an Italian Jew who settled in London. She was first taught singing by Charles Dibdin and began to sing small parts at his Royal Circus in 1782; she later sang at Dublin. In 1790 she married George Bland, Mrs. Dorothy (Dora) Jordan's brother, and they had several children; but he left her and went to America. Physically unprepossessing—she was short, fat, nearsighted, and pitted with smallpox—she excelled in simple songs, using no ornaments (Phillips). Nevertheless, she was capable of performing in Italian opera. Both Haydn and Pleyel praised her (Kelly, II, 72). A sketch of her by Kenrick in 1821 (BS, Sept.) states that "her voice has hitherto suffered no diminution of its early beauty, but is listened to with as much satisfaction as ever."

She made her Drury Lane debut in Burgoyne's *Richard* in 1786 and stayed with the company forty years. She "continued to render Antonio a character of some importance. She sung the air . . . 'The merry dance I dearly love' with great taste and correctness" (C; Parke). She was praised as Cicely in *Haunted Tower* (1789), and as Nina in the *Prisoner* (1792) she performed "a smart little drummer—her appearance alone excited repeated bursts of laughter, and her adroit *rub-a-dub* accompaniment to a very charming air, produced repeated peals of applause" (Este). At the Little Theatre in 1793, as Josephine in *Children of the Wood*, she "sings the old ballad, with a captivation that subdues every heart" (C). In a "spirited duet" with her husband in *Auld Robin Grey* (1794), when she played Mogy, they "were once more, on the Stage at least, in *unison*" (T). Later that year, as Winifred in *Cherokee*, she sang "the most favourite air of the piece," which her husband had composed for her (C). In 1795 the *Oracle*, reviewing

Three and the Deuce, wrote cryptically that she "experienced more of the public resentment than we had expected." She played Fanny in a *Maid of the Mill* revival in 1798, when "her vocal powers were as fascinating as on any former occasion, but her acting went far beyond her usual exertions" (T), and later that year she drew general praise as Moola in *Captive of Spilburg* (P; T).

In 1798 she made her only appearance at the King's—in *Schiave* as a substitute for the indisposed Banti—by "permission" of Drury Lane Theatre. "We congratulate her on her success," wrote the *Chronicle*. "Her whole performance was distinguished by the warmest approbation" and she had two encores. The *Post* declared:

> Until very lately, to insinuate that a second-rate performer, at one of our winter Theatres, was capable of filling the place of the first comic woman at the Anglo-Italian Opera, would have been attributed to some sinister motive; but . . . we feel no hesitation in averring the fact. Mrs. Bland spoke the Italian with the most perfect propriety. Her songs were given with taste, and a degree of ease infinitely delightful to those who have so often suffered from the apparent agonies . . . which most Italian singers exhibit in calling forth all the powers of voice.

Even Mount-Edgcumbe admitted she performed "very creditably" and that few English singers at the King's had her command of the language in recitative. A different report comes from Parke, who stated that her substitution "did not afford the gratification which the subscribers required." Perhaps he was right; she never again appeared at the King's.

In 1802 she "sang with a most heavenly air" (C) as Fanny in *House to be Sold* and was encored (P). She had two encores in *Matrimony* in 1804. In 1805 she was admired in *Soldier's Return* (T; C) as well as in *Youth, Love, and Folly* (C). In 1806 she sang in a trio in Corri's *Travellers* with "extraordinary powers" (C), and she was encored in a duet in *Forty Thieves* (Cr). In 1807 she "sang with her usual sweetness" in *False Alarms* (C).

These notices suggest that while Bland was effective and popular in her simple songs, she was cast in roles that required little or no acting. Thereafter, reports of her were more sporadic. In 1810 she was "enchanting" in *Maniac* (MM), and was encored in *Oh! This Love* (C). In 1815 Hunt wrote that her "style has a sort of gentle-hearted, dairy-maid simplicity with it, that would set all the people in a village listening to nothing else every summer's evening" (Feb. 12). In 1817 she "sang delightfully" in *Elphi Bey* (TI), and as Margery in *Love in a Village*—"an old favourite with the musical world"—"there cannot be a more natural unpretending singer; but she delivers her songs with a propriety and truth of feeling that performers of a higher rank might copy with advantage" (T).

In 1818, as Jenny in another old revival, *Lionel and Clarissa*, she "proved that her vocal powers have not lost their accustomed sweetness" (T). But in 1820 the *Inquisitor*, at a revival of *Artaxerxes*, declared: "We cavil at nothing in this opera but Mrs. Bland's grotesque appearance as a youthful princess"; yet they could not fault her singing in Moncrieff's *Giovanni in London*, when she was encored (TI; TO).

In 1823 she suffered a "complete breakdown" (N.O.), but by 1826 she filled the role of Puck in *Oberon* at Covent Garden (T). Two years later, at age fifty-nine, she reappeared at Drury Lane and was applauded in a trio in *Love in Wrinkles* (T)—her last appearance on any stage (N.O. states her last stage performance was in June 1822).

Billington

With Elizabeth Billington we come to an English opera singer who, as we have seen, made a capable prima donna assoluta at the King's. (She was also a prominent recitalist.) She made her English opera debut as Rosetta at Covent Garden in *Love in a Village* in 1786, when the *Register* wrote:

> This lady possesses very extraordinary vocal abilities. She is a perfect and scientific mistress of instrumental music, and sings with infinite taste and critical judgment. Her person is neat, her deportment easy, her face beautiful and expressive. She appears to possess great sensibility, and has good action; but, from being used to act in a small theatre [Dublin], her speaking did not yesterday evening sufficiently fill the house, though it improved considerably in fullness and audibility during the progress of her acting. (Feb. 14)

Of that performance Burney stated that at first she had some difficulties but totally overcame them. Boaden wrote that her "In love should you meet a fond pair" "produced an effect which literally haunted the ear" (I, 311); and Parke stated she sang her songs in an unaccustomed way but so brilliantly she delighted the house.

The following month she appeared as Coraly in the premiere of *Peruvian*. The *Register* complained: "We highly disapprove the partiality shewn to Mrs. Billington, for though she executed her songs with infinite taste and judgment, and an astonishing power of voice, it is prejudicial both to her and to the other performers, to cast such a quantity of the musical business into her part; . . . she had no less than four solo airs and parts in six duets, &c." But the *Chronicle* had no such objections: "We recollect not to have witnessed so much of taste and skill, in respect to execution, allied to so much natural ability, and so much sweetness of voice. Mrs. Billington possesses an elegant figure, and a beautiful face. . . . When she has from practice acquired a more easy disposition of her arms, and a more proper mode of speaking dialogue, she will be one of the most valuable singing actresses that ever trod the English stage."

Still later that year, she sang Berengalia in the Macnally *Richard*, where she had only three songs to sing but sang them "exquisitely, and in the Anfossi composition, she may almost be said to have outdone Al[l]egranti herself" (C, Oct. 19). She "enraptured the audience, who almost manifested a species of phrenzy in their applause" (LC, Oct. 14–17). And at a November revival of *Love in a Village* that year, she again played Rosetta "in a style of superior excellence," she had "infinite sprightliness," and she was worthy "the first Opera Stage in Europe" (UR).

In 1787 she first appeared as Mandane in *Artaxerxes*, and the audience was so impetuous to get into the theatre that there were several injuries. She sang the opening duet with Leoni[19] "in a charming style—[in several airs] she displayed the graces and beauties of singing—which distinguish her performance, with the most advantageous effect." Her encored "Soldier tir'd" was "repeated with those little variations and beauties with which no singer can so successfully embellish as Mrs. Billington" and "the superiority [of her recitative] placed the other singers at an unpleasant distance" (H; UR, Jan. 22).

At a 1788 revival of that opera she "was far from being depressed by a very indifferent House" and "executed her wonderful talents with more than usual spirit and animation." Her "Soldier tir'd" was "encored with unanimous and repeated acclamation" (T). She also sang the title role of *Marian* that year, and she sang Theresa in *Magician no Conjurer* in 1792, but she received trivial praise in both.

Burney wrote of her during this period: "But besides these powers [of execution], which the bad taste of the public tempts or obliges her to exercise . . . the natural tone of her voice is so exquisitely sweet, her knowledge of music so considerable, her shake so true, her closes and embellishments so various and her expression so grateful, that nothing but envy or apathy can hear her without delight" (II, 1021). In 1794 she went to Italy, where she sang successfully for several years in Italian operas, returning to England in 1801. Her later singing was confined to the King's or to concerts. In ill health, she retired from the stage in 1810 and died at her estate near Venice in 1818.

Mountain

A better singer than actress was Sara Mountain, née Wilkinson (c. 1768–1841), called "Rosomon" after the name of the proprietor at Sadler's Wells, where her parents were circus performers. Charles Dibdin trained her at his Royal Circus Theatre. Mountain had a few minor parts at the Little Theatre in 1782 and made a successful debut in 1786 at Covent Garden. In 1787 she married the violinist John Mountain. In 1788 she sang in a revival of *Inkle and Yarico* and "made so much of the little character of Narcissa as to have been entitled to a better dress" (T).

In 1798 she left the stage briefly after a dispute with the management and studied singing with Rauzzini. In 1800 she returned to the Little Theatre as Leonora in *What a Blunder!* She "sang charmingly" (LC), had "the only airs worth notice," and "for their success they were indebted to her superior voice, taste, and science" (P; MM). In 1802 Mountain sang Polly in the *Beggar's Opera* (Covent Garden) and "appears to have every requisite for giving interest to the character. That gentle timidity which is so strongly contrasted with the boldness and assurance of Lucy, she is of all others most qualified to represent; and her voice is, perhaps, more appropriate than that of any other Performer on the stage. . . . She displayed just sufficient science to improve that melody ["Cease your funning"] without destroying it." (T; P).

Despite such notices, she apparently did not perform again until 1805, when she sang in *Soldier's Return* at Drury Lane; her duet with Mrs. Bland was "enthusiastically and deservedly applauded" (T; C). The next month she was supportive in *Youth, Love, and Folly* (C). In 1806, in Corri's *Travellers*, she was cited, with Braham, as being among the fine singers who could give London "a national Opera" under the right direction (C). In 1807 she appeared as the lead, Lady Gayland, in *False Alarms* and again was admired in a duet with Bland (C); in one air she accompanied herself on a harp (H), and also "displayed some delightful acting" (MM). Three months later, in *Young Hussar*, she performed some "worthy" singing and acting (T). The following year, as Leila, the female lead in *Kais*, she "sung her airs and performed with great animation, but she had nothing worthy of her talents" (C; MM). Later that season, as Zelma in *Jew of Magadore*, she "sung her several airs with exquisite sweetness" (MM).

More active at the Lyceum in 1809, she performed in *Up All Night* and "sung and looked gracefully" (C); this was followed by her performance of Clara in *Duenna*, where "her fine talents were never developed more happily, nor with greater effect" (UM). In *Russian Impostor* she "gave us all the '*Mountain honey*' of her lips in 'Oh! roses are sweet,'" but was thrust into a character (a captain) she could not act (MM; C). She then sang in *Safe and Sound*, and her "mellow pipe was in excellent tune" (C). In 1810, again at the Lyceum, Mountain sang and acted Lauretta, the lead in *Maniac*, with distinction (C; EM). "With her delicate taste," Hunt thought she "did full justice to the Maniac's singing, but it is a mere joke to see her playing the Octavian among mountains" (E). DuBois (MM), however, was caustic:

> In her share of the character, with tattered garb and dishevelled locks, she formed a true picture of a dairy-fed lady, who having appeared as Ophelia at a masquerade, was late in the morning, after a *row*, returning all on foot, and considerably overtaken with liquor, to her lodgings in *Howland-Street*. Such an appearance with corresponding action, we may safely say with Johnson, 'takes away all dignity from distress, and makes *calamity ridiculous*.'

At the end of 1812 she was back at Drury Lane in a revival of the *Cabinet*. "Mrs. Mountain's voice was firmer than before, and her acting in Floretta had all the animation which could be given to that [character]: her whole performance was received with great favour" (T). In 1813 she also was admired in a revival of *Lodoiska* (T). She apparently was ill that year; of her performance in *Who's to Have Her*, the *Universal Magazine* wrote: "Mrs. Mountain sang with uncommon excellence. Her health appears to be perfectly restored, and her voice is as powerful and melodious as it has ever been." This was perhaps her last regular performance, however. In 1815 she took leave of the stage at a farewell at the King's.

Storace

Although she did not have the brilliant vocal resources of Billington, Nancy Storace, whom we have also met in Italian opera, was a far better singing actress and became as much at home on the English stage as at the King's. All her singing before 1800, however, was confined to her brother's English operas.

Two years after her King's debut, she first appeared at Drury Lane as Adela in the *Haunted Tower* (1789). We question the *New Grove*'s assertion that her Italian accent on that occasion proved to be a handicap; adaptation to the different demands of English opera did, however, cause initial difficulties, as Este reported:

> *Signora Storace* — an old favourite of all the fashionable operatical circles — though new to the English stage, was so evidently overcome by that diffidence, ever the companion of real merit — that she was for

some time unable to give utterance to her most exquisite powers—and the symphony was obliged to be repeated—the applause however soon had its proper effect, and she went through her part with that nicety of accent—marked propriety of emphasis—and truth of character—as agreeably to surprise those who expected only fine singing and bad English from the *Signora*—who, though brought up in Italy, is completely English. (T)

The *Herald* agreed, saying she "delivered the dialogue very articulately, and the humour lost not its points: her first song showed embarrassment, but the *acting* in it was good;—Her second was charmingly sung."

In *Siege of Belgrade* (1791), "the comic powers of Storace were perhaps never exhibited more advantageously—her Lilla was throughout a most perfect portrait of pure nature—the dancing air was alone sufficient to give any Opera a *run*. It was *twice* repeated" (Este). As Daphne in *Cave of Triphonius* later that year, she was in "high song" (LC). As Fabulina in the *Pirates* (1792), she received an encore for her finale lullaby: "She ran up her divisions with as much ease as the most finished Italian singer that ever trod the stage" (T, Nov. 26). Her duet with Mrs. Crouch in *Cherokee* (1794), when she played Eleanor, "cannot be too highly praised" (T). And in 1796, in *Mahmoud*, she "accompanied [Braham] in a *duo* of extreme difficulty with great precision, if not equal sweetness" (OPA).

During these years she was also singing at the King's. In 1796 she resigned from Drury Lane; following the death of her brother, they had no music director she could respect (N.G.). In 1797 she made a concert tour of the Continent with Braham; though he was seven years her junior, they became lovers, and she bore him a son in 1802.

Storace returned to the English stage in 1801, making her Covent Garden debut as Zulima in *Chains for the Heart*. She was, however, less than a total success. The *Post* declared that "this lady is equally qualified to appear in either department of sense or sound, and maintain the lead in both. She had several opportunities of displaying this versatility in Zulima, and did not fail to take advantage of them." And the *Times* reported: "Although occasionally affected with a hoarseness," she "sung and acted with spirit." But the *Chronicle* noted: "She would please more, however, if she attempted to do less. There is a graceful elegance of manner which gives to gaiety its proper zest, and in this Madame Storace is not always successful. Her *naivete* is of a more humourous cast. She leaves nothing to the imagination to conceive."

In 1802 she made a hit as Floretta in the *Cabinet* (T). DuBois (MM) wrote: "The archness and true *Buffa* of Madame Storace are unusually effective. . . . Her 'No, no, no, not you' is fascination itself." Later that year she was also successful as Susan in *Family Quarrels* (T, Dec. 20). In 1803 a trio by Storace, Braham, and Eliza Atkins[20] in *English Fleet* brought the house down (C), and DuBois (MM) admired the "sort of French catechism" in which she "so charmingly displays her peculiar naivete as a comic actress." She was not quite as effective as Braham in *Thirty Thousand* in 1804 (T).

In 1805 she sang at the King's but returned to Drury Lane the next year in Corri's *Travellers*. She "was by no means happy in her character. Neither nature nor habits have qualified her for an Italian fine Lady; but her first song had point, and was uncommonly droll" (C). Shortly after, she returned to the King's; but early in 1807 she was again at Drury Lane in *False Alarms* and played Susan with much comic effect (MM).

Her voice must have declined markedly by 1808. That year she appeared as Rozella in *Kais*, and the *Times* and the *Chronicle*, perhaps out of politeness, failed to comment on her performance. But Hunt, noting she was cast as "a Circassian beauty," stated: "I did not think the Managers possessed such powers of irony" (E). DuBois (MM) agreed: one of her songs "was to the last degree absurd. The coarseness of her look and manner, and the imperfection of her voice, makes such attempts preposterous." And in the *Jew of Magadore* later that year, a duet with Braham "would have been a treat, if the cracked voice of Signora Storace had not frequently destroyed the sweetness of the harmony," and she was "quite over-done" in her other songs (MM). She again repeated her role as Zulima, but Hunt was acerbic: "Who can refrain from disgust, when he sees an unwieldly matron attempting all the personal giddiness and tricksome levity of a skittish girl. . . . [She] shakes her whole frame with huge enjoyment. . . . The galleries always applaud with proportionate vehemence, for they are well pleased with their own likeness" (E).

She retired after making a farewell performance in her brother's *No Song, No Supper* on May 30, 1808. She and Braham quarreled in 1816; she died the following year. In speaking of her accomplishments on the English stage, Edwards stated that she had raised English opera to "new heights," and Boaden (II, 14) wrote: "Storace was certainly one of the most effective burletta singers in the world. She took business as a pleasure, and seemed always happy when employed. In the discharge of her public duty, she was highly exemplary; laughed at colds and nervous complaints; used her shoes in the dry, and her pattens in the wet, to convey her to and from the theatre, and had not a grain of affectation about her."

Dickons

Maria Caroline Dickons was also one of the few English opera singers capable of holding her own at the King's. She was even capable of composing her own songs on occasion, and sometimes she accompanied herself on the pianoforte. She made her Covent Garden debut as Ophelia in 1793, primarily to sing Purcell's "Mad Bess" song (John Taylor, TI, "Sketch," Feb. 1819) — Catherine Stephens was hissed off the stage for a similar attempt in 1814. The following year she was "uncommonly successful in both her Bravuras" in Bate Dudley's *Travellers in Switzerland* (T; C). She later appeared in the provincial theatres, but she married in 1800 and retired from the stage.

Her husband, however, ran into financial problems, and she returned to Covent Garden in 1807 as a successful Mandane in *Artaxerxes*. Later that year she appeared in the *Beggar's Opera*, and the *Times* thought she was "by no means to be applauded as the *performer* of Polly Peacham, however she may be admired as the *singer*. She did not understand her character to be at all ludicrous. . . . [But] her style of singing, although it still wants somewhat of feeling, suits much better with those strains of which flourishes are the dress, than with those of which they are the body."

Still later that year, Dibdin got Harris to sign her on as the lead — Claudine — in his *Two Faces*, and she composed two of the airs herself. "If her execution had been less brilliant, we should sometimes have been inclined to think it redundant; but in several instances she had an opportunity for the display of all her science," and she had two encores (C). DuBois (MM) waxed rapturous: "[Last month] we said, *par excellence, 'she can sing.'* This was now proved by such a display of brilliant execution, as the English stage can scarcely parallel. In her first air 'Why did he come? Why did he go?' she shared the glory with [Shield] — nothing in composition or execution could be more exquisitely delightful. . . . Indeed, the ease and propriety of [her] acting surprised us almost as much as her masterly manner of singing."

In 1808 Dickons sang in a revival of the *Travellers*; Hunt noted she "was in excellent voice, and exhibited her usual scientific variety in all it's playfulness and power" (E). She also appeared as Catherine in the *Exile* (Covent Garden company at King's Theatre) and "sang in a stile amply worthy of the musical theatre in which she stood" (C). She was "a perfect eclipse to all other singing. In '*Once on a time*,' she shewed much playfulness, and in 'Hope, her support,' all her extraordinary powers" (MM). Hunt agreed, though he noted "an occasional vehemence in her attitudes and trippings somewhat too nearly approaching to a copy of Signora Storace" (E).

She was apparently inactive until 1811, when, in Bishop's *Knight of Snowdoun* (Covent Garden), "the warblings of Mrs. Dickons seemed to become more grateful, and to acquire new melody by the ability of the composer" (C). She "sang with great excellence" (BWM). And in 1812, at Drury Lane, she sang "with great taste" (C) in *Devil's Bridge*; in her role of Countess Rosalvina she was "excellent both as an actress and a singer; indeed, in all she does, there is so much simplicity, modesty, and effective science, that she is deservedly deemed the most popular performer of the stage" (BWM). This may have been the year in which she sang Clarissa in a revival of *Lionel and Clarissa*. S. D. ("Chronicles"), writing years later of that occasion, stated: "As an actress, Mrs. Dickons was above mediocrity; those who remember her representation of Clarissa, in Bickerstaff's opera, must remember also that, though no longer young or handsome, the deep feeling of Mrs. Dickons, in her last scene, often drew tears from many unwilling eyes."

Later that year she sang at the King's and remained there three seasons. But in July of 1813 she sang at the Lyceum in the *Jovial Crew* and exerted herself "with considerable spirit" (TI, Aug.), and at the end of that year, in between engagements at the King's, she returned to Drury Lane, repeating her excellent performance in the *Devil's Bridge* (T).

After her recovery from a nearly fatal fever and a tour of the Continent with Catalani, she returned to Drury Lane in 1815, singing Celestina in the *Unknown Guest*. But she began to run into quite adverse notices. "Mrs. Dickons was, as usual, not a very bad actress, and not a very bad singer; but, upon the whole, disagreeable in the extreme. Pride and self-conceit are so visible in her manner, that it requires some patience to endure her" (TI). Hazlitt (E) complained: "Mrs. Dickons never appeared to us as anything but an ordinary musical instrument, and at present, she is very much out of tune." Hunt, in "Musical Sketches" (E, Feb. 12, 1815), wrote:

> Mrs. Dickons is the best [singer] we have after Braham, and is perhaps as correct a one as any living: she has also considerable power, and may be called upon the whole a very useful and effective singer, a pitch above mediocrity. By many indeed she is thought to possess a good deal of taste; but this we conceive to be one of the impositions arising from the bravura and florid style. To us, besides her unpleasant readiness of voice, there is a coarse, flaunting air in her very best manner; and on no account should she ever undertake to be fascinating.

In August she sang the lead, Elfrida, in *King's Proxy* at the Lyceum, but the *Inquisitor*, still calling her Miss Poole, found her "as insipid and conceited as ever." Still later that year, at Drury Lane, she again sang Polly, and "made us forget every thing but her voice, which was in its highest excellence" (T). But the *Inquisitor* saw it otherwise: she was not only too mature for the role, but her "style of singing the character" was faulty; "the notes 'played round the head, but never reach the heart.' Her trills and quavers are, perhaps, very scientific, and doubtless very difficult; we wish . . . they were impossible. She is, moreover, insufferably confident and conceited in her acting."

Yet when she returned to Covent Garden in 1818, the reviewers greeted her almost as though she were a debutant. She appeared as Rosina in the Englished *Barber of Seville*, in which she accompanied herself on the piano. Sterling (T) was enthusiastic: "As an English singer, there are few, if any, superior to this lady: her style is bold and determined, her taste is correct, and her execution possesses singular neatness and articulation; she seldom or never offends the ear by any of those deviations from strict tune; . . . her shake is close and distinct, and her expression admirably dramatic and characteristic." The *Chronicle* agreed: she "acquitted herself with considerable talent throughout, not only as a vocal, but as a dramatic personage." And the *Champion* wrote: "Mrs. Dickons has decidedly improved since she has appeared on the London boards. To a voice of singular clearness and flexibility, she unites unusual brilliancy of execution and admirable taste. She appears to have lost a little of her *embonpoint* during her abode in France, and there is infinitely more *naivete* and spirit in her manner than we ever before observed. She is indeed the only singing actress on the English stage."

Hunt, however, thought she "has not got rid of the old error of overloading an air with ornaments; we really prefer, at any time, the heart and sentiment of Paisiello to the vocal millinery of the greatest singers in Europe" (E). The *Gazette* admitted: "We do not, indeed, find in her voice those tones which fall with inexpressible sweetness upon the ear. . . . But in taste, brilliancy, skill, and execution, she is not surpassed." And Kenrick (BS) averred: "She does not seem in possession of those extremely soft or moving tones that send criticism to sleep; nor on the other hand does her execution of Bravuras deserve a higher praise than that of being correct."

In March of 1819 she sang the countess in the Englished *Marriage of Figaro*. Comparisons with Catherine Stephens (see below), who sang Susanna, were inevitable, and Sterling thought any preference would be "a matter of individual taste." The former had "matured experience, perfect science, and a high degree of refinement," while to the latter belonged "a voice of the utmost strength and purity, combined with native graces." But the *Inquisitor* thought Stephens's vocal performance "certainly not equal to that of Mrs. Dickons," who was "a perfect mistress of her art" with "a delivery of taste and a high finish in her execution."

At the end of the year, still at Covent Garden, she sang in a poor revival of *Lodoiska* and "her great talents were . . . wasted on the role," for which Anna Maria Tree (see below) would have been a more popular choice (TI). She retired from the stage the following year.

Vestris

One of the finest singing actors of either sex in our period was Lucia Vestris, a contralto, who, as we have seen, made her debut at the King's in 1815. She sang there successfully—off and on—until 1827, but from 1820 to 1826, she sang mainly at the English theatres and was there exclusively after 1827.

She made her debut at Drury Lane on February 19, 1820, as Lilla in a revival of *Siege of Belgrade*, and Hunt gave her a warm welcome:

> The lover of singing, who is unacquainted with the Italian opera, may have an opportunity, in hearing [in Vestris] the true Italian style of singing on his native stage, and be able to distinguish it from the other without feeling it to be too violent a contrast. . . . There is nothing foreign in her pronunciation. Neither does she Italianize her ballads or lighter songs, unless a certain southern air of warmth and vivacity be said to throw a little more sunshine over them than usual. It is in her more elaborate songs . . . that she gives specimens of the more decided Italian style,—a certain syllabical marking in the pronunciation, and breathing passion in the voice; as if the spirit were divided between the earnest cordiality of it's sensations, and the pleasure of hearing itself utter them. . . .
>
> Her voice comes from her, riding upon it's own glad breath. . . . Her graces also, though truly graceful, are of no easy or cheap kind. . . . They are either passages worth the display of their composition, or pure graces of feeling, revolving upon a thought which they do not like to quit. (E)

The *London* added: "Her voice is a light mezzo soprano, clearer and more extended in its upper tones than is usual with the limited compass of such a scale. Her style is rather of expression than execution; and while below the modern standard of excellence, in agility and mechanical facility, she rises far above it in grace, sweetness, and pathos."

Artaxerxes, in which she sang the title role, soon followed. This production retained at least some of the recitative, in which her experience "in the Italian style gave her great advantage over the other performers," while her rendition of "In infamy" "was chaste and touching, and may almost be adduced as a specimen of the true style of simple singing" (T). But the *Inquisitor* thought it "decidedly inferior" to that of others and added: "Her singing is simplicity itself, for she cannot manage the most transient shake, or the slightest *cadenza*; and this we deeply regret, as there is a rawness in her higher notes which the greatest dexterity is wanted to conceal."

Her choice of this trouser role signaled her penchant for such roles in many of her English opera vehicles. It was quickly followed, for example, by *Giovanni in London*, in which she played the Don. In his sketch of this performer, Kenrick wrote (BS, Jan. 1821): "The bait succeeded; the town ran in crowds to see Madame Vestris's legs, though they had been somewhat lukewarm about her singing; and hundreds . . . discovered that her proportions were most captivating when set off to advantage by a tight pair of elastic pantaloons."

> The *Inquisitor* waxed furiously moralistic:
> The disgusting woman who undertook this libertine character at its outset, prepared us very fully for the only result that can ever be drawn, in the nicest hands, from its loathsome repetition; and we, therefore, feel bound to treat it as a part which no female should assume till she has discarded every delicate scruple by which her mind or her person can be distinguished.

But the *London*, probably prompted by this review, had no such reservations on that score; rather, she was *too* feminine:

> Madame Vestris played, sung, and looked the incorrigible Don John very prettily and spiritedly; but, we confess, we had rather see her petticoated than in a Spanish doublet and hose, hat and feather. . . . There is a pulpy softness and ripeness in her lips, a roseate hue, like the leaves of the damask rose, a lucious honeyed sound in her voice, depth and fulness too, . . . a languid archness, an Italian lustre in her eye, an enchanting smile, a mouth—shall we go on?

In 1821 she appeared in the all-sung *Dirce*; she acted "with spirit" and sang "with more than usual power" (LG), but she could not save it. In his "Sketch" (BS, Jan. 1821), Kenrick noted striking improvements in her voice and stage confidence over her early years at the King's. In a brief note that year, Bacon (QMM, III, 385) thought she "has been generally over-rated: her natural gifts are not extraordinary. . . . Voice, intonation, and execution are all imperfect; yet still the simplicity of her style has gained her great favor with the public at large."

In 1822 she appeared in the *Pirate*. Regarding her singing and acting, Sterling wrote: "Madame Vestris has the rare merit of uniting both talents, and in a high degree of perfection; yet what but some strange fatality or perversity of taste could select her for the serious Minna." She was "not exactly the Minna of [Scott's] novel, yet her sweet voice rendered her not less pleasing" (LitC). She repeated her triumph as *Artaxerxes* (T), and as Lilla in a revival of the *Siege of Belgrade* the *Examiner* found her "far better" than Storace in the role, "especially in the acting."

In 1823 she sang two songs "very charmingly" in *Sweethearts and Wives* at the Little Theatre (T). She played Laura, the rejected niece, "with great sprightliness, and sang still better" (E; LG), singing "with admirable archness" (Har). She also played Macheath there, which Sterling thought "indelicate and ridiculous" (July 10) and had "little dash or spirit" (Jan. 2, 1824). But she followed this up a few days later as Annette in a revival of *Lord of the Manor* and sustained that part "uncommonly well. She sang charmingly, and her acting was eminently distinguished by *gaieté de coeur*" (T).

In 1824, still at Drury Lane, she appeared in *Philandering* and "very archly enacted the sprightly paysanne Pauline . . . but her attire . . . did not please us. She sang . . . with great naiveté and sweetness" (E). At the Little Theatre she performed another trouser role, Don Felix, in *Alcaid*, and "although she was sufficiently unlike a student of Salamanca, yet as she sung better than any male the establishment could produce, one must be content" (T). The *London* was again enthusiastic: "Madame Vestris enacted Don Felix in a good loose dashing rakehelly fashion. She is the best bad young man about town, and can stamp a smart leg in tight whites, with the air of a fellow who has an easy heart and a good tailor."

She was at the King's in 1825, but the next year appeared at Covent Garden as Fatima in *Oberon*. She had but two songs to sing in this small role and got only routine praise (T; C; LG; EM). In its revival there that fall she sang with her "accustomed excellence" (T); "even Miss Paton scarcely excels her" (C). In 1827 she sang a trouser role in the *White Maid* and "looked as manly and as handsome as she is wont to do on such occasions" (LitC). Her appearance was "rendered extremely effective by her acting and very playful execution of the first air, 'Ah what delight the soldier knows'" (E). She "played right gallantly the hero, and sang in excellent taste" (NM).

At the Little Theatre that summer she appeared as Justine in *Rencontre*, and Sterling proclaimed her "the very queen of actresses for English vaudevilles; . . . she could play five or six in a night, of her own skill and popularity, and without any assistance at all. There is not a performer in town that so perfectly commands the stage while she is upon it." Talfourd (NM) agreed, adding: "Where she attempts too much, or too hastily, her good looks and good humour made us prefer her failure to the success of others." At the end of the year, she played Blonda, a waiting-maid in the *Seraglio*, and won the only singing encore of the evening, though she "sang unusually flat" (LG). She was "as usual, all smiles, and songs, and sauciness" (At), and provided "the real support of the piece" (Har).

In her only 1828 performance for which we find a review, she appeared in a revival of *Native Land*. Hunt wrote in the *Companion*: "Madame Vestris, though she does not insinuate a sufficient stock of sentiment through her gaieties to complete the proper idea of a charmer to our taste, is always charming after her fashion.... The song of 'Is't art, I pray, or nature' she gave with too little vivacity; and her part in the *bolero* she seemed to go through more as a duty than a pleasure—which is anything but boleresque." In 1829 she appeared as Eglantine in Dimond's *Nymph of the Grotto*, and "had the best songs in the piece" (T), though the part had "nothing worthy of her" (LG). But "for the first time in our remembrance" she "sang out of tune" (E) and was not "in her usual voice" (At). In a dispute with the management over another singer, she refused to sing beyond the ninth night—a loss to the theatre (Genest).

In 1830, back again at Drury Lane, she was delightful in *National Guard* (LG), but she "had not recovered the purity of intonation, for which she has till of late been remarkable" (Holmes). She had the same problem two months later in *The Beggar's Opera* (At; E). As Josephine in *Hofer*—another breeches role and "a real female sharpshooter"—she had "little opportunity" for acting, but she sang well (T; NM) and was in excellent voice (At).

Before the year ended, she was already indicating some impatience with theatre managers and an interest in the minors. She performed Annette in a revival of *Lord of the Manor* at the Tottenham Street Theatre (Royal West London), and in his *Tatler* review, Hunt summed up her accomplishments and defects as he saw her then:

> Her notes had less sweetness than we had given them credit for, and were not always in tune. We remember hearing her sing, "In infancy our hopes and fears" ... when the house was as silent as if every note was a jewel.... She sees nothing beyond the better part of "the town." She knows what would be thought sensible by this judicious old gentleman, and tasteful by that, and pretty by another; but she brings nothing from the stores of the cordial and ideal.... If she goes out of her way, it is not to do something affecting, but something daring. She puts on the breeches, and then is at the top of her attraction.

Hunt tells us she was "angry that the Managers" of the majors "have resolved not to pay large sums by the night," and "we are glad of the gain of the minor theatres." From 1831 until 1838, she took control of the Olympic and "made it one of the most refined theatres in London" (N.). In the latter year she married Charles Mathews junior, and together they managed Covent Garden from 1839 to 1842 — where she occasionally mounted fine operas in English — and the Lyceum from 1847 to 1855. Chorley, in his obituary of her, regretted that she did not have enough patience to be the greatest contralto of all.

Carew

A not inconsiderable figure who sang from 1816 to 1822, but who has been overlooked by music historians, is a Miss Carew (1799–?). She was born in London of an Irish family; her grandfather was a captain in the navy and her father was a lowly government official. She early gave intimations of musical ability, and at age 12 she was articled to James Welsh. At fourteen she sang in the Covent Garden chorus and occasionally had walk-on parts. Her big chance came early in 1816, when she served as replacement on four hours' notice for the indisposed Catherine Stephens in the role of Lucy Bertram in a revival of *Guy Mannering*; she performed it with "complete success" ("Sketch," TI, Aug. 1818). She continued to replace her as Sophia in a revival of *Lord of the Manor* and "looked and acted wonderfully like Miss Stephens" — long the reigning favorite (TI). She also succeeded as Sylvia in *Cymon*, and that summer she was first singer at the Little Theatre, as a consequence of which some of her songs appeared in printed music the next year, "as sung by Miss Carew at the Haymarket" (BS, Sept.).

In the fall of 1816, although depressed by being again "harnessed to the drudgery" of minor theatrical chores (TI, Nov.), Carew did get a small part in *Slave*, and with others, she was encored in a glee (C; Ch). In 1817 she was very successful at the English Opera House as Clara in *Duenna* and as Polly in *Beggar's Opera*. In 1818 she distinguished herself in the *Americans*, according to J. D. Collier (C), and "was repeatedly encored, and sometimes in songs of too much difficulty and labour, to be made the subjects of such compliment. We do not remember to have heard her in better voice, or animated by so much self-possession." Sterling admitted she "may now fairly rank as the *prima donna* of the English opera. Her acting, too, is very pretty and graceful." There was, however, a "constant appearance of effort" that should be avoided.

She "charmed the audience with some fine specimens of vocal power" (T) in *Jealous on all Sides*. She replaced Miss Kelly on short notice as Sophia, a difficult role in the *Privateer*; but "she played from her own conception, and that conception was natural and feeling, and never failed to produce the strongest impressions" (EM). (Both works were minor English Opera House productions.) In August of that year, the *Inquisitor* wrote that she "has now no occasion to look back in the world; she has broken the ice.... This lady's voice is a clear, powerful, and sweet soprano, of considerable compass, which has been formed and cultivated in the purest school; her performance is rather remarkable for a fascinating simplicity, a depth of feeling, and a correctness of taste, than for a brilliancy of execution."

Anent the English Opera House 1819 season opening, the *Inquisitor* cited Carew as a "respectable support" of the music department but claimed that "as a leading singer [she] cannot be highly prized." Nevertheless, she moved on to Drury Lane that fall, playing Lady Bertram in a revival of *Guy Mannering*, and gave a satisfactory performance (T). In a revival of *Fontainbleau*, she "sustained" Rosa, the lead, and "sang with customary sweetness" (T; TI, Oct.). She was also commended for her Leah in *Fisherman's Hut*.

In 1820 Carew sang Mandane in *Artaxerxes* and "distinguished herself in a more than usual manner. Her voice in the slow passages, and when exerted to its full strength, lost its distinctness... but this defect was repaid by the correctness and delicacy with which she gave some of the more elaborate airs" (T). But later that year she was miscast in *Giovanni in London*: "We saw Miss Carew with regret in the paltry character to which her talents were condemned, though her delightful execution of a popular air atoned... for the indignity a sordid manager [Elliston] inflicted" (TI, Jan.).

At the English Opera House in 1822, she sang the lead in *Love Among the Roses*—an unoperatic production by Beazley—and the *Literary Chronicle* called her "one of the best vocal performers on the stage." The *Examiner* noted she "both acts and sings with taste and feeling; and gave all the interest to a truthful heroine of this every day description, which it is capable of receiving—appropriate appearance, and easy and graceful delivery." She later sang in *Gil Blas* and, with Kelly and Povey, "braced up our ears like tonics" (LM, Sept.). Finally, in our last notice of her, she sang the lead in *Fair Gabrielle*, acted well, and "sang the old French air of 'Charmante Gabrielle,' unaccompanied, very impressively" (E).

In 1823 Bacon (QMM, V, 475–78) summed up her accomplishments:

> Miss Carew's voice is sufficiently powerful to fill a large room, or even a theatre, but it is certainly below that standard which dramatic command implies. [Yet] in point of execution Miss Carew is exceedingly neat, brilliant, and easy. She can do all that is necessary to be done

with facility, though she has none of that wonderment about her singing, which disgusts as many general auditors as it pleases.

> But the chief characteristic of this young lady's performance is, that rare combination of excellence—fine taste.... Her style is masterly, her expression pure though sensitive, her ornaments pleasing yet scientific, and her general manner nicely suited to the occasion.

He pointed out that she had sung at many public and private concerts, both in London and in the provinces but concluded with the unexplained statement: "She has of late seceded from the stage, and is occupied in teaching and singing at concerts." She was perhaps too much of a lady to be quite happy in the burly atmosphere of the playhouses.

Tree

Ann Maria Tree (1801–62),[21] daughter of an East India House merchant, began singing lessons at age fourteen under Lanza and for a time sang in the Drury Lane chorus. Later she made the acquaintance of Madame Fodor, through whom she was thrust into a minor role at the King's in 1817; Bacon (LG, Mar. 15) growled: "To put Miss Tree into any but chorus parts is doing no service to her or the audience." Later she was trained by T. S. Cooke, and in 1818 she made her debut as Polly in *Beggar's Opera* at Bath, with flattering notices (TI, Oct. 1819). Following another success as Patty in *Maid of the Mill*, she was awarded a three-year contract by Covent Garden.

Tree made her London debut there, in 1819, as Rosina in a revival of the *Barber*, and had a "brilliant success." "Her rich and easy tones smack most delightfully of taste and tenderness," and she evinced "unblemished symptoms of ultimate superiority" (TI). Hunt wrote: "She seems to be quite at home in songs that hold the middle place between the ballad and the scientific" (E, Sept. 19). She followed this with Philidel in *Arthur and Emmeline* and "surprised and delighted the audience by her perfect command of the old English songs. She is superior, we think, in that style, to any that she has hitherto attempted" (T; E). The *Champion* noted her "admirable execution of the simple and delightful music of Purcell and Arne." Her Philidel "must rank among the happiest of that lady's assumptions," and she has "the warmest corroboration our 'delighted spirit' can connect with her exquisite exertions" (TI).

Tree concluded her very full first year as Luciana in the *Comedy of Errors* and was deemed "the best second on the English stage" (T). "She grows in our estimation daily; she has true feeling, as well as a cultivated taste for music" (C),. and she "surprised us, by pleasing us so much" (LG). The

Champion declared that, in her, "we have, what on the English stage is a perfect phenomenon, the excellencies of the singer and the actress, united in the same person." She "supported an unimportant character with uncommon spirit," and her "ease, elegance, and propriety of demeanour" were observed (TI). Hunt (E) admired her deep tones: "If they have any fault, it is that they are occasionally too luscious, and contrasted with her upper. But they are exquisitely true. Her ear indeed throughout is one of the finest we ever witnessed."

In 1820, as a "young French rustic bride" in *Henri Quatre*, Tree "was nearly as happy in her acting as in her singing" (T; LM). The next month Hazlitt cited her in a review of *Artaxerxes*: "What is it that gives such a superiority to her singing? Nothing but its truth, its seriousness, its sincerity. She has no caprices, plays no fantastic tricks; but seems as much in the power, at the mercy of the composer, as a musical instrument: her lips transmit the notes she has by heart . . . and her voice seems to brood over, and become enamoured of the sentiment" (LM, June).

She then "charmed every one" as Viola in *Twelfth Night*, as Bacon (LG) wrote: "She performed well, and sung enchantingly, both in her solos and in her second to Olivia. Her melody is delicious." It was the "best character" she "has hitherto sustained. There was a zeal and animation in the manner of Miss Tree while giving many capital passages" (TI). Hunt (E) wrote: "There is a strength and fullness in the lower notes, which being unusual in a female, appeared to fall in with the character she had assumed as a male." Then he took particular notice of her leg: "And (as such subjects are eminently critical) we must be allowed to say that her leg is the very prettiest leg we ever saw on the stage. . . . It is a right feminine leg, delicate in foot, trim in ancle, and with a calf at once soft and well-cut, distinguished and unobtrusive. . . . It is fit for a statue; still fitter for where it is."

The *European* thought she "exhibited a superior ease and spirit in her acting, that, added to her sweet voice, made her a favourite from the beginning" (EM). And later that year Bacon again took notice of her (QMM, II, 377–78): "The novelty of the year is Miss M. Tree, a young singer whose merits have already raised her to a high degree of favour with the public. . . . Her execution is brilliant, but reduced in effect (particularly to English ears) by the too frequent and too forceful use of the *portamento* or glide. There is no ornament so dangerous, particularly in English singing, as this."

In 1821 her singing of Julia in *Two Gentlemen of Verona* was "uncommonly beautiful" (T). "Never in our life did we witness a female more calculated than Miss Tree to fill up the idea of devoted female loveliness, of which our old dramatists were so fond" (E). In 1822 she appeared "to great advantage as Zaide" in *Law of Java*: "Both in action and in song she gives full effect to the character." Indeed, only her "exquisite pathos" render the work passable; she "breathes out the accents of conjugal tenderness with an apparent absence of all effort—with such delicate yet distinctive marking—that a very common scene of leave-taking was rendered most beautifully effective" (E; Ch). That fall she repeated her Viola and sang well but "neglect[ed] distinctness of articulation"—"the words of the part are lost" (T). As Rosa, in a revival of *Fontainbleau*, she "was particularly happy in her execution of a Rossini aria" (T).

She completed the year with Matilda, the lead in *Maid Marian*. "Her playing was distinguished by the most bewitching *naivete*; her singing by taste and science." "A duet between her and Master Longhurst,[22] 'Come hither, come hither, my merry foot page,' demands the highest praise" (T; C). But the *Herald* thought she "had not the vigour for the character," and the *Gazette* found her middle tones "not so perfect." The *Examiner* reported she "very delightfully executed" Bishop's "Let us seek the yellow shore" but regretted a bravura: "The effort was powerful, but it was not an effort for Miss Tree." Yet the *London* was most enthusiastic: "She was Maid Marian to the life. When she sang, and when she spake, the forest of Sherwood spread its green boughs in the air, the herd went trooping by, and the ear seemed to feel the noise of the foresters, and the rustling of the forest leaves come swooning upon the air as in the very days of the merry merry Outlaw—Bold Robin Hood!"

In 1823 a dispute between her and Mary Anne Paton arose over the casting of *Figaro*: "Miss Paton intended to introduce *Bid me discourse*, which has been sung by Miss Tree, into the part of the Countess. Miss Tree pleaded her right. Miss Paton replied, by claiming the part of Susanna as her own, by a similar right, and then Miss Tree became *indisposed*" (LM, Feb.). After this affair had blown over, Tree took another lead—Clari in Payne's opera. Sterling reported she "sang with taste and feeling, and acted with delicacy and without offense; but she is unequal in melodramatic situations which she has to fill." He was the only one to think so. The *Chronicle* and the *Examiner* found she excelled in just those situations, and the *Herald* wrote that she was encored in "Home, Sweet Home"—"the word 'home' she gave with a peculiar sweetness and pathos." The *Gazette* found her acting admirable throughout: "No female songstress is at all equal to her in this respect," and "she did such justice to her part in every point as to merit the highest praise." The *Drama Magazine* also agreed: "The slow encroachment of agitation, the hurried and fluttering efforts to keep down her passionate emotions, and the final outbreak of irrepressible feeling in one wild cry of agony, were exhibited with uncommon ability and success. That scene alone was sufficient to place Miss Tree very high in the serious part of her profession." Ayrton thought her acting was "the salvation of the piece," and the *London* admired her "deeply pathetic" portrayal of the role.

The next year she was again singing with Paton, who had the lead in *Native Land*. Sterling noted: "We are sorry to observe the retiring and pensive Miss Tree in such a part as Biondina, where she has to put off the qualities of a sex which she adorns, and assume the foppery and dress of a male coxcomb," even though only for some scenes. And Talfourd (NM) deplored the practice: "These assumptions [of male attire] are now becoming common nuisances. There is not an opera, a melodrama, hardly even a farce free from them." But the *Examiner* saw it otherwise: "The jewel of the evening . . . was the mock cavalier and bridegroom of Miss Tree. It was not only light, airy, and elegant, as intended, but impregnated with a portion of that ethereal spirit, which gives feeling even to coxcombry, and impressiveness to bagatelle. Her roguishness, vivacity, courtship, dancing, and fencing, were all inimitable." The *London* of course thoroughly agreed.

In 1825 she upheld the role of Miriam in an unoperatic melodrama, *The Hebrew Family* (E, Apr. 10). But two months later she took her farewell benefit at Covent Garden, after which she married James Bradshaw, a politician; thereafter she made only concert appearances. Talfourd (NM, July) wrote:

> Notwithstanding the immediate loss to ourselves, we are glad that her public career has come to so fortunate and so timely an end. For a few years longer she might have continued on the stage with undiminished attraction and improved powers; but just when she had attained her greatest excellence the town would have discovered that she was no longer young, and would have turned from her to bestow its capricious favour on the first pretty girl whom the manager might draw from Bath or Dublin.

Chorley called her "a singer with a cordial, expressive mezzo-soprano voice and much real feeling." The D.N.B. states she succeeded because of "pathos of voice."[23]

Paton

Tree's competitor, Mary Anne Wood (née Paton) (1802–64), was born in Scotland and as a child took lessons on the piano and violin and in singing; she began to perform in public at eight.[24] She made her adult debut in 1822 in *Artaxerxes* at Covent Garden, but she first comes to our notice at the

Little Theatre that summer as Lydia in *Morning, Noon and Night*. She "even surpassed her former efforts. Her powers unfold themselves as she gains confidence upon the stage." She sang a Scottish ballad "without music, and was rapturously encored" (T; C). "She combined the flights of science with simple melody so harmoniously, as to prove how well and how deeply she has studied" (LitC). The *Examiner* agreed: "We have already hazarded an opinion that this lady will become an excellent actress; and we have been further confirmed in it by the ease with which she assumed the accent and *naivete* of a cultivated Scottish lassie. It was delightfully bland and delicate." This was quickly succeeded by her Polly in *Beggar's Opera*: "Take Miss Stephens from the boards, and this lady stands at the head of the English dramatic vocal corps. She sang with great expression. There was no dissonance between sentiment of the part and strain of the composer" (T).

In 1823 Paton successfully performed Adriana in the *Comedy of Errors*. "We particularly admire that sensitiveness of expression which accompanies the harmony of her voice and renders it doubly agreeable" (H). Later she had a leading role in *Cortez*; she "was in excellent voice, and the music was well calculated to set it off to advantage." She performed an encore of a "most difficult passage" with "uncommon spirits" (C). The *Herald* wrote that she was fine in some duets but was "most eminently successful" in her solos, and "her triumph was a bravura air . . . over which she diffused a richness of melody with an exercise of power over the musical scale, which . . . acted with an electric touch upon the audience. She displayed . . . that infusion of soul and feeling . . . in which Italian singers so particularly excel." She concluded the year as Floretta in a revival of the *Cabinet*, which "was charmingly played; full of archness and vivacity, but perhaps a little overacted in the cunning of the character. Her singing . . . was as characteristic as her dialogue" (T).

In 1824 "Miss Paton, who always looks a lady, also acted one (as Clymante) with no small animation, in the single animated scene which was given to her" in *Native Land* (E). She "certainly will add to her reputation by the very brilliant execution of her bravuras" (T; EM). But the *London* wrote that she "sings as though she were wrestling with the music. The talents . . . for singing and dancing do not meet in this young lady." At the Little Theatre she sang Susanna in *Figaro*, but it "is not, perhaps, her happiest character: it requires rather more acting than she is able to give it" (T). This was followed by *Alcaid*, in which "she sang very delightfully" and was frequently encored but "had nothing at all to act" (T). The *London* stated she had requested a newspaper editor to contradict his report that she had "acquired a title by marriage" — she had, becoming Lady Lennox — "on the grounds of its being injurious to her professional pursuits." Unlike

Miss Tree's, however, her marriage seems not at all to have affected her career.

Paton sang in the Covent Garden *Freischütz*[25] that fall, taking over the role of Bertha. Though not in good voice, she executed her "exquisite scena" with "chasteness and feeling," and her last-act cavatina was "beautifully expressive of devout resignation" (E; LG). *Drama Magazine* declared: in the "execution of *bravura* singing she "is without a rival on the English stage." In 1825 she represented Preciosa in Weber's opera, which failed. There was only a single song in the work (the rest were choruses), though it was "ill suited" to her (LitC). Yet the *Examiner* found her effective—"especially in the scene in which she 'improvisatrices'—the only opportunity afforded." That summer she sang for the first time at the English Opera House—as Ninetta in *Tarrare*—and "was happily conspicuous in a sort of seraglio waiting woman, and put off her songs and duets to advantage" (T; C). She "sang with great sweetness and variety of intonation," (E) but was getting "rather stout" (LitC). Talfourd (NM) thought her "the most scientific and perfect, though not the sweetest of English singers."

In 1826 Paton sang Reiza in *Oberon*, and J. P. Collier (C) noted: "There is always great propriety about her manner of speaking, and less languor and indifference than usually belongs to singers." The *Gazette* said she "displayed her accustomed brilliancy and spirit in the execution of the difficult passages." But she also "sang with great delicacy" (NM) and "possibly never appeared to better advantage" (E). Planché, who admired her fine voice, considered her no actress in this role, however. At the English Opera House she appeared in a revival of *Tarrare* and sang and acted well, "although there is a dash of affectation about" her acting, "which, the sooner she throws aside the better" (T). Next, she and Miss Kelly "saved" a revival of *Lord of the Manor* by their fine singing (T).

This was followed by *The Oracle*, in which she performed the lead role of Myra, the Inca's daughter, and had repeated encores, though the management had tried to suppress them (T). She sang well in concerted numbers as well as in a rondo, "sung with the most enchanting tenderness of expression." And her "mad scena could not be exceeded. It was full of the most impassioned expression, given in the most finished style of excellence" (C). The *Gazette* wrote: "Miss Paton, on whom the chief weight falls, sustained it like an Atlas, or rather like an Angel. It is hardly possible to image a more exquisite treat." Her acting was admirable, too, except for occasional "facial exaggeration"—"the eyes looking war to the music and the words, the brows rapidly elevating and contracting, and the face undergoing changes the opposite of the agreeable." (Was this not appropriate in a "mad" scene?) Others (E; NM; Har) had only the highest praise for her. That fall Paton appeared as Alice Bridgeworth in Pocock's *Peveril*. She did much for the play (T; C; LitC) and gave her inferior songs "a charm almost approaching to that of originality" (E).

Paton began 1827 with Mandane (*Artaxerxes*) and, according to Sterling, "was one of the finest since the days of Billington. She is little inferior to that celebrated singer in power and execution, but far behind her in sentiment and passion, which are the soul of music." But she soon had a "fracas" with the manager of Covent Garden, "in consequence of which she retired from that theatre" (At, May 13). That fall she reappeared at Drury Lane as Annette in *Lord of the Manor* and "sustained the character with great ability as a singer—as an actress she was not sufficiently spirited.... Her gait was staid, her actions prim, and her most lively sentence uttered with very little animation" (T). And after a "severe indisposition," she repeated her role as Mandane, but both her acting and singing "betray strong symptoms of languor and lassitude"—she was still obviously unwell (T).

Because of her health, she was absent from the boards in 1828, but she returned to Covent Garden in 1829, apparently having made peace with the manager, and she repeated her Reiza in *Oberon*. Though she still showed some effects of her illness, "she went through her long and trying part with uncommon energy, and sang with her accustomed good taste, scientific skill and precision.... We never feel pain for her on account of incompetence; and ... she very rarely makes a slip in her intonation" (E). She next sang Rebecca in the *Maid of Judah*—the only woman in the cast. Sterling wrote that she "had a great deal of vocal execution assigned to her part, [and] a more competent representative of the character could not be met with on the English stage. It is, we believe, the first time that this lady has appeared in an opera, the music of which is entirely of Italian composition, and we can only regret that the attempt is likely to prove of a temporary nature" (T). J. D. Collier (C) agreed and was surprised by the "energy and effect" she gave to the dialogue. She "out-Sontag'd Sontag in her flights and fancies" (LG).

In 1830 Paton performed the title role in *Ninetta* and sang with "neatness and brilliancy" and showed much dramatic talent (T; LG; Ath). Her singing, "for truth of intonation, high polish of style, and judicious discrimination, was all but perfect of its kind" (E). And Holmes (At) wrote: "When we consider how coarse is the preference of audiences at the great theatres; how much they delight in excess, and violent contrasts ... we shall esteem it no small praise to the first dramatic singer of England, that she has attained her high popularity without resorting to such poor expedients." Ayrton, too, found her admirable but wished she would "spare human ears the torture of listening to chromatic scales."

This was followed by her *Cinderella*, which she played "with a good deal of natural simplicity" (T). There was "one passage in her part . . . which appeared to us a masterpiece of narrative singing; we were delighted both with her manner, style, and articulation" (E). Holmes, too, was impressed, though admitted Sontag or Blasis at the King's "may, perhaps, execute the bravura music of the original better than Miss Paton." At the Little Theatre that summer, she appeared as Rosina in a revival of *Barber* and sang a bravura "with extraordinary effect and power" (T). And in a revival of *Clari* (cut down to an afterpiece) the same evening, she sang "Home, Sweet Home" with "intense feeling" and "her acting was extremely pathetic." (T). But Hunt, in the *Tatler* review the same day, saw quite a different performer:

> Miss Paton is a fine singer of a certain order, but not we think of the finest; and she is a better actress than we had supposed her, but entirely of the artificial kind. Her acting seems to have been taught her, and she has learnt it well; but the "system" is displayed at every turn: she is obvious and declamatory; loud or low, indignant or patient, as the surface of the feeling suggests, her face being all the while singularly devoid of expression. In short, she is a very good self-possessed actress, for a singer; and shows how little real feeling of a character is required to attain the conventional style of performance. . . .
>
> When she sings, the thought of the singing-book so much predominates with her over the sentiment, that she makes absolute grimaces . . . and now and then plunges at them with a sort of fury, as if she would get through them tooth and nail. What is even more offensive to us than this, she cares as little . . . about the demands of a beautiful melody, full of expression, as the most common-place executionists of the day.

The following week he thought her little improved as Susanna in a revival of *Figaro* (see part I, appendix 2).

In 1833 she and her husband went on a musical tour of the United States, and they retired to Yorkshire in 1843. Weber, who considered Vestris the only singer who could act, thought Paton a singer "of the very first rank," which he attributed to her "good Italian training" (Warrack, p. 333).

Stephens

Our final singer, Catherine Stevens (1794–1882), not only held the English stage longer than any other singer, but by most accounts she was regarded as the first woman singer on the English stage. From numerous "Sketches"[26] we learn something of her early background. She was the daughter of a "respectable tradesman" ("carver" and "gilder" according to Phillips) and had an older sister who made a successful debut at Drury Lane in 1798 as Polly and sang a small role in Houlton's *Wilmore Castle* there in 1800 — the last we hear of her. Meanwhile, Catherine, in 1807, was articled to Gesualdo Lanza for five years, though he gave her only twenty-seven lessons.

In 1812 Thomas Welsh happened to hear her at a private concert and immediately felt she had extraordinary talent. He took her on as a pupil and, the same year, sang with her at the Manchester concerts. She had already changed her stage name to "Stephens" when she sang a small role in Mozart's *Figaro* at the Pantheon (May 2). Her person was described by Kenrick (BS, Jan. 1817) as "extremely pleasing. Her countenance, if not beautiful, irresistably commands the regard and admiration of the spectator by its placid and good-tempered expression. These feelings are inexpressibly strengthened by the evident diffidence which pervades all she says and does."

In 1813 she made her debut at Covent Garden as Mandane in *Artaxerxes* and, until 1823, sang only leading roles there. Our single review of that occasion was cautious: "A first trial is insufficient for a judgment" (T). The debut was quickly followed by her performance of Clara in *Duenna*. Sterling wrote that she was "beyond all doubt, deserving of encouragement. Her voice is sweet, distinct, and feminine: without a rage for ornament, it has the evidence of tasteful training. Her song of 'Adieu, thou Dreary Pile,' combined all its good and ill. It was delicate and tender, it was occasionally tame and negligent: its lengthened tones were sometimes protracted till they were inaudible; and its embellishments lost their beauty in their incorrectness" (T).

She concluded her very ambitious first year as Rosetta in *Love in a Village*. Hazlitt wrote of her in the *Chronicle*: "She gave the songs in this character with a charm, a truth, and a simplicity, which nothing could surpass.... In some of them we think she displayed greater power and depth of voice than in her other characters. Her manner of acting the part was beautiful; it was ease and nature itself. The sprightliness and *naivete* with which she sang the comic sings with Justice Woodcock, had the most fascinating effect." In their "Memoirs" of her that December, the *Inquisitor* stated:

> Her voice is powerful, yet, mellifluous; her intonation rich and various, yet, in the highest degree articulate, and pathetic; her conception of character [is] as correct as her expression of the conception is

effective.... Her faults ... are the faults of timidity, inexperience, and the novelty of the characters she has found it expedient to sustain. We hail her appearance as an epoch in the history of the musical world, as a corrective of the Italian taste so obtrusive on the English stage, and as compensating beyond our hopes for the absence of a Billington.

In 1814 she sang Mrs. Cornflower in Dibdin's *Farmer's Wife* and was encored in a polacca and a bravura (T; BWM), though the latter "was not in harmony with the scene" (C). "The artless modesty of her deportment, and her apparent unconsciousness of her own excellence, form a pleasing contrast to the coquettish airs and grins of self-satisfaction with which [the character of] Miss Matthews endeavours to win her audience" (TI). At the end of the season, she appeared in *John of Paris* and "delightfully executed" Boieldieu's airs (C); she "could not fail of commanding the applause of the house" (EM). At some time during the year, she apparently performed Ophelia and was hissed for introducing Purcell's "Mad Bess" into the part (N.G.).

In 1815 she sang Donna Isadora in Dimond's *Brother and Sister* and was "very happy in her execution of an echo song" (EM), which was "loudly encored" (UM). Later, she performed Sylvia in *Cymon*: "We have never heard Miss Stephens in more delightful voice. With her restored health, it seems to have caught even greater freshness and vigour" (T; C). "Too much cannot be said in praise of the manner in which she executed" the air "What's life without passion" (TI).

She began 1816 with *Midsummer Night's Dream* and was "impressive in sentiment" (EM; T). "The first air she gave, had a beautiful simplicity in it, which was even somewhat increased by the voice that breathed it" (Ch). She "most sweetly" represented Lucy Bertram in *Guy Mannering*. "This young lady is the most interesting female performer on the stage; her voice is soft and melodious—her looks are always modest and expressive.... She never strayed into an unbecoming wildness in her singing, and her tones are exquisitely simple and sweet" (Ch). She also appeared in *Your's or Mine* and sang a bravura "with inimitable skill and expression" (T). And she concluded the year as Zelinda in Morton's *Slave* and was "the perfect syren" (EM). Her song of the mockingbird was "a charming bravura" (T), and "nothing could be more fascinating than the simple and affecting sweetness with which she executed this air" (C). Her last song, "Sons of Freedom," "we think has seldom been surpassed for tone, sensibility, and sweetness of expression" (T). Hunt wrote of this performance: "There is only one note in her voice that seems at all harsh or reedy; the rest is clear, easy, and delicious. The notes drop from her undistorted lips, like the pearls of the little girl in the fairy tale" (E).

In 1817 she played Zerlina in *Libertine* "most captivatingly," though she omitted "Batti, batti" at one performance (BS). The *Times*, however, considered her a failure in the role, as did Hazlitt: "She undoubtedly sung her songs with much sweetness and simplicity, but her simplicity had something of insipidity in it" (E). Still later that year, she "made an interesting Lilla" in a revival of *Siege of Belgrade*, "but did not infuse that spirit into the part which we were accustomed to admire in Storace" (T; BS). This was followed by *Duke of Savoy*, in which she played the small role of Nanette and sang "some agreeable airs in the sweetest possible manner" (C), and was encored in a duet (TI); indeed, she may have saved the piece from disaster (BS). At the end of the year, she appeared as Floretta in a revival of the *Cabinet* and sang well, but "her comic powers are not great. . . . Simplicity, and not archness, is her forte" (EM). In his "Sketch" (BS, Jan. 1817) Kenrick wrote that she "has no equal either in compass and sweetness of voice, or brilliancy and correctness of execution," though he admitted that, as an actress, "she certainly is not possessed of powers sufficient to entitle her to be ranked with first-rate performers."

Stephens began 1818 with a repetition of Mandane: "With the exception of Madame Mara and Mrs. Billington, she is the best we have ever heard" (T). She next performed the lead role in Didbin's *Zuma*; her "echo duet"[27] with Braham "was rapturously received and encored" (TI). As Diana Vernon in *Rob Roy Macgregor*, she "did great justice to the beautiful national airs of Scotland" (T; C). But the *European* found her love scenes with Sinclair uninteresting, and the *Inquisitor* wrote that she "neither looked or talked like the romantic, fox-hunting, resistless Diana Vernon; she was the meek filial devoted daughter but nothing more, and in this instance her usual excellencies were, by misapplication, converted into faults."

In 1819 she sang Susanna in *Figaro*. Sterling thought she complemented Mrs. Dickons as the countess with her voice "of utmost strength and purity, combined with native graces 'beyond the reach of art.'" The *Inquisitor* agreed: her Susanna, "though somewhat deficient in vivacity, was nevertheless exceedingly pleasing; and she gave a pretty, though faint portrait of the spirited soubrette." Yet "her performance of the music was certainly not equal to that of Mrs. Dickons. . . . It is in warbling the pure melodies of less artificial construction, that her fascination is irresistible." But Kenrick (BS) went so far as to opine "that the great composer would not have desired a voice or a style more deliciously in unison with his own divine strain." She wound up the year performing Adriana in *Comedy of Errors*: "Miss Stephens, by her skill, experience, and now mature talents, is justly entitled to take the lead" (T); the *Inquisitor* agreed she sang well but noted her "maukish deportment."

She sang the lead in the unoperatic *Henri Quatre* with the usual plaudits in 1820—perhaps her only appearance that year. But in 1821 she was praised for her acting, beginning with Rosetta (*Love in the Village*); the *Literary Chronicle* wrote: "In the whole range of her characters, there is not one more adapted to her talents. The music of the opera has always been one of her triumphs. The union of the simple and scientific, the pastoral and the refined, which characterize it, display, with a peculiar charm, the power, richness, and sweetness of her voice." And Hazlitt (LM) reported: "We care . . . but little for Rosetta, excepting only when Miss Stephens is the representative. *She* is indeed a pleasant quean, and we shall not readily forgive ourselves for not having discovered until lately her comic talent. Her naivete is quite delightful, and she throws off a piquant saying as if she had a true relish for it." As Dorinda in the *Tempest* her acting was "almost the best thing in the play" (T). It "deserved our most favourable mention. It has been so long usual for our first rate singers to neglect every thing beside singing, that we have the most pleasure in noticing those exertions which are an exception to so arbitrary an exclusion" (EM).

Kenrick (BS), in the last of his "Sketches," found her "still unrivalled." She has "all in all the most perfect female voice which we have heard on any stage," though he admitted she was no bravura singer and should never "condescend" to sing them. Bacon (QMM, III, 58–64) also had some reservations:

> Her voice is powerful and rich beyond most others. . . . Her taste is pure and her general manner exceedingly chaste. Granting her these attributes, we have never perhaps heard a singer who moved the high affections less, yet did so little to reprehend. . . .
>
> Miss Stephens's imagination . . . has been cooled rather than heated in the tempering; and whether she sings upon the boards of the theatre or in the orchestra [i.e., at concerts], her whole performance appears to us subdued somewhat below the point necessary to fine expression. . . .
>
> [She] seems to pour her notes with such ease, such fullness, and such unvarying richness, that it is quite impossible to imagine her labouring under the distress she is endeavouring to pourtray. . . . Miss Stephens is never guilty of any extravagance in art. Genius is certainly excess.

In 1822 she sang a minor role effectively in *Laws of Java* (E) and was "arch and captivating" (LG), but illness prevented her reappearance until February of 1823, when she sang Lady Bartram in a revival of *Guy Mannering* and was greeted "with stunning cheers." She seemed fully recovered and sang with "sweetness and pathos" (LitC). She was even invited to the King's in June, when she sang "Auld Robin Grey" between the acts of a Rossini opera and was encored (H). Apparently unhappy at Covent Garden, she switched to Drury Lane in 1824 and remained there until 1828. In May she appeared there in a revival of *Lord of the Manor*: "Though rather too demure for the lively part of Annette," she "went through the character very pleasantly" (EM).

Early in 1824 she was "in fine voice" in *Philandering* (LG), "sang spiritedly," (E) and was "loudly encored" in Carafa's song, "Souvenir" (DM). That summer she made her first appearance at the English Opera House in *Freischütz*, which had opened the previous month, taking the place of a Miss Noel, who showed "modesty and good sense" in relinquishing the role of Agnes," (T) "thus exhibiting a striking exception to the usual humours of the green room" (NM). Two songs, previously omitted, were now restored: "Nothing could exceed the general taste and simplicity of her execution nor the liquid sweetness with which she poured forth the delightful Scena, which in this opera is the crown of the female vocal performance" (E). But the Talfourd (NM) thought her "not most at home in German music," and the *European* reported she overcharged one song "to such a degree as to change the effect and destroy its meaning." That fall she again excelled as Lilla in *Siege of Belgrade:* "We scarcely imagined that Miss Stephens could unite so much comic humour with so much exquisite harmony" (T). She "sang most spiritedly" (E).

In 1825 she was "an arch and pleasant Lauretta" in *Fall of Algiers* and had two encores (T); she sang "with exquisite feeling and spirit" (LM); and much of the work's success was due to her (Har). She returned to the English Opera House as Polly and "displayed her almost unrivalled powers of voice and skill (LitC); in *Broken Promises* she "sang in a delightful manner" (T) and was "in full song" (LM; Har).

She began 1826 in a revival of *Figaro*—"Miss Stephens, as well by her arch acting as her beautiful singing, makes Susannah a very charming personage" (T)—and of *Lord of the Manor*, in which she repeated her role as Annette and displayed "a good deal of playful humour," though "sprightly characters" were not her forte and she was not in good voice (T). She next sang the lead in *Malvina* "with the most exquisite sweetness and pathos" (C; T). She "played and sang with taste and feeling," though her music (by Cooke) was poor (LG). In the song of "Roslyn Castle," which she sang without accompaniment, "every tone went to the heart" and it alone was worth the price of admission (LitC). In May she sang the lead, a trouser role, in *Aladdin* "and charmed the audience almost as much by the archness of her manners in the light early scenes, and the feeling which she threw into those of a serious character as the opera advances, as by her chaste, simple, and expressive type of singing. Her first air to a pleasing melody, 'Are you angry, mother? No!' ... breathed the very spirit of gentleness and affection" (T; C). She "improves vastly as an actress" (LitC); indeed, "a more beautiful performance, in the way of acting, has rarely been seen on the stage" (NM; LG). She completed the year with a "bewitching" performance in an unoperatic melodrama, *Knights of the Cross* (LG, June 3), and her "tones made even in indifferent music appear tolerable" (C, May 30).

Stephens did not sing again until brief appearances in 1828, when she was back at Covent Garden—and then not again until May 1830. Apparently these absences were owing to ill health, which had plagued her periodically in earlier years, though they may have been due, in part, to disputes with the management. Sterling was strangely silent on her performance of Blanche in *Carron Side*, but Talfourd (NM) reported she "plays the love-less maiden with touching delicacy," and she "shone conspicuously in her grand scene and recitative, 'The die is cast,' which is altogether written in the classic style of the Italian school." Holmes (At) wrote: "Her voice was in excellent order ... and she appears to us completely to have recovered that command of it which we feared she had lost in the great theatres; she now rarely sings too sharp."

In 1830, back again at Drury Lane, she repeated her role of Polly, and the *Eaminer* remarked on her warm and enthusiastic reception; they "were sorry, however, to perceive traces of indisposition, not only in the thinness of her appearance ... but in the deterioration of the quality of her voice," which was now "comparatively weak and unsteady" and was occasionally marked with faulty intonation; her "piano" tones, however, were "still of incomparable beauty." But Holmes, after fulsome praise of her past performance, was brutally frank: "The truth is, Miss Stephens now sings so sharp ... that many of her notes are shocking to a well trained ear. ... It must be attributed to its real cause, physical weakness. ... The present voice is but the ruin of the former. ... We would have this lady avoid the great theatres, where even a good voice must be forced in order to please the public."

But Ayrton, in a *volte-face*, noted that "though her voice has not the youthful clearness, or all the high notes it once possessed, it is still a lovely organ. ... Indeed, what it has lost in the upper part of the scale, has been gained in the lower, so that its actual extent is not diminished" (Har). Ward (Ath) was also displeased, but in quite a different way: "It is very shocking ... to see Polly Peacham represented by a ladylike concert-singing refinedly-speaking person, such as Miss Stephens, with a white satin dress, resembling in its delicacy the character and manners of the wearer. But then

Miss Stephens sings so charmingly . . . that we think only of the gratification of one scene, and send the judgment for the time to Coventry."

The next month she appeared in *Hofer* and "sang with her accustomed delicacy and sweetness" (T), though Talfourd (NM) noted her "diminished power." Holmes found her "less defective in intonation than usual," but the *Examiner* reported she "sang the whole evening so perseveringly out of tune, as to destroy the effect of every concerted piece in which she bore a part."

Stephens retired in 1835 and three years later married the Earl of Essex. Phillips thought she was "not very thoroughly grounded in music" and was "unreliable in concerted numbers," though the latter may have referred to her later years. Weber wrote a song for her—his last composition.

CHORUS, ORCHESTRA, COSTUME, AND SCENERY

Though fairly frequent references were made by critics to choruses in our period, most of them—as in Italian opera criticism—referred to the composition, not the performances. Indeed, there were few comments on the latter until the 1820s. One exception occurred in 1794, however, in a review of *Cherokee* (Drury Lane) by James Gray (C): "Few things are more fatiguing to the spirits than the drilling of choruses for the stage; and we never heard, on a first night, choruses that, upon the whole, were better performed; neither do the singers, as formerly, stand motionless, with their hands clasped, their bodies stiff, and nothing moving but the contortions of their countenance. At present the chorus has assumed animation, and even passion."

Not until *Freischütz* (Covent Garden, 1824) was there further favorable comment: the choruses were "excellently performed" (TO); and later Covent Garden productions were also praised. In *Oberon* (1826) "the chorus of friends, and that most voluptuous dance and chorus in the last act, are sung and received *con amore*—nothing can surpass them" (TO). In 1829 the *Examiner*, remarking on the difficult choruses in the *Robber's Bride*, wrote: "We have seldom heard any which (the abstruseness of the modulation considered) went off so well." Sterling concurred, noting that the chorus performed admirably there under the direction of Samuel Wesley.[28] And of *Ninetta* in 1830, the *Examiner* declared: "Much praise is due to the master of the chorus for the manner in which his department has been conducted."

Even a minor theatre like the English Opera House came in for much praise. At the *Freebooters* there in 1827, Talfourd (NM) declared: "Of the choruses and the whole instrumental department, it is impossible to speak too highly; the time is admirably kept." And at a revival of *Freischütz* there the following month, the *Examiner* reported: "The choruses testify the lynx-eyed surveillance of Mr. Hawes; the consequence is, they are performed with correctness and precision, and we perceive, by other theatres, how little is to be done without constant attention."

But late commentaters could be negative as well. At *Oberlin's Oath* (Drury Lane) in 1816, the *Times* found the choruses "so badly executed as to justify considerable disapprobation; several of the minor voices being equally out of time and out of tune." And the next year the "chorus beauties" of *Guy Mannering* (Covent Garden) were "barbarously mangled" (TI). In 1829, at a Covent Garden revival of *Oberon*, the *Examiner* castigated the "director of the chorusses; for the manner in which they performed was disgraceful. In the first chorus the singers were in confusion. . . . We should think it probable that there had been no rehearsal previous to the performance. . . . Such slovenly work would not have occurred under the ferret-like dominion of Mr. Hawes, at the English Opera House."

The orchestras at the majors were comparable to the one at the King's. As early as 1760, Covent Garden had an orchestra of nineteen players—larger than those in Paris theatres; and after 1775 Drury Lane had an orchestra of twenty-four: sixteen strings, four woodwinds, two horns, and keyboard, with drums and trumpets added later (Fiske, pp. 180–81). After 1808, according to Wyndham, Covent Garden had an orchestra of six or eight first violins, six or eight second violins, two tenors, two cellos, three or four basses, an oboe, a flute, two clarinets, two horns, two bassoons, a trumpet, piano, bells, and drums. An engraving of Drury Lane dated 1812 clearly shows thirty players, and in 1825 it had an orchestra of thirty-one members.[29] W. H. Kearns, a composer and leader at Covent Garden, earned 14s. a night; Parke, an oboist, 10s 6d; and the leader of the second violins, 8s. 4d. Other theatre orchestras, especially the one at the English Opera House, were comparable. In fact, Parke thought the orchestra at Vauxhall one of the finest in Europe.

Early on, there were few references to the orchestra and its members. At Drury Lane, Thomas Shaw, already cited as composer, was the leader during our early years. The *Register* welcomed him in 1785 (Dec. 15), and on the occasion of his successful *Island of St. Marguerite* (1789) the *Herald* praised him as leader and added, "We never heard an Orchestra more brilliant, accurate, and expressive." As late as 1813, long after he had left Drury Lane, he was praised as leader of the orchestra at the new Pantheon Theatre (T, July 23). Charles Dibdin thought him a better leader than Baumgarten. Some time after 1813, Shaw went to Paris to avoid debts, and he died there about 1830.

Karl Friedrich Baumgarten[30] (1740–1824), a violinist, was leader at

Covent Garden from 1780 to 1794 and also composed occasional music. His overture to *Robin Hood* (1785) possessed "infinite merit" (UR), and the next month the obbligato parts were "executed with a strength and taste, that cannot be equalled but by the nervous [i.e., strong] and finished manner in which [they were performed] by the Orchestra, Baumgarten's violin, Parke's hautboy, and Sarjeant's trumpet" (UR, Nov. 16). The "band, and Sarjeant's trumpet" again drew praise in 1787 (UR, Jan. 22), and the next year Baumgarten "led the band with great spirit and the accompaniments went in exceeding good order" (H, Nov. 7).

William Thomas Parke (1762–1847), frequently cited for his *Musical Memoirs*, was singing in the Drury Lane chorus in 1773 at age eleven, and in 1776 he was engaged at Vauxhall Gardens. At the recommendation of his lifelong friend Shield, he took the post of first oboe in the Covent Garden orchestra (his brother John was also a fine oboist at Drury Lane), which he filled for forty years.[31] He played the flute as well and occasionally appeared at concerts (UR, Jan. 11, 1785). He was also something of a composer, and Shield requested overtures from him for *Netley Abbey* (1794) and *Lock and Key* (1796); the one for the latter "brought him good credit" (T). Indeed, between 1808 and 1821 he composed many songs and occasional music for Vauxhall. Shield wrote difficult concertante parts for him, and he was frequently cited for his brilliant obbligato playing.[32] Mrs. Margaret Martyr (see appendix 17) was his mistress until her death in 1807.

Later comments on the orchestra were usually negative. In 1822, at a performance of the *Pirate*, the *Times* noted that the Drury Lane orchestra was "in a state of very imperfect discipline: in accompanying the songs, the voice of the singer, instead of being supported, is uniformly overpowered by the instruments. We know the evil is not peculiar to this theatre, but reform has to begin somewhere, and no person [is] so fitted to effect it . . . as the leader[33] of the Drury-lane orchestra" (Jan. 16). And in 1824 Bacon (QMM, VI, 389) wrote: "Our theatrical orchestras must . . . be materially improved, before they will be able to give effect to fine music. Those of the London *theatres*, though a few good performers may be found in them, are a discredit to the metropolis. When I was in town last autumn, I visited the Haymarket [Little] theatre, the band of which would disgrace a country barn."

In 1825, at the Drury Lane production of the *Fall of Algiers*, Ayrton found the band "not strong enough" for performing Cherubini's *Anacréon* overture: "The weakness is chiefly observable in the violins, which ought to be unusually strong to do justice to so good a work." In 1827, however, the orchestra there was found to be "much improved" in *Turkish Lovers*. Covent Garden fared somewhat better. Early in 1824 the *Examiner* noted the fine performance there of the overture to Rossini's *Ricciardo* (Feb. 15). And that fall, at the premiere of *Freischütz*, the *Chronicle* wrote: "Too much praise cannot be given to the orchestra department; we never in an English theatre heard a band to so much advantage; this excessively difficult music was now performed with an accuracy and effect that could hardly be exceeded at the Italian Opera" (Oct. 15). About the same time, Parke, at a performance of Mozart there, noted that the band "would have done honour to the Opera House."

By 1827 the Covent Garden orchestra was under the direction of George Smart, who "has aimed at the general improvement of his department. . . . There has been more energy, more passion, in the general execution of the music" (QMM, IX, 60). At the *Night Before the Wedding* in 1829, Ayrton noted that the orchestra powerfully contributed to the success of the opera." But in 1830 the *Examiner*, at a revival there of *Cinderella* wrote: "We must protest the vehemence with which the concerted pieces in this opera are accompanied. In the quintette . . . the voices were so overborne, that they were to be heard only at intervals."

The orchestra at the English Opera House garnered most of the plaudits, however. In 1827, in the *Freebooters*, the band appeared "as but one instrument" (NM). And in 1828, in *Tit for Tat*, much praise was "due to the orchestra for its share, an important one, in the performance." In 1829 the *Examiner*, at a performance of the *Robber's Bride* at the English Opera House, wrote: "The band also, under Mr. Wagstaff, in many critical passages displayed care and precision unusual in the theatrical orchestras of the metropolis." Talfourd (NM) agreed: "We must thank Mr. Arnold for his admirable band, and for the good taste by which fine concerted pieces are provided every evening between the dramatic entertainments." Yet J. D. Collier (C), in a rare comment on conducting, disagreed:

> We ought not to omit some notice of a very principal performer, Mr. Hawes, who seemed resolved to shew that his musical directorship is no sinecure, and beat time too loudly and vehemently with his hand and scroll, not merely during the chorusses, but while some of the singers were giving some of the best airs, that (he must excuse us for saying) he materially injured their effect, and attracted to himself a vast deal too much attention.

At a performance of *Sylvania* at the Adelphi Theatre that fall, Holmes (At) was quite acerbic: "In forming a judgment of the composition, we were obliged to listen to the author through a prodigious accumulation of blunders. Mr. MacLaughlin, the bassoon player, in particular, laboured under the most delusive notions; while Messrs. Southern, Polglaze, &c.

(the horns), being neither fiery nor apprehensive, fumbled about in all parts of their instruments for the right notes." But the *Examiner* reviewer, seeing it a week later, departed from his usual unison with the *Atlas*. Noting the fine support of the management for the opera, he cited "the liberal complement of orchestral performers—thirty-two by number—and this at a *minor* theatre." The orchestra at the Little Theatre was called "meagre and spiritless" in 1824 (NM)—the only comment we find on that theatre.

In costuming and scenery, the English opera reviewers expressed far more interest than those at the King's. Garrick had forced some improvements in costuming, but "the Catos and Tammerlanes were still in periwigs" in the 1780s (Peake, II, 13n). From the beginning of our period, the press was critical of costumes.

The "dresses" of the knights in the Drury Lane *Richard* (1785) "were properly and strikingly distinguished, and in each the *costume* is strictly observed" (UR). Yet in the same year we find that in the part of Stella in *Robin Hood*—"a representation of simple nature in a rustic situation"—"a French head dress is very improper for the character" (UR). In *Strangers at Home*, also in 1785, the appearance of Mr. King "in brown and gold, is offending egregiously against propriety. Black is the professional die for the habit of lawyers all over Europe" (UR). Also that year Mrs. Bannister, in *Turk and No Turk*, "was ill dressed, by her handkerchief being too much of the Queen Elizabeth ruff."

Mrs. Mountain's dress in an *Inkle* revival (1788) "had not half splendour enough for a Governor's daughter" (T); and in the *Prophet* (1788) the female slaves "should have been habited alike" (T, Dec. 15). "Mr. Duffy's dress was infinitely worse than his address" in a *Castle of Andalusia* revival the next year (T). Also in 1789 the *Herald* pointed out that there was "too much frippery in [Kelly's] dress for his gloomy situation" in the *Island of St. Marguerite*. At a revival of the *Haunted Tower* (1790), the *Times* asked "why had not Romanzini a habit more suitable to her situation and figure—she is much too young for a Duenna."

By the 1790s, though, most comments were positive. In the *Crusade* (1790) "the Dresses are all made up from the plates in the British Museum" (T). And the dresses for the *Woodman* (1791) and the *Pirates* (1792)—the latter "extremely costly and rich"—received high praise (T). In the *Cherokee* (1794) the costumes, "at once appropriate and magnificent, are observed with the utmost precision" (T). In 1794 the entire cast for *Auld Robin Gray* appeared in Scottish dress.

For a time after 1800, interest in costuming slackened, but in the *Travellers* (1806), the costuming of the different nations was found to be "correct." In 1810 DuBois (MM) deplored Miss Lyons for "walking about in her flannel petticoat." And in 1815 the *Chronicle* noted the "attention to ancient costume" in the *King's Proxy* at the English Opera House, but thought it "ought ever to be accompanied by an equal regard to tasteful embellishment."

In the 1820s interest again quickened. In *Tarrare* at the English Opera House in 1825, the *Chronicle* found the dresses "of the most magnificent description." (Phillips thought Braham's costume "ridiculous," though he admitted Braham looked "elegant.") And in the production of the *Oracle*, which immediately followed, the *New Monthly* thought the "processions, scenery, dresses" were "in the highest degree superb." At the *Maid of Judah* (Covent Garden, 1829) the *Examiner* noted: "In their costume, the managers of our classical theatres are ambitious of being as appropriate as possible." And in the *Vampyr* (English Opera House) "the costume of the characters was both elegant and correct" (E).

But reviewers were not always in agreement. In 1827 the costuming in the *Seraglio* at the Covent Garden was "perfect" for the *Gazette*, but the *Atlas* condemned its "confusion of costume." In 1829, at the *Nymph of the Grotto*, also at Covent Garden, the dresses were "uniformly beautiful" (LG), but the *Theatrical Observer* asked why does the nurse in it "wear such a hideous cap? It is neither correct to the costuming of the period [n]or becoming."

In his *Recollections* Planché cited his *King John* of 1823—in which the costumes had "real historical accuracy"—as a turning point for the "reform" of the stage in that department. He also explained that he got "accurate" costumes for his *Der Vampyr* (1830) from a Dr. Welsh and that, in one melodrama, he experimented with tableaux imitating well-known engravings that were very popular. But Planché merely intensified a trend already established much earlier in our period, when the "appropriateness" and "precision" of costuming relative to time and place were noted and when, as we have seen, some costumes had even been modeled from plates in the British Museum. In 1830 the *Theatrical Observer* noted that Mrs. Keeley's dress, at the *National Guard* at Drury Lane, was "neither appropriate nor becoming"—this at a Planché production![34]

"Romantic" scenery had become a stage art at least as early as 1771, when Philip Jones De Loutherbourg was hired by Garrick for Drury Lane, though he was less a scene painter than a designer of stage effects. By 1785 Covent Garden had ten full- and part-time painters, and "spectacles" were mounted well before then.[35] At Drury Lane *Richard* that year the *Register* (Este) wrote: "Considered as a *spectacle* [designed by Thomas Greenwood senior] we have not for a long time seen anything superior. . . . To have been merely *splendid* would have been in the power of any manager; but perfectly to have united *splendour* with the *character* of the times, reflects great credit on those who were concerned in its preparation." Indeed, even before the theatres were enlarged, much expense was lavished on scenery. In the *Crusades* (Covent Garden, 1790), for instance, the scenery (not credited) "must be ranked with the most superlative efforts of the art—the storm and shipwreck, prison, and scaling of the Tower, with its different views, must be seen, for they surpass description" (T).

Scenic effects received growing emphasis toward the end of the century. The scenery both for *Mahmoud* (Drury Lane, 1796) and *Blue-Beard*[36] (Drury Lane, 1798) was highly praised, though the *Times* objected to the introduction of a skeleton, "which was clearly intended to improve on the present rage in favour of sepulchral scenes and sepulchral appearances." At the "spectacle" of *Ramah Droog* (Covent Garden, 1798), designed by John Inigo Richards, the scenery was "entitled to the highest praise. More perfect specimens of stage painting have rarely been seen, and . . . the pencil of the artist has been judiciously employed on locality. The colouring is naturally finished, and the . . . perspective is delightfully realized. . . . The mechanism of the elephant and buffaloes, is admirably contrived and well executed" (T). But at the *Captive of Spilburg* (Drury Lane), also 1798, there was a shade of criticism: "The Painter has exerted his talents in a manner truly picturesque and striking; . . . and had the rules of *Gothic* architecture been more strictly attended to, the effect would have been greater" (T).

Some reviewers were beginning to find that spectacles were receiving too much emphasis, even at the Little Theatre. At a production there of *Red Cross Knights* (1799), the *Times* wrote: "We can only attribute [the manager's] rashness in bringing out this miserable exhibition, to the present fondness for the . . . glare of theatrical pageantry, and the fascinations of sound and decoration." DuBois (MM) had noted the problem in *Ramah Droog* (Covent Garden, 1798): "Of the author of a piece like this, it is difficult to speak in a manner satisfactory to criticism . . . for a writer whose design is necessarily crippled by the intervention of his coajutors, is entitled to great allowances when we come to disencumber his story from the decorations to which he has, perhaps, rendered himself chiefly subservient." The following year he ironically complimented the "authors" of *Feudal Times* (Drury Lane):

> We have to congratulate the town on the acquisition of three admirable dramatic writers, in the persons of Mr. Johnston [a machinist], Mr. Greenwood, and Miss Rein, who have exhibited a specimen of the SUBLIME and BEAUTIFUL. . . . This is one of those annual tri-

umphs of the painter, the machinist, and the fancy-dress maker, with which it has been long the custom of [Drury Lane], at infinite expense, and with astonishing liberality, to furnish the public."37 (Jan.)

And in 1801 DuBois thought Hoare (*Chains of the Heart*, Covent Garden) "would have been more honorably and successfully employed in a service which demanded the exertions of the intellect rather than the drudgery of furnishing materials for the carpenter and the scene-painter."

Occasionally, as we just saw, individual artists were credited by reviewers for their efforts. At Drury Lane, in Cobb's *Love in the East* (1788), the first scene was "an exact representation of Calcutta, taken from a design of Mr. [William] Hodges; it is so exact a resemblance as to give an idea of each particular house belonging to the principal inhabitants. . . . The last scene affords a picturesque and elegant view of an Indian garden. The grove of Bettle trees is novel and striking" (T).

But Drury Lane's outstanding scenic artist before 1795 was Thomas Greenwood the Elder (?–1797), who was also a well-known portrait painter. In 1789 the scenery for the *Island of St. Marguerite* was praised: "Greenwood has outdone his usual outdoings" (T). The next month, in the *Haunted Tower*, Greenwood "had the opportunity of displaying the wonders of his magic pencil." His scenes were "an equal to the best we have seen of Loutherbourg" (T). The *Siege of Belgrade* (1791), "as a spectacle," was "the most splendid one . . . that our Theatres ever produced;—the Scenes, and there are twelve, form a succession of beautiful and correct views of Belgrade, and the surrounding country, in which Mr. Greenwood has fully evinced his wonderful skill in perspective—displaying what may truly be termed a splendid exhibition of paintings" (T).

For *Dido* (1792) the portico of the palace and the Temple of Neptune were the "very happy efforts of Mr. Greenwood's pencil" (PA). And in 1794, *Lodoiska* was "got up with a degree of magnificence, with respect to scenery, machinery, and decoration, unequalled in the annals of the stage." The manager called upon the services of Malton, and his assistants Lupino and D'Maria, who painted the scenes for act I, as well as Greenwood, who did acts II and III; the "Castle on Fire shows off the genius of Cobranel for complicated machinery to great perfection" (T).

At Covent Garden, John Inigo Richards (d. 1810), R. A., a landscape painter, became the principal scene painter in 1777 and painted there many years. In the *Woodman* (1791) the "prospect of the country and the mill . . . is a most picturesque scene, and worthy the masterly pencil of Mr. Richards" (LC). Richards's scenery for *Midnight Wanderers* (1793) was widely praised, and in *Travellers in Switzerland* (1794) he "has made the most of his subject; a more beautiful and picturesque succession of scenery has hardly ever graced a Theatre" (T). For his *Netley Abbey* (1794) Pearce reported that Richards created "the most picturesque Portrait of a Gothic Ruin that the hand of Science ever produced." Others, too, got credit. In his dedication to *Hartford Bridge* (Covent Garden, 1792), Pearce acknowledged his obligations to Mr. Wigstead for the accurate scenery (N., III, 29). Even the Little Theatre had noteworthy scenery; in *New Spain* (1790) it "did great credit to the Pencil of Rooker" (T).[38]

For a time after 1800, fears over the intrusion on the dramatic by the spectacular seemed to be forgotten, and Drury Lane productions were praised. In 1806 *Forty Thieves*, with a budget of £5,000 for dresses and scenery, had "the most splendid decoration which we ever witnessed" (C).[39] In the same year, Drury Lane was thought to be superior in scenic effects because of the younger Greenwood's artistry (C, Jan. 23). Greenwood also drew praise for his work on *Kais* in 1803 (MM) and *Godolphin* in 1815 (C).

Even the Lyceum came in for praise of its scenery on one occasion (T, May 8, 1812). In general, however, it was productions at Covent Garden that drew most praise in the middle years. In 1800, for example, *Bondocani* provided a rich spectacle with "appropriate" scenery (T), and in 1803 Richards and Phillips were commended for stage effects there (T, Dec. 14). In 1806 "the machinist, the painter and the *decorateur*, all have bestowed all their care on" the *Deserts of Arabia* (MM). In 1811 the scenery of *Knight of Snowdoun* was "the most wild, varied, and romantic we have ever seen" (T), and it "fully indemnifie[d] for the wearisome insipidity of the dialogue" (BWM). And in 1812 the reviewers were stirred by a storm, accompanied by a violent earthquake, in *Virgin of the Sun*: "The plantains and lofty palms were seen waving in the wind, and as the tempest swells, are torn up and laid prostrate—the whole stage, by machinery of a singular construction, rocks and swells like a sea; and the splendid domes of the Temple of the Sun are dashed in fragments over the ground" (C). It "surpasses all that we had hitherto ever conceived of stage capabilities" (T). Scenery at the Lyceum also received praise the next year (T, May 8).

After 1815 Covent Garden continued to garner most of the kudos in this department. At the revival of *Cymon* there that year, Sterling wrote: "The scenery is new and splendid—the palace of *Urganda*, and surrounding landscape—the final scene of rocks and cataracts, with Sylvia's prison—and the change to her triumphal entry with Cymon, were grand proofs of the superior excellence to which this (humbler) department of the modern drama has attained." In 1820, at *Twelfth Night*, Sterling observed: "The mask [from the *Tempest*] is a beautiful spectacle, and the descents of Iris, Juno, and Venus, with the rising of the Nereid in her shell from the ocean, will be numbered among the triumphs of the stage mechanism. Unfortunately, it is worse than useless in that place, and unseasonably interrupts the progress of the drama." Hunt agreed.

In 1823 the *Chronicle* noted at *Cortez* that "no expence has been spared" and complimented "Mr. Grieve and his assistants"[40] for the scenery:

> The horse-riders bore the palm in the several processions and engagements. One of them, after a sharp engagement with an individual of the opposite party, was thrown from his horse. The successful assailant mounted in his turn, and after riding with the fury of a savage up a steep ascent, was thrown over a bridge and tumbled down a precipice. This well contrived fall had a most terrific effect, it was too like a real accident not to give rise to unpleasant sensations. . . . The destruction of the Spanish Fleet by fire was another admirable specimen of the combined powers of painting and mechanism. They blazed in the water, illuminating the waves until they burnt to the very edge, and then fell to pieces and disappeared.

(Not to be outdone, Drury Lane was also displaying horses on stage at the same time.)

Competition between the majors was particularly keen in the scenery for the various productions of *Freischütz* in 1824, as well as in 1826, when both winter houses mounted *Oberon*. The scenery for the latter at Covent Garden "was important, and Messrs. Grieve and Co. have done wonders in this particular" (EM, May). "The water scene, with the change of lights . . . is particularly fortunate" (T, Apr. 14). In fact, Talfourd (NM) thought it "too gorgeous . . . to be absolutely pleasing: the moonlights are a shade too blue, the rivers too icy, and the sun-lights too glowing." Moreover, the scene-shifters were "refractory" and "the machinists clumsy" (LG). Covent Garden also enjoyed the services of David Roberts (1796–1864) (R.A., 1841), who, after early theatrical experience at Edinburgh, worked for a time at both majors. His scenery for the *Seraglio* (Covent Garden, 1827) was "a Stupendous task for an individual" (T) and "has probably never been surpassed on the stage" (E).

But Drury Lane also reaped considerable praise from later critics, as Roberts joined William Clarkson Stanfield[41] there for several productions. In 1824 both were highly praised (T; C) for their scenery for *Freischütz* as well as in 1825 for the *Fall of Algiers* (T). In 1826 — a busy year for both scenic artists — Talfourd (NM) asserted, at *Malvina*, that he had "never beheld scenery more exquisite even from Mr. Stanfield's pencil," and Sterling praised Roberts as well. Both were admired for the scenic effects in Macfarren's *Oberon*, produced in competition with Weber's opera at Covent

Garden (T). The *Literary Chronicle* (May 1) declared that Stanfield's panorama of Tunis was, "perhaps, the finest painting for truth, effect, and magical illusion ever exhibited within the walls of a theatre."

Roberts and Stanfield also drew praise (T: LitC) for *Aladdin* (Drury Lane, 1826), though Talfourd thought some scenes by Stanfield "interfered unpleasantly with previous impressions." And again "the machinery work[ed] badly, and the scene-shifters [were] very profuse with their mistakes" (LG). But J. P. Collier (C), like some earlier critics cited above, was concerned about so much emphasis on the *scenic*:

> It is singular that that which in the best age of our Drama was nothing, when a chalked board indicated the place represented, has now become the most important part of the representation. . . . Dennis, writing on the Italian Opera, more than a century ago, maintained that 'music had driven out poetry from among the people.' This was partly true, & Scenery has since added its assistance to injure & weaken the imagination. Poetry has no enemy like refinement. Stanfield's views are painted in the best style of this department of the art, for he has raised Scene painting to a rank which enables it to take that place.

In 1827 Sterling especially admired Stanfield's "bird's-eye view of the Bay and Port of Malta" and an interior view of the island for *Isadore de Merida* at Drury Lane. It was "worthy his high character" (E). And in 1830 *Hofer* was "aided by all the appliances of picture and grouping which Stanfield and Wallack can supply" (NM); the scenes were "exceedingly good" (T; C).

With the generally high praise bestowed on the orchestra, costume, and scenery—and sometimes even the chorus during the latter part of our period—it is something of a shock to note Henry F. Chorley's comments in 1862: "The orchestra in 1830 was, compared with what it is now, meagre and ill disciplined; the chorus was an ear-torment rather than an ear-pleasure; the scenery and appointments were shabby to penury."[42] One must deduce that Chorley's recollections were less accurate than his need to dispraise an earlier period in order to enhance later accomplishments.

Themes and Currents

NOT SURPRISINGLY, there were jabs at Italian opera from time to time in English opera criticism, though they had effectively ceased before the turn of the century. In their panegyric on Shield, for example, Este in the *Register* (Nov. 16, 1785) urged him to "prove to your prejudiced countrymen that they need not go to the fertile plains of *Italia* for matured fruit, when thy blossoms promise so rich an harvest in their own country." Several complaints were on stage mannerisms. In 1786 the *Chronicle* wrote of Billington in the *Peruvian*: "Her manner exemplifies all the superior graces of an Italian singer, without any portion of the monstrous affectation that disgraces the Signoras, and disgusts the spectator at the Opera House." When a Miss Waters, who had sung briefly at the King's, appeared in *Ramah Droog* (1798), DuBois (MM) noted "her manner is affectedly *Italianized*." Even Boaden (II, 37) stated that the Covent Garden singers "were sure of the admiration of all those (no small body) who boasted themselves superior to all foreign tricks and sophistication." But sometimes critics tried to be impartial. When French dancers from the King's appeared at a Drury Lane benefit for Storace's widow, DuBois observed: "John Bull forgot his natural antipathy, and applauded the *foreigners* as they deserved" (May 1796).

Few voices were raised against opera itself—a view that was strongest among the literary weeklies in reviewing opera books. In their review of the *Woodman* (1791), for example, the *Theatrical Guardian* complained:

> There was neither wit to excite gratitude of mind, plot to induce interest, or language to command admiration: but in this tyranny of perverted taste, when indecency is substituted for wit, and sense is sacrificed to sound, nothing more is thought necessary in the composition of an opera, than a ligature of dialogue, answering the single purpose of introducing musical support, and brilliant scenery on which the success is to depend. Such subordination is derogatory to the respectability of an author; it is a servile submission to the despotic usurpation of sister powers, instituted originally as secondary attendants to assist and enforce the effusions of [literary] genius.

Similarly, the *Analytical Review* wrote on *Lodoiska* (1794): "It is not in the power of custom ever to reconcile the judgment to so extravagant a deviation from every principle of sound criticism, as the introduction of songs by the persons of the drama in their most impassioned parts."

OPERA TYPES

The press speculated very little on the category of drama assigned by the advertisements and playbills. But these categories, which received brief comment early in "The Operas," part III, need closer attention here. From the accompanying table, "Opera Types and Their Popularity," which is based on appendix 10 and has more detail than the second part of appendix 12, it will be noted that in our forty-five-year period there were a total of 204 productions of English opera premieres, or an average of approximately 4.5 each season. (Not included in these figures are an average of about two revivals each season from 1785 to 1812 and of approximately five revivals each season from 1813 to 1830.) The table shows that 164 of these 204 productions were successes, and 40, or about 23 percent, were failures. While at least 9 performances constituted success for a new production, 38 of these successes were "superhits," having at least 20 performances (two—Cobb-Storace's *Haunted Tower* and the Drury Lane *Freischütz*—chalked up over 70).

By far, the most popular type was the comic opera, though musical drama, opera, and farce were also common. By and large, it would seem that both the romances and the operettas belong with the comic opera type, and that both dramatic opera and the one drama belong with the opera type. (One romantic opera, by Weber, was not included because its success is unknown.) Of course none of these designations is rigid. For example, the Reynolds-Bishop *Virgin of the Sun* (1824)—classified by Nicoll as a dramatic opera—was called a play by some reviewers and an operatic drama by others. *Malvina* (1826), a dramatic opera, was designated a "National Ballad Opera" by one critic and referred to as a melodrama by others. *Rosina* was listed as both a pastoral opera and a comic opera.

There were some shifts in taste: farces—very popular in the eighteenth century—fell off drastically after 1809; all but two of the entertainment type were produced before 1807; and the interlude was abandoned after 1793. The melodrama is rare before 1790, becomes very strong for some years, but then drops off sharply after 1825. Aside from the superhit *Beggar's Opera*, the ballad opera was scant throughout the period, while the operetta was a late influence (1822 and 1828).

With the later shifting of operatic types—especially the melodrama—

Opera Types and Their Popularity

Types	Total	No. of Successes (20+ perf.)	No. of Failures
Comic opera	68	(9)	14
Romance (a)	7	–	–
Operetta	3	–	–
Musical drama (b)	28	(11)	9
Opera	20	(4)	8
Dramatic opera (c)	4	(4)	–
Drama	1	–	–
Farce (d)	17	(7)	6
Entertainment (e)	8	(1)	1
Miscellaneous (f)	8	(2)	2
	164	(38)	40

(a) Includes comic, dramatic, operatic romance, and semiserious; (b) is also called melodrama, but sometimes includes operas; (c) includes operatic drama; (d) includes operatic farce and musical farce; (e) includes musical and operatic entertainment; (f) includes five ballad operas (one a failure), two interludes, one masque, one pastoral, and one burletta (a failure).

some critics complained that the works under discussion were not really operas. In 1822 the *Examiner* wrote: "The phrase Musical Drama must be kept in mind, for [Dimond's] *The Pirate* is certainly not in any sense an opera." In 1826 J. P. Collier (C), commenting on *Peveril of the Peak*—a musical drama—cautioned that it "was brought upon this stage . . . in the shape of an Opera." And in 1827 Hazlitt (At) severely castigated "two Operas—as we now call melodrame with songs" (Dec. 2).

There was no discussion of the operetta beyond the fact that it designated a one- or two-act opera of French derivation. By the late 1820s, too, the term "vaudeville" turned up—usually related to French translations of slender productions. The two-act opera *Carron Side* (1828) was "a production of the kind which are sometimes called operas at our national theatres, but which resemble much more what our neighbours call *vaudevilles*" (T).

To return to our table, the overall failure rate was nearly one out of five productions. Comic opera, at 21 percent, did somewhat better, but opera, at 40 percent, was much worse. Except for the perennial favorite *Artaxerxes*, no operas at all were produced from 1793 to 1807; it is not surprising to note that six of the failures in this category occurred after 1818, since productions of operas more than doubled after 1815.

Perhaps the most astonishing of all the failures was *Duke of Savoy* (1817), produced by that successful team Reynolds and Bishop. Bacon's review (LG) was savage—the "worst piece of nonsense" he had "ever sat through"—and he reveals that the management, anticipating the worst, had not printed a book of songs (expected at *all* performances) and even started a rumor that Holman, not Reynolds, was the true author, whereas, Bacon pointed out, Holman was then in America; indeed, a report of his death there had just come to hand!

PRESS VERSUS PUBLIC

Now a somewhat different analysis provides another perspective. To make a reasonably fair evaluation of the attitudes of press and public toward opera productions (exclusive of English adaptations), I have selected a list of English opera *premieres* during our period that were reviewed by at least two critics and that contained comment on both the libretto and the music—a list that comprises a total of some eighty-eight productions. The reviews of each have been roughly evaluated (i.e., irrespective of quality) for positive, negative, or mixed comments on the librettos and on the music, and the success or failure of the production (most Lyceum/English Opera House productions have again been eliminated).

In this evaluation we find that a large percentage of productions was successful regardless of any adverse criticism, with seventy-eight successes and only ten failures (12 percent). This indicates more emphatically the popularity of musicals during our period. Moreover, music had power over the critics too: of these eighty-eight productions, they gave fifty-eight positive and only seven negative responses to the music, while they voiced mixed opinions on twenty-three others.

But the press was not at all that happy about the librettos, with positive responses to twenty-five, negative responses to thirty, and mixed opinions to about thirty-three. Comparing this to our success rate, it becomes apparent that the reviews probably had little influence over the opera-going public and that the critics showed independence and determination to write what they thought about the productions regardless of public indifference or disagreements with each other. In some instance the reviews were *markedly* divergent, showing obviously differing tastes, though in a few cases the differences may have reflected shifting political views or professional jealousy among the various journals.

It is not easy to account for the ten failures that are scattered throughout our forty-five years. Possibly the negative rating on two of Holcroft's operas was a factor, but production problems clearly indicated the failure of an opera by Hoare and one by Colman. Dibdin's only failure was no doubt due in part to his writing a "serious" opera with Bishop—it was just not his style—and there were sharp divergences on the libretto. Boaden's only opera failed, I believe, because it was too literary for an opera (he wrote many successful plays). The two operas by Thompson that failed got negative or mixed reviews; this was also true of a failure by Reynolds despite a competent cast. Planché's failure is also a puzzle—critics praised both libretto and music—but it was produced late in the season.

Other examples beyond just this special grouping tell a similar story. Early on, *Orpheus* (1792), highly praised by the *Times*, had but one performance, and *Cave of Triphonius* (1791) got a good press but failed. On the other hand, Walter's *Hide and Seek* (1789) handily survived not only a cabal but the opposition of all the morning papers (T). The press was hard on *Netley Abbey* (1794) and *Abroad and At Home* (1796), but both were successful. If an opera failed, the reviewers were much more inclined to blame the book than the music, as, for example, in St. John's *Island of St. Marguerite* (1789), Merry's *Magician* (1792), Cumberland's *Armourer* (1793), Hoare's *Mahmoud* (1796), and William Linley's *Honey Moon* (1797). The same situation prevailed in later years.

We must not overemphasize the differences between the playgoers and the press (the latter's attitude toward the public is discussed below). Two-thirds of the reviews on librettos were either positive or mixed (there were many positive reviews in this large category). And most operas that were awarded the highest marks for both drama and music succeeded. Moreover, in later years, when the reviews were outstanding, as in *Native Land*, *Turkish Lovers*, and *Cinderella*, the number of performances tended to soar, while operas strongly condemned by the press, such as *Zuma*, *Dirce*, and *Wedding Present*, often failed. Yet, here, too, the pattern persists, for though *Libertine*, *Figaro*, and *Barber* got fairly low marks from the critics, they proved very popular indeed. There is no doubt that on the whole the public did not object to inferior dramas as long as the music was pleasing.

In considering the popularity of operas, it should not be forgotten that certain works gained enormously from certain aspects of the performance, such as the appearance of a popular singer in a new trouser role, the appeal of a child singer, the rage to see animals on stage, or spectacular scenic effects. These factors were not always stressed by the press, and sometimes the drawing power of such a singer as Braham was evident in the face of rising criticism in the press. For example, in our special grouping cited above, we find that "spectacle" saved not only seven productions that had received mixed reviews on librettos or music, but it also saved two others that drew *only* negative criticism. At least one production was saved because of the popularity of Scott's romances, and two others were saved by individual performers (Braham and Tree). There is no doubt that it was the performance, rather than any other aspect of a work, that had most effect on its popularity.

QUALITY OF LIBRETTOS AND LYRICS

Critics early in our period showed a willingness to suspend dramatic "rules" when it came to opera. Because of the heterogeneous nature of Holman's plot for *Strangers at Home*, wrote the *Register* in 1785, "we think the author was prudent in converting his piece into an Opera, which does not require that strict adherence to nature, and easy rise of incident, indispensably necessary to a comedy" (Dec. 9). And in 1786 they even thought Macnally had been *overcritical* in writing his *Richard Coeur de Lion*:

> The author, we observe, has sacrificed much to the taste of the fastidious critics, by leaving out the allusions to the business of the present day. . . . If this had been a regular Tragedy or Comedy, we should readily have . . . applauded his compliance; but in a Musical Piece, as in a Pantomime, we think that strictness of method, and the refinement of Aristotle, should be exiled together, as injurious to the natural pleasantry of the scene. (Oct. 19)

In *Highland Reel* (1788), O'Keeffe "has given to this the title of a *Comic Romance*"—though it was called an opera—"intimating thereby, as we apprehend, that it is wild, eccentric, and not to be judged by the strict rules that govern the legitimate drama. It certainly would not bear such a scrutiny. There is a romantic air through the whole which, while it is not strictly reconcilable to sound reason, does not fail to interest and exhilarate the mind" (LC). Anent Cobb's *Haunted Tower* in 1789, one critic (Hazlitt) noted that in modern comic operas "custom has sanctioned a slight, irregular, and unconnected fable." The drama is "merely a sketch" and not to be subjected to the "vigour and strictness of critical investigation." Other critics pointed out, however, that even operas required intelligent librettos. In 1792 the *Times* cautioned Cobb for taking his libretto (*Pirates*) too lightly, for it "had not that fine stamina of writing that gives vigour to the sentiments of the mind, and which is requisite in Opera as in Comedy." And in 1793 they pointed out that the dialogue for Cumberland's *Armourer* was "written with grammatical accuracy, but without that point requisite to Comic Opera. It therefore appeared as a *Sentimental* Comedy interspersed with Songs" (T).

A growing number of reviewers after 1800 were concerned with a perceived decline in the literary and dramatic qualities in English opera, as well as their possible effect on the decline of legitimate drama. In 1801 the *Chronicle* complained: "From the complexion of our late dramatic pieces, it appears that writing for the *stage* is rendered far more easy than could have been expected. An author thinks himself privileged to write any thing, in the firm confidence that the public will bear with any thing, and that his defects, even where most obvious, will be covered by the *musician*, the *painter*, or the *carpenter*" (May 6). And the *Times* also strongly protested attempts to turn failed plays into operas (Sept. 4, 1807; Aug. 24, 1812). In 1813 one writer, surveying the decline in drama, cited those who

> impute the decline of comedy to the rage for music. We are become, say they, a singing race; and though the taste for theatrical music is as gross and uncultivated as in private society, the taste for vocal harmony is classical and refined, yet nothing will go down but opera and burlettas on the stage. It is this love of music that encourages so many new theatres upon license for music and dancing. . . . [In France, too] the genuine drama has fallen a sacrifice to the most trumpery music. (TI, Oct.)

And in 1816 Sterling wrote of *Slave*: "That it is unnatural and improbable is sufficiently answered that it is a melodrama, an opera, a romance."

We have noted the *Critical Review*'s strong critique on Kenney's *False Alarms* in 1807. In that year and 1808, Barron Field in the *Times* and his friend Hunt in the *Examiner* turned to the problem; Field, confirming the decline in the drama, wrote: "Which of us, in calling to mind the literary men of the present century, would once think of the names of Holcroft, Reynolds, Hoare, Dibdin, Cherry, or Hook?" He also denied that the press was to blame for "the taste of the town" and challenged the public, with some pomposity, "to look grave at every clap-trap, to be deaf to German sentiment, and blind to Parisian spectacle. . . . *The Times* shall do its duty: let the public look to theirs" (Sept. 4).

Hunt, writing of Hook's *Siege of San Quintin* in late 1808, thought the situation had improved:

> Within these two or three years, the public have certainly lost a great deal of respect for those huge farces, which they were good-natured enough to call operas and comedies. I recollect the time when Messrs. Reynolds, Cobb and Dibdin never wrote a play, but it was panegyrized

in all the newspapers and magazines. . . . Now however the case is considerably altered: Punch is no longer a specimen of polite learning: some of the periodical works have changed their tone because they have changed their critics. (Nov. 13)

Already noted were Hunt's 1809 comments that much better writing and composing were needed to reform public taste.

But not all the productions of "the Dibdins and the Cobbs" were mere "vehicles," as we have seen. DuBois (MM) was careful to point out that Dibdin's *Cabinet* "is by no means to be regarded as a mere vehicle for the music" (Mar. 1802), and the *Times* also noted its unity of time. Even Cherry was not utterly condemned for the *Travellers*: "We shall not try Mr. Cherry by rules which we know he meant to violate" (MM, Jan. 1806). In fact, in 1804 the *Chronicle* admitted the Aristotelian unities were "little relished" in England.

There was no agreement on the effects of melodramatic elements entering into librettos (as well as into quite unoperatic entertainment). True, Hunt, Field, and some others objected to the "mummeries" and "pageants" typical of the melodrama, but other reviewers relished them and could regard a comic opera as "just as good a drama" as contemporary comedies. Reynolds, who had written a typical melodrama in *The Caravan* in 1803, declared in his *Life* that "the hue and cry against modern comedy now [c. 1808] increased to a formidable height," and he turned to further novelty in "the melodramatic opera"—*The Exile* (actually designated an "Opera"); it was presumably because of these developments that he was called "the founder of the modern school" by *Bell's*. Yet DuBois (MM), although giving him "the highest credit for *his* school of comedy," complained: "But where is he that loves the stage and knows its proper end, who can see the abuse with which it is covered and surrounded, without striving . . . to restore it to the state of happier days?" (Nov. 1808).

The quality of the lyrics was occasionally censured—even by early critics. The *Chronicle* was happy to note, in 1793, that Pearce, in *Midnight Wanderers*, "thinks that even yet the Music of a Song is not likely to be worse for being set to words that have sense and poetry." The special difficulty of writing good songs for music already composed—something about which Sheridan, Burgoyne, and Bate Dudley had complained—was recognized (UR, Oct. 25, 1786), as well as the "detached condition" of songs due to changes in the book (MM, Dec. 1796). The supplanting of favorite numbers with new lyrics was also frowned upon (T, Oct. 23, 1788).

With respect to the airs, the *New Oxford History of Music* states that Shield, Arnold, and Storace borrowed only about one-quarter of their songs from Italian opera and that "new music was the draw" (VII, p. 264). But the early reviewers were certainly as much interested in the borrowed airs as in the newly composed ones: they preferred a balance between the two. In 1785 the *London Chronicle* thought it "no derogation" to Dr. Arnold's merits if he borrowed more airs for his *Turk and No Turk*. And in 1797, in a review of William Linley's *Honey Moon*, Boaden (OPA) observed: "We have no living composer who could, or who *ought*, to compose an entire Opera. — Since Arne, there has not been *versatility* and *science* enough, to do it well. Storace has succeeded best; but though he wrote *originally* with great force and taste, yet he knew it was wisdom to compile the greater part; which made his works not 'a composition of drugs and sediment, like a bad tavern's worst wine;' for he knew how to 'steal with taste.'"

Later critics were also annoyed at tamperings with the songs in revivals, whether managers, composers, or leading singers were to blame. At an 1817 revival of the *Siege of Belgrade*, Sterling noted that some of the old songs were removed and others substituted, "but no benefit was derived from the change; they did not rise above mediocrity." At a revival of *Lord of the Manor* in 1823, he was dismayed that "nearly all" of Jackson's music was omitted, and "the *hiatus* is filled up by a variety of hackneyed introduction." And in 1824, at a revival of *Maid of the Mill*, he pointed out that the work was "almost denuded of the original music" because "the talent of this house [Drury Lane], either in the vocal or acting department, is not sufficiently vigorous to give due effect to the extensive range of characters, serious and comic, which the opera comprises" — a statement that suggests there was either a decline in the quality of the performers in later years or reviewers had grown more critical. In 1826, at a Covent Garden revival of *Guy Mannering*, Sapio "introduced several songs, some of which have no relation whatever to the character he was playing. . . . This is a custom which should not be permitted" (LG). Even Weber's *Sylvania* did not escape tampering in 1826, when Phillips introduced two airs (E). Holmes (At) wrote: "We forbear to say more at present of a practice which is both impudent and dishonest. . . . Such freedoms with an original piece will, if not checked, soon destroy the confidence of the public."

The problem of borrowings and insertions aside, Holmes also recognized (*pace* Boaden) the artistic limitations imposed on an opera that required more than one composer. In an 1827 review of *Isidore de Merida* (the opera had five composers), for instance, he pointed out:

> Every reasonable being must be aware that an opera, to be symmetrical should be the result of one man's thinking and feeling (unless friend-

ship and intimacy make two minds grow into one).... [But in] these joint-stock affairs, resulting from that detested system of theatrical finesse which demands an Opera to be made ready against a certain hour to foil certain rival schemes, or to make a hit with a new singer, all design is lost, and the music is a mere stalking horse to the more serious object of the managers.

And in an 1829 review of Dimond's *Nymph of the Grotto*, composed by Liverati and Lee (the music failed to please), Holmes wrote: "The number of hands now usually employed on a new piece is a satire on the present state of dramatic music. We find partly on this account that the movements in modern English opera have so little connexion or relation one with another."

RECITATIVE

We have seen the grudging acceptance and the occasional abandonment of recitative in *Artaxerxes*. Attempts to introduce "the horrible accompaniment of nonsensical recitative" in *Dido* and *Orpheus* (both 1792) resulted in total failures, though Storace's "musical conversation" in the *Cherokee* (H, 1794) was quite acceptable.

The "English" point of view was best expressed in this period by Burgoyne in his preface to the printed libretto (1781) of *Lord of the Manor* (1780). He admitted that music was "the very soul of Italian opera," and, "provided it be well maintained in composition and execution, every inconsistency in fable, conduct, or character, is not only always pardoned, but often applauded." He also admitted that music was "a powerful aid to drama" on the English stage. But recitative was "incongruous" to the English language; moreover, it

> diverts the mind from sense to sound and . . . destroys the delusion and charm of fancy which invokes the situations before us. [Therefore] music should be confined to expressing the feelings of the passions, but never to express the exercise of them. Song, in any action in which reason tells us it would be unnatural to sing must be preposterous. [In English opera it] should always be the *accessory* not the *principal* subject of the drama.

There were mixed views on the Italianization of opera during the middle years. In 1806 the *Times* was annoyed with Reynolds and Lanza for imitating Italian opera in their *Deserts of Arabia*, and they found the recitative "insupportably tedious." Yet the same year Corri had "boldly" modeled the *Travellers* on the style of Italian opera and had shown what

English opera "might be" (C). In 1808 DuBois (MM, Feb.) expressed distaste for the abruptness of the transition from dialogue to song that was characteristic of English opera. And in 1810 the libretto for *Gustavus Vasa* was found to be properly subservient to the music (C).

Later reviews also wrestled with the problem. The recitatives in *Artaxerxes* were found distasteful in 1818 (T, Jan. 9) and 1820 (C, Apr. 6). At Weber's *Preciosa* in 1825 Sterling wrote: "An attempt to give effect to simple recitation by musical accompaniment . . . was not, we think, successful; the common recitative [i.e., spoken dialogue] of the musical drama would have answered better" (Apr. 25). But in 1828, anent Wiegl's *Pirate of Genoa*, Sterling thought it necessary to caution: "It must be remembered that, in recitative, many an insignificant dialogue will pass, which, in words, appears intolerable." And in 1826 Weber was praised for the "variety and vigorous expression" of his recitative in *Oberon*.

The problem of recitative in English opera was also given broader treatment in several passages. The earliest occurred in an *Inquisitor* article (1818) by "E. T." dealing mainly with Italian opera. "Recitative," he wrote, "possesses decided superiority over that wretched heterogeneous anomaly an English opera; music is admitted as the medium of expression, in the one, all is regular and consequential; but to hear a man make a speech first, and then epitomize or illustrate it by a song, is, indeed, a violation to the intellect" (Feb.). The second passage was a comment the following year by Bacon (QMM, II, p. 67) on recitative and other elements of opera with respect to Bishop's production of the Englished *Barber*. Noting the current "public appetite" for "works of foreign composers in their entire state," he pointed to features of Italian comic opera "of a kind our language, actions, and habits are not acceptable of . . . an elegance which our comic opera has seldom if ever sustained." He added: "The Italians depend almost wholly on the effect of the music; we blend the other and not seldom more prominent attractions of intricate plot, dialogue, scenery, and show, with the music. In a word, we are not yet nationally speaking musical enough to melt down our other senses & faculties into the one reigning delight of combined melody & harmony to be satisfied with 'the concord of sounds alone.'"

Bacon again championed sung recitative in his review (LM) of the ill-fated production of *Dirce* in 1821:

> We are glad to perceive any attempt made to change the jumble of music and dialogue, which disgraces the English stage, to a better style. Whether music be, or be not, a suitable vehicle for dramatic incident, is not a question now to be argued: the demand for operas has settled that

point. It remains for us of this age, only to choose between a mixed jargon of discourse and song, and a complete musical drama. Now there arises to our minds no possible reason, why the more conversational parts of a performance should not be supported by music, as well as those which are held to be more strictly lyrical. At all events, it seems more consonant with common sense, that the singing should be continuous rather than interrupted; for if, in the most impassionate parts of the representation . . . the dramatis personae can be permitted to stop, not only to sing, but to pace the scene during long symphonies: if the imagination, we say, can make allowance for such absurdities, surely the one consistent notion of an entire action, expressed by music and poetry, with their conjoint influences and powers, may be more easily embraced. The time will come, we are persuaded, when such an arrangement will be preferred; but, at present, the ears of an English audience are not reconciled to recitative, and poor *Dirce* passed from life to death without distinction, and almost without notice.

Finally, Holmes (At) also explored this problem in a review of Lacy's *Maid of Judah* in 1829:

The necessity of making some characters sing, and others talk, reduces this sort of production below the grade of the melodrame, which, with all its violations of nature, is nevertheless consistent in its mode of awakening emotion. In the melodramatic opera, one event is explained in a chromatic run, and another in a piece of declamation that assumes the office of the regular drama. Just as you begin to take an interest in the plot, your enjoyment is interrupted by a song; and just as you become pleased with the music, it is dismissed for a scene of rant. There is no regularity in these attacks on our nerves; the illusion is destroyed by its uncertainty; for people cannot shift their feelings as rainbows do their colours. Let music and dialogue keep their own provinces, but it is in vain to hope that an audience can be found to relish an entertainment which changes every ten minutes the means and character of its excitement.

But playwright William Dimond thought it possible to raise English opera to the operatic without recourse to recitative, and in the preface to the printed edition of his successful opera, *Native Land* (1824), he attempted a definition of opera as he saw it. (Possibly Dimond's reason for writing the preface was his annoyance with critics who did not understand opera, although most reviewers had been quite favorable to *his* opera.) He wrote:

It has now been a *fashion* in this country, of nearly a century's growth, among the never-dying race of hyper-critics — those skilful masters of the ugliest art—to bastinado, be-pummel, and be-devil, without mercy or remorse, each devoted author of an *Opera*, purely upon the grounds of his not accomplishing objects which never were, nor ought to have been, within his contemplation to attempt.

    These awful erudite persons are for ever informing the obsequious town, that such serious scenes and characters lack the due elevation and intenseness of *Tragedy*. . . . That is, they abuse an Opera because it is *not* that which it makes no pretension to be, and because it *is* precisely the very thing it calls itself.

Dimond continued with his prescription for writing an English opera:

> Opera has its own rules of composition, which, at this time, are very tolerably established and defined. In its *Plot*, it may be either serious or sprightly, or it may combine both qualities, *ad libitum*, with just a sufficient interest to excite attention and to banish *ennui* during the necessary spaces between song and song, but never so vividly to stimulate the feelings of an Audience, as to make the recurrence of Music be felt as an impertinent interruption. The *Incidents* are not required to be strictly probable; nevertheless they certainly ought to be *just possible*, and at no time to degenerate into the downright extravagances of fantastic Melodrame or of buffoon Farce. . . . Above all, the MUSICAL SITUATIONS ought to spring with spontaneity out of the very necessities of the Scene; never betraying themselves to be labored introductions for the mere purpose of exhibiting vocal talent, but always to appear so many integral portions and indispensable continuations of the Story.

He then came to the heart of his thesis:

> Music must not be a mere embroidery upon the surface of the piece, liable to be picked out again at pleasure, but actually woven up in the very woof of the web, and inextricably thence without destruction to the entire texture. . . . Many a Drama may be so constructed, as to comprise twenty or thirty songs within its compass, yet be no *Opera*. O'Keeffe's humorous *Fontainbleau*, and the exquisitely pathetic *Inkle and Yarico* of Mr. Colman, are instances in point. Each of these pieces has been entitled an "Opera," by its Author, yet, as I think, improperly. . . . As a proof of this assertion, *Inkle and Yarico* may be entirely divested of its lyrical portions (even as I have often seen it performed upon provincial stages), and without the addition of a single sentence to its dialogue, the story will remain intelligible and perspicuous to the most obtuse capacities. Such a Piece may be *better* than an Opera, nevertheless, "Opera" it is *not*.

The application of such a narrow definition would have limited our consideration to perhaps less than a dozen works—mostly failures—during our entire period; indeed, it is not clear in *Native Land* how Dimond's language, fitted to Rossini arias selected by Bishop, provided "the very woof of the web" required of musico-dramatic productions! Moreover, his *Pirate* was deemed "no opera" at all by one critic, and his earlier productions were inconsistent. In *Adrian* and *Orilla* (1806), for example, he did not "connect the songs properly" to the piece; yet in *Gustavus Vasa* (1810) "everything was made subservient to the music."

Similar problems were cited by various writers for the *Quarterly Musical*, by far the most persistent and outspoken organ (in our later years) of the shortcomings of English opera and the importance of reforming it. In 1821, for example, in an article entitled "On the Means of Giving an Opera to the English" (III, 157), a correspondent wrote: "I quite agree with you [the editor] in the opinion that our own Opera is an insult to common sense as well as good taste, and that until the entire performance be moulded into one consistent *musical* whole, the English nation will still remain under the disgrace of possessing little or nothing beyond melodramatic plays or farces—certainly nothing like genuine opera."

In 1823 another correspondent, writing on "Opera," concluded: "There are few I believe who have seen half a dozen Italian musical dramas, that do not perceive and would not prefer regular opera to the interrupted jargon of speech and song" (V, 281–91). And in his "State of Music in London" for 1827, Bacon complained:

> We never recur to the music of the English houses but with regret at the recollection of how little is done or attempted for the true interests of the art, or for their own exaltation as lyric theatres. . . . No nearer approach has been made for almost a century to the establishment of a legitimate opera, and we feel persuaded that so long as the present miserable jargon of dialogue and song is continued, so long as the taste of the English public is treated as if it were incapable of understanding and relishing the highest species of musical drama, so long will the whole train of musical perceptions be lowered and kept down in the nation generally. (VIII, 139)

Against these views we may consider an excerpt from the *Champion* as representing a protest against the trend toward the more operatic and as a justification for the status quo in English opera. It was a preamble to their review of Arnold's *King's Proxy* in 1815:

> Where music is the primary object, many sacrifices must be made in the other essentials of poetry, character, and interest in the conduct of the plot. . . . But unfortunately, music is not calculated to excite such protracted feeling; the ear grows weary by being kept so long upon the stretch, while the mind, not being at all acted upon, becomes equally listless from inactivity. In addition to this, the language of music is indistinct; it may perhaps express the extremes of any particular passion, but this is the extent of its influence. . . .
>
> By making music only a secondary consideration, much is gained, and nothing is lost. . . . [The mind] is always fresh because variously employed; and the composer is not at all fettered in his efforts by following the track of the poet, though the poet is always cramped into dullness by being bound to the composer. Upon this principle we must think the system of English Opera infinitely preferable to that of the Italian.

It was of course against such prevailing attitudes that innovations on the English musical stage had to contend.

ADAPTATIONS

A few of the later reviewers commented on the significance of performing adaptations of foreign operas in English. Hazlitt (At), in a review of *Turkish Lovers* in 1827, stated, perhaps ironically, that he did not *want* to understand the translation at all:

> We are able to say very little about the literary merit of this Opera; we make a point of never looking at an Opera-book, and put our trust in the singers, that we may not hear the words. It is in vain to expect sense in an Opera—therefore the more sense is sacrificed to sound the better. When unfortunately a phrase does come articulately on the ear, it spoils the conception we had formed of the expressions appropriate to the action, and generally gives an insignificant meaning to a lofty sound. In a concerted piece, we heard in this Opera seven or eight persons each repeating in different tones and parts, with great vehemence and apparent feeling, a certain phrase, which sounded uncommonly well—at length it came distinctly upon the ear, and proved to be nothing but "Passion assailing, passion assailing." This half-English, half nonsense, destroyed the effect of the situation. This will explain the relish with which the Italian Opera is heard in English.

Yet Hazlitt—often unpredictable—was moved to exclaim at a performance of *Love in Wrinkles* the next year: "We do not see what is to prevent our having all the treasures of the Italian comic operas laid out for us at the theatre, since in the translation of words and adaptations of the music, which have been successfully performed in two or three experiments, we find the whole *gusto* of the original."

One problem with English translations was touched on by Ward (Ath) in a review of the *Maid of Judah*: "The fault of the vocal music we think generally to be in the quantity of words which are forced into the air [of a quartet], and which necessarily break up very much the softness and continuous flow of the music." And in 1829 Ayrton noted, in reviewing the *Robber's Bride*, a defect "too commonly the case in music arranged for our theatres"—"the superbundance of words. It requires some skill, we confess, to restrain a translation within the syllabic compass of the original, but this ought to be done; for, unless accomplished, a sort of *chattering* will be produced, wholly at variance with musical effect."

The English translations, too, presented problems. Rossini's grand finale in the Englished *Barber* was "adapted to words which must have occasioned no little torture to the unfortunate man [Terry, in this instance], whose brains were tasked to find syllables of tolerable meaning to suit such various musical rhythm." And the *European*, in a preface to their review of *Oberon* in 1826, explored other problems of the playright:

> Have our readers any idea of the duty that the unfortunate wretch, who is satirically called the author, has to undergo? In the first place, he is retained to the establishment at a regular salary, whether he works by "time or *piece*".... So many times in the season he is called upon to work on tragedy, comedy, opera, farce, melodrama, or occasionally, by way of a change, pantomime. When done, don't fancy his job is over.... Oh, no! the manager, or the manager's friend, takes time to look at it; if he approves of it, the musical composer is called in; he declares the dialogue too heavy—this character too airy—and the next not airy enough; in fact, that the piece is not adapted to his music.... The aspirant for fame having the fear of the King's Bench and an empty stomach before his eyes, dares not rebel; and after enduring the tortures of Tantalus, he at last succeeds in satisfying the composer. Next come the performers. Mr. A— — declares he would rather pay the fine than play the part set down for him. Mr. B— — don't care if he does, provided it is entirely re-written. Mrs. C— — says she has too much to do, and Mrs. D— — has too little. ... None of the ladies and gentlemen are of one opinion, except that the author is a dolt.

SINGING AND ACTING

Criticism of singing in English opera was, not surprisingly, more superficial than that of singing in Italian opera, especially during the earlier years. Falsetto singing generally seemed to be acceptable, even essential, though on one occasion Sterling thought Sinclair "employed it too frequently to satisfy English ears, which require a more direct and enthusiastic style" (Feb. ll, 1824). Interestingly, there were relatively few complaints of insufficient volume in singers, although they had to sing in houses comparable in size to the King's.

Vocal ornamentation was barely mentioned by early reviewers, even in critiques on Billington.[2] But it came in for much criticism in later years. In addition to the many instances noted of Braham's singing, for instance, we find that the *Times* chastised a Miss Hughes for "vulgar and unreasonable ornaments" in her singing of Mandane and in *John of Paris* (1814). At the opening of Weber's *Sylvania* at the Surrey, the *Examiner* could not say much for the singers there: "Their style is formed in the fast declining school of roulade and hacknied ornament, excluding the effect, sentiment, and intention of the composer." And in 1830 they complained: "The constant desire to produce effects by surprise, violent contracts, and *roulades* is the cause of our possessing so few genuine singers of the *cantabile* style" (Apr. 18).[3]

Regarding the *shake* (trill), however, there were mixed feelings. At the debut of a Miss Byrne in the *Haunted Tower* in 1817, Sterling observed: "We think her shake not so perfect as it might be." But at Miss Povey's debut in *Guy Mannering* in 1819, Hunt commended her for "being able to deny herself even the pleasure of a shake, where it would be no real ornament. Singers in general seem no more able to resist a shake when they are getting out of a song, than a dog when he gets out of the water" (E). In 1826, at the opening of the *Oracle*, J. P. Collier (C), speaking of a duet with Miss Paton and Sapio, declared: "It is too much the fashion to introduce a shake on the English stage on every occasion, and in this instance the effort was too laborious to be pleasing." But Parke noted of Vestris's performance in the *Seraglio*: "It is to be regretted that this excellent singer is deficient in that essential requisite, a good shake, as there are few instances in the English style of stage-singing of vocalists making their closes in a finished manner without it."

A degree of competence in acting by the singers—at least in certain roles—was also expected fairly early in our period. In 1798 the *Times* provided two reviews of revivals that displayed a strong interest in acting and characterization. The first was of *Inkle and Yarico*: "This part [Yarico] requires the united merits of the Singer and the Actress, to impress that peculiar degree of interest which the Author clearly meant it should convey. The perfect combination of sense and sound, is, however, an excellence but rarely displayed on our stage, or on that of any other country." The second was of the *Maid of the Mill*: "Bickerstaff has drawn but a faint sketch of rustic humour in the character [of Ralph], and the Actor is necessarily called upon to fill the outlines in a masterly manner, and to embellish them with a richness of colouring peculiarly his own. It has therefore fallen to the lot of very few Performers to excite more than common interest in [the role]."

In 1808 DuBois (MM) complained of the poverty of acting in English operas, and most reviewers in the middle years were pleased to note a well-played part, though a brilliant singer like Braham or Billington blinded them for a time to their wooden acting. Of course, many of the smaller operatic roles at that time made little demand on acting ability; in some cases the basic personality of the singer was regarded by reviewers as a more important asset than vocal strength.

Occasionally, managers were blamed for the incompetent acting, as the *Inquisitor* averred regarding *Comus* in 1815: "The truth is, if the performers do not themselves know what is right, they may act wrong; there is nobody to direct them. Thus it happens that Mr. Young turns every character into a monk, and Mr. Liston always plays the ideot." Sometimes the vehicle made impossible demands, as in Dibdin's *Zuma* in 1818, when roles "requiring great pathos and power of acting are thrown upon a class of performers who are accustomed to delight us by efforts of a different kind, and consequently fail almost entirely in dramatic effects" (T).

In 1824 at a revival of *Maid of the Mill*, Sterling noted of the lead role of Lord Aimworth that "there is no character in English opera that more emphatically demands the union, very rarely seen, of the talents of a good actor with those of an excellent singer." And in 1830 he admitted: "But it is not indispensible that great singers should be very distinguished actresses; and on the English stage especially we have not yet been taught to look for a union of both qualifications in the same person" (Dec. 18).[4]

There were differing views about the level of competency of English singers. In his heyday Braham was widely regarded as the "finest tenor in Europe." But by 1818 Sterling pointed out that "our English school of singing is already sufficiently low in the estimation of foreigners" (Sept. 10). Yet the following month he noted, of a soprano, that "not one of her songs was given in the perfect manner which is expected at a London Theatre."

Later, with the mounting of English versions, comparisons with singers at the King's arose, and in his review of *Cinderella*, Holmes (At) gave strong support to the English singers: "Sontag, or Blasis, may, perhaps, execute the bravura music of the [Rossini] original better than Miss Paton; Donzelli is unquestionably *preferable* to Wood; but the support given to the inferior characters at the [King's] is not equal to that of Miss Hughes, and the two Misses Cawse, at the English theatre." But in 1821 Bacon (QMM, III, 61) explained the failure of even the leading English opera singers to achieve dramatic power:

> To train a singer for the serious [i.e., Italian] opera is to court the highest attributes of the art. Such a code of instruction appears by the universal powers of almost every legitimate Prima Donna, to include the qualities of an actress as well as the highest cultivation of the vocal requisites.... Our singers, on the contrary, who are trained for the stage, consider only one branch of the profession. If they vocalize well, it is, they think, sufficient; and they seldom care to remember that singers who aspire to move the affections of their hearers must accomplish their end very much by means which are common to acting as well as singing—in short, by dramatic force, dramatic fire, dramatic feeling, dramatic elocution—and all these refined by the highest cultivation, science, and polish of vocal superiority.

"SCIENCE"

"Science" during our early years of English opera had none of the pejorative connotation found in Italian opera criticism. In 1786 the *Register* declared Billington "a perfect and scientific mistress of instrumental music" (Feb. 14); by contrast, Hook's music for the *Peruvian*, though commendable, "will not stand the critical test of a scientific judgment." In 1785 they several times praised the science in Shield's music. In 1797 the *Times* found "more *science* than *fashion*" at a performance of *Artaxerxes* (Dec. 1), and in *Travellers in Switzerland* (1794) Shield's "accompaniments to the several Airs, as well as many of the airs themselves, evince an happy union of Science, Taste, and Fancy" (T). Kelly's music for *Feudal Times* (1799) curiously "had much science" but insufficient attention to harmony (T). In 1798 Mazzinghi's "accompaniments" in *Ramah Droog* were "truly scientific" (T), as were Dussek's choruses in *Captive of Spilburg*, which were "without exception, as perfect specimens of scientific taste as we can find" (T).

In the middle years, however, simple melody was still prized: "The melodies with which [the *Beggar's Opera*] abounds seem to have been caught by simplicity from the voice of nature; and they appeal with irresistible force to the soul" (T, Oct. 1, 1802). Parke, with considerable hindsight, noted (c. 1801) that Boyce's duet, "Together let us range the field," "ought to convince the mere theorists of the day that science and melody may be united by genius." Commenting on Charles Dibdin's death in 1814, he wrote that Dibdin was "noted for fine melody, even in those scientific days when science has almost turned poor melody out of doors." Yet we find that some old-fashioned melodies would no longer satisfy. In 1812 the *Times* complained that the songs in Arnold's *Privateer* (the music included borrowings from Stevenson, Webbe, and Handel), "as selections from 'simple old melodies,' as we think they are quaintly styled by the composer, have none of the grace, delicacy, nor even popularity which might entitle them to the notice of a musician . . . and are of a most meagre and unattractive order."

Later views were also mixed. In one instance in 1822, Sterling thought Bishop's music too scientific for a light vehicle like *Maid Marian*, but in 1826, at the *Oracle*, he found Winter's music—thought to be too scientific for English taste—no problem even for the galleries. In 1832 Hunt opted strongly in favor of the simplicity of *Artaxerxes* over "German science" (*Tatler*, Jan. 3, 7).

MUSICAL TASTE

The attitude of reviewers toward the public, cited earlier with respect to successful productions, shifted considerably over the years. Early on it was generally commendatory—sometimes even fawning; such was the attitude of the *Post* (Dec. 14, 1803). In 1808 the *Chronicle* wrote of the *Exile*: "We never remember to have been the spectators of a success more . . . creditable to the discernment of an audience." Yet as early as 1796, the *Chronicle* could observe that, "depraved as the publick taste is now a days," the "manliness and spirit of a British audience" must "maintain their claim of deciding for themselves" the merit of a production (Feb. 23). And at his debut in 1787, Kelly was "much too good for the generality of an English audience" (UR).

Sometimes the public was a patsy for theatrical influences generally: in 1800 *Wilmore Castle* was "not degraded by the miserable buffoonery which has of late, in the exchange of sense for sound, forced itself upon the multitude" (T). In the same year, the *Dramatic Censor*, referring to a ballad sung by Mrs. Jordan, declared that it "affords convincing proof of the frivolity and depraved taste of the age . . . and possesses no other recommendation, but *Namby Pamby* insipidity" (July). The *Chronicle* thought the audience "really resembled so many Egyptian mummies," and in 1805 Hook's *Soldier's Return* "was not only endured" by the audience "but occasionally applauded!!!"

To be sure, early in 1807 DuBois (MM), rejoicing at *False Alarms*, said: "That the public do but sleep, and are not dead to what rational creatures ought to applaud is amply proved by the event." But later that year he found the "jingle" of Reeve and Braham appealed to the "senseless multitude" (Nov.), and in 1808 he asserted that Reynolds, in the *Exile*, "condescended, in compliance with prevailing taste, to furnish the stage with something nearer and nearer approaching pantomime." At Moore's *M.P.* in 1811, the *Times* thought that if his musical "'science' was not uniformly hissed, it was only because it was not understood, meagre as it was, by a tenth of the audience" (Sept. 10). And in 1813 the *Inquisitor* complained: "Of the inmates of a theatre, constituted as we now are, nine tenths know little and care less about dramatic excellence: they have no ear but for music, no eyes but for processions" (Dec.).

Still later reviewers were somewhat more articulate in their comments on public taste, though they, too, had divergent attitudes. Some writers, for example, saw considerable improvement in public taste toward English opera, especially with regard to the foreign adaptations. In 1820 Bacon noted an increase in the appetite of audiences for "whole operas" and believed the operas of Mozart had done much to raise English taste (QMM, II, 73, 77). In 1824 the *Gazette* approved of the "recent intensification" of interest in opera among the English (Feb. 14). At the premiere of *Tit for Tat* (*Cosi*) in 1828, Sterling, J. P. Coller (C), and Talfourd (NM) remarked on the improvement in public taste. In 1830 the *Theatrical Observer* thought English taste for "really good music" had been increased by the influence of Rossini. And at the premiere of *Cinderella* that year, Ward (Ath) wrote: "We are glad that adaptations of sterling Italian operatic music are found to give delight to our purely English audiences. It both proves and advances a better taste with regard to musical productions, and we do not despair of seeing perfect operatic performances popular in our national theatres, as well as the heterogeneous amalgamations still too much in vogue." Parke, writing some years later of the production of *Figaro* (1819), stated: "It is gratifying to observe the advance music has made in this country during the last fifty years, particularly in our English theatres, where now it is listened to with attention and its beauties felt and applauded, even by those in the galleries" (II, 146–47).

But also among later critics there were widespread comments on the inferiority of musical taste in the English theatres, intensifying the independent stance of some of the earlier critics. In 1814, for instance, J. D. Collier (C) deplored some songs in "that trite, hacknied stile which has so long disgusted the cultivated ear, and which we trust to see assigned to the mere Burletta Theatres" (Feb. 2). And in 1816 Sterling observed that Shield's music was perhaps "more calculated for a concert room, and an assembly of amateurs, than for the less cultivated ear of a mixed English audience" (Sept. 24). In 1822 he commented on the public's need for "immediate gratification" with regard to Scott adaptations (Jan. 16), and he deplored the encore of an overture by those who "would have suffered the finest overture of Mozart to pass by unregarded" (Dec. 4). That year the *Examiner* observed: "People seem to us no longer to frequent the theatre to exercise judgment, but rather with a contrary view — to abandon themselves to a sort of dissipation of the mind" (Sept. 15).

In 1825 Sterling noted: "The town has become familiarized to irregularity [of drama] and will accept a whimsical or pathetic situation, without much caring what has preceded or what is to follow it" (Sept. 9). The *European* averred: "The more vulgar and common-place a song is, the more it is generally applauded in our theatres" (Sept.). And Ayrton, commenting in 1823 on poor English operas that were well received by the public, declared: "When I hear of the musical taste of the public, I cannot help smiling at such a misapplication of the term. The *taste* of the public is a mere chimera; it is true that boxes, pit, and gallery, have their enthusiasm desperately excited by a long shake on the octave-flute; but further than this, deponent saith not" (Har, III, 223–24).

In 1826 a song that "ought to be hissed from the stage" was encored (T, Jan. 27). That year J. P. Collier (C) wrote: "It may be very truly remarked . . . that the 'English public' are not esteemed very competent judges" of Weber's music for *Oberon*, and he alluded to *Freischütz* being "murdered" by young ladies on the pianoforte (Apr. 13).

At the *Seraglio* in 1827, the exasperated *Literary Chronicle* declared:

> The English are certainly an unmusical selfish people. Let any one of tolerable musical feelings go to an opera with the intention of hearing the overture, they will find out what is meant; few think of listening to the most inspired passages, and the few that try to listen, find so many illustrations of the dog in the manger around them, that they give up the attempt in hopeless disgust.

In 1828 critic Y of the *Examiner* was contemptuous of a public that "still tolerates" cuts and substitutions in adapted Mozart operas, and he was glad to find in Elliston, at the Surrey, a manager who could *lead*, not merely follow, public taste. Sterling hoped one singer would not "prematurely suffer herself to be blinded by that silly and indiscriminate applause of shallow audiences" (July 1). In 1830 Holmes (At) wrote: "When we consider how coarse is the preference of audiences at the great theatres; how much they delight in excess, and violent contrasts, either at shouting in full cry, or a *piano* scarcely audible; we shall esteem it no small praise to the first dramatic singer of England, that [Paton] has attained her high popularity without resorting to such poor expedients" (Feb. 7).

Many years later James Planché⁵ commented on the backward taste of the period, although, like Chorley, he may have drawn a darker picture than necessary. With reference to his *Cortez* (1823), he noted that "such was the state of music" at that time that when Bishop tried to introduce concerted pieces and a finale to the second act, "more in accordance with the rules of true operatic construction, it had proved, in spite of all the charm of Bishop's melody, a signal failure." And he added: "A dramatic situation in music was . . . inevitably received with cries of 'cut it short!' from the gallery. . . . Nothing but the Huntsman's Chorus and the diablerie in 'Der Freischutz' saved that fine work from immediate condemnation in England." This latter point, however, lacks the support of contemporary reviews of that opera.

LATER VIEWS

Public taste aside, later reviewers occasionally voiced strong objections to the mediocrity of English opera. In 1816 J. D. Collier (C), in a prefatory passage to his review of Morton's *Slave*, wrote:

> We are certainly no friends to Operas, — at least to such as have been produced for the last few years, and are still being produced daily. . . . In the first place, a Modern Opera makes a direct and most outrageous attack upon the ears and eyes, by dint of inexplicable shew and noise: — it deals in nothing but spangles and thunder. The characters are always gorgeously dressed, delectably silly, and overpoweringly sentimental: — The plot is full of love, danger, and confusion: — and the dialogues are merely the sprigs on which the songs are hung; — they are the little dark combustible trains, by which the airs are exploded. . . . The music is generally unmeaningly noisy, or affectedly pathetic: but how should it be otherwise, when it is but the accompaniment of dull verses about "war's alarms," and "the loving heart."

In 1823 Ayrton (III, 223–24) wrote: "The operas of the present day are not required to possess any peculiar musical merit; they are mere accompaniment to something of more interest which is to be passing on the stage." And in 1826 Sterling protested the "Gothic nonsense" of most operas and pleaded for a revival of the older type of English operas, which were better written and more profitable than the current craze (July 26).

Even the production of English adaptations did not help. In 1827

Hazlitt (At), commenting on both the *Seraglio* and *Isidore de Merida*, was altogether out of sorts with English opera:

> This species of exhibition is compounded by glare of scenery, dazzle of light, uproar of music, confusion of costume, bustle of action, silly verse, bombastic prose. . . . If our remarks on such pieces should appear deficient in that discrimination which we of course think ordinarily distinguishes them, we candidly declare that we are not able to see the scenery for the light—that we cannot hear the singing for the music—that the brilliant dresses confound our vision—that the rhyme we do not understand; and the absence of all reason in plot, character, and incident, puts us out of patience with author, fiddler, singer, dancer, machinist, and manager. A critic should, above all things, be cool; but who can be cool amidst the stew of a Grand English Opera. (Dec. 2)

In the same year, Bacon (QMM, IX, 62) pointed out that the movement toward foreign adaptations—however it may have affected public taste—did very little for true English opera:

> If then it should be enquired what advance has been made this season towards the most desirable improvement in the music of the country, the establishment of really good opera?—we are afraid we must answer—but very little. . . . At all the Theatres we perceive the talent of Europe borrowed to piece out our own. . . . They have taught our countrymen that good music may be patched in with flippant, poor, or absurd dialogue, and that one may help out the other, while mere novelty is pro tempore, a short-lived attraction.

In two essay-type passages, Holmes (At) explored the problems a commercial milieu imposed on a serious English opera composer. The first (1828) dealt specifically with song writing:

> Theatrical songs are now completely matters of money-making speculation, produced through the conjunction of singer, musicseller, and tunemonger; and the musician who was formerly, as the writer of a song, the most important personage concerned in it, is now the least so of the three. Songs are composed, not because the composer feels a disposition to write, but because Vestris and Braham are in fashion, and the audience is all for love or war. . . . There are Messrs. ———, the music-sellers, seated in the second circle, who have already bought the copyright of the song, and who have brought all their shopmen, kindred, and acquaintance, relative and collateral, to clap and vociferate. Thus the noble triumvirate plays a sure game. . . . For this reason,

good composers and good music have long since bid adieu to the theatres. (Jan. 20, p. 44)

The second, an attack on English adaptations written in 1830, was even more bitter:

> The occupation of the dramatic composer, a situation which brought honour and emolument to Shield, to Storace, to Bishop, and others, is now dismissed from the stage; and, instead of his labours, foreign ready made scores are found, and the leader of the band and his journeymen are set to hack them *ad libitum*. Original music is thus obtained without expense, and success is almost certain to attend it—for nothing is chosen but such a piece as has already had popularity elsewhere. (Feb. 14, p. 105)

Despite this bleak picture, Bacon (QMM, IX, 62) thought the time ripe for experiments: "What we wish to see tried is a good and legitimate lyric drama, supported throughout by good music, and we cannot help believing, first, that there is talent in this country to produce both, and taste in the country to relish and support them." Composer George Rodwell tried to launch such an experiment in his *Letter to the Musicians of Great Britain* (1832), containing a prospectus for a proposed "Grand National Opera."[6] In his opening letter he complained:

> No English composer can now get an engagement at either of our great theatres but as an adaptor of foreign music—a most mortifying situation for any man with one spark of genius. . . . English composers are now no longer paid but by the publishers; so that, should a composer . . . find it pleasant to eat as well as to write, he must study more particularly what will be acceptable at the boarding-school, than what will be admired by the scientific of the musical world.

In an accompanying letter to the king, he solicited his "royal prerogative for the protection and encouragement of English music and grant . . . a patent, under which they might open a New Grand National Opera, whose aim should be science—whose end charity." He proposed to raise £40,000 by donations, to be administered by several directors and a committee. Operas would be selected by committee for presentation at nightly performances, to include a grand opera and one two-act opera or two one-act operas. Equal payments to authors and composers would be based on 12 percent of the gross nightly receipts, estimated at £8 each for a grand opera and £4 for an afterpiece.

The outcome of this proposal was sorely recounted by Edward Fitzball in his memoirs (1859):

> It makes my heart ache when I think on the *neglected* talent in *this* country, which only requires a *few* rays of sunshine to render it equal, if not superior, to that of any other land in the world. George Rodwell some time ago, made a laudable attempt to establish *something* like a national opera; and published a prospectus to that effect; but his endeavours, so zealously, and so praiseworthily set about, were seconded by professors themselves with so much apathy and supineness, and so much *selfishness*, that the outsetting champion retired from the field in disgust, and the whole affair fell, from inertia, to the ground. (p. 231)

Thus English opera slowly struggled on with its detractors — and champions — among the literati, music scholars, and the more serious critics. Most reviewers, however, took little notice of what they likely regarded as an esoteric subject anyway, and their attitude seems to have coincided with that of the theatre-going public, who supported most of these musicals, by whatever name, provided they were well produced.

To be sure, John Barnett's *Mountain Sylph* in 1834, and Irishman Michael Balfe's *Bohemian Girl* in 1843 — both claimed as the most successful "true" operas since *Artaxerxes* — showed sporadic development; but in comic opera it would take the genius of Gilbert and Sullivan in late Victorian times to invest the form with renewed vigor, and not until the twentieth century would composers arise who were ready to create *drammas per musica* in English.

Appendix 10

Annual Listing of Performances and Reviews

SINCE THIS IS AN ANNUAL LISTING, it should be kept in mind that the season for the winter theatres (DL—Drury Lane; CG—Covent Garden) ran from about September to about June and for the summer theatres (LT—Little Theatre in the Haymarket and, after 1808, the LYC/EOH—Lyceum Theatre/English Opera House) from about June to about September, though this varied from season to season. (The English Opera House had performances throughout the year while the Drury Lane company was there: 1809–12.)

Operas are listed in two groups for each year. In the first group are the premieres, with titles in all capitals, and the *earliest* revivals (after 1784) for which we have reviews, with titles in initial capitals. Both types are listed chronologically by date of performance. The revival entries show, in brackets following the name of the composer, the theatre and year of its first performances, and both entries show the years in which revivals took place up to 1801. The second group lists *later* revivals alphabetically, indented, and below the first group, with titles in initial capitals and with cross-references to the year of earliest listing in this appendix.

The main entries are as follows: (1) theatre; (2) date of premiere; (3) opera type (in parentheses), followed by "-A" if an afterpiece; (4) title of the opera; (5) the number of performances (in parentheses), if known; (6) author; and (7) composer(s). (If the work is an English adaptation of a foreign opera, the place and year of the original premiere are provided.) Then there follows a chronological listing of periodicals, by date of review of the opera, then alphabetically for a given day. A periodical shown in parentheses indicates a verbatim reprint of a review that appeared in the immediately preceding periodical. Finally, productions having revivals are next listed by year (in italic) followed by the reviews, if any. (Pagination is provided for most weekly or monthly reviews, as indicated at the end of part I.)

Abbreviations of opera types are:

Ba	burletta	MF	musical farce
BO	ballad opera	MR	musical romance
CO	comic opera	O	opera
CR	comic romance	Oa	operetta
D	drama	OC	operatic comedy
DO	dramatic opera or operatic drama	OEnt	operatic entertainment

DR dramatic romance
Ent entertainment
Int interlude
MD musical drama or melodrama

OF operatic farce
OR operatic romance
PO pastoral opera
RO romantic opera
S-C semicomic opera

Other abbreviations used are:

ad. adaptation
alt. altered
arr. arrangements

l. libretto
m. music

sel. selection(s)
tr. translation

1785

DL Feb 8 (CO) *LIBERTY HALL; or, A Test of Good Fellowship* (11), C. Dibdin (words and music). Feb 10–12 LC (UM).

CG May 12 (CO) *THE CAMPAIGN; or, Love in the East Indies* (3), Jephson; m. Tenducci. May 13 UR.

LT July 9 (CO) *TURK AND NO TURK* (13), Colman the Younger; m. Dr. Arnold. July UM; 11 H, PA (LC), UR; 18 UR. *1786.*

CG Oct 7 (CO) *Fontainbleau; or, Our Way in France* (14), O'Keeffe; m. Shield [CG, 1784; rev. 1785–1800]. Oct 8 H, UR. *1788*: Sep 27 T. *1819*: Oct TI p217f; 19 T; 23 LG p685. *1822*: Oct 19 T.

CG Oct 21 (CO) *Robin Hood; or, Sherwood Forest* (15), Macnally; m. Shield [CG, 1784; rev. 1785–1800]. 1784: Apr. 17 LM. *1785*: Oct 22 UR. *1787*: Oct 19 UR. *1813.*

CG Nov 10 (CO) *THE CHOLERIC FATHERS* (7), Holcroft; m. Shield. Nov 11 PA, UR; 12 H, UR; 10–12 LC; 16 UR; Dec 8 WH.

DL Dec 8 (CO) *THE STRANGERS AT HOME* (21), Cobb; m. T. Linley the Elder [rev. 1786–87, 1789–92, 1799–1800]. Dec 9 H, UR; 10 UR; 8–10 LC; 12 UR. *1789*: Mar 10 T.

1786

CG Feb 13 (CO) *Love in a Village,* Bickerstaffe; m. Arne and sel. 16 composers [CG, 1762; rev. 1763–98]. Feb 14 UR; Nov 14 UR. *1787*: May 12 H, UR. *1788*: Jan 16 T. *1808*: Sep 25 E. *1810*: June MM p466. *1813*: Dec 8 C. *1816*:

Aug TI p145f; 18 E; Oct 2 T. *1817*: July 27 E; Nov 6 T; 16 E. *1820*: Sep 29 T; Oct TI p306f; 1 E. *1821*: Mar 2 T; 10 LitC; Apr LM p435f. *1822*: Nov 25 T. *1823*: Dec 17 T. *1827*: Aug NM p333; Nov 21 T; Har (V, 249). *1828*: Sep 6 LG p573.

CG Mar 18 (CO) THE PERUVIAN (7), Anon, "by a Lady," ad. from a French sour; m. Hook. Mar 20 C (LC), UR.

LT Aug 12 (CO) THE SIEGE OF CURZOLA (7), O'Keeffe; m. Arnold. Aug 14 C (LC), PA, UR; 19 G. *1787*.

CG Oct 16 (CO) RICHARD COEUR DE LION (13), Macnally, ad. Sedaine; m. Shield. Oct 17 C, PA; 14–17 LC; 19 C, G, UR; 17–19 LC; 23 UR.

DL Oct 24 (MD) RICHARD COEUR DE LION (43), Burgoyne, ad. Sedaine; m. Grétry, arr. T. Linley the Elder [rev. 1787–89, 1791–93, 1797]. Oct 25 C, PA, UR.

1787

CG Jan 13 (O) *Artaxerxes*, Arne (words and music; ad. Metastasio) [CG, 1762; rev. 1763–1800]. Jan 15 G, H, UR; 22 UR; Oct 26 UR; Dec 1 UR. *1788*: Apr 8 H; Oct 25 T. *1792*: May 24 C; Nov 12 T. *1796*: May MM p53. *1813*: Sep 24 T; Oct 17 E. *1815*: Sep 23 T. *1816*: July 21 E; Nov TI p359f. *1817*: July 6 E. *1818*: Jan 9 T; Mar BS p60f. *1820*: Apr TI p236f; 6 T, 16 E; June LM p69f. *1821*: Mar LM p330. *1822*: Dec 9 T. *1827*: Feb 28 T; Oct 24 T; Nov 12 T.

LT Aug 4 (CO) INKLE AND YARICO (21), Colman the Younger; m. Dr. Arnold. [rev. 1788–1800]. Aug 6 H, PA, UR; 4–7 LC. *1788*: Oct 23 T. *1789*: Oct 14 PA. *1790*: Aug 24 D. *1793*: May 18 D. *1798*: Sep 27 P, T. *1821*: Aug LM p199. *1822*: Sep EM p271.

CG Oct 31 (OF-A) THE FARMER (19), O'Keeffe; m. Shield. [rev. 1788–1800]. Nov 1 PA, UR.
 —*Love in a Village*, Bickerstaffe, see 1786.
 —*Robin Hood*, Macnally, see 1785.

1788

DL Feb 25 (CO) LOVE IN THE EAST; or, Adventures of Twelve Hours (9), Cobb; m. T. Linley the Elder Feb 26 H, T; 26–28 LC; AR.

CG May 22 (CO) MARIAN (12), Brooke; m. Shield. [rev. 1789–90, 1792–95, 1798, 1800]. May 23 PA, T; 22–24 LC.

DL Oct 25 (OF-A) *THE DOCTOR AND THE APOTHECARY* (18), Cobb; m. Storace, ad. Ditter's *Doktor und Apotheker* (Vienna, 1786). [rev. 1789–92, 1796–98]. Oct 27 PA; 28 H (LC), T.

CG Nov 6 (CR) *THE HIGHLAND REEL* (11), O'Keeffe; m. Shield. [rev. 1789–1800]. Nov 7 PA, H, T; 6–8 LC.

CG Dec 13 (CO) *THE PROPHET* (11), Bentley; m. Shield. [rev. 1789]. Dec 15 PA, T; 16 T.
—*Artaxerxes*, Arne, see 1787.
—*Fontainbleau*, O'Keeffe, see 1785.
—*Inkle and Yarico*, Colman, see 1787.
—*Love in a Village*, Bickerstaffe, see 1786.

1789

CG Feb 24 (OF-A?) *HIDE AND SEEK; or, The Slippers* (7), Walter II; m. Crouch. Feb 25 PA, T; 24–26 LC; Mar 11 T.

DL Oct 13 (CO) *The Tempest; or, The Enchanted Island* (6), Kemble, ad. Dryden's ad. Shakespeare; m. T. Linley the Younger and sel. Purcell and Arne. [rev. 1790–93?]. Oct 14 PA, T; 13–15 LC; *see also* Reynolds's *Tempest*, 1821.

CG Oct 24 (Int-A) *Thomas and Sally; or, The Sailor's Return*, Bickerstaffe; m. Arne [CG, 1760; rev. 1761–75, 1777, 1780, 1783–84, 1787, 1789, 1791, 1793, 1797]. Nov 30 T.

CG Sep 23 (CO) *The Castle Of Andalusia* (39), O'Keeffe; m. Dr. Arnold [CG, 1781; rev. 1782–1800, alt. for 1788]. Sep 24 T. *1812*: Dec 18 T. *1815*: July 20 T. *1816*: June 21 T; Sep 1 E. *1817*: Aug TI p139; Nov EM p457. *1819*: Dec 18 LG p813.

DL Nov 13 (O-A) *THE ISLAND OF ST. MARGUERITE* (33), St. John; m. Shaw. [rev. 1790–91, 1798]. Nov UM p271; 14 H, T.

DL Nov 24 (CO) *THE HAUNTED TOWER* (70), Cobb; m. Storace. [rev. 1790–94, 1796–98, 1800]. Nov UM p271f; 25 H, T; 24–26 LC; *Whitehall Evening Post* (I, 715); WH p715. *1790*: Sep 13 T; WH p109f. *1793*: Dec 18 PA. *1797*: Oct 20 T. *1817*: Oct 15 T; 19 E. *1819*: Dec TI p333f. *1829*: Har (VII, 205). *1832*: Feb 5 Plain Dealer.
—*The Strangers at Home*, Cobb, see 1785.

1790

DL Apr 16 (OF-A) *NO SONG, NO SUPPER* (25), Hoare; m. Storace. [rev. 1791–1800]. Apr 19 T. *1803*: May 4 T. *1819*: Oct TI p216f. *1830*: Dec 15 *Tatler*.

CG May 6 (MD) *THE CRUSADE* (12), Reynolds; m. Shield. [rev.1791]. May 7 PA, T.

LT July 16 (CO) *NEW SPAIN; or, Love in Mexico* (9), Scawen; m. Dr. Arnold. July 17 T; 15–17 LC.
—*The Haunted Tower*, Cobb, see 1789

1791 (DL at KT)

DL Jan 1 (CO) *THE SIEGE OF BELGRADE* (47), Cobb; m. Storace (see also Burghersh, 1830). [rev. 1792–1800]. Jan UM p66; 3 C, PA, T; 4 G, 1–4 LC; *Whitehall Evening Post* (I, 155–57); WH. *1811*: Apr 14 E. *1813*. *1816*: July 2 C. *1817*: Oct 24 T; Nov EM p456f, 16 E. *1820*: Feb 27 E; Apr LM p441f. *1822*: Apr 28 E; Nov 22 T, 24 E. *1824*: Dec 2 T. *1829*: Mar 18 TO.

CG Feb 26 (CO) *THE WOODMAN* (28), Bate Dudley; m. Shield. [rev. 1792–93, 1795–97, 1800]. Feb 28 C, G, T; Feb 26-Mar 1 LC; CR p349; *Theatrical Guardian* (I,11–14); WH p337–39. *1808*: Feb EM, MM p129; 7 E.

DL May 3 (Ent-A) *THE CAVE OF TRIPHONIUS* (7), Hoare; m. Storace. [rev. 1792]. May 3–5 LC.

LT July 30 (MD-A) *THE SURRENDER OF CALAIS* (28), Colman the Younger; m. Dr. Arnold. [rev. 1792–1800]. Aug 1 PA, T.

CG Dec 28 (CO) *The Duenna*, Sheridan; m. T. Linley the Elder and T. Linley the Younger [CG,1775; rev. 1776–98, 1800]. Dec 29 C, T. *1800*: Oct 21–23 LC. *1809*: Aug UM p148f. *1813*: Nov 17 T. *1819*: June 20 E. *1820*: Sep TI p237f. *1828*: Dec 13 T.

1792 (DL at KT)

CG Feb 2 (CO) *THE MAGICIAN NO CONJURER* (4), Merry; m. Mazzinghi. Feb 3 C (LC, UM), T; Aug LitM; WH p259–60.

CG Feb 28 (O) *ORPHEUS AND EURYDICE* (1), Cadell; m. sel. Gluck pasticcio. Feb 29 T.

CG May 10 (CO) *JUST IN TIME* (9), Hurlstone; m. Carter. *1793*: Oct 29 C (LitM), T; 27–30 LC.

DL (KT) May 23 (O) *DIDO, QUEEN OF CARTHAGE* (5), Hoare; m. Storace. May 24 C, D, G, H, PA (LC); June LitM.

DL (KT) Oct 18 (MD) *THE PRISONER* (27), Rose, ad. de Monuel's *Raoul sire de crequi*; m. Attwood. [rev. 1793, 1796–99]. Oct 19 C (LitM), T; 18–20 LC.

CG Nov 3 (OF-A) *HARTFORD-BRIDGE; or, The Skirts of the Camp* (36), Pearce; m. Shield. [rev. 1793, 1796–99]. Nov LitC; 6–8 LC (UM). *1793*: Jan BC, MR.

DL (KT) Nov 21 (CO) *THE PIRATES* (36), Cobb; m. Storace. [rev. 1793–98]. Nov UM 393; 2 C, T; 22–24 LC; 26 T. *1793*: Jan *Thespian Mag*, p169.
—*Artaxerxes*, Arne, see 1787.

1793 (DL at KT and LT)

CG Feb 25 (CO-A) *THE MIDNIGHT WANDERERS* (13), Pearce; m. Shield. [rev. 1794–95]. Feb. 26 D, T, TB; 27 C, D, H; BC (I, 340); MR p346; May *Thespian Mag*. (II, 253); WH p350. *1794*: CR p103.

DL Mar 7 (MD-A) *OZMYN AND DARAXA* (5), Boaden; m. Attwood. Mar 8 C (LC), D, H, *Star, English Chronicle, Whitehall Evening Post* (*General Evening Post*).

DL Mar 11 (OF-A) *THE PRIZE; or, 2, 5, 3, 8* (20), Hoare; m. Storace. [rev. 1794–1800].

CG Apr 4 (CO) *THE ARMOURER* (3), Cumberland; m. Capt. Warner, an "amateur." Apr LitM; 5 Cr, D, H, T, TB; 4–6 LC.

CG May 11 (CO) *SPRIGS OF LAUREL* (15), O'Keeffe; m. Shield (alt. as *Rival Soldiers*, 1797). [rev. 1794–98, 1800]. May UM p389; 13 C, T, TB; 14–16 LC; AR (VI, 494); BC (I, 453), CR p349f, MR p347.

DL Oct 1 (Int-A) *THE CHILDREN IN THE WOOD* (75), Morton; m. Dr. Arnold. [rev. 1794–1800]. Oct 2 C (LC), T.

DL Dec 16 (MF-A) *MY GRANDMOTHER* (47), Hoare; m. Storace. [rev. 1794–1800]. Dec 17 TB (17–19 LC).
—*The Haunted Tower*, Cobb, see 1789.
—*Incle and Yarico*, Colman, see 1787.
—*Just in Time*, Hurlstone, see 1792.
—*The Pirates*, Cobb, see 1792.

1794

CG Feb 22 (CO) *THE TRAVELLERS IN SWITZERLAND* (21), Bate Dudley; m. Shield. [rev. 1795, 1797]. Feb 24 C (LC), T; AR (I, 85–87); MR p350. *1808*: Mar 27 E.

CG Apr 10 (OF-A) *NETLEY ABBEY* (10), Pearce; m. Shield. [rev. 1795–1800]. Apr 11 T.

DL June 9 (MD) *LODOÏSKA* (45), Kemble; m. Storace. [rev. 1795, 1797, 1800]. June 10 T, C; AR (XX, 478–81). 1795: CR, p108–9. *1813*: Apr 20 T. *1819*: Dec TI p381.

LT July 26 (PO) *AULD ROBIN GREY* (9), Arnold; m. Dr. Arnold. [rev. 1795]. July 28 T, TB.

DL Dec 20 (CO) *THE CHEROKEE* (41), Cobb; m. Storace. [rev. 1795, 1798]. Dec 22 C, T (UM), TB (20–23 LC). *1795*: WH p39.
—*The Midnight Wanderers*, Pearce, see 1793.

1795

DL May 6 (CO) *JACK OF NEWBURY* (9), T. Hook; m. J. Hook. May UM p368; 7 OPA, P, T, TB; 7–9 LC.

LT Sep 2 (CO) *THE THREE AND THE DEUCE* (12), Hoare; m. Storace. [rev. 1796]. Sep EM; 3 OPA, P, T, TB; 1–3 LC; 4 OPA.

1796

CG Feb 2 (OF-A) *LOCK AND KEY* (38), Hoare; m. Shield. [rev. 1797–1800]. Feb 3 OPA, T, TB.

DL Mar 12 (MD) *THE IRON CHEST* (6), Colman the Younger; m. Storace. [rev. 1797–98, 1800]. Mar 14 OPA, *Star*, T, TB (12–15 LC); Aug 30 T.

DL Apr 30 (MD) *MAHMOUD* (16), Hoare; m. Storace. [rev. 1797–98]. May MM p51f, 320; 2 H, OPA, T, TB (3–5 LC); WH p27f.

CG Nov 19 (CO) *ABROAD AND AT HOME* (33), Holman; m. Shield. [rev. 1797, 1799–1800]. Nov 21 OPA, T, TB (19–22 LC); Dec MM p500, UM p438f. 1797: Jan BC, MR p102, WH p101–4.

DL Dec 10 (MEnt-A) *THE SHIPWRECK* (21), Arnold; m. Dr. Arnold. [rev. 1797–1800]. Dec MM p500, UM; 12 OPA, T, TB. *1798*: May BC.
—*Artaxerxes*, Arne, see 1787.

1797

DL Jan 7 (CO) *THE HONEY MOON* (1), William Linley (words and music). Jan MM p56; 9 OPA, T; 7–10 LC.

CG Feb 9 (CO-A) *A FRIEND IN NEED Is a Friend Indeed* (11), Hoare; m. Kelly. Feb UM p148; 10 OPA, T.

CG Apr 25 (CO) *THE ITALIAN VILLAGERS* (6), Hoare; m. Shield. [rev. 1798–1800]. Apr 26 OPA; 27–29 LC.

LT June 26 (OF) *THE IRISH LEGACY* (3), Arnold; m. Dr. Arnold. June 27 OPA; July MM p54.
—*The Haunted Tower*, Cobb, see 1789.

1798

DL Jan 16 (DR) *BLUE-BEARD; or, Female Curiosity* (64), Colman the Younger; m. Kelly. [rev. 1799–1800]. Jan 17 OPA, P, T.

CG Sep 27 (CO) *The Maid of the Mill*, Bickerstaffe; m. sel. Bickerstaffe and Dr. Arnold. [CG, 1765; rev. 1766–1798]. Sep 28 T. *1814*. *1824*: Nov 8 T.

CG Nov 12 (CO) *RAMAH DROOG* (35), Cobb; m. Mazzinghi and W. Reeve. [rev. 1799–1800]. Nov MM (p.378); 13 H, P, T; Dec MM p365. *1800*: June MM p353; July *Anti-Jacobin Rev.*; Sep AR (VII, 61); MR; Oct CR. *1801*: Apr BC. *1816*: Dec TI p433f, 22 E. *1817*: Jan BS p8f.

DL Nov 14 (MD) *THE CAPTIVE OF SPILBURG* (19), Hoare, ad. Marsollier's *Camille*; m. Dussek, Kelly. Nov MM p308f; 15 P, T (LC).
—*Inkle and Yarico*, Colman, see 1787.

1799

DL Jan 19 (MD-A) *FEUDAL TIMES; or, the Banquet Gallery* (58), Colman the Younger; m. Kelly. Jan MM p47; 21 C, T; Feb MM p113.

CG Apr 2 (MF) *THE OLD CLOATHSMAN* (3), Holcroft; m. Attwood. Apr MM p242; 3 P, T; 2-4 LC.

LT Aug 21 (MD) *THE RED-CROSS KNIGHTS* (8), Holman; m. Attwood. Aug 22 T.

CG Oct 7 (MEnt) *THE NAVAL PILLAR* (12), T. Dibdin; m. Moorehead. Oct MM p237f; 8 T.

1800

DL Feb 1 (OF-A) *OF AGE TOMORROW* (39), T. Dibdin; m. Kelly. Feb 3 T.

CG May 1 (MD) *PAUL AND VIRGINIA* (13), Cobb; m. Mazzinghi and W. Reeve. May 2 T.

LT Aug 14 (CO) *WHAT A BLUNDER!* (10), Holman; m. Davy. Aug MM p111ff, UM p143f; 15 P, T; 14-16 LC.

DL Oct 21 (CO-A) *WILMORE CASTLE* (5), Houlton; m. Hook. Oct MM; 22 P, T, TB (21-23 LC). *1801*: Apr MM p260.

CG Nov 15 (MD) *IL BONDOCANI; or, The Calif Robber* (27), T. Dibdin, ad. *Arabian Tales*; m. Attwood and Moorehead. Nov 17 P, T (LC); Dec MM p400.
 —*The Duenna*, Sheridan, see 1791.
 —*Ramah Droog*, Cobb, see 1798.

1801

CG Oct 17 (MEnt-A) *THE ESCAPES; or, The Water-Carrier* (12), Holcroft; m. Attwood, ad. Cherubini's *Les deux journees* (1800). Oct 15 C, P, T.

CG Dec 9 (CO) *CHAINS OF THE HEART; or, The Slave by Choice* (15), Hoare; m. Mazzinghi and W. Reeve. Dec MM p423-25; 10 C, P; 12 T.
 —*Wilmore Castle*, Houlton, see 1800.

1802

CG Feb 9 (CO) *THE CABINET* (30), T. Dibdin; m. Moorehead, W. Reeve, Davy, Corri and Braham. Feb 10 C, P, T; 11 T; Mar MM p203f. *1804*: Feb 6 P. *1805*: July CR; Sep BC. *1806*: May MM p333. *1807*: Feb MM p141. *1808*: Jan 24 E; 31 E; May MR. *1812*: Dec 25 T. *1813*: July 23 T. *1817*: July EM p66; 13 E; Dec EM p548f. *1823*: Apr 12 LitC; Nov 20 T; Dec LM p640; 4 T; 12 T. *1825*: Jan LM.

CG Sep 30 (BO) *The Beggar's Opera*, Gay; m. arr. Pepusch (1728). New arr. T. Linley the Elder, 1771. Oct 1 P, T. *1807*: Oct 24 T. *1812*: Sep 13 E. *1813*: Oct 23 C. *1814*: Jan TI p10. *1815*: June 18 E; Sep 29 T; Oct TI p312–15; Nov 5 E. *1816*: July 26 T; 28 E; Aug 23 T. *1817*: Oct BS p146–48. *1819*: Feb 7 E. *1820*: July TI p18f, 80–83; Sep EM p259f; 24 E; Oct BS p292. *1821*: Oct 24 T. *1822*: Sep 28 T; Oct 29 T. *1825*: July 9 LitC. *1829*: June 17 Ath p380f. *1830*: Apr 17 Ath p237; 18 At p250, E: Har (VIII, 224).

DL Nov 17 (OF-A) *A HOUSE TO BE SOLD* (11), Cobb, ad. Duval's *La maison à vendre*; m. Kelly. Nov MM p345; 18 C, H, P, T.

CG Dec 18 (CO) *FAMILY QUARRELS* (22), T. Dibdin; m. Moorehead, W. Reeve, Davy and Braham. Dec 20 C, P, T. *1803*: Jan MM p54–56; 5 T. *1805*: Nov BC.

1803

DL Feb 19 (MD) *HERO OF THE NORTH* (20), Dimond, ad. *Gustavus Vasa*, 1810; m. Kelly. Feb 21 T.

LT July 25 (OF-A) *LOVE LAUGHS AT LOCKSMITHS* (30), Colman the Younger, ad. Bouilly's *Un folie*; m. Kelly. July MM p58f; 26 C, P, T.

DL Nov 1 (MD) *THE WIFE OF TWO HUSBANDS* (34), Cobb; m. Mazzinghi. Nov 2 T.

CG Dec 13 (CO) *THE ENGLISH FLEET IN 1342* (36), T. Dibdin; m. Braham. Dec 14 C, P, T. *1804*: Jan MM p56f. *1805*: May CR. *1808*: May MR. —*No Song, No Supper*, Hoare, see 1790.

1804

DL Nov 20 (OF-A) *MATRIMONY* ("successful"), Kenney, ad. Marsollier's *Adolphe et Clare*; m. King. Nov MM p349f; 21 C, T. *1805*: Jan CR p349.

CG Dec 10 (CO) *THIRTY-THOUSAND; or, Who's the Richest?* (11), T. Dibdin; m. Davy, W. Reeve and Braham. Dec 11 C; 12 T. 1805: Feb MM p131.
—*The Cabinet*, Dibdin, see 1802.

1805

CG Feb 28 (OF-A) *OUT OF PLACE; or, The Lake of Lausanne* (17), Reynolds; m. Reeve and Braham. Mar 1 T.

CG Apr 23 (CO) *THE SOLDIER'S RETURN; or, What can Beauty do?* (?), T. Hook; m. J. Hook. Apr 24 C, H, T.

DL May 24 (CO-A) *YOUTH, LOVE, AND FOLLY* ("failed"), Dimond; m. Kelly. May 27 C.

1806

DL Jan 22 (MEnt) *THE TRAVELLERS; or, Music's Fascination* (30), Cherry; m. Corri. Jan MM p57f; 23 C (Cr), T. *1823*: May EM p471; Har (I, 85).

DL Feb 8 (BO) *THE BROKEN GOLD* ("failed"), C. Dibdin (words and music). Feb 10 Cr, H, T.

DL Apr 8 (OR) *THE FORTY THIEVES* (25), Colman the Younger; m. Kelly. Apr MM p264, UM p226; 9 C, Cr, T; 16 H.

CG Apr 10 (MD) *THE WHITE PLUME; or, The Border Chieftains* (5), T. Dibdin; m. W. Reeve. Apr MM p264–66, UM; 11 C, Cr, H, T.

CG Nov 15 (MD) *ADRIAN AND ORRILA* (11), Dimond (alt. of *Youth, Love, and Folly*, 1805); m. Attwood and Kelly. Nov MM p346f; 17 C, H. T.

CG Nov 20 (OENT-A) *THE DESERTS OF ARABIA* (15), Reynolds; m. Lanza. Nov MM p347; 21 C, H, T; Dec UM p527f; 1807 June 24 T.

CG Dec 11 (OF) *ARBITRATION; or, Free and Easy* (11), Reynolds; m. Lanza. Dec 12 T.
—*The Cabinet*, Dibdin, see 1802.

1807

DL Jan 12 (CO) *FALSE ALARMS; or, My Cousin* (21), Kenney; m. King and Braham. Jan EM, MM p67–70, UM p61; 13 C, H, T; Feb CR; June 24 T.

DL Mar 12 (CO-A) *THE YOUNG HUSSAR; or, Love and Mercy* (12), Dimond; m. Kelly. Mar 13 T; 16 H.

CG May 8 (CO) *PETER THE GREAT; or, The Wooden Walls* (5), Cherry; m. Jouve. May EM p375f, MM p359f; 9 Cr, T; June 6 T.

CG Nov 17 (CO) *TWO FACES UNDER A HOOD* (19), T. Dibdin; m. Shield, W. Reeve and Braham. Nov MM p362–65, UM p426f; 18 C, T.
 —*The Beggar's Opera*, Gay, see 1802.
 —*The Deserts of Arabia*, Reynolds, see 1806.

1808

DL Feb 11 (O) *KAIS; or, Love in the Desarts* (19), Brandon, ad. I. D'Israeli's *Mejnoun and Leila*; m. Reeve and Braham. Feb MM p126–28, UM p141f; 12 C, T; 14 E.

DL Mar 1 (OF) *IN AND OUT OF TUNE* ("failed"), Cherry (ad. Dennis Lawler?); m. Corri. Mar 2 T; 6 E.

DL May 3 (CO) *THE JEW OF MOGADORE* (5), Cumberland; m. Kelly. May MM p394–98; 4 C, T; 8 E.

CG (at KT) Nov 10 (O) *THE EXILE; or The Deserts of Siberia* (42), Reynolds; m. Mazzinghi and Bishop. Nov EM p391f, MM p324–26, UM p400–2; 11 C, 13 BWM p366f, E. *1813*: Sep 10 T. *1821*: Oct 19 TO; Nov 12 T.

DL Nov 10 (MD) *THE SIEGE OF SAN QUINTIN; or, Spanish Heroism* (9), T. Hook; m. J. Hook. Nov MM p316, UM p461f; 11 C, T; 13 BWM p366f, E.
 —*The Cabinet*, Dibdin, see 1802.
 —*Love in a Village*, Bickerstaffe, see 1786.
 —*The Travellers in Switzerland*, Bate, see 1794.
 —*The Woodman*, Bate, see 1791.

1809 (DL at LYC after Feb. 23)

DL Feb 23 (O) *THE CIRCASSIAN BRIDE* (1), Ward; m. Bishop. Feb 24 T (DL burned).

DL June 26 (CO) *UP ALL NIGHT; or, The Smuggler's Cave*, Arnold; m. King. June 27 C, T (Cr), BWM; July EM p46, MM p48–51; 2 E (UM). *1812*: Sep TI. *1816*: June 17 C (Cr), T.

LT July 1 (OF) *KILLING NO MURDER* (35), T. Hook; m. J. Hook. June 27 C; July EM p47.

LYC July 22 (O) *THE RUSSIAN IMPOSTOR; or, The Siege of Smolensko* (14), Siddons, alt. Arnold; m. Addison. July 23 T; 24 C; 30 E; Aug MM p121–23.

LYC Aug 28 (CO) *SAFE AND SOUND*, T. Hook; m. J. Hook. Aug 29 C, T; Sep MM p188–91, UM p236f; 8 E.
 —*The Duenna*, Sheridan, see 1791.

1810 (DL at LYC)

LYC Mar 13 (S-C) *THE MANIAC; or, Swiss Bandetti* (26), Arnold; m. Bishop. Mar EM p219f, MM p232–36; 14 C, T; 18 E (UM).

LYC June 12 (CO) *OH! THIS LOVE; or, The Masqueraders*, Kenney; m. King. June MM p467–70, UM p499f (EM); 13 C; 17 BMW p191, E; 25 T.

LYC Sept 9 (CO-A) *TRICKS UPON TRAVELLERS*, Burges[s]; m. Horn and W. Reeve. July MM p73–76; 10 T; 15 BWM p221 (UM), E.

CG Nov 29 (O) *GUSTAVUS VASA* (14), Dimond, ad. his *Hero of the North*, 1803; m. Kelly. Dec 1 C, T; 2 BWM p381.
 —*Love in a Village*, Bickerstaffe, see 1786.

1811 (DL at LYC)

LYC Jan 31 (DO) *THE PEASANT BOY* (24), Dimond; m. Kelly. Feb EM p130, UM; 1 C; 3 BWM p37.

CG Feb 5 (MD) *THE KNIGHT OF SNOWDOUN* (23), Morton, ad. Scott's *Lady of the Lake*; m. Bishop. Feb EM p130f; 6 C, T; 10 BWM p44, E (UM); June 16 E. *1823*: July 19 LitC.

LYC Apr 27 (CO) *THE AMERICANS*, Arnold; m. King and Braham. Apr 29 C. *1818*: July 31 C, T; Aug EM p158.

LYC Sep 9 (CO) *M. P.; or, The Bluestocking*, Moore (words and music) and m. Horn. Sept EM p211f, UM p239f (BWM); 10 C, T; 13 T; 15 E.
 —*The Siege of Belgrade*, Cobb, see 1791.

1812 (DL at LYC)

CG Jan 31 (DO) *THE VIRGIN OF THE SUN* (33), Reynolds, ad. Kotzebue; m. Bishop. Feb EM p121; 1 C; 2 BWM p37; 3 T.

LYC May 6 (OR) *THE DEVIL'S BRIDGE; or, The Piedmontese Alps*, Arnold; m. Horn and Braham. May 7 C, T; 8 T; 10 BWM p149, E; June EM p473f. *1813*: Nov 15 T. *1815*: July 18 T. *1826*: Oct 23 T.

LYC Aug 22 (CO) *THE PRIVATEER*, Arnold, ad. Cumberland's *The Brothers*; m. Arnold (sel.). Aug 24 T; Sep TI p513. *1818*: Sep EM p257.
 —*The Beggar's Opera*, Gay, see 1802.
 —*The Cabinet*, Dibdin, see 1802.
 —*The Castle of Andalusia*, O'Keeffe, see 1789.
 —*Up All Night*, Arnold, see 1809.

1813

EOH June 16 (BO) *The Jovial Crew*, Brome, Cancanen, and Sir William Yonge (six ed. 1731–67) based on Richard Brome's prototype play (1641). Aug TI p58–61. *1819*: July TI p55; 4 E.

DL Oct 12 (MD) *GODOLPHIN; or, The Lion of the North* (3), Thompson; m. Horn. Oct EM p334f, TI, UM; 13 C, T; 17 BMW.

CG Oct 21 (MD-A) *THE MILLER AND HIS MEN* (50), Pocock; m. Bishop. Oct EM p235, UM; 23 T; Nov TI.

DL Nov 22 (OF) *WHO'S TO HAVE HER?* (13), T. Dibdin; m. W. Reeve and Whittaker. Nov UM p410f.
 —*Artaxerxes*, Arne, see 1787.
 —*The Cabinet*, Dibdin, see 1802.
 —*The Devil's Bridge*, Arnold, see 1812.
 —*The Duenna*, Sheridan, see 1791.
 —*The Exile*, Reynolds, see 1808.
 —*Lodoiska*, Kemble, see 1794.
 —*Love in a Village*, Bickerstaffe, see 1786.
 —*The Siege of Belgrade*, Cobb, see 1791.
 —*Robin Hood*, Macnally, see 1785.

1814

CG Feb 1 (CO) *THE FARMER'S WIFE* (16), C.I.M. Dibdin; m. Bishop, Davy, W. Reeve and Addison. Feb EM p139f, TI p125–27, UM p143f; 2 C, Cr, T; 6 BWM p45; 12 Ch p53.

CG Nov 12 (CO) *JOHN OF PARIS* (17), Pocock, ad. St. Just's *Jean de Paris*; m. Bishop, ad. Boieldieu. Nov EM p434, TI p340f; 14 C, T; 20 BWM. *1815*: Oct 10 T.
 —*The Maid of the Mill*, Bickerstaffe, see 1798.

1815

CG Feb 1 (OF-A) *BROTHER AND SISTER* (17), Dimond (lyrics by C.I.M. Dibdin); m. Bishop and W. Reeve. Feb EM p133, UM p151; 2 T; 5 Ch p45. *1821*: Nov 22 T.

DL Mar 29 (MD) *THE UNKNOWN GUEST* (11), Arnold; m. Kelly and Braham. Mar 30 T; Apr TI p303f; 2 E.

CG May 17 (Masque-A) *Comus* (15), Colman the Elder, ad. J. Dalton; ad. Milton; m. Arne and Bishop. May TI p390–92.

Lyc Aug 19 (CO) *THE KING'S PROXY; or, Judge for Yourself*, Arnold; m. Cooke. Aug TI p155–57; 21 C, T; 27 Ch p278. *1816*: Sep TI p209f.

CG Nov 20 (DR) *Cymon* (15), Garrick; m. Michael Arne (DL, 1767); revived Dec. 31, *1791* (DL at KT), m. Storace and Shaw (no ref. Arne); *1815*: m. arr. Bishop. Nov TI p407–9; 21 C, T.
 —*Artaxerxes*, Arne, see 1787.
 —*The Beggar's Opera*, Gay, see 1802.
 —*The Castle of Andalusia*, O'Keeffe, see 1789.
 —*The Devil's Bridge*, Arnold, see 1812.
 —*John of Paris*, Pocock, see 1814.

1816

CG Jan 17 (CO) *A MIDSUMMER NIGHT'S DREAM* (18), Reynolds, ad. Shakespeare; m. Bishop. Jan EM p57; 18 T; 21 Ch p21.

CG Mar 12 (MD) *GUY MANNERING* (18), Terry (assisted by Scott); m. Bishop, Davy, Cooke, Whittaker and Braham. Mar 13 T; 17 Ch p854. *1817*: Feb

TI p152. *1818*: Sep 10 T; Oct EM p353. *1819*: Apr TI p310; Oct (DL) 8 T; 10 E. *1821*: July 31 T; Aug LM; 4 LitC. *1822* (DL): Dec 2 T; 7 LG p779. *1825* (DL): Dec 12 T. *1826* (CG): Oct 14 LG p653. *1827*: Oct 22 T. *1828* (DL): Nov 12 T. *1830* (DL): Mar 24 T.

DL May 21 (MD) *OBERON'S OATH; or, The Paladin and the Princess* (5), Thompson, ad. tr. Sotheby of Wieland; m. Parry. May EM, 22 C, T.

LT July 15 (CO) *The Lord of the Manor*, Burgoyne, ad. Marmontel; m. Jackson [DL, 1780]. *1816*: Aug TI p144. *1823*: Sep 24 T. *1824*: May EM p466. *1825*: May 14 TO. *1826*: Jan 27 T. *1827*: Oct 17 T. *1829*: Feb 2 T. *1830*: Nov 16 *Tatler*

CG Sep 23 (OF-A) *YOUR'S OR MINE?* (6), Tobin; m. Shield. Sep 24 T; 29 E.

CG Nov 12 (MD) *THE SLAVE* (32), Morton; m. Bishop. Nov EM p455f, TI p371–75; 13 C, T (Cr); 17 Ch p265, E. *1817*: Mar BS p59f. *1822*: Apr 20 TO.

DL Dec ? (CO) *Lionel and Clarissa*, Bickerstaffe; m. Dibdin the Elder (DL, 1768). Dec 8 E. *1818*: Oct EM p252; 19 T; Nov BS p246.
 —*Artaxerxes*, Arne, see 1787.
 —*The Beggar's Opera*, Gay, see 1802.
 —*The Castle of Andalusia*, O'Keeffe, see 1789.
 —*The King's Proxy*, Arnold, see 1815.
 —*Love in a Village*, Bickerstaffe, see 1786.
 —*Ramah Droog*, Cobb, see 1798.
 —*The Siege of Belgrade*, Cobb, see 1791.
 —*Up All Night*, Arnold, see 1809.

1817

CG Apr 15 (CO) *THE CONQUEST OF TARANTO; or, St. Clara's Eve* (6), Dimond; m. Kelly. Apr 20 Ch p125; June TI p448f.

DL Apr 17 (MD) *ELPHI BEY; or, The Arab's Faith* (3), Hamilton; m. Attwood, Horn, and Smart. Apr EM p346f, TI p304–6; 18 T.

CG May 20 (MD) *THE LIBERTINE* (20), Pocock, ad. da Ponte; m. Bishop, ad. Mozart's *Don Giovanni*. May 21 T; 25 E; June BS p132; July TI p59f; Aug BS p172f.

CG July 3 (BO-A) *The Gentle Shepherd*, Ramsay; m. Scottish tunes collected by W. Thompson (Edinburgh, 1725). July 6 E.

CG Sep 29 (MD) *THE DUKE OF SAVOY; or, Wife and Mistress* (2), Reynolds, ad. Marsollier's *Les deux petites Savoyards*; m. Bishop. Sep 30 C, T; Oct BS p226f, TI p308f; 4 LG p221f; 5 E.

DL Dec 13 (CO) *OUTWITTED AT LAST* (4), Earle; m. Lanza. Dec EM p548; 15 C, T; 20 LG p396f.
 —*Artaxerxes*, Arne, see 1787.
 —*The Beggar's Opera*, Gay, see 1802.
 —*The Cabinet*, Dibdin, see 1802.
 —*The Castle of Andalusia*, O'Keeffe, see 1789.
 —*Guy Mannering*, Terry, see 1816.
 —*The Haunted Tower*, Cobb, see 1789.
 —*Love in a Village*, Bickerstaffe, see 1786.
 —*The Siege of Belgrade*, Cobb, see 1791.
 —*The Slave*, Morton, see 1816.

1818

CG Feb 21 (O) *ZUMA; or, The Tree of Health* (6), T. Dibdin, ad. Mme de Genlis; m. Bishop and Braham. Feb 23 C, T (EM,TI); 28 LG p141f; Mar BS p62f.

CG Mar 12 (MD) *ROB ROY MACGREGOR* (34), Pocock, ad. Scott; m. Davy. Mar EM p253, TI p217–20; 13 C, T; 15 E. *1819*: Sep 30 T. *1820*: Oct TI p307f. *1823*: Nov DM; 17 H, T. *1826*: Jan 6 T. *1827*: Oct 6 T.

CG Oct 13 (CO) *THE BARBER OF SEVILLE* (20), Terry and Fawcett; m. Bishop and ad. Rossini's and Paisiello's *Barbiere*. Oct TI p309–11; 14 C (EM), T; 18 Ch p662, E; 22 LG p669; Nov BS p249f. 1819: QMM (II, 67–80). *1824*: July 5 T. *1830*: Sep 22 T, *Tatler*; 24 *Tatler*.
 —*The Americans*, Arnold, see 1811.
 —*Artaxerxes*, Arne, see 1787.
 —*Guy Mannering*, Terry, see 1816.
 —*Lionel and Clarissa*, Bickerstaffe, see 1816.
 —*The Privateer*, Arnold, see 1812.

1819

CG Mar 6 (CO) *THE MARRIAGE OF FIGARO* (15), Bishop, ad. Holcroft's *Follies of the Day*, 1784; m. Bishop, ad. Mozart's *Figaro*. Mar EM p260f, TI p228–32; 8 T; 21 E; Apr BS p118–20. *1823*: Mar LM p356f; 1 LitC; July 7 T; 9 H; 12 LG p446. *1824*: July 21 T; Har (I,41); Oct 25 T. *1826*: Jan 7 T. *1828*: Aug 3 E. *1830*: Sep 27 *Tatler*.

DL Oct 20 (MD) *THE FISHERMAN'S HUT* (3), Tobin; m. G.(?) Reeve. Oct EM p351f, TI p218–21; 21 C, T; 23 LitC, LG p685f; 24 Ch p683.

CG Oct 26 (Ent) *Arthur and Emmeline*, Anon. (DL, 1784), ad. Garrick's *King Arthur* (DL, 1770), ad. Dryden; m. Purcell ad. Arne. [rev. c. 1803.] Oct 27 T; 31 Ch, E; Nov EM p453, TI p277–80. *1827*: July 3; Aug NM p332; Har (V, 172). *1828*: Aug 24 At p540.

CG Dec 11 (CO) *THE COMEDY OF ERRORS* (27), Reynolds, ad. Shakespeare; m. Bishop. Dec EM p540f, TI p339f; 13 C, T; 18 LitC, LG p43; 19 Ch; 26 E. 1820: Feb LM p171. *1823*: Feb 19 H.
—*The Beggar's Opera*, Gay, see 1802.
—*The Castle of Andalusia*, O'Keeffe, see 1789.
—*The Duenna*, Sheridan, see 1791.
—*Fontainbleau*, O'Keeffe, see 1785.
—*Guy Mannering*, Terry, see 1816.
—*The Haunted Tower*, Cobb, see 1789.
—*The Jovial Crew*, Brome, see 1813.
—*Lodoiska*, Kemble, see 1794.
—*No Song, No Supper*, Hoare, see 1790.
—*Rob Roy Macgregor*, Pocock, see 1818.

1820

DL June 17 (O) *DAVID RIZZIO* (5), Hamilton; m. Attwood, Cooke, Braham, G. (?) Reeve. June EM p532f, TI p398–400; 17 T; 24 LitC; July LM p92f.

DL June 30 (OExt) *GIOVANNI IN LONDON; or, The libertine Reclaimed* (ad. ?) Moncrieff; m. sel. Mozart (from Olympic Pavilion, 1817). June TI p393–95; 4 E; July LM p92f. *1821*: Jan BS p33ff.

LT Oct ? (CO-PO) *Rosina*, Brooke; m. Shield. [CG, 1782]. Oct 15 E. *1825*. *1828*: Nov 6 T. *1830*: Sep 9 *Tatler*.

CG Nov 8 (CO) *TWELFTH NIGHT* (17), Reynolds, ad. Shakespeare; m. Bishop. Nov EM p451f, TI p335–38; 9 C, T; 11 LG p734f; 12 E. *1821*: Mar LM p31f. *1822*: Oct 2 T.
—*Artaxerxes*, Arne, see 1787.
—*The Beggar's Opera*, Gay, see 1802.
—*The Duenna*, Sheridan, see 1791.
—*Love in a Village*, Bickerstaffe, see 1786.

—*Rob Roy Macgregor*, Pocock, see 1818.
—*The Siege of Belgrade*, Cobb, see 1791.

1821

CG May 15 (CO) *THE TEMPEST* (15), Reynolds, ad. Shakespeare; m. Bishop. May: DM, EM p455; 16 T; 18 LitC; June LM p670f. *1822*: Jan 28 T.

DL June 2 (O) *DIRCE; or, The Fatal Urn* (7), Anon., ad. Metastasio's *Demofoonte*; m. Horn and Braham. June DM; 9 LG p364; July BS p207–9, LM p90.

CG Nov 29 (CO) *THE TWO GENTLEMEN OF VERONA*, Reynolds, ad. Shakespeare; m. Bishop. Nov 30 T; Dec 1 Ch p760f; 2 E.
—*Artaxerxes*, Arne, see 1787.
—*The Beggar's Opera*, Gay, see 1802.
—*Brother and Sister*, Dimond, see 1815.
—*Guy Mannering*, Terry, see 1816.
—*The Exile*, Reynolds, see 1808.
—*Inkle and Yarico*, Colman, see 1787.
—*Love in a Village*, Bickerstaffe, see 1786.
—*Twelfth Night*, Reynolds, see 1820.

1822

DL Jan 15 (MD) *THE PIRATE* (9), Dimond, ad. Scott; m. Cooke. Jan EM p74f; 16 T; 19 LitC; 20 E; Feb NM p58f.

CG May 11 (MD) *THE LAW OF JAVA* (11), Colman the Younger, ad. his *Iron Chest*, 1796; m. Bishop. May 18 LG p315; 19 Ch p316, E; June LM p580f.

EOH Sept 5 (Oa-A) *THE FAIR GABRIELLE*, Planché; m. Livius and G. Reeve. Sep DM; 6 T; 8 E; 15 E; Oct LM p375.

LT Sept 9 (CO) *MORNING, NOON AND NIGHT; or, The Romance of a Day* (12), T. Dibdin; m. Perry. Sep DM, EM p269f; 10 C, T; 14 LitC; 15 E; Oct LM p375–77.

CG Dec 3 (O) *MAID MARIAN; or, The Huntress of Arlingford* (27), Planché, ad. Peacock; m. Bishop. Dec DM; 4 C, H, T(EM); 7 LitC, LG p779f; 8 E. 1823: Jan LM p101f, NM p8f.
—*Artaxerxes*, Arne, see 1787.

—*The Beggar's Opera*, Gay, see 1802.
—*Fontainbleau*, O'Keeffe, see 1785.
—*Guy Mannering*, Terry, see 1816.
—*Inkle and Yarico*, Colman, see 1787.
—*Love in a Village*, Bickerstaffe, see 1786.
—*The Siege of Belgrade*, Cobb, see 1791.
—*The Slave*, Morton, see 1816.
—*The Tempest*, Reynolds, see 1821.
—*Twelfth Night*, Reynolds, see 1820.

1823

CG May 8 (O) *CLARI; or, The Maid of Milan* (12), Payne; m. Bishop. May DM, EM p471f; 9 C, H, T; 10 LG p301; 11 E; June LM p694,705f, NM p251f; Har (I, 85). *1830*: Sep 15 T, *Tatler*; Nov 28 *Tatler*.

LT July 9 (OC) *SWEETHEARTS AND WIVES* (51), Kenney; m. Cooke, Whittaker, Nathan, and Perry. July DM, EM; 8 C, H; 10 T; 12 LG p445; 13 E; Aug LM p45; Sep LM p321f; Har (I,115). *1829*: Aug NM p344.

CG Nov 5 (MD) *CORTEZ; or, The Conquest of Mexico* (12), Planché; m. Bishop. Nov DM, EM p469; 6 C, H; 7 H; 8 LG p718; 9 E; Dec LM p641f, NM p538f, Har (I, 201).
—*The Cabinet*, Dibdin, 1802.
—*The Comedy of Errors*, Reynolds, see 1819.
—*The Knight of Snowdoun*, Morton, see 1811.
—*The Lord of the Manor*, Burgoyne, see 1816
—*Love in a Village*, Bickerstaffe, see 1786.
—*The Marriage of Figaro*, Holcroft-Bishop, see 1819.
—*Rob Roy Macgregor*, Pocock, see 1818.
—*The Travellers*, Cherry, see 1806.

1824

DL Jan 13 (CO) *PHILANDERING; or, The Rose Queen* (10), Beazley; m. Horn. Jan DM, EM p77f; 14 C, T; 17 LG p43f, LitC; 18 E; Har (II, 32).

CG Feb 10 (DO) *NATIVE LAND; or, The Return from Slavery* (20), Dimond; m. Bishop. Feb DM, EM p172f; 11 T; 14 LG p108f; 15 E; Mar LM p311f, NM (XII, 107–9), Har (II, 53). *1828*: Jan 14 C; 16 *Companion* p14–16, Har (VI, 48).

CG Feb 20 (CO) *THE MERRY WIVES OF WINDSOR*, Reynolds, ad. Shakespeare; m. Bishop. Feb 21 T; 29 E.

EOH July 22 (MD) *DER FREISCHUTZ; or, The Seventh Bullet*, tr. Logan (with Kerr?), ad. F. Kind; m. Weber (Berlin, 1821), arr. Hawes. July DM; 23 C, T; 24 LG p477; 25 E; 26 T; Aug EM p176f, LM p199f; 16 T; Sep NM (XII, 391f), Har (II, 167–72); Oct 16 LG p670. *1829*: Aug 2 E; Har (VII, 233).

LT Aug 10 (CO) *THE ALCAID; or, The Secrets of Office* (9), Kenney; m. Nathan. Aug DM, EM p176f; 11 C, T; 14 LG p525, LitC; Sep LM p312f, NM (XII, 342–44).

CG Oct 14 (MD) *DER FREISCHUTZ; or The Black Huntsman of Bohemia* (52), Planché, ad. Kind; m. Weber, arr. Livius. Oct DM; 15 C, T; 16 LG p670, LitC; 17 E; Har (II, 214). *1825*: Apr 9 LG p238. *1829*: (in German) June 3 Ath p365.

DL Nov 10 (O) *DER FREISCHUTZ* (72), Soane, ad. Kind; m. Weber, arr. Bishop. Nov EM p461f, LM p134; 11 C, T; 14 E; Dec LM p647f, NM (XII, 535f), Har (II, 233). *1831*: Mar 18 *Tatler*.
—*The Lord of the Manor*, Burgoyne, see 1816.
—*The Maid of the Mill*, Bickerstaffe, see 1798.
—*The Marriage of Figaro*, Holcroft-Bishop, see 1819.
—*The Siege of Belgrade*, Cobb, see 1791.

1825

DL Jan 19 (O) *THE FALL OF ALGIERS* (10), Walker (also attributed to Payne); m. Bishop. Jan 20 T; Feb LM p288f, Har (III, 38).

DL Apr 4 (CO-A) *ABOU HASSAN; or, The Sleeper Awakened* (31), Dimond, ad. Hiemer; m. Weber, arr. Cooke (Munich, 1811). Apr DM; 5 C, T; 9 LitC, LG p237f; 10 E; May LM p145; Har (III, 90).

CG Apr 28 (O) *PRECIOSA* (1), Soane, ad. Wolff?; Weber (Berlin, 1821), arr. Hawes. Apr 29 T; 30 LitC; May 1 E.

EOH July 5 (BO) *BROKEN PROMISES; or, The Colonel, the Captain and the Corporal*, Arnold; m. Hawes. July 6 C, T; 9 LitC; 10 E; Har (III, 144); Aug LM p603f; Sep EM p79.

EOH Aug 15 (O) *TARRARE; or, The Tartar Chief*, Arnold, ad. Beaumarchais' *Tarare* (Paris, 1787); m. Salieri, arr. Hawes. Aug 16 C, T; 20 LitC, LG p542; 21 E; Sep EM p80, LM p132–34, NM (XV, 390f), Har (III, 166). *1826*: Sep 3 T.

DL Oct 28 (CO) *THE WEDDING PRESENT* (5), Kenney; m. Horn. Oct 29 C, T.
— *The Beggar's Opera*, Gay, see 1802.
— *Der Freischütz*, Planché, see 1824.
— *Guy Mannering*, Terry, see 1816.
— *The Lord of the Manor*, Burgoyne, see 1816.
— *Rosina*, Brooke, see 1820.

1826

DL Jan 28 (DO) *MALVINA* (28), Macfarren; m. Cooke. Jan 30 C, T; Feb 4 LitC, LG p77f; Mar EM p305f, NM (XIIX, 101f).

CG Apr 12 (O) *OBERON; or, The Elf-King's Oath* (31), Planché, ad. tr. Sotheby of Wieland; m. Weber. Apr 12 T, 13 C, T; 15 LitC, LG p236f; 16 E; May EM p528–30, NM (XIIX, 191); June EM p634–36, NM (XIIX, 238–40), Har (IV, 146); Nov 20 C, T. *1829*: Feb 25 T; Mar 1 E.

DL Apr 29 (O) *ALADDIN* (10), Soane; m. Bishop. Apr 1 LG p206; May 1 C, T; 6 LitC, LG p285; 7 E; June EM p636–40, NM (XIIX, 235f).

EOH Aug 7 (S-C) *THE ORACLE; or, The Interrupted Sacrifice*, Anon., ad. Huber; m. Winter (*Das unterbrochene Opferfest*, Vienna, 1796), arr. Hawes. Aug 8 C, T; 12 LitC, LG p509f; 13 E; Sep NM (XIIX, 336f), Har (IV, 176–80, 186). *1827* (CG): Feb Har (V, 58).

DL Oct 9 (MR-A) *THE WHITE LADY; or, The Spirit of Arenel* (9), Beazley, ad. Scribe's *La dame blanche*; ad. Scott; m. Boieldieu, arr. Cooke. Oct 10 C, T; 14 LG p653; 15 E.

CG Oct 21 (MD) *PEVERIL OF THE PEAK* (9), Pocock, ad. Scott; m. Horn. Oct 23 C, T; 28 LitC, LG p685f; 29 E; Nov NM (XIIX, 455).

DL Oct 30 (CO) *THE TWO HOUSES OF GRENADA* (11), Wade (words and music) and sel. Braham. Nov 1 T; 4 LG p701; Har (IV, 250); QMM (IX, 61).
— *The Devil's Bridge*, Arnold, see 1812.
— *Guy Mannering*, Terry, see 1816.
— *The Lord of the Manor*, Burgoyne, see 1816.

—*The Marriage of Figaro*, Holcroft-Bishop, see 1819.
—*Rob Roy Macgregor*, Pocock, see 1818.
—*Tarrare*, Arnold, see 1825.

1827

CG Jan 2 (O) *THE WHITE MAID* (5), Payne, ad. Scribe; ad. Scott; m. Boieldieu (*La dame blanche*, Paris, 1825), arr. unknown. Jan 3 T; 6 LitC; 7 E; Feb NM (XXI, 54f), Har (V, 38).

DL May 1 (O) *THE TURKISH LOVERS* (10), Lacy; m. Rossini (*Il Turco in Italia*), arr. Lacy and sel. Braham. May 2 T; 6 At p282, E; June NM (XXI, 238f).

LT July 12 (CO) *THE RENCONTRE; or, Love will find out the Way* (59), Planché; m. Bishop. July 13 T; 14 LitC; 15 At, E; Aug NM (XXI, 333); Har (V, 196).

EOH Aug 20 (O) *THE FREEBOOTERS*, Napier, ad. Anelli; m. Paer (*I fuorusciti di Firenze*, Dresden, 1802); arr. Hawes. Aug 21 T; 25 LitC; 26 E; Oct NM (XXI, 421f); Har (V, 196). *1828*: June 6 [for 7] At p425.

CG Nov 24 (O) *THE SERAGLIO* (21), Dimond; m. Mozart (*Die Entführung aus dem Serail*, Vienna, 1782), arr. Kramer. Nov 26 T; Dec 1 LitC, LG p780f; 2 At p761–64, E; Har (V, 249). *1828*: Har (VI, 24).

DL Nov 29 (D) *ISIDORE DE MERIDA; or, The Devil's Creek* (18), Dimond, ad. Cobb's *Pirates*; m. Storace, Cooke and Braham. Nov 30 T; Dec 1 LitC, LG p780; 2 At p261, 264, E; 3 T; Har (VI, 24).
  —*Artaxerxes*, Arne, see 1787.
  —*Arthur and Emmeline*, Anon., see 1819.
  —*Guy Mannering*, Terry, see 1816.
  —*The Lord of the Manor*, Burgoyne, see 1816.
  —*Love in a Village*, Bickerstaffe, see 1786.
  —*The Oracle*, Anon., see 1826.
  —*Rob Roy Macgregor*, Pocock, see 1818.

1828

CG May 27 (O-A) *CARRON SIDE; or, The Fête Champêtre* (7), Planché; m. Liverati. May 28 T; 30 LitC; 31 LG p349; June 1 At p345, E; July NM XXIV, 295–98).

EOH July 29 (Oa) *TIT FOR TAT*, Arnold; m. Mozart (*Così fan Tutte*), arr. Hawes. July 30 C, T; Aug 2 LG p493, Sp p75; 3 At p489, E; Har (VI, 214); Sep NM (XXIV, 390f).

Surrey Sep 2 (RO) *SYLVANIA*, Somerset, ad. Hiemer; m. Weber (Frankfort, 1810), arr. Blewitt. Sep 3 C, T; 6 LG p573, Sp p156; 7 At p569, 572; 14 E.

EOH Sep 5 (CO) *THE PIRATE OF GENOA*, Wade, ad. de Gamerra; m. Weigl (*Gli amori mariani*, Vienna, 1797), arr. Wade. Sep 6 C, T; 7 At p569, 572; 14 E; Har (VI, 238).

DL Dec 4 (Oa-A) *LOVE IN WRINKLES; or, The Russian Stratagem* (11), Lacy, ad. Scribe; m. Fétis (*La vieille*, Paris, 1826), arr. Lacy. Dec 5 C, T; 6 LG p781f; 7 At p777, E; Har (VII, 23).
— *Arthur and Emmeline*, Anon., see 1819.
— *The Duenna*, Sheridan, see 1791.
— *The Freebooters*, Napier, see 1827.
— *Guy Mannering*, Terry, see 1816.
— *Love in a Village*, Bickerstaffe, see 1786.
— *The Marriage of Figaro*, Holcroft-Bishop, see 1819.
— *Native Land*, Dimond, see 1824.
— *Rosina*, Brooke, see 1820.

1829

CG Jan 15 (O) *THE NYMPH OF THE GROTTO; or, A Daughter's Vow* (10), Dimond; m. Liverati and Lee. Jan 16 C, T; 17 LG p45f; 18 At p42, E.

CG Mar 7 (O) *MAID OF JUDAH; or, The Knights Templars* (17), Lacy. ad. Scott; m. Rossini, arr. Lacy. Mar 9 C, T; 14 LG p180, Sp p164; 15 At p169, E; 18 Ath 183f.

EOH July 15 (MD) *THE ROBBER'S BRIDE*, Fitzball, ad. Ries's *Die Rauberbraut*, Frankfurt, 1828; m. Ries, arr. Hawes. July 16 C, T; 18 Sp p458; 19 E; 22 Ath p416f; Aug NM (XXVII, 342f); Har (VII, 205, 233).

EOH Aug 18 (MEnt) *THE SPRING LOCK*, Peake; m. Rodwell. Aug 19 C, T; 23 At p553f, E; 26 Ath p536; Sep NM (XXVII, 389); Har (VII, 234).

EOH Aug 25 (O) *DER VAMPYR*, Planché, ad. Wohlbruch; m. Marschner (Leipzig, 1828), arr. unknown. Aug 26 C, T; 29 LG, Sp; 30 At p570, E; Sep 2 Ath p552f; Oct NM p431f, Har (VII, 261). *1830:* Sep 21 *Tatler*.

CG Nov 17 (OF) *THE NIGHT BEFORE THE WEDDING, and the Wedding Night* (4), Fitzball, ad. Scribe, ad. Bouilly; m. Boieldieu (*Les deux nuits*, Paris, 1829), arr. Bishop. Nov 18 T; 22 E; 25 Ath; Har (VII, 313).
—*The Beggar's Opera*, Gay, see 1802.
—*Der Freischütz*, Logan, see 1824.
—*The Haunted Tower*, Cobb, see 1789.
—*The Lord of the Manor*, Burgoyne, see 1816.
—*Oberon*, Planché, see 1826.
—*The Siege of Belgrade*, Cobb, see 1791.
—*Sweethearts and Wives*, Kenney, see 1823.

1830

DL Feb 4 (CO-A) *THE NATIONAL GUARD; or, Bride and No Bride* (14), Planché, ad. Scribe; m. Auber (*La fiancée*, Paris, 1829), arr. Cooke. Feb 6 LG p92; 7 Ath p78, E; 14 At p105; Nov 15 *Tatler*; 20 Ath.

CG Feb 4 (O) *NINETTA; or, The Maid of Palaiseau* (12), Fitzball; m. Rossini (*La Gazza Ladra*), arr. Bishop. Feb 5 T; 6 LG p92, Sp; 7 Ath p77f, At p89, E; Har (VIII, 135).

CG Apr 13 (CO) *CINDERELLA; or, The Fairy Queen and the Glass Slipper* (22), Lacy; m. Rossini (*La Cenerentola*), arr. Lacy. Apr 14 T; 17 Ath p237f, Sp p245; 18 At p250, E; Dec 15 T, *Tatler*; 18 Ath p796f, T; 26 E.

DL May 1 (O) *HOFER; or, The Tell of the Tyrol* (12), Planché; m. Rossini (*Guillaume Tell*, Paris, 1829), arr. Bishop. May 3 C, T; 8 Sp p293, TO; 9 At p298, E; June NM (XXX, 238); Nov 12 *Tatler*.

EOH (at Adelphi) May 7 (Ba) *DON JUAN*, Buckstone; m. Mozart, arr. Hawes. May 6 T; June 10 Ath p428f.

KT-Concert Room Nov 6 (CO) *CATHERINE; or, The Austrian Captive*, Burghesh (words and music; ad. Cobb's *The Siege of Belgrade*). Nov 8 T; Dec NM (XXX, 515f).
—*Clari*, Payne, see 1823.
—*The Barber of Seville*, Terry, see 1818.
—*Guy Mannering*, Terry, see 1816.
—*The Lord of the Manor*, Burgoyne, see 1816.
—*The Marriage of Figaro*, Holcroft-Bishop, see 1819.
—*No Song, No Supper*, Hoare, see 1790.
—*Rosina*, Brooke, see 1820.
—*Der Vampyr*, Planché, see 1829.

Appendix II

New and Revived Operas: Productions and Performances By Year and Theatre[1]

Year	Drury Lane Premieres			Covent Garden Premieres			Little Theatre Premieres			Lyceum/EOH		Total	
	Productions	Performances	Revivals	Productions	Performances	Revivals	Productions	Performances	Revivals	Productions	Revivals	Productions	Revivals[2]
1785	2	32	—	4	39	—	1	13	—	—	—	7	—
1786	1	43	—	2	20	1	1	7	—	—	—	4	1
1787	—	—	—	1	19	3	1	21	—	—	—	5	4
1788	2	27	—	3	34	1	—	—	1	—	—	5	4
1789	2	103	2	1	7	2	—	—	—	—	—	3	4
1790	1	25	1	1	12	1	1	9	—	—	—	2	2
1791[3]	2	54	—	1	28	1	1	28	—	—	—	4	1
1792[3]	3	68	—	4	50	—	—	—	—	—	—	7	1
1793	4	147	2	3	61	2	—	—	—	—	—	7	4
1794	2	117	—	2	31	1	1	9	—	—	—	5	1
1795	1	9	—	—	—	—	1	12	—	—	—	2	—
1796	3	43	—	2	71	—	—	—	—	—	—	5	1
1797	1	1	1	2	17	—	1	3	—	—	—	3	1
1798	2	83	—	1	35	1	—	—	1	—	—	3	2
1799	1	58	—	2	15	—	1	8	—	—	—	4	—
1800	2	44	—	2	40	2	1	10	—	—	—	5	2
1801	—	—	1	2	27	—	—	—	—	—	—	2	1
1802	1	11	—	2	52	1	—	—	—	—	—	3	1
1803	2	54	1	1	36	—	1	30	—	—	—	4	1
1804	1	9?	—	1	11	1	—	—	—	—	—	2	1
1805	1	6?	—	2	26?	—	—	—	—	—	—	3	—
1806	3	61?	—	4	42	1	—	—	—	—	—	7	1
1807	2	33	—	2	24	1	—	—	—	—	—	4	2
1808[4]	4	39	—	1	42	3	—	—	—	—	—	5	4
1809[5]	2	15	—	—	—	—	1	35	—	2	—	5	1
1810[5]	1	16	—	1	14	—	—	—	—	2	—	4	1
1811[5]	1	24	1	1	23	—	—	—	—	2	—	4	1
1812[5]	—	—	—	1	33	2	—	—	—	2	1	3	4
1813	2	16	2	1	50	2	—	—	—	—	2	3	8

(Continued on next page)

(Appendix II—Continued)

Year	Drury Lane Premieres			Covent Garden Premieres			Little Theatre Premieres			Lyceum/EOH		Total	
	Productions	Performances	Revivals	Productions	Performances	Revivals	Productions	Performances	Revivals	Productions	Revivals	Productions	Revivals[2]
1814	—	—	—	2	33	—	—	—	—	—	—	2	1
1815	1	11	—	1	17	4	—	—	—	1	2	3	8
1816	1	5	1	4	74	3	1	?	1	—	2	6	9
1817	2	7	—	3	28	6	—	—	—	—	—	5	9
1818	—	—	1	3	60	1	—	—	—	—	2	3	5
1819	1	3	1	2	42	5	—	—	—	—	1	3	11
1820	2	14	—	1	17	1	1	?	—	—	—	3	6
1821	1	7	1	2	24?	3	—	—	—	—	1	3	8
1822	1	9	1	2	38	5	1	12	1	1	—	4	10
1823	—	—	1	2	24	5	1	51	—	—	—	3	8
1824	2	82	—	3	81	2	1	9	—	1	—	7	4
1825	3	46	1	1	1	1	—	—	—	2	—	6	5
1826	4	58	1	2	40	2	—	—	—	1	2	7	6
1827	2	28	1	2	26	1	1	59	—	1	1	6	7
1828	1	11	1	1	7	2	—	—	—	2	1	5	8
1829	—	—	—	3	31	3	—	—	1	3	—	6	6
1830	2	36	2	2	34	3	—	—	—	1	1	5	8
Total	72	1141	25	86	1436	73	18	316	4	21	17	197	169
(Avg.)	(1.6)	(32)	(.6)	(2)	(32)	(1.6)	(.4)	(7.0)		(1)[6]	(.8)[6]	(4.4)	(3.8)

Notes: 1. No. of performances of all revivals unknown and no. of performances of new productions at LYC/EOH unknown. 2. Revivals of operas in public domain, such as *Beggar's Opera, Artaxerxes*, and so on, are included in this column in addition to revivals assigned to particular theatres. 3. DL at KT. 4. CG at KT. 5. DL at LYC except for summer productions. 6. Averages for LYC/EOH based on twenty-one years, 1809–1830. ? = number of performances uncertain.

Appendix 12

Premiere Productions: By Theatre and Type

Number of "Successful" Premiere Productions
By Theatre

	Drury Lane	Covent Garden	Little Theatre	Total
Nine or more	67	55	14	136
Eight or fewer	19	17	4	40
Total	86	72	18	176
"Failure" rate	22%	24%	22%	

Types of Premiere Productions
By Period

	Comic Operas	Operatic Farces	Musical Drama or Melodrama	Operas	All Others
1785–1799	35	12	12	3	7
1800–1814	24	10	10	5	7
1815–1830	21*	4	16*	20	10**
Total all Theatres	45	34	38	28	24

*Some of these were called operas.
**Includes domestic operas, operettas, and even dramas.

Appendix 13

Operas by Known Playwrights: Major and Minor Theatre Performances By Five-Year Periods, 1760–1830

Period	Major Theatres	Minor Theatres	Total
1760–1764	8	—	8
1765–1769	13	—	13
1770–1774	11	4	15
1775–1779	25	6	31
1780–1784	29	11	40
1785–1789	20	6	26
1790–1794	25	8	33
1795–1799	28	8	36
1800–1804	29	12	41
1805–1809	24	12	36
1810–1814	12	16	28
1815–1819	34	17	51
1820–1824	26	28	54
1825–1830	45	17	62

Appendix 14

Productions* by Composer: In Three-Year Periods

Composers	1785–1787	1788–1790	1791–1793	1794–1796	1797–1799	1800–1802	1803–1805	1806–1808	1809–1811	1812–1814	1815–1817	1818–1820	1821–1823	1824–1826	1827–1830	Total
Arne	4	2	1	1	—	—	—	1	1	2	5	4	4	—	5**	30
Shield	4	5	4	4	2	—	—	5	—	—	—	3	1	1	—	20
Arnold, Dr.	3	2	2	2	1	—	—	—	—	3	3	2	2	1	—	21
Linley (E)	2	1	1**	—	—	1	—	—	1	1	—	2	—	—	1	10
Storace	1	4	3	4	1	—	1	—	1	2	—	3	1	1	4**	26
Shaw	—	1	—	—	—	—	—	—	—	—	—	—	—	—	—	1
Carter	—	—	2	—	—	—	—	—	—	—	—	—	—	—	—	2
Attwood	—	—	1	—	2**	1	—	—	—	—	—	—	—	—	—	4
Gay/Linley (E)	—	—	1	—	—	1	1	—	—	—	3	2	2	—	1	11
Hook, J.	—	—	—	1	—	1	—	1	2	—	—	—	—	—	—	5
Kelly	—	—	—	—	4**	2	2	5**	2	—	2	—	—	—	—	17
Mazzinghi	—	—	—	—	1**	2**	1	1**	—	1	2	—	1**	—	—	9
Reeve, W.	—	—	—	—	1**	4**	3**	5**	1**	4**	4**	—	2**	—	—	24
Dussek	—	—	—	—	1	—	—	—	—	—	—	—	—	—	—	1
Moorehead	—	—	—	—	1	3**	1**	2	—	2**	1**	—	—	1**	—	9
Davy	—	—	—	—	—	3**	2**	1**	—	3**	2**	3	2**	1**	2**	19
Braham	—	—	—	—	—	2**	4**	5	1**	4	4**	1	1**	2**	1**	25
Corri	—	—	—	—	—	1**	1**	3	—	2	1**	—	2**	—	—	10
King	—	—	—	—	—	—	1	1**	3	1	1	—	—	—	—	7
Lanza	—	—	—	—	—	—	—	2	—	—	—	—	—	—	—	2
Bishop	—	—	—	—	—	—	—	1**	2	4	8	6	13	8**	7	42
Addison	—	—	—	—	—	—	—	—	1	1**	—	—	—	—	—	2
Horn	—	—	—	—	—	—	—	—	1	2**	1	—	—	2	—	6
Moore	—	—	—	—	—	—	—	—	1	—	—	—	—	—	—	1
Whittaker	—	—	—	—	—	—	—	—	—	1**	1**	—	1**	—	1**	4
Cooke	—	—	—	—	—	—	—	—	—	—	2**	—	2**	3	3**	10
Perry	—	—	—	—	—	—	—	—	—	—	3**	—	2**	—	1**	6
Nathan	—	—	—	—	—	—	—	—	—	—	—	—	1**	1	1**	3
Livius	—	—	—	—	—	—	—	—	—	—	—	—	—	1	—	1
Hawes	—	—	—	—	—	—	—	—	—	—	—	—	—	5	6	11
Wade	—	—	—	—	—	—	—	—	—	—	—	—	—	1	1	2
Lacy	—	—	—	—	—	—	—	—	—	—	—	—	—	—	4	4
Kramer	—	—	—	—	—	—	—	—	—	—	—	—	—	—	1	1
Liverati	—	—	—	—	—	—	—	—	—	—	—	—	—	—	1	1
Lee	—	—	—	—	—	—	—	—	—	—	—	—	—	—	1	1

*Includes all known revivals and all premieres with nine or more performances but excludes most LYC/EOH productions.
**Shared composership.

Appendix 15

Productions* by Librettist: In Three-Year Periods

Librettists	1785–1787	1788–1790	1791–1793	1794–1796	1797–1799	1800–1802	1803–1805	1806–1808	1809–1811	1812–1814	1815–1817	1818–1820	1821–1823	1824–1826	1827–1830	Total
Dibdin, C.	1	—	—	—	—	—	—	—	—	—	—	—	—	—	—	1
Colman (Y)	2	1	1	1	3	—	1	1	—	—	—	2	3	—	—	15
O'Keefe	2	2	—	—	—	—	—	—	—	1	3	1	1	—	—	10
Macnally	3	—	—	—	—	—	—	—	1	—	—	—	—	—	—	4
Cobb	1	5	2	1	2	4	1	—	—	—	5	2	1	2	—	26
Burgoyne	1	—	—	—	—	—	—	—	—	—	1	—	1	3	2	8
Bickerstaffe	2	2	—	—	2	—	—	1	1	2	1	2	1	1	2	18
Brooke	—	1	—	—	—	—	—	—	—	—	—	1	—	1	2	5
Bentley	—	1	—	—	—	—	—	—	—	—	—	—	—	—	—	1
St. John	—	1	—	—	—	—	—	—	—	—	—	—	—	—	—	1
Hoare	—	1	2	3	2	1	—	—	—	—	—	1	—	—	—	10
Reynolds	—	1	—	—	—	—	1	4	—	2	2	2	7	—	—	19
Scawen	—	1	—	—	—	—	—	—	—	—	—	—	—	—	—	1
Bate Dudley	—	1	1	1	—	—	—	2	—	—	—	—	—	—	—	5
Hurlstone	—	—	2	—	—	—	—	—	—	—	—	—	—	—	—	2
Pearce	—	—	2	2	—	—	—	—	—	—	—	—	—	—	—	4
Sheridan	—	—	1	—	—	1	—	—	1	1	—	2	—	—	1	7
Rose	—	—	1	—	—	—	—	—	—	—	—	—	—	—	—	1
Morton	—	—	1	—	—	—	—	—	—	—	—	—	—	—	—	1
Arnold	—	—	—	2	—	—	—	—	3	4	5	2	—	3	1	20
Kemble	—	—	—	1	—	—	—	—	—	—	—	—	—	—	—	1
Hook, T.	—	—	—	1	—	—	—	1	2	—	—	—	—	—	—	4
Holman	—	—	—	1	—	1	—	—	—	—	—	—	—	—	—	2
Dibdin, T.	—	—	—	—	1	4	2	3	—	3	1	1	—	1	—	16
Holcroft	—	—	—	—	—	1	—	—	—	—	—	—	1	2	2	6
Dimond	—	—	—	—	—	—	1	2	2	—	1	—	2	1	4	13
Kinney	—	—	—	—	—	—	1	1	—	—	—	—	1	1	1	5
Cherry	—	—	—	—	—	—	—	1	1	—	—	—	1	—	—	3
Brandon	—	—	—	—	—	—	—	1	—	—	—	—	—	—	—	1
Morton	—	—	—	—	—	—	—	—	1	—	2	—	1	—	—	4
Pocock	—	—	—	—	—	—	—	—	—	2	2	3	1	1	1	11
Dibdin, C.I.M.	—	—	—	—	—	—	—	—	—	1	—	—	—	—	—	1
Terry	—	—	—	—	—	—	—	—	—	—	2	3	—	—	—	5
Colman (E)	—	—	—	—	—	—	—	—	—	—	1	—	—	—	—	1

638

Appendixes

Librettists	1785–1787	1788–1790	1791–1793	1794–1796	1797–1799	1800–1802	1803–1805	1806–1808	1809–1811	1812–1814	1815–1817	1818–1820	1821–1823	1824–1826	1827–1830	Total
Planché	—	—	—	—	—	—	—	—	—	—	—	—	2	3	6	11
Payne	—	—	—	—	—	—	—	—	—	—	—	—	1	—	1	2
Soane	—	—	—	—	—	—	—	—	—	—	—	—	—	2	—	2
Walker	—	—	—	—	—	—	—	—	—	—	—	—	—	1	—	1
Macfarren	—	—	—	—	—	—	—	—	—	—	—	—	—	1	—	1
Wade	—	—	—	—	—	—	—	—	—	—	—	—	—	1	1	2
Logan	—	—	—	—	—	—	—	—	—	—	—	—	—	1	—	1
Lacy	—	—	—	—	—	—	—	—	—	—	—	—	—	—	4	4
Fitzball	—	—	—	—	—	—	—	—	—	—	—	—	—	—	2	2
Napier	—	—	—	—	—	—	—	—	—	—	—	—	—	—	2	2
Buckstone	—	—	—	—	—	—	—	—	—	—	—	—	—	—	1	1
Peake	—	—	—	—	—	—	—	—	—	—	—	—	—	—	1	1

*Includes known revivals and all premieres with nine or more performances but excludes most LYC/EOH productions.

Appendix 16

Operas by Librettist/Dramatist: With Composer

By year of premiere or earliest known revival; asterisk indicates a published libretto (*National Union Catalog*)

ANONYMOUS: 1786: *The Peruvian* (Hook). 1819: *Arthur and Emmeline* (see Garrick). 1821: *Dirce* (Horn and Braham). 1826: *The Oracle* (Hawes).
ARNE (words and music): 1787: **Artaxerxes*.
ARNOLD, S.J.: 1794: *Auld Robin Grey* (Dr. Arnold). 1796: **The Shipwreck* (Dr. Arnold). 1797: *The Irish Legacy* (Dr. Arnold). 1809: **Up All Night* (King). 1810: **The Maniac* (Bishop). 1811: *The Americans* (King and Braham). 1812: **The Devil's Bridge* (Horn and Braham); *The Privateer* (Dr. Arnold). 1815: *The Unknown Guest* (Kelly and Braham); **The King's Proxy* (Cooke). 1825: *Broken Promises* (Hawes); *Tarrare* (Hawes/Salieri). 1828: *Tit for Tat* (Hawes/Mozart).
BATE DUDLEY: 1791: **The Woodman* (Shield). 1794: **Travellers in Switzerland* (Shield).
BEAZLEY: 1824: **Philandering* (Horn). 1826: *The White Lady* (Cooke/Boieldieu).
BENTLEY: 1788: **The Prophet* (Shield).
BICKERSTAFFE: 1786: **Love in a Village* (Arne). 1789: **Thomas and Sally* (Arne). 1798: *The Maid of the Mill* (Dr. Arnold). 1816: **Lionel and Clarissa* (C. Dibdin).
BOADEN: 1793: *Ozmyn and Doraxa* (Attwood).
BRANDON: 1808: **Kais* (Reeve and Braham).
BROME, et al.: 1813: **The Jovial Crew* (ballads).
BROOKE: 1784: **Rosina* (Shield). 1788: **Marian* (Shield).
BUCKSTONE: 1830: **Don Juan* (Hawes/Mozart).
BURGES[S]: 1810: *Tricks Upon Travellers* (Horn and Reeve).
BURGOYNE: 1786: **Richard Coeur de Lion* (T. Linley the Elder/Grétry). 1816: **The Lord of the Manor* (Jackson).
CADELL: 1792: *Orpheus and Eurydice* (past. Gluck).
CHERRY: 1806: **The Travellers* (Corri). 1807: **Peter the Great* (Jouve). 1808: *In and Out of Tune* (Corri).
COBB: 1785: **Strangers at Home* (Linley, Sr.). 1788: **Love in the East* (Linley, Sr.); **The Doctor and the Apothecary* (Storace). 1789: **The Haunted Tower* (Storace). 1791: **The Siege of Belgrade* (Storace). 1792: **The Pirates* (Storace). 1794: **The Cherokee* (Storace). 1798: **Ramah Droog* (Mazzinghi and Reeve). 1800: **Paul and Virginia* (Mazzinghi and

Reeve). 1802: *A House to be Sold (Kelly). 1803: *The Wife of Two Husbands (Mazzinghi).

COLMAN the Elder: 1815: *Comus (Arne, Bishop, Shaw?).

COLMAN the Younger: 1785: Turk and No Turk (Dr. Arnold). 1787: *Inkle and Yarico (Dr. Arnold). 1791: The Surrender of Calais (Dr. Arnold). 1796: *The Iron Chest (Storace). 1798: *Blue-Beard (Kelly). 1799: *Feudal Times (Kelly). 1803: *Love Laughs at Locksmiths (Kelly). 1806: *The Forty Thieves (Kelly). 1822: *The Law of Java (Bishop).

CUMBERLAND: 1793: The Armourer (Warner). 1808: *The Jew of Mogadore (Kelly).

DIBDIN, C.I.M.: 1814: *The Farmer's Wife (Bishop, Davy, Reeve, Addison).

DIBDIN, C. (words and music): 1785: Liberty Hall. 1806: The Broken Gold

DIBDIN, T.: 1799: *Naval Pillar (Moorehead). 1800: *Of Age Tomorrow (Kelly); *Il Bondocani (Attwood and Moorehead). 1802: *The Cabinet (Reeve, Moorehead, Davy, Braham); *Family Quarrels (Moorehead, Reeve, Davy, Braham). 1803: *The English Fleet (Braham). 1804: *Thirty-Thousand (Davy, Reeve, Braham). 1806: The White Plume (Reeve). 1807: *Two Faces Under a Hood (Shield, Reeve, Braham). 1813: *Who's to have Her? (Reeve and Whittaker). 1818: *Zuma (Bishop and Braham). 1822: *Morning, Noon and Night (Perry).

DIMOND: 1803: *The Hero of the North (Kelly). 1805: *Youth, Love, and Folly (Kelly). 1806: *Adrian and Orrila (Attwood and Kelly). 1809: *The Young Hussar (Kelly). 1810: *Gustavus Vasa (Kelly). 1811: *The Peasant Boy (Kelly). 1815: *Brother and Sister (Bishop and Reeve). 1817: *The Conquest of Taranto (Kelly). 1822: The Pirate (Cooke). 1824: *Native Land (Bishop). 1825: *Abou Hassan (Cooke/Weber). 1827: *The Seraglio (Kramer/Mozart); Isidore de Merida (Storace, Cooke, Braham). 1829: *The Nymph of the Grotto (Liverati and Lee).

EARLE: 1817: Outwitted at Last (Lanza).

FAWCETT (with Terry): 1818: *The Barber of Seville (Bishop/Rossini, Paisiello).

FITZBALL: 1829: The Robber's Bride (Hawes/Ries); The Night before the Wedding (Bishop/Boieldieu). 1830: *Ninetta (Bishop/Rossini).

GARRICK: 1815: *Cymon (M. Arne, Bishop, Shaw?).

GAY: 1802: *The Beggar's Opera (mostly ballads arr. Pepusch).

HAMILTON: 1817: *Elphi Bey (Attwood, Horn, Smart). 1820: *David Rizzio (Cooke, Attwood, Braham, W. [?] Reeve).

HOARE: 1790: *No Song, No Supper (Storace). 1791: The Cave of Triphonius (Storace). 1792: *Dido, Queen of Carthage (Storace). 1793: *My Grandmother (Storace); *The Prize (Storace). 1795: *The Three and the Deuce (Storace). 1796: *Mahmoud (Storace; Kelly); *Lock and Key (Shield). 1797: A Friend in Need (Kelly); *The Italian Villagers (Shield). 1798:

The Captive of Spilburg (Dussek and Kelly). 1801: *Chains of the Heart* (Mazzinghi and Reeve).

HOLCROFT: 1785: *The Choleric Fathers* (Shield). 1799: *The Old Cloathsman* (Attwood). 1801: *The Escapes* (Attwood/Cherubini). 1819: *The Marriage of Figaro* (*Follies of a Day*) (Bishop/Mozart).

HOLMAN: 1796: *Abroad and at Home* (Shield). 1799: *The Red-Cross Knights* (Attwood). 1800: *What a Blunder!* (Davy).

HOOK, T.: 1795: *Jack of Newbury* (J. Hook). 1805: *The Soldier's Return* (J. Hook). 1808: *The Siege of San Quintin* (J. Hook). 1809: *Killing No Murder* (J. Hook); *Safe and Sound* (J. Hook).

HOULTON: 1800: *Wilmore Castle* (J. Hook).

HURLSTONE: 1792: *Just in Time* (Carter).

JEPHSON: 1785: *The Campaign* (Tenducci).

KEMBLE: 1789: *The Tempest* (T. Linley the Younger). 1794: *Lodoiska* (Storace).

KENNEY: 1804: *Matrimony* (King). 1807: *False Alarms* (King and Braham). 1810: *Oh! This Love* (King). 1823: *Sweethearts and Wives* (Cooke Whittaker, Nathan, Perry). 1824: *The Alcaid* (Nathan). 1825: *The Wedding Present* (Horn).

KERR (with Logan?): 1824: *Der Freischütz* (Hawes/Weber).

LACY (words and music): 1827: *The Turkish Lovers* (ad. Rossini). 1828: *Love in Wrinkles* (ad. Fétis). 1829: *The Maid of Judah* (ad. Rossini). 1830: *Cinderella* (ad. Rossini).

LINLEY, W. (words and music): 1797: *The Honey Moon*.

LOGAN (with Kerr?): 1824: *Der Freischütz* (Hawes/Weber).

MACFARREN: 1826: *Malvina* (Cooke).

MACNALLY: 1785: *Robin Hood* (Shield). 1786: *Richard Coeur de Lion* (Shield).

MERRY: 1792: *The Magician No Conjurer* (Mazzinghi).

MONCRIEFF: 1820: *Giovanni in London* (Anon./Mozart).

MOORE: 1811: *M.P.* (Moore with Horn).

MORTON: 1793: *The Children in the Wood* (Dr. Arnold). 1811: *The Knight of Snowdoun* (Bishop). 1816: *The Slave* (Bishop).

NAPIER: 1827: *The Freebooters* (Hawes/Paer).

O'KEEFFE: 1785: *Fontainbleau* (Shield). 1786: *The Siege of Curazola* (Dr. Arnold). 1787: *The Farmer* (Shield). 1788: *The Highland Reel* (Shield). 1789: *The Castle of Andalusia* (Dr. Arnold). 1793: *Sprigs of Laurel* (Shield).

PAYNE: 1823: *Clari* (Bishop). 1827: *The White Maid* (anon./Boieldieu).

PEAKE: 1829: *The Spring Lock* (Rodwell).

PEARCE: 1792: *Hartford-Bridge* (Shield). 1793: *The Midnight Wanderers* (Shield). 1794: *Netley Abbey* (Shield).

PLANCHÉ: 1822: *The Fair Gabrielle (Livius and G. Reeve); *Maid Marian (Bishop). 1823: *Cortez (Bishop). 1824: *Der Freischütz (Livius/Weber). 1826: *Oberon (Weber). 1827: *The Rencontre (Bishop). 1828: Carron Side (Liverati). 1829: Der Vampyr (Marschner). 1830: The National Guard (Cooke/Auber); Hofer (Bishop/Rossini).
POCOCK: 1813: *The Miller and his Men (Bishop). 1814: *John of Paris (Bishop/Boieldieu). 1817: *The Libertine (Bishop/Mozart). 1818: *Rob Roy Macgregor (Davy). 1826: *(also complete MS at Brit.Libr.) Peveril of the Peak (Horn).
RAMSAY: 1817: *The Gentle Shepherd (ballads).
REYNOLDS: 1790: *The Crusade (Shield). 1805: *Out of Place (Reeve and Braham). 1806: Arbitration (Lanza); The Deserts of Arabia (Lanza). 1808: *The Exile (Mazzinghi and Bishop). 1812: *The Virgin of the Sun (Bishop). 1815: A Midsummer Night's Dream (Bishop). 1817: The Duke of Savoy (Bishop). 1819: The Comedy of Errors (Bishop). 1820: Twelfth Night (Bishop). 1821: The Tempest (Bishop); Two Gentlemen of Verona (Bishop). 1824: The Merry Wives of Windsor (Bishop).
ROSE: 1792: *The Prisoner (Attwood).
ST. JOHN: 1789: *The Island of St. Marguerite (Shaw).
SCAWEN: 1790: *New Spain (Dr. Arnold).
SHERIDAN: 1791: *The Duenna (T. Linleys).
SIDDONS (ad. Arnold): 1809: The Russian Impostor (Addison).
SOANE: 1824: *Der Freischütz (Bishop/Weber). 1825: Preciosa (Hawes/Weber). 1826: *Aladdin (Bishop).
SOMERSET: 1828: Sylvania (Blewitt/Weber).
TERRY: 1816: *Guy Mannering (Bishop, Davy, Cooke, Braham, Whittaker). 1818: (with Fawcett) *The Barber of Seville (Bishop/Rossini/Paisiello).
THOMPSON: 1813: Godolphin (Horn). 1816: *Oberon's Oath (Parry).
TOBIN: 1816: *Your's or Mine? (Shield). 1819: The Fisherman's Hut (G. Reeve).
WADE (words and music): 1826: The Two Houses of Grenada (sel. Braham). 1828: The Pirate of Genoa (ad. Weigl).
WALKER: 1825: The Fall of Algiers (Bishop).
WALTER II: 1789: Hide and Seek (Crouch).
WARD: 1809: The Circassian Bride (Bishop).

Appendix 17

Operas By Composer: With Librettist/Dramatist

By year of premiere or earliest known revival; asterisk indicates published score, usualy vocal (*National Union Catalog*)

ADDISON: 1809: *The Russian Impostor* (Arnold). 1814: *The Farmer's Wife* (C.I.M. Dibdin).
ANONYMOUS: 1792: *Orpheus and Eurydice* (Cadell). 1820: *Giovanni in London* (Moncrieff). 1827: *The White Maid* (Payne). 1829: *Der Vampyr* (Planché).
ARNE, M.: 1815: **Cymon* (Garrick).
ARNE, T.: 1786: **Love in a Village* (Bickerstaffe). 1787: **Artaxerxes*. 1789: **Thomas and Sally* (Bickerstaffe). 1815: **Comus* (Colman the Elder). 1819: **Arthur and Emmeline* (Garrick/Anon.).
ARNOLD, Dr.: 1785: **Turk and No Turk* (Colman the Younger). 1786: **The Siege of Curazola* (O'Keeffe). 1787: **Inkle and Yarico* (Colman the Younger). 1788: **The Castle of Andalusia* (O'Keeffe). 1790: **New Spain* (Scawen). 1791: **The Surrender of Calais* (Colman the Younger). 1793: **Children in the Wood* (Morton). 1794: **Auld Robin Grey* (Arnold). 1796: **The Shipwreck* (Arnold). 1797: *The Irish Legacy* (Arnold). 1798: **The Maid of the Mill* (Bickerstaffe). 1812: *The Privateer* (Arnold).
ATTWOOD: 1792: **The Prisoner* (Rose). 1793: *Oxmyn and Doraxa* (Boaden). 1799: **The Old Cloathsman* (Holcroft); **The RedCross Knights* (Holman). 1800: **Il Bondocani* (T. Dibdin). 1801: **The Escapes* (Holcroft). 1806: *Adrian and Orrila* (Dimond). 1817: **Elphi Bey* (Hamilton). 1820: *David Rizzio* (Hamilton).
BISHOP: 1808: **The Exile* (Reynolds). 1809: **The Circassian Bride* (Ward). 1810: **The Maniac* (Arnold). 1811: *The Knight of Snowdoun* (Morton). 1812: **The Virgin of the Sun* (Reynolds). 1813: **The Miller and his Men* (Pocock). 1814: **John of Paris* (Pocock); **The Farmer's Wife* (C.M.I. Dibdin). 1815: *Comus* (Colman the Elder); *Cymon* (Garrick); **Brother and Sister* (Dimond). 1816: *The Slave* (Morton); *Guy Mannering* (Terry); **A Midsummer Night's Dream* (Reynolds). 1817: *The Duke of Savoy* (Reynolds); **The Libertine* (Pocock). 1818: **The Barber of Seville* (Terry); **Zuma* (T. Dibdin). 1819: **The Comedy of Errors* (Reynolds); **The Marriage of Figaro* (Holcroft). 1820: *Twelfth Night* (Reynolds). 1821: *The Tempest* (Reynolds); **Two Gentlemen of Verona* (Reynolds). 1822: **The Law of Java* (Colman the Younger); **Maid Marian* (Planché). 1823: **Clari* (Payne); **Cortez* (Planché). 1824: *The Merry Wives of*

Windsor (Reynolds); **Native Land* (Dimond); **Der Freischütz* (Soane); *The Fall of Algiers* (Walker). 1826: **Aladdin* (Soane). 1827: **Rencontre* (Planché). 1829: *The Night Before the Wedding* (Fitzball). 1830: *Ninetta* (Fitzball); *Hofer* (Planché).

BLEWITT: 1828: *Sylvania* (Somerset).

BRAHAM: 1802: **The Cabinet* (T. Dibdin); *Family Quarrels* (T. Dibdin). 1803: **The English Fleet* (T. Dibdin). 1804: *Thirty-Thousand* (T. Dibdin). 1805: *Out of Place* (Reynolds). 1807: *Two Faces under a Hood* (T. Dibdin); **False Alarms* (Kenney). 1808: **Kais* (Brandon). 1811: *The Americans* (Arnold). 1812: *The Devil's Bridge* (Arnold). 1815: *The Unknown Guest* (Arnold). 1816: *Guy Mannering* (Terry). 1818: **Zuma* (T. Dibdin). 1820: *David Rizzio* (Hamilton). 1821: *Dirce* (Anon.). 1826: *The Two Houses of Granada* (Wade). 1827: *Isidore de Merida* (Dimond).

BURGHERSH: 1830: *Catherine*.

CARTER: 1792: **Just in Time* (Hurlstone).

COOKE: 1815: *The King's Proxy* (Arnold). 1816: *Guy Mannering* (Terry). 1820: *David Rizzio* (Hamilton). 1822: *The Pirate* (Dimond). 1823: *Sweethearts and Wives* (Kenney). 1825: *Abou Hassan* (Dimond). 1826: **Malvina* (Macfarren); *The White Lady* (Beazley). 1827: *Isidore de Merida* (Dimond). 1830: *The National Guard* (Planché).

CORRI: 1802: **The Cabinet* (T. Dibdin). 1806: **The Travellers* (Cherry). 1808: *In and Out of Tune* (Cherry).

CROUCH: 1789: *Hide and Seek* (Walter II).

DAVY: 1800: **What a Blunder!* (Holman). 1802: **The Cabinet* (T. Dibdin); *Family Quarrels* (T. Dibdin). 1804: *Thirty-Thousand* (Dibdin). 1814: *The Farmer's Wife* (C.M.I. Dibdin). 1816: *Guy Mannering* (Terry). 1818: *Rob Roy Macgregor* (Pocock).

DIBDIN, C.: 1785: **Liberty Hall*. 1806: *The Broken Gold*. 1816: **Lionel and Clarissa* (Bickerstaffe).

DUSSEK: 1798: *The Captive of Spilburg* (Hoare).

HAWES: 1824: **Der Freischütz* (Logan). 1825: *Broken Promises* (Arnold); *Tarrare* (Arnold); *Preciosa* (Soane). 1826: *The Oracle* (Anon.). 1827: *The Freebooters* (Napier). 1828: *Tit for Tat* (Arnold). 1829: *The Robber's Bride* (Fitzball). 1830: *Don Juan* (Buckstone).

HOOK, J.: 1786: **The Peruvian* (Anon.). 1795: **Jack of Newbury* (T. Hook). 1800: *Wilmore Castle* (Houlton). 1805: **The Soldier's Return* (T. Hook). 1808: *The Siege of San Quintin* (T. Hook). 1809: *Killing No Murder* (T. Hook); *Safe and Sound* (T. Hook.).

HORN: 1810: *Tricks upon Travellers* (Burges). 1811: *M.P.* (Moore), with Moore. 1812: **The Devil's Bridge* (Arnold). 1813: *Godolphin* (Thompson). 1817: *Elphi Bey* (Hamilton). 1821: *Dirce* (Anon.). 1824:

Philandering (Beazley). 1825: *The Wedding Present* (Kenney). 1826: *(also MS in Brit.Libr.) *Peveril of the Peak* (Pocock).
JACKSON: 1816: **The Lord of the Manor* (Burgoyne).
JOUVE: 1807: *Peter the Great* (Cherry).
KELLY: 1797: **A Friend in Need* (Hoare). 1798: *The Captive of Spilburg* (Hoare); **Blue-Beard* (Colman the Younger). 1799: **Feudal Times* (Colman the Younger). 1800: **Of Age Tomorrow* (T. Dibdin). 1802: **A House to be Sold* (Cobb). 1803: **Love Laughs at Locksmiths* (Colman the Younger); *Hero of the North* (Dimond). 1805: **Youth, Love, and Folly* (Dimond). 1806: *Adrian and Orrila* (Dimond); *Forty Thieves* (Colman the Younger). 1807: *The Young Hussar* (Dimond). 1808: *The Jew of Mogadore* (Cumberland). 1810: *Gustavus Vasa* (Dimond). 1811: **The Peasant Boy* (Dimond). 1815: *The Unknown Guest* (Arnold). 1817: *The Conquest of Taranto* (Dimond).
KING: 1804: *Matrimony* (Kenney). 1807: **False Alarms* (Kenney). 1809: **Up All Night* (Arnold). 1810: *Oh! This Love* (Kenney). 1811: *The Americans* (Arnold).
KRAMER: 1827: **The Seraglio* (Dimond).
LACY (words and music): 1827: *The Turkish Lovers*. 1828: *Love in Wrinkles*. 1829: **Maid of Judah*. 1830: *Cinderella*.
LANZA: 1806: *Arbitration* (Reynolds); *The Deserts of Arabia* (Reynolds). 1817: *Outwitted at Last* (Earle).
LEE: 1829: *The Nymph of the Grotto* (Dimond).
LINLEY, T. the Elder: 1785: **Strangers at Home* (Cobb). 1786: *Richard Coeur de Lion* (Burgoyne). 1788: **Love in the East* (Cobb). 1791: **The Duenna* (Sheridan).
LINLEY, T. the Younger: 1789: **The Tempest* (Kemble). 1791: **The Duenna* (Sheridan).
LINLEY, W. (words and music): 1797: *The Honey Moon*.
LIVERATI: 1828: *Carron Side* (Planché). 1729: *The Nymph of the Grotto* (Dimond).
LIVIUS: 1822: *Fair Gabrielle* (Planché). 1824: **Der Freischütz* (Planché).
MAZZINGHI: 1792: *Orpheus and Eurydice* (Cadell); **The Magician no Conjurer* (Merry). 1798: **Ramah Droog* (Cobb). 1800: **Paul and Virginia* (Cobb). 1801: **Chains of the Heart* (Hoare). 1803: *The Wife of Two Husbands* (Cobb). 1808: **The Exile* (Reynolds).
MOORE (words and music): 1811: **M.P.* (with Horn).
MOOREHEAD: 1799: **Naval Pillar* (T. Dibdin). 1800: **Il Bondocani* (T. Dibdin). 1802: **The Cabinet* (T. Dibdin); *Family Quarrels* (T. Dibdin).
NATHAN: 1823: *Sweethearts and Wives* (Kenney). 1824: *Alcaid* (Kenney).
PARRY: 1816: *Oberlin's Oath* (Thompson).

PEPUSCH (accompaniments): 1802: *The Beggar's Opera* (Gay).
PERRY: 1822: *Morning, Noon, and Night* (T. Dibdin). 1823: *Sweethearts and Wives* (Kenney).
REEVE, G.: 1819(?): *The Fisherman's Hut* (Tobin). 1822: *The Fair Gabrielle* (Planché).
REEVE, W.: 1798: **Ramah Droog* (Cobb). 1800: **Paul and Virginia* (Cobb). 1801: **Chains of the Heart* (Hoare). 1802: **The Cabinet* (T. Dibdin); *Family Quarrels* (T. Dibdin). 1804: **Thirty-Thousand* (T. Dibdin). 1805: *Out of Place* (Reynolds). 1806: *The White Plume* (T. Dibdin). 1807: *Two Faces under a Hood* (T. Dibdin). 1808: **Kais* (Brandon). 1810: *Tricks upon Travellers* (Burges). 1813: *Who's To Have Her?* (T. Dibdin). 1814: *The Farmer's Wife* (C.M.I. Dibdin). 1815: *Brother and Sister* (Dimond).
RODWELL: 1829: *The Spring Lock* (Peake).
SHAW: 1789: **The Island of St. Marguerite* (St. John).
SHIELD: 1785: **The Choleric Fathers* (Holcroft); **Robin Hood* (Macnally); **Fontainbleau* (O'Keeffe). 1786: *Richard Coeur de Lion* (Macnally). 1787: **The Farmer* (O'Keeffe). 1788: **The Highland Reel* (O'Keeffe); **The Prophet* (Bentley); **Marian* (Brooke). 1790: **The Crusade* (Reynolds). 1791: **The Woodman* (Bate Dudley). 1793: **Hartford-Bridge* (Pearce). 1793: **The Sprigs of Laurel* (O'Keeffe); **The Midnight Wanderers* (Pearce). 1794: **Netley Abbey* (Pearce); **Travellers in Switzerland* (Bate Dudley). 1796: **At Home and Abroad* (Holman); **Lock and Key* (Hoare). 1797: *The Italian Villagers* (Hoare). 1807: *Two Faces under a Hood* (T. Dibdin). 1816: *Your's or Mine* (Tobin). 1820: *(also MS in Brit.Libr.) Rosina* (Brooke).
SMART: 1817: **Elphi Bey* (Hamilton).
STORACE: 1788: **The Doctor and the Apothecary* (Cobb). 1789: **The Haunted Tower* (Cobb). 1790: *(also MS in Brit.Libr.) No Song, No Supper* (Hoare). 1791: *The Cave of Triphonius* (Hoare); **The Siege of Belgrade* (Cobb). 1792: *Dido* (Hoare); **The Pirates* (Cobb). 1793: **My Grandmother* (Hoare); **The Prize* (Hoare). 1794: **The Cherokee* (Cobb); **Lodoiska* (Kemble). 1795: **The Three and the Deuce* (Hoare). 1796: **Mahmoud* (Hoare); **The Iron Chest* (G. Colman the Younger). 1827: *Isidore de Merida* (Dimond).
TENDUCCI: 1785: *The Campaign* (Jephson).
WADE (words and music): 1826: *The Two Houses of Grenada*. 1828: *The Pirate of Genoa*.
WARNER: 1793: *The Armourer* (Cumberland).
WEBER: 1826: *Oberon* (Planché).
WHITTAKER: 1813: *Who's To Have Her?* (T. Dibdin). 1816: *Guy Mannering* (Terry). 1823: *Sweethearts and Wives* (Kenney).

Appendix 18

English Adaptations:
With Composer and Arranger

1786: Grétry, *Richard Coeur de Lion*: *Richard Coeur de Lion* (arr?).
1788: Ditters, *Doktor und Apotheker*: *The Doctor and the Apothecary* (Storace).
1792: Gluck pastiche *Orfeo*: *Orpheus and Eurydice* (arr.?).
1794: Cherubini, *Lodoïska*: *Lodoiska* (Storace).
1801: Cherubini, *Les deux journées*: *The Escapes* (Attwood).
1814: Boieldieu, *Jean de Paris*: *John of Paris* (Bishop).
1817: Mozart, *Don Giovanni*: *The Libertine* (Bishop).
1818: Rossini/Paisiello, *Il Barbiere di Siviglia*: *The Barber of Seville* (Bishop).
1819: Mozart, *Le Nozze di Figaro*: *The Marriage of Figaro* (Bishop)
1824: Weber, *Der Freischütz*: *Der Freischutz* (Hawes; Livius; Bishop).
1825: Weber, *Abou Hassan* (Cooke); *Preciosa* (Hawes);
Salieri, *Tarare*: *Tarrare* (Hawes).
1826: Winter, *Das Unterrochene Opferfest*: *The Oracle* (Hawes);
Boieldieu, *La Dame Blanche*: *The White Lady* (Cooke).
1827: Rossini, *Il Turco in Italia*: *The Turkish Lovers* (Lacy);
Paer, *I Fuorusciti di Firenze*: *The Freebooters* (Hawes);
Mozart, *Die Entführung aus dem Serail*: *The Seraglio* (Kramer).
1828: Mozart, *Così fan Tutte*: *Tit for Tat* (Hawes);
Weber, *Sylvania* (Blewitt);
Weigl, *Gli Amori Mariani*: *The Pirate of Genoa* (Wade);
Fétis, *La Vieille*: *Love in Wrinkles* (Lacy).
1829: Ries, *Die Rauberbraut*: *The Robber's Bride* (Hawes);
Marschner, *Der Vampyr* (arr.?);
Boieldieu, *Les Deux Nuits*: *The Night Before the Wedding* (Bishop).
1830: Auber, *La Fiancée*: *The National Guard* (Cooke);
Rossini, *La Gazza Ladra*: *Ninetta* (Bishop); *Cenerentola*: *Cinderella* (Lacy); *Guillaume Tell*: *Hofer* (Bishop);
Mozart, *Don Giovanni*: *Don Juan* (Hawes).

Appendix 19

The Minor Singers

These singers are here arranged chronologically, like the major singers, according to their appearances at the theatres.

THE MALE SINGERS

OF THE MALE SINGERS in this period, John Henry JOHNSTONE (1749–1828), a tenor, had one of the longest stage careers though he was never an outstanding singer. Born in Ireland, he joined the cavalry early on, but by 1773 he was singing in Dublin's Smock Alley Theatre and remained on the Irish stage for seven years. He came to Covent Garden in 1783 and sang there until 1802, when he switched to Drury Lane. Although he appeared on stage in 1820, he all but disappears from press notices after 1808. His greatest roles were of comic Irishmen, and in *Campaign* (1785), his performance bore "strong marks of native and characteristic humour" (T). As Edwin in *Robin Hood* the same year, he sang both humorous and pathetic songs "with peculiar grace" (T), and in 1786 he was much applauded for his Blondel in Macnally's *Richard Coeur de Lion*. As the male lead in *Rosina* (1788), he displayed a large "share of skill and taste in giving the songs of Edward," and he sang a duet with Mrs. Billington "most exquisitely" (LC). In *Inkle and Yarico* he "would have been more at home in Inkle, could he banish the frequent smile which sits rather ungracefully on the prudent trader" (T). That he could also hold his own in serious opera, however, is evident in the *Times* review of *Artaxerxes* two days later, in which they noted that the cast "might be considerably improved" with Johnstone as Rimenes. The next month he appeared as Sandy in *Highland Reel*, in which he "had a very elegant melody allotted to him, which he sung with much taste" (LC; H). But he was rapped for forgetting some of his lines in a 1789 revival of *Castle of Andalusia* (T). In 1792 a number of his airs "very happily adapted to the character" were encored in *Just in Time* (C), and the next year, in the title role of the *Armourer*, he "rendered the character interesting, though he delivered the words . . . with more than necessary precipitancy" (D). In *Netley Abbey* (1794), as a fiddling barber—"a kind of Irish Tully at second hand"—he "had an Hiberian air, deservedly encored, in which the accompaniments were very happily adapted to the 'tune of his fiddle'" (T). He had two encores in *Matrimony* (1804) and received special praise in the *Soldier's Return* (1805). He last comes to notice in the *Jew of Magadore* (1808), in which only the lead "makes any attempt at character: Mr. Johnstone, indeed, acts an 'Irishman', but this Irishman is a national, not an individual character, and differs in no respect from the Irishmen who have so long kept possession of our stage" (C). Two songs were "full of drollery well suited to the character, and were given with admirable effect by Mr. Johnstone" (M). The press apparently took no notice of his "fine falsetto" (Kelly, I, 293).

John QUICK (1748–1831), a comedian who played in the provinces, came to the Little Theatre in 1767, but most of his career (he retired in 1798) was at Drury Lane. He was cited for his performance in the *Armourer* (1793), when "he was frequently interrupted by applause, due both for what the author has done for him and to what he has done for the author" (H).

Thomas BLANCHARD, Jr., first on stage in 1783, made a good appearance as Hodge in *Love in a Village* (1787), and in *Marian* (1793) "his 'Patty Clover' will probably be as popular as his 'Whistling Ploughboy'" (LC); but in *Midnight Wanderers* (1793) "his song we should wish to see omitted" (H). He ceased performing the next year.

Richard SUETT (c. 1758–1805) sang in the Westminister Abbey choir at St. Paul's and, after 1769, at Ranelegh Gardens. Because of his musical skills and training (he even wrote some of his own songs), he was particularly successful in English opera. After several years in the provinces, he joined Drury Lane in 1780, singing there and at the Little Theatre the rest of his life. He was very popular in low-comedy parts but was seldom cited in the press; Boaden tells us he drank too much. He "made the most" of his lead in *Auld Robin Grey* (1794) (T), was a hit in *My Grandmother* (1793) (Fiske), and apparently contributed one of his own songs to the *Cave of Triphonius* (LC, 1791). In *Three and the Deuce* (1795), the last we hear of him, he was "to be admired for his musical adroitness" (OPA).

John EDWIN the Younger (c. 1769–1805), son of a notable theatrical singer, was playing comic roles in the Little Theatre by 1778. He was warmly welcomed as Jeremy in *Fontainbleau* (1785), where his "antient Briton was truly laughable, and his imitative song excellent" (H); Parke called his song "In London my life is a ring of delight" a "ne plus ultra of comic singing." As Pedro in *Choleric Fathers* the same year, he was "highly entertaining in a ludicrous duet . . . with the mock cantabile" (H). His character of Cricola in the *Siege of Curzola* (1786) was "well sustained" (C), and as Trudge in *Inkle and Yarico* (1787) he was "perhaps the most incomparable comic actor now on the stage"; all his songs were encored (UR). As Gubbins in the *Battle of Hexam* (1789) he performed the best comic singing "on any stage" (Parke). Yet we hear nothing further of him.

Thomas KING (1730–1805), a tenor, ran away as a boy to join a travelling company. He first appeared at Drury Lane in 1748, managed the company for a time after Garrick's death, and sang there almost until his own death. He was author of some farces. He had the lead, Aldobrand, in *Strangers at Home* (1785), but the part "certainly is not a character in his cast" (UR). He was "no actor" as Mandane in *Love in a Village* (1786), and in 1787 the *Herald* complained of his performance in *Artaxerxes*: "His voice is a good tenor,— and if he assumed a little animation—he would be a decent singer." The D.N.B. called him a "fair singer," but there seems little basis for Boaden's assertion that he was equal to Morelli.

A considerably finer actor, if not singer, than any of the above was John "Jack" BANNISTER, Jr. (1760–1836), a bass and son of an actor and singer. He studied painting at the Royal Academy but was soon drawn to the theatre. In 1778 he was performing at the Little Theatre and the next year at Drury Lane, from which he retired in 1815. Hunt called him "the first low comedian of the stage." Although he could not read a note of music, he began to take singing roles in 1784 (Saxe notes he had to have the Covent Garden pianist parrot the songs to him in *Robin Hood*). But he had great range, a fine ear, and was "one of the best comic singers" (Adolphus). Parke called him a fine rich mellow bass. As Lawrence in *Strangers at Home* (1785), he deserved "the first tribute of communication for the uncommon merit displayed by him, not only in the acting of his character, but in his singing of the drunken song" (LC). The next year, in the Burgoyne *Richard Coeur de Lion*, he ably supported his noncomic role of Sir Owen (C). His last song, "Old England," in *Highland Reel* (1788), when he played "Serjeant Jack," was "admirably suited to his powers" (LC). As Edward in the *Haunted Tower* (1789), he "leaves Edwin far behind; last night afforded a specimen, more *comic*, without descending to the Buffoon" (H). The same season, as Jonas in *Island of St. Marguerite*, he "made so much of his several songs, that the audience encored him in every one of them" (UM). His acting was enormously praised as Walter in *Children in the Wood* (1793), but apparently he sang no songs (C; T). His singing and acting as Jack Average in *Cherokee* (1794) were "very superior" (T). He "contributed effectually" (LC) as Cassan in *Mahmoud* (1796). He was encored in *Wilmore Castle* (1800) (P), and in 1805 he was still included among "the greatest part of the vocal powers of Drury Lane" (C, Apr. 24). In 1807 his performance in *False Alarms* was "full of life and spirit" (MM, Jan.)—our last notice of him, though he did not leave the stage until 1815.

William BARRYMORE, né Blewit (1759–1830), who sang the role of Meadows in *Love in a Village* at Drury Lane in 1782, was active at that theatre until 1809 but had only minor roles for many years. When he played Montano in *Strangers at Home* (1785), his stage whiskers kept falling off, but "he went through the rest of his part with very considerable approbation, particularly in his execution of a trumpet song" (UR). In the Burgoyne *Richard Coeur de Lion* (1786), he "did everything to bring Blondel forwards on the dramatic canvas" (C). And as Artabanes at a revival of *Artaxerxes* (1787), "he exceeded by far our expectations" (UR). Yet we hear no more of him.

Thomas SEDGWICK (d. 1803) was a singer and actor, "an ironmonger who discovered he had a voice" (H). He sang in glee clubs, was apparently more of a serious singer than most of our early male performers, and appeared at the Anacreontic and other concerts. In 1787 he made his Drury Lane debut in the trying part of Artabanes in *Artaxerxes*, and the *Register* (Oct. 26) "seldom witnessed a more respectable first appearance, although, in one song he executed rather with more *feeling* than *taste*.... His action wants considerable improvement—the *arms* were stuck to the *sides* like *fixtures*." As Charles in the *Haunted Tower* (1789), he had a fine voice: "He is young enough to cultivate it, and acquires besides a talent for acting" (H). He sang Aristo in *Cave of Trophonius* (1791), and his "Invocation was given in a very capital style indeed" (LC). In 1792 he sang creditably in the all-sung *Dido* and as Pasquil in the *Prisoner* (T). Though he was still performing after 1800, we last hear of him as Duncan in Arnold's *Auld Robin Grey* (1794), when "his fine voice added to the vocal strength of the cast, though his demeanor by no means bespoke the 'gracious' Duncan" (T).

Joseph Shepherd MUNDEN (1758–1832) left his law apprenticeship to join a strolling company. In 1790 he began singing at Covent Garden to fill Edwin's roles after his death. Performing there and at the Little Theatre until 1811, he became the most celebrated comedian in London, and at the apex of his career, he knew up to three hundred character parts. He quarreled with the Covent Garden management and shifted to Drury Lane in 1813. He became ill by 1822 and retired two years later. Primarily a comedian, he was also called upon to sing in many of his roles. As the Marquis de Morelle in *Midnight Wanderers* (1793), he was praised "for his execution of two excellent songs," which were encored (T), and he sang well as Friar Domenic in the *Armourer* (D). But one song he sang as Oakland in *Netley Abbey* (1794) "gave great disgust" (T). In *Lock and Key* (1796), "never were an author's thought furthered with finer powers than were exhibited by" him and Fawcett (OPA). As a drunken sailor in *English Fleet* (1803), he "gave all the native whim, spirit, and humour of a British Tar; and his song *I have lived a life of some few years*, was loudly encored" (P). The same year his song "Gaffer Grist" in *Family Quarrels* "produce[d] great effect" (MM). In 1806 he was "very successful" and was encored for his songs in *Forty Thieves* (MM) and *White Plume* (C). As late as 1817, in the *Beggar's Opera*, he gave an "inimitable picture" as Peachum (BS). The following year, in a revival of *Lionel and Clarissa*, "that old and deserving favourite of the town, Munden, played the part of Colonel Oldboy with his accustomed humour. We were highly gratified to observe, that the ravages of time, which have certainly rendered him somewhat infirm in person, have not extended to his spirits, which happily retain their wonted buoyancy" (BS). This is our last notice of him.

A popular bass-singing comedian who also had a long career on the stage despite a poor voice was John FAWCETT (1768–1827). Son of an actor and a pupil of Dr. Arne, he ran away from his apprenticeship to a linen-draper and joined a provincial troupe. He made his London debut in 1791 at Covent Garden, where he remained most of his life. He had a character of "bluff honesty" and a high reputation among actors. He was also, for a time, stage manager of the Little Theatre and later of Covent Garden. He wrote several farces, some in collaboration with Dibdin. In 1794 he delivered a "buffo song" in a "masterly manner" in *Travellers*. In *Irish Mimic* (1795) he was encored in an "excellent" imitation of Giovanni Morelli, and at *Lock and Key* (1796) the *Oracle* declared he "has long had the fame of English burletta singing, superior to all competition." In 1800 Fawcett had the lead—Dashington—in *What a Blunder!* at the Little Theatre and "did honour to his profession by his whim and versatility of powers" (T). As the "Cadi of Bagdat"—the lead in *Bondocani*—he acted well and was "the life and soul of the performance," and his whimsical songs provided "ample scope for his inimitable comic talents" (MM). In 1802 he was "truly great" (C) as Michelli in the *Escapes* and "essentially contributed to the success of the piece" (T). In 1802 he was creditable in the *Cabinet*. In 1806 his comic songs were given "with great humour" (C) in *White Plume*. In *Two Faces* (1807) he was "the most effective character: he played it with infinite spirit" and "with great accuracy both of intonation and articulation" (C; MM).

In his *Critical Essays* that year, Hunt praised Fawcett's "readiness of ear for harmony, and his peculiar skill in burlesque comedy." He was also effective as a Siberian apothecary in the *Exile* (1808). We hear nothing further of him until 1812, when he contributed "all his power" to *Privateer* at the Lyceum (TI), and in 1815 he was effective in *Brother and Sister* (UM). Negative criticism began in 1818, when he was not happy in the role of Doctor Bartolo in the *Barber* (MM). In the *Marriage of Figaro* in 1819 "he personated a drunken gardener" with a voice "which is the perfect antidote to any thing like music" (MM; BS). He was not "congenial" (TI) as

Touchstone in *Twelfth Night* (1820), and he forgot his lines in *Cortez* (1823). But in 1826 he was praised for his function as stage manager at Covent Garden in the production of *Oberon* (T). At his farewell benefit in 1830, the house was "crowded to the roof," and Talfourd (NM, June) declared he "will very long be remembered and talked of as one of the most pleasant and most perfect comedians of our time."

Little is known of Thomas PHILLIPS (1774–1841), a native of Dublin who sang at Bath early on and by 1796 was singing in London (possibly at concerts). He made his English opera debut in *Up All Night* at the Lyceum in 1809, in the role of Young Hartwell. The *Chronicle* wrote that his "fame had excited a lively expectation of superior talents. . . . His voice is flexible and clear, his stile chaste, and he has the never-failing charm of perfect articulation. . . . His defects arise from imitation. . . . He has caught the jerks of Mr. Braham. But we trust he will get confidence in his own powers." Kenrick (MM) was commendatory but thought that "as an actor he has much to learn. . . . His voice is between a tenor and contralto." The next month Phillips appeared as Colonel Risberg in *Russian Impostor* and was "loudly encored" in the ballad "I was on the Wolga rolling dark" (C), but the songs "were not adapted to his style of singing" (MM). He also sang Don Carlos in a revival of the *Duenna*, and the *Universal Magazine* was most enthusiastic. As Lindor in *Safe and Sound*, he "sung with his usual ability and distinct articulation." And the *European* was pleased "because he is a singer who can act." In 1810, still at the Lyceum, he sang well (T; C); Hunt agreed: "He is always playful and pleasing, and occasionally exhibits much feeling; but he should avoid Mr. Braham's style."

In 1811 he appeared in *Peasant Boy* and "expiated his sins of acting, by the taste and science of his singing" (C). But in *M.P.* he was less satisfactory (C). Yet in *Jovial Crew* (1813) his acting was "still more admirable than his singing" (TI). As Egbert in *Godolphin* he "succeeded in some songs but lacked simplicity in others," and he should "cultivate his art under a good Master" (C). Apparently shortly after this he retreated to Crow Street Theatre in Dublin (TI, Feb. 1817). Later he toured America, returning to London and Covent Garden in 1819. On that occasion Hunt remarked that he had "lost much of the voice he had, and he never had much. . . . The passage between his natural voice and falsetto, has that unpleasant gurgle to jump over, which is common enough, but which in Mr. Phillips is more than usually prominent to the ear. He has to slip over it, like a bump on the ice." Phillips turned up once more in 1824, when he sang the count in the *Barber* at the English Opera House. Sterling (T) wrote: "He did once sing better than he does; but even now he sings better than all the singers of which this theatre has had to boast for some years past." But he complained that Phillips was "deficient in the article of teeth. . . . To play a lover, and a singing lover too, without his teeth, here in London, where a man may buy teeth as easily as he may buy a walking stick, is a fault which cannot be overlooked."

Thomas Ludford BELLAMY (1770–1843), a bass, was taught singing by his father and by a Dr. Cooke. Although he sang at Covent Garden for five years (c. 1806–12), there are few references to him; later he sang at Drury Lane. Phillips tells us he was *primo basso* at the Ancient Concerts. When he made his opera debut is unknown: our first reference shows him winning several encores in *Adrian and Orrila* in 1806 (T). He also drew encores in *Peter the Great* in 1807 (EM), and later that year he was in excellent voice in *Two Faces* (C). In 1813 at Drury Lane he appeared in *Godolphin* and "sang with that pure and unadulterous taste which always distinguishes him" (C).

James HILL, a tenor, appeared at Covent Garden in 1798 as one of the Indians in *Ramah Droog*: "We cannot avoid noting a Solo by Mr. Hill, which he executed with much sweetness and melody" (P). This was apparently his London debut, for the *Mirror* tells us he was from Bath: "His voice is a fine counter-tenor; equable, clear, and extremely pleasing. We are no great admirers of *falsetto*, but we must allow him to be the most perfect we ever heard." In 1800, in *Bondocani*, he rendered a song "in a very pleasing manner" (MM). And in 1806, the last we hear of him, he appeared "to great advantage" (C; Cr) as a Scottish chieftan in *White Plume*.

Charles MAT[T]HEWS (1776–1835) was a less important comic actor who could also put over a comic song when required. In Colman's *Love Laughs at Locksmiths* in 1803, "a song by Mathews, in which he anticipates the joys of a farmer, and imitates the noises made by all the animals in a farm-yard, set the House in a roar, and was encored" (P). He sang the "best song" in *Circassian Bride* in 1809 (T). He performed well in *Maniac* the next year, but his one song "did not tell" (EM). In *Farmer's Wife* in 1814, the last we hear of him, he played Dr. Pother, the village apothecary: "He is a sort of person perpetually fond of story-telling. He has a song, describing the transactions of a debating society, which was rather too long; but on being encored, after a considerable struggle, this truly whimsical actor gave one entirely different from the first, except as to the subject, and received unbounded applause" (Cr).

A Mr. PYNE comes to notice in 1812, when he was commended for singing in the *Privateer* at the Lyceum (T). In 1815 he sang a duet "with considerable elegance" in the *King's Proxy* (T). In 1818 he even sang the lead in *Guy Mannering* at Covent Garden, but "his talents as a vocal performer are by no means of the first class [and] is far from being qualified to sustain a leading part in our national operas" (T). Yet this was followed by his performance of Fiorello in the *Barber*, when he "sang some of the exquisite airs with truth and feeling" (LG) and "in a style which entitles him to rank as a singer of the first order" (TI). Yet his name surfaces only once more, in 1823, when he was singing minor roles at Covent Garden.

Another singer who was better as a composer than as a performer was Dublin-born Thomas Simpson COOKE, whom we have already met as a composer. Though he sang tenor roles (in falsetto?), his voice must have been low, as his good friend Phillips called him a bass. His first London appearance was in a revival of Cobb's *Siege of Belgrade* at the Lyceum on July 13, 1813. The following year the *Inquisitor*, in a profile (June, p. 340–42), commented on his very "capable" voice with "much compass and flexibility" and warmly welcomed him to the stage. In 1815, still at the Lyceum/English Opera House, he sang Count Belino in *Devil's Bridge*. The *Times* wrote: "This gentleman sings well—with some powerful tones, derived from nature, and much assiduous cultivation of the vocal gifts she has bestowed. His lower notes have considerable strength. He is rather too much given to decoration in his music. . . . Mr. Cooke's acting is nearly the worst sample on the stage." The *Inquisitor* agreed: "In pity to his feelings we shall say nothing of his acting, and in his singing he does not appear much improved" as Athelwold in *King's Proxy*. Yet in parts he displayed "the most touching tenderness" (C).

That fall he made his Drury Lane debut as Macheath in the *Beggar's Opera*. The *Times* was enthusiastic: "We prefer his Macheath to that of any of his contemporaries. . . . He sung last night in a purer taste, and in a more unadorned style than he often indulges, and we were certainly gainers by the change. . . . [Moreover] he articulates better than any musician we ever heard." They objected only to his "Hibernicisms" when he attempted to speak. The *Inquisitor* agreed, though they thought his acting "still wants more spirit and boldness." But when he appeared in a revival of *Ramah Droog* at the end of 1816, they wrote: "Mr. T. Cooke becomes more tolerable, as we have less opportunity to look or listen for his crudities." He returned to Macheath in 1817 and succeeded, though "we wish Mr. Cooke could 'screw his courage to the sticking place,' and assume a little more spirit; his Macheath at present is far from being a 'gay bold-faced villain'" (BS). At the end of the year, Hazlitt (T) thought he "clipped his words too much" in *Outwitted at Last*. This was not quite his last stage appearance.

From 1820 on he was increasingly in demand as composer and music director at Drury Lane. But in 1824 he "re-ascended from the Orchestra to the Stage, and with his skill and judicious estimate of his own powers gave the music set down for Adolph," in the Drury Lane *Der Freischütz*, "much to the satisfaction of the audience" (E). Sterling (T) agreed: "His scientific knowledge enabled him to execute the difficult music of the part with truth and feeling. His voice appeared to be deeper and mellower than when we last heard him sing"—"many years ago." Ayrton also concurred, but the *London* found him no match for Braham. He continued to sing occasionally until 1835. Phillips admitted Cooke lacked a powerful voice but called him an excellent musician.

John Pritt HARLEY (1786–1858) was apprenticed at first to a linen-draper and later as a law clerk, but he became involved in amateur theatricals in 1802 and was playing at provincial theatres by 1806. In 1815 he made his London debut at the Lyceum/English Opera House, where Arnold hired him for his *Devil's Bridge*. He was praised as a fine commedian then as well as in *Castle of Andalusia* and *King's Proxy* later that year, but first reference to his singing occurred in 1817, when he was hissed (T, Apr. 18). At the close of that year, in *Outwitted at Last*, he was encored in a duet and dance with Mrs. Alsop (T; EM). In 1818 the *Times* thought the production of the *Americans* at the English Opera House was "much indebted to the exertions of Harley" (Planché tells us he "pulled through" many a worthless piece at Drury Lane) and that Harley "sung some comic songs . . . with great humour and vivacity" (C), one of which was heartily encored (EM). In 1820 he was "unexceptionably fortunate in the briskness of Leporello" in *Giovanni in London* (T). He does not appear to have had another singing role again until 1824, when he was commended for a comic song in *Philandering* (C) at Drury Lane, as well as in the *Alcaid* at the Little Theatre (T). He finished off the year as Leopold in a revival of the *Siege of Belgrade*, a character he "admirably sustained," and he held his own in a duet with Miss Stephens (T). The next year he played Zabone in Weber's *Abou Hassan*—"the best character in the opera"—"with much comic excellence" (T), though apparently he did not sing; he also made much of his part in the *Wedding Present* (T). In 1826 he again won plaudits in a Drury Lane revival of the *Devil's Bridge* (T)—our last notice of him. Harley stayed at Drury Lane until 1835, moving that year with Braham to the St. James Theatre. He acted right up to his death, which occurred from a paralyzing stroke as he was making a stage exit.

J. ISAACS, otherwise unknown, made his first London appearance in 1816 in an English Opera House revival of *Up All Night*. The *Times* noted his "extraordinary organic power; and when he had been drilled out of the awkwardness of his manner, he will be a valuable acqusition to the English Opera." And later they again noted he "sung with great force and depth of organ" in a revival of *Castle of Andalusia*. In 1817 he sang with "much effect" (EM) in another revival, the *Siege of Belgrade*, but the *Times* reported: "He has a good voice; but has much to learn, and much to unlearn, before he can take any rank as a singer." In 1818 he sang *Zuma* at Covent Garden and "was encored in one song, but not without much opposition" (BS). He sang well in the *Americans* (C; EM) and was still singing in 1823 in *Clari* and *Cortez*, but in our last notice of him the next year, in the Covent Garden *Freischütz*, he did not seem "to comprehend thoroughly the nature of the music, and therefore did not perform it with confidence and spirit" (Har).

An example of managers pushing nonsingers into singing roles occurred in a revival of Arnold's *Up All Night* (1816), when George BARTLEY (1782–1858), stage manager at the English Opera House, played Admiral Blunt: "It ought to have been recollected that the Admiral had some songs to encounter and that Mr. Bartley had laid in amongst his sea-stock but a very short allowance of voice—and of musical ear still more scanty provision. The consequence was, that the solo songs of the character were spoiled—that the harmonies, where he had to sing in concert, were ruined—and that Mr. Bartley . . . was treated with marks of ill-humour by the audience" (T). Bartley went on to become a first-rate comedian.

Another comedian—a great rustic—occasionally given comic songs was John LISTON (c. 1776–1846); once, for example, he was thrust into the role of Leporello in the *Libertine* (1817), and "the deficiency of his voice was woefully apparent" (BS). But his wife was a beautiful singer and his daughter married composer George Rodwell.

William PEARMAN (1792–?) was a true tenor but never presented any challenge to Braham. Born in Manchester, Pearman was frustrated by his parents' unwillingness to permit him to follow a stage career, so he joined the navy at age fourteen, was wounded at Copenhagen, and retired at age sixteen. By 1810 he was singing nautical songs at Sadler's Wells and was playing small roles in the provinces. He achieved some notice at Newcastle and especially at Bath, where, by 1816, he even "enjoyed an extensive patronage among the politest circles" (TI "Sketch," Aug. 1817). In London, already married, he took some singing lessons from John Addison and made his first appearance at the Little Theatre as Orlando in a revival of the *Cabinet*. The *European* wrote: "This Gentleman possesses a sweet tenor; his lower-tones, firm and musical; and his falsetto good. Braham electrified us by the power of his execution; and after such a master, the attempt at Orlando was daring: but Mr. Pearman seemed determined to be every thing or nothing—and boldly risked his fame on *that* which might establish his claim to metropolitan patronage. He was most favourably received throughout." He also sang that summer at the English Opera House in an opera, *Fire and Water*, and his voice, "though not extremely powerful, is inexpressibly sweet, and has in some degree rescued the theatre from the imputation of being an opera-house without singers" (BS, Sept.). In 1818, in a revival of the *Americans* at the same theatre, he lacked "power for such songs as the 'Death of Nelson,' but some of the subdued, *sottovoce* passages possess peculiar merit" (T). He was "successful as usual" in an afterpiece, *Jealous on all Sides* (T; EM).

At the English Opera House opening of the 1819 season, Pearman was regarded as a "respectable support," but he "cannot be highly prized" as a leading singer (TI, June). Yet in *Jovial Crew* he was encored in three songs, "was in good voice, and sang with taste and feeling" (TI). In a season review that year Hunt called him "a singer with a delicate and sweet voice" and "by no means destitute of feeling" (E, July 12). That fall, he seems to have sung for the first time at a winter theatre: *No Song, No Supper* was produced for him at Drury Lane, and as Frederick he "made no ordinary addition to the vocal strength of this Theatre. Mr. Pearman is a firm, though not a finished singer, and with few pretensions to the graceful deportment of his art" (TI). Following this, he "sustained" the lead, Lord Winlove, in a Covent Garden revival of *Fontainbleau* (T).

In 1820 he was successful in an early version of Planché's *Vampire* (TI, Aug.), but he does not seem to have appeared in 1821. Pearman was very active, however, in 1822, beginning with *Gil Blas* at the English Opera House, when "his acting was tinged with vulgarity" (T; E). And in *Gretna Green*, a melodramatic afterpiece, the *London* noted "a dash of coarseness in his manner. . . . Still, Pearman is the best acting singer on the stage . . . and his voice is of that sound quality which only wants the aid of science to be really excellent." That fall he played Henry in *Fontainbleau* at Covent Garden and sang "tastefully" but should "adhere to the soft and plaintive" songs (T). He also sang Macheath in "a pleasing rather than a bold style" (T). As Young Gamwell in *Maid Marian*, he "sang with considerable feeling" (T), but "scientifically, this singer has much to learn" (E).

In 1823 he sang a small role in *Clari* with "good effect" (H). But Bacon (QMM, V, 265) declared: "Mr. Pearman, at Covent Garden, is a living proof of the dearth of exalted ability." The following year he took the role of

Wilhelm (Randolph) in the Covent Garden *Freischütz*, but "though a singer of much merit" he "is not quite equal to the principal tenor parts of such an opera" (C; T). Ayrton agreed, but the *Gazette* thought "he took considerable pains" with it and the *Examiner* reported he "succeeded very passably." Pearman does not again turn up until 1827, when he "distinguished" himself in *Arthur and Emmeline* (T; NM). He then played Edwards in *Freebooters* and "managed a bounded power with considerable skill and feeling" (E). Talfourd (NM) thought he "sung in a chaste and impressive style." This is our last notice of him. A small man of limited power and range, he never quite fulfilled his potential.

A Mr. THORNE, otherwise unknown, first comes to notice (though it was not his debut) as Captain Fairfield in *Broken Promises* (1825) at the English Opera House, where he "sung two dull songs 'indifferent well;' but he was certainly on the wrong side of the hedge when histrionic talent was dealt out" (EM). The *Literary Chronicle*, however, stated that he "developed, occasionally, a capability to *act*, as well as to sing, that must render him a great acquisition." He then turned to Macheath, when "his voice is peculiarly sweet, and possesses considerable power" (LitC). This was followed by a minor role in *Tarrare*, when he "sang in a very pleasing manner" (C) and "made a *serious* effort to be comical. He succeeded in making us very miserable" (EM). In 1827 he sang in *Arthur and Emmeline* at the English Opera House. He "plays the devil much better than the lover, and subdues his voice to the appropriate growl with commendable boldness" (NM). At the same house the next summer, he sang Guglielmo in *Tit for Tat* and was "extremely successful" (T). He "both sang and acted as if he understood the part and relished the music" (C). The *Examiner* agreed, though found him "sometimes flat." In 1829, in *Der Vampyr*, he executed his part in a very meritorious manner" (LG).

Paul BEDFORD (1792–1871), a bass, got his start in the provinces and in Dublin. In 1824 Bishop brought him to London, where he made his debut at Drury Lane in a revival of *Love in a Village*. The *Times* thought his Giles, "though rather obstreperous, had merit. He has not yet learned the due modulation of his tones, which are, in consequence, sometimes harsh and discordant." He played Bernhard in the Drury Lane *Freischütz*; his acting was "respectable" (E), and his vocal efforts "heightened the general effect of the opera" (NM). He "possesses a good, deep bass voice, and sung in this opera with judgment and apparent knowledge" (Har). In 1825 he sang the Calif in *Abou Hassan*, and the humorous role "was not a little aided by the deep tones and assumed gravity of Mr. Bedford" (T). In 1826 he sang Rashly in a revival of *Lord of the Manor*, but the role "could not have been placed in worse hands" (T); he failed in the same role in 1827 (T) and yet again in 1829 (T). In 1830 he sang Haspinger in *Hofer*, and "in most of the concerted pieces during the evening, Mr. Bedford did good service" (T; C; At). The D.N.B., citing his "portly figure," stated that his later success was principally due to his "vocal capacity" rather than his comic acting.

The press had difficulty making up its collective mind about a Mr. WOOD, a tenor, about whom little is known. He first appeared at Covent Garden in 1828 as the lead in *Native Land*, which was revived for him soon after his debut in *Love in a Village*, and he was repeatedly encored (C). Hunt (*Companion*) wrote: "Mr. Wood has great sweetness of voice, with taste and sensibility; and the sweetness is manly." But Ayrton was more critical: "He has not the true *voce di petto*, for . . . it does not come pure from the chest, but is rather modified in its passage, and . . . partakes of the nasal. His intonation, also, is not perfect." The *New Monthly* praised him in *Carron Side*, but Holmes (At) found that he was "totally unskilled in the management of his voice, sings out of tune, bawls to the galleries, and commits other enormities." And Holmes also reported he did "not seem to understand the music he sings" in the *Freebooters*.

Yet as Ferrando in *Tit for Tat* at the English Opera House, he was, with others, "extremely successful" (T; At), and though the *Chronicle* found him "obviously not much at home," the *Examiner* was thoroughly surprised: "To Mr. Wood we owe our sincere congratulation. . . . He performed his part creditably, and assisted in the concerted pieces with considerable correctness." As Povimante in the *Pirate of Genoa*, he was faulty in execution and in places seemed "a little at a loss" (C), but the *Examiner* was supportive. As Ferdinand in a revival of the *Duenna* he sang his songs very well (T). At Covent Garden in 1829 he sang Sir Huon in a revival of *Oberon*, but the part was "too arduous a character in every respect" for him (E). As Hyppolite in *Nymph of the Grotto*, he executed his music "with an unusual degree of finish," but "his carriage was awkward" (C; T). Yet his articulation was "remarkably distinct" (E), and the *Atlas* declared that "his singing is now more sensible and chaste, as well as in tune, than it used to be." He then sang in *Maid of Judah*; he "was very efficient in his heroic part, and we have seldom heard him sing better" (C). But the *Gazette* thought the music "quite out of his style"; the *Athenaeum* agreed. He then sang the Grand Duke of Florence in *Spring Lock*; he was "extremely pleasant" in his songs and and was encored (C; T). In a brief retrospective, the *New Monthly* (Aug.) thought that, "with a few affectations laid aside," he "would be incomparably the best male ballad singer we have had since Incledon." In 1830 he had a difficult role—Adolphe, the lover in *Ninetta*—and though he did his best, "he was many times sadly flat" (E). He followed this with another difficult role—the prince in *Cinderella*—but was "not effective" and again sang "sadly out of tune" (E).

One G. PENSON, also unknown, seems to have made his debut as Figaro at the English Opera House in 1826 and was "much approved" (E, Oct. 29). He later sang Sherasmin in *Oberon* at Covent Garden and was "very lively, and made more both of the singing and acting of the part than either of his predecessors" (C). "His voice and science gave great value to several pieces," and he "cannot fail to be of great assistance in operas generally, to the theatre" (T, Nov. 20). At the English Opera House in 1827, "Gianni, the merry talkative servant" in *Freeboothers* "was represented in a lively and pleasant manner by Mr. G. Penson. He gave the *buffa* recitative and air, 'Adieu: adieu: my beauty' not only with great comic force, but with very considerable musical skill" (T; E; NM). But as Osmyn in the *Seraglio*, he was "altogether inadequate to the character" (Har). In 1828, as Solfeggio, a deaf music-master in *Pirate of Genoa*, he "employed both his comic and vocal powers to some purpose" (T). He "astonished us with the richness of humour he threw into the part. He looked perfectly old and infatuated" (At, pp. 569, 572). In 1830 he played the part of Cinderella's father "in good rich fooling. He is a thriving graft from the true Neapolitan buffo stock" (E). He was cast as Leporello in an adaptation of *Giovanni* at the Adelphi, but "we think a more efficient one, *much more efficient*, could have been found in the company" (Ath, July 10). Yet in another revival of *Cinderella*— the last we hear of him—Hunt thought he "acquitted himself very well" (*Tatler*).

THE FEMALE SINGERS

Mrs. (Margaret?) Farrell (after 1779, Mrs. KENNEDY) (?–1793), a native of Ireland who had studied under Arne, first sang at Covent Garden in 1776. A contralto, her chief successes were in male parts, but she also sang in concerts and in the oratorios. As Mrs. Casey in *Fontainbleau*, (1785) she was "in full voice" (H). She had the breeches part (Blanford) in the *Peruvian* (1786) and "looked like a very pretty fellow; her singing is always pleasant and [she] was almost the only person . . . that could be heard distinctly" (C). In the Macnally *Richard*, she "sung one air admirably [and] did every thing for Margery, that the character would admit of" (LC, Oct. 14–17). As Mandane in *Artaxerxes* (1787), she "kept her ground with considerable credit" (H). And in 1788 she was encored as Peggy in *Marian* (LC). Parke called her "one of the finest counter-tenor voices we ever heard."

Anna Marie CROUCH, née Phillips (1763–1805), gave strong support to English opera from 1780 to 1801, though Hogarth thought her powers not sufficiently cultivated. She had a sweet coloratura voice and studied under Linley and later under Michael Kelly, with whom she was intimate for several years. She spent most of her career at Drury Lane, making her debut there as Mandane (*Artaxerxes*) in 1780, but she could play nonsinging comic and tragic roles as well. In 1785 she married Rawlings Edward Crouch, and she first comes to our notice that year in *Strangers at Home*, where she sang the lead, Viola, "with her usual excellence" (UR, Dec. 9; H) and "with abundant grace and power of execution" (LC). She ably supported her role as Laurette in the Burgoyne *Richard Coeur de Lion* (C, 1786), and in 1787 in *Love in a Village*, she "threw an archness and spirit into the part of Rosetta, which we thought her incapable of assuming—she sang all her airs elegantly and correctly" (UR). The *Herald* added that she "sings in a style to shrink from no comparison, and came alternately recommended by characteristic animation, and refined sensibility." As Mandane (*Artaxerxes*) later that year, Mrs. Crouch "never appeared to more advantage. . . . Her manner of executing this *break-neck* air ["Soldier tir'd"] well deserved the compliment" of an encore (UR, Oct. 26). In another revival of that opera the next year, she was an excellent Arbaces and was encored in "Water parted from the sea" (H). Also in 1788, as Ormellina in *Love in the East*, she sang several of her songs well but "was, however, too much frightened to do [a bravura] the justice it merits" (H). As Anna in *Doctor and Apothecary*, she was encored in "The summer heats bestowing" (H). As Miranda in the *Tempest* (1789), she "played and sung with more than usual inspiration" (LC). A month later, as Lady Elinore in the *Haunted Tower*, she had "never sung better; and her first air by *Pleyel* was most applauded. We recommend her to forbear as much as possible the *outrageous swell*, with which her cadence in *bravura* singing, are always distinguished" (H). She excelled as Caroline in *Island of St. Marguerite* the same year. We next hear of her in 1792, when she was "exceedingly happy" as Anaeus in the all-sung *Dido* (PA); she "never played to more advantage or sung with greater melody and sweetness" (D). Later that year she "looked and sang delightfully" (T) as Clara in the *Prisoner*. Her air, "As wrapt in sleep I lay," in the role of Donna Aurora in the *Pirates* was "divinely sung, and with justice encored" (T, Nov. 22).

About 1793 Mrs. Crouch was injured in a coach accident and her voice was permanently affected, but she continued her career. Presumably it was to this that the *Post* referred in reviewing *Jack of Newbury* (1795): "Mrs. Crouch, though in an early stage of convalescence, from her late severe indisposition, sang sweetly, and is much improved in her voice." In 1798 her voice "has considerably improved since last season," and as Eufenia in *Captive of Spilbury*, she sang her airs "with taste and feeling," and her acting in the last scene "was deservedly applauded" (T; LC; P). She retired in 1801. Though a stiff actress at first, she evidently improved considerably under Kelly's tutelage. Fiske says she could reach high F ("Queen of the Night").

Mrs. Margaret MARTYR, née Thornton (?–1807), was a rival of Mrs. Crouch at Covent Garden, where she made her debut in 1779 as Rosetta in *Love in a Village*. She married a "Captain" Martyr in 1780, but he died in King's Bench prison in 1783. She had two illegitimate children by oboist William Parke. She first comes to notice in 1785 as Celia in *Fontainbleau* (1785), when she was "as lively as ever" (H). When she sang Jacquelina in *Choleric Fathers* that year, her "laughing song was performed with uncommon powers of imitation" (H), and in a "sprightly style" (UR, Nov. 16). In *Marian* (1788) she "did all for Patty that the part would allow" (LC). Later that year, in *Inkle and Yarico*, she "looks Wowsky extremely well—to the songs she is by no means equal—and we hope in the next representation she will not smack her lips so much when recounting the fate of the poor ship wrecked tars" (T).

In 1791 she appeared as Dolly in the *Woodman*, and the *Theatrical Guardian* (I, 11-13) regretted "that the audience were prevented from doing justice to the abilities of Mrs. Martyr, by the indecent tendency of her song . . . which, as an excellent actress, she was obliged to accompany with corresponding gesture." She was competent as Kate in the *Armourer* (D, 1793). In 1796 she had "not often been more fortunate" than in her role in *Lock and Key* (OPA). In *Abroad and at Home* that year, she "gave the part of Kitty every possible effect; her first scene with Young Testy, was an admirable performance" (LC). In 1797 she "contributed in no small degree to the entertainment" as Annetta in *Italian Villagers* (LC). And in our final notice of her, she was "all alive in the animated Wowski" (P) in a revival of *Inkle and Yarico* (1798). She was a very popular performer, but the press seemed much more interested in her acting than in her voice.

Mrs. Elizabeth BANNISTER, née Harper (c. 1757–1849), was singing at the Little Theatre after 1778 and made her Covent Garden debut in 1781. In 1785 her song "Sweet Anna frae the seabeach come" in *Turk and no Turk*, when she played Emily at the Little Theatre, was "delightfully pathetic" (H), and she "never appeared in a trio with more applause" (PA). She sang well as Rosa in *Fontainbleau* at Covent Garden, and as Angelina she "touched the heart" in the ballad "I traversed Judas barren sand" in *Robin Hood*. In *Choleric Fathers* she ably performed pathetic songs (UR, Nov. 16) and sang a bravura well, but she was imperfect in a Shield air. In 1786 "her presence in an opera" was "universally wished for," and "her absence universally regretted" (UR, Mar. 20). And she sang "most successfully" that year as Stella in *Siege of Curzola* (C). I find no further mention, though she sang until 1792, when she retired because of her large family.

Perhaps the best comic actress among the early singers was Mrs. Dorothy (Dora) JORDAN, née Bland (1762–1816), who became mistress of the Duke of Clarence and had ten children by him. She was also very active on the Drury Lane stage until two years before her death. Not a regular singer at all, she occasionally introduced simple, sometimes unaccompanied ballads in her performances. Hazlitt had tongue-in-cheek when he called her singing "like the twang of Cupid's bow." In 1785 she sang in the breeches part of Rosa in *Strangers at Home* at Covent Garden; "the air of Ally Croker, assisted by accompaniments, was sung by her in slow time, and was encored. It is impossible to over-rate her address, style, and manner in the song" (H). She also sang well as Matilda in Burgoyne's *Richard* (UR, 1786), but thereafter we hear nothing of her singing until *Matrimony* at Drury Lane in 1804, when her acting "entirely saved the piece. Her spirit, her *naivete*, her matchless humour, and her song, which, by the way, is better *sung* than *set*, kept the house in excellent humour" (MM). She was last on the London stage in 1814.

Giovanna SESTINI, whom we met at the King's, also sang briefly in English opera, appearing at Covent Garden in 1782 and in the *Siege of Curzola* at the Little Theatre in 1786. She sang "most successfully" in O'Keeffe's *Curzola* (1789) and, with others in the cast, "lifted molehills with the strength of Atlas; lemon juice characters were perhaps never so powerfully played" (C). She "*acted* her airs with all the animation which distinguishes her at the Opera-house" (G).

Mrs. William (Elizabeth) CLENDENING, née Arnold (1768–99), who made her stage debut in Bath in 1770, made her London debut in 1792 at Covent Garden and was "rather overburdened" with songs in the *Armourer* (1793) but "acquitted herself creditably" (LC). In *Sprigs of Laurel* that year she sang well and "played with much vivacity" (LC). She was "too powdered for a *nightly wanderer*" in *Midnight Wanderers* (1792). In *Travellers in Switzerland* (1794) she "introduced with charming effect her favourite Air from Giordani, of 'Silly Fan'" (T), and she was "happy in her part" (LC) in *Italian Villagers* (1797). Her last years were plagued by illness.

Maria Theresa KEMBLE, née De Camp (1774–1838), appeared at age six as a cupid in a ballet at King's Theatre and was taught singing by Charles

Dibdin. She made her Drury Lane debut at twelve in Burgoyne's *Richard* in 1786, when the *Register* remarked on "the astonishing abilities of this little enchantress; who, both from the peculiar sweetness of her voice, her surprising taste and judgment in singing, and her wonderful graces, agility, and exertions in dancing . . . excited our applause and admiration" (Oct. 25). Her first success as an adult was in the role of Macheath (*Beggar's Opera*) at the Little Theatre in 1792. In 1794 she sang in *Auld Robin Grey* in another trouser part and "evinced considerable improvement of skill in 'music's art'" (T). In 1796 she sang in *Shipwreck* at Drury Lane and was cited for a duet with Master Welsh (T). In 1800 she pleased in *Wilmore Castle* (P). Again in the *Beggar's Opera* in 1802, "the spirit and fire of Miss De Camp" as Lucy "keeps our attention tremblingly alive to the fate of her hero" (T). She "has long been allowed to be the best Lucy on the stage" (P). Later that year she sang Charlotte in *A House to be Sold* and was "the life of the performance. She danced, sung, and acted the romp in the most captivating style" (C; H). In 1805 she was cited in *Soldier's Return* (C), and in *Youth, Love, and Folly* she had another trouser role: "She looked extremely well in the *leathers*, and was much applauded for her alternate flippancy and pathos" (C). In 1806 she performed the lead in *Forty Thieves* at Drury Lane; she "exerted herself with her usual address" and "performed the murder of the thieves with eclat" (C; H; Cr). That year she married Charles Kemble, who became manager of Covent Garden in 1822, and appeared there under his management but not, apparently, in operas.

Elizabeth Sarah LYON (1787–1831) made her debut at Drury Lane in 1808 in *Kais* and drew forth a brief lecture on musical science from the *Chronicle*: "Miss Lyon's most mellifluous voice would be irresistible in its influence over the heart if she could be taught the importance of being articulate." The *Mirror* noted an encored air and a duet with Braham "with a very delicate and pleasing effect." The next year she "excelled" in Bishop's *Circassian Bride* at Drury Lane in February (T). In April she became Mrs. Henry Bishop. In July she appeared in *Up All Night* at Lyceum, where she was "certainly an acquisition to this theatre, but there is no symptom of improvement in either her acting or singing" (MM). And in August she sang in *Safe and Sound* but had "no character" in her part (MM). In 1810 she was "in fine voice" in *Maniac* (T), but she was "walking about in her flannel petticoat, with a head and body dress that defies all description" (MM). We hear nothing further of her. She became the mother of two sons and a daughter; she died in childbirth.

A weak singer but a very fine actress—and undoubtedly the most beloved performer of the time—was Frances Maria KELLY (1790–1882).

Better known as Fanny, she was a niece of Michael Kelly, who trained her as a child for the stage. She made her debut as an adult performer at Drury Lane in 1809 and remained there some thirty-six years. Personally most attractive, she was twice fired on from the pit (and fortunately missed) by frustrated suitors (Charles Lamb was an ardent but less violent one). She was mainly an actress, performing many Shakespearean heroines and many other leading roles, both serious and comic; she was not, however, reluctant to perform minor characters, which she often raised to prominence by her performances. While she appeared in many operas at the Lyceum/English Opera House, she sang little and sometimes not at all in them. She first comes to notice as a singer in 1810, when she sang "her little pathetic songs" in *Oh! this Love* at the Lyceum, "and it gave us a new idea of the powers of this interesting young actress" (T). In 1815 she had a demanding singing role as Lucy in the *Beggar's Opera*: "This character . . . she has raised to . . . importance. . . . Though her voice has scarcely sufficient compass to do justice to the songs, yet she sung them with exquisite taste and propriety. . . . Miss Kelly possesses in a remarkable degree the art of giving importance to trifles" (TI). But almost without exception references to her singing in many operas up to 1830 were trivial. She retired from the stage in 1835, and later lost all her savings in speculation on an experimental theatre. She died at ninety-two, still single.

Our first notice of a Miss MAT[T]HEWS, is in the *Farmer's Wife* at Covent Garden in 1814, and "every now and then [she] stepped on the stage very opportunely to charm away the disgust of a bad pun" (TI). She "acquitted herself very respectably" in *John of Paris* later that year (EM), and in 1815 was encored in an air in *Brother and Sister* (EM). In 1816 she performed well as Annette in *Lord of the Manor* (TI). But as Katherine in the *Siege of Belgrade* (1817), she "had too much singing and too little acting, to be admired as she deserves" (T). As Lucy Bertram in *Guy Mannering* the next year, she "succeeded better than we expected" (T).

We have already met Miss HUGHES, later Mrs. GATTIE, who sang briefly at the King's from 1817 to 1821. She made her stage debut in Dublin on February 18, 1815, and was hailed by public and press as a "first-rate singer and a good actress" (TI, "Sketch," Mar. 1816). Late in 1815 she made her Covent Garden debut as Mandane in *Artaxerxes*: "Her voice is naturally piercing in its upper notes, harsh in the middle, and weak and bodiless below. She has a copious general knowledge of music, but we think she is not gifted with refinement of ear or taste to sense the more mysterious beauties of the Italian school. . . . Her acting is overloaded with false and ungrateful movement as her singing is with vulgar and unseasonable ornaments" (T). The following month she sang the Princess of Navarre in *John of Paris* (in which she had made her Dublin debut), but the *Times* was of the same opinion. She followed this with the role of Urganda in *Cymon*, and she "sung with more success than she ever did before: and in one instance proved herself capable of that pure and simple style of song" (T). But the *Chronicle* noted she "has not an organ for the delivery of dialogue. Her *bravura* in music is her talent." The *Inquisitor* noted she "sang with that brilliancy so peculiar to herself." Doubtless she was dismayed by this critical reception. She did not sing in 1816, and in 1817 she was singing at the King's.

A Miss BYRNE, granddaughter of the "famous" Edward Byrne of Dublin, had been in society until her father lost his inheritance. She made a successful stage debut in Dublin (TI, "Sketch," Jan. 1818), and in her Drury Lane debut in 1817, as Adela in the *Haunted Tower*, she showed herself an accomplished singer and had a good compass and execution but was rather deficient in volume; she also lacked a good shake and introduced "injudicious ornaments" but she was a "very agreeable actress" (T). As Rosetta in *Love in a Village* the next month, she was less secure in the more demanding music (T), but Hazlitt thought her performance in *Outwitted at Last* satisfactory (T). In our last report of her, in a repetition of the *Haunted Tower* in 1819, the *Inquisitor* was outraged that she had used their favorable "Sketch" to a "promotion of her career": "We will resign the dictates of honest anger for the guidance of sober contempt, and denominate Miss Byrne, with inveterate frigidity, as one of the vilest screechers by which vocal science has ever been invaded."

Emma Sarah LOVE (1801–?), a contralto, gained some notice in the 1820s. Her father, Lieutenant F. L. Love, "in his majesty's service," died about 1812. She is said to have had a good education and at an early age was articled "to a musician of competent talent." After some juvenile parts, she blossomed into adult singing roles in the 1822–23 season, when she first appeared in *Maid Marian* at Covent Garden and "treated us with a few beautiful deep-tones in a Glee and Chorus" (LG). As a waiting-maid in *Clari*, she "showed a great deal more animation and *naivete* than usual" (Har). She "displayed much native humour, and sang a song . . . with richness and eclat" (E; LG). At the Little Theatre that summer, she was "entitled to praise" (C) as Susan in *Sweethearts and Wives*. Her Peggy in *Lord of the Manor* was "not deficient in spirit" (T). As a replacement for Ann Marie Tree on short notice as Marina in *Cortez* at Covent Garden, she "sang the songs with exquisite taste and expression" and impressed with her acting as well (E; C; H; LG). The *Harmonicon* found her voice "remarkable for its depth and beauty; but she should never sing above C." In 1824 she sang in *Native Land*, and she, Tree, and Mary Ann Paton "literally vied with each other who should be the most captivating and the most amusing" (LG). Her comedy was "anything but imitation" (E). She "is becoming shrewder and shrewder every hour; she will anon be able to throw an *arch* over the Thames," though "she *cries* too much" (LM). Later she impersonated the "damsel confident" (Agathe) in the Covent Garden *Freischütz* and "sang with unusual finish and lightsomeness, while her acting was the very essence of simple-hearted *naiveté*" (E), but the *Harmonicon* disagreed, reporting that she did not seem "to comprehend the nature of the music [which was] imperatively necessary in singing every note of this opera."

In 1827 she sang Arbaces in *Artaxerxes* at Drury Lane, but her voice was unsuited to the music (T). In 1828 she appeared as Countess Sterloff in *Love in Wrinkles* and "played and sang with much judgment," though was really too young for such a mature part (T; C). But Holmes (At) disliked her singing: "She has no taste, no style, no tone; we neither like the squeak of her upper notes, nor the quality of her lower ones." Our last reference to her occurs in 1829, when she sang Adele in Lacy's *Casket*—still at Drury Lane—and was "was successful in her singing, but her acting was coarse; her attempts at playfulness and simplicity are the most unlucky that can be imagined" (T, Mar. 11; E). Phillips commented on her great depth of voice.

A Miss POVEY, otherwise unknown, was a principal singer at the Catholic chapel in Moorfields. She studied with T. S. Cooke and made her Drury Lane debut in 1820 in a revival of *No Song, No Supper*, and immediately afterwards she appeared as Jaffa Mannering in a revival of *Guy Mannering* "with a degree of success still more marked than on her first appearance. Her voice seems more flexible and steady than at first, and some of her upper notes were sustained with remarkable strength and clearness" (T). In a minor role in *Fontainbleau*, she "made a fresh advance upon public admiration. The upper notes . . . are pre-eminently beautiful, but we think a little less art in displaying their peculiar qualities, would not detract from their collective impression" (TI). In 1820 she "exerted the upper tones of her voice, with popular effect" in *Giovanni in London*, and she supported a small role in *David Rizzio* "with that ease and sprightliness which time will ripen into value" (TI, June).

In 1821 she sang another small role in a revival of *Love in a Village*. The *Times* thought that "she always displays a steadiness and judgment which entitle her to praise," while the *London* found her "a very promising young vocalist" with "a voice almost as rich as any one upon the stage." That year Bacon reported (QMM, III, 385–86): "Her natural organ is fine, powerful, and considerable, and she is proceeding soberly and by just degrees to excellence. Her tone is pure, rich, and sweet in its quality, and with as much brilliancy as consists with the fullness. Her compass is extensive, and the notes are equal and alike throughout." In 1822 at English Opera House, she excelled in concerted numbers in *Fair Gabrielle* (T), as well as in a Covent Garden revival of *Gil Blas*. Her Julia Mannering was "worthy of considerable praise" (T). When she played Diana Vernon in *Rob Roy* the following year, the *Times* complained: "This young lady is a sweet and pleasing singer; but her talents do not at all qualify her for the situation of *prima seria donna*."

In the English Opera House *Freischütz* in 1824, she did justice to a very minor role (C; T), and the *Harmonicon* found her "a very useful person in a musical drama; she wants a little refinement certainly, but has a clear voice and sings in tune," but the *Examiner* disagreed. Later she successfully sang Theodosia in *Maid of the Mill* (T); and still later, as Rose in the Drury Lane *Freischütz*, she "sang with her usual sweetness" (C). In 1825, the last year she comes to notice, she "agreeably represented" the countess in a revival of *Figaro* at Drury Lane (T), and in a minor role in *Malvina* she was "in excellent voice" (C). She also performed Tenda, Genius of the Ring, in *Aladdin*, and "dear little Povey did all that could be done with the materials" (EM).

A Miss HALLANDE sang at least two seasons late in our period. In 1821 she "added to her already considerable reputation" (T) as Miranda in the Covent Garden *Tempest*; her voice was "clear, and ravishing, and musical, as is the lute of Apollo" (LM). She played Sylvia in *Two Gentlemen from Verona* the same year, and her voice had "more of the character of richness than that of any other competitor on the stage" (Ch). In *Clari* (1823) she sang in her "happiest style" (C) and "displayed her extraordinary voice to great advantage in a minor character and both looks and acts charmingly" (LG) — but this is the last we hear of her.

Another late singer who became well known was Harriet WAYLETT, née Cooke (1798–1851), whose uncle was a member of the Drury Lane company. She had early instruction in music at Bath, where she was born, and she sang there and at other provincial theatres in 1816 and 1817. She married Waylett, an actor, in 1819, and from 1820 to 1823 sang at the minors and in the provinces. A favorite in the country (N.G.), she was particularly successful in *Guy Mannering* at Birmingham in 1823. The next year she made her Drury Lane debut in *Love in a Village* (I have not found a review; the D.N.B. states it played Dec. 4 at Drury Lane, but advertisements state another work was produced there that night). She followed this up with the role of Fanny in *Maid of the Mill*, which she played "exceedingly well" (T). She later performed at the Little Theatre, as well as at Dublin, where she was successful, but she did not reappear in London until 1828, when she sang the countess in *Figaro* at the Little Theatre: "We are sorry to find," the *Times* observed, "that her voice was not in its proper pitch; for, notwithstanding her being encored, she contrived to sing out of tune throughout the opera."

In 1830 she substituted for Vestris in an 1830–31 revival of *National Guard*. "We sought in vain in Mrs. Waylett's performance for the fire and spirit which marked that of Madame Vestris in the comic parts, and there was the same comparative tameness in the more pathetic passages.... We must recommend her to learn the words of her songs: singers have no right to *improvise* nonsense verses" (Ath). But Hunt thought she "sang her songs, and played her part too, in a very pleasing style of simplicity" (*Tatler*). In the same year, she began a liaison with composer George Alexander Lee, which led to marriage after the death of her husband; Lee composed many songs for her, and she was on stage till the mid-1840s. According to N.G. she was one of the best soubrettes of the day and was almost as popular as Vestris. We see little inkling of this in the few reviews before 1831, but Fitzball declared (1859) that "we have no more warblers like Mrs. Waylett"—singers now have "only heavy, deep voices."

A Miss GRADDEN (1804–c. 54), later Mrs. Gibbs, who studied under Cooke and sang at Vauxhall in 1822, had her Drury Lane debut in 1824 as Susanna in *Figaro*, but it was a rocky beginning. The *Times* thought her powers "very moderate.... The figure of Miss Gradden is *petite*, her features are intelligent if not handsome. The quality of her voice is good, but its compass is not calculated for a large theatre. Her shake ... is feeble and undecided. She so attenuated her cadences, that ... they are barely audible," and she has "no pretentions whatever" as an actress. Yet as Linda (Bertha) in the Drury Lane *Freischütz*, she "made a most favourable impression," and her style compensated for her limited compass (T; C). But the *Examiner* found her too lacking in confidence, and the *Harmonicon* thought her inadequate. As Catherine in a revival of *Siege of Belgrade*, she was improved and sang a very spirited bravura (T). In 1825 she gave "some serious airs with much taste and feeling" in the *Fall of Algiers* (LM); and she performed a duet in *Abou Hassan* that was "worthy of Weber's fire and genius" (T; E). She tastefully executed one song in *Wedding Present* late that year (T). In 1826 she performed well in *White Lady* (T; LG; E). She also upheld her role in the *Devil's Bridge* but was cautioned to mind her articulation (T). She also sang well in *Two Houses of Grenada* (T). In 1828 she failed in a trouser role—Count Rudolph—in *Sylvania* (T; C); we hear no more of her.

Among later arrivals were the CAWSE sisters. Phillips states that Harriet (apparently the elder) was a mezzo and a pupil of Sir Henry Smart, and that Mary was a high soprano. Both sang together in some productions. Harriet made her debut in 1825 at Covent Garden in a melodrama, the *Hebrew Family*, and "sang a lightsome and effective ballad of Whittaker's with highly promising refinement of taste and execution. Her voice is very good, and her manner most prepossessing" (E). The *London*, describing her as "*little*," reported she "sung with great skill and spirit." In 1826 she sang Puck in *Oberon*; the *Times* observed: "We have no doubt this opera will increase the estimation of this charming little performer" (Apr. 12), but the *Chronicle* reported she "went through her character with less spirit than it certainly required," and the *Gazette* noted "she did not gain ground." In 1827 she replaced the indisposed Paton as Louise in the *White Maid*; she performed "with considerable spirit" and "some little improvement in articulation," and she "sang very sweetly" (E). Though no match for Paton, she "got through her task with considerable ability" (Har). She also sang with her sister Mary in the *Seraglio*, and both were "rather pleasing singers" (Har).

In 1828 Harriet performed a minor role in *Carron Side* and "danced and flourished around [the stage] as she sang, because Madame Vestris does so. We are quite satisfied with Madame Vestris, without wishing to see her imitated" (E). She followed this with the role of Dorabella in *Tit for Tat* at the English Opera House and performed "with great effect" (T), though she and Miss Betts "have the same defects—a little hardness of voice" (At; E). She finished the year in a trouser role in *Pirate of Genoa* and was "extremely correct and pleasing" (Har). In 1829, still at Covent Garden, she appeared in *Nymph of the Grotto* and one song was "extremely well sung" by her (T). At the English Opera House again she sang in *Robber's Bride* and "deserved more applause than [she] received" (C). This was followed by the *Vampyr*, when she again sang with her sister Mary and was "most delightful as the village bride," Liska. "Her first song was sung with a feeling and expression that called forth an immediate *encore*" (C). She was "quite a hit" (LG), and the *Atlas* found her "the most delightful village maiden that has appeared on the stage since the Zerlina of Mozart." She sang "with a touching grace it would be hard to parallel" (NM).

In 1830 both sisters performed in *Cinderella*. The *Examiner* disliked Mary's singing—"her tones were ever hard, sharp, and sudden, and come upon the ear like detonating balls"—but Harriet "possesses both a better style and taste, and had she more physical power, would become a valuable singer." Harriet repeated her role in a revival of the *Vampyr* and was "perfectly satisfactory" (E). She also sang Rosina in the *Barber*, and Hunt "stayed till the half price, in order to refresh ourselves with the sweet tones and imposing manners of Miss H. Cawse, whose charming natural smile we shall not scruple again to praise, because we think she is too clever to spoil it by affectation. We beg to say (critically speaking) we are in love with it" (*Tatler*).

Mary Anne GOWARD (1805–99) made her Dublin debut in 1823 and her London debut at the English Opera House as Rosina in the *Barber* in 1824, when the *Times* found her voice "by no means powerful," yet it was "sweet and flexible" and she was very successful in a number of songs; moreover, she played Rosina "in an intelligent and delicate manner." In 1825 she sang the Child of the Temple in *Tarrare*: She "tempers her vivacity so as to look the mere passive instrument of fate, till she sings out Tarrare's name in inspirant tones" (NM). In 1826 Weber chose her for the sea nymph in *Oberon* at Covent Garden—apparently her only appearance at the majors. She may have had trouble being heard (N.G.), but our single reference to her on that occasion, the *Examiner*, expressed only delight in her song. In 1827 "the spirit of Philadel was agreeably represented by Miss Goward, who is considerably improved both in her acting and singing," in a revival of *Arthur and Emmeline* at the English Opera House (T). She played it "very prettily, and sings it not only sweetly, but with great care and precision" (NM). Following this she appeared in *Freebooters*: "Miss Goward, in the character of an arch country girl, performed with her usual vivacity; and although evidently frightened, executed a sprightly and very characteristic air . . . with spirit and precision" (E). The *New Monthly* found her "pert and piquant." In 1828 she married Robert Keeley. In later years she became more actress than singer (N.G.).

A Miss BETTS, otherwise unknown, sang on the English stage from 1827 to 1830—and probably later. She made her debut at the English Opera House as Rosetta in *Love in a Village*, and "as a singer she has considerable power and taste," but "as an actress she has everything to learn" (NM). As Isabella in *Freebooters* "she sang correctly and tastefully. In some instances there was a degree of spirit in her expression, which augured exceedingly well for her future career. Her acting we cannot praise. It was tameness itself" (T; E; NM). In 1828 she sang Fiordiligi in *Tit for Tat* "with great effect" (T), but "to some degree" she "wanted expression" (C). Although she and Harriet Cawse were "too hard and too loud in concerted pieces," they sang "with more feeling and in better taste altogether than we have hitherto heard them" (E; At). In 1829 she performed in the *Casket* at Drury Lane; "she showed herself more of an actress than heretofore; her voice is powerful and flexible; and she executed her songs with great force and success" (T; C). She introduced a bravura in D from *Idomeneo* and "sung her difficult song extremely well" (At). At the English Opera House she appeared in *Robber's Bride* and was "an exceedingly efficient representative of Laura. She sang with great truth and power, and she acted with more nature and feeling than vocalists are accustomed to display" (T; C). But the *Examiner* wrote: "Miss Betts will never gain the *feeling* necessary to a great singer; but her acquirements will always command the respect of musicians." The *Athenaeum* concurred. She next sang Henrika in the *Vampyr*: she "has improved both as a singer and performer; she screams less, and is more easy and animated than is her wont" (E; At; LG; Har). In 1830 she was back at Drury Lane in *National Guard*, and she sang well (At). At the Adelphi *Figaro*, Hunt noted "a general want of tone and softness and [a] defect even in ear . . . though she has a good deal of execution occasionally, and a shake singularly good and liquid for a voice so uneasy in its general character" (*Tatler*).

A Miss FERON (also called Madame FEARON and Mrs. GLOSSOP), who had trained under a violinist named Cobham, first sang in public about 1814. Bacon (QMM, IX, 351–54) wrote in 1827: "Madam Feron is now probably at that middle and best period of life, when all her faculties, vocal and intellectual, might be expected to be found in their fullest vigour. . . . Her voice, however, but too clearly manifests the injurious tendency of over-exertion: the tone lacks quality—that fullness and that brilliancy, which the Italians denominate *metallo*." That year she appeared at Drury Lane as a waiting woman in *Isidore de Merida* and was warmly received. "She possesses very considerable power of voice, but her tones are sharp and wiry" (T). The *Examiner* noted "some inadequacy in volume and fulness of tone," while admiring her execution, and Holmes (At) was quite negative: "Her voice is eminently high, loud, and harsh; the tone appears squeezed and strained through too small an aperture." Ayrton agreed, but Bacon (QMM) observed that she had "little opportunity" for the display of her ability: "In the *Lullaby*, a song of pure English ballad expressiveness, she failed, both in the conception and the execution, and it was in the *arie d'agilita* alone that she shone." In 1828 she played Despina in *Tit for Tat* at the English Opera House and "sung as perfectly as every one would expect" (T), but she "looks as fat and round as a barrel-organ, pouring out her pleasing notes" (LG). She followed this with Claretta in *Pirate of Genoa*: she failed as an actress, and though she sang well in "a buffa style," she "cannot sustain her voice sufficiently for serious music" (C). The *Harmonicon* declared flatly that she was "anything in the world but agreeable."

Another Miss HUGHES (not Mrs. Gattie), who was a pupil of Mr. Watson, a chorus director at Covent Garden, gained early experience at the provincial theatres and especially in Dublin. She made her London debut as Mandane in 1827 at Covent Garden and "played it admirably. Her features are not strongly marked, but there is about them much of gentleness, of kindness, and of intelligence. Her figure is excellent. . . . Her voice is less powerful than many . . . but we recollect none more melodious" (T). She next played Costanza in the *Seraglio* and "proved that she is capable of executing with taste and facility, very difficult music" (T; E). But the *Harmonicon* was quite negative. That year Bacon (QMM, IX, 354–55) noted: "She possesses a voice of sufficient volume, compass, and flexibility, to have made a singer of high rank, though not we think of the very first class. . . . [But] her intonation . . . has been found to fail in the progress of her exertions." In 1828 she took the lead in a revival of *Native Land*; the *Harmonicon* was again negative: "Her greatest defect is that of ear; she too often sings a quarter of a note too sharp. This is, we fear, an irremediable fault." In 1830 she sang one of the sisters in the Englished *Cinderella*; the *Atlas* thought the singer of that role at the King's was inferior to her.

Notes

Selected Bibliography

Photographic Credits

Index

Notes

Preface

1. *New Oxford History of Music*, VIII, 376n1. On surviving librettos and scores for English operas for this period, see app. 15 and 16.
2. Note that "Romanticism reached articulate expression in literature at least a generation earlier than in music" (*NOHM*, VIII, 36) — even earlier in the case of English literature.
3. Robert D. Hume, in "English Drama and the Theatre, 1660–1800: New Directions in Research," *Theatre Survey*, 23, no. 1 (1982), 92–94, though noting the "growing recognition of the importance of music in the theatrical life of London," has pointed out the need for much more study of both English and Italian opera in London in the eighteenth century.
4. My readings in the press have been guided by the *New Cambridge Bibliography of English Literature* (vols. II and III), as well as by the bibliographies of W. S. Ward and of K. K. Weed and R. P. Bond. The period actually perused in each journal is indicated in my bibliography for primary sources. Although most of the 2,500-odd reviews scrutinized for this period are recorded in appendixes 3 and 10, a large number that contribute little or no material strength to the study remain uncited in the text.

Part I

Overview

1. Michael Winesanker, in "Musico-Dramatic Criticism of English Comic Opera, 1750–1800," *Journal of American Musicological Society*, II (1949), 87–96, quotes liberally from an excellent opera review in the *British Magazine* for June 1760, i, 349–50. For an overview of stage criticism from 1776 to 1800, see the Introduction by Charles Beecher Hogan, ed., *The London Stage. Part 5: 1776–1800* (Carbondale, Ill., 1968), clxxv-clxxx.
2. Raymond Williams, *The Long Revolution* (London, 1961), 135.
3. Ten other newspapers, published in London in the 1780s, were intended mainly for provincial distribution and were published two or three times a week; most of them had a very small circulation.

4. H. R. Fox Bourne, *English Newspapers: Chapters in the History of Journalism* (London, 1887), I, 289.

5. Williams, 189.

6. Nov., X, 305, quoted by Winesanker, 95.

7. Maurice J. Quinlan, *Victorian Prelude: A History of English Manners, 1700–1830* (New York, 1941), 160–61; see also Richard D. Altick, *The English Common Reader* (Chicago, 1957), 41, 82–83.

8. Arthur Aspinal, *Politics and the Press, 1780–1850* (London, 1949), 63, 283–87. Despite government subsidies, advertising was of course the only way a journal could survive well into the nineteenth century. See Ivon Asquith, "Advertisement and the Press in the Late Eigheenth and Early Nineteenth Centuries: James Perry and the *Morning Chronicle*, 1790–1821," *Historical Journal*, 18, no. 4 (1975), 703–24.

9. F. Knight Hunt, *The Fourth Estate: A History of Newspapers and the Liberty of the Press* (London, 1850), I, chap. 6.

10. *The History of British Journalism* (London, 1859), II, 82.

11. See Theodore Fenner, "Edward Quin and the *Traveller*," *Studies in Romanticism* (Spring, 1975), 146–47.

12. A reference to the so-called Peterloo Massacre of 1819.

13. *Edinburgh Review* (1823), 349–78.

14. Perhaps it *was not* such an advantage; Hazlitt, in the survey cited above, didn't think deadlines affected the quality of criticism: "Where there is the necessary stimulus for making the effort, what is given from a first expression, what is struck off at a blow [his own style] is in many respects better than what is produced on reflection, and at several heats."

15. Leanne Langley, in *The English Musical Journal in the Early Nineteenth Century* (dissertation) (Ann Arbor, Mich., 1893), 112, states that "roughly half of the editors who can be identified by name also served as principal writer in their journals."

16. Henry Phillips, *Musical and Personal Recollections* (London, 1864), 120, 163.

17. Joan Reilly, "Winston's Braham Scrapbook," *Theatre Notebook*, 36, no. 2 (1982), 52–55. Sources and dates are not usually cited.

18. Richard Brindsley Peake, *Memoirs of the Colman Family* (London, 1841), I, 424.

19. John O'Keeffe, *Recollections* (London, 1826), II, 119.

20. Charles H. Gray, *Theatrical Criticism in London to 1795* (New York, 1931), 303–4.

21. *The Life and Times of Frederic[k] Reynolds* (London, 1826), I, 319–20.

22. *Thirty-five years of a Dramatic Author's Life* (London, 1859), ix.

23. Quoted by Henry Saxe Wyndham, *The Annals of Covent Garden Theatre from 1832 to 1897* (London, 1906), II, 56.

24. At the conclusion of a performance, the manager, stage manager, or a leading performer came forward to ask the audience's pleasure on the piece — should it be repeated — as indicated by their applause or hisses. Sometimes opposing patrons came to blows over the decision.

25. Cecil J. L. Price, *Theatre in the Age of Garrick* (Totowa, N.J., 1973), 141, and L.S., I, clxxix.

26. *Records of My Life* (London, 1832), II, 102.

27. No. 8, March 23, 1784, cited by Frederick C. Petty, *Italian Opera in London, 1760–1800* (Ann Arbor, Mich., 1980), 214–15.

28. L.S., I, clxxix, also cites Goöde's *Stranger in England* (II, 201–2) as presuming that the managers paid for their favorable reviews but finds him mistaken.

29. *Memoirs of Lorenzo Da Ponte* (New York, 1929), 120–21, 169, 143. Hunt admitted Badini had a good idiomatic English style but was of "low character."

30. TC, May 15; quoted by Petty, 260.

31. Leslie A. Marchand, *The Athenaeum: A Mirror of Victorian Culture* (Chapel Hill, N. C., 1941), 105n.

32. Ian R. Christie, in *Myth and Reality in Late Eighteenth-Century British Politics and Other Papers* (Berkeley, 1970), 322, states that reporters were paid four guineas a week c. 1800; John Campbell was paid one hundred guineas a year by James Perry in 1803 and considered it "very liberal" (Mary Hardcastle, *The Life of John, Lord Campbell* [London, 1881], I, 126).

33. Leanne Langley, 112.

34. *Composer and Critic: Two Hundred Years of Musical Criticism* (New York, 1945), xi, 240.

35. *Critic at the Opera* (London, 1957), xi.

36. *Music in Western Civilization* (New York, 1941), 985.

37. Quoted by Winton Dean, "Criticism," in N.G.

38. These dates indicate the life of the journal; the bibliographic citation indicates the inclusive dates of the journal actually perused. To avoid confusion I have usually cited only the title by which the journal was generally known during the period perused, though a number of them modified their titles somewhat from time to time.

39. For that very reason, though, John Campbell, who also reported on parliament, thought him a bad reporter—he didn't convey *"meaning"* (Hardcastle, I, 111).

40. James Perry came to the Chronicle with considerable experience; he had served on the *General Advertiser* (1777), the *London Evening Post*, the *European Magazine* (1782–83), and he also edited the Whiggish *Gazetteer* (1783–89). He was an early supporter of Fox.

41. See Henry Crabb Robinson, *Diary, Reminiscences, and Correspondence of Henry Crabb Robinson*, 3 vols. (London, 1869), II, 117. Robinson was a widely experienced journalist and on intimate terms with the Colliers.

42. Christie (356) states that Hazlitt joined the staff in 1813 and wrote theatricals in 1814, but Perry was unhappy that his "damned stuff" filled up the paper "at the height of the advertisement season"; in any event Hazlitt, meanwhile also writing for the *Examiner*, left the *Chronicle* in 1817.

43. Wilfrid Hindle, *The Morning Post, 1772–1937* (Westport, Conn., 1974), 5.

44. Sources are in conflict as to just when he left the *Post* and how long he was in jail.

45. See Boaden, I, 241n, 328; II, 32–33. Steevens, also a critic for the *St. James's Chronicle*, was an editor of Shakespeare and a lover of practical jokes (Taylor, II, 44–45, 289). Este toured the Continent in 1793 and published an account of it in 1794.

46. *The History of "The Times"* (New York, 1935); see vol. I: *The Thunderer in the Making, 1785–1841*, 75.

47. T. H. S. Escott, *Masters of English Journalism* (London, 1911), 147.

48. "Thomas Massa Alsager, Esq.: A Beethoven Advocate in London," *Nineteenth Century Music*, IX, no. 2 (Fall, 1984), 119–27.

49. Specimens in the 1790s of other dailies, such as the *Diary, or Woodfall's Register* (1789–1793), the *General Evening Post* (1733–1807), the evening *Star* (c. 1788), and Taylor's evening *Sun* (1792–1876), are too scant to characterize except to observe that they reviewed both Italian and English opera. The same is true of the thrice-weekly *Whitehall Evening Post*, which later merged with the *English Chronicle* (1779–1843) and the *St. James's Chronicle* (1761–1806). But as a morning thrice-weekly of eight pages, the *London Chronicle* (1757–1823) is an exception. Gray tells us they had some dramatic criticism in 1757–58 that ranked with Hunt and Hazlitt in literary quality. Library holdings are complete after 1770, giving welcome coverage in opera criticism before 1800, when surviving dailies other than the *Times* are often widely scattered; however, many if not all of its reviews were copied from other dailies, particularly the *Times*, the *Chronicle*, and after 1793 the *True Briton*.

50. Deeply divided British political interests are reflected in these periodicals, many of which appeared briefly in the 1790s.

51. These included the thrice-weekly *Flowers of Literature* (1803–10), the weeklies *Town Talk* (1811–14) and *Weekly Magazine* (1816)—the latter carried some articles on Italian opera—and the following monthlies: Gilbert Stuart's *English Review* (1783–95), for which Thomas Holcroft wrote some outstanding criticism (Gray); *Carlton Houe Magazine* (1792–96); *Literary Review and Historical Journal* (1794–95); *Monthly Visitor* (1797–1800); *New London Review* (1799–1800); *Literary Journal . . . a Review* (1803–6); *Oxford Review* (1807–8); and *New Monthly Magazine* (1814–15—not to be confused with a later series). Three annuals also reviewed librettos: the *Poetical Register* (1802–11); *Annual Review* (1802–1808); and *New Annual Register* (1781–1826), which was quite negative on opera.

52. Several weekly, semiweekly, and monthly periodicals of this type—*Theatrical Guardian* (1791), *Monthly Recorder* (1792), *Thespian Magazine* (1792–94), *Drury Lane Theatrical Gazette* (1798–1820), *Dramatic Censor* (1800–1801), *Covent Garden Theatrical Gazette* (1816–17—also under other titles), and *Opera Glass* (1826–27)—are too fugitive to have any value.

53. The oldest monthly in this category, the *Universal Magazine of Knowledge and Pleasure* (1747–1815), was perhaps the weakest. It carried no reviews until about 1785, and their reviews before 1800, some copied from the *London Chronicle*, were very brief and trivial.

54. See Winesaker, *passim*, and Langley, 443–45.

55. The *Examiner* signed Leigh Hunt's writings with an indicator symbol (fist

with pointing index finger); John Hunt's articles were unsigned; other contributors were signed with the writer's initials.

56. Benjamin Robert Haydon, *The Diary of Benjamin Robert Haydon*, ed. Willard P. Pope (Cambridge, Mass., 1960); entry for October 25, 1816.

57. Theodore Fenner, *Leigh Hunt and Opera Criticism: The "Examiner" Years, 1808–1821* (Lawrence, Kan., 1972), 66–67. Percy Young goes even further in declaring that there are "few more competent critics" in musical journalism: "Leigh Hunt—Music Critic," *Music and Letters*, XXV, no. 2 (1944), 87.

58. Langley (484–85) cites evidence of Bacon's connection with the journal in 1818; internal evidence shows that Bacon contributed in 1817 as well.

59. *The Autobiography of William Jerdan* (London, 1852), II, 179.

60. *English Music in the XIXth Century* (New York, 1902), 32. See also Langley, 489–94.

61. Another weekly in this category was *The Literary Chronicle* (1819–1828). Despite their avowed literary interests, their reviews were weak and trivial. They reviewed both Italian and English opera and carried articles of theatrical interest. W. H. Perry, whose name we find assigned to some of these in 1819, may have been the author of most of them.

62. This journal should not be confused with the *London Magazine, or gentleman's Monthly Intelligencer* (1732-June 1783) or a new series, the *London Magazine* (July 1783–85).

63. See Josephine Bauer, *The London Magazine, 1820–1829* (Copenhagen, 1953), I, 64, 90, 303.

64. Cyrus Redding, *Literary Reminiscences and Memoirs of Thomas Campbell* (London, 1860), I, 202. Redding replaced Campbell as editor in the 1830s.

65. Bacon wrote some articles for the journal, but this criticism is not his style. George Hogarth or G. L. Engelbach, both of whom contributed musical articles to the journal, may have written this criticism.

66. James Croy Kassler, *The Science of Music in Britain, 1714–1830* (New York and London, 1979), 35.

67. Langley, 114, 342. Kassler (1231) cites the "manly and impartial" reviews of Hogarth, which have "contributed greatly to the improvement in taste." Elsewhere we have noted his invaluable *Memoirs of the Musical Drama* (1838).

68. Perhaps it was for this reason that Hunt objected to the "transparent honesty" of the journal (Langley, 399).

69. Holmes in the *Atlas*, (see text below) took him to task for this criticism (*Atlas*, June 7, 1829).

70. Langley (366) surely had the "Review of Music" in view when she cited Ayrton's "unprecedented attention to detail"; this would not have applied to his "Drama" column. Elsewhere she finds his criticism comprehensive but superficial.

71. Hazlitt's writings for the *Atlas*, as well as that for the *Examiner* of May 7, 1826, and no doubt others, are not included in P. P. Howe's *Complete Works*.

72. Langley, 539–42. See also Leslie A. Marchand, *The Athenaeum: A Mirror of Victorian Culture* (Chapel Hill, N.C., 1941), chap. I.

73. Such literary heavyweights as the monthly *Gentleman's Magazine* and *Edinburgh Magazine*, and the *Quarterly Review*—the latter two politically oriented—carried no theatrical reviews, though the *Gentleman's* occasionally printed "fables" of the operas.

74. For a perceptive contemporary review of Mount-Edgcumbe's 1834 edition see *The Works of Thomas Love Peacock*, vol. 9, "Critical and Other Essays" (New York, 1967), 223–52.

75. Boaden's *Life of Mrs. Jordan* (London, 1831) is occasionally useful, and my references to it are always documented in the notes, whereas notes on the *Kemble*, cited in the Abbreviations, are merely inserted in the text.

76. The quality of that rise is evident from the course of this volume. Less obvious is the fact of the increase in the length of reviews. The new weeklies and monthlies had more space for longer reviews, but the dailies also expanded in size, adding additional columns and shifting to smaller type. The average review of an Italian opera premiere in the *Times*, for example, was about four hundred words in the 1790s and more than fifteen hundred words in the 1820s.

77. Hunt wrote briefly for Edward Quinn's *Traveller* in 1804 under the pseudonym Mr. Town, but no numbers for that year have survived. Barron Field was a Templar.

78. See James R. Thompson, *Leigh Hunt* (Boston, 1977), 61, and my *Leigh Hunt*, 58–59.

79. Writing of late-eighteenth-century developments in musical journalism, which addressed "a larger public than aristocratic connoisseurs and amateurs," Lang has observed: "This new public demanded a new manner of writing" (726). It is interesting to note that, though Germany had some musical journals of the early eighteenth century, the first traces of significant newspaper musical criticism, written by Frederich Relstab, appeared in the Berlin *Vossische Zeitung* at the identical period of the *Examiner*—1808–13 (Graf, 116; Lang, 979–80).

80. Paul Johnson, in the *Birth of the Modern: World Society (1814–1830)*, provides a breathless account of the arts and literature, science and technology, industry and economics during his period. Not devoid of errors, and more interested in colorful anecdotes than in a careful and coherent development, Johnson does nevertheless provide strong evidence of the cultural forces at work in those years, and we find him linking the poet William Wordsworth (in the country) and the essayist Charles Lamb (in the city) as fearing, along with many others, the portents of the new age they were witnessing.

81. Casts for most Italian and English operas up to 1800 are available in the *London Stage*. William C. Smith, in *Italian Opera and Contemporary Ballet in London: 1789–1820* (London, 1955), provides casts for some Italian operas from 1800 to 1822. John Genest, in *Some Account of the English Stage* (1832) usually provides casts for English operas at the Theatres Royal, but he provides nothing at all on the Lyceum/E.O.H.

82. The *Examiner* is an exception, owing to the frequency of quotations from it and to its wide availablity on microfilm.

83. Researchers interested in library holdings of periodicals in this period may want to consult the *Center for Research Libraries Catalogue* (Chicago, 1972; 2 vols.); the *National Registr of Microform Masters*; the *National Union Catalog*; and the Library of Congress *Newspapers in Microform: Foreign Countries: 1948–1983* (Washington, 1984), which lists only newspapers, not other serials, and is not up-to-date. The latter cites Research Publication Incorporated's "Early English Newspapers," available on microfilm, that includes a dozen or so serials in our period, though incomplete runs were filmed for some titles, and other sources may need to be consulted as well. Researchers might also want to consult the *Union List of Serials in the Libraries of the United States and Canada* (3d ed., 1965; 5 vols.), though long out-of-date.

Information as to current library holdings is best ascertained with the assistance of a reference or research librarian, who could help determine titles and library holdings; after that, a researcher would deal with the interlibrary loan staff. Some libraries even encourage patrons to conduct the search themselves, with access to online databases, such as the widely available international OCLC, maintained by the Online Computer Library Center in Ohio. For those seeking a complete run of a serial, it should be added that sometimes indicated holdings are only of scattered numbers and that missing numbers may need to be sought elsewhere or indeed may not be available anywhere.

Fortunately, most library holdings of serials in the United States are now available on microfilm through interlibrary loan. But some journals are not yet on microfilm; such is the case with some of the holdings of *Bell's Weekly*, for instance, which must be consulted at the New York Public Library's Newspaper Annex, and with the *Atlas* up to 1830, which is available at Yale (the numbers for 1829, however, are missing and must be consulted at the British Library Newspaper Library). Microfilms of some journals, such as the *London Gazette*, may be available only at the New York Public Library or through the Library of Congress, which will not lend microfilms to most libraries. I have tried to assist researchers by indicating, in my bibliography for primary sources, the origin of a number of long runs I was successful in obtaining, many through the cooperation of area facilities; microfilms of the *Times* and the *Examiner* are complete and readily available in many libraries.

For the preservation of most extant newspapers of the period we are of course ultimately indebted to the assiduity of Charles Burney—not Dr. Burney, the music historian, as stated by *Newspapers in Microform*, but his son—whose collection was left to the British Museum.

Part II

Introduction

1. William B. Boulton, *The Amusements of Old London* (London, 1901), I, 271–72.
2. *An Essay on the operas after the Italian manner* . . . (London, 1706).

3. See Frederic C. Petty, *Italian Opera in London, 1760–1800* (Ann Arbor, Mich., 1980), 72–74; Dennis Arundell, *Critic at the Opera* (London, 1957), 226.

4. Quoted by Percy M. Young, *A History of British Music* (London, 1967), 344n.

5. *Considerations of the past and present state of the stage* (London, 1809), anonymous pamphlet. For other instances, see Petty, chap. I.

6. *Anecdotes of Music* (London, 1814), I, 509.

7. The "Oratorios," which originated in 1760 at Covent Garden Theatre and were presented at the playhouses every Lenten season when their usual dramatic fare was suspended, had degenerated under John Astley in 1795 to nothing more than a kind of singing concert in which favorite arias taken from oratorios as well as from Italian operas (even including ballads and songs from English operas) were presented helter-skelter fashion; sometimes instrumental numbers were included. They were very popular.

8. Donald J. Grout, *A Short History of Opera* (New York, 1955), I, 190; Manfred F. Bukofzer, *Music in the Baroque Era* (New York, 1947), 239.

9. They were somewhat anticipated by composers Niccolo Jormelli and Tommaso Traetta, who, however, had little influence.

The Theatres

1. In June many patrons returned to their country estates, but since most boxes were subscribed in advance, this did not represent an intolerable burden to the management. In a King's Theatre ad in 1783, subscribers were notified that all of their fifty performances had been completed by May 3.

2. Based on the treasurer's book for 1786–87; see L.S., I, xxviii. For further details on the theatre generally, see *Survey of London*, XXIX, chap. VIII, 223–50.

3. Judith Milhous, "Lighting at the King's Theatre Haymarket, 1780–82," *Theatre Research International*, XVI, no. 3 (1991), 213–36.

4. Frederic C. Petty, *Italian Opera in London, 1760–1800* (Ann Arbor, Mich., 1980), 41.

5. Herbert Weinstock, *Rossini: A Biography* (New York, 1968), 131.

6. In addition to L.S. and *Survey of London*, details for this chapter are drawn from William C. Smith, *Italian Opera and Contemporary Ballet in London, 1789–1820* (London, 1955), 4–6, Daniel Nalbach, *The King's Theatre, 1704–1867* (London, 1972), 67–77 — his details for this period vary somewhat from Smith's; and John Ebers, *Seven Years of the King's Theatre* (London, 1828). My very brief sketch depends mainly on items in the periodical press.

7. Cecil J. L. Price, "Thomas Harris and the Covent Garden Theatre," *The Eighteenth Century Stage*, ed. Kenneth Richards and Peter Thompson (London, 1972), 115–16.

8. See *Survey of London*, XXXI, chap. XVIII, "Pantheon." See also Nalbach, 77–78, 97–100; Smith, 10–12, 16–18, 22; see also the *Times* for Apr. 10, Apr. 21, and July 29, 1790; Jan. 2 and Mar. 28, 1791; and Jan. 16 and Jan. 21, 1792.

9. Haydn's last opera, *L'amina del filosofo*, though paid for, was not given "because *Sig*. Gallini didn't receive the license from the King, and never will," he

wrote on Jan. 14, 1792 (H. C. Robbins Landon, ed., *Collected Correspondence and London Notebooks of Joseph Haydn* [Fairlawn, N.J.: 1959], III, 122). Adalbert Gyrowetz's *Semiramide* was written for production at the Pantheon, but the score perished in the fire.

10. Fortunately the Pantheon Papers survived in the destruction of the theatre; see Curtis Alexander Price's invaluable "Italian Opera and Arson in Late Eighteenth-Century London," *Journal of the American Musicological Society*, XLII (1989), 55–107, for a detailed account.

11. Curtis Price, Judith Milhous, and Robert D. Hume, "The Rebuilding of the King's Theatre, Haymarket, 1789–1791," *Theatre Journal*, 43, no. 4, December 1991.

12. Gallini's losses at the King's were not severe. He gained considerable wealth in remodeling the Hanover Square Rooms for the Bach and Able concerts in 1775 and was impresario there many years. He died a rich man in 1805. His children, to whom he left most of his estate, endowed a chapel in his memory at the Church of Our Lady, St. John's Wood. See Highfill and R. Ralph, "Sir John Gallini," *About the House*, V, no. 9 (1979), 30–37.

13. Da Ponte, né Emanuele Conegliano (1749–1838), was a baptised Jew who briefly became a priest but who was something of a libertine like his friend Casanova. Most famous for his libretto in Mozart's *Don Giovanni*, he wrote many successful librettos during the ten years he was in Vienna. In London he was arrested some thirty times in 1800 because he had foolishly signed a document backing Taylor's debts. When later creditors pursued him, he sailed for Philadelphia in April 1805, winding up as a distinguished professor of Italian at King's College (Columbia University) in New York. See Highfill and Alfred Loewenberg, "Lorenzo da Ponte in London," *Music Review*, IV (1943), 178–79.

14. The Duke of Sussex; Marquis of Headford; Earl of Cholmondelay; Earl of Seston; Viscount Hampden; Thomas Wynn Belasyse, Esq.; and William Ogelvie, Esq.

15. Feb. 4, 1806; see also Smith, 84. The press greatly exaggerated her salary (see "Veritas," 33–39). Of course she attracted a large following, but in 1808 when she sang all sixty nights, "towards the close of the season, empty benches and a miserable box account, told the manager his error" ("Chronicles," 73).

16. Smith, 113. The amount does seem high; in 1797 upper-tier "Green" boxes, seating four, could be taken for the night for four guineas; this compares with two guineas for a single box seat in 1787 (L.S., I, xxvii). The discrepancy is probably owing to the different types of boxes and whether by season or for a single night.

17. Though no house poet was officially designated on the roster from da Ponte's departure in 1805 until 1816, Serafino Buonaiuti certainly acted in that capacity in 1809. He was probably brought to London by composer Vincenzo Pucitta since the librettist and he produced no less than five premieres that season. Buonaiuti may also have remained for the 1810 season when they produced another premiere and when Buonaiuti wrote librettos for two or three premieres by P. C. Guglielmi. Buonaiuti also wrote a libretto for an opera premiere by Felice Radicati in 1811.

18. The *London Magazine* called Bochsa "a man of various and extraordinary talents."

19. The rent, which had been £8,500 in 1828, was doubled in 1829 (Letter to the Editor, T, Jan. 30). An "impartial observer" thought the rent should be no more than £9,000 (LG, Jan. 20, 1828, 48).

The Audience

1. *A Foreigner's Opinion of England* . . . (London, 1821), 407.
2. Letter to the Editor, T, Jan. 30, 1829. On the King's audience generally, see L.S., I, cxcvii and ccvi–ccviii.
3. *A History of Music in England* (London, 1952), 248–49.
4. Donald J. Grout, *A Short History of Opera* (New York, 1955), I, 200; Michael F. Robinson, *Naples and Neapolitan Opera* (Oxford, 1972), 9.
5. Southerland Edwards, *History of the Opera* (London, 1862), II, 135.
6. The King and the Prince of Wales had their separate boxes on either side of the stage. George III, before his illness, gave "Command Performances" at the King's and at the major playhouses. The Prince of Wales, later George IV, also occasionally attended Italian opera (the well-known rivalry between father and son extended to Italian opera, as we have seen). The cello was his favorite instrument; in his Sunday concerts, he and the Duke of Gloucester played together, accompanied by the Duke of Cumberland on the violin (Parke). He had a large music library, and it was owing to his possession of the score of Mozart's *La Clemenza di Tito* that the opera received its King's premirere in 1806.
7. This is slightly above the 18*p* a day average for wages in the London area: Adam Smith, *An Inquiry into the Nature and Causes of the Wealth of Nations* (New York, 1937), 75; 1st ed. London, 1776. Paul Johnson in *Birth of the Modern* shows that in 1815–30 the average annual wage of constables was £60 and of skilled artisans was £75, which would bring opera tickets well within reach.
8. Quoted by Frederic C. Petty, *Italian Opera in London, 1760–1800* (Ann Arbor, 1980), 155f. The cabal was also cited in a letter by Stephen Storace; see Eric Walter White, *A History of English Opera* (London, 1983), 218.
9. Cited by H. C. Robbins Landon, *Haydn in England, 1791–1795* (Bloomington, Ind., 1976), 128. Giardini (1716–96), a violinist, made a successful debut in London in 1751 and for the next twenty years was variously the King's leader and manager, concert impresario, and composer of operas and instrumental works. For a time he received powerful support from the Prince of Wales, who favored the "modern school" while his father favored Handel. See Simon McVeigh, "Felici Giardini: A Violinist in Late Eighteenth-Century London," *Music and Letters*, 64, no. 3–4 (July–Oct. 1983), 162–72.
10. See Lorenzo da Ponte, *Memoirs* (New York, 1929), 251.
11. Daniel Nalbach, *The King's Theatre, 1704–1865* (London, 1972), 5.
12. Robinson, 10. At the premiere of *Figaro,* every piece was encored, nearly doubling the length of the performance, and the King forbade further encores (Kelly). In a letter to his wife, Mozart recounted the encores in his *Magic Flute,*

adding, "But what always gives me most pleasure is the *silent approval*" (*The Letters of Mozart and his Family*, ed. Emily Anderson [New York, 1966], II, 966–67).

13. Curtain calls were illegal in Paris in the 1820s; see Howard Bushnell, *Maria Malibran* (University Park, Penn., 1979), 73f.

14. These were the Duchess of Devonshire, Duke of Cumberland, Lady Clarges, Duke of Dorset, Lady Cadogan, Duke of Marlborough, Lady Anne Linsey, Lord Abingdon, Lady Margaret Fordyce, and Duke of Queensbury (P, Jan. 11). Kelly reports that the Duke of Essex was a "great patron," and in 1787 Lord Cowper, long a resident of Florence and a "trusted scout" for Gallini, brought a Paisiello score to London (H, Feb. 19). Lord Exeter was probably a connoisseur (T, Jan. 8, 1787), and later amateurs included the Duke of Wellington (Chorley) and the Duke of Devonshire, who gave Rossini a letter of introduction to people in London. The Earl of Sandwich and Viscount Fitzwilliam were also "leading amateurs" (Davey). The list also no doubt included the Earl of Buckingham, who laid the first stone for the new King's Theatre, and the Duke of Bedford, who was the power behind the Pantheon affair.

15. "In Italy," Stendhal reported, "there are certain distinguished *dilettanti* who, although few in number, will always manage in the end to determining public opinion in the arts" (*Rome, Naples and Florence in 1817* [London, 1818], 37).

16. See Arthur Loesser, *Men, Women & Pianos* (New York, 1954), 230–35.

The Operas

1. See Frederick C. Petty, *Italian Opera in London, 1760–1800* (Ann Arbor, Mich., 1980), 374–78.

2. *The Tenth Muse* (New York, 1970), 161.

3. See Edward J. Dent, *The Rise of Romantic Opera* (London, 1976), 139–40. Romanticism in *music*, which is marked by a loosening of the "solid architecture" of classical music and the introduction of tone color, was not much in evidence before Weber, whose first opera was written in 1800, and probably no Romantic opera music reached England before his *Der Freischütz* in 1824.

4. Paul Henry Lang, *Music in Western Civilization* (New York, 1941), 786, 791–92.

5. John Ebers, in accounting for his 1821 season in *Seven Years of the King's Theatre*, shows, for example, that his "payments for engagement" totaled £8,631 for opera, £10,678 for ballet, £3,231 for the orchestra, and £5,372 for costumes and scenery painting. Against these costs his receipts were £20,316 for the boxes, £9,714 for the pit, and £1,261 for the galleries. He lost £7,073 for the season, which had seven productions and forty-five performances—both well below average.

6. According to Stendhal a successful run in Italy, under the *stagione* system, was regarded as thirty consecutive performances, which were offered (without ballets) every night but Friday. The season comprised eighty to one hundred performances, as against the King's sixty or sixty-five. See his *Life of Rossini*, tr. Richard N. Coe (New York, 1957), 443–45.

7. Perhaps one of the few Handel works to be presented almost unchanged at the oratorios was *Acis and Galatea*, performed at Drury Lane on February 28, 1789. The *Times* called it "one of the lightest and most captivating works of this master" (Mar. 7). Selections from Handel also found their way into the pasticcio *Orfeo* (1785) and a few English operas: the *Farmer* (1787), *Marian* and *Highland Reel* (1788), *Crusade* (1790), and *Midsummer Night's Dream* (1816).

8. Bach was "completely devoted to opera seria, without paying any particular attention to its dramatic aspects" (*NOHM*, VII, 46).

9. English opera borrowings included *Maid of the Mill* (1765), *Flitch of Bacon* (1778), and *Strangers at Home* (1785).

10. The press especially admired the bravura "Non é la mia speranza" and a second-act duet.

11. Petty shows 1791 as the work's premiere.

12. On Feb. 17, not Apr. 9 as shown by Nicoll.

13. English opera borrowings are found in *Strangers at Home* (1785), *The Prophet* (1788), *Rosina* (1789), and *Hartford-Bridge* (1792).

14. Admired numbers were "Sono in mar," "Alla selva," "Per costume," the rondo "Deh! Vien meco amato bene," and the "*recitativo instrumental* in the prison-scene."

15. Julius Sabinus pretended to derive his lineage from Julius Caesar and attempted a revolution in Gaul but was defeated by Titus; he hid in a cave many years but was finally discovered and put to death by Vespasian.

16. It opened on Apr. 14, not Apr. 18 as listed by Petty.

17. A pasticcio *Medonte* with music by Sarti was produced by the King's in 1783 (Petty).

18. Arias praised were "Mellanimoso[?] tromba," "Tremante gelosa," and "Odi grand'ombra," the last by Benelli.

19. Admired numbers were "Quel fabbro adorato," "Scherza il nocchier talora," "Se libera non sono," and "Luci del caro bene."

20. The opera combines Italian melody with "the delicate imagination, simplicity, lyricism and rhythmic finesse" of the French (Donald J. Grout, *A Short History of Opera* [New York, 1965], I, 259).

21. Perhaps the work was too "serious" for the English; as Karen Pendle reports, Grétry "set particular importance on the truth of musical declamation" in the opera, yet he "did so in a genre which was patently artificial." See "The Operas Comique of Grétry and Marmontel," *Musical Quarterly*, LXII, no. 3 (July 1976), 409–34.

22. "It was characteristic of the traditional operatic outlook" of Bach that he supplied additional airs for *Orfeo* (Reinhard G. Pauley, *Music in the Classical Period* [Englewood Cliffs, N.J., 1965], 173).

23. Gluck's great innovation was the "uniquely simple character of his melodies" (*NOHM*, VII, 83). Aside from *Orpheus and Euridice* (1792), English opera borrowings occurred in *No Song, No Supper* (1790) and *A Friend in Need* (1797).

24. Cleonice, Queen of Syria, forced to choose a mate, loves only the low-born

Alcestes, but the final revelation of his true nobility makes marriage possible.

25. Margery Stomne Selden, "Cherubini and England," *Musical Quarterly*, LX (1974), 421–34.

26. Arias praised by reviewers were "L'onda placida e tranquilla," "Quel amabile Visino," "Altezza eccellentissima," "Idol mio se tu non vivi," "A tanto amore," and "Come potesti ingrato core."

27. Not listed in N.G. or N.O.

28. Basil Deane, in *Cherubini* (London, 1965), 1–2, finds this opera and *Sabino* conventional for their time though they showed somewhat richer orchestration and more interest in ensembles than current *opere serie*. Cherubini "lacked melodic invention," but he compensated for this "by developing a style at once rhetorical and orchestrally massive" (*NOHM*, VIII, 38).

29. His work was basically classical, however; see Lang, 187–91, and Dent, 63. Deane, 4–5, calls *Lodoïska* "entirely original in its depth of psychological insight, dramatic tension, and musical depth," though it owed something to Grétry's *Richard*.

30. Stephen Storace (1766–96) was born in London and his main career there belonged to English opera, but he produced one of his Italian operas at the King's—*La Cameriera Astuta*—in 1788. It received mixed reviews and failed.

31. The critics admired a second-act quintet, "A la rabbia mi diova [for "dove"?]"; the aria "Dispensar a mio talento" (encored); and the rondo "Partirò dal caro sposo," which "raised admiration to a kind of enthusiasm" (P).

32. Angelo Tarchi (1760–1814) had very modest success at the King's despite his presence there from 1787 to 1789.

33. Cimarosa had a keen dramatic sense and an "ability to enhance comedy by musical caricature and apt portrayal of playfulness in his characters." His later operas had more expressiveness and warmer melodies, and his reputation in his last years was unparalleled except by Rossini (N.G.). He rivaled Mozart for melody and spontaneity but was "lacking in Mozart's profundity" (Grout, I, 254).

34. Cited were "Vedrete un ciglio nero," "Perche togliermi la sposa," "L'innalzi un Mausolco," the duet "Dell'odiosa mia Rival," and a last-act trio.

35. La Locandiera convinces the credulous Don Polidoro that a certain Miss Harriet carries about her a peculiar stone that can render her invisible, a situation that gives rise to many humorous developments (H).

36. The *Herald* and the *Times* (Jan. 15) praised especially the duet "Con quelle tue manine."

37. "Sento in petto un freddo gelo," "Dal tuo core," and the duet were praised.

38. Hogarth stated the opera was "not to be equalled even by the productions of Mozart"; "Chronicles" called the work a masterpiece.

39. In addition to the overture, they commended "Nel vedervi" in the first act, and "Ah mainer [for "manier"?] crudel" and a duet in the second.

40. Dent (*Romantic Opera*, 97) thinks the opera was treated too much in the style of opera buffa.

41. Encored were a trio, "O dolce e caro istante?", and a cavatina, "Quelle pupille tenere."

42. Hugh Canning, in "Cimarosa's Gli Orazi e i Curiazi," *Opera*, 32 (March 1981), 248–51, reports that Cimarosa's music in this seria is comparable to his *Matrimonio* in buffa style. Arias like "Quelle pupille tenere" and "Se pieta nel cor serbate" look to the past, while his prominent choruses and other arias "foreshadow the great 19th century operas."

43. The duet "La mia tenera" and the cavatina "Il mio bene" (from Paisiello's *Nina*, "Il mio ben quando"?) were admired. There were additional numbers by Mazzinghi and others, including Mozart's "Dite almeno in che maniera," based on a theme from his quartet K. 479.

44. They cited the duet "Pace caro mio sposo," already a favorite in Storace's *The Siege of Belgrade*, among other "worthy numbers." Mozart used a witty quotation from the first-act finale of *Cosa Rara* (1786) in the supper scene of *Don Giovanni*.

45. Roy Jesson, writing of this opera in the *Musical Times* (109, 609–11), states that Martín "commands a rich variety of rhythmic idioms and has an unfailing sense of theatrical timings in employing them."

46. Loewenberg, 178. The duet, "Quel tuo visetto amabile," was taken from *Orlando Paladino* (1782).

47. L.S., which does not identify this as a King's premiere, states: "In subsequent bills occasionally entitled, as originally, *L'Arbore di Diana*. The *Times* stated: "A magical tree is the center of a ceremonial test of virtue; it glows with light, and beautiful music is heard, if chastity prevails."

48. Jesson states that da Ponte provided "a well balanced sequence of arias, recitatives, and ensembles" in this opera and that Martín's music "distinguishes carefully" between the various characters: "music and text are inseparable" (*Musical Times*, 113 [June 1972], 551–53). Andrew Porter, however, finds the libretto weak (*New Yorker*, 54 [June 26, 1978], 95–98).

49. Martín's "popular" duet, "Ochietto furbetto," was praised, as was Mozart's aria, "Batti, batti" from *Don Giovanni*, apparently sung to the words "Bella rosa porporina." Also praised were a trio, "Mandina amabile," based on his K. 480; "Dite almeno in che maniera"; and Susanna's "Deh vieni, non tardar," from the last act of *Figaro*. See Petty, 277, and Loewenberg, 165.

50. "A compir già ve' l'impresa." Other airs praised were the aria "Ah non rai" and the duet "Dal tua caro."

51. Mount-Edgcumbe called it the most popular opera at the King's; it did not come even close to Piccinni's *Buona Figliuola*.

52. Joseph Haydn, *Collected Correspondence and London Notebooks*, ed. H. C. Robins Landon (London, 1959), 293. Another pastoral that also failed the same year was *Ati e Cibele*, by Gian Battista Cimador (1761–1805), Italian violinist, pianist, singer, composer, and music publisher, who came to London in 1791 and settled there for the rest of his life. This was his only opera at the King's; it had but one performance and was not reviewed.

53. Petty's date for this review is transposed; it should read 1798.

54. The *Courier* critic cited the sextet at the end of the first act, one second-act aria by Banti, and a trio, "Ah, se Re, se giusto sei," which had "exquisite taste" and was encored.

55. The plot, taken from Tasso (also set by Sacchini and Morlacchi), concerns "the magical skills of Armida, who holds Rinaldo enchanted on her isle and forgetful of war and glory, until two friends summon him and he effectively defies her 'Infernal Powers.'"

56. Da Ponte cut it to two acts in 1794 and added new lyrics, one of which was set by Domenico Corri. *Frascatana* was the first opera in Paisiello's mature style (I.L. Hunt, *Giovanni Paisiello* [n.p., 1975], 13).

57. Paisiello's music has less melodic ornamentation than his predecessors, and he did much to curb abuses by singers (N.G.).

58. This song first appeared in Burgoyne's comedy, *The Heiress*, which opened at Drury Lane on Jan. 14—just twelve days before this review appeared; it was the most popular English song ever derived from Italian opera.

59. Petty believes this was a first performance. Unaccountably, neither I. L. Hunt (even in the "works of uncertain ascription") nor N.G. lists this opera. Possibly it could have been his *Lo sposo burlato*, libretto by Casti (St. Petersburg, 1779), reworked for London following Paisiello's return to Naples in 1784.

60. On April 30 they pointed to the duet "Piche cornacchie e nottole" as a special favorite (Petty).

61. Theodor Neuhof (c.1686–1756), whose "kingdom" lasted less than a year, was rescued from debtors' prison in 1749 by Horace Walpole. A hero to Londoners, he was buried in St. Anne's, Soho. Einstein (*Essays on Music*, 191–96) called the libretto Casti's masterpiece and stated he had "one hundred times da Ponte's talent."

62. An unidentified review (TC) remarked especially on the song of the dream, "Non era ancora sorta l'aurora," which was "generally considered abroad as [Paisiello's] masterpiece" (Dec. 17).

63. This premiere (Mar. 10), which took place at the Little Theatre, is omitted by Smith.

64. T; I. L. Hunt, 42.

65. "Addio rinanti in pace," "Sognai tormenti, affani," "Che ascolto mai, che miro!", "Deh numi pietosi," "Nuove ognor funeste pene," and "Non temer fra pochi istanti," the last by Anfossi.

66. "Cara borza," a trio by Guglielmi; "Da questi lineamenti" by Salieri; and "Sospiro e mi vergogno" by Ferrari. I. L. Hunt lists the opera as *Gli Zingieri*.

67. One of these was "Mi perdo, si, mi perdo."

68. Rossini's "Di piacer mi balza il cor" and an old air, "Malbroug s'en va t'en guerre," were introduced into the opera that season.

69. The story was about a young, sensitive girl driven to madness by unrequited love and restored by the musical ministrations of her repentant loved one. *NOHM* (VIII, 391) notes that this reduction of a serious character to a plebeian

level was a fine example of the new semiseria opera and had a strong influence on Paer's later operas.

70. He was one of the first to introduce ensemble finales in opera seria; his tragedies are now thought too light and frivolous (N.G.).

71. According to Anglo-Saxon anecdote, King Edgar commissioned Athelwold to visit the fair Elfrida, and if he found her to answer to the elogiums on her beauty, to demand her hand in marriage. The plot turns on the deception practiced by Athelwold toward Edgar when Elfrida becomes Athelwold's ambitious and vengeful wife. The story was popular in several versions on the English stage in plays by A. Hill (1710); W. Meson (1752); T. Dibdin (1822); and in Arnold's opera, *The King's Proxy* (1822).

72. None of the reviewers recognized Paisiello's innovations—the use of concerted numbers rather than choruses, the insertion of recitative-like passages in the concerted numbers, and the avoidance of ornament—intended to increase the opera's dramatic effect. See I. L. Hunt, 42.

73. Borrowings from him occurred in *Marian* (1788), *Doctor and the Apothecary* (1788), *Siege of Belgrade* (1791), *Cave of Triphonius* (1791), and *Freebooters* (1827), among others. His music for *Barbiere* was the basis for a production of an English *Barber* in 1789.

74. The opera was produced with the assistance of Christian Cramer (Jeremy Commons, *One Hundred Years of Italian Opera*, I, 28).

75. The duet "Vaghi colli, ameni prati" and the airs "Paga fui lieta un di" and "O Giove omnipossente" were outstanding (TI). Kelly (II, 194–95) also praised Grassini's cavatina "Che farò senza la madre?" and Billington's "Apri la madre il core" as "brilliantly executed" and "long remembered."

76. Set in Palestine at the time of the Crusades, the opera ends with two deaths on stage—"a feature which would not have been tolerated in Italy for another ten years" (Commons, I, 33).

77. His *Opferfest* could not be performed at the King's, but an English translation was arranged by Hawes.

78. The librettists for most of Guglielmi's operas at the King's are unknown; probably they were all by Buonaiuti—see E, Feb. 25, 1810.

79. Especially praised was "Per quest' amore luguime [for "lacrime"?]."

80. N.G. lists only *La Caccia* and *Adolpho* of the Pucitta operas premiering in London.

81. Henry IV "loses his way in the chace, and after encountering fatigue, hunger, and storm, is sheltered in the house of a peasant, where he is hospitably entertained and gratified by being an unknown hearer of the praises of *Le Bon Henri*" (T).

82. "Viva Furico" was "rapturously encored." Commons states that Pucitta thoroughly understood the genre.

83. Boadicea, queen of the ancient Britons, taking advantage of the absence of Suetonius Paulinus, attacked the Roman legions and almost destroyed them.

84. Cited arias were "Son Regina" and "Ah non lasciarmi."

85. Cited numbers were the trio "Quel che piace a mio marito," the duet "Veder lo sol bramo," and the arias "L'angel che sta sul nido" and "Voi par foste, O care piume."

86. The plot, based on Emilie Opie's novel *Father and Daughter* (1801), concerns Agnes, daughter of Neapolitan nobleman Count Hubert, who elopes with Ernesto; consequently Hubert goes insane and is placed in confinement. After seven years she leaves her inconstant lover and returns home with her young daughter. "The most impressive scene in the whole piece is that which follows her introduction to her father's apartment. In one part of it Hubert, unconscious of the presence of Agnes, is endeavouring, but in vain, to recollect the words of a song which in happier days his daughter used to sing to him. Agnes, observing his distress, supplies them—the strongest emotion is excited—he appears to recognize her for a moment, but relapses into distraction; a mental conflict ensues, which his frame can no longer support—he faints—Agnes kneels at his feet kissing his hands, and the act closes" (T). In the final act Agnes's song, accompanied by a harp, restores Hubert's reason, and she is again reconciled to Ernesto, who pleads for forgiveness.

87. Cited were a cavatina by Agnes, "Tutto è silenzio intorno"; a duet, "Quel Sepolcro"; an air, "Quando la trovero"; and finest of all, "La vita umana è un mare." LM (Aug. 1820) also cited "O come è barono" and a duet "O cielo che questo."

88. Stendhal thought *Agnese* much too gruesome. He ranked *Sargino* (1803)—not performed at the King's—far above Paer's other operas. See Coe, *Rossini*, 27.

89. *The Freebooters*, essentially a translation of Angelo Anelli's libretto for Paer's *I fuorusciti di Firenze*, was produced on the English stage in 1827.

90. "Don Fedro is a nobleman of fortune whose love of music surpasses all bounds of reasonable moderation. The whole of his house is converted into a musical laboratory. No servant is admitted into his house who is not learned in the 'incomparable science.' He plays upon most instruments, sings in all kinds of voices, and pretends to superior skill in composition. But his daughter and her lover, a count, don't share his enthusiasms. Dismissed by the father, the count reappears in the disguise of a maestro of great celebrity, to whom Don Fedro is happy to give his daughter in marriage" (T, Jan. 7, 1829).

91. Jeremy Commons calls *Adelasia* "one of Mayr's strongest operas" (*One Hundred Years of Italian Opera*, vol. II, 7), and Stendhal thought Mayr's "E deserto il bosco intorno" in this opera his "finest achievement."

92. Irving Kolodin, in the *Saturday Review of Literature*, 52 (Dec. 20, 1969), 46–47, notes the influence of Gluck (philosophically) and Mozart (musically) in the opera and admires the libretto, stating that the music has "harmonic colorations beyond the common range of Italian resourcefulness." Yet Mayr was not a good melodist—the only factor that made the work less than a "major" production (Herbert Weinstock, *Opera*, 21 [Nov. 1970], 233).

93. The arias "Sento encore, mio dolce amor," "Si crudo e il mio destino," "Coi suoi frequenti palpiti," and the trio "La notte vicina," were cited as outstanding.

Carafa's "beautiful air" of "Mi vedrai nel ciglio ancor" was also introduced (T).

94. Commons (vol. II) sees Romani's fine libretto of *Rosa bianca* as responding to new Romantic currents of interest in medieval life.

95. The reviewers saw none of the "early romanticism in all its most extravagant vitality" attributed to the work by Commons (II, 28).

96. One other composer who had a single opera produced at King's Theatre during this period was Ferdinando Orlandi (1774–1848), an Italian composer and singing teacher who was active mostly in Milan, Munich, and Stuttgart, though his first opera was composed for Parma (1800). He apparently never came to London. A composer of some twenty-six operas between 1800 and 1820, he has been termed a "facile melodist"; S. D. ("Chronicles") links him with Pucitta as being an "insipid" composer. Yet his *La Dama Soldato* (librettist Mazzolà), which had its premiere at the King's in 1813, did fairly well and was revived in 1814 and 1815. But the *Chronicle* called it a "mélange" and undistinguished at that.

97. Fiske (506) surmises the Storaces brought back with them from Vienna some of the music for *Figaro* and possibly for *Don Giovanni*, since arias from them appeared in English and Italian operas before they were published on the Continent. A score for *Don Giovanni* was already available for amateur productions in 1809.

98. "Chronicles," 71n.

99. Reviewers praised the arias "Deh prendi un dolce amplesso" and "Deh perdona."

100. An anonymous amateur singer—see "Autobiography of an Amateur Singer"—wrote that a Mr. Howard "lent us his floor-cloth manufactory to perform in" and that the performances were "oratorio fashion, without action, amidst the mingled effluvium of canvas, oil, and turpentine." Yet an English translation of the libretto was available, and there was even a small band led by Spagnoletti. *Don Giovanni* was the first, followed by *Tito* and *Figaro*. No dates are cited, but Loewenberg ("'Don Giovanni' in London," *Music and Letters*, 24 [1943], 164–68) discovered that *Giovanni* was performed on May 23, 1809. The leads, however, were not amateurs at all. Sophia Dussek sang Donna Elvira; Maria Bland, Zerlina; Mrs. Hughes, Donna Anna; Charles Horn, the Don; John Braham, Attavio; Thomas Bellamy, the Commendatori; a Sr. Miarteni "of the King's," Leporello; and Gesualdo Lanza, Mazetto—all professionals. Even Billington sang some interpolated numbers.

There were also two concert performances of *Giovanni* in April and May of 1809, one in the Hanover Square Rooms and another in the Old London Tavern. See Alexander Hyatt King, "'Don Giovanni' in London before 1817," *Musical Times*, 27 (Sept. 1986), 487–93.

101. Arias cited as outstanding were "La mia Dorabella," "Di scrivermi," "Serva sia il vento," and "Un aura amorosa."

102. Catalani had introduced an aria from this opera in her performance of Fioravanti's *Virtuoso* in 1808 (T, June 1). The first performance was advertised as *Die Zauberflöte*, but of course it was sung in Italian. On March 29, 1806, the *Times*

advertised a performance (in German?) of Mozart's "The Enchanted Flute" to be performed at the San Souci German Theatre (cited by Dennis Arundell).

103. They were sung, respectively, by Rovedino and Griglietti, but without critical comment.

104. George Hogarth stated (II, 257) that "in the Italian version" the allegorical matter "is got rid of, and the piece is reduced to a childish and insipid fairy tale"—an objection that no doubt applied to all the King's productions through 1830.

105. This is the first instance I find of German sung at the King's—in violation of the legal restriction to Italian. Sontag, as we shall see, introduced excerpts from other German operas in the same season. These prefigure the production there, in 1832, of Beethoven's *Fidelio*, sung in German (Covent Garden presented an English version in 1835).

106. It was first advertised as "Le Mariage de Figaro," after Beaumarchais.

107. Cf. my *Leigh Hunt and Opera Criticism* (Lawrence, Kan., 1972), 202–6. In 1830 Tomas Love Peacock, reviewing a performance of the opera for the *Globe and Traveller* (May 7), noted that "the curtain fell amidst a shower of hisses, a well-merited complement to the more than usual bungling as the paltry *diablerie* at the end, to which Mozart's magnificent conclusion has been so strangely sacrificed." And at an 1832 performance, the work "ended as it should, with no dance of the devils" (*Works*, IX, 404, 432). Hogarth, too, regretted the "low buffooneries" of this scene (II, 248).

But Pauly (108) states that in the 1788 version (Vienna) Mozart "strangely" allowed some of the earlier "slapstick" elements of the story to be reintroduced. And Patrick Smith (*The Tenth Muse*, 164) claims that Gazzinga's tragicomedy *Don Giovanni Tenorio* (King's Theatre, 1794) was the immediate source for da Ponte's libretto, which lost dramatic power by the interlarding comic scenes and the "buffo" finale.

108. Even before 1800 selections from his operas found their way into the *Prisoner* (1792), *Ozmya and Doraxa* (1793), *Caernarvon Castle* (1793), and the *Mariners* (1793); see Loewenberg, "'Don Giovanni' in London," 164–68. Later interpolations occurred in *Elphi Bey* (1817), *Artaxerxes* (1818), and *Comedy of Errors* (1819), among others. And whole operas were adapted to the English stage, including the *Seraglio* (1827), *Tit for Tat* (1828), and the *Casket* (1829), as well as several versions of *Don Giovanni* and *Figaro* in the 1820s (see part III). Planché Englished the *Flute* for London in 1838, but Norwich could boast of an English adaptation as early as 1829.

109. Meyerbeer's theatre "became a sort of grand spectacle where the most bizarre figures paraded to the accompaniment of cleverly calculated music," and the popularity of Grand Opera continued to 1900 despite the works of Wagner, Verdi, and Debussy (Lang, *Music in Western Civilization*, 830ff.).

110. The story concerns love and treachery when some Knights of Rhodes are captured by Saracens during a Crusade.

111. Quoted by Arundell. Singled out for praise were "Giovinetto Cavalier" and

a quintet, "Sogni ridenti." Despite Ayrton's direction Garcia substituted an air of his own for Meyerbeer's "Pace ci reca?"

112. Though a mature Meyerbeer dismissed the opera as a fault of his youth, Robert Schumann admired *Crociato* much above any of his later operas. See John W. Klein ("Meyerbeer and 'Il Crociato,'" *Musical Times*, 113 [Jan. 1972], 39–40) writes: "The brilliant, often pompous orchestration . . . helps to camouflage the numerous defects of an inane libretto."

113. The story concerned Margaret's intrigues and defeat and the death of her son and heir in the War of the Roses (following the death of her husband, Henry VI); it also concerned her ultimate ransom by Louis XI of France. Unlike German critics, the French thought Mercadante's historical operas "as true as history itself" (Lang). *NOHM* (VIII, 441) regards Romani as "the best librettist of the age."

114. The arias "Se sfidai per voi," "Mio pianto rasciuga," and "Odo di belli concenti"; the duet "Sposa adorabile"; and the chorus "Che bell' alba!" drew special praise. The finales were excellent.

115. Dennis Libby, in "Spontini's Early French Operas," *Musical Times*, 117 (Jan. 1976), 23–24), calls the work "an Italian opera with French words," though Spontini "found the formula for the successful synthesis" of both styles. Luigi Bellingardini, in *Opera*, 24 (Aug. 1973), 727–29, notes that "the orchestration is exemplary, full of surprising and extraordinary solutions. . . . Such a work requires a first-class production." Berlioz, who "revered" the work, was imbued by the spirit of Gluck and *tragedie lyrique* through Spontini (N.G.).

116. "The opera begins with the Pirate's wreck on the seashore, his reception there by his former mistress, the jealousy of her husband, and his own distraction on finding her married to another. He then resolves on murdering her child, after which he fights with her husband, who falls his victim. He is condemned to death, and Imogen dies distracted" (E).

117. Dent, citing *Pirata* as a Romantic opera because it contained no *secco* recitative, states: "The imitations of Rossini leap to the eyes, but there are many scenes that have a charm and sensibility that are entirely Bellini's" ("Bellini in England," in *Selected Essays*, ed. Hugh Taylor [London, 1979], 167).

118. Lang states that the *Barbiere*, "sadly disfigured in modern performances," is "worthy of standing close to Mozart."

119. Quoted by Arundell, 299–300.

120. In all his operas after 1815, Rossini wrote out his ornaments and cadenzas (not excessive for the period), rather than leaving these to the abuse of the singers (Grout, I, 354).

121. In *Elisabetta*, all recitatives had orchestral accompaniment. Rossini was criticized in Italy (c. 1816–17) as "too German," overwhelming the voice with instrumentation, though he did not regard himself as of the German school (see Herbert Weinstock, *Rossini: A Biography* [New York, 1968], 50, 77–78). Yet he "had all his life an admiration, amounting almost to reverence, for German music" (*NOHM*, VIII, 415).

122. Dent (*Romantic Opera*, 117) calls Rossini a Romantic because his serious and comic styles are the same.

123. Highlights were the duets "Perche mai destin crudele"; "Non bastan quelle lagrime"; and "Ritorna al mio seno"; the recitative "Che pensa desolata Regina"; and the quartet "Se mi serbasti il soglio" (T; TI).

124. Luigi Bellingardini calls the opera "a bridge genially vaulting a whole neo-classic culture and leading directly to the Romantic image." It reformed opera seria by fusing in it buffa elements in earnestness for the first time; all recitative was orchestra-accompanied, and all ornament was written out for the first time (not in *Tancredi*) ("'Queen Elizabeth'—Its Style and Originality," *Opera* 23 [Aug. 1972], 686–91). *NOHM* (VIII, 415) finds the figures in the opera "too shallow."

125. The first-act trio "Cenerentola vien quà" and the arias "Una volta c' era un Re" and "Tutto è deserta"; the second-act arias "Fra tante angoscie e palpiti" (encored), "Signori, una parola," and "Ah! sempre fra le cenere," as well as the quintets "Ne tu più mormori" and "Sprezzo quel don che versa"; and the finales.

126. The success of *Tancredi*, which contained many ensembles, made Rossini's name international after 1817.

127. Stendhal greatly admired the opera and this aria, noting its *"originality* of style" and the "unexpected accompaniments, which perpetually stung the ear into wakefulness" (see Coe, 62).

128. Ebers reported this "difficult" music required one month for rehearsals. Rossini "took pains" with the orchestration to win over the pro-German Milanese (Weinstock, 75). All recitatives were *accompagnato.* Stendhal thought Rossini "sank deeper into German harmony" to compensate for Colbran's voice, which had markedly declined after 1816.

129. One Selim, a travelling Turk arriving in Naples, "is smitten . . . with the charms of Fiorilla, who, although fettered by the marriage tie, and also, after the received fashion in Italy, by the attention of a *cavalier servent[e]*, does not disdain his princely passion" (C).

130. Weinstock, 83–84. The opera was revived for Paris (1827) as *Moïse et Pharaon, ou Le passage de la Mer Rouge.*

131. Especially praised were the quartet "Mi manca la voce," the aria "Tutto me ride interno," and the chorus "All' etta, al ciel," plus, of course, the prayer.

132. Dent (*Romantic Opera*, 115) thinks Rossini was closest to Romanticism in *Otello* and *Donna del Lago.*

133. Rossini was drawn toward opera buffa, but he had little choice: impresarios thrust seria librettos on him (Weinstock, 120).

134. Argorante, an African prince, has seized upon Zoraide, a "beautiful female," who is betrothed to Ricciardo, a young and enterprising soldier. But the lovers are finally united (T).

135. Highlights were the quartet "Cessi omai" and sestet "Confusa, smarrita" in the first-act finale, and the second-act trio "Sara l'alma" and duet "Proteggi amore."

136. It is not clear if he "presided" at the piano for this performance, at which his wife sang Zoraide. The *New Monthly* noted at the 1829 one-act performance that the "recent curtailments" had been made by Rossini himself; the composer had prepared a one-act version for Vienna.

137. Corradino, a knight, lives in a great castle, dislikes women, and terrifies the countryside with his ferocity, but he is at last tamed by the beauty of Matilda.

138. Weinstock (III) has noted the opera's "careful composition" and "unity of style."

139. Drawn by Tottola from a tragedy by Belloy, the story relates "the dethronement of Palidoro, Prince of Lesbos, who is saved from destruction by his daughter Zelmira till the return of her husband, Ilo, who, at the head of his devoted followers, destroys Antenore, the usurper, and restores his father-in-law to the throne" (E).

140. Numbers praised were the arias "Terra amica," accompanied by chorus, and "Cora, deh attendimi"; a chorus of priests, "Di luce sfavillante"; a duet, "Perche mi guardi"; and three quintets, "Ah! che diffendi?", "La sorpresa, lo stupore," and "Nei lasci miei cadesti."

141. Rossini's music was "often inappropriate to character and situation" (NOHM, VIII, 425).

142. Contemporary Parisian critic Auguste Laget complained of loudness in Rossini's later operas (Weinstock, 166).

143. The *London*, annoyed by the English wealth bestowed on Rossini, wrote: "He has refused to put pen to paper for less than 100 guineas, and demands the very trifling compensation of 1,200*l*. for the copyright of the opera he proposes, *Deo volente*, to compose." But the work, partially paid for, was never completed and perhaps never even begun.

144. Exceptions were a second-act duet, "Quella ricordante," "which is distinguished by profound feeling," and "Ah! Sconvolia nell' ordine eterno" from the first-act finale.

145. Henry F. Chorley, *Thirty Years' Musical Recollections* (London, 1862), I, 25.

146. Other Rossini adaptations to the English stage were *Barber of Seville* (1818 and 1824), *Cinderella* (1830 and 1837), *Ninetta* (1830 and 1835), *Italian in Algiers* and *Othello* (1844). Some of his music was used in *Israelites in Egypt* (1833), *Fair Gabrielle* (1822), *Native Land* (1824), *Taming of the Shrew* (1828), and *Maid of Judah* (1829); see part III.

The Performances

1. Paul Henry Lang, *George Frederic Handel* (New York, 1966), 670. We have made no attempt, incidentally, to ascertain all the roles sung by particular singers herein—only those that were reviewed.

2. This was between Faustina Bordoni and Francesca Cuzzomi; see Lang (*Handel*) 182, and Dennis Arundell, *The Critic at the Opera* (London, 1957), 232.

3. Quoted by Edward J. Dent, *The Rise of Romantic Opera* (London, 1976), 26.

4. Paul Henry Lang, *Music in Western Civilization* (New York, 1941), 709.

5. Quoted by Lang, *Handel*, 670. "The extreme virtuosity of the solo parts" was "a regular feature of all *opere serie* of the period" (*NOHM*, VIII, 386).
6. Donald J. Grout, *A Short History of Opera* (New York, 1965), I, 190–92.
7. John Ebers, *Seven Years of the King's Theatre* (London, 1828), 110.
8. Cf. William C. Smith, *Italian Opera and Contemporary Ballet in London: 1789–1820* (London, 1955), 3–4; Arundell, *passim*.
9. At the 1828 York Festival, Sontag was paid £840 *per annum* at the chapel of the King of Prussia (Parke).
10. Frederic C. Petty, *Italian Opera in London, 1760–1800* (Ann Arbor, 1980), 13.
11. Quoted by Richard B. Peake, *Memoirs of the Colman Family* (London, 1841), I, 95.
12. James Boaden, *Memoirs of John Philip Kemble* (London, 1825), I, 447.
13. The aria was by Gioacchino Alberti, not Tarchi; see Petty, 240n16.
14. Quoted by Smith, 15.
15. He went to Paris in 1801, but the trip did not interfere with a full season at the King's. N.G. states that he "reached top rank" at Naples in 1797; if so, he *still* managed a full season at the King's.
16. Ayrton added this footnote: "The exquisite beauty of Braham's singing on the Italian stage will not easily be forgotten by the present age, and ought not to be overlooked by the future musical historian. No less entitled to the highest praise are his performances in... Handel's oratorios.... If in the English theatre he occasionally sacrifices to the *gods*, who are certainly infernal deities, though seated on high, he only does that which every man who knows the value of independence would, in his situation, do, if he could be sure of equal success.... 'Those who please to live must live to please.'"
17. Cremona, in Lombardy, where the finest violins were made.
18. Naldi later assisted Morelli in his financial difficulties (Kelly).
19. These reviews refute the assertion in "Chronicles" that his debut was "not particularly effective."
20. His name was taken from his stepfather; he never knew his natural father.
21. Cf. Stendhal: "Garcia, as Otello, shows unusual powers, not only as a remarkable singer, but as a considerable tragic actor; no one could show a finer grasp of every thread in that infinitely subtle web of thought and feeling which goes to make up" his character (quoted by Howard Bushnell, *Maria Milibran* [London, 1979], 8).
22. This astonishing attack was repeated in another indictment on July 2 (T).
23. The Duke of Wellington and Lord Maryborough were prominent supporters of Velluti (T).
24. Ebers, on the contrary, noted Velluti's "highly mobile features," which were sensitive to dramatic situations.
25. On August 15 the *Times* carried a long rebuttal to its critics and stated they had intended no personal attack on Velluti.
26. This was also pointed out by Ayrton (Har, III, 166).
27. A year later, a J. Russell, singing in English opera at the Little Theatre,

"gave an excellent imitation" of Velluti — "in our opinion no caricature, though it convulsed the house with laughter" (At, Aug. 23). Stendhal (Coe, 265) strongly defended Velluti's style, which "gives us a whole, coherent speech, every line of which is conceived *in the same character*."

28. First cited in the press as "di Begni."

29. In "Musical Chit Chat" for May 1828 the *London* wrote with tongue-in-cheek about a paternity suit: "The talents of Signor Curioni have never been so highly rated by the Opera pit as since his little affair with the parish officers of Mary-la-bonne, and his masterly endeavours to prevent the escheat of his lands for want of an heir. His paternal dignity is thought to become him."

30. Nancy, if not her brother, retained the Italian pronunciation of her name; in 1808 Genest referred to her as "Storache."

31. Some reviewers do not support this criticism.

32. Cf. "Chronicles," 13; they and Mount-Edgcumbe state that she nearly failed at first, but she performed *Vergine* ten times that season.

33. "Chronicles," however, asserted her voice "exceeded not the usual compass, the two octaves between B flat and B flat." At her debut her brother accompanied her on a *"vox humane."* Though played with skill, however, it "added no brilliancy" (H).

34. Which aria was not stated, but it could hardly have been an asset to Guglielmi's opera, which had but four performances.

35. Even at a Bath concert, considerable opposition to her was apparent in the fashionable audience (T, Nov. 15, 1809).

36. Mount-Edgcumbe, II, 97–100; see also Hogarth, II, 243.

37. "Chronicles." She had opened a small theatre in Paris but was unsuccessful. Sutherland Edwards, who heard her, stated she had most of her success in England, and the least in Italy (*History of the Opera* [London, 1862], II, 21). A fine, life-size sculpture of the standing diva at the Victoria and Albert Museum reveals a figure actually petite; one wonders where all that vocal power came from.

38. She is said to have "saved the opera" that season after the withdrawal of Mme Colbran (Scott, "Rossini in England," *Opera*, 27 [May 1976], 439). In 1821 she sang at a concert attended by the nobility and the amateurs and was reviewed by the *London Chronicle* (Aug.). Henry Phillips stated that at a concert she sang "Comfort ye" "very flat" (*Musical and Personal Recollections during half a century* [London, 1864], II, 63).

39. It would appear that she was even more successful in 1816 than in 1815, despite N.G.'s views to the contrary.

40. Variously called de Begni, di Begni, de Begnis, and Ronzi by her first London critics, who later settled on Madame de Begnis. After her separation she used Ronzi as her stage name.

41. On April 15, not April 19 as reported in N.G.

42. They carried a full account of her continental successes and reported her King's terms were about £250 a night, with liberty to sing six concerts.

43. I find no record of *Der Freischütz*, or even a scene from it, being performed at the King's before 1831.

44. Sontag's sister Nina sang Papagena; Madame Roser, the Queen; Mr. Schutz, Papageno; and Mr. Vellaner, Sarastro.

45. This likely reflects a growing Romanticism in the musical taste of the French.

46. The *Examiner*. See also "The Plain Speaker," *The Complete Works of William Hazlitt*, ed. P. P. Howe (London, 1930–34), XII, 324–35.

47. "Mi vedrai nel ciglio ancor" and "Cara memoria."

48. Pasta played Otello at the King's in the 1829 revival, according to Bushnell (132).

49. Henry F. Chorley, *Thirty Years of Musical Recollections* (London, 1862), 88–89.

50. Bushnell overlooks Ayrton's review (Har) of her Rosina (though he cites his other reviews frequently) as well as other reviews that show García-Malibran's first King's season was considerably less enthusiastic than he describes.

51. Quoted by Petty, 301–2.

52. *Music in the Classic Period* (Englewood Cliffs, N.J., 1965), 89.

53. See H, Jan. 7, 1784; PA, Feb. 28, 1785; P, Jan. 5, 1796, for example.

54. Some years after Salomon's death, Edward Holmes, marking the decline of the Philharmonic, wrote: "It was Salomon who first made the distinction between *fiddling* and playing the violin. . . . He gave the first fillip to instrumental music in this country. . . . In successive seasons of the Philharmonic, the spirit has evaporated; the fiddlers are now glad to turn over the leaves of their music-books, and the conductor is anxious for his lobster-sallad at home" (At, Sept. 7, 1828).

55. PA, Feb. 28, 1785; TC, June 3, 1786; P, Apr 16, 1800.

56. C, Jan. 16, 1804; C, Mar. 26, 1804; T, Mar. 29, 1804; Cr, Jan. 27, 1806; and T, Apr. 29, 1811, respectively.

57. The orchestra of the Royal Academy of Music attracted favorable notices (T, Dec. 7 and 14, 1829; Ath, Dec. 9, 1829).

58. Daniel Nalbach, *The King's Theatre, 1704–1867* (London, 1972), 116.

59. Aglio replaced Marinari in 1804. See Sybil Rosenfeld, *Georgian Scene Painters and Scene Painting* (Cambridge, 1981).

Themes and Currents

1. A particularly malevolent attack occurred in a review by the *New Spectator* for March 23, 1784, quoted by Frederic C. Petty, *Italian Opera in London, 1760–1800* (Ann Arbor, Mich., 1986), 214.

2. T, Feb. 23, 1787, and July 23, 1797, for example.

3. "Chronicles"; see also Michael F. Robinson, *Naples and Neapolitan Opera* (Oxford, 1972), 61.

4. Holmes (At) declared in 1827 that "shakes are odious, and only fit for the galleries of Covent Garden and Drury Lane" (May 13).

5. Apparently George IV still had a strong influence at the King's.
6. As indicated earlier, Rossini himself would scarcely have agreed to this.
7. For the full review, see *The Complete Works of William Hazlitt*, ed. P. P. Howe, "Dramatic Criticism," XII, 395–98.
8. See my *Leigh Hunt and Opera Criticism* (Lawrence, Kan., 1972), 178–81.
9. The public taste was denegrated in these reviews: C, June 8, 1816; TI, Aug, 1819; T, Jan. 2, 1824; At, Apr. 26, 1830; and Ath, Mar. 20, 1830. And it was praised in these reviews: LG, Apr. 26, 1817, T, May 28, 1817, Aug. 4 and Dec. 22, 1828; and NM, Feb. 1827.
10. Stendhal noted: "It is a sad, but probably true reflection, that, in music at least, the *ideal* conception of beauty changes every thirty years" (*Rossini*, trans. Coe, 14).
11. Barnett (1802–90) was the son of a Prussian diamond merchant who changed his name and settled in England. He "sang like a bird" as a child and at eleven performed at the Lyceum. Taking lessons from C. E. Horn and others, he remained on stage until age eighteen, when he began composing. He wrote much incidental theatre music (1826–36), "not of a high standard" (N.G.), and by 1830 had written nothing operatic.

In that year he had three productions, however. In the first, a two-act romantic drama, *Robert the Devil, Duke of Normandy* (Covent Garden, Feb. 2), the play (attributed by Nicoll to Lacy but by the *Chronicle* and Genest to Robert J. Raymond) was dismissed, though the music was thought to be "worthy of a better fate" (LG); some airs were "extremely pretty" (C), and "the overture and first chorus were far from being despicable" (E). The music, "but a slight effort," was by a few degrees better than "current theatre music" (At). In September the Adelphi produced a "new" *The Deuce is in Her* (perhaps adapted from Planché's 1820 work), and Hunt wrote: "Mr. Barnett, we believe, has written many popular songs, and we are told, many indifferent ones. We only know him by the one before us, and the *Light Guitar*, which was an odd mixture enough of chaunt and bolero, but pleasant too. We are persuaded, however, that he has the right stuff in him, if he will take pains to work it" (*Tatler*, Sept. 4). At another production two months later, though, Hunt was sorry he could not praise his music: "There is occasionally much ostentation in it of dramatic effect and orchestral potency; but the vigour is more 'loud than deep'; the accompaniments appeared to us to be at once noisy and barren, the melodies neither new nor flowing, and the whole music disjointed, and wanting in purpose" (Nov. 1). And Wade (Ath, Nov. 6) noted further plagiarism: "Does Mr. Barnett think that music is like a kiss, sweetest when stolen? He should not do such things, for he has given repeated evidences of being a very delightful composer."

But his *Mountain Sylph* (1834), libretto by T. J. Thackeray, was very successful. Its musical importance lay in the cumulative effect of dramatic scenes (with few strophic songs), showing the influence of Weber (N.G.).

12. See Edward P. Mackerness, "Leigh Hunt's Musical Journalism," *Monthly Musical Record*, LXXXIII (1956), 219–22, for a fuller account of the controversy.

13. The N.G. states that he "admired" *Artaxerxes*.

14. Yet reviews by writers who are not musicians or musicologists are not unwelcome even today! Adrian Wintle, who admires Shaw's music criticism—it bears many stylistic resemblances to Hunt's—writes: "I believe that criticism ought primarily to be a pleasure to read. Though I am a musician as well as a critic, I would far rather read a sensitive report by a man whose perception was but faintly matched by knowledge of technical terms, than criticism by some ardent, eminent, jerky-styled pedant" ("In Defence of Musical Criticism," *Musical Opinion*, vol. 87 [Dec. 1963], 149).

Part III

Introduction

1. *Foundations of English Opera* (London, 1928), 233.
2. Delius's *Koanga* (1897) and *A Village Romeo and Juliet* (1901), Dame Ethel Smyth's *The Wreckers* (1906), and Vaughan Williams's *Sir John in Love* (1929) and *Riders to the Sea* (1937) might be regarded as exceptions. Weber did not consider *Oberon*, which he hoped to translate into German, a true opera.
3. *The History of English Opera* (London, 1983), 7.
4. John Dennis, *An Essay on the Opera's after the Italian Manner* (London, 1706).
5. Quoted by Paul Henry Lang, *George Frederic Handel* (New York, 1966), 613.
6. *A Short History of Opera* (New York, 1965), I, 141.
7. *The Critic at the Opera* (London, 1957), 279; see also Fiske, 274–75.
8. "Theatre Music, 1800–1834," *Music in Britain: The Romantic Age, 1800–1914*, ed. N. Temperley (London, 1981), 292.
9. "The English Romantic Opera," *Victorian Studies*, 9 (Mar. 1966), 296.
10. "'Gothic' Literature and Dramatic Music in England," *Journal of the American Musicological Society*, XV, no. 1 (Spring 1962), 52–53.
11. "Victorian Musical Theatre," *Opera*, 29, no. 2 (1972), 138.
12. See David Mayer, "Nineteenth Century Theatre Music," *Theatre Notebook*, 30, no. 3 (1976), 116; his comments were based on Fiske's first edition.
13. From 1775 to 1800 only William Jackson's *Lord of the Manor* (1780) and Stephen Storace's *No Song No Supper* (1790) were published in full orchestral score. Some are available in manuscript, but upwards of one hundred were published as vocal scores—not always reliable as a guide to the complete work. Theatre managers, fearful of pirating, were reluctant to publish successful works (see *NOHM*, VII, 264).

Appendix 14 indicates opera scores (usually vocal) that are known to have been published, and appendix 15 indicates librettos that are known to have been published.

14. See White, 68–76, and Curtis A. Price, *Henry Purcell and the London Stage* (Cambridge, 1984), 39.

15. Price, 296–97.

16. Most of Purcell's stage works are semioperas, a type of "heroic" Restoration drama with singing and dancing that emphasized spectacle and masque-like scenes somewhat akin to the French divertissement, sometimes with supernatural beings. Elkanah Settle's *The Empress of Morocco* (1673) established the type.

17. Curtis Price, 6. *Dido and Aneas*, which Price regards as derivative, never had a public performance in Purcell's lifetime (it was politically unwelcome), and until 1895 much of the music was lost; yet some did survive and was well known in our period.

18. *Music in Western Civilization* (New York, 1941), 515–16, 682.

19. *A History of English Drama*, II, 238–39.

20. Until recently, it still had long runs. In 1928 Kurt Weill wrote new music to lyrics by Bertolt Brecht in *Die Dreigroschenoper*, a popular German opera based on Gay's work.

21. For a study of the work and its history, see Edmund M. Gagey, *Ballad Opera* (New York, 1937)

22. In his *Harmonious Meeting* (London, 1965), Wilfrid Mellers, who finds little to admire in English music after the Restoration, writes: "The virtual disappearance, as a creative force, of both opera and drama from 19th century England is not fortuitous. On the contrary, it is a direct sequel to the negativism of *The Beggar's Opera*: which was in turn an extension of the lyricism inherent in Restoration society" (283). And he adds that theatre music after Handel "is decadent in that it has ceased to be *inherently* dramatic. It is pretty music attached to a drama" (266).

23. As pointed out at the end of part II, John Barnett's successful *Mountain Sylph* (1834) was long thought—erroneously—to be an all-sung opera. Michael Balfe's even more popular *Bohemian Girl* (1843) also had spoken dialogue; his *Catherine Grey* (1837) and *Falstaff* (1838) *were* all-sung but had limited success.

24. *Music and Nationalism: A Study of English Opera* (London, 1911), chap. VI.

25. Nicoll (III) cites only Colman the Younger and Holcroft among the best of the playwrights who produced librettos, while Burgoyne, Cumberland, and Reynolds were among the runners-up for "genuine stock pieces." After 1800 (IV), however, he commended the dramas of Cobb and Hoare.

26. Aubrey S. Garlington junior, in "'Gothic' Literature and Dramatic Music in England" (JAMS, XV, 59), states that Busby "composed some vivid music to illustrate many of the scenes."

27. Smith also makes the interesting observation that, just as Metastasian opera seria viewed abstracted emotions from an "empyrean plane," especially in the "exit arias," so the melodrama "carried over this emotional highlighting" and "made it exaggeratedly human as the opera seria had been exaggeratedly ideal. . . . Thus the neurotic, the febrile—and, pre-eminently, the outright insane—became an integral part of the stock operatic scene" (*The Tenth Muse*, 193).

28. *Sheridan to Robertson* (Cambridge, Mass., 1926), 349–54.

29. See Cecil J. L. Price, ed., *The Letters of Richard Brinsley Sheridan* (London, 1966), I, 89, 91.

30. Richard Brindsley Peake, *Memoirs of the Colman Family* (London, 1841), II, 287.

31. Edward Fitzball (né Ball), *Thirty-five years of a Dramatic Author's Life* (London, 1859), I, 196, 203.

32. John O'Keeffe, *Recollections of the Life of John O'Keeffe* (London, 1826), II, 15, 323.

33. *The Reminiscences of Thomas Dibdon* (London, 1827), I, 240–41.

34. This was the arrangement for Bickerstaffe's operas; see Cecil J. L. Price, *Theatre in the Age of Garrick* (Totowa, N.J., 1973), 114f.

35. See also the *Examiner*, Dec. 21, 1828.

The Theatres

1. See *Survey of London*, XXXV, chap. 1.

2. Londoners themselves often confused the King's Theatre with the so-called "little" theatre opposite it—both in the Haymarket—as the "Haymarket theatre." I have referred to the latter—the Theatre-Royal Haymarket—as the "Little Theatre" throughout. Another point of confusion is a reference to the King's Theatre as "The English Opera House" (Marc Baer, *Theatre and Disorder in Late Georgian London* [Oxford, 1992], 47), confounding it with Samuel Arnold's "English Opera House," formerly the Lyceum Theatre.

3. Quoted by Ernest B. Watson, *Sheridan to Robertson* (Cambridge, Mass., 1926), 13.

4. The successful playwright/librettist Frederic Reynolds, as might be expected, thought the magnificence of the scenic effects compensated for other problems; but even William Hazlitt saw no theatrical falling off "to an alarming degree" (Josephine Bauer, *The London Magazine, 1820–1829* [Copenhagen, 1953], 64).

5. *Theatrical Repertory*, no. II, Sept. 26, 1801.

6. Fiske, 171–72.

7. *Tatler*, April 11, 1832.

8. In this struggle the *Times* and *Post* supported Kemble, the *Chronicle* the O.P.'s. In addition to the price increases of about six pence, the playgoing public was incensed over the replacement of a number of their regular seats with new boxes, for which the theatre could charge more. They were also vexed because Madame Catalani was to sing there on opening night (Baer, 110). The riots led to the withdrawal of aristocratic patrons, and "all critics complained that [these patrons] could find no good in anything dramatic that was not of foreign origin" (Watson, 12).

9. Many lawsuits ensued, for example, leaving the theatre bankrupt by 1829. Some earlier seasons were profitable; T. Dibdin tells us their receipts for 1816 were £58,000, leaving a profit of £11,000.

10. Arnold's productions were limited to the summer season. From 1809 to 1812

the theatre housed the Drury Lane company while their theatre was being rebuilt.

11. Details on the performances have been drawn from Fiske, 254ff; L.S., I, Introduction; and Watson.

12. Henry Saxe Wyndham, *The Annals of Covent Garden Theatre from 1732 to 1897* (London, 1906), I, 202.

The Audience

1. See also Marc Baer, *Theatre and Disorder in Late Georgian London* (Oxford, 1991), *passim*; on the playhouse audiences generally, see L.S., I, cxcv–ccviii, and Nicoll on "Audience" in vols. III and IV.

2. They could of course see the afterpiece entire; and some plays were written so that a character would briefly summarize the foregoing plot for the benefit of latecomers.

3. Ernest B. Watson, *Sheridan to Robertson* (Cambridge, Mass., 1926), 13–14.

4. H. C. Robbins Landon, *Collected Correspondence and London Notebooks of Joseph Haydn* (Fair Lawn, N.J., 1959), 273f.

5. Obviously, the theatrical situation had changed considerably from the mid-eighteenth century, when the majors were not regarded as so different from the minors and when no portion of the audience, including those in the boxes, "was the exclusive preserve of any social group" (Marvin Carlson, "Theatre Audiences and the Reading of Performance," *Interpretation of the Theatrical Past*, Thomas Postlewait and Bruce A McConachie, eds. [Iowa City, 1989], 167). Also, in Garrick's day, "playgoers of quality vied for a seat in the pit, content to rub shoulders with butcher and barber" (George Rowell, *The Victorian Theatre, 1792–1942* [Cambridge, 1978], 4).

6. The colors of Charles Fox's Whig party—probably an allusion to the Prince of Wales; in 1792 his box was decorated in blue and silver (T, Dec. 29). Yellow was the Tory color.

The Operas

1. *The Rakish Stage: Studies in English Dram, 1660–1800* (Carbondale, Ill., 1983), 238.

2. Leigh Hunt, *Autobiography* (London, 1948), 42.

3. *The Life of Mrs. Jordan* (London, 1831), II, 88f.

4. A rewrite of his review for the *Chronicle* (Oct. 23, 1813). In July, the *Inquisitor* reviewed Gay's *Polly* (1728), a sequel to *The Beggar's Opera* that so offended Sir Robert Walpole it went unperformed until 1777.

5. Sheridan thought critics were "greater prudes than ladies in the boxes" (Cecil J. L. Price, ed., *The Letters of Richard Brinsley Sheridan* [Oxford, 1966], I, 86).

6. Fiske, 181. A 1789 revival included "Pace caro mio sposa" from *Cosa Rara*; Petty cites six editions of the song.

7. Paul Henry Lang, in *George Frederic Handel* [New York, 1966], 319), has

noted Handel's interest in Arne's music because, although quite un-Handelian, "there is a felicity and domestic security present that is as attractive as it is thoroughly middle-class English."

8. Charles Dibdin, who admired Purcell, gave Arne's adaptation high praise.

9. Cited were "Fairest isle, all isles excelling," "Come, if you dare, our trumpets sound," "Britons, strike home," and "Rule Britannia."

10. The "Prospect of Winter in Frozen Countries," a masque in act III later known as the "Frost Scene," occasionally mounted as a separate work, was regarded in the eighteenth century as "one of Purcell's greatest works" (Curtis A. Price, *Henry Purcell and the London Stage* [London, 1984], 303).

11. Eric Walter White, *A History of English Opera* (London, 1983), 140.

12. *Anecdotes of Music* . . . (London, 1814), III, 408.

13. The *Inquisitor* (Dec. 1816) even doubted Bickerstaffe's guilt.

14. *General History of Music* (New York, 1935), II, 1016.

15. Percy M. Young, *A History of British Music* (London, 1967), 357.

16. Cf. Hunt's criticism of Mr. Scriven in the similar role of Hodge in *Love in a Village*: Scriven "did nothing, or in other words he invented nothing for his author, and this is . . . bad work for Mr. Bickerstaff" (E, Sept. 25, 1808).

17. When Dibdin deserted Covent Garden for Drury Lane in 1768, he rewrote the music for the new singers. Some English composers were as careful as the Italians to style their songs for particular singers.

18. Bishop "refurbished" the score for an 1818 Covent Garden production. At a revival of the opera in 1965, M. D. Hastings noted that the music "repays revival and increases the many pleasures of the comedy," adding that "the advantages of the original piece is good proportion between play and music: sufficient action has the complement of musical repose (though the 'repose' is gay and lively)" ("Touched-Down Dibdin," *Musical Opinion*, 88 [Sept. 1975], 727–28).

19. The "Woodman" is a somewhat mythic figure, at whose hut and "Hop Ground" the tangled love interests of four principals are satisfactorily resolved (LC). Fiske calls it a "drab" rehash of *Rosina*.

20. Fiske admires the music and choruses of the last act but finds too many glees in earlier acts.

21. John Taylor, MM, January 1798, 13.

22. Fiske (453–54) reports that Arnold produced the work himself for Covent Garden for £700 since the management had "no confidence" in it. Despite its success, Arnold never wrote another piece for Covent Garden.

23. John O'Keeffe, *Recollections of the Life of John O'Keeffe* (London, 1826), II, 70–71.

24. Fiske, 462. O'Keeffe got £600 for the opera, out of which he paid Shield £20 and gave him publication rights to the music.

25. The plot, laid on the island of Col in Scotland, involves the matrimonial prospects of Jenny, an orphan raised by the unregenerate steward, M'Gilpin, and who loves the peasant Sandy (the Laird's son in disguise), but the latter is bought off by a recruiting sergeant. The timely arrival of the Laird of Col sets all straight (LC).

26. "Old England" was adapted to Bannister's powers; other national tunes were "Maggie Lawder," "Donald," and "The lad with the white cockade"—a "favorite Highland reel."

27. I mistakenly followed Hunt's ascription of the music to Dr. Arnold in my *Leigh Hunt and Opera Criticism* (Lawrence, Kan., 1972), 129; undoubtedly Shield was responsible for the music, and either he borrowed some of Arnold's airs or they were inserted by singers.

28. In 1966 London Records issued a recording of the opera under the direction of Richard Bonynge. *Rosina* is Shield's only orchestrated manuscript to survive.

29. Edward is forbidden to marry Marion by her father until it is learned that Edward's mother had recovered her estate, of which she had been deprived by the artifices of her uncle.

30. Patrick Smith, in *The Tenth Muse* (New York, 1970), 136, states that the "recognition scene" in the Sedaine-Grétry original "became one of the celebrated moments in French opera."

31. Many of these songs were apparently rescued from the failed *Campaign* of Robert Jephson and Giusto Ferdinando Tenducci.

32. Two choleric old fathers fall out over plans to unite their families through marriage, but this is finally accomplished through the scheming of Pedro, an arch rogue of a valet.

33. "The wayward tongue fond love repelling" was especially praised. This critic was obviously more experienced than the reporter four days earlier, who admitted his knowledge of music was "insufficient to discriminate particular beauties or slight faults; we judge from *feeling* more than from *science*" (UR, Nov. 12).

34. It was a medley of quotations, including a fandango from Gluck's *Don Juan*, "Nel cor più non mi sento" from Paisiello's *Molinara*, and a Russian folk tune (Fiske, 550). The "Traveling song" ("Thro' France, Thro' all the German regions") was "declamatory and comic" (MM, Jan. 1798). Fiske calls the score "animated . . . with a good deal of fifing and drumming and more quotations than usual."

35. A French family, forced to flee from their chateau to Spain, is set upon by robbers but saved by a Spanish gentleman whose son falls in love with the French daughter (T).

36. "The Seaman's Home" was cited as well as "The Waving Willow," and "The Rosery" became very popular; Shield borrowed the overture from J. H. Naumann's *Amphion* (Fiske).

37. Parke wrote that the "bustle and variety in this piece kept the spectacle continually alive." And Boaden thought the prose "more pointed and of a better tone than usual."

38. Fiske (557) cites "Ah, Divinité," from Gluck's *Alceste*, as the most interesting borrowing and states that "the absence of glees and the fewness of strophic songs" show "some seriousness of purpose." This opera may mark some decline in the quality of Shield's theatrical music (N.G.), though reviews of his later operas were still supportive.

39. One song, "On board the Arethusa," sung by Incledon, was praised.

40. The plot, set in Renaissance Italy, concerned Valentine, a favorite of the Duke of Urbino, and his love for Isabel, whose father has been banished from the court. Boaden found it written "rather in Shakespearean language."

41. A posthumous production of Shield, with a libretto by John Tobin, who died in 1804, surfaced in 1816 — *Your's or Mine?* It failed, although critics still praised Shield's music.

42. R. Crompton Rhodes, *The Plays and Poems of Richard Brinsley Sheridan* (New York, 1962), I, 248–54.

43. N.G. At seven he studied with William Boyce and began composing. He was on stage briefly (Covent Garden, 1767), then went to Italy and met Mozart and Burney. In 1771 he became violinist leader at Bath, and from 1773 to 1778 he was a regular performer in the Drury Lane orchestra. In his last five years he produced an "astonishing amount" of music with a "high and consistent merit" (Gwilym Beechez, "Thomas Linley, Junior, 1756–1778," *Musical Quarterly*, 54, 73–82).

44. William Jackson "of Exeter" (1730–1803), a composer, organist, essayist, painter, was the son of a grocer. He studied music at Exeter and London, becoming organist at Exeter Cathedral in 1777. He began to compose successful songs in 1755, and his first dramatic composition was for *Lycidas* in 1767. His *Metamorphoses* (Drury Lane, 1783), for which he also wrote the words, failed. He was a fine melodist and tried to revive the "true English tradition of opera without Italian opera borrowings," which became the subject of a feud with Burney (N.G.). He deplored the influence of Handel as detrimental to English composers.

45. "My Anna's urn" and "When first this humble roof" were retained. As early as 1812 Bishop had "refurbished" the score for Covent Garden.

46. Winton Dean, writing of this opera in the *Musical Times*, 119 (Apr. 1978), 348, has noted Romantic trends in the work as a "rescue" opera and in using "a leading motif for dramatic ends, and local color," but he points out that it "leaves important episodes like ceremonial entries without any music at all," and Richard sings only three of seventeen numbers.

47. Boaden noted cryptically that Grétry's music was so "beautiful, expressive, and impassioned, as to beget the attitude of disparagement toward French opera." In 1776 Linley set Sir George Collier's *Selima and Azor*, based on Grétry's *Zemire ed Azor* (1770), which, as we have seen, didn't reach the King's until 1796.

48. The "strangers" are two Florentines of the indeterminate past who, having been captured by Algerian pirates, are at length released; upon their return they are obliged to employ numerous ruses and stratagems to win back their loves and their estates that had been unscrupulously wrested from them in their absence.

49. Fiske, noting the mounting influence of Haydn on Linley, sees in this opera "an intelligent awareness of new continental trends" (449).

50. Fiske finds "little to admire in the way the situations are handled" (452).

51. The new airs cited were: "Ah! when safe at home," "Hear me, O God of love," "I love my massa kind," "Hope bids pleasure," and "Oh! no accusing sigh

shall rise." "Hark I hear, I hear him coming" had "in particular great *acting merit*" (H). The compiled songs included "We be three poor mariners"; "John said to Jean," a catch; and Paisiello's "The guardian, dear sir" ("one of the most beautiful compositions we ever heard" [H]).

52. Another son, William Linley (1771–1835), composed both words and music for *The Honey-Moon* (Drury Lane, 1797), but the *Oracle* thought him "too young for the task," and the opera was withdrawn after a single performance. He was, according to Kelly (II, 114), subject to an "unjust cabal, which was clearly proved to exist on the night of its performance"; the reviewers make no reference to it.

53. Apparently Attwood, in Vienna from 1785 to 1787, was at that time Mozart's "first and only pupil for theory and composition." The manuscript of his studies with Mozart is in the British Library. See Erich Hertzman, "Mozart and Attwood," *Journal of the American Musicological Society*, XII (1959), 178–84.

54. Thomas Welsh (c. 1780–1848), English bass and composer, was a chorister at Wells Cathedral at age six and was singing at Bath concerts in 1792. Attwood's *Prisoner* was written to display his talents; he also sang in Storace's *Lodoiska*. He wrote theatre music from 1810 to 1816, but his greatest achievement was as a singing teacher; his pupils included Sinclair, Horn, Stephens, and Mary Ann Wilson, whom he married in 1827.

55. One of the borrowed numbers was "Non più andrai," sung to the words, "When the Banners of Glory are streaming." Two of the songs were encored. Giornovichi assisted Attwood in the finale (C. B. Oldman, "Attwood's Dramatic Works," *Musical Times*, 107 [Jan. 1966], 23).

56. Twelve numbers were by Attwood and five were borrowed, including Mozart's "In diesen heil'gen Hallen," sung to the words "Why swells my wavy, burnish'd grain." The *Chronicle* (May 10) wrote that the music was "in some instances pleasing. Its general defect is a tameness of manner and expression, which neither interests nor exhilarates" (Oldman, 23).

57. One number was apparently written by Holcroft and "corrected by Shield" (Oldman, 25).

58. Attwood composed some music for Holman's five-act melodrama, *The Red-Cross Knights* (Little Theatre, 1799), based on Schiller's *Die Rauber*. The drama was castigated by the press, but the air of Mrs. Bland "and the glee and chorus [are] composed with considerable taste, and the compilations are judiciously selected" (T). Attwood selected another Mozart number—"Bei Mannern," from *Die Zauberflöte*. The work did not quite succeed.

59. The story "introduces a lively and eccentric English Officer and a humorous Hiberean" in a Spanish setting, where the "blunder" consists of a mistaken identity in a love triangle.

60. The surviving piano score shows tight musical development with "adventurous modulations," and the overture is "among the best of its time" (N.G.). Young (392) reports it had an energy and drive reminiscent of Beethoven.

61. He did produce two more comedies there in 1804 and 1811; an operatic farce of 1812 is also attributed to him.

62. This may have been Thomas Cadell the Elder (1742–1802), a bookseller, publisher, and one-time member of the Johnson circle; he retired in 1793 "with a fortune." But the D.N.B. states nothing about his playwrighting, and more likely the piece was by his son, Thomas Cadell the Younger (1772–1836). If so, he was also probably the author, with M. P. Andrews, of *Fire and Water* (1780), and of some ballet scenarios for playhouses from 1796 to 1800. Incidentally, the L.S. index does not list this production.

63. Jeremu Felix Bagster-Collins, *George Colman the Younger, 1762–1836* (New York, 1946), 94–95.

64. The skimpy plot told of the deception practiced by the impecunious Young Ramble, who affected a Turkish disguise before his London friends and his lover, upon his return from "an extravagant tour to many parts of the globe," and of the discovery of his disguise and his reconciliation with his father. The L.S. index lists this production as anonymous.

65. These included "Done over taylor," "Sweet Annie frae the sea beach come," and "British Grenadiers," the first stanza of which reads:

> Some talk of Cherokees, Sir, and some of Catabaws,
> And some of iny Indians, carousing with their squaws;
> But what are Gentoo generals, or tawny chiefs so queer?
> For shapes, and dress, and war, give me a jolly grenadier.

66. Inkle, affianced to the daughter of the governor of Barbados, is driven by storm to a coastal wilderness where his shipmates abandon him. He finds an Indian girl, Yarico, asleep in a cave and soon falls in love with her. After some months he obtains passage back to Barbados, taking Yarico with him. But after they arrive, Inkle's greed prompts him to try to sell her. He finally "acknowledges his principles had been polluted by the errors of education, and renouncing the narrow-minded system of profit and gain, bestows his hand on the Indian maid" (LC). Their baby, found in the original story in Ligon's *True and Exact History of the Island of Barbados* (1673) and repeated by Steele in the *Spectator*, was suppressed in the play (Fiske).

67. Songs especially praised were "Freshly now" and "Remember when," but not cited was the sprightly "Come let us dance and sing," from the finale, which became a hit.

68. John Adolphus, *Memoirs of John Bannister, Comedian* (London, 1839), II, 127.

69. Kelly complained about critics' charging him with lack of originality and even denying him authorship of his own songs. But he never tried to conceal his musical debts (Peake, II, 16).

70. Charles W. Ward, Sheridan's brother-in-law, was given carte blanche to write a piece, and he had much elaborate scenery prepared. But at the green-room reading, Sheridan saw the play was worthless and got Kelly to persuade Colman to salvage it (Genest).

71. *The Africans* (Little Theatre, 1808) was their last opera.

72. The comic situations arise from various impersonations. The tower is said to be haunted by the servants, who use it to conceal their nightly carousals. The deceptions are unraveled and the story concludes with a double wedding.

73. The *Herald* cited the following English titles as deserving special notice: an opening chorus by Storace; "From Hope's fond dream," "Septello" (a "charming composition"), and "My native land," by Storace. Borrowed music included: "Tho' pity I cannot deny," by Pleyel; "Whither, my love," by Paisiello; "Love from the heart," by Martín; "Dangers unknown impending," by Sarti; "As now we're met," a catch by Purcell; "Come then sweet sounds," by Mellico; "Tho' time had from," a French air; and "Nature to women still so kind," an Irish air.

74. The commander of the Turkish troops defending Belgrade has captured and placed in his seraglio the wife of a colonel of the Austrians, who are besieging the town. The colonel, in disguise, enters the Turkish camp and finds his wife, but he is betrayed and thrown into a dungeon. During an attack by the Austrians, the colonel escapes, assists in the defeat of the Turks, and regains his wife. The underplot involved Lilla, a peasant girl, who is frustrated by her brother in her love for a rustic.

75. The story, set in Naples, involves the need of the hero, Don Altador, to retrieve his lady from the hands of the unscrupulous Don Gaspero, into whose charge the dying father had entrusted her. The capture of the young couple by pirates and their release from a castle furnished scenic interest. A magic lantern was used in the last act.

76. Fiske, 529. Some Cherokees had been brought to London in 1762 and again in 1782. This production had seven rehearsals for music, twelve for action, and three for dialogue and business (L.S.).

77. Colonel Blandford, an English officer serving in colonial America, loses his wife, Harriet, and their son to the Cherokees. Malooko, their chief, unsuccessfully woos her and threatens the son unless she consents, but another Indian rescues the boy and returns him to the colony. During the hostilities Blandford is captured, discovers his wife, and is confined to a cavern. The son learns of his capture and, with bow and arrow, effects their escape. In a subsequent action, Blandford kills Malooko and rescues his wife.

78. At the close of their review, they remarked that the drama "was a very reprehensible practice . . . to encourage national prejudices, and to teach the vulgar to despise whatever is not English."

79. "Glory Firing" and other songs and duets—especially Mrs. Bland's song, "A shepherd once," said to be composed by her husband—were praised.

80. The Indian chorus "is full of vigorous and almost Handelian counterpoint, and unlike anything else in English opera of the period" (Fiske, 530).

81. A detachment of British troops sent to dispossess a usurper near Malabar are surprised and made prisoners. Luffy, the sergeant, disguises himself as a physician and cures the Rajah with a potato. Another detachment attacks the fortress of Ramah Droog, and Zelma, the rightful princess, is united with her prince. Fiske notes a strain of racism in the story.

82. MM, July 1800; N.G., however, asserts that it was manager Harris who, not trusting Mazzinghi, consented to his assistance only if he worked with Reeve.

83. In a Polish setting, Lodoiska, betrothed to Count Floreski, is confined to the castle of Baron Lovinski, to whom her father had entrusted her. With the help of the besieging Tartars, Floreski storms the castle, and the lovers are united. Directions for the final catastrophe read: "Shouts, Drums, Trumpets, and Cannon. An engagement commences between the Polanders and the Tartars; the Tartars having stormed the castle, which they fire in various places, the battlements and towers fall in the midst of loud explosions," and so on.

84. "Biographical Sketch" by John Taylor in MM (Aug. 1796), 195–200.

85. *Memoirs of John Bannister, Comedian* (London, 1839), I, 229.

86. The L.S. Index doesn't even cite Hoare and credits the libretto to Joseph Reed, whose *Dido, Queen of Carthage* was first produced in 1767. But the main entry in the *Stage* (II, 1457) states that Hoare merely adapted Metastasio's *Didone Abbandonata*. On the other hand, a Drury Lane production of *The Queen of Carthage* in 1797 was a revival of the Reed prototype.

87. Jack Bannister excelled in "whimsicalities — an ingredient Hoare sketched for his powers" (Boaden), and he "got complete possession of the audience" (EM).

88. Bacon especially praised "Five times by the taper's light" (*Iron Chest*), "At your feet thus lowly bending" (*Mahmoud*), "Hear, oh hear a simple story" (*Pirates*), and "Hope a distant joy disclosing" (*No Song*). In 1820 Storace's music was used by Kitchener in Beazley's opera *Ivanhoe*.

89. Eugenia, secretly married to Korowitz, is rescued from the bandetti by Canzemar, his nephew, who courts her unsuccessfully, but he releases her on the promise never to divulge his name. But her husband's jealousy is aroused by her silence, and he places her in his dungeon. He is arrested by the prince for her supposed murder, but Canzemar confesses, and Eugenia is again rewed and restored to her husband.

90. Some of his music found its way into Guglielmi's *L'amor fra le Vendemmie* (TB, Dec. 7, 1796), and he wrote the overture and entr'act music for *Pizarro* (May 24, 1798).

91. Of this work Boaden (II, 226) wrote cryptically: "Dussek, sitting in society at the piano forte, and improvising upon the *progress* and *succession* of the *passions*, was an object of perfect astonishment, and never to be forgotten."

92. The story was founded on the expedition of the Portuguese, under Prince Henry, against Centa, on the coast of Africa, where some years earlier the Moors had imprisoned Spanish and Portuguese captives.

93. Benjamin Haydon, *Diary*, chap. 2. Haydon described Hoare as a "delicate, feeble-looking man, with a timid expression of face, and when he laughed heartily he almost seemed to be crying."

94. He probably knew Robert Merry (1755–98), who wrote five works for the stage, including a comic opera, *Magician no Conjurer* (1792), which was panned by the press — Boaden thought he had become "politicized" — and failed, though

Mazzinghi's music drew praise. For a time Merry was chief poetaster of the Della Cruscans, for which he was savagely attacked by William Gifford, editor of the *Anti-Jacobin*, in two long satirical poems, *The Baviad* (1791) and *The Maviad* (1795).

95. Kelly (302) wrote that while composing one unnamed opera of his, "it struck me that there was a good opportunity to introduce . . . a duet; and I fixed upon the celebrated Italian duet of Nasolini, 'Pace, cara miea sposa,' which created a great sensation at Vienna. . . . The English words put to it, 'Oh, thou wert born to please me,' were very good . . . ; it was always called for three times, and no performance was allowed to go on in which it was not introduced."

96. Samuel Birch (1757–1841), a politician, dramatist, and pastry-cook, produced several musical-drama afterpieces from 1795 to 1798, some composed by Attwood. In 1815 he was elected Lord-Mayor of Dublin.

97. Though we have no figures from Genest on the Lyceum/English Opera House performances, Arnold was a superb reader of public sentiment and was probably successful with most of his productions there, regardless of what the press thought of them.

98. Miss Sedley, a friend of Lady Gayland, is instrumental in the reconciliation of Sir Damon Gayland, a jealous old rake, with his young bride through a series of intrigues and disguises.

99. Domenico's daughter, Sophia Giustina Corri (1775–1828), a singer, married composer Jan L. Dussek in 1792 and sang briefly at the King's. Domenico's son, Montague Phillip Corri (1784–1849), a composer, assisted his father in music publishing. Domenico's brother Natale was father of Francesca, whose career we have followed at the King's, and of Angelina and Rose, who were also singers.

100. Stephen Jones, *Biographia Dramatica* (London, 1812), II, 321. In a letter to the *Examiner*, Lawler protested that Cherry "stole" the farce.

101. Siddons (1774–1815), an actor and playwright, was an indifferent performer at the majors from 1800 to 1809, after which he managed an Edinburgh theatre. He wrote only a few plays.

102. Parry (1776–1851) was a Welsh instrumentalist and composer. He studied the harp, clarinet, and several other instruments, and he became master of a militia band in 1795. By 1807 he was teaching the flageolet in London and was composing for Vauxhall—often ballads with a Celtic flavor. He retired from composing in 1837 and served as music critic for the *Morning Post* from 1834 to 1849.

103. Sir John Stevenson (1761–1833), an Irish composer, was knighted in 1803.

104. He was an illegitimate son of Charles Dibdin and full brother of Charles Isaac Mungo Dibdin, known as Charles Dibdin the Younger, also illegitimate. The mother of both was Miss Pitt, a sometime actress at Covent Garden who took the name of Mrs. Davenet.

105. "The opening chorus of Persian Guards and Janissaries and the Finale are adapted from the Chorus of Janissaries in the Finale of Mozart's *Die Entführung*" (C. B. Oldham, "Attwood's Dramatic Works," *Musical Times*, 107 [Jan. 1966], 26).

106. The first quatrain from a song by Corri, sung by Floretta (Storace) reads:

> The bird in yonder cage confin'd,
>   Sings but to lovers young and true;
> Then pray approach if you can find
>   The picture suit, ah! no not you.

And one by Orlando (Braham):

> When absent from her, whom my soul holds most dear,
>   What medley of passion invade!
> In this bosom what anguish, what hope, and what fear
>   I endure for my beautiful maid.

107. Curvoso, an avaricious Italian count, has promised his daughter Constantia in marriage to Prince Orlando, but upon the sudden loss of his estates, Curvoso engages her to an old French marquis, whom of course Constantia rejects. With the assistance of six additional characters and innumerable complexities, the lovers are finally united. Nicoll states the opera observed the unities.

108. CR and BC (1805), MM (May, 1806), MR (1808).

109. An odd description of William, who was then forty-seven if his date of birth is correct; perhaps the *Inquisitor* erred in stating that his son George did not begin composing until 1813.

110. Especially admired were the trio, "Ah! how can I leave," a duet, "In the morn I ring the bell," and an aria, "All in the silent convent cell," with an organ accompaniment.

111. Charles Isaac Mungo Dibdin (1768–1833) also wrote a large number of miscellaneous musical pieces, mainly for Sadler's Wells Theatre, of which he was proprietor until 1819. Thomas brought him to Covent Garden to provide new songs for a revival of *Lord of the Manor*; they were so successful he was commissioned to write a full-length comic opera, *The Farmer's Wife*, produced there in 1814. He concealed his authorship to avoid adverse critical response to his connection with one of the minors (*Memoirs*, 108), but his name leaked out anyway. The *Times* was fairly supportive, but the *Chronicle* thought it had "too many cooks," for Dibdin had called upon Bishop, Davy, Reeve, Addison, Condell, and Welsh for the settings. The *Champion* thought the piece "beneath criticism," but many of the songs were encored, and the work had nineteen performances.

112. A brother, Giuseppe, born in London, was also a singing teacher and composer, but he returned to Naples in 1819.

113. Bruce Carr, "Theatre Music, 1800–1834," *Music in Britain: The Romantic Age, 1800–1914*, ed. Nicholas Temperley (London, 1981), 295.

114. The story was based on the "beautiful" novel *Elizabeth*, by Sophie Cottin (1770–1807). Count Ulrick is banished to Siberia by state intrigues, and Alexina, his daughter, undertakes a journey to Moscow, in the hope of procuring his pardon. Romanoff, secretly loyal to the count but disguised as an Indian to aid his intrigues, saves her from perils on the journey, assists in obtaining the pardon

from the Empress Elizabeth, and, throwing off his disguise, marries Alexina (C).

115. Fawcett's two songs, "The night was three months long" and "Young Lobski," were encored, as were Dickons's "Once on a time" and "Hope, her support."

116. Cora, Priestess of the Sun, breaks her vows and elopes from the Temple with Alonzo, whom she marries. They are caught and condemned to death under the law. But a rejected lover, Rolla, foments a rebellion to save her, which Cora succeeds in preventing; for her heroism she and Alonzo are pardoned.

117. The song begins:

> Oh! the merry *table d'hote*
> Where different tongues displaying,
> Guests of nations most remote;
> All sit, the world pourtraying;
> > Where gay Monsieur
> > And dry Mynheer,
> > Where Spanish Don
> > And English John,
> > Pole and Prussian,
> > German, Russian,
> > Italian, Swiss,
> > Madame and Miss.

118. Nicoll cites the *Theatrical Repertory* (VIII, Nov. 7, 1801) as protesting an operatic version of the *Tempest*. Curtis Price, in *Henry Purcell and the London Stage* (Cambridge, 1984), 320, tends to side with more recent critics who see the operatic adaptation of Shakespeare as a "function of the production" rather than as a desecration of the bard.

119. See, for example, Lamb's "On the Tragedies of Shakespeare" (1818).

120. Richard John Samuel Stevens (1758–1837), an English composer known mainly for his glees. Kelly states that Storace (in Vienna, c. 1784) produced a successful Italian opera based on Da Ponte's translation of Shakespeare's *Comedy of Errors*, using some of the music from his *Equivoci*; Kelly later suggested the subject to Sheridan for an English adaptation at Drury Lane, but he never acted on the suggestion.

121. These songs included: "Since first I saw your face," "We be three poor mariners," "Now is the month of Maying," and "From the fair Lavinian shore." Thomas Morley (1557–1602) was a composer of madrigals; Thomas Ford (d. 1648), was a composer and viol player; and Thomas Ravenscroft (c. 1596–1633), was a composer of madrigals.

122. They added that the music, which also included a selection from Jeremy Savile (fl. 1652–65) consisted of seven songs, two duets, five glees, several choruses, and an overture.

123. This included Braham's echo duet, saved from Dibdin's failed *Zuma*.

124. Most of the songs were taken from the sonnets; borrowings included

"Pray, Goody," from *Midas*; "If e'er the cruel tyrant Love" (Arne); and numbers by Rossini (E).

125. Bruce Carr, who has examined some of these operas, reports that they had from ten to twenty vocal numbers each and that only rarely were they integrated with the plot.

126. "The Maniac is a young Lady, who having been seduced from her father's house by a treacherous lover, hears that her father has died of a broken heart; in consequence of which she . . . wanders distracted among the rocks and woods" (C). But all ends well.

127. Songs selected for praise were "When absent from the lad I love"; "When deeds of fame"; the duet, "Say, fair one, has thy virgin heart"; and the comic "In England they tell us."

128. Several extra male and female characters were added, but the leading characters did not sing; Scottish airs were included. See Jerome Mitchell, *The Walter Scott Operas* (University of Ala. Press, University, Ala., 1977), 10.

129. William Charles Macready (1793–1873), an actor, made his London debut in 1816, and by 1819 he had become a tragedian of first rank. He managed Covent Garden from 1836 to 1839 and Drury Lane from 1841 to 1843.

130. "The action of the piece arises from Captain Clifton's having formed an ardent attachment to Zelinda, a slave belonging to Col. Lindenburg . . . who won from Clifton the money he had procured to emancipate Zelinda and her child. — Clifton arrives at Surinam while it is in possession of the English and finds the settlement endangered by the Negro rebellion. . . . He commands a successful attack against the rebels, in which his life is saved by his African rival, Gambia; and on the Governor's granting Clifton the privilege of emancipating a slave, he sacrifices his feelings for Zelinda to a sense of duty and gratitude, and gives freedom to Gambia. At this time Lindenburg arrives, and hearing that Clifton's mistress and child are his slaves, he exults in his power over them, and contrives to have Clifton thrown into prison for debt. But Gambia sells himself to Lindenburg, and restores Clifton to freedom. Lindenburg demands of the Governor possession of Zelinda and her child, and attempts the chastity of Zelinda. Gambia interposes, and in the struggle he discovers the brand of a thief on the colonel's breast. Meanwhile Zelinda has made her escape and joined Clifton. Gambia, while heroically saving the child, is captured; but Lindenburg emancipates him, Zelinda, and the child" (T). There was, in addition, a long underplot!

England abolished the slave trade in 1807.

131. John Gabriel Stedman, *The Narrative, of five ears' expedition* . . . (London, 1796). Several pizarros and oroonokos were popular at the time; Sheridan's *Pizarro* (1799) was perhaps the best. In many *Examiner*s Hunt was outspoken on behalf of Negroes.

132. A reference to B. Thompson's *Rolla* (1800), after Kotzebue.

133. Cited were the opening glee for five voices, "Blow, gentle gales"; the "Mocking Bird"; the first-act finale, with music by Boieldieu and Bishop, which

"would not disgrace even a Mozart"; a duet, "In joyful peace disarming"; and a ballad, "Pity the slave." "The sostenuto accompaniments, judiciously given to the wind Instruments, add greatly to the beauty of the song" (C).

134. The book was serious; the playbills, however, advertised it as a comic opera, which the *British Stage* thought inappropriate.

135. *Zuma* was "so transformed, transposed, and altered in various ways, through all its incidents and situations, for the sake, no doubt, of improved musical subjects" that it is "completely metamorphosed" (T).

136. The Peruvians are bound by oath to destroy the entire generation of that person who reveals the virtues of Quinquina, or the Jesuits' bark, to their detested conquerors, the Spaniards. But Zuma secretly obtains the bark for her ill mistress, the wife of a benevolent viceroy, and Zuma and her husband, also implicated, are condemned to the stake. They are saved by the Vice Queen, who has recovered her health, while the Indians, relenting, reveal the secret of the Tree of Life.

137. Praised numbers included a "clever" overture; a march and chorus of Indians; an air, "No voice endearing"; and a glee in the finale—all by Bishop. Other numbers praised included a song, "His dearest mother's joy" and an echo duet, "Whither is he straying," both by Braham. Some of these were apparently borrowed, however.

138. Thus the "foolish" *Post*, according to the *British Stage*: "We appeal to any one who was present, to declare whether this is not a gross falsehood."

139. A bravura was "stolen almost without disguise from the 'Soldier tired,'" and English words were supplied for the "exquisite 'Di tanti palpiti' of Rossini" (E).

140. "A Genoese Noble, Aurelio di Montalti, betrothed to Clymonte, having been taken prisoner by the Barbary corsairs, in vain endeavours to make his situation known in his native land, all his letters being intercepted and destroyed by his roguish guardian Giuseppo. . . . The piece opens with the spirited and well-imagined incident of a return of the Christian captives from Moorish slavery" (E). Giuseppo is found out, and the couple are united in marriage.

141. These included two borrowings: "Aurora che sorgerai" of Rossini and "Questo sol" of Zingarelli.

142. In 1805 he married Miss Howells, a Covent Garden actress by whom he had several children and with whom he occasionally sang in operas.

143. Nicoll is silent on Lambe but cites one W. Rooke for the music.

144. The *Gazette*, cited by Dimond, contemptuously inquired whether he had married Cobb's widow, since he had also recently adapted Cobb's *Love in the East* (in *Englishmen in India*).

145. They especially admired two songs, however: "Old Time today twines flowers" and "the well-imagined tune 'Sailor's Lullaby.'"

146. George Alexander Lee (1802–51), an English composer and tenor, trained in Dublin (1822) and was engaged as a singer at the Little Theatre in 1826. The next year he began composing for the stage, producing *Sublime and Beautiful* for

Covent Garden in 1828 (the *Atlas* called his music "beneath criticism"). Altogether he wrote music for about twenty plays. He was also a theatre manager in the 1840s. He formed a liaison with Mrs. Waylett about 1830 and married her on the death of her husband in 1840. Planché called him a clever composer and an agreeable singer.

147. A reference to the European political settlement (1815) following the fall of the Napoleonic empire.

148. Cited by the press were: "The Love that follows fair"; "Let us seek the yellow shore"; "Oh well do I remember"; the duet "Come hither"; the glee and chorus in the first-act finale; an act-two glee; and a sestet "O bold Robin Hood."

149. The story opens with the mutiny of the Spaniards against their leader and the arrival of the Mexican embassy. "Cortez destroys his fleet, to prevent the retreat of his troops, and leads them against the Tlascalans, whom he subdues, and enters into an alliance with. The Mexicans endeavour to entrap the Spaniards at Cholula, but the plot is discovered by a Tlascalan, whose life Cortez has saved; and the Spaniards are enabled to defeat their purpose, and arrive at the great Temple in time to save Mariana, the faithful and loving Mexican girl, so famous in Spain to this day. . . . The piece concludes with a triumphal entry of Cortez into Mexico [City]" (C).

150. They provided the following specimens:

> O! 'tis great at noon to study
> By the Carron's winding way,
> Where the silver birches shiver
> O'er the deeply dimpling river,
> Which, like some coy beauty flies
> Trembling, to that shady cover,
> From the sun, her glorious lover;
> Who, down the cloudless sky,
> Rushing through the leafy bower,
> Woos her in a golden shower,
> As of old his father Jove
> Won the maid of Argos' love!
> . . . .
> Boot and saddle, bonnie Scot,
> The foe! the foe's in sight, man!
> Out wi' sword, and in wi' shot,
> And shew that ye can fight, man!
> See the saucy flag unfold,
> Where Scotland's lion 'ramps in gold.'

151. Especially praised were an opening rondo, "A Robe like its wearer"; a trio, "Oh 'tis sweet at noon to stray"; a "boat song," "Knight to his Leddy"; another trio, "Now, as we loved in childhood's morn"; a duet, "O'er the billows let me roam"; and a "grand scene and recitative, 'The die is cast,' which is altogether written in the classic style of the Italian school."

152. Mitchell (359) states: "Many a situation in Scott is either eminently operatic in itself or easily altered into something operatic."

153. According to the piano score—"composed and arranged for the Piano Forte by Thos. Attwood and Henry Bishop"—two songs, "Lord Henry" and "The Love that's born of gratitude," were by Attwood; the playbill does not even mention Bishop, though the reviewers do. See C. B. Oldman, "Attwood's Dramatic Works," *Musical Times*, 107 (Jan. 1966), 26

154. John Whittaker (also spelled Whitaker) (1776–1847), a composer, was in the music-publishing business with J. S. Button from 1808 to 1819, and from then to 1824 he was sole proprietor. He wrote occasional songs and glees for the stage from 1807 to 1825, of which the best known is perhaps "Fly away, dove" from the anonymous *Hebrew Family* (1825).

155. "Ye dear paternal scenes, farewell" (Davy), "Oh! slumber my darling" (Whittaker), "In ancient times, in Britain's isle" (Attwood), "The chough and crow to roost are gone," "Gipsey" solo and chorus (Bishop), and "Follow him, follow him" (Cooke).

156. Isaac Pocock (1782–1835) also provided some successful operatic adaptations of Scott and others. His afterpiece, *The Miller and his Men* (1813), music by Bishop, was enormously popular. More operatic was their successful *John of Paris* (1814), adapted from St. Just's opera *Jean de Paris*, set by Boieldieu, some of whose music Bishop borrowed. Pocock's *Peveril of the Peak* (from Scott), set by Horn in 1826, barely succeeded; see Mitchell (260–69), who finds much of the music uninteresting. A vocal score was published, and the complete text in manuscript is in the British Library. On Pocock see also Pieter Van Der Merwe, "The Ingenious Squire: New Aspects of Isaac Pocock (1782–1835)" in *Theatre Notebook* 31, no. 21 (1977), 12–18.

157. This was probably *Woman's Will—A Riddle*, by Edmund L. Swift (1820).

158. Only one song from this opera survives (N.G.). Three of Attwood's songs were published separately.

159. Even less successful was *David Rizzio*, a serious opera by Colonel Ralph Hamilton, with music by Attwood, Braham, Cooke, and W. Reeve; the work was found too serious for an opera, although Attwood's contribution was praised (T).

160. Nicoll lists the work as Planché's, but with a note that it was also credited to Payne. Loewenberg (*Annals*); the *Dictionary of American Biography*; and Willis T. Hanson junior, in *The Early Life of John Howard Payne* (Boston, 1913) all attribute *Clari* to Payne. The press is altogether silent on Planché, but the *Chronicle* and others called it Payne's translation, while the *Examiner*, *Drama*, and *New Monthly* called it Payne's production and the *London* flatly declared: "Clari is the work of Mr. Howard Payne, the American Roscius; and certainly... in this instance a *very American* Roscius"; they found the language of the drama "French-English, which is not the best of styles." This strikes me as the best evidence that both translation *and* play were Payne's, not Planché's.

In 1829, a sequel, *Home, Sweet Home* (Somerset/Bishop) was produced at Covent Garden.

161. Clari, daughter of a farmer, Rolamo, elopes with a duke and is conducted to his mansion, where, however, she refuses his dishonorable proposals. Making her escape, she returns home and is reconciled to her parents. The now penitent duke offers her marriage and wealth, which she accepts. The piece was fraught with melodramatic confrontations.

162. Parke reported the melody came from "a German opera." The confusion probably arose because Bishop had first used it in *Who Wants a Wife?* (1816) and published it as "a Sicilian Air" in *National Airs*, which he edited in 1821. It was not joined with Payne's familiar words until *Clari*. Hanson also attributes it to Payne and states that Goulding & Co., music publishers, realized a fortune from the song, which was not credited to Payne since he had sold his manuscript outright and had no further claims on it.

163. Payne's *'Twas I*, an operatic farce (composer unnamed), opened at Covent Garden December 3, 1825; the *Times* (Dec. 5) thoroughly panned it, and the *London* called it "the very climax of stupidity" but reported it was very successful.

164. Bishop wrote to Bacon in a later number that year denying any competition between himself and Weber and complaining that Elliston, the manager, had long kept him in the dark as to who would be in the cast, that he had to appeal to Soane to get a copy of the libretto, and that the opera was produced prematurely — it needed at least one more month of rehearsals (QMM, VIII, 242–52). With all its faults, Bacon found much to admire in the opera. See also Trevor Fawcett, "Bishop and Aladdin," *Musical Times*, 113 (Nov. 1972), 1076f. In still another letter, Bishop complained that Drury Lane refused to supply extra orchestra performers, "which were essentially requisite" (White, 258).

165. See Bacon (QMM, VI, 286) for another fine estimate of the composer.

166. Thomas Hardy enjoyed Bishop's "Should he upbraid" at a concert in 1878.

167. *The Stage: Both before and behind the Curtain* (London, 1840), III, 7.

168. *Anecdotes of Music* (London, 1814), III, 499.

169. Bruce Carr (p. 193) writes that some of Bishop's songs are "quite attractive in a sub-Mozartian way" but "his charm is often vitiated by a 'tonic-bound' quality." He goes on to note that Bishop had little talent for music without words and that he could characterize classes of people on the stage but not persons.

170. *Thirty-Five Years of a Dramatic Author's Life* (London, 1859), 153.

171. *A History of Music in England* (London, 1952), 286–87.

172. In 1825 he produced *The Wedding Present*, with music by Horn, for Drury Lane; it had a bad press, however, and played but five times. He also produced a romantic drama — really a melodrama — *Benyowsky* (Drury Lane, 1826); the music was by Horn (who sang in it), Cooke, and Livius, with selections by Kelly and Stevenson. It received only passing notice and the play was barely successful.

173. Samuel Beazley, Jr. (1786–1851), son of an architect, wrote farces as a schoolboy; himself an architect, he designed many theatres in London and elsewhere. In 1816 he began producing a number of operettas for the English Opera House, but many were too slight even to be reviewed. In 1820 he hopped on the Scott bandwagon and produced a three-act musical drama for Covent

Garden—*Ivanhoe; or, the Knights Templar*. Some seven versions of the Ivanhoe story were produced at the minors in the 1820s as well as *Guy Mannering* and *Rob Roy*, already cited. Beazley's work opened on the same night as Soane's drama, *The Hebrew*, at Drury Lane.

The music for *Ivanhoe* was selected by Dr. William Kitchiner (c. 1775–1827), who enjoyed a large inheritance and took his doctorate in medicine at Glasgow, though he never practiced it. He became interested in cooking for his health, and his epicurean lunches and dinners became famous. He wrote a cookbook; studied optics; and played and sang "with considerable feeling," publishing some of his songs. Singer Henry Phillips, a stalwart friend, enjoyed his sauces. He also composed Beazley's *Love among the Roses*. The reviewers (T; TI; LM) were unhappy with *Ivanhoe* and said nothing of the singing or the music, which included borrowings from Storace. In 1826 Beazley did produce one piece at Drury Lane, *Knights of the Cross*, a romantic drama, with music by Bishop; it failed badly.

174. Henri-Montan Berton (1767–1844), a French opera composer; Frederick Heinrich Himmel (1765–1814), a German opera composer.

175. "The First Performance of Mozart's Entführung in London," *Essays on Music* (New York, 1956), 206–16.

176. For a complete understanding of the limitations that inadequate or totally lacking (bass) singers imposed on Kramer in making these changes, Einstein's article should be read in conjunction with a very full and detailed explanation of the changes in a QMM article (IX, 1827), 520–29; the writer (perhaps Bacon) was certainly quite familiar with Mozart's score.

177. Citing his adaptations of Mozart and Rossini, Robert Rushmore, in "The Unholy Bishop," *Opera News*, 34 (Dec. 20, 1969), 6–7, writes: "For sheer brass in tampering with the sacred, this musician . . . seems to have had no equal." But his flippant article is scant on facts, citing Bishop's *Sinbad*, rather than *Aladdin*, as the competition to Weber's *Oberon*.

178. "Vedrai, carino" (the only one encored), "Batti, batti," "Fin ch'an dal vino," "Là ci darem," "Deh vieni," "Giovinette che fate," and "Madamina il catalogo." One duet was borrowed from another Mozart opera.

179. The first of these, a one-act "Operatic Extravaganza," *Giovanni in London*, by William Thomas Moncrieff (1794–1857), with at least one song by Whittaker, appeared at the Olympic Pavilion in 1817 and found its way to Drury Lane in 1820. It was founded on the idea that the Don was "dismissed from hell, on account of his exceeding wickedness" and that he continued his intrigues in contemporary London society. It received excoriating notices, mostly on account of its "immorality," but it succeeded nevertheless and was followed by his *Giovanni in Ireland*.

180. John Baldwin Buckstone (1802–79), an actor and playwright, first appeared at Drury Lane in 1823 and wrote a large number of burlettas and other operatic types—mostly for the minors—from 1825 to 1850 and later. In 1853 he became manager of the Little Theatre.

181. These included "Se a caso madama," "Sull' aria," "Non so più cosa son,"

"Se vuol ballare," "Voi che sapete," "Cinque dieci," "Venite inginocchiatevi," and possibly others; also, a considerable part of the first finale was introduced, but from the second, Bishop included only the exchange between Figaro and the disguised Susanna (T).

182. The *Post* and the *Sun* had trivial reviews (see Dennis Arundell, *The Critic at the Opera* [London, 1957], 300–301), as did the *Literary Chronicle*. Puckler-Maskau exaggerated the defects by erroneously claiming that "neither Count, Countess, or Figaro sang" and placing it at Drury Lane rather than at Covent Garden (*Tour of a German Prince*, III, Letter 6 [Dec. 1, 1826] [London, 1832]).

183. Mozart's singspiel, *Die Entführung aus dem Serail* (Vienna, 1782) was not performed in London until 1842, but the story was known to 1827 audiences through an English translation, *The Illustrious Bossa*, of a novel by Madeleine du Scudery (E) as well as through a translated French play, *L'Enlèvement du Serail* (LG).

184. Numbers included from Mozart's operas were the aria "War ein Liebchen hat gefunden" ("much curtailed for want of a good bass voice"); the chorus "Singt dem grossen Bossa lieder"; the aria "Ach, ich liebte"; the trio "Marsch! Marsch! Marsch!"; Blonda's opening air in act II and a duet for her and Osmin followed by a recitative and aria for Constanza; another air for Blonda; the aria "Constanza!"; the duet "Vivat Bacchus" (arranged as a trio); and "Ach, Belmonte" (altered into a quintet).

185. In 1829 Michael Lacy (see text, below) also produced *The Casket* (Drury Lane), based on music from Mozart, including at least one number from *Idomeneo*. For the plot Lacy drew on the French play, *Les premières amours*. The *Times* thought the musical adaptations skillful but "the great fault in the opera" was a "want of spirit and case in the dialogue." The *Examiner* reported the piece "halts dreadfully in the progress." The music was quite "secondary" (LM). The performances were only fair, and the opera closed after the second performance.

186. Bacon (QMM, II, 67–80) provides the following detailed record of the numbers in sequence. Overture (Bishop). Act I: first air and chorus (Rossini); "For tenderness formed" (Paisiello); the duet "All' idea di quel metallo" (Rossini); "Una voce poco fà" (Rossini — "very effective in English"); "Woman kind" (Bishop — based on a trio from Paisiello's *Zingari in Fiera*); finale (Rossini — "cut down with great judgment"). Act II: a Venetian air, "An old man would be wooing" (Mrs. Dickons's borrowing — "particularly effective"); a comic song (Bishop); "The rose on beauty's cheeks" (Bishop); a bravura (Bishop); "Zitti, Zitti" (Rossini — "adroitly" Englished and the most successful piece in the opera); and the finale (Rossini — "with abridgments").

187. On July 3, 1824, the English Opera House mounted another *Barber*, by unknown hands, which was not remotely an English adaptation. Besides Rossini's music, there was music by Mozart, Fioravanti, Dibdin, and others.

188. According to the *Times*, *Semiramide* provided the overture, a chorus, and scena; *Torvaldo e Dorliska* (Rome, 1815), an aria and scena ("sung by Pasta in concerts"); and *Le Comte Ory*, a drinking chorus. There were also borrowings

from *Maometto Secondo* (Naples, 1820), *Armida* (Naples, 1817), and other Rossini operas.

189. His surname was Ball, to which he prefaced his mother's name, Fitz, to distinguish himself from another contemporary writer named Ball.

190. *NOHM* (VIII, 105) states that, because of its revolutionary nature, *Tell* "was constantly mutilated by the censorship, especially in Italy and Russia; the hero variously metamorphosed into Andreas Hoffer, Charles the Bold," and others.

191. "Uberto dei Ardinghelli is driven into banishment [from Florence] by his hereditary opponent Edoarde dei Ligozzi and becomes chief of a company of Freebooters, who have established their head-quarters in the fortress of the Alps. As the story opens the band have just captured Isabella on her way to join her husband at Rome. Uberto treats her with the greatest consideration and is determined to set her free. Meanwhile Edoarde, in the guise of a shepherd, endeavours to gain tidings of his wife and is also seized by the banditti. While they attempt escape, Uberto runs to stab his hated enemy, but being prevented by Isabella, his noble nature gradually triumphs, and he determines that to spare a prostrate foe will be the most signal vengeance. Isabella turns out to be Uberto's lamented daughter; mutual forgiveness is exchanged; and the band and Uberto agree to return to the bosom of Honourable society" (E).

192. According to N.G.; but the press (except the *Harmonicon*) pluralized the original as *Gli Amori Marinari*.

193. Mitchell (45), however, calls Scribe's libretto "excellent."

194. *NOHM*, remarking that Boieldieu's style—based on Grétry—has "pliancy and charm" in contrast to Cherubini's "rigidity," notes that this was the first opera to reflect the influence of Weber. They add that Boieldieu's music "offers a light vein of poetry and sentiment, amorous rather than passionate, a technique sufficient but never pedantic, and a gift of graceful entertainment not to be taken too seriously" (VIII, 98–101).

195. The earliest *Masaniello* was the "Drama" by Soane and Bishop (Drury Lane, 1825), but in 1829, in addition to a King's ballet of that name, there were adaptations by Livius (Drury Lane), Milner (Coburg), and Kenney (Covent Garden). All but the first had some of Auber's music; none was very operatic. The *Athenaeum* (May 6), reviewing the Drury Lane production, wrote, "If the music were not already known to all, we should be tempted to say a good deal in its praise," adding that the composer was "able to diversify the character of the parts without changing the tone of the whole."

196. It would be hard to dispute this; Arnold's production of *Freischütz* in 1824 came very close, of course, but it was not quite the "complete" original.

197. "The scene lies in Peru, where Faulkland, an English gentleman . . . has performed great exploits for the country in the war, and is to be rewarded with the hand of . . . the Inca's daughter. By the machinations of a jealous commander of the Peruvian army and a Spanish lady to whom he has formally been contracted, Faulkland's wedding is broken off, and he is sentenced to be burned alive for

holding disrespectful opinions about the sun. In the end, it of course appears that the charge has been got up from interested purposes, the Englishman is released and married: and so the piece concludes." Talfourd (NM) relished one joke, in Faulkland's denial of any irreverence: "I am sure I have always shown the highest respect for the Sun—I respect the Sun as if he were my father—I never walk on the shady side of the way."

198. Nicoll lists the title as *Die Rauberbraut, or The Robber's Bride*, but the reviewers call it *The Robber's Bride*, which was also the title of the work after it had moved to Covent Garden (Oct. 22), with further adaptations in the story by Pocock.

199. Nothing is known of Logan (LitC), or of one John Kerr, to whom Nicoll attributes the book, and who had only half a dozen works produced between 1820 and 1845.

200. Boosey & Co., London music publishers, had the complete score on sale twelve months before it appeared at the English Opera House (QMM, VII, 195n).

201. Braham was chided for introducing some German airs that "did not accord with the music." Bacon (QMM, VII, 196–97) thought the music of the opera "had but a slight share in fixing its popularity." He added: "Weber has displayed a strong and original turn of mind in his *Freyschutz* [sic], but there is nothing in his works, taken as a whole, that can justify the attempt thus to make him an idol, and an idol to the exclusion of all other worship."

202. At a 1829 English Opera House revival, the "final" finale was included, but Ayrton thought it should have been dropped—"It is *de trop*,—a mere piece of garrulity."

203. *NOHM* (VIII, 496–98) states: "Weber's achievement was to make the supernatural theatrically credible and symbolically significant. . . . For the first time in opera supressed and half understood aspirations are given musical utterance on a level with acknowledged emotional and intellectual content." The weaknesses in the opera, they noted, stem from the libretto. John W. Kline, in "Der Freischutz—a Revaluation" (*Musical Opinion*, 87 [Dec. 1963], 147–48), asserts: "Its virtues are great virtues: sincerity, spontaneity, colour and a directness of appeal that at crucial moments is surely irresistible."

204. For a time *Euryanthe* was passed over, probably because of its failure (Vienna, 1823). But Covent Garden produced it in German in 1833, and an English adaptation appeared at the Prince's Theatre in 1840.

205. *NOHM* (VIII, 490) states that this was the only one of Weber's operas to "achieve a satisfactory balance of music and drama."

206. Nicoll cites a previous *Preciosa* at the English Opera House, August 26, 1824, but *Freischütz* was playing there that night, and I have been unable to trace it.

207. Blewitt (1780–1850) wrote music for pantomimes and was music director of Sadler's Wells in 1828–29. In 1830 the *Atlas* wrote that his music was "more like that of a man who understands his art than any that is now heard at the great theatres" (Mar. 14). Nothing is known of Somerset.

208. *NOHM* (VIII, 492), finding the score "very uneven," notes that the opera is "a hotchpotch of all elements integrated into Romantic opera, except for the supernatural."

209. Weber was to receive £500 for the opera, £250 for conducting it twelve nights, and £125 for conducting selections of *Freischütz* at the Philharmonic and at the Oratorios (see David Reynolds, ed., *Weber in London, 1826* (London, 1976). He was also promised £1,000 for a piano arrangement of the opera. He was to conduct a complete *Freischütz* for his benefit the day he died; Einstein errs in stating he conducted that opera at Covent Garden; it was not even revived in 1826.

210. *The Recollections and Reflections of J. R. Planché* (London, 1872), I, 76f

211. The *Chronicle* (Aug. 8) thought the "laborious, but futile, attempt at prejudgment and dictation" by the management "did the Opera serious injury on its first performance."

212. John H. Warrack, *Carl Maria von Weber* (London, 1962), 312n. The Drury Lane *Oberon*, called a fairy tale and written by Macfarren, used essentially the same story but was not very operatic: Cooke selected music from Cherubini (overture to *Lodoïska*), Winter, and Mozart. It received a mixed press but had twenty-eight performances—nearly as many as Weber's.

213. Weber wrote to his wife: "My English is tripping merrily off my tongue, and the English are amazed by it" (Robin Langley, "Weber in England," *Musical Times*, 117 [June 1976], 477–83).

214. *Carl Maria von Weber*; quoted by White, 254–55.

215. *Musical Recollections of the Last Half-Century*.

216. George Smart (1776–1867), an organist, violinist, and composer, was a chorister at the Chapel Royal who studied under Ayrton and for some years conducted the Lenten oratorios at the winter theatres and at festivals. He also conducted the Philharmonic Society, of which he was a founder. He taught singing to Sontag and Lind. Busby states that as a conductor he "stands alone" in superiority. He was knighted by the Lord Lieutenant of Ireland in 1811. He visited Beethoven and conducted his "Mount of Olives" in London in 1814; he also visited Weber, to whom he bore Kemble's offer to compose *Oberon*.

217. "The English Romantic Opera," *Victorian Studies*, 9 (Mar. 1966), 296–97.

The Performances

1. On singing at the playhouses before 1800, see L.S., I, lxxxii–lxxxviii.

2. Thomas Dibdin, *The Reminiscences of Thomas Dibdin* (London, 1827), II, 142.

3. See also Henry Saxe Wyndham, *The Annals of Covent Garden from 1732 to 1897* (London, 1906), 204.

4. John O'Keeffe, *Recollections of the Life of John O'Keeffe* (New York, 1960, I, 343.

5. On salaries of actors before 1800, see L.S., I, xcix–c.

6. *Life of Mrs. Jordan* (London, 1831), I, 350f.

7. The press could not even agree on this; the *Inquisitor* said "three times," and the *British Stage*, "once." The latter pointed out that the words were a parody

reflecting a recent political event in the Commons and reported that the "foolish" *Courier* was "styling the song an incentive to a rebellion, revolution, and everything terrible."

8. The *London* erroneously reported (Apr.) that "Braham (very wisely) has not sung this season."

9. The next month he sang Fenton in a production of the *Merry Wives of Windsor* but "fortunately did not have to act" (T, Feb. 21).

10. NM, December 1824. In January 1825 the *London* (probably Bacon), noting his place there was taken by Sapio—a bass!—wrote: "There can be no question in the mind of any judge of art, that Mr. Braham *can be* the finest singer England produced;... there is also no question that Mr. Braham often is below mediocrity. This however is the fault of the public in some degree—of himself in a greater.... Mr. Braham has made a large fortune... and if he were now to see his error and seek to retrace his steps (he has done so of late), there would be much difficulty in overcoming the judgment he has brought upon his own head."

11. The most thorough report on Braham was a very long "Sketch" in the *London* for July 1821 (62–65). Braham, who had a large Jewish following, was the occasional victim of anti-Semitic barbs—see LM, June 1821.

12. John H. Warrack, *Carl Maria von Weber* (London, 1968), 333.

13. In a one-act *Barber* at the Little Theatre that summer, he was loudly applauded in a duet with Miss Paton (T, Sept. 22).

14. *Midas* (1759), a spoof on Italian opera, was the most successful production of Kane O'Hara (c.1714–82).

15. Not to be confused with a Mr. Sapio, bass or baritone, who made an undistinguished debut at the King's in 1828.

16. QMM, IV, 60–64; *A Dictionary of Musicians*.

17. James Bartleman (1769–1821), a baritone and bass, sang at the Ancient and other concerts but apparently not on the English stage. Dr. Callcott and Crotch wrote songs for him.

18. Though the *Atlas* and *Examiner* reviewers sometimes differed sharply, there are other instances, such as this one, to demonstrate that these Sunday reviewers at the very least compared notes after performances.

19. Michael Leoni [Myer Lyon] (1755–97), a tenor and composer, made his debut in *Artaxerxes* in 1775 and sang in *Duenna* in 1776, but he failed to find favor in either London or Dublin and emigrated to Jamaica. He composed a number of small pieces for the Jewish ritual, although he was dismissed from his synagogue for having sung in *Messiah*. Probably most important was his being both uncle and teacher of John Braham, whom he introduced to the Royalty Theatre.

20. Mrs. William Atkins (née Warnell), later Mrs. Hill, flourished from 1787 to 1808. She made her London debut as Rosina at the Little Theatre on August 17, 1797, and she later sang at Covent Garden.

21. D.N.B.; a TI "Sketch" (Oct. 1819) states she was born in August of 1802.

22. Master Longhurst was a popular singer at Covent Garden in the early 1820s. In 1820, when he was twelve, the *Times* called him a "clever child" (Apr. 24).

23. Probably an equally fine actress, if not singer, was her sister Ellen Tree. She made a brief appearance at Covent Garden with Ann Maria in 1823 (LitC, May 24), began performing at Drury Lane in 1826, and moved to Covent Garden in 1829. She married Charles Kean in 1842 and had a long stage career.

24. Her younger sisters Eliza and Isabel were both singers, the latter appearing briefly at Drury Lane in 1826.

25. N.G. states she was a "great success" in the English Opera House *Freischütz*, but she did not even sing in that production.

26. TI, Dec. 1813; BS, Jan. 1817; Feb. 1819; June 1821.

27. The lyrics were by C. M. I. Dibdin; an example follows:

> What airy sound floats sweetly round,
>   Some spirit seems to play!
> How did that note on aether float,
>   And steal my soul away!
> Still, all I hear the changeful strain,
> It mocks, it echoes me again.
>   Is't fairy ground — are spirits round?
> Still, still I hear the changeful strain,
> It mocks, it echoes me again!

28. Samuel Sebastian Wesley (1810–76), a composer and organist, was the illegitimate son of the more famous Samuel Wesley (1776–1837).

29. Bruce Carr, "Theatre Music, 1800–1834." In *Music in Britain*, ed. N. Temperley (London, 1981), 290.

30. He was apparently unrelated to Samuel Christian Baumgarten (1729–98), who played bassoon at the King's from 1789 to 1791.

31. Parke, speaking of the high degree of perfection of the Covent Garden orchestra early in our period, cited these outstanding players: Pieltain and Bartélémon, violin; Crosdill and Cervetto, cello; Fischer and the elder Parke, oboe; Clementi, Schroeter, and Dance at the keyboard; Florio and Graeff, flute; Schutz and Holmes, bassoon; Abel, viol de gamba; Mahon, clarinet; Sarjeant, trumpet; and Stamstz and Shield, tenor (viola).

32. See, for example, T (May 23, 1788); H and T (Nov. 7, 1788), C and T (Feb. 28, 1791).

33. This was no doubt John Mountain, husband of Rosomon, who also lead Philharmonic Society concerts. At the Drury Lane *Freischütz* later that season, the *Times* noted: "The band was ably led by the veteran Mountain."

34. C. Goëde wrote that "an absurd costume is perfectly fashionable on the English Stage" (*A Foreigner's Opinion of England* [London, 1821], 427).

35. See Sybil Rosenfeld, *Georgian Scene Painters and Scene Painting* (Cambridge, 1981), 8, 75.

36. The scenery for *Blue-Beard* was painted by Thomas Greenwood the Younger, then age nineteen.

37. Rosenfeld (38) credits the younger Greenwood, Thomas Banks, and William Chalmers with the scenery, which provoked considerable criticism in *Gentleman's Magazine* for its faults.

38. This was Michael Rooker (1732–1800), R.A., an engraver and water colorist who did book illustrations in addition to scene painting at the Little Theatre for several years.

39. Painted by John Henderson Grieve (1770–1824) and Thomas (or Samuel) Lupino.

40. Apparently the most important of these was Thomas Grieve (1799–1882), son of John Henderson Grieve. Another son, William Grieve (1800–1844), became famous at Drury Lane and had an unprecedented curtain call for his scenery for *Robert le Diable* in 1832.

41. Stanfield (1793–1867) was apprenticed to a painter but spent many of his early years at sea, which he loved. He began painting scenery at Coburg and Drury Lane in 1822 and became very successful, but he gave it up for easel painting in 1834. One of his paintings brought £1,000 in 1840, and he gained a great reputation as a marine painter.

42. *Thirty Years' Musical Recollections* (London, 1862), I, 3.

Themes and Currents

1. C. 1803–4, when he was writing for the *News*.

2. In *The Bee* (1758–59) Oliver Goldsmith had decried the vocal gymnastics of singers in introduced numbers.

3. "Gracing is now carried to such an excess, that knowledge and taste are more shown by forbearance" (*A Dictionary of Musicians*, "Sapio," II, 414).

4. Again C. Goëde, a harsh critic who wrote on the state of acting in general (not just in operas) that prevailed at the London theatres at this time, cited the "frigid manner that borders on the incredible," while even the best actors did not know "how to handle natural, common feelings"; instead, they "tend to rant" (*A Foreigner's Opinion of England* [London, 1821], 426ff).

5. *The Recollections and Reflections of J. R. Planché* (London, 1872 I, 79–80.

6. The later Royal Academy of Music, founded in 1822, supported English performers in *Italian* opera, not in English. Indeed, the Academy was thought to have been harmful to English opera; see *Harmonicon* (VII, 24) in 1829 and *Athenaeum* (Dec. 18) in 1830.

Selected Bibliography

PRIMARY SOURCES

An asterisk indicates interrupted runs or missing numbers; sometimes the subordinate title [in square brackets] changes or is just dropped with a new series; entries are numbered to facilitate cross-references between journals. Abbreviations used are (d) daily; (sw) semiweekly; (t) triweekly; (w) weekly; (m) monthly; (a) annual; [E.E.N.] Early English Newspapers; [NYPL] New York Public Library.

1. *Analytical Review* (m), 1792–95.
2. *Annual Register* (a), 1805–6 (see 48).
3. *Annual Review* (a), 1805–6.
4. *Anti-Jacobin Review and Magazine* (m), 1800, 1805.*
5. *Athenaeum* [*and Literary Chronicle*] (w), 1828–30 (see 33).
6. *Atlas* (w), 1826–30. [Original at Yale, but for 1829 see British Library Newspaper Library, Colindale Ave.]
7. *Bell's Weekly Messenger* (w), 1808–14.* [Original at NYPL, Newspaper Annex.]
8. *British Critic* (m), 1793–1813.
9. *British Stage and Literary Cabinet* (m), 1817–22. [Original at Columbia Univ.]
10. *Carlton House Magazine* (m), 1795.*
11. *Champion* (w), 1814–22.
12. *Companion* (w), 1828.
13. *Courier* [*and Evening Gazette*] (d), 1804–9; 1814–16.*
14. *Covent Garden Monthly Recorder* (m), 1792.*
15. *Covent Garden Theatre Gazette* (sw), 1816–17.*
16. *Critical Review* (m), 1791–1805.
17. *Daily Advertiser* (d) (see 29 and 55).
18. [*Daily*] *Gazetteer* (see 29).
19. [*Daily*] *Universal Register* (see 75 and 79).
20. *Diary, or Woodfall's Register* (d), 1792.*
21. *Drama or Theatrical* [*Pocket*] *Magazine* (m), 1821–25. [NYPL, Lincoln Center.]
22. *Dramatic Censor,* [*or Weekly Theatrical Report*] (w), 1800–1801.*

23. *Drury Lane Theatre Gazette* (sw), 1817.*
24. *English Chronicle [and Whitehall Evening Post]* (t), 1793* (see 83).
25. *English Review* (m), 1791–94.*
26. *European Magazine* (m), 1789–1826.
27. *Examiner* (w), 1808–30.
28. *Flowers of Literature* (w), 1806.*
29. *Gazetteer [and New Daily Advertiser]* (d), 1785–97* (see 17 and 55).
30. *General Advertiser* (d), 1788.*
31. *General Evening Post* (d), 1793.*
32. *Harmonicon* (m), 1823–30. [Republished.]
33. *Literary Chronicle* (w), 1819–28* (see 5).
34. *Literary Gazette* (w), 1817–30. [Original at NYPL.]
35. *Literary Journal . . . A Review* (m), 1805* (see 52).
36. *Literary Review and Historical Journal* (m), 1794* (see 62).
37. *London Chronicle* (t), 1785–1800. [Temple Univ.]
38. *London Magazine* (m), 1820–29.*
39. *London Magazine and Gentleman's Intelligencer* (m), 1781–June, 1783; n.s. *London Magazine*, July, 1783–85. [Univ. of Connecticut.]
40. *Monthly Magazine [and British Register] [Supplement]* (m), 1796, 1801–1807* (see 51 and 52).
41. *Monthly Mirror* (m), 1795–1811* [Hamilton Coll.] (see 72).
42. *Monthly Musical Journal* (m), 1800–1801.*
43. *Monthly Review* (m), 1793–1811.*
44. *Monthly Visitor* (m), 1797.*
45. *Morning Chronicle [and London Advertiser]* (d), 1781–87*; 1790–95*; 1800–1830 [Bowdoin Coll., Harvard Univ., Columbia Univ.].
46. *Morning Herald* (d), 1782–1807*; 1822–23* [E.E.N., Bowdoin Coll., Duke Univ.]
47. *Morning Post* (d) 1795–1804* [Univ. of Wisconsin; Harvard Univ.]
48. *New Annual Register* (a), 1806 (see 2).
49. *New Lady's Magazine* (m), 1794.*
50. *New London Review* (m), 1800.*
51. *New Monthly Magazine* (m), 1814–15* (see 40 and 52).
52. *New Monthly Magazine and Literary Journal* (m), 1822–30 [Original at Columbia Univ.] (see 35, 40, and 51).
53. *Opera Glass* (w), 1826.*
54. *Oracle [and Bell's New World]* (d), 1789–94 (see 55 and 56).
55. *Oracle [and Daily Advertiser]* (d), 1798–1800 (see 17, 29, 54, and 56).
56. *Oracle [and Public Advertiser]* (d), 1794–98 (see 54, 55, and 60).
57. *Oxford Review* (m), 1807.*
58. *Plain Dealer* (w), 1832. [Columbia Univ.]
59. *Poetical Register* (a), 1801–11.
60. *Public Advertiser* (d), 1781–94* [E.E.N., S.U.N.Y., Buffalo; Yale Univ.] (see 56).

61. *Quarterly Musical Magazine and Review*, 1818–28. [Hamilton Coll.]
62. *Register of the Times and the Literary Review*, 1795* (see 36).
63. *St. James's Chronicle* (t), 1789, 1791.*
64. *Satirist, or Monthly Meteor* (m), 1808.*
65. *Spectator* (w), 1828–30.
66. *Star* (d), 1793–95.
67. *Sun* (d), 1794, 1796.*
68. *Tatler* (d), 1830–32. [Original at Columbia Univ. Special Collections.]
69. "Theatrical Cuttings; Clippings from British Newspapaers, 1711–1862." [NYPL, Lincoln Center Special Collections.]
70. *Theatrical Examiner* (w), 1823–31.
71. *Theatrical Guardian* (w), 1791.
72. *Theatrical Inquisitor* [*and Monthly Mirror*] (m), 1812–20 (see 41).
73. *Theatrical Observer* (d), 1821–23. [Cornell Univ.]
74. *Thespian Magazine and Literary Repository* (m), 1793.
75. *Times* (d), 1788–1830 (see 19 and 79).
76. *Town Talk* (w), 1811.*
77. *True Briton* (d), 1793–96, 1799–1800.*
78. *Universal Magazine* [*of Knowledge and Pleasure*] (m), 1783–1815. [Univ. of Rochester.]
79. [*Daily*] *Universal Register* (d), 1785–87 (see 19 and 75).
80. *Walker's Hibernian Magazine* (m), 1783–97. [Univ. of North Carolina, Chapel Hill.]
81. *Weekly Magazine* (w), 1816.*
82. *Westminister Magazine* [*or the Pantheon of Taste*] (m), 1778–82. [Bowdoin Coll.]
83. *Whitehall Evening Post* (d), 1791 (see 24).
84. *World* (d), 1787–89.

SECONDARY SOURCES

Adolphus, John. *Memoirs of John Bannister, Comedian*. 2 vols. London: Richard Bentley, 1839.

Algarotti, Francesco. *An Essay on the Opera*. London, 1767. Translation of his *Saggio sopra l'opera in musico*, 1755.

Andrews, Alexander. *The History of British Journal, from the Foundation of the Newspaper Press in England, to the Repeal of the Stamp Act in 1855, with sketches of Press Celebrities*. 2 vols. London: Richard Bentley, 1859.

Arundell, Dennis. *The Critic at the Opera*. London: Ernest Benn, Ltd., 1957.

Aspinall, Arthur. *Politics and the Press, 1780–1850*. London: Holm & Van Thal, 1949.

Asquith, Ivon. "Advertisement and the Press in the Late Eighteenth and Early Nineteenth Centuries: James Perry and the 'Morning Chronicle,' 1790–1821." *Historical Journal*, 18 (1975), 703–24.

"Autobiography of an Amateur Singer." *Harmonicon*, IX (1831), 106–7, 135–37.

Baer, Marc. *Theatre and Disorder in Late Georgian London*. London: Oxford Univ. Press, 1992.
Bagster-Collins, Jeremu Felix. *George Colman the Younger, 1762–1836*. New York: Kings Crown Press, 1946.
Baker, Henry Barton. *History of the London Stage and its Famous Players, 1576–1903*. New York: Benjamin Blom, Inc., 1969. 1st ed., London, 1904.
Bauer, Josephine. *The London Magazine, 1820–1829*. Copenhagen: Rosenkilde and Bagger, 1953.
Beechey, Gwilym, "Thomas Linley, Junior, 1756–1778." *Musical Quarterly*, 54 (Jan. 1968), 74–82.
Bellingardini, Luigi. "Rossini's 'Queen Elizabeth'—Its Style and Originality." *Opera*, 23 (Aug. 1972), 686–91.
———. "Spontini's 'La Vestale.'" *Opera*, 24 (Aug. 1973), 727–29.
Beyle, Henri (The Count de Stendhal). *Life of Rossini*. Translated by Richard N. Coe. New York: Criterion Books, 1957. 1st ed., Paris, 1823.
———. *Rome, Naples and Florence, in 1817*. London: Henry Colburn, 1818. 1st ed., Paris, 1817.
Boaden, James. *Life of Mrs. Jordan*. 2 vols. London: E. Bull, 1831.
———. *Memoirs of John Philip Kemble*. 2 vols. London: n.p., 1825.
"James Boaden, Esq." Obituary in *Gentleman's Magazine*. April 1839, 436–37.
Boulton, William B. *The Amusements of Old London*. 2 vols. London: John Nimmo, 1901.
Bourne, Henry Richard Fox. *English Newspapers: Chapters in the History of Journalism*. 2 vols. London: Chatto and Windus, 1887.
Brown, Edmund. *The London Theatre, 1811–1866; Selections from the Diary of Henry Crabb Robinson*. London: Society for Theatre Research, 1966.
Bukofzer, Manfred F. *Music in the Baroque Era*. New York: W. W. Norton & Co., Inc., 1947.
Bunn, Alfred. *The Stage: Both Before and Behind the Curtain*. 3 vols. London: Richard Bentley, 1840.
Burgh, Allatson. *Anecdotes of Music, Historical and Biographical*. 3 vols. London: Longman, 1814.
[Burgoyne, John.] *The Lord of the Manor, a Comic Opera as it is Performed at the Theatre Royal, Drury-Lane, with a Preface by the Author*. Philadelphia: William Spotswood, 1790.
Burney, Charles. *General History of Music from the Earliest Ages to the Present Time*. 2 vols. New York: Harcourt, Brace, Jovanovich, 1935. 1st ed., London, 1789.
Busby, Thomas. *A General History of Music from the Earliest Times*. New York: Da Capo Press, 1968. 1st ed., London, 1819.
Bushnell, Howard. *Maria Malibran*. University Park: Pennsylvania State Univ. Press, 1979.
Canning, Hugh. "Cimarosa's 'Gli Orazi e i Curiazi.'" *Opera*, 32 (Mar. 1981), 248–51.
Carlson, Marvin. "Theatre Audiences and the Reading of Performance." In *Interpretation of the Theatrical Past*, edited by Thomas Postlewait and Bruce

A. McConachie. Iowa City: Univ. of Iowa Press, 1989.
Carr, Bruce. "Theatre Music, 1800–1834." In *Music in Britain: The Romantic Age, 1800–1914*, edited by Nicholas Temperley. London: Athlone Press, 1981.
———. "The First All-sung English 19th Century Opera." *Musical Times*, 115, 1572 (Feb. 1974), 125–26.
Chorley, Henry F. *Thirty Years' Musical Recollections*. 2 vols. London: Hurst & Blackett, 1862.
Christie, Dan R. *Myth and Reality in Late Eighteenth-Century British Politics and Other Papers*. Berkeley: Univ. of California Press, 1970.
"Chronicles of the Italian Opera in England." by S. D., *Harmonicon*, VIII (1830), 10–338 passim.
Commons, Jeremy. Notes on recordings: *A Hundred Years of Italian Opera 1800–1810*, vols. I and II; and *A Hundred Years of Italian Opera, 1810–1820*. London: Opera Rara Ltd.
Considerations of the Past and Present State of the Stage. London: n.p., 1809.
Da Ponte, Lorenzo. *Memoirs of Lorenzo Da Ponte*. Translated by Elizabeth Abbott. Edited and with an introduction by Arthur Livingston. New York: Orion Press, 1929.
Davey, Henry. *History of English Music*. 2d ed. New York: Da Capo Press, 1969.
Dean, Winton. "Richard Coeur de Lion." *Musical Times*, 119 (Apr. 1978), 348.
Deane, Basil. *Cherubini*. London: Oxford Univ. Press, 1965.
Dennis, John. *An Essay on the Opera's after the Italian Manner*. London: J. Nutt, 1706.
Dent, Edward J. "Bellini in England." In *Selected Essays*, edited by Hugh Taylor. London: Cambridge Univ. Press, 1979.
———. *Foundations of English Opera*. London: Cambridge Univ. Press, 1928.
———. *The Rise of Romantic Opera*. Edited by Winton Dean. London: Cambridge Univ. Press, 1976.
Dibdin, Charles. *Professional and Literary Memoirs of Charles Dibdin the Younger*. Edited by George Speaight. London: The Society for Theatre Research, 1956. 1st ed., London, 1803.
Dibdin, Thomas. *The Reminiscences of Thomas Dibdin*. London: H. Colburn, 1827.
Dictionary of Musicians. 2 vols. London: Sainsbury & Co., 1824.
Dimond, William. *Native Land, or The Return from Slavery*. New York: E. M. Murden, 1824.
Ebers, John. *Seven Years of the King's Theatre*. London: n.p., 1828.
Edwards, Sutherland. *History of the Opera*. 2 vols. London: Wm. H. Allen & Co., 1862.
Einstein, Alfred. *Essays on Music*. New York: W. W. Norton, 1956.
Escott, T. H. S. *Masters of English Journalism*. London: T. Fisher Unwin, 1911.
Fawcett, Trevor. "Bishop and *Aladdin*." *Musical Times*, 113 (Nov. 1972), 1076–77.
Fenner, Theodore. "Edward Quin and the *Traveller*." *Studies in Romanticism*, 14 (Spring 1975), 137–64.
———. *Leigh Hunt and Opera Criticism: The "Examiner" Years 1808–1821*. Law-

rence: Univ. Press of Kansas, 1972.
Fétis, F. J., ed. *Biographie Universale Des Musiciens e Bibliographie Generale de la Musique*. 2d ed. Paris: Fermin-Didot, 1878–80.
Fiske, Roger. *English Theatre Music in the Eighteenth Century*. New York: Oxford Univ. Press, 1986.
Fitzball [Ball], Edward. *Thirty-five Years of a Dramatic Author's Life*. London: T. C. Newby, 1859.
Forsyth, Cecil. *Music and Nationalism: A Study of English Opera*. London: Macmillan and Co., 1911.
Freeman, James. "Pietro Generali in Sicily." *Music Review*, 34 (1973), 231–40.
Fuller-Maitland, J. A. *English Music in the XIXth Century*. New York: E. P. Dutton and Co., 1902.
Gagey. Edmond M. *Ballad Opera*. New York: Columbia Univ. Press, 1937.
Garlington, Aubrey S. "'Gothic' Literature and Dramatic Music in England." *Journal of the American Musicological Society*, XV, no. 1 (Spring 1962), 48–64.
Genest, John. *Some Account of the English Stage*. 10 vols. Bath: T. Rodd, 1832.
Goëde, Christian Augustus G. *A Foreigner's Opinion of England, Englishmen, Englishwomen, English morals* . . . . Translated by Thomas Horne. Boston: Wells and Lilly, 1822. 1st ed., London, 1821.
Graf, Max. *Composer and Critic: Two Hundred Years of Musical Criticism*. New York: W. W. Norton, 1946.
Gray, Charles H. *Theatrical Criticism in London to 1795*. New York: Columbia Univ. Press, 1931.
Grout, Donald J. *A Short History of Opera*. 2d ed. 2 vols. New York: Columbia Univ. Press, 1965.
Grove, Sir George, ed. *A Dictionary of Music and Musicians*. London: Macmillan, 1890.
Hardcastle, Mary. *The Life of John, Lord Campbell*. 2 vols. London: 1881.
Hastings, M. D. "Touched-Down Dibdin." *Musical Opinion*, 88 (Sept. 1965), 727–28.
Hauser, George. "Victorian Musical Theatre." *Opera*, 29 (1978) no. 2, 135–39; no. 3, 266–69.
Haydon, Benjamin Robert. *The Diary of Benjamin Robert Haydon*. Edited by Willard B. Pope. Cambridge, Mass.: Harvard Univ. Press. vols. 1–2, 1960; vols. 3–5, 1963.
Hazlitt, William. *The Complete Works of William Hazlitt*. 21 vols. Edited by P. P. Howe. London: J. M. Dent and Sons, 1930–34.
———. "The Periodical Press." *Edinburgh Review*, 38 (1823), 349–78.
Hertzman, Erich. "Mozart and Attwood." *Journal of the American Musicological Society*, XII (1959), 178–84.
Highfill, Philip H., Jr., Kalman A. Burnim, and Edward A. Langhans. *A Biographical Dictionary of Actors, Actresses, Musicians, Dancers, Managers, and Other Stage Personnel in London, 1660–1800*. Carbondale: Southern Illinois Univ. Press, 1973–93.

Hogarth, George. *Memoirs of the Musical Drama.* 2 vols. London: Richard Bentley, 1838.
Houghton, Walter E., ed. *The Wellesley Index to Victorian Periodicals, 1824–1900.* 4 vols. Toronto: Univ. of Toronto Press, 1979.
Houlton, Robert. *A Review of the Musical Drama of the Theatre Royal, D[rury] L[ane], for the Years 1797–1800.* London: Wesley, Stuart, and Co., 1801.
Hudson, Derek. *Thomas Barnes of "The Times."* London: Cambridge Univ. Press, 1931.
Hume, Robert D. *London Theatre Worl 1660–1800.* Carbondale: Southern Illinois Univ. Press, 1980.
———. *The Rakish Stage: Studies in English Drama, 1660–1800.* Carbondale: Southern Illinois Univ. Press, 1983.
———. "Studies in English Drama, 1660–1800." *Philological Quarterly* (1976), 451–87.
Hunt, F. Knight. *The Fourth Estate: A History of Newspapers and of the Liberty of the Press.* 2 vols. London: David Brogue, 1850.
Hunt, Ino Leland. *Giovanni Paisiello, His Life as an Opera Composer.* N.p.: National Opera Association, 1975.
Hunt, Leigh. *The Autobiography of Leigh Hunt.* Edited by Jack E. Morpurgo. London: Cresset Press, Ltd., 1948. 1st ed., London, 1850.
———. *Critical Essays on the performers of the London Theatres, including general observations on the practice and genius of the stage by the author of the Theatrical Criticism in the weekly paper called the News.* London: John Hunt, 1808.
Jackson, William. *Observations on the Present State of Music in London.* London: n.p., 1789.
Jerdan, William. *The Autobiography of William Jerdan.* 4 vols. London: Arthur Hall, Virtue, & Co., 1852.
Jesson, Roy. "Martin's 'L'arbore di Diana.'" *Musical Times,* 113 (June 1972), 551–53.
———. "Una Cosa Rara." *Musical Times,* 109 (July 1968), 619–21.
Johnson, Paul. *The Birth of the Modern: World Society 1815–1830.* New York: HarperCollins, 1991.
Jones, Stephen. *Biographia Dramatica.* 4 vols. London: Longman, Hurst, 1812.
Kassler, Jamie Croy. *The Science of Music in Britain, 1714–1830.* 2 vols. New York: Garland Publishers, Inc., 1979.
[Kelly, Michael.] *Reminiscences of Michael Kelly, of the King's Theatre and Theatre Royal Drury Lane, including a period of nearly half a century; with original anecdotes of many distinguished persons, political, literary, and musical.* 2d ed. 2 vols. London: Henry Colburn, 1826.
King, Alexander Hyatt. "*Don Giovanni* in London before 1817." *Musical Times,* 127 (Sept. 1986), 487–93.
Klein, John W. "Der Freischutz—A Revaluation." *Musical Opinion,* 87 (Dec. 1963), 147–49.
———. "Meyerbeer and 'Il Crociato.'" *Musical Times,* 113 (Jan. 1972), 39–40.
Kolodin, Irving. "Music to my Ears." *Saturday Review,* 52 (Dec. 20, 1969), 46–47.

Landon, H. C. Robbins, ed. *Collected Correspondence and London Notebooks of Joseph Haydn*. Fairlawn, N.J.: Essential Books, 1959.
Landon, H. C. Robbins. *Haydn in England, 1791–1795*. Vol. III, *Haydn: Chronicle and Works*. Bloomington: Indiana Univ. Press, 1976.
Lang, Paul Henry. *George Frideric Handel*. New York: W. W. Norton, 1966.
———. *Music in Western Civilization*. New York: W. W. Norton, 1941.
Langley, Leanne. *The English Musical Journal in the Early Nineteenth Century*. Ann Arbor, Mich.: Univ. Microfilms, 1983.
Langley, Robin. "Weber in England." *Musical Times*, 117 (June 1976), 477–83.
Leacroft, Richard. *The Development of the English Playhouse*. Ithaca: Cornell Univ. Press, 1973.
Levy, David B. "Thomas Massa Alsager, Esq.: A Beethoven Advocate in London." *Nineteenth Century Music*, IX, no. 21 (Fall 1985), 119–27.
Libby, Dennis. "Spontini's Early French Operas." *Musical Times*, 117 (Jan. 1976), 23–24.
Loesser, Arthur. *Men, Women & Pianos: A Social History*. New York: Simon & Schuster, 1954.
Loewenberg, Alfred. *Annals of Opera: 1597–1940*. 3d ed. 2 vols. Introduction by Edward J. Dent. Totowa, N.J.: Rowman and Littlefield, 1978.
———. "'Don Giovanni' in London." *Music and Letters*, 24 (1943), 164–68.
———. "Lorenzo da Ponte in London." *Music Review*, IV (1943), 171–89.
Lynch, James J. *Box, Pit and Galler: Stage and Society in Johnson's London*. Berkeley: Univ. of California Press, 1953.
Mackerness, Eric D. "Leigh Hunt's Musical Journalism." *Monthly Musical Record*, LXXXVI (Nov.–Dec. 1956), 212–22.
McVeigh, Simon. *The Violinist in London's Concert Life, 1750–1784: Felice Giardini and His Contemporaries*. New York: Garland Publishing, 1989.
Marchand, Leslie A. *The Athenaeum: A Mirror of Victorian Culture*. Chapel Hill: Univ. of North Carolina Press, 1941.
Mayer, David. "Nineteenth Century Theatre Music." *Theatre Notebook*, 30, no. 3 (1976), 115–22.
Mellers, Wilfrid. *Harmonious Meeting, a Study of the Relationship between English Music, Poetry and Theatre, c. 1600–1900*. London: Dennis Dobson, 1965.
Milhous, Judith. "Lighting at the King's Theatre Haymarket, 1780–1782." *Theatre Research International*, 16, no. 3 (1991), 215–36.
Mitchell, Jerome. *The Walter Scott Operas*. University, Ala.: Univ. of Alabama Press, 1977.
Morison, Stanley. *John Bell, 1745–1831, bookseller, printer, typesetter, Journalist, &c.* Cambridge: Univ. of Cambridge Press (printed for author), 1930.
Mount-Edgcumbe, Richard. *Musical Reminiscences, containing an account of Italian opera in England, from 1773*. 4th ed., London, 1834. New York: Da Capo Press, 1973.
Nalbach, Daniel. *The King's Theatre, 1704–1867*. London: Society for Theatre Research, 1972.

New Cambridge Bibliography of English Literature. Edited by George Watson. Vol. II, 1660–1800 (1972); vol. III, 1800–1900 (1969).
New Grove Dictionary of Music and Musicians. 20 vols. Edited by Stanley Sadie. London: Macmillan, 1980.
New Grove Dictionary of Opera. Edited by Stanley Sadie. 4 vols. London: Macmillan, 1992.
New Oxford History of Music. Vol. VII, *The Age of Enlightenment, 1745–1790*, Edited by Egon Wellesz and Frederick Sternfeld. London, 1973); vol. VIII, *The Age of Beethoven, 1790–1830*, edited by Gerald Abraham. London, 1982.
Nicholson, Watson. *The Struggle for a Free Stage in London.* London: Archibald Constable and Co., 1906.
Nicoll, Allardyce. *A History of English Drama, 1660–1900.* 6 vols. Vol. III, *Late Eighteenth Century Drama, 1750–1800*; vol IV, *Early Nineteenth Century Drama, 1800–1850.* London: Cambridge Univ. Press, 1955.
O'Keeffe, John. *Recollections of the Life of John O'Keeffe.* 2 vols. New York: Benjamin Blom, Inc., 1961. 1st ed., London, 1826.
Oldman, C. B. "Attwood's Dramatic Works." *Musical Times*, 107 (Jan. 1966), 23–26.
Parke, William T. *Musical Memoirs.* 2 vols. London: H. Colburn and R. Bentley, 1830.
Pauley, Reinhard G. *Music in the Classic Period.* Englewood Cliffs, N.J.: Prentice Hall, 1965.
Peacock, Thomas Love. *The Works of Thomas Love Peacock.* Vol. 9, *Critical and Other Essays.* New York: AMS Press, Inc., 1967.
Peake, Richard Brindsley. *Memoirs of the Colman Family.* London: Richard Bentley, 1841.
Pendle, Karin. "The Opéras Comiques of Grétry and Marmontel." *Musical Quarterly*, LXII (July 1976), 409–34.
Petty, Frederick C. *Italian Opera in London, 1760–1800.* Ann Arbor, Mich.: UMI Research Press, 1980.
Phillips, Henry. *Musical and Personal Recollections During Half a Century.* 2 vols. London: Charles J. Skeet, 1864.
Planché, James R. *The Recollections and Reflections of J. R. Planché, a Professional Autobiography.* 2 vols. London: Tinsley Bros., 1872.
Price, Cecil John Layton, ed. *The Letters of Richard Brinsley Sheridan.* 3 vols. London: Oxford Univ. Press, 1966.
Price, Cecil John Layton. *Theatre in the Age of Garrick.* Totowa, N.J.: Rowan and Littlefield, 1973.
———. "Thomas Harris and the Covent Garden Theatre." In *Eighteenth-Century Stage*, edited by Kenneth Richards and Peter Thompson. London: Methuen & Co., 1972, 105–22.
Price, Curtis Alexander. *Henry Purcell and the London Stage.* London: Cambridge Univ. Press, 1984.
———. "Italian Opera and Arson in Late Eighteenth-Century London." *Journal*

of the American Musicological Society, XLII, no. 1 (Spring, 1989), 55–107.

———. "Music as Drama." In *London Theatre World, 1660–1800*, edited by Robert D. Hume. Carbondale: Southern Illinois Univ. Press, 1980.

———. "Turner at the Pantheon Opera House, 1791–92." *Turner Studies*, VII (Winter 1987), 2–8.

Price, Curtis Alexander, Judith Milhous, and Robert D. Hume. "The Rebuilding of the King's Theatre, Haymarket, 1789–1791." *Theatre Journal*, vol. 43 (Dec. 1991), 421–44.

Quinlan, Maurice J. *Victorian Prelude: A History of English Manners, 1700–1830*. New York: Columbia Univ. Press, 1941.

Ralph, Richard. "Sir John Gallini," *About the House*, V, no. 9 (1979), 30–37.

Rapp, Merton H. "Frederick Reynolds and the English Drama, 1785–1840." Ph.D. diss., State University of Iowa, 1939.

Redding, Cyrus. *Literary Reminiscences and Memoirs of Thomas Campbell*. 2 vols. London: Charles J. Skeet, 1860.

Reilly, Joan. "Winston's Braham Scrapbook." *Theatre Notebook*, 36, no. 2 (1982), 52–55.

Reynolds, David, ed. *Weber in London, 1826*. London: Oswald Wolff, Ltd., 1976.

Reynolds, Frederic. *The Life and Times of Frederick [sic] Reynolds, Written by Himself*. 2 vols. London: H. Colburn, 1826.

Rhodes, R. Crompton. *The Plays and Poems of Richard Brinsley Sheridan*. New York: Russell & Russell, 1962.

Robinson, Michael F. *Naples and Neapolitan Opera*. London: Oxford Univ. Press, 1972.

Rodwell, G. Herbert. *A Letter to the Musicians of Great Britain; containing a prospectus of a proposed plan for the better encouragement of native music talent and for the erection and management of a grand national opera in London*. London: James Fraser, 1833.

Rosenfeld, Sybil. *Georgian Scene Painters and Scene Painting*. London: Cambridge Univ. Press, 1981.

Rosenthal, Harold D. *Two Centuries of Opera at Covent Garden*. New York: Putnam, 1958.

Rowell, George. *The Victorian Theatre, a Survey*. 2d ed. London: Cambridge Univ. Press, 1978.

Rushmore, Robert. "The Unholy Bishop." *Opera News*, 34 (Dec. 20, 1969), 6–7.

Saint, Andrew, et al. *A History of the Royal Opera House Covent Garden, 1732–1982*. London: Royal Opera House Covent Garden Ltd., n.d.

Savage, James. *An Account of London Daily Papers*. London: n.p., 1811.

Schneider, Ben Ross, Jr., comp. *Index to "The London Stage, 1660–1800."* Carbondale: Southern Illinois Univ. Press, 1979.

Scott, Michael. "Rossini in England." *Opera*, 27 (Mar., May 1976), part 1, 210–14; part 2, 434–39.

Selden, Margery Stomne. "Cherubini and England." *Musical Quarterly*, 60, 421–34.

Shaw-Taylor, Desmond. *Covent Garden*. New York: Chanticleer Press, 1948.
Smith, Patrick J. *The Tenth Muse: A Historical Study of the Opera Libretto*. New York: Knopf, 1970.
Smith, William Charles. *Italian Opera and Contemporary Ballet in London: 1789–1820*. London: Society for Theatre Research, 1955.
Spettacolo, Enciclopedia dello. 9 vols. Rome: Casa Editrice le Maschere, 1954–62.
Survey of London. Vols. XXIX, XXX, XXXI. London County Council Staff. Edited by F. W. Sheppard et al. New York, 1970.
Taylor, John. *Records of my Life*. 2 vols. London: Bull, 1832.
Temperley, Nicholas. The English Romantic Opera." *Victorian Studies*, 9 (Mar. 1966), 293–301.
The Thespian Dictionary; or Dramatic biography of the eighteenth century containing sketches of the Lives, Productions &c &c of all the Principal Managers, Dramatists, Composers. London: T. Hurst, 1802.
Thomas, William Beach. *The Story of the Spectator, 1828–1928*. London: Methuen & Co. Ltd., 1928.
Thompson, Oscar, ed. *The International Cyclopedia of Music and Musicians*. 9th ed. New York: Dodd, Mead & Co., 1964.
Van Der Merwe, Pieter. "The Ingenious Squire: New Aspects of Isaac Pocock (1782–1835)." *Theatre Notebook*, 31, no. 21 (1977), 12–18.
"Veritas." *Opera House. A Review of this Theatre from the Period Described by the Enterprizer*. London: n.p., 1818.
Walker, Ernest. *A History of Music in England*. 3d ed. London: Oxford Univ. Press, 1952. 1st ed., London, 1924.
Ward, William Smith. *British Periodicals: Index and Finding List of Serials Published in the British Isles, 1789–1832*. Lexington: Univ. of Kentucky Press, 1953.
Warrack, John H. *Carl Maria von Weber*. London: H. Hamilton, 1968.
Watson, Ernest B. *Sheridan to Robertson: A Study of the Nineteenth Century London Stage*. Cambridge, Mass.: Harvard Univ. Press, 1926.
Weed, Katherine Kertley, and Richmond Pugh Bond. *Studies of British Newspapers and Periodicals from Their Beginnings to 1800 — A Bibliography*. Chapel Hill: Univ. of North Carolina Press, 1946.
Weinstock, Herbert. "Medea in Corinto," *Opera*, 21 (Nov. 1970), 223.
———. *Rossini: A Biography*. New York: Knopf, 1968.
Werkmeister, Lucyle. *A Newspaper History of England, 1792–93*. Lincoln: Univ. of Nebraska Press, 1967.
White, Eric Walter. *A History of English Opera*. London: Faber and Faber, 1983.
Wiles, R. M. "Periodical Publications." In *New Cambridge Bibliography of English Literature*, vol. II (1660–1800). Edited by George Watson. London: Cambridge Univ. Press, 1971.
Williams, Raymond. *The Long Revolution*. London: Chatto and Windus, 1961.
Winesanker, Michael. "Musico-Dramatic Criticism of English Comic Opera, 1750–1800." *Journal of American Musicological Society*, II (1949), 87–96.

———. "The Record of English Musical Drama, 1790–1800." Ph.D. diss. Cornell University, 1944.

Wyndham, Henry Saxe. *The Annals of Covent Garden Theatre from 1732 to 1897.* 2 vols. London: Chatto and Windus, 1906.

Young, Percy M. *A History of British Music.* London: Ernest Benn, Ltd., 1967.

Photographic Credits

The author and publisher wish to thank the following individuals and institutions for kindly permitting us to reproduce the photographs in this book.

Frontispiece. From E. W. Brayley, *Historical and Descriptive Accounts of the Theatres of London* (1826).
 1. From Edmund C. Blunden, *Leigh Hunt, a Biography* (London: Cobden-Sanderson Ltd., 1930).
 2. From Catherine M. Maclean, *Born under Saturn* (New York: Macmillan, 1944).
 3. From Percy A. Scholes, *Oxford Companion to Music*, 9th ed. (Oxford Univ. Press, 1955).
 4. Courtesy of The Bettmann Archive.
 5. From H. C. Robbins Landon, *Haydn in London, 1791–1795*, vol. III (Bloomington: Indiana Univ. Press, 1976). Courtesy of H. C. Robbins Landon.
 6. Courtesy of Opera Rara, Ltd.
 7. From Herbert Weinstock, *Rossini, a Biography* (New York: Alfred A. Knopf, 1968).
 8. Courtesy of Opera Rara, Ltd.
 9. Courtesy of Opera Rara, Ltd.
 10. Courtesy of Opera Rara, Ltd.
 11. From *British Stage* (Feb. 1818).
 12. Courtesy of the Music Division, The New York Public Library for the Performing Arts, Astor, Lenox and Tilden Foundations.
 13. Courtesy of the Music Division, The New York Public Library for the Performing Arts, Astor, Lenox and Tilden Foundations.
 14. Courtesy of Opera Rara, Ltd.
 15. From Herbert Weinstock, *Rossini, a Biography* (New York: Alfred A. Knopf, 1968).
 16. From H. C. Robbins Landon, *Haydn in London, 1791–1795*, vol. III (Bloomington: Indiana Univ. Press, 1976). Courtesy of H. C. Robbins Landon.
 17. From H. C. Robbins Landon, *Haydn in London, 1791–1795*, vol. III (Bloomington: Indiana Univ. Press, 1976). Courtesy of H. C. Robbins Landon.
 18. From a portrait by John Hoppner in Heinemann Gallery, Munich. Courtesy of Paul McCarron Portraits and Drawings, New York City.

19. Courtesy of the Music Division, The New York Public Library for the Performing Arts, Astor, Lenox and Tilden Foundations.
20. Courtesy of Opera Rara, Ltd.
21. Courtesy of the Music Division, The New York Public Library for the Performing Arts, Astor, Lenox and Tilden Foundations.
22. Courtesy of the Music Division, The New York Public Library for the Performing Arts, Astor, Lenox and Tilden Foundations.
23. From John Ebers, *Seven Years of the King's Theatre* (1828).
24. From Herbert Weinstock, *Rossini, a Biography* (New York: Alfred A. Knopf, 1968).
25. From Herbert Weinstock, *Rossini, a Biography* (New York: Alfred A. Knopf, 1968).
26. From E. W. Brayley, *Historical and Descriptive Accounts of the Theatres of London* (1826).
27. From *The Microcosm of London* (1809).
28. Courtesy of Berg Publications Ltd.
29. From *The Beggar's Opera* (1978 edition). Courtesy of Dover Publications.
30. From *Monthly Mirror* (Jan. 1803).
31. From *Monthly Mirror* (Dec. 1807).
32. From *Monthly Mirror* (Aug. 1796).
33. From *Monthly Mirror* (Dec. 1795).
34. From John H. Warrack, *Carl Maria von Weber* (London: Hamish Hamilton, 1968).
35. From Harold D. Rosenthal, *Two Centuries of Opera at Covent Garden* (New York: Putnam, 1958).
36. From Henry Saxe Wyndham, *Annals of Covent Garden Theatre* (London: Chato and Windus, 1906).
37. From Henry Saxe Wyndham, *Annals of Covent Garden Theatre* (London: Chato and Windus, 1906).
38. From Henry Saxe Wyndham, *Annals of Covent Garden Theatre* (London: Chato and Windus, 1906).
39. Courtesy of the Music Division, The New York Public Library for the Performing Arts, Astor, Lenox and Tilden Foundations.
40. From *British Stage* (Dec. 1817).
41. By courtesy of the Board of Trustees of the Victoria & Albert Museum.
42. Courtesy of Opera Rara, Ltd.
43. From Ernest B. Watson, *Sheridan to Robertson* (1928). Copyright © 1928 by Harvard University Press. Reprinted by permission of Harvard University Press.
44. From Autumn 1983 Imprint, vol. 8, no. 2, of the *Journal of the American Historical Print Collectors Society*. Courtesy of the Maryland Historical Society, Baltimore.
45. Courtesy of Berg Publications Ltd.

46. From Harold D. Rosenthal, *Two Centuries of Opera at Covent Garden* (New York: Putnam, 1958).
47. Courtesy of Berg Publications Ltd.

Index

In entries for English operas, the virgule (/) separates names of dramatist and composer; for English opera adaptations, it also separates the names of musical adapter and primary composer.

In the appendixes and notes, only the names of arias and of major titles and figures have been indexed.

Abbreviations: (ad.) adaptation from or by; (c.) composer; (d.) dramatist; (j.) journalist; (l.) librettist; (mgr.) theatre manager; (s.) singer; and (sel.) selections from or by.

Abel, Karl Friedrich (c., viola de gamba), 381, 687, 730
Abou Hassan (Dimond ad. Heimer/ Cooke/Weber), 506–7, 628
Abroad and At Home (Holman/ Shield), 395, 615
Aci e Galatea (Bianchi), 88, 115, 282
Acis and Galatea (Handel/Gay), 373, 690
Addison, John (c.), 392, 436. See also *Farmer's Wife, The; Russian Impostor, The*
Addison, Joseph, 66. See also *Rosamond*
Adelasia e Aleramo (Mayr), 131, 293
Adelina (Generali), 298
Adolfo e Chiara (Pucitta), 128, 293
Adolphe et Clare (Marsollier), 450
Adopted Child, The (Birch/Attwood), 402
Adrian and Orrila (Dimond/ Attwood; Kelly), 426, 618. See also *Youth, Love, and Folly*
Aglio, Augustino (scene painter), 703
Agnese, L' (Paer), 130, 294
Aladdin (Soane/Bishop), 58–59, 475–76, 629

Albero di Diana, L'. See *Arbore di Diana, L'*
Albert and Adelaide (Birch/ Attwood), 402, 429
Albert (Bonet) (s.), 324
Alcaid, The (Kenney/Nathan), 479, 628
Alceste (Cherubini), 105
Alceste (Gluck), 71, 104, 282
Alceste (Gresnich), 103, 278
Alessandro e Timoteo (Sarti), 102, 285
Alessandro nelle Indie. See *Generosità d'Alessandro, La*
Allegranti, Maddalena Teresa (s.), 329
Alsager, Thomas Massa (j.), 16, 24, 35, 41, 55
Alzira (Bianchi), 91, 116, 286
Amanti Consolati, Gli. See *Contrattempi Amorosi, I*
Amateurs. See Aristocracy; English opera audience; King's Theatre audience; Major theatres
Ambrogetti, Giuseppe (s.), 177–81
Americans, The (Arnold/King; Braham), 430, 620
Amina del filosofo, L' (Haydn), 686

749

Amor Contrasto, L' (Paisiello), 75. See also *Molinarella, La*
Amor fra le Vendemmie, L' (P. A. Guglielmi), 284, 715
Amori mariani, Gli (Weigl). See *Amor marinaro, L'*
Amori piacevole d'Ergasto, Gli (Greber), 65
Amor marinaro, L' (Weigl), 493–94. See also *Pirate of Genoa, The*
Amor Vuol Gioventù (P. C. Guglielmi?), 290
Andrei, Antonio (l.), 108, 279. See also *Ninetta*
Andreozzi, Gaetano (c.), 91, 286. See also *Principessa Filosofa, La; Teodolinda; Vergine del Sol, La*
Andrews, M. P. (d.), 713. See also *Fire and Water*
Andromaca (Nasolini), 280
Anelli, Angelo (l.), 284, 294–95. See also *Griselda; Italiana in Algieri, L'*
Anfossi, Pasquale (c.), 75, 100–101. See also *Curioso Indiscreto, Il; Didone Abbandonata; Nitteti; Viaggiratori Felici, Il*
Angelelli (Correr) (s.), 331
Angiolina, L' (Salieri), 107, 286. See also *Matrimonio Segreto, Il* (Fioravanti)
Angrisani, Carlo (s.), 323
Anseaume, L. (l.), 421
Antigona (Bianchi), 115, 283
Arbitration (Reynolds/Lanza), 618
Arbore di Diana, L' (Martín y Soler), 114, 284
Argenide e Serse (Portogallo), 126, 288
Arias. See English and French vocal numbers; English opera songs; Italian and German vocal numbers
Aristocracy, 65, 85–86, 92, 271–72; and amateurs, 86; interference of, 83; limited interest in opera, 85; not well behaved, 86; private concerts of, 66, 85, 159, 233–34. See also English opera audiences; King's Theatre audiences; Middle and lower classes
Aristodamo (Pucitta), 128, 293
Armida (Bianchi), 117, 286, 430
Armida (Mortellari), 278
Armida (Sacchini), 68, 100, 280
Armourer, The (Cumberland/Warner), 613
Arne, Michael (c.), 455, 613. See also *Cymon*
Arne, Thomas (c.), 346, 350–51, 376–82. See also *Artaxerxes; Arthur and Emmeline; Comus; Love in a Village; Olympiade, L'; Thomas and Sally*
Arnold, Dr. Samuel (c.), 31, 41, 99, 361, 382–83, 406–7. See also *Auld Robin Grey; Battle of Hexam, The; Castle of Andalusia, The; Children in the Wood; Inkle and Yarico; Irish Legacy, The; Maid of the Mill, The; Mountaineers, The; New Spain; Privateer, The; Shipwreck, The; Siege of Curazola, The; Surrender of Calais, The; Turk and No Turk; Two to One*
Arnold, Samuel James (d., mgr.), 361, 363, 427–30, 436–37, 465, 480–81, 488–89, 494–95, 498–99. See also *Americans, The; Auld Robin Grey; Broken Promises; Devil's Bridge, The; Irish Legacy, The; King's Proxy, The; Maniac, The; Privateer, The; Shipwreck, The; Terrare; Tit for Tat; Up All Night*
Arsinoe, Queen of Cyprus (Clayton), 346
Artaserse (Cherubini—pasticcio), 105, 277
Artaxerxes (T. Arne/T. Arne), 345, 351, 356, 378–79, 610
Arthur and Emmeline (Anon.; Gar-

rick ad. Dryden/Purcell; T. Arne), 43, 377, 625. See also *King Arthur*
Arvire et Evelina. See *Evelina*
Assedio di Corinto, L' (Rossini), 157
Astley's Ampitheatre, 427
Astuzie Fallacie, Le (Fioravanti), 294
Astuzie Femminili, Le (Cimarosa), 110-11, 287
Atalida (P. C. Guglielmi), 4, 291
Ati e Cibele (Cimador), 282, 692
Attwood, Thomas (c.), 401–4, 440–41, 470–72. See also *Adopted Child, The; Adrian and Orrila; Albert and Adelaide; Bondocani, Il; Britain's Brave Tars!; Caevarnon Castle; David Rizzio; Day in Rome, A; Elphi Bey; Escapes, The; Fast Asleep; Irish Tar, The; Mariners, The; Old Cloathman, The; Oxmyn and Doraxa; Prisoner, The; Packet Boat, The; Red-Cross Knights, The*
Auber, Daniel-François-Ésprit (c.), 497–98. See also *Fiancée, La; National Guard, The*
Auld Robin Grey (Arnold/Dr. Arnold), 427, 614
Aureliano in Palmira (Rossini), 155, 299
Avison, Charles (c.), 384
Ayrton, William (j., and musical director), 4, 15, 17, 37, 41–43, 54, 68, 80, 81

Babbini, Matteo (s.), 164–65
Bach, Johann Christian (c.), 87, 99, 687. See also *Clemenza di Scipione, La*
Bacon, Richard Mackenzie (j.), 15, 36-39, 54
Badini, Carlo Francesco (j., l.), 9, 20, 31, 100, 277–80. See also *Alceste; Andromaca; Generosità d'Alessandro, La; Inglese in Italia, L'; Vestale, La*

Baker, Thomas (j.), 66
Baldwin, Robert (j.), 38
Balelli, Antonio (s.), 317
Balfe, Michael (c.), 516, 706. See also *Bohemian Girl, The*
Ball, Edward. *See* Fitzball, Edward
Ballad opera. *See* English opera
Ballet and dance, 4, 67, 72, 75–76
Balocchi, G. L. (l.), 289. See also *Virtuoso in Puntiglio, Il*
Bandettino, Teresa (l.), 281. See also *Odenato and Zenobia*
Banditti, The (O'Keeffe), 388
Banks, Thomas (scene painter), 731
Bannister, John ("Jack"), Jr. (s.), 651
Bannister, Mrs. Elizabeth (s.), 664–65
Banti, Brigida (s.), 74, 100–101, 103, 114–15, 202–6
Barber of Seville, The (Terry; Fawcett/Bishop/Rossini/Paisiello), 57–58, 489, 624
Barbiere di Siviglia, Il (Paisiello), 33, 119, 146, 279
Barbiere di Siviglia, Il (Rossini), 33, 144–46, 295
Barnes, Thomas (j.), 19, 22–24, 26, 31, 33
Barnett, John (c.), 16, 274–75. See also *Mountain Sylph, The*
Barone di Dolsheim, Il (Pacini), 296
Barrymore, William (s.), 651–52
Barsene, Regina di Lidia (Portogallo), 126, 293
Barthélémon, François Hyppolyte (c.), 398, 730
Bartley, George (s.), 658
Bartolozzi, Francesco, 216
Bate Dudley, William (j., d.), 19–20, 384. See also *Flitch of Bacon, The; Travellers in Switzerland; Woodman, The*
Battista, Giovanni (impresario), 65
Battle of Hexam, The (Colman the Younger/Dr. Arnold), 407

Baumgarten, Karl Friedrich (violinist and leader), 572
Baumgarten, Samuel Christian (c., bassoonist), 392
Beaumarchais, Pierre Augustin de (d.), 393
Beazley, Samuel, Jr. (d.), 715, 723. See also *Knights of the Cross, The; Philandering; White Lady, The*
Bedford, Duke of, 73, 74
Bedford, Paul (s.), 660–61
Beethoven, Ludwig van, 24, 449, 728
Beggar's Opera, The (Gay; arr. Pepusch), 345, 351, 373–76, 617
Begnis, Giuseppe de (s.), 188–89
Begnis, Ronzi de (s.), 226–29
Begrez, Pierre Ignace (s.), 322
Bell, John (j.), 19–20, 31
Bell, Robert (j.), 43–45
Bella Arsene, La (Monsigny), 104, 283
Bellamy, Thomas Ludford (s.), 655
Bella Pescatrice, La (P. A. Guglielmi), 112, 280
Belle et la bête, La. See *Zemire ed Azor*
Bellini, Vincenzo (c.), 143–44. See also *Capuletti ed i Montecchi, I; Pirata, Il; Puritani, I; Somnambula, La*
Belloc (Bellochi), Teresa (s.), 222–24
Benelli, Antonio (s.), 319
Benelli, Giovanni Battista (mgr.), 81–82
Benincasa, Bartolomeo (l.), 279. See also *Disertore, Il*
Benini, Anna (s.), 330
Bentley, Richard (d.), 611. See also *Prophet, The*
Benucci, Francesco (s.), 318
Benyowsky (Kenney/Horn; Cooke; Livius), 505, 723
Beria di Salsa, Marchese Francesco (l.), 297. See also *Otello; Ricciardo e Zoraide*

Bertati, Giovanni (l.), 279–80, 287. See also *Don Giovanni Tenorio; Locanda, La; Matrimonio Segreto, Il; Vendemmia, La; Villanella Rapita, La*
Bertinotti-Radicati, Teresa (s.), 78, 135, 335
Berton, Henri-Montan (c.), 724
Bertoni, Ferdinando Giuseppe (c.), 280. See also *Quinto Fabio*
Betterman, Thomas, 65
Betts, Miss (s.), 673–74
Beyle, Henri. See Stendhal
Bianchi, Francesco (c.), 76, 114–18. See also *Aci e Galatea; Alzira; Antigona; Armida; Cinna; Erfile; Ines de Castro; Merope; Morte di Cleopatra, La; Piramo e Tisbe; Semiramide; Villanella Rapita, La*
Bianchi, Francesco (s.), 324
Bianchi, Jane (s.), 334
Bickerstaffe, Isaac (d.), 120, 346, 380–84. See also *Lionel and Clarissa; Love in a Village; Maid of the Mill, The; Thomas and Sally*
Billington, Elizabeth (s.), 4, 99, 206–8, 542–43
Billington, Thomas (j.), 37
Birch, Samuel, Jr. (d.), 402, 429, 716. See also *Adopted Child, The; Albert and Adelaide; Fast Asleep; Mariners, The; Packet Boat, The*
Bishop, Henry Rowley (c.), 115, 350, 354–55, 448–60, 466–78, 484–86, 489, 491–92, 496, 505. See also *Aladdin; Barber of Seville, The; Brother and Sister; Cicasian Bride, The; Clari; Comedy of Errors, The; Comus; Cortez; Cymon; Duke of Savoy, The; Exile, The; Fall of Algiers, The; Farmer's Wife, The; Freischütz, Der; Guy Mannering; Hofer; Home, Sweet Home; John of Paris; Knight of Snowdoun, The;*

Knights of the Cross, The; Law of Java, The; Libertine, The; Maid Marian; Maniac, The; Marriage of Figaro, The; Merry Wives of Windsor, The; Midsummer Night's Dream, A; Miller and his Men, The; Native Land; Night before the Wedding, The; Ninetta; Rencontre; Slave, The; Tempest, The; Twelfth Night; Two Gentlemen of Verona, The; Virgin of the Sun, The; Zuma
Black, John (j.), 17, 19
Blanchard, Thomas, Jr. (s.), 650
Bland, Maria Teresa (s.), 540–42
Blewitt, Jonathan (c.), 507–8, 727. See also *Sylvania*
Blockade, 22, 49, 77
Blue-Beard, The (Colman the Younger/Kelly), 408, 615
Boaden, James (d., j.), 5, 21, 46, 360, 402–3. See also *Ozmyn and Doraxa*
Boadicea (Pucitta), 78, 128, 292
Bocciardini, M. (l.), 291. See also *Zaïra*
Bochsa, Nicholas Charles (c.), 82, 84, 143. See also *Messicani, I*
Boggio, Giandomenico (l.), 281. See also *Teodolinda*
Bohemian Girl, The (Balfe), 706
Boieldieu, François-Adrien (c.), 495–96. See also *Dame blanche, La; Deux nuits, Les; John of Paris; White Lady, The*
Bolla, Maria (s.), 332
Bondocani, Il (T. Dibdin/Attwood; Moorehead), 440–41, 616
Bonduca (Purcell), 378
Bonet, Albert. *See* Albert
Bonfanti, Luigi (s.), 88
Bordogni, Giulio (s.), 327
Borselli, Fausto (s.), 202
Bottarelli, Giovanni C. (l.), 277, 288. See also *Clemenza di Scipione, La*
Bouilly, Jean Nicolas (l.), 409. See also *Folie, Un*
Boyce, William (c.), 397
Braham, John (s., c.), 5–6, 103, 168–70, 356, 427, 430–32, 436–37, 439, 441–42, 464, 471, 479, 518–25. See also *Americans, The; Cabinet, The; David Rizzio; Devil's Bridge, The; Dirce; English Fleet, The; False Alarms; Family Quarrels; Guy Mannering; Isidore de Merida; Kais; Out of Place; Thirty-Thousand; Two Faces under a Hood; Two Houses of Granada, The; Unknown Guest, The; Zuma*
Brambilla, Marietta (s.), 339
Brandon, Isaac (d.), 6, 347, 619. See also *Kais*
Brecht, Bertolt (d.), 706. See also *Dreigroschenoper, Die*
Britain's Brave Tars! (Attwood), 403
Broadwood, John, 92
Broken Gold, The (C. Dibdin/C. Dibdin), 618
Broken Promises (Arnold/Hawes), 480–82, 628
Brome, Richard (d.), 621. See also *Jovial Crew, The*
Brooke, Frances (d.), 391–92. See also *Marian; Rosina*
Brother and Sister (Dimond; C. I. M. Dibdin/Bishop; W. Reeve), 462, 622
Brothers, The (Cumberland), 619
Bruni, Domenico Luigi (s.), 317
Brutus (Payne), 473
Buckingham, James Silk (j.), 45
Buckstone, John Baldwin (d.), 484, 724. See also *Don Juan*
Bulwer-Lytton. *See* Lytton, Edward Bulwer
Bunn, Alfred (mgr.), 6
Buona Figliuola, La (Piccinni), 277
Buonaiuti, Serafino (l.), 126, 285–86, 290–92, 687. See also *Atalida;*

Boadicea; Caccia d'Enrico IV, La; Due Svizzeri, I; Eroina di Raab, L' (?); *Morte di Cleopatra, La; Phædra; Quattro Nazioni, La; Romeo e Giulietta; Sadigero; Scommessa, La; Serva Raggiratrice, La; Vestale, La; Villeggiatori Bizzarri, I*
Buonavoglia, L. (l.), 294. See also *Agnese, L'*
Burbero di Buon C[u]ore, Il (Martín y Soler), 113, 282
Burges[s], Sir James Bland (d.), 435–36. See also *Tricks upon Travellers*
Burgh, Allatson (critic), 67
Burghesh, Lord (c., l.), 412. See also *Catherine*
Burgoyne, John (d.), 398–99. See also *Lord of the Manor, The; Maid of the Oaks, The; Richard Coeur de Lion*
Burla Fortunata, La. See *Adolfo e Chiara*
Burletta, 360
Burney, Dr. Charles (music historian), 16, 27, 71, 435
Busby, Thomas (c., j.), 15, 27, 31, 353. See also *Tale of Mystery, A*
Butturini, Matteo (l.), 285. See also *Fratelli Rivali, I; Merope e Polifante*
Byrne, Miss (s.), 668
Byron, George Gordon, Lord, 32, 478

Cabinet, The (T. Dibdin/Moorehead; W. Reeve; Davy; Corri; Braham), 355, 441–42, 611
Caccia d'Enrico IV, La (Pucitta), 127, 290
Cadell, Thomas, the Younger (d.), 405. See also *Fire and Water; Orpheus and Erydice*
Caernarvon Castle (Rose/Attwood), 402
Callcott, John Wall (j.), 27

Calvesi, Vincenzo (s.), 119, 310
Calypso. See *Grotta di Calypso, La*
Calzabigi, Ranieri de' (l.), 68, 282, 284. See also *Alceste; Elfrida*
Cameriera Astuta, La (Storace), 278, 410
Camilla (Fioravanti), 288
Camilla (Paer), 94, 129, 292
Camille (Marsollier), 423
Campaign, The (Jephson/Tenducci), 609
Campbell, John, Lord (j.), 5, 9, 18, 25, 48
Campbell, Thomas (j., poet), 29, 40
Camporese, Violante (s.), 83, 224–26
Cancanen (d.), 620. See also *Jovial Crew, The*
Capriccio Drammatico, Il (Cimarosa), 110, 282
Capricciosa Pentita, La (Fioravanti), 290
Captive of Spilburg, The (Hoare/Dussek; Kelly), 423, 615
Capuletti ed i Montecchi, I (Bellini), 143
Caradori-Allan, Maria (s.), 229–32
Carafa, Prince Michele di Colobrano (c.), 118
Caravan, The (Reynolds), 447
Caravita, Giuseppe (l.), 288, 291. See also *Camilla; Climème; Tre Sultane, Le*
Carew, Miss (s.), 555–57
Caritea, regina di Spagna. See *Donna Caritea*
Carolan, Turlough (c.), 389
Carpani, Giuseppe (l.), 288, 292. See also *Camilla* (Fioravanti; Paer); *Nina*
Carron Side (Planché/Liverati), 469, 630
Carter, Thomas (c.), 613. See also *Just in Time*
Casentini, Anna (s.), 11, 47, 331

Casket, The (Lacy/Lacy/Mozart), 725
Casoli, F. (l.), 287. See also *Vergine del Sol, La*
Castellani Burlati, I [due] (Fabrizi), 133, 279
Castelli, Mme. Ignez (s.), 339
Casti, Giovanni (l.), 278, 419. See also *Re Teodoro, Il; Tutor Burlato, Il* (?)
Castle of Andalusia, The (O'Keeffe/ Dr. Arnold), 353, 388, 611
Castle Spectre, The (Lewis), 353
Catalani, Angelica (s.), 77, 82–83, 89–90, 102, 127, 129, 210–15
Catherine (Burghesh; Cobb/Burghesh), 632
Cause, Harriet (s.), 672–73
Cause, Mary (s.), 672–73
Cauvini, Signor (s.), 320
Cauvini, Signora (s.), 320
Cave of Triphonius, The (Hoare/Storace), 14, 419, 612
Cenerentola, La (Rossini), 55, 148–49, 295. See also *Cinderella*
Cervetto, James (cello), 249, 730
Chains of the Heart (Hoare/Mazzinghi; W. Reeve), 424, 616
Challoner, Neville Butler (j.), 45
Chalmers, A. (j.), 20
Chalmers, William (scene painter), 731
Cherokee, The (Cobb/Storace), 413, 614
Cherry, Andrew (d.), 25, 433–35. See also *In and Out of Tune; Peter the Great; Spanish Dollars; Travellers, The*
Cherubini, Luigi (c.), 76, 105. See also *Artaserse; Demetrio; Finta Principessa, La; Gulio Sabino; Ifigenia in Aulide*
Chesterfield, Earl of, 66
Chiari, Petro (l.), 277. See also *Marchese Tulipano, Il*

Children of the Wood (Morton/Dr. Arnold), 394, 459, 613
Chi originale. See *Fanatico per la Musica, Il*
Choleric Fathers, The (Holcroft/Shield), 394, 609
Chorley, Henry (impresario), 45
Christie, Thomas (j.), 27
Cibber, Colly, 65
Cifra, La (Salieri), 107, 284
Cimador, Gian Battista (c.), 282, 692. See also *Ati e Cibele*
Cimarosa, Domenico (c.), 107–12. See also *Astuzie Femminili, Le; Capriccio Drammatico, Il; Due Baroni, I; Giannina e Bernardone; Locandiera, La; Matrimonio Segreto, Il; Ninetta; Olimpiade, L'; Orazi ed Curiazi, Gli; Penelope; Pittor Parigino, Il; Traci Amanti, I; Trame Delusi, La; Villana Riconcosciuta, La*
Cinderella (Lacy/Lacy/Rossini), 490–91, 632
Cinna (Bianchi), 115, 284
Cipriani, Lorenzo Angelo (s.), 11, 47, 317
Circassian Bride, The (Ward/Bishop), 619
Clandestine Marriage, The (Colman the Elder; Garrick), 109
Clari (Payne/Bishop), 473–75, 637
Clark, Charles Cowden (j.), 43
Clayton, Thomas (c.), 346
Clement, W. J. (j.), 17
Clementgi, Museo (keyboard), 730
Clemenza di Scipione, La (Bach), 99, 288
Clemenza di Tito, La (Mozart), 133–35, 288, 696
Clendening, Mrs. William (Elizabeth) (s.), 665
Climène (Trento), 291
Clowes, W. (j.), 41

Cobb, James (d.), 399–401, 409–17.
  See also *Cherokee, The; Doctor and the Apothecary, The; Haunted Tower, The; House to be Sold, A; Humourist, The; Love in the East; Paul and Virginia; Pirates, The; Ramah Droog; Siege of Belgrade, The; Strangers at Home; Wife of Two Husbands, The*
Coccia, Carlo (c.), 82, 143. See also *Maria Stuarda*
Colbran-Rossini, Isabella (s.), 339
Colburn, Henry (j.), 36, 40, 45
Coleridge, Samuel Taylor, 11, 18, 23
Collier, John Dyer (j.), 17–18, 23
Collier, John Payne (j.), 13, 17, 19, 41, 58
Collini, Signora (s.), 334
Colman, George, the Elder (d., mgr.), 8, 376. See also *Clandestine Marriage, The; Comus*
Colman, George, the Younger (d., mgr.), 5–6, 8, 361, 406–7, 418–19, 451–54, 459. See also *Battle of Hexam, The; Blue-Beard; Feudal Times; Forty Theves, The; Inkle and Yarico; Iron Chest, The; Law of Java, The; Love Laughs at Locksmiths; Mountaineers, The; Surrender of Calais, The; Turk and No Turk; Two to One; Ways and Means*
Comedy of Errors, The (Reynolds ad. Shakespeare/Bishop), 452, 625
Comus (Colman the Elder ad. Dalton ad. Milton/Arne; Bishop), 622
Comus (Dalton ad. Milton/Arne), 376–77
Concert of Ancient Music, 215, 334, 463
Concerts. See Concert of Ancient Music; Hanover Square Rooms; Philharmonic Society; Royal Academy of Music
Confusioni della somiglanza o siano, La. See *Due Gobbi, I*

Conquest of Taranto, The (Dimond/Kelly), 427, 623
Consiglio Imprudente, Il (Bianchi), 115, 284
Contadini Bizzarri, I (Sarti), 101, 281. See also *Gelosie Villane, Le*
Conte Ori, Il (Rossini), 155, 300
Conte Ridicolo, Il (Paisiello), 75. See also *Re Teodoro in Venezia, Il*
Contrattempi Amorosi, I (Sarti), 102, 290
Cooke, Henry (c.), 349
Cooke, Thomas Simpson (s., c.), 463–66, 470–72, 478–80, 497–98, 506–7, 656. See also *Abou Hassan; David Rizzio; Guy Mannering; Isidore de Merida; King's Proxy, The; Malvina; National Guard, The; Sweethearts and Wives; White Lady, The*
Corri, Domenico (c.), 71, 434–35, 441–42, 693, 716. See also *Cabinet, The; In and Out of Tune; Travellers, The*
Corri, Montague Phillip (c.) (son of Domenico), 716
Corri, Natale (s.) (brother of Domenico), 716
Corri, Sophia Giustina. See Dussek, Sophia
Corri-Paltoni, Francesca (s.), 338
Cortez (Planché/Bishop), 10, 467, 627
Cosa Rara, La (Martín y Soler), 113, 279, 412
Così fan Tutte (Mozart), 135–36, 291. See also *Tit for Tat*
Covent Garden Theatre, 65, 73, 358, 360; audience at, 366; under Thomas Harris, 9, 22, 359; under Charles and John Kemble, 361; and "O.P." riots, 361. *See also* Aristocracy; English opera audiences; English opera theatres; Major theatres

Cowper, Lord, 118
Cox, John Edmund (j.), 31
Cramer, Franz (leader), 248
Cramer, John Baptist (violinist and leader), 248
Cramer, Wilhelm (violinist), 248
Crescentini, Girolamo (s.), 317
Critic, The (Sheridan), 5, 360
Criticism: characteristics of, 14, 20–21; coverage of, 13, 27; critics on, 272–74; and English opera, 586; length of reviews, 14; and musical taste, 274–75; between periodicals, 3, 4; and the public, 7, 585–87; and puffery, 7, 22; and the rise of opera, 47–50; and Romanticism in, 49; theatrical, 4, 7, 9, 1–12, 47
Critics, 47: anonymity of, 11–12; identity of, 13; musical judgments of, 23–24; musical taste of, 274–75; no competent judges, 603; salaries of, 12; and style of, 14–15.
Crivelli, Gaetano (s.), 80, 176–77
Crociato in Egitto, Il (Meyerbeer), 35, 82, 95, 141, 298
Croly, George (j.), 23, 26
Crosdill, John (cello, violin), 730
Crouch, Anna Marie (s.), 663–64
Crouch, William (c.), 611. See also *Hide and Seek*
Crow Street Theatre (Dublin), 463
Crusade, The (Reynolds/Shield), 447, 612
Cumberland, Richard (d.), 619. See also *Armourer, The; Brothers, The; Jew of Mogadore, The*
Cupid and Death (Locke), 349
Curioni, Alberico (s.), 83, 192–95
Curioso Indiscreto, Il (Anfossi), 100, 276
Cymon (Garrick/M. Arne; Storace; Shaw; Bishop), 455, 622

Dalton, John (d.), 376–77
Dama Pastorella, La. See *Cifra, La*

Dama Soldato, La (Orlandi), 292, 696
Dame blanche, La (Boieldieu; Scribe), 495–96
Dance, William (c., keyboard), 730
Daphne and Amintor (Bickerstaffe), 381
Da Ponte, Lorenzo (Emmanuele Conegliano) (l.), 9, 76, 139, 279, 282–84, 286–88, 291–92, 294. See also *Antigona; Arbore, L'; Burero di Buon C[u]ore, Il; Calypso; Capriccio Dramatico, Il; Casa Rara, La; Cifra; Cinna; Consiglio Imprudente, Il; Così fan Tutte; Don Giovanni; Isola del Piacere, L'; Merope; Nozze di Figaro, Le; Ratto di Proserpina, Il; Scuola dei Meritati, La; Tesoro, Il; Trionfo, Il; Zaïra*
Darta. See D'Orta, Rochele
Davenant, Sir William (d., mgr.), 358. See also *Siege of Rhodes, The*
David Rizzio (Hamilton/Attwood; Cooke; Braham; Reeve), 625, 722
Davy, John (c.), 404–5, 434, 441–43, 470–72. See also *Cabinet, The; Family Quarrels; Farmer's Wife, The; Guy Mannering; Rob Roy Macgregor; What a Blunder!; Woman's Will*
Day in Rome, A (Attwood), 403
De [or di] Angeli, Signor (s.), 327
Death of Abel, The (Perry), 461
De Begnis. See Begnis, De
Defranceschi, C. P. (l.), 286, 291. See also *Angiolina; Matrimonio per Susurro, Il*
D'Egville, James (dancer, balletmaster), 77, 441
Delestre-Poirson, C. G. (l.), 300, See also *Conte Ori, Il*
Delicati, Margherita (s.), 330
Della Cruscans, 716
De Loutherbourg, Philip James (scene painter), 576

Demetrio (Cherubini—pasticcio), 105, 277
Demofoonte (Metastasio), 472
Dennis, John (critic), 66, 346
Deserts of Arabia, The (Reynolds/Lanza), 447–48, 618
Deux journees, Les (Cherubini), 403
Deux nuits, Les (Boieldieu), 496. See also *Night Before the Wedding and the Wedding Night, The*
Devil's Bridge, The (Arnold/Horn; Braham), 436–37, 621
Dibdin, Charles (c., d.), 28, 383–84. See also *Broken Gold, The; Liberty Hall; Lionel and Clarissa*
Dibdin, Charles, the Younger. See Dibdin, Charles Isaac Mongo
Dibdin, Charles Isaac Mungo (d., mgr.), 462. See also *Brother and Sister; Farmer's Wife, The*
Dibdin, Thomas (d.), 5–6, 25, 28, 352, 355, 440–46, 460–62. See also *Bondocani, Il; Cabinet, The; English Fleet, The; Family Quarrels; Morning Noon and Night; Naval Pillar; Of Age Tomorrow; Thirty-Thousand; Two Faces under a Hood; White Plume, The; Who's to Have Her?; Zuma*
Dickens, Charles, 34
Dickons, Maria Caroline (s.), 215–16, 548–51
Dido, Queen of Carthage (Hoare/Storace), 420, 613
Dido and Aneas (Tate/Purcell), 350
Didone, La (Mercadante), 300
Didone, La (Paisiello), 123, 285
Didone Abbandonata, La (Anfossi—pasticcio), 100, 277
Didone Abbandonata, La (Paer), 129, 293
Dilke, Charles Wentworth (j.), 12
Dimond, William Wyatt (d.), 4, 352, 425–27, 462–63, 86–88, 506–7. See also *Abou Hassan; Adrian and Orrila; Brother and Sister; Conquest of Taranto, The; Gustavus Vasa; Hero of the North; Isidore de Merida; Native Land; Nymph of the Grotto, The; Peasant, The; Pirate, The; Seraglio, The; Young Hussar, The; Youth, Love, and Folly*
Diodati, Giuseppe Maria (l.), 281–82, 294. See also *Penelope; Trame Deluse, La*
Dirce (Anon; Metastasio/Horn; Braham), 472–73, 626
Discordia Conjugale, La (Paisiello), 10, 47, 121, 281
Disertore, Il (Tarchi), 279
D'Israeli, I. (l.), 619. See also *Mejnoun and Leila*
Ditters von Dittersdorf, Carl (c.), 410. See also *Doctor and the Apothecary, The*
D'Maria, I. (scene painter), 578
Doctor and the Apothecary, The (Cobb/Storce/Ditters), 410, 611
Don Giovanni, [Il] (Mozart), 33, 49, 93, 130, 138–40, 294, 696. See also *Don Juan; Giovanni in London; Libertine, The*
Don Giovanni Tenorio (Gazzaniga), 94, 281
Don Juan (Buckstone/Hawes/Mozart), 484, 632
Donna Caritea (Mercadante), 301
Donna del Lago, La (Rossini), 95, 152–53, 297
Donzelli, Domenico (s.), 195–98
D'Orta, Rochele (Rosina) (s.), 329
Dragonetti, Domenico (double bass), 83, 251
Dramatist, The (Reynolds), 447
Dreigroschenoper, Die (Weill/Brecht), 706
Drury Lane, 358, 360. *See also* English opera audiences; Kemble,

John; Major theatres; Sheridan, Richard Brinsley
Dryden, John, 349, 377. See also *Indian Queen, The; King Arthur*
DuBois, Edward (j.), 29, 39
Dudley Bate. *See* Bate, William
Due Baroni, I (Cimarosa), 110, 287
[Due] Castellani Burlati, I. See Castellani Burlati, I
Due Contesse, Le (Paisiello), 118
[Due] Fratelli Rivali, I (Winter), 123, 245
Due Gobbi, I (Portogallo), 283
Duenna, The (Sheridan/Linley the Elder; Linley the Younger), 360, 398, 441, 443, 612
Due Nozze ed un Sol Marito, I (P. C. Guglielmi), 125, 288
Due Pretendi, I. See Pretendenti, I
Due Svizzeri, I (Ferrari), 285
Duke of Savoy, The (Reynolds/Bishop), 450, 624
Duni, Egidio Ronoaldo (c.), 383
Duruset, John (s.), 531–33
Dussek, Jan Ladislaw (c.), 423–24, 715. See also *Captive of Spilburg, The*
Dussek, Sophia (s.), 334
Duval, Alexander (d.), 416. See also *Maison à vendre, La*

Ebers, John (impresario), 81–83
Edwin, John, the Younger (s.), 388, 650
Elfrida (Paisiello), 94, 122, 284
Elisabetta, Regina d'Inghilterra (Rossini), 146, 295
Elisa e Claudio (Mercadante), 297
Ellison, Ralph W. (mgr.), 363, 723
Elphi Bey (Hamilton/Attwood; Horn; Smart), 623
Empress of Morocco, The (Settle), 706
Encores, 89–90, 108, 130, 367–69. See also English opera performances; King's Theatre performances

Engelbach, G. L. (j.), 683
Englese in Italia, L' (Anfossi), 101
English and French vocal numbers: "Adieu, Adieu, my native shore," 632–662; "Ah, Divinite," (Gluck), 710; "Ah! how can I leave" (Shield), 717; "Ah! when safe at home" (Linley), 711; "All in the silent convent cell" (Shield), 717; "Ally Croker" (Linley adapt. of Larry Grogan, 1725), 400; "Are you angry, mother? No!" 570; "As now we're met" (Purcell), 714; "At your feet thus lowly bending" (Storace), 715; "Auld Lang Syne" (folk; Shield), 391; "Aux armes, mes citoyens," 460; "Battle Song," 534; "Bay of Biscay" (Davy), 404, 419, 472; "Beaux yeux," 201; "Blow, gentle gales" (Bishop), 719; "British Grenadiers" (Arnold), 713; "Britons, strike home" (Arne), 709; "Cease your funning" (*Beggar's Opera*), 544; "The chogh and crow to roost are gone" (Bishop), 721; "Come hither" (Bishop), 721; "Come, if you dare, our trumpets sound" (Arne), 709; "Come let us dance and sing" (Arnold), 713; "Come then sweet sounds" (Mellico), 714; "Dangers unknown impending" (Sarti), 714; "Daughter of error," 46; "The death of Abercrombie," 444; "The death of Nelson," 659; "The die is cast" (Liverati), 721; "Donald" (Scotch air), 710; "Done over taylor" (Arnold), 713; "Fairest Isle all Isles excelling" (Purcell), 709; "Farewell! thou coast of glory!" (Rossini), 463; "Five times by the taper's light" (Storace), 715; "Fly, soft ideas" (Arne), 379; "Follow him, follow him" (Cooke), 722; "For

Tenderness Form'd" (Paisiello), 118; "For thee I live my dearest" (T. Arne), 379; "Freshly now" (Arnold), 713; "From Hope's fond dream" (Storace), 714; "From the fair Lavinian shore" (Bishop?), 718; "The Guardian, dear Sir" (Paisiello; Kelly), 712; "Gipsey" (Bishop), 722; "Glory Firing" (Storace), 714; "Hark I hear, I hear him coming," 712; "Hear me, O God of love" (Linley), 711; "Hear, oh hear a simple story" (Storace), 715; "His dearest mother's joy" (Braham), 720; "Home, Sweet Home" (*see* "Sweet Home"); "Hope a distant joy disclosing" (Storace), 716; "Hope bids pleasure" (Linley), 711; "Hope her support" (Bishop), 718; "Hope told a flattering tale" (Paisiello), 175; "Hours of Love," 465; "If e'er the cruel tyrant Love" (Arne), 719; "I love my massa kind" (Linley), 711; "In ancient times, in Britain's isle" (Attwood), 722; "In England they tell us" (Bishop), 719; "In joyful peace disarming" (Bishop), 720; "In infamy" (Arne), 551; "In the morn I ring the bell" (Shield), 717; "Is't art, I pray, or nature" (Bishop), 463; "I traversed Judah sand," 664; "Just like love" (Davy), 472; "Knight to his Leddy" (Scotch air), 721; "The lad with the white cockade," 710; "Let us seek the yellow shore" (Bishop), 721; "Lord Henry" (Attwood), 722; "Love from the heart" (Martín y Soler), 714; "The Love that follows fair" (Bishop), 721; "The love that's born of gratitude" (Attwood), 722; "Lo! when showers descending" (Bishop), 463; "Mad Bess" (Purcell), 548, 566; "Maggie Lawder," 710; "Malbroug s'en va t'en guerre," 693; "Man was born to sorrow" (Whittaker), 419; "Marseilles hymn," 532; "May we ne'er want a friend" (Davy), 472; "Mild as the moonbeam" (Braham), 379; "Mocking Bird" (Bishop), 719; "My Anna's urn" (Jackson), 711; "My native land" (Storace), 714; "Nature to women still so kind" (Irish air), 714; "The night was three months long" (Bishop?), 718; "No voice endearing" (Bishop), 720; "Now, as we loved in childhood's morn" (Liverati), 728; "Now is the month of Maying" (Morley), 718; "O bold Robin Hood" (Bishop), 721; "O'er the billows let me roam" (Liverati), 721; "Oh! no accusing sigh shall rise" (Linley), 711; "Oh! slumber my darling" (Whittaker), 722; "Oh! the merry *table d'hote*" (Bishop?), 718; "Oh, thou wert born to please me" (Kelly ad. Nasolini's "Pace, cara mie sposa"), 716; "Oh 'tis sweet at noon to stray" (Liverati), 721; "Oh well do I remember" (Bishop), 721; "Old England" (based on "Old England forever"), 651, 710; "An old man would be wooing" 725; "Old Time today twines flowers" (Storace or Braham), 720; "On board the Arethusa" (Shield), 711; "Once upon a time" (Bishop), 718; "O pescator dell' onda" (a popular song), 485; "Pity the slave" (Bishop), 720; "Pray, Goody" (from *Midas*), 719; "Remember when" (Arnold), 713; "A Robe like its wearer" (Liverati), 721; "The Rosary" (Shield), 710; "The Rose on beauty's cheeks"

(Bishop), 725; "Roslyn castle," 569; "Rule Britannia" (Arne), 709; "Said a Smile to a Tear" (Braham), 432–33; "Sailor's Lullaby" (1794 Storace?), 720; "Say, fair one, has thy virgin heart" (Bishop), 719; "Scots wha hae," 521; "The Seaman's Home" (Shield), 710; "Septello" (Storace), 714; "A shepherd once" (Bland), 714; "Should he upbraid" (Bishop), 723; "Silly fan," 665; "Since first I saw your face" (Bishop?), 718; "The Smuggler" (Davy), 472; "The Soldier tir'd," 543, 663; "Sons of Freedom," 556; "Souvenir," (Carafa), 569; "Sweet Annie frae the sea beach come" (Arnold), 664, 713; "Sweet Home" (Bishop), 474, 1078; "Tho' pity I cannot deny" (Pleyel), 714; "Tho' time had from" (French air), 714; "Traveling song," 710; "Water parted from the sea," 663; "The Waving Willow" (Shield), 710; "The Wayward tongue fond love repelling," 710; "We be three poor mariners" (*Deuleromelia*, 1609), 712; "When absent from the lad I love" (Bishop), 719; "When deeds of fame" (Bishop), 719; "When first this humble roof" (Jackson), 532, 711; "When the Banners of Glory are streaming" ("Non più andrai"), 712; "Whistling cowboy," 650; "Whither is he straying" (Braham), 720; "Whither, my love" (Paisiello), 714; "Why are you wandering here, I pray" (Nathan), 479; "Why did he come, when did he go? (Shield), 548; "Why swells my wavy, burnish'd grain" ("In diesen heil'gen Hallen" Mozart), 712; "Wine, rosy Wine" (Attwood), 427; "Within a Mile of Edinburgh" (Hook), 425; "With plaintive wit" (street song), 419; "Woman kind" (Bishop/Paisiello), 725; "Ye dear paternal scenes, farewell" (Davy), 722; "You gave me last week a young linnet" (Arne), 531; "Young Lobski" (Bishop?), 718. *See also* English opera at the playhouses: musical borrowings; English opera songs; Italian and German vocal numbers

English Fleet in 1342, The (T. Dibdin/Braham), 335, 443, 617

English opera: all-sung opera vs. plays with music, 345–46, 349; ballad opera, 351; definition of, 345, 592–96; dialogue in, spoken, 346, 350; dramatist/librettist vs. composer in, 350; early history of, 349–51; and the English language, 346; growth of, 370; nonsingers in leading roles of, 348; music in, 345, 347, 350; recitative in, 346, 349, 379–80, 349; and *style galant*, 351; and translations of Italian opera, 351; types of, 348, 371, 583–85. *See also* English opera adaptations; English opera at the playhouses; English opera audiences; English opera composers; English opera librettists; English opera librettos; English opera performers and performances; English opera songs

English opera adaptations, 596–97; detractors of, 483, 606; and influence of Italian opera, 482; and musical taste, 482–83, 604; and problems for composers and librettists, 597; translations of, 597. *See also* English opera

English opera at the playhouses: attacks on English opera in, 582; and commercialism, 355, 605–6; critical coverage of, 357; and French music, 408; and German influence on, 423, 448; improvements sought in, 606–7; Italian influence on, 423, 448; mediocrity in, 604; melodrama in, 25, 351, 371, 423, 450, 457–58; more operatic, 411–13, 431; musical borrowings, 372, 381, 590; original music in, increasing, 372–73; pasticci, 381; productions of, new and revived, 373; prudery in, 375; quality of music in, declining, 373; and recitative, 379, 420, 472–73, 498–99, 491–96; resistance to all-sung operas, 370, 405, 420; revivals of, 373; and "science" in, 600–601; shared composership of, 590; *Sturm und Drang* in, 353; successes and failures of, 371, 584–85; and "superhits," 372, 583. *See also* English opera; Major theatres

English opera audiences: amateurs, 366–69; cabals, 366, 400; changes in, 365; claqueurs, 367; musical taste of, 428, 601–4; orders for, 367; riots, 364–65; views of average Englishman, 345. *See also* Encores; English opera; Major theatres

English opera composers: competition from foreigners and librettists, 350, 354; remuneration for, 356. *See also* English opera librettists; English opera songs

English Opera House Theatre (formerly Lyceum), 362–63

English opera librettists: and "Book of Songs," 355; and composers, 354; fitting words to music, 354, 356, 386, 399; problems of, 597; remuneration for, 355–56. *See also* English opera composers

English opera librettos: criticism of, 352, 585; and decline of drama, 351–52, 588; vs. legitimate drama, 352; melodramatic elements in, 353, 589; quality of, 352, 587–91; recent attacks on, 352; and the unities, 407, 466, 587; words out of place, 420. *See also* English opera; English opera songs

English opera performers and performances: acting in, 413, 460, 513, 598–99; critical interest in, 515; falsetto singing in, 598; inadequate performers, 413, 513; in *Oberon*, 511; personality of singers, 513; pitfalls of singers, 514–15; playhouse orchestra instruments, 572; playhouse orchestras vs. King's, 572, 599–600; playhouse singers vs. King's, 600; popular aspects of, 586; productions of, careless, 354; rehearsals, 364; roles adapted to singers, 513–14; salaries of, 514; and singers' careers, 515; singers' lack of power, 600; and "taking measure," 514; tampering with songs in, 590; two casts required, 513; vocal ornamentation in, 598. *See also* Aristocracy; Encores; English opera; English opera songs; Major theatres

English opera songs: ballads, 351; "Book of Songs," 355; folk songs, 391; and leading singers, 390; not well adapted, 590; and quality of lyrics, 589; sales of, 356; strophic, 347; through-composed, 547. *See also* English and French vocal numbers; English opera

Entführung aus dem Serail, Die (Mozart), 486, 488, 630. *See also Seraglio, The*

Equi, Gli (Storace), 410

Erfile (Bianchi), 117, 288

Ero e Leandro (Paer), 129

Eroina di Raab, L' (Ferrari), 292

Escapes, The (Holcroft/Attwood), 403, 615

Este, Charles (j.), 21–22, 24
Euryanthe (Weber), 727
Evelina (Sacchini), 100, 284
Evelyn, John (diarist), 346
Exile, The (Reynolds/Mazzinghi; Bishop), 448–49, 619

Fabrizi, Vincenzo (c.), 279. See also *Castellani Burlati, I*
Fair Gabrielle, The (Planché/Livius; G. Reeve), 626
Fairy Festival, The (Rose/Attwood), 402
Fairy Queen, The (Settle, ad. Shakespeare/Purcell), 349, 709
Fall of Algiers, The (Walker/Bishop), 628
False Alarms (Kenney/King; Braham), 431–33, 619
Family Quarrels (T. Dibdin/Moorehead; W. Reeve; Davy; Braham), 5, 443, 617
Fanatico in Berlina, Il. See *Locanda, La*
Fanatico per la Musica, Il (Mayr), 131, 289
Farinelli, Carlo Broschi (c.), 290, 293. See also *Rito D'Efeso, Il*; *Teresa e Claudio*
Farington, Joseph (diarist), 22
Farmer, The (O'Keeffe/Shield), 390, 610
Farmer's Wife, The (C. I. M. Dibdin/Bishop; Davy; W. Reeve; Addison), 436, 622, 717
Farrari, F. G. (l.), 288. See also *Argenide e Serse*
Fast Asleep (Birch, Jr./Attwood), 402
Favart, Charles (l.), 283. See also *Bella Arsene, La*
Fawcett, John (s., d.), 6, 653
Fearon, Madame. *See* Feron, Miss
Federici, C. (l.), 295. See also *Elisabetta*
Federici, Francesco ("Chevalier") (c.), 291. See also *Zaïra*
Federici, Vincenzo (c.), 76, 112, 284. See also *Odenato and Zenobia*; *Usurptor Innocente, L'*
Federico, Gennaro (l.), 482. See also *Serva Padrona, La*
Fedra. See *Phædra* (Radicati)
Ferdinand IV (king of Naples), 118
Ferlendis, Alexandre (tenoroon), 250
Ferlendis, Camilla (s.), 336
Fernando nel Messico (Portogallo), 126, 287
Feron, Miss (Mrs. Glossop) (s.), 674–75
Ferrari, Giacomo Gotifredo (c.), 78, 285. See also *Due Svizzeri, I*; *Eroina di Raab, L'*; *Rinaldo d'Asti*; *Sbaglio Fortunato, Il*
Ferretti, Giacomo (l.), 295, 297. See also *Cenerentola, La*; *Matilde e Corradino*
Feste d'Iside, La (Nasolini), 289
Fetís, François-Joseph, (c., author), 496–97. See also *Love in Wrinkles*
Feudal Times (Colman the Younger/Kelly), 408, 616
Fiancée, La (Auber), 497. See also *National Guard, The*
Fidelio, 94, 345, 697
Field, Barron (j.), 23, 25, 29
Fineschi, Vincenzo (s.), 317
Finta Principessa, La (Cherubini), 105, 277
Finte Contesse, Le. See *Marchese Tulipano, Il*
Fioravanti, Valentino (c.), 288–91. See also *Astazie Fallacie, Le*; *Camilla*; *Capricciosa Pentita, La*; *Furbo contra il Furbo, Il*; *Matrimonio per Susurro, Il*; *Virtuoso in Puntiglio, Il*
Fire and Water (Cadell [the Younger?]/Andrews), 713
Fischer, Johann Christian (c., oboist), 730

Fischer, Joseph (s.), 320
Fischer, Ludwig (s.), 320
Fisherman's Hut, The (Tobin/G. Reeve), 625
Fitzball, Edward (d.), 6, 354, 491, 496, 499–500. See also *Night before the Wedding, The; Ninetta; Robber's Bride, The*
Five Miles Off (Colman the Younger), 6
Flauto Magico, Il (Mozart), 136–37, 291. See also *Zauberflöte, Die*
Flitch of Bacon, The (Bate/Shield), 384
Florio, Charles Hainen (s., c., flutist), 730
Fodor-Mainvielle, Joséphine (s.), 80, 134, 219–22
Folie, Un (Bouilly), 409
Follies of the Day (Holcroft), 393
Fonblanque, Albany (j.), 43
Fontainbleau (O'Keeffe/Shield), 389, 609
Foote, Samuel (mgr.), 361
Foppa, Giuseppe (l.), 282, 290, 295, 298. See also *Aci e Galatea; Inganno Felice, L'; Romeo e Giulietta; Teresa e Claudio*
Ford, Thomas (c.), 718
Forlivesi, Giuseppe (s.), 316
Forty Thieves, The (Colman, the Younger/Kelly), 409, 618
Fra due Litiganti il terzo gode. See *Rivali Delusi, I*
Franchi, Angelo (s.), 164
Frascatana, La (Paisiello), 10, 118, 279
Fratelli Rivali, Il. See *Due Fratelli Rivali, Il*
Freebooters, The (Napier ad. Anelli/Hawes/Paer), 492–93, 630, 695
Freischütz, Der (Logan; Kind/ Hawes/ Weber), 503–5, 628
Freischütz, Der (Planché; Kind/Livius/Weber), 505–6, 628

Freischütz, Der (Soane; Kind /Bishop/Weber), 506, 628
Freischütz, Der (Weber), impact of, 372
Friend in Need, A (Hoare/Kelly), 615
Fuorusciti di Firenze, I (Paer). See *Freebooters, The*
Furbo contra il Furbo (Fioravanti), 289

Gabrielli, Adriana (s.), 329
Gallet, Sébastien (balletmaster), 75
Galli, Filippo (s.), 326
Gallini, John (impresario), 71–72, 74
Gamerra, Giovanni de (l. and translator), 27, 278, 280, 285, 288. See also *Armida* (Mortellari, Sacchini); *Erfile; Flauto Magico, Il; Medonte; Perseo; Piro*
García, Manuel del Poppolo Vincente (s), 181–85
García-Malibran, Maria Felicita (s.), 83, 90, 242–46
Gardner, William (j.), 135
Gare Generose, Le. See *Schiavi per Amore, Gli*
Garrick, David (d., mgr.), 8, 19, 360, 377, 455. See also *Cymon; Clandestine Marriage, The*
Gastone e Bajardo (Liverati), 296
Gattie, Mrs. See Hughes, Miss
Gay, John (d., poet), 351, 373–76. See also *Acis and Galatea; Beggar's Opera, The; Polly*
Gazza Ladra, La (Rossini), 37, 94, 149, 296. See also *Ninetta*
Gazzaniga, Giuseppe (c.), 281. See also *Don Giovanni Tenorio; Vendemmia, La*
Gelosie Villane, Le (Sarti), 101. See also *Contadini Bizzarri, I*
Generali, Pietro (c.), 298. See also *Adelina*
Generosità d'Alessandro, La (Tarchi), 279

Genest, John (chronicler), 387
Geni, Signor (s.), 321
Gentle Shepherd, The (Ramsay/W. Thompson), 623
George III (king of England), 71, 131, 698
Gerbini, Lugia (s.), 333
Gherardini, Giovanni (l.), 296. See also *Gazza Ladra, La*
Giannina e Bernardone (Cimarosa—pasticcio), 107, 278
Giannone, Signor (l.), 299. See also *Maria Stuarda*
Giardini, Felici (violinist), 248, 688
Gifford, John (j.), 26
Gifford, William (j. and poet), 716
Gilbert, W. S. (l.), 607
Ginevra di Scozia (Pucitta), 292
Gini. *See* Geni, Signor
Giorgi, Signora. *See* D'Orta, Rochele
Giornovichi, Giovanni (c.), 76
Giovanni in London (Moncrieff/Whittaker; sel. Mozart), 625, 724
Giovannini, Pietro (l.), 277, 279. See also *Gilio Sabino*
Giuliani, Cecilia (s.), 159, 330
Giulio Cesare in Egitto (Handel), 99, 278
Giulio Sabino, [Il] (Cherubini), 105, 277
Giulio Sabino, [Il] (Sarti), 47, 101, 279
Giuochi D'Agrigento, Il (Paisiello), 121, 281
Glossop, Mrs. *See* Feron, Miss
Gluck, Christoph Willibald von, 68, 95, 104–5. See also *Alceste; Ifigenia in Tauride; Orfeo*
Godolphin, or The Lion of the North (Thompson/Horn), 437, 621
Godwin, William, 418
Goëde, Christian Augustus (critic), 681
Goldoni, Carlo (l.), 68, 120, 227, 282. See also *Buona Figliuola, La; Rivali Delusi, I*

Goldsmith, Oliver, 392
Goold, Francis (mgr.), 76–77
Goward, Mary Anne (s.), 673
Graam, Signor (s.), 321
Gradden, Miss (s.), 671–72
Graeff, Johann Georg (c., violist, violinist, flutist), 730
Grandi, Tommaso (l.), 281. See also *Contadini Bizzarri, I*
Grassini, Joséphine (s.), 91, 208–10
Gray (or Grey), James (j.), 16, 18
Greber, Jacob (c.), 65. See also *Amori piacerole d'Ergasto, Gli*
Green, James R. *See* Gifford, John (pseud.)
Greenwood, Thomas (j.), 37
Greenwood, Thomas, the Elder (portrait and scene painter), 578
Greenwood, Thomas, the Younger (scene painter), 519, 730–31
Gresnich, Antoine-Frédéric (c.), 103. See also *Alceste*
Grétry, André Ernest Modeste (c.), 103, 408, 421. See also *Richard Coeur de Lion; Zemira ed Azor*
Grey, James. *See* Gray, James
Griesbach, Friedrich (oboist), 250
Grieve, Thomas (scene painter), 580, 731
Grieve, William (scene painter), 580, 731
Griffith, Ralph (j.), 27
Griglietti, Signora (s.), 334
Griselda (Paer), 94, 130, 294
Grotta di Calypso, La (Winter), 124, 287
Guadagni, Sga. (?) (s.), 104
Guerra aperta, La. *See Scommessa, La*
Guglielmi, Pietro Alessandro (c.), 112, 280, 284. See also *Amor Fra le Vendemmie; Bella Pescatrice, La; Pastorella Nobile, La; Virtuosa in Margellina, La*
Guglielmi, Pietro Carlo (c.), 79, 125–

26. See also *Atalida; Due Nozze ed un Sol Marito, I; Romeo e Gilietta; Scommessa, La; Serva Raggiratrice, La; Sidagero*
Guillard, Nicolas (l.), 283–84. See also *Evelina; Ifigenia in Tauride*
Guillaume Tell (Rossini), 157. See also *Hofer*
Gustavus Vasa (Dimond/Kelly), 426, 620. See also *Hero of the North*
Guy Mannering (Terry ad. Scott/Bishop; Davy; Cooke; Whittaker; Braham), 471–72, 622
Gyrowetz, Adalbert (c.), 73, 687

Hallande, Miss (s.), 670
Hamilton, Col. Ralph (d.), 623, 625. See also *Ephis Bey; David Rizzio*
Hamilton, Sir William, 166
Handel, George Frederic, 65–67, 99, 158, 442, 690. See also *Acis and Galatea; Giulio Cesare in Egitto*
Hanover Square Rooms, 73, 687, 696
Harley, John Pritt (s.), 657
Harris, Thomas (mgr.), 9, 22, 71, 360, 443
Hartford-Bridge (Pearce/Shield), 395, 613
Haunted Tower, The (Cobb/Storace), 353, 410, 611
Hawes, Marie (s.), 780
Hawes, William (c.), 378, 380–82, 484, 488–89, 492–94, 498–500, 503–5, 507. See also *Broken Promises; Don Juan; Freebooters, The; Freischütz, Der; Oracle, The; Preciosa; Robber's Bride, The; Tarrare; Tit for Tat*
Haydn, Joseph, 68, 73, 95, 113, 115, 248, 449, 686. See also *Anima del filoso, L'*
Haym, Nicola Francesco (c., l.), 278. See also *Giulio Cesare in Egitto*

Hazlitt, William, 3, 11, 18, 25, 31, 33–35, 39–41, 43–44
Heidegger, John Jacob (mgr.), 65
Henri Quatre (Morton/Bishop), 459
Heriot, John (j.), 26
Hérold, Louis (c.), 469
Hero of the North (Dimond/Kelly), 426, 617
Hessey, James (j.), 38
Hide and Seek (Walter, Jr./Crouch), 611
Hiemer, Franz Karl (l.), 628
Highland Reel, The (O'Keeffe/Shield), 389, 611
Hill, James (s.), 655
Hill, Thomas (j.), 23, 29
Himmel, Frederich Heinrich (c.), 481
Hoare, Prince (d.), 355, 396–97, 419–23. See also *Captive of Spilburg, The; Cave of Triphonius, The; Chains of the Heart; Dido, Queen of Carthage; Friend in Need, A; Italian Villagers, The; Lock and Key; Mahmoud; My Grandmother; No Song No Supper; Price, The; Three and the Deuce, The*
Hodges, William (scene painter), 578
Hofer (Planché/Bishop/Rossini), 491–92, 632
Hoffmann, Mr. (author), 297
Hogarth, George (critic), 42, 46, 352
Holcroft, Thomas (d.), 393–94, 403–4, 484–86. See also *Choleric Fathers, The; Escapes, The; Marriage of Figaro, The; Noble Peasant, The; Old Cloathsman, The; Tale of Mystery, A*
Holman, Joseph George (d.), 395–96, 404–5. See also *Abroad and At Home; Red-Cross Knights, The; What a Blunder!*
Holmes, Edward (j., musician), 4, 15, 37, 43–44, 46, 60, 356
Holmes, Mr. (bassoonist), 730

Home, Sweet Home (Somerset/ Bishop), 722
Honey-Moon, The (W. Linley), 615, 712
Hood, Thomas (poet, j.), 40
Hook, James (c.), 425. See also *Jack of Newbury; Killing No Murder; Peruvian, The; Safe and Sound; Siege of San Quintin, The; Soldier's Return, The; Wilmore Castle*
Hook, Theodore E. (d.), 29, 40, 46, 425. See also *Jack of Newbury; Killing No Murder; Safe and Sound; Siege of San Quintin, The; Soldier's Return, The*
Horn, Charles Edward (s., c.), 435–37, 438, 472–73, 525–27. See also *Devil's Bridge, The; Dirce; Elphi Bey; Godolphin; M.P.; Peveril of the Peak; Philandering; Tricks upon Travellers; Wedding Present, The*
Horsley, Jane M. (j.), 37
Horsley, William (c.), 37
Houlton, Robert (d.), 425. See also *Wilmore Castle*
House to be Sold, A (Cobb/Kelly), 416, 617
Huber, F. X. (l.), 629
Hughes, Miss (not Mrs. Gattie) (s.), 675
Hughes, Miss (later Mrs. Gattie) (s.), 337, 667–68
Huguenots, Les (Meyerbeer), 142
Humourist, The (Cobb), 400
Hunt, John (j.), 31–34
Hunt, Leigh (j., poet), 3–4, 6–7, 11, 15–16, 23, 25, 28–29, 31–35, 40, 43, 48–49, 60, 133
Hunt, Robert (j.), 31
Hunt, Thornton (j.), 46
Hurlstone, Dr. Robert (d.), 613. See also *Just in Time*

Idalide; Ossia, La Vergine del Sole (Sarti), 102, 280
Ifigenia in Aulide (Cherubini), 106, 279
Ifigenia in Tauride (Gluck), 105, 283
Impresario in Augustie, L'. See *Capriccio Drammatico, Il*
In and Out of Tune (Cherry/Corri), 435, 619
Incledon, Charles (s.), 515–17
Indian Queen, The (Dryden/Purcell), 349
Ines de Castro (Bianchi), 88, 115, 285
Inganno Felice, L' (Rossini), 147, 295
Inglese in Italia, L' (Anfossi), 278
Inguista Gelosia, L' (Tramezzani), 291
Inkle and Yarico (Colman the Yonger/Dr. Arnold), 406, 610
Ipermestra (Sarti—pasticcio), 102, 284
Irish Legacy, The (Arnold/Dr. Arnold), 429, 615
Irish Tar, The (Attwood), 403
Iron Chest, The (Colman the Younger/Storace), 353, 418, 614. See also *Law of Java, The*
Isaacs, J. (s.), 657–58
Isidore de Merida (Dimond ad. Cobb/Storace; Cooke; Braham), 413, 464, 630
Island of St. Margerite, The (St. John/Shaw), 611
Isola del Piacere, L' (Martín y Soler), 114, 282
Italiana in Algieri, L' (Rossini), 147, 295
Italiana in Londra, L'. See *La Locandiera*
Italian and German vocal numbers: "Ach, Belmonte" (Mozart), 725; "Ach, ich liebte" (Mozart), 725; "A compir già ve' l'impresa" (Bianchi), 692; "Addio rinanti in pace" (Paisiello), 693; "Ah! che diffendi?" (Rossini), 700; "Ah che nel petto" (Paisiello), 199; "Ah mainer

[for "manier"?] crudel" (Cimarosa), 691; "Ah non lasciarmi" (Paer), 694; "Ah non rai" (Bianchi), 692; "Ah! per noi bella Aurora," 236; "Ah! Sconvolia nell' ordine eterno" (Rossini), 700; "Ah! sempre fra le cenere" (Rossini), 699; "Ah, se Re, sa giusto sei" (Bianchi), 693; "A la rabbia mi diova [for "dove"?]" (Salieri), 691; "Alla selva" (Anfossi), 690; "Alla selva" (Cherubini), 690; "All' etta, al ciel" (Rossini), 699; "All' idea di quel metallo" (Rossini), 725; "Altezza eccellentissima" (Cherubini), 691; "L'angel che sta sul nido" (Paer), 695; "Apri la madre il core" (Winter), 694; "A tanto amore," 691; "Aurora che sorgerai" (Rossini), 720; "Batti, batti" (Mozart), 567, 692; "Bei Mannern" (Mozart), 712; "Bella rosa porporina" ("Batti, batti") (Mozart), 692; "La Calunnia" (Paisiello), 145; "Cara borza" (P. A. Giglielmi), 693; "Cara memoria" (Cafra), 703; "Lo caro mio tu sei," 112; "Cenerentola vien quà" (Rossini), 699; "Cessi omai" (Rossini), 699; "Che ascolto mai, che miro!" (Paisiello), 693; "Che bell' alba!" (Meyerbeer), 698; "Che farò senza la madre?" (Winter), 694; "Che ne dici tu Taddeo" (Paisiello), 165; "Che pensa desolata Regina" (Rossini), 699; "Chi mi mostra" (Paisiello), 201; "La ci darem" (Mozart), 72; "Cinque dieci" (Mozart), 725; "Coi suoi frequenti palpiti" (Mayr), 695; "Come potesti ingrato core" (Cherubini), 691; "Come scoglio" (Mozart), 135; "Come ti piace" (Mozart), 182; "Confusa, smarrita" (Rossini), 699; "Con quelle tue manine" (Cimarosa), 691; "Constanza" (Mozart), 725; "Cora, deh attendimi," 700; "Dal tua cara" (Bianchi), 692; "Dal tuo core" (Cimarosa), 691; "Dal tuo stellato soglio" (Rossini), 151; "Da questi lineamenti" (Salieri), 693; "Deh numi pietosi" (Paisiello), 693; "Deh perdona" (Mozart), 696; "Deh prendi un dolce amplesso" (Mozart), 696; "Deh s'affretti" (Gluck), 199; "Deh vieni, non tardar" (Mozart), 692, 724; "Deh! Vien meco amato bene" (Anfossi), 690; "Dell'odiosa mia Rival" (Cimarosa), 691; "Di luce sfavillante" (Rossini), 700; "Di piacer mi balza il cor" (Rossini), 693; "Di scrivermi" (Mozart), 696; "Dispensar a mio talento" (Salieri), 691; "Di tanti palpiti" (Rossini), 149, 760; "Dite almeno in che maniera" (Mozart), 692; "La dove prendi" (Mozart), 223; "Dove sono" (Mozart), 485; "E amore un ladroncello" (Mozart), 135; "Fidi amanti voi vedete" (Tarachi?), 162; "Finch'han dal vino" (Mozart), 724; "Fra tante angoscie e palpiti" (Rossini), 699; "Fuggi, crudele, fuggi!," 228, 338; "Gente e accellatore" (Mozart), 137; "Già fan ritorno," 137; "Giovinetta che fate" (Mozart), 724; "Giovinetto Cavalier" (Myerbeer), 697; "Idol mio se tu non vivi" (Cherubini), 691; "Idolo mio, questa alma Amante" (Tarchi), 162; "In che accendi" (Rossini), 149; "Ingrato! perfido!" (Rossini), 240; "Il mio bene" (Paisiello), 692; "Io parto mio bene!" (Portogallo), 167; "La mia Dorabella" (Mozart), 696; "La mia tenera" (P. A. Guglielmi), 692; "La notte vicinia" (Paer), 696; "La Rachelina" ["Nel cor più me sento"] (Paisiello), 120; "La sorpresa, lo stupore" (Rossini), 700; "La vita umana è un mare" (Paer), 695; "L'innalzi un Mausolco" (Cimarosa), 691; "L'onda placida e tranquilla" (Cherubini), 691; "Luci del caro bene" (Gresnich), 690; "Madamina il catalogo" (Mozart), 724; "Mandina amabile" Mozart), 692; "Marsch! Marsch! Marsch!" (Mozart), 725; "Mellanimoso tromba" (Sarti), 690; "Mi manca la voce" (Rossini), 152, 699; "Mio pianto rasciuga" (Meyerbeer), 698; "Mi perdo, si, mi perdo" (Paisiello), 693; "Misero che farò" (Zingarelli), 184; "Nei lasci miei cadesti" (Rossini), 700; "Nel cor più [non] mi sento" (Paesiello), 120; "Nel vedervi" (Cimarosa), 621; "Ne tu più mormori" (Rossini), 699; "Non bastan quelle lagrime" (Rossini), 699; "Non è la mia speranza" (Sacchini), 198, 690; "Non era ancora sorta l'aurora" (Paisiello), 693; "Non più di fioni" (Mozart), 133; "Non so più cosa son" (Mozart), 724; "Non temer fra pochi istanti" (Anfossi), 693; "Nuove ognor funeste pene" (Pasiello), 693; "O! cara armonia" (Rossini?), 235; "Ochietto furbetto" (Martín y Soler), 692; "O cielo che questo" (Paer), 695; "O come è barono" (Paer), 695; "Odi grand'ombra" (Sarti or Benelli), 690; "Odo di belli concenti" (Meyerbeer), 698; "O dolce e caro istante?" (Cimarosa), 692; "O Giove omnipossente" (Winter), 694; "Oh Dei, di tanti affanni miei" (Sarti), 101; "Pace caro mio sposo" (Martín y Soler or Nasolini), 692; "Pace ci reca" (Meyerbeer), 698; "Paga fui lieta un di", 694; "Partirò dal caro sposo" (Sacchini or Salieri), 691; "Perche mai destin crudele" (Rossini), 699; "Perche mi guardi" (Rossini), 700; "Perche togliermi la sposa" (Cimarosa), 601; "Per costume" (Anfossi), 690; "Per pietà" (Bianchi), 135; "Per quest' amore luguime [for "lagrime"?]" (Portogallo), 694; "Piche, cornacchie e nottole" (Paisiello), 693; "Porgi amor" (Mozart), 135, 351; "Pria che spunti" (Cimarosa), 196; "Pria che spunti in ciel l'aurora" (Cimarosa), 103; "Proteggi amore" (Rossini), 699; "Qual pallor! qual silenzio" (Cimarosa), 111; "Quando la trovero" (Paer), 695; "Quel amabile visino" (Cherubini), 691; "Quel che piace a mio marito" (Paer), 695; "Quel fabbro adorato" (Gresnich), 690; "Quella ricordante" (Rossini), 700; "Quelle pupille tenere" (Cimarosa), 692; "Quel Sepolcro" (Paer), 695; "Quel tuo visetto amabile", 692; "Questo sol" (Zingarelli), 760; "La Rachelina" ["Nel cor più me sento"] (Paisiello), 120; "Ritorna al mio seno" (Rossini), 699; "Saper bramate" (Paisiello), 118; "Sara l'alma" (Rossini), 699; "Scherza il nocchier talora" (Gresnich), 690; "Se a caso Madama" (Mozart), 714; "Se fiato in corpo avete" (Cimarosa), 192; "Se il ciel divide" (Piccinni), 311; "Se inclinassi a prender moglie" (Rossini), 147; "Se libera non sono" (Gresnich), 690; "Se mi serbasti il soglio" (Rossini), 699;

"Sento encore, mio dolce amor" (Mayr), 695; "Sento in petto un freddo gelo" (Cimarosa), 691; "Se pieta nel cor serbate" (Cimarosa), 697; "Serva sia il vento" (Mozart), 696; "Se sfidai per voi" (Meyerbeer), 698; "Se vuol ballare" (Mozart), 725; "Si crudo e il mio destino" (Mayr), 695; "Signori, una parola" (Rossini), 699; "Singt dem grossen Bossa lieder" (Mozart), 765; "Si ti perco" (Bach), 207; "Sognai tormenti, affani" (Paisiello), 693; "Sogni ridenti" (Meyerbeer), 698; "Sono in mar" (Anfossi), 690; "Son Regina" (Sacchini), 322, 420; "Sospiro e mi vergogno" (Ferrari), 693; "Sposa adorabile" (Meyerbeer), 698; "Sprezzo quel don che versa" (Rossini), 699; "Sul' aria" (Mozart), 724; "Terra amica," 700; "Tremante gelosa" (Sarti), 690; "Tutto è deserta" (Rossini), 699; "Tutto è silenzio intorno" (Paer), 695; "Tutto me ride interno" (Rossini), 699; "Un aura amorosa" (Mozart), 696; "Una voco poco fà" (Rossni), 145, 725; "Una volta c'era un Re" (Rossini), 699; "Un segreto," 322; "Vaghi colli, ameni prati" (Winter), 694; "Veder lo sol bramo" (Paer), 695; "Vedrai, Carino" (Mozart), 724; "Vedrete un ciglio nero" (Cimarosa), 691; "Venite ingiocchiatevi" (Mozart), 725; "Viva Furico" (Pucitta), 694; "Vivat Bacchus," (Mozart), 725; "Voi chè sapete" (Mozart), 725; "Voi par foste, O care piume" (Paer), 695; "War ein Liebchen hat gefunden" (Mozart), 725; "Zitti, Zitti" (Rossini), 725

Italian language, 65–66, 121; and audiences, 92; best for singing, 67; objections to, 67; translations of, 92. *See also* Italian opera librettos and librettists

Italian opera: baroque opera, 67; beginnings in London, 65–67; castratos in, 66; comic operas and plots in, 66, 68–69, 94; da capo arias, 67–68; English vs. foreign composers of, 66; Gluck's reforms of, 68; Neapolitan opera, 68; opera buffa, 68; opera of the nobility, 65; opera seria, 67, 94; pasticci and opera seria, 67–68; realism and romance in, 69; recitative in, 67; resistance to, 66–67; ridicule of, in English opera, 66; songs in, 67, 69; and style galant, 68. *See also* Aristocracy; Criticism; Italian opera at King's Theatre; Italian opera librettos and librettists; King's Theatre audiences; King's Theatre performers and performances; Middle and lower classes

Italian opera at King's Theatre: action finales in, 68; artistic success in, 80, 259; dancing in, 148; detractors of, 257; growth of *farsa and melodramma sentimentale* in, 94; growth of German vs. Italian influence on, 95, 109–10, 120, 122, 132–33, 146, 154–55, 266–69; musical borrowings in, 97; musical "science" in, 265–66; and nature of opera, 258; neoclassical chill in, 103; recitative in, 69, 130, 262–63; repertory of, changes in, 94; Romanticism in, 94; shift toward semiserious in, 94; theme of madness in, 94. *See also* Italian opera

Italian opera librettos and librettists: 145, 260–61; changes in, 67; condemned, 66, 109, 134, 136, 147, 261; and pasticci, 67; Romanticism

in, 94; translations of, 70, 261–62.
See also Italian opera
Italian Villagers, The (Hoare/
Shield), 397, 615
Ivanhoe (Beazley/Kitchiner), 715

Jack of Newbury (T. Hook/J. Hook), 614
Jackson, William (j.), 20
Jackson, William ("of Exeter") (c.),
399, 711. See also *Lord of the Manor,
The*
Jarvis, J. (l.), 313. See also *Orfeo*
Jean de Paris (St. Just/Boieldieu), 622
Jennings, S. Clayton (j.), 35
Jephson, Robert (d.), 609. See also
Campaign, The
Jerdan, William (j.), 36, 45
Jewell, William (mgr.), 78
Jew of Mogadore, The (Cumberland/
Kelly), 619
John of Paris (Pocock/ Bishop/Boieldieu), 483, 622
Johnson, Charles (d.), 381. See also
Village Opera, The
Johnson, Dr. Samuel, 66
Johnston, Alexander (carpenter, machinist, painter, etc.), 577
Johnstone, John Henry (s.), 649
Jonson, Ben, 286
Jordan, Mrs. Dorothy (Dora) (s.),
400, 655
Jouve, J. (c.), 619
Jouy, V. J. Etienne de (l.), 313. See
also *Vestale, La*
Jovial Crew, The (Brome; Cancanen;
Yonge), 621
Just in Time (Hurlstone/Carter), 613

Kais (Brandon/W. Reeve; Braham),
6, 18, 342, 446, 619
Kean, Charles (mgr.), 722
Kean, Edmund (actor), 6, 360
Kearns, William Henry (violinist,
leader), 378

Keats, John, 44
Kelly, Earl of (c.), 383
Kelly, Frances Maria "Fanny" (s.),
427, 513, 666–67
Kelly, Michael (s., c., stage mgr.), 5,
8, 46, 76, 78, 166–67, 407–9, 416–
17, 421, 423, 425–28, 517–18. See also
*Adrian and Orilla; Blue-Beard,
The; Captive of Spilburg, The; Conquest of Taranto, The; Feudal
Times; Forty Thieves; Friend in
Need, A; Gustavus Vasa; Hero of the
North; House to be Sold, A; Jew of
Mogadore, The; Love Laughs at
Locksmiths; Of Age Tomorrow; Peasant, The; Unknown Guest, The;
Young Hussar, The; Youth, Love,
and Folly*
Kemble, Charles (d., mgr., actor),
360, 417. See also *Lodoiska; Tempest, The*
Kemble, John Philip (actor), 377, 418,
451
Kemble, Maria Theresa ("Fanny,"
née de Camp) (s., dancer, actress),
665–66
Kennedy, Mrs. Margaret Farrell (s.),
662
Kenney, James (d.), 430–33, 478–80.
See also *Alcaid, The; False Alarms;
Matrimony; Oh! This Love; Sweethearts and Wives; Wedding Present,
The*
Kenrick, Thomas (j.), 4, 29
Kenrick, William (d.), 425. See also
Raising the Wind
Kerr, John (d.), 727. See also
Freischütz, Der
Killigrew, Thomas (mgr.), 358
Killing No Murder (T. Hook/J.
Hook), 620
Kind, Friedrich (l.), 503. See also
Freischutz, Der
King, Matthew Peter (c.), 429–33.

See also *Americans, The; False Alarms; Matrimony; Oh! This Love; Up All Night*
King, Thomas (s.), 651
King Arthur (Garrick ad. Dryden/Purcell), 349–50, 377
King John (Planché), 466
King's Proxy, The (Arnold/Cooke), 480, 622
King's Theatre: admission to, 70; advertising for, 9; best attended in years, 74; boxholders, 81, 85; a commercial house, 69; competition from playhouses, 77; vs. Continental houses, 74; damaged by fire, 72–73; early history of, 65; and European premieres, 69; "fop allies," 85; a foreign concern, 83; galleries, 70, 87; house composers and poets, 68, 75–76; lighting of, 70, 79; performances at, 70; pit, 87; poor productions at, 71; rebuilding of, 73–74, 82; stalls in, 79; and theatrical criticism, 9. See also Aristocracy; Criticism; Italian opera; Italian opera at King's Theatre; King's Theatre audience; King's Theatre management; King's Theatre performers and performances; Middle and lower classes
King's Theatre audience: amateurs, 90–91, 269–70, 689; and cabals, 66–67, 80, 92–93, 251; musical taste of, 83, 85, 93, 270, 704; no competent judges, 91–92; persons onstage, 74, 86–87; press vs. public, 270–72; riots, 72, 74, 76, 78. See also Amateurs; Aristocracy; Encores; Italian opera at the King's Theatre; King's Theatre; Middle and lower classes
King's Theatre management: audiences, problems with, 72–74; claqueurs, 83, 87–88, 115; financial problems, 71–72, 74–76, 78, 80–81; fire problems, 72, 74; and the Lord Chancellor, 72; overuse of orders, 83; and "premieres," false, 75; and prima donnas, 77, 80; productions, blamed for poor, 75, 77, 84; productions, praised for good, 72, 76; subscriptions, 76. See also King's Theatre
King's Theatre performers and performances: acting, 263–64; benefits for, 70; castratos, 161, 185–88; choruses, 83, 246–47; costuming, 252–54; curtain calls, 90; domination by leading singers, 80, 158–59; falsetto singing, 68; leaders and composers, 247–48, 251–52; orchestra, 75, 81, 82, 154, 247–52; prima donnas and "right of the book," 68, 97, 158; rehearsals, 71; scenery, 254–56; singers and audience, 159; singers in Italian vs. English opera, 265; singers, large fees for, 159; tamperings of songs by singers, 68, 259; vocal ornamentation, 85, 158, 264–65; voice, tenor and bass, 68. See also Encores; Italian opera; King's Theatre
Kitchiner, Dr. William (c.), 715
Knight of Snowdoun, The (Morton/Bishop), 456–57, 620
Knights of the Cross, The (Beazley, Jr./Bishop), 724
Kotzebue, Auguste von (d.), 353, 450
Kramer, Christian (c.), 486–88. See also *Seraglio, The*
Kreutzer, Rodolphe, 417

Lablache, Luigi (s.), 328
Lacy, Michael Rophino (c.), 352, 489–91, 496–97. See also *Cinderella; Love in Wrinkles; Maid of Judah; Turkish Lovers, The*
Lady of the Lake, The (Scott), 297

Lalande, Henrietta Meric (s.), 340
Lamb, Charles, 11, 18, 23, 32, 40–41
Lanza, Gesualdo (c.), 447–48. See also *Arbitration; Deserts of Arabia, The; Outwitted at Last*
Laporte, Pierre (mgr.), 79
Laurenti, Marinna (s.), 332
Lawes, Henry (c.), 349, 376
Lawler, Dennis (d.), 716. See also *In and Out of Tune*
Law of Java, The (Colman the Younger/Bishop), 459, 626
Lazzarini, Gustavo (s.), 11, 47, 318
Lee, George Alexander (c., s.), 465–66, 469, 720. See also *Nymph of the Grotto, The*
Lee, Sophia (author), 295
Leoni, Michael (Myer Lyon) (s., c.), 168, 729
LeSage, René (writer), 402
Levasseur, Nicholas (s.), 321
Lewis, Mathew Gregory "Monk" (d.), 353
Libertine, The (Pocock; da Ponte/Bishop/Mozart), 483–84, 623
Liberty Hall (C. Dibdin/C. Dibdin), 609
Lindley, Robert (cellist, violinist, leader), 83, 249, 251
Linley, Thomas, the Elder (c.), 374, 397, 401. See also *Duenna, The; Love in the East; Richard Coeur de Lion; Strangers at Home*
Linley, Thomas, the Younger (c.), 397–98. See also *Duenna, The; Tempest, The*
Linley, William (d., c.), 615, 712. See also *Honey-Moon, The*
Lionel and Clarissa (Bickerstaffe/C. Dibdin), 354, 383, 623
Liston, John (actor), 658
Litchfield, John (j.), 30
Little Theatre, 5, 73, 358, 361
Liverati, Giovanni (c.), 296, 465–66, 469. See also *Gastone e Bajardo; Selvaggi, I*
Livigni, Filippo (l.), 277–79, 289. See also *Castellani Burlati, I; Finta Principessa, La; Frescatana, La; Giannina e Bernardone; Principe di Toranto, Il; Viaggiatori Felici, Il*
Livius, B. (c.), 505–6. See also *Fair Gabrielle; Freischütz, Der*
Locanda, La (Paisiello), 121–280
Locandiera, La (Cimarosa), 108, 278
Lock and Key (Hoare/Shield), 396, 614
Locke, Matthew (c.), 349. See also *Cupid and Death*
Lockhart, John Gibson (j.), 38
Lodoïska (Cherubini), 94, 106, 417
Lodoïska (Kemble/Storace), 18, 417, 614
Lodoïska (Kreutzer), 417
Logan, W. McGregor (d.). See *Freischütz, Der*
Longhurst, Master (s.), 729
Lord of the Manor, The (Burgoyne/Jackson), 347, 398–99, 623, 705
Lorenzi, G. B. (l.), 281, 283. See also *Discordia Conjugale, La; Modeste Raggiratrice, La; Nina*
Love, Emma Sarah (s.), 668–69
Love among the Roses (Beazley, Jr./Kitchiner), 724
Love in a Village (Bickerstaffe/Arne), 346, 381, 609
Love in the East (Cobb/Linley), 400, 610
Love in Wrinkles (Lacy; Scribe/Lacy/Fétis), 496–97, 631
Love Laughs at Locksmiths (Colman the Younger/Kelly), 409, 617
Love, Youth, and Folly (Dimond/Kelly), 426, 618
Lupino, Thomas (tailor), 731
Lyceum Theatre, 361–62, 427. See also English Opera House Theatre

Lyon, Elizabeth Sarah (s.), 666
Lyon, Meyer. *See* Lioni, Michael
Lytton, Edward Bulwer (author), 40

Macfarren, George (d.), 629. See also *Malvina*
Mackintosh, John (bassoonist, violinist), 251
MacLaughlin, Mr. (bassoonist), 574
Macnally, Leonard (d.), 392–93. See also *Richard Coeur de Lion*; *Robin Hood*
Macready, William Charles (actor, mgr.), 457, 719
Magician No Conjurer, The (Merry/Mazzinghi), 612, 715
Mahmoud (Hoare/Storace), 421–22, 615
Mahon, John (c., clarinetist, violinist), 730
Maid Marian (Planché ad. Peacock/Bishop), 26, 58, 466–67, 626
Maid of Judah, The (Lacy ad. Scott/Lacy/Rossini pastiche), 490, 631
Maid of the Hill, The (Bickerstaffe/Dr. Arnold), 120, 382–83, 615
Maid of the Oaks, The (Burgoyne/Barthélémon), 398
Maison à vendre, La (Duval), 416
Major theatres (Covent Garden, Drury Lane), 358; competition between, 358–59, 362; dramas, not operas, hurt by size, 358; enlargement of, 358; expense of star players, 359; galleries, 366; "half prices" at, 364–65; and Lenten oratorios, 363; lighting, 364; orders, abuse of, 363; performances at, 363–64; scenery at, changing, 364; "waiting music," 364. *See also* Minor theatres
Malibran. *See* García-Malibran
Malton, Thomas (scene painter), 578

Malvina (Macfarren/Cooke), 629
Manchester massacre, 22
Maniac, The (Arnold/Bishop), 455, 620
Mara, Gertrude (s.), 47, 72, 89, 99–100, 103, 198–200, 420
Marchese, Luigi (s.), 101, 162–63
Marchese Giardiniera, Il (Anfossi), 164
Marchese Tulipano, Il (Paisiello), 118, 277
Margherita D'Anjou (Meyerbeer), 56–57, 142, 300
Mariage de Figaro, Le (Beaumarchais), 393–94
Mariage de Figaro, Le (Mozart). See *Nozze di Figaro, Le*
Marian (Brooke/Shield), 392, 610
Maria Stuarda, Regina di Scozia (Coccia), 143, 299
Marinari, Gaetano (scene painter), 254
Mariners, The (Birch/Attwood), 402, 697
Marlybone Gardens, 425
Marmontel, Jean-François (d.), 283, 473. See also *Zemira ed Azor*
Marriage of Figaro, The (Bishop ad. Holcroft/Bishop/Mozart), 60–61, 484–86, 624
Marschner, Heinrich August (c.), 500–502. See also *Vampyr, Der*
Marsollier, B. J. (d.), 423, 450. See also *Adolpho e Chiara*
Martini, Vincente. *See* Martín y Soler
Martín y Soler, Vincente (c.), 76, 113–14. See also *Arbore di Diana, L'*; *Burbero di Buon C[u]ore, Il*; *Casa Rara, La*; *Isola del Piacere, L'*; *Nozze dei Contadini, Le*; *Scuola dei Meritati, La*
Martyr, Mrs. Margaret (s.), 573, 664
Marzocchi, Signor (s.), 321

Masaniello (Soane/Bishop), 497–98. See also *Muette de Portici, La*
Masque, 349
Matilde di Shabran. See *Matilde e Corradino*
Matilde e Corradino (Rossini), 153–54, 297
Matrimonio per Susurro, Il (Fioravanti), 291
Matrimonio Segreto, Il (Cimarosa), 35, 109, 281
Matrimony (Kenney/King), 431, 617
Mat[t]hews, Charles (s.), 29, 655
Mat[t]hews, Miss (s.), 667
Mayr, Johann Simon (c.), 131–32. See also *Adelasa e Alaramo*; *Chi originale*; *Fanatico per la Musica, Il*; *Medea in Corinto*; *Rosa Bianca e la Rosa Rossa, La*
Mazzinghi, Joseph (c.), 66, 71, 76, 100, 113, 414–15, 416–21, 424–25. See also *Chains of the Heart*; *Exile, The*; *Magician No Conjurer, The*; *Orpheus and Eurydice*; *Paul and Virginia*; *Ramah Droog*; *Tesoro, Il*; *Wife of Two Husbands, The*
Mazzini, C. (l.), 283. See also *Due Gobbi, I*
Mazzolà, Caerino (l.), 277, 288, 292. See also *Clemenza di Tito, La*; *Dama Soldato, La*; *Scola del Gelosi, La*
Medea in Corinto (Mayr), 132, 299
Medonte (Sarti), 102, 285
Mejnoun and Leila (I. D'Israeli), 619
Melodrama. See English opera; English opera librettos; Italian opera at King's Theatre
Mengozzi, Bernardo (s.), 317
Mercadante, Saverio (c.), 141. See also *Didone*; *Donna Caritea*; *Elisa e Claudio*
Merope (Bianchi), 115, 284
Merope [e Polifante] (Nasolini), 286

Merry, Robert (d.), 715. See also *Magician No Conjurer, The*
Merry Wives of Windsor, The (Reynolds ad. Shakespeare/Bishop), 454, 628
Messicani, I (Bochsa—pasticcio), 143, 301
Metastasio, Pietro (l.), 66–68, 27–78, 280, 284–85, 288, 293, 300, 472. See also *Artaserse*; *Demetrio*; *Didone (Abbandonata)*; *Ipermestra*; *Nitteti*; *Olimpiade, L'*; *Usurpator Innocente, L'*; *Zenobia*
Meyerbeer, Giacomo (c.), 141–42. See also *Crociato in Egitto, Il*; *Margherita d'Anjou*
Midas (O'Hara), 719, 729
Middle and lower classes, 66–67, 80, 92–93, 257
Midnight Wanderers, The (Pearce/Shield), 395, 613
Midsummer Night's Dream, A (Reynolds ad. Shakespeare/Bishop), 451–52, 622
Miller and his Men, The (Pocock/Bishop), 621
Milton, John, 621
Minor theatres and places of amusement, 359–60, 363. *See also* Adelphi Theatre; Astley's Ampitheatre; Crow Street Theatre (Dublin); Marlebone Gardens; Olympic Pavilion; Olympic Theatre; Royal Circus; Royal Coburg Theatre; Sadler's Wells; Surrey Theatre; Vauxhall Gardens
Modista Raggiratrice, La (Paisiello), 121, 283
Molinara, La. See *Molinarella, La*
Molinarella, La (Paisiello), 54, 75, 120, 280
Moncrieff, William Thomas (d.), 625, 724. See also *Giovanni in London*
Monsigny, Pierre-Alexander (c.), 104.

See also *Bella Arsène, La*
Monuel, M de (d.), 613
Moore, Thomas (poet, d.), 19, 438–39. See also *M.P.*
Moorehead, Alexander (leader), 440
Moorehead, John (c.), 439–43. See also *Bondocani, Il*; *Cabinet, The*; *Family Quarrels*; *Naval Pillar*
Morelli, Giovanni (s.), 72, 165
Moretti, Ferdinando (l.), 280, 282. See also *Idalide*; *Ifigenia in Aulide*; *Semiramide*
Mori, Miss (s.), 5, 337
Mori, Nicholas (violinist), 5
Morichelli, Anna (s.), 113, 331
Morigi, Andrea (s.), 316
Morlacchi, Francesco (c.), 429. See also *Tebaldo e Isolina*
Morley, Thomas (c.), 718
Morning, Noon and Night (T. Dibdin/Perry), 461, 626
Morte di Cleopatra, La (Bianchi), 286
Morte di Cleopatra, La (Nasolini), 288
Morte di Mithridate, La (Portogallo), 126, 289
Morte di Mit[h]ridate, La (Nasolini), 286
Morte di Semiramide, La. See *Semiramide* (Portogallo)
Mortellari, Nichele (c.), 141, 278. See also *Armida*
Morton, Thomas (d.), 25, 456–59. See also *Children in the Wood, The*; *Knight of Snowdoun, The*; *Slave, The*
Mosca, Giuseppe (c.), 297. See also *Pretendenti Delusi, I*
Mosè in Egitto (Rossini), 151. See also *Pietro l'Eremita*
Mountain, John (violinist and leader), 730
Mountain, Sara (s.), 544–45
Mountaineers, The (Colman the Younger/Dr. Arnold), 353, 407
Mountain Sylph, The (Barnett), 704, 706
Mount-Edgcumbe, Richard, Earl of (c., critic), 46. See also *Zenobia*
Mozart, W. A., 24, 34, 68–69, 84, 91, 95, 109, 129, 132–41, 145, 169, 401, 407, 413, 457, 477, 483–89, 510, 521, 688. See also *Clemenza di Tito, La*; *Don Giovanni*; *Così Fan Tutte*; *Flauto Magico, Il*; *Nozze di Figaro, Le*; *Zauberflöte, Die*
M.P.; or, The Bluestocking (Moore/Horn), 19, 438–39, 621
Muette de Portici, La (Auber), 497–98
Munden, Joseph Shepherd (s.), 652–53
Murphy, Arthur (d.), 6
My Grandmother (Hoare/Storace), 420, 614

Naldi, Giuseppe, 138, 172–75
Napier, N. (d.), 492–93. See also *Freebooters, The*
Napoleon, 118
Nasolini, Sebastiano (c), 280, 286, 288–89. See also *Andromaca*; *Feste D'Iside, La*; *Merope e Polifonte*; *Morte di Cleopatra, La*; *Morte di Mit[h]ridate, La*
Nathan, Isaac (c.), 478–80. See also *Alcaid, The*; *Sweethearts and Wives*
National Guard, The (Planché ad. Scribe/Cooke/Auber), 497–98, 632
Native Land (Dimond/Bishop), 462–63, 627
Naval Pillar, The (T. Dibdin/Moorehead), 440, 616
Netley Abbey (Pearce/Shield), 394, 614
New Spain (Scawen/Dr. Arnold), 612
Newspapers, 1–14, 16–26. See also Periodicals

Night before the Wedding and the Wedding Night, The (Fitzball/ Bishop/Boieldieu), 496, 632
Nina (Paisiello), 63, 162, 284
Nina, Pazza per Amore. See *Nina*
Ninetta (Fitzball/Bishop/Rossini), 491, 632
Ninetta, La (Cimarosa), 108, 279
Nitteti (Anfossi), 100, 277
Noble Peasant, The (Holcroft/Shield), 394
No Song, No Supper (Hoare/Storace), 419, 429, 612, 705
Novello, Mary, 32, 43
Novello, Vincent (music publisher), 16, 32, 41, 43
Noverre, Jean-Georges (balletmaster), 72
Novosielski, Michael (architect), 73
Nozze dei Contadini, Le (Martín y Soler), 282
Nozze di Dorina, Le (Sarti). See *Rivali Delusi, I*
Nozze di Figaro, Le (Mozart), 54, 91, 137–38, 292, 394, 696
Nymph of the Grotto, The (Dimond/ Liverati; Lee), 465–66, 639

Oberon (Planché; Sotheby/Weber), 37, 475–76, 508–12, 629, 705
Oberon's Oath (Thompson/Parry), 437–38, 508, 623
Odenato and Zenobia (V. Federici— pasticcio), 281
Of Age Tomorrow (T. Dibdin/Kelly), 616
O'Hara, Kane (d.), 719, 729. See also *Midas*
Oh! This Love (Kenney/King), 433, 620
O'Keeffe, John (d.), 5, 8, 24, 389–91. See also *Castle of Andalusia, The*; *Farmer, The*; *Fontainbleau*; *Highland Reel, The*; *Poor Soldier, The*; *Rival Soldiers, The*; *Shamrock, The*;

Siege of Curazola, The; *Sprigs of Laurel*
Old Cloathsman, The (Holcroft/ Attwood), 403, 616
Olimpiade, L' (Arne), 87
Olimpiade, L' (Cimarosa), 108, 279
Olimpiade, L' (Sacchini), 99
Olympic Pavilion, 724
Olympic Theatre, 527, 555
Oracle: or The Interrupted Sacrifice (Arnold/Hawes/Winter), 498–99, 629
Oratorios, 65, 67, 686
Orazi e[d] I Curiazi, Gli (Cimarosa), III, 288
O'Reilly, Robert Bray (mgr.), 73
Orfeo (Gluck), 68, 104, 124, 277
Orfeo (Gluck—pasticcio), 277, 690. See also *Orpheus and Eurydice*
Orgoglio Arvilito, L'. See *Capricciosa Pentita, La*
Orlandi, Ferdinando (c.), 696. See also *Dama Soldato, La*
Orpheus and Eurydice (Cadell [the Younger?]/Gluck—pasticcio), 405, 420, 612
Otello (Rossini), 34, 95, 151–52, 297
Out of Place (Reynolds/W. Reeve; Braham), 618
Outwitted at Last (Earle/Lanza), 448, 624
Ozmyn and Daraxa (Boaden/ Attwood), 402, 613

Pachieratti, Gasparo (s.), 72
Pacini, Giovanni (c.), 296, 299. See also *Barone di Dolsheim, IL*; *Schiava di Bagdad, La*
Packet Boat, The (Birch/Attwood), 402
Paer, Fernando (c.), 129–31. See also *Agnese, L'*; *Camilla*; *Didone Abbandonata, La*; *Griselda*; *Principe di Toronto, Il*

Paisiello, Giovanni (c.), 73, 76, 118–23. See also *Barbiere di Seviglia, Il*; *Didone*; *Discordia Conjugale, La*; *Elfrida*; *Giuochi D'Agrigento, I*; *Locanda, La*; *Marchese Tulipano, Il*; *Modesta Raggiratice, La*; *Molinarella, La*; *Nina*; *Pirro*; *Re Teodoro in Venezia, Il*; *Schiavi per Amore, Gli*; *Serva Padrona, La*; *Tutor Burlato, Il*; *Zingari in Fiera, I*
Palma, Silvestro (l.), 281. See also *Discordia Conjugale, La*
Palomba, Giovanni (l.), 278, 280–81, 283–84, 287, 290. See also *Amore Fra le Vendemmie*; *Astuzi Femmineli, Le*; *Due Baroni, I*; *Molinarella, La*; *Ninetta, La*; *Schiavi per Amore, Gli*; *Traci Amanti, I*; *Villana Riconosciuta, La*; *Zingari in Fiera, I*
Pantheon Theatre, 23, 73–74, 78
Parke, William Thomas (oboist, chronicler), 47, 573
Parry, John (c.), 42, 437–38, 716. See also *Oberlin's Oath*
Pasta, Giuditta (s.), 4, 41, 83, 236–42
Pastorella Nobile, La (P. A. Guglielmi), 75, 112, 133, 280
Paton, Mary Anne (s.), 560–64
Paul and Virginia (Cobb/Mazzinghi; W. Reeve), 616
Payne, John Howard (d.), 473–75, 495–96. See also *Clari*; *White Maid, The*
Peacock, Thomas Love (novelist), 466
Peake, Richard Brinsley (d.), 631. See also *Spring Lock, The*
Pearce, William (d.), 394–95. See also *Hartford-Bridge*; *Midnight Wanderers, The*; *Netley Abbey*
Pearman, William (s.), 658–60
Peasant Boy, The (Dimond/Kelly), 427, 620

Pedrazzi, Prospero (s.), 320
Pellegrini, Felice (s.), 326
Penelope (Cimarosa), III, 294
Penson, G. (s.), 662
Pepoli, Alessandro (l.), 281–82. See also *Ati e Cibelle*; *Giuocchi d'Agrigento, I*
Pepusch, Johann Christoph (c.), 374. See also *Beggar's Opera, The*
Periodicals, 26–27; *Analytical Review*, 27; *Annual Review*, 682; *Anti-Jacobin Review*, 27; *Athenaeum*, 12, 36; *Atlas*, 4, 15, 33, 35, 42–46; *Bell's Weekly Messenger*, 6, 9, 19, 31; *Blackwood's Edinburgh Magazine*, 38; *British Critic*, 27; *British Magazine*, 697; *British Review*, 1; *British Stage*, 3–4, 21, 28; *Carlton House Magazine*, 682; *Champion*, 23, 35–36, 43; *Companion*, 34; *Courier*, 3, 4, 21; *Covent Garden Theatrical Gazette*, 682; *Critical Review*, 18–19, 28; *Daily Gazetteer*, 8, 21; *Day*, 2, 9; *Diary*, 9, 11, 16; *Drama or Theatrical [Pocket] Magazine*, 28; *Dramatic Censor*, 602; *Drury Lane Theatrical Gazette*, 602; *Edinburgh Magazine*, 684; *Edinburgh Review*, 680; *Edinburgh Weekly Journal*, 42; *English Chronicle*, 682; *English Review*, 682; *European Magazine*, 4, 30; *Examiner*, 3–4, 6, 15, 24, 31–35, 42–44, 48; *Flowers of Literature*, 682; *Gazetteer* (see *Daily Gazetteer*); *General Evening Post*, 682; *Gentleman's Magazine*, 684; *Harmonicon*, 4, 15, 37–38, 41–43; *Liberal*, 31; *Literary Chronicle*, 71; *Literary Gazette*, 23, 36–37, 48; *Literary Journal, a Review*, 683; *Literary Magazine*, 28; *Literary Review and Historical Journal*, 682; *London Chronicle*, 1, 14; *London Magazine*, 3–4, 30, 37–39; *London Magazine*

and Intelligencer, 7–8, 683; *Monthly Advertiser*, 2; *Monthly Magazine*, 2, 27, 31, 40; *Monthly Mirror*, 3, 15, 26, 29–30, 48; *Monthly Musical Journal*, 15; *Monthly Recorder*, 682; *Monthly Register*, 18; *Monthly Review*, 27–28; *Monthly Visitor*, 682; *Morning Chronicle*, 2–5, 9, 13, 16–19, 24, 37, 42; *Morning Herald*, 6, 10, 20; *Morning Post*, 3, 8, 9, 19–21, 687; *Musical Times*, 43; *New Annual Register*, 682; *New Lady's Magazine*, 28; *New London Review*, 682; *New Monthly Magazine*, 3, 39, 682; *News*, 6, 32; *New Spectator*, 8; *New Times*, 3, 23; *Norwich Mercury*, 37; *Opera Glass*, 682; *Oracle*, 11, 18, 21; *Oracle and Daily Advertiser*, 26; *Oxford Review*, 682; *Plain Dealer*, 607; *Poetical Register*, 682; *Public Advertiser*, 5, 8, 21, 47; *Public Ledger*, 2; *Quarterly Musical Magazine*, 3, 15, 36–38; *Quarterly Review*, 684; *Reflector*, 25; *Register of the Times*, 28; *St. James's Chronicle*, 8, 682; *Satirist*, 28; *Spectator*, 42, 45–46; *Star*, 682; *Sun*, 5, 26, 682; *Tatler*, 16, 28, 34; *Theatrical Examiner*, 28; *Theatrical Guardian*, 682; *Theatrical Inquisitor*, 4, 9, 30; *Theatrical Observer*, 4, 28; *Thespian Magazine*, 682; *Times*, 2–4, 6, 9, 11, 15, 18–19, 21–26, 37, 47–48; *Town Talk*, 682; *Traveller*, 2, 32; *True Briton*, 3, 26; *Universal Magazine*, 7, 682; *Universal Register*, 22; *Walker's Hibernian Magazine*, 27; *Weekly Magazine*, 682; *Whitehall Evening Post*, 682; *World*, 21. See also Newspapers
Perry, George Frederick (c.), 461, 478–80. See also *Morning, Noon, and Night*; *Sweethearts and Wives*
Perry, James (j.), 5, 9, 16, 21, 30–31
Perry, W. H. (j.), 681
Perseo (Sacchini), 99, 277
Peruvian, The (Anon./Hook), 610
Peter Grimes (Britten), 345
Peter the Great (Cherry/Jouve), 619
Peter the Hermit. See *Pietro l'Eremita*
Petracchi, Signor (mgr.), 81
Petrosellini, Giuseppe (l.), 277–79, 284. See also *Barbiere di Siviglia, Il*; *Cifra, La*; *Locandiera, La*; *Pittor Parigino, Il*
Peveril of the Peak (Pocock ad. Scott/Horn), 629
Pezzi, V. (l.), 299. See also *Schiava di Bagdad, La*
Phædra (Radicati), 291
Philandering (Beazley, Jr./Horn), 627
Philharmonic Society, 41, 249–50
Philidor, François-André (c.), 383
Phillips, Henry (s.) 5, 427, 535–40
Phillips, Mr. (scene painter), 579
Phillips, Thomas (s.), 654
Piccinni, Niccolò (c.), 118, 277. See also *Buona Figliuola, La*
Pieltain, Dieudonné Pascal (c., violin, viola), 730
Pieltain, Marie (s.), 330
Pietro l'Eremita (Rossini), 151, 297
Piramo e Tisbe (Bianchi), 115, 283
Pirata, Il (Bellini), 143, 301
Pirate of Genoa, The (Wade ad. de Gamerra/Wade/Weigl), 493–94, 631
Pirate, The (Dimond ad. Scott/Cooke), 464, 626
Pirate, The (Scott), 464
Pirates, The (Cobb/Storace), 412, 464, 613. See also *Isidore de Merida*
Pirro (Paisiello), 94, 120, 280
Pistrucci, Signor (l.), 301. See also *Messicani, I*
Pittor Parigino, Il (Cimarosa), 107, 277
Placci, Gennaro (s.), 323
Planché, James Robinson (d.), 466–70, 491–92, 497–98, 500–502, 508–

12. See also *Carron Side*; *Cortez*; *Fair Gabrielle, The*; *Freischütz, Der*; *Hofer*; *Maid Marian*; *National Guard, The*; *Oberon*; *Recontre, The*; *Vampyr, Der*
Plots! or The North Tower (Arnold/King), 430
Pocock, Isaac (d.), 472, 483, 500. See also *John of Paris*; *Libertine, The*; *Peveril of the Peak*; *Rob Roy Macgregor*
Pola, G. (l.), 301. See also *Donna Caritea*
Polly (Gay), 708
Ponte, da. See Da Ponte, Lorenzo
Poor Soldier, The (O'Keeffe/Shield), 388
Porter, Walsh (d.), 713
Porto, Mathieu (s.), 83, 189–90
Portogallo, Marcos Antonio (c.), 126–27. See also *Argenide e Serse*; *Barsene, Regina di Lidia*; *Due Gobbi, I*; *Fernando nel Messico*; *Morte di Mithridate, La*; *Principe Spezzacamino, Il*; *Semiramide*
Portugal, Marcos Antonio. See Portogallo, Marcos Antonio
Povey, Miss (s.), 669–70
Preciosa (Soane/Hawes/Weber), 507, 628
Pretendenti Delusi, I (Mosca), 56, 297
Principe Spezzacamino, Il (Portogallo), 285
Principe di Taranto, Il (Paer), 129, 289
Principessa Filosofa, La (Andreozzi), 91, 286
Prisoner, The (Rose/Attwood), 401, 613
Privateer, The (Arnold/Dr. Arnold), 621
Prividali, L. (l.), 297. See also *Pretendenti Delusi, I*
Prize, The (Hoare/Storace), 420–21, 613

Prophesy, The (Wade/Wade), 493
Prophet, The (Bentley/Shield), 611
Prophète, Le (Meyerbeer), 141
Pucitta, Signora (s.), 334
Pucitta, Vincenzo (c.), 17, 79, 127–28, 687. See also *Adolfo e Chira*; *Aristodamo*; *Boadicea*; *Caccia D'Enrico IV, La*; *Ginevra di Scozia*; *Quattro Nazioni, Le*; *Tre Sultane, Le*; *Villeggiatori Bizzarri, I*
Purcell, Henry (c.), 43, 67, 349, 377, 398. See also *Dido and Aeneas*; *Fairy Queen, The*; *Indian Queen, The*; *King Arthur*
Puritani, I (Bellini), 143–44
Pygmalion (Rousseau), 353
Pyne, Mr. (s.), 655

Quattro Nazioni, Le (Pucitta), 290
Quick, John (s.), 650
Quinto Fabio (Bertoni), 280

Racine, Jean, 280
Radicati, Felice (c.), 291, 310. See also *Phædra*
Raising the Wind (Kenney), 431
Ramah Droog (Cobb/Mazzinghi; Reeve), 414, 615
Ramsay, Allan (lyricist), 623. See also *Gentle Shepherd, The*
Raoul sire de crequi (de Monuel), 613
Raphael, 441
Ratto di Prosperpina, Il (Winter), 76, 124–25, 287
Rauberbraut, Die (Ries), 499–500. See also *Robber's Bride, The*
Rauzzini, Venanzio (c.), 88. See also *Regina di Golconde, La*; *Vestale, La*
Ravenscroft, Thomas (c.), 718
Recitative. See English opera; Italian opera
Red-Cross Knights, The (Holman/Attwood), 616
Redding, Cyrus (j.), 29

Re di Epiro. See *Medonte* (Sarti)
Reeve, George (c.), 446, 717. See also *Fair Gabrielle, The*; *Fisherman's Hut, The*
Reeve, William (c.), 414–15, 424, 435–36, 439, 441–43, 462–63, 717. See also *Brother and Sister*; *Cabinet, The*; *Chains of the Heart*; *Family Quarrels*; *Farmer's Wife, The*; *Kais*; *Out of Place*; *Paul and Virginia*; *Ramah Droog*; *Thirty-Thousand*; *Tricks Upon Travellers*; *White Plume, The*; *Who's to Have Her?*
Regina di Golconda, La (Rauzzini), 8
Remorini, Ranieri (s.), 326
Rencontre, The (Planché/Bishop), 469, 630
Re Teodora in Venezia, Il (Paisiello), 71, 75, 94, 119, 278
Retorno di Serse, Il. See *Argenide e Serse*
Reviewers and reviews. See Critics and criticism
Reynolds, Frederic (d.), 5–6, 25, 356, 446. See also *Arbitration*; *Caravan, The*; *Crusade, The*; *Deserts of Arabia, The*; *Dramatist, The*; *Duke of Savoy, The*; *Exile, The*; *Merry Wives of Windsor, The*; *Midsummer Night's Dream, A*; *Out of Place*; *Tempest, The*; *Twelfth Night*; *Two Gentlemen of Verona, The*; *Virgin of the Sun, The*
Ricciardo e Zoraide (Rossini), 153, 297
Richard Coeur de Lion (Burgoyne/Linley the Elder/Grétry), 353, 399, 610
Richard Coeur de Lion (Macnally/Shield), 392–93, 610
Richards, John Inigo (scene painter), 577
Richards, R. D. (j.), 35
Richardson, Joseph (j.), 19
Ries, Ferdinand (c.), 499–500. See also *Robber's Bride, The*
Righi, Pietro (s.), 320
Rinaldo d'Asti (Ferrari), 286
Rintoul, Robert Stephen (j.), 43
Rito [Riti] d'Efeso, Il (Farinelli), 293
Rivali Delusi, I (Sarti), 101, 227
Rival Soldiers, The (O'Keeffe), 390. See also *Sprigs of Laurel*
Road to Ruin, The (Holcroft), 403
Robber's Bride, The (Fitzball/Hawes/Reis), 499–500, 631
Robber's Wife, The. See *Robber's Bride, The*
Robert le Diable (Meyerbeer), 142
Roberto l'Assassino (Trento), 289
Roberts, David (scene painter), 580
Robertson, Francis (j.), 32
Robertson, Henry (j.), 4, 24, 32–33, 48–49
Robert the Devil (Barnett), 704
Robin Hood (Macnally/Shield), 347, 392, 609
Robinson, Henry Crabb (j.), 22–23, 41
Rob Roy Macgregor (Pocock ad. Scott/Davy), 472, 624
Rodwell, George (c.), 631. See also *Spring Lock, The*
Romanelli, Luigi (l.), 290, 293, 296–97, 299. See also *Adelasia e Aleramo*; *Aureliano in Palmira*; *Capricciosa Pentita, La*; *Elisa e Claudio*
Romani, Felice (l.), 296, 299–301. See also *Barone di Dolsheim, Il*; *Magherita d'Anjou*; *Medea in Corinto*; *Pirata, Il*; *Rosa Bianca e la Rosa Rossa, La*; *Turco in Italia, Il*
Romanticism, 679, 689, 703
Romeo e Giulietta (P. C. Guglielmi), 4, 126, 290
Romeo e Giulietta (Zingarelli), 298
Romero, Signor (s.), 324
Rooker, Michael (scene painter), 731

Rosa Bianca e la Rosa Rossa, La (Mayr), 95, 132, 300
Rosamond (Addison), 66
Rose, John (d.), 401–2. See also *Caevarnon Castle*; *Fast Alseep*; *Prisoner, The*
Roselli, Agrippino (s.), 318
Rosina (Brooke/Shield), 391, 625
Rossi, Gaetano (l.), 286, 289, 292, 296, 298–99. See also *Alzina*; *Crociato in Egitto, Il*; *Feste d'Iside, La*; *Ginevra di Scozia*; *Semiramide* (Rossini); *Tebaldo e Isolina*
Rossini, Gioacchino Antonio, 33–34, 45, 68, 144–57, 463, 489–92. See also *Assedio di Corinto, L'*; *Aureliano in Palmira*; *Barbiere di Seviglia, Il*; *Cenerentola, La*; *Conte Ori, Il*; *Donna del Lago, La*; *Elisabetta*; *Gazza Ladra, La*; *Inganno Felice, L'*; *Italiana in Algieri, L'*; *Matilde e Corradino*; *Otello*; *Pietro L'Eremita*; *Ricciardo e Zoraide*; *Semiramide Tancredi, Il*; *Turco in Italia, Il*; *Zelmira*
Rousseau, J. J., 353. See also *Pygmalion*
Rovedino, Carlo (s.), 319
Royal Academy of Music (1719–28), 65, 278; (1822–present), 703, 731
Royal Circus, 461
Royal Coburg Theatre, 461
Royal Theatre, 729
Rubens, Peter Paul, 24
Rubinelli, Giovanni (s.), 99, 161–62
Russian Impostor, The (Siddons; Arnold/Addison), 436, 620

Sacchini, Antonio (c.), 76, 88, 99, 400. See also *Armida*; *Evelina*; *Perseo*
Sadler's Wells, 355, 446
Safe and Sound (T. Hook/J. Hook), 425, 620

St. John, The Honorable (d.), 611. See also *Island of St. Marguerite, The*
St. Just (d.), 722. See also *Jean de Paris*
Salieri, Antonio (c.), 106–7, 494–95. See also *Angiolina*; *Cifra, La*; *Scuola dei Gelosi, La*
Salomon, Johann Peter (violinist, leader, impresario), 73, 248–49
Sanctis, Luigi de (l.), 285. See also *Jean de Paris*
San Suci [German] Theatre, 697
Santani [Vincenzo-Felici?] (s.), 327
Sapio, Mr. (s.), 533–35
Sarjeant, Mr. (trumpet), 593
Sarti, Giuseppe (c.), 101–3. See also *Alessandro e Timoteo, I*; *Contadini Bizzarri, I*; *Contrattempi Amorosi*; *Giulio Sabino*; *Idalide*; *Ipermestra*; *Medonte*; *Rivali Delusi, I*
Savile, Jeremy (c.), 718
Sbaglio Fortunato, Il [Lo] (Ferrari), 294
Scawen, John (d.), 612. See also *New Spain*
Schiava di Bagdad, La (Pacini), 299
Schiavi per Amore, Gli (Paisiello), 119, 278
Schikaneder, Emanuel (l.), 291. See also *Flauto Magico, IL*; *Zauberflöte, Der*
Schmidt, G. (l.), 295. See also *Elisabetta*
Schroeter, Johann Samuel (c., s., keyboard), 730
Schutz, Herr (s.), 340
Schutz, Herr (bassoon), 730
Schutz, Mme. (s.), 340
Schweizerfamilie, Die (Wiegl), 493
Scommessa, La (P. C. Guglielmi), 125, 290
Scott, John (j.), 23, 38
Scott, Sir Walter, 94, 152, 445, 456, 460, 470, 495. See also *Guy Man-*

nering; *Ivanhoe*; *Peveril of the Peak*; *Pirate, The*; *Lady of the Lake*; *Lay of the Last Minstrel*; *Rob Roy Macgregor*
Scribe, Augustin Eugen (l.), 300. See also *Conte Ori, Il*
Scuola dei Gelosi, La (Salieri), 106, 277
Scuola dei Maritati, La (Martín y Soler), 114, 282
Sedaine, Jeab-Marie (l.), 393. See also *Richard Coeur de Lion*
Sedgwick, Thomas (s.), 652
Selvaggi, I (Liverati), 293
Semiramide (Gyrowitz), 687
Semiramide (Portogallo), 289
Semiramide (Rossini), 155, 298
Semiramide; La Vendetta di Nino (Bianchi), 115, 282
Seraglio, The (Dimond/Kramer/Mozart), 37, 480–87
Sertor, Gaetano (l.), 283. See also *Piramo e Tisbe*; *Zenobia in Palmira*
Serva Astuta, La (anon.), 288
Serva bizzari, La. See *Serva Raggiratrice, La*
Serva Padrona, La (Paisiello), 121, 282
Serva Raggiratrice, La (P. C. Guglielmi), 125, 290
Sessi, Morianna (s.), 336
Sestini, Giovanna (s.), 328, 388, 665
Settle, Elkanah (d.), 706. See also *Empress of Morocco, The*; *Fairy Queen, The*
Shadwell, Thomas (d.), 483
Shakespeare, 451–54; *As You Like It*, 397; *The Comedy of Errors*, 452; *Hamlet*, 451; *Macbeth*, 451; *Measure for Measure*, 451; *The Merchant of Venice*, 451; *The Merry Wives of Windsor*, 454; *A Midsummer Night's Dream*, 451; *Othello*, 451; *Romeo and Juliet*, 5, 451; *The Tempest*, 451; *Twelfth Night*, 453; *The Two Gentlemen of Verona*, 454

Shamrock, The (O'Keeffe), 388
Shaw, Thomas (c., leader), 455, 572. See also *Island of St. Marguerite, The*
Shelley, Percy Bysshe, 32
Sheridan, Elizabeth, 397
Sheridan, Richard Brinsley (d., mgr.), 5, 71, 360, 397–98. See also *Critic, The*; *Duenna, The*
Shield, William (c., tenor), 24, 30, 350, 356, 366, 384–97, 422, 445–48, 730. See also *Abroad and At Home*; *Choleric Fathers, The*; *Crusade, The*; *Farmer, The*; *Fontainbleau*; *Hartford-Bridge*; *Highland Reel, The*; *Italian Villagers, The*; *Lock and Key*; *Marian*; *Midnight Wanderers, The*; *Netley Abbey, The*; *Prophet, The*; *Richard Coeur de Lion*; *Robin Hood*; *Rosina*; *Sprigs of Laurel, The*; *Travellers in Switzerland, The*; *Two Faces under a Hood*; *Woodman, The*; *Your's or Mine?*
Shipwreck, The (Arnold/Dr. Arnold), 428, 615
Shoberl, Frederic (j.), 40
Shuter, Ned (j.), 4
Siboni, Giuseppe (s.), 92, 320
Sidagero (P. C. Guglielmi), 125, 290
Siddons, Henry (d., actor), 436, 716. See also *Russian Imposter, The*
Siddons, Sarah (actress), 360
Siege of Belgrade, The (Cobb/Storace), 354, 411, 612. See also *Catherine*
Siege of Curzola, The (O'Keefe/Dr. Arnold), 388, 610
Siege of Rhodes, The (Davenant/Lawes, etc.), 349, 351
Siege of San Quintin, The (T. Hook/J. Hook), 425, 619
Sinclair, John (s.), 527–30
Slave, The (Morton/Bishop), 457, 623
Smart, George (c., leader), 511–12,

574, 728. See also *Elphi Bey*
Smugglers, The (Attwood), 402
Soane, George (d.), 475–76, 507. See also *Aladdin; Freischütz, Der; Preciosa*
Soane, Sir John (architect), 475
Sografi, Simeone Antonio (l.), 286, 288. See also *Morte di Cleopatra, La; Morte de Mit[h]ridate, La; Orazi ed Curiazi, Gli; Principessa Filosofa, La*
Soldier's Return, The (T. Hook/J. Hook), 618
Somerset, Charles A., 722. See also *Home, Sweet Home; Sylvania*
Somnambula, La (Bellini), 144
Songs. See English and French vocal numbers; English opera songs; Italian and German vocal numbers
Sontag, Henrietta (s.), 232–36
Sotheby, William (translator), 623
Southern, Henry (j.), 38
Spagnoletti, Paolo (violinist, leader), 250
Spalding, the Reverend William (author), 12
Spanish Barber, The (Goldoni), 120
Spanish Dollars (Cherry/Davy), 404, 433
Spankie, Robert (j.), 18
Spohr, Ludwig (c.), 45
Spontini, Gaspare (c.), 143. See also *Vestale, La*
Sposo Burlato, Lo (Paisiello), 693
Sposo malcontenti (Storace), 410–13
Sprigs of Laurel (O'Keeffe/Shield), 390, 613
Spring Lock, The (Peake/Rodwell), 631
Stametz, Carl Phillip (c., violinist, tenor), 730
Stanfield, William Clarkson (scene painter), 580–81, 731
Steevens, George, 5, 21

Stendhal (né Beyle), 40, 699, 701, 704
Stephens, Catherine (s.), 564–71
Sterbini, Cesare (l.), 295. See also *Barbiere di Seviglia, Il*
Sterling, Edward (j.), 22, 26, 57–58
Stevens, Richard John Samuel (c.), 716
Stevenson, John, Sir (c.), 438, 716
Storace, Nancy (s.), 72, 168, 201–2, 545–48
Storace, Stephen (c.), 71, 75–76, 115, 133, 350, 356, 409–14, 417–23, 455, 464. See also *Cave of Triphonius, The; Cherokee, The; Dido; Doctor and the Apothecary, The; Haunted Tower, The; Iron Chest, The; Isidore de Merida; Lodoïska; Mahmoud; My Grandmother; No Song No Supper; Pirates, The; Prize, The; Siege of Belgrade, The; Three and the Deuce, The*
Stranger, The (Thompson), 437
Strangers at Home, The (Cobb/Linley the Elder), 400, 609
Street, T. G. (j.), 21
Stuart, Charles (j.), 8
Stuart, Daniel (j.), 20, 21
Stuart, Peter (j.), 20
Suett, Richard (s.), 650
Sullivan, Arthur (c.), 667
Surrender of Calais, The (Colman the Younger/Dr. Arnold), 407, 612
Surrey Theatre, 363
Sweethearts and Wives (Kenney/Cooke; Whittaker; Nathan; Perry), 42, 478–79, 627
Swift, Edmund L. (d.), 472. See also *Woman's Will*
Swift, Jonathan, 66, 472
Sylvania (Somerset ad. Heimer/Blewitt/Weber), 507–8, 631

Tale of Mystery, A (Holcroft/Busby), 353

Talfourd, Thomas Noon (j.), 39–41, 48
Tancredi, Il (Rossini), 149, 296
Tarare (Beaumarchais). See *Tarrare*
Tarare (Salieri), 107, 494–95
Tarchi, Angelo (c.), 691. See also *Disertore, Il*; *Generosità d'Alessandro, La*; *Virginia*
Tarducci, F. (l.), 287. See also *Fernando nel Messico*
Tarrare (Arnold/Hawes/Salieri), 628
Tasca, Luigi (s.), 316
Tasso, Torquato (poet), 290
Taylor, Edward (j.), 42, 45–46
Taylor, John (j.), 8, 15, 20, 26, 30, 38–39
Taylor, William (impresario), 9, 71–72, 74–80
Tebaldo e Isolina (Morlacchi), 299
Tempest, The (Kemble/Linley the Younger), 611
Tempest, The (Purcell), 350
Tempest, The (Reynolds ad. Shakespeare/Bishop), 454, 626
Tenducci, G. F. (c., s.), 609. See also *Campaign, The*
Teodolinda (Andreozzi), 281
Teresa e Claudio (Farinelli), 290
Terry, Daniel (d.), 470–72, 489. See also *Barber of Seville, The*; *Guy Mannering*
Tesoro, Il (Mazzinghi—pasticcio), 113, 283
Theatres. See Concerts; Covent Garden Theatre; Crow Street Theatre (Dublin); Drury Lane Theatre; English Opera House; Little Theatre; Lyceum Theatre; Major theatres; Minor theatres; Olympic Pavilion; Olympic Theatre; Pantheon Theatre; San Souci Theatre; Surey Theatre; York Theatre
Thelwall, John (j.), 35
Thirty-Thousand (T. Dibdin/Davy; W. Reeve; Braham), 355, 444–45, 618
Thomas and Sally (Bickerstaffe/Arne), 381, 611
Thompson, Benjamin (d.), 437. See also *Godolphin*; *Oberon's Oath*
Thompson, W. (collector of Scottish tunes), 437, 623
Thorne, Mr. (s.), 660
Three and the Deuce, The (Hoare/Storace), 421, 614
Threepenny Opera, The. See *Dreigroschenoper, Die*
Tit for Tat (Arnold/Hawes/Mozart), 60, 488–89, 631
Tobin, John (d.), 623. See also *Fisherman's Hut, The*; *Your's or Mine?*
Toniolo, Girolamo (l.), 280. See also *Locanda, La*
Topham, E. (j.), 21
Torre di Rizzonico, Gastone della (l.), 285. See also *Alessandro e Timoteo*
Torri, Alberto (s.), 325
Toso-Puzzi, Giacinta (s.), 340
Tottola, Andrea Leone (l.), 289, 297–98. See also *Donna del Lago, La*; *Furbo contra il Furbo, Il*; *Zelmira*
Traci Amanti, I (Cimarosa), 110, 115, 283
Trame Deluse, Le (Cimarosa), 108, 281
Tramezzani, Diomiro (s., c.), 170–72. See also *Inguista Gelosia, L'*
Travellers, The (Cherry/Corri), 434–35, 618
Travellers in Switzerland, The (Bate/Shield), 386, 614
Tree, Ann Maria (s.), 557–60
Tree, Ellen (s.), 730
Trento, Vittorio (c.), 289. See also *Climène*; *Roberto L'Assassino*
Tresham, Henry (artist), 264
Tre Sultane, Le (Pucitta), 128, 291
Tricks upon Travellers (Burges/Horn; W. Reeve), 435, 620

Trionfo del'amor Fraterno, Il (Winter), 76, 124, 287
Trionfo della Belta, Il. See *Matilde e Corradino*
Trionfo de Rosselane, Il. See *Tre Sultane, Le*
Turco in Italia, Il (Rossini), 150–51, 296
Turk and No Turk (Colman the Younger/Dr. Arnold), 406, 609
Turkish Lovers, The (Lacy/Lacy/Rossini; sel. Braham), 489–90, 630
Turner, Joseph M. W., 254
Tutor Burlato, Il (Paisiello), 108, 118, 278
'Twas I (Payne), 723
Twelfth Night (Reynolds ad. Shakespeare/Bishop), 453, 625
Two Faces under a Hood (T. Dibdin/Shield; W. Reeve; Braham), 355, 445, 619
Two Gentlemen of Verona, The (Reynolds ad. Shakespeare/Bishop), 454, 626
Two Houses of Grenada, The (Wade; sel. Braham), 629
Two to One (Colman the Younger/Dr. Arnold), 406

Unknown Guest, The (Arnold/Kelly; Braham), 427, 622
Unterbrochene Opferfest, Das (Winter), 498–99
Up All Night (Arnold/King), 429, 620
Usurpator Innocente, L' (V. Federici), 112, 280

Vampyr, Der (Planché; Wohlbruch/Marschner), 500–502, 631
Vanbrugh, John, 65, 72
Vane Gelosie, Le. See *Discordia Conjugale, La*
Vauxhall Gardens, 425, 466

Velluti, Giovanni Battista (s.), 40, 82, 142, 185–88
Vendemmia, La (Gazzaniga), 133, 279
Vendetta di Nino, La. See *Semiramide* (Bianchi)
Verazzi, Signor (translator), 283
Vergine del Sol, La (Andreozzi), 287
Vestale, La (Pucitta), 77–78, 127–28, 291
Vestale, La (Rauzzini), 278
Vestale, La (Spontini), 82, 143, 299
Vestris, Armand (balletmaster), 217
Vestris, Gaetano (balletmaster), 217
Vestris, Lucia (s.), 216–19, 356, 551–55
Vestris, Stephen (l., translator), 296. See also *Gastone e Bajardo*
Viaggiatori Felici, I (Anfossi), 75, 100, 277
Vieille, La (Fétis), 496–97, 617. See also *Love in Wrinkles*
Viganoni, Giuseppe (s.), 167
Village Opera, The (Johnson), 381
Villana Riconosciuta, La (Cimarosa), 108, 279
Villanella Rapita, La (Bianchi), 88, 115, 280
Villeggiatori Bizzarri, I (Pucitta), 127, 290
Vinci, Mariana (s.), 333
Viotti, Giovanni Battista (violinist, violist), 248–49
Virginia (Tarchi), 278
Virgin of the Sun, The (Reynolds/Bishop), 450, 621
Virtu, La. See *Griselda*
Virtuosa in Margellina, La (P. A. Guglielmi), 289
Virtuosi Ambulanti, I. See *Virtuoso in Puntaglio, Il*
Virtuoso in Puntiglio, Il (Fioravanti), 289
Voltaire, 119, 149, 282, 284, 289

Wade, Joseph Augustine (c., l.), 45, 493–94. See also *Pirate of Genoa, The*; *Two Houses of Granada, The*
Wagstaff, Mr. (leader), 574
Wales, Prince of, 26, 31, 73–74, 90, 133, 360, 401, 688
Walker, C. E. (d.), 628. See also *Fall of Algiers, The*
Walter, John (I) (j.), 22
Walter John (II) (j., d.), 19, 22–25. See also *Hide and Seek*
Ward, C. (d.), 713. See also *Circassian Bride, The*
Warner, Capt. ("amateur" c.), 613. See also *Armourer, The*
Waters, Edmund (mgr., impresario), 77–80
Waylett, Harriet (s.), 670–71, 721
Ways and Means (Colman), 5
Weber, Carl Maria von (c.), 502–12. See also *Abou Hassan*; *Euryanthe*; *Freischütz, Der*; *Sylvania*
Wedding Present, The (Kenney/Horn), 629, 723
Weichsel[l], Carl (father of Charles) (oboist), 249
Weichsell, Charles (violinist and leader), 249
Weigl, Joseph (c.), 493–94. See also *Pirate of Genoa, The*
Weill, Kurt (c.), 706. See also *Drigroschenoper, Die*
Welsh, Thomas (c., s.), 402, 712, 717
Wesley, Samuel Sebastian (c.), 571, 730
What a Blunder! (Holman/Davy), 404–5, 616
Wheble, John (j.), 19
White Lady, The (Beazley, Jr. ad. Scott/Cooke/Boieldieu), 629
White Maid, The (Payne ad. Scott/Boieldieu), 495–96, 630
White Plume, The (T. Dibdin ad. Scott/Reeve), 445, 618

Whittaker (or Whitaker), John (c.), 470–72, 478–80, 722, 724. See also *Guy Mannering*; *Sweethearts and Wives*; *Who's to Have Her?*
Who's to Have Her? (T. Dibdin/W. Reeve; Whittaker), 621
Wieland, Christoph Martin (poet), 623. See also *Oberon*
Wife of Two Husbands, The (Cobb/Mazzinghi), 415, 617
Wigstead, Mr. (scene painter), 579
Wilkinson, Miss (j.), 37
Williams, Tate (mgr.), 7
Wilmore Castle (Houlton/Hook), 425, 616
Winter, Peter von (c.), 78, 123–25, 498–99. See also *Gratta di Calypso, La*; *Fratelli Rivali, I*; *Ratto di Proserpina, Il*; *Zaira*
Wohlbruch, Wilhelm Auguste (l.), 500–502. See also *Vampyr, Der*
Wolff, P. A. (l.), 626. See also *Preciosa*
Woman's Will — A Riddle (Swift/Davy), 472
Wood, Mr. (s.), 661–62
Woodfall, Henry Sampson (j.), 21
Woodfall, William "Memory" (j.), 5, 8, 10
Woodman, The (Bate/Shield), 385, 612
Wyatt, James (architect), 73

Yonge, Sir William (d.), 621. See also *The Jovial Crew*
Young Hussar, The (Dimond/Kelly), 619
Your's or Mine? (Tobin/Shield), 623, 711
Youth, Love, and Folly (Dimond/Kelly), 618

Zaïra (F. Federici), 291
Zaïra (Winter), 76, 124, 288
Zarzuela, 346

Zauberflöte, Die (Mozart), 65, 137, 291, 345, 696–97. See also *Flauto Magico, Il*
Zelmira (Rossini), 91, 154, 298
Zémira ed Azor (Grétry), 103, 283
Zeno, Apostolo (l.), 67. See also *Quinto Fabio*
Zenobia (Mount-Edgcumbe), 285
Zenobia in Palmira (Anfossi), 101, 282

Zingarelli, Niccolo Antonia (c), 298. See also *Romeo e Giulietta*
Zingari in Fiera, I (Paisiello), 121, 281
Zini, Salvario (l.), 280, 289. See also *Bella Pescatrice, La*; *Pastorella Nobile, La*; *Virtuosa in Margellina, La*
Zucchelli, Carlo (s.), 190–92
Zuma (T. Dibdin/Bishop; Braham), 460, 624, 718